ENGLISH
STUDY
DICTIONARY

PETER COLLIN PUBLISHING

First published in Great Britain in October 2000

Published by Peter Collin Publishing Ltd
1 Cambridge Road, Teddington, Middlesex, TW11 8DT

© Copyright PH Collin, F Collin, SMH Collin 2000

British Library Cataloguing-in-Publication Data

A catalogue record for this book is available from the British Library

ISBN 1-901659-63-1

Text processing and computer typesetting by PCP
Printed and bound in Finland by WS Bookwell

General editor
PH Collin

Preface

The aim of this dictionary is to provide a modern vocabulary of English for the intermediate student.

The vocabulary of over 15,000 entries has been selected carefully according to various word frequency counts and syllabuses for national and international examinations.

Each word or term is clearly defined, and examples of each word and phrase are given in simple illustrative contexts (over 28,000 in all) , so as to show how the words can be used in practice.

Layout of the Dictionary

We have tried to lay the dictionary out as clearly as possible, in order to make it as easy as possible for the student to use.

Each entry begins with a main word, followed by the pronunciation in international phonetic symbols; this is followed by the part of speech. Entries where the same word occurs as two or more different parts of speech are split by numbers. Within each entry, major differences of meaning are highlighted by letter divisions.

The meanings of the words are written as simply as possible, using only a small defining vocabulary, supplemented as necessary by other words which appear in the dictionary. All word have examples of usage, and for the commonest words we give very many examples, all set in contexts which are easy to understand. Common idiomatic expressions and collocations are highlighted, explained, and examples are given for them also.

Throughout the book, usage notes (beginning with the word NOTE:) give irregular forms, constructions, words which can be confused, etc. These notes are also used to give information about the countries of the world which appear as entries.

Some words have fuller encyclopaedic comments in boxes, and these give more information than can be given within a simple definition.

Word frequency grading

Each entry word is preceded by a number. These refer to the frequency of the main word according to reliable international word counts. The most common 1,500 words are ①, the next 1,500 words are ②, the next 1,500 are ③ and the 3,500 remaining words are ④.

Phonetics

The following symbols have been used to show the pronunciation of the main words in the dictionary.

Stress has been indicated by a main stress mark ('), but these are only guides as the stress of the word may change according to its position in the sentence.

Vowels		*Consonants*	
æ	back	b	buck
ɑː	harm	d	dead
ɒ	stop	ð	other
aɪ	type	dʒ	jump
aʊ	how	f	fare
aɪə	hire	g	gold
aʊə	hour	h	head
ɔː	course	j	yellow
ɔɪ	loyalty	k	cab
e	head	l	leave
eə	fair	m	mix
eɪ	make	n	nil
ə	abroad	ŋ	bring
əʊ	float	p	post
əʊə	lower	r	rule
ɜː	word	s	save
iː	keep	ʃ	shop
ɪ	fit	t	take
ɪə	near	tʃ	change
u	supreme	χ	loch
uː	pool	θ	theft
ʊ	book	v	value
ʌ	shut	w	work
		z	zone
		ʒ	measure

Aa

A, a
[eɪ]
first letter of the alphabet, followed by B; *do you mean 'dependant' spelt with an 'a' or with an 'e'?*; **from A to Z** = completely, all the way through; **the A to Z** = street guide for a town, especially one for London; *you can find our road in the A to Z*

a, an
[eɪ or æn] *article*
(a) one; *I want a cup of tea*; *she's bought a new car*; *an enormous hole*; *we had to wait an hour for the bus*; *a useful guidebook*
(b) for each or to each; *apples cost 50p a kilo*; *the car was travelling at 50 kilometres an hour*; *he earns £100 a day* (NOTE: **an** is used in front of words beginning with **a, e, i, o, u** and with **h** if the **h** is not pronounced **(an apple; an hour)**; **a** is used in front of all other letters and also in front of **u** where **u** is pronounced [juː] **(a useful guidebook)**)

abandon
[əˈbændən] *verb*
(a) to leave; *he abandoned his wife and children*; *the crew abandoned the sinking fishing boat*
(b) to give up, to stop doing something; *the company has decided to abandon the project*; *we abandoned the idea of setting up a London office*

abandoned
[əˈbændənd] *adjective*
no longer used or lived in; *two families of refugees moved into the abandoned house*

abbreviation
[əbriːvɪˈeɪʃn] *noun*
short form of a word; *'Ltd' is the abbreviation for 'Limited'*

ability
[əˈbɪlɪti] *noun*
(a) having the force to do something; *he has many abilities but singing isn't one of them* (NOTE: plural in this meaning is **abilities**)
(b) being clever; *he's a man of great or outstanding ability*; **I'll do it to the best of my ability** = I'll do it as well as I can

able
[ˈeɪbl] *adjective*
to be able to do something = to have the capability or chance to do something; *she wasn't able to breathe*; *will you be able to come to the meeting?*; *they weren't able to find the house* (NOTE: **able** is only used with **to** and a verb)

aboard
[əˈbɔːd] *adverb & preposition*
on a ship or vehicle; *the truck ran into a bus with twenty passengers aboard*; *the passengers went aboard the 'Queen Elizabeth' at 10 p.m.*; *when the ship docked, customs officers came aboard to inspect the cargo*; **all aboard!** = everyone get on, please!

abolish
[əˈbɒlɪʃ] *verb*
to get rid of (a law, a right); *Parliament voted to abolish capital punishment*

abortion
[əˈbɔːʃn] *noun*
ending of a woman's pregnancy; *she did not want the baby, so asked to have an abortion*

about
[əˈbaut]
1 *preposition*
(a) referring to; *he told me all about his operation*; *what do you want to speak to the doctor about?*; *she's worried about her heart problems*
(b) **to be about to do something** = to be just going to do something; *we were about to go home when you arrived*
(c) in the process of doing something; *while you're about it, can you post this letter?*
(d) *(informal)* **how about** *or* **what about** = what do you think; *we can't find a new secretary for the club - what about Sarah?*; **how about a cup of tea?** = would you like a cup of tea?
2 *adverb*
(a) approximately; *the table is about two metres long*; *I've been waiting for about four hours*; *she's only about fifteen years old*
(b) in various places; *there were papers lying about on the floor*; *there is a lot of flu about during the winter months*

above
[əˈbʌv]
1 *preposition*
(a) higher than; *the plane was flying above the clouds*; *the temperature in the street was above 30 degrees*; *at prices above £6.00, nobody will buy it*; *if you are above 18, you have to pay the full fare*
(b) louder than; *I couldn't hear the telephone above the noise of the drills*

(c) earlier on (in a book); higher up (on a page); *see the section on computers on page 25 above*

2 *noun*

the above = people mentioned earlier; *all the above have passed the test*

abroad
[ə'brɔ:d] *adverb*

in another country; to another country; *he travels abroad a lot on business*; *they've gone abroad on holiday*; *holidays abroad are more and more popular*; *she lives abroad and only comes back to England for her holidays*

abrupt
[ə'brʌpt] *adjective*

(a) sudden; *he made an abrupt change of plan*; *the bus made an abrupt turn to the right*

(b) not very polite; *his reply was abrupt and to the point*

absence
['æbsɪns] *noun*

(a) being away from a place; *she did not explain her absence from the meeting*; *the former president was sentenced in his absence*; **in the absence of** = without someone being there; *in the absence of the chairman, his deputy took the chair*; **leave of absence** = permission to be away from work; *he asked for leave of absence to visit his wife in hospital*

(b) lack of something; *in the absence of any map of the town we had to ask our way*

absent
['æbsɪnt] *adjective*

not there; *the chairman was absent from the meeting*; *ten of the staff are absent with flu*; *let's drink a toast to absent friends*

absolute
['æbsɪlu:t] *adjective*

complete, total; *the general assumed absolute power*; *he's an absolute fool - he should have accepted the offer immediately*; **absolute majority** = majority over all the others; *the government has an absolute majority of fifteen*; **absolute zero** = the lowest possible temperature

absolutely
['æbsɪlu:tli] *adverb*

completely, totally; *I am absolutely sure I left the keys in my coat pocket*

absorb
[əb'zɔ:b] *verb*

(a) to take in (a liquid, etc.); *the liquid should be absorbed by the paper*; *salt absorbs moisture from the air*

(b) to reduce a shock; *the car's springs are supposed to absorb any shock from the road surface*

(c) **absorbed in** = totally interested in; *he was so absorbed in his newspaper that he didn't notice that the toast had burnt*

abstract
['æbstrækt]

1 *adjective*

(a) which exists only in the mind; *she has lots of abstract theories about how to reorganize society*

(b) **abstract art** = art which does not reproduce something exactly; *an abstract painting by Picasso*

2 *noun*

(a) something which exists in your mind only; **in the abstract** = in a general way

(b) an abstract painting; *he started by painting abstracts and then turned to portraits*

(c) short form of a report or document; *he was asked to make an abstract of the report*

absurd
[əb's3:d] *adjective*

silly; *it's absurd to rely on winning the lottery*

abuse
1 *noun*

[ə'bju:s]

(a) bad use; *the minister's action is an abuse of power*; *demonstrators are protesting against abuses of human rights in various parts of the world*

(b) rude words; *the strikers shouted abuse at the police*; **a term of abuse** = a rude word

(c) very bad treatment; *she suffered physical abuse in prison*; *sexual abuse of children* (NOTE: no plural for meanings (b) and (c))

2 *verb*

[ə'bju:z]

(a) to make the wrong use of; *he abused his position as finance director*; **he abused my confidence** = he took advantage of my trust in him

(b) to treat very badly, usually sexually; *as a child, she was abused by her uncle*

(c) to say rude things about someone; *the crowd sang songs abusing the president's wife*

academic
[ækɪ'demɪk]

1 *adjective*

(a) referring to study at a university; *members of the academic staff received a letter from the principal*; **academic year** = school year or university year, period which starts in September and finishes in August; *the new academic year starts next week*

(b) theoretical; *it is only of academic interest*

2 *noun*

a university teacher; *she teaches at a university and all her friends are academics*

academy
[ə'kædəmi] *noun*

(a) college where specialized subjects are taught; *a military academy*; *an academy of music*

(b) *(in Scotland)* secondary school which selects students by their exam results; *he went to Stirling Academy*

(c) private society for the study of art or science; *the Russian Academy of Sciences*; **the Royal Academy of Arts** = private London society for teaching art and putting on art exhibitions

④ **accelerate**
[æk'seləreɪt] *verb*
(a) to go faster; *he pressed down on the pedal and the car accelerated; don't accelerate when you get to traffic lights*
(b) to make something go faster; *the drug accelerates the heart rate*

④ **accent**
['æksɪnt] *noun*
(a) particular way of saying words; *she has an Irish accent; he speaks with an American accent*
(b) sign over a printed letter; **an acute accent** = sign sloping forwards over a vowel, such as é; *'résumé' has two acute accents*
(c) stress in speaking; *in the word 'accelerate' the accent is on the 'cel'*
(d) general stress; *the accent of the government's programme is on youth unemployment*

① **accept**
[ək'sept] *verb*
(a) to take a present; *we hope you will accept this little gift*
(b) to say 'yes' or to agree to something; *she accepted the offer of a job in Australia; I invited her to come with us and she accepted*
(c) to agree to handle something; *various European currencies are accepted on the ferry; 'all major credit cards accepted'; do you accept traveller's cheques?* (NOTE: do not confuse with **except**)

③ **acceptable**
[ək'septəbl] *adjective*
easily accepted; *a small gift of flowers would be very acceptable; the offer is not acceptable to the people selling the house*

③ **acceptance**
[ək'septəns] *noun*
(a) taking something which is offered; *he indicated his acceptance of the offer*
(b) agreement; *we received her letter of acceptance this morning*

③ **accepted**
[ək'septɪd] *adjective*
which is taken as correct by most people; *this is not an antiseptic in the accepted sense of the word*

① **access**
['ækses]
1 *noun*
(a) way of getting to a place; *the concert hall has access for wheelchairs; at present there is no access to the site*
(b) to have (easy) access to = to be able to get easily; *the company has access to substantial funds*
2 *verb*

to get information from a computer; *she tried to access the address list*

① **accident**
['æksɪdɪnt] *noun*
(a) something which happens by chance; *he discovered the missing papers by accident*
(b) unpleasant thing which happens and causes damage; *the accident happened or took place at a dangerous corner; she was involved in a car accident and had to go to hospital; thirty people were killed in the air accident; he missed his flight, because his bus had an accident on the way to the airport;* **industrial accident** = accident which takes place at work

④ **accidental**
[æksɪ'dentl] *adjective*
which happens by accident; *the police think his death was not accidental*

④ **accidentally**
[æksɪ'dentli] *adverb*
by chance; *he discovered the missing papers accidentally*

② **accommodation**
[əkɒmə'deɪʃn] *noun*
(a) place to live; *all the available accommodation in the town has been taken by journalists; visitors have difficulty in finding hotel accommodation during the summer; they are living in furnished accommodation*
(b) compromise, agreement; *he reached an accommodation with his creditors*
(c) accommodation address = address used for receiving messages but which is not the real address of a company (NOTE: no plural in British English but American English uses **accommodations** in the first meaning)

② **accompany**
[ə'kʌmpni] *verb*
(a) to go with; *he accompanied his wife to the hospital; the pain was accompanied by high temperature; turkey is served accompanied by roast potatoes*
(b) to play a musical instrument, when someone else plays or sings; *she sang and was accompanied on the piano by her father* (NOTE: accompanied **by** someone *or* something)

④ **accomplish**
[ə'kʌmplɪʃ] *verb*
to achieve something successfully; *what do you hope to accomplish at the meeting?; I don't think he has accomplished very much in his first year as head of the museum*

④ **accord**
[ə'kɔːd]
1 *noun*
(a) agreement; *they are still discussing the terms of the accord but we hope it will be signed today;* **with one accord** = with the agreement of everyone

(b) of your own accord = without being ordered or forced by anyone; *of his own accord he decided to sell his business and retire to a Greek island*

2 *verb*

(a) *(formal)* to give as an honour; *he was accorded a civic reception*

(b) to accord with = to agree with; *his way of behaving does not accord with his principles*

① according to
[ə'kɔːdɪŋ tu] *adverb*

(a) as someone says or writes; *the washing machine was installed according to the manufacturer's instructions; according to the witness, the car was going too fast*

(b) in relation to; *the teachers have separated the children into classes according to their ages*

④ accordingly
[ə'kɔːdɪŋli] *adverb*

as a result of something just mentioned; *we have received your letter and have changed your flight booking accordingly; he's an experienced cook and should be paid accordingly*

① account
[ə'kaʊnt]

1 *noun*

(a) bank account = arrangement which you make with a bank to keep your money safely; *I put all my savings into my bank account; this type of bank account pays 10% interest;* **to open a bank account** = to start keeping money in a bank; **to close a bank account** = to stop keeping money in a bank; **current account** *or* **cheque account** *US* **checking account** = account which pays little or no interest but from which the customer can withdraw money when he wants by writing cheques; **deposit account** = account which pays interest but on which notice usually has to be given to withdraw money; **savings account** = account where you put money in regularly and which pays interest, often at a higher rate than a deposit account

(b) *(in a shop)* arrangement which a customer has to buy goods and pay for them later; *put it on my account or charge it to my account; (of a customer)* **to open an account** = to ask a shop to supply goods which you will pay for later; *(of a shop)* **to open an account** *or* **to close an account** = to start *or* to stop supplying a customer on credit; **to settle an account** = to pay all the money owed on an account

(c) on account = as part of a total bill; **to pay money on account** = to pay to settle part of a bill

(d) on account of = because of, due to; *the trains are late on account of the fog; we don't use the car much on account of the price of petrol*

(e) I was worried on her account = I was afraid something might happen to her; **on no account** = not under any circumstances

(f) to take something into account *or* **to take account of something** = to consider something; *we have to take the weather into account*

(g) story; *they were amused by his account of the journey;* **by all accounts** = as everyone says; *by all accounts, she is a very attractive woman*

(h) the accounts of a business *or* **a company's accounts** = detailed records of a company's financial affairs; **to keep the accounts** = to write each sum of money in the account book; **profit and loss account (P&L account)** = statement of company expenditure and income over a period of time, showing whether the company has made a profit or loss; **accounts department** = department in a company which deals with money paid, received, borrowed or owed

2 *verb*

to account for = to explain; *he was asked to account for all his expenditure*

④ accountancy
[ə'kaʊntənsi] *noun*

study of the work of being an accountant; *he is studying accountancy or he is an accountancy student* (NOTE: American English uses **accounting** in this meaning)

③ accountant
[ə'kaʊntənt] *noun*

person who deals with accounts; *I send all my tax queries to my accountant; she has an appointment with her accountant to go over her tax form*

④ accounting
[ə'kaʊntɪŋ] *noun*

work of recording money paid, received, borrowed or owed (NOTE: the word **accounting** is used in the USA to mean the subject as a course of study, where British English uses **accountancy**)

④ accuracy
['ækjʊrəsi] *noun*

being correct in every detail; *accuracy is very important when drawing maps; the police doubt the accuracy of the witness' statements*

② accurate
['ækjʊrət] *adjective*

correct in all details; *are the figures accurate?; we asked them to make an accurate copy of the plan of the house*

④ accurately
['ækjʊrɪtli] *adverb*

correctly; *the weather forecast accurately predicted the storm; it is very difficult to reproduce the sound of an owl accurately*

④ accusation
[ækjʊ'zeɪʃn] *noun*

statement that someone has done wrong; *the secretary made an accusation against her boss; he denied the accusations which were made against him*

③ accuse
[ə'kjuːz] *verb*

to say that someone has done something wrong; *the police accused her of stealing the money;*

she was accused of stealing from the shop where she worked (NOTE: you accuse someone of a crime or of doing something)

④ **accused**
[əˈkjuːzd] *noun*
the accused = person or people charged with a crime; *all the accused pleaded not guilty; the police brought the accused into the court* (NOTE: can be singular or plural: **the six accused all appeared in court**)

④ **ace**
[eɪs] *noun*
(a) playing card with one spot; *he played the ace of spades*
(b) someone who is brilliant at doing something; *he's our ace salesman*
(c) *(in tennis)* service which the opposing player cannot touch; *Henman has served four aces so far*

① **achieve**
[əˈtʃiːv] *verb*
to succeed in doing something; *what do you hope the achieve by writing to your MP?; the theatre company has achieved great success in the USA; he achieved all his objectives*

② **achievement**
[əˈtʃiːvmənt] *noun*
thing which has been done successfully; *coming sixth was a great achievement, since he had never raced before; she is excessively modest about her achievements*

② **acid**
[ˈæsɪd]
1 *noun*
liquid chemical substance containing hydrogen, which burns; *the muggers threw acid in her face*
2 *adjective*
(a) sour; *the acid taste of lemons*
(b) **acid rain** = polluted rain which kills trees; *acid rain often falls a long distance away from the source of the pollution*

③ **acknowledge**
[əkˈnɒlɪdʒ] *verb*
(a) to say that something has been received; *I am writing to acknowledge receipt of your letter of the 15th; he has still not acknowledged my letter of the 24th*
(b) to admit that something is true; *in the end, they acknowledged defeat or they acknowledged that they were beaten; he acknowledged that what she said was true*

④ **acquaintance**
[əˈkweɪntəns] *noun*
(a) knowing someone; **to make the acquaintance of someone** = to get to know someone for the first time; *I made her acquaintance when we were at college together*
(b) person you know; *she has many acquaintances in the newspaper industry but no real friends*

② **acquire**
[əˈkwaɪə] *verb*
to obtain or to get; *she has acquired a large collection of shoes;* **acquired taste** = something which you come to like after a time; *hot curry is something of an acquired taste*

③ **acquisition**
[ækwɪˈzɪʃn] *noun*
(a) act of acquiring; *his acquisition of half the shares in the company shocked the staff*
(b) thing which has been acquired; *you simply must see his latest acquisition - a pink Rolls Royce!*

④ **acre**
[ˈeɪkɪ] *noun*
measure of land, 4840 square yards or 0.4047 hectares (NOTE: the plural is used with figures, except before a noun: **he has bought a farm of 250 acres** *or* **he has bought a 250-acre farm**)

① **across**
[əˈkrɒs]
1 *preposition*
(a) from one side to the other; *he helped the old lady across the street; don't run across the road without looking to see if there are any cars coming*
(b) on the other side; *he called to her from across the street;* **their house is across the street from ours** = it is just opposite our house
2 *adverb*
from one side to the other; *the river is only twenty feet across; the stream is very narrow - you can easily jump across*

① **act**
[ækt]
1 *noun*
(a) thing which is done; *he didn't forget the many acts of kindness she had shown him over the years;* **we caught him in the act** = we caught him as he was doing it
(b) part of a play, of a show; *Act II of the play takes place in the garden; the circus has acts with lions and elephants; (informal)* **to get your act together** = to organize yourself properly; *if they don't get their act together, they'll miss the last date for entries to the competition*
(c) law passed by Parliament; *an act to ban the sale of weapons*
2 *verb*
(a) to take part in a film, play, etc.; *she's acted on TV many times; he acted the part of Hamlet in the film*
(b) to do something; *you will have to act quickly if you want to stop the fire; she acted in a very responsible way;* **to act on behalf of** = to represent; *the lawyer is acting on behalf of the old lady's family;* **to act as** = to do the work of; *the thick curtain acts as a screen to cut out noise from the street*
(c) to behave; *he's started acting very strangely*

④ **acting**
['æktɪŋ]
1 *adjective*
taking the place of someone who is absent; *Mr Smith is the acting chairman while Sir James is in hospital*
2 *noun*
profession of an actor; *he has decided to make his career in acting*

① **action**
['ækʃɪn] *noun*
(a) doing something; *what action are you going to take to prevent accidents?*; **out of action** = not working; *the car has been out of action for a week*; *the goalkeeper broke his leg and will be out of action for some time*; **to take industrial action** = to do something (usually to go on strike) to show that you are not happy with conditions at work
(b) what happens in a play, film, etc.; *the action of the play takes place in a flat in London*
(c) instruction to start filming; *camera, lights, action!*
(d) case in a law court where someone sues someone else; *an action for libel or a libel action*; *to bring an action for damages against someone*; **to take legal action against someone** = to sue someone

② **active**
['æktɪv] *adjective*
(a) energetic or positive; *my grandmother is still very active at the age of 88*; *he didn't play an active part in the attack on the police station*
(b) *(volcano)* which is erupting; *scientists think the volcano is no longer active*
(c) **on active service**; *US* **on active duty** = serving in the armed services in time of war; *he was killed on active service*
(d) form of a verb which shows that the subject is doing something (NOTE: if you say 'the car hit him' the verb is active, but 'he was hit by the car' is passive)

② **actively**
['æktɪvlɪ] *adverb*
in an active way; *the store is actively recruiting new staff*

③ **activist**
['æktɪvɪst] *noun*
person who vigorously supports a political party; *the meeting was disrupted by an argument between the chairman and left-wing activists*

① **activity**
[æk'tɪvɪtɪ] *noun*
(a) being active; *there was a lot of activity on the stock market*
(b) occupation, thing you do to amuse yourself; *children are offered various winter holiday activities - sailing, skating, skiing, etc.*; **activity holiday** = planned holiday where you do certain things (such as painting, climbing rocks, etc.) (NOTE: plural in this meaning is **activities**)

③ **actor** *or* **actress**
['æktɪ or 'æktrɪs] *noun*
person who acts in the theatre, in films, on television; *a famous TV actor* (NOTE: the plural of **actress** is **actresses**)

① **actual**
['æktjʊɪl] *adjective*
real; *it looks quite small but the actual height is 5 metres*; *her actual words were much ruder than that*; **in actual fact** = really; *in spite of what the newspapers said, in actual fact he did sell his shares*

① **actually**
['æktjʊɪlɪ] *adverb*
really; *it looks quite small, but actually it is over 5 metres high*; *he told his boss he was ill, but actually he wanted to go to the football match*

④ **acute**
[ə'kjuːt] *adjective*
(a) serious illness or pain which starts suddenly and lasts for a short time; *he felt acute chest pains*; *the pain was very acute*; *compare* CHRONIC
(b) **acute angle** = angle which is less than 90°
(c) keen; *dogs have an acute sense of smell*
(d) **acute accent** = mark sloping forwards over a vowel, indicating a change of sound; *'café has an acute accent on the 'e'*

③ **ad**
[æd] *noun*
(informal) = ADVERTISEMENT; *if you want to sell your car quickly, put an ad in the paper*; **classified ads** = newspaper advertisements which are listed under special headings, such as 'jobs wanted' or 'household items for sale'; *look in the classified ads if you want a cheap cooker*; **small ads** = small advertisements for jobs, for things for sale; *I was just looking through the small ads when I saw that they wanted a gardener*

③ **adapt**
[ə'dæpt] *verb*
(a) to change something so that it fits; *the play has been adapted for the cinema*; *she adapted the story for TV*; *the car has been adapted for the disabled*
(b) to change to become more suitable; *the country will have to adapt to the new political system*

① **add**
[æd] *verb*
(a) to make a total of numbers; *if you add all these numbers together it should make fifty* (NOTE: **add** is usually shown by the plus sign + : **10 + 4 = 14**: say 'ten add four equals fourteen')
(b) to join to something else; *interest is added to the account monthly*; *add two cupfuls of sugar*; *put a tea bag into the pot and add boiling water*; *by building the extension, they have added thirty rooms to the hotel*; *this paint is too thick - add some water to it*

(c) to say or to write something more; *I have nothing to add to what I put in my letter; she added that we still owed her some money for work she did last month*

④ **addict**
['ædɪkt] *noun*
person who cannot stop doing something, especially taking drugs; **drug addict** = person who takes drugs as a habit; *a centre for drug addicts*

④ **addicted**
[ə'dɪktɪd] *adjective*
(person) who cannot stop doing something; *people addicted to alcohol can be treated at the centre*

④ **addiction**
[ə'dɪkʃn] *noun*
not being able to stop doing something; *he hopes to cure her drug addiction*

① **addition**
[ə'dɪʃn] *noun*
(a) action of adding figures to make a total; *you don't need a calculator to do a simple addition*
(b) thing or person added; *the latest addition to the family; he showed us the additions to his collection of paintings*
(c) in addition = also; **in addition to** = as well as; *there are twelve registered letters to be sent in addition to this parcel*

② **additional**
[ə'dɪʃənl] *adjective*
more; *additional duty will have to be paid*

② **additionally**
[æ'dɪʃɪnli] *adverb*
in addition; *the price includes the camera, its case and additionally six free films*

① **address**
[ə'dres]
1 *noun*
(a) details of the number of a house, the name of a street and the town where someone lives or works; *what is the doctor's address?; he wrote his address on a piece of paper; our address is: 1 Cambridge Road, Teddington, Middlesex;* **accommodation address** = address used for receiving messages but which is not the real address of a company; **business address** = address of a business (as opposed to private address); *my business address and phone number are printed on the card;* **home address** *or* **private address** = address of a house or flat where someone lives; *please send the plane tickets to my home address;* **address book** = special notebook, with columns printed in such a way that names, addresses and phone numbers can be entered; **address list** = list of addresses
(b) formal speech; *he made an address to the Parliament* (NOTE: plural is **addresses**)
2 *verb*
(a) to write the details of name, street, town, etc., on a letter or parcel; *that letter is addressed to me - don't open it!*

(b) to speak to, to write to; *please address your inquiries to the information office; teachers are not normally addressed as 'Sir' in the USA*
(c) to make a formal speech; *the chairman addressed the meeting*
(d) to examine a problem; *this is an important issue which must be addressed at the next meeting; the committee failed to address the question of sexual harassment*

③ **adequate**
['ædɪkwɪt] *adjective*
enough; *his salary is barely adequate to support his family; we don't have adequate supplies for the whole journey*

① **adjective**
['ædʒektɪv] *noun*
word which describes a noun; *in the phrase 'a big black cloud', 'big' and 'black' are both adjectives*

① **adjust**
[ə'dʒʌst] *verb*
(a) to make a slight change to; *if the trousers are too tight, we can easily adjust the fitting*
(b) to adjust to = to change and adapt to; *it's difficult adjusting to living in a tropical climate*

④ **administer**
[əd'mɪnɪstə] *verb*
(a) *(a country, an office, a company)* to manage, to organize; *the province was administered by Portugal for many years*
(b) *(formal)* to give; *to administer a drug to a patient*
(c) *(formal)* **to administer an oath** = to make someone swear an oath

② **administration**
[ədmɪnɪ'streɪʃn] *noun*
(a) action of organizing; *hospital administration must be improved; who's in charge of administration here?*
(b) the administration = the government; *the Major Administration*
(c) the administration of justice = providing justice

③ **administrative**
[əd'mɪnɪstrətɪv] *adjective*
referring to administration; *his duties are almost entirely administrative; administrative expenses are rising all the time; there are more administrative staff than workers*

④ **admiration**
[ædmɪ'reɪʃn] *noun*
respect for; *I have great admiration for her; everyone looked on in admiration as she showed us how to skate*

③ **admire**
[əd'maɪə] *verb*
to look at someone *or* something with respect; *we admired his garden; everyone admires her paintings; he was admired for his skill as a rally driver; a much-admired chief minister*

admission
[əd'mɪʃn] *noun*
(a) being allowed to enter; *there is a £1 admission charge; admission to the exhibition is free on Sundays; my friend was refused admission to the restaurant because he was not wearing a tie*
(b) statement saying that something is true; *his admission of fraud; her admission that she had taken the watch*

admit
[əd'mɪt] *verb*
(a) to allow someone to go in; *children are admitted free, but adults have to pay; this ticket admits three persons*
(b) to say that something is true; *he admitted stealing the car; she admitted she had taken the watch* (NOTE: admitting - admitted)

adolescent
[ædɪ'lesɪnt]
1 *adjective*
referring to the period between being a child and being an adult; *she teaches a class of adolescent boys*
2 *noun*
young person between 12 and 18; *all adolescents rebel against the authority of their parents*

adopt
[ə'dɒpt] *verb*
(a) to take legally as a son or daughter; *they have adopted a little boy*
(b) to take; *the opposition parties have adopted a different line of argument; he adopted an air of deep depression*
(c) to tell all students to use; *the book has been adopted for use in all English classes*
(d) *(of a political party)* to choose a candidate; *James Black was adopted as the candidate for our constituency*

adult
['ædʌlt]
1 *adjective*
(a) fully grown; *an adult lion*
(b) referring to grown-up people; **adult education** = teaching people over the age of 20
2 *noun*
grown-up person; *children are admitted free, but adults have to pay*

advance
[əd'vɑːns]
1 *noun*
(a) movement forwards; *the police have made some advances in their fight against crime*
(b) in advance = early; *if you want to get good seats for the play, you need to book three weeks in advance; you must phone well in advance to make an appointment; they asked us to pay £200 in advance*
(c) money paid as a loan or as a part of a payment to be made later; *she received an advance from the purchaser; can I have an advance of £50 against next month's salary?*
2 *verb*
(a) to go forward; *the police slowly advanced across the square*
(b) to pay as a loan; *he advanced me £100*
(c) to bring a date forward; *the date of the meeting has been advanced by a week*
(d) to move a clock to a later time; *when crossing from England to France, watches should be advanced by one hour; see also* PUT FORWARD

advanced
[əd'vɑːnst] *adjective*
(a) which is studied after studying for several years'; *he is taking advanced mathematics; she is studying for an advanced degree;* **advanced level examination (A level)** = examination taken at about 18, at the end of secondary school, which is used as a basis for entry to university or college
(b) which has moved forward; *in an advanced state of decay*

advantage
[əd'vɑːntɪdʒ] *noun*
thing which will help you to be successful; *being able to drive a car is an advantage; knowledge of two foreign languages is an advantage in this job; she has several advantages over the other candidates for the job;* **to take advantage of** = to profit from; *they took advantage of the cheap fares on offer;* **to take advantage of someone** = to cheat someone; *he took advantage of the old lady;* **to advantage** = to make someone look perfect; *her dress shows off her figure to advantage;* **to use to great advantage** = to use in a way which helps you win

adventure
[əd'ventʃə] *noun*
new, exciting and dangerous experience; *I must tell you about our adventures in the Gobi desert*

adverb
['ædvɜːb] *noun*
word which modifies a verb, an adjective, another adverb or a whole sentence; *in the phrase 'he walked slowly, because the snow was very thick', 'slowly' and 'very' are both adverbs*

advertise
['ædvɪtaɪz] *verb*
to make sure that people know that something is for sale, that something is going to happen, that a show is on; *there are posters all over the town advertising the circus; I sent away for a watch which I saw advertised in the paper; did you see that the restaurant is advertising cheap meals on Sundays?; the company is advertising for secretaries*

③ **advertisement**
[əd'vɜːtɪzmənt] *noun*
announcement which tries to make sure that people know that something is for sale, that something is going to happen, that a show is on; *he put an advertisement in the paper*; *she answered an advertisement in the paper*; **classified advertisements** = advertisements listed in a newspaper under special headings, such as 'property for sale' or 'jobs wanted'

① **advertising**
['ædvɪtaɪzɪŋ] *noun*
the action of making sure that people know that something is for sale, that something is going to happen, that a show is on; *they spent millions on the advertising campaign*; *the company has increased the amount of money it spends on advertising*; **advertising agency** = agency which organizes advertisements for other companies

① **advice**
[əd'vaɪs] *noun*
saying what should be done; *he went to the bank manager for advice on how to pay his debts*; *they would not listen to the doctor's advice*; *my grandfather gave me a very useful piece of advice*; *his mother's advice was to stay in bed*; *she took or followed the doctor's advice and stopped smoking* (NOTE: no plural: **some advice**; for one item say **a piece of advice**)

① **advise**
[əd'vaɪz] *verb*
to suggest what should be done; *he advised her to put all her money into a deposit account*

① **advise against**
[əd'vaɪz ə'genst] *verb*
to suggest that something should not be done; *he advised against buying the house*

③ **adviser** *or* **advisor**
[əd'vaɪzə] *noun*
person who gives advice; *he is consulting his financial adviser*

④ **advocate**
1 *noun*
['ædvɪkɪt] person who pleads for a cause; *the advocates of capital punishment*
2 ['ædvɪkeɪt] *verb*
to recommend; *she advocates the introduction of capital punishment*

① **affair**
[ə'feə] *noun*
(a) thing which concerns someone; *that's his affair - it's nothing to do with me*; *it's an affair for the police*; *she's always sticking her nose into other people's affairs*; *his business affairs were very complicated*
(b) (love) **affair** = sexual relationship; *he's having an affair with his boss's wife*
(c) **state of affairs** = general situation; *the present state of affairs*
(d) **affairs of state** = government business

① **affect**
[ə'fekt] *verb*
to have an influence on, to change; *the new regulations have affected our business*; *train services have been seriously affected by the strike*

④ **affection**
[ə'fekʃn] *noun*
liking or love; *she felt great affection for her youngest grandson*

① **afford**
[ə'fɔːd] *verb*
to have enough money to pay for; *we can't afford to run a large car these days*; *he couldn't afford the time to take a holiday* (NOTE: only used after **can, cannot, could, could not, able to**)

① **afraid**
[ə'freɪd] *adjective*
(a) to be afraid of something = to be frightened of something; *I am afraid of snakes*; *she is afraid of going out alone*; *he's too afraid to climb the ladder*
(b) to be afraid (that) = to be sorry to say; *I'm afraid that all the cakes have been sold*; *you can't see the boss - I'm afraid he's ill*; *have you got a pocket calculator? - no, I'm afraid not* (NOTE: **afraid** cannot be used in front of a noun: **the girl's afraid** but **a frightened girl**)

① **Africa**
['æfrɪkə] *proper noun*
large continent, to the south of the Mediterranean, between the Atlantic Ocean and the Indian Ocean; *they want to go to Africa on holiday*; *after ten days at sea, they saw the coast of North Africa in the distance*

① **African**
['æfrɪkən]
1 *adjective*
referring to Africa; *the African jungle*; **African elephant** = type of elephant with large ears (the other type is the Indian elephant)
2 *noun*
person from Africa; *the guitarist is an African*

④ **African-American**
['æfrɪkənˈmerɪkən] *noun*
black person living in the United States

① **after**
['ɑːftɪ]
1 *preposition*
(a) following or next in order; *what's the letter after Q in the alphabet?*; *if today is Tuesday, the day after tomorrow is Thursday*; *they spoke one after the other*; **after you** = you go first; **after you with the milk** = pass me the milk when you have finished with it
(b) later than; *we arrived after six o'clock*; *he should be in bed - it's after ten o'clock*; *we don't let the children go out alone after dark*

(c) to be after someone = (i) to be looking for someone; (ii) to be angry with someone; *the police are after him*; *if you leave mud all over the kitchen floor, your mother will be after you*; *what's she after?* = what does she want?

2 *conjunction* later than a time; *after the snow fell, the motorways were blocked*; *after the driver had got in, the coach started*; *phone me after you get home* (NOTE: **after** is used with many verbs: **look after**, **take after**, etc.)

ⓘ **after all**
['ɑːftɪ 'ɔːl] *adverb*

(a) in spite of everything; *she changed her mind and decided to come with us after all*

(b) the fact is; *I think I'll go out in the car - after all, it's a fine day and I've finished my work*

ⓘ **afternoon**
[ɑːftɪ'nuːn] *noun*

time between lunchtime and the evening; *he always has a little sleep in the afternoon*; *the shop is closed on Wednesday afternoons*; *can we meet this afternoon?*; *there is an afternoon flight to Paris*; *I'm playing tennis tomorrow afternoon*; **afternoon tea** = meal taken in the afternoon, usually with small sandwiches, cakes, and tea

ⓘ **afterwards** *US* **afterward**
['ɑːftɪwɪdz or 'ɑːftɪwɪd] *adverb*

later; *we'll have lunch first and go shopping afterwards*; *she felt fine before dinner but was ill afterwards*

ⓘ **again**
[ə'gen] *adverb*

(a) another time, once more; *he wrote again to say he was ill*; *we'd love to come to see you again*; *he had to take his driving test again*

(b) back as you were before; *although I like going on holiday, I'm always glad to be home again*; *she brought the jeans back to the shop again because they didn't fit*

◊ **once again**
['wʌns 'gein] another time; *once again, the train was late*

◊ **yet again**
['jet ə'gein] once more after many times; *she's taking her driving test yet again*

ⓘ **against**
[ə'genst] *preposition*

(a) touching; *he was leaning against the wall*; *she hit her head against the low doorway*

(b) not as someone suggests; **it's against the rules** *or* **against the law** = it's not as the rules say *or* as the law says; *it's against the law to drive in the dark without lights*; *you mustn't hold the football in your hands - it's against the rules*; *what do you have against the plan?* = why don't you agree with the plan?; *she was against the idea of going to the cinema*

(c) opposite; *England is playing against South Africa tomorrow*; *it's hard cycling uphill against the wind*

(d) as part of; *can I have an advance against next month's salary?*

ⓘ **age**
[eidʒ] *noun*

(a) the number of years which you have lived; *what age will he be on his next birthday?*; *she is thirty years of age*; *he looks younger than his age*; **old age** = period when you are old; **under age** = younger than the legal age to do something; *the government is taking action against under-age drinking*

(b) **ages** = a very long time; *I've been waiting here for ages*; *it took us ages to get served*

ⓘ **aged**
adjective

(a) [eidʒd] with the age of; *a girl aged nine*; *she died last year, aged 83*

(b) ['eidʒid] very old; *an aged man* (NOTE: in this meaning, it comes before the noun)

ⓘ **agency**
['eidʒinsi] *noun*

office which represents another firm; *we have the agency for Ford cars*; *an advertising agency*; **estate agency** = office which arranges for the sale of houses, flats, etc.; **travel agency** = office which sells air tickets, organizes tours, etc. (NOTE: plural is **agencies**)

ⓘ **agenda**
[ə'dʒendə] *noun*

list of points for discussion; *we will now take item five on the agenda*; *after two hours we were still discussing the first item on the agenda*; *what's on the agenda?* = what are we going to discuss?

ⓘ **agent**
['eidʒint] *noun*

person who works for or represents someone else; *our head office is in London but we have an agent in Paris*; **travel agent** = person who sells tickets, organizes tours, etc.; *I bought my plane tickets at the travel agent's*

ⓘ **aggressive**
[ə'gresiv] *adjective*

ready to attack; *she's very aggressive towards her family*; *the team played an extremely aggressive game and were warned by the referee*

ⓘ **ago**
[ə'gəʊ] *adverb*

in the past; *he phoned a few minutes ago*; *she came to England two years ago*; *this all happened a long time ago* (NOTE: **ago** always follows a word meaning time)

ⓘ **agree**
[ə'griː] *verb*

(a) to say yes; *we asked her to come with us and she agreed*; *he nodded to show that he agreed*;

most of the group agreed with her suggestion;
after some discussion he agreed to our plan
(NOTE: you agree **to** or **on** a plan)
(b) to agree with someone = to think the same
way as someone; *I agree with you that most*
people drive too fast
(c) not to agree with someone = to make
someone ill; *all this rich food does not agree*
with me
(d) to agree to do something = to say that you
will do something; *she agreed to baby-sit for us;*
the bank will never agree to lend the company
£250,000

① **agreement**
[ə'gri:mənt] *noun*
(a) thinking the same; *to reach an agreement or*
to come to an agreement on salaries;
agreement between the two sides is still a long
way off; **they are in agreement with our plan** =
they agree with our plan; *we discussed the plan*
with them and they are in agreement
(b) contract; *we signed an agreement with the*
Italian company; **to draw up** or **to draft an**
agreement

② **agricultural**
[ægrɪ'kʌltʃɪrl] *adjective*
referring to agriculture; *agricultural machinery*

② **agriculture**
['ægrɪkʌltʃɪ] *noun*
growing crops or raising animals on farms; *not*
many people work in agriculture compared
with fifty years ago; the country's agriculture is
based on rice

③ **ah**
[ɑ:] *interjection showing surprise; Ah! Wilkins,*
how nice to see you!; the circus audience let
out 'oohs' and 'ahs' as they watched the lions

① **ahead**
[ə'hed] *adverb*
in front; *our team was losing, but now we are*
ahead again; run on ahead and find some seats
for us; you need to go straight ahead, and then
turn left; **full steam ahead!** = go forwards as
fast as possible; **to draw ahead** = to become the
leader in a race, etc.

① **ahead of**
[ə'hed 'ɒv] *preposition*
(a) in front of; *ahead of us was a steep hill; you*
have a mass of work ahead of you; they ran on
ahead of the others
(b) *(informal)* before; *they drafted in extra*
police ahead of the international match

② **aid**
[eɪd] *noun*
(a) help; *aid to Third World countries; aid*
agency; aid worker
(b) first aid = help for injured people; *we keep a*
first aid kit in the office
(c) in aid of = to help; *we give money in aid of*
the Red Cross; they are collecting money in aid
of refugees; (informal) **what's all this in aid of?**
= what's all the fuss about?

(d) device which helps; *he wears a hearing aid;*
food processors are useful aids in the kitchen

② **aim**
[eɪm]
1 *noun*
what you are trying to do; *his aim is to do well at*
school and then go to university; one of our
aims is to increase the speed of service
2 *verb*
(a) to plan to do something; *we aim to go on*
holiday in June
(b) to point a weapon at something; *he was not*
aiming at the target

① **air**
[eə]
1 *noun*
(a) mixture of gases (mainly oxygen and
nitrogen) which cannot be seen, but which is all
around us and which every animal breathes; *his*
breath was like steam in the cold air; the
mountain air feels cold; he threw the ball up
into the air
(b) method of travelling (or sending goods)
using aircraft; **air fares** = different types of fares
charged for travel on aircraft; **air letter** = a
special sheet of thin blue paper which when
folded can be sent by air mail without an
envelope
(b) little tune; *she played an air by Bach*
(c) appearance or feeling; *there was an air of*
gloom over the meeting
2 *verb*
to make (a room, clothes, etc.) fresher; *let's open*
the windows to air the bedroom

◊ **by air**
['baɪ 'eə]
in an aircraft; *we are going to France by ferry,*
not by air; send the letter by air if you want it to
arrive before Christmas

④ **air-conditioner**
['eə kɪn'dɪʃɪnɪ] *noun*
device which cools the air in a room; *how can*
we turn the air-conditioner off?

④ **air-conditioning**
['eə kɪn'dɪʃɪnɪŋ] *noun*
system of controlling the temperature in a room
or office or train, etc.; *if you hire a car in Texas,*
make sure it has air-conditioning; **to turn the**
air-conditioning on = to start the making the air
cooler; **to turn the air-conditioning off** = to
stop the air being cooled; **to turn the**
air-conditioning down = to make a room
warmer; **to turn the air-conditioning up** = to
make a room cooler

② **aircraft**
['eəkrɑ:ft] *noun*
machine which flies in the air; *the passengers*
got into the aircraft; the airline has a fleet of
ten aircraft; the president came down the
aircraft steps (NOTE: plural is **aircraft: one**
aircraft, six aircraft)

④ **air force**
['eɪ 'fɔːs] *noun*
the organization that runs a country's fighting planes; *he's joined the Belgian Air Force*; *American Air Force fighters*

② **airline**
['eɪlaɪn] *noun*
company which runs air services; *which airline are you flying with?*; *he's an airline pilot*; *the airline has been voted the most popular with business travellers*

③ **airmail**
['eɪmeɪl]
1 *noun*
way of sending letters or parcels by air; *we sent the package by airmail*; **airmail envelope** = very light envelope for sending airmail letters; **airmail sticker** = blue sticker with the words 'by air mail' which can be stuck to an envelope or packet to show it is being sent by air
2 *verb*
to send letters or parcels by air; *we airmailed the documents to New York*

④ **airplane**
['eɪpleɪn] *noun*
US aircraft; *the president came down the airplane steps*

② **airport**
['eɪpɔːt] *noun*
place where aircraft land and take off; *you can take the underground to the airport*; *we are due to arrive at London Airport at 6 p.m.*; *we leave from London Airport at 10.00*; **airport bus** = bus which takes passengers to and from an airport; *there is an airport bus which takes passengers to the centre of town*

② **alarm**
[ə'lɑːm]
1 *noun*
(a) loud warning; *an alarm will sound if someone touches the wire*; **to raise the alarm** = to warn everyone of danger; *it was only a false alarm* = it was only a wrong warning
(b) burglar alarm = device which rings if a burglar enters a building; **fire alarm** = bell which sounds if there is a fire; **alarm bell** = bell which rings to warn people; **alarm (clock)** = clock which can be set to ring a bell at a certain time to wake you up; *I set my alarm for 5.30 because I had to catch the 7 o'clock plane*
(c) being afraid; *the expression on his face increased her alarm*; *there's no cause for alarm, the injection won't hurt at all*
2 *verb*
to warn or frighten; *I don't want to alarm you, but the police say a dangerous criminal has been seen in the village*

③ **album**
['ælbɪm] *noun*
(a) large book; *an album of photos* or *a photo album*; *he showed me his stamp album*

(b) collections of songs on a CD, cassette, etc.; *this is her latest album*

③ **alcohol**
['ælkɪhɒl] *noun*
liquid, such as beer, wine, etc., which can make you drunk; *they will not serve alcohol to anyone under the age of 18*

④ **alcoholic**
[ælkɪ'hɒlɪk]
1 *adjective*
referring to alcohol; *they served alcoholic drinks as well as fruit juice*
2 *noun*
person who is addicted to alcohol; *she went to a clinic for alcoholics*

④ **alert**
[ə'lɜːt]
1 *adjective*
(a) able to think clearly; *after a short sleep he was bright and alert*
(b) watching carefully; *the guard must remain alert at all times*
2 *noun*
warning signal; *he gave the alert*; **to be on the alert** = to watch out for something
3 *verb*
to alert someone to = to warn someone of something; *she was alerted to the dangers of smoking*

② **A Level**
['eɪ 'levɪl] = ADVANCED LEVEL
examination taken at about 18, at the end of secondary school; *if you pass your A Levels, you can go on to university*

④ **alien**
['eɪliɪn]
1 *adjective*
foreign, different; *speaking foreign languages is alien to the British way of life*
2 *noun*
foreigner, a person who is not a citizen of the country; *aliens are not permitted to travel outside the capital*; *when you arrive at the airport, you must go through the door marked 'aliens'*

④ **alike**
[ə'laɪk] *adjective*
very similar; *the two sisters are very alike*

② **alive**
[ə'laɪv] *adjective*
(a) not dead; *he was still alive when he was rescued, even though he had been in the sea for hours*; *when my grandfather was alive, there was no television* (NOTE: alive cannot be used in front of a noun: the fish is alive but a live fish)
(b) lively; *the fishing village is rather dead during the day time, but really comes alive at night*

① **all**
[ɔːl]
1 *adjective & pronoun*
everything *or* everyone; *did you pick all (of) the*

tomatoes?; *where are all the children?*; *they all like coffee or all of them like coffee*; *all trains stop at Clapham Junction*; *let's sing the song all together* = everyone at the same time

2 *adverb*

(a) completely; *the ground was all white after the snow fell*; *I forgot all about her birthday*

(b) all by yourself = all alone; *you can't do it all by yourself*; *I'm all by myself this evening - my girlfriend's gone out*; *he drove the lorry all by himself*

◊ **not at all**

['nɒt ət 'ɔːl]

certainly not; *do you mind waiting for a few minutes? - not at all!*; *she wasn't at all annoyed*

◊ **all along**

['ɔːl ə'lɒŋ] *adverb*

(a) along the whole length of; *police were stationed all along the route of the procession*

(b) right from the beginning; *I knew all along that he was cheating me*; *we suspected all along that something was wrong*

◊ **all at once**

['ɔːl ət 'wʌns]

suddenly; *all at once the telephone rang*

◊ **all the same**

['ɔːl ðɪ 'seɪm] *phrase*

(a) in spite of this; *I'm not really keen on horror films, but I'll go with you all the same*

(b) it's all the same = it makes no difference; *if it's all the same to you, I won't come to the party*

④ **allegation**

[ælɪ'geɪʃn] *noun*

suggestion that someone has possibly done something wrong; *she made several allegations about her boss*; *he denied the allegations made against him*

④ **allege**

[ə'ledʒ] *verb*

to suggest that someone may have done something wrong; *the police alleged that the accused was inside the building when the theft took place*

④ **alleged**

[ə'ledʒd] *adjective*

suggested; *the alleged victim refused to make a statement to the police*

④ **allergy**

['ælədʒi] *noun*

bad reaction to a substance; *she has an allergy to household dust*; *the baby has a tomato allergy*

③ **alliance**

[ə'laɪəns] *noun*

formal link between two groups or countries; *the alliance between England and France*

① **allied**

['ælaɪd] *adjective*

(a) linked in an alliance; *the allied powers*

(b) allied to = linked with; *his poor health allied to his age means that he will not be able to run the marathon*

③ **all in**

['ɔːl 'ɪn] *adjective*

(a) including everything; *they quoted us an all-in price of £250.00*

(b) *(informal)* tired out; *after moving all my stuff to my new flat I was all in*

② **allocate**

['æləkeɪt] *verb*

to give out to various people; *we have allocated £2,500 to buying furniture for the office*; *our group were allocated rooms at the back of the hotel*

③ **all over**

['ɔːl 'əʊvə] *phrase*

(a) everywhere; *his trousers were dirty all over*

(b) finished; *the show was all over by nine o'clock*

① **allow**

[ə'laʊ] *verb*

(a) to let someone do something; *she allowed me to borrow her book*; *smoking is not allowed in the restaurant*; *you are allowed to take two pieces of hand luggage onto the plane*

(b) to give; *we will allow you a discount*

(c) to agree or to accept legally; *to allow a claim for damages*

① **allowance**

[ə'laʊəns] *noun*

(a) money paid regularly; *she gets a weekly allowance from her father*

(b) something which is allowed; **baggage allowance** = weight of baggage which an air passenger is allowed to take free when he or she travels

(c) amount of money which you are allowed to earn without paying tax; *allowances for married couples have been increased in the budget*

(d) to make allowances for = to take something into account; *you must make allowances for his age*

① **all right**

['ɔːl 'raɪt]

1 *adjective*

well; *she was ill yesterday but is all right now*

2 *interjection (meaning 'yes')*

all right, here's your money; *will you answer the telephone for me? - all right!* (NOTE: **OK** and **no problem** are often used in this meaning)

③ **ally**

1 *noun*

['ælaɪ] person who is on the same side; *he's a close ally of the leader of the opposition*; *when one of our allies is attacked, we have to come to their defence* (NOTE: plural is **allies**)

2 *verb*

[ə'laɪ]

to **ally yourself with** *or* to someone = to join forces with someone; *the nationalists have allied themselves with the government party*

① **almost**
['ɒlmɪʊst] *adverb*
nearly; *London is almost as far from here as Paris; she's almost as tall as I am; she'll eat almost anything; hurry up, it's almost time for the train to leave*

① **alone**
[ə'ləʊn]
1 *adjective*
with no one else; *she lives alone with her cats; he was all alone in the shop; we don't let the children go out alone after dark;* **I want to talk to you alone** = just the two of us together
2 *adverb*
(a) to **leave someone alone** = not to bother someone; *leave that cat alone and come and have your tea*
(b) **let alone** = and certainly not; *he can't ride a bike let alone drive a car*

① **along**
[ə'lɒŋ]
1 *preposition*
(a) by the side of; *he has planted fruit trees along both sides of the garden path; the river runs along one side of the castle*
(b) from one end to the other; *she ran along the pavement; walk along the street until you come to the post office*
2 *adverb (with verbs)*
(a) to **get along with someone** = to agree with or to work well with someone; *she doesn't get along very well with her new boss; they don't get along very well together*
(b) to go with, to come with, etc.; *come along to the party; after the accident, she was taken along to the police station*

③ **alongside**
[əlɒŋ'saɪd]
1 *preposition* beside; *the ship was tied up alongside the wharf*
2 *adverb*
beside; *we had stopped at a red light when a police car pulled up alongside*

④ **aloud**
[ə'laʊd] *adverb*
in a voice which can be heard; *she read the poem aloud; he insists on reading the football scores out aloud*

④ **alphabet**
['ælfɪbet] *noun*
series of letters in order, A, B, C, etc.; *A is the first letter of the alphabet, and B is the second; G comes before L in the alphabet; if you're going to Greece on holiday, you ought to learn the Greek alphabet*

④ **alphabetical**
[ælfɪ'betɪkl] *adjective*
referring to the alphabet; **in alphabetical order** = in order of the first letter of each word; *the*

words in the dictionary are in alphabetical order; the computer will sort out the addresses into alphabetical order

① **already**
[ɔːl'redɪ] *adverb*
(a) before now, before a certain time; *I've already done my shopping; it was already past ten o'clock when he arrived;* **I have seen that film already** = I've seen that film before
(b) sooner than expected; *have you finished your work already?*

① **also**
['ɔːlsɪʊ] *adverb*
too, as well as; *she sings well and can also play the violin; they came to visit us, and their children also came*

③ **alter**
['ɒltɪ] *verb*
to change; *they wanted to alter the terms of the contract after they had signed it; he has altered so much I didn't recognize him*

④ **alternate**
1 *adjective*
[ɔːl'tɜːnɪt] every other one; *we see each other on alternate Sundays*
2 *verb*
['ɔːltɪneɪt] to put something in place of something, then switch them round; *fill the pot with alternating slices of potato and onion; she alternated between excitement and despair as she waited for her exam results*

② **alternative**
[ɔːl'tɜːnɪtɪv]
1 *adjective*
(a) in place of something else; *if the plane is full, we will put you on an alternative flight*
(b) following a different way from usual; **alternative energy** = energy produced by tides, the wind, etc.; **alternative medicine** = treating diseases by means which are not normally used by doctors (such as medicines made from herbs, etc.); **alternative source of energy** = means of providing energy from the tide, the wind, the sun, etc., rather than by using coal, oil or nuclear power
2 *noun*
something which takes the place of something else; *now that she's got measles, do we have any alternative to calling the holiday off?;* **there is no alternative** = there is nothing else we can do

① **although**
[ɔːl'ðɒʊ] *conjunction*
in spite of the fact that; *although it was freezing, she didn't put a coat on; I've never been into that shop although I've often walked past it*

① **altogether**
[ɔːltɪ'geðɪ] *adverb*
(a) taking everything together; *the food was £10 and the drinks £5, so that makes £15 altogether; the staff of the three shops come to 200 altogether*

(b) completely; *he's altogether a happier man since he got married*; *their situation is altogether different from ours*

④ **aluminium** *US* **aluminum**
[ælju'minjim or ə'luːminəm] *noun*

extremely light silver metal; *we were given a set of aluminium saucepans for our wedding* (NOTE: Chemical element: chemical symbol: **Al**; atomic number: **13**)

① **always**
['ɔːlweɪz] *adverb*

(a) every time; *she is always late for work*; *why does it always rain when we want to go for a walk?*

(b) continually; *it's always hot in tropical countries*

(c) again and again; *she's always asking me to lend her money*

① **am**
[æm] *see* BE

① **a.m.** *US* **A.M.**
['ei 'em] *adverb*

in the morning, before 12 o'clock; *I have to catch the 7 a.m. train to work every day*; *telephone calls made before 6 a.m. are charged at the cheap rate* (NOTE: **a.m.** is usually used to show the exact hour and the word **o'clock** is left out)

④ **amateur**
['æmɪtɪ]

1 *noun*

(a) sportsman who is not paid to play; *the golf tournament is open to amateurs*

(b) someone who does something because he likes doing it; *for an amateur he's a very good painter*

2 *adjective*

(a) not paid; *he plays for the local amateur football team*

(b) doing something as a hobby rather than to earn money; *he's an amateur painter*; *our amateur theatre club is putting on 'Henry V'*

④ **amaze**
[ə'meiz] *verb*

to surprise very much; *your attitude amazes me*; *they were amazed at the sounds and colours of the market*

② **amazing**
[ə'meizɪŋ] *adjective*

(a) very surprising; *it was amazing that she never suspected anything*

(b) extremely interesting and unusual; *it was an amazing experience, sailing down the Nile*

④ **ambassador**
[æm'bæsɪdɪ] *noun*

the representative of a country in another country; *His Excellency, the French Ambassador*

④ **ambition**
[æm'bɪʃn] *noun*

desire to become great, rich or famous, or to do something special; *his great ambition is to ride on an elephant*

① **ambulance**
['æmbjulns] *noun*

van which carries sick or injured people; *when she fell down the stairs, her husband called an ambulance*; *he pulled into the side of the road when he saw the ambulance coming*

④ **ambush**
['æmbuʃ]

1 *noun*

surprise attack by people who have been hiding; *the guerrillas lay in ambush beside the path* (NOTE: plural is **ambushes**)

2 *verb*

to wait hidden and attack someone by surprise; *the soldiers were ambushed as they went along the mountain path*

③ **amend**
[ə'mend] *verb*

to change for the better; *the Prime Minister amended the text of the speech in several places*

③ **amendment**
[ə'mendmənt] *noun*

(a) change; *he has made several amendments to the text*

(b) proposed change to a law, to a proposal; *to propose an amendment to the constitution*; *see also* FIFTH

① **America**
[ə'merikə] *proper noun*

(a) one of two large continents between the Atlantic and Pacific Oceans; *in the year 1492 Columbus discovered America*; *they went to America by boat across the Atlantic*; *see also* CENTRAL AMERICA, NORTH AMERICA, SOUTH AMERICA

(b) the United States; *she spent all her savings on a holiday in America*; *send your furniture to America by sea - it would be much too expensive by air*

① **American**
[ə'merikən]

1 *adjective*

referring to America or to the United States of America; *an American dollar*; *the American president*; *I'm letting my house to an American family for the summer*; *I'm reading about the American presidential election*; *his wife is American*

2 *noun*

person from the United States of America; *I met a group of Americans on the train*; *the Americans won several gold medals at the Olympics*

④ **amid**
[ə'mɪd] *preposition (formal)*
in the middle of; *the family stood amid the ruins of their shop*

④ **ammunition**
[æmju'nɪʃn] *noun*
bullets, shells, etc.; *they fought all day until they started to run out of ammunition*; *the football fans used bottles as ammunition against the police* (NOTE: no plural)

① **among** *or* **amongst**
[ə'mʌŋ or ə'mʌŋst] *preposition*
(a) surrounded by, in the middle of; *to make a camp, we put up tents among the trees*; *among the people at the party was a woman who does the TV weather forecasts*; *he was standing amongst a crowd of tourists*
(b) between various people in a group; *the Christmas cake was divided among the class of children*; *we had to share one towel amongst the three of us*

① **amount**
[ə'maʊnt] *noun*
quantity of something, such as money; *the amount in my bank account has reached £1,000*; *this make of car uses by far the least amount of petrol*; **a certain amount** = some; *the storm did a certain amount of damage*; *painting the house will take a certain amount of time*

① **amount to**
[ə'maʊnt tu] *verb*
(a) to make a total of; *the total bill amounts to over £100*
(b) **to amount to the same thing** = to mean the same, to be the same; *whether he took cash or free holidays, it all amounts to the same thing*

④ **ample**
['æmpl] *adjective*
plenty, enough; *we have ample funds to pay for the development programme*; *four hours should be ample time to get to Glasgow*

④ **amuse**
[ə'mju:z] *verb*
(a) to make someone laugh; *the story about the Prime Minister's cat will amuse you*; *I was amused to hear that you and Jim are sharing an office*
(b) to make the time pass in a pleasant way; **to amuse yourself** = to play, to get pleasure from what you are doing; *the children amused themselves quietly while their parents talked*

④ **amusement**
[ə'mju:zmənt] *noun*
(a) pleasure; *when rain stopped the tennis match, the group sang for the crowd's amusement*; **amusement park** = open-air park with various types of entertainment, such as roundabouts, shooting galleries, etc.
(b) **to someone's amusement** = making someone laugh; *much to her amusement, the band played 'Happy Birthday to you!'*

(c) **amusements** = things which amuse people; *there are all sorts of amusements on cross-Channel ferries*

④ **amusing**
[ə'mju:zɪŋ] *adjective*
which makes you laugh; *it was amusing to hear about your journey*; *he stayed late, telling us amusing stories about his life in the army*

① **an**
[æn or ən]
see A

④ **anaesthetic** *US* **anesthetic**
[ænɪs'θetɪk] *noun*
substance given to a patient to remove feeling, so that he or she can have an operation without feeling pain; **general anaesthetic** = substance given to make a patient lose consciousness so that a major operation can be carried out; *you will have to be given a general anaesthetic for this operation*; **local anaesthetic** = substance which removes the feeling in a certain part of the body only; *she had an operation to her leg under local anaesthetic*; *this operation can be carried out under local rather than general anaesthetic*

③ **analyse** *or* **analyze**
['ænɪlaɪz] *verb*
to examine closely and scientifically; *to analyse the market for computer games*; *when the food was analysed it was found to contain bacteria*

① **analysis**
[ə'nælɪsɪs] *noun*
close examination; *to make an analysis of the sales or a sales analysis*; *to carry out an analysis of the market* (NOTE: plural is **analyses** [ə'nælɪsi:z])

④ **analyst**
['ænɪlɪst] *noun*
(a) person who carries out analyses; *political analysts are examining the results of the election*; **systems analyst** = person who examines computer systems
(b) doctor who is trained in analysing the psychology of patients; *my analyst says I haven't got an Oedipus complex*

④ **ancestor**
['ænsestɪ] *noun*
member of your family a long time ago; *his ancestors built a castle here in the 13th century*

④ **anchor**
['æŋkɪ]
1 *noun*
large metal hook which holds a ship in place; *the ship was at anchor in the harbour*; **to drop anchor** = to let the anchor fall to the bottom of the sea to hold a ship in the same place; *the ship dropped anchor in the harbour*
2 *verb*
(a) *(of ship)* to drop an anchor to stay in the same place; *the ship anchored in the mouth of the river*

(b) to hold firm; *the hot air balloon was anchored to the ground with cables*

② **ancient**
['eɪnʃɪnt] *adjective*
very old; *she's studying ancient history; he was riding an ancient bicycle; see also* MONUMENT

① **and**
[ænd or nd] *conjunction; used to join two words or phrases*
all my uncles and aunts live in the country; use a knife and fork to eat your meat; the children were running about and singing; come and sit down next to me (NOTE: **and** is used to say numbers after 100: **seven hundred and two = 702**)

① **and so on**
[nd 'sɪʊ ɒn] *adverb*
with other things; *he talked about plants: flowers, vegetables, and so on*

④ **angel**
['eɪndʒl] *noun*
(a) being who lives in the sky; *she dreamt she was flying in the sky with the angels*
(b) *(informal)* sweet, kind person; *be an angel and get me my slippers*
(c) *(informal)* person who backs a new business or a theatre production financially; *the play failed and the angels lost all their money*

③ **anger**
['æŋgɪ]
1 *noun*
being annoyed; *I felt no anger, only great disappointment*
2 *verb*
to make someone annoyed; *her being late angered him*

③ **angle**
['æŋgl] *noun*
(a) corner between two lines; *she planted the tree in the angle of the two walls*; **acute angle** = angle less than 90°; **right angle** = 90° angle
(b) point of view; *what's the government's angle on the story?*

④ **angrily**
['æŋgrɪli] *adverb*
in an angry way; *he shouted angrily when the children climbed over his fence*

① **angry**
['æŋgri] *adjective*
upset and annoyed, and sometimes wanting to harm someone; *the shopkeeper is angry with the schoolchildren because they broke his window; he gets angry if the post is late; I am angry that the government is doing nothing to prevent crime; when the taxi still hadn't arrived by 3 o'clock the boss got angrier and angrier* (NOTE: **angrier - angriest**)

① **animal**
['ænɪml] *noun*
living and moving thing (but usually not people); *I like to have animals about the house: we have two dogs and three cats; the football crowd behaved like animals*

④ **ankle**
['æŋkɪl] *noun*
part of the body, where your leg joins your foot; *I couldn't swim, the water only came up to my ankles; she twisted her ankle when she slipped on the stairs*; **ankle socks** = short socks

① **anniversary**
[ænɪ'vɜːsɪri] *noun*
the same date as an important historical event; *the fiftieth anniversary of the end of the Second World War; 1966 was the nine-hundredth anniversary of the Battle of Hastings*; **wedding anniversary** = date which is the date of a wedding; *see also* GOLDEN, SILVER (NOTE: plural is **anniversaries**)

① **announce**
[ə'naʊns] *verb*
to say officially or in public; *he announced his resignation; she announced that she would be standing for parliament; she announced the results of the competition*

① **announcement**
[ə'naʊnsmənt] *noun*
statement made in public; *the managing director made an announcement to the staff; there were several announcements about flight changes*

③ **annoy**
[ə'nɔɪ] *verb*
to make someone irritated; *you can tell he's annoyed by the way his ears go red; he gets very annoyed if you keep him waiting; try not to annoy your father*

① **annoyed**
[ə'nɔɪd] *adjective*
angry; *he was annoyed with his neighbours for cutting down one of his trees; I was annoyed to find someone had stolen my car; we came back from holiday to find some very annoyed letters from the gas company because we hadn't paid our bill*

① **annoying**
[ə'nɔɪɪŋ] *adjective*
which makes you angry; *it is highly annoying to have to try and get my car back from the police station; I find it very annoying that the post doesn't come before 10 o'clock; how annoying! - I've got to go back to the supermarket because I forgot to buy some milk; the baby has an annoying cough which won't go away*

② **annual**
['ænjʊɪl] *adjective*
happening once a year; *the school play is an annual event; I get annual interest of 6% on my savings account*

④ **anonymous**

[ə'nɒnɪməs] *adjective*

without giving a name; *the police have received several anonymous phone calls*; *the club has had a donation from a businessman who wants to remain anonymous*; **anonymous letter** = letter with no name or signature

① **another**

[ə'nʌðə] *adjective and pronoun*

(a) one more (like others); *would you like another drink?*; *I'd like another one of those cakes, please*; *there is only another week before we go on holiday*

(b) a different (one); *he's bought another car*; *can I have another plate, please, this one's dirty?*; *she tried on one dress after another, but couldn't find anything she liked*; *see also* EACH OTHER, ONE ANOTHER

① **answer**

['ɑːnsɪ]

1 *noun*

reply, letter or conversation after someone has written or spoken to you, asking you a question; *I phoned his office but there was no answer*; *have you had an answer to your letter yet?*; **in answer to** = as a reply to; *I am writing in answer to your letter of October 6th*

2 *verb*

(a) to reply, to speak or write words when someone has spoken to you or asked you a question; *he never answers my letters*; *when he asked us if we had enjoyed the meal we all answered 'yes'*

(b) to answer the phone = to lift the telephone when it rings and listen to what the caller is saying; *when I called, it was his secretary who answered the phone*; **to answer the door** = to open the door when someone knocks or rings; *he leapt out of the bath and answered the door dripping wet with a towel round his waist*

① **answerphone**

['ɑːnsɪfɪʊn] *noun*

machine which answers the telephone automatically when someone is not in the office or at home, and allows messages to be recorded; *I left a message for him on his answerphone*

④ **ant**

[ænt] *noun*

small insect; *I found some ants in our kitchen*

④ **antibiotic**

[æntɪbaɪ'ɒtɪk]

1 *adjective*

which kills bacteria; *she's taking a new antibiotic drug*

2 *noun*

substance which kills bacteria; *the doctor prescribed some antibiotics*; *he was given a course of antibiotics*

③ **anticipate**

[æn'tɪsɪpeɪt] *verb*

to expect something to happen; *we are anticipating bad weather*; *I don't anticipate taking a later flight*

④ **antique**

[æn'tiːk]

1 *adjective*

old and valuable; *an antique Chinese bowl*

2 *noun*

valuable old object; *their house if full of antiques*; **antique shop** = shop which sells antiques

③ **antiseptic**

[ænti'septɪk]

1 *adjective*

which prevents germs spreading or a wound becoming infected; *she put an antiseptic dressing on his knee*; *she washed her mouth out with an antiseptic solution*

2 *noun*

substance which prevents germs growing or spreading; *the nurse painted his knee with antiseptic*

③ **anxiety**

[æŋ'zaɪti] *noun*

(a) nervous worry about something; *her anxiety about her job prospects*

(b) being eager to do something; *in his anxiety to get away quickly, he forgot to lock the door*

③ **anxious**

['æŋkʃɪs] *adjective*

(a) nervous and very worried about something; *she's anxious about the baby*

(b) eager to do something; *the shopkeeper is always anxious to please his customers*

① **anxiously**

['æŋkʃɪsli] *adverb*

in a nervous worried way; *she peered anxiously through the window*; *they are waiting anxiously for the results of the tests*

① **any**

['eni]

1 *adjective and pronoun*

(a) it doesn't matter which; *take any book you like*; *I'm free any day next week except Tuesday*; *I don't like any of the paintings in the exhibition*

(b) a quantity; *have you any money left?*; *is there any food for me?*; *would you like any more to eat?*; *will any of your friends be there?*

(c) not...any = none; *there isn't any food left - they've eaten it all*; *can you lend me some money? - sorry, I haven't got any*

2 *adverb*; used to emphasize comparatives; **not...any** = not even a little (more); *can't you sing any louder?*; *he can't cycle any faster*; *she's been in hospital for two weeks and isn't any better*

① **anybody**

['enɪbɒdɪ]

see ANYONE

① **anyhow**
['enɪhaʊ] *adverb*
1 in a careless way; *he piled up the books anyhow*
2 = ANYWAY

③ **any more**
[enɪ'mɔː] *adverb*
(a) a certain number more; *do you have any more books on gardening?*
(b) not ... any more = no longer; *we don't go there any more*

① **anyone** *or* **anybody**
['enɪwʌn *or* 'enɪbɒdi] *pronoun*
(a) it doesn't matter who; *anyone can learn to ride a bike*; *anybody could tell you that*
(b) *(after questions, negatives)* any person; *can anybody lend me some money?*
(c) some person; *did anyone telephone while I was out?*; *we didn't meet anybody we knew* = we met no one we knew; **hardly anybody came to the meeting** = very few people came to the meeting

③ **anyplace**
['enɪpleɪs] *adverb*
US = ANYWHERE; *anyplace you want to go, she'll want to go too*

① **anything**
['enɪθɪŋ] *pronoun*
(a) it doesn't matter what; *you can eat anything you want*; *our dog will bite anything that moves*
(b) *(in questions, negatives)* something; *did you do anything interesting during the weekend?*; *did you hear anything make a noise during the night?*; *has anything happened to their plans for a long holiday?*; *do you want anything more to drink?*; *he didn't eat anything* = he ate nothing

① **anything else**
['enɪθɪŋ 'els] *pronoun*
any other thing; *do you want anything else to drink?*; *is there anything else you would like to know about?*; *she must have a doll which closes its eyes - anything else won't do*

① **anyway**
['enɪweɪ] *adverb*
in any case; *I'm not supposed to drink during office hours, but I'll have a beer anyway*; *I think it's time to leave - anyway, the last bus is at 11.40*

① **anywhere**
['enɪweə] *adverb*
(a) it doesn't matter where; *put the chair anywhere*
(b) *(in questions, negatives)* somewhere; *did you go anywhere at the weekend?*; *is there anywhere where I can sit down?*; *I can't see your wallet anywhere* (NOTE: American English is also anyplace)

① **apart**
[ə'pɑːt] *adverb*
(a) separated; *the two villages are about six miles apart*

(b) not living together; *they were married but now they're living apart*
(c) in separate pieces; **the watch came apart** = the watch came to pieces; *he took the watch apart*
(d) to tell something *or* **someone apart** = to identify two things or people that are similar; *the twins are very alike - how can you tell them apart?*

① **apart from**
[ə'pɑːt frɒm] *phrase*
except, other than; *do you have any special interests apart from your work?*; *I'm feeling fine, apart from a slight cold*

② **apartment**
[ə'pɑːtmənt] *noun*
separate set of rooms for living in; *she has an apartment in downtown New York*; **an apartment block** *or* **a block of apartments** = large building divided into many apartments; **apartment house** = large house which has been divided up into apartments; **a studio apartment** = apartment with one main room, plus kitchen and bathroom (NOTE: British English is usually flat)

② **apologize**
[ə'pɒlədʒaɪz] *verb*
to say you are sorry; *did you apologize to your mother for what you said?*; *he shouted at her and then apologized*; *she apologized for being late*

② **apology**
[ə'pɒlədʒi] *noun*
saying sorry; *he wrote a letter of apology*; *I enclose a cheque for £10 with apologies for the delay in answering your letter*; *my apologies for being so late*; *I expect we will receive an apology in due course* (NOTE: plural is apologies)

④ **apostrophe**
[ə'pɒstrəfi] *noun*
printing sign: ' ; *"it's" written with an apostrophe means "it is"*

> COMMENT: an apostrophe either shows that a letter has been left out (weren't) or is used with 's' to show possession: before an 's' with singular words, after the 's' with plural words (a boy's coat, the girls' team)

④ **apparatus**
[æpɪ'reɪtɪs] *noun*
scientific or medical equipment; *he dropped an expensive piece of apparatus in the lab this morning*; *the firemen had to wear breathing apparatus to enter the burning building* (NOTE: no plural: for one item say **a piece of apparatus**)

② **apparent**
[ə'pærənt] *adjective*
obvious, which seems to be; *it was apparent to everyone that there had been an accident*; *there is an apparent mistake in the accounts*

① **apparently**
['əpærəntli] *adverb*
as it seems; *apparently she took the last train home and then disappeared*; *he didn't come to work today - apparently he's got a cold*

② **appeal**
[ə'piːl]
1 *noun*
(a) asking for help; *the police have made an appeal for witnesses*; *the hospital is launching an appeal to raise £50,000*
(b) legal request to look at a decision again to see if it was correct; *his appeal was rejected*; *the verdict was overturned on appeal*; **Court of Appeal** *or* **Appeal Court** = law court which decides on appeals
(c) attraction; *the appeal of Greece as a holiday destination*; **sex appeal** = being attractive to the opposite sex
2 *verb*
(a) to appeal for = to ask for; *they appealed for money to continue their work*
(b) to appeal against a verdict = to make a legal request for a court to look again at a verdict; *he has appealed against the sentence*
(c) to appeal to = to attract; *these CDs appeal to the teenage market*; *the idea of working in Australia for six months appealed to her*

① **appear**
[ə'piə] *verb*
(a) to start to be seen; *a ship appeared through the fog*
(b) to seem; *there appears to be a mistake*; *he appears to have forgotten the time*; *she appeared rather cross*
(c) to play a part in a film or play; *his dream is to appear on Broadway*

① **appearance**
[ə'piːərɪns] *noun*
(a) look; *you could tell from his appearance that he had slept badly*
(b) being present, being there; *this is her second appearance in a film*; **to put in an appearance** = to arrive at, to come to a meeting, etc.

① **appearances**
[ə'piːərɪnsɪz] *noun*
looks; *by all appearances, the house is empty*; **to keep up appearances** = to try to show that you are still as rich or important as you were before

④ **appetite**
['æpɪtaɪt] *noun*
wanting to eat; *going for a long walk has given me an appetite*; *he's not feeling well and has lost his appetite*; **good appetite** = interest in eating food; *the baby has a good appetite*; **poor appetite** = lack of interest in eating food

④ **applaud**
[ə'plɔːd] *verb*
to bang your hands together to show that you like something; *the audience applauded the singers at the end of the concert*

④ **applause**
[ə'plɔːz] *noun*
banging your hands together; *at the end of the concert there was a storm of applause*

① **apple**
['æpl] *noun*
(a) common hard round sweet fruit, growing on a tree; *don't eat those green apples - they'll make you ill*; **cooking apple** = sour apple which is good for cooking, not for eating raw; **eating apple** = apple which is good to eat raw, rather than to be cooked
(b) apple (tree) = tree which apples grow on; *there's an old apple tree behind our house*

④ **appliance**
[ə'plaɪəns] *noun*
machine, especially an electrical machine used in the home, such as a washing machine; *household appliances should be properly earthed*

④ **applicant**
['æplɪkɪnt] *noun*
person who applies for something; *applicants for visas will have to wait at least two weeks*

① **application**
[æplɪ'keɪʃn] *noun*
(a) putting on (of medicine); *several applications of the cream will be necessary*; **for external application only** = to be used on the skin only
(b) applying for a job, etc.; *he wrote a letter of application*; *we've received dozens of applications for the job of van driver*; **application form** = form to be filled in when applying; *she filled in an application form*

① **apply**
[ə'plaɪ] *verb*
(a) to apply for a job = to ask for a job; *she applied for a job in the supermarket*; *he's applying for a job as a teacher*; **to apply to take a course** = to ask to be admitted to a course; *it's an encouraging sign that so many students have applied to take the course*
(b) to put on (paint); *wait until the first coat of paint is dry before you apply the second*
(c) to apply to = to affect or to relate to; *this rule only applies to people coming from outside the European Union*

① **appoint**
[ə'pɔɪnt] *verb*
to give (a job) to someone; *he was appointed (as) manager or to the post of manager*; *we want to appoint someone to manage our sales department* (NOTE: you appoint a person **to** a job)

① **appointment**
[ə'pɔɪntmənt] *noun*
(a) being given a job; **on her appointment as manager** = when she was made manager; *she had a rise on her appointment as manager*
(b) agreed time for a meeting; *I want to make an appointment to see the doctor*; *she was late for her appointment*; *I have an appointment*

with Dr Jones; **a dentist's appointment** = arrangement to see a dentist; **appointments book** = book in which you write down the time and place of meetings

① **appreciate**
[ə'priːʃieɪt] *verb*
(a) to recognize the value of; *most people appreciate shops which give good value*; *customers don't appreciate having to wait to be served*
(b) to increase in value; *the pound has appreciated against the dollar*

④ **appreciation**
[əpriːʃi'eɪʃn] *noun*
(a) showing that you recognize the value of something; *the company presented him with a watch in appreciation of his years of service*
(b) increase in value; *the appreciation of the pound against the dollar*

② **approach**
[ə'prəʊtʃ]
1 *noun*
(a) coming closer; *with the approach of winter we need to get the central heating serviced*
(b) way which leads to; *the approaches to the city were crowded with buses*; **approach road** = road leading to a main road
(c) way of dealing with a situation; *his approach to the question was different from hers*
(d) proposal; *he made approaches to her to leave her job and come to work for him* (NOTE: plural is **approaches)**
2 *verb*
(a) to come near; *the plane was approaching London airport when the lights went out*
(b) to deal with a problem; *he approached the question in an entirely new way*
(c) to make a proposal; *our company was approached with a takeover bid*; *he approached his bank with a request for a loan*

① **appropriat**
1 *adjective*
[ə'prəʊprɪɪt] suitable; *that short skirt is not really appropriate for gardening*; *we leave it to you to take appropriate action*
2 *verb*
[ə'prəʊprɪeɪt]
(a) to seize property; *the authorities appropriated the land to build a new hospital*
(b) to put a sum of money aside for a special purpose; *they appropriated £100,000 to the reserve fund*

② **approval**
[ə'pruːvəl] *noun*
(a) agreeing with; *does the choice of colour have your approval or meet with your approval?*; *the committee gave their approval to the scheme*; **approval rating** = points system showing how many people approve of

something, usually of a politician's work; *the Prime Minister's approval rating has fallen to a new low*
(b) **on approval** = (merchandise) taken by a customer to use and see if he or she likes it; *the shop let us have the machine for two weeks on approval*

② **approve**
[ə'pruːv] *verb*
(a) **to approve of** = to think something is good; *he doesn't approve of loud music*
(b) to agree to something officially; *the committee approved the scheme*

④ **approximate**
1 *adjective*
[ə'prɒksɪmət] more or less correct; *the approximate cost will be £600*; *these figures are only approximate*
2 *verb*
[ə'prɒksɪmeɪt] to be nearly correct; *the cost of the sports stadium will approximate to two million pounds*

① **approximately**
[ə'prɒksɪmətli] *adverb*
roughly; *it takes approximately 35 minutes to get to central London from here*

① **April**
['eɪprɪl] *noun*
the fourth month of the year, the month after March and before May; *her birthday is in April*; *we went on holiday last April*; *today is April 5th US April 5*; **April 1st;** *see* APRIL FOOL'S DAY (NOTE: **April 5th** or **April 5:** say 'the fifth of April' or 'April the fifth'; American English: 'April fifth')

① **April Fools' Day**
['eɪprɪl 'fuːlz deɪ] *noun*
April 1st, the day when you play tricks on people

④ **aptitude**
['æptɪtjuːd] *noun*
skill or ability in doing something; *she shows great aptitude for French*; **aptitude test** = test of someone's ability; *twenty young people will take the aptitude test this month*

③ **arch**
[ɑːtʃ] *noun*
(a) round structure forming a roof or doorway; *the church roof is formed of tall stone arches*
(b) **triumphal arch** = large building over a road, to celebrate a victory; *there are the ruins of a triumphal arch in the centre of the square* (NOTE: plural is **arches)**

③ **architect**
['ɑːkɪtekt] *noun*
person who designs buildings; *which architect designed the new town hall?*; *we've asked a local architect to draw up plans for a new house*

③ **architecture**
['ɑːkɪtektʃɪ] *noun*
design of buildings; *she is studying architecture or she's an architecture student*; *he doesn't like modern architecture*

① **are**
[ɑː]
see BE

① **area**
['eɪrɪɪ] *noun*
(a) space; *the whole area round the town hall is going to be developed*; *we always sit in the 'no smoking' area*
(b) measurement of the space taken up by something (calculated by multiplying how long it is by how wide it is); *the area of the room is four square metres*; *we are looking for a shop with a sales area of about 100 square metres*
(c) subject; *it's a problem area for the government*; *he's an expert in the area of crowd control*
(d) district, part of a town or country; *our house is near the commercial area of the town*; *the factory is in a very good area for getting to the motorways and airports*; **the London area** = the part of England round London; *houses in the London area are more expensive than elsewhere in the country*

① **area code**
['eɪrɪɪ'kɪʊd] *noun*
special telephone number which is given to a particular area; *the area code for central London is 0207*

> COMMENT: area codes always start with 0, and may have three further figures for large towns (Central London is 020 7, Liverpool is 0151) or several figures for smaller towns (Oxford is 01865). These are spoken as 'oh two oh seven, oh one eight six five,' etc.

④ **arena**
[ə'riːnə] *noun*
building with seats for spectators, where sports and fights are held; *the boys went skating at the school arena*

① **aren't**
[ɑːnt]
see BE

① **argue**
['ɑːgjuː] *verb*
to discuss without agreeing; *they argued over the prices*; *she argued with the waiter about the bill*; *I could hear them arguing in the next room* (NOTE: you argue with someone about or over something)

① **argument**
['ɑːgjuːmɪnt] *noun*
quarrel; *nobody would back her up in her argument with the boss*; *the argument took place in the restaurant*; *to get into an*

argument with someone = to start to argue with someone; *he got into an argument with the customs officials*

② **arise**
[ə'raɪz] *verb*
(a) to start, to appear; *a problem has arisen in connection with the tickets*
(b) **to arise from** = to result from, to happen because of; *the misunderstanding arose from a mistake in her instructions* (NOTE: arising - arose [ə'rəʊz] - arisen [ə'rɪzn])

① **arm**
[ɑːm]
1 *noun*
(a) part of your body which goes from your shoulder to your hand; *he held the parcel under his arm*; *she tripped over the pavement and broke her arm*; *lift your arms up above your head*; **arm in arm** = with their arms linked; *they walked down the street arm in arm*; **to welcome someone with open arms** = to welcome someone eagerly; *the villagers welcomed the UN soldiers with open arms*; **to cost an arm and a leg** = to be very expensive; *see also* COST
(b) sleeve, the part of a coat, shirt, etc., which you put your arm into; *there was a hole under the arm of her favourite T-shirt*
(c) part of a chair which you can rest your arms on; *he put his coffee cup on the arm of his chair*
2 *verb*
to equip with weapons; *the farm workers have all been armed because of possible attacks*; *the soldiers were armed with guns*

④ **armchair**
['ɑːmtʃeɪ] *noun*
chair with arms; *each room in the hotel is furnished with two armchairs and a TV*; *she settled down in a comfortable armchair to read*

③ **armed**
[ɑːmd] *adjective*
(person) carrying weapons; *most British policemen are not armed*; *armed police guarded the house*; **the armed forces** = the army, navy and air force of a country; *(informal)* **armed to the teeth** = carrying lots of weapons; *the robbers were armed to the teeth*

④ **armour** *US* **armor**
['ɑːmɪ] *noun*
(a) metal clothes worn by medieval soldiers as protection; *knights wore suits of armour*
(b) thick metal covering to protect ships or tanks; *the gun is capable of piercing a tank's steel armour*

④ **armoured** *US* **armored**
['ɑːmɪd] *adjective*
protected by armour; **armoured car** = military vehicle which is protected by thick metal; **armoured column** = series of armoured cars or tanks in a line; *the armoured column moved off down the road*

① **arms**
[ɑːmz] *noun*

(a) weapons, such as guns or bombs; *he's a well-known arms dealer*; *they were selling arms to African countries*

(b) up in arms about = very annoyed about; *they are up in arms about the new bus timetable*

① **army**
['ɑːmi] *noun*

all the soldiers of a country, trained for fighting on land; *he left school at 16 and joined the army*; *an army spokesman held a news conference* (NOTE: plural is **armies**)

① **around**
[ə'raʊnd]

1 *preposition*

(a) going all round something; *she had a gold chain around her neck*; *the flood water was all around the village*; *the police car drove around the town*

(b) close to, nearby; *a few boys hung around the bus stop*

(c) in various places; *we have lots of computers scattered around the office*; *it's hard to find your way around Rome without a map*

(d) more or less; *it will cost around £200*; *around sixty people came to the meeting*

2 *adverb*

(a) in various places; *papers were lying around all over the floor*; *the restaurants were all full, so we walked around for some time*

(b) all round; *a castle with water all around*

(c) close to, nearby; *the children stood around waiting for the bus*; *it's the only swimming pool for miles around*

(d) in existence; *she's one of the best eye surgeons around*; *the new coins have been around for some weeks now*

④ **arouse**
[ə'raʊz] *verb*

(a) to excite someone's emotions; *she only wanted to arouse our sympathy*; *he is easily aroused* = it is easy to make him angry

(b) to make someone interested, excited, etc.; *the proposal has aroused a lot of opposition among the people of the village*; *the painting has aroused the interest of several collectors*

② **arrange**
[ə'reɪndʒ] *verb*

(a) to put in order; *the chairs are arranged in rows*; *the books are arranged in alphabetical order*; *the ground floor is arranged as an open-plan area with a little kitchen at the side*

(b) to organize; *let's arrange to meet somewhere before we go to the theatre*; *the tour has been arranged by the travel agent*; *she arranged for a taxi to meet him at the airport*; *I've arranged with my mother that she will feed the cat while we're away*

(c) to adapt a piece of music for different instruments; *the piece was written for the piano, but it has been arranged for full orchestra* (NOTE: you arrange **for** someone to do something; you arrange **for** something to be done; or you arrange **to** do something)

② **arrangement**
[ə'reɪndʒmənt] *noun*

(a) putting into an order; *the arrangement of the pictures in a book*

(b) organizing; *all the arrangements for the wedding were left to the bride's mother*

(c) general agreement; *we have an arrangement by which we meet for lunch every Tuesday*

③ **arrest**
[ə'rest]

1 *noun*

holding someone for breaking the law; *the police made several arrests at the demonstration*; **under arrest** = held by the police; *after the demonstration, three people were under arrest*

2 *verb*

to hold someone for breaking the law; *the police arrested two men and took them to the police station*; *he ended up getting arrested as he tried to leave the country*; *he was arrested for stealing, but the judge let him off with a fine*

① **arrival**
[ə'raɪvl] *noun*

(a) action of reaching a place; *we announce the arrival of flight AB 987 from Tangiers*; *the time of arrival is 5 p.m.*; *we apologize for the late arrival of the 14.25 express from Edinburgh*; **on arrival** = when you arrive; *on arrival at the hotel, members of the party will be allocated rooms*

(b) person who has arrived; *he's a new arrival on our staff*

(c) arrivals = part of an airport that deals with passengers who are arriving; *I'll wait for you in arrivals*; *compare* DEPARTURES

(d) birth of a baby; *the arrival of their son was announced in the newspapers*

① **arrive**
[ə'raɪv] *verb*

to reach a place; *the train from Paris arrives in London at 5 p.m.*; *when we arrived at the cinema we found it was full*; *they arrived home tired out* (NOTE: that you arrive **in a town** or **in a country** but **at a place**)

④ **arrogant**
['ærɪgənt] *adjective*

very proud in an unpleasant way; *because he was so arrogant, the people in his department refused to have anything to do with him*; *you should not treat customers in that arrogant way!*

④ **arrow**
['ærɪʊ] *noun*
(a) piece of wood with a sharp point, shot into the air with a bow; *King Harold was killed by an arrow at the Battle of Hastings*
(b) printed sign which points to something; *follow the arrows to the exhibition*

① **art**
[aːt] *noun*
painting, drawing, etc.; *she is taking art lessons; he went to an exhibition at the local art college; when you're in Washington, don't miss the Museum of Modern Art*; **art gallery** = museum of paintings, sculptures, etc.; *see also* ARTS

④ **artery**
['aːtɪrɪ] *noun*
tube carrying blood from the heart round the body; *a main artery runs down the side of the neck; compare* VEIN (NOTE: plural is **arteries**)

① **article**
['aːtɪkl] *noun*
(a) report in a newspaper; *there's an interesting article on fishing in the newspaper; did you read the article on skiing holidays in yesterday's paper?*
(b) section of a legal agreement; *see article 8 of the treaty*
(c) object, thing; *several articles of clothing were found near the road*
(d) one of the parts of speech; *'the' is the definite article; 'a' is the indefinite article*

③ **artificial**
[aːtɪ'fɪʃl] *adjective*
not real; *she was wearing artificial pearls*; **to give someone artificial respiration** = to revive someone who is almost dead by blowing air into their lungs

② **artist**
['aːtɪst] *noun*
person who paints, draws, etc.; *he collects paintings by 19th-century artists*; **pavement artist** = artist who draws pictures on the pavement with coloured chalks

④ **artistic**
[aː'tɪstɪk] *adjective*
with feeling for art; *her aunt is very artistic; he comes from an artistic family*

③ **arts**
[aːts]
(a) all work connected with art; *the Arts Minister or the Minister for the Arts*
(b) subject taught which is not a science; *she has an arts degree*

① **as**
[æz]
1 *conjunction*
(a) because; *as you can't drive, you'll have to go by bus; as it's cold, you should wear a warm coat*
(b) at the same time as; *as he was getting into the bath, the telephone rang; the little girl ran into the road as the fire engine was turning the corner*
(c) in this way; *leave everything as it is; you should take a holiday as the doctor told you*
2 *preposition*
(a) in a certain job; *he had a job as a bus driver*
(b) because you are; *as a doctor, he has to know the symptoms of all the common diseases*
(c) like; *she was dressed as a nurse; they treated him as a friend of the family*

◊ **as...as**
[æz] *(making comparative)*
like; *she is as tall as I am; as black as coal; I can't run as fast as you*

◊ **as for**
['æz 'fɔː] *preposition*
referring to; *as for him - he will have to take the bus; you play cards if you want to - as for me, I'm going to watch TV*

◊ **as from**
['æz 'frɒm] *preposition*
from a time; **as from next Friday** = starting from next Friday

◊ **as if** *or* **as though**
[əz 'ɪf or əz 'ðɪʊ]
in the same way as; *it looks as if it is going to be fine for the cricket match; she looked as if she was going to cry; he spoke very slowly, as though he was talking to a little child*

◊ **as well**
['æz 'wel] *phrase*
in addition, also; *she came to have tea and brought her sister as well; we visited the castle and swam in the pool as well*

◊ **as well as**
[əz 'wel æz] *phrase*
in addition to, together with; *he has a cottage in the country as well as a flat in town; as well as being a maths teacher, he is a part-time policeman*

④ **ash**
[æʃ] *noun*
(a) grey dust left after a fire, the eruption of a volcano, etc.; *there was a pile of black ash left after we burnt the rubbish; a thick layer of ash from the volcano*
(b) tree growing in the northern part of Europe; *ash trees have black buds and are the last trees to have leaves in spring*

③ **ashamed**
[ə'ʃeɪmd] *adjective*
embarrassed and sorry (for what you have done or not done); *I am ashamed to say that I have never been to the Tate Gallery; she was ashamed of herself; being proud of your family nothing to be ashamed of*

③ **ashtray**
['æʃtreɪ] *noun*
little dish for cigarette ash; *there was no ashtray, so he asked the waiter for one*

① **Asia**
['eɪʒɪ] *noun*
large continent running from the east of Europe to China and Japan; *the Trans-Siberian Railway crosses the deserts of central Asia*

① **Asian**
['eɪʒn]
1 *adjective*
referring to Asia; *we went to a concert of Asian music*
2 *noun*
person coming from one of the countries of Asia; *more than half the children in the class are Asians*

③ **aside**
[ə'saɪd] *adverb*
(a) to one side; *he took me aside and whispered in my ear*; **to put aside** *or* **to set aside** = to save money; *he is putting £50 aside each week to pay for his car*
(b) *(usually US)* **aside from** = apart from; *aside from a minor infection, his health has been remarkably good*

① **ask**
[ɑːsk] *verb*
(a) to put a question to get information; *she asked a policeman the way to the hospital; she went to the railway station to ask about cheap tickets; ask her how much her shoes cost*
(b) to put a question to get someone to do something; *ask your father to teach you how to drive; can I ask you not to make so much noise?*
(c) to invite; *we asked them round for dinner*; **to ask someone out** = to ask someone to go out to a restaurant, to a film, etc., with you; *don't ask her out - she always orders the most expensive things on the menu*

① **ask for**
['ɑːsk 'fɔː] *verb*
to say that you want something; *he asked Father Christmas for a new bike; she asked her boss for more money; someone came into the shop and asked for the manager*; **he asked for his book back** = he said that he wanted to have the book that he had lent

① **asleep**
[ə'sliːp] *adjective*
sleeping; *he was asleep and didn't hear the fire alarm; they were lying asleep on the ground;* **she fell asleep** = she began to sleep; *see also* FAST ASLEEP (NOTE: **asleep** cannot be used in front of a noun: **the cat is asleep** but **a sleeping cat**)

① **aspect**
['æspekt] *noun*
(a) way of considering a situation, a problem; *I will examine several aspects of the problem*
(b) direction which a house faces; *the living room has a south-facing aspect*

① **aspirin**
['æsprɪn] *noun*
(a) common drug, used to stop the symptoms of flu, colds, headaches, etc.; *she always keeps a bottle of aspirin in her bag*
(b) one tablet of aspirin; *take a couple of aspirins and lie down*

③ **ass**
[æs] *noun*
(informal) stupid person; *don't be such an ass!*; *he's an ass - he should have accepted straight away* (NOTE: plural is **asses**)

④ **assassinate**
[ə'sæsɪneɪt] *verb*
to kill a famous person for political reasons; *do you remember the day when the President was assassinated?*

③ **assault**
[ə'sɔːlt]
1 *noun*
attack; *troops are getting ready for the assault; he was accused of assault on a police officer*
2 *verb*
to attack; *he was arrested for assaulting a police officer*

④ **assemble**
[ə'sembl] *verb*
(a) to come together; *the fans assembled at the gates of the football ground*
(b) to put various pieces together; *the cars are assembled in Scotland*

② **assembly**
[ə'semblɪ] *noun*
(a) meeting; *the General Assembly of the United Nations*; **school assembly** = meeting of all the children in a school, normally at the beginning of the morning, when prayers are said, and notices read out (NOTE: plural in this meaning is **assemblies**)
(b) putting together; *the parts are shipped to Scotland for assembly*; **assembly line** = moving line in a factory, where the product moves slowly past workers who add pieces to it as it goes past; *he works on an assembly line or he is an assembly line worker*

② **assess**
[ə'ses] *verb*
(a) to calculate an amount to be paid; *damages were assessed at £1m*
(b) to calculate the value of; *how do you assess United's performance today?; teachers have to assess each student once a term*

② **assessment**
[ə'sesmənt] *noun*
(a) calculation of an amount to be paid; *assessment of the damages will take about a week*

(b) calculation of value; *what's your assessment of United's performance today?*; *student assessments showed that some were falling behind*

② **asset**
['æsɪt] *noun*
(a) valuable quality; *knowing several languages is an asset*
(b) assets = valuable things which are owned; *they will have to sell some of their assets to repay the debt*

④ **assign**
[ə'saɪn] *verb*
(a) to assign someone to = to put someone in a position; *she was assigned to the ear, nose and throat section of the hospital*; *we are assigning you to work in the accounts department*
(b) to assign something to someone = to give something to someone; *he was assigned the job of cleaning the kitchen*; *she was assigned a bedroom on the ground floor*

① **assignment**
[ə'saɪnmənt] *noun*
(a) appointment of someone to a job; *Inspector Murray's assignment to the investigation did not please everyone*
(b) job of work; *he was given the assignment of reporting on the war*
(c) written work given to a student; *I have two assignments which must be in by the end of the week*

③ **assist**
[ə'sɪst] *verb*
(formal) to help; *he assists me with my income tax forms*; *I will be assisted in my work by Miss Smith* (NOTE: you assist someone in doing something or with something)

② **assistance**
[ə'sɪstəns] *noun*
help; *he was trying to change the wheel, when a truck drew up and the driver offered his assistance*; *he asked if he could be of any assistance*; *she will need assistance with her luggage*; *financial assistance* = help in the form of money

② **assistant**
[ə'sɪstənt] *noun*
person who helps; *his assistant works in the office next door*; *shop assistant* = person who serves the customers in a shop; *assistant manager* = person who is second, after a manager

② **associate**
1 [ə'səʊsɪeɪt] *verb*
to associate with = to be linked with, to work with; *I don't want you to associate with that family - they've all been in trouble with the police*; *the government is closely associated with the project*
2 [ə'səʊsɪɪt] *noun*
person who works in the same business; *she is a business associate of mine*

① **associated**
[ə'səʊsɪeɪtɪd] *adjective*
linked with; *the sales division and all associated departments*

① **association**
[əsəʊsɪ'eɪʃn] *noun*
(a) official group, group of companies in the same trade; *an association offering support to victims of street violence*; *the Association of British Travel Agents*
(b) connection between things; *for some people, a black cat has an association with luck*; *Manchester has strong family associations for him*
(c) in association with = together with, sponsored by; *the guidebook is published in association with the local tourist board*; *this programme is brought to you in association with British Airways*

① **assume**
[ə'sjuːm] *verb*
(a) to suppose; *let's assume that he is innocent*; *I assume you have enough money to pay for the meal?*
(b) to take on; *when she was twenty-one, she assumed complete control of the family business*; *he has assumed responsibility for fire safety*

② **assumption**
[ə'sʌmpʃn] *noun*
(a) supposing something is true; *we must go on the assumption that she was murdered*
(b) *(formal)* assumption of office = starting your duties

④ **assurance**
[ə'ʃʊrəns] *noun*
(a) promise; *he gave her an assurance that he would not do it again*
(b) guarantee; *there is no assurance that he will ever pay the damages*
(c) life assurance = insurance which pays if someone dies; *she took out a life assurance policy* (NOTE: **assurance** is used in Britain for insurance policies relating to something which will certainly happen, such as death; otherwise, **insurance** is used)
(d) calm, with a feeling of being sure; *his air of assurance hid the fact that he was very worried*

② **assure**
[ə'ʃʊə] *verb*
(a) to state definitely; *I can assure you we will do everything to try to find your missing daughter*
(b) to make sure; *you are assured of a warm welcome in that hotel*
(c) to insure; *to assure someone's life*

④ **asthma**
['æsmɪ] *noun*
breathing difficulty, often caused by an allergy; *she has chronic asthma*; *a new drug to help asthma sufferers or sufferers from asthma*

ⓐ **astonished**
[ə'stɒnɪʃt] *adjective*
very surprised; *we were astonished to learn that he had died*; *she stood on a table and started to dance, watched by an astonished crowd*

ⓐ **astonishing**
[ə'stɒnɪʃɪŋ] *adjective*
very surprising; *they spent an astonishing amount of money buying Christmas presents*; *for an eight-year-old, the way she plays the piano is astonishing*

ⓐ **astonishingly**
[ə'stɒnɪʃɪŋli] *adverb*
very surprisingly; *the teacher was astonishingly calm considering she was surrounded by screaming children*

ⓐ **astonishment**
[ə'stɒnɪʃmənt] *noun*
great surprise; *she could not hide her astonishment at the news*; *to my great astonishment they paid the bill in full*

ⓐ **astronomer**
[ə'strɒnəmɪ] *noun*
person who studies the stars and planets; *a group of astronomers met to observe the new star*

① **at**
[æt] *preposition*
(a) *(showing time) we'll meet at eleven o'clock*; *you must put your lights on when you drive at night*; *at the weekend, we went to see my mother*; *we went to Paris at Easter*
(b) *(showing place) meet us at the post office*; *she's got a job at the supermarket*; *he's not at home, he's at work*
(c) *(showing speed) the train was travelling at 200 kilometres an hour*
(d) *(showing direction) they threw rotten eggs at the speaker* (NOTE: **at** is often used after verbs: **look at, point at,** etc.)

◊ **at least**
['æt 'liːst] *phrase*
(a) *(mentioning one good thing in a bad situation) it rained all day but at least we have brought our umbrellas*; *the children were very naughty but at least no windows were broken*
(b) *(to correct a statement) she lives in Liverpool - at least, she used to*
(c) *as a minimum; try to tidy yourself up, at least comb your hair*
(d) *not less than; at least a third of the children are ill*; *she can't be sixty - she looks at least eighty*

◊ **at length**
['æt 'leŋθ] *phrase*
(a) *for a long time and using many words; he spoke at length about the results of the election*
(b) *with a lot of details; she explained at great length how the machine worked*
(c) *in the end; at length he arrived, having taken a later train than we expected*

◊ **at once**
['æt 'wɒns] *adverb*
(a) *immediately; come here at once!*; *the ambulance came at once*
(b) *at the same time; don't all speak at once!*
(c) *all at once = suddenly; all at once the phone rang*

① **ate**
[eɪt]
see eat

ⓐ **athlete**
['æθliːt] *noun*
sportsman who competes in races, etc.; *the Olympic athletes marched round the stadium*

ⓐ **athletic**
[æθ'letɪk] *adjective*
(a) referring to sport; *the athletic events start at 2.30*
(b) fit, because you do a lot of sport; *her very athletic younger brother*

ⓐ **athletics**
[æθ'letɪks] *noun*
organized sports; *at school I hated athletics*; *we spent the afternoon watching athletics on TV*

ⓐ **Atlantic (Ocean)**
[ət'læntɪk 'əʊʃɪn] *noun*
ocean between the Americas and Europe and Africa; *she sailed across the Atlantic on her own*

② **atmosphere**
['ætmɪsfɪɪ] *noun*
(a) air around the earth; *the atmosphere surrounds the earth to a height of several hundred kilometres*
(b) general feeling; *the atmosphere in the office was tense*; *I like the friendly atmosphere in our college*

③ **atom**
['ætɪm] *noun*
(a) basic bit of matter; *all substances are composed of atoms*; *splitting an atom releases energy*
(b) very small thing; *there's not an atom of evidence against him*

③ **atomic**
[ə'tɒmɪk] *adjective*
referring to atoms; **atomic bomb** = bomb using nuclear energy; **atomic energy** = energy created during a nuclear reaction, as in a nuclear power station; **atomic number** = number of positive electric charges in an atom which giving the element its place in the table of elements

② **attach**
[ə'tætʃ] *verb*
(a) to fasten; *the gate is attached to the post*; *I am attaching a copy of my previous letter*
(b) to consider that something has a particular quality; *she attaches great importance to food safety*

④ **attachment**
[ə'tætʃmənt] *noun*

(a) thing which can be attached to something; *the camera has several attachments*; *I don't use half the attachments which come with the food processor*

(b) affection, liking for someone; *he formed an attachment to the girl next door*

① **attack**
[ə'tæk]

1 *noun*

(a) trying to hurt someone or something; *they made an attack on the town*; **under attack** = being attacked; *the town is under attack from guerrillas*

(b) criticism; *he launched an attack on the government*

(c) sudden illness; *she had a heart attack*

2 *verb*

to try to hurt someone or something; *three men attacked her and stole her watch*; *the old lady was attacked by robbers*; *they attacked the enemy camp*

① **attempt**
[ə'tempt]

1 *noun*

try; *he failed in his attempt to climb Mount Everest*; *all his attempts to get a job have failed*; *we closed down one shop in an attempt to cut costs*; *she passed her driving test at her second attempt*

2 *verb*

to try; *she attempted to commit suicide*

② **attend**
[ə'tend] *verb*

to be present at; *she attended the wedding*; *they organized a protest meeting but only one or two people attended*

④ **attendance**
[ə'tendəns] *noun*

(a) *(formal)* being present at a ceremony; *your attendance at the opening ceremony is required*; **in attendance** = being present as helper; *the Queen unveiled the memorial, with Major Jones in attendance*

(b) the number of people present at a ceremony; *there was huge attendance on the first day of the show* (NOTE: no plural)

④ **attendant**
[ə'tendənt] *noun*

(a) person on duty; *ask the lavatory attendant if he found your purse*; **flight attendant** = person who looks after passengers on a plane; *press the button to call the flight attendant*

(b) person on duty in a museum; *the attendant asked her to open her bag*

(c) person who helps someone during a ceremony; *one of the bride's attendants tripped over*

① **attention**
[ə'tenʃən] *noun*

(a) careful thinking; *don't distract the driver's attention*; **for the attention of** = words written on a letter to show that a certain person must see it and deal with it; *mark your letter 'for the attention of the Managing Director'*; **to pay attention to** = to note and think about something carefully; *pay attention to the instructions in the leaflet*; *don't pay any attention to what she says!*

(b) position of a soldier, standing straight, with heels together and looking straight ahead; *the guards stood to attention at the entrance of the palace*

④ **attentive**
[ə'tentɪv] *adjective*

(a) listening carefully; *the students were very attentive as the teacher explained the problem*

(b) being careful when dealing with someone; *the manager was very attentive to her needs*

④ **attentively**
[ə'tentɪvli] *adverb*

in an attentive way; *the children listened attentively while their teacher told them what to do*

① **attitude**
['ætɪtjuːd] *noun*

(a) way of standing, sitting, etc.; *his portrait shows him in a thoughtful attitude*

(b) way of thinking; *what is the government's attitude to the problem?*

② **attorney**
[ə'tɜːni] *noun*

(a) *(especially US)* lawyer; *after his arrest he tried to call his attorney*; *see also* DISTRICT ATTORNEY

(b) **power of attorney** = written document, which gives someone power to act on behalf of someone else; *she's going to the solicitor's today to sign the power of attorney*

② **attract**
[ə'trækt] *verb*

to make someone come near; *the shops are lowering their prices to attract more customers*; *the exhibition attracted hundreds of visitors*; *we must see if we can attract more candidates for the job*; **to be attracted to someone** = to feel a sexual interest in someone; *I can't understand why she's attracted to him*

③ **attraction**
[ə'trækʃən] *noun*

(a) the ability to attract; *the attraction of a large salary*; *what is the attraction of cricket?*

(b) something which attracts people; *the Tower of London is a great tourist attraction*

(c) *(in physics)* act of attracting something; *the attraction of magnets*

② **attractive**

[ə'træktɪv] *adjective*

(a) pleasant-looking; *they found the Lake District very attractive*; *she's an attractive young girl*

(b) which attracts; *there are some attractive bargains on offer*; *the rival firm made him a very attractive offer*; **attractive salary** = good salary to make sure many people will apply for the job

④ **auction**

['ɔːkʃn]

1 *noun*

sale to the person who makes the highest bid in public; *the house was sold by auction*; *I bought the painting at an auction*; **to put something up for auction** = to offer something for sale at an auction

2 *verb*

to sell to the person who makes the highest bid in public; *they are auctioning all grandmother's possessions*; *the princess's dresses will be auctioned for charity*

② **audience**

['ɔːdiɪns] *noun*

(a) people at a theatre, cinema, concert hall, or watching TV or listening to the radio; *members of the audience cheered*; *there was a huge audience on the first night of the play*

(b) allowing you to speak to someone; *the ambassador had an audience with the President*

④ **audio**

['ɔːdɪʊ] *prefix* referring to sound; **audio tape** = special magnetic tape on which sounds can be recorded

④ **audit**

['ɔːdɪt]

1 *noun*

official check of a company's accounts; *the auditors are carrying out the annual audit*

2 *verb*

to check accounts officially; *the accounts have not yet been audited*

④ **auditor**

['ɔːdɪtɪ] *noun*

accountant who checks a company's accounts officially; *the company's auditors are going through last year's accounts*

① **August**

['ɔːgɪst] *noun*

eighth month of the year, the month after July and before September; *my birthday is in August*; *I left my job last August*; *today is August 15th US August 15* (NOTE: **August 15th** or **August 15:** say 'August the fifteenth' or 'the fifteenth of August'; American English: 'August fifteenth')

① **aunt**

[ɑːnt] *noun*

sister of mother or father; wife of an uncle; *say goodbye to Aunt Anne*; *she lives next door to my aunt*

① **Australia**

[ɒs'treɪliɪ] *proper noun* large country, covering a whole continent in the south west of the Pacific Ocean; *they went to Australia by boat*; *she spent all her savings on a holiday in Australia* (NOTE: capital: **Canberra**; people: **Australians**; language: **English**; currency: **Australian dollar**)

① **Australian**

[ɒs'treɪliɪn]

1 *adjective*

referring to Australia; *an Australian dollar*; *the Australian Prime Minister*; *I'm letting my house to an Australian family for the summer*; *his wife is Australian*

2 *noun*

person who lives in or comes from Australia; *we beat the Australians at cricket last year*; *I met an Australian in the train*

① **Austria**

['ɒstrɪ] *noun*

country in central Europe, south of Germany and east of Switzerland; *we often go skiing in Austria*; *they are moving to Austria as her father has a business in Vienna* (NOTE: capital: **Vienna**; people: **Austrians**; language: **German**; currency: **schilling, euro**)

① **Austrian**

['ɒstrɪɪn]

1 *adjective*

referring to Austria; *you can get Austrian wine in some supermarkets*; *an Austrian family has bought the house next door to us*

2 *noun*

person from Austria; *the group was made up mainly of Germans and Austrians*

② **author**

['ɔːθɪ] *noun*

writer; *the books are written under the name 'Mr Big', and no one knows who the author is*; *she is the author of a popular series of children's books*

① **authority**

[ɔː'θɒrɪtɪ] *noun*

(a) power to do something; *he has no authority to act on our behalf*

(b) permission to do something; *he signed without having my authority to do so*

(c) source of information; *what is his authority for the story?*

(d) ruling organization; *the education authority pays teachers' salaries*; **local authority** = council which runs a town or country area; **the authorities** = the government; *the authorities have cancelled his visa*

(e) expert; *he's an authority on Greek literature* (NOTE: plural is **authorities**)

④ **authorization**
[ɔːθɪraɪˈzeɪʃn] *noun*
official permission; *she wrote the letter without our authorization*; *do you have authorization for this expenditure?*; *he has no authorization to act on our behalf*

④ **authorize**
[ˈɔːθɪraɪz] *verb*
to give permission for something to be done; *to authorize payment of £10,000*; *to authorize someone to act on the company's behalf*

① **auto**
[ˈɔːtʊ] *noun*
car; *he runs a small auto spares store*; **auto insurance** = insurance covering a car, its driver and others

④ **autobiography**
[ɔːtɪbaɪˈɒɡrɪfi] *noun*
story of the life of a person written by himself or herself; *he's writing his autobiography*; *I'm reading the autobiography of a cabinet minister*

① **automatic**
[ɔːtɪˈmætɪk]
1 *adjective*
which works by itself; *there is an automatic device which cuts off the electric current*; **automatic pilot** = device which flies a plane, allowing the pilot to rest
2 *noun*
(a) gun which goes on firing as long as the trigger is being pulled; *the robbers opened fire with automatics*
(b) car which has automatic gear change; *I prefer driving automatics to manual models*

① **automatically**
[ɔːtɪˈmætɪkli] *adverb*
working by itself; *the doors open automatically when someone comes near them*

④ **automobile**
[ˈɔːtɪmɪbiːl] *noun*
(especially US) car; *Ford is one of the main companies in the automobile industry*

① **autumn**
[ˈɔːtɪm] *noun*
season of the year between summer and winter; *in autumn, the leaves turn brown*; *we went on a walking holiday last autumn*; *they say the building will be finished next autumn*; *I'll be starting my new job in the autumn* (NOTE: in American English this is **the fall**)

① **available**
[əˈveɪləbl] *adjective*
(a) which can be obtained; *the tablets are available from most chemists*
(b) to make yourself available = to arrange to be free to do something; *I can make myself available to meet you next week*; *the manager is never available when customers want to complain*

③ **avenue**
[ˈævɪnjuː] *noun*
wide street in a town, often with trees along the side; *a suburban avenue lined with trees*; **Fifth Avenue** = famous shopping street in New York; *we went into the stores on Fifth Avenue* (NOTE: in names of streets, usually shortened to **Ave: 15 Laurel Ave**)

① **average**
[ˈævɪrɪdʒ]
1 *noun*
(a) number calculated by adding several figures and dividing by the number of figures added; *the temperature has been above the average for the time of year*; *the average for the last three months* or *the last three months' average*
(b) on average = as a rule; *on average, £15 worth of goods are stolen every day*
2 *adjective*
(a) ordinary; *it was an average working day at the office*; *their daughter is of above average intelligence*
(b) calculated by dividing the total by the number of quantities; *his average speed was 30 miles per hour*
3 *verb*
to work out as an average; *price increases have averaged 10% per annum*

① **avoid**
[əˈvɔɪd] *verb*
(a) to keep away from; *travel early to avoid the traffic jams*; *aircraft fly high to avoid storms*; *you must avoid travelling on Friday evenings*
(b) to try not to do something; *he's always trying to avoid taking a decision* (NOTE: you avoid something or avoid **doing** something)

④ **await**
[əˈweɪt] *verb*
(formal) to wait for; *we are awaiting the decision of the court*; *your order is in the warehouse awaiting collection*

① **awake**
[əˈweɪk]
1 *verb*
(a) to stop somebody sleeping; *he was awoken by the sound of the telephone*
(b) to wake up; *he awoke when he heard them knocking on the door*; *they awoke to find a rabbit in their tent* (NOTE: **awaking - awoke** [əˈwəʊk] **- has awoken**)
2 *adjective*
not asleep; *I can't get to sleep - it's 2 o'clock and I'm still awake*; **wide awake** = completely awake (NOTE: **awake** cannot be used in front of a noun)

① **award**
[əˈwɔːd]
1 *noun*
(a) prize; *the coffee machine has won a design award*; *the school has been nominated for an award*; *we all went to London for the award-giving ceremony*

(b) decision which settles a dispute; *the latest pay award has been announced*
2 *verb*
to give compensation, a prize, etc., to someone; *he was awarded first prize*; *she was awarded damages*

① **aware**
[ə'weə] *adjective*
knowing; *is he aware that we have to decide quickly?*; *I am not aware of any problem*; *not that I am aware of* = not as far as I know; *has there ever been an accident here before? - not that I am aware of*

③ **awareness**
[ə'weənɪs] *noun*
being aware; *the police are trying to increase public awareness of car crime*

① **away**
[ə'weɪ]
1 *adverb*
(a) at a distance; *they've gone away on holiday*; *the nearest shop is three kilometres away*; *go away! - I don't want to see you*; *we all waved as the bus moved away*
(b) *(as emphasis, after verbs)* without stopping; *the birds were singing away in the garden*
(c) not here, somewhere else; *the managing director is away on business*; *my secretary is away sick*
(d) *(in sports)* at your opponents' sports ground; *our team is playing away next Saturday* (NOTE: the opposite is **at home**)

2 *adjective*
away game = game played at your opponents' sports ground (NOTE: the opposite is **a home game**)

① **awful**
['ɔːfʊl] *adjective*
very bad, very unpleasant; *turn off the television - that programme's awful!*; *she felt awful about missing the party*; *he's got an awful cold*

① **awfully**
['ɔːflɪ] *adverb (informal)*
very; *I'm awfully sorry to have to disturb you*; *she was awfully upset by the news*; *it was awfully cold in Moscow*

① **awkward**
['ɔːkwɪd] *adjective*
(a) difficult to do; *I couldn't reach the handle - it's in a very awkward position*; *the lock is awkward and stiff*
(b) embarrassing; *it's awkward for us to invite him and his second wife, when his first wife is a friend of my sister*; *when he asked for the loan the bank started to ask some very awkward questions*
(c) not convenient; *next Thursday is awkward for me - what about Friday?*

① **awoke, awoken**
[ə'wəuk or ə'wəukn]
see AWAKE

Bb

① **B, b**
[biː]
second letter of the alphabet, between A and C; *he initialled the document with a large 'BB' for Ben Brown*

③ **B & B** *or* **b. & b.**
['biː ənd 'biː] *noun*
= BED AND BREAKFAST; *we want to find a B & B away from the main road* (NOTE: plural is **B & Bs**)

① **baby**
['beɪbɪ] *noun*
(a) very young child; *most babies start to walk when they are about a year old*; *I've known him since he was a baby*; **to have a baby** = to give birth to a baby; *she's going into hospital to have her baby*; *see also* BATH WATER

(b) very young animal; *a baby rabbit* (NOTE: plural is **babies;** note also that if you do not know if a baby is a boy or a girl, you can always call it **it:** *the baby was sucking its thumb*)

③ **baby-sit**
['beɪbɪsɪt] *verb*
to look after a child or children in a house, while their parents are out; *she baby-sits for me while I go to my evening classes*; *I'm baby-sitting my little brother tonight* (NOTE: **baby-sitting - baby-sat**)

③ **baby-sitter**
['beɪbɪsɪtɪ] *noun*
person who baby-sits; *we have to find a baby-sitter for next Thursday evening*

① **back**
[bæk]
1 *noun*
(a) part of your body which is not in front; *she*

went to sleep lying on her back; *he carried his son on his back; don't lift that heavy box, you may hurt your back; she stood with her back to the wall*; he did it behind my back = he did it without telling me; **we were glad to see the back of him** = we were glad to see him leave; **to put someone's back up** = to annoy someone; **we've broken the back of the work** = we've done most of the work

(b) the opposite part to the front; *he wrote his address on the back of the envelope; she sat in the back of the bus and went to sleep; the dining room is at the back of the house*; **he knows London like the back of his hand** = he knows London very well; **he put his trousers on back to front** = he put them on the wrong way round

(c) *(in many sports)* person who defends the goal area; *(in rugby)* one of the attacking players immediately behind the forwards; *the backs should stay back to defend the goal*

2 *adjective*

(a) on the opposite side to the front; *he knocked at the back door of the house; the back tyre of my bicycle is flat*

(b) referring to the past; **back pay** = salary which has not been paid; *I am owed £500 in back pay*

3 *adverb*

(a) towards the back; *he stepped back from the edge of the platform; she leant back in her armchair; can you please sit back, I can't see the screen*

(b) in the state where things were before; *put the telephone back on the table; she watched him drive away and then went back into the house; she gave me back the money she had borrowed; I'll phone you as soon as I get back to the office*

(c) in the past; *back in the 1950s, life was much less complicated than it is today*

4 *verb*

(a) to go backwards; to make something go backwards; *he backed (his car) down the drive*; **to back away from** = to go backwards from something frightening; *the little girl backed away from the dog*

(b) to support with money; *she is backing her son's restaurant*

(c) to bet on something happening; *we're backing the Prime Minister to win the election* (NOTE: **back** is often used after verbs: **to give back, to go back, to pay back**, etc.)

② **background**
['bækgraund] *noun*

(a) part of a picture which seems farther away; *the photograph is of a house with mountains in the background; his white shirt stands out against the dark background*

(b) **background music** = music played quietly in a film, restaurant, etc.; *the background music was too loud, so we asked for it to be turned down*

(c) past life or experience; *he comes from a working class background; do you know anything about her background?; his background is in the restaurant business*

(d) past details; *he explained the background of the claim for damages*

③ **backing**
['bækɪŋ] *noun*

(a) financial support; *he has the backing of a French bank*

(b) action of going backwards; *backing your car round corners is always difficult*

(c) music played to accompany a singer; *she sings with an Irish backing group*

③ **backpack**
['bækpæk] *noun*

large bag carried on the back when walking; *I'll have to take something out of my backpack - it's much too heavy*

③ **backpacker**
['bækpækɪ] *noun*

person who goes walking, carrying a backpack; *we picked up two backpackers who were hitching a lift into the Rockies*

③ **backpacking**
['bækpækɪŋ] *noun*

going on a long distance walk, carrying a backpack; *we went backpacking round Greece*

③ **back up**
['bæk 'ʌp] *verb*

(a) to help someone; *nobody would back her up when she complained about the service; will you back me up in the vote tomorrow?*

(b) to make a copy of a computer file; *don't forget to back up your work before you go home in the evening*

(c) *US* to make a car go backwards; *can you back up, please? I want to get out of the parking lot* (NOTE: British English for this is simply to **back**)

④ **backward**
['bækwɪd]

1 *adjective*

(a) not as advanced as is normal; *he is backward for his age*

(b) not having much industrial development; *poor and backward countries*

2 *adverb*

US = BACKWARDS

① **backwards** *US also* **backward**
['bækwɪdz] *adverb*

from the front towards the back; *don't step backwards; 'tab' is 'bat' spelt backwards; she looked backwards at the next person in the queue*; **backwards and forwards** = in one direction, then in the opposite direction; *the policeman was walking backwards and forwards in front of the bank*; *(informal)* **to bend over backwards** *or* **to lean over backwards to do something** = to do everything you can to be helpful; *we bent over backwards* *to get her a mortgage, and then she decided not to buy the house; the social services leant over backwards to help the family*

③ **bacon**
['beɪkɪn] *noun*
salted or smoked meat from a pig, usually cut in thin slices; **bacon and eggs** = fried bacon and fried eggs (served at breakfast) (NOTE: no plural: **some bacon; a pound of bacon;** for a single piece say **a rasher**)

COMMENT: bacon is cured in salt water for several days; some bacon is also smoked by hanging in smoke, which improves its taste; bacon which has not been smoked is also known as 'green' bacon

④ **bacteria**
[bæk'tɪɪriɪ] *noun*
tiny organisms, which can cause disease; *the cleaning liquid will kill harmful bacteria in the toilet; bacteria can move and reproduce very rapidly* (NOTE: the word is plural; the singular is **bacterium** [bæk'tɪɪriɪm])

① **bad**
[bæd] *adjective*
(a) not good; *eating too much fat is bad for you; I think it would be a bad idea to go on holiday in November*
(b) of poor quality; *he's a bad driver; she's good at singing but bad at playing the piano*
(c) unpleasant; *he's got a bad cold; she's in a bad temper; I've got some bad news for you; the weather was bad when we were on holiday in August*
(d) serious; *he had a bad accident on the motorway*
(e) *(food)* which is not fresh, which has started to rot; *the meat we bought yesterday has started to go bad* (NOTE: **bad - worse** [wɜːs] **- worst** [wɜːst])

◊ **not bad**
['nɒt 'bæd] quite good; *the food in this restaurant isn't bad; what did you think of the film? - not bad!*

④ **badge**
[bædʒ] *noun*
small sign pinned to someone's clothes (to show who he or she is, what company he or she belongs to, etc.); *all the staff at the exhibition must wear badges*

① **badly**
['bædli] *adverb*
(a) not well; *she did badly in her driving test*
(b) seriously; *he was badly injured in the motorway accident*
(c) very much; *his hair badly needs cutting* (NOTE: **badly - worse** [wɜːs] **- worst** [wɜːst])

① **bag**
[bæg]
1 *noun*
(a) container made of paper, plastic, etc., in which you can carry things; *he put the apples in a paper bag; (informal)* **to let the cat out of the bag** = to tell a secret by accident; *her husband let the cat out of the bag and it was all over the newspapers the following morning; (informal)* **it's in the bag** = the deal has been agreed; **carrier bag** = large paper or plastic bag with handles, for carrying shopping, often given by a shop, with the shop's name on it; *have you got a carrier bag for all this shopping?*; **doggy bag** = bag in which you can put food which you didn't eat in a restaurant to take home; **shopping bag** = bag for carrying your shopping in; **shoulder bag** = bag which you carry on a strap over your shoulder; **sleeping bag** = comfortable warm bag for sleeping in, often used by people camping; **string bag** = bag made like a net
(b) what is contained in a bag; *a bag of potatoes; a small bag of flour; (informal)* **bags of** = a large amount of; *let him pay the bill if he wants to - he's got bags of money*
(c) = HANDBAG; *my keys are in my bag*
(d) suitcase, piece of luggage; *I always pack my bags at the last minute; (informal)* **to tell someone to pack their bags** = to tell someone to leave, to sack someone; *when he got home, she told him to pack his bags*
2 *verb*
(informal)
(a) to catch, kill or destroy; *we bagged several rabbits; he bagged three enemy planes*
(b) **bags I go first** = let me go first, I claim the right to go first (NOTE: **bagging - bagged**)

④ **baggage**
['bægɪdʒ] *noun*
luggage, cases and bags which you take with you when travelling; *she brought a huge amount of baggage with her*; **excess baggage** = cases which weigh more than you are allowed when travelling by air, and for which you must pay extra; **baggage allowance** = weight of baggage which an air passenger is allowed to take free when he or she travels; *US (at airport)* **baggage cart** = little cart with wheels which you use to carry your luggage at an airport; *there's a row of baggage carts near where you claim your baggage* (NOTE: British English for this is **luggage trolley**); *US* **baggage room** = room at a railway station, coach station, ferry terminal or airport where suitcases, bags and parcels can be left (NOTE: British English for this is **left luggage office**. Note also **baggage** has no plural; to show one suitcase, etc., you can say **a piece of baggage**. Note also that British English uses **luggage** more often than **baggage**)

④ **bail**
[beɪl]
1 *noun*
(a) money paid to a court as guarantee that a prisoner who is released will return to the court to stand trial; *she was released on bail of £5000;*

to jump bail = not to appear in court after being released on bail; *the police are afraid he will jump bail*
(b) bails = two pieces of wood on top of the stumps in cricket
2 *verb*
to scoop water out of a boat; *we're filling up with water - start bailing!*

④ **bail out**
['beɪl 'aʊt] *verb*
(a) to help someone in difficulty; *when he couldn't pay his rent, he asked his father to bail him out*
(b) to pay money to a court to have a prisoner released; *he phoned his lawyer to see if someone could bail him out*
(c) to scoop water out of a boat; *I'll try to plug the hole, if you start to bail out*

④ **bait**
[beɪt]
1 *noun*
something used to attract fish or animals so that you can catch them; *we must put down some more bait to try to get rid of the mice*; **to rise to the bait** *or* **to take the bait** = to let yourself to get caught by a tempting offer
2 *verb*
to attach bait (to a hook); *he baited his line with a worm*

③ **bake**
[beɪk] *verb*
to cook in an oven; *Mum's baking a cake for my birthday*; *do you like baked potatoes?*; *bake the pizza for 35 minutes*

③ **baked beans**
['beɪkt 'biːnz] *noun*
dried white beans cooked in tomato sauce; *we had baked beans on toast for supper*; *when you go shopping, can you get me a tin of baked beans?*

④ **baking**
['beɪkɪŋ]
1 *noun*
cooking in an oven, especially bread and cakes; *there was a wonderful smell of baking coming from the kitchen*; **baking dish** = dish which goes into the oven
2 *adjective*
(informal) very hot; *it's baking (hot) in here - can you open the window?*

② **balance**
['bæləns]
1 *noun*
(a) staying steady; *the cat needs a good sense of balance to walk along the top of a fence*; **to keep your balance** = not to fall over; **to lose your balance** = to fall down; *as he was crossing the river on the rope bridge he lost his balance and fell*
(b) money left in an account; *I have a balance of £25 in my bank account*; **balance of payments** = the difference in value between a

country's imports and exports; *the government is trying to reduce the balance of payments deficit*
(c) money left to be paid; *you can pay £100 down and the balance in three instalments*; *the remaining balance to pay is now £5000*
(d) the result is hanging in the balance = you cannot tell which way the result will turn out
2 *verb*
(a) to stand without falling; *the cat balanced on the top of the fence*
(b) to make something stand without falling; *the waiter balanced a pile of dirty plates on his arm*
(c) to make accounts balance *or* **to balance the accounts** = to make income and expenditure equal in accounts

④ **balanced**
['bælɪnst] *adjective*
(a) which does not contain too much of something; *children need a balanced diet*
(b) not in profit or loss; *we are aiming for a balanced budget this year*
(c) sensible, not extreme; *to express a balanced opinion*

④ **balcony**
['bælkɪnɪ] *noun*
(a) small floor sticking out from the upper level of a building; *the flat has a balcony overlooking the harbour*; *breakfast is served on the balcony*
(b) upstairs rows of seats in a theatre or cinema; *we booked seats at the front of the balcony*
(NOTE: plural is **balconies**)

④ **bald**
[bɔːld] *adjective*
(a) who has no hair; *his grandfather is quite bald*; *he is beginning to go bald*
(b) straightforward, without any explanation; *after the fire, the police issued a bald statement*
(c) a bald tyre = a tyre which has been worn smooth

① **ball**
[bɔːl] *noun*
(a) round thing for throwing, kicking, playing games, etc.; *they played in the garden with an old tennis ball*; *he kicked the ball into the goal*; *he threw the ball and I caught it*; **to keep the ball rolling** = to keep everything moving, especially a conversation; *John kept the ball rolling by telling a long story about his trip to Egypt*; **I'll start the ball rolling** = I'll start things going; **he's on the ball** = he knows his job, he's clever in business; *I'll ask Mary to do it - she's been here a long time and is really on the ball*; **they won't play ball** = they won't cooperate with us
(b) any round thing; *a ball of wool*; *he crushed the paper up into a ball*
(c) formal dance; *Cinderella lost her shoe at the ball*; *(informal)* **to have a ball** = to enjoy yourself; *the children don't want to go home - they're having a ball*

④ **ballet**
['bæleɪ US bæ'leɪ] *noun*
(a) type of dance, given as a public entertainment, where dancers perform a story to music; *she's taking ballet lessons or she's going to ballet school*
(b) a performance of this type of dance; *they are putting on Tchaikovsky's ballet 'Swan Lake' at Covent Garden*; *we went to the ballet last night*

③ **balloon**
[bɪ'lu:n] *noun*
large ball which is blown up with air or gas; *he was blowing up balloons for the party*; **hot-air balloon** = very large balloon which rises into the air as the air inside it is heated, with people travelling in a basket attached underneath; *we went for a ride in a hot-air balloon*

④ **ballot**
['bælɪt]
1 *noun*
way of voting where voters mark papers with a cross; **postal ballot** = ballot where the votes are sent by post; **ballot box** = box for putting voting papers into; **ballot paper** = paper on which the voter marks a vote
2 *verb*
(a) to get people to vote on something; *the union is balloting its members on the strike*
(b) to vote by marking papers with a cross; *they balloted for the place on the committee*

③ **ban**
[bæn]
1 *noun*
order which forbids something; *the government has introduced a ban on smoking in cinemas*; *they imposed a ban on cycling in the park*
2 *verb*
to forbid; *smoking has been banned in cinemas*; *she was banned from driving for three years* (NOTE: **banning - banned**)

④ **banana**
[bɪ'nɑ:nɪ] *noun*
(a) long yellow, slightly curved fruit which grows in hot countries; *she was peeling a banana*; *can I have a banana milk shake?*; **banana split** = dessert made of a banana with ice cream, cream and chocolate sauce; usually served in a long dish
(b) *(informal)* **to go bananas** = to go mad, to get very annoyed; *when he saw what they had done to his car, he went bananas*

② **band**
[bænd]
1 *noun*
(a) **elastic band** *or* **rubber band** = thin circle of rubber for holding things together; *the roll of papers was held together with a rubber band*; *put a band round the cards to stop them getting mixed*
(b) group of people; *bands of drunken football fans wandered around the streets*
(c) group of people who play music together; *the soldiers marched down the street, following the band*; *the dance band played all night*
(d) range of things taken together; *he's in the £50 - 60,000 salary band*; *we're looking for something in the £10 - £15 price band*
2 *verb*
to band together = to form a group; *they banded together to form a pressure group*

③ **bandage**
['bændɪdʒ]
1 *noun*
cloth for putting round a wound, an injured leg, etc.; *the nurse put a bandage round his knee*; *his head was covered in bandages*
2 *verb*
to put a cloth round a wound, an injured leg, etc.; *she took him to the hospital and the nurse bandaged his knee*

③ **BandAid**
['bændeɪd] *noun*
US *(trademark)* small strip of cloth which can be stuck to the skin to cover a wound; *let me put a BandAid on your finger* (NOTE: British English is **sticking plaster**)

③ **bang**
[bæŋ]
1 *noun*
sudden noise like that made by a gun; *the car started with a series of loud bangs*; *there was a bang and the tyre went flat*
2 *verb*
to hit hard, so as to make a loud noise; *can't you stop the door banging?*; *he banged (on) the table with his hand*
3 *interjection;* *(showing the something makes a sudden noise)* *a firework suddenly went bang*; **bang in the middle** = right in the middle; *bang in the middle of the film, someone's mobile phone started to ring*

④ **banger**
['bæŋɪ] *noun*
(a) *(slang)* old car; *I'm surprised his old banger is still on the road*
(b) *(slang)* sausage; **bangers and mash** = fried sausages and mashed potatoes

① **bank**
[bæŋk]
1 *noun*
(a) business which holds money for its clients, which lends money at interest and trades generally in money; *I must go to the bank to get some money*; *how much money do you have in the bank?*; *she took all her money out of the bank to buy a car*; *see also* BOTTLE BANK
(b) land along the side of a river; *he sat on the river bank all day, trying to catch fish*; *there is a path along the bank of the canal*
(c) long heap of earth, sand, snow, etc.; *the road was blocked by banks of snow blown by the wind*
2 *verb*

(a) to put money away into a bank; *have you banked the money yet?*; *I banked the cheque as soon as it arrived*

(b) to pile up in a long mound; *the snow was banked up along both sides of the road*

② **bank account**
['bæŋk ə'kaʊnt] *noun*

arrangement which you make with a bank to keep your money safely, where you can deposit and withdraw money as you want; *I put all my savings into my bank account*; **to open a bank account** = to start keeping money in a bank; *he opened a bank account when he started his first job*; **to close a bank account** = to stop having an account with a bank

④ **banker**
['bæŋkɪ] *noun*

person who has a senior post in a bank; *he works as a banker in the City*

① **bank holiday**
['bæŋk 'hɒlɪdeɪ] *noun*

special day when most people do not go to work and the banks are closed; *Christmas Day is a bank holiday*

COMMENT: bank holidays in England and Wales are: New Year's Day, Good Friday, Easter Monday, the first Monday in May (May Day), the last Monday in May (Spring Bank Holiday), the last Monday in August (Summer Bank Holiday), Christmas Day and Boxing Day (December 26th). In Scotland, the first Monday in August and January 2nd are also Bank Holidays, but Easter Monday and the last Monday in August are not. In the USA, New Year's Day, 21st January (Martin Luther King Day), February 12th (Lincoln's Birthday), the third Monday in February (Washington's birthday), the last Monday in May (Memorial Day), July 4th (Independence Day), the first Monday in September (Labor Day), the second Monday in October (Columbus Day), 11th November (Veterans' Day), the fourth Thursday in November (Thanksgiving) and Christmas Day are public holidays nationally, although there are other local holidays

③ **banking**
['bæŋkɪŋ] *noun*

(a) the profession of working in a bank; *he is planning a career in banking*

(b) the business of working in a bank; *some supermarkets now offer banking services*; **banking hours** = time when a bank is open for its customers; *you cannot get money out of the bank after banking hours unless you go to a cash machine*

④ **banknote**
['bæŋknɪʊt] *noun*

piece of paper money; *he pulled out a pile of new banknotes*; *the new design of the banknotes makes them difficult to forge* (NOTE: American English is **bill**)

③ **bankrupt**
['bæŋkrʌpt]
1 *adjective*

not able to pay your debts; *he was declared bankrupt, with debts totalling more than £1m*
2 *noun*

person who cannot pay his debts; *a bankrupt cannot be a Member of Parliament*

④ **bankruptcy**
['bæŋkrʌptsɪ] *noun*

being bankrupt; *when his business failed he faced bankruptcy*; *the number of bankruptcies increased during the recession* (NOTE: plural is **bankruptcies**)

④ **banner**
['bænɪ] *noun*

(a) long flag; *they hung banners from the tops of buildings for the festival*

(b) large piece of cloth with a slogan on it; *the demonstrators carried banners with the words 'Power to the People'*

(c) **banner headline** = newspaper headline printed in very large letters

① **bar**
[bɑː]
1 *noun*

(a) long piece of something hard; *the yard was full of pieces of wood and metal bars*

(b) solid piece of material; *put a new bar of soap by the bath*; *she was eating a bar of chocolate*

(c) long piece of wood or metal which closes a door or window; **bars** = pieces of metal in front of a prison window; *the prisoners escaped by sawing through the bars*; **behind bars** = in prison; *he was put behind bars for several years*

(d) long metal or plastic key on a typewriter or computer keyboard; **space bar** = long bar at the bottom of the keyboard on a typewriter or computer which inserts a single space into text

(e) place in a hotel or pub where you can buy and drink alcohol; *let's meet in the bar before dinner*; *the salesmen met in the bar of the hotel*

(f) small shop where you can buy food; **coffee bar** = small restaurant which sells coffee, cakes and sandwiches; **sandwich bar** = small shop which mainly sells sandwiches; **snack bar** = small restaurant where you can eat simple meals; *she bought a piece of pizza in the snack bar at Waterloo Station*

(g) thing which prevents something happening; *not having the right qualifications could be a bar to your promotion*; **colour bar** = using the colour of someone's skin as a reason to stop them doing something

(h) the profession of a barrister; **to be called to the bar** = to become a barrister

(i) division within a piece of music; *let's play the first few bars again*

2 *preposition* except; *all of the suppliers replied bar one*; *all bar two of the players in the team are British*

3 *verb*

(a) to block; *the road was barred by the police*; *the path is barred to cyclists*

(b) to bar someone from doing something = to prevent someone doing something; *she was barred from entering the USA* (NOTE: barring - barred)

③ **barbecue**

['bɑːbɪkjuː]

1 *noun*

(a) food cooked on a metal grill; *here is a recipe for chicken barbecue*

(b) meal or party where food is cooked out of doors on a metal grill; *we had a barbecue for twenty guests*; *let's have a barbecue in our back yard*; *they've been invited to a barbecue*

(c) metal grill for cooking out of doors; *light the barbecue at least half an hour before you start cooking*

2 *verb*

to cook on a metal grill; *she was barbecuing sausages for lunch when it started to rain*

③ **bare**

['beɪ]

1 *adjective*

(a) naked, with no clothes on; *he walked on the beach in his bare feet*

(b) with no leaves on, no furniture inside, etc.; *in winter, the trees are all bare*; *they slept on the bare boards*; *they saw the bare bones of dead animals in the desert*

(c) a bare living = just enough to live on; *he makes a bare living selling T-shirts to tourists*; **bare minimum** = the smallest amount needed; *the flat is furnished with the bare minimum of furniture*

2 *verb*

to make part of the body bare by removing clothes; *men should bare their heads on entering the church* (NOTE: do not confuse with bear)

③ **barely**

['beɪli] *adverb*

scarcely, almost not enough; *she barely had enough money to pay the bill*; *he barely had time to get dressed before the police arrived*

③ **bargain**

['bɑːgɪn]

1 *noun*

(a) an agreed deal; **to strike a bargain** = to agree terms; *we shook hands and the bargain was struck*; *he drives a hard bargain* = he is a tough negotiator

(b) into the bargain = as well as other things; *the plane was late and they lost my suitcase into the bargain*

(c) something bought more cheaply than usual; *the car was a real bargain at £500*; **bargain basement** = cheap department in the basement of a shop; *you'll find cheaper items in the bargain basement*; **bargain offer** *or* **bargain sale** = sale at a specially low price

2 *verb*

(a) to negotiate terms; *after bargaining with the man at the door, we managed to get into the club*

(b) to discuss a price; *if you bargain with the man in the carpet shop, you'll probably get him to reduce the price*

(c) to bargain for something = to expect something to happen; *I hadn't bargained for him being away and leaving me to do all the work*; **I got more than I bargained for** = the deal had unpleasant results which I did not expect (NOTE: you bargain **with** someone **over** *or* **about** *or* **for** something)

④ **barge**

[bɑːdʒ]

1 *noun*

cargo boat on a river or canal; *we watched the barges go past along the Rhine*

2 *verb*

to barge in = to interrupt; *we were having a quiet chat when he came barging in*

> COMMENT: barges on English canals are also called 'narrow boats' because they are long and narrow

④ **bark**

[bɑːk]

1 *noun*

(a) hard outer layer of a tree; *the rough bark of an oak tree*; *the bark of birch trees comes off in strips*

(b) call of a dog; *the dog gave a bark to greet us as we came into the house*; *his bark is worse than his bite* = he is not as frightening as he seems; *don't be afraid of Aunt Bessie - her bark is much worse than her bite*

2 *verb*

to make a call like a dog; *the dog barks every time he hears the postman*; **to bark up the wrong tree** = to be mistaken; *they don't know what the problem is - they're barking up the wrong tree*

④ **barn**

[bɑːn] *noun*

large farm building for storing produce; *the barn is full of wheat*

④ **barracks**

['bærɪks] *noun*

building where soldiers live; *the soldiers marched into their barracks*; *the barracks were built in the 19th century* (NOTE: barracks is both singular and plural)

③ **barrel**
['bærɪl] *noun*
(a) round wooden container for liquid; *a barrel of beer*; *we sell wine by the barrel*; *he's got me over a barrel* = I'm placed in very awkward situation
(b) amount contained in a barrel; *the price of oil has reached $30 a barrel*; *the oil well produces thousands of barrels of oil per day*
(c) firing tube of a gun; *you need to clean the barrel of your gun very carefully*

③ **barrier**
['bærɪɪ] *noun*
bar which blocks the way; thing which prevents the spread of a disease, the import of goods, etc.; *he lifted the barrier and we drove across the border*; **crush barriers** = metal fences which are put up to control crowds; *the fans simply climbed over the crush barriers to get at the pop group's car*; **customs barriers** *or* **trade barriers** = special taxes to prevent imports; *to impose trade barriers on certain goods*

④ **barrister**
['bærɪstɪ] *noun*
GB lawyer who can present cases in court; *they hired one of the top barristers to defend them*; *see also* BAR (NOTE: the term is not used in the USA; also called a **counsel**)

> COMMENT: barristers are instructed by solicitors, and never by the client whom they are representing. Important barristers are nominated to become QCs

① **base**
[beɪs]
1 *noun*
(a) bottom part; *the table lamp has a flat base*
(b) place where you work from; *he lives in London but uses Paris as his base when travelling in France*; **a military base** = a camp for soldiers; *he was posted to an air base in East Anglia*
(c) one of the marked spots in baseball where a player is safe; *players have to run from base to base*; **to touch base with someone** = to get in touch with someone again; *I'm calling because I wanted to touch base with you*
2 *verb*
to use as a base; *the company is based in Paris, it is not London-based as you might expect*; *he based his article on work done at Harvard University*

② **baseball**
['beɪsbɔːl] *noun*
(a) American game for two teams of nine players, in which a player hits a ball with a bat and players from the other team try to catch it; he scores points by running round the field from base to base (there are four bases in all); *we went to the baseball game last Saturday*; **baseball cap** = soft cotton cap with a large peak; *she was wearing a baseball cap back to front*

(b) the hard ball used in playing baseball; *we lost yet another baseball in the river*

④ **basement**
['beɪsmɪnt] *noun*
floor in a building below the ground level; *we keep the washing machine in the basement*; *she lives in a basement flat in Kensington*; *see also* BARGAIN (NOTE: also called **lower ground floor**)

④ **bash**
[bæʃ]
1 *noun*
(a) knock; *I see your car has had a bash*
(b) *(informal)* **have a bash** = go on, try to do it; *driving a bus looks fun - do you think I could have a bash at it?*
(c) *(informal)* big party; *are you going to Jane's bash tomorrow?* (NOTE: plural is **bashes**)
2 *verb*
to hit hard; *he bashed her over the head with a stick*; *she was bashing stakes into the ground with a hammer*

① **basic**
['beɪsɪk] *adjective*
very simple, at the first level; *being able to swim is a basic requirement if you are going sailing*; *knowledge of basic Spanish will be enough for the job*; **basic vocabulary** = most common words in a language

① **basically**
['beɪsɪkli] *adverb; (used when stating the simplest fact)* at the simplest level; *basically, he's fed up with his job*

④ **basin**
['beɪsɪn] *noun*
large bowl; *mix the flour and butter in a basin*; **wash basin** = large bowl in the bathroom, used for washing your hands and face

① **basis**
['beɪsɪs] *noun*
(a) general facts on which something is based; *what is the basis for these proposals?*; **on the basis of** = based on; *the calculations are done on the basis of an exchange rate of 1.6 dollars to the pound*
(b) general terms of an agreement; *she is working for us on a freelance basis*; *many of the helpers at the children's home work on a voluntary basis* (NOTE: plural is **bases** ['beɪsiːz])

② **basket**
['bɑːskɪt] *noun*
container made of thin pieces of wood, wire, grass, etc., woven together; **shopping basket** = basket used for carrying shopping; *if you're going shopping, don't forget your shopping basket*; **wastepaper basket** = container into which paper or pieces of rubbish can be put; *he threw the letter into the wastepaper basket*

② **basketball**
['bɑːskɪtbɔːl] *noun*
(a) game played by two teams of five players; *he plays in the college basketball team*

(b) the ball used when playing basketball

④ **bass**
[beɪs]
1 *adjective*
referring to a low-pitched voice or music; *he has a pleasant bass voice*; **bass guitar** = guitar which plays a lower range of notes; *he plays bass guitar in a pop group*
2 *noun*
(a) singer with deep voice; *the famous Russian bass*
(b) (double) bass = very large musical instrument like a big cello; *she plays the double bass in the city orchestra* (NOTE: plural is **basses**; do not confuse with **base**)

③ **bastard**
[ˈbɑːstɪd]
1 *adjective*
with parents who are not married; *the bastard son of the last king*
2 *noun*
(a) person whose parents are not married; *many children are born bastards nowadays*
(b) *(informal) (generally offensive)* nasty person, nasty thing; *the bastard walked out of the restaurant without paying*; *the written driving test is a real bastard*

③ **bat**
[bæt]
1 *noun*
(a) piece of wood used for hitting a ball; *a baseball bat*; *a cricket bat*; **he did it off his own bat** = he decided to do it himself without asking anyone
(b) little animal, similar to a mouse, which can fly; *bats were flying all round the trees in the garden*; *bats hang upside down*
2 *verb*
(a) *(in cricket)* to be one of the two players or to be the team which is hitting the ball; *Atherton is batting*; *England batted all day*
(b) *(in baseball)* to be the player who is hitting the ball; *I watched him batting on TV his afternoon*
(c) he never batted an eyelid = he showed no surprise at all (NOTE: **batting - batted**)

④ **batch**
[bætʃ] *noun*
number of things made at one time; *she baked a batch of cakes*; *the department processed a batch of orders*; **batch number** = number printed on a batch of units made at one time; *when making a complaint, please quote the batch number on the packet* (NOTE: plural is **batches**)

② **bath**
[bɑːθ]
1 *noun*
(a) large container in which you can sit and wash your whole body; *there's a wash basin and a bath in the bathroom*; *the bath has not been cleaned properly*

(b) washing your whole body; *he had a bath when he came home from work*; *my father has a cold bath every morning*; *(informal)* **to throw the baby out with the bath water** = to get rid of something good and useful at the same time as you are getting rid of something useless
(c) public baths = large building belonging to a local council, with an indoor swimming pool; **swimming baths** = large building with a swimming pool; *he goes to the municipal swimming baths every day before breakfast* (NOTE: you say **one bath** [bɑːθ] but **two baths** [bɑːðz])
2 *verb*
to wash all over; *she's bathing the baby* (NOTE: do not confuse with **bathe**; note also **baths** [bɑːθs] - **bathing** [ˈbɑːθɪŋ] - **bathed** [bɑːθt])

④ **bathe**
[beɪð]
1 *noun*
act of swimming in a pool, a river, the sea, etc.; *we all went for a bathe before breakfast*
2 *verb*
(a) to wash a wound carefully; *the nurse bathed his wound before applying a dressing*
(b) US to have a bath; *I just have enough time to bathe before my dinner guests arrive*
(c) *(formal)* to go swimming in a pool, lake, the sea, etc.; *on summer evenings, we like to bathe in the lake behind our house* (NOTE the pronunciation (and compare to **bath**): **bathes** [beɪðz] - **bathing** [ˈbeɪðɪŋ] - **bathed** [beɪðd])

② **bathroom**
[ˈbɑːθruːm] *noun*
(a) room in a house with a bath, a washbasin and usually a lavatory; *the house has two bathrooms*
(b) (said instead of) toilet; *where's the bathroom?*; *can I use your bathroom, please?*

④ **bathtub**
[ˈbɑːθtʌb] *noun*
(especially US) bath, the large container in which you can sit and wash your body; *I'd rather have a shower than a bathtub in the bathroom* (NOTE: British English uses simply **bath**)

④ **batsman**
[ˈbætsmɪn] *noun*
(in cricket) the player who is batting; *the last batsman batted on for two hours* (NOTE: plural is **batsmen**; compare also **batter**)

④ **batter**
[ˈbætɪ]
1 *noun*
(a) liquid mixture of flour and milk; *the fish are coated in batter and fried*
(b) *(in baseball)* the player who has the bat and hits the ball; *compare* BATSMAN
2 *verb*
to hit someone often; *he was accused of battering the baby to death*

② **battery**

['bætɪri] *noun*

(a) little device for storing electric energy; *my calculator needs a new battery*; *the battery has given out so I can't use my mobile phone*

(b) series of small cages in which thousands of chickens are kept; **battery chicken** = chicken which spends its life confined in a small cage; *we never eat battery chicken, only free-range* (NOTE: plural is **batteries**)

> COMMENT: battery farming is a very efficient method of egg production; it is criticized, however, because of the quality of the eggs, the possibility of disease and also on the grounds of cruelty because of the stress caused to the birds

② **battle**

['bætl]

1 *noun*

(a) important fight between armed forces; *many of the soldiers died in battle*; *Napoleon was beaten at the Battle of Waterloo*; *Nelson was killed at the Battle of Trafalgar*; **pitched battle** = battle where the opposing sides stand and face each other; **running battle** = battle which moves around; *the police were engaged in running battles with the protesters*

(b) fight against something; *the government's constant battle against inflation*; *he lost his battle against cancer*

2 *verb*

to battle against = to fight against; *she had to battle against the other members of the board*; *his last years were spent battling against cancer*

④ **battlefield**

['bætlfiːld] *noun*

site where a battle took place; *we went to visit the battlefields of northern France*

③ **bay**

[beɪ] *noun*

(a) large curve in a coast; *the Bay of Biscay*

(b) **bay window** = window which sticks out from a flat wall; *can we sit at that table in the bay window?*

(c) **loading bay** = place for loading lorries in a warehouse; **parking bay** = place for one car in a car park; *you can park in the visitors' parking bay*

(d) **to keep someone at bay** = to stop someone attacking; *he tried to keep the bank manager at bay by promising to repay the loan in ten days' time*; *farmers use guns to protect their lambs and keep foxes at bay*

(e) shrub with leaves used in cooking; *add a bay leaf to the soup*

① **BBC**

[biːbiːˈsiː] = BRITISH BROADCASTING CORPORATION; *we were listening to the BBC news* or *to the news on the BBC*; *the BBC broadcasts to many countries in the world*; *a BBC reporter wanted to interview her*

① **be**

[biː]

1 *verb*

(a) *(describing a person or thing)* *our house is older than yours*; *she is bigger than her brother*; *lemons are yellow*; *the soup is hot*; *are you tired after your long walk?*; *put on your coat - it is cold outside*; *I'm cold after standing waiting for the bus*

(b) *(showing age or time)* *he's twenty years old*; *she will be two next month*; *it is nearly ten o'clock*; *it is time to get up*; *September is the beginning of autumn*

(c) *(showing price)* *onions are 80p a kilo*; *the cakes are 50p each*; *my car was worth £10,000 when it was new*

(d) *(showing a job)* *his father is a bus driver*; *she wants to be a teacher*

(e) *(showing size, weight, height, etc.)* *he's 1.70m tall*; *the room is three metres square*; *our house is ten miles from the nearest station*

(f) *(meaning to add up to)* *two and two are four*

(g) *(showing that something exists)* *where are we?*; *there's your hat!*; *there was a crowd of people waiting for the shop to open*; *there were only two people left on the bus*

(h) *(meaning to go or visit)* *the police have been into every room*; *have you ever been to Spain?*; *we have been to see the film three times*

2; *(making part of a verb)*

(a) *(making a present tense)* *don't make a noise when he's watching the football on TV*; *I'm waiting for the bar to open*; *we are hoping to go on holiday in June*

(b) *(making a past tense)* *he was singing in the bath*; *we were walking towards the post office when we met her*

(c) *(making a future tense)* *we will be going to Germany next week*

(d) *(showing a passive)* *he was killed by a train*; *the children were sent home by the teacher*

② **beach**

[biːtʃ]

1 *noun*

area of sand or little stones by the edge of the sea; *let's go to the beach this afternoon*; *many of the beaches are covered with oil from the tanker*; *we walked along the beach and looked for shells*; **beach towel** = large towel normally used on the beach; *she was wrapped in a bright blue and yellow beach towel*; **beach umbrella** = large coloured umbrella to use on a beach (NOTE: plural is **beaches**)

2 *verb*

to bring onto a beach; *they beached the boat near the harbour*; *at high tide we will try to return the beached whale to the sea*

④ **beam**
[biːm]
1
(a) long block of wood or metal which supports part of a building, especially a roof; *you can see the old beams in the ceiling*
(b) ray of light; *beams of sunlight came through the windows of the church*; *the beam from the car's headlights shone into the room*; **dipped beam** = lowered headlights of a car
2 *verb*
to give a wide smile; *the little girl beamed at him*

③ **bean**
[biːn] *noun*
(a) long thin green vegetable, of which you eat the outside or the seeds; *we had fish with chips and French beans or green beans*; *(informal)* **full of beans** = full of energy; *she's full of beans today*; *(informal)* **I haven't got a bean** = I have no money at all; *see also* BAKED BEANS, SPILL
(b) coffee beans = seeds of the coffee bush, which are roasted and ground to make coffee; **soya beans** = beans of the soya plant, which have a high protein and fat content and are low in carbohydrates; *soya sauce is made from soya beans*

① **bear**
[beə]
1 *noun*
large wild animal covered with fur; *they say that bears like honey*; *there are bears near the camp in the mountains*; **polar bear** = big white bear which lives in the snow near the North Pole; *the explorers were attacked by polar bears*; **teddy bear** = toy bear; *she came carrying her favourite teddy bear* (NOTE: usually simply called a **teddy**); *(informal)* **like a bear with a sore head** = in a very bad temper; *what's the matter with him, he's like a bear with a sore head this morning*
2 *verb*
(a) to carry, to produce; *this apple tree has borne fruit every year for the last twenty years*; *a bond which bears interest at 5%*
(b) not to bear = not to like; *I can't bear the smell of cooking fish*
(c) to turn slightly; *bear right at the crossroads* (NOTE: **bearing - bore** [bɔː] **- has borne** [bɔːn])

③ **beard**
[biːd] *noun*
hair growing on a man's chin; *Father Christmas has a long white beard*

③ **bearing**
['beərɪŋ] *noun*
(a) (ball) bearings = set of little balls inside which a wheel turns; *the bearings in the bicycle wheel had to be replaced*

(b) calculation to show where you are; **to get your bearings** = to find out where you are; *give me a few moments to get my bearings*; **to lose your bearings** = to get lost; *I'm sorry I'm late, but I didn't have a map and lost my bearings*
(c) bearing on something = connection to something; *the letter had no bearing on the result of the trial*

② **beat**
[biːt]
1 *noun*
(a) regular sound; *the patient's heart has a beat which is not regular*
(b) *(in music)* regular sound of a piece of music; *they danced to the beat of the steel band*
(c) area patrolled by a police officer on foot; *here policemen on the beat have to go round in pairs*
2 *verb*
(a) to do better than someone else, than another team in a game; *they beat their rivals into second place*; *our football team beat France 2 - 0*; *they beat us by 10 goals to 2*; *we beat the Australians at cricket last year*
(b) to make a regular sound; *his heart was still beating when the ambulance arrived*; *her heart beat faster as she went into the interview*
(c) to hit hard; *the boy was taken away and beaten by a gang of youths*; *she hung the carpet on the line and beat it with a stick to remove the dust*
(d) *(informal)* **beat it!** = go away! (NOTE: beating - beat - has beaten)

③ **beaten**
['biːtɪn] *adjective*
(a) defeated; *the beaten team was very disappointed*
(b) off the beaten track = in a place which is away from main roads and not normally visited by many people; *our village is off the beaten track and so is very quiet*

③ **beating**
['biːtɪŋ] *noun*
act of hitting or defeating; *they gave our team a beating*

② **beat up**
['biːt 'ʌp] *verb*
to attack someone; *three muggers beat him up and stole his credit cards*

① **beautiful**
['bjuːtɪful] *adjective*
very nice, especially to look at; *the beautiful colours of the autumn leaves*; *Mr Smith and his three beautiful daughters*; *what beautiful weather!*; *they have a beautiful house in the country*

④ **beautifully**
['bjuːtɪfuli] *adverb*
in a very pleasing way; *she sang the song beautifully*

② beauty
['bjuːtɪ] *noun*
(a) quality of being beautiful; *her beauty was famous*; *the beauty of the autumn trees against the background of the blue lake*
(b) beautiful woman; beautiful thing; *at 18 she was a real beauty*; *his motorbike is a beauty - I must buy one like it*; *look at these apples, they're real beauties*

① became
[bɪ'keɪm]
see BECOME

① because
[bɪ'kɒz] *conjunction* for this reason; *I was late because I missed the train*; *the dog's wet because he's been in the river*; *just because I'm lending you my car this time, it doesn't mean you can borrow it when you like*

① because of
[bɪ'kɒz ɒv] *preposition*
on account of, due to; *the trains are late because of the fog*; *we don't often use the car because of the price of petrol*

① become
[bɪ'kʌm] *verb*
(a) to change to something different; *the sky became dark and the wind became stronger*; *they became good friends*; *as she got older she became rather deaf*; *it soon became obvious that he didn't understand a word of what I was saying*
(b) to start to work as; *he wants to become a doctor*
(c) **to become of** = to happen to; *I never saw her brother again, I wonder what became of him* (NOTE: **becoming - became** [bɪ'keɪm] - **has become**)

① bed
[bed]
1 *noun*
(a) piece of furniture for sleeping on; *lie down on my bed if you're tired*; **double bed** = bed for two people; **single bed** = bed for one person; **to go to bed** = to get into your bed for the night; *she always goes to bed at 9 o'clock*; **to be in bed** = to be sitting or lying in bed; *she's in bed with a cold*; *he was sitting up in bed drinking a cup of coffee*; **to make a bed** = to make it tidy or change the sheets after someone has slept in it; *have you made your bed?*; *you can't go into your hotel room because the beds haven't been made*; **to get out of bed on the wrong side** = to start the day badly
(b) piece of ground specially for plants; *a strawberry bed*; *a bed of roses*; *her life isn't a bed of roses* = she leads a life full of difficulties
(c) ground at the bottom of water; *the sandy bed of a river*
2 *verb*
to bed out plants = to put plants into a garden bed; *it's still too cold to start bedding out the summer flowers*

① bed and breakfast (b. & b. *or* **B & B)**
['bed n 'brekfɪst] *noun*
(a) staying for a night in a hotel, etc., and having breakfast but no other meals; *I only want to have bed and breakfast*
(b) private house offering accommodation and breakfast; *we got a list of bed and breakfasts from the tourist office*

① bedroom
['bedruːm] *noun*
room where you sleep; *my bedroom is on the first floor*; *the hotel has twenty-five bedrooms*; *shut your bedroom door if you don't want to be disturbed*

④ bedside
['bedsaɪd] *noun*
the side of a bed; *his wife was sitting at his bedside*; *there's a small lamp on the bedside table*; **bedside manner** = way in which a doctor behaves towards a patient, especially a patient who is in bed; *he has a good bedside manner* = he comforts and reassures his patients

③ bedtime
['bedtaɪm] *noun*
time when you go to bed; *10 o'clock is my bedtime*; *she read the children a bedtime story*; **go to bed - it's past your bedtime** = it's later than the time when you normally go to bed

④ bee
[biː] *noun*
insect which makes honey, and can sting you if it is annoyed; *the bee moved from flower to flower*

COMMENT: in a bee colony, the main female bee is the **queen;** the other females are the **workers,** and the males are the **drones**

③ Beeb
[biːb]
the Beeb = BRITISH BROADCASTING CORPORATION

④ beef
[biːf]
1 *noun*
meat from a cow or bull; *a plate of roast beef and vegetables* (NOTE: no plural)
2 *verb*
(informal) **to beef about** = to grumble about; *what's he beefing on about, tell him to shut up!*; **to beef up** = to make bigger or stronger; *we will have to beef up our advertising budget*

① been
[biːn] *see* BE

② beer
[bɪɪ] *noun*
(a) alcoholic drink made from grain and water; *can I have a glass of beer?*; *British beer is flavoured with hops*
(b) a glass of beer; *three beers, please* (NOTE: the plural **beers** is used to mean **glasses of beer**)

④ **beetle**
['biːtl] *noun*
insect with hard covers on its wings; *there were black beetles in the kitchen*

④ **beetroot**
['biːtruːt] *noun*
vegetable with a dark red root, eaten cooked with vinegar to make a salad; **as red as a beetroot** = very red in the face; *he went as red as a beetroot when we asked him about his girlfriend* (NOTE: American English is simply **beet**)

① **before**
[bɪ'fɔː]
1 *adverb*
earlier; *why didn't you tell me before?*; *I didn't see him last week, I saw him the week before*
2 *preposition*
earlier than; *they should have arrived before now*; *you must be home before 9 o'clock*; *G comes before H in the alphabet*
3 *conjunction*
earlier than; *before you sit down, can you switch on the light?*; *the police got there before I did*; *think carefully before you start to answer the exam questions*; *wash your hands before you have your dinner*

③ **beforehand**
[bɪ'fɔːhænd] *adverb*
in advance; *you must tell me beforehand if you want to borrow any more money*

④ **beg**
[beg] *verb*
(a) to ask for money, food, clothes, etc.; *she sat begging on the steps of the station*; *children were begging for food*
(b) to ask someone in an emotional way to do something, to give something; *his mother begged him not to go*; *he begged for more time to find the money*
(c) to beg a favour of someone = to ask someone to do something for you
(d) I beg your pardon! = excuse me, forgive me; *I beg your pardon, I didn't hear what you said*; *I do beg your pardon - I didn't know you were busy* (NOTE: **begging - begged**)

① **began**
[bɪ'gæn]
see BEGIN

① **begin**
[bɪ'gɪn] *verb*
to start; *the children began to cry*; *she has begun to knit a red pullover for her father*; *the house is beginning to warm up*; *his surname begins with an S*; *the meeting is due to begin at ten o'clock sharp*; **to begin again** = to start a second time; *he forgot to save his file and had to begin keyboarding all over again* (NOTE: **beginning - began** [bɪ'gæn] - **has begun** [bɪ'gʌn])

③ **beginner**
[bɪ'gɪnɪ] *noun*
person who is starting; *he can't paint well, he's only a beginner*

① **beginning**
[bɪ'gɪnɪŋ] *noun*
first part; *the beginning of the film is rather boring*; *hurry up if you want to see the beginning of the news*

① **begun**
[bɪ'gʌn]
see BEGIN

④ **behalf**
[bɪ'hɑːf] *noun*
(a) on behalf of = acting for someone; *she is speaking on behalf of all the businesses in the association*; *he was chosen to speak on behalf of the other workers in the factory*
(b) acting on my behalf = acting as my representative; *the solicitor acting on my behalf*
(c) don't worry on my behalf = don't worry about me

③ **behave**
[bɪ'heɪv] *verb*
to act in a certain way with someone; *he behaved very pleasantly towards his staff*; *she was behaving in a funny way*; *(of children)* **to behave (yourself)** = to be good; *if you don't behave (yourselves) you won't have any ice cream*

① **behaviour** *US* **behavior**
[bɪ'heɪvjɪ] *noun*
way of doing things; *his behaviour was quite natural*; *visitors complained about the behaviour of the football fans*

① **behind**
[bɪ'haɪnd]
1 *preposition*
(a) at the back of; *they hid behind the door*; *I dropped my pen behind the sofa*; *he was second, only three metres behind the winner*; *she's behind the rest of class* = not as advanced as the others; *see also* TIME
(b) responsible for; *the police believe they know who is behind the bombing campaign*
(c) supporting; *all his colleagues were behind his decision*; *we're behind you!*
2 *adverb*
(a) at the back; *he was first, the rest of the runners were a long way behind*; **he left his umbrella behind** = he forgot to take his umbrella with him; **when the others went out, he stayed behind to watch TV** = he stayed at home when the others went out
(b) later than you should be; *I am behind with my correspondence*; *the company has fallen behind with its deliveries*
3 *noun*

(informal) part of the body which you sit on; *there was some water on the chair and my behind's all wet*; *I'll kick his behind if he doesn't get a move on*; *he's so lazy! - he needs a good kick up the behind*

① **being**
['biːɪŋ]
see HUMAN, TIME

③ **Belgian**
['beldʒɪn]
1 *adjective*
referring to Belgium; *Belgian chocolates are very popular in England*; *all Belgian motorways are lit up at night*
2 *noun*
person from Belgium; *there were ten people at the meeting, and two of them were Belgians*

③ **Belgium**
['beldʒɪm] *noun*
country on the North Sea, between France and Holland; *if you're driving to Denmark, it is quicker to drive through Belgium into Germany* (NOTE: capital: **Brussels**; people: **Belgians**; languages: **Flemish, French**; currency: **Belgian franc, euro**)

② **belief**
[bɪ'liːf] *noun*
feeling sure that something is true; *his firm belief in the power of law*; *her strong belief in God*; **it is my belief** = I believe; *it's my belief that the problems with the engine are caused by the rain*; **to the best of my belief** = as far as I know; *to the best of my belief, no one else has seen this document*; **beyond belief** = quite incredible; *that she did not know that there were drugs in the parcel is quite beyond belief*

① **believe**
[bɪ'liːv] *verb*
(a) to be sure that something is true, although you can't prove it; *people used to believe that the earth was flat*; *don't believe anything he tells you*
(b) not to be absolutely sure; *I don't believe I have ever met your father*; *I believe I have been here before*
(c) to believe in = to be sure that something exists; *do you believe in flying saucers?*; *some people believe in miracles*
(d) can't *or* **couldn't believe your eyes** *or* **ears** = be very surprised to see *or* hear something; *I couldn't believe my ears when I heard my name read out as the winner*; *she couldn't believe her eyes when she saw the car he had bought her*

② **bell**
[bel] *noun*
(a) metal object, like a cup, which makes a ringing noise when hit; electric device which makes a ringing noise if you push a button; *the alarm bell rings if you touch the door*; *the postman rang the door bell*; *you ought to have a bell on your bicycle*; *they rang the church*

bells at the wedding; **that rings a bell** = that reminds me of something; *does the name Forsyth ring a bell?*
(b) *(informal)* **to give someone a bell** = to phone someone; *I'll give you a bell when we've sorted out the details*

③ **belly**
['beli] *noun*
(informal) stomach and the front part of the body below the chest; *the little boy lifted his T-shirt and showed his round belly* (NOTE: plural is **bellies**)

① **belong**
[bɪ'lɒŋ] *verb*
(a) to belong to someone = to be the property of someone; *does the car really belong to you?*
(b) to belong to a group or club = to be a member of a group or club; *which tennis club do you belong to?*
(c) to belong with = to be part of, to be stored with; *these plates belong with the big dinner service*

④ **belongings**
[bɪ'lɒŋɪŋz] *noun*
personal property; *her belongings were scattered all over the room*; *please be sure to take all personal belongings with you when you leave the aircraft*

④ **beloved**
[bɪ'lʌvɪd] *adjective*
(person or place) which someone loves very much; *she doesn't want to leave her beloved childhood home*; *he was very upset at the death of his beloved grandfather*

① **below**
[bɪ'ləʊ]
1 *adverb*
lower down; *standing on the bridge we looked at the river below*; *these toys are for children of two years and below*
2 *preposition* lower down than; *the temperature was below freezing*; *in Singapore, the temperature never goes below 25°C*; *can you see below the surface of the water?*; *do not write anything below this line*; *these tablets should not be given to children below the age of twelve*

② **belt**
[belt]
1 *noun*
(a) strap which goes round your waist (to hold up a skirt or trousers); *she wore a bright red belt*; *this silver belt comes from Japan*
(b) seat belt *or* **safety belt** = belt which you wear in a car or a plane to stop you being hurt if there is an accident; *please fasten your seat belts as we are preparing to land*; *the police caught him driving without a seat belt*
(c) zone around something; **commuter belt** = area round a large town, where commuters live; *they live in the Surrey commuter belt*; **Green Belt** = area of farming land or woods and parks,

which surrounds a town, and on which building is restricted or completely banned; *they can't put houses in Old Oak Wood, it's Green Belt land*

2 *verb*

(informal)

(a) to travel fast; *the car was belting along the motorway at over 100 miles an hour*

(b) to belt out = to sing very loudly; *the fans were belting out football songs*

② **bench**
[bentʃ] *noun*

(a) long wooden seat; *we sat down on one of the park benches*

(b) (work) bench = table in a workshop at which someone works; *the shoe repairer was standing at his bench*

(c) the bench = magistrates sitting in court; *he was up before the bench for speeding*

(d) *(in Parliament)* long seats in the House of Commons; **front bench** = seat where ministers sit; *he's hoping for a seat on the front bench*; **back benches** = seats where ordinary MPs sit (NOTE: plural is **benches**)

② **bend**
[bend]

1 *noun*

(a) curve (in a road, line, etc.); *don't drive too fast, there's a sudden bend in the road*; *the pipe under the sink has an awkward S-bend*

(b) *(informal)* **round the bend** = mad; *he's completely round the bend*; *she'll go round the bend when she hears that*; *that music is driving me round the bend*

2 *verb*

(a) to make something curved; *you will have to bend the pipe to fit round the corner*

(b) to curve; *the road bends sharply after the bridge* (NOTE: **bending - bent** [bent])

② **bend down** *or* **bend over**
['bend 'daʊn or 'əʊvɪ] *verb*

to bend your body so that your head is lower than your waist; *he dropped his pen and bent down to pick it up*; *she was bending over the sink*; *see also* BACKWARDS

② **beneath**
[bɪ'niːθ]

1 *adverb*

underneath; *from the bridge we watched the river flowing beneath*

2 *preposition*

(a) under; *there are dangerous rocks beneath the surface of the lake*; *the river flows very fast beneath the bridge*

(b) not suitable, not important enough; *he thinks it is beneath him to make the coffee himself*

④ **beneficial**
[benɪ'fɪʃl] *adjective*

which helps, which is a benefit; *a regular walk every morning is beneficial to your general health*

① **benefit**
['benɪfɪt]

1 *noun*

(a) advantage; *what are the benefits of joining the club?*

(b) payment made by the state; *he receives unemployment benefit*

2 *verb*

(a) to be useful to someone; *the book will benefit anyone who is planning to do some house repairs*

(b) to benefit from *or* **by something** = to get an advantage from; *British tourists will benefit from the strong pound*; *pensioners can benefit from free bus passes*

② **bent**
[bent]

1 *adjective*

(a) curved; *these nails are bent so we can't use them*; *see also* BEND

(b) to be bent on = to be very keen on doing something; *he is bent on buying the car even if he can't afford it*

2 *noun*

instinct; *she has a natural bent to be a nurse*; *he followed his bent and joined the navy*

④ **berry**
['berɪ] *noun*

small fruit; *they spent the afternoon picking berries in the woods* (NOTE: plural is **berries;** do not confuse with **bury**)

② **beside**
[bɪ'saɪd] *preposition*

(a) at the side of someone or something; *come and sit down beside me*; *the office is just beside the railway station*; **it's beside the point** = it's got nothing to do with the main subject; *whether or not the coat matches your hat is beside the point - it's simply too big for you*

(b) to be beside yourself with = to be mad with; *the parents were beside themselves with worry when their daughter did not come home from school*; *she was beside herself with grief*

② **besides**
[bɪ'saɪdz]

1 *preposition* as well as; *they have two other cars besides the big Ford*; *besides the football team, our town also has a hockey team*; *besides managing the shop, he also teaches in the evening*

2 *adverb*

(a) as well; *he paints, plays chess and has lots of other interests besides*

(b) in any case; *I don't want to go for a picnic - besides, it's starting to rain*

① **best**
[best]

1 *adjective*

(a) very good, better than anything else; *she's my best friend*; *what is the best way of getting to London from here?*; *he put on his best suit to go to the interview*

(b) for the best part of = for most of; *she's been in bed for the best part of a week*

2 *noun*

(a) thing which is better than anything else; *the picture shows her at her best*; **to do your best** = to do as well as you can; *she did her best, but didn't win*

(b) to make the best of something = to take what advantage you can from something; *they say it will rain this afternoon, so we'd better make the best of the sunshine while it's here*; **to make the best of a bad job** = to do something in spite of terrible conditions; *it was raining when we stopped for a picnic, so we made the best of a bad job and had our sandwiches in the car*

(c) *(informal)* best clothes; *the children were all in their Sunday best*

(d) *(informal)* best bitter beer; *two pints of best, please!*

3 *adverb*

in the best way; *which of you knows London best?*; *the engine works best when it's warm*; *oranges grow best in hot countries*; **as best you can** = in the best way you can, even though this may not be perfect; *he repaired the dent in the car door as best he could* (NOTE: **best** is the superlative of both **good** and **well**)

① **best man**
['best 'mæn] *noun*

man who helps the bridegroom at a wedding; *the best man had put the wedding rings in his pocket*; *the best man gave a speech and told some funny stories about the bridegroom when he was a student*

① **best wishes**
['best 'wɪʃɪz] *noun*

greeting sent to someone; *give my best wishes to your father*

① **bet**
[bet]

1 *noun*

money which is risked by trying to say which horse will come first in a race, which side will win a competition, etc.; *he placed a bet on his friend's horse but lost his bet when the horse came last*; *I've got a bet on England to win the next World Cup*; **safe bet** = bet which you are not likely to lose; *it's a safe bet that if we decide to go camping it will rain*

2 *verb*

to risk money by saying which horse you think will come first in a race, which team will win, etc.; *he bet me £10 the Prime Minister would lose the election*; **I bet you she's going to be late** = I am quite sure she's going to be late; *(informal)* **you bet!** = of course; *do you want to go to the pub? - you bet!* (NOTE: **betting - bet**)

④ **betray**
[bɪ'treɪ] *verb*

(a) to harm someone by telling a secret about them; *he was betrayed to the enemy by his best friend*; *the scientist was accused of betraying secrets to the enemy*

(b) to show a feeling which you want to keep hidden; *the tears in her eyes betrayed her emotion*

① **better**
['betɪ]

1 *adjective*

(a) good when compared to something else; *the weather is better today than it was yesterday*; *his latest book is better than the first one he wrote*; *she's better at maths than English*; *brown bread is better for you than white*; *we will shop around to see if we can get a better price*

(b) healthy again; *I had a cold last week but I'm better now*; *I hope your sister will be better soon*

2 *adverb*

well as compared to something else; *she sings better than her sister*; *my old knife cuts better than the new one*; **to think better of something** = to decide that something is not a good idea; *he was going to drive to London, but thought better of it when he heard the traffic report on the news* (NOTE: **better** is the comparative of both **good** and **well**)

3 *noun*

to get the better of someone = to beat someone; *no one can get the better of him at cards*; **for the better** = which makes the situation better; *he's earning more money now, and his financial situation has changed for the better*; **he took a turn for the better** = his health began to improve

◊ **had better**
['hæd 'betɪ] *phrase*

it would be a good thing if; *you had better wear a coat - I think it's starting to snow*; *she'd better go to bed if she's got flu*; *hadn't you better answer the phone?*

② **betting**
['betɪŋ]
see BET

① **between**
[bɪ'twiːn] *preposition*

(a) placed with things on both sides; *there's only a thin wall between his office and mine, so I hear everything he says*; *don't sit between him and his girlfriend*

(b) connecting two places; *the bus goes between Oxford and London*

(c) in the interval separating two times; *I'm have a meeting between 10 o'clock and 12*; *can you come to see me between now and next Monday?*

(d) in the space separating two amounts; *the parcel weighs between four and five kilos*; *cherries cost between £2 and £3 per kilo*

(e) showing a difference; *she's colour-blind - she can't tell the difference between red and green*

(f) sharing; *we only had £10 between the three of us*

(g) among; *she could choose between courses in German, Chinese or Russian*

(h) between you and me = speaking privately; *between you and me, I don't think he's very good at his job*

◊ **in between**
[ɪn bɪ'twiːn]
in the middle, with things on both sides; *the hotel looks over the river, with a railway line in between*; *he had two meetings in the morning but managed to fit in a game of tennis in between*

④ **beware**
[bɪ'weɪ] *verb*
watch out for; *beware of the dog!*; *beware of pickpockets!*

① **beyond**
[bɪ'jɒnd]
1 *preposition*
(a) further away than; *the post office is beyond the bank*; **it is beyond my means** = it is too expensive for me to buy it; *I'd love to buy a sports car, but I think it would be beyond my means*

(b) later than; *the party went on till beyond midnight*
2 *adverb*
further away, on the other side; *she stared through the window at the fields beyond*

④ **bias**
['baɪəs] *noun*
fixed opinion in favour of something or against something; *the judges in the beauty competition were accused of bias*; *the Prime Minister had a bias against men with beards*

④ **biased**
['baɪəst] *adjective*
too much in favour of something or against something; *we felt the decision was biased*; *the court was biased in favour of the president's daughter*

③ **Bible**
['baɪbl] *noun*
(a) Christian and Jewish book of holy writing; *he reads from the Bible every evening*

(b) important and useful reference book; *she keeps an old French cookery book in the kitchen - it's her bible*

> COMMENT: the Bible is formed of the Old Testament (the Jewish holy book) and New Testament, the writings concerned with the life and works of Christ and the early Christian church

③ **bicycle**
['baɪsɪkl] *noun*
vehicle with two wheels which is ridden by one person who makes it go by pushing on the pedals; *he goes to school by bicycle every day*; *she's going to do the shopping on her bicycle*; *he's learning to ride a bicycle*; **bicycle pump** = small hand pump for blowing up bicycle tyres; *we blew up the mattress with a bicycle pump*; *see also* BIKE (NOTE: also called a **bike**. The person who rides a bicycle is a **cyclist**. Note also that to show the difference with a motorcycle, a bicycle is sometimes called a **push bike**)

③ **bid**
[bɪd]
1 *noun*
(a) offer to buy at an auction; *his bid for the painting was too low*

(b) attempt to do something; **he made a bid for power** = he tried to seize power; **takeover bid** = attempt to take over a company by offering to buy most of its shares
2 *verb*
(a) to make an offer to buy something at an auction; *he bid £500 for the car* (NOTE: **bidding - bid**)

(b) *(formal)* to wish; *he bade me farewell* (NOTE: **bid** *or* **bade** [bæd] **- has bidden**)

① **big**
[bɪg] *adjective*
of a large size; *I don't want a small car - I want a big one*; *his father has the biggest restaurant in town*; *I'm not afraid of him - I'm bigger than he is*; *we had a big order from Germany*; **big toe** = the largest of your five toes (NOTE: **bigger - biggest**)

① **Big Ben**
['bɪg 'ben] *noun*
clock and bell at the top of the tower of the Houses of Parliament in London; *Big Ben strikes the hours for the TV news*

① **big deal**
['bɪg 'diːl] *noun*
(a) important business transaction; *it's one of the biggest deals we have ever signed*

(b) *(informal)* **big deal!** = that's not a very good deal; *he offered me £20 for the car - big deal!*

② **bike**
[baɪk] *noun*
(informal) = BICYCLE; *he goes to school by bike*; *she was knocked off her bike by a car*; *although he is over eighty he still rides a bike or goes for a bike ride every day*; **exercise bike** = bicycle fixed to the floor, which you can pedal on as exercise; *he does ten minutes on his exercise bike before breakfast*; **mountain bike** = strong bicycle with wider tyres, used for country cycling; *she rode her mountain bike along the hill paths*; **push bike**; *see note at* BICYCLE

① **bill**
[bɪl] *noun*

(a) piece of paper showing the amount of money you have to pay (in a restaurant, for repairs, etc.); *the total bill came to more than £200*; *does the bill include VAT ?*; *ask the waiter for the bill*; *don't forget to pay the gas bill* (NOTE: in American English in a restaurant or hotel, this is a **check**)

(b) hard part of a bird's mouth; *the bird was picking up food with its bill*

(c) *US* piece of paper money; *a 10-dollar bill* (NOTE: British English for this is **note: a 10-pound note**)

(d) proposed act of parliament which, if passed by parliament, becomes law; *Parliament will consider two bills this week*; *he has drafted a bill to ban the sale of guns*

④ **billiards**
['bɪljɪdz] *noun*

game where two players with long cues hit their own white ball against a red ball or the opponent's ball, scoring points; *they played a game of billiards*; *the club has bought a new billiard table*; *compare* SNOOKER (NOTE: the word **billiards** loses the 's' when it is in front of another noun)

> COMMENT: The game is played on a table covered with smooth green cloth and with raised edges (or 'cushions') and six small net bags (or 'pockets') at each corner and in the middle of the two long sides

④ **billion**
['bɪljɪn] *noun*

(a) one thousand million; *(sometimes)* one million million; *the government raises billions in taxes each years*

(b) a great many; *billions of Christmas cards are sent every year* (NOTE: in American English it has always meant one thousand million, but in British English it formerly meant one million million, and it is still sometimes used with this meaning. With figures it is usually written **bn: $5bn** say 'five billion dollars')

② **bin**
[bɪn]

1 *noun*

(a) metal box for keeping things; **bread bin** = metal box for keeping bread in

(b) container for putting rubbish; *don't throw your litter on the floor - pick it up and put it in the bin*; **pedal bin** = container for rubbish which opens with a pedal

2 *verb*

(informal) to throw away into a rubbish bin; *he just binned the letter asking for payment* (NOTE: **binning - binned**)

② **bind**
[baɪnd] *verb*

(a) to force someone to do something; *the contract binds him to make regular payments*

(b) to put a cover on a book; *the book is bound in blue leather*

(c) to tie; *they bound her to the tree with ropes*; *see also* BOUND (NOTE: **binding - bound** [baʊnd])

④ **binding**
['baɪndɪŋ] *adjective*

which has legal power; *this contract is binding on both parties*

④ **biography**
[baɪ'ɒgrɪfi] *noun*

the story of someone's life; *have you read the new biography of Churchill?*; *she's the author of a biography of Henry VIII* (NOTE: plural is **biographies**)

④ **biological**
[baɪɪ'lɒdʒɪkl] *adjective*

(a) referring to living things; *the biological balance in the North Sea*

(b) using bacteria; *a treaty to ban biological warfare*

(c) biological mother = mother who gave birth to a child (as opposed to a parent who adopts)

④ **biologist**
[baɪ'ɒlɪdʒɪst] *noun*

scientist who specializes in biology; *Darwin was a famous biologist*

③ **biology**
[baɪ'ɒlɪdʒi] *noun*

study of living things; *she took biology and chemistry as exam subjects*; *biology students spend some of their time in the research lab*

④ **birch**
[bɜːtʃ] *noun*

silver birch = northern tree, with small leaves and white bark; *the birch forests of Russia*; *the bark of birch trees comes off in strips* (NOTE: plural is **birches**)

② **bird**
[bɜːd] *noun*

(a) animal with wings and feathers; *most birds can fly, but some can't*; *she keeps a little bird in a cage*; **a little bird told me** = someone told me the secret, but I can't tell you who it was; **a bird in the hand is worth two in the bush** = be satisfied with what you have, rather than hope for something better which may never come; *see also* EARLY

(b) *(informal)* person; *she's a funny old bird*

(c) *(informal)* girl; *who's that new bird in the accounts department?*; *did you see the bird he was with last night?*

② **birth**
[bɜːθ] *noun*

being born; *he was a big baby at birth*; **to give birth to** = to have a baby; *she gave birth to a boy last week*; **birth certificate** = official document which says when and where someone was born; **date of birth** = day, month and year when a person was born; *he put his date of birth as 15th June 1985*

② **birthday**
['bɜːθdeɪ] *noun*
date on which you were born; *April 23rd is Shakespeare's birthday*; *my birthday is on 25th June*; *what do you want for your birthday?*; **he'll be 10 years old next birthday** = on his next birthday he will be 10 years old; **birthday cake** = cake made specially for a birthday and decorated with icing, candles, etc.; **birthday card** = card sent to someone to wish him or her good luck on their birthday; *remind me to send her a birthday card, it's her birthday next Tuesday*; **birthday party** = party held for a birthday; **birthday presents** = presents given to someone for his or her birthday; *the watch was a birthday present from my father*

◊ **Happy Birthday**
['hæpi 'bɜːθdeɪ]
greeting said to someone on their birthday; **'Happy Birthday to you!'** = song sung at a birthday party; *we all sang 'Happy Birthday to you' and then she blew out the candles on her cake*

③ **biscuit**
['bɪskɪt] *noun*
small flat hard cake, usually sweet; *a packet of chocolate biscuits*; **cheese and biscuits** = cheese served with biscuits (which are not sweet); *they had cheese and biscuits after the meal* (NOTE: American English for sweet biscuits is **cookies**)

③ **bishop**
['bɪʃɪp] *noun*
(a) Christian church leader; *the Bishop of London*
(b) piece in chess, which looks like a bishop's hat; *she took both his bishops in three moves*

① **bit**
[bɪt]
1 *noun*
(a) little piece; *he tied the bundle of sticks together with a bit of string*; *would you like another bit of cake?*; **to come to bits** = to fall apart; *the chair has come to bits*; **to take something to bits** = to put it in pieces to mend it; *he's taking my old clock to bits*
(b) **a bit** = a little; *the painting is a bit too dark*; *let him sleep a little bit longer*; *have you got a piece of wood a bit bigger than this one?*; *can you wait a bit, I'm not ready yet*; **a bit much** = not fair; *being told it was my fault when I wasn't even there is a bit much*; **not the slightest bit** = not at all; *she didn't sound the slightest bit worried*
(c) tool which fits into a drill, used for making holes; *have you seen the bit for the drill anywhere?*
(d) metal rod which is in a horse's mouth, and which the rider uses to control the horse
2 *verb*
see BITE

◊ **bit by bit**
['bɪt baɪ 'bɪt] *phrase*
not all at the same time, little by little; *he paid back the money he owed, bit by bit*; *he inched forward, bit by bit, towards the edge of the cliff*

① **bite**
[baɪt]
1 *noun*
(a) mouthful; *all I had for lunch was a bite of bread and cheese*; *she took a big bite out of the sandwich*
(b) place where someone has been bitten; **insect bite** = sting caused by an insect which goes through the skin and hurts; *some insect bites can be very painful*; *her arms were covered with mosquito bites*
2 *verb*
(a) to cut with your teeth; *the dog tried to bite the postman*; *she bit a piece out of the pie*
(b) *(of an insect)* to sting; *she's been bitten by a mosquito* (NOTE: biting - bit [bɪt] - has bitten ['bɪtn])

① **bitten**
['bɪtn]
see BITE

③ **bitter**
['bɪtɪ]
1 *adjective*
(a) not sweet; *this black coffee is too bitter*
(b) angry and annoyed; *she was very bitter about the way the boss treated her*; **to the bitter end** = to the very end; *they resisted the changes to the bitter end*
(c) very cold; *a bitter December night*; *bitter weather coming from the Arctic*
2 *noun*
ordinary pale British beer which is not sweet; *a pint of bitter, please* (NOTE: usually no plural; **bitters** means glasses of bitter: **two bitters and a packet of crisps, please**)

④ **bitterly**
['bɪtɪli] *adverb*
(a) deeply; *he bitterly regrets what he said*
(b) **bitterly cold** = very cold; *it was bitterly cold in the tent*

④ **bizarre**
[bɪ'zɑː] *adjective*
very strange; *I find it bizarre that no one told her that the house had been sold*; *she's started to wear the most bizarre clothes*

① **black**
[blæk]
1 *adjective*
(a) very dark colour, the opposite to white; *he was wearing a black suit*; *a black and white photograph*; **black coffee** = coffee with no milk in it; *do you want your coffee black or white?*
(b) **black economy** = goods and services which are paid for in cash, and not declared to the income tax authorities

(c) with a dark-coloured skin; *many black people work in the car industry* (NOTE: blacker - blackest)

2 *noun*

(a) the colour of black; **in the black** = in credit, in profit; *the company went into the black last year*; *my bank account is still in the black*

(b) person whose skin is dark coloured

3 *verb*

to forbid trading in certain goods or with certain suppliers; *three firms were blacked by the government*

blackberry
['blækbɪri] *noun*

(a) small black fruit that grows on a bush; *for dessert we're having blackberry and apple pie*

(b) the bush this fruit grows on; *we had to struggle through blackberry bushes which had grown over the path*

blackbird
['blækbɜːd] *noun*

common garden bird with black feathers and a yellow bill; *listen to the blackbird singing*

blackboard
['blækbɔːd] *noun*

dark board on the wall of a classroom, etc., which you can write on with chalk; *he wrote the instructions for the exam on the blackboard*; *some dishes are not on the menu, but are written on a blackboard*

blackcurrant
[blæk'kʌrɪnt] *noun*

(a) garden fruit with little black berries which are usually eaten cooked; *a jar of blackcurrant jam*; *the blackcurrants need more sugar - they're very sour*

(b) the small bush this fruit grows on; *I planted six blackcurrants in the garden*

blackmail
['blækmeɪl]

1 *verb*

to threaten to harm someone unless a demand is met, to threaten to reveal a secret unless money is paid; *her former cook tried to blackmail her*; *they tried to blackmail the government into releasing prisoners of war*

2 *noun*

act of blackmailing; *the government will not give in to terrorist blackmail*

black market
['blæk 'mɑːkɪt] *noun*

buying and selling goods in a way which is not allowed by law (as when goods are rationed); *we bought some gold coins on the black market*

blade
[bleɪd] *noun*

(a) sharp cutting part; *the blades of a pair of scissors*; *be careful - that knife has a very sharp blade*

(b) shoulder blade = one of two large flat bones covering the top part of your back; *he fell when skiing and broke his shoulder blade*

(c) thin leaf of grass; *she sat in the shade of an apple tree, chewing a blade of grass*

(d) long piece of wood with a flat part at the end, used for rowing

blame
[bleɪm]

1 *noun*

criticism for having done something (even if you did not do it); *I'm not going to take the blame for something I didn't do*; **to get the blame for** = to be accused of; *who got the blame for breaking the window? - me, of course!*

2 *verb*

to blame someone for something or **to blame something on someone** = to say that someone is responsible for something; *blame my sister for the awful food, not me*; *he blamed the accident on the bad weather*; **I don't blame you** = I think you're right to do that; *I don't blame you for being annoyed, when everyone else got a present and you didn't*; **he has only himself to blame** = no one else is responsible for what happened; *he has only himself to blame if he missed the chance of a free ticket to Thailand*; **to be to blame for** = to be responsible for; *the manager is to blame for the bad service*

bland
[blænd] *adjective*

(a) without much flavour; *some people don't like rice because they find it too bland*; *the sauce needs more herbs - it's far too bland*

(b) dull and not very interesting, not giving any information; *he gave a bland reply to the questions from the reporters*

blank
[blæŋk]

1 *adjective*

(a) (paper) with no writing on it; *she took a blank piece of paper and drew a map*

(b) he looked blank = he didn't seem to know anything about it; *when she mentioned the money he owed, he just looked blank*

2 *noun*

(a) empty space (on a piece of paper); *just fill in the blanks on the form*

(b) my mind is a blank = I can't remember anything about it; **to draw a blank** = to get no result; *when she tried to trace her father, she drew a blank*

3 *verb*

to blank out = to cover up something (which has been written); *he showed her the letter with the signature blanked out*

blanket
['blæŋkɪt]

1 *noun*

(a) thick cover which you put over you to keep warm; *he woke up when the blankets fell off the bed*; *she wrapped the children up in blankets to keep them warm*; **wet blanket** = miserable person who spoils a party, etc.; *don't ask her to your birthday - she's such a wet blanket*

(b) thick layer; *a blanket of snow covered the fields*; *the motorway was covered in a blanket of fog*

2 *verb*

to cover with something; *the whole area was blanketed with snow*

④ **blast**

[blɑːst]

1 *noun*

(a) explosion; *windows were broken by the blast*

(b) strong wind; *a cold blast from the north*

(c) sharp blow on a signal or whistle; *three blasts of the alarm means that passengers should go on deck*

(d) going full blast = going at full power; *they kept the heating going full blast even in summer*

2 *verb*

(a) to destroy with an explosive or bullets; *the burglars blasted their way into the safe*; *they blasted their way out of the police trap*

(b) to ruin; *the accident blasted his hopes of a sporting career*

④ **blaze**

[bleɪz]

1 *noun*

(a) large bright fire; *five fire engines were called to the blaze*

(b) to work like blazes = to work very hard; *they worked like blazes to get the house ready*

2 *verb*

(a) to burn fiercely; *the camp fire was blazing and everyone sang songs*

(b) to blaze away = to shoot fiercely; *they blazed away at the enemy for several minutes*

④ **blazer**

['bleɪzɪ] *noun*

jacket which is worn with trousers of a different material, often with a club badge stitched to the pocket; *she was wearing a blue blazer with brass buttons*; **school blazer** = blazer of a special colour with the badge of the school on it; *a crowd of boys and girls in school blazers got onto the bus*

④ **bleak**

[bliːk] *adjective*

(a) cold and miserable; *the path led across bleak mountains*

(b) showing no sign of hope or encouragement; *she gave him a bleak stare*; *with no qualifications, his job prospects are bleak* (NOTE: bleaker - bleakest)

④ **bled**

[bled]

see BLEED

④ **bleed**

[bliːd] *verb*

to lose blood; *his chin bled after he cut himself while shaving*; *he was bleeding heavily from his wound* (NOTE: bleeding - bled ['bled])

④ **blend**

[blend]

1 *noun*

mixture; *different blends of coffee*

2 *verb*

(a) to mix; *blend the eggs, milk and flour together*

(b) *(of colour)* to go well together, not to contrast with each other; *the grey curtains blend with the pale wallpaper*

③ **bless**

[bles] *verb*

(a) to make holy by prayers, etc.; *the church was blessed by the bishop*

(b) to bring happiness or good fortune; *their marriage was blessed with two fine sons*

(c) *(informal) (said when someone sneezes)* *bless you!* (NOTE: blessing - blessed [blest])

② **blew**

[bluː]

see BLOW

② **blind**

[blaɪnd]

1 *adjective*

(a) not able to see; *he's not only blind, he's also very deaf*; **to turn a blind eye to something** = not to bother about something, even if you know it exists; *we turn a blind eye to minor cases of theft in the office*

(b) *(informal)* none at all; *he didn't pay a blind bit of notice to the regulations*; *it didn't make a blind bit of difference*

2 *noun*

(a) covering over a window that can be pulled up and down; *they must still be asleep - their blinds are closed*; *he pulled down the blind to keep out the sun*

(b) the blind = people who cannot see; *the town hall has excellent facilities for the blind*

3 *verb*

to make someone unable to see; *she was blinded by the bright lights of the cars*

③ **blink**

[blɪŋk]

1 *noun*

(informal) **on the blink** = not working, out of action; *the telephone's on the blink*

2 *verb*

(a) to close your eyelids very quickly; *he blinked when the light was switched on*; *she watched the bull come towards her without blinking*

(b) *(of lights)* to go on and off; *the alarm light is blinking*

② **block**

[blɒk]

1 *noun*

(a) large building; *they live in a block of flats*

(b) *US* section of buildings surrounded by streets; *he lives two blocks away*

(c) large piece; *blocks of ice were floating in the river*

(d) group of things together; *they booked a block of seats in the middle of the plane*; **block vote** = casting of a large number of votes at the same time by one person who represents a large number of people at a meeting

2 *verb*

to prevent something passing along something; *the pipe is blocked with dead leaves*; *the crash blocked the road for hours*; *what can I take for my blocked nose?*

③ **bloke**

[bləʊk] *noun*

(informal) man; *I bought the car from a bloke I know at work*

③ **blond**

[blɒnd] *adjective*

fair, or with fair hair; *is her blond hair natural?*; *two little blond children*

③ **blonde**

[blɒnd]

1 *adjective*

fair, or with fair hair; *she has lovely long blonde hair*

2 *noun*

woman with fair hair; *he came to the party with a gorgeous blonde*

① **blood**

[blʌd] *noun*

red liquid in the body; *blood was pouring out of the wound on his head*; *she can't stand the sight of blood*

COMMENT: blood is mainly formed of red and white cells. It circulates round the body, going from the heart and lungs around the body and back again. As it moves round the body, blood takes oxygen to the tissues and removes waste matter which is cleaned through the kidneys. An adult has about six litres of blood in his or her body

② **blood pressure**

['blʌd 'preʃɪ] *noun*

pressure at which the heart pumps blood; *he has to take pills for his high blood pressure*

④ **bloodstream**

['blʌdstriːm] *noun*

flow of blood round the body; *the antibiotics are injected into the bloodstream*; *hormones are carried by the bloodstream to various parts of the body*

③ **bloody**

['blʌdɪ] *adjective*

(a) with much blood; *a bloody battle*

(b) *(slang)* awful, terrible; *stop that bloody noise!* (NOTE: **bloodier - bloodiest**)

④ **bloom**

[bluːm]

1 *verb*

to have flowers; *the cherry trees are blooming in the park*

2 *noun*

flower; **the apple trees are in full bloom** = the apple trees are in flower

④ **blossom**

['blɒsɪm]

1 *noun*

mass of flowers on trees; *the hedges are covered with blossom*; *the trees are in full blossom*

2 *verb*

(a) to flower; *the roses were blossoming round the door of the cottage*

(b) to do well; *she's really blossomed since she got married*

① **blow**

[bləʊ]

1 *noun*

knock or punch; *he received a blow to the head in the fight*

2 *verb*

to make air move; *the wind had been blowing hard all day*; *blow on your soup if it's too hot*; **to blow your nose** = to clear a blocked nose by blowing down it into a handkerchief; *she has a cold and keeps having to blow her nose* (NOTE: **blowing - blew** [bluː] **- has blown** [bləʊn])

① **blow away**

['bləʊ ə'weɪ] *verb*

(a) to go away by blowing; *his hat blew away*

(b) to make something go away by blowing; *the wind will blow the fog away*

① **blow down**

['bləʊ 'daʊn] *verb*

(a) to make something fall down by blowing; *six trees were blown down in the storm*

(b) to fall down by blowing; *the school fence has blown down*

① **blow off**

['bləʊ 'ɒf] *verb*

to make something go away by blowing; *the wind blew his hat off*; *the wind has blown all the leaves off the trees*

① **blow out**

['bləʊ 'aʊt] *verb*

to make something go out by blowing; *she blew out the candles on her birthday cake*

① **blow up**

['bləʊ 'ʌp] *verb*

(a) to make something get bigger by blowing into it; *he blew up balloons for the party*; *your front tyre needs blowing up*

(b) to destroy something in an explosion; *the soldiers blew up the railway bridge*

(c) to make a photograph bigger; *the article was illustrated with a blown-up picture of the little girl and her uncle*

(d) to make something seem more important than it really is; *the story has been blown up by the papers*

① **blue**

[bluː]

1 *adjective*

(a) coloured like the colour of the sky; *he wore a*

pale blue shirt; they live in the house with the dark blue door; all their children have got blue eyes

(b) sad or miserable; *when you're feeling blue just sing a song and you'll feel better* (NOTE: **bluer - bluest**)

2 *noun*

(a) the colour of the sky; *have you a cloth of a darker blue than this?; she was dressed all in blue; (informal)* **the boys in blue** = the police

(b) **out of the blue** = suddenly; *out of the blue came an offer of a job in Australia*

④ **blunt**
[blʌnt]

1 *adjective*

(a) not sharp; *he tried to cut the meat with a blunt knife;* **blunt instrument** = something used as a weapon such as a piece of wood or hammer, which is not sharp; *the doctor says the wounds were caused by a blunt instrument*

(b) almost rude (way of speaking); *his blunt manner made people think he was being rude* (NOTE: **blunter - bluntest**)

2 *verb*

to make blunt; *using the knife to open tins has blunted it*

④ **blur**
[blɜ:]

1 *verb*

to become less clear, to make less clear; *his vision became blurred; the paper printed a rather blurred photograph of the house* (NOTE: **blurring - blurred**)

2 *noun*

picture which is not very clear; *he was hit on the head, and everything became a blur; he tried to take a picture of the plane as it flew past but it was just a blur*

① **board**
[bɔ:d]

1 *noun*

(a) long flat piece of wood, etc.; *the floor of the bedroom was just bare boards;* **ironing board** = long narrow table for ironing; **board games** = games (like chess) which are played on a flat piece of wood

(b) blackboard; *the teacher wrote on the board*

(c) food; **board and lodging** = meals and accommodation; **full board** = rate for bedroom and all meals in a hotel; **half board** = rate for breakfast and dinner at a hotel, but not lunch

(d) group of directors; *she was asked to join the board; the board meets every month*

(e) **to go on board** = to go on to a ship, train, plane, etc.; *we went on board at 9.30 and the ship sailed at 12.00*

2 *verb*

to go on to a ship, train, plane, etc.; *six passengers boarded at Belgrade; customs officials boarded the ship in the harbour; the 16.50 train to Paris is now ready for boarding at platform 5*

④ **boast**
[bɪust]

1 *noun*

act of boasting; *their proudest boast is that they never surrendered*

2 *verb*

(a) **to boast of** *or* **about something** = to say how good, etc., you are; *he was boasting of how he had climbed the three mountains in a day*

(b) to have something good; *the house boasts an indoor swimming pool; the town boasts an 18-hole golf course*

① **boat**
[bɪut] *noun*

small ship; *they sailed their boat across the lake; they went to Spain by boat; when is the next boat to Calais?;* **a rowing boat** *US* a **rowboat** = small boat which is rowed with long wooden blades; *we hired a rowing boat and went down the river;* **a sailing boat;** *US* a **sailboat** = boat which has sails; *two sailing boats sank during the race;* **a fishing boat** = boat used for catching fish at sea; *the fishing boats are back, let's go down to the harbour and buy some fish; (informal)* **we're all in the same boat** = we're all in the same situation; *it's a shame about the redundancies, but if the firm goes bust we'll all be in the same boat*

① **the Boat Race**
[ðɪ 'bɪut 'reɪs] *noun*

the annual race on the Thames between rowing eights from Oxford and Cambridge universities; *we watched the Boat Race on TV*

COMMENT: the race is rowed each year over a course of 4 miles, 374 yards, on the Thames between Putney and Mortlake in the west of London. The race has been rowed each year since 1864, and to date Cambridge have won 75 times and Oxford 69 times, with one dead heat. The fastest time for the race is 16 minutes, 45 seconds

① **body**
['bɒdi] *noun*

(a) the whole of a person or of an animal; *he had pains all over his body; the dead man's body was found in the river*

(b) the main part of an animal or person, but not the head and arms and legs; *she was beaten on the arms and the upper part of her body*

(c) the main part of a car, plane, text, etc.; *the car has an all-steel body; the body of the text is printed in black* (NOTE: plural is **bodies** for meanings (a), (b) and (c))

(d) being strong or solid; *the conditioner will give your hair body; the wine has a good body*

③ **bodyguard**
['bɒdɪgɑ:d] *noun*

(a) person who guards someone; *the attacker was grabbed by the president's bodyguards*

(b) group of people who guard someone; *he has a bodyguard of six people* or *a six-man bodyguard*

③ **boil**
[bɔɪl]
1 *noun*
(a) infected swelling; *he has a boil on the back of his neck*
(b) when water is boiling; **the kettle is on the boil** = the water in the kettle is boiling; **bring the water to the boil** = to heat the water until it boils
2 *verb*
(a) *(of water or other liquid)* to bubble and change into steam or gas because of being very hot; *put the egg in when you see that the water's boiling*; *don't let the milk boil*; *the kettle's boiling* = the water in the kettle is boiling
(b) to heat water (or another liquid) until it changes into steam; *can you boil some water so we can make tea?*; *boil the water before you drink it*
(c) to cook (vegetables, eggs, etc.) in boiling water; *small potatoes do not take long to boil*; *would you like a boiled egg for breakfast?*; **soft-boiled egg** = egg cooked by boiling in water until it is hot, but with the yolk still more or less liquid; **hard-boiled egg** = egg that has been boiled until it is hard; *I need two hard-boiled eggs for the salad*

③ **boiler**
[ˈbɔɪlɪ] *noun*
apparatus for boiling water; heater for central heating; *naturally the boiler broke down just before Christmas*

③ **boiling**
[ˈbɔɪlɪŋ]
1 *noun*
action of heating a liquid to the point where it becomes steam or gas; *boiling water for five minutes will kill germs in it*
2 *adjective*
(a) which has started to boil (i.e., for water, at 100°); *put the potatoes in a pan of boiling water*
(b) very hot; *it is boiling in this room*
3 *adverb*
boiling hot = very hot; *it's boiling hot in our office*; *a pan of boiling hot oil fell on her foot*

④ **boiling point**
[ˈbɔɪlɪŋ ˈpɔɪnt] *noun*
temperature at which a liquid boils, i.e. when it turns into steam or gas; *100°C is the boiling point of water*

③ **boil over**
[ˈbɔɪl ˈʊvɪ] *verb*
(of liquid) to rise up when boiling and run over the side of the pan; *the milk boiled over and made a mess on the cooker*

④ **bold**
[bɪʊld]
1 *adjective*
(a) strong in colour or design; *she likes bold colours*; *the wallpaper is a bold design of dark green leaves*
(b) brave; *she was bold enough to say 'no' to the Prime Minister*; *may I be so bold as to ask if you are free for dinner this evening?* (NOTE: **bolder - boldest**)
2 *noun*
printing type with thick black letters; *the main words in this dictionary are printed in bold*; *compare* ITALIC

④ **bolt**
[bɪʊlt]
1 *noun*
(a) long metal rod with a screw thread, fastened with a nut; *the top of the table is attached to the legs with bolts*
(b) long metal rod which is pushed into a hole to close a door firmly; *she looked through the window and after a long pause pulled back the bolts*
(c) flash of lightning; *he had taken shelter under a tree that was hit by a bolt of lightning*; **it came as a bolt from the blue** = it came as a complete surprise
(d) **to make a bolt for** = to rush towards; *at the end of the show everyone made a bolt for the door*; **to make a bolt for it** = to run away; *when the guards weren't looking two prisoners tried to make a bolt for it*
2 *verb*
(a) to fasten with a bolt; *he bolted the door when he went to bed*; *the tables are bolted to the floor*
(b) to run fast, to escape; *the horse bolted*
(c) to eat quickly; *don't bolt your food*
3 *adverb*
sitting bolt upright = sitting with your back very straight

② **bomb**
[bɒm]
1 *noun*
(a) weapon that explodes, dropped from an aircraft or placed by hand; *the bomb was left in a suitcase in the middle of the station*; *they phoned to say that a bomb had been planted in the main street*; *enemy aircraft dropped bombs on the army base*
(b) *(informal)* **it went like a bomb** = it went very well indeed; **it costs a bomb** = it costs a lot of money
2 *verb*
(a) to drop bombs on something; *enemy aircraft bombed the power station*
(b) *(informal)* to go very fast; *we bombed down the motorway to Bristol*

④ **bomber**
[ˈbɒmɪ] *noun*
(a) person who plants bombs; *the bombers managed to escape after planting the bomb*

(b) aircraft for dropping bombs; *the bombers were out during the night, attacking enemy targets*

③ **bond**
[bɒnd]
1 *noun*

(a) document showing a loan to the government; *government bonds are a very safe form of investment*; **premium bond** = government bond which gives a prize in a draw, instead of paying interest

(b) link between two people; *there is a close bond between her and her sister*

(c) contract; *his word is his bond*

(d) goods in bond = goods which are held by customs until duty has been paid

2 *verb*

to stick together tightly; *cover the two surfaces with glue and hold them tightly until they bond*

② **bone**
[bɪun]
1 *noun*

(a) one of the solid pieces in the body, which make up the skeleton; *he fell over and broke a bone in his leg*; *be careful when you're eating fish - they have lots of little bones*; *the two dogs were fighting over a bone*; **I've got a bone to pick with you** = I want to complain about something you have done

(b) bone dry = extremely dry; *don't put your shirt on until it is bone dry*

2 *verb*

to remove bones from meat; *a boned leg of lamb*

④ **bonfire**
['bɒnfaɪɪ] *noun*

outdoor fire; *he put the dead leaves on the bonfire*; *they sat around the bonfire singing songs*; **Bonfire Night** = 5th November, when the attempt by Guy Fawkes to blow up the Houses of Parliament in 1605 is remembered

COMMENT: bonfires are burnt with a figure of a man on top (the guy) and fireworks are set off. Children collect money in advance by standing with the guy, and asking for a 'penny for the guy'

② **bonus**
['bɪunɪs] *noun*

(a) extra money; *salesmen earn a bonus if they sell more than their quota*; **no claims bonus** = reduced insurance premium because no claims have been made against the policy; *the insurance premium is £300 but I have a 50% no claims bonus*; *because of the accident, he lost his no claims bonus*

(b) advantage; *it was an added bonus that the plane arrived early, as we were able to catch an earlier bus home* (NOTE: plural is **bonuses**)

① **book**
[bʊk]
1 *noun*

(a) sheets of printed paper attached together, usually with a stiff cover; *I'm reading a book on the history of London*; *he wrote a book about butterflies*; **coffee table book** = heavy expensive book with many illustrations, which can be left on a table for people to look at; **phone book** *or* **telephone book** = book which lists names of people and businesses in alphabetical order with their addresses and telephone numbers; *he looked up the number of the company in the phone book*; **picture book** = book with mainly pictures and not much text; *the book shop has a few picture books for the under twos*; **reference book** = book (such as a dictionary or directory) where you can look up information; **school book** = book used when learning a subject in school; *I've lost one of my school books*

(b) sheets of paper attached together; **account book** = book which records sales and purchases; **chequebook** *US* **checkbook** = set of blank cheques attached together in a cover; *don't leave your chequebook on the counter*; **a book of stamps** = several stamps attached inside a little paper cover; **a book of matches** = set of cardboard matches attached together in a paper cover; *he collect books of matches*

(c) books = business records; *her job its to keep the firm's books up to date*; *we have no one on our books with that name*; *we have ten houses for sale on our books*

2 *verb*

(a) to reserve a place, a seat, a table in a restaurant or a room in a hotel; *we have booked a table for tomorrow evening*; *I want to book two seats for Friday evening*; *I'm afraid the dentist is fully booked until the end of next week*; *I'm sorry, the concert is sold out - all the seats have been booked*

(b) to charge someone with an offence; *the police officer booked him for speeding*

② **booking**
['bʊkɪŋ] *noun*

reservation of seats, places, etc.; *we had to cancel our booking and travel the next day*; **to make a booking** = to reserve a room, a seat, a table, etc.; *we tried to make a booking for the week beginning May 1st, but the hotel was full*

② **booking office**
['bʊkɪŋ 'ɒfɪs] *noun*

office in a cinema, theatre, etc., where you can buy tickets in advance; *phone the booking office to see if there are any seats left for tonight*

② **booklet**
['bʊklɪt] *noun*

book of information with only a few pages; *you'll find booklets about the town at the Tourist Information Office*

② **bookshop**
['bʊkʃɒp] *noun*

shop which sells books; *the local bookshop has books on local history* (NOTE: American English is usually **bookstore**)

② **bookstore**
['bʊkstɔː] *noun*
US store which sells books; *there's a good bookstore just across the street from our apartment* (NOTE: British English is **bookshop**)

③ **boom**
[buːm]
1 *noun*
(a) increase in wealth for everyone; *the economy is improving and everyone is forecasting a boom for next year*
(b) loud noise, like a deep bang; *there was such a loud boom that everyone jumped*
(c) long rod for holding a microphone over the heads of speakers)
2 *verb*
(a) to become more prosperous, to increase; *sales to Europe are booming*
(b) to make a loud deep noise; *his voice boomed across the square*

④ **boost**
[buːst]
1 *noun*
help or increase; *the advertising campaign gave a boost to our sales*
2 *verb*
to help to increase; *the TV commercial should boost our sales*

③ **boot**
[buːt]
1 *noun*
(a) strong shoe which covers your foot and goes above your ankle; *the policemen were wearing long black boots*; *put on your boots if you're going to dig the garden*; *bring walking boots with you as we will be climbing in the hills*; **football boots** = boots to wear when playing football; **ski boots** = boots to wear when skiing
(b) the space at the back of a car where luggage is put; *put the cases in the boot*; *this box won't fit into the boot* (NOTE: American English for this is the **trunk**)
2 *verb*
(informal) **to boot someone out** = to throw someone out; *he was booted out of the police force for taking bribes*

③ **booth**
[buːð] *noun*
(a) small place for one person to stand or sit; **polling booth** = small enclosed space in a polling station, where the voter goes to mark his ballot paper in private; **phone booth** = public box with a telephone; *there's a phone booth near the supermarket - we can phone from there*; **ticket booth** = place outdoors where a person sells tickets

(b) *US* separate section of a commercial fair where a company shows its products or services; *the American publisher wants us to meet him at his booth* (NOTE: British English for this is a **stand**)

② **border**
['bɔːdɪ]
1 *noun*
(a) frontier between countries; *they managed to cross the border into Switzerland*; *there was nothing to show that we had crossed the border*; *the enemy shelled several border towns*; *he was killed by the border guards*
(b) edge; **flower border** = flower bed by the side of a path or lawn
2 *verb*
to be along the edge of something; *the path is bordered with rose bushes*

④ **bore**
[bɔː]
1 *noun*
(a) thing which makes you bored; *he went on talking non-stop and in the end it became a bit of a bore*; **what a bore!** = what a nuisance
(b) dull person who is not very interesting; *I don't want to sit next to him, he's such a bore*
(c) measurement of the inside of a pipe or gun barrel; *a small-bore gun*
2 *verb*
(a) to make a round hole in something; *bore three holes two centimetres apart*
(b) to make someone fed up with what you are saying or doing; *I won't bore you with the details of my operation*
(c) *see also* BEAR

② **bored**
[bɔːd] *adjective*
fed up, not interested in what is happening; *you get very bored having to do the same work every day*; *I'm bored - let's go out to the club*; **bored with** = fed up with; *I'm bored with this programme, can't we change to another channel*; *(informal)* **bored stiff** = very bored; *can't we switch on the TV? - I'm bored stiff waiting for the rain to stop* (NOTE: do not confuse with **board**)

② **boring**
['bɔːrɪŋ] *adjective*
dull, not interesting; *I don't want to watch that boring TV programme*

① **born**
[bɔːn] *verb*
to be born = to begin to live; *he was born in Scotland*; *she was born in 1956*; *he's American-born but was brought up in the UK*; *the baby was born last week*; *(informal)* **I wasn't born yesterday** = I'm not as stupid as you think (NOTE: **born** is usually only used with **was** or **were**)

③ **borne**
[bɔːn]
see BEAR

borough

['bʌrɪ] *noun*

large town run by a town council; *the borough council is responsible for roads*

> COMMENT: a borough is an officially incorporated town, which has a charter granted by Parliament. A borough is run by an elected council, with a mayor as its official head. Most boroughs are represented in Parliament by at least one MP

borrow

['bɒrɪʊ] *verb*

(a) to take something for a short time, usually with the permission of the owner; *can I borrow your car to go to the shops?*; *she borrowed three books from the school library*; *he wants to borrow one of my CDs*

(b) to take money for a time, usually paying interest; *he borrowed £10 from me and never paid it back*; *companies borrow from banks to finance their business*; *she borrowed £100,000 from the bank to buy a flat*; *compare* LEND

borrower

['bɒrɪʊwɪ] *noun*

person who borrows; *the interest rate for borrowers is 18.5%*

borrowing

['bɒrɪʊwɪŋ] *noun*

(a) action of taking money for a time; **borrowing power** = amount of money which a company or person can borrow; *he has enormous debts, so his borrowing power is very limited*

(b) **borrowings** = money which is borrowed; *the company has borrowings of over £200,000*

boss

[bɒs]

1 *noun*

(informal) person in charge, owner (of a business); *if you want a day off, ask the boss*; *I left because I didn't get on with my boss* (NOTE: plural is **bosses)**

2 *verb*

to boss someone about or **around** = to tell someone what to do all the time; *she's always bossing her little brother about*; *stop bossing me around!*

both

[bɪʊθ] *adjective & pronoun*

(a) two people together, two things together; *hold on to the handle with both hands*; *both my shoes have holes in them*; *both her brothers are very tall*; *she has two brothers, both of them in Canada*; *she and her brother both go to the same school*; *I'm talking to both of you*

(b) *(for emphasis)* *she is both clever and modest*

bother

['bɒðɪ]

1 *noun*

trouble or worry; *we found the shop without any bother*; *it was such a bother getting packed that we nearly didn't go on holiday*

2 *verb*

(a) to annoy, to cause trouble; *stop bothering me, I'm trying to read*; **to be hot and bothered** = to be annoyed and nervous about something

(b) **to bother to do something** = to take the time or trouble to do something; *don't bother to come with me to the station - I can find my way easily*

(c) **can't be bothered to** = don't have the time to, don't have the energy to; *I can't be bothered to iron the sheets*; *he couldn't be bothered to answer my letters*

3 *interjection; (informal)*

used to show you are annoyed; *bother! I've left my umbrella on the train*

bottle

['bɒtl]

1 *noun*

(a) tall plastic or glass container for liquids; *he bought two bottles of red wine*; *she drank the water straight out of the bottle*; *he bought his wife a bottle of perfume*

(b) **hot water bottle** = rubber bottle filled with hot water, for warming the bed

(c) *(informal)* courage; *he hasn't got the bottle to do it*

2 *verb*

(a) to put in bottles; *the wine is bottled in Germany*; *only bottled water is safe to drink*; *she perfected a process for speeding up the bottling system*

(b) *(informal)* **to bottle out** = to decide not to do something because you are afraid; *he was ready to jump but bottled out at the last minute*

bottle bank

['bɒtɪl 'bæŋk] *noun*

place where you can throw away empty bottles for recycling; *there's a box of bottles in the kitchen ready to be taken to the bottle bank*

bottom

['bɒtɪm]

1 *noun*

(a) lowest point; *is there any honey left in the bottom of the jar?*; *the ship sank to the bottom of the sea*; *turn left at the bottom of the hill*; *he's bottom of his class* = he gets the worst marks; **to get to the bottom of a problem** = to find the real cause of a problem

(b) far end; *go down to the bottom of the street and you will see the post office on your left*; *the greenhouse is at the bottom of the garden*

(c) part of the body on which you sit; *if you are naughty again, you will get a smack on your bottom*; *see also* BEHIND

(d) lower part of a piece of clothing; *he was wearing just his track suit bottom*; *I can't find the bottom of my swimming costume*

(e) from the bottom of my heart = deeply and sincerely; *I want to thank you all from the bottom of my heart*

2 *adjective*

lowest; *the jam is on the bottom shelf; he was standing on the bottom rung of the ladder*

① **bought**
[bɔːt]
see BUY

③ **bounce**
[baʊns]
1 *noun*

(a) movement up and down; *he hit the ball on the second bounce*

(b) energy; *she's always full of bounce*

2 *verb*

(a) to spring up and down or off a surface; *the ball bounced down the stairs; he kicked the ball but it bounced off the post*

(b) *(informal)* **his cheque bounced** = there was not enough money in his account to pay the sum on the cheque

② **bound**
[baʊnd]
1 *noun*

great jump; **in leaps and bounds** = very rapidly; *the project is going forward in leaps and bounds*

2 *adjective*

(a) bound for = on the way to; *a ship bound for the Gulf*

(b) tied up; *the boy was left bound to a tree; the burglars left him bound hand and foot; a bundle of old letters bound in pink ribbon*

(c) obliged; *he felt bound to help her; he is bound by the contract he signed last year*

(d) very likely; *they are bound to be late*

(e) *see also* BIND

3 *verb*

to leap; to run fast; *she bounded into the room; he bounded out of his chair; the dog bounded into the bushes*

② **boundary**
['baʊndri] *noun*

limit of property, knowledge, etc.; *the white fence marks the boundary between our land and his*; **the boundaries of knowledge** *or* **of science** = the furthest point in human knowledge; *scientists are trying to push back the boundaries of human knowledge*; *(in cricket)* **to hit a boundary** = to hit the ball beyond the edge of the playing field (and score four runs) (NOTE: plural is **boundaries**)

④ **bout**
[baʊt] *noun*

(a) fight or contest, especially a boxing match; *Lewis won that bout*

(b) attack of illness; *she had a bout of flu*

③ **bow**
1 ['bəʊ] *noun*

(a) ribbon knotted in a shape like a butterfly; *the parcel was tied up with red bows*; **bow tie** = tie which is tied in the shape of a butterfly; *he always wears a bow tie*

(b) piece of wood with strings, used for playing a string instrument; *he slowly drew the bow across the strings of his double bass*

2 [baʊ] *noun*

(a) bending the body forward as a mark of respect; *he made a deep bow to the queen*; **to take a bow** = to step forward on a stage and bow to the audience to thank them for their applause; *the actors took their bows one after the other*

(b) *(also;* **bows**) front part of a ship; *the captain posted a sailor in the bow(s) to look out for rocks*; **bow wave** = big wave which forms at the front of a boat

(c) the person rowing who sits nearest to the bow of a boat; *he rowed bow for Cambridge*; *compare* STROKE

3 [baʊ] *verb*

to bend forward in salute; *he bowed to the queen*

④ **bowels** *or* **bowel**
['baʊəlz] *noun*

(a) the tube from the stomach in which food is digested as it passes through; **bowel movement** = action of passing solid waste matter from the bowel; *the patient had a bowel movement this morning*

(b) in the bowels of the earth = deep underground

② **bowl**
[bəʊl]
1 *noun*

(a) wide container for food, water, etc.; *put the egg whites in a bowl and beat them*; **salad bowl** = special bowl for salad; **soup bowl** = special bowl for soup

(b) the food or liquid contained in a bowl; *he was eating a bowl of rice; give the dog a bowl of water; a bowl of hot thick soup is just what you need in this cold weather*

(c) large heavy ball, used for playing the game of bowls or the game of bowling; *she picked up the bowl and stepped up to take her turn* (NOTE: the proper name for it is a **wood**)

2 *verb*

(a) *(especially in cricket)* to throw a ball (to a batsman); *just as the bowler ran up to bowl, a pigeon landed on the pitch; it's your turn to bowl*

(b) *(in a game of bowls)* to roll a bowl (to try to get close to the target)

④ **bowler**
['bəʊlə] *noun*

(a) person who plays bowls

(b) *(in cricket)* person who throws the ball to the batsman; *one of the England fast bowlers*

④ **bowling**
['bɪʊlɪŋ] *noun*
game where your roll a large ball to knock down a set of pieces of wood standing at the end of a wooden stage; *we're going bowling tomorrow night*

③ **bowls**
[bɪʊlz] *noun*
game played on grass, where teams of players roll large balls towards a small ball thrown as a target; *their team are the bowls champions*

① **box**
[bɒks]
1 *noun*
(a) container made of wood, plastic, metal, etc., with a lid; *she put the cakes into a cardboard box*; **cash box** = metal box for keeping cash in
(b) a container and its contents; *he took a box of matches from his pocket*; *he gave her a box of chocolates for her birthday*
(c) **letter box** *or* **pillar box** = container for posting letters; *she posted her cards in the letter box on the corner*; **P.O. box number** = address with a number at a post office
(d) **callbox** = small shelter with a public telephone inside; *not a single callbox at the station was free*
(e) line running round a section of text or an illustration; *in this dictionary, the comments are in boxes*
(f) small separate section in a theatre; *they took a box for the performance of the 'Marriage of Figaro'*; **royal box** = special section in a theatre where a king or queen sits (NOTE: plural is **boxes)**
(g) tree with very small leaves, used to make hedges; *the beds of flowers are edged with box* (NOTE: no plural in this meaning)
2 *verb*
to fight by punching; *he learnt to box at a gym in the East End*

④ **boxer**
['bɒksɪ] *noun*
fighter who fights by punching; *the two boxers came together in the ring*; **boxer shorts** = men's underwear shaped like sports shorts

④ **boxing**
['bɒksɪŋ] *noun*
sport in which two opponents fight each other in a ring by punching with thick gloves; **boxing gloves** = thick padded gloves, laced at the wrist, worn for boxing; **boxing ring** = square area, surrounded with a rope fence, in which boxing matches take place; *the two boxers climbed into the (boxing) ring*

COMMENT: a fight lasts a certain number (usually 10 or 15 in professional boxing) of 3-minute rounds with a 1-minute rest between rounds, the object being to knock out or score more points than your opponent. Blows must land above the waist on the front and sides of the body and on the head. A referee in the ring supervises the fight. If one boxer is knocked down he is allowed ten seconds, counted out loud by the referee, to get up; if at the end of ten seconds he is still down, he is counted out and as a result he is declared to have lost by being knocked out

② **Boxing Day**
['bɒksɪŋ 'deɪ]
26th December, the day after Christmas Day; *we're going to see my grandparents on Boxing Day*

COMMENT: traditionally, Boxing Day was the occasion when gifts in the form of Christmas boxes were given to workers and staff. The Boxing Day holiday is moved to the Monday if the 26th December falls on a Saturday or Sunday

① **boy**
[bɔɪ] *noun*
(a) male child; *a boy from our school won the tennis match*; *when I was a boy, hardly anyone in the village had a television set*; *I knew him when he was a boy*; **paper boy** = boy who delivers newspapers to your house; *the paper boy comes every morning at seven o'clock*; **a boys' school** = a school for boys only; *see also* OLD BOY
(b) a son; *her three boys are all at university*

④ **boycott**
['bɔɪkɒt]
1 *verb*
to refuse to deal with someone, usually for political reasons; *we are boycotting all food imports from that country*
2 *noun*
action of refusing to deal with someone, usually for political reasons; *the boycott of the company lasted three months*

② **boyfriend**
['bɔɪfrend] *noun*
man, usually young, that a girl is having a relationship with; *she's got a new boyfriend*; *she brought her boyfriend to the party*; *compare* GIRLFRIEND

④ **bra**
[brɑː] *noun*
(informal) a piece of clothing worn by women to hold the breasts; *don't wear a black bra under that white shirt*

④ **brace**
[breɪs]
1 *noun*
(a) support which makes a bone straight; *he had his leg in a brace*; *she wears braces on her teeth*
(b) **braces** = straps over your shoulders to hold up your trousers; *he wore bright red braces with his jeans* (NOTE: American English is **suspenders)**

(c) **a brace of** = two, a pair of (NOTE: only used with birds which have been killed)

(d) **a brace and bit** = a drill, the tool holding a bit

2 *verb*

to brace yourself for = to prepare yourself for something nasty to happen; *when the phone rang, she braced herself for the shock of hearing his voice again*; *the pilot told us to brace ourselves for a crash landing*

③ **Braille**

['breɪl] *noun*

system of writing using raised dots on paper to show the letters, which allows a blind person to read by passing his or her fingers over the page; *the book has been published in Braille*

② **brain**

[breɪn] *noun*

(a) nerve centre in the head, which controls all the body; *the brain is the most important part of the body*

(b) intelligence; **use your brain** = think hard; **she's got brains** *or* **she's got a good brain** = she's intelligent

③ **brake**

[breɪk]

1 *noun*

device for stopping a vehicle or making it go slower; *put the brake on when you go down a hill*; *the brakes aren't working!*; **hand brake** = brake which is worked by hand; *he managed to stop the car safely using the hand brake*; *release the hand brake before you start*; **foot brake** = brake which is worked by foot, using a pedal; **brake lights** = red lights at the back of a car which light up when you put the brakes on; *do you know that one of your brake lights isn't working?*; **brake pedal** = pedal in a car which you press with your foot to make the brakes work; *see also* JAM

2 *verb*

to slow down by pressing the brakes; *the driver of the little white van braked hard* (NOTE: do not confuse with **break**)

① **branch**

[brɑːnʃ]

1 *noun*

(a) thick part of a tree, growing out of the trunk; *he hit his head against a low branch*

(b) local office of an organization; *he's the manager of our local branch of Lloyds Bank*; *the store has branches in most towns in the south of the country* (NOTE: plural is **branches**)

2 *verb*

to branch off = to come off a main road; *drive along for about a mile and you will see a small road branching off on the left*; **to branch out** = to start to do something different, as well as what you normally do; *the corner shop has branched out and now sells flowers*

④ **brand**

[brænd]

1 *noun*

(a) product with a name; *a well-known brand of soap*

(b) mark burnt with a hot iron on an animal's skin, to show who owns the animal

2 *verb*

(a) to name in public; *he was branded as a thief*; *the minister was branded a crook in the newspaper*

(b) to mark an animal's skin with a hot iron; *the cattle were branded before being sent to market*

③ **brand-new**

[brænd'njuː] *adjective*

completely new; *these shoes are brand-new - I bought them for the wedding*

④ **brass**

[brɑːs] *noun*

(a) mixture of copper and zinc; *the doctor has a brass name plate on his door*

(b) musical instruments made of brass; *a brass band led the parade*; **the brass section** *or* **the brass** = section of an orchestra with brass instruments; *compare* STRINGS, WIND

④ **brassiere**

['bræzɪɪ] *noun*

(formal) a piece of clothing worn by women to hold the breasts (NOTE: usually simply called a **bra**)

③ **brave**

[breɪv]

1 *adjective*

full of courage; *it was very brave of him to dive into the river to try to rescue the little girl* (NOTE: **braver - bravest**)

2 *verb*

to be brave enough to do something dangerous; *the ambulance braved the snowstorm to answer the 999 call*

③ **breach**

[briːtʃ]

1 *noun*

breaking the law, or a promise; *this is a breach of the promise they made last year*; **breach of the peace** = noisy behaviour; *they were arrested for a breach of the peace*; **breach of faith** = going back on a promise; **in breach of** = breaking; *in breach of their agreement, they started negotiating with our rivals behind our backs* (NOTE: plural is **breaches**)

2 *verb*

(a) to go against rules, etc.; *the pay settlement has breached the government's rules*; *he was arrested for breaching the peace*

(b) to make a hole; *the enemy guns breached the town's defences*

① **bread**

[bred] *noun*

food made from flour and water baked in an oven; *can you get a loaf of bread from the supermarket?*; *she cut thin slices of bread for sandwiches*; **bread and butter** = slices of bread covered with butter; **brown bread** = bread made from brown flour; **white bread** = bread made from white flour; **French bread** = bread in the form of a long thin stick (NOTE: do not confuse with **bred**; note also there is no plural: **some bread**; for one piece say **a loaf of bread, a slice of bread**, etc.)

④ **breadcrumbs**
[ˈbredkrʌmz] *noun*
little pieces of dried bread; *the fish is covered in breadcrumbs and then fried*

① **break**
[breɪk]
1 *noun*
(a) space; *you can see blue sky through a break in the clouds*
(b) short rest; *there will be a 15-minute break in the middle of the meeting*; **they worked for three hours without a break** = they worked without stopping; **to take a break** = to have a short rest; *we'll take a break now, and start again in fifteen minutes*; **coffee break** *or* **tea break** = short rest in the middle of work when you drink coffee or tea; *we'll have a coffee break now*
(c) *(in schools)* **morning break** *or* **afternoon break** = short period for rest and play in the middle of the morning and afternoon; *we couldn't go out during the morning break because it was raining*
(d) short holiday; **weekend break** = short holiday over a weekend; *we went away for a weekend break in Brighton*; **city break** = short holiday in a large and famous town; *we took a city break in Prague*
(e) move away from someone or something; *I thought they were in love, so the break came as a surprise; it's not always easy to make a break with the past*
(f) *(commercial)* **break** = short period between TV programmes or parts of programmes when advertisements are shown; *we will continue with the news after this break*
(g) crack in a broken bone, piece of china, etc.; *the break is clean so it should heal quite quickly*
(h) stop in something regular; *there's a break in the pattern which shouldn't be there*
(e) **he had a lucky break** = his bad luck changed
2 *verb*
(a) to make something come apart in pieces; *he dropped the plate on the floor and broke it; she broke her leg when she was skiing*
(b) to come apart in pieces; *the clock fell on the floor and broke*
(c) **to break a record** = to do better than a previous record; *he broke the record for the 2000 metres*

(d) **to break your journey** = to stop for a while before going on; *we'll break our journey in Edinburgh*
(e) **to break a silence** = to make a noise; *the silence was broken by a mobile phone*; **to break your silence** = to talk about something which has been kept secret for a long time; *at long last he broke his silence about the affair*
(f) **to break with the past** = to cut your links with people you used to know, places you used to visit; *they decided to break with the past and go to live in New Zealand*
(g) to fail to carry out the duties of a contract; *the company has broken its agreement*; **to break a promise** = not to do what you had promised to do; *he broke his promise and wrote to her again*; **to break a contract** = to cancel a contract
(h) to start; *we woke up as day was breaking*
(i) **to break it to someone** *or* **to break the news to someone** = to tell someone bad news; *we will have to break it to her as gently as possible* (NOTE: do not confuse with **brake**; note also **breaking - broke** [brʊk] **- has broken** [ˈbrʊkn])

① **break down**
[ˈbreɪk ˈdaʊn] *verb*
(a) *(of machine)* to stop working; *the lift has broken down again; the car broke down and we had to push it*
(b) to show all the items in a total list; *can you break down this invoice into travel costs and extras?*

③ **breakdown**
[ˈbreɪkdaʊn] *noun*
(a) failure of a system to work properly; *there has been a breakdown in communications between them*
(b) collapse of the body or mind; **nervous breakdown** = severe depression; *he had a breakdown after he was sacked*
(c) *(of machine)* stopping working; *we had a breakdown on the motorway; a breakdown truck came to tow the car to the garage*
(d) showing details item by item; *give me a breakdown of the travel costs*

② **breakfast**
[ˈbrekfɪst] *noun*
first meal of the day; *I had a boiled egg for breakfast; she didn't have any breakfast because she was in a hurry; the hotel serves breakfast from 7.30 to 9.30 every day*; **breakfast TV** = TV show at breakfast time; **working breakfast** = breakfast where you discuss business; **continental breakfast** = light breakfast of rolls, toast, and coffee (as opposed to a 'full English breakfast'); **full English breakfast** *or* **cooked breakfast** = meal with bacon, eggs, sausages, etc.; *see also* WEDDING

COMMENT: a traditional 'full English breakfast' may include cereals or cooked fruit, and a choice of grilled fish, bacon and eggs, sausages, fried tomatoes or mushrooms and fried bread, followed by toast and marmalade and tea or coffee

① **break in**
['breɪk 'ɪn] *verb*
to break in or **to break into a building** = to use force to get into a building; *burglars broke into the office during the night*

④ **break-in**
['breɪkɪn] *noun*
burglary; *they had a break-in when they were on holiday*; *the police reported a series of break-ins during the weekend*

④ **breakthrough**
['breɪkθruː] *noun*
sudden success; *we have had* or *have made a breakthrough in our search for a cure for cancer*

① **break up**
['breɪk 'ʌp] *verb*
(a) to come to pieces; *the oil tanker was breaking up on the rocks*
(b) to stop being together; *we broke up last year*; *their marriage broke up after 25 years*
(c) to stop being in a group; *the meeting broke up at 3 p.m.*; *the group broke up when the lead singer left*
(d) **school breaks up next week** = the school holidays start next week
(e) **come on, break it up!** = stop fighting!

④ **breakup**
['breɪkʌp] *noun*
coming to pieces, stopping being together; *the board has recommended the breakup of the company*; *the breakup of their marriage was a surprise to everyone*

③ **breast**
[brest] *noun*
(a) one of two parts on a woman's chest which produce milk; **breast cancer** = tumour in the breast; **breast stroke** = swimming stroke where you face downwards, pushing your arms out in front and bringing them back to the sides while your feet are kicking; *she won the 200m breast stroke*
(b) meat from the front part of a bird; *do you want a wing or a slice of breast?*; *we bought some chicken breasts to fry*

② **breath**
[breθ] *noun*
(a) air which goes into and out of the body through the nose or mouth; *you should smell his breath - he must have been eating onions last night*; **out of breath** or **gasping for breath** = having difficulty in breathing; *he ran all the way to the station, got there out of breath, and then saw the train leaving*; **to get your breath back** = to breathe normally again, after exercise; *first get your breath back, then tell me all about it*; **to hold your breath** = to keep air in your lungs to go under water, as a test or because you are afraid that something will happen; *she held her breath under water for a minute*; *we're all holding our breath to see if he wins* = we're all waiting anxiously to see if he wins; **to take a deep breath** = to breathe in as much air as you can; *take a deep breath for the X-ray*; **to take someone's breath away** = to make someone very surprised; *the view of the mountains took my breath away*; **under your breath** = quietly; *he cursed under his breath*; **breath test** = test for a driver to see if he has been drinking; *the police stopped him and made him take a breath test*; *the breath test showed he was way over the limit*
(b) **a breath of wind** = slight movement of air; *there wasn't a breath of wind all day*

③ **breathe**
[briːð] *verb*
to take air into the lungs or let it out; *take your hand off my mouth, I can't breathe*; *I want to listen to your chest, so breathe in and then out when I tell you to*; *do you know how fish breathe?*; *she breathed a sigh of relief*; **breathe deeply** = take in a lot of air; **he's breathing down my neck all the time** = he's always watching how I'm working

③ **bred**
[bred]
see BREED (NOTE: do not confuse with **bread**)

③ **breed**
[briːd]
1 *noun*
race of animal or plant; *Alsatians and other large breeds of dog*
2 *verb*
(a) to produce young (animals); *rabbits breed very rapidly*
(b) **I was born and bred in the country** = I was born and grew up in the country; **well-bred** = polite, well-educated
(c) to raise new plants; *they are breeding new varieties of wheat* (NOTE: breeding - bred [bred])

④ **breeder**
['briːdɪ] *noun*
person who breeds animals or plants; *a pigeon breeder*

④ **breeze**
[briːz]
1 *noun*
slight wind; *a cool breeze is welcome on a hot day like this*; **a stiff breeze** = a strong wind; *there was a stiff breeze blowing from the south*
2 *verb*
to walk around looking very pleased with yourself; *he breezed into the meeting carrying a cup of coffee*

brew
[bru:]
1 *verb*

(a) to make beer; *they've been brewing beer in this town for over two hundred years*

(b) to make tea or coffee; *let's brew some tea before we sit down and talk*

(c) there's trouble brewing = there will soon be trouble; *the police moved in when they felt trouble brewing in the crowd*

2 *noun*

(informal) **a brew** = a cup of tea; *he makes a good strong brew; do you fancy a brew?*

bribe
[braɪb]
1 *noun*

illegal payment to someone to get something done; *he offered me a bribe to say nothing to the police*

2 *verb*

to give an illegal payment to someone; *she planned to bribe customs officials to get her case through customs*

brick
[brɪk] *noun*

hard block of baked clay used for building; *you'll need more than eighty bricks to build a wall*

bride
[braɪd] *noun*

woman who is getting married; *the bride wore white; the bride was given away by her father; it is usual for the bride to arrive a few minutes late*

bridegroom
['braɪdgru:m] *noun*

man who is getting married; *the bridegroom and best man waited nervously in the church; the parents of the bridegroom came all the way from New Zealand*

bridesmaid
['braɪdzmeɪd] *noun*

girl who is one of the bride's attendants at a wedding; *three bridesmaids followed the bride into the church* (NOTE: a boy who does the same is a **page**)

bridge
[brɪdʒ] *noun*

(a) construction built over a road, river, etc., so that you can walk or drive from one side to the other; *there are a dozen bridges across the River Thames in London;* **railway bridge** = bridge which carries railway lines

(b) part of a ship where the captain and crew can keep watch and steer; *the captain was on the bridge when the accident occurred*

(c) card game for four people; *they played bridge until midnight*

brief
[bri:f]
1 *adjective*

short; *he wrote a brief note of thanks; the meeting was very brief; tell me what happened, but be brief as we don't have much time*

2 *noun*

instructions given to a professional person; *his brief was to modernize the accounts system*

3 *verb*

(a) to give information or instructions to someone; *he briefed the staff on the latest stage in the negotiations; she was briefed to look for new office premises*

(b) to give a case to a lawyer and explain the details; *my solicitor will brief the lawyers tomorrow morning*

briefcase
['bri:fkeɪs] *noun*

thin case for carrying papers, documents, etc.; *he put all the files into his briefcase*

briefly
['bri:fli] *adverb*

for a short time; *she spoke briefly about the work of the hospital*

brigade
[brɪ'geɪd] *noun*

(a) fire brigade = group of fire fighters; *she called the fire brigade when she saw smoke coming out of the windows*

(b) section of the army; *the general sent a brigade to the region*

bright
[braɪt] *adjective*

(a) shining strongly; *bright sunshine*

(b) with a very strong colour; *they have painted their front door bright orange*

(c) intelligent; *he's a bright little boy; both their children are very bright; she's the brightest of the class;* **bright idea** = clever thought; *I've had a bright idea - let's all go to the beach!*

(d) clear and sunny; *there will be bright periods during the afternoon*

(e) cheerful; *she gave me a bright smile* (NOTE: **brighter - brightest**)

brightly
['braɪtli] *adverb*

(a) in a bright way; *a children's book with brightly painted pictures; the streets were brightly lit for Christmas*

(b) cheerfully; *she smiled brightly as she went into the hospital*

brilliant
['brɪljənt] *adjective*

(a) extremely clever; *he's the most brilliant student of his year; she had a brilliant idea*

(b) (*informal*) very good; *the graphics on this computer package are brilliant*

(c) shining brightly; *she stepped out into the brilliant sunshine*

brilliantly
['brɪljəntli] *adverb*

in a brilliant way; *the gold roofs of the temples shone brilliantly in the sun; he did brilliantly at university*

① **bring**
[brɪŋ] *verb*
to come with someone or something to this place; *she brought the books to school with her*; *he brought his girlfriend home for tea*; *are you bringing any friends to the party?* (NOTE: bringing - brought [brɔːt])

④ **brink**
[brɪŋk] *noun*
edge; **on the brink of** = very close to; *the company is on the brink of collapse*; *she was on the brink of a nervous breakdown*

④ **brisk**
[brɪsk] *adjective*
rapid; *we went for a brisk walk along the beach* (NOTE: brisker - briskest)

① **Britain**
['brɪtɪn] *noun*
(Great) Britain = country formed of England, Scotland and Wales (which with Northern Ireland makes up the United Kingdom); *we sometimes go abroad for our holidays, but we mostly stay in Britain*; *in 1814 Britain was at war with France or Britain and France were at war*; *in Britain, cars drive on the left hand side of the road*; *see also* GREAT BRITAIN, UNITED KINGDOM (NOTE: the word **England** is often used instead of Britain, and this is a mistake, as England is only one part of Britain; note also the capital: **London**; people: **British**; language: **English**; currency: **pound sterling (£)**)

① **British**
['brɪtɪʃ]
1 *adjective*
referring to Great Britain; *a British citizen*; *the British army*; *the British press reported a plane crash in Africa*; *the ship was flying a British flag*; **the British government** = the government of the United Kingdom; **the British Isles** = the islands which make up Great Britain and Ireland (NOTE: the word **English** is often used instead of British, and this is a mistake, as England is only one part of Great Britain; you say **the British Prime Minister** and not **the English Prime Minister**)
2 *noun*
the British = the people of Great Britain

① **British Broadcasting Corporation (BBC)**
['brɪtɪʃ 'brɔːdkɑːstɪŋ kɔːpɪ'reɪʃn] *noun*
British national radio and TV company (NOTE: usually called by the initials **BBC**, but also sometimes called **the Beeb**)

② **broad**
[brɔːd] *adjective*
(a) very wide; *a broad river*
(b) *(as an emphasis)* **in broad daylight** = when it is light during the day; *the gang attacked the bank in broad daylight*; **a broad Irish accent** = a strong Irish accent
(c) broad beans = large flat pale green beans (NOTE: broader - broadest)

④ **broadcast**
['brɔːdkɑːst]
1 *noun*
radio or TV programme; *the broadcast came live from outside Buckingham Palace*; **outside broadcast** = programme not done in the studio
2 *verb*
(a) to send out on radio or TV; *the programme will be broadcast on Monday at 8 p.m.*; *the police broadcast an appeal for information*
(b) to tell everyone; **don't broadcast the fact** = keep it a secret (NOTE: broadcasting - broadcast)

④ **broadcasting**
['brɔːdkɑːstɪŋ] *noun*
sending out on radio or TV; *many companies now have broadcasting licences*

④ **broadly**
['brɔːdlɪ] *adverb*
widely; *he smiled broadly as he handed her the parcel*; **broadly speaking** = speaking in a general way; *broadly speaking, you can calculate that 10 francs equals one pound*

④ **brochure**
['brəʊʃɪ] *noun*
small publicity leaflet; *I picked up a brochure about ferry services*; *can you get some holiday brochures from the travel agent's?*

② **broke**
[brəʊk] *adjective*
(informal) with no money; *it's the end of the month and, as usual, I'm broke*; **to be flat broke** = to have no money at all; *see also* BREAK

① **broken**
['brəʊkɪn] *adjective*
(a) in pieces; *she tried to mend the broken cup*; **a broken home** = a family where the parents have separated; *the girl comes from a broken home*
(b) not working; *they came to mend the broken TV*; *we can't use the lift because it's broken*
(c) not complete; *after so many broken nights, she's looking forward to the day when the baby will sleep all night without waking*
(d) broken English = English spoken with a foreign accent and mistakes; *he only spoke broken English when he arrived, but was soon speaking like a native*
(e) discouraged; *he was pardoned, but came out of prison a broken man*; *see also* BREAK

④ **broker**
['brəʊkɪ] *noun*
dealer in shares or insurance; *he works as an insurance broker*; **to play the honest broker** = to try to solve the problems of other people

④ **bronze**
[brɒnz] *noun*
(a) mixture of copper and tin; *they put up a bronze statue of the emperor on a horse*

(b) bronze (medal) = medal given to someone who finishes third in a race or competition; *Britain won a gold and three bronzes at the athletics meeting*; see also GOLD, SILVER

① **brother**
['brʌðɪ] *noun*
boy or man who has the same mother and father as someone else; *my brother John is three years older than me*; *she came with her three brothers*

① **brought**
[brɔːt]
see BRING

④ **brow**
[braʊ] *noun*
(a) forehead; *she wrinkled or knit her brow as she tried to understand the guidebook*; *by the sweat of your brow* = with a lot of hard work; *he became a millionaire by the sweat of his brow*
(b) top of a hill; *having reached the brow of the hill they stopped to look at the view*

① **brown**
[braʊn]
1 *adjective*
with a colour like the earth or wood; *she has brown hair and blue eyes*; *it's autumn and the leaves are turning brown*; *he's very brown - he must have been sitting in the sun*; *I like brown bread better than white* (NOTE: **browner - brownest**)
2 *noun*
the colour brown; *I'd prefer a darker brown than this*
3 *verb*
to cook until brown; *brown the onions in a little butter*

④ **bruise**
[bruːz]
1 *noun*
dark, painful area on the skin, following a blow; *she had bruises all over her arms*
2 *verb*
(a) to make a bruise; *she bruised her knee on the corner of the table*
(b) to bruise easily = to get bruises easily because your skin is delicate; *she bruises easily, even a little blow gives her a bruise*; *peaches are delicate fruit - they bruise easily*

③ **brush**
[brʌʃ]
1 *noun*
(a) tool made of a handle and hairs or wire, used for cleaning, painting, etc.; *you need a stiff brush to get the mud off your shoes*; *she used a very fine brush to paint the details*; *he was painting the front of the house with a large brush* (NOTE: plural is **brushes**)
(b) act of cleaning with a brush; *she gave the coat a good brush*
(c) land covered with bushes or low trees; *they walked through the brush for several miles*

(d) near miss, when something nearly happens to harm you; *they had a brush with death on the motorway*
(e) short argument or fight with someone; *he's had several brushes with the police recently*
2 *verb*
(a) to clean with a brush; *he brushed his shoes before going to the office*; *always remember to brush your teeth before you go to bed*
(b) to go past something touching it gently; *she brushed against me as she came into the café*

④ **brutal**
['bruːtɪl] *adjective*
cruel and violent; *the police said it had been a particularly brutal murder*

③ **bubble**
['bʌbl]
1 *noun*
(a) ball of air or gas trapped in liquid; *bubbles of gas rose to the surface of the lake*; *he blew bubbles in his drink*; *bubble bath* = bath with special liquid soap which makes lots of bubbles; *she relaxed in a hot bubble bath*
(b) *(informal)* bubble and squeak = fried potatoes and cabbage
2 *verb*
to make bubbles, to have bubbles inside; *the soup was bubbling in the pan*; *to bubble up* = to come to the surface as bubbles; *gas was bubbling up out of the hot mud*

① **buck**
[bʌk]
1 *noun*
(a) male animal; *a buck rabbit*
(b) *US (informal)* dollar; *it'll cost you ten bucks*; *you couldn't lend me 100 bucks, could you?*; *to make a quick buck* = to get rich quickly; *all he wants is to make a quick buck*
(c) *(informal)* to pass the buck = to pass responsibility to someone else; *the manager is a very weak character, he's always passing the buck*; *the buck stops here* = I am the person who is responsible
2 *verb*
(a) to buck the trend = to go against the trend; *sales of health books have bucked the trend and risen sharply*
(b) *(of horse)* to jump in the air; *the horses bucked at the sound of the gun*

① **bucket**
['bʌkɪt]
1 *noun*
(a) round container with a handle but no lid, used mainly for liquids; *throw the water on the fire and pass the empty bucket back to me*; *(informal)* to kick the bucket = to die; *don't worry - I don't intend to kick the bucket just yet!*; *to come down in buckets* = to pour with rain; *you should have seen the rain - it was coming down in buckets!*

(b) the contents of a bucket; *he brought a bucket of water from the river; they threw buckets of water on the fire*

2 *verb*

(informal) to pour with rain; *it's bucketing down outside*

④ **bud**

[bʌd] *noun*

place where a new shoot comes on a plant; *it was spring and the buds on the trees were beginning to open*; **in bud** = flower which has not yet opened; *the roses are in bud*; *(informal)* **to nip something in the bud** = to stop something before it develops any further; *we must try to nip the student protests in the bud*

① **budget**

['bʌdʒɪt]

1 *noun*

(a) proposed expenditure; *there isn't enough money in the household budget to pay for a new carpet*; **publicity budget** = money allowed for expected expenditure on publicity; *we've increased the publicity budget by 50%*

(b) the Budget = the government's plans for spending and tax

2 *adjective*

cheap; **budget prices** = low prices; **budget travel** = cheap travel

3 *verb*

to plan how you will spend money in the future; *they are having to budget carefully before going on holiday in Greece*; **to budget for** = to plan to spend money on something; *we're budgeting for a 10% increase in electricity prices*

③ **bug**

[bʌg]

1 *noun*

(a) insect; *what are these bugs on the roses?*

(b) *(informal)* germ; *she got a stomach bug on holiday*

(c) hidden microphone; *the secret services left a bug in her bedroom*

(d) error in a computer program; *you need a special program to remove the bugs in the system*

2 *verb*

(a) *(informal)* to plant a hidden microphone; *they met in Hyde Park because he was afraid his flat had been bugged*

(b) *(informal)* to annoy, to bother; *what's bugging him?* (NOTE: **bugging - bugged**)

① **build**

[bɪld]

1 *noun*

shape of the body; *a girl of slight build; he has the same build as his father*

2 *verb*

to make something by putting things together; *the house was only built last year; they are planning to build a motorway across the field; the children built sand castles on the beach* (NOTE: **building - built** [bɪlt])

③ **builder**

['bɪldɪ] *noun*

person who builds houses, blocks of flats, etc.; *he works for a local builder; the builders are starting work on the kitchen today*

① **building**

['bɪldɪŋ] *noun*

(a) something which has been built, such as a house, railway station, factory, etc.; *the flood washed away several buildings; his office is on the top floor of the building; they will have to knock several buildings down to build the new motorway*

(b) *(used in names of large office blocks)* **the Shell Building**

(c) action of constructing something; *the building of the church must have taken many years*

③ **building society**

['bɪldɪŋ sɪ'saɪɪtɪ] *noun*

organization which pays interest on deposits and lends money to people buying houses or flats; *he put his savings in the building society; how much do you have in your building society account?*

③ **bulb**

[bʌlb] *noun*

(a) fat underground part of a plant, from which leaves and flowers grow; *she planted bulbs all round the house*

(b) glass ball which gives electric light; *you'll need a ladder to change the bulb*; *see also* CLEAR, PEARL

④ **bulk**

[bʌlk] *noun*

large amount; **in bulk** = in large quantities; *it is cheaper to buy stationery for the school in bulk*; **bulk purchase** = buying in large quantities; *bulk purchase is much cheaper*; **the bulk of** = most of; *the bulk of our sales are in Europe; she finished the bulk of the work before lunch*

④ **bulky**

['bʌlkɪ] *adjective*

awkward and large; *the post office does not take very bulky parcels* (NOTE: **bulkier - bulkiest**)

④ **bull**

[bʊl] *noun*

(a) male animal of the cow family; *be careful when you cross the field - there's a bull in it*; *(informal)* **to take the bull by the horns** = to tackle a difficult problem; *he decided to take the bull by the horns and tell his father that he was leaving the family firm*

(b) male of some other animals; *a bull elephant*

④ **bullet**
['bolɪt] *noun*
piece of metal fired from a gun; *he loaded his gun with bullets*; *two bullets had been fired*

④ **bulletin**
['bolɪtɪn] *noun*
information given to the public about a situation; *the hospital issued a daily news bulletin on the condition of the accident victims*

④ **bulletin board**
['bolɪtɪn 'bɔːd] *noun*
(a) *US* board on which notices can be pinned (NOTE: British English is **noticeboard**)
(b) *(on the Internet)* system of sending messages, advertising events, etc.; *she advertised the concert on a bulletin board*

④ **bully**
['boli]
1 *noun*
person who hurts or is not kind to weaker people; *he's a bully and is always trying to frighten the smaller children* (NOTE: plural is **bullies**)
2 *verb*
to treat someone who is weaker badly; *she was bullied by the other children in school* (NOTE: **bullying - bullied**)

③ **bump**
[bʌmp]
1 *noun*
(a) slight knock; *the boat hit the dock wall with a bump*
(b) raised place; *drive slowly, the road is full of bumps*
(c) raised place on your body, where something has hit it; *he has a bump on the back of his head*
2 *verb*
to hit; *he's crying because he bumped his head on the door*

④ **bumper**
['bʌmpɪ]
1 *adjective*
very large; *a bumper crop of corn*; *we're publishing a bumper edition of children's stories*; *last year was a bumper year for sales of mobile phones*
2 *noun*
protective bar on the front and rear of a car; *he backed into a tree and bent his rear bumper*; *there was a mile-long traffic jam with cars standing bumper-to-bumper*

② **bunch**
[bʌntʃ] *noun*
(a) group of things taken together; *he carries a bunch of keys attached to his belt*; *he brought her a bunch of flowers*; *I work with a nice bunch of people*
(b) cluster of fruit on the same stem; *a bunch of grapes*; *a bunch of bananas* (NOTE: plural is **bunches**)

④ **bundle**
['bʌndl]
1 *noun*
parcel of things wrapped up or tied up together; *a bundle of clothes was all she possessed*; *he produced a bundle of papers tied up with green string*; *she left her clothes in a bundle on the floor*
2 *verb*
(a) to put things somewhere roughly; *he bundled the papers into a drawer*; *she bundled the children off to school*; *the police bundled him into the back of their van*
(b) to sell a software programme at the same time as you sell hardware, both sold together at a special price; *the word processing package is bundled with the computer*

② **bungalow**
['bʌŋgɪlʊ] *noun*
house with only a ground floor; *my grandparents have bought a bungalow by the sea*

④ **bunk**
[bʌŋk] *noun*
(a) bed attached to a wall, as in a ship, etc.; *he climbed up into his bunk and fell asleep*; *do you want the top bunk or the bottom one?*; **bunk beds** = two beds one on top of the other, with a ladder to climb to the top one; *we put the children in bunk beds because they take up less space*
(b) *(informal)* **to do a bunk** = to run away; *as soon as they saw the police van, they did a bunk across some waste land*

③ **bunny**
['bʌni] *noun*
child's name for a rabbit; *what a sweet little bunny!*; *look at all the bunnies in the field* (NOTE: plural is **bunnies**)

③ **burden**
['bɜːdn]
1 *noun*
(a) heavy load; *he relieved her of her burden*
(b) something hard to bear; *I think he finds running the office at his age something of a burden*; **to make someone's life a burden** = to make someone's life difficult
2 *verb*
to weigh down with a load; *the whole town was burdened with grief*; *the company is burdened with debt*

④ **bureau**
['bjʊrɪʊ] *noun*
(a) office; *he filed the report from the New York bureau*; **computer bureau** = office which does computer work for other offices; **(tourist) information bureau** = office which gives information to tourists; *ask for a list of bed and breakfasts at the information bureau*
(b) *US* chest of drawers; *my socks are in the bureau in the bedroom*

(c) *US* department of the government; *the Federal Bureau of Investigation* (NOTE: plural is **bureaux** ['bjʊrɪəuz])

④ **bureaucracy**
[bjʊɪ'rɒkrɪsɪ] *noun*
(a) official system that is run by civil servants; *red tape and bureaucracy slow down our export business*; *I'm fed up with all this bureaucracy, just to get an export licence*
(b) group of officials working for central or local government, or for an international body; *the investigation of complaints is in the hands of the local bureaucracy*

④ **bureaucrat**
['bjʊɪrɪkræt] *noun*
civil servant; *bureaucrats in Brussels are still trying to decide on what to do*

③ **burger**
['bɜːgɪ] *noun*
chopped beef grilled and served in a toasted roll; *the children want burgers and French fries for lunch* (NOTE: also called **hamburger**)

③ **burglar**
['bɜːglɪ] *noun*
person who tries to get into a building to steal; *burglars broke in during the night*; *she saw the burglar as he was climbing out of the window*; **burglar alarm** = device which rings a loud bell if someone enters a building

④ **burglary**
['bɜːglɪrɪ] *noun*
robbery by a burglar; *he was charged with burglary*; *there are many more burglaries during the summer holidays when houses are empty*

④ **burgle**
['bɜːglɪ] *verb*
to enter a building and steal things from it; *their flat was burgled while they were on holiday*; *someone tried to burgle our house*

① **burn**
[bɜːn]
1 *noun*
burnt area of the skin or a surface; *she had burns on her face and hands*; *there's a burn on the edge of the table where he left his cigarette*
2 *verb*
(a) to damage or destroy by fire; *all our clothes were burnt in the hotel fire*; *she burnt her finger on the hot frying pan*; *the house was burnt to the ground last year*; *look, you've burnt the bacon* = you've cooked it too much, so that it is black; *(informal)* **to burn the candle at both ends** = to work much too hard; *he gets up early to go to the office, and comes home late - he's burning the candle at both ends*; *see also* MONEY
(b) to be on fire; *the firemen were called to the burning school*
(c) to use as a fuel; *the cooker burns gas*; *a* **wood-burning stove** = heater which burns wood (NOTE: **burning - burnt** [bɜːnt] *or* **burned**)

③ **burnt**
[bɜːnt] *adjective*
black with fire; *the kitchen smells of burnt toast*; *all that remained of the house were some burnt walls*

① **burst**
[bɜːst]
1 *noun*
(a) sudden loud sound; *there was a burst of shooting and then silence*; *bursts of laughter came from the office*
(b) sudden effort or activity; *he put on a burst of speed*; *in one of her bursts of efficiency she sorted out the old stock*
2 *verb*
to explode suddenly; *a water main burst in the High Street*; *when she picked up the balloon it burst* (NOTE: **bursting - burst**)

④ **bury**
['berɪ] *verb*
to put into the ground; *he was buried in the local cemetery*; *they buried the gold in the garden*; *(informal)* **to bury your head in the sand** = to pretend that a danger or problem doesn't exist (NOTE: do not confuse with **berry**)

① **bus**
[bʌs] *noun*
large motor vehicle which carries passengers; *he goes to work by bus*; *she takes the 8 o'clock bus to school every morning*; *we missed the last bus and had to walk home*; *the number 6 bus goes to Oxford Street*; **airport bus** = bus which takes passengers between a town and an airport; **school bus** = bus which takes schoolchildren to school; *the children were waiting for the school bus* (NOTE: plural is **buses**)

④ **bush**
[bʊʃ] *noun*
(a) small tree; *an animal was moving in the bushes*; *a holly bush with red berries* (NOTE: plural is **bushes**)
(b) *(in Africa, India, etc.)* **the bush** = land covered with bushes or low trees; *they walked through the bush for several days before finding a village* (NOTE: no plural in this meaning)

① **business**
['bɪznɪs] *noun*
(a) occupation or trade, the work of buying or selling things; *she works in the electricity business*; *they do a lot of business with European countries*; **business college** *or* **business school** = place where commercial studies are taught; *he's going to a business school in September*; **business letter** = letter about business matters; **business trip** = trip to do with your business; *he's on a business trip to France*; **on business** = on commercial work; *the sales director is in Holland on business*
(b) commercial company; *she runs a photography business*; *he runs a secondhand car business*; **business address** = details of

number, street and town where a company is located; **business card** = card showing a businessman's name and the name and address of the company he works for; **business hours** = time (usually 9 a.m. to 5.30 p.m.) when a business is open (NOTE: plural in this meaning is **businesses**)

(c) affair, concern; **it's none of your business** = it's nothing to do with you

④ **businessman, businesswoman**
['bɪznɪsmæn or 'bɪznɪswʊmɪn] *noun*
person who is engaged in business, who runs a business; *the early morning flights to Frankfurt are full of businessmen* (NOTE: plural is **businessmen, businesswomen**)

① **bus stop**
['bʌs 'stɒp] *noun*
place where a bus stops and passengers can get on or off; *there were ten people waiting at the bus stop*

④ **bust**
[bʌst]
1 *noun*
(a) sculpture of the head and shoulders of a person; *there's a bust of Shakespeare in Stratford church*
(b) woman's breasts; **bust size** *or* **bust measurement** = measurement round a woman's breasts
2 *adjective*
(informal)
(a) broken; *the washing machine's bust*
(b) **to go bust** = to fail, to be bankrupt; *thousands of people lost their savings when the bank went bust*
3 *verb*
(informal) to break; *she's bust my precious Chinese bowl!; he hit the ball hard and it bust a window* (NOTE: **busting - busted** *or* **bust**)

① **busy**
['bɪzi]
1 *adjective*
working on something, doing something; *he was busy mending the car; I was too busy to phone my aunt; the busiest time for shops is the week before Christmas; the line's busy at the moment* = someone is using the phone line (NOTE: **busier - busiest**)
2 *verb*
to busy yourself with something = to occupy yourself, to keep yourself busy with something; *my sister likes to busy herself with the garden now she's retired*

① **but**
[bʌt]
1 *conjunction; (coming before a contrast)*
he is very tall, but his wife is quite short; we would like to come to your party, but we're doing something else that evening; I'm sorry, but there are no seats left
2 *preposition*

except; *everyone but me is allowed to go to the cinema; they had eaten nothing but apples*

③ **butcher**
['bʊtʃɪ]
1 *noun*
man who prepares and sells meat; *ask the butcher for some lamb chops; the butcher's* = shop where you can buy meat; *can you get me some sausages from the butcher's?*
2 *verb*
to kill in a brutal way; *the soldiers set fire to the village and butchered the people living in it*

① **butter**
['bʌti]
1 *noun*
yellow fat made from cream, used on bread or for cooking; *could you pass the butter, please?; don't spread the butter so thick; fry the mushrooms in butter* (NOTE: no plural: **some butter; a knob of butter**)
2 *verb*
(a) to spread butter on something; *she was busy buttering slices of bread for the sandwiches*
(b) *(informal)* **to butter someone up** = to flatter someone, to praise someone without really believing it to be true; *just butter up the boss a bit - tell him how good his golf is*

③ **butterfly**
['bʌtɪflaɪ] *noun*
(a) insect with large brightly coloured wings which comes out in daylight; *butterflies come out in the sunshine*
(b) *(informal)* **to have butterflies in the stomach** = to be very nervous; *she had butterflies in the stomach before the interview* (NOTE: plural is **butterflies**)

① **button**
['bʌtɪn]
1 *noun*
(a) little round disc for fastening clothes; *the wind is cold - do up the buttons on your coat; a button's come off my shirt*
(b) little round disc which you push to ring a bell, etc.; *press the 'up' button to call the lift; push the red button to set off the alarm; push the button marked 'black' if you want coffee without milk*
(c) **button mushroom** = small round white mushroom
2 *verb*
to fasten with buttons; *he buttoned (up) his coat because it was cold*

① **buy**
[baɪ]
1 *verb*
to get something by paying money; *I bought a newspaper on my way to the station; she's buying a flat; she bought herself a pair of ski boots; what did you buy your mother for her birthday?* (NOTE: **buying - bought** [bɔːt])
2 *noun*

a good buy = something which you have bought which is worth the money spent; *that camera you bought was a very good buy*

③ **buyer**
['baɪə] *noun*
person who buys; *there were no buyers for his house*; *she works as shoe buyer in a department store*; **head buyer** = most important buyer in a store; **a buyer's market** = market where products are sold cheaply because there are more sellers than buyers; *compare* SELLER'S MARKET

④ **buzz**
[bʌz]
1 *noun*
(a) noise like the noise made by a bee; *I can hear a buzz but I can't see the bee*; *the buzz of an electric saw in the garden next door*
(b) *(informal)* excitement; *she gets a buzz from skiing fast downhill*
(c) *(informal)* telephone call; *give me a buzz tomorrow* (NOTE: plural is **buzzes**)
2 *verb*
(a) to make a noise like a bee; *flies were buzzing round the jam*
(b) *(informal)* **to buzz off** = to go away; *we stood and watched the men painting the fence until they told us to buzz off*

① **by**
[baɪ]
1 *preposition*
(a) near; *the house is just by the bus stop*; *sit down here by me*
(b) before, not later than; *they should have arrived by now*; *you must be home by eleven o'clock*; *we must finish this piece of work by Friday*
(c) *(showing means or way)* send the parcel by airmail; *get in touch with the office by phone*; *they came by car*; *she caught a cold by standing in the rain*; *she paid by cheque, not by credit card*

(d) *(showing the person or thing that did something)* a painting by Van Gogh; *'Hamlet' is a play by Shakespeare*; *a CD recorded by our local group*; *the postman was bitten by the dog*; *she was knocked down by a car*
(e) **by yourself** = alone; *don't sit at home all by yourself*; *she made the hat all by herself*; *can he find his way to the station by himself?*
(f) *(showing how much)* we sell tomatoes by the kilo; *eggs are sold by the dozen*; *prices have been increased by 5%*; *they won by 4 goals to 2*
(g) *(showing dimensions)* the table is 60cm long by 25 wide
2 *adverb*
past; *she drove by without seeing us*

◊ **by and large**
['baɪ n 'lɑːʒ]
in general; *by and large, the trains run on time*

◊ **by the way**
['baɪ ðɪ 'weɪ]
(used to mention something not very important) by the way, did you see the TV programme on cars yesterday?; *by the way, I shall be home late tonight*

① **bye** or **bye-bye**
[baɪ or 'baɪbaɪ] *interjection*
goodbye; *bye! see you next week!*

④ **bypass**
['baɪpɑːs]
1 *noun*
(a) road round a town; *take the bypass if you want to avoid hold-ups in the town centre*
(b) **heart bypass** = operation to put pieces of vein around a part near the heart which is not functioning properly; *she had a heart bypass ten years ago and is still going strong*
2 *verb*
to go round a town, avoiding the centre; *it would be better if you could bypass the town centre on market day*; *the main road bypasses the town centre*

Cc

① **C, c**
[siː]
third letter of the alphabet, between B and D; *remember the rhyme: I before E except after C: so write 'receive' and not 'recieve'*

④ **cab**
[kæb] *noun*
(a) taxi, a car which takes people from one place to another for money; *he took a cab to the*

airport; *can you phone for a cab, please?*; *the office is only a short cab ride from the railway station*; *cab fares are very high in New York*; **black cab** = London taxi
(b) separate section for a driver in a large vehicle, such as a truck; *the truck driver climbed into his cab and started the engine*

④ **cabbage**
['kæbɪdʒ] *noun*
vegetable with large pale green or red leaves which you eat; *we had red cabbage with our lunch*; *the school always smells of boiled cabbage*; *he was planting cabbages in his garden* (NOTE: as food, **cabbage** does not have a plural: **some cabbage**; **a helping of cabbage**; as plants you can count **one cabbage**, **two cabbages**, etc.)

④ **cabin**
['kæbɪn] *noun*
(a) small room on a ship; *we booked a first-class cabin on the cruise*; *she felt sick and went to lie down in her cabin*
(b) small hut; *he has a cabin by a lake where he goes fishing*
(c) inside of an aircraft; *the aircraft is divided into three separate cabins*; *the first-class cabin is in the front of the plane*; **the cabin crew** *or* **cabin staff** = the stewardesses and stewards on a plane

② **cabinet**
['kæbɪnɪt] *noun*
(a) piece of furniture with shelves; *a china cabinet*; **filing cabinet** = piece of office furniture with drawers for storing files
(b) committee formed of the most important members of a government; *the cabinet met at 10 o'clock this morning*; *there's a cabinet meeting every Thursday morning*; **shadow cabinet** = senior members of the opposition who cover the areas of responsibility of the actual cabinet, and will form the cabinet if their party is elected to power

③ **cable**
['keɪbl] *noun*
(a) wire for carrying electricity; *he ran a cable out into the garden so that he could use his electric saw*
(b) thick rope or wire; *the ship was attached to the dock by cables*; *the cable snapped and ten passengers died when the cable car fell to the floor of the valley*; **cable railway** = railway where the carriages are pulled by a cable
(c) wire for sending messages underground or under the sea; *they've been digging up the pavements to lay cables*; **cable TV** = TV where the programmes are sent along underground wires

③ **cable car**
['keɪbl 'kɑː] *noun*
(a) vehicle which goes up a mountain, hanging on a wire cable; *ten people were killed when the cable car fell to the floor of the valley*
(b) *US* *(in San Francisco)* type of tram which is pulled by a metal cable set in a channel in the road; *we took the cable car down to Fisherman's Wharf*

④ **café**
['kæfeɪ] *noun*
small restaurant selling snacks or light meals; *we had a snack in the station café*

③ **cage**
[keɪdʒ] *noun*
box made of wire or with metal bars for keeping birds or animals so they cannot get out; *the rabbit got out of its cage*; *don't put your hand into the cage*

② **cake**
[keɪk]
1 *noun*
(a) food made by mixing flour, eggs, sugar, etc., and baking it; *a piece of cherry cake*; *she had six candles on her birthday cake*; *have another slice of Christmas cake*; *would you like some chocolate cake?*; **wedding cake** = special cake made with dried fruit, covered with icing, eaten at a wedding reception; **cake mix** = main ingredients for a cake which are bought ready mixed in a packet; *(slang)* **it's a piece of cake** = it's very easy; *the exam was a piece of cake - I finished it in half-an-hour!*; **you can't have your cake and eat it** = you can't benefit from two opposing things (NOTE: as food, cake sometimes has no plural: **some cake, a piece of cake**; when it means one single item of food it can have a plural: **she made twenty cakes; a plate of cakes; there are no cakes left in the shop**)
(b) small round or square piece of something; *a cake of soap*
(c) food made by mixing ingredients together into small round pieces which are then fried; *a meal of fish cakes and chips*
2 *verb*
to dry and form a hard crust; **to be caked with** = to be covered with something that has dried hard; *his boots were caked with mud*

③ **calcium**
['kælsiːm] *noun*
(a) chemical element which is a major component of bones and teeth; *their diet does not have enough calcium* (NOTE: chemical symbol: Ca; atomic number: 20)
(b) white substance found in water, which makes a white deposit; *calcium deposits form inside pipes and kettles*

> COMMENT: calcium is an important element in a balanced diet. Milk, cheese, eggs and certain vegetables are its main sources

② **calculate**
['kælkjuːleɪt] *verb*
to find the answer to a problem using numbers; *the bank clerk calculated the rate of exchange for the dollar*; *I calculate that we have enough money left for a meal*; *he calculated that it would take us six hours to get to Madrid*

④ **calculated**
['kælkjuleɪtɪd] *adjective*
planned; *his speech was calculated to make his opponents very angry*; **a calculated insult** =

insult which was made on purpose; **a calculated risk** = risk which you think you can afford to take

② **calculation**
[kælkju'leɪʃn] *noun*
act of calculating; *according to my calculations, we have enough fuel left for only twenty kilometres*; **rough calculation** = approximate answer to a problem using numbers; *I made some rough calculations on the back of an envelope*

③ **calculator**
['kælkjuleɪtɪ] *noun*
machine for doing sums; *he worked out the price on his calculator*; **pocket calculator** = small calculator which you can put in your pocket

④ **calendar**
['kælɪndɪ] *noun*
paper showing the days and months of the year, which can be pinned on a wall; *he pinned the calendar to the wall next to his desk*; *turn over to the next page of the calendar - today is November 1st*; **calendar month** = month from the first day to the last; **calendar year** = twelve months from January 1st to December 31st

① **call**
[kɔːl]
1 *noun*
(a) telephone conversation; trying to get in touch with someone by telephone; *were there any calls for me while I was out?*; **local call** = call to a number in the same area; **long-distance call** = call to a number in a different area; **overseas call** *or* **international call** = call to another country; **to make a call** = to dial and speak to someone on the telephone; *she wanted to make a (phone) call to Australia*; **to take a call** = to answer the telephone
(b) telephone call or shout to wake someone; *he asked for an early morning call*; **I want a call at 7 o'clock** = I want someone to wake me at 7 o'clock
(c) visit; *the doctor made three calls on patients this morning*; **on call** = available for duty
2 *verb*
(a) to say something loudly to someone who is some distance away, to tell someone to come; *call the children when it's time for tea*; **call me at 7 o'clock** = wake me up at 7; **to call a taxi** = to shout to a taxi to come
(b) to give someone or something a name; *they're going to call the baby Sam*; *his name is John but everyone calls him Jack*; *our cat's called Felix*; *what do you call this computer programme?*
(c) to telephone; *if he comes back, tell him I'll call him when I'm in the office*; *Mr Smith is out - shall I ask him to call you back?*; *call the police - the shop has been burgled!*; *can you call me a cab, please?*

(d) to visit; *the doctor called at the house, but there was no one there*; *the whole family called round to see if she was better*

③ **callbox**
['kɔːlbɒks] *noun*
public telephone box; *I'm phoning from the callbox outside the post office* (NOTE: plural is **callboxes**)

④ **caller**
['kɔːlɪ] *noun*
(a) person who comes to visit; *she can't see any callers today*
(b) person who telephones; *I picked up the phone and the caller asked for my father*

③ **call for**
['kɔːl 'fɔː] *verb*
(a) **to call for someone** = to fetch someone before going somewhere; *he called for me to take me to the theatre*
(b) **to call for help** = to shout to ask for help; *we could hear people calling for help from under the ruins*
(c) to need or to require; *rescuing people with a helicopter calls for particular flying skills*

③ **call off**
['kɔːl 'ɒf] *verb*
to decide not to do something which had been planned; *he called off the visit to the museum*; *the picnic has been called off because it is raining*; *when the chairman heard about the deal he called it off*

③ **call on**
['kɔːl 'ɒn] *verb*
(a) to visit someone; *she called on her mother to see how she was*
(b) to ask someone to do something; *the police have called on everyone to watch out for the escaped prisoner*

③ **call up**
['kɔːl 'ʌp] *verb*
to tell someone to join the army, navy or air force; *thousands of men were called up at the beginning of the war*

③ **calm**
[kɑːm]
1 *adjective*
quiet, not rough or excited; *the sea was perfectly calm and no one was sick*; *keep calm, everything will be all right* (NOTE: **calmer - calmest**)
2 *noun*
period of quiet; *the calm of the Sunday afternoon was broken by the sound of jazz from the house next door*
3 *verb*
to calm (down) = to make someone quieter; to become quieter and less annoyed; *she stroked his hand to try to calm him down*; *after shouting for some minutes he finally calmed down*

④ **calorie**
['kælɪri] *noun*
(a) unit of measurement of energy in food; *she's counting calories to try to lose weight*; *there are 250 calories in a pint of beer*
(b) unit of measurement of heat or energy (the heat needed to raise the temperature of 1g of water by 1°C)

① **came**
[keɪm]
see COME

④ **camel**
['kæml] *noun*
desert animal with long legs and one or two humps; *when we were on holiday in Kuwait we went to camel races in the desert*

> COMMENT: there are two breeds of camel: the Bactrian camel has two humps and lives in Asia; the Arabian camel has one hump, and is common in North Africa and the Arab countries

② **camera**
['kæmrɪ] *noun*
machine for taking photographs; *he took a picture of the garden with his new camera*; *they went on holiday and forgot to take their camera*; *did you remember to put a film in your camera?*

③ **camp**
[kæmp]
1 *noun*
place where people live in tents in the open air; *we set up camp halfway up the mountain*; **camp fire** = small bonfire at a camp; **holiday camp** = place where people go to spend their holidays in little wooden houses or tents
2 *verb*
to spend a holiday or a period of time in a tent; *we go camping in Sweden every summer*; *they had camped by the side of the lake*

① **campaign**
[kæm'peɪn]
1 *noun*
(a) organized military attack; *Napoleon's Russian campaign of 1812*
(b) organized attempt to achieve something; *a publicity campaign or an advertising campaign*; *he's organizing a campaign against the new motorway*; *the government's anti-smoking campaign*
2 *verb*
to work in an organized way to achieve something; *they are campaigning for a new bypass*; *the party is to campaign against nuclear reactors*

④ **campaigner**
['kæmpeɪni] *noun*
person who campaigns; *the anti-road campaigners are protesting on the village green*; *she's a well-known campaigner for women's rights*

③ **camping site** *or* **campsite**
['kæmpɪŋ saɪt *or* 'kæmpsaɪt] *noun*
area specially arranged for camping and caravans, with special places for tents, washing and toilet facilities, etc.; *there are several well-equipped campsites near the lake*

④ **campus**
['kæmpɪs] *noun*
land on which a university or college is built, and the buildings on it; *the campus covers an area of about 25 square miles*; **to live on campus** = to live in accommodation for students; *all students live on campus during their first year at university* (NOTE: plural is **campuses**)

① **can**
[kæn]
1 *noun*
(a) round metal container for food or drink; *he opened a can of lemonade*; *empty beer cans were all over the pavement*; *can you open a can of beans?* (NOTE: British English also uses **tin** to mean a container of food, but not of drink)
(b) *(informal)* **to carry the can for something** = to take responsibility or blame for something; *they all ran away and left me to carry the can*
(c) **watering can** = container similar to a bucket, with a long tube for pouring, used to give water to plants
2 *verb used with other verbs*
(a) *(to mean 'be able')* *he can swim well but he can't ride a bike*; *she can't run as fast as I can*; *can you remember what the doctor told us to do?*; *I can't bear to watch this film any longer*
(b) *(to mean 'be allowed')* *children under 18 can't drive cars*; *he says we can go in*; *the policeman says we can't park here*
(c) *(in asking politely)* *can we come in, please?*; *can you shut the door, please?* (NOTE: negative: **cannot**, usually **can't**; past: **could, could not**, usually **couldn't**; **can** and **could** are only used with other verbs, and are not followed by the word **to**)
3 *verb*
to put food in cans; *the town has a factory where they can peas* (NOTE: **canning - canned**)

① **Canada**
['kænɪdɪ] *noun*
very large country in North America, to the north of the United States; *they live in Canada, though his family comes from France* (NOTE: capital: **Ottawa**; people: **Canadians**; languages: **English, French**; currency: **the Canadian dollar**)

① **Canadian**
[kɪ'neɪdjɪn]
1 *adjective*
referring to Canada; *his mother is Canadian and so is he*; *she is a Canadian citizen*; *the ticket costs 250 Canadian dollars*
2 *noun*
person from Canada; *how many Canadians are there living in London?*

④ **canal**
['kɪ'næl] *noun*
(a) artificial river made to allow boats to go from one place to another; *you can take a boat trip round the canals of Amsterdam*
(b) tube in the body

② **cancel**
['kænsl] *verb*
(a) to stop something which has been planned; *the singer was ill, so the show had to be cancelled; there is no refund if you cancel less than three weeks before the date of departure; the trip was cancelled because the weather was too bad*
(b) to mark a postage stamp with a rubber stamp to show that it has been used (NOTE: British English: **cancelling - cancelled** but American spelling is **canceling - canceled**)

② **cancer**
['kænsɪ] *noun*
disease in which cells grow in a wrong way; *she developed skin cancer; he died of lung cancer*

② **candidate**
['kændɪdɪt] *noun*
(a) person who applies for a job; *there are six candidates for the post of assistant manager; we have asked three candidates to come for an interview*
(b) person who is standing for election; *the candidate went round the constituency talking to voters*
(c) person who has entered for an examination; *all candidates should answer three questions; candidates are given three hours to complete the exam*

③ **candle**
['kændl] *noun*
stick of wax with a thread in the centre, which you light to make a flame; *he blew out all the candles on his birthday cake; we lit a candle in her memory*

③ **candy**
['kændi] *noun*
US
(a) sweet food, made with sugar; *eating candy is bad for your teeth* (NOTE: no plural in this meaning)
(b) one piece of this food; *she bought a box of candies* (NOTE: plural in this meaning is **candies**; British English for this is **sweets**)

④ **cane**
[keɪn] *noun*
(a) walking stick cut from the stem of a plant; *she was leaning on a cane as she walked up the path*
(b) strong stem of a plant, especially used of tall thin plants; *a field of sugar cane*

④ **cannon**
['kænɪn] *noun*
(a) large gun; *the sailors hauled a huge cannon across the ship's deck;* (*informal*) **a loose cannon** = someone who is not easily controlled and may do or say things which are not officially approved; *he described the minister as a loose cannon in the government*
(b) **water cannon** = machine for spraying water against demonstrators, etc.; *the police turned the water cannon on the group of protesters* (NOTE: plural is usually **cannon**)

① **cannot**
['kænɒt]
see CAN

③ **can opener**
['kæn 'ɪupnɪ] *noun*
US device for opening cans; *there's a can opener on the wall of the kitchen by the telephone* (NOTE: the British equivalent is **tin opener**)

① **can't**
[kɑːnt] *see* CAN

④ **canvas**
['kænvɪs] *noun*
(a) thick cloth for making tents, sails, etc.; *he was wearing a pair of old canvas shoes;* **a holiday under canvas** = a camping holiday in a tent (NOTE: no plural in this meaning)
(b) a painting; *three canvases by Picasso* (NOTE: plural is **canvases**)

③ **cap**
[kæp]
1 *noun*
(a) flat hat with a flat hard piece in front; *the bus driver was wearing an old black cap; an officer's cap with a gold badge;* **England cap** = cap worn by a sportsman who has played for England in an international match
(b) top which covers something; *screw the cap back on the medicine bottle; a red pen with a black cap*
2 *verb*
(a) to put a cap on top of something; to fix a cover on something to stop it leaking; *they tried to cap the broken pipe*
(b) to name someone to play for his country in an international match; *he has been capped five times for Wales* (NOTE: **capping - capped**)

③ **capability**
[keɪpɪ'bɪlɪti] *noun*
being able to do something; **beyond your capabilities** = too difficult for you to do; *I'm afraid this job is way beyond my capabilities* (NOTE: plural is **capabilities**)

③ **capable**
['keɪpɪbl] *adjective*
competent, able to work well; *she's an extremely capable secretary;* **capable of** = able to do something; *the car is capable of very high speeds; she isn't capable of running the department on her own* (NOTE: you are capable **of** something or **of doing** something)

② **capacity**
[kɪ'pæsɪti] *noun*
(a) amount which something can hold; *this barrel has a larger capacity than that one; the*

cinema was filled to capacity; **a capacity audience** = an audience which fills a cinema, theatre, etc.; **seating capacity** = number of seats in a bus, cinema, etc.; **to work at full capacity** = to do as much work as possible

(b) engine capacity = output of an engine or electric motor

(c) being able to do something easily; *he has a capacity for making friends with anyone he meets*

(d) position; *acting in his capacity as manager* = acting as a manager; **speaking in an official capacity** = speaking officially (NOTE: no plural)

④ **cape**
[keɪp] *noun*
(a) piece of high land sticking out into the sea; *we rounded the cape on June 21st at 8 a.m.*; **the Cape (of Good Hope)** = the point at the very south of the African continent; *they almost sank in a storm when they were rounding the Cape*

(b) long piece of clothing with no sleeves; *she wrapped her cape more tightly around her*

COMMENT: the cape at the southern tip of South America is Cape Horn

① **capital**
['kæpɪtl]
1 *noun*
(a) main city of a country, usually where the government is based; *the capital is in the eastern part of the country*; *Madrid is the capital of Spain*; *the Italian capital is full of tourists at Easter*; *the capital's traffic has ground to a halt*

(b) money which is invested; *company with £10,000 capital or with a capital of £10,000*; **capital gains** = profit made when selling shares or other investments

(c) carved top part of a column; *we visited the cathedral and looked at the carvings on the capitals*

(d) block capitals = capital letters, letters written as A, B, C, D, etc., and not a, b, c, d; *write your name in block capitals at the top of the form*

2 *adjective*
(a) capital letters = letters written as A, B, C, D, etc., and not a, b, c, d; *write your name in capital letters at the top of the form*

(b) capital punishment = killing someone as a punishment for a crime; *capital punishment still exists in many countries*

④ **capitalism**
['kæpɪtlɪzm] *noun*
economic system based on the ownership of resources by individuals or companies and not by the state; *capitalism gives us all greater freedom*

④ **capitalist**
['kæpɪtlɪst]
1 *noun*
(a) person who supports the theory of capitalism; *capitalists are in favour of free enterprise*

(b) businessman who invests money in a business; *he's a young capitalist who is only twenty-one, but on the way to becoming a millionaire*

2 *adjective*
working according to the principles of capitalism; *a capitalist economy*; *the capitalist system*

③ **capping, capped**
['kæpɪŋ or kæpt]
see CAP

③ **captain**
['kæptɪn] *noun*
(a) person in charge of a team; *the England captain*; *the two captains shook hands at the beginning of the match*

(b) person in charge of a ship or of an aircraft; *go and see the captain if you want to use the radio phone*; *Captain Smith is flying the plane*

(c) rank in the army above a lieutenant and below a major; *a lieutenant has to report to his captain* (NOTE: used as a title with names, and often shortened to **Capt.**)

④ **caption**
['kæpʃn] *noun*
words printed beneath a picture; *the caption read 'England manager to resign'*

③ **capture**
['kæptʃɪ]
1 *noun*
being captured; *we must do everything to avoid capture*

2 *verb*
(a) to take someone *or* something as a prisoner; *they captured the enemy capital very quickly*; *four soldiers were captured in the attack*

(b) to take a share of sales from another company; *they have captured 10% of the market*

① **car**
[kɑː] *noun*
(a) small private vehicle for carrying people; *she's bought a new car*; *my car was stolen while I was shopping*; *he drove his car into the garage*; *he goes to his office every morning by car*; **company car** = car owned by a company and lent to a member of staff to use for business or other purposes; **car ferry** = boat which carries vehicles and passengers from one place to another

(b) wagon on a railway; *is there a restaurant car on the train?*; **observation car** = special wagon with a glass roof, so that passengers can see more of the scenery

④ **caravan**
['kærɪvæn] *noun*
(a) van with beds, table, washing facilities, etc., which can be towed by a car; *we got stuck behind a caravan on a narrow mountain road*; *we rent a caravan in a caravan park* (NOTE: American English is **trailer** *or* **mobile home**)
(b) group of animals or vehicles travelling together, one behind the other; *a caravan of camels crossing the desert*; *we joined a caravan of lorries going to Romania*

③ **carbohydrate**
[kɑːbʊ'haɪdreɪt] *noun*
chemical substance containing carbon, hydrogen and oxygen; *she eats too many carbohydrates*

> COMMENT: carbohydrates are found in particular in sugar, potatoes and bread; they provide the body with energy. Compare proteins

④ **carbon**
['kɑːbɪn] *noun*
(a) chemical element found in coal; *carbon is an essential part of all living matter* (NOTE: Chemical element: chemical symbol: **C**; atomic number: **6**)
(b) **carbon (paper)** = paper with a black coating on one side, used for making copies; *you forgot to put a carbon in the typewriter*
(c) carbon copy; *make a top copy and two carbons*

④ **carbon copy**
['kɑːbɪn 'kɒpɪ] *noun*
copy made with carbon paper; *give me the original, and file the carbon copy*

④ **carbon paper**
['kɑːbɪn 'peɪpɪ] *noun*
paper with a black coating on one side, used for making copies; *you forgot to put any carbon paper in the typewriter*; *he put the carbon paper in the typewriter the wrong way round*

① **card**
[kɑːd] *noun*
(a) flat piece of card (often with a picture on one side) which you send to someone with a short message on it; *they sent us a card from Italy*; *how much does it cost to send a card to Australia?*; *see also* POSTCARD
(b) piece of stiff paper, folded so that a message can be written inside; **birthday card** = card which you send someone to wish them a happy birthday; **Christmas card** = card which you send someone at Christmas
(c) piece of stiff paper with a picture or pattern on it, used to play games; *a pack of cards*; *they were playing cards in the bar*; *would you like a game of cards?*
(d) piece of stiff paper with your name and address printed on it; *he gave me his business card*

(e) piece of stiff plastic used for payment; *do you want to pay cash or with a card?*; **cash card** = plastic card used to obtain money from a cash machine; **charge card** = plastic card which you use for buying things (you pay off the total sum charged at the end of each month); **cheque (guarantee) card** = plastic card from a bank which guarantees payment of a cheque up to a certain amount, even if the user has no money in his account; **credit card** = plastic card which allows you to buy goods without paying for them immediately; *he paid for the hotel with his credit card*; **smart card** = credit card with a chip, used for withdrawing money from cash machines or for buying at automatic terminals; **store card** = credit card issued by a department store which can only be used for purchases within that store; *see also* PHONECARD
(f) **filing card** = card with information written on it, used to classify information in correct order; **index card** = card used to make a card index; *she tipped all the index cards out onto the table*

④ **cardboard**
['kɑːdbɔːd] *noun*
thick card; *have you got a piece of cardboard which I can use to make this model?*; *we put the glasses into cardboard boxes*; *(informal)* **cardboard city** = place where homeless people build themselves shelters out of pieces of cardboard (NOTE: no plural: **some cardboard; a piece of cardboard**)

① **care**
[keɪ]
1 *noun*
(a) serious attention; *he handled the glass with great care*; **to take care** = to be very careful; *take care when you cross the road*; *he took great care with the box of glasses*; *take care not to be late*
(b) *(on a letter)* **care of** = words to show that the person is living at the address, but only as a visitor; **Mr Brown, care of Mrs Green** = to Mr Brown at the address of Mrs Green (NOTE: usually written **c/o** on the envelope)
(c) looking after someone; *the care of the elderly*; **child care** = looking after children; *the council has several children in care*; **to take care of someone** = to look after someone; *who will take care of mother while I'm away?*
2 *verb*
to be worried; *I don't care if my car is dirty*; *she cares a lot about the environment*; *he couldn't care less* = he doesn't worry at all about it

② **career**
[kɪ'rɪɪ]
1 *noun*
life of professional work; *she is starting her career as a librarian*; *he gave up his career as a civil servant and bought a farm*; *go and see the school careers adviser - she will give you advice on how to become a dentist*; **career woman** *or*

girl = woman who is working and does not plan to stop working to look after the house or children

2 *verb*

to rush forward out of control; *the car careered off the road into a ditch*

ⓘ **care for**
['keɪ 'fɔ:] *verb*

(a) to like; *would you care for another cup of coffee?*; *I don't care for this music very much*

(b) to look after; *nurses cared for the injured people after the accident*; *people who have to care for their elderly relatives should get a grant from the state*

ⓘ **careful**
['keɪful] *adjective*

taking care; *be careful not to make any noise, the baby is asleep*; *be careful when you're packing those glasses, they're very valuable!*; *she is very careful about what she eats*; *the project needs very careful planning*

ⓘ **carefully**
['keɪfɪli] *adverb*

with great care; *carry the box of eggs carefully!*; *drive more carefully in future!*; *it poured with rain and spoilt her carefully arranged hair*

② **careless**
['keɪlɪs] *adjective*

without taking care; *he is careless about his work*; *he made several careless mistakes when he took his driving test*

④ **caretaker**
['keɪteɪkə] *noun*

person who looks after a building; *go and ask the caretaker to replace the light bulb in the entrance hall*

④ **cargo**
['kɑ:gɪʊ] *noun*

goods carried (especially on a ship); *the ship was taking on cargo*; *cargo boat or cargo ship or cargo plane* = ship *or* plane which carries only cargo and not passengers (NOTE: plural is **cargoes**)

③ **caring**
['keɪrɪŋ] *adjective*

loving and helping; *she's a very caring person*; *his caring attitude towards his students*

④ **carnival**
['kɑ:nɪvl] *noun*

festival, often with music, dancing and eating in the open air; *the carnival procession arrived in the main square of the town*; *Notting Hill Carnival* = big carnival held every year in August in Notting Hill, in the west of London; *thousands of people take part in the Notting Hill Carnival every year*

ⓘ **car park**
['kɑ: pɑ:k] *noun*

special public place where you can leave a car when you are not using it; *there's a free car park next to our office*; *if you're going shopping, you can park your car in one of the car parks in the centre of town* (NOTE: in American English, this is a **parking lot**)

③ **carpet**
['kɑ:pɪt]

1 *noun*

thick material for covering the floor, stairs, etc.; *he spilt his coffee on our new white dining-room carpet*

2 *verb*

(a) to cover with a carpet; *a thickly carpeted hotel room*

(b) to cover with something as if with a carpet; *the path through the woods is carpeted with wild flowers*

③ **carriage**
['kærɪdʒ] *noun*

(a) cost of carrying goods; action of carrying goods; *carriage is 15% of the total cost*; *how much do they charge for carriage?*; **carriage free** = deal where the customer does not pay for the transport of goods; **carriage paid** = deal where the price paid includes transport

(b) **horse-drawn carriage** = open vehicle pulled by a horse; *the queen rode in an open carriage*

(c) **railway carriage** = railway wagon for passengers; *he was sitting in a first-class carriage although he only had a second-class ticket*

ⓘ **carried, carries**
['kærɪd or 'kærɪz]

see CARRY

④ **carrier**
['kærɪi] *noun*

(a) thing or person that carries; *a procession of water carriers with jars on their heads*; **luggage carrier** = metal shelf on the back of a bicycle on which you can carry a bag or box; **carrier bag** = large paper or plastic bag with handles, for carrying shopping, often given by a shop, with the shop's name on it; *her carrier bag split and all her shopping fell onto the pavement*

(b) person who carries the germ of a disease without showing any signs of it, and who can infect others with it; *the disease is transmitted by a carrier through infected food or drink*

(c) **aircraft carrier** = large ship which carries aircraft; *we sent an aircraft carrier to the Mediterranean*

④ **carrot**
['kærɪt] *noun*

vegetable with a long orange root which can be eaten; *boiled carrots*; *carrot soup*

ⓘ **carry**
['kæri] *verb*

(a) to take something and move it to another place; *they had to carry the chest of drawers up the stairs*; *the plane was carrying 120 passengers*; *that suitcase is too heavy for me to carry*

(b) to vote to approve; **the motion was carried** = the motion was accepted after a vote; *her proposal was not carried*

(c) to keep in stock; *a supermarket will carry about 5,000 different lines of goods*

(d) *(of sound)* to be heard at a distance; *the sound of the church bells carried across the marsh*

③ **carry on**
['kæri 'ɒn] *verb*

to go on doing something; *when the policeman came into the restaurant, they all carried on talking as if nothing had happened*; *they carried on with their work even though the office was on fire*

③ **cart**
[kɑ:t]
1 *noun*

(a) vehicle pulled by a horse; *a cart piled high with furniture*; **to put the cart before the horse** = to deal with things the wrong way round

(b) *US* **baggage cart** = metal holder on wheels, on which baggage can be placed to be moved easily in an airport, train station, etc.; **shopping cart** = metal basket on wheels, used by shoppers to put their purchases in as they go round a supermarket (NOTE: British English for these is **luggage trolley** and **shopping trolley** *or* **supermarket trolley**)

2 *verb*

to carry a big or heavy thing; *why do we have to cart this folding bed around with us?*; *they carted all their equipment up three flights of stairs*; *the police came and carted him off to jail*

③ **cartoon**
[kɑ:'tu:n] *noun*

(a) funny, often political, drawing in a newspaper; *he draws a cartoon for the 'Evening Standard'*

(b) film made of moving drawings; *I like watching Tom and Jerry cartoons*

④ **carve**
[kɑ:v] *verb*

(a) to cut a large piece of meat up at table; *who's going to carve?*; *Father sat at the end of the table, carving a chicken*

(b) to cut stone or wood to make a shape; *he carved a bird out of wood*

④ **carving**
['kɑ:vɪŋ] *noun*

(a) cutting up cooked meat; **carving knife** = large sharp knife, used for carving; *it would be easier to carve the chicken with a proper carving knife*

(b) art of cutting stone or wood into shapes; *stone carving is an option at art school*

(c) an object which has been made by carving; *he gave me a wood carving for my birthday*; *the stone carvings in the old church date from the 15th century*

① **case**
[keɪs] *noun*

(a) suitcase, a box with a handle, for carrying your clothes, etc., in when travelling; *she was still packing her case when the taxi came*; *my plane went to Chicago, but my case went to New York by mistake*; *the customs made him open his case*

(b) special box for something; *put the gun back in its case*; *I've lost my red spectacle case*

(c) large wooden box for goods; *he bought a case of wine*; **a packing case** = large wooden box for carrying items which can be easily broken; *the removal men are bringing their packing cases tomorrow*

(d) situation, way in which something happens; *your case is very similar to mine*; *it was a case of first come, first served*

(e) **court case** = legal action or trial; **the case is being heard next week** = the case is coming to court next week

◊ **in any case**
[ɪn 'eni 'keɪs]

anyway, whatever may happen; *she missed the bus but in any case it didn't matter because the film started late*; *they scored a late penalty, but it didn't matter, we were losing 3 - 0 in any case*

◊ **in case**
[ɪn 'keɪs]

because something might happen; *take your gloves in case it's cold on the mountain*; *I always carry an umbrella in case it rains*; **in case of fire, break the glass** = if there is a fire, break the glass; **just in case** = because something might happen; *it's still sunny, but I'll take my umbrella just in case*

◊ **in that case**
[ɪn 'ðæt 'keɪs]

if that happens or if that is the situation; *there is a strike on the underground - in that case, you'll have to take a bus*

① **cash**
[kæʃ]
1 *noun*

money in coins and notes, not in cheques; *we don't keep much cash in the house*; *I'd prefer to use up my spare cash, rather than pay with a credit card*; **cash box** = metal box for keeping cash; **cash machine** = machine which gives out money when a special card is inserted and instructions given; **cash on delivery (COD)** = payment in cash when goods are delivered; **cash register** = machine at a cash desk where you pay, with a drawer for cash (NOTE: no plural)

2 *verb*

to cash a cheque = to change a cheque into cash; *he tried to cash a cheque for seven hundred pounds*

③ **cash desk**
['kæʃ 'desk] *noun*
place in a store where you pay for the goods you are buying; *take your purchases to the nearest cash desk*

③ **cash flow**
['kæʃ 'fləʊ] *noun*
rate at which money comes into and is paid out of a business; **the company is suffering from cash flow problems** = cash income is not coming in fast enough to pay the cash expenditure going out

③ **casket**
['kɑːskɪt] *noun*
(a) box for jewels; *the thief stole a casket from beside her bed*
(b) *(mainly US)* long wooden box in which a dead person is buried; *they watched in silence as the casket was lowered into the ground* (NOTE: British English prefers **coffin**)

④ **cassette**
[kɪ'set] *noun*
(a) magnetic tape in a plastic case which can fit directly into a playing or recording machine; *do you want it on cassette or CD?*; *he bought a cassette of folk songs*; **cassette player** = machine which plays cassettes; **cassette recorder** = machine which records and plays back cassettes
(b) film in a plastic case which fits directly into a camera; *she quickly put a new cassette into her camera*

③ **cast**
[kɑːst]
1 *noun*
all the actors in a play or film; *after the first night the cast went to celebrate in a restaurant*
2 *verb*
(a) to make a metal or plaster object from a mould; *he cast the statue in copper*
(b) to choose actors for a play *or* film; *he was cast as a soldier in 'Henry V'*
(c) **to cast a vote** = to vote; *the process of counting all the votes cast in the election has just begun*
(d) *(formal)* to throw; **to cast doubts on** = to say that you are doubtful about something; *he cast doubts on the whole proposal*; **to cast light on something** = to make something easier to understand; *the papers cast some light on how the minister reached his decision* (NOTE: casting - cast)

③ **castle**
['kɑːsl] *noun*
(a) large building with strong walls; *the Queen is spending the week at Windsor Castle*; *the soldiers shut the castle gate*; *see also* SAND CASTLE
(b) one of two pieces used in chess, shaped like a little castle tower; *she took my last castle*

④ **casual**
['kæʒjʊəl] *adjective*
not formal; *he just walked in without knocking in a very casual way*; *she tried to appear casual at the interview, even though she was very nervous*; **casual labour** = temporary workers; **casual shoes** = light shoes, which are not office shoes; **casual work** = work where workers are hired for a short period

④ **casualty**
['kæʒjʊəlti] *noun*
(a) person injured or killed in a battle or in an accident; *casualties were taken to hospital by ambulance and helicopter*; *the radio reported that there had been heavy casualties*; **casualty department** = department in a hospital for accident victims (NOTE: plural is **casualties**)
(b) *(informal)* casualty department in a hospital; *the accident victim was rushed into casualty*

① **cat**
[kæt] *noun*
animal with soft fur and a long tail, kept as a pet; *she asked her neighbours to feed her cat when she went on holiday*; *don't forget to get some tins of cat food* (NOTE: cats are often called **Puss** or **Pussy**; a baby cat is a **kitten**)

③ **catalogue** *US* **catalog**
['kætɪlɒg]
1 *noun*
list of things for sale or in a library or museum; *look up the title in the library catalogue*; *an office equipment catalogue*; *we got the latest catalogue of greenhouses*
2 *verb*
to make a list of things that exist somewhere; *she spent months cataloguing his correspondence*

③ **catastrophe**
[kɪ'tæstrɪfi] *noun*
disaster, very bad accident; *it's a natural catastrophe on the same scale as the earthquake last year*; *this is the latest catastrophe to hit the family*

① **catch**
[kætʃ]
1 *noun*
(a) thing which has been grabbed or taken; *the boat brought back a huge catch of fish*
(b) action of grabbing a ball in the air; *he made a marvellous catch*; *he dropped an easy catch*
(c) hidden disadvantage; *it seems such a good deal, there must be a catch in it somewhere*; **catch 22** = circle of events which you cannot escape from
(d) little hook which holds a door shut (NOTE: plural is **catches**)
2 *verb*
(a) to grab hold of something moving in the air; *can you catch a ball with your left hand?*; *when he knocked a glass off the table he managed to catch it before it hit the floor*

(b) to grab hold of something; *she caught him by the sleeve as he turned away*; *as he slipped, he caught the rail to stop himself falling*; **to catch someone's eye** = to look at someone who is looking at you; *she caught his eye and nodded towards the door*

(c) to get hold of an animal, especially to kill it; *he sat by the river all day but didn't catch anything*; *our cat is no good at catching mice: she's too lazy*

(d) to get on a bus, plane, train, etc., before it leaves; *you will have to run if you want to catch the last bus*; *he caught the 10 o'clock train to Paris*

(e) to get an illness; *he caught a cold from standing watching the rugby match*; *the baby has caught measles*

(f) to find someone doing something wrong; *she caught the boys stealing in her shop*; *the police caught the burglar as he was climbing out of the window*

(g) to arrest someone; *after months of searching, the police finally caught the gang*

(h) to hear; *I didn't quite catch what she said* (NOTE: **catching - caught** [kɔːt] **- has caught**)

② **category**
['kætɪgɪrɪ] *noun*
classification of things or people; *we only sell the most expensive categories of watches*; *if there is no room in the hotel mentioned in the leaflet, we will put you into a similar category of hotel* (NOTE: plural is **categories**)

④ **cater for**
['keɪtə 'fɔː] *verb*
(a) to supply food and drink at a party, etc.; *our firm caters for receptions of up to 250 guests*
(b) to provide for; *the college caters mainly for older students*; *we cater for private individuals as well as for groups*

③ **caterpillar**
['kætɪpɪlɪ] *noun*
(a) insect worm with many legs, which turns into a moth or butterfly; *caterpillars have eaten most of the leaves on our trees*
(b) caterpillar track = metal belt running round wheels on a tank, etc.; **caterpillar tractor** = tractor with a metal belt round its wheels

③ **cathedral**
[kɪ'θiːdrɪl] *noun*
large church where a bishop sits; *we went on a tour of cathedrals in the Midlands*; *you can see the cathedral tower from miles away*; *Canterbury Cathedral is one of the oldest in England*

③ **catholic**
['kæθlɪk]
1 *adjective*
(a) Catholic = referring to the Roman Catholic Church; *the Catholic communion service is called a mass*; *our local Catholic priest is leaving to go to Serbia*; *there's a French Catholic church near Leicester Square*

(b) wide, general (taste); *his interests have always been quite catholic*
2 *noun*
a Catholic = a member of the Roman Catholic Church; *she became a Catholic when she married*; *the war between Protestants and Catholics*

④ **cattle**
['kætl] *noun*
animals of the cow family; *a herd of cattle*; *cattle farmers are complaining about the high cost of foodstuffs*; *the cattle were brought inside for the winter* (NOTE: the word is plural)

① **caught**
[kɔːt]
see CATCH

④ **cauliflower**
['kɒlɪflauɪ] *noun*
vegetable with hard white flowers, which are eaten cooked; *would you like some more cauliflower?*; **cauliflower cheese** = dish of cauliflower cooked in the oven with a white sauce and cheese on top (NOTE: no plural when referring to the food: **some cauliflower; we had cauliflower with the meat**)

① **cause**
[kɔːz]
1 *noun*
(a) thing which makes something happen; *what is the chief cause of traffic accidents?*; *the police tried to find the cause of the fire*
(b) organization which people support; *she is fighting for the cause of working mothers*
2 *verb*
to make something happen; *the accident caused a traffic jam on the motorway*; *the loud bang caused her to drop the cup she was carrying*

④ **caution**
['kɔːʃn]
1 *noun*
(a) care; *the pavement is covered with ice - please proceed with great caution* (NOTE: no plural in this meaning)
(b) warning not to do something again; *the magistrate let him off with a caution*
2 *verb*
to warn; *he was cautioned by the police*; *the doctor cautioned him against working too hard*

④ **cautious**
['kɔːʃɪs] *adjective*
careful, not rushing; *we were warned to be cautious when driving through the crowded streets of the old town*; *she's a very cautious driver*; *he has adopted a cautious approach to his investments*

④ **cautiously**
['kɔːʃɪslɪ] *adverb*
in a cautious way; *she walked cautiously along the top of the wall*

④ **cave**
[keɪv]
1 *noun*
large underground hole in rock or earth; *when the tide went out we could explore the cave*; **cave paintings** = paintings done by ancient peoples on the walls of caves
2 *verb*
to cave in = to collapse; *the beam cracked and the roof caved in*

④ **CD**
['siː 'diː]
abbreviation for compact disc; *I don't like his new CD - do you?*; *some CDs are expensive so I borrow them from the music library*; *you can get it on CD or cassette*; **CD player** = machine which plays CDs

② **CD-ROM**
['siː diː 'rɒm] *noun*
= COMPACT DISC READ ONLY MEMORY
small plastic disc which can store data, sounds or pictures; **CD-ROM drive** = disc drive that allows a computer to read data stored on a CD-ROM; *most PCs have CD-ROM drives*

③ **cease**
[siːs] *verb*
to stop; *at long last the drilling noise has ceased*; **to cease to exist** = to stop being in existence; *the pub on the corner ceased to exist some time ago*

④ **ceasefire**
['siːsfaɪə] *noun*
agreement to stop shooting (in a war); *they agreed a two-week ceasefire to allow negotiations to start*

③ **ceiling**
['siːlɪŋ] *noun*
(a) inside roof over a room; *he's so tall, he can easily touch the ceiling*; *flies can walk on the ceiling*; *he painted the kitchen ceiling*; *watch out when you go into the bedroom - it has a very low ceiling*
(b) highest point, such as the highest interest rate, the highest amount of money which you can invest, etc.; *output has reached its ceiling*; *there is a ceiling of £20,000 on the amount you can hold in premium bonds*

③ **celebrate**
['selɪbreɪt] *verb*
(a) to have a party or do special things because something good has taken place, or because of something that happened in the past; *our team won, so we're all going out to celebrate*; *today we celebrate the five-hundredth anniversary of the founding of our school*; *they celebrated their wedding anniversary quietly at home with their children*
(b) to perform a religious ceremony; *the priest was celebrating Mass*

③ **celebration**
[selɪ'breɪʃn] *noun*
action of celebrating something; *we had my birthday celebration in the local pub*; *after our team won, the celebrations went on late into the night*

④ **celery**
['selɪri] *noun*
plant with a white or green stem, eaten as a vegetable or raw as a salad; *she bought a bunch of celery in the market*; **a stick of celery** = a piece of the stem of the celery plant (often served raw with cheese) (NOTE: no plural)

① **cell**
[sel] *noun*
(a) room in a prison; *he was arrested in the centre of town and spent the night in the police cells*; **condemned cell** = room for prisoners condemned to death
(b) basic unit of an organism; *you can see the cancer cells under a microscope* (NOTE: do not confuse with **sell**)

④ **cello**
['tʃeləʊ] *noun*
large stringed musical instrument smaller than a double bass; *a quartet made up of two violins and two cellos* (NOTE: plural is **cellos**)

③ **Celsius**
['selsiəs] *adjective & noun* scale of temperature where the freezing point of water is 0° and the boiling point is 100°; *do you use Celsius or Fahrenheit in the weather forecasts?*; *what is 75° Fahrenheit in Celsius?* (NOTE: used in many countries, but not in the USA, where the Fahrenheit system is still preferred. Normally written as a **C** after the degree sign: **32°C** (say: 'thirty-two degrees Celsius'). It was formerly called **centigrade**)

> COMMENT: to convert Celsius temperatures to Fahrenheit, multiply by 1.8 and add 32. So 20°C is equal to 68°F. To convert Fahrenheit to Celsius, subtract 32 and divide by 1.8

④ **cement**
[sɪ'ment]
1 *noun*
(a) powder made from lime and clay, which is mixed with water and dries hard; *he was mixing cement to make a path round the house*
(b) strong glue; *she stuck the handle back on the cup with cement*
2 *verb*
to attach strongly; *he cemented some stones on the top of the wall*; *the two halves should be cemented together*

③ **cemetery**
['semɪtri] *noun*
place where people are buried; *he is buried in the cemetery next to the church*; *there are two cemeteries in the city* (NOTE: plural is **cemeteries**)

④ **census**
['sensɪs] *noun*
official count of a country's population; *the next census will be taken in ten years' time* (NOTE: plural is **censuses)**

① **cent**
[sent] *noun*
(a) small coin, one-hundredth part of a dollar; *the stores are only a 25-cent bus ride away*; *they sell oranges at 99 cents each* (NOTE: do not confuse with **sent, scent; cent** is usually written **c** in prices: **25c,** but not when a dollar price is mentioned: **$1.25)**
(b) *see also* PER CENT

③ **centigrade**
['sentɪgreɪd] *noun*
scale of temperature where the freezing point of water is 0° and the boiling point is 100°; *do you use centigrade or Fahrenheit in the weather forecasts?*; *what is 75° Fahrenheit in centigrade?*; *see note at* CELSIUS

③ **centimetre** *US* **centimeter**
['sentɪmiːtɪ] *noun*
measure of length, one hundredth part of a metre; *I need a short piece of string - about 25 centimetres long* (NOTE: written **cm** with numbers: **25cm:** say: 'twenty-five centimetres')

① **central**
['sentrl] *adjective*
in the centre; *the hall has one central pillar*; *his offices are very central*; **central government =** the main government of a country, as opposed to local government; **central heating =** heating of a whole house from one main heater and several radiators; *the house has gas central heating*; **central reservation =** section of road or grass, bushes, etc., between the two sections of a major road; *the lorry crashed through the central reservation and hit a car coming in the opposite direction*

③ **Central America**
['sentrl ə'merɪkə] *noun*
part of the American continent between North and South America, containing Mexico, Costa Rica, etc.; *our cruise took us to several ports in Central America*

① **centre** *US* **center**
['sentɪ]
1 *noun*
(a) middle; *they planted a rose bush in the centre of the lawn*; *the town centre is very old*; *chocolates with coffee cream centres*; **centre of gravity =** the point in an object at which it will balance; *a bus has a very low centre of gravity*
(b) large building containing several different sections; *an army training centre*; **health centre** *or* **medical centre =** building with various doctors and specialists; **sports centre =** place where several different sports can be played; **shopping centre =** several shops in one big building

(c) important town; *Nottingham is the centre for the shoe industry*
(d) group or political party, such as the Liberals or Democrats, between the left and right; *the centre combined with the right to defeat the proposal*; *the cabinet is formed of right-of-centre supporters of the Prime Minister*
(e) jobcentre = government office which advertises jobs which are vacant
2 *verb*
(a) to put something in the middle; *make sure you centre the block of wood on the work bench*
(b) to concentrate on; *the opposition's attack was centred on the government's reorganization of the social services*; *our report centres on some aspects of the sales team*

① **century**
['sentʃɪri] *noun*
(a) one hundred years; **the seventeenth century =** the period from 1600 to 1699; *a 17th-century church*; *the church dates from the 17th century*
(b) score of 100, especially in cricket; *he scored a century, including four fours and two sixes* (NOTE: plural is **centuries;** note also that the number of a century is always one more than the date number: so the period from **1900 to 1999** is the **20th century,** and the period starting in the year **2000** is the **21st century)**

③ **cereal**
['sɪərɪəl] *noun*
(breakfast) cereal = food made from corn, oats, etc., eaten with milk for breakfast; *would you like some cereal for breakfast?* (NOTE: do not confuse with **serial)**

④ **ceremony**
['serɪmɪni] *noun*
important official occasion when something special is done in public; *they held a ceremony to remember the victims of the train crash*; **to stand on ceremony =** to be formal and not relaxed; *don't stand on ceremony* (NOTE: plural is **ceremonies)**

① **certain**
['sɜːtɪn] *adjective*
(a) sure; *are you certain that you locked the door?*; *I'm not certain where she lives*; **to make certain that =** to do something to be sure that something with happen; *he put the money in his safe to make certain that no one could steal it*
(b) without any doubt; *our team is certain to win the prize*
(c) a certain quantity *or* **a certain amount =** some; *the fire did a certain amount of damage*; *rebuilding the house took a certain amount of time*; *you need to add a certain quantity of water to the paint*
(d) which you don't know or are not sure about; *the manager is a certain Mr Arbuthnot*; *certain mushrooms can make you ill if you eat them*

① **certainly**
['sɜːtɪnli] *adverb*
(a) *(after a question or order)* of course; *can you give me a lift to the station? - certainly*; *tell him to write to me immediately - certainly, sir*; *give me a kiss - certainly not!*
(b) definitely; *she certainly impressed the judges*; *he certainly knows how to score goals*

③ **certificate**
[sɜːˈtɪfɪkɪt] *noun*
official document which proves or shows something; *she has been awarded a certificate for swimming*; *he has an advanced certificate in English*; **birth certificate** = official paper showing the date on which someone was born, together with details of the parents; **death certificate** = paper signed by a doctor which shows that someone has died and what was the cause of death; **insurance certificate** = document from an insurance company showing that an insurance policy has been issued; **marriage certificate** = official paper to confirm that two people are married; **savings certificate** = document showing you have invested money in a government savings scheme; **share certificate** = document proving that you own shares

② **chain**
[tʃeɪn]
1 *noun*
(a) series of metal rings joined together; *she wore a gold chain round her neck*; *he stopped when the chain came off his bike*; **chain reaction** = series of reactions which follow on from an event; **chain saw** = saw made of a chain with teeth in it, which turns very fast when driven by a motor
(b) series of stores, restaurants, pubs, hotels, etc., belonging to the same company; *a chain of hotels* or *a hotel chain*; *a do-it-yourself chain*; *she runs a chain of shoe shops*
(c) row (of large mountains); *the Rockies are a chain of mountains running down from Canada through the western states*
(d) series of people, each buying another's house; *there is a chain of six families involved, so the sale will take some time*
2 *verb*
to attach with a chain; *I chained my bike to the fence*

① **chair**
[tʃeɪ]
1 *noun*
(a) piece of furniture which you can sit on, with a back; *someone has been sitting in my chair, said the father bear*; *he pulled up a chair and started to write*; *these dining-room chairs are very hard*; **easy chair** = comfortable chair; *see also* ARMCHAIR

(b) the chairman, the person who presides over a meeting; *please address all your comments to the chair*; **Mr Jones took the chair** = Mr Jones presided over the meeting
(c) position of professor at a university; *he has been appointed to the chair of English*
2 *verb*
to preside over a meeting; *the meeting was chaired by Mrs Smith*

① **chairman**
['tʃeɪmɪn] *noun*
(a) person who is in charge of a meeting; *Mrs Jones was the chairman at the meeting*
(b) person who presides over a board of directors; *the chairman of the bank* (NOTE: plural is **chairmen**)

④ **chalk**
[tʃɔːk]
1 *noun*
(a) type of soft white rock made of calcium; *the white cliffs of Dover are formed of chalk*; *(informal)* **they're as different as chalk and cheese** = they are totally different
(b) stick of white or coloured material for writing on a blackboard; *he wrote the dates on the board in coloured chalk*
2 *verb*
to mark or write with chalk; *she chalked the menu for the day on the blackboard*

② **challenge**
['tʃælɪndʒ]
1 *noun*
(a) test of skill, strength, etc.; *the action by the union is another challenge to the authority of the government*; **to pose a challenge to someone** = to be a difficult task; *getting the piano up the stairs will pose a challenge to the removal men*
(b) invitation to a fight or match; *our team accepted the challenge to play another game*; **to take up a challenge** = to agree to fight
2 *verb*
(a) to ask someone to prove that he is right; *when challenged, he admitted that he had seen her get into a car*; *the committee's conclusions have been challenged by other experts*
(b) **to challenge someone to a fight** = to ask someone to fight

③ **chamber**
['tʃeɪmbɪ] *noun*
(a) official room; **council chamber** = room where a council meets
(b) **chambers** = office of a judge or a lawyer; *we went to see our lawyer in his chambers*
(c) **chamber music** = music for a few instruments which can be played in a small room; **chamber orchestra** = small orchestra which plays chamber music
(d) empty space inside the heart; *blood collects inside the chambers of the heart and is then pumped out*

④ **champagne**
[ʃæmˈpeɪn] *noun*
sparkling white wine from the north-east of
France; *they opened a bottle of champagne to
celebrate the birth of the baby*

② **champion**
[ˈtʃæmpiɪn]
1 *noun*
best in a particular competition; *a champion
cow*; *she was champion two years running*;
he's the world champion in the 100 metres
2 *verb*
to champion a cause = to support a cause
strongly; *they are championing the cause of
women's rights*

② **championship**
[ˈtʃæmpiɪnʃɪp] *noun*
(a) contest to find who is the champion; *the
schools' tennis championship was won by a
boy from Leeds*
(b) support for a cause; *her constant
championship of the homeless*

① **chance**
[tʃɑːns]
1 *noun*
(a) possibility; *has our team any chance of
winning? - yes, I think they have a good
chance*; *is there any chance of our getting
home tonight?*; *there is no chance of rain in
August*; *what are their chances of survival in
this weather?*
(b) opportunity; *I've been waiting for a chance
to speak to the Prime Minister*; *I wish I had the
chance to visit South Africa*
(c) luck; *it was pure chance or it was quite by
chance that we were travelling on the same bus*
(NOTE: the meanings: **chance of +ing** =
possibility of doing something; **chance to** =
opportunity to do something)
2 *verb*
(a) to do something by chance; *he chanced to
look round as she came up to him*; *the car in
front of us chanced to turn right*
(b) to chance it = to try to do something which
is risky; *the sky looks grey, but I think I'll
chance it without an umbrella*
(c) to chance upon = to find something by
accident; *as he was searching in the library he
chanced upon an unknown play by
Shakespeare*

◊ **by any chance**
phrase
by luck, by accident; *do you by any chance
happen to know where the nearest post office
is?*; *have you by any chance seen my glasses?*

② **chancellor**
[ˈtʃɑːnsɪlɪ] *noun*
(a) important official; *he became chancellor of
the university in 1996*
(b) *(in Germany or Austria)* head of the
government (= Prime Minister); *Chancellor
Kohl of Germany*

② **Chancellor (of the Exchequer)**
[ˈtʃɑːnsɪlɪr əv ðiː ɪksˈtʃekə] *noun*
chief finance minister in the British government;
*newspapers always carry pictures of the
Chancellor on Budget day* (NOTE: in most
countries, this job is called the **Minister of
Finance**; the American equivalent is the **Secretary
of the Treasury**)

① **change**
[tʃeɪnʒ]
1 *noun*
(a) making something different or becoming
different; *there was a last-minute change of
plan*; *we've seen a lot of changes over the
years*; *I think it's a change for the better* = I
think it has made things better than they were
(b) something different; *we usually go on
holiday in summer, but this year we're taking a
winter holiday for a change*; *a cup of tea is a
nice change after all those glasses of orange
juice*; *a change of job will do you good*; **he took
a change of clothes with him** = he took a set of
clean clothes with him
(c) money in coins or notes; *I need some
change for the parking meter*; *have you got
change for a £5 note?*; **small change** = coins,
especially ones with a low value; *I have only
two £10 notes - I have no small change at all*
(d) money which you get back when you have
given more than the correct price; *the book is
£3.50, so if you give me £5, you should get
£1.50 change*; *the shopkeeper gave me the
wrong change*; **keep the change** = keep it as a
tip (said to waiters, etc.) (NOTE: no plural for
meanings (c) and (d))
(e) to ring the changes = to try various things to
see which is best; *I don't always buy the same
newspaper, I prefer to ring the changes
between 'The Times', 'The Independent' and
'The Guardian'*
2 *verb*
(a) to make something different; to become
different; *living in the country has changed his
attitude towards towns*; *London has changed a
lot since we used to live there*; *he's changed so
much since I last saw him that I hardly
recognized him*; **I've changed my mind** = I've
decided to do something different
(b) to put on different clothes; *I'm just going
upstairs to change or to get changed*; *go into
the bathroom if you want to change your dress*;
changing room = room where you can change
into or out of sports clothes; **to change a bed** =
to put clean sheets, etc., on a bed; *the girl has
come in to change the beds*
(c) to use or have something in place of
something else; *you ought to change your car
tyres if they are worn*; *can we change our room
for one with a view of the sea?*; *she's recently
changed her job or changed jobs*; **to change
trains** *or* **to change buses** = to get off one train

or bus and onto another to continue your journey; *to get to Stratford you will have to change (trains) at Birmingham*

(d) to change gear = to change from one gear to the next when driving a car (NOTE: American English is to **shift gears**)

(e) to give smaller coins or notes for a larger one; **can you change a £20 note?** = can you give me small change for it?

(f) to give one type of currency for another; *to change £1,000 into dollars*; *we want to change some traveller's cheques*

② **channel**
['tʃænl]
1 *noun*

(a) piece of water connecting two seas; **the (English) Channel** = the sea between England and France; *many people use the Channel Tunnel to get to France; the boat only takes 50 minutes to cross the Channel*

(b) way in which information or goods are passed from one place to another; *the matter was sorted out through the normal diplomatic channels*; **channels of communication** = ways of communicating

(c) green channel = way through customs for people who have nothing to declare; **red channel** = way through customs for people with something to declare

(d) frequency range for radio or TV; station using this range of frequencies; *we're watching Channel 4; can you switch to Channel 1 for the news?; the new chat show is scheduled to compete with the gardening programme on the other channel*

2 *verb*

to send in a certain direction; *they are channelling their funds into research; the money from the sale of the farm has been channelled into the building project* (NOTE: **channelling - channelled** but American spelling is **channeling - channeled**)

④ **chaos**
['keɪɒs] *noun*

confusion; *there was total chaos when the electricity failed*; **Chaos Theory** = theory that things happen at random, and one should plan for the unexpected to happen

③ **chap**
[tʃæp]
1 *noun*

(informal) man; *he's a really nice chap; I bought it from a chap at work*
2 *verb*

(of the skin) to crack; *rub an ointment on your chapped lips* (NOTE: **chapping - chapped**)

④ **chapel**
['tʃæpl] *noun*

(a) separate part of a large church; *there are three chapels on the west side of the cathedral*

(b) small church; *the chapel is an ancient monument and is protected; they were buried in the prison chapel*

① **chapter**
['tʃæptɪ] *noun*

(a) division of a book; *the first chapter is rather slow, but after that the story gets exciting; don't tell me how it finishes - I'm only up to chapter three*; *see also* VERSE

(b) a chapter of accidents = a series of accidents

(c) group of priests who run a cathedral; **chapter house** = special room where a chapter meets

① **character**
['kærɪktɪ] *noun*

(a) the part of a person which makes him or her different from all others; *his character is quite different from yours; she is a very strong character*

(b) person in a play or novel; *the leading character in the film is an old blind man*

(c) letter or symbol used in writing or printing; *the book is printed in Chinese characters*

② **characteristic**
[kærɪktɪ'rɪstɪk]
1 *adjective*

special, typical; *you can recognize him by his characteristic way of walking; that is characteristic of this type of flower* (NOTE: something is characteristic **of** something)

2 *noun*

typical feature; *the two cars have very similar characteristics*

③ **characterize**
['kærɪktɪraɪz] *verb*

(a) to be a typical feature of something; *the northern coast is characterized by tall cliffs and tiny beaches*

(b) to describe something as; *he didn't like to be characterized as weak and inefficient; how would you characterize her reaction to the film?*

① **charge**
[tʃɑːdʒ]
1 *noun*

(a) money which you have to pay; *there is no charge for delivery; we make a small charge for rental*; **we will send the parcel free of charge** = without asking you to pay for postage; **admission charge** *or* **entry charge** = price to be paid before going into an exhibition, etc.; **service charge** = charge added to a bill in a restaurant to pay for service; *a 10% service charge is added; does the bill include a service charge?*

(b) claim by the police that someone has done something wrong; *he was kept in prison on a charge of trying to blow up the Houses of Parliament*

(c) in charge = being in control of; *he is in charge of the sales department*; *who's in charge here?*; **to take charge of something** = to start to be responsible for something; *he took charge of the class while the teacher was out of the room*; **charge nurse** = senior male nurse in charge of a ward; *the charge nurse told me my son was getting better* (NOTE: the female equivalent is a **sister**)

(d) electric current; *he was killed by an electric charge from the wires*

(e) running attack; *the captain led the charge against the enemy camp*

2 *verb*

(a) to ask someone to pay; *the restaurant charged me £10 for two glasses of water*; *how much did the garage charge for mending the car?*; *can I charge the restaurant bill to my room number?*; **to charge the packing to the customer** = to ask the customer to pay for the packing

(b) *(of the police)* to say that someone has done something wrong; *he was charged with stealing the jewels*

(c) to attack while running; *the police charged the group of protesters*; *if the elephant charges, run as fast as you can!*

(d) to run violently; *the children charged into the kitchen*

(e) to give someone responsibility; *she was charged with organizing the club's dinner dance*

(f) to put electricity into a battery; *you can charge your phone battery by plugging it into the mains overnight*; *my mobile phone doesn't work - the battery probably needs charging*

② **charity**
['tʃærɪti] *noun*

(a) organization which collects money to help the poor or support some cause; *charities do not pay tax*; **charity shop** = shop run by a charity, where you can take old clothes, china, etc., which are then sold and the money given to the charity (NOTE: plural is **charities**)

(b) help, usually money, given to the poor; *he lost his job and his family have to rely on the charity of neighbours* (NOTE: no plural in this meaning)

④ **charm**
[tʃɑːm]

1 *noun*

(a) being attractive; *she has great personal charm*; *the charm of the Devon countryside*

(b) object which is supposed to be magic; *she wears a lucky charm round her neck*

2 *verb*

(a) to put under a spell; *the old man played a pipe and charmed a snake out of its basket*

(b) to attract someone, to make someone pleased; *he always manages to charm the girls at the office*; *I was charmed by their tiny cottage in the country*

③ **charming**
['tʃɑːmɪŋ] *adjective*

attractive; *she looks charming in her pink dress*; *he was such a charming young man*; *the effect of the little lights in the trees was charming*

③ **chart**
[tʃɑːt]

1 *noun*

(a) map of the sea, a river or a lake; *you will need an accurate chart of the entrance to the river*

(b) diagram showing statistics; *a chart showing the increase in cases of lung cancer*; **bar chart** = diagram where quantities are shown as thick columns of different heights; **pie chart** = diagram where information is shown as a circle cut up into sections of different sizes

(c) the charts = list of the most popular records; *his single is going up in the charts*; **chart show** = TV or radio show where records which are in the charts are played

2 *verb*

(a) to make a map of the sea, a river or lake; *he charted the coast of southern Australia in the 18th century*

(b) to describe or make a diagram of something to show information; *the book charts the rise of the new political party*

③ **charter**
['tʃɑːtə]

1 *noun*

(a) charter flight = flight in an aircraft which has been hired specially; *our charter flight for Marbella was ten hours late*; **charter plane** = plane which has been chartered

(b) legal document giving rights or privileges to a town or a university; *the university received its charter in 1846*

2 *verb*

to hire an aircraft, bus or boat for a particular trip; *we chartered a boat for a day trip to the island*

③ **chase**
[tʃeɪs]

1 *noun*

running after someone to try to catch him; *he was caught after a three-hour chase along the motorway*; **to give chase** = to run after someone; *the robbers escaped and the police gave chase*; *see also* WILD GOOSE CHASE

2 *verb*

(a) to run after someone to try to catch him; *the policeman chased the burglars down the street*; *the postman was chased by a dog*

(b) to try to speed up work by asking how it is getting on; *we are trying to chase the accounts department for your cheque*; *I will chase up your order with the production department*

④ **chassis**
['ʃæsi] *noun*
(a) metal framework of a car; *the car's chassis was damaged in the accident*
(b) wheels of an aircraft; *the aircraft radioed to say that the chassis had failed* (NOTE: plural is **chassis** ['ʃæsɪz])

② **chat**
[tʃæt]
1 *noun*
casual friendly talk; *he likes to drop in for a cup of coffee and a chat; I'd like to have a chat with you about your work*
2 *verb*
to talk in a casual and friendly way; *they were chatting about their holidays when the bus arrived; (informal)* **to chat someone up** = to talk to someone to try to make friends; *he tried to chat up the girl he met in a bar* (NOTE: **chatting - chatted**)

② **chat show**
['tʃæt 'ʃʊ] *noun*
TV show where famous people talk to the host; *she has been invited to appear on the new chat show*

① **cheap**
[tʃiːp]
1 *adjective*
which does not cost a lot of money; *if you want a cheap radio you ought to shop around; why do you go by bus? - because it's cheaper than the train; buses are by far the cheapest way to travel;* **dirt cheap** = extremely cheap; *oranges are dirt cheap in the street markets* (NOTE: **cheaper - cheapest**)
2 *adverb*
at a low price; *I bought them cheap in the local market*

② **cheaply**
['tʃiːpli] *adverb*
without paying much money; *you can live quite cheaply if you don't go out to eat in restaurants*

③ **cheat**
[tʃiːt]
1 *noun*
person who acts in an unfair way in order to win; *I won't play cards with him again, he's a cheat*
2 *verb*
(a) to act in an unfair way in order to be successful; *they don't let him play any more since they found he was cheating; they are sure he cheated in his exam, but can't find out how he did it*
(b) **to cheat someone out of something** = to get something by tricking someone; *he was furious, saying that he had been cheated out of the first prize*

① **check**
[tʃek]
1 *noun*
(a) examination or test; *the police are carrying out checks on all cars; a routine check of the*

fire equipment; **baggage check** = examination of passengers' baggage to see if it contains bombs or other dangerous devices
(b) *US (in a restaurant)* bill; *I'll ask for the check*
(c) *US* = CHEQUE
(d) *US* mark on paper to show that something is correct; *make a check in the box marked 'R'* (NOTE: British English is **tick**)
(e) **in check** = under control; *we must keep our spending in check*
(f) **check (pattern)** = pattern made of small squares; *the restaurant has red check tablecloths*
2 *verb*
(a) to make sure; to examine; *I'd better check with the office if there are any messages for me; did you lock the door? - I'll go and check; you must have your car checked every 10,000 miles*
(b) *US* to mark with a sign to show that something is correct; *check the box marked 'R'*
(c) to bring someone or something to a halt; *bad weather checked the expedition's progress* (NOTE: British English is **tick**)

② **checkbook**
['tʃekbʊk] *see* CHEQUEBOOK

① **check in**
['tʃek 'ɪn] *verb*
(a) *(at a hotel)* to arrive at a hotel and sign for a room; *he checked in at 12.15*
(b) *(at an airport)* to give in your ticket to show you are ready to take the flight; *please check in two hours before your departure time*
(c) **to check baggage in** = to pass your baggage to be put on the plane for you; *my bag hasn't been checked in yet*

② **check-in**
['tʃekɪn] *noun*
place where passengers give in their tickets and baggage for a flight; *the check-in is on the first floor; holders of valid tickets can go straight through the check-in;* **check-in counter** *or* **desk** = counter where passengers check in; **check-in time** = time at which passengers should check in

① **check out**
['tʃek 'aʊt] *verb*
(a) *(at a hotel)* to leave and pay for a room; *we will check out before breakfast*
(b) to take luggage out of safe keeping; *the ticket shows that he checked out his bag at 9.15*
(c) *US* to see if something is all right; *I thought I heard a noise in a kitchen - I'll just go and check it out*

② **checkout**
['tʃekaʊt] *noun*
(a) *(in a supermarket)* cash desk where you pay for the goods you have bought; *there were huge queues at the checkouts*
(b) *(in a hotel)* **checkout time is 12.00** = time by which you have to leave your room

② **checkup**
['tʃekʌp] *noun*
(a) test to see if someone is fit; general examination by a doctor or dentist; *he had a heart checkup last week*; *he made an appointment with the dentist for a checkup*
(b) general examination of a machine; *I'm taking the car to the garage for its six-monthly checkup*

① **cheek**
[tʃiːk] *noun*
(a) fat part of the face on either side of the nose and below the eye; *a baby with red cheeks*; *see also* TONGUE
(b) *(informal)* being rude and unpleasant; *he had the cheek to ask for more money* (NOTE: no plural in this sense)

③ **cheer**
['tʃiə]
1 *noun*
shout of praise or encouragement; *when he scored the goal a great cheer went up*; **three cheers** = three shouts of praise for someone; *three cheers for the captain! hip! hip! hooray!*
2 *verb*
to shout encouragement; *the crowd cheered when the first cyclists appeared*

② **cheerful**
['tʃiːfʊl] *adjective*
happy; *you're looking very cheerful today*; *'hi!' he said in a cheerful voice*

④ **cheerfully**
['tʃiːfʊli] *adverb*
in a happy way; *they marched cheerfully along, singing songs*

③ **cheerio**
[tʃiːri'əʊ] *interjection; (informal)*
goodbye; *she shouted 'cheerio!' as the bus pulled out*

③ **cheers!**
['tʃiəz] *interjection; (informal)*
(a) thank you!; *can I help you with your bag? - cheers, mate!*
(b) *(when drinking)* good health!; *they all lifted their glasses and said 'cheers!'*

③ **cheer up**
['tʃiə 'ʌp] *verb*
to become happier; **cheer up!** = don't be miserable!; **to cheer someone up** = to make someone happier; *she made him a good meal to try to cheer him up*

② **cheese**
[tʃiːz] *noun*
solid food made from milk; *she ordered a cheese sandwich and salad*; *at the end of the meal we'll have biscuits and cheese*; *can I have a pound of Cheshire cheese, please?*; **cream cheese** = soft white cheese; **blue cheese** = cheese with blue mould in it; *(informal)* **'say cheese!'** = asking people to smile when their photo is being taken; *the photographer got us all in a line and then told us to 'say cheese!'*

(NOTE: the plural **cheeses** is only used to mean different types of cheese or several large round whole blocks of cheese; usually there is no plural: **some cheese; a piece of cheese**)

③ **chef**
[ʃef] *noun*
cook in a restaurant; *they've got a new chef at the 'King's Head' and the food is much better*; **chef's special** = special dish, sometimes one which the chef is famous for, which is listed separately on the menu

③ **chemical**
['kemɪkl]
1 *adjective*
referring to chemistry; *if you add acid it sets off a chemical reaction*
2 *noun*
substance which is formed by reactions between elements; *rows of glass bottles containing chemicals*; *chemicals are widely used in agriculture*

③ **chemist**
['kemɪst] *noun*
(a) person who sells medicines and also prepares them; *ask the chemist to give you something for your stomach pains*; **the chemist's** = shop where you can buy medicine, toothpaste, soap, etc.; *go to the chemist's and get me some cough medicine* (NOTE: in American English this is usually a **drugstore**)
(b) scientist who studies chemical substances; *he works as a chemist in a nuclear laboratory*

③ **chemistry**
['kemɪstri] *noun*
(a) science of chemical substances and their reactions; *she's studying chemistry at university*; *he passed his chemistry exam*
(b) **personal chemistry** = reaction of one person to another; *the personal chemistry of the two leaders was very good* (NOTE: no plural)

① **cheque** *US* **check**
[tʃek] *noun*
note to a bank asking for money to be paid from one account to another; *I paid for the jacket by cheque*; *he made out the cheque to Mr Smith*; *he's forgotten to sign the cheque*; **pay cheque** *or* **salary cheque** = monthly cheque by which an employee is paid; **traveller's cheque** = cheque which you buy at a bank before you travel and which you can then use in a foreign country; *most shops in the USA accept traveller's cheques*; *the hotel will cash traveller's cheques for you*; *the bank guarantees to replace stolen traveller's cheques* (NOTE: the American spelling is **traveler's checks**)

② **chequebook** *US* **checkbook**
['tʃekbʊk] *noun*
set of blank cheques attached together in a cover; *I need a new chequebook*

③ **cherry**
['tʃeri] *noun*
small sweet red fruit, growing usually in pairs on a tree; *she ate half a pound of cherries; a pot of cherry jam;* **cherry tree** = the tree which grows this fruit; *we have a beautiful cherry tree in the middle of the lawn* (NOTE: plural is **cherries**)

③ **chess**
[tʃes] *noun*
game for two people played on a board with sixteen pieces on each side; *would you like a game of chess?; they played chess all evening* (NOTE: no plural)

> COMMENT: the game is played on a board with 64 black and white squares. Each player has sixteen pieces: eight pawns, two castles, two knights, two bishops, one queen and one king. The object is to capture and remove your opponent's pieces, and finally to put your opponent's king in a position where he cannot move without being captured

② **chest**
[tʃest] *noun*
(a) the top front part of the body, where the heart and lungs are; *if you have pains in your chest or if you have chest pains, you ought to see a doctor; she was rushed to hospital with chest wounds;* **he has a 48-inch chest; to get something off your chest** = to speak frankly about a problem
(b) piece of furniture, like a large box; *he keeps his old clothes in a chest under the bed;* **chest of drawers** = piece of furniture with several drawers for clothes

④ **chew**
[tʃuː] *verb*
to make something soft with your teeth; *you must chew your meat well, or you will get pains in your stomach; the dog was lying in front of the fire chewing a bone*

② **chewing gum**
['tʃuːɪŋ gʌm] *noun*
sweet substance which you chew but do not swallow; *would you like a piece of chewing gum?; I've got some chewing gum stuck under my shoe*

④ **chick**
[tʃɪk] *noun*
baby bird, especially a baby hen; *all the chicks hatched on the same day; the chicks came running along in a line behind the mother hen*

② **chicken**
['tʃɪkɪn] *noun*
(a) young hen; *chickens were running everywhere in front of the farmhouse*
(b) meat from a hen; *we're having roast chicken for lunch; would you like another slice of chicken?; we bought some chicken salad sandwiches* (NOTE: no plural for this meaning: **some chicken; a piece** *or* **a slice of chicken**)

② **chief**
[tʃiːf]
1 *adjective*
most important; *he's the chief planner in the local authority; what is the chief cause of air accidents?*
2 *noun*
(a) person in charge in a group of people or in a business; *he's been made the new chief of our department; the fire chief warned that the building was dangerous*
(b) the leader of a tribe; *all the chiefs came together at a meeting; (informal)* **too many chiefs and not enough Indians** = situation in a company where there are too many managers, but not enough people to do the actual work

④ **chiefly**
['tʃiːflɪ] *adverb*
mainly; *our town is famous chiefly for its pork pies*

① **child**
[tʃaɪld] *noun*
(a) young boy or girl; *there was no TV when my mother was a child; here is a photograph of the Prime Minister as a child; a group of children were playing on the beach;* **child's play** = something which is very easy; *building a wall may look like child's play, but it's not as easy as you think*
(b) son or daughter; *whose child is that?; how many children have they got?; they have six children - two boys and four girls* (NOTE: plural is **children** ['tʃɪldrɪn])

③ **childhood**
['tʃaɪldhʊd] *noun*
time when someone is a child; *he spent his childhood in the country; she had a happy childhood living on a farm in Canada; she's had all the usual childhood diseases - measles, etc.; he married his childhood girlfriend*

④ **chimney**
['tʃɪmni] *noun*
tall brick column for taking smoke away from a fire; *the house has two tall chimneys; if you look up the chimney in an old house you can see the sky; (informal)* **he smokes like a chimney** = he smokes cigarettes all the time

③ **chin**
[tʃɪn] *noun*
front part of the bottom jaw; *she suddenly stood up and hit him on the chin;* **to keep your chin up** = to stay confident; *even if everything seems to be going wrong, try to keep your chin up!*

④ **china**
['tʃaɪnɪ] *noun*
fine white cups, plates, etc.; *she got out her best china tea service because she had visitors; a china cup and saucer; all our china was broken when we moved house* (NOTE: no plural)

① **China**

['tʃaɪnɪ] *noun*

very large country in Asia; *we went to China on business last year*; *visitors to China always go to see the Great Wall* (NOTE: capital: **Beijing**; people: **the Chinese**; language: **Chinese**; currency: **renminbi** *or* **yuan**)

① **Chinese**

[tʃaɪ'niːz]

1 *adjective*

referring to China; *her husband is Chinese*; *we often go to a Chinese restaurant in the evening*

2 *noun*

(a) person from China; *the Chinese are very good at mathematics* (NOTE: plural is **Chinese**)

(b) language spoken in China; *she had been taking Chinese lessons for some weeks*; *the book has been translated into Chinese*

② **chip**

[tʃɪp]

1 *noun*

(a) long thin piece of potato fried in oil; *he ordered chicken and chips and a glass of beer*; **fish and chips** = traditional British food, obtained from special shops, where portions of fried fish are sold with chips; *we're having fish and chips for dinner*; **fish-and-chip shop** = shop selling cooked fish and chips, and usually other food, such as pies (NOTE: in the USA, chips are called **French fries**. Note also that a **fish-and-chip shop** can also be called a **chip shop**)

(b) *US* thin slice of potato, fried till crisp and eaten cold as a snack; *he ordered a beer and a packet of chips* (NOTE: In British English, this is called a **crisp**)

(c) small piece of something hard, such as wood or stone; *chips of stone flew all over the studio as he was carving the statue*; **chocolate chip** = small piece of hard chocolate, used in ice cream, biscuits or cakes; *a chocolate chip biscuit*; *mint chocolate chip ice cream*

(d) a computer chip = a small piece of a substance which can store data, used in a computer; *computer chip manufacturers are doing very well*

(e) a chip on your shoulder = a feeling of being constantly annoyed because you feel you have lost an advantage; *he's got a chip on his shoulder because his brother has a better job than he has*

(f) counter, piece of plastic or metal which stands in for money in gambling; *he put a pile of chips on the table*; *(informal)* **when the chips are down** = when the situation is serious and important decisions have to be made

2 *verb*

to break a small piece off something hard; *he banged the cup down on the plate and chipped it* (NOTE: **chipping - chipped**)

② **chocolate**

['tʃɒklɪt] *noun*

(a) sweet brown food made from the crushed seeds of a tropical tree; *can I buy a bar of chocolate?*; *her mother made a chocolate cake*; **dark chocolate** *or* **plain chocolate** = dark brown chocolate which is quite bitter; **milk chocolate** = light brown sweet chocolate

(b) a single sweet made from chocolate; *there are only three chocolates left in the box*; *who's eaten the last chocolate?*

(c) drink made from chocolate powder and milk; *I always have a cup of hot chocolate before I go to bed*

(d) dark brown colour, like chocolate; *we have a chocolate-coloured carpet in the sitting room* (NOTE: no plural, except for meaning (b))

① **choice**

[tʃɔɪs]

1 *noun*

(a) thing which is chosen; *Paris was our first choice for our honeymoon*

(b) act of choosing something; *you must give the customer time to make his choice*

(c) range of items to choose from; *the store has a huge choice of furniture*; **I hadn't any choice** *or* **I had no choice** = there was nothing else I could do

2 *adjective*

specially selected food; *choice meat*; *choice peaches*

④ **choir**

['kwaɪə] *noun*

group of people who sing together; *he sings in the church choir*

④ **choke**

[tʃəʊk]

1 *noun*

(in a car engine) valve which increases the flow of air to the engine; *this model has an automatic choke*

2 *verb*

(a) to block a pipe, etc.; *the river was choked with weeds*

(b) to stop breathing properly because you have swallowed something which blocks your throat; *don't talk with your mouth full or you'll choke*; *he choked on a piece of bread* *or* *a piece of bread made him choke*

① **choose**

[tʃuːz] *verb*

(a) to pick something which you like best; *have you chosen what you want to eat?*; *they chose him as team leader*; *don't take too long choosing a book to read on holiday*; *there were several good candidates to choose from*; *you must give customers plenty of time to choose*

(b) to decide to do one thing when there are several things you could do; *in the end, they chose to go to the cinema* (NOTE: **choosing - chose** [tʃəʊz] - **has chosen** ['tʃəʊzn])

① **chop**
[tʃɒp]
1 *noun*
piece of meat with a bone attached; *we had lamb chops for dinner*
2 *verb*
(a) to cut into small pieces; *he spent the afternoon chopping wood for the fire*
(b) to chop and change = to do one thing, then another; *he keeps chopping and changing and can't make his mind up* (NOTE: chopping - chopped)

① **chop down**
['tʃɒp 'daun] *verb*
to cut down a tree, etc.; *they chopped down hundreds of trees to make the motorway*

① **chop off**
['tʃɒp 'ɒf] *verb*
to cut off; *he chopped off the dead branch*; *the table was too high for the children, so we chopped 6cm off the legs*

① **chop up**
['tʃɒp 'ʌp] *verb*
to cut into pieces; *chop the vegetables up into little pieces*

③ **chose, chosen**
[tʃɪuz or 'tʃɪuzɪn]
see CHOOSE

③ **Christ**
[kraɪst]
1 *noun*
Jesus Christ, the person on whose life and teachings the Christian religion is based
2 *interjection; (informal)*
showing that you are annoyed; *Christ! it's eight o'clock already and I haven't started cooking dinner*

③ **Christian**
['krɪstʃn]
1 *noun*
person who believes in the teaching of Christ and follows the Christian religion; *the early Christians were victims of the Roman emperors*
2 *adjective*
referring to the teachings of Jesus Christ; *there are several Christian churches in the town*; *she practises all the Christian virtues*

④ **Christianity**
[krɪstɪ'ænɪti] *noun*
religion based on the teaching of Jesus Christ and followed by Christians ever since; *the course on religious studies covers both Christianity and Islam*

③ **Christian name**
['krɪstʃn 'neɪm] *noun*
a person's first name, the special name given to someone as a child; *I know his surname's Smith, but what's his Christian name?*

① **Christmas**
['krɪsmɪs] *noun*
Christian festival on December 25th, the birthday of Jesus Christ; *have you opened your Christmas presents yet?*; *we're going to my grandfather's for Christmas Day*; **what did you get for Christmas?** = what presents were you given?; **Christmas cake** = special fruit cake eaten at Christmas time; **Christmas card** = special card sent to friends at Christmas to wish them a happy time; **Christmas pudding** = special pudding eaten at Christmas time; **Christmas stockings** = large coloured stockings, which children hang up by their beds or under the Christmas tree, and which are filled with presents by Father Christmas; **Christmas tree** = green tree which is brought into the house at Christmas and decorated with coloured lights; **Father Christmas** = man in a long red coat, with a big white beard, who is supposed to bring presents to children on Christmas Day; **Happy Christmas!** *or* **Merry Christmas!** = way of greeting someone on Christmas Day

③ **Christmas Eve**
['krɪsmɪs 'iːv] *noun*
(a) 24th December, the day before Christmas Day; *the office is closed on Christmas Eve*
(b) the evening of the 24th December; *a Christmas Eve party*

④ **chronic**
['krɒnɪk] *adjective*
(a) (illness, etc.) which is continual, which comes back often; *chronic asthma sufferers need to use special drugs*; *compare* ACUTE
(b) always very bad; *we have a chronic shortage of skilled staff*

② **chuck**
[tʃʌk]
1 *noun*
part of a drill which holds the bit; *he released the chuck and put in a bigger bit*
2 *verb*
(informal) to throw; *chuck me that newspaper, can you?*; *she chucked the book out of the window*

① **church**
[tʃɜːtʃ] *noun*
building where Christians go to pray; *we usually go to church on Sunday mornings*; *the oldest building in the village is St Mary's Church*; *the times of the church services are given on the board outside* (NOTE: plural is **churches**)

③ **CID**
[siːaɪ'diː]   *abbreviation   for* CRIMINAL INVESTIGATION DEPARTMENT

② **cigarette**
[sɪgɪ'ret] *noun*
chopped dried tobacco rolled in very thin paper which you can light and smoke; *a packet or pack of cigarettes*; *he's trying to cut down on the number of cigarettes he smokes*; *the room was full of cigarette smoke*; **cigarette machine** =

machine which sells packets of cigarettes when you put the right money in; *have you any change for the cigarette machine?*

③ **cinema**

['sɪnɪmɪ] *noun*

building where you go to watch films; *we went to the cinema on Friday night*; **what's on at the cinema this week?** = which film is being shown? (NOTE: American English for this is **movie theater**)

② **circle**

['sɜːkl]

1 *noun*

(a) line forming a round shape; *he drew a circle on the blackboard*

(b) thing forming a round shape; *the children sat in a circle round the teacher*; *the soldiers formed a circle round the prisoner*

(c) group of people or society; *she went to live abroad and lost contact with her old circle of friends*; *he moves in the highest government circles*

(d) row of seats above the stalls in a theatre; *we got tickets for the upper circle*

2 *verb*

to go round in a ring; *big birds were circling in the air above the dead deer*

③ **circuit**

['sɜːkɪt] *noun*

(a) trip around something; *his first circuit of the track was very slow*

(b) path of electricity; *he's designed a circuit for a burglar alarm*; **printed circuit board** = card with metal tracks printed on it, which forms a connection when other electronic elements are fitted onto it; **short circuit** = electrical fault where two wires touch or where the electric current passes through another channel; *the fallen electricity cable caused a short circuit that blacked out half the town*

② **circular**

['sɜːkjʊlɪ]

1 *adjective*

round in shape; *a circular table*

2 *noun*

publicity leaflet; *the restaurant sent round a circular offering a 10% discount*

③ **circulate**

['sɜːkjʊleɪt] *verb*

(a) to send round to various people; *they circulated a new list of prices to all their customers*

(b) to move round; *blood circulates round the body*; *waiters circulated round the room carrying trays of drinks*

(c) *(informal)* to go round a party, talking to people; *let's talk later - I've got to circulate*

③ **circulation**

[sɜːkjʊ'leɪʃn] *noun*

(a) act of circulating; *the circulation of the new price list to all departments will take several days*; **banknotes which are in circulation** = notes which have been issued and are in use

(b) movement of blood round the body; *rub your hands together to get the circulation going*; *he has poor circulation*

(c) number of copies of a magazine, newspaper, etc., which are sold; *the new editor hopes to increase the circulation*

① **circumstances**

['sɜːkɪmstænsɪz] *noun*

(a) way in which something happened; *he described the circumstances leading up to the accident*; *she died in very suspicious circumstances*; **in the circumstances** *or* **under the circumstances** = as this is the case; *under the circumstances, it would probably be wiser to cancel the meeting*

(b) state of your finances; *she's been in difficult circumstances since the death of her husband* (NOTE: usually used in the plural)

④ **circus**

['sɜːkɪs] *noun*

(a) travelling show, often given under a large tent, with animals and other entertainments; *we went to the circus last night*; *the circus is coming to town for the bank holiday weekend*

(b) busy road junction in the centre of a large town; *Oxford Circus is where Oxford Street crosses Regent Street* (NOTE: plural is **circuses**)

④ **cite**

[saɪt] *verb*

(a) to quote a reference, a person, etc., as proof; *she cited several passages from his latest book*

(b) to call someone to appear in court; *he was cited to appear before the magistrates* (NOTE: do not confuse with **sight, site**)

② **citizen**

['sɪtɪzɪn] *noun*

(a) person who comes from a certain country or has the same right to live there as someone who was born there; *all Australian citizens have a duty to vote*; *he was born in Germany, but is now a British citizen*; **senior citizen** = old retired person

(b) person who lives in a certain city; *the citizens of London complained about their taxes*

① **city**

['sɪti] *noun*

(a) large town; *walking around the hot city streets can be very tiring*; *which is the largest city in Germany?*; *traffic is a problem in big cities*; **the city centre** = the central part of a town; *he has an office in the city centre* (NOTE: plural is **cities**)

(b) **the City** = the main financial district in London; *he works in the City*

④ civic

['sɪvɪk] *adjective*

referring to a city; *we must try to encourage a sense of civic pride*; **civic centre** = building with social and sports facilities for a town; **civic authorities** = the town council, and the directors of various municipal departments

② civil

['sɪvɪl] *adjective*

(a) belonging to the general public and not to the armed forces; *he left the air force and became a civil airline pilot*; **civil engineer** = person who builds roads, bridges, etc.

(b) referring to ordinary people; *there have been civil disturbances again today*; **civil defence** = defence of a country by ordinary civilians; **civil law** = laws relating to people's rights and agreements between individuals (NOTE: the opposite, laws relating to crimes against the law of the land punished by the state, is **criminal law**); **civil rights** = rights of an ordinary citizen; *she campaigned for civil rights in the 1980s*; **civil rights movement** = campaign for equal rights for all citizens; **civil war** = situation inside a country where groups of armed people fight against each other or against the government

(c) polite; *she wasn't very civil to the policeman*; **please keep a civil tongue in your head** = please be polite

④ civilian

[sɪ'vɪljən]

1 *adjective*

not in the armed forces; *both the military and civilian personnel will be involved*; *the civilian population was advised to take shelter underground*

2 *noun*

ordinary private citizen who is not in the armed forces; *it is certain that ordinary civilians will be affected by the war*; *many civilians were killed in the air raids*

② civilization

[sɪvɪlaɪ'zeɪʃn] *noun*

society or way of organizing society; *the civilization of Ancient Greece*; *she is studying Chinese art and civilization*

③ civil servant

['sɪvɪl 'sɜːvɪnt] *noun*

person who works in a government department; *as a cleaner in a government office I am considered to be a civil servant*

COMMENT: the words 'civil service' and 'civil servant' only refer to government or local government departments. People such as teachers, lawyers, policemen, soldiers, etc., although they are paid by the government, do not consider themselves to be 'civil servants'. This is different from the situation in many other countries

③ civil service

['sɪvɪl 'sɜːvɪs] *noun*

the organization and its staff who administer a country; *you have to pass an examination to get a job in the civil service or to get a civil service job*; *see* COMMENT *above*

① claim

[kleɪm]

1 *noun*

(a) asking for money; *his claim for a pay increase was turned down*; **wage claim** = asking for an increase in wages

(b) statement; *his claim that the car belonged to him was correct*

(c) demand for money against an insurance policy; *after the floods, insurance companies received hundreds of claims*; **no claims bonus** = lower insurance premium paid because no claims have been made against the insurance policy; *it's not worth making a small claim as you'll lose your no-claims bonus*; **to put in** *or* **to submit a claim** = to ask the insurance company officially to pay damages; *to put in a claim for repairs to the car*; *she submitted a claim for £250,000 damages against the driver of the other car*

2 *verb*

(a) to demand as a right; *steel workers have claimed huge pay rises*; *if the machine doesn't work properly you must claim a refund*

(b) to state, but without any proof; *he claims he never received the letter*; *she claims that the car belongs to her*

(c) to say you own something which has been left behind or lost; *no one has claimed the umbrella found in my office, so I am going to keep it*

③ claimant

['kleɪmɪnt] *noun*

(a) person who claims; *benefit claimants will be paid late because of the bank holiday*

(b) person who starts a legal action against someone in the civil courts; *she's the claimant in a libel action*; *the court decided in favour of the claimant* (NOTE: this is the new term; it used to be called a **plaintiff**; the other party in an action is the **defendant**)

③ claim back

['kleɪm 'bæk] *verb*

to claim something which you owned before; *his car was towed away and he had to go to the police station to claim it back*

④ clash

[klæʃ]

1 *noun*

(a) loud noise of metal things hitting each other; *she heard a loud clash like two saucepans being banged together*

(b) battle, argument; *there were clashes outside the football ground between supporters of the two teams*; *we are getting reports of clashes between government forces and guerrillas* (NOTE: plural is **clashes**)

2 *verb*

(a) to bang together making a loud noise; *he clashed the two dustbin lids together*

(b) to argue violently; *she clashed with her mother about wearing a ring in her nose*; *the opposition deputies clashed with the government*

(c) to fight; *rioting fans clashed with the police*

(d) to happen at the same time as something else; *the party clashes with a meeting I have to go to*; *unfortunately, the two meetings clash, so I'll have to miss one*

(e) *(of colours)* to shock when put side by side; *that bright pink tie clashes with your green shirt*

① **class**

[klɑːs] *noun*

(a) group of people (usually children) who go to school or college together; *there are 30 children in my son's class*

(b) group of people who were at the same school or college at the same time in the past; *she's organizing a dinner for the class of '76*

(c) lesson; **evening classes** = lessons given in the evening (usually to adults); *I am going to evening classes to learn German*; *we have two maths classes a week*

(d) people of the same group in society; *people from different social classes mixed at the reception*; **working class** = people who mainly work with their hands; **middle class** = people who have taken exams for their jobs, such as doctors, teachers, etc., or people in business

(e) certain level of quality; *always buy the best class of product*; *these peaches are Class 1*; **first-class** = very good; *he is a first-class tennis player*; **second-class** = not as good as first class

(f) quality of seats or service on a plane, train, etc.; **first class** = best quality (and most expensive); *if you travel first class on the train to France, you get free drinks*; **business class** = less expensive than first class; **economy class** *or* **tourist class** = cheapest; *they are staying in a first-class hotel*; *first-class passengers get free drinks with their meal*; *the tourist-class fare is much less than the first-class*; *I travel economy class because it is cheaper* (NOTE: plural is **classes**)

③ **classic**

['klæsɪk]

1 *noun*

(a) great book, play, piece of music, etc.; *'the Maltese Falcon' is a Hollywood classic*; *we have to study several classics of English literature for our course*

(b) Classics = study of the languages, literature, philosophy, etc., of Ancient Greece and Rome; *she studied Classics at Oxford*; *he has a Classics degree from Edinburgh*

2 *adjective*

(a) (style) which is elegant and traditional; *the classic little black dress is always in fashion*; *the style of the shop is classic, simple and elegant*

(b) *(style of architecture)* which is based on that of Greek or Roman architecture; *the British Museum is built in classic Greek style*

(c) typical; *it was a classic example of his inability to take decisions*

③ **classical**

['klæsɪkl] *adjective*

(a) which is elegant and based on the style of Greek or Roman architecture, literature, etc.; *a classical eighteenth century house*

(b) referring to Ancient Greece and Rome; *classical Greek literature*

(c) referring to traditional, serious music; *a concert of classical music*

④ **classification**

[klæsɪfɪ'keɪʃn] *noun*

way of arranging things into categories; *the classification of social classes into various categories*; *the hotel has been classified with three stars, under the new classification system*

③ **classified**

['klæsɪfaɪd] *adjective*

(a) which has been put into a category; **classified ads** *or* **classified advertisements** = newspaper advertisements which are listed under special headings, such as 'jobs wanted' or 'household goods for sale'; *look in the classified ads if you want a cheap cooker*; **classified directory** = directory of business addresses listed under various headings, such as 'hairdressers', 'bookshops', etc.; *look for his address under 'builders' in the classified directory*

(b) secret; **classified documents** *or* **classified information** = documents or information marked 'secret'; *he left a box of classified documents in the back of his car*; *this is classified information, and only a few people can see it*

③ **classify**

['klæsɪfaɪ] *verb*

to arrange things into groups; *the hotels are classified according to a star system*; *now that these plants have been classified, please write a label for each one*

④ **classroom**

['klɑːsrʊm] *noun*

room in a school where children are taught; *when the teacher came into the classroom all the children were shouting and throwing books*

② **clause**
[klɔːz] *noun*
(a) paragraph in a treaty or legal document; *according to clause six, payments will not be due until next year*
(b) part of a sentence; *the sentence has two clauses, separated by the conjunction 'and'*; **main clause** = main part of a sentence; **subordinate clause** = clause which depends on the main clause

③ **clay**
[kleɪ] *noun*
(a) stiff soil found in river valleys; *the soil in our garden has a lot of clay in it*
(b) stiff soil used for making bricks or china; *he put a lump of clay onto his wheel and started to make a pot*

① **clean**
[kliːn]
1 *adjective*
(a) not dirty; *wipe your glasses with a clean handkerchief; the bedrooms must be clean before the guests arrive; tell the waitress these cups aren't clean; the girl forgot to put clean towels in the bathroom*; *(informal)* **to come clean** = to confess to a crime, etc.; *he came clean and owned up to stealing the watch*
(b) with no record of offences; *candidates should hold a clean driving licence*
(c) fair, according to the rules; *we played a good clean of football* (NOTE: **cleaner - cleanest**)
2 *verb*
to make clean, by taking away dirt; *remember to clean your teeth every morning; she was cleaning the kitchen when the telephone rang; he cleans his car every Saturday morning*
3 *adverb; (informal)*
completely; *I clean forgot to send the letter*
4 *noun*
(informal) action of cleaning; *the restaurant kitchen needs a good clean*

③ **cleaner**
['kliːnɪ] *noun*
(a) machine which removes dirt; **vacuum cleaner** = machine which sucks up dirt from floors
(b) substance which removes dirt; *this new oven cleaner doesn't get rid of the worst stains; can you buy another bottle of toilet cleaner?*
(c) person who cleans (a house, office, etc.); *the cleaners didn't empty my wastepaper basket*

③ **cleaner's**
['kliːnɪz] *noun*
(a) shop where you take clothes to be cleaned; *when I got my suit back from the cleaner's there was a button missing*
(b) *(slang)* **to take someone to the cleaner's** = to take all someone's money; *I played cards last night and got taken to the cleaner's*

② **clean up**
['kliːn 'ʌp] *verb*
(a) to make everything clean and tidy after a party, etc.; *it took us three hours to clean up after her birthday party*
(b) to remove corruption; *the police are going to have a hard job cleaning up this town*
(c) *(informal)* to make a lot of money; *David cleaned up at the races*

④ **clean-up**
['kliːnʌp] *noun*
making clean; *after the floods had gone down the clean-up took weeks*

① **clear**
[klɪɪ]
1 *adjective*
(a) with nothing in the way; *you can cross the road - it's clear now; from the window, she had a clear view of the street*
(b) with no clouds, mist, etc.; *a clear blue sky; on a clear day, you can see the other side of the lake*
(c) easily understood; *she made it clear that she wanted us to go; the instructions on the computer screen are not very clear; will you give me a clear answer - yes or no?*
(d) which is not covered and which you can easily see through; *a clear glass window*; **clear light bulb** = bulb which you can see through (NOTE: a bulb with a pale white coating is a **pearl bulb**)
(e) whole period of time; *it will take a clear week to process the information*; **three clear days** = three whole working days; *allow three clear days for the cheque to be paid into the bank* (NOTE: **clearer - clearest**)
2 *verb*
(a) to remove something which is in the way; *ploughs cleared the railway line of snow or cleared the snow from the railway line; we'll get a plumber to clear the blocked pipe in the bathroom*; **to clear the table** = to take away knives, forks, plates, etc., after a meal
(b) *(of a bank)* **to clear a cheque** = to pass a cheque through the banking system, so that the money is transferred from one account to another; *the cheque took ten days to clear or the bank took ten days to clear the cheque*
(c) to sell cheaply in order to get rid of stock; *'demonstration models to clear'*; *if we reduce the price we'll clear the stock in no time*
(d) *(of a court)* to find that someone is not guilty; *the court cleared him of all the charges*
(e) to go over the top of something without touching it; *she cleared 1.3m in the high jump*
3 *adverb*
not close; *stand clear of the doors, please; I would advise you to stay clear of that dog*

clearing

['klɪːrɪŋ] *noun*

(a) act of removing things that are in the way; *the clearing of the wreckage from the railway track will take several days*

(b) area in a wood where the trees have been cut down; *they set up camp in a clearing in the middle of the forest*

(c) **clearing bank** = bank which issues and processes cheques; *two of the major clearing banks have decided to merge*

clearly

['klɪːli] *adverb*

(a) in a way which is easily understood or heard; *he didn't speak clearly, and I couldn't catch the address he gave*

(b) obviously; *he clearly didn't like being told he was too fat*

clear up

['klɪː 'ʌp] *verb*

(a) to tidy and clean completely; *the cleaners refused to clear up the mess after the office party*

(b) to solve a problem; *in the end, we cleared up the mystery of the missing computer disk*

(c) to get better; *I hope the weather clears up because we're going on holiday tomorrow; he has been taking aspirins, but his cold still hasn't cleared up*

clerk

[klɑːk *US* klɜːk] *noun*

person who works in an office; *a ticket clerk; a bank clerk*

clever

['klevɪ] *adjective*

intelligent, able to learn quickly; *he's the cleverest person in the family; she's very clever with money; he is very clever at spotting bargains*; **he's clever with his hands** = he's good at making things with his hands (NOTE: **cleverer - cleverest**)

cleverly

['klevɪli] *adverb*

in a clever way; *the dog had cleverly worked out how to open the door*

click

[klɪk]

1 *noun*

short sharp sound; *she heard a click and saw the door start to open*

2 *verb*

(a) to make a short sharp sound; *the cameras clicked as she came out of the church; he clicked his fingers to attract the waiter's attention*

(b) *(informal)* to become clear and easily understood; **suddenly everything clicked** = suddenly it all became clear

(c) to press the button on a mouse quickly to start a computer function; *the menu is displayed by clicking on the menu bar at the top of the screen; click twice on the mouse to start the program*

client

['klaɪnt] *noun*

person who you give a service to; *a personal trainer who visits his clients in their own homes; how often do your salesmen visit their major clients?*

cliff

[klɪf] *noun*

steep or vertical face of rocks, usually by the sea; *he went for a walk along the top of the cliffs; their first view of England was the white cliffs of Dover; huge heads of presidents are cut into the cliff face*

climate

['klaɪmɪt] *noun*

(a) general weather conditions in a certain place; *the climate in the south of the country is milder than in the north; the climate in Central Europe is hot in the summer and cold and dry in the winter*

(b) general atmosphere; *the current economic climate makes an interest rate rise very likely; she wants to change jobs - she thinks she could do with a change of climate*

climax

['klaɪmæks] *noun*

most important and exciting point; *the celebrations reached their climax with a parade through the centre of the town; the film was reaching its climax when the electricity failed* (NOTE: plural is **climaxes**)

climb

[klaɪm]

1 *noun*

going up; *it's a steep climb to the top of the hill*

2 *verb*

(a) to go up (or down) using arms and legs; *the cat climbed up the apple tree; the burglars climbed over the wall; he escaped by climbing out of the window*

(b) to go up; *the road climbs up to 1,000m above sea level*

(c) to go up mountains as a sport; *when you have climbed Everest, there is no higher mountain left to climb; he goes climbing every weekend*

climb down

['klaɪm 'daun] *verb*

(a) to come down a mountain, a ladder, etc.; *he climbed down from the roof; the firemen helped the hotel guests climb down the ladder*

(b) not to do what you had previously insisted on doing; *in the end, the government had to climb down and admit that a mistake had been made*

climber

['klaɪmɪ] *noun*

person who climbs mountains; *the climbers roped themselves together and set off up the mountain*

③ **clinch**
[klɪntʃ]
1 *noun*
(a) position where two people hold each other tightly; *he found his girlfriend in a clinch with another man*
(b) *(in boxing)* position where both boxers hold on to each other; *the referee tried to separate the two boxers who were in a tight clinch* (NOTE: plural is **clinches**)
2 *verb*
to settle (a deal); *he offered an extra 5% to clinch the deal*

④ **cling**
[klɪŋ] *verb*
to cling (on)to something = to hold tight; *she survived by clinging onto a piece of wood*; *he clung tightly to his mother's arm* (NOTE: **clinging - clung** [klʌŋ])

③ **clinic**
['klɪnɪk] *noun*
specialized medical centre or hospital; *a family planning clinic*; *she had treatment in a private clinic in Switzerland*

③ **clinical**
['klɪnɪkl] *adjective*
(a) medical; **clinical medicine** = treatment of patients in a hospital or a doctor's surgery (as opposed to an operating theatre); *I'm more interested in clinical medicine than in surgery*
(b) to look at things in a clinical way = to look at something in a cool way, without any prejudices

④ **clip**
[klɪp]
1 *noun*
(a) paper clip = piece of bent wire for attaching papers, etc., together; *he attached the cheque to the letter with a paper clip*
(b) *(especially US)* piece of jewellery which clips onto your clothes; *he wore a gold clip on his tie*; *she has a diamond clip on her dress*
(c) *(informal)* short piece of film; *here is a clip of the president getting into the car*
(d) *(informal)* **a clip round the ear** = a smack on the side of the head; *stop that noise or you'll get a clip round the ear*
2 *verb*
(a) to attach things together with a clip; *she clipped the invoice and the cheque together and put them in an envelope*; *these earrings are made to clip onto your ears*
(b) to cut with scissors; *the dog has its fur clipped once a month*; *he carefully clipped the article out of the newspaper*
(c) to hit slightly; *the wing of the plane clipped the top of the tree before it crashed* (NOTE: **clipping - clipped**)

① **clock**
[klɒk]
1 *noun*
large instrument which shows the time; *the station clock is always right*; *your clock is 5 minutes slow*; *the office clock is fast*; *the clock has stopped - it needs winding up*; **alarm clock** = clock which can be set to ring a bell at a certain time to wake you up; *see also* GRANDFATHER, O'CLOCK (NOTE: a small instrument for showing the time, which you wear, is a **watch**)
2 *verb*
to clock in or **on** = to arrive for work and register by putting a card into a timing machine; **to clock out** *or* **off** = to leave work and register by putting a card into a timing machine

① **close**
1 [kləus] *adjective*
(a) very near, just next to something; *our office is close to the railway station*; *this is the closest I've ever been to a film star!*
(b) where only a few votes separate the winner from the other candidates; *the election was very close*; *it was a close contest*
(c) hot, with no air; *it's very close in here, can someone open a window?*
2 [kləus] *adverb*
very near; *keep close by me if you don't want to get lost*; *go further away - you're getting too close*; *they stood so close (together) that she felt his breath on her cheek*; *the sound came closer and closer* (NOTE: **closer - closest**)
3 [kləuz] *verb*
(a) to shut; *would you mind closing the window, there's a draught?*; *he closed his book and turned on the TV*
(b) to make something come to an end; *she closed her letter by saying she was coming to see us*; **to close a meeting** = to end a meeting
(c) to come to an end; *the meeting closed with a vote of thanks*
(d) to close an account = to take all the money out of a bank account and stop the account; *he closed his building society account*
(e) to close on someone = to come closer to someone, to catch someone up; *the horse in second place was closing on the leader*
4 [kləuz] *noun*
end, final part; *the century was drawing to a close*; **at close of play** = when a cricket match stops for the day

① **closed**
[kləuzd] *adjective*
shut; *the shop is closed on Sundays*; *the office will be closed for the Christmas holidays*; *there was a 'closed' sign hanging in the window*

③ **close down**
['kləuz 'daun] *verb*
to shut a business; *they're going to close down the factory because they haven't enough work*

① closely

['kləʊsli] *adverb*

(a) with a lot of attention; *she studied the timetable very closely*

(b) very close together; *the photographers moved in closely around the car*; *the prisoners were closely guarded by armed soldiers*

③ close-up

['kləʊsʌp] *noun*

photograph taken very close to the subject; *flowers are ideal subjects for close-up photography*; *he has a framed close-up of his daughter on his desk*; *using a zoom lens can give you close-ups of lions from quite a long way away*

④ cloth

[klɒθ] *noun*

(a) material; *her dress is made of cheap blue cloth*; *this cloth is of a very high quality*

(b) piece of material for cleaning; *he wiped up the spill with a damp cloth*

(c) piece of material which you put on a table to cover it; *the waiter spread a white cloth over the table*; *she split some red wine on the cloth*

② clothes

[kləʊðz] *noun*

(a) things (such as shirts, trousers, dresses, etc.) which you wear to cover your body and keep you warm; *he walked down the street with no clothes on or without any clothes on*; *the doctor asked him to take his clothes off*; *the children haven't had any new clothes for years*

(b) clothes horse = frame for hanging wet clothes on to dry; **clothes line** = rope for hanging wet clothes on to dry; **clothes peg** *(US & Scotland)* **clothes pin** = little clip for attaching wet clothes to a line; **clothes rail** = rail for hanging clothes on in a shop

④ clothing

['kləʊðɪŋ] *noun*

clothes; *take plenty of warm clothing on your trip to the mountains*; *an important clothing manufacturer* (NOTE: no plural: **some clothing; a piece of clothing**)

① cloud

[klaʊd] *noun*

(a) mass of white or grey mist floating in the air; *do you think it's going to rain? - yes, look at those grey clouds*; *the plane was flying above the clouds*

(b) *(informal)* **on cloud nine** = very happy; *they were on cloud nine when she won the lottery*; **under a cloud** = suspected of having done something wrong; *he was under a cloud for some time after the thefts were discovered*; *see also* LINING

(c) similar mass of smoke; *clouds of smoke poured out of the burning shop*

② cloudy

['klaʊdi] *adjective*

(a) with clouds; *the weather was cloudy in the morning, but cleared up in the afternoon*; *when it's very cloudy it isn't easy to take good photographs*

(b) not clear, not transparent; *this beer is cloudy*; *the water in the tank turned cloudy and the fish died* (NOTE: **cloudier - cloudiest**)

① club

[klʌb] *noun*

(a) group of people who have the same interest or form a team; *an old people's club*; *I'm joining a tennis club*; *our town has one of the top football clubs in the country*

(b) place where a club meets; *the sports club is near the river*; *he goes to the golf club every Friday*

(c) club class = specially comfortable class of seating on a plane, though not as luxurious as first class

(d) clubs = one of the black suits in a pack of cards, shaped like a leaf with three parts; *he had the five of clubs in his hand* (NOTE: the other black suit is **spades; hearts** and diamonds are the red suits)

(e) large heavy stick; *she was knocked to the ground by a blow from a club*; **a golf club** = stick for playing golf (NOTE: **a golf club** can either mean the place where you play golf, or the stick used to hit the ball)

2 *verb*

(a) to hit with a club; *she was clubbed to the ground*

(b) *(of several people)* **to club together** = to contribute money jointly; *they clubbed together and bought a yacht*

(c) *(informal)* **to go clubbing** = to go out to night clubs; *on Saturday evenings we go out clubbing in the West End* (NOTE: **clubbing - clubbed**)

② clue

[klu:] *noun*

information which helps you solve a mystery or puzzle; *the detective had missed a vital clue*; **I haven't a clue** = I don't know at all; *the police still haven't a clue who did it*

④ clumsy

['klʌmzi] *adjective*

who frequently breaks things or knocks things over; *don't let Ben set the table - he's so clumsy, he's bound to break something* (NOTE: **clumsier - clumsiest**)

③ clung

[klʌŋ] *verb*

see CLING

④ cluster

['klʌstɪ]

1 *noun*

group of objects close together; *he photographed a cluster of stars*

2 *verb*

to cluster (together) = to form a group; *they clustered round the noticeboard to read their exam results*

④ **clutch**
[klʌtʃ]
1 *noun*
(a) holding tight; *she felt the clutch of his fingers on her sleeve*; **in the clutches of** = under the control of; *if the company were to get into their clutches it would be a disaster*
(b) mechanism for changing gear in a car; *the car has just had a new clutch fitted*; **clutch pedal** = pedal which operates the clutch and allows the driver to change gear; **to let in the clutch** = to make the clutch engage the gears; *let the clutch in slowly, or you'll stall the car* (NOTE: plural is **clutches**)
2 *verb*
to grab hold of; *she clutched my arm as we stood on the edge of the cliff*

③ **cm**
see CENTIMETRE; *yesterday we had 3cm of rain*; *25cm of snow had fallen during the night*

③ **co.**
[kɪʊ or ˈkʌmpɪnɪ] *abbreviation for* COMPANY; *J. Smith & Co.*

③ **c/o**
[ˈsiːˈɪʊ]
(in addresses) = CARE OF; *Jane Smith, c/o Mr & Mrs Jonas, 4 Willowbank Road*

③ **coach**
[kɪʊtʃ]
1 *noun*
(a) large bus for travelling long distances; *there's an hourly coach service to Oxford*; *they went on a coach tour of southern Spain*; **coach driver** *fell asleep while driving*; **coach party** = group of people travelling together in a coach; *there were no seats left in the restaurant as a coach party had arrived just before us*; **coach station** = place where coaches and buses begin and end their journey; *we had to wait at the coach station for an hour*
(b) passenger carriage on a train; *the first four coaches are for Waterloo*
(c) *US* category of seat on a plane which is cheaper than first class; *we went coach to Washington*
(d) person who trains tennis players, etc.; *the coach told them that they needed to spend more time practising*; *he's a professional football coach* (NOTE: plural is **coaches**)
2 *verb*
(a) to train tennis players, football players, etc.; *she was coached by a runner who won a gold medal in the Mexico Olympics*
(b) to give private lessons to someone; *all the actors had to be coached separately*

③ **coal**
[kɪʊl] *noun*
black substance which you can burn to make heat; *it's getting cold in here - put some more*

coal on the fire*; *I do love a good coal fire!*; **coal-fired power station** = electric power station which burns coal (NOTE: no plural: **some coal; a bag of coal; a piece of coal** *or* a lump of coal)

③ **coalition**
[kɪʊɪˈlɪʃn] *noun*
combination of several political parties to form a government; *they formed a coalition government*; *a coalition of the Labour and Liberal parties*

④ **coarse**
[kɔːs] *adjective*
(a) not fine, not small; *coarse grains of sand*; *a coarse net*
(b) rough, not polite; *he gave a coarse laugh*; *he could hear her coarse voice booming down the corridor*
(c) rude (joke); *he made a coarse gesture and walked out*; *don't make any coarse remarks in front of my mother*
(d) **coarse fishing** = fishing for fish in rivers or lakes, not in the sea; *the coarse fishing season opens next week* (NOTE: **coarser - coarsest**; do not confuse with **course**)

③ **coast**
[kɪʊst] *noun*
land by the sea; *after ten weeks at sea, Columbus saw the coast of America*; *the south coast is the warmest part of the country*; *let's drive down to the coast this weekend*; **from coast to coast** = from the sea on one side of a country to the sea on the other side; *he crossed the USA from coast to coast*

④ **coastline**
[ˈkɪʊstlaɪn] *noun*
edge of land along a coast; *the rocky coastline of Cornwall*

② **coat**
[kɪʊt]
1 *noun*
(a) piece of clothing which you wear on top of other clothes when you go outside; *you'll need to put your winter coat on - it's just started to snow*; *she was wearing a black fur coat*
(b) **coat of paint** = layer of paint covering something; *that window frame needs a coat of paint*; **we gave the door two coats of paint** = we painted the door twice
2 *verb*
to cover with a layer of something; *we coated the metal disc with silver*

③ **Coca-Cola**
[ˈkɪʊkɪ ˈkɪʊlɪ] *noun*
trademark for a popular fizzy soft drink; *two Coca-Colas, please, and a pint of beer* (NOTE: often just called **coke: two cokes, please**)

④ **cock**
[kɒk] *noun*
male domestic chicken; *we were woken by the cocks on our neighbour's farm* (NOTE: American English is **rooster**)

④ **cockroach**
['kɒkrɪʊtʃ] *noun*
big black or brown insect, a common household
pest; *in hot damp climates, cockroaches are
often found in kitchens* (NOTE: plural is
cockroaches)

④ **cocktail**
['kɒkteɪl] *noun*
(a) mixed alcoholic drink; *a Bloody Mary is a
cocktail with tomato juice*; **cocktail lounge** =
smart bar in a hotel; **cocktail party** = party
where drinks and snacks are served, but not a
full meal; **cocktail snacks** = little snacks eaten
with drinks
(b) mixture of various things; *she died after
taking a cocktail of drugs*; **fruit cocktail** =
mixture of little pieces of fruit

④ **coconut**
['kɪʊkɪnʌt] *noun*
(a) large nut from a type of palm tree; *I won a
coconut at the fair*; **coconut shy** = place at a fair
where you throw balls at coconuts balanced on
posts, trying to knock them off
(b) white flesh from a coconut; *a coconut cake*;
I don't like biscuits with coconut in them
(NOTE: no plural in this meaning)

② **code**
[kɪʊd]
1 *noun*
(a) set of laws, rules of behaviour; *the hotel has
a strict dress code, and people wearing jeans
are not allowed in*; **the Highway Code** = rules
for driving on the road; **code of practice** =
general rules for a group of people, such as
lawyers
(b) secret words or system agreed in advance for
sending messages; *we're trying to break the
enemy's code*; *he sent the message in code*;
code word = secret word which allows you to
do something
(c) system of numbers or letters which mean
something; *the code for Heathrow Airport is
LHR*; *what is the code for phoning
Edinburgh?*; **area code** = numbers which
indicate an area when telephoning; **bar code** =
system of lines printed on a product which can
be read by a computer to give a reference
number or price; **international dialling code** =
numbers which indicate a country when
telephoning; *what's the international dialling
code for France?*; *see also* POSTCODE, ZIP
CODE

③ **code of conduct**
['kɪʊd əv 'kɒndʌkt] *noun*
informal (sometimes written) rules by which a
group of people work

① **coffee**
['kɒfi] *noun*
(a) bitter drink made from the seeds of a tropical
plant; *would you like a cup of coffee?*; *I always
take sugar with my coffee*; *the doctor told me to
avoid tea and coffee*; **black coffee** = coffee

without milk in it; **instant coffee** = drink which
you make by pouring hot water onto a special
coffee powder; **white coffee** = coffee with milk
or cream in it; **coffee machine** = automatic
machine which gives a cup of coffee or other
drink when you put in a coin and press a button;
coffee spoon = very small spoon, used with
small cups of coffee
(b) a cup of coffee; *I'd like a white coffee,
please*; *three coffees and two teas, please*
(c) pale brown colour, like white coffee; *we
have a coffee-coloured carpet in our sitting
room* (NOTE: usually no plural; **coffees** means
cups of coffee)

③ **coffee shop**
['kɒfi 'ʃɒp] *noun*
small restaurant (often in a hotel) serving tea,
coffee and snacks; *it will be quicker to have
lunch in the coffee shop than in the main
restaurant*

③ **coffin**
['kɒfɪn] *noun*
long wooden box in which a dead person is
buried; *they watched in silence as the coffin
was lowered into the ground* (NOTE: American
English prefers **casket**)

③ **coin**
[kɔɪn]
1 *noun*
piece of metal money; *I found a 50p coin in the
street*; *he hid the gold coins under his bed*; *this
machine only takes 10p coins*
2 *verb*
to invent a new word or phrase; *they coined the
phrase 'surfing the net' to mean searching for
information on the Internet*; (*informal*) **to coin
a phrase** = to emphasize that you are saying
something which everyone says; *'it never rains
but it pours' - to coin a phrase*

④ **coincide**
[kɪʊɪn'saɪd] *verb*
to coincide with something = to happen by
chance at the same time as something else; *this
year, my exams don't coincide with my
birthday*; *do our trips to Frankfurt coincide? -
if they do, we can meet while we're both there*

③ **coincidence**
[kɪʊ'ɪnsɪdɪns] *noun*
two things happening at the same time by
chance; *the two of us happening to be at the
same party was pure coincidence*; *by
coincidence, she was at the chemist's too*; *what
a coincidence, I went to that school too!*

③ **coke**
[kɪʊk] *noun*
(a) fuel processed from coal, which produces a
very strong heat; *the steel is produced in coke
ovens* (NOTE: no plural in this meaning)
(b) (*informal*) Coca-Cola, trademark for a type
of fizzy soft drink; a glass of this drink; *he
drinks nothing but coke*; *three cokes, and a
beer, please* (NOTE: plural is **cokes**)

④ **cola**
['kəʊlə] *noun*
fizzy sweet drink made from the seeds of a tropical tree; *the kids would like two colas please*

① **cold**
[kəʊld]
1 *adjective*
(a) with a low temperature; not hot or not heated; *they say that cold showers are good for you; the weather turned colder after Christmas; it's too cold to go for a walk; if you're hot, have a glass of cold water; start eating, or your soup will get cold; he had a plate of cold beef and salad; put your slippers on if your feet are cold; (informal)* **to give someone the cold shoulder** = not to give someone a friendly welcome; **to get cold feet** = to begin to feel afraid that a plan is too risky; *we wanted to buy an old house and start a hotel business, but my husband got cold feet*
(b) not friendly; *he got a very cold reception from the rest of the staff; she gave him a cold nod* (NOTE: **colder - coldest**)
2 *noun*
(a) illness, when you sneeze and cough; *he caught a cold by standing in the rain at a football match; my sister's in bed with a cold; don't come near me - I've got a cold*
(b) cold temperature (outdoors); *he got ill from standing in the cold waiting for a bus; house plants can't stand the cold;* **to be left out in the cold** = not to be part of a group any more

③ **collapse**
[kə'læps]
1 *noun*
(a) sudden fall; *the collapse of the old wall buried two workmen*
(b) sudden fall in price; *the collapse of the dollar on the foreign exchange markets*
(c) sudden failure of a company; *investors lost thousands of pounds in the collapse of the bank*
2 *verb*
(a) to fall down suddenly; *the roof collapsed under the weight of the snow*
(b) to fail suddenly; *the company collapsed with £25,000 in debts*

② **collar**
['kɒlə]
1 *noun*
part of a shirt, coat, dress, etc., which goes round your neck; *I can't do up the top button on my shirt - the collar's too tight; she turned up her coat collar because the wind was cold; he has a winter coat with a fur collar;* **to get hot under the collar** = to get angry or worried about something
2 *verb*
to catch hold of someone; *I managed to collar him as he was leaving the hotel*

② **colleague**
['kɒliːg] *noun*
person who works in the same company, office, school, etc. as you; *his colleagues gave him a present when he got married; I know Jane Gray - she was a colleague of mine at my last job*

① **collect**
[kə'lekt]
1 *verb*
(a) to fetch something or bring things together; *your coat is ready for you to collect from the cleaner's; the mail is collected from the postbox twice a day; I must collect the children from school*
(b) to buy things or bring things together as a hobby; *he collects stamps and old coins*
(c) to gather money for charity; *they're collecting for Oxfam*
(d) to come together; *a crowd collected at the scene of the accident*
2 *adverb*
US **to call collect** = to ask the person being phoned to pay for the call; *if you don't have any money you can always try calling collect* (NOTE: British English for this is **to reverse the charges**)

① **collection**
[kə'lekʃɪn] *noun*
(a) group of things brought together as a hobby; *he allowed me to see his stamp collection; the museum has a large collection of Italian paintings*
(b) money which has been gathered; *we're making a collection for Oxfam*
(c) action of bringing things together; **debt collection** = collecting money which is owed
(d) fetching of goods; *your order is in the warehouse awaiting collection*
(e) taking of letters from a postbox or post office for dispatch; *there are four collections a day from the postbox at the corner of the street; the last collection is at 6 p.m.*

① **collective**
[kə'lektɪv]
1 *adjective*
done together; *they had a meeting and soon reached a collective decision;* **collective bargaining** = wage negotiations between management and unions
2 *noun*
business run by a group of workers; *the owner of the garage sold out and the staff took it over as a workers' collective*

① **college**
['kɒlɪdʒ] *noun*
(a) teaching institution (for adults and young people, but not children); *she's going on holiday with some friends from college; he's studying accountancy at the local college; the college library has over 20,000 volumes;* **college of education** = college where teachers are trained;

college of further education = teaching establishment for students after secondary school

(b) *US* teaching institution for young people and adults, which grants degrees at BA level (NOTE: in British English this is a **university**)

④ **collide**
[kɪ'laɪd] *verb*
to collide with something = to bump into something; *he lost control of the car and collided with a bus*

④ **collision**
[kɪ'lɪʒɪn] *noun*
action of bumping into something; *two people were injured in the collision*; *a collision between a truck and a bus closed the main road for some time*

④ **colonel**
['kɜːnl] *noun*
officer in the army, a rank above lieutenant-colonel; *he married the colonel's daughter*; *is Colonel Davis in?* (NOTE: used as a title before a surname: **Colonel Davis**; often shortened to **Col.: Col. Davis**)

④ **colonial**
[kɪ'lɪʊnɪəl] *adjective*
referring to a colony; *Britain was once an important colonial power*; *the colonial status of Hong Kong ended in 1997*

④ **colonize**
['kɒlɪnaɪz] *verb*
to take possession of an area or country and rule it as a colony; *the government was accused of trying to colonize the Region round the South Pole*

④ **colony**
['kɒlɪnɪ] *noun*
(a) territory ruled by another country; people who live in this territory; *Roman colonies were established in North Africa and along the shores of the Black Sea*; *the former French colonies in Africa are now all independent countries*
(b) group of animals or human beings living together; *a colony of ants*; *an artists' colony* (NOTE: plural is **colonies**)

① **colour** *US* **color**
['kʌlɪ]
1 *noun*
(a) shade which an object has in light (red, blue, yellow, etc.); *what colour is your bathroom?*; *I don't like the colour of his shirt*; *his socks are the same colour as his shirt*; **to be off-colour** = to feel unwell; *he's a bit off-colour today, so he won't be coming to the party*
(b) not black or white; *the book has pages of colour pictures*
(c) shade of a person's skin; *people must not be discriminated against on grounds of sex, religion or colour*; **colour bar** = using the colour of someone's skin as an obstacle to something

(d) water colour(s) = paint which is mixed with water; *I used to paint in oils but now I prefer water colours*
(e) local colour = amusing or unusual details which go with a certain place; *elephants working in the forests lend some local colour to the scene*
(f) with flying colours = with great success; *she passed her test with flying colours*
2 *verb*
to add colour to something; *the children were given felt pens and told to colour the trees green and the earth brown*

④ **colour-blind** *US* **color-blind**
['kʌlɪ blaɪnd] *adjective*
not able to tell the difference between certain colours, such as red and green; *he can't become a pilot because he's colour-blind*

① **coloured** *US* **colored**
['kʌlɪd] *adjective*
(a) in colour; *a coloured postcard*; *a book with coloured illustrations*
(b) with a skin that is not white; *coloured children make up over 90% of this class*

② **colourful** *US* **colorful**
['kʌlɪful] *adjective*
(a) with bright colours; *I'm trying to create a bed of flowers which will remain colourful all year round*; *she tied a colourful silk scarf round her hair*
(b) full of excitement and adventure; *she lived a colourful existence as a dancer in an Egyptian club*; *a colourful account of life in Vienna before the First World War*

② **column**
['kɒlɪm] *noun*
(a) tall pillar; *there is a row of huge columns at the entrance to the British Museum*; *Nelson's Column is in Trafalgar Square*
(b) thing which is tall and thin; *a thin column of smoke rose from the bonfire*; **control column** = handle for steering an aircraft; **steering column** = the pillar which holds a steering wheel in a car, bus, etc.
(c) line of people, one after the other; *a column of prisoners came into the camp*; *columns of refugees crossed the border*
(d) *(in the army)* line of soldiers, tanks, etc., moving forward; *two columns of soldiers advanced towards the enemy positions*; *a column of tanks entered the town*
(e) thin block of printing going down a page; *his article ran to three columns on the first page of the paper*; *'continued on page 7, column 4'*
(f) series of numbers, one under the other; *to add up a column of figures*; *put the total at the bottom of the column*
(g) regular article in a newspaper; *she writes a gardening column for the local newspaper*; *regular readers of this column will know about*

my problems with drains; **gossip column** = regular article about famous people and their private lives

⊕ **columnist**
['kɒlɪmɪst] *noun*

journalist who writes a regular column for a paper; *our regular columnist is on holiday, so the editor had to write the motoring feature this week*; **gossip columnist** = person who writes a gossip column

④ **comb**
[kɪʊm]

1 *noun*

instrument with long teeth used to make your hair straight; *her hair is in such a mess that you can't get a comb through it*

2 *verb*

(a) to smooth your hair with a comb; *she was combing her hair in front of the mirror verb*

(b) to search; *police combed the woods for clues*

④ **combat**
['kɒmbæt]

1 *noun*

fighting; *these young soldiers have no experience of combat*; *they exercise with periods of unarmed combat*

2 *verb*

to fight against; *they have set up a special police squad to combat drugs*

② **combination**
[kɒmbɪ'neɪʃn] *noun*

(a) several things taken together; *a combination of cold weather and problems with the car made our holiday in Germany a disaster*

(b) series of numbers which open a lock; *the safe has a combination lock*; *I've forgotten the combination to my case*

② **combine**

1 *noun*

['kɒmbaɪn]

(a) large financial or commercial group; *a German industrial combine*

(b) large farm machine which cuts corn, takes out and keeps the seeds and throws away the straw; *a row of combines moved across the huge field*

2 *verb*

[kɪm'baɪn]

to combine with = to join together with; *the cold weather combined with high winds has made it a dreadful harvest*

① **come**
[kʌm] *verb*

(a) to move to or towards this place; *come and see us when you're in London*; *the doctor came to see him yesterday*; *some of the children come to school on foot*; *don't make any noise - I can hear someone coming*; *come up to my room and we'll talk about the problem*

(b) to happen; *how did the door come to be open?*; *(informal)* **how come?** = why?; *how come the front door was left open?*

(c) to occur; *what comes after R in the alphabet?*; *P comes before Q*; *what comes after the news on TV?* (NOTE: **coming - came** [keɪm] **- has come**)

③ **come across**
['kʌm ə'krɒs] *verb*

to find by chance; *we came across this little restaurant when we were out walking*

③ **come along**
['kʌm ə'lɒŋ] *verb*

(a) to go with someone; *if you walk, the children can come along with us in the car*

(b) to hurry; *come along, or you'll miss the bus*

③ **come apart**
['kʌm ə'pɑːt] *verb*

to break into pieces; *the toy simply came apart in my hands*

③ **come back**
['kʌm 'bæk] *verb*

to return; *they left the house in a hurry, and then had to come back to get their passports*; *they started to walk away, but the policeman shouted at them to come back*

④ **comedy**
['kɒmɪdi] *noun*

play or film which makes you laugh; *'A Midsummer Night's Dream' is one of Shakespeare's comedies* (NOTE: plural is **comedies**)

③ **come in**
['kʌm 'ɪn] *verb*

to enter; *please come in, and make yourself at home*; *why didn't you ask him to come in?*

③ **come off**
['kʌm 'ɒf] *verb*

(a) to stop being attached; *the button has come off my coat*; *I can't use the kettle, the handle has come off*

(b) to be removed; *the paint won't come off my coat*

(c) to do well or badly; *our team came off badly in the competition*

③ **come on**
['kʌm 'ɒn] *verb*

(a) to hurry; *come on, or we'll miss the start of the film*

(b) to arrive; *a storm came on as we were fishing in the bay*; *night is coming on*; *she thinks she has a cold coming on*

③ **come to**
['kʌm 'tuː] *verb*

(a) to add up to; *the bill comes to £10*

(b) to become conscious again; *when he came to, he was in hospital*

comfort
['kʌmfɪt]
1 *noun*
(a) thing which helps to make you feel happier; *it was a comfort to know that the children were safe*
(b) state of being comfortable; *they live in great comfort; you expect a certain amount of comfort on a luxury liner; she complained about the lack of comfort in the second-class coaches; see also* CREATURE
2 *verb*
to make someone happier, when they are in pain or miserable, etc.; *she tried to comfort the little girl; he felt comforted by the gentle words of the priest*

comfortable
['kʌftɪbl] *adjective*
(a) soft and relaxing; *this chair isn't very comfortable - it has a wooden seat; there are more comfortable chairs in the lounge*
(b) to make yourself comfortable = to relax; *she made herself comfortable in the chair by the fire*

comfortably
['kʌmftɪbli] *adverb*
(a) in a comfortable or relaxing way; *if you're sitting comfortably, I'll explain to you what the work involves; make sure you're comfortably dressed because it is rather cold outside*
(b) comfortably off = having plenty of money; *her husband left her comfortably off when he died*

comic
['kɒmɪk]
1 *noun*
(a) children's paper with cartoon stories; *he spends his pocket money on comics and sweets*
(b) man who tells jokes to make people laugh; *he's a well-known TV comic*
2 *adjective*
funny; *US* comic book = children's book with cartoon stories

coming
['kʌmɪŋ]
1 *adjective*
which is approaching; *their coming silver wedding anniversary; the newspaper tells you what will happen in the coming week in Parliament*
2 *noun*
arrival; comings and goings = lots of movement; *the photographers watched the comings and goings at the palace*

comma
['kɒmɪ] *noun*
punctuation mark (,) showing a break in the meaning of a sentence; *use a comma between each item listed in this sentence;* inverted commas = printing signs (« «), which are put round words which are being quoted, or round titles; *you can put this French word in italics or in inverted commas; the title Pickwick Papers should be in inverted commas*

command
[kɪ'mɑ:nd]
1 *noun*
(a) order; *the general gave the command to attack;* in command of = in charge of; second-in-command = person serving under the main commander
(b) knowledge (of a language); *she has a good command of French*
2 *verb*
(a) to order; *he commanded the troops to open fire on the rebels*
(b) to be in charge of; *he commands a group of guerillas*

commander
[kɪ'mɑ:ndɪ] *noun*
officer in charge of a group of soldiers or a ship; *the commander must make sure that all his soldiers know exactly what they must do*

comment
['kɒment]
1 *noun*
(a) words showing what you feel about something; *his comments were widely reported in the newspapers; the man made a rude comment accompanied by some very offensive gestures;* 'no comment' = I refuse to discuss it in public
(b) discussion of a question; *the scandal aroused considerable comment in the press; it is a sad comment on modern values that we spend more money on arms than on helping the poor* (NOTE: no plural in this meaning)
2 *verb*
to comment on something = to make a remark about something; *he commented on the lack of towels in the bathroom*

commentary
['kɒmɪntri] *noun*
(a) spoken report on a football match, horse race, etc.; *the match is being shown on Channel 4 with live commentary also on the radio*
(b) remarks about a book, a problem, etc.; *for intelligent commentary on current events you should read this magazine* (NOTE: plural is commentaries)

commentator
['kɒmɪnteɪtɪ] *noun*
person who reports events as they happen, on the radio or TV; *radio commentators are much better at describing details than those on TV*

commerce
['kɒmɜ:s] *noun*
business, the buying and selling of goods and services; *a trade mission went to South America to boost British commerce in the region*

② **commercial**
[kɪˈmɜːʃl]
1 *adjective*
(a) referring to business; *he is a specialist in commercial law*; **commercial college** = college which teaches business studies; **commercial course** = course where business skills are studied
(b) used for business purposes, not private or military; *he left the air force and became a commercial airline pilot*; *the company makes commercial vehicles such as taxis and buses*
(c) profitable; *our commercial future looks doubtful*; **not a commercial proposition** = not likely to make a profit
2 *noun*
advertisement on television; *our TV commercial attracted a lot of interest*

① **commission**
[kəˈmɪʃn]
1 *noun*
(a) group of people which investigates problems of national importance; *the government has appointed a commission to look into the problem of drugs in schools*
(b) order for something to be made or to be used; *he received a commission to paint the portrait of the Prime Minister*
(c) percentage of sales value given to the salesman; *she gets 15% commission on everything she sells*; *he charges 10% commission*
(d) order making someone an officer; *he has a commission in the Royal Marines*
(e) out of commission = not working; *the lift's out of commission so you'll have to use the stairs*
2 *verb*
(a) to authorize an artist or architect, etc., to do a piece of work; to authorize a piece of work to be done; *the magazine commissioned him to write a series of articles on Germany*
(b) to make someone an officer; *he was commissioned into the guards*

④ **commissioner**
[kəˈmɪʃn]
(a) representative of authority; **commissioner of police** = highest ranking police officer
(b) **commissioner for oaths** = person, such as a solicitor, who is authorized to take sworn statements

② **commit**
[kəˈmɪt] *verb*
(a) to carry out a crime; *the gang committed six robberies before they were caught*; *he said he was on holiday in Spain when the murder was committed*
(b) to commit suicide = to kill yourself
(c) to commit someone for trial = to send someone for trial; *she has been committed for trial at the Central Criminal Court*

(d) to commit funds to a project = to agree to spend money on a project; *the party pledged to commit more funds to the health service*
(e) to commit yourself = to promise to do something; to give your opinion; *he refused to commit himself*; *I can't commit myself to anything until I have more details* (NOTE: **committing - committed**)

② **commitment**
[kəˈmɪtmənt] *noun*
(a) promise to pay money; *he has difficulty in meeting his commitments*
(b) agreement to do something; *she made a firm commitment to arrive for work on time in future*; *we have the fax machine on one week's trial, with no commitment to buy*

① **committee**
[kəˈmɪti:] *noun*
official group of people who organize or discuss things for a larger group; *the town council has set up a committee to look into sports facilities*; *committee members will be asked to vote on the proposal*; **to be on a committee** = to be a member of a committee; *he's on the finance committee*

④ **commodity**
[kəˈmɒdɪti] *noun*
thing sold in very large quantities, especially raw materials (such as silver and tin) and food (such as corn or coffee); **basic commodities** = food and raw materials; *the country's basic commodities are coffee and timber*; *because of the drought, even basic commodities have to be imported* (NOTE: plural is **commodities**)

① **common**
[ˈkɒmɪn]
1 *adjective*
(a) which happens often, which you find everywhere; *the plane tree is a very common tree in towns*; *it's very common for people to get colds in winter*; **it is common knowledge** = everyone knows it; *it is common knowledge that he is having an affair with his secretary*
(b) belonging to two or more people; *the two countries have a common border*; *blue eyes are not common to all the members of our family*; **common ownership** = ownership of a property by a group of people; **in common** = shared by two or more people; *they have two things in common - they are both Welsh and they are both left-handed* (NOTE: **commoner - commonest**)
2 *noun*
land which belongs to a community; *we went walking on the common* (NOTE: now mainly used in names of places: **Clapham Common, Wimbledon Common**, etc.)

③ **commonly**
[ˈkɒmɪnli] *adverb*
often; *rabbits are commonly found in sandy soil*; *mobile phones are commonly used in restaurants*

common sense
['kɒmɪn 'sens] *noun*
ordinary good sense; *use some common sense - switch the machine off before you start working on it with a screwdriver; at least she had the common sense to call the police*

commonwealth
['kɒmɪnwelθ] *noun*
the (British) Commonwealth = an association of independent countries linked to Britain; *the Queen is the head of the Commonwealth*

communicate
[kɪ'mjuːnɪkeɪt] *verb*
(a) to send or give information to someone; *although she is unable to speak, she can still communicate by using her hands; he finds it impossible to communicate with his staff; communicating with our office in London has been quicker since we installed the fax; he communicated his wishes to his children*
(b) to connect with; **communicating rooms** = rooms with a connecting door between them; **communicating door** = door between two rooms; *the communicating door is kept locked at all times*

communication
[kɪmjuːnɪ'keɪʃn] *noun*
(a) passing of information; *email is the most rapid means of communication; it is not a happy school - there is no communication between the head teacher and the other members of staff;* **to enter into communication with someone** = to start discussing something with someone, usually in writing; *we have entered into communication with their solicitors*
(b) official message; *we had a communication from the local tax inspector*
(c) **communications** = being able to contact people; *after the flood all communications with the outside world were cut off*

communism
['kɒmjunɪzm] *noun*
political and social system in which all property is owned and shared by the society as a whole and not by individual people

communist
['kɒmjunɪst]
1 *adjective*
referring to communism; *the Communist Party is holding its annual meeting this weekend*
2 *noun*
person who believes in communism; member of the Communist Party; *he was a Communist all his life; the Communists have three seats on the city council*

community
[kɪ'mjuːnɪti] *noun*
(a) group of people living in one area; *the local community is worried about the level of violence in the streets;* **rural community** = people living in a small area of the countryside; *rural communities will suffer most from the reduced bus service;* **urban community** = a town's inhabitants; **community centre** = building providing sports or arts facilities for a community; *flood victims are being housed in the local community centre*
(b) **the Community** or **the European (Economic) Community** = THE EUROPEAN UNION (NOTE: plural is **communities**)

commute
[kɪ'mjuːt] *verb*
(a) to travel to work from home each day; *he commutes from Oxford to his office in the centre of London*
(b) to reduce a legal penalty; *the prison sentence was commuted to a fine; his death sentence was commuted to life imprisonment*
(c) to exchange one type of payment for another; *his pension has been commuted to a lump sum payment*

commuter
[kɪ'mjuːtɪ] *noun*
person who travels to work in town every day; *commuters face a 10% increase in rail fares;* **commuter belt** = area round a town where commuters live; *house prices in London's commuter belt have increased by 10% over the last year;* **commuter train** = train which commuters take in the morning and evening; *the commuter trains are full every morning*

compact
1 *adjective*
[kɪm'pækt] small; close together; *the computer system is small and very compact*
2 *noun*
['kɒmpækt]
(a) small family car; *they sold the four wheel drive and bought a compact*
(b) *(formal)* agreement; *the two companies signed a compact to share their research findings*
(c) **powder compact** = small box with face powder in it; *she always carries a compact in her handbag*

compact disc (CD)
['kɒmpækt 'dɪsk] *noun*
metal recording disc, which can hold a large amount of data, pictures or music, and which is read by a laser in a special player; *the sound quality on CDs is better than on old records*

companion
[kɪm'pænjɪn] *noun*
person or animal who lives with someone; *his constant companion was his old white dog;* **travelling companion** = person who travels with someone; *he and his travelling companions were arrested as they tried to cross the border*

company
['kʌmpni] *noun*
(a) commercial firm; *it is company policy not to allow smoking anywhere in the offices; the*

company has taken on three secretaries; *she runs an electrical company*; *he set up a computer company* (NOTE: usually written **Co.** in names: **Smith & Co.** Note also the plural **companies** in this meaning)

(b) company car = car which belongs to a company and is lent to an employee to use for business or other purposes; **company director** = person appointed by the shareholders to help run a company; **company doctor** = doctor who works for a company and looks after sick workers; **Companies House** = office of the Registrar of Companies, who makes sure that companies are properly registered, and that they report their accounts and other information on time; *the company failed to lodge their accounts with Companies House*

(c) being together with other people; *I enjoy the company of young people*; *she went to Paris in company with* or *in the company of three other girls from college*; **he is good company** = he's a very entertaining person to be with; **to keep someone company** = to be with someone to prevent them feeling lonely; *would you like to come with me to keep me company?*; **to part company** = to split up; *we all set off together, but we parted company when we got to Italy*

(d) group of people who work together; **a ship's company** = the crew of a ship; **a theatre company** = the actors and directors of a theatre

(e) *(in the army)* a group of men commanded by a captain

④ **comparative**
[kəmˈpærɪtɪv]
1 *adjective*
when considered next to something else; *judged by last year's performance it is a comparative improvement*
2 *noun*
form of an adjective or adverb showing an increase in level compared to something else; *'happier', 'better' and 'more often' are the comparatives of 'happy', 'good' and 'often'*

COMMENT: comparatives are usually formed by adding the suffix -er to the adjective: 'quicker' from 'quick', for example; in the case of long adjectives, they are formed by putting 'more' in front of the adjective: 'more comfortable', 'more expensive', and so on

③ **comparatively**
[kəmˈpærɪtɪvli] *adverb*
to a certain extent, more than something else; *the country is comparatively rich in minerals*; *she is comparatively well-off*; *comparatively speaking, he's quite tall*

① **compare**
[kəmˈpeɪ] *verb*
(a) to compare something with or **to something else** = to look at two things side by side to see how they are different; *if you compare the situation in France with that in Britain*
(b) to compare something with or **to something else** = to say that something is like something else; *he compared his mother's cake to a brick*

① **compared**
[kəmˈpeɪd] *adjective*
compared to or **with** = when you compare it to; *compared with my Rolls Royce, your car is tiny*; *compared to last year, this summer was cold*

① **comparison**
[kəmˈpærɪsɪn] *noun*
act of comparing; *this year, July was cold in comparison with last year*; **there is no comparison between them** = one is much better than the other

④ **compassion**
[kəmˈpæʃn] *noun*
feeling of sympathy for someone who is in an unfortunate situation; *the soldiers showed no compassion in separating families and driving them away from their homes*

④ **compatible**
[kəmˈpætɪbl] *adjective*
(a) compatible with something = able to fit or work with something; *make sure the two computer systems are compatible*
(b) compatible with someone = able to live or work happily with someone; *how their marriage has lasted so long no one knows - they're not at all compatible*

④ **compensate**
[ˈkɒmpenseɪt] *verb*
to compensate someone for something = to pay for damage, for a loss; *they agreed to compensate her for damage to her car*; *the airline refused to compensate him when his baggage was lost*

③ **compensation**
[kɒmpenˈseɪʃn] *noun*
(a) payment for damage or loss; *the airline refused to pay any compensation for his lost luggage*; *you must submit a claim for compensation to the insurance company within two weeks*; **compensation for loss of office** = payment made to someone who is asked to leave a company before his or her contract ends
(b) something that makes up for something bad; *working in the centre of London has its compensations*; *four weeks' holiday is no compensation for a year's work in that office*

③ **compete**
[kəmˈpiːt] *verb*
to compete with someone = to try to beat someone in sport, trade, etc.; *he is competing in both the 100 and 200 metres*; *we have to compete with cheap imports from the Far East*

④ **competent**
[ˈkɒmpɪtənt] *adjective*
(a) efficient; *she is a very competent manager*

(b) quite good, but not brilliant; *he's quite competent at maths; she's a competent golfer*

(c) legally able to do something; **the court is not competent to deal with this case** = the court is not legally able to deal with the case

① **competition**
[kɒmpɪˈtɪʃn] *noun*

(a) sport or game where several teams or people enter and each tries to win; *France were winners of the competition*; *he won first prize in the piano competition*; *the competition is open to everybody* (NOTE: plural in this meaning is **competitions**)

(b) trying to do better than someone in business; *our main competition comes from the big supermarkets*; *we have to keep our prices low because of competition from cheap imports*

(c) **the competition** = people or companies who are trying to do better than you; *we have lowered our prices to try to beat the competition*; *the competition is or are planning to reduce their prices* (NOTE: singular in this meaning, but can take a plural verb)

② **competitive**
[kəmˈpetɪtɪv] *adjective*

(a) liking to win competitions; *he's very competitive*; **competitive sports** = sports which are based on competition between people or teams

(b) **competitive prices** = prices which are lower or no higher than those of rival firms; *we must keep our prices competitive if we want to stay in business*

④ **competitor**
[kəmˈpetɪtɪ] *noun*

(a) person who enters a competition; *all the competitors lined up for the start of the race*

(b) company which competes; *two German firms are our main competitors*

② **complain**
[kəmˈpleɪn] *verb*

to say that something is no good or does not work properly; *the shop is so cold the staff have started complaining*; *she complained about the service*; *they are complaining that our prices are too high*; *she complained that no one spoke English in the hotel* (NOTE: you complain **to** someone **about** something or **that** something is no good)

② **complaint**
[kəmˈpleɪnt] *noun*

(a) saying that something is wrong; *she sent her letter of complaint to the managing director*; *you must file your complaint with the relevant department*; **complaints department** = department which deals with complaints from customers

(b) illness; *she was admitted to hospital with a kidney complaint*

① **complete**
[kəmˈpliːt]
1 *adjective*

with all its parts; *he has a complete set of the new stamps*; *we have to study the complete works of Shakespeare*

2 *verb*

(a) to finish; *the builders completed the whole job in two days*

(b) to fill in a form; *when you have completed the application form, send it to us in the envelope provided*

① **completely**
[kʌmˈpliːtli] *adverb*

totally; *the building was completely destroyed in the fire*; *I completely forgot about my dentist's appointment*

④ **completion**
[kəmˈpliːʃn] *noun*

act of finishing; *the bridge is nearing completion*

② **complex**
[ˈkɒmpleks]
1 *adjective*

complicated; *the committee is discussing the complex problem of the site for the new hospital*; *the specifications for the machine are very complex*

2 *noun*

(a) series of buildings; *the council has built a new sports complex*; *an industrial complex is planned on the site of the old steel works*

(b) *(in the mind)* group of ideas which are based on an experience that you had in the past, and which influence the way you behave; *he has a complex about going bald*; *stop talking about her height - you'll give her a complex about it* (NOTE: plural is **complexes**)

④ **complexion**
[kəmˈplekʃn] *noun*

colour of the skin on your face; *she has a beautiful pale complexion*

① **complicated**
[ˈkɒmplɪkeɪtɪd] *adjective*

with many small details; difficult to understand; *it is a complicated subject*; *it's all getting too complicated - let's try and keep it simple*; *chess has quite complicated rules*; *the route to get to our house is rather complicated, so I'll draw you a map*

④ **complication**
[kɒmplɪˈkeɪʃn] *noun*

(a) illness occurring because of or during another illness; *she appeared to be getting better, but complications set in*

(b) trouble, complicated problem; *it all seems quite simple to me - what's the complication?*; *all these forms which we have to fill in just create further complications*

② **compliment**

1 *noun*

['kɒmplɪmɪnt]

(a) remark which praises someone *or* something; *she turned red when she read his compliments on her dancing*; **to be fishing for compliments** = to try to get someone to say nice things about you; **to pay someone a compliment** = to praise someone, to do something which shows you appreciate someone; *they paid her the compliment of asking her to speak to the meeting*

(b) compliments = good wishes; **send him my compliments** = give him my good wishes; **with the compliments of Apple Co. Ltd** = with good wishes from Apple Co. Ltd; *a box of chocolates with the compliments of the manager or with the manager's compliments*; *please accept these flowers with my compliments*

2 *verb*

['kɒmplɪment]

to praise; *the management compliments the staff on an excellent turnover this year*; *I would like to compliment the chef on an excellent meal*

② **complimentary**

[kɒmplɪ'mentɪrɪ] *adjective*

(a) that praises; *he was very complimentary about her dress*; *the reviews of his book are very complimentary*

(b) complimentary ticket = free ticket, sent to a friend or business associate; *the club does not allow you to sell complimentary tickets*

④ **comply (with)**

[kɪm'plaɪ] *verb*

(a) to observe a rule; *does it comply with all the EU regulations?*

(b) to obey an order; *if you fail to comply with the court order you may be prosecuted*

② **component**

[kɪm'pɪʊnɪnt]

1 *adjective*

which forms part of a larger machine, etc.; *they supply component parts for washing machines*

2 *noun*

small piece in a larger machine; *a components manufacturer*; *the assembly line stopped because they ran out of components*

④ **compose**

[kɪm'pɪʊz] *verb*

(a) to write a piece of music; *it took Mozart only three days to compose this piece*; *who composed the music to 'Doctor Zhivago'?*

(b) to write something, using your intelligence; *he sat down to compose a letter to his family*

④ **composer**

[kɪm'pɪʊzɪ] *noun*

person who writes music; *Elgar, Copland and other British and American composers*; *that was a marvellous piece, but who was the composer?*

③ **composition**

[kɒmpɪ'zɪʃn] *noun*

(a) how something is made up; *scientists are trying to establish the composition of the rock sample from the moon*

(b) something which has been composed, a poem, piece of music, etc.; *we will now play a well-known composition by Dowland*

(c) essay, piece of writing on a special subject; *we had three hours to write a composition on 'pollution'*

③ **compound**

1 *adjective*

['kɒmpaʊnd] made up of several parts; **compound interest** = interest calculated on the original total plus any previous interest; *compare* SIMPLE INTEREST

2 *noun*

['kɒmpaʊnd]

(a) chemical made up of two or more elements; *water is a compound of hydrogen and oxygen*

(b) buildings and land enclosed by a fence; *guard dogs patrol the compound at night*; *soldiers were guarding the embassy compound*

3 *verb*

[kɪm'paʊnd]

(a) to make something worse; *the plane's late arrival was compounded by fog at the airport*; *the problems of getting across London will be compounded by today's bus strike*

(b) to agree with creditors to pay part of the money owed

③ **comprehensive**

[kɒmprɪ'hensɪv] *adjective*

which includes everything; *she was given a comprehensive medical examination before being allowed back to work*; *the police made a comprehensive search of all the files*; *the list is really comprehensive - I don't think we've left anything out*; **comprehensive (school)** = state school for children of all abilities; **comprehensive education** = education system for all children without any selection according ability; **comprehensive insurance** = insurance policy which covers you against all risks which are likely to happen

④ **compress**

1 *noun*

['kɒmpres] pad of cloth, sometimes soaked in hot or cold liquid, placed on the skin to relieve pain or to force infected matter out of a wound; *she applied a cold compress to the bruise*; *the nurse applied a dry compress to his bleeding knee* (NOTE: plural is **compresses**)

2 *verb*

[kɪm'pres]

(a) to squeeze into a small space; *the garden centre sells soil compressed into plastic bags*; *I tried to compress the data onto one page, but couldn't do it*

(b) compressed air = air under pressure; *the cleaning machine uses a jet of compressed air*

comprise
[kəm'praɪz] *verb*

to be made up of; *the course comprises three years at a British university and one year's study abroad*; **to be comprised of** = to be made up of; *the exam is comprised of two written papers and an oral*

compromise
['kɒmprəmaɪz]

1 *noun*

agreement between two opposing sides, where each side gives way a little; *they reached a compromise after some discussion*; *there is no question of a compromise with the terrorists*

2 *verb*

(a) to come to an agreement by giving way a little; *he asked £15 for it, I offered £7 and we compromised on £10*; *the government has refused to compromise with the terrorists*

(b) to put someone in a difficult position; *now that he has been compromised, he has had to withdraw as a candidate*

(c) to do something which reveals a secret; *the security code has been compromised*

compulsory
[kəm'pʌlsəri] *adjective*

which everyone is forced to do; *a compulsory injection against a tropical disease*; *it is compulsory to wear a crash helmet on a motorcycle*

computer
[kəm'pju:tə] *noun*

electronic machine which calculates and keeps information automatically; *all the company's records are on computer*; **personal computer (PC)** *or* **home computer** = small computer which can be used in the home; *he wrote his book on his home computer*; **computer bureau** = office which does computer work for other offices; **computer error** = mistake made by a computer; **computer file** = section of information on a computer, such as a list of addresses, a letter, etc.; **computer game** = game which you can play on a computer, using a special program; *the boys spent the weekend playing computer games*; **computer program** = instructions to a computer, telling it to do a particular piece of work

computerize
[kəm'pju:təraɪz] *verb*

(a) to equip a business, school, etc., with computers; *the school is being computerized, but we still have only one computer per class*; *all our supermarket checkouts are fully computerized*

(b) to change from a manual system to one using computers; *our booking system has been completely computerized*; *we get computerized pay cheques*

computing
[kəm'pju:tɪŋ] *noun*

using a computer; *all children learn computing at school*; *computing is a very important skill*

conceal
[kən'si:l] *verb*

to hide something, to put something where it cannot be seen; *she concealed the loss from her manager*; *he tried to conceal the camera by putting it under his coat*

concede
[kən'si:d] *verb*

(a) to admit that you are wrong; *she conceded that this time she had been mistaken*

(b) **to concede defeat** = to admit that you have lost; *with half the votes counted, the presidential candidate conceded defeat*; *after sixteen moves, the chess champion had to concede defeat*

conceive
[kən'si:v] *verb*

(formal)

(a) to imagine; *I can't conceive of any occasion where I would wear a dress like that*; *it is difficult to conceive how people can be so cruel*

(a) to become pregnant; *after two years of marriage she began to think she would never conceive*; *(of a child)* **to be conceived** = to start existence inside the mother; *our little girl was conceived during a power cut in New York*

concentrate
['kɒnsɪntreɪt]

1 *verb*

(a) to be very attentive; *the exam candidates were all concentrating hard when someone started to giggle*; **to concentrate on something** = to pay special attention to something; *don't talk - he's trying to concentrate on his homework*; *the salesmen are supposed to concentrate on getting orders*

(b) to put everything together in one place; *the enemy guns are concentrated on top of that hill*

2 *noun*

substance which is concentrated, after water has been removed; *lemon concentrate*

concentrated
['kɒnsɪntreɪtɪd] *adjective*

(a) (juice) from which water has been removed, so giving a very strong taste; *a bottle of concentrated orange juice*

(b) very determined to do something; *with a little concentrated effort we should be able to do it*

concentration
[kɒnsɪn'treɪʃn] *noun*

(a) thinking carefully about something; *a loud conversation in the next room disturbed my concentration*; *his concentration slipped and he lost the next two games*

(b) grouping of a lot of things in one area; *the concentration of computer companies in the south of Scotland*; *the concentration of wild animals round the water hole makes it easy for lions to find food*

(c) concentration camp = harsh camp, often for political prisoners

② **concept**
['kɒnsept] *noun*

philosophical idea; *it is difficult for some countries to grasp the concept of democratic government*; *the concept of grammar is completely foreign to her*; *our children have absolutely no concept of what peace and quiet is*

① **concern**
[kɪn'sɜːn]

1 *noun*

(a) worry; *she's a cause of great concern to her family*

(b) interest; *my main concern is to ensure that we all enjoy ourselves*; *the teachers showed no concern at all for the children's safety*; **it is no concern of yours** = it's nothing to do with you; *I don't care what they do with the money - it's not my concern*

(c) company, business; *a big German chemical concern*

2 *verb*

(a) to have as the subject; **the letter concerns you** = the letter is about you; **that does not concern him** = it has nothing to do with him; **as far as money is concerned** = referring to money; **to concern yourself with** = to deal with; *you needn't concern yourself with cleaning the shop*

(b) to worry; *it concerns me that he is always late for work*

① **concerned**
[kɪn'sɜːnd] *adjective*

worried; *she looked concerned*; *I could tell something was wrong by the concerned look on her face*; *we are concerned about her behaviour - do you think she is having problems at school?*

① **concerning**
[kɪn'sɜːnɪŋ] *preposition* dealing with; *can you answer some questions concerning holidays?*; *I'd like to speak to Mr Robinson concerning his application for insurance*; *anyone with information concerning this person should get in touch with the police*

② **concert**
['kɒnsɪt] *noun*

programme of music played in public; *I'm sorry, the concert is sold out*; *I couldn't go to the concert, so I gave my ticket to a friend*; **concert hall** = large building where concerts are given

④ **concession**
[kɪn'seʃn] *noun*

(a) allowing someone do something that you do not really want them to do; *we insist that the children are home by 8 p.m. on weekdays, but as a concession, we let them stay out until 11 on Saturdays*

(b) to make concessions to someone = to change your plans so as to please someone; *the Prime Minister has said that no concessions will be made to the terrorists*

② **conclude**
[kɪn'kluːd] *verb*

(a) to end; to come to an end; *he concluded by thanking all those who had helped arrange the exhibition*; *the concert concluded with a piece by Mozart*

(b) to come to an opinion; *the police concluded that the thief had got into the building through the kitchen window*

(c) to conclude an agreement with someone = to arrange an agreement or treaty with someone

② **conclusion**
[kɪn'kluːʒn] *noun*

(a) end; *at the conclusion of the trial all the accused were found guilty*

(b) opinion which you reach after careful thought; *she came to or reached the conclusion that he had found another girlfriend*; *what conclusions can you draw from the evidence before you?*

③ **concrete**
['kɒŋkriːt]

1 *noun*

mixture of cement and sand, used in building; *concrete was invented by the Romans*; *the pavement is made of blocks of concrete*

2 *adjective*

(a) made of cement and sand; *a concrete path*

(b) real, important; *he had no concrete proposals to offer*; *the police are sure he is guilty, but they have no concrete evidence against him*

④ **condemn**
[kɪn'dem] *verb*

(a) to say that you do not approve of something; *she condemned the local council for the delay*

(b) to sentence a criminal; *he was condemned to death*

(c) to declare a house to be not in good enough state to live in; *the whole block of flats has been condemned and will be pulled down*

① **condition**
[kɪn'dɪʃn] *noun*

(a) state that something is in; *the car is in very good condition considering it is over thirty years old*; *he was taken to hospital when his condition got worse*

(b) state of the surroundings in which someone is living or working; *conditions in the refugee camps are very bad*; *the 7 o'clock news forecast poor weather conditions*

(c) illness; *he is being treated for a heart condition*

(d) term of a deal; something which has to be agreed before something else is done; *they didn't agree with some of the conditions of the contract; one of conditions of the deal is that the company pays all travel costs*; **on condition that** = only if; *I will come on condition that you pay my fare*

④ **conditioner**
[kən'dɪʃnɪ] *noun*

(a) liquid which puts hair into good condition; *the hairdresser asked me if I wanted some conditioner after the shampoo; I always use a combined shampoo and conditioner*

(b) **fabric conditioner** = substance which makes fabrics softer after washing or cleaning; *add some fabric conditioner to the wash*; *see also* AIR-CONDITIONER

② **conduct**
1 *noun*
['kɒndʌkt] way of behaving; *his conduct in class is becoming a cause of concern; her conduct during the trial was remarkably calm; he was arrested for noisy conduct in the High Street*
2 *verb*
[kən'dʌkt]

(a) to guide; *the guests were conducted to their seats*; **conducted tour** = tour led by a guide

(b) to direct an orchestra; *the orchestra will be conducted by a Russian conductor*

(c) to allow electricity, heat, etc., to pass through; *copper conducts electricity very well*

(d) to carry out; *they are conducting an experiment into the effect of TV advertising*

(e) to lead, to direct; *the chairman conducted the negotiations very efficiently*; **to conduct a meeting** = to be chairman of a meeting; *as he was going away on business, he asked his deputy to conduct the meeting*

③ **conductor**
[kən'dʌktɪ] *noun*

(a) metal, or other substance which conducts heat or electricity; *copper is a good conductor but plastic is not*; **conductor rail** = the electric rail for trains

(b) person who directs an orchestra; *as the orchestra reached the end of the piece, the conductor started to sing; the orchestra will be conducted by a Russian conductor*

(c) **bus conductor** = person who sells tickets on a bus

(d) *US* person in charge of a train (NOTE: British English is **railway guard**)

① **conference**
['kɒnfɪrɪns] *noun*

(a) discussion; *the managers had a quick conference to decide what action to take*; **to be in conference** = to be in a meeting; **conference phone** = telephone link arranged that several people can speak into it at the same time from

different places; **press conference** = meeting where newspaper, radio and TV reporters are invited to hear news of something or to talk to a famous person; *he gave a press conference on the steps of Number Ten*; **sales conference** = meeting of sales managers, representatives, publicity staff, etc., to discuss future sales plans

(b) meeting of a group or society; *the annual conference of the Electricians' Union; the conference agenda or the agenda of the conference was drawn up by the secretary; 2000 people attended the conference on the effects of global warming*

④ **confess**
[kən'fes] *verb*

(a) to admit that you have done something wrong; *he confessed to having stolen the watch; she confessed that she had forgotten to lock the door*

(b) to admit your sins to a priest; *she went to church to confess to the priest*

④ **confession**
[kən'feʃn] *noun*

(a) admission of fault; *the prisoner said his confession had been forced from him by the police*

(b) **to make your confession** = to admit your sins to a priest

② **confidence**
['kɒnfɪdɪns] *noun*

(a) feeling sure; *the staff do not have much confidence in their manager; I have total confidence in the pilot*; *see also* VOTE

(b) being secret; **in confidence** = as a secret; *he showed me the report in confidence*

(c) **confidence trick** = a trick to get money by making someone believe something

② **confident**
['kɒnfɪdɪnt] *adjective*

sure that you or something will be successful; *I am confident (that) the show will go off well; she's confident of doing well in the exam*

③ **confidential**
[kɒnfɪ'denʃl] *adjective*

secret, private; *please mark the letter 'Private and Confidential'*; **confidential secretary** = secretary who deals with her employer's private matters

③ **confine**
[kən'faɪn] *verb*

(a) to keep in one small place; *the tigers were confined in a small cage with no room to move around*; **confined to bed** = forced to stay in bed; *she wanted to get up, but the doctor has confined her to bed*

(b) to restrict; *make sure you confine your answer to the subject in the question*

② **confirm**
[kən'fɜːm] *verb*

(a) to say that something is certain; *the dates of the concerts have been confirmed by the pop group's manager; the photograph confirmed that the result of the race was a dead heat; we have been told that she left the country last month - can you confirm that?*

(b) to confirm someone in a job = to say that someone is now permanently in the job; **to be confirmed in office** = to be kept in your job by a new management

(c) to be confirmed = to be made a full Christian by a bishop; *he was confirmed when he was twelve*

④ **confirmation**

[kɒnfɪˈmeɪʃn] *noun*

(a) making sure; *we are awaiting official confirmation of the figures*

(b) document which confirms something; *we have had confirmation from the bank that the payment has been made*

(c) ceremony where a person is made a full Christian by a bishop; *when is your daughter's confirmation?*

② **conflict**

1 *noun*

[ˈkɒnflɪkt]

(a) fighting; *the army is engaged in armed conflict with rebel forces; the border conflict escalated into an full-scale war*

(b) angry situation between people; *the demand for equal treatment for all classes can lead to social conflict;* **to come into conflict with someone** = to start to fight someone; *the decision brought the union into conflict with the management;* **conflict of interests** = situation where a person may profit personally from decisions which he takes as an official

2 *verb*

[kɪnˈflɪkt] **to conflict with** = to contradict; *the defendant's version of events conflicts with that of the witness;* **conflicting advice** = pieces of advice from different people which are the opposite of each other

④ **confront**

[kɪnˈfrʌnt] *verb*

(a) to try to tackle someone; *don't confront a burglar on your own - he may be armed*

(b) to confront someone with the evidence = to show the evidence to someone; *when the police confronted him with the photographs he confessed*

④ **confrontation**

[kɒnfrʌnˈteɪʃn] *noun*

angry meeting between opposing sides; *to avoid confrontation, the fans of the two opposing teams will be kept as far apart as possible; there have been some violent confrontations between students and the police*

④ **confuse**

[kɪnˈfjuːz] *verb*

to muddle; *she was confused by all the journalists' questions; I always confuse him with his brother - they are very alike*

③ **confused**

[kɪnˈfjuːzd] *adjective*

not clear in your mind; *I'm a bit confused - did we say 8.00 p.m. or 8.30?; grandmother used to get rather confused in her old age*

③ **confusing**

[kɪnˈfjuːzɪŋ] *adjective*

which is difficult to make clear; *she found the instructions on the computer very confusing*

③ **confusion**

[kɪnˈfjuːʒn] *noun*

disorder; *there were scenes of confusion at the airport when the snow stopped all flights*

④ **congratulate**

[kɪnˈɡrætjʊleɪt] *verb*

to give someone good wishes on a special occasion or for having done something; *he congratulated them on their silver wedding anniversary; I want to congratulate you on your promotion*

③ **congratulations**

[kɪnɡrætjuːˈleɪʃnz] *noun*

good wishes to someone who has done well; *congratulations - you're our millionth customer!; congratulations on passing your exam!; the office sent him their congratulations on his wedding*

④ **congress**

[ˈkɒŋɡres] *noun*

meeting of a group; *the annual congress of a scientific society; this year's Conservative Party congress will be held in Blackpool*

③ **Congress**

[ˈkɒŋɡres] *noun*

legislative body of the USA, formed of the House of Representatives and the Senate; *the President has to persuade Congress to pass his budget*

③ **congressional**

[kɪnˈɡreʃɪnl] *adjective*

referring to the US Congress; *a congressional hearing*

④ **congressman** *or* **congresswoman**

[ˈkɒŋɡresmɪn *or* ˈkɒŋɡrɪwʊmɪn] *noun*

member of the United States House of Representatives (NOTE: plural is **congressmen, congresswomen**; note also that it can be used as a title with a name: **Congressman Smith, Congresswoman Murphy**)

④ **conjunction**

[kɪnˈdʒʌŋkʃn] *noun*

word which links different words together to make phrases or sentences; *'and' and 'but' are conjunctions*

② **connect**

[kɪˈnekt] *verb*

(a) to join; *the computer should have been connected to the printer; has the telephone been connected yet?; connect the two red wires together*

(b) to link up with; **the flight from New York connects with a flight to Athens** = the plane from New York arrives in time for passengers to catch the plane to Athens; **this train connects with the 12.45** = this train allows passengers to catch the 12.45

② **connection**
[kɪ'nekʃn] *noun*
(a) link; *there is a definite connection between smoking and lung cancer; he said that there was no connection between how much he had had to drink and his falling over in the street;* **in connection with your visit** = referring to your visit
(b) train, plane, etc., which you catch after getting off another train or plane; *my train was late and I missed my connection to Birmingham*
(c) connections = people you know; *he has business connections in Argentina*

④ **conquer**
['kɒŋkɪ] *verb*
to defeat with an army; *England was conquered by the Normans in 1066; the Romans conquered most of Europe as far east as Romania*

③ **conscience**
['kɒnʃns] *noun*
feeling which you have that you have done right or wrong; *I can say with a clear conscience that I have done nothing wrong; why can't you look me in the eye - have you got a guilty conscience?; he refused to serve in the army as a matter of conscience*

② **conscious**
['kɒnʃs] *adjective*
aware of things happening around you; *she was conscious during the whole operation;* **a conscious decision** = a decision which you have thought about; *refusing the offer was a conscious decision on his part; he made a conscious decision to try to avoid her in future*

③ **consciousness**
['kɒnʃsnɪs] *noun*
being conscious; **to lose consciousness** = to become unconscious; **to regain consciousness** = to become conscious again; *he never regained consciousness after the accident*

④ **consecutive**
[kɪn'sekjʊtɪv] *adjective*
one after the other; *the bank sent him reminders for two consecutive weeks*

③ **consent**
[kɪn'sent]
1 *noun*
agreement; *doctors must obtain a patient's consent before operating;* **to withhold your consent** = not to agree; *her parents withheld their consent to the marriage;* **the age of consent** = age at which someone can legally agree to have sex
2 *verb*

to consent to something = to agree to something; *the judge consented to the prosecution's request*

② **consequence**
['kɒnsɪkwɪns] *noun*
(a) something which follows, a result; *we walked all day in the rain, with the consequence that all of us got colds*
(b) importance; **it is of no consequence** = it is not important

③ **consequently**
['kɒnsɪkwɪntli] *adverb*
because of this; *we walked all day in the rain and consequently all caught colds*

③ **conservation**
[kɒnsɪ'veɪʃn] *noun*
saving of energy, natural resources, old buildings, etc.; *the company is spending more money on energy conservation;* **a Conservation Area** = area of a town where the buildings are of special interest and cannot be altered or destroyed

③ **conservative**
[kɪn'sɜːvɪtɪv]
1 *adjective*
(a) not wanting to change; *he has very conservative views*
(b) *(politics)* **the Conservative party** = political party which is in favour of only gradual change in society and is against government involvement in industry and welfare
(c) probably too low; *a conservative estimate of sales; at least two hundred people came to the flower show, and that is a conservative estimate*
2 *noun*
a Conservative = a member of the Conservative Party; *the Conservatives lost their majority in Parliament*

① **consider**
[kɪn'sɪdɪ] *verb*
(a) to think carefully about something; *please consider seriously the offer which we are making; we have to consider the position of the children after the divorce*
(b) to think; *do you consider him the right man for the job?; she is considered (to be) one of the best lawyers in town*
(c) all things considered = on the whole; *all things considered, the flower show went off quite well*

① **considerable**
[kɪn'sɪdrɪbl] *adjective*
quite large; *he lost a considerable amount of money at the horse race*

① **considerably**
[kɪn'sɪdrɪbli] *adverb*
quite a lot; *it is considerably hotter than it was last week*

① **consideration**
[kɪnsɪdɪ'reɪʃn] *noun*
(a) careful thought; *we are giving serious consideration to the possibility of moving the*

head office to Scotland; **to take something into consideration** = to think about something when making a decision; *the age of the children has to be taken into consideration*; **under consideration** = being thought about; *the matter is under consideration*
(b) thing which has an effect on a decision; *the safety of the children is our most important consideration*
(c) *(formal)* small sum of money; **for a small consideration** = for a small fee or payment

① **considering**
[kən'sɪdrɪŋ] *conjunction & preposition*
when you think about it; *he plays the piano extremely well, considering he's only five*; *he ought to be more grateful, considering the amount of help you have given him*

③ **consist**
[kən'sɪst] *verb*
(a) to consist of = to be formed of; *the package tour consists of air travel, six nights in a luxury hotel, all meals and visits to places of interest*
(b) to consist in = to be, to mean; *for him, dieting consists in having two chocolates instead of three*

③ **consistent**
[kɪ'sɪstənt] *adjective*
(a) consistent with something = which does not contradict something; *the measures taken must be consistent with government policy*
(b) always at the same level; *some of his work is very good, but he's not consistent*

④ **consolidate**
[kən'sɒlɪdeɪt] *verb*
(a) to make firm or sure; *having entered the market, the company spent a year consolidating its position*; *the team consolidated their lead with a second goal*
(b) to join together to make one single unit or one single shipment; *the two businesses consolidated to form one group*; *the shipment to India is being consolidated, and will leave the docks on Tuesday*

④ **consonant**
['kɒnsɪnɪnt] *noun*
letter representing a sound which is made using the teeth, tongue or lips; *'b' and 't' are consonants, while 'e' and 'i' are vowels*

> COMMENT: the five vowels are 'a', 'e', 'i', 'o' and 'u'. All the other letters of the alphabet are consonants

④ **constable**
['kʌnstɪbl] *noun*
ordinary member of the police; *the inspector was accompanied by a sergeant and three constables*; *the constable on duty raised the alarm*; *an off-duty police constable happened to be in the bank when the robbers came in* (NOTE: British English only; American English uses **officer**)

② **constant**
['kɒnstɪnt]
1 *adjective*
(a) not changing or stopping; *the constant noise of music from the bar next door drives me mad*
(b) always there; *his dog was his constant companion*
(c) with a value which does not change; *the calculations are in constant dollars*
2 *noun*
number or thing which does not change; *the speed of light is a constant*; *death and taxes are the only constants in life*

② **constantly**
['kɒnstɪntli] *adverb*
all the time; *he is constantly changing his mind*; *the telephone rang constantly all morning*

③ **constituency**
[kən'stɪtjuːnsi] *noun*
area of the country which elects a Member of Parliament; *he represents a Welsh constituency*; *MPs from the North of England have to live in London and can only visit their constituencies at weekends* (NOTE: plural is **constituencies**)

③ **constitute**
['kɒnstɪtjuːt] *verb*
to be or form; *selling the photographs to a newspaper constitutes a serious breach of security*; *women now constitute the majority of the committee*

② **constitution**
[kɒnstɪ'tjuːʃn] *noun*
(a) ability of a person to stay healthy; *she has a very strong constitution*; *(informal)* **to have the constitution of an elephant** = to be tough, to have a very strong constitution; *Aunt Maud has the constitution of an elephant*
(b) laws and principles under which a country is ruled, which give the people rights and duties, and which give the government powers and duties; *unlike most states, Britain does not have a written constitution*; *freedom of speech is guaranteed by the American Constitution*
(c) written rules or regulations of a society, club, etc.; *under the society's constitution, the chairman is elected for two years*

③ **constitutional**
[kɒnstɪ'tjʃɪnl]
1 *adjective*
(a) according to a country's constitution; *such action by the Minister of Defence is not constitutional*; **constitutional monarchy** = system of government where a king or queen is the head of state, but the country is ruled by an elected government
(b) according to a society's constitution; *the election of the chairman for a third term of office is not constitutional*
2 *noun*

short walk which you think is good for your health; *after a big lunch I went for a constitutional*; *he always takes his early morning constitutional in the park*

③ **constraint**
[kın'streınt] *noun*

something which limits your ability to act; *the financial constraints placed on a country by the international banking system*; *the legal constraints of my position do not allow me to make any comment*

③ **construct**
[kın'strʌkt] *verb*

to build; *we have tendered for the contract to construct the new airport*; *the wings are constructed of light steel*

② **construction**
[kın'strʌkʃn] *noun*

(a) the act of building; *the construction of the new stadium took three years*; **construction company** = company which specializes in building; **under construction** = being built; *the airport is under construction*

(b) thing which has been built; *the new stadium is a magnificent construction*; *planning regulations ban any construction more than 20m high in the old part of the town*

④ **constructive**
[kın'strʌktıv] *adjective*

which aims to help or improve; *she made some constructive suggestions for improving the design of the shop*

③ **consult**
[kın'sʌlt] *verb*

(a) to ask someone for advice; *he consulted his accountant about his tax*; **consulting room** = room where a doctor sees his patients

(b) to look at something to get information; *after consulting the map they decided to go north*; *he consulted his watch and said that they had enough time to catch the train*

③ **consultant**
[kın'sʌltınt] *noun*

(a) medical specialist attached to a hospital; *we'll make an appointment for you to see a consultant*

(b) specialist who gives advice; *his tax consultant advised him to sell the shares*

③ **consultation**
[kɒnsʌl'teıʃn] *noun*

(a) act of consulting; *after consultations with the police, the government has decided to ban the protest march*; *a 30-minute consultation with my lawyer cost me more than I earn in a week!*

(b) act of visiting a doctor for advice; *she had a consultation with an eye surgeon*

④ **consume**
[kın'sjuːm] *verb*

(a) to eat or drink; *the guests consumed over 100 hamburgers*

(b) to use up; *the factory consumes a vast quantity of energy*

② **consumer**
[kın'sjuːmı] *noun*

person or company that buys goods or services; *gas consumers are protesting at the increase in prices*; *consumers are buying more from supermarkets and less from small shops*; **consumer goods** = goods bought by members of the public

③ **consumption**
[kın'sʌmpʃn] *noun*

(a) act of consuming; *the meat was condemned as not fit for human consumption*; *the consumption of alcohol on the premises is not allowed*

(b) quantity consumed; *unless you reduce your consumption of fat, you risk having a heart attack*; **petrol consumption** = amount of petrol used by a car to go a certain distance; *a car with a low petrol consumption*

② **contact**
['kɒntækt]

1 *noun*

(a) touch; *avoid any contact between the acid and the skin*; *anyone who has been in physical contact with the patient must consult their doctor immediately*; **contact lenses** = tiny lenses worn on the eye

(b) act of communicating with someone; *we don't have much contact with our old friends in Australia*; **to get in contact with someone** = to communicate with someone you have not spoken to or written to; **he put me in contact with a good lawyer** = he told me the name and address of a good lawyer; **I have lost contact with them** = I do not communicate with them any longer; **contact number** = phone number which you can call to speak to someone

(c) person whom you know; *he has a lot of contacts in the newspaper world*; *who is your contact in the ministry?*

2 *verb*

to get into communication with someone; *he tried to contact his office by phone*; *can you contact the ticket office immediately?*

④ **contagious**
[kın'teıdʒıs] *adjective*

(a) (*disease*) which can be passed by touching an infected person or objects which an infected person has touched; *did you have any contagious diseases when you were a child?*; *your child is no longer contagious and can go back to school* (NOTE: compare **infectious**)

(b) which can be passed on to someone else; *he's a great music teacher and his enthusiasm for music is very contagious*

① **contain**
[kən'teɪn] *verb*
(a) to hold, to have inside; *the bottle contains acid*; *the envelope contained a cheque for £1000*; *a barrel contains 250 litres*; *I have lost a bag containing important documents*
(b) to restrict; *the army tried to contain the advance of the enemy forces*; *the party is attempting to contain the revolt among its members*

③ **container**
[kən'teɪnɪ] *noun*
(a) box or bottle, etc., which holds something else; *we need a container for all this rubbish*; *the gas is shipped in strong metal containers*
(b) special very large case for easy loading onto a ship, lorry, etc.; *the crane was loading the containers onto the ship*; *we had our furniture shipped out to Singapore in a container*; a **container-load of spare parts** = a shipment of spare parts sent in a container; **container port** = port which only deals with containers; **container ship** = ship which only carries containers

④ **contaminate**
[kən'tæmɪneɪt] *verb*
to make something dirty by touching it or by adding something to it; *supplies of drinking water were contaminated by refuse from the factories*; *a party of tourists fell ill after eating contaminated food*

② **contemporary**
[kən'tempɪrɪ]
1 *adjective*
(a) contemporary with someone *or* **something** = existing at the same time as someone *or* something; *most of the people I was contemporary with at college have already got jobs*
(b) modern, present-day; *a museum of contemporary art*
2 *noun*
person who lives at the same time as someone; *he is one of my contemporaries from school*; *Shakespeare and his contemporaries lived and worked in London*

④ **contempt**
[kən'tempt] *noun*
feeling of not respecting someone; *you have shown contempt for the feelings of our family*; *the reviewer had nothing but contempt for the author of the novel*; **to hold someone in contempt** = not to respect someone; *they hold all foreigners in contempt and won't have anything to do with them*

② **content**
1 *adjective*
[kən'tent]
content to = happy to; *she was content to sit in the sun and wait*; **content with** = satisfied with; *if you are not content with the way the car runs, bring it back and we will look at it again*

2 *noun*
(a) [kən'tent]
satisfaction; **to your heart's content** = as much as you want; *you can play billiards to your heart's content*; *living by the sea, they can go sailing to their heart's content*
(b) ['kɒntent]
thing or amount which is contained; *dried fruit has a higher sugar content than fresh fruit*; **the mineral content of water** = the percentages of different minerals contained in a sample of water

② **contents**
['kɒntents] *noun*
things which are inside something, which are in a container; *he dropped the bottle and the contents spilled onto the carpet*; *the burglars took the entire contents of the safe*; *the customs officials inspected the contents of the packing case*; *she kept the contents of the letter secret*; **table of contents** = list of chapters in a book, usually printed at the beginning of the text

④ **contest**
1 *noun*
['kɒntest] fight, competition; *only two people entered the contest for the party leadership*; **beauty contest** = competition to see which girl is most beautiful
2 *verb*
[kən'test]
(a) to fight an election; *there are four candidates contesting the seat*
(b) to query a will, or argue that a will is invalid; *when she died and left all her money to a cats' home, her family contested the will*

① **context**
['kɒntekst] *noun*
phrase in which a word occurs which helps to show what it means; *even if you don't know what a word means, you can sometimes guess its meaning from the context*; **taken out of context** = quoted without surrounding text; *my words have been taken out of context - if you read the whole speech you will see that I meant something quite different*

④ **continent**
['kɒntɪnɪnt] *noun*
(a) one of the major land areas in the world (Africa, North America, South America, Asia, Australia, Europe, etc.)
(b) *(in Britain)* **the Continent** = the rest of Europe, as opposed to Britain itself, which is an island; **on the Continent** = in Europe; **to the Continent** = to Europe; *when you drive on the Continent remember to drive on the right*; *they go to the Continent on holiday each year, sometimes to France, sometimes to Switzerland*

④ **continental**
[kɒntɪ'nentl]
1 *adjective*
(a) referring to a continent; **continental climate** = climate of hot dry summers and very cold

winters; *Germany has a continental climate which is quite different from ours in Britain*; **continental shelf** = area of shallow sea round the edges of a continent; *oil companies are keen to explore the waters of the continental shelf*
(b) referring to Europe (excluding the British Isles); *we've decided to take a continental holiday this year*; **continental breakfast** = light breakfast of toast and coffee (as opposed to a 'full English breakfast') *US* **continental plan** = hotel tariff including accommodation and a continental breakfast
2 *noun*
(informal) **a Continental** = a European; *the Continentals seem to play a different type of football from us*

② **continual**
['kɪn'tɪnjuɪl] *adjective*
which goes on all the time; *I am getting fed up with her continual complaints*; *the computer has given us continual problems ever since we bought it*

④ **continually**
[kɪn'tɪnjʊu:li] *adverb*
very often, again and again, almost all the time; *the photocopier is continually breaking down*

① **continue**
[kɪn'tɪnju:] *verb*
to go on doing something or go on happening; *he continued working, even though the house was on fire*; *the engine continued to send out clouds of black smoke*; *the meeting started at 10 a.m. and continued until 6 p.m.*; *the show continued with some children's dances*

② **continuous**
[kɪn'tɪnjuɪs] *adjective*
with no break; *she has been in continuous pain for three days*; *a continuous white line means that you are not allowed to overtake*; **continuous stationery** = long sheet of computer paper; **continuous tense** = form of a verb showing that something is going on and has not stopped; *'is going' is a continuous form of the verb 'to go'*; *continuous tenses in English are formed using the ending -ing*

④ **continuously**
[kɪn'tɪnjuɪsli] *adverb*
without stopping; *the children behind me ate sweets continuously during the film*; *the Prime Minister was on the platform continuously for four hours*

④ **contraceptive**
[kɒntrɪ'septɪv]
1 *adjective*
which prevents pregnancy; *the contraceptive pill is available from doctors and clinics*
2 *noun*
drug or device which prevents pregnancy; *the chemist sells various types of contraceptives*; *an oral contraceptive such as the pill*

① **contract**
1 ['kɒntrækt] *noun*
legal agreement; *I don't agree with some of the conditions of the contract*; **under contract** = bound by the terms of a contract; *the company is under contract to a French supermarket*; **breach of contract** = breaking the terms of a contract; *the company is in breach of contract* = the company has failed to do what was agreed in the contract
2 [kɪn'trækt] *verb*
(a) to agree to do some work under a legally binding contract; *to contract to supply spare parts or to contract for the supply of spare parts*
(b) to sign an agreement with a contractor; *the corporation has contracted the refuse collection service to a private company*
(c) to become smaller; *metal contracts when it gets cold, and expands when it is hot*

④ **contractor**
[kɪn'træktɪ] *noun*
person who does work according to a signed agreement; *a building contractor; an electricity contractor*

④ **contradict**
[kɒntrɪ'dɪkt] *verb*
to say that what someone else says is not true; to be different from what has been said before; *why do you always contradict me?*; *the witness contradicted herself several times*; *what you have just said contradicts what you said yesterday*

④ **contradiction**
[kɒntrɪ'dɪkʃn] *noun*
stating or being the opposite; *there is a basic contradiction between the government's policies and what it actually does*; **a contradiction in terms** = phrase which is formed of two parts which contradict each other, and so have no meaning; *a politician who tells the truth is a contradiction in terms*

④ **contrary**
['kɒntrɪrɪ]
1 *adjective*
(a) opposite; *most people agreed with the speaker, but one or two expressed contrary views*; **contrary winds** = winds blowing in the opposite direction; *the ship could not leave harbour because of contrary winds*
(b) **contrary to** = in opposition to; *contrary to what you would expect, the desert gets quite cold at night*
(c) [kɪn'treɪrɪ]
always doing the opposite of what you want; *she's such a contrary child*
2 *noun*
the contrary = the opposite; **on the contrary** = just the opposite; *I'm not annoyed with her - on the contrary, I think she has done the right thing*; **to the contrary** = stating the opposite; *we will go on with the plans for the exhibition*

unless we hear to the contrary; smoking used to be considered harmless, but now the evidence is to the contrary

② **contrast**
1 *noun*
['kɒntrɑːst] sharp difference between two things; *the contrast in weather between the north and the south of the country*; **in contrast to** = as opposed to; *he is quite short, in contrast to his sister who is very tall; the north of the country is green and wooded in contrast to the south which is dry and sandy; the two cities are in sharp contrast*
2 *verb*
[kɪn'trɑːst] to be quite obviously different from; *his rude letter contrasted with his friendly conversation on the telephone*

② **contribute**
[kɪn'trɪbjuːt] *verb*
(a) to help towards; *the government's policies have contributed to a feeling of worry among teachers*
(b) to give money to; *we were asked to contribute to a charity; everyone was asked to contribute to the secretary's leaving present*
(c) to contribute to a magazine = to write articles for a magazine

② **contribution**
[kɒntrɪ'bjuːʃn] *noun*
(a) money, etc., given to help something; *she makes monthly contributions to the Red Cross*; **National Insurance contributions (NIC)** = money paid each month to the government by a worker and the company he or she works for, to go towards the costs of looking after the sick, poor and unemployed
(b) article submitted to a newspaper; *the deadline for contributions is December 1st*

① **control**
[kɪn'trʊl]
1 *noun*
(a) keeping in order, being able to direct something; *the club is under the control of three shareholders; he lost control of his business and resigned; the teacher has no control over the class*; **control button** = on a TV, radio, etc., the button which switches it on, changes channel, increases volume, etc.; **control column** = handle for steering an aircraft; **control key** = key on a computer which works part of a program
(b) restricting something; **under control** = restricted; *we try to keep expenses under tight control*; **to bring something under control** = to reduce or restrict something; *the firemen quickly brought the fire under control*; **out of control** = not restricted; *the car ran down the hill out of control; our spending has got out of control; the fire started in the roof and quickly got out of control; football fans got out of control and started breaking windows in the centre of town*

(c) control group = group against which the results of a test on another group can be compared
2 *verb*
(a) to keep in order, to direct or restrict; *the police couldn't control the crowds; there was nobody there to control the traffic; we must try to control the sales of foreign cars; the government controls the price of meat*
(b) to control a business = to have the power to direct the way a business is run; *the business is controlled by a company based in Luxembourg*
(NOTE: **controlling - controlled**)

④ **controller**
[kɪn'trʊlə] *noun*
person who controls; **air traffic controller** = person who directs planes from a control tower; *the strike by air traffic controllers disrupted air services*

④ **controversial**
[kɒntrə'vɜːʃl] *adjective*
which starts violent discussions; *he made a highly controversial speech; making drugs legal is a very controversial issue; she has controversial views on abortion*

④ **controversy**
[kɪn'trɒvɪsi] *noun*
sharp discussion; *there is a lot of controversy about the funding of political parties*

④ **convenience**
[kɪn'viːnɪns] *noun*
(a) being convenient; *I like the convenience of working from home; we bought the house because of the convenience of the area for shopping*; **at your earliest convenience** = as soon as you can easily do it; *please return this form at your earliest convenience*
(b) public conveniences = public toilets; **all modern conveniences** = all modern facilities such as central heating, telephone, electricity, etc.; *the flat is advertised for sale with all mod cons*
(c) convenience food = food which is prepared by the shop before it is sold, so that it needs only heating to be made ready to eat; *sales of convenience food are booming*; **convenience shop** *or* **convenience store** = small local shop which stays open long hours and stocks a wide range of necessary goods

③ **convenient**
[kɪn'viːnɪnt] *adjective*
which does not cause any practical problems; *6.30 in the morning is not a very convenient time for a meeting; a bank draft is a convenient way of sending money abroad*

② **convention**
[kɪn'venʃn] *noun*
(a) the usual way of doing things; *it is a convention that the bride wears a white dress to her wedding*
(b) contract or treaty; *an international convention on human rights*

(c) general meeting of an association or political party; *they are holding their annual convention in Chicago*; **convention centre** = building with a series of meeting rooms, hotel bedrooms, restaurants, etc., built specially for holding large meetings

③ **conventional**
[kən'venʃnɪl] *adjective*
ordinary, usual; *we are planning a conventional Christmas at home*; *he arrived at the office wearing a very conventional grey suit*; **conventional weapons** = ordinary weapons such as guns, not nuclear weapons

① **conversation**
[kɒnvɪ'seɪʃn] *noun*
talk; *we had a long conversation with the bank manager*; *why did he suddenly change the subject of the conversation?*; **to carry on a conversation with someone** = to talk to someone; *she tried to carry on a conversation with him while he was working*; *it's difficult to carry on a conversation with Uncle Harry because he's deaf*

④ **conversion**
[kən'vɜːʃn] *noun*
(a) changing of one thing into another; *the conversion of the old shed into an artist's studio*; *I need a calculator to work out the conversion of £500 into pesetas*
(b) turning of a person to another set of ideas or religion; *she underwent a sudden conversion to Islam*
(c) *(in Rugby)* act of converting a try; *his attempted conversion failed, and the scores remained level*

③ **convert**
1 *noun*
['kɒnvɜːt] person who has changed his ideas or religion; *he has become a convert to Islam*
2 *verb*
[kən'vɜːt]
(a) to turn or to make someone turn from one set of ideas or religion to another; *when she got married she converted to Islam*; *she tried to convert her husband to becoming a vegetarian*; *see also* PREACH
(b) to change; *we are converting the shed into a studio*; *these panels convert the heat of the sun into electricity*
(c) *(in Rugby)* **to convert a try** = to earn extra points by kicking the ball over the bar between the posts after a try has been scored; *if he converts the try the scores will be level*
(d) to change money of one country for money of another; *we converted our pounds into Swiss francs*

④ **convertible**
[kən'vɜːtɪbl]
1 *noun*
car with a roof which folds back or can be removed; *you can hire a small convertible for $100 a day*

2 *adjective*
(especially of a currency) which can easily be changed into another currency; *the dollar, the yen and other convertible currencies can be bought easily at banks*

④ **convict**
1 *noun*
['kɒnvɪkt] criminal who has been sent to prison; *the police are searching for two escaped convicts*
2 *verb*
[kən'vɪkt] to find someone guilty; *she was convicted of theft*

③ **conviction**
[kən'vɪkʃn] *noun*
(a) being found guilty; *his lawyers are appealing against his conviction*
(b) being certain that something is true; *it was a common conviction in the Middle Ages that the earth was flat*; *her religious convictions do not allow her to eat pork*
(c) being likely, able to convince someone; *she gave a string of excuses which completely lacked conviction*

③ **convince**
[kən'vɪns] *verb*
to convince someone of something = to persuade someone that something is true; *the lawyer has to convince the jury that his client is innocent*; *at an interview, you have to convince the employer that you are the right person for the job*

③ **convinced**
[kən'vɪnst] *adjective*
very certain; *I am convinced that she knows something about the robbery*; *I'm still not convinced she is telling the truth*

① **cook**
[kʊk]
1 *noun*
person who gets food ready; *she worked as a cook in a pub during the summer*; *he's a very good cook* = he makes very good food
2 *verb*
(a) to get food ready for eating, especially by heating it; *if you want to learn how to cook Chinese food, watch the TV programme*; *don't bother your mother when she's cooking the dinner*; *how do you cook cabbage?*; *see also* BAKE, BOIL, FRY, etc.
(b) *(of food)* to be got ready by heating; *the chicken is cooking in the oven*; *how long do these vegetables take to cook?*

③ **cooker**
['kʊkɪ] *noun*
device run on gas, electricity, coal, etc., for cooking food; *we have a fridge, a dishwasher and a gas cooker in the kitchen* (NOTE: also called a **stove**)

③ **cookie**
['kʊki] *noun*
(usually US) biscuit, a small flat hard sweet cake; *she bought a packet of cookies*; **chocolate chip cookie** = sweet biscuit made with little pieces of hard chocolate inside

③ **cooking**
['kʊkɪŋ] *noun*
(a) action of getting food ready to eat, especially by heating it; *he does the cooking, while his wife serves in the restaurant*; **cooking apple** = sour apple which can be cooked but not eaten raw
(b) particular way of preparing food; *the restaurant specializes in French provincial cooking*

④ **cookout**
['kʊkaʊt] *noun*
US meal or party where food is cooked out of doors; *we had a cookout for twenty guests*; *let's have a cookout in our back yard*; *they've been invited to a cookout*

③ **cool**
[kuːl]
1 *adjective*
(a) quite cold; *blow on your soup to make it cool*; *it was hot on deck but cool down below*; *wines should be stored in a cool place*; *it gets cool in the evenings in September*
(b) not enthusiastic; *I got a cool reception when I arrived half an hour late*; *the management was quite cool towards the proposal*
(c) calm; *the nurses remained cool and professional when dealing with all the accident victims* (NOTE: **cooler - coolest**)
2 *verb*
to make cool; to become cool; *she boiled the jam for several hours and then put it to one side to cool*
3 *noun*
(a) colder area which is pleasant; *after the heat of the town centre, it is nice to sit in the cool of the garden*
(b) *(informal)* state of being calm; *as soon as the reporters started to ask her questions she lost her cool*

③ **co-op**
['kɪʊɒp] *noun*
(informal) cooperative store; *we do all our shopping at the local co-op*

④ **cooperate**
[kɪʊˈɒpɪreɪt] *verb*
to cooperate with someone = to work with someone; *several governments are cooperating in the fight against international drug smuggling*

② **cooperation**
[kɪʊɒpɪˈreɪʃn] *noun*
action of working together with someone else; *the school is run with the cooperation of the local church*; *he wrote the book in cooperation with one of his students*

③ **cooperative**
[kɪʊˈɒprɪtɪv]
1 *adjective*
(a) working with the profits shared between the workers; *a cooperative farm*; *a cooperative store*
(b) helpful, willing to work with someone; *the bank manager was not at all cooperative when I asked for a loan*
2 *noun*
business which works on the basis that all profits are shared; *a workers' cooperative*

④ **coordinate**
1 *verb*
[kɪʊˈɔːdɪneɪt] to make people or things work together or fit in with each other; *his job is to coordinate with the work of the various relief agencies*; *the election campaign was coordinated by the party headquarters*
2 *noun*
[kɪʊˈɔːdɪnɪt] set of figures which fix a point on a map or graph; *what are the coordinates for that hill? I don't think it is marked on the map*; *draw the X - Y coordinates*

④ **coordination**
[kɪʊɔːdɪˈneɪʃn] *noun*
(a) action of coordinating people or things; *better coordination between departments would have allowed everyone to know what was happening*
(b) being able to move parts of your body at the same time properly; *she has excellent coordination for a little girl who is only two years old*

③ **cop**
[kɒp] *noun*
(informal) policeman; *he was stopped by a cop*; *when the cops came to arrest him he had disappeared*; *watch out! there's a cop coming*

② **cope**
[kɪʊp] *verb*
to cope with something = to manage to deal with something; *she can cope perfectly well on her own*; *we are trying to cope with a sudden mass of orders*

④ **copper**
['kɒpɪ] *noun*
(a) reddish metal which turns green when exposed to air; *copper is a good conductor of electricity*; *the end of the copper wire should be attached to the terminal* (NOTE: Chemical element: chemical symbol: **Cu**; atomic number: **29**)
(b) *(informal)* policeman; *watch out! there's a copper coming*
(c) small coin made of copper or other brown metal; *it only costs a few coppers*; *she was begging for any spare coppers*

① **copy**
['kɒpi]
1 *noun*
(a) something made to look the same as

something else; *this is an exact copy of the painting by Picasso*; **carbon copy** = copy made with carbon paper

(b) one book; one newspaper; *where's my copy of today's 'Times'?*; *I lent my old copy of Shakespeare to my brother and he never gave it back*; *can I borrow your copy of the telephone directory?*

(c) text written to be used in a newspaper or advertisement; *he sent in his copy three days late*; *we need more copy for this page* (NOTE: plural is **copies** in meanings (a) and (b))

2 *verb*

to make something which looks like something else; *to knit the pullover, just copy this pattern*; *I get very annoyed because he copies everything I do*; **copying machine** = a machine which copies

④ **copyright**

['kɒpɪraɪt] *noun*

an author's right to publish a book, put on a play, etc., and not to have it copied without permission; *who holds the copyright for the play?*; *she is being sued for breach of copyright*; **book which is in copyright** = book which is protected by the copyright laws; **book which is out of copyright** = book by a writer who has been dead for more than seventy years and which anyone can publish

④ **cord**

[kɔːd] *noun*

strong thin rope; *the box was tied with cord*; *in an emergency, pull the cord to stop the train*

③ **core**

[kɔː]

1 *noun*

central part; **apple core** = hard part in the middle of an apple, containing the seeds; *he threw the apple core into the lake*; **rotten to the core** = completely rotten; *the local police force is rotten to the core*; **to take a core sample** = to cut a long round sample of soil or rock for testing

2 *verb*

to cut out the central part of an apple, etc.; *peel and core the apples before putting them in the oven*

④ **cork**

[kɔːk]

1 *noun*

(a) piece of light wood from the bark of a tree, which closes wine bottles; *he pulled the cork out of the bottle*; *the little boat went up and down on the surface of the water like a cork*

(b) material made from the very light bark of a type of oak tree; *she placed little cork mats on the table to stop the wine glasses marking it*; **cork oak** = type of oak tree with thick light bark; *cork oaks are common in Spain and Portugal*

2 *verb*

to put a cork into a bottle; *when they had drunk half the bottle, she corked it up to use the following day*

③ **corn**

[kɔːn] *noun*

(a) cereal plants such as wheat, etc.; *a field of corn*

(b) in particular, a widely grown very tall cereal crop; **sweet corn** = sweet variety of corn, which you can eat as a vegetable; **corn cob** = head of corn with seeds; **corn on the cob** = a piece of corn, with seeds on it, boiled and served hot, with butter and salt

(c) hard painful lump of skin, usually on your foot, where something, such as a tight shoe, has rubbed it; *he has a corn on his little toe*

① **corner**

['kɔːnɪ]

1 *noun*

(a) place where two walls, sides or streets meet; *the bank is on the corner of London Road and New Street*; *put the plant in the corner of the room nearest the window*; *the number is in the top right-hand corner of the page*; *the motorbike went round the corner at top speed*; **to paint yourself into a corner** = to get yourself into a situation that you cannot get out of; **to turn the corner** = (i) to go round a corner; (ii) to get better after being ill or in difficulties; *as she turned the corner she saw the bus coming*; *he has been in bed for weeks, but he seems to have turned the corner*; **corner shop** = small general store in a town on a street corner; *I still use the local corner shop for newspapers and cigarettes*

(b) *(in games, such as football)* free kick taken from the corner of the field near the opponent's goal

2 *verb*

(a) to turn a corner; *this new model corners very well*

(b) **to corner the market** = to own most or all of the supply of a certain thing and so control the price; *the group tried to corner the market in silver*

④ **corporal**

['kɔːprɪl]

1 *adjective*

referring to the body; **corporal punishment** = punishment by beating someone; *corporal punishment is illegal in state schools*

2 *noun*

rank in the army below sergeant; *the major ordered the corporal to take down the flag* (NOTE: can be used with the surname: **Corporal Jones**)

② **corporate**

['kɔːpɪrɪt] *adjective*

referring to a body such as a company; *corporate responsibility rests with the whole management*; *corporate profits are down this year*; **corporate plan** = plan for a whole company

② **corporation**
[kɔːpɪˈreɪʃn] *noun*
(a) town council; *the corporation has contracted the refuse collection service to a private company*; *the corporation swimming pool is closed on Mondays*
(b) large firm; *working for a big corporation can pay better that working for a small family firm*; **corporation tax** = tax on profits made by companies

④ **corpse**
[kɔːps] *noun*
dead body; *after he had killed her he didn't know what to do with the corpse*

① **correct**
[kɪˈrekt]
1 *adjective*
right; without any mistakes; *can you tell me the correct time?*; *you have to give correct answers to all the questions if you want to win first prize*; *you are correct in thinking that the weather in Greece is hot*; *would it be correct to say that the shop has not made a profit for years?*
2 *verb*
to take away mistakes in something; *the boss had to correct the letter which his secretary had typed*; *you must try to correct your driving mistakes, or you will never pass the test*; *the computer keeps switching itself off - can you correct this fault?*

④ **correction**
[kɪˈrekʃn] *noun*
showing a mistake in something, making something correct; *he made a few small corrections to the letter*

② **correctly**
[kɪˈrektli] *adverb*
in a correct way; *you must answer all the questions correctly if you want to win the prize*

④ **correspond**
[kɒrɪˈspɒnd] *verb*
(a) **to correspond to** = to fit with; *the findings correspond to my own research*
(b) **to correspond with someone** = to write letters to someone; *she corresponded for years with this man living in New York whom she had never met*

④ **correspondence**
[kɒrɪˈspɒndɪns] *noun*
letters; *they had been carrying on a correspondence for years*; *she was told by her father to break off the correspondence*; **correspondence course** = lessons given by post; **business correspondence** = letters concerned with a business; **to be in correspondence with someone** = to write

letters to someone and receive letters back; *I have been in correspondence with the company about a refund but with no success*

④ **correspondent**
[kɒrɪˈspɒndɪnt] *noun*
(a) journalist who writes articles for newspapers or reports for TV or radio on a particular subject; *he is the Paris correspondent of the 'Telegraph'*; *the report comes from the BBC's correspondent in the area*; *a report from our football correspondent*
(b) person who writes letters; *a correspondent in Australia sent us an email*

④ **corresponding**
[kɒrɪˈspɒndɪŋ] *adjective*
which corresponds; *the approach of winter brings a corresponding rise in the number of people wanting to go on holiday to warm countries*

② **corridor**
[ˈkɒrɪdɔː] *noun*
long, narrow passage; *the ladies' room is straight ahead at the end of the corridor*; *there is an underground corridor to the next building*

④ **corrupt**
[kɪˈrʌpt]
1 *adjective*
(a) who is not honest, who takes bribes; *the Prime Minister promised to sack any officials who were found to be corrupt*
(b) (data on a computer disk) which is faulty; *he sent us a disk with corrupt data*
2 *verb*
(a) to make dishonest; *he was corrupted by his rich friends from college*; *'power corrupts, absolute power corrupts absolutely'*
(b) to make data faulty; *the data on this disk has been corrupted*

④ **corruption**
[kɪˈrʌpʃn] *noun*
(a) paying money or giving a favour to someone (usually an official) so that he does what you want; *government corruption is difficult to control*; *corruption in the civil service will be rooted out*
(b) making data faulty; *you have to watch out for corruption of data*

④ **cosmetic**
[kɒzˈmetɪk]
1 *adjective*
which improves someone's *or* something's appearance; *she uses a cosmetic cream to remove the lines round her eyes*; *the changes to the organization were purely cosmetic*; **cosmetic surgery** = surgery to improve the appearance of someone
2 *noun*
cosmetics = substances like skin cream, which improve your appearance; *my wife keeps all her cosmetics in a little bag*

① cost

[kɒst]

1 *noun*

(a) price which you have to pay for something; *what is the cost of a return ticket to London?*; *computer costs are falling each year*

(b) costs = expenses involved in a court case; **to pay costs** = to pay the expenses of a court case; *he lost his case and was ordered to pay costs*; **the judge awarded costs to the defendant** = the judge said that the defendant would not have to pay the cost of the case

2 *verb*

to have a price; *potatoes cost 20p a kilo*; *petrol seems to cost more all the time*; **what does it cost?** = how much is it?; **to cost the earth** = to be very expensive; *tropical fruit costs the earth in winter*; **to cost an arm and a leg** = to be very expensive; *don't buy your kitchen there - it'll cost you an arm and a leg*; *the repairs to his car cost him an arm and a leg*; *see also* FORTUNE, SMALL (NOTE: **costing - cost - has cost**)

④ costly

['kɒstli] *adjective*

very expensive; *our new car is not very costly to run*; **costly mistake** = mistake which results in a lot of money being spent; *telling them we would pay all their expenses was a costly mistake* (NOTE: **costlier - costliest**)

③ cost of living

['kɒst əv 'lɪvɪŋ] *noun*

money which has to be paid for food, heating, rent, etc.; *higher interest rates increase the cost of living*; **cost-of-living increase** = increase in salary to allow it to keep up with the increased cost of living; **cost-of-living index** = way of measuring the cost of living which is shown as a percentage increase on the figure for the previous year

④ costume

['kɒstjuːm] *noun*

(a) **bathing costume** *or* **swimming costume** = clothing worn by women or children when swimming; *bother! we forgot to bring the swimming costumes*

(b) set of clothes worn by an actor or actress in a play or film or on TV; *the costumes for 'Henry V' are magnificent*

(c) **national costume** = special clothes worn by people of a certain country; *they all came to the wedding in national costume*

④ cottage

['kɒtɪdʒ] *noun*

little house in the country; *we have a weekend cottage in the mountains*; *my mother lives in the little cottage next to the post office*; **cottage cheese** = type of moist white cheese; **cottage pie** = chopped meat cooked in a dish with a layer of potatoes on top (NOTE: also called **shepherd's pie**)

④ cotton

['kɒtɪn] *noun*

(a) thread from the soft seed heads of a tropical plant; *she put a new reel of cotton on the sewing machine*

(b) cloth made of cotton; *he was wearing a pair of cotton trousers*; *I bought some cotton material to make a skirt*

③ cotton wool

['kɒtɪn 'wʊl] *noun*

cotton fibres used to clean wounds, to clean the skin, to apply cream, etc.; *she dabbed the cut with cotton wool*; *the nurse put a pad of cotton wool over the graze*

④ couch

[kaʊtʃ] *noun*

long comfortable seat with a soft back; *she lay down on a couch in the lounge*; *(informal)* **couch potato** = person who lies on a sofa all day, watching TV or videos (NOTE: plural is **couches**)

③ cough

[kɒf]

1 *noun*

sending the air out of your lungs suddenly, for example when you are ill; *take some cough medicine if your cough is bad*; *he ought to see the doctor if his cough is no better*; *he gave a little cough to attract the waitress's attention*; **cough sweet** = sweet with medicine in it against coughs; *she always carries a tube of cough sweets in her bag*

2 *verb*

to send air out of your lungs suddenly because your throat hurts; *the smoke from the fire made everyone cough*; *people with flu go around coughing and sneezing*

① could

[kʊd] *verb used with other verbs*

(a) *(meaning 'was or would be able')* the old lady fell down and couldn't get up; *you could still catch the train if you ran*

(b) *(meaning 'was allowed')* the policeman said we could go into the house

(c) *(in asking)* could you pass me the salt, please?; could you shut the window?

(d) *(meaning 'might happen')* the new shopping centre could be finished by Christmas

(e) *(making a suggestion)* you could always try borrowing money from the bank (NOTE: negative is **could not**, usually **couldn't**; note also that could is the past of can; could is only used in front of other verbs and is not followed by the word **to**)

① council

['kaʊnsɪl] *noun*

(a) elected committee; **town council** = elected committee which runs a town; *the town council has decided to sell off the old swimming pool*; *you need to ask the council for planning permission*; **council flat** *or* **council house** = flat *or* house belonging to a town council which is let to a tenant; *they live in a council house, but are hoping to save up enough money to buy a flat*; *see also* SECURITY COUNCIL

(b) official group chosen to advise on a problem; **consumer council** = group representing the interests of consumers (NOTE: do not confuse with **counsel**)

Ⓒ **councillor**
['kaʊnsɪlɪ] *noun*

elected member of a town council; *the mayor is elected from among the councillors*; *the local paper has exposed corruption among the councillors* (NOTE: do not confuse with **counsellor**)

Ⓓ **counsel**
['kaʊnsl]
1 *noun*

lawyer, barrister; *counsel for the defence* or *defence counsel*; *counsel for the prosecution* or *prosecution counsel*; *GB* **Queen's Counsel (QC)** = senior lawyer; *she was represented by a leading QC* (NOTE: no plural; do not confuse with **counsel**)

2 *verb*

to advise; *she counselled us against buying the house* (NOTE: British English **counselling - counselled** but American English **counseling - counseled**)

Ⓓ **counsellor** *US* **counselor**
['kaʊnsɪlɪ] *noun*

adviser; *he was advised to see a counsellor about his drink problem*; **marriage counsellor** = person who gives advice to couples whose marriage is in difficulties (NOTE: do not confuse with **councillor**)

Ⓘ **count**
[kaʊnt]
1 *noun*

(a) action of counting or of adding; **to lose count** = to no longer have any idea of how many there are; *I tried to add up all the sales figures but lost count and had to start again*; *I've lost count of the number of times he's left his umbrella on the train*

(b) adding up the votes after an election; *the candidates paced up and down during the count*

(c) large amount of something, calculated in a scientific way; *today there is a high pollution count*

(d) accusation, charge read out against someone in court; *she was found guilty on two counts of theft*

2 *verb*

(a) to say numbers in order (1, 2, 3, 4, etc.); *she's only two and she can count up to ten*; *count to five and then start running*; **to count backwards** = to say numbers in the opposite order (9, 8, 7, 6, etc.)

(b) to find out a total; *did you count how many books there are in the library?*; *he counted up the sales for the twelve months*

(c) to include when finding out a total; *there were sixty people in the boat if you count the children*; *did you count my trip to New York as part of my expenses?*; **not counting** = not including; *there are three of us, not counting the baby*; *we have three computers, not counting the old ones that don't work any more*

(d) to be important; *your appearance counts for a lot in an interview; every little bit of energy saved counts*

Ⓒ **counter**
['kaʊntɪ]
1 *noun*

(a) long flat surface in a shop for displaying goods, or in a bank for placing money; *she put her bag down on the counter and took out her cheque book*; *the cheese counter is over there*; **bargain counter** = counter where things are sold cheaply; **ticket counter** = place where tickets are sold; **sold over the counter** = sold without a prescription; *some drugs are sold over the counter, but for most you need a prescription*

(b) small round disc used in games; *you've thrown a six - you can move your counter six places*; *she placed a pile of counters on the board*

2 *verb*

to reply in an opposing way; *he accused her of theft and she countered with an accusation of sexual harassment*

Ⓓ **counterpart**
['kaʊntɪpɑːt] *noun*

person who has a similar job or who is in a similar situation; *the Foreign Secretary had talks with his French counterpart*; **John is my counterpart at Smith's** = John has the same job at Smith's as I have here

Ⓒ **count on**
['kaʊnt 'ɒn] *verb*

to be sure that someone will do something; *can I count on you to help wash the dishes?*; *don't count on having fine weather for the cricket match*

Ⓘ **country**
['kʌntri] *noun*

(a) land which is separate and governs itself; *the countries of the EU*; *some African countries voted against the plan* (NOTE: plural in this meaning is **countries**)

(b) land which is not the town; *he lives in the country*; *we went walking in the hill country*; *road travel is difficult in country areas* (NOTE: no plural in this meaning)

(c) **country music** or **country and western** = style of music popular in the south-eastern United States, especially Tennessee; *she's the queen of the country and western*

② **countryside**

['kʌntrısaıd] *noun*

land away from towns, with fields, woods, etc.; *the beautiful English countryside in spring; the countryside is in danger of being covered in new houses* (NOTE: no plural)

① **county**

['kaʊntı] *noun*

administrative district; *the southern counties of England; they come from County Down, in Northern Ireland;* **county court** = court which hears minor civil cases; **county town** = main town of a county, where the administrative offices are; *Dorchester is the county town of Dorset* (NOTE: plural is **counties**)

④ **coup**

[kuː] *noun*

(a) the overthrow of a government by force; *the army took over after yesterday's coup; the officers who planned the failed coup were all executed*

(b) great success, successful move; *getting the Minister of Education to open the school exhibition was a coup for the organizers*

① **couple**

['kʌpl]

1 *noun*

(a) two things together; **a couple of** = (i) two; (ii) a few; *I have a couple of jobs for you to do; can you move the chairs a couple of metres to the left?; do you mind waiting a couple of minutes while I make a phone call?; the film lasted a couple of hours*

(b) two people together; *they are a charming couple; several couples strolled past hand in hand;* **married couple** = husband and wife

2 *verb*

(a) to link; *high tides coupled with strong winds caused flooding along the coast*

(b) to join two machines together; *couple the trailer to the back of the truck*

④ **coupon**

['kuːpɒn] *noun*

piece of paper which is used in place of money or in place of a ticket; *cut out the six coupons from the paper and send them to this address to receive your free travel bag; collect all seven coupons and cross the Channel for £1!;* **gift coupon** = coupon from a store which is given as a gift and which must be exchanged in that store

④ **courage**

['kʌrıdʒ] *noun*

being brave when in a dangerous situation; *she showed great courage in attacking the burglar* (NOTE: no plural)

① **course**

[kɔːs] *noun*

(a) **in the course of** = during; *he's got much richer in the course of the last few years*

(b) series of lessons; *I'm taking a maths course; she's going on a painting course; she has finished her computing course; the hotel offers weekend courses in art*

(c) series of treatments, medicines, etc; *he's taking a course of antibiotics*

(d) separate part of a meal; *a five-course meal; the first course is soup, and then you can have either fish or roast lamb*

(e) **golf course** = area of land specially designed for playing golf; *there is a golf course near the hotel*

◊ **in due course**

[ın 'djuː 'kɔːs]

after a certain amount of time; *if you study for several years at college, in due course you will get a degree; put a coin in the slot and in due course the machine will produce a ticket*

◊ **of course**

[ɒf 'kɔːs]

(a) *(used to say 'yes' or 'no' more strongly)* are *you coming with us? - of course I am!; do you want to lose all your money? - of course not!*

(b) naturally; *he is rich, so of course he lives in a big house*

① **court**

[kɔːt]

1 *noun*

(a) tribunal where a judge tries criminals, sometimes with a jury; *the court was packed for the opening of the murder trial; please tell the court what you saw when you opened the door; the defendant was in court for three hours;* **court case** = legal action or trial; *the court case is expected to last two weeks;* **to take someone to court** = to tell someone to appear in court to settle an argument

(b) area where a game of tennis, basketball, etc., is played; *the tennis courts are behind the hotel;* **to be on court** = to be playing tennis; *they were on court for over three hours;* **Centre Court** = the main tennis court at Wimbledon

(c) group of people living round a king or queen; *the people at court were very cold towards the young princess; it was dangerous to be a pretty young girl at the court of Henry VIII*

2 *verb*

(a) *(old)* to try to persuade a woman to marry you; *King Henry courted Anne Boleyn for some months*

(b) to be often together before getting married; *do you remember when we were courting and you took me to see the sun setting over the sea at Brighton?; they've been courting for three years, and there are still no signs of them getting married*

(c) to try to get someone to support you; *he has been courting the shareholders to win their approval for the scheme*

(d) **to court disaster** = to risk disaster happening; *you are courting disaster if you try to drive a sports car without a licence*

④ **courtesy**
['kɜːtɪsi] *noun*
(a) being polite, having good manners; *the hotel staff showed us every courtesy*; *she might have had the courtesy to apologize*; *children should show some courtesy towards their grandparents*
(b) (by) courtesy of = as a gift from; with the kind permission of; *a box of chocolates by courtesy of the management*; *he arrived home two hours late, courtesy of the train service*; **courtesy bus** *or* **car** *or* **coach** = bus *or* car *or* coach which is provided for people free of charge as a service; *a courtesy coach will pick you up at the airport*; *the garage lent me a courtesy car to use while mine was being repaired*

④ **courtroom**
['kɔːtrum] *noun*
room where a judge presides over a trial; *the jury left the courtroom to decide their verdict*

③ **cousin**
['kʌzɪn] *noun*
son or daughter of your uncle or aunt; *our cousins from Canada are coming to stay with us for Christmas*; *we didn't have a Christmas card from Cousin Charles this year*

① **cover**
['kʌvɪ]
1 *noun*
(a) thing put over something to keep it clean, etc.; *keep a cover over your computer when you are not using it*; *put a cover over the meat to keep the flies off*
(b) front and back of a book, magazine, etc.; *she read the book from cover to cover*
(c) place where you can hide or shelter; *they ran for cover when it started to rain*; **under cover** = under a roof, not in the open air; *if it rains the meal will be served under cover*; **under cover of night** *or* **of darkness** = at night, when everything is hidden; *they crept out of the city under cover of darkness*; *the Marines attacked under cover of night*; **to take cover** = to shelter; *it started to rain and they took cover under a tree*; *when the robbers started shooting, the policeman took cover behind a wall*
(d) *(in a restaurant)* **cover charge** = charge per person in addition to the charge for food; *there is a £3.00 cover charge*
(e) envelope; **to send something under separate cover** = in a separate envelope; **to send a magazine under plain cover** = in an ordinary envelope with no company name printed on it
2 *verb*
(a) to put something over something to keep it clean, etc.; *you should cover the furniture with sheets before you start painting the ceiling*
(b) to hide something; *he covered the hole in the ground with leaves*; *she covered her face with her hands*

(c) to provide enough money to pay for something; *the damage was covered by the insurance*; *the prize covers all the costs of the holiday*
(d) to write a report on an event for a newspaper, radio programme, etc.; *the journalists covering the story were briefed by the police*
(e) to travel a certain distance; *they made good progress, covering twenty miles a day*

④ **coverage**
['kʌvrɪdʒ] *noun*
press coverage or **media coverage** = amount of space or time given to an event in newspapers or on TV; *the company had good media coverage for the launch of its new car*; *coverage of Wimbledon continues on BBC2* (NOTE: no plural)

④ **covering**
['kʌvrɪŋ] *noun*
(a) thing which covers; *there was a light covering of snow*; *you need a really hard floor covering in a kitchen*
(b) covering letter = letter explaining what is enclosed with it; *further details of the job are given in the covering letter*

③ **cover note**
['kʌvɪ 'nɪut] *noun*
letter giving agreement for an insurance sent before the policy is issued; *this cover note is valid until the day you receive your policy*

② **cow**
[kau] *noun*
(a) large female farm animal, kept to give milk; *a field of cows*; *the farmer was milking a cow*; *(informal)* **until the cows come home** = for a very long time; *you can wait until the cows come home before getting paid*
(b) female of other animals; *a cow elephant*; *a cow whale* (NOTE: the meat from a cow is **beef**)

③ **cowboy**
['kaubɔɪ] *noun*
(a) man who looks after cows in the west of the USA; **a cowboy film** = film about the west of the USA in the late 19th century; **a cowboy hat** = large wide-brimmed hat worn by cowboys
(b) *(informal)* workman who does bad work and charges a high price; *the people we got in to paint the house were a bunch of cowboys*

③ **crack**
[kræk]
1 *noun*
(a) sharp sound; *the crack of a branch behind her made her turn round*
(b) long thin break in something hard; *a crack appeared in the ceiling*; *her ring fell down a crack in the pavement*; *the field is so dry it is full of cracks*; **at (the) crack of dawn** = as soon as it starts to be light; *if we want to miss the traffic we must set off at (the) crack of dawn*
(c) *(informal)* **to have a crack at something** = to try to do something; *I've never tried sailing before but I'm willing to have a crack at it*

(d) *(informal)* joke; *she made a nasty crack about his bald patch*

2 *verb*

(a) to make a sharp sound; *a piece of wood cracked as he stepped on it*

(b) to make a long thin break in something; *the stone cracked the glass*

(c) to crack jokes = to tell jokes; *he spent the entire lunch break cracking jokes*

(d) *(informal)* **get cracking!** = get going!, start now!; *if you don't get cracking you'll never finish on time*

(e) to find out how to read a secret code; *they spent months trying to crack the enemy codes*

④ **cracker**
['krækɪ] *noun*

(a) dry biscuit made of flour and water; *after the main course they served cheese and crackers*

(b) (Christmas) cracker = colourful paper tube which makes a little bang when it is pulled, given at Christmas parties; *we had mince pies and pulled crackers*; *what did you get in your cracker? - a paper hat and a puzzle*

> COMMENT: Christmas crackers have little presents inside them; usually folded paper hats, small plastic toys, and pieces of paper with bad jokes written on them

④ **craft**
[krɑ:ft] *noun*

(a) using skills to make something by hand; *he learnt the craft of furniture-making as a boy*; *we went to a demonstration of traditional country crafts*

(b) *(formal)* ship; *his little craft slipped out of harbour*; *all sizes of craft took part in the rescue* (NOTE: plural in this meaning is **craft**)

③ **crafty**
['krɑ:fti] *adjective*

planning something in secret; *I could tell from the crafty look on her face that she was going to play a trick on me*; *I have a crafty plan for making a lot of money* (NOTE: **craftier - craftiest**)

④ **crane**
[kreɪn]

1 *noun*

tall metal construction for lifting heavy weights; *the container slipped as the crane was lifting it onto the ship*; *they had to hire a crane to get the piano into the upstairs room*

2 *verb*

to crane your neck = to stretch your neck; *he craned his neck to try to see the soldiers*

③ **crash**
[kræʃ]

1 *noun*

(a) accident where cars, planes, etc., are damaged; *he was killed in a train crash*; *none of the passengers were hurt in the coach crash*; *his car was badly damaged in the crash*; **crash barrier** = strong fence by the side of a road to prevent cars from running off the road; **crash helmet** = hard hat worn by motorcyclists, etc.; *it is illegal to ride a motorbike without a crash helmet*

(b) loud noise when something falls over; *the ladder fell down with a crash*; *he said he would go and do the washing up, and then there was a crash in the kitchen*

(c) collapse of a company; *he lost all his savings in the bank crash*

(d) complete breakdown of a computer (NOTE: plural is **crashes)**

2 *verb*

(a) *(of vehicles)* to hit something and be damaged; *the bus crashed into a wall*; *the plane crashed six kilometres from the airport*

(b) to move, making a loud noise; *the wall came crashing down*; *the ladder crashed onto the floor*

(c) *(of a company)* to collapse; *he lost all his savings when the bank crashed*

(d) *(of a computer)* to stop working; *the hard disk has crashed but we think the data can be saved*

3 *adjective*

crash course = course of rapid, hard study; *he took a crash course in German*

④ **crawl**
[krɔ:l]

1 *noun*

very slow speed; *the traffic on the motorway was reduced to a crawl* (NOTE: no plural)

2 *verb*

(a) to move around on your hands and knees; *the baby has just started to crawl*

(b) to go along slowly; *the traffic was crawling along*

(c) to be crawling with = to be covered with (insects, etc.); *the place was crawling with ants*; *the streets were crawling with police*

③ **crazy**
['kreɪzi] *adjective*

(a) mad; *it was a crazy idea to go mountain climbing in beach shoes*; **to drive someone crazy** = to have an effect on someone so that they become very annoyed; *the noise is driving me crazy*; *all this work is driving her crazy*; **crazy about** = very enthusiastic about; *he's crazy about her*; *she's crazy about Indian dancing*

(b) crazy paving = odd-shaped paving stones (NOTE: **crazier - craziest)**

④ **cream**
[kri:m]

1 *noun*

(a) top part of milk, full of fat; *I like strawberries and cream*; **single cream** = liquid cream, with a lower fat content; **double cream** = thick cream with a high fat content; **whipped cream** = cream, beaten until it is stiff, flavoured with sugar; **cream cake** = any cake or pastry filled with whipped cream; **cream cheese** = rich soft cheese; **cream tea** = afternoon tea, with cakes, thick cream and jam

(b) soft stuff for cleaning, oiling, etc.; *face cream*; *shaving cream*; *shoe cream*

(c) the top few; *the cream of the medical students*

2 *adjective*

coloured like cream, a very pale brown; *he was wearing a cream shirt*; *do you like our new cream carpet?*

① **create**
[krɪ'eɪt] *verb*
to make, to invent; *do you believe that God created the world?*; *a government scheme which aims at creating new jobs for young people*

① **creation**
[krɪ'eɪʃn] *noun*
(a) thing which has been made; *for dessert they served some sort of chocolate and cream creation*; *the model appeared wearing a pink and blue creation*

(b) act of creating; *the aim is the creation of new jobs for young unemployed people*; **job creation scheme** = government scheme to encourage new jobs for the unemployed

③ **creative**
[krɪ'eɪtɪv] *adjective*
full of ideas; always making something; *he's a very creative child*

④ **creator**
[krɪ'eɪtə] *noun*
person who makes or invents something; *he's the creator of the radio which doesn't use electric power*

③ **creature**
['kriːtʃɪ] *noun*
(a) *(formal)* animal; *lift any stone and you'll find all sorts of little creatures underneath*; *we try not to harm any living creature*; *some sea creatures live in holes in the sand*

(b) **creature comforts** = things which make life comfortable for you; *he likes his little creature comforts - his pipe and his glass of beer*

④ **credible**
['kredɪbl] *adjective*
which can be believed; *the jury did not find the witnesses' stories at all credible*; *the plot of the film is not entirely credible*

② **credit**
['kredɪt]
1 *noun*
(a) praise for something which is well deserved; *the professor took all the credit for the invention*; *to his credit, he owned up immediately*; **it does you credit** = you must be proud of it; *your daughter does you both credit*; **he's a credit to the school** = he's done well and this gives honour to the school where he studied

(b) time given to pay; *we give customers six months' credit with no interest to pay*; **credit check** = check on a customer's credit rating; **credit controller** = member of staff whose job is to try to get payment of invoices; **on credit** = without paying immediately; *we bought the dining room furniture on credit*

(c) side of an account showing money in hand or which is owed to you; *we paid in £100 to the credit of Mr Smith*; **credit note** = note showing that money is owed; *she took the jumper back to the shop and got a credit note*; *the company sent the wrong items and had to issue a credit note*

(d) **credits** = list of people who helped to make a film, TV programme, etc.; *she sued the company when her name did not appear in the credits*

2 *verb*
(a) **to credit someone with** = to say that someone has done something good; *he has been credited with making the company profitable again*

(b) to believe; *I find that hard to credit*; *would you credit it? - she's got married again!*

(c) to pay money into an account; *to credit an account with £100* or *to credit £100 to an account*

④ **credit card**
['kredɪt 'kɑːd] *noun*
plastic card which allows you to borrow money and to buy goods without paying for them immediately; *how do you want to pay - cash, cheque or credit card?*; *I bought a fridge and put it on my credit card*

② **creditor**
['kredɪtɪ] *noun*
person who is owed money; *he is trying to pay off his creditors*

④ **creep**
[kriːp]
1 *verb*
(a) to move around quietly; *they crept softly down the stairs*; **to creep up on someone** = to come up close behind someone without making any noise; *the idea is to creep up on the gang as they are loading the stolen goods into the lorry*

(b) to go along slowly; *the traffic was creeping along the motorway because of the fog* (NOTE: **creeping - crept** [krept])

2 *noun*
(a) *(informal)* unpleasant person who does things in secret

(b) **to give someone the creeps** = to make someone shiver with disgust; *I don't like that bank manager - he gives me the creeps*

③ **crew**
[kruː] *noun*
people who work on a boat, aircraft, bus, etc.; *the helicopter rescued the crew of the sinking ship*; *the plane was carrying 125 passengers and a crew of 6*; **stage crew** = workers who

move things around on a theatre stage; *the stage crew worked all night to get the set ready for the following morning*

① **cricket**
['krɪkɪt] *noun*

(a) game played between two teams of eleven players using bats and a hard ball; *we haven't played much cricket this year - the weather has been too bad*; *we are going to a cricket match this afternoon*; *when did we last beat the Australians at cricket?*

(b) *(informal)* **it's not cricket** = it is not fair

COMMENT: the game is played between two teams of eleven players with a wicket made up of three sticks at either end of a 22-yard pitch. The aim is for each team to score runs by hitting a ball with a wooden bat while the other team tries to get them out. One team bats, using two batsmen at a time (one at either end of the pitch) and a run is scored when they change ends. All 11 members of the opposing team stand in the field and try to prevent the batsmen scoring runs. One member of the fielding side bowls the ball at the batsman and a different bowler takes over from the opposite end after six balls (or an 'over') have been bowled. Matches start at 11.30 in the morning and continue until the early evening with breaks for lunch and tea; most matches go on for several days

① **cried, cries**
[kraɪd or kraɪz]
see CRY

② **crime**
[kraɪm] *noun*

illegal act or acts; *we must try to reduce the levels of crime in the inner cities*; *the government is trying to deal with the problem of teenage crime* or *with the teenage crime problem*; *more crimes are committed at night than during the day*

② **criminal**
['krɪmɪnl]

1 *adjective*

referring to illegal acts; *he has a criminal record*; *stealing is a criminal offence*; *the criminal justice system*; **Criminal Investigation Department (CID)** = department of the police which investigates serious crimes; **criminal law** = laws which deal with crimes against the law of the land, which are punished by the state (NOTE: the opposite, actions relating to people's rights and freedoms, and to agreements between individuals, is **civil law**)

2 *noun*

person who commits a crime; *the police think two well-known criminals did it*

④ **cripple**
['krɪpl]

1 *noun*

person who is disabled and has difficulty in walking; *cripples sat outside the hotel, begging for money from tourists*

2 *verb*

(a) to make someone disabled; *he was crippled in a mining accident*

(b) to prevent something from working; *the explosion crippled the tanker and she drifted towards the rocks*; *the bus and rail strike has crippled the capital's transport system*

② **crisis**
['kraɪsɪs] *noun*

serious situation where decisions have to be taken quickly; *an international crisis*; *a banking crisis*; **to take crisis measures** = to take measures rapidly to stop a crisis developing; *the government had to take crisis measures to stop the collapse of the currency* (NOTE: plural is **crises** ['kraɪsiːz])

④ **crisp**
[krɪsp]

1 *adjective*

(a) hard, which can be broken into pieces easily; *these biscuits are not crisp any more, they have gone soft*; *pick an apple off the tree, they're really very crisp*

(b) sharp and cold; *it was a beautiful crisp morning, with snow on the mountains*; *she could see her breath in the crisp mountain air* (NOTE: **crisper - crispest**)

2 *noun*

(potato) crisps = slices of potato fried until they are dry and break easily; *we always take packets of crisps with us on picnics* (NOTE: American English for these is **chips**)

② **criterion**
[kraɪ'tɪəriən] *noun*

standard by which things are judged; *does the candidate satisfy all our criteria?*; *this is not a reliable criterion on which to base our decision* (NOTE: plural is **criteria**)

③ **critic**
['krɪtɪk] *noun*

(a) person who examines something and comments on it, especially a person who writes comments on new plays and films for a newspaper; *she's the TV critic of the 'Times'*; *the film was praised by all the critics*

(b) person who says that something is bad or wrong; *the chairman tried to answer his critics at the meeting*

② **critical**
['krɪtɪkl] *adjective*

(a) dangerous and difficult; *with the enemy attacking on all sides, our position was becoming critical*

(b) extremely important; *he made a critical decision to break off the negotiations*; *critical relief supplies have been held up at customs*

(c) very serious; *the driver of the car was in a critical condition last night; the hospital said that her condition was critical; after the accident, she was on the critical list for some hours*

(d) which criticizes; *the report was highly critical of the minister*

② **criticism**
['krɪtɪsɪzm] *noun*
(a) comment; *if you have any constructive criticisms to make, I shall be glad to hear them*; **literary criticism** = criticism of works of literature
(b) comment which criticizes; *there was a lot of criticism of the government's plan*

③ **criticize**
['krɪtɪsaɪz] *verb*
to say that something *or* someone is bad or wrong; *she criticized the sales assistant for not being polite; the design of the new car has been criticized*

④ **crook**
[krʊk] *noun*
dishonest person, a criminal; *I don't trust the government - they're a bunch of crooks; that secondhand car dealer is a bit of a crook*

④ **crooked**
['krʊkɪd] *adjective*
(a) bent, not straight; *that picture is crooked; I don't think the wallpaper has been put on straight - it looks crooked to me*
(b) *(informal)* dishonest; *the police chief promised to remove any crooked officers in his force*

③ **crop**
[krɒp]
1 *noun*
plants, such as vegetables or cereals, grown for food; *the bad weather has set the crops back by three weeks; we had a wonderful crop of potatoes or a wonderful potato crop this year; see also* GENETICALLY
2 *verb*
(a) to cut short; *the photograph had to be cropped to fit the space on the page*
(b) *(of plant)* to have fruit; *the pear trees cropped heavily this year* (NOTE: **cropping - cropped**)

③ **crop up**
['krɒp 'ʌp] *verb*
to happen suddenly; *get in touch if any problem should crop up; a little difficulty has cropped up - we've lost the key to the safe*

② **cross**
[krɒs]
1 *adjective*
(a) angry, annoyed; *the teacher will be cross with you for missing school; don't be cross - the children were only trying to help*
(b) opposed; *they were at cross purposes =* they were in total disagreement
2 *noun*

(a) shape made where one line goes straight across another; *write your name where I have put a cross; there is a cross on the top of the church tower*; **the Red Cross** = international organization which provides medical help; *Red Cross officials have been allowed into the war zone*
(b) breed of plant or animal which comes from two different varieties; *a cross between two types of cattle* (NOTE: plural is **crosses**)
3 *verb*
(a) to go across to the other side; *she just crossed the road without looking to see if there was any traffic coming; he crossed the lake in a small boat; the road crosses the railway line about 10km from here; Concorde only takes three hours to cross the Atlantic*
(b) to put one thing across another; *he crossed his arms and looked annoyed; she sat down and crossed her legs*; **crossed line** = fault on a telephone line, where you can hear a conversation from another line; *I can't hear you properly - we've got a crossed line; see also* FINGER
(c) to breed a new animal or plant, etc., from two varieties; *he crossed two strains of rice to produce a variety which is resistant to disease*

③ **crossing**
['krɒsɪŋ] *noun*
(a) action of going across to the other side of an area of water; *how long is the crossing from England to Germany?*; **they had a rough crossing** = the sea was rough when they travelled
(b) place where you go across safely; *cars have to take care at the railway crossing*; **level crossing** *US* **grade crossing** = place where a road crosses a railway line without a bridge or tunnel; *the level crossing gates opened when the train had passed*; **zebra crossing** = place marked with black and white lines where you can walk across a road; *it's safer to use a zebra crossing when you're crossing a main road*

③ **cross off** *or* **cross out**
['krɒs 'ɒf or 'krɒs 'aʊt] *verb*
to draw a line through something which has been written to show that it should not be there; *he's ill, so you can cross him off the list for the party; I had difficulty reading her letter - she'd crossed out so many words; she crossed out £250 and put in £500*

④ **crossroads**
['krɒsrɪʊdz] *noun*
place where one road crosses another; *turn right at the next crossroads*

④ **crossword**
['krɒsw3:d] *noun*
puzzle where small squares have to be filled with letters to spell words; *I can't do today's crossword - it's too hard; he finished the crossword in 25 minutes*

② **crowd**
[kraʊd]
1 *noun*

mass of people; *she was cut off from her friends by a crowd of school children*; *after the election, the crowds were dancing in the streets*; *someone in the crowd threw an egg at the speaker on the platform*; *if you travel early, you will avoid the crowds of Christmas shoppers*

2 *verb*

to group together; *all the rugby fans crowded into the pub*; *the children were crowding round their teacher*

② **crowded**
['kraʊdɪd] *adjective*

with a large number of people; *the town gets very crowded during the holiday season*; *the stands were crowded before the game started*

③ **crown**
[kraʊn]
1 *noun*

(a) gold hat decorated with jewels, worn by an emperor, king, queen, etc.; *the bishop placed the crown on the head of the young king*; *the queen received the ambassadors wearing a heavy gold crown*

(b) *(in Britain)* king or queen representing the state; *in England, all swans belong to the crown*; *the Crown Jewels are kept in the Tower of London*; **counsel for the Crown** = lawyer representing the state in a trial; *the Crown's case was that the defendant passed secrets to an enemy*

(c) false top attached to a broken tooth; *I'm going to the dentist to have a crown fitted*

2 *verb*

(a) to make someone king, queen, emperor, etc., by placing a crown on his or her head; *the Queen was crowned in Westminster Abbey*

(b) to be a splendid end to something; *to crown it all, he won the lottery*

(c) to attach a false top to a broken tooth; *the dentist said that the tooth was so badly broken that he would have to crown it instead of trying to fill it*

② **crucial**
['kruːʃl] *adjective*

extremely important; *it is crucial that the story be kept out of the papers*

④ **crude**
[kruːd]
1 *adjective*

(a) not processed; *beaches were covered in crude oil from the tanker*

(b) rude, with no manners; *he made some crude gestures at the fans* (NOTE: cruder - crudest)

2 *noun*

raw oil, taken from the ground; *the price of Arabian crude has fallen*

③ **cruel**
['kruːl] *adjective*

who causes pain, who makes a person or animal suffer; *you must not be cruel to your new puppy*; *it was cruel of him to mention her weight problem* (NOTE: crueller - cruellest but American spelling is crueler - cruelest)

④ **cruelty**
['kruːlti] *noun*

act of being cruel; *the zoo keeper was accused of cruelty to animals*; *cases of cruelty to children are increasing*; **mental cruelty** = being cruel to someone in a way that does not hurt them physically

④ **cruise**
[kruːz]
1 *noun*

long voyage in a ship calling at different places; *when he retired he went on a cruise round the Mediterranean*

2 *verb*

(a) to go in a boat from place to place; *they spent May cruising in the Mediterranean*; *the ship cruised from island to island*

(b) to travel at an even speed; *the car cruises very comfortably at 160 kilometres an hour*

(c) to win without much difficulty; *he cruised to victory in the race*

④ **crunch**
[krʌntʃ]
1 *noun*

(a) sound of something dry being crushed; *the crunch of dry snow under his boots*

(b) *(informal)* crisis point; *the crunch will come when the firm has no cash to pay the wages*; **if it comes to the crunch** = if crisis point is reached; *when it came to the crunch, the other side backed down*

2 *verb*

(a) to crush something dry; *the snow crunched under his boots*

(b) to chew something hard which makes a noise when you are eating; *she was crunching an apple when the phone rang*

④ **crush**
[krʌʃ]
1 *verb*

(a) to press flat; *she was crushed against the wall by the car*; *crush a piece of garlic and add it to the soup*

(b) to end completely; *government troops crushed the student rebellion*; *all her hopes of getting a better job were crushed by the report of the interview board*

2 *noun*

(a) mass of people; *she was hurt in the crush of people trying to get to the exit*; *he lost his case in the crush on the train*; **crush barriers** = metal fences which are put up to control crowds; *the fans simply climbed over the crush barriers to get at the pop group's car*

(b) *(informal)* **to have a crush on someone** = to have a feeling of love for someone you do not know very well; *she had a crush on her tennis coach*

④ **crust**
[krʌst] *noun*
hard outside layer of bread, the earth, etc.; *you can cut the crusts off the sandwiches*; *the earth's crust is over 30km thick*

① **cry**
[kraɪ]
1 *noun*
(a) loud shout; *no one heard her cries for help*
(b) sharp sound made by a bird or animal; *the cry of the birds overhead*; *we could hear the cries of monkeys in the trees* (NOTE: plural is **cries**)
2 *verb*
(a) to have tears coming out of your eyes; *the baby cried when her mother took away her toys*; *cutting up onions makes me cry*; *many people were crying when they left the cinema*; *(informal)* **to cry over spilt milk** = to be upset because of something which you couldn't prevent; *it's no use crying over spilt milk - what's happened has happened*
(b) *(formal)* to call out; *'hello there', she cried*

④ **crystal**
['krɪstl] *noun*
(a) solid chemical substance with a regular shape; *the salt formed crystals at the bottom of the jar*
(b) very clear bright glass; *a crystal wine glass*; **crystal clear** = very clear and simple to understand; *I want to make this crystal clear: anyone who gets into trouble with the police will be sent home immediately*

④ **cube**
[kjuːb]
1 *noun*
(a) shape where all six sides are square and join each other at right angles; *the design for the library is nothing more than a series of cubes*
(b) piece of something shaped like a cube; *he put two cubes of sugar in his tea*; *put the ice cubes in the glasses and then add orange juice*
(c) *(mathematics)* the result when a number is multiplied by itself twice; *27 is the cube of 3*; **cube root of a number** = number which when multiplied twice by itself will equal the number; *the cube root of 1728 is 12 (12 x 12 x 12 = 1728)*
2 *verb*
(a) to cut into little cubes; *wash, peel and then cube the potatoes*
(b) to multiply a number twice by itself; *if you cube 6 the result is 216 (6 x 6 x 6)*

③ **cubic**
['kjuːbɪk] *adjective*
measured in volume by multiplying length, depth and width; *the packing case holds six*

cubic metres (NOTE: cubic is written in figures as sup3 **6msup3=** six cubic metres; **10ftsup3=** ten cubic feet)

④ **cucumber**
['kjuːkʌmbɪ] *noun*
long dark green vegetable used in salads; *we had cucumber sandwiches for tea*; *(informal)* **as cool as a cucumber** = very calm and relaxed; *he walked out of the prison as cool as a cucumber*

④ **cue**
[kjuː] *noun*
(a) *(in a play)* words after which you have to speak or act; *he missed his cue and had to be prompted*; *the sound of the gun is your cue to rush onto the stage screaming*; **to take your cue from someone** = to do as someone does; *watch the managing director during the negotiations and take your cue from him*
(b) long stick for playing billiards or snooker; *before playing his shot, he put some chalk on the tip of his cue*; **cue ball** = the white ball which a snooker player hits with his cue (NOTE: do not confuse with **queue**)

④ **cult**
[kʌlt] *noun*
small religious group; *I'm worried about my daughter - she left joined a cult two years ago and we haven't heard from her since*; **cult hero** = person who is admired by a group

④ **cultivate**
['kʌltɪveɪt] *verb*
(a) to dig and water the land to grow plants; *fields are cultivated in early spring, ready for sowing seeds*
(b) to grow plants; *this field is used to cultivate new strains of wheat*

④ **cultivated**
['kʌltɪveɪtɪd] *adjective*
(a) who has been well educated in music, art, literature, etc.; *the new head teacher is a really cultivated person*
(b) *(land)* prepared on which crops are grown; *from the air, the cultivated fields were a pattern of brown and green*

④ **cultivation**
[kʌltɪ'veɪʃn] *noun*
(a) act of cultivating land or plants; *the weather can affect the cultivation of soft fruit*; **land under cultivation** = land which is being cultivated; *he has sixty acres under cultivation*
(b) good education; *his lack of cultivation was apparent as soon as he began to speak*

② **cultural**
['kʌltʃɪrl] *adjective*
referring to culture; *a French cultural delegation visited the exhibition*; *his cultural interests are very wide-ranging - from Mexican art to 12th century Greek paintings*

① **culture**
['kʌltʃɪ] *noun*
(a) a country's civilization, including music, art, literature, etc.; *he is taking a course in Russian*

culture; *is a TV in every home really the peak of western culture?*; **culture shock** = shock which you feel when moving from one type of society to another which is very different; *going from California to live with hill tribes in India was something of a culture shock*

(b) cultivation of plants; *the culture of some greenhouse plants must be done in warm damp conditions*

(c) bacteria grown in a laboratory; *the first part of the experiment is to grow a culture in the lab*

① **cup**
[kʌp] *noun*

(a) small bowl with a handle, used for drinking tea, coffee, etc.; *she put out a cup and saucer for everyone*; **a tea cup** = a large cup for drinking tea; **a coffee cup** = a small cup for drinking coffee

(b) liquid in a cup; *he drank two cups of coffee*; *can I have a cup of tea?*; **to make a cup of tea** = to prepare tea, usually in a pot; *I'll make you all a cup of tea*; *(informal)* **it's not my cup of tea** = it's not something I like very much; *modern art isn't really my cup of tea*

(c) tall silver bowl given as a prize for winning a competition; *he has won three cups for golf*; **cup final** = last game in a football or rugby competition, where the winning side is given the cup; *the winners of the two semi-finals will meet in the cup final on May 4th*; **cup tie** = football or rugby game where the winning side will go on to the next round of the competition; *our star player will miss the cup tie because of injury*

① **cupboard**
['kɪbɪd] *noun*

piece of furniture with shelves and doors; *put the jam in the kitchen cupboard*; *the best plates are in the dining room cupboard*; *she painted the cupboard doors white*

④ **curb**
[kɜːb]
1 *noun*

(a) something which holds something back; *the company needs to put a curb on its spending*

(b) US stone edge to a pavement; *he sat on the curb and watched the cars go past*; *try not to hit the curb when you park* (NOTE: British English is **kerb**)

2 *verb*

to hold back; *she needs to curb her enthusiasm to spend money*

④ **cure**
[kjuːɪ]
1 *noun*

something which makes a disease better; *doctors are still trying to find a cure for colds*

2 *verb*

(a) to make a patient or a disease better; *I don't know what's in the medicine, but it cured my cough very fast*

(b) to preserve meat, by putting it in salt; *a piece of cured ham*; *this bacon has been cured in salt water*

④ **curfew**
['kɜːfjuː] *noun*

period when no one is allowed out into the street; *the town council is proposing to impose a curfew for young people*

④ **curiosity**
[kjuɪrɪ'ɒsɪti] *noun*

wanting to know about something; *I just asked out of sheer curiosity* (NOTE: no plural)

③ **curious**
['kjuɪrɪɪs] *adjective*

(a) strange; *she has a curious high-pitched voice*

(b) wanting to know; *I'm curious to know if anything happened at the party*

③ **curl**
[kɜːl]
1 *noun*

(a) lock of hair which twists; *the little girl looked so sweet with her golden curls*

(b) twist in the hair; *my hair has a natural curl*

2 *verb*

(a) to make hair twist round; *she curled her hair round her finger*; *she went to the hairdresser's to have her hair curled*

(b) to twist; *my hair curls naturally*

③ **curly**
['kɜːli] *adjective*

curly hair = hair with natural waves in it; *she has naturally curly hair* (NOTE: **curlier - curliest**)

② **currency**
['kʌrɪnsi] *noun*

(a) money used in a certain country; *I want to change my pounds into French currency*; **foreign currency** = the money of other countries; *the bank will change your foreign currency for you*; **hard currency** = money which is stable and is easily exchanged for foreign currency; *people in some countries will do anything to get hold of hard currency*; *developing countries need to sell raw materials for hard currency*; **soft currency** = currency of a country with a weak economy, which is cheap to buy and difficult to exchange for other currencies

(b) *(formal)* state of being known or accepted; **to gain currency** = to become better known or more accepted; *the idea that the world was round began to gain currency in the later Middle Ages*

① **current**
['kʌrɪnt]
1 *noun*

(a) flow of water or air; *don't go swimming in the river - the current is very strong*; *a warm current of air is flowing across the country*; *big black birds were circling in rising currents of warm air*

(b) flow of electricity; *switch the current off at the mains*

2 *adjective*

(a) referring to the present time; *what is your current position?*; *who is the current Prime Minister of Japan?*; *do you have a current timetable? - mine is out-of-date*; **the current rate of exchange** = today's rate of exchange; *the current rate of exchange is 1.50 dollars to the pound*

(b) widely believed; *the idea that the world was flat was current in the Middle Ages*

③ **current account**
['kʌrɪnt ə'kaʊnt] *noun*
bank account from which you can take money at any time; *he deposited the cheque in his current account*; *her salary is paid directly into her current account*

> COMMENT: current accounts often do not pay any interest, but you can write cheques on them

① **currently**
['kʌrɪntli] *adverb*
at the present time; *he is currently the manager of our Paris office*; *we are currently in the process of buying a house*

② **curriculum**
[kɪ'rɪkjʊlɪm] *noun*
subjects studied in a school, etc.; *I am very glad that music and drama have been added to the curriculum*; *the National Curriculum is followed by all British schools*

③ **curriculum vitae (CV)**
[kɪ'rɪkjʊlɪm 'viːtaɪ] *noun*
summary of the details of a person's life, especially details of education and previous jobs; *please apply in writing, enclosing a current curriculum vitae*; *please enclose a curriculum vitae with your application form* (NOTE: plural is **curriculums** or **curricula vitae**. Note also that the American English is **résumé**)

③ **curry**
['kʌri]
1 *noun*
(a) curry powder *or* **paste** = hot spicy powder *or* paste, used to make Indian dishes; **curry house** = restaurant serving Indian food
(b) Indian food prepared with spices; *I would like a mild curry, please*; *we ordered chicken curry and rice* (NOTE: plural is **curries**)
2 *verb*
to curry favour with someone = to try to please someone; *he's just trying to curry favour with the boss by coming in at seven o'clock in the morning*

③ **curse**
[kɜːs]
1 *noun*
(a) swear word; *he threw the letter down with a curse*

(b) magic word to make something unpleasant happen to someone; *the wicked sister put a curse on the whole family*
(c) something which causes you problems; *being on call 24 hours a day is the curse of being a doctor*; *pollution is the curse of industrial societies*
2 *verb*
(a) to swear; *he cursed under his breath and marched out of the room*
(b) to cast an evil spell on someone; *we must be cursed - everything we do seems to go wrong*

② **curtain**
['kɜːtɪn] *noun*
(a) long piece of cloth hanging in front of a window, etc.; *can you close the curtains, please?*; **to draw the curtains** = (i) to open the curtains; (ii) to close the curtains; *draw the curtains - it's getting cold*
(b) long piece of cloth hanging in front of the stage at a theatre; **the curtain will go up at 8.30** = the play begins at 8.30; **safety curtain** = special curtain in front of the stage in a theatre, which protects against fire; *the safety curtain is lowered and raised at the beginning of each performance*; **it will be curtains for him** = he will be sacked, ruined, etc.

③ **curve**
[kɜːv]
1 *noun*
(a) round shape like part of a circle; *the road makes a sharp curve to the left*
(b) rounded shape on a graph; **learning curve** = gradual process of learning; **a steep learning curve** = having to learn new skills fast; **sales curve** = graph showing how sales increase or decrease
2 *verb*
to make a rounded shape; *the road curves round the side of the mountain*

② **cushion**
['kʊʃɪn]
1 *noun*
(a) bag filled with feathers, etc., for sitting or leaning on; *feel how soft this cushion is*; *put a cushion behind your back if you find your chair is too hard*
(b) money which allows you to get through a difficult period; *we have a little reserve in the bank which is a useful cushion when money is tight*
2 *verb*
to make soft something which could be hard or painful; *luckily when he fell off the ladder there was a hedge underneath to cushion his fall*; *she made no attempt to cushion the blow, but just told them straight out that they were all being sacked*

④ **custody**
['kʌstɪdi] *noun*
(a) keeping; *the jewels were in the custody of the manager, and he had placed them in the*

hotel safe; **to take someone into custody** = to arrest someone; *the three fans were taken into police custody*

(b) right of keeping and looking after a child; *when they were divorced, she was granted custody of the children* (NOTE: no plural)

③ **custom**
['kʌstɪm] *noun*

(a) habit, thing which is usually done; *it's a local custom in this part of the world*

(b) *(formal)* use of a shop; *if the assistants are rude to me again I will take my custom elsewhere*; **to lose someone's custom** = to do something which makes a regular customer go to another restaurant, shop, etc.; *the little corner shops will lose a lot of custom when the new supermarket is built*

(c) custom-built *or* **custom-made** = made to order for a customer; *he drives a custom-built sports car*

① **customer**
['kʌstɪmə] *noun*

(a) person who buys something in a shop; *the shops are lowering their prices to attract customers*; *she was locking up the shop when a customer came in*; *his shop is always full of customers*; **a satisfied customer** = someone who is happy with what he has bought

(b) person who uses a service, such as a train passenger; *we apologize to customers waiting on Platform 5 for the late arrival of their train*

② **customs**
['kʌstɪmz] *noun*

(a) Customs and Excise = the British government department which organizes the collection of taxes on goods coming into a country (and also collects VAT); *he was stopped by customs*; *her car was searched by customs*; *the customs officer asked her to open her bag*; **customs duty** = tax which you have to pay to take goods into a country; *you may have to pay customs duty on goods imported from outside the EU*

(b) office of this department at a port or airport; **to go through customs** = to pass through the area of a port or airport where customs officials examine goods; *when you come into the country, you have to go through customs*; **to take something through customs** = to carry something through the customs area without always declaring it; *she said that her boyfriend had asked her to take the case through customs for him*

① **cut**
[kʌt]
1 *verb*

(a) to make an opening using a knife, scissors, etc.; to remove something using a knife, scissors, etc.; *the meat is very tough - I can't cut it with my knife*; *he needs to get his hair cut*; *there were six children, so she cut the cake into six pieces*

(b) to hurt yourself by making a wound in the skin; *she cut her finger on the broken glass*; *he cut himself while shaving*

(c) to reduce the size of something; *we are trying to cut the number of staff*; *accidents have been cut by 10%*; *the article is too long, so I asked the author to cut 500 words*

(d) to cut across *or* **to cut through** = to take a short cut to get somewhere; *it's quicker if you cut across or through the park*

(e) to cut a corner = to try to go round a corner quickly, by driving on the pavement; *he was trying to cut the corner and hit a fence*; **to cut corners** = to do things rapidly and cheaply; *she tried to cut corners and the result was that the whole job had to be done again*

(f) to look at someone and pretend not to recognize him or her; *when I held out my hand she cut me dead*

(g) to miss (a lecture); *she cut her history lecture and went shopping* (NOTE: **cutting - cut - has cut**)

2 *noun*

(a) place which bleeds when your skin has been broken; *she had a bad cut on her leg*; *put some sticking plaster on your cut*

(b) short cut = shorter way; *he took a short cut through the park*

(c) sudden lowering of a price, salary, etc.; *price cuts or cuts in prices*; **job cuts** = reductions in the number of jobs; *the union is forecasting huge job cuts*; *he took a cut in salary or a salary cut* = he accepted a lower salary

(d) stopping the supply of water, electricity, etc.; *there were power cuts again during the night*

(e) piece of meat; *you can use a cheaper cut of meat if you cook it slowly*

(f) *(informal)* share (of profits, etc.); *each salesman gets a cut of what he can sell for cash*

(g) *(computing)* **cut and paste** = taking a section of text from one point and putting it in at another

③ **cut back**
['kʌt 'bæk] *verb*

to reduce spending; *we are having to cut back on staff costs*

③ **cut down**
['kʌt 'daʊn] *verb*

(a) to make a tree fall down with a saw, etc.; *he cut the tree down or he cut down the tree*

(b) to cut down (on) = to reduce; *we are trying to get him to cut down the number of cigarettes he smokes each day*; *she's trying to cut down on chocolates*

③ **cute**
[kjuːt] *adjective*

(informal) nice; *what a cute little cottage!*; *Doreen may look cute now, but you should see her when she's in a temper*

③ **cut off**
['kʌt 'ɒf] *verb*
(a) to take away a small part of something using a knife, etc.; *she cut off a little piece of string*; *he cut off two slices of ham*
(b) to stop someone from being with someone or reaching a place; *she was cut off from her friends by a crowd of policemen*; *the village was cut off by the snow*; *the tide came in and cut off a party of schoolchildren*
(c) to stop a phone call before it is finished; *we were cut off in the middle of our conversation*
(d) to stop electricity or water from reaching someone; *he didn't pay the bill, so the company cut off his electricity*; *the lightning hit the cable and caused the electricity to be cut off*

③ **cut out**
['kʌt 'aʊt] *verb*
(a) to remove a small piece by cutting it from a large piece (of paper, etc.); *she cut an advertisement out of the newspaper*; *he used a pair of scissors to cut out the picture*
(b) to stop doing or eating something; *she's decided to cut out sweet things so as to lose weight*; *cut it out!* = stop doing that!
(c) *(of an engine)* to stop working; *one of the engines cut out as the plane came in to land*
(d) to be cut out for = to be ideally suited for; *I don't think he's cut out for a job in the post office*

④ **cut-price**
['kʌt 'praɪs] *adjective*
sold at a cheaper price than usual; *supermarkets attract customers with cut-price petrol*; **cut-price store** = store selling goods at cheaper prices

④ **cutting**
['kʌtɪŋ]
1 *noun*
(a) small piece of paper cut out of a newspaper; **press cuttings** = references to a person or thing cut out of newspapers or magazines; *she has a file of press cuttings about her son*
(b) little piece of a plant which will grow roots if it is pushed into the ground; *the cuttings I took from your plant are all growing well*
2 *adjective*
cutting remark = sharply critical remark

③ **cut up**
['kʌt 'ʌp]
1 *verb*
(a) to make into small pieces by cutting; *she cut the old towel up into little pieces*; *can you cut up the meat for the children?*

(b) *(informal)* to drive suddenly in front of another car; *did you see how the little white car cut up the black Audi?*
2 *adjective*
(informal) upset, annoyed; *she's rather cut up because her dog has disappeared*

③ **CV** *or* **cv**
[siː'viː] *noun*
= CURRICULUM VITAE; *please apply in writing, enclosing a current CV*; *please enclose a CV with your application form*

③ **cycle**
['saɪkl]
1 *noun*
(a) bicycle; *if your bike's got a flat tyre, take it to the cycle shop*; **cycle path** = special path for cyclists; *there are thousands of cycle paths in Holland*
(b) period during which something develops and then returns to its starting point; *global warming is starting to affect the natural cycle of the seasons*; *the washing machine broke down in the middle of the spin cycle*; **business cycle** *or* **economic cycle** *or* **trade cycle** = period during which trade expands, then slows down, then expands again; **life cycle** = life of an animal or plant from birth to death, which is repeated by the next generation
2 *verb*
to go on a bicycle; *it's hard cycling against the wind*; *he thinks nothing of cycling ten miles to work every day*

③ **cyclist**
['saɪklɪst] *noun*
person who rides a bicycle; *the police told the crowds to stand back as the cyclists were passing*

④ **cyclone**
['saɪkləʊn] *noun*
tropical storm in the Indian Ocean and Pacific, where the air moves very fast in a circle round a central area; *according to the shipping forecasts, a cyclone is approaching Sri Lanka* (NOTE: in the Far East this is called a **typhoon**; in the Caribbean a **hurricane**)

④ **cylinder**
['sɪlɪndɪ] *noun*
(a) object shaped like a round tube closed at both ends; **gas cylinder** = metal tube containing gas; *the divers carried oxygen cylinders on their backs*
(b) part of an engine; *the car has a six-cylinder engine*; *the engine seems to lack power - maybe it's not firing on all six cylinders*

Dd

③ **D, d**
['diː]
fourth letter of the alphabet, between C and E;
you don't spell 'riding' with two d's

③ **DA**
['diː 'eɪ] = DISTRICT ATTORNEY

① **dad** *or* **daddy**
[dæd *or* 'dædɪ] *noun*
child's name for father; *Hi Daddy! look at my
exam results!*; *my dad has bought me a new
bike*; *compare* MUM, MUMMY

② **daily**
['deɪli]
1 *adjective*
happening every day; *daily newspapers such as
'The Times' and 'Daily Mail'*; *the cooker has
been in daily use for ten years*; *there's a daily
flight to Washington*
2 *noun*
newspaper published every weekday; *the story
was carried on the front page of most of the
dailies* (NOTE: plural is **dailies**)
3 *adverb*
every day; **twice daily** = two times a day

④ **dairy**
['deɪri] *noun*
place where milk, cream and butter are
processed or sold; *you can buy butter and
cheese from the dairy*; **dairy farm** = farm
which produces milk, cheese, etc.; **dairy
produce** = milk, butter, cream, etc. (NOTE: plural
is **dairies**)

④ **dam**
[dæm]
1 *noun*
wall of earth or concrete which blocks a river to
make a lake; *after the thunderstorm people
were afraid the dam would burst*
2 *verb*
to block a river with a wall of earth or concrete;
*when they built the power station, the river had
to be dammed* (NOTE: **damming - dammed**)

② **damage**
['dæmɪdʒ]
1 *noun*
(a) harm (done to things not to people); *the
storm did a lot of damage*; *it will take us
months to repair the damage to the restaurant*;
the fire caused damage estimated at £100,000;
fire damage = damage caused by a fire; **flood
damage** = damage caused by a flood; **storm**

damage = damage caused by a storm; **to suffer
damage** = to be harmed; *the car suffered
serious damage in the accident* (NOTE: no plural
in this meaning)
(b) **damages** = payment to someone who has
been hurt or whose property has been damaged;
*the accident victim claimed £200,000 in
damages*; *after his operation went wrong, he
sued the hospital for damages*; *the court
awarded the girl damages against the driver of
the car*
2 *verb*
to harm something; *a large number of shops
were damaged in the fire*; *glasses need to be
packed carefully as they are easily damaged*

③ **damp**
[dæmp]
1 *adjective*
rather wet; *she'd just had a shower and her hair
was still damp*; *the basement room has cold
damp walls* (NOTE: **damper - dampest**)
2 *noun*
moisture in the air, on a surface; *the damp
makes my rheumatism worse*; **rising damp** =
damp which enters the walls of houses and
damages them (NOTE: no plural)

② **dance**
[dɑːns]
1 *noun*
(a) way of moving in time to music; *she teaches
dance or she's a dance teacher*; *we learnt a new
dance today*; *Scottish dances are very lively*
(b) evening entertainment for a group of people
where you can dance; *the club is holding a New
Year's dance*; *they met at a youth club dance*;
dance floor = specially polished floor for
dancing on
2 *verb*
(a) to move in time to music; *there he is - he's
dancing with that tall girl*; *she often goes to
clubs but never dances*
(b) to move or jump around happily; *she danced
into the room and announced she's got the job*;
football fans were dancing in the streets

⑤ **dancer**
['dɑːnsɪ] *noun*
person who dances; *she trained as a dancer*; *the
dancers hold hands and form a circle*

② **dancing**
['dɑːnsɪŋ] *noun*
action of moving to music; *she teaches dancing; she goes to dancing classes; she's taking dancing lessons* (NOTE: no plural)

④ **Dane**
[deɪn] *noun*
person from Denmark; *Danes are often tall and blond*

② **danger**
['deɪnʒɪ] *noun*
possibility of damage, failure, getting hurt, etc.; *when it rains, there's a danger of flooding; the broken window is a danger to office security; there's a danger we won't get there in time; we were warned of the dangers of travelling alone in the desert;* danger money = payment for a dangerous job; *the workers said the job was very dangerous and asked for danger money;* out of danger *or* off the danger list = not likely to die; *she was very ill, but she's off the danger list now*

◊ **in danger**
['ɪn 'deɪndʒɪ] *phrase*
likely to be harmed; *get an ambulance - her life is in danger; I don't think the children are in any danger; the whole building was in danger of catching fire*

② **dangerous**
['deɪnʒɪrɪs] *adjective*
which can cause injury or damage; *be careful - those old stairs are dangerous!; these electric wires are dangerous; children are warned that it is dangerous to go out alone at night*

④ **dangerously**
['deɪnʒɪrɪsli] *adverb*
in a dangerous way; *she was standing dangerously close to the edge of the cliff;* to be dangerously ill = to be very ill

① **Danish**
['deɪnɪʃ]
1 *adjective*
referring to Denmark; Danish pastry = sweet pastry cake with jam or fruit folded in it (NOTE: also called simply a Danish: an apple Danish)
2 *noun*
language spoken in Denmark

③ **dare**
['deɪ]
1 *verb*
(a) to be brave enough to do something; *I bet you wouldn't dare put your hand into the cage and stroke that tiger;* I dare say = very probably; *I dare say you're right*
(b) *(negative) I dare not go out into the street or I don't dare go out into the street while that man is standing there*
(c) to challenge someone to do something by suggesting he is too afraid to do it; *I dared him to go the meeting in his pyjamas*
2 *noun*

act of challenging someone to do something; *he only climbed on the roof for a dare*

① **dark**
[dɑːk]
1 *adjective*
(a) with little or no light; *the sky turned dark and it started to rain; can you switch the light on - it's getting too dark to see; in Scotland in the summer it gets dark very late*
(b) not a light colour; *her eyes are dark; she was wearing a dark blue coat;* a dark horse = someone who may succeed unexpectedly
(c) with black or brown hair; *he's quite dark, but his sister has red hair*
(d) to keep something dark = to keep something a secret; *they kept their plans dark from the rest of the family* (NOTE: darker - darkest)
2 *noun*
(a) absence of light; *little children are afraid of the dark; they say cats can see in the dark; in the dark, everything looks different;* after dark = during the night time; *you must put on your car lights after dark*
(b) in the dark = not knowing anything about something; *I'm completely in the dark about the whole business; we want to keep everyone in the dark about our plans*

③ **darkness**
['dɑːknɪs] *noun*
not having any light; *the cat's eyes glowed in the darkness; the sun had set and the darkness was closing in;* the building was in complete darkness *or* in total darkness = there were no electric lights on in the building (NOTE: no plural)

④ **darling**
['dɑːlɪŋ]
1 *adjective*
which you can love; *what a darling little baby!*
2 *noun*
(a) name used to talk to someone you love; *Darling! I'm back from the shops*
(b) person who is loved; *she's an absolute darling!; be a darling and fetch me the newspaper*

④ **dart**
[dɑːt]
1 *noun*
(a) small heavy arrow with plastic feathers, used for playing the game of darts; *each player takes turn to throw his three darts*
(b) darts = game for two or more people, played by each player throwing three darts in turn at a round target; *they had a game of darts; I'm not very good at darts; he plays darts every evening in the pub* (NOTE: not plural, and takes a singular verb)
2 *verb*
to rush; *the little boy darted across the street; we sat by the river and watched the fish darting about chasing flies*

④ **dash**

[dæʃ]

1 *noun*

(a) little line written to joint two figures or phrases; *the reference number is one four six dash seven (146-7)*

(b) sudden rush; *there was a mad dash to buy tickets*; *while the policeman wasn't looking she made a dash for the door*

(c) small amount; *a tomato juice with a dash of sauce* (NOTE: plural is **dashes**)

2 *verb*

to rush; *I can't stop now - I must dash to catch the last post*; *I dashed home to watch the football on television*; *she dashed into a shop so that he wouldn't see her*

① **data**

['deɪtɪ] *noun*

information in the form of statistics; *the data is stored in our main computer*; *we spent months gathering data on hospital waiting times*; *the data shows that, on average, a murder is committed every two weeks*; **data bank** = store of information on a computer; **data protection** = making sure that information on a computer does not get into the wrong hands (NOTE: **data** is usually singular: **the data is easily available**)

② **database**

['deɪtɪbeɪs] *noun*

data stored in a computer, which can be used to provide information of various kinds; *we can extract the lists of possible customers from our database*; *I'll just add your details to our customer database*

③ **data processing**

['deɪtɪ 'prɪʊsesɪŋ] *noun*

selecting and examining data in a computer to produce special information; *she's a data processing manager*

① **date**

[deɪt]

1 *noun*

(a) number of a day in a month or year (when something happens or happened); *put today's date on the cheque*; *what's the date next Wednesday?*; *the dates of the exhibition have been changed*; *the date of the next meeting has been fixed for Wednesday, June 10th*; *do you remember the date of your girlfriend's birthday?*; **date of birth** = date on which someone was born; *please write your date and place of birth on the registration form*; **arrival date** *or* **date of arrival** = day on which you arrive; **departure date** *or* **date of departure** = day on which you leave

(b) time agreed for a meeting, usually between a boy and a girl; *we made a date to meet at the Italian restaurant*; *he asked her out for a date*; **blind date** = meeting arranged between two people who have never met before

(c) small sweet brown fruit of the date palm; **date palm** = a tall tropical tree with very large leaves and sweet fruit

2 *verb*

(a) to write the date on something; *the cheque was dated the 15th of June*; *you forgot to date the cheque*

(b) **to date from** = to exist since; *this house dates from* or *dates back to the seventeenth century*

(c) to give the date of a old piece of wood, a monument, an antique, etc.; *the bowl has been dated to 1500 BC*

(d) *(especially US)* to agree to meet someone of the opposite sex regularly; *he's dating my sister*

◊ **out of date**

['aʊt əv 'deɪt]

not containing recent information; *this guidebook is out of date*; *the information in it is two years out of date*

◊ **up to date**

['ʌp tɪ 'deɪt]

containing very recent information; *the new telephone directory is completely up to date*; *he is bringing the guidebook up to date*; **to keep someone up to date on** *or* **with something** = to tell someone all the latest information about something; *while I'm on holiday, you must keep me up to date on what's happening at the office*

① **daughter**

['dɔːtɪ] *noun*

girl child of a mother or father; *they have two sons and one daughter*; *my daughter Mary goes to the local school*

④ **dawn**

[dɔːn]

1 *noun*

beginning of a day, when the sun rises; *we must set off for the Pyramids at dawn, so you'll have to get up very early*; **at the crack of dawn** = as soon as it starts to be light; *the plane leaves at 6.30 a.m. - it means I'll have to get up at the crack of dawn*

2 *verb*

(a) *(of day)* to begin; *the day of the cricket match dawned wet and windy*

(b) **it dawned on him that** = he began to realize that; *it gradually dawned on him that someone else was going to get the job he had applied for*

① **day**

['deɪ] *noun*

(a) period of time lasting 24 hours; *there are 365 days in a year and 366 in a leap year*; *New Year's Day is January 1st*; *they went on a ten-day tour of Southern Spain*; *I spoke to him on the phone the day before yesterday*; *we are planning to meet the day after tomorrow*; **what day is it today?** = is it Monday, Tuesday, etc.

(b) **every other day** = every two days (i.e., on Monday, Wednesday, Friday, etc.); *he phones his mother every other day*; **the other day** =

quite recently; *the other day I went for a walk by the river*; **one day** or **some day** = at some time in the future; *one day we'll have enough money to go on holiday*

(c) period from morning until night, when it is light; *he works all day in the office, and then helps his wife with the children in the evening*; *it took the workmen four days to build the wall*; **day tour** or **day trip** = tour which leaves in the morning and returns the same day in the evening

(d) work period from morning to night; *she took two days off* = she did not come to work for two days; *he works three days on, two days off* = he works for three days, then has two days' holiday; **to work an eight-hour day** = to spend eight hours at work each day; **to work a four-day week** = to work four days each week

(e) days = time in the past; *in the days of Henry VIII kings were very powerful*; **those were the days** = they were good times we had in the past; *do you remember spending all night going round the bars in Hamburg? - ah! those were the days!*

◊ **a day**
[ə ˈdeɪ]
every day; *an apple a day keeps the doctor away*; *you should drink a litre of water a day*

◊ **all day**
[ˈɔːl ˈdeɪ]
the whole day; *it's been raining hard all day*

④ **daylight**
[ˈdeɪlaɪt] *noun*
light from the sun during the day; *he pulled back the curtains to let in the daylight*; **in broad daylight** = openly, in the middle of the day; *three men robbed the bank in broad daylight* (NOTE: no plural)

① **dead**
[ded]
1 *adjective*
(a) not alive any more; *his parents are both dead*; *dead fish were floating in the water*; *he brushed the dead leaves into piles*; *six people were dead as a result of the accident*; *(informal)* **wouldn't be seen dead in** = would not ever want to be seen in; *I wouldn't be seen dead in a hat like that*; *our teacher wouldn't be seen dead in a bar*; *(informal)* **as dead as a dodo** = completely dead, no longer able to function; *the plan is as dead as a dodo now that the banks have refused their support*; **to drop dead** = to die suddenly; *he dropped dead in the middle of the High Street*
(b) complete; *there was dead silence in the exam room*; *the train came to a dead stop*
(c) not working; **the line went dead** = the telephone line suddenly stopped working; *I was talking on the phone when suddenly the line went dead*
2 *adverb*
(a) completely; *he was dead tired after his long walk*

(b) exactly; *you're dead right*; *the train arrived dead on time*
3 *noun*
(a) the dead = dead people; *a list of the names of the dead of the two world wars*
(b) the dead of night = the middle of the night; *he woke up in the dead of night and thought he heard a noise downstairs*

④ **deadline**
[ˈdedlaɪn] *noun*
date by which something has to be done; *we've been given an October deadline to finish the job*; **to meet a deadline** = to finish something in time; *I don't think we can meet the deadline*; **to miss a deadline** = not to finish something in time; *they worked as fast as they could but missed the deadline by two days*

③ **deadly**
[ˈdedlɪ] *adjective*
(a) which will kill; *don't eat those mushrooms - they're deadly poisonous*; *the female spider is deadlier than the male*
(b) very serious or bitter; *they are deadly rivals*; *he was deadly serious* (NOTE: **deadlier - deadliest**)

③ **deaf**
[def]
1 *adjective*
(person) who cannot hear, who has difficulty in hearing; *the old lady is going deaf*; *he's deafer than he used to be*; **stone deaf** = completely deaf (NOTE: **deafer - deafest**)
2 *noun*
the deaf = people who cannot hear; *their son goes to a school for the deaf*

① **deal**
[diːl]
1 *noun*
(a) a good deal or **a great deal** = much; *he's feeling a good deal better after two days off work*; *she didn't say a great deal*; **a good deal of** or **a great deal of** = a lot of; *he made a good deal of money from his business*; *there's a great deal of work still to be done*
(b) business affair, agreement, contract; *we've signed a deal with a German firm*; *they did a deal to supply envelopes*; *the sales director set up a deal with a Russian bank*; **bad deal** or **rough deal** or **raw deal** = bad treatment; *she got a rough deal from the firm*; **package deal** = agreement where several different items are agreed at the same time
2 *verb*
(a) to deal in = to buy and sell; *she deals in carpets and rugs imported from India*
(b) to hand out cards to players; *it's my turn to deal*; *he dealt me two kings* (NOTE: **dealing - dealt** [delt])

③ **dealer**
[ˈdiːlə] *noun*
person who buys and sells; *he bought his car from a secondhand car dealer*; *she's an*

antiques dealer with a shop in Brighton; **drug dealer** = person who sells illegal drugs to other people

③ **deal with**
['di:l 'wɪθ] *verb*
to concern yourself with, to handle; *the job involves dealing with the public; leave it to the filing clerk - he'll deal with it; we will deal with your order as soon as we can; the government has to deal with the problem of teenage crime*

① **dear**
[dɪ]
1 *adjective*
(a) well liked, loved; *she's a very dear friend of mine; we had a letter from dear old Mrs Smith*
(b) *(used at the beginning of a letter)* **Dear Sir** or **Dear Madam** = addressing a man or woman whom you do not know, or addressing a company; **Dear Sirs** = addressing a company; **Dear Mr Smith** or **Dear Mrs Smith** or **Dear Miss Smith** = addressing a man or woman whom you know; **Dear James** or **Dear Julia** = addressing a friend or a person you do business with
(c) costing a lot of money; *fresh fruit is always dearer in the winter; that restaurant is too dear for me* (NOTE: **dearer - dearest**)
2 *interjection; (meaning how annoying)*
oh dear! it's started to rain; dear me! is that how late it is!
3 *noun*
(way of referring to someone you like) *be a dear, and pass me my glasses; did you have a good day at the office, dear?*; **old dears** = old people (NOTE: do not confuse with **deer**)

① **death**
[deθ] *noun*
(a) act of dying; *she never got over her mother's death; road accidents caused over 1,000 deaths last year*; **death rate** = percentage of deaths per thousand of population; *the region has a death rate of 15 per thousand; an increase in the death rate due to accidents*
(b) *(informal)* **to death** = completely; *he was bored to death sitting watching football on television; she's sick to death of always having to do the housework*

① **debate**
[dɪ'beɪt]
1 *noun*
formal discussion; *the Prime Minister spoke in the Commons debate on capital punishment; after his talk the scientist had a lively debate with the students; there has been some debate among experts about whether global warming is really taking place*
2 *verb*
to discuss; *we sat in the rain and debated what to do next; the House of Commons will debate the Crime Bill next week*

④ **debit**
['debɪt]
1 *noun*
money which is paid out, or taken out of an account; *your bank statement gives a list of credits and debits at the end of each month*
2 *verb*
to debit money to an account = to deduct money from an account; *the whole bill was debited to my account or my account was debited with the whole bill*; *see also* DIRECT

④ **debris**
['debri *US* dɪ'bri:] *noun*
pieces of a building which is being knocked down, aircraft which has crashed, etc.; *debris from the crash littered the ground; she was hit by flying debris* (NOTE: no plural)

② **debt**
[det] *noun*
money owed to someone; *her debts are mounting up*; **to be in debt** = to owe money; *he is in debt to the tune of £2500*; **to get into debt** = to start to owe money; **to be out of debt** = not to owe money any more; *see also* RED; **debt collector** = person who collects money owed to other people

④ **debut**
['deɪbju:] *noun*
first appearance of an actor, etc.; *she made her debut on the stage in the role of Ophelia*

② **decade**
['dekeɪd] *noun*
period of ten years; *during the last decade of the 20th century*

④ **decay**
[dɪ'keɪ]
1 *noun*
rotting, falling into ruin; *the government has plans to deal with inner city decay; tooth decay is specially bad in children who eat sweets; you must treat the wood to prevent decay* (NOTE: no plural)
2 *verb*
to rot, to fall into ruin; *sugar makes your teeth decay; the jungle path was blocked by decaying branches*

④ **deceive**
[dɪ'si:v] *verb*
to trick someone, to make someone believe something which is not true; *he deceived everyone into thinking that he was a policeman*

① **December**
[dɪ'sembɪ] *noun*
twelfth and last month of the year, after November and before January; *she was born in December; his birthday is December 25th - Christmas Day!; they always go on a skiing holiday in December; today is December 6th US December 6* (NOTE: **December 6th** or **December 6:** say 'the sixth of December' or 'December the sixth'; American English: 'December sixth')

② **decent**
['di:sɪnt] *adjective*
(a) honest; *the boss is a hard-working decent man*
(b) quite good; *she earns a decent salary*
(c) *(informal)* properly dressed, wearing clothes; *you can't come in yet - I'm not decent*

① **decide**
[dɪ'saɪd] *verb*
to make up your mind to do something; *have you decided which restaurant to go to?; they decided to stay at home and watch TV; she decided not to spend her money on a new car*

① **decide against**
[dɪ'saɪd ə'genst] *verb*
to make up your mind not to do something; *we've decided against going to France this year*

④ **decimal**
['desɪml]
1 *adjective*
decimal system = system of counting based on the number 10
2 *noun*
fraction expressed as tenths, hundredths and thousandths; *three-quarters is 0.75 in decimals*; **to three places of decimals** *or* **to three decimal places** = with three figures shown after the decimal point; *67 divided by 13 gives 5.154 to three places of decimals*; **decimal point** = dot used to show the division between whole numbers and parts of numbers; *to multiply by ten, simply move the decimal point one place to the right* (NOTE: three and a half is written: 3.5 (say 'three point five')

> COMMENT: the decimal point is used in the USA and Britain. In most European countries a comma is used to show the decimal, so 4,75% in Germany is written 4.75% in Britain

① **decision**
[dɪ'sɪʃn] *noun*
act of making up your mind to do something; **to come to a decision** *or* **to reach a decision** *or* **to take a decision** = to decide to do something; *they talked for hours but didn't come to any decision; he thought about the job offer, but, in the end, took the decision to stay where he was*; **the decision-making process** = the process involved in making up your mind to do something; *we involve all the staff in the decision-making process*

③ **decisive**
[dɪ'saɪsɪv] *adjective*
(a) firm (tone of voice); *he was nervous but tried to sound decisive*
(b) which brings about a result; *the second and decisive round of voting takes place next Sunday; her action was decisive in obtaining the release of the hostages*

④ **deck**
[dek] *noun*
(a) floor of a ship, bus, etc.; *I'll stay on deck because I feel sick when I'm inside the ship; the sailors were washing down the deck; let's go up to the top deck of the bus - you can see the sights better from there*; **main deck** = deck on a ship with the most important facilities, such as the restaurant, bars, etc.
(b) *US* set of playing cards; *she shuffled the deck* (NOTE: British English is **pack of cards**)
(c) wooden platform outside a house; *we had drinks outside on the deck*

③ **declaration**
[deklɪ'reɪʃn] *noun*
official statement; *the minister's declaration was broadcast at 6 o'clock; we had to fill in a customs declaration form*; **VAT declaration** = statement declaring VAT income to the VAT office

② **declare**
[dɪ'kleɪ] *verb*
(a) to state officially; *Mr Clinton declared his intention to run for President; she was declared dead on arrival at hospital; it was declared that Mrs Broom was elected chairman by 46 votes*; **to declare war on a country** = to state formally that a war has begun with a country
(b) *(at customs)* **to declare goods to customs** = to list the goods you are carrying on which you may need to pay customs duty; *the customs officials asked him if he had anything to declare; go through the green channel if you have nothing to declare*

② **decline**
[dɪ'klaɪn]
1 *noun*
going downwards; *sales figures have gone into a sharp decline; the decline in the value of the franc; a welcome decline in the number of cases of pollution*
2 *verb*
(a) to refuse or to turn down (an invitation); *she declined their request; he declined to come to lunch*
(b) to become weaker; *he declined rapidly after he went into hospital*
(c) to become less in numbers or amount; *our sales declined over the last year; the fish population has declined sharply*

③ **decorate**
['dekɪreɪt] *verb*
(a) to paint (a room or a building); to put new wallpaper in (a room); *she can't come to the phone - she's decorating the kitchen*; **interior decorating** = arranging and decorating the inside of a house (curtains, paint, wallpaper, carpets, etc.)
(b) to cover something with pretty or colourful things to make it look attractive, or to celebrate an occasion; *the streets were decorated with flags*

(c) to put coloured icing on a cake; *Christmas cakes are decorated with green leaves and red berries*

(d) to award someone a medal; *he was decorated for his brave rescue of the children*

③ **decoration**
[dekɪ'reɪʃn] *noun*
(a) action of decorating; *she is charge of the decoration of the church for the wedding*
(b) action of painting a room, etc.; *the decoration of the town hall took over a year*
(c) things added to make something more attractive; *the only decoration allowed was a pattern of red and blue squares*
(d) decorations = flags or lights, etc., used to celebrate an occasion; *we put up the Christmas decorations at the beginning of the holidays*; *we must go to see the Christmas decorations in Regent Street*
(e) medal; *he went to Buckingham Palace to receive his decoration from the Queen*; *old soldiers were wearing their decorations for the November 11th parade*

④ **decorative**
['dekɪrɪtɪv] *adjective*
pleasant to look at; serving as a decoration; *she stuck a decorative border round the edge*

④ **decrease**
1 *noun*
['diːkriːs] falling, becoming less; *a decrease in traffic*; *sales show a 10% decrease on last year*; *there has been a decrease of 20% in applications to join the club*; **to be on the decrease** = to be falling; *road accidents are on the decrease*
2 *verb*
[diː'kriːs] to fall, to become less; *the number of road accidents is decreasing*; *applications to join have decreased by 20 %*

④ **decree**
[dɪ'kriː]
1 *noun*
legal order which has not been voted by a Parliament; *the President has issued a decree banning short dresses*
2 *verb*
to state as a legal order; *the President has decreed that everyone must work on Saturdays*

④ **dedicate**
['dedɪkeɪt] *verb*
(a) to spend all your life doing something; *she dedicated her life to the service of the poor*
(b) to name a church after a saint; *the chapel was dedicated to St Christopher in the 13th century*
(c) to offer a book to someone as a mark of respect or love; *he dedicated his collection of poems to his wife*

④ **deduct**
[dɪ'dʌkt] *verb*
to remove something from a sum of money; *we took £60 at the sale, but if we deduct our expenses, we only made £25*; *the landlord deducted some money from our deposit to cover broken items*; **tax deducted at source** = tax which is removed from wages, interest payments, etc., before the money is paid

④ **deduction**
[dɪ'dʌkʃn] *noun*
(a) sum of money which is taken away from a total sum; *there is an automatic deduction for insurance*; *net wages are wages after deduction of tax and social security payments*; **tax deductions** = money removed from your salary to pay tax
(b) conclusion which is reached; **by a process of deduction** = by looking at the evidence and reaching a conclusion

③ **deed**
[diːd] *noun*
legal document; **title deeds** *or* **the deeds of a house** = legal documents showing who owns a house; *we have deposited the deeds of the house in the bank*

① **deep**
[diːp]
1 *adjective*
(a) which goes a long way down; *the water is very deep in the middle of the river*; *this is the deepest lake in North America*; *in the shallow end of the pool, the water is only a few centimetres deep* (NOTE: the use with figures: **the pool is six feet deep; a lake 50m deep**)
(b) dark (colour); *a deep brown carpet*
(c) felt very strongly; *we want to express our deepest thanks for what you have done*; *she sat in a corner, deep in thought*
(d) low-pitched, bass (voice); *who's been sitting on my chair, said Father Bear in his deep voice* (NOTE: **deeper - deepest**)
2 *adverb*
a long way down; *the mine goes deep under the sea*

④ **deepen**
['diːpɪn] *verb*
(a) to make something become deeper; *they're going to deepen the channel so that bigger boats can use the harbour*
(b) to become deeper; *the water deepened as he walked out into the lake*

③ **deeply**
['diːpli] *adverb*
(a) very much; *we deeply regret having to put so many people out of work*
(b) to sleep deeply = to sleep without waking; *after taking the drug she slept deeply for ten hours*

④ **deer**
[dɪ] *noun*
wild animal of which the male has long horns, often hunted; *there is a herd of red deer in the park* (NOTE: do not confuse with **dear**; the plural is **deer**)

COMMENT: there are three species of deer which live wild in the UK. The largest is the red deer, found in Scotland and the West Country

④ **default**
[dɪ'fɒlt]
1 *noun*
(a) he is in default = he has failed to carry out the terms of the contract
(b) by default = because someone else fails to do something; *his opponent withdrew and he won by default*
(c) *(computers)* set way of working; **default drive** = the drive which is accessed first
2 *verb*
to fail to carry out the terms of a contract; **to default on payments** = not to make payments which are due; *he paid his mortgage regularly for six months and then defaulted*

③ **defeat**
[dɪ'fiːt]
1 *noun*
loss of a fight, a vote, a game; *the government suffered a defeat in Parliament last night*; *it was the team's first defeat for two years*
2 *verb*
to beat someone in a fight, game or vote; *the proposal was defeated by 10 votes to 3*; *the ruling party was heavily defeated in the presidential election*; *our team has not been defeated so far this season*

④ **defect**
1 *noun*
['diːfekt]
fault; *there must be a defect in the computer programme*
2 *verb*
[dɪ'fekt]
to defect (to the enemy) = to leave your country and join the enemy; *she defected while on a tour of South-East Asia*

① **defence** *US* **defense**
[dɪ'fens] *noun*
(a) protection against attack, infection, etc.; *several people ran to her defence when she was attacked by muggers*; *these tablets offer a limited defence against the disease*
(b) protection provided by the armed forces; *some countries spend more on defence than on education*; **the Ministry of Defence** = government department dealing with the army, navy and air force
(c) *(in games)* part of a team whose job is to protect the goal; *the England defence came under attack from the Brazilian forwards*
(d) defences = strong walls, etc., which are built to protect something; *the town is strengthening its defences by building thicker walls*; **when your defences are down** = when you are not

prepared for an attack; *burglars often strike when you're relaxing and your defences are down*
(e) *(in a law court)* **the defence** = lawyers acting for the accused person; **defence counsel** = lawyer who represents the defendant in a lawsuit (NOTE: the opposing side in a court is the **prosecution**)

① **defend**
[dɪ'fend] *verb*
(a) to protect someone who is being attacked; *he jumped forward to defend his wife against the robbers*; *she couldn't defend herself against the muggers*
(b) *(in a law court)* to speak on behalf of an accused person; *he hired the best lawyers to defend him*; *the lawyer who is defending my uncle*; **to defend a lawsuit** = to appear in court to state your case when accused of something

② **defendant**
[dɪ'fendɪnt] *noun*
(in a law court) person who is accused of doing something illegal; person who is sued in a civil case; *the defendant says he is innocent*

COMMENT: in a civil case, the defendant faces a complaint from the claimant. In a criminal case, the defendant (also called the accused) is being prosecuted for a crime by the prosecution

① **defense**
[dɪ'fens]
US = DEFENCE

④ **defensive**
[dɪ'fensɪv]
1 *adjective*
which protects; *they built a defensive wall around the camp*
2 *noun*
to be on the defensive about something = to feel you need to give reasons for having done something; *she's always on the defensive when newspapers mention her huge salary*

④ **deficiency**
[dɪ'fɪʃɪnsi] *noun*
lack of; *their diet has a deficiency in vitamins or has a vitamin deficiency*

④ **deficit**
['defɪsɪt] *noun*
amount by which expenditure is more than receipts in a company's or a country's accounts; *the company announced a two-million pound deficit*; **to make good a deficit** = to put money into an account to balance it; **balance of payments deficit** *or* **trade deficit** = situation when a country imports more than it exports; *the UK's balance of payments deficit has fallen by £2bn*

② **define**
[dɪ'faɪn] *verb*
(a) to explain clearly, to give the meaning of something; *how would you define*

environmental?; the memo tried to define the way in which the two departments should work together

(b) to indicate the limits of something; *the police operate within limits that have been clearly defined*

③ **definite**
['defɪnɪt] *adjective*

(a) very clear, very sure; *I need a definite answer; he was quite definite that he had seen the girl at the bus stop*

(b) definite article = 'the' (as opposed to the indefinite article 'a' or 'an')

① **definitely**
['defɪnɪtli] *adverb*

certainly, surely; *I'll definitely be there by 7 o'clock*

② **definition**
[defɪ'nɪʃn] *noun*

(a) clear explanation (of a word); *an English-German dictionary doesn't give definitions, only translations; look up the definition of 'democracy' in the dictionary*

(b) *(of a photograph)* being clear and with sharp lines; *the portrait shots are clear, but your landscape photos lack definition* (NOTE: no plural in this meaning)

④ **definitive**
[dɪ'fɪnɪtɪv] *adjective*

final and best, which cannot be made better; *this is the definitive production of 'Macbeth'*

④ **defrost**
[diː'frɒst] *verb*

(a) to melt ice which has formed; *I must defrost the freezer*

(b) *(frozen food)* to stop being frozen; *a large turkey will take 24 hours to defrost*

④ **defy**
[dɪ'faɪ] *verb*

(a) to refuse to obey the law; *he should never have tried to defy the university authorities*

(b) *(formal)* to defy someone to do something = to challenge someone to do something; *I defy you to jump higher than that*

① **degree**
[dɪ'griː] *noun*

(a) division of a scale; *the temperature of the water is above 20 degrees; an angle of 80°* (NOTE: with figures, **degree** is usually written °: **25°)**

(b) level; *to what degree do you think the driver was to blame for the accident?*; **to a certain degree** = partly; *it's his own fault to a certain degree*

(c) diploma from a university; *she has a degree in mathematics from Oxford*

② **delay**
[dɪ'leɪ]
1 *noun*

length of time that something is late; *there will be a delay of ten minutes before the meeting starts; we are sorry for the delay in replying to your letter*

2 *verb*

(a) to make late; *the train has been delayed by fog; he was delayed because his taxi had an accident*

(b) to put something off until later; *we will delay making a decision until we see the result of the election; the company has delayed payment of all invoices*

④ **delegate**
1 *noun*

['delɪgət] person who represents others at a meeting; *the minister met delegates from the union*

2 *verb*

['delɪgeɪt] to pass authority or responsibility on to someone else; *she finds it difficult to delegate; he delegated the job of locking up the shop to the junior manager*

④ **delegation**
[delɪ'geɪʃn] *noun*

(a) group of representatives; *the minister met a union delegation*

(b) passing authority or responsibility to someone else; *the secret of good management is delegation* (NOTE: no plural in this meaning)

③ **deliberate**
1 *adjective*

[dɪ'lɪbərɪt]

(a) done on purpose; *it was a deliberate attempt to spoil her birthday party; the fans came with the deliberate intention of stirring up trouble*

(b) slow and thoughtful in speaking or doing something; *she has a very deliberate way of signing her name*

2 *verb*

[dɪ'lɪbəreɪt]

(a) to debate, to discuss; *the council were deliberating all morning; the jury left the courtroom to deliberate*

(b) to think carefully about something; *I'll need some time to deliberate on the possible ways of solving the problem*

③ **deliberately**
[dɪ'lɪbərɪtli] *adverb*

(a) on purpose; *it was an accident - I didn't hit her deliberately; he deliberately left the cage door open; the police think that the fire was started deliberately*

(b) slowly and carefully; *she walked deliberately up the steps onto the platform*

④ **delicate**
['delɪkɪt] *adjective*

(a) easily damaged; *a delicate china bowl*

(b) liable to get illnesses; *little babies are very delicate*

(c) very soft and fine; *a delicate silk dress*

(d) possibly difficult; *he is in a delicate situation*

④ **delicious**
[dɪ'lɪʃɪs] *adjective*
which tastes very good; *can I have another piece of that delicious cake?*

④ **delight**
[dɪ'laɪt]
1 *noun*
pleasure; *their singing was a pure delight*; *the news was greeted with delight by the waiting crowd*; **to take great delight in something** = to take great pleasure in something
2 *verb*
to delight in something = to take great pleasure in something; *she delights in teasing her little brother*

② **delighted**
[dɪ'laɪtɪd] *adjective*
very pleased; *she's delighted with her present*; *we are delighted that you were able to come*; *I'm delighted to meet you at last*

② **delightful**
[dɪ'laɪtful] *adjective*
very pleasant; *we had a delightful picnic by the river*

② **deliver**
[dɪ'lɪvɪ] *verb*
(a) to bring something to someone; *has today's newspaper been delivered?*; *he delivered the letter himself so as to save buying a stamp*
(b) to deliver a baby = to help a mother when a baby is born; *the twins were delivered by the nurse*
(b) to deliver a speech = to make a speech; *this is the full text of the speech the President delivered at the meeting*

② **delivery**
[dɪ'lɪvrɪ] *noun*
(a) bringing something to someone; *there is no charge for delivery within the London area*; *use the rear entrance for deliveries*; *the next delivery will be on Thursday*; **delivery van** = goods van for delivering goods to retail customers
(b) birth of a child; *the doctor supervised the delivery*

① **demand**
[dɪ'mɑːnd]
1 *noun*
(a) asking for something; *they made a demand for payment*; *her latest demands are quite impossible to meet*; **final demand** = last reminder from a supplier, after which he will sue for payment or cut off supplies; *we had a final demand from the gas company*
(b) need for goods or services at a certain price; **to meet a demand** *or* **to fill a demand** = to supply what is needed; *the factory had to increase production to meet the extra demand*; *we cannot keep up with the demand for our services*; **there is not much demand for this item** = not many people want to buy it; **this item is in great demand** = many people want to buy

it; **law of supply and demand** = general rule that the amount of a product which is available is linked to the amount which is wanted by customers
2 *verb*
to ask for something in a firm way; *she demanded a refund*; *I demand an explanation*

③ **demanding**
[dɪ'mɑːdɪŋ] *adjective*
which takes up much time and energy; *he has a very demanding job*; *looking after little children is very demanding*

② **democracy**
[dɪ'mɒkrɪsɪ] *noun*
(a) country governed by elected representatives of the people; *we live in a democracy* (NOTE: plural is **democracies**)
(b) system of government by elected representatives of the people; *the people want democracy, not a military government* (NOTE: no plural in this meaning)

③ **democrat**
['demɪkræt] *noun*
(a) person who believes in democracy; *all true democrats will unite against the military rulers*
(b) *US* **a Democrat** = a member of the Democratic Party; *the Democrats lost the election to the Republicans*

② **democratic**
[demɪ'krætɪk] *adjective*
referring to democracy; *they promised to restore democratic government*

③ **Democratic Party**
[demɪ'krætɪk 'pɑːtɪ] *noun*
one of the two main political parties in the USA, which is in favour of some social change and state help for poor people; *the Democratic Party's candidate for the presidency*; *compare* REPUBLICAN PARTY

② **demonstrate**
['demɪnstreɪt] *verb*
(a) to show; *this demonstrates how little he has changed*; *he demonstrated how the machine worked*
(b) to demonstrate against something = to protest against something in public; *a group were demonstrating against the new motorway*

③ **demonstration**
[demɪn'streɪʃn] *noun*
(a) showing (how something works); *can you give me a demonstration of how it works?*; **demonstration model** = car, or other piece of equipment, which has been used by a shop to show how it works, and is then sold at a lower price
(b) crowd of people who are protesting against something; *we went shopping and got mixed up in a demonstration in Trafalgar Square*; *they staged demonstrations against the government in several towns*

③ **demonstrator**
['demɪnstreɪtɪ] *noun*

(a) person who shows how to do something or how pieces of equipment work; *the demonstrator showed how to work the electric saw*

(b) person who marches, or who forms part of a crowd protesting against something; *a crowd of demonstrators blocked the road*; *the police used tear gas to clear demonstrators from in front of the Parliament building*

④ **denial**
[dɪ'naɪl] *noun*
statement that something is not true; *despite his repeated denials, people still suspect he is the man responsible for planting the bomb*; *the company issued a denial that it was planning to close down the factory*

① **Denmark**
['denmɑːk] *noun*
country in northern Europe, south of Sweden and Norway, and north of Germany; *Legoland is one of the tourist attractions of Denmark* (NOTE: capital: **Copenhagen**; people: **the Danes**; language: **Danish**; currency: **Danish krone**)

④ **dense**
[dens] *adjective*
(a) very thick; *dense fog closed the airport*
(b) crowded together; *they tried to find their way through dense forest*; *I find it difficult to read through 100 pages of dense text*
(c) *(informal)* stupid; *how can anybody be so dense?* (NOTE: **denser - densest**)

④ **dental**
['dentl] *adjective*
referring to teeth; *he's a dental student*; dental surgery = a dentist's office

② **dentist**
['dentɪst] *noun*
person who looks after your teeth; *she had to wait for an hour at the dentist's*; *he hates going to the dentist*; *the dentist filled two of my teeth*

② **deny**
[dɪ'naɪ] *verb*
(a) to state that something is not correct; *you were there, weren't you? - don't deny it!*; *she denied that she had ever seen him*; *he denied stealing the car*
(b) to deny someone something = to prevent someone having something; *he was denied access to the secret government papers*; to deny oneself = not to eat, not to do something, which you would like to do; *she denied herself a holiday in order to earn enough to pay off her mortgage*

④ **depart**
[dɪ'pɑːt] *verb*
(a) to go away, to leave; *the coach will depart from Victoria Coach Station at 0900*
(b) to depart from the normal procedure = to act in a different way from the normal practice

① **department**
[dɪ'pɑːtmɪnt] *noun*
(a) specialized section of a large company; *he is in charge of the marketing department*; *write to the complaints department about the service*; accounts department = section in a company which deals with money paid or received, borrowed or owed; *if you have a query about your bill, ask to speak to the accounts department*
(b) one of the sections of the government; *the Department for Education and Employment*; *the Department of Transport*
(c) part of a large shop; *if you want cheese you must go to the food department*; *you will find beds in the furniture department*

③ **department store**
[dɪ'pɑːtmɪnt 'stɔː] *noun*
a large shop with many departments; *Selfridges is one of the largest department stores in London*

③ **departure**
[dɪ'pɑːtʃɪ] *noun*
(a) leaving; *the departure time is 3 o'clock*; *the plane's departure was delayed by two hours*
(b) departures = (i) list of trains, planes, etc., which are leaving; (ii) part of an airport terminal which deals with passengers who are leaving; departure lounge = waiting area at an airport for people who are about to leave
(c) departure from = working in a different way from usual; this is a departure from our usual practice = we are doing something in a different way from the usual one

① **depend**
[dɪ'pend] *verb*
(a) to happen because of something or someone; *the success of the book will depend on the publicity campaign*; *I can't be sure that we will come to lunch - it depends on what time we get home from the party the night before*; *(informal)* it (all) depends = it is not certain; *we may go to France on holiday, or Spain, it all depends*
(b) to depend on someone *or* something = to rely on someone *or* something, to be sure of someone *or* something; *you can't depend on Jack - he's always too busy to help*; *you can depend on her to do her best*

③ **dependent**
[dɪ'pendɪnt] *adjective*
(a) supported with money by someone; *she has five dependent relatives*
(b) relying on someone else; *the patients become very dependent on the hospital staff*

① **depending**
[dɪ'pendɪŋ] *adjective*
depending on = which varies according to something; *it takes around one hour to drive to the centre of London, depending on the traffic*

④ **deport**
[dɪ'pɔːt] *verb*
to expel someone from a country; *the refugees were ordered to be deported*

deposit
[dɪˈpɒzɪt]

1 *noun*

(a) money placed (in a bank); *her deposits in the bank had grown over the years*; **deposit account** = bank account which pays an interest if you leave money in it for some time; *compare* CURRENT ACCOUNT, SAVINGS ACCOUNT; **deposit slip** = piece of paper stamped by the bank to prove that you have paid money into your account; **on deposit** = in a deposit account; *the money is on deposit in his bank account*

(b) money given in advance so that the thing which you want to buy will not be sold to someone else; *she had to pay a deposit on the watch*; *can you leave £50 as deposit?*; *I paid a 30% deposit and don't have to pay anything more for six months*

(c) layer of mineral in the ground; *coal deposits occur in several parts of the country*; *the North Sea oil deposits yield 100,000 barrels a month*

2 *verb*

to put money into a bank account; *he deposited £100 in his current account*; *the cheque arrived at long last, and I deposited it immediately*

depressed
[dɪˈprest] *adjective*

(a) sad, miserable; *she's been feeling depressed since the accident*

(b) **depressed area** = part of a country where people are poor and unemployed and living conditions are bad

depressing
dɪˈpresɪŋ] *adjective*

gloomy; *a depressing November day*; *that film is deeply depressing - it just made me want to cry*

depression
[dɪˈpreʃn] *noun*

(a) mental state where you feel miserable and hopeless; *he was in a state of depression after the exams*; *she is subject to fits of depression*

(b) low pressure area bringing bad weather; *the depression coming from the Atlantic will bring rain to most parts of the country*; *winds move rapidly round the centre of a depression*

(c) economic crisis; *an economic depression*; **the (Great) Depression** = the world economic crisis of 1929-1933; *all economies suffered during the Depression*

(d) place which is lower than the area round it; *a pool of water had formed in a depression in the rocks*

deprive
[dɪˈpraɪv] *verb*

to deprive someone of something = to take something away from someone, not to let someone have something; *as an artist, it was dreadful for him to be deprived of his paints in prison*

dept.
= DEPARTMENT

depth
[depθ] *noun*

(a) how deep something is; *the depth of the lake is 20m*; *the submarine dived to a depth of 200m*

(b) deepest or most extreme point; *in the depth of the Russian winter, temperatures can reach -45°C*; *they have a house in the depths of rural Wales*; **the depths of despair** = complete lack of hope; *when he lay in bed in the depths of despair and thought of committing suicide*

◊ **out of your depth**
phrase

(a) to be in deep water and not be able to touch the bottom; *she got out of her depth and had to be rescued by the beach guards*

(b) to be unable to understand; *he's quite out of his depth in discussions about monetary theory*

deputy
[ˈdepjuti] *noun*

person who can take the place of another person; *he appointed her as his deputy*; *she's acting as deputy chairman while the chairman is in hospital*

derive
[dɪˈraɪv] *verb*

(a) **to derive from** *or* **to be derived from** = to come from originally; *the name of the plant 'fuchsia' is derived from the name of the German scientist, Fuchs*

(b) *(formal)* to get; *the local people derive a good deal of pleasure from watching the tourists riding on camels*

descend
[dɪˈsend] *verb*

(a) to go down (a ladder, etc.); *the president seemed to trip as he descended the steps from the plane*

(b) **to descend from someone** = to have someone as an ancestor; *he is descended from one of William the Conqueror's knights*

(c) **to descend on** = to visit in large numbers; *my wife's family descended on us for Christmas*; *crowds of children descended on the ice cream van*

describe
[dɪˈskraɪb] *verb*

to say or write what something *or* someone is like; *can you describe the car which hit the old lady?*; *she described how the bus suddenly left the road*; *he described the mugger as a tall man with a black beard*; *the police asked him to describe what happened*

description
[dɪˈskrɪpʃn] *noun*

saying or writing what something *or* someone is like; *she gave the police a clear description of the car*; **job description** = official document from a company which says what a job involves

desert
1 [ˈdezɪt] *noun*

very dry area of the world; *from Los Angeles you can drive into the Mojave Desert; she plans to cross the Sahara Desert on a motorbike; it hardly ever rains in the desert; we watched a TV programme on desert animals* (NOTE: do not confuse with **dessert**)

2 *verb*

[dɪ'zɜːt]

(a) to leave the armed forces without permission; *the general ordered that all soldiers who had deserted should be captured and shot*

(b) to leave someone all alone; *he deserted his wife when she was expecting their second child*

② **deserve**

[dɪ'zɜːv] *verb*

to earn something because of what you have done; *he didn't deserve to win because I think he cheated; I've been on my feet all day - I think I deserve a rest; I'm sure she deserved to be punished; see also* TURN

① **design**

[dɪ'zaɪn]

1 *noun*

(a) plan or drawing of something, before it is made or built; *here are the designs for the book cover; the architect has produced the designs for the new town hall*

(b) to have designs on something = to plan to try to take something; *I think he has designs on my job*

2 *verb*

to draw plans for the shape or appearance of something before it is made or built; *he designed the new university library; she designs garden furniture*

③ **designer**

[dɪ'zaɪnɪ] *noun*

artist who plans the shape or appearance of goods, clothes, rooms, etc.; *we've chosen an interior designer to plan the inside of the house;* **designer clothes** = clothes designed by a famous designer; *she was wearing designer jeans;* **designer label** = label attached to clothes made by a famous designer; *see also* INTERIOR DESIGNER

④ **desirable**

[dɪ'zaɪrɪbl] *adjective*

which a lot of people want; *this has become a very desirable part of the town to live in*

② **desire**

[dɪ'zaɪ]

1 *noun*

something that you want very much; *it's difficult to satisfy the public's desire for information; she had a sudden desire to lie down and go to sleep*

2 *verb*

(a) *(formal)* to want; *he will get you anything you desire*

(b) to leave a lot to be desired = not to be of the right standard, not to be acceptable; *the bathrooms in the hotel leave a lot to be desired*

② **desk**

[desk] *noun*

(a) table for writing (often with drawers); *he put the papers away in his desk drawer; she was sitting at her desk when the telephone rang;* **desk pad** = pad of paper kept on a desk for writing notes

(b) cash desk *or* **pay desk** = place in a shop where you pay for the goods bought; *please pay at the cash desk*

(c) section of a newspaper, of a government department; *he works on the City desk; she on the Central Europe desk in the Foreign Office*

④ **despair**

[dɪ'speɪ]

1 *noun*

lack of hope; *he was in despair when he lost his job and his girlfriend left him;* **the depths of despair** = complete lack of hope (NOTE: no plural)

2 *verb*

to despair of something = to give up all hope of something; *after two months in the jungle, he despaired of ever being rescued*

③ **despatch**

[dɪs'pætʃ]

see DISPATCH

③ **desperate**

['desprɪt] *adjective*

(a) hopeless; *food ran out and the situation on the ship was becoming desperate*

(b) urgent; *there is a desperate need of medical supplies*

(c) wild with despair; *when he didn't phone she became desperate with worry*

④ **despise**

[dɪ'spaɪz] *verb*

to look down on someone, to think someone is not worth much; *I despise people who always agree with the boss; she despised his attempts to speak French when ordering food in a restaurant*

① **despite**

[dɪ'spaɪt] *preposition*

in spite of; *despite the wet weather we still enjoyed our holiday*

④ **dessert**

[dɪ'zɜːt] *noun*

sweet course at the end of a meal; *the meal will end with a dessert of strawberries and cream; what's for dessert?;* **dessert menu** = special separate menu for desserts in a restaurant; *can I see the dessert menu please?;* **dessert spoon** = spoon which is larger than a teaspoon, but smaller than a soup spoon, used for eating desserts (NOTE: do not confuse with **desert;** the word **dessert** is mainly used in restaurants. At home, this part of the meal is usually called **the sweet** *or* **pudding**)

④ **destination**
[destɪˈneɪʃn] *noun*
place to which a person or vehicle is going; *we reached our destination at eight o'clock*; *the destination is shown on the front of the bus*

④ **destiny**
[ˈdestɪnɪ] *noun*
(a) what will happen to you in the future; *the war affected the destinies of many people*
(b) power that controls what happens to you in the future; *you never know what destiny has in store for you*

② **destroy**
[dɪˈstrɔɪ] *verb*
to ruin completely; *the bomb destroyed several buildings*; *a lot of private property was destroyed in the war*

② **destruction**
[dɪˈstrʌkʃn] *noun*
action of ruining completely, of causing a lot of damage; *the volcano caused enormous destruction*; *the destruction of the village by enemy bombs*; *after the bomb attack there was a scene of total destruction* (NOTE: no plural)

④ **destructive**
[dɪˈstrʌktɪv] *adjective*
which destroys, which causes a lot of damage; *the destructive power of an earthquake*

① **detail**
[ˈdiːteɪl]
1 *noun*
(a) small item of information; *send in your CV including full details of your past experience*; *can you give me further details of when the accident took place?*; *I can't make out the details in the photo because the light is bad*
(b) in detail = with plenty of details; *the catalogue lists all the furniture in detail*; *please describe the circumstances of the accident in as much detail as possible*
2 *verb*
(a) to list all the small items; *he detailed the work which had to be done*
(b) to detail someone to do something = to tell someone to do a job; *he was detailed to wash the kitchen floor*

② **detailed**
[ˈdiːteɪld] *adjective*
in detail, giving a lot of details; *we need a detailed list of the items which have been stolen*; *the police issued detailed descriptions of the two men*

③ **detect**
[dɪˈtekt] *verb*
to discover; to notice; *a little device detects the presence of smoke*; *if breast cancer is detected early enough, it can be cured*; *do I detect a note of optimism in your report?*

③ **detective**
[dɪˈtektɪv] *noun*
policeman who investigates crimes; *detectives have interviewed four suspects*; **private**

detective = detective who is not part of a police force, and works for a fee; *we hired a private detective to track them down*

④ **deter**
[dɪˈtɜː] *verb*
to deter someone from doing something = to put someone off doing something; *the heavy rain didn't deter the tourists from visiting the castle*; *we have installed cameras to deter shoplifters* (NOTE: deterring - deterred)

④ **deteriorate**
[dɪˈtɪərɪəreɪt] *verb*
to become bad; to get worse; *her health has deteriorated since the accident*; *deteriorating weather conditions make driving difficult*

④ **determination**
[dɪtɜːmɪˈneɪʃn] *noun*
strong wish to do something, and not to let anyone stop you doing it; *his determination to win the prize*; *the government needs to show more determination in their fight against drugs* (NOTE: no plural)

① **determine**
[dɪˈtɜːmɪn] *verb*
(a) to fix (a date, etc.); *the meeting will be at a date still to be determined*
(b) *(formal)* **to determine to do something** = to make up your mind to do something; *I determined not to make the same mistake again*

③ **determined**
[dɪˈtɜːmɪnd] *adjective*
decided; *he had a very determined expression on his face as he entered the ring*; *she is determined to win the prize*

④ **deuce**
[djuːs] *noun*
score of 40 - 40 in tennis; *see note at* TENNIS

④ **devastating**
[ˈdevɪsteɪtɪŋ] *adjective*
(a) causing a lot of damage; *the country has still not recovered from the devastating effects of the storm*
(b) which shocks or upsets; *the news from Paris was devastating*

① **develop**
[dɪˈveləp] *verb*
(a) to grow and change; *eventually, that little plant will develop into a giant oak*
(b) to make larger; *she does exercises to develop her leg muscles*
(c) to start a disease, etc.; *she developed a cold from standing in the rain*
(d) to produce and fix a photograph from film; *we can develop your film in an hour*
(e) to plan and produce; *to develop a new product*
(f) to plan and build; *they are planning to develop the site as an industrial estate*; *the company is developing a chain of motorway service stations*

developer

[dɪ'veləpə] *noun*

(a) person or company that plans and builds roads, airports, houses, factories or office buildings; *the land has been acquired by developers for a housing estate*; **property developer** = person who plans and builds property

(b) liquid for developing photographs; *she put the film into a bath of developer*

developing

[dɪ'veləpɪŋ] *adjective*

(a) growing; *his rapidly developing network of contacts in government*; *her developing knowledge of the English language*

(b) **developing countries** = countries with industries which are growing

development

[dɪ'veləpmɪnt] *noun*

(a) growth; *the development of the little plant takes place rapidly*; **economic development** = process by which a country's economy changes and its industries grow; **industrial development** = planning and building of new industries in special areas

(b) **developments** = things which happen; *the police are waiting for further developments in the case*

(c) planning the production of a new product; *the development of new drugs will take some time*

(d) planning and building on an area of land; *they are planning a large-scale development on the site of the former docks*; **development plan** = plan drawn up by a government or local council showing how an area will be developed over a long period; **housing development** = group of houses built at the same time

device

[dɪ'vaɪs] *noun*

(a) small useful machine; *he invented a device for screwing tops on bottles*; *the engineers brought in a device for taking samples of soil*

(b) **left to your own devices** = left to do whatever you want, left to look after yourself; *their parents were away and the children were left to their own devices*

devil

['devl] *noun*

(a) powerful evil spirit; *he believes in ghosts and devils and all that sort of thing*

(b) *(informal: showing surprise)* **what the devil?** = what on earth?; *what the devil has been going on here while we've been away?*

(c) *(informal)* person; *he's won the lottery, lucky devil!*; *poor devil! I must go and see him in hospital*; **little devil** = naughty child; *that little devil has been pulling the cat's tail*

devise

[dɪ'vaɪz] *verb*

to think up, to invent; *we've devised a new timetable for the summer term*; *he devised a plan for making more money out of the farm*

devote

[dɪ'vəʊt] *verb*

to devote time to something = to spend precious time on something; *don't you think you've devoted enough time to your model trains?*; **to devote yourself to** = to spend all your time on; *she devoted herself to looking after refugee children*

devoted

[dɪ'vəʊtɪd] *adjective*

(a) **devoted to someone** = loving someone; *he is devoted to his children*; *he died suddenly, leaving his devoted wife and six children*

(b) **devoted to something** = spending all your time on something; *she's devoted to her charity work*

diabetes

[daɪə'biːtiːz] *noun*

illness where the body cannot control the rate at which sugar is absorbed; *some people with diabetes give themselves daily injections* (NOTE: no plural)

diabetic

[daɪə'betɪk]

1 *adjective*

referring to diabetes; *the hospital provides a special diet for diabetic patients*; *he's on a strict diabetic diet*; **diabetic food** = special food with a low sugar content which can be eaten by people with diabetes

2 *noun*

person with diabetes; *she is a diabetic and has to be careful about what she eats*

diagnose

[daɪəg'nəʊz] *verb*

to identify a patient's illness by examining him or her and noting symptoms; *the doctor diagnosed cancer*

diagnosis

[daɪəg'nəʊsɪs] *noun*

action of identifying an illness; *tests confirmed the doctor's diagnosis*; *the doctor's diagnosis was cancer, but the patient asked for a second opinion* (NOTE: plural is **diagnoses**)

diagram

['daɪəgræm] *noun*

sketch, plan or accurate drawing; *she drew a diagram to show how to get to her house*; *the book gives a diagram of the circulation of blood*

dial

['daɪl]

1 *noun*

round face of a clock, meter, telephone, etc.; *modern telephones don't have dials - just buttons*

2 *verb*

to call a telephone number; *to call the police you must dial 999*; *dial 9 to get an outside line*; **to dial direct** = to contact a phone number yourself without asking the operator to do it for you; *you can dial New York direct from London* (NOTE: **dialling - dialled**, but American spelling is **dialing - dialed**)

④ **dialogue** *US* **dialog**
['daɪɒlɒg] *noun*
(a) conversation between two people; *the next exercise on the tape is a dialogue between a shopkeeper and a customer*
(b) spoken words in a film or TV drama; *turn the volume up so that we can hear the dialogue more clearly*
(c) political talks or negotiations; *the government is trying to encourage greater dialogue in the Middle East*

④ **diameter**
[daɪ'æmɪtɪ] *noun*
distance across the centre of a circle; *each tube is one centimetre in diameter*

③ **diamond**
['daɪmɪnd] *noun*
(a) very hard precious stone; *he gave her a diamond ring*; *diamonds sparkled on her crown*; **diamond wedding** = 60th anniversary of a wedding day
(b) one of the red suits in a pack of cards; *he held the ten of diamonds* (NOTE: the other red suit is **hearts**; **clubs** and spades are the black suits)

③ **diaper**
['daɪpɪ] *noun*
US cloth which is wrapped round a baby's bottom; *she changed the baby's diaper* (NOTE: British English for this is **nappy**)

③ **diary**
['daɪrɪ] *noun*
(a) description of what has happened in your life day by day; *he kept a diary for years*; *she kept a diary of the places she visited on holiday*
(b) small book in which you write notes or make appointments for each day of the week; *I've noted the appointment in my desk diary*; *I can't fix the date immediately because I haven't got my diary with me* (NOTE: plural is **diaries**)

④ **dice**
[daɪs]
1 *noun*
small cube with one to six dots on each side, used for playing games; *shake the dice in the cup and then throw them onto the board*; *he lost hundreds of pounds playing dice* (NOTE: plural is **dice**)
2 *verb*
(a) to cut food into small cubes; *a cup of diced potato*
(b) *(informal)* **to dice with death** = to do something very risky; *running across the main road is dicing with death*

④ **dictate**
[dɪk'teɪt] *verb*
(a) to say something to someone who writes down your words; *she dictated a letter to her secretary*; *he dictated his address to me over the phone*
(b) to tell someone what to do; *the army commander dictated the terms of the surrender*; *she's always trying to dictate to us how to run the business*

③ **dictation**
[dɪk'teɪʃn] *noun*
act of speaking something which is to be written down; *I got nine out of ten for French dictation*; **to take dictation** = to write down what someone is saying; *the secretary was taking dictation from the managing director*

④ **dictator**
[dɪk'teɪtɪ] *noun*
person who rules a country alone; *the country was ruled by a military dictator*

④ **dictionary**
['dɪkʃɪnrɪ] *noun*
book which lists words, giving their meanings or translations into other languages; *look up the word in the dictionary if you don't know what it means*; **a French dictionary** = book which gives English words with their French translations, and French words with their English translations; *if you want to find the French translation of this word, look it up in a French dictionary*; **pocket dictionary** = small dictionary which you can put in your pocket (NOTE: plural is **dictionaries**)

① **did, didn't**
[dɪd or dɪdnt]
see DO

① **die**
[daɪ] *verb*
to stop living; *his mother died in 1995*; *she died in a car crash*; *if you don't water the plants they'll die*; *see also* DYING (NOTE: do not confuse with **dye**; note also **dies - dying**)

① **die out**
['daɪ 'aʊt] *verb*
to disappear gradually; *the habit of having a cooked breakfast is dying out*; *this butterfly is likely to die out unless measures are taken to protect it*

② **diet**
['daɪɪt]
1 *noun*
(a) kind of food you eat; *he lives on a diet of bread and beer*; *during the war, people were much healthier than now because their diet was simpler*
(b) eating only certain types of food, either to become thinner or to cure an illness; *the doctor told her to follow a strict diet*; *because she is pregnant she has to follow a diet*; **salt-free diet** = diet which does not contain salt; **to be on a diet** = to eat only certain types of food,

especially in order to become thin or to deal with an illness; *he's been on a diet for some weeks, but still hasn't lost enough weight*; **to go on a diet** = to start to eat less; *she went on a diet before going on holiday*
2 *verb*
to eat less food or only one sort of food; *she dieted for two weeks before going on holiday*; *he is dieting to try to lose weight*

③ **differ**
['dɪfɪ] *verb*
(a) not to be the same as something else; *the two machines differ considerably - one has an electric motor, the other runs on oil*; **to differ from** = to be different from, not to be the same as; *this car differs from the earlier model*; *their business differs from ours in one important way*
(b) I beg to differ = I do not agree

① **difference**
['dɪfrɪns] *noun*
(a) way in which two things are not the same; *can you tell the difference between an apple and a pear with your eyes shut?*; *what is the difference in price between these two cars?*; **it doesn't make any difference** = it's not important; *you can use any colour you like - it doesn't make any difference*; **to split the difference** = to agree on a figure which is half way between two figures suggested; *twenty's too many, ten's not enough, let's split the difference and say fifteen*; *you are offering £20 and he wants £40, so why don't you split the difference and settle on £30?*
(b) differences = arguments between people; *they had a meeting to try to settle their differences*

① **different**
['dɪfrɪnt] *adjective*
not the same; *living in the town is very different from living in the country*; *I went to three different clothes shops but I couldn't find anything in my size*; *he looks different now that he has a beard*; **that's quite a different matter** = it's not at all the same thing

④ **differently**
['dɪfrɪntli] *adverb*
not in the same way; *the same subject is treated quite differently in the three paintings*

① **difficult**
['dɪfɪkʌlt] *adjective*
not easy; which is hard to do; *the German examination was very difficult - half the class got low marks*; *finding a parking space is difficult on Saturday mornings*; *the company is finding it difficult to sell their cars in the European market*; *it's difficult for me to judge my own sister from an objective point of view*; **to make things** *or* **life difficult for someone** = to create problems for someone; *his main aim at the office seems to be to make life as difficult as possible for his assistants*

① **difficulty**
['dɪfɪkʌlti] *noun*
(a) to have difficulty with something *or* **in doing something** to find it hard to do something; *she has difficulty in paying the rent*
(b) problem; *the difficulty is that nobody has a driving licence*; *he is in financial difficulties*; *she went swimming in the rough sea and got into difficulties*; **to create** *or* **make difficulties for someone** = to make problems for someone; *she doesn't realize that going on holiday now is going to make difficulties for everyone* (NOTE: plural is **difficulties**)

③ **dig**
[dɪg]
1 *verb*
to make a hole in the ground (with a spade); *she's been digging in the garden all morning*; *the prisoners dug a tunnel to try to escape*; *digging holes in the ground is hard work* (NOTE: **digging - dug** [dʌg] **- has dug**)
2 *noun*
(a) making holes in the ground to find something old; *they are working on a dig to find the remains of a Roman town*
(b) funny attack in words; *the song is a dig at the Prime Minister*

④ **digest**
[daɪ'dʒest] *verb*
(a) to break down food in the stomach and convert it into elements which can be absorbed by the body; *I find cabbage salad difficult to digest*
(b) to think about something and understand it fully; *give me time to digest the news*

④ **digest**
[daɪ'dʒest] *verb*
(a) to break down food in the stomach and convert it into elements which can be absorbed by the body; *I find cabbage salad difficult to digest*
(b) to think about something and understand it fully; *just give me a few moments to digest the news*

④ **digestion**
[dɪ'dʒestʃɪn] *noun*
process by which food is broken down and the elements in it are absorbed into the body; *brown bread helps the digestion*

④ **dignified**
['dɪgnɪfaɪd] *adjective*
solemn, looking important; *a dignified old gentleman came out of the bank*; *she was walking at a dignified pace*

③ **dig up**
['dɪg 'ʌp] *verb*
(a) to find by digging; *we dug up a Roman coin in the garden*
(b) to break a solid surface by digging; *the workmen had to dig the road up to mend the gas pipe*

(c) to find information with difficulty; *he managed to dig up some old government statistics*

④ **dilemma**
[dɪ'lemɪ] *noun*
serious problem, where a choice has to be made between several alternatives none of which is really acceptable; *how can we ever solve this awful dilemma?*; **in a dilemma** = not sure what action to take

④ **dilute**
[daɪ'ljuːt] *verb*
(a) to add a liquid, usually water, to another liquid to make it weaker; *dilute the acid with water*
(b) to make something weaker and less effective; *the minister's proposals were thought too radical and so had to be diluted before being announced to the press*

④ **dim**
[dɪm]
1 *adjective*
(a) weak (light); *the lights grew dimmer*; **to take a dim view of something** = to disapprove of something; *the boss takes a very dim view of people who arrive late for work*
(b) rather stupid; *he must be the dimmest sales manager we've ever had* (NOTE: **dimmer - dimmest**)
2 *verb*
(a) to make a light less bright; *they dimmed the cabin lights before the plane took off*
(b) to become less bright; *the cinema lights dimmed before the programme started* (NOTE: **dimming - dimmed**)

③ **dimension**
[daɪ'menʃn] *noun*
(a) **dimensions** = measurements of length, height, etc.; *what are the dimensions of the hall?*
(b) size of a problem; *the international dimension of the refugee issue*; *the task is taking on huge dimensions*

④ **diminish**
[dɪ'mɪnɪʃ] *verb*
(a) to make something smaller or weaker; *nothing will ever diminish his enthusiasm for fast cars*
(b) to become smaller or weaker; *my income has diminished over the last few years*

④ **dine**
[daɪn] *verb*
(formal) to have dinner; *we normally dine at 8.30*; **to dine out** = to have dinner away from home; *we're dining out tonight*

③ **dining room**
['daɪnɪŋ 'ruːm] *noun*
room in a house or hotel where you usually eat; *we were sitting in the dining room having supper*; *he was doing his homework on the dining room table*

① **dinner**
['dɪnɪ] *noun*
(a) main meal of the day (usually eaten in the evening); *we were having dinner when the telephone rang*; *would you like to come to dinner on Saturday?*; *he ate his dinner quickly because there was a TV programme he wanted to watch*; *what are we having for dinner?* or *what's for dinner?*; *the restaurant is open for dinner* or *serves dinner from 7.30 to 11.30*; **dinner party** = private dinner to which guests are invited; **dinner plate** = wide flat plate for serving the main course on
(b) formal evening meal; *the club is organizing a dinner and dance on Saturday*; **dinner jacket** = a man's formal black jacket (worn with a bow tie)
(c) meal eaten in the middle of the day (especially at school); *school dinners are awful*; **dinner lady** = woman who helps serve dinners at a school (NOTE: if you call the meal in the middle of the day **dinner,** then you call the evening meal **tea** or **supper**; if you call the evening meal **dinner** then you call the meal in the middle of the day **lunch.** In schools, the meal in the middle of the day is always called **dinner;** in offices, it is always called **lunch**)

③ **dinnertime**
['dɪnɪtaɪm] *noun*
time when you usually have dinner; *hurry up, it's almost dinnertime*

④ **dinosaur**
['daɪnɪsɔː] *noun*
large animal that lived many millions of years ago, and whose bones are found in rock; *at the time when dinosaurs lived, England was covered with tropical forests*

③ **dip**
[dɪp]
1 *noun*
(a) sudden drop of a road, of land; *watch out - there's a dip in the road which makes it difficult to see cars coming in the opposite direction*
(b) soft food into which biscuits, etc., can be dipped as snacks; *a bowl of smoked salmon dip*
(c) short bathe or swim; *we went for a quick dip before breakfast*; *are you coming for a dip in the pool?*
(d) sudden small fall; *last year there was a dip in our sales*
2 *verb*
(a) **to dip something into** = to put something quickly into a liquid; *she dipped the biscuit into her coffee*; *he dipped his hand into the stream*
(b) to fall suddenly; *shares dipped sharply on the stock exchange*; *the bird flew overhead then dipped behind the trees*
(c) **to dip your headlights** = to lower the beam of the headlights of your car; *please drive with dipped headlights in the tunnel* (NOTE: **dipping - dipped**)

diploma
[dɪˈpləʊmə] *noun*

document which shows that a person has reached a certain level of skill in a subject; *she has a diploma in personnel management; he is studying for a diploma in engineering; at the end of the course she was awarded a diploma*

diplomacy
[dɪˈpləʊməsɪ] *noun*

art of negotiating between different sides, especially between different countries; *civil servants skilled in diplomacy are dealing with the negotiations*; **shuttle diplomacy** = going backwards and forwards between countries to try to solve an international crisis (NOTE: no plural)

diplomat
[ˈdɪpləmæt] *noun*

person (such as an ambassador) who represents his country abroad and discusses matters with representatives from other countries; *the ambassador had invited diplomats from other countries to the reception*

diplomatic
[dɪpləˈmætɪk] *adjective*

(a) referring to diplomats; *we are looking for a diplomatic solution to the crisis, rather than sending in troops*; **diplomatic immunity** = being outside the control of the laws of the country you are living in because of being a diplomat; *he refused to pay his parking fines and claimed diplomatic immunity*; **the Diplomatic Service** = the government department concerned with relations with other countries; *he has decided on a career in the Diplomatic Service*

(b) careful not to give offence; *it wouldn't be very diplomatic to arrive late for the wedding*

direct
[daɪˈrekt]

1 *adjective*

(a) straight, without any bends or stops; *this phone number will give you a direct line to the minister*; **direct flight** = flight without any stops; *there are direct flights every day to London*

(b) not involving another person or organization; **direct debit** = system where a customer allows a company to charge costs to his bank account automatically and where the amount charged can be increased or decreased with the agreement of the customer; *I pay my electricity bills by direct debit*; **direct mail** = selling something by sending publicity material to possible buyers through the post; **direct taxation** = tax, such as income tax, which is paid straight to the government

(c) not trying to hide the meaning or make a meaning weaker; *I want a direct answer to a direct question*

2 *verb*

(a) to manage or to organize; *he directs our London operations*; *the policeman was directing the traffic*

(b) to aim towards a point; *can you direct me to the nearest post office?*; *he directed his remarks to the head of the complaints department*

(c) to tell someone to do something; *the spray has to be used as directed on the bottle*; *he did as he had been directed, and took the plane to Birmingham*

3 *adverb*

(a) straight, without stopping; *you can telephone New York direct from here*; *the plane flies direct to Anchorage*

(b) not involving other people; *they sell insurance direct to the public*

direction
[dɪˈrekʃn] *noun*

(a) point towards which you are going; *you are going in the wrong direction if you want to get to the station*; *the post office is in the opposite direction*; **in all directions** = everywhere; *the wind was blowing bits of old newspapers in all directions*; *see also* SENSE OF DIRECTION

(b) **directions** = instructions how to do something; *we couldn't find the railway station, so we asked a policeman for directions*; *I can't start the computer because there are no directions telling me how to put it together*; **directions for use** = instructions showing how to use something

(c) organizing or managing; *he took over the direction of the group*

directly
[daɪˈrektlɪ]

1 *adverb*

(a) straight, without anything or anyone between; *this door opens directly into the kitchen*; *she reports directly to the managing director himself*

(b) soon; *I'll be with you directly*

2 *conjunction*

as soon as; *I will write the letter directly I get home*

director
[daɪˈrektə] *noun*

(a) person who is appointed by the shareholders to help run a firm; *the sales director gave a report on sales*; *there are four directors on the board of the company*; **managing director** = director in charge of a company

(b) person in charge of an organization, a project, an official institute, etc.; *she's just started her job as director of an international charity*; **director-general** = person in charge of a large organization; *the Director-General of the BBC*

(c) person in charge of making a film or a play; *who was the first female director to win an Oscar?*

COMMENT: a director organizes the actual making of the film or play, giving instructions to the actors, dealing with the lighting, sound, etc. The producer is in general charge, especially of the finances of the film or play, but does not deal with the technical details

③ **directory**
[daɪˈrektɪri] *noun*
book giving lists of professional people, organizations or businesses with their addresses and telephone numbers; **classified directory** = book listing companies classified into groups; **street directory** = map of a town with all the streets listed in an index; **telephone directory** = book which lists names of people and businesses with their phone numbers and addresses; *look up his number in the telephone directory*; *his number must be in the London directory*; **directory enquiries** = telephone service which finds phone numbers which you do not know or cannot find; *call directory enquiries on 192*

③ **dirt**
[dɜːt] *noun*
(a) mud; earth; *children were playing in the dirt*; *his clothes were covered with dirt from handling potatoes*
(b) *(informal)* **dirt cheap** = very cheap; *I got the shoes dirt cheap in the market*

① **dirty**
[ˈdɜːti] *adjective*
(a) not clean; *playing rugby gets your clothes dirty*; *after the party, someone has to wash all the dirty plates*; *don't come into the kitchen with your dirty boots on*
(b) not honest, not done according to the rules; *he never uses violence himself, he just gets other people to do his dirty work for him*; *there was some dirty play from the other team*; *he's one of the dirtiest players in Football League*
(c) referring to sex; *he keeps the dirty magazines on the top shelf*; *he makes his money selling dirty postcards to tourists*; *(informal)* **dirty old man** = old man who shows a lot of interest in sex (NOTE: **dirtier - dirtiest**)

③ **dirty trick**
[ˈdɜːti ˈtrɪk] *noun*
(a) nasty action that upsets someone; *that was a dirty trick to play on an old lady*
(b) method of spoiling someone's plans or of ruining his reputation by spreading rumours; *they mounted a dirty tricks campaign against the rival company*

④ **disability**
[dɪsɪˈbɪlɪti] *noun*
physical handicap; *being deaf is a disability which affects many old people*; *people with severe disabilities can claim grants from the government*; **learning disability** = mental handicap, being unable to learn as fast as others

③ **disabled**
[dɪsˈeɪbld]
1 *adjective*
(a) physically handicapped; *a hospital for disabled soldiers*; *the car crash left him permanently disabled*
(b) not able to work properly; *a tug went to the help of the disabled cruise ship*
2 *noun*
the disabled = handicapped people; *the library has facilities for the disabled*; **access for the disabled** = entrances with sloping paths instead of steps, which are easier for people in wheelchairs to use; **disabled toilets** = public toilet with a larger room than usual to make it easier for people in wheelchairs to use (NOTE: more polite or formal terms for the **disabled** are **people with disabilities** *or* **people with special needs**)

④ **disadvantage**
[dɪsədˈvɑːntɪdʒ] *noun*
factor which makes someone *or* something less likely to succeed; *her main disadvantage is her lack of experience*; *it was a disadvantage not to be able to get to the airport quickly*; *there are certain disadvantages to leaving at 5.30 in the morning*; **at a disadvantage** = handicapped by something, suffering from a disadvantage; *we are at a disadvantage compared with our competitors because we have no salesmen*

② **disagree**
[dɪsəˈɡriː] *verb*
(a) not to agree, to say that you do not think the same way as someone; *we all disagreed with the chairman*; *they all disagreed about what to do next*
(b) **to disagree with someone** = to make someone feel ill; *raw onions disagree with me*

③ **disagreeable**
[dɪsəˈɡriːəbl] *adjective*
unpleasant; *he's a very disagreeable old man*; *we had a disagreeable meeting with the tax inspectors*

② **disagreement**
[dɪsəˈɡriːmɪnt] *noun*
argument; *they had a disagreement about who should sit in the front row*; *nothing could be decided because of the disagreement between the chairman and the secretary*

② **disappear**
[dɪsəˈpɪə] *verb*
to vanish, not to be seen any more; *he hit the ball hard and it disappeared into the bushes*; *there was a bottle of orange juice in the fridge this morning and now it's disappeared*; *the two boys disappeared on their way home from school*

③ **disappointed**
[dɪsəˈpɔɪntɪd] *adjective*
sad, because things did not turn out as expected; *she is disappointed with her exam results*; *he*

was disappointed because his ticket didn't win a prize; you should have seen the disappointed expression on his face

③ **disappointing**
[dɪsɪˈpɔɪntɪŋ] *adjective*
which makes you sad because it does not turn out as expected; *the results of the tests were disappointing; it's disappointing to see so few young people come to our meetings*

③ **disappointment**
[dɪsɪˈpɔɪntmɪnt] *noun*
(a) sadness because what was expected did not take place; *she tried hard not to show her disappointment; to his great disappointment, he didn't win anything on the lottery* (NOTE: no plural in this meaning)
(b) something that disappoints someone; *it was a disappointment to his parents when he failed his exam; after many disappointments she finally won a race*

④ **disapproval**
[dɪsɪˈpruːvɪl] *noun*
act of disapproving; *the Speaker showed her disapproval of the way the MPs behaved*

④ **disapprove**
[dɪsɪˈpruːv] *verb*
to disapprove of something = to show that you do not approve of something, that you do not think something is good; *the head teacher disapproves of members of staff wearing jeans to school*

② **disaster**
[dɪˈzɑːstɪ] *noun*
(a) catastrophe, very bad accident; *the disaster was caused by fog or due to fog; ten people died in the air disaster; insurance companies are paying out millions for flood disaster damage; we're insured against natural disasters such as storms and floods*
(b) something that is completely unsuccessful; *the advertising campaign was a disaster - our sales went down; if it rains on Saturday the village fair will be a complete disaster*
(c) financial collapse; **the company is heading for disaster** *or* **is on a disaster course** = the company is going to collapse

④ **disastrous**
[dɪˈzɑːstrɪs] *adjective*
very bad; *there have been disastrous floods in the region before; the country had a disastrous harvest; it would be disastrous if the car didn't start just when we need to get to the church on time*

② **disc**
[dɪsk] *noun*
(a) round flat object, such as a music record; *the setting sun was a huge orange disc on the horizon;* **disc jockey (DJ)** = person who plays recorded music at a night club; *the DJ played another track from the album*

(b) flat round bone which links with others to make the spine; **slipped disc** = painful back, caused by a disc having moved out of line (NOTE: British English prefers **disc**, but American English is usually **disk**)

④ **discard**
[dɪsˈkɑːd] *verb*
to put something on one side because it is no longer useful, to throw something away; *discard any damaged or burnt items*

④ **discharge**
1 *verb*
[dɪsˈtʃɑːdʒ]
(a) to get rid of waste; *the factory is discharging waste water into the river*
(b) to send someone away; *the judge discharged the jury;* **he was discharged from hospital** = he was sent home from hospital
(c) to let a prisoner go free; *the prisoners were discharged by the judge; he was discharged after having served eleven months in jail*
(d) *(formal)* to dismiss, to sack; *he was discharged for being late*
2 *noun*
[ˈdɪstʃɑːdʒ]
(a) liquid which comes out of a pipe, etc.; *the discharge from the factory flows into the river*
(b) release (of a prisoner); *he was arrested again within a month of his discharge from prison*

② **discipline**
[ˈdɪsɪplɪn]
1 *noun*
(a) keeping people under control; *the tour leaders are trying to keep discipline among the teenagers; we need to enforce stricter discipline in the school* (NOTE: no plural in this meaning)
(b) branch of learning; *chemistry and other related disciplines*
2 *verb*
to control someone, to punish someone; *as a result of the investigation, one employee was dismissed and three were disciplined; she was disciplined for swearing at her supervisor*

④ **disclose**
[dɪsˈkluːz] *verb*
to reveal a secret; *the journalists refused to disclose their sources to the police; the bank has no right to disclose details of my account to the tax people*

④ **disco**
[ˈdɪskɪʊ] *noun*
(informal) place where people dance to recorded music; *they spent the evening in the disco next door; you can't have a conversation in the disco because the music is too loud* (NOTE: plural is **discos**)

④ **discomfort**
[dɪsˈkʌmfɪt] *noun*
lack of comfort; *we suffered acute physical discomfort on the flight back from our vacation because it was so crowded*

③ discount

1 *noun*

['dɪskaʊnt] percentage by which a full price is reduced to a buyer by the seller; *the store gives a discount on bulk purchases*; *we give a discount on summer holidays booked before Christmas*; **to sell goods at a discount** *or* **at a discount price** = to sell goods below the normal price; **10% discount for cash** *or* **10% cash discount** = you pay 10% less if you pay in cash; **student discount** = reduction in price to students; **discount store** = shop selling cheap goods

2 *verb*

[dɪs'kaʊnt]

(a) to reduce a price; *we are discounting many items in our January sales*

(b) not to pay any attention to something; *don't discount all his advice - he is very experienced*

④ discourage

[dɪs'kʌrɪdʒ] *verb*

not to encourage; *we try to discourage people from coming in without tickets*; *don't be discouraged if people in the audience start to go to sleep*

③ discourse

['dɪskɔːs] *noun*

(formal) talk, speech; *we listened politely to a lengthy discourse on the history of the southern States*; *grammar mistakes are common in spoken discourse*

① discover

[dɪs'kʌvɪ] *verb*

to find something new; *in the year 1492 Columbus discovered America*; *who discovered aspirin?*; *we discovered that the estate agent had sold the house twice*; *the auditors discovered some errors in the accounts*

③ discovery

[dɪs'kʌvɪri] *noun*

(a) act of finding something new; *they congratulated him on his discovery of a new planet*; *her discovery that someone had been in her house while she was away*

(b) new thing which has been found; *the first discovery they made was that the lake contained salt water*; *look at his latest discovery - an old oak table which he found in a shed*

④ discretion

[dɪs'kreʃn] *noun*

(a) power to decide or choose what to do; **I leave it to your discretion** = I leave it for you to decide what to do; *tips are left to the discretion of the customer*

(b) wisdom, or good sense; *he showed great discretion in his handling of the family crisis*

(c) ability to keep a secret, not to give information about someone; *the chairman's secretary is known for her discretion* (NOTE: no plural)

③ discriminate

[dɪs'krɪmɪneɪt] *verb*

to distinguish; **to discriminate between** = to treat two things in different ways; *the board must not discriminate between men and women candidates*; *we discriminate between part-time and full-time staff*; **to discriminate against** = to be biased against; *she accused the management of discriminating against female members of staff*

④ discrimination

[dɪskrɪmɪ'neɪʃn] *noun*

(a) treating people in different ways because of class, religion, race, language, colour or sex; *we try to avoid discrimination against older applicants*; **racial discrimination** = bad treatment of someone because of their race; **sexual discrimination** *or* **sex discrimination** *or* **discrimination on grounds of sex** = treating men and women in different ways

(a) judgement, good taste; *the shop sells gifts which appeal to people of discrimination* (NOTE: no plural)

> COMMENT: in Britain, sexual and racial discrimination are against the law. The Equal Opportunities Commission deals with cases of sexual discrimination and the Commission for Racial Equality deals with cases of racial discrimination

① discuss

[dɪs'kʌs] *verb*

to talk about a serious matter or problem; *the point of the meeting is to discuss how to save money*; *they spent hours discussing the details of the wedding*

① discussion

[dɪs'kʌʃn] *noun*

talking about a serious matter or problem; *most problems can be solved by discussion*; *the next programme will feature a discussion between environmental experts*; *the discussion led to a violent argument*; *she had a heated discussion with the bus driver*

① disease

[dɪ'ziːz] *noun*

serious illness (of people, animals, plants, etc.); *hundreds of people caught the disease*; *it is a disease that can be treated with antibiotics*

③ disgrace

[dɪs'greɪs]

1 *noun*

(a) having lost someone's respect because of errors, scandal, corruption, etc.; *the minister's disgrace followed the discovery of the papers in his office*; **the minister fell into disgrace** = he became out of favour

(b) thing which brings shame; *he's a disgrace to the teaching profession*; *it was a disgrace to see her lying on the pavement like that*; *you say it is acceptable behaviour - I would term it a disgrace* (NOTE: no plural)

2 *verb*

to bring shame on; *he disgraced all his family by arriving drunk at the tea party*; **to disgrace yourself** = to do something which brings shame on you; *he disgraced himself by throwing sandwiches at the speakers at the conference*

④ **disgraceful**
[dɪsˈɡreɪsfʊl] *adjective*
which you should be ashamed of; *people living near the football stadium complained about the disgraceful behaviour of the fans*; *it's disgraceful that you have to pay £1 for a cup of tea in the museum café*

④ **disguise**
[dɪsˈɡaɪz]
1 *noun*
clothes, false hair, etc., to make a person look like someone else; *I didn't recognize him as he was wearing a disguise*; **in disguise** = dressed to look like someone else; *the burglar turned out to be a policeman in disguise*
2 *verb*
to dress so as to look like someone else; *he entered the country disguised as a student*; *she had her hair cut short to disguise her appearance*

④ **disgust**
[dɪsˈɡʌst]
1 *noun*
(a) strong dislike, feeling sick; *the sight of the flies on the meat in the market filled her with disgust*
(b) strong feeling of being annoyed; *to my disgust, my girlfriend passed her driving test and I didn't*; **in disgust** = because you are upset and annoyed; *she walked out of the interview in disgust*
2 *verb*
to give someone a strong feeling of dislike or disapproval; *the smell of cooking disgusted her*; *the rudeness of the waiters disgusts me*

② **disgusting**
[dɪsˈɡʌstɪŋ] *adjective*
that fills you with disgust; *there's a disgusting smell in the passage*; *a disgusting display of violence on the part of the fans*

② **dish**
[dɪʃ] *noun*
(a) large plate for serving food; *she carefully arranged the slices of meat on a dish*
(b) **dishes** = plates and cups, etc.; **to wash the dishes** *or* **to do the dishes** = to wash plates, glasses, knives and forks, etc., after a meal; *he's offered to do the dishes*; *can you dry the dishes for me?*
(c) part of a meal; plate of prepared food; *we are trying a new Mexican dish*; **side dish** = small dish served on a side plate; *he had a green salad as a side dish*
(d) round device, shaped like a plate, used to get signals from satellites; *almost every house in the street has a satellite dish on the roof* (NOTE: plural is **dishes**)

④ **dishonest**
[dɪsˈɒnɪst] *adjective*
not honest; *it was quite dishonest of him to tell his wife that he'd given up smoking*; *he has a record of dishonest business deals*

③ **dish out**
[ˈdɪʃ ˈaʊt] *verb*
(informal) to hand out roughly and in large quantities; *he dished out a piece of bread and a bowl of soup to anyone who asked for it*; *they were dishing out free tickets for the concert*; *they dished out leaflets to everyone at the meeting*; *at the end of the school year, they dish out prizes to the best students*

③ **dish up**
[ˈdɪʃ ˈʌp] *verb*
(informal) to serve food; *she dished up the food with a large spoon*; *he was dishing up the meal*

③ **dishwasher**
[ˈdɪʃwɒʃɪ] *noun*
machine for washing dishes, knives, forks, spoons, etc.; *I never put the saucepans in the dishwasher* (NOTE: a machine for washing clothes is a **washing machine**)

④ **disintegrate**
[dɪsˈɪntɪɡreɪt] *verb*
to fall to pieces; *the library book had been borrowed so much that its cover was disintegrating*; *most satellites disintegrate when they enter the Earth's atmosphere*

② **disk**
[dɪsk] *noun*
any round flat object, especially a piece of plastic used in computers to record information; *all the data is on two floppy disks*; **floppy disk** = small disk which can be inserted and removed from a computer; **hard disk** = large fixed disk; *see also* DISC

③ **diskette**
[dɪˈsket] *noun*
small floppy disk; *the data came on a diskette*

③ **dislike**
[dɪsˈlaɪk]
1 *noun*
(a) not liking something *or* someone; *she had never felt such a dislike for someone before*; **to take a dislike to** = to hate; *their dog took a sudden dislike to the postman*
(b) thing which you do not like; *we try to take account of the likes and dislikes of individual customers*
2 *verb*
not to like; *I dislike it when the people behind me at the cinema start whispering*; *my father dislikes having to get up early on Monday mornings*; **I don't dislike Mozart** = I quite like Mozart

④ **dismay**

[dɪsˈmeɪ]

1 *noun*

horror, great disappointment; *to her dismay she couldn't find her passport*; *to the dismay of the supporters, the team played extremely badly*

2 *verb*

to strike someone with horror; *his reaction to her letter dismayed her*; *she was dismayed to find that her passport had been stolen*

③ **dismiss**

[dɪsˈmɪs] *verb*

(a) **to dismiss an employee** = to remove an employee from a job; *he was dismissed for being late*; *when they found him taking money from the cash box he was dismissed immediately*

(b) to send someone away; *at the end of the interview he dismissed her with a brief 'good afternoon'*

(c) to refuse to consider an idea; *her plan was dismissed as being quite impossible*; *all his suggestions were dismissed by the MD*

(d) to refuse a request; *they dismissed my application for a loan*

④ **dismissal**

[dɪsˈmɪsɪl] *noun*

removal from a job; *he had only been working there three months when he received notice of dismissal*; **unfair dismissal** = removing of a person from his job for reasons which do not appear to be reasonable; *he appealed to the tribunal on the grounds of unfair dismissal*

③ **disorder**

[dɪsˈɔːdɪ] *noun*

(a) lack of order; *the whole office is in a state of disorder*

(b) riot, disturbance in the streets; *violent public disorders broke out in the streets*

(c) illness; *she suffers from a stomach disorder*; *a doctor who specializes in disorders of the kidneys or in kidney disorders*

④ **dispatch**

[dɪsˈpætʃ]

1 *noun*

(a) sending; *dispatch of the goods will be delayed until Monday*; **dispatch note** = note to say that goods have been sent

(b) message sent; *the reporters send regular dispatches from the war zone*; *we received a dispatch from our Calcutta office*; **dispatch box** = box with government papers (NOTE: plural is **dispatches**)

2 *verb*

(a) to send; *they dispatched the message to all commanding officers*; *the goods were dispatched to you first thing this morning*

(b) to finish doing something quickly; *she set to work on the files and dispatched most of them by lunchtime*

④ **dispenser**

[dɪsˈpensɪ] *noun*

machine which automatically provides something, when money is put in or a button is pushed; *there is a liquid soap dispenser in the gents' toilets*; **cash dispenser** = machine which gives out money when a special card is inserted and instructions given

④ **disperse**

[dɪsˈpɜːs] *verb*

(a) to clear away; *the sun will soon disperse the mist*; *the police were called in to disperse the crowds of angry fans*

(b) to scatter in different directions; *the crowd dispersed rapidly once the parade was over*

② **display**

[dɪsˈpleɪ]

1 *noun*

(a) show, exhibition; *they have a fine display of Chinese art*; *a display of local crafts*; **air display** = show of new aircraft; **display case** *or* **display unit** = glass case for showing goods for sale

(b) **on display** = shown in an exhibition or for sale; *the shop has several car models on display*

2 *verb*

(a) to put something on show; *she is displaying her collection of Persian carpets at the antique fair*

(b) to show; *he displayed considerable courage in meeting the rebel troops*; *make sure your parking ticket is clearly displayed on the windscreen*

④ **disposable**

[dɪsˈpɪuzɪbl] *adjective*

which can be used and then thrown away; *burgers are sold in disposable boxes*

④ **disposal**

[dɪsˈpɪuzɪl] *noun*

(a) getting rid of something; *the disposal of refuse is a problem for large cities*

(b) **my car is at your disposal** = you can use my car if you want to

④ **dispose**

[dɪsˈpɪuz] *verb*

to dispose of something = to get rid of something; *how are we going to dispose of all this waste paper?*; *his objections are easily disposed of*

② **dispute**

[dɪsˈpjuːt]

1 *noun*

argument; *he tried to mediate in the dispute*; *there was a little dispute over who would pay the bill*; **industrial dispute** *or* **labour dispute** = argument between management and workers; **in dispute** = not agreed; *the ownership of the land is in dispute*

2 *verb*

to argue that something is not correct; *I dispute her version of what happened*; *there is no disputing the fact that Sarah is the best qualified of the candidates*

④ **disrupt**
[dɪs'rʌpt] *verb*
(a) to stop a service running normally; *the snowstorm has disrupted bus services throughout the country*
(b) to break up or to interrupt a meeting; *we are not used to having our meetings disrupted by protesters*

④ **dissolve**
[dɪ'zɒlv] *verb*
(a) to put a solid substance into a liquid so that it becomes part of the liquid; *dissolve the sugar in half a litre of boiling water*; *the powder should be completely dissolved in warm water*
(b) to become part of a liquid; *the sugar dissolved quite quickly*; *stir the mixture until the sugar dissolves*
(c) to bring to an end; *to dissolve a partnership or a company or a marriage*; **to dissolve Parliament** = to close the Parliament, and call new elections

② **distance**
['dɪstɪns]
1 *noun*
(a) space from one point to another; *what is the distance from London to Paris?*; *the furthest distance I have travelled by train is 800km*; *the railway line goes underground for a short distance*; **within walking distance** = near enough to walk to; *the hotel is within walking distance of the town centre*
(b) **in the distance** = a long way away; *I caught sight of the mountain in the distance*; *we could hear guns firing in the distance*
(c) **distance learning** = studying in your own time away from the place where the course is organized, using radio or TV; *the government is putting a lot of resources into distance learning projects*
2 *verb*
to distance yourself from = to show that you are some distance away from; *the police chief took pains to distance himself from the remarks made by the President*

③ **distant**
['dɪstɪnt] *adjective*
(a) far away; *we could hear the sound of distant guns*; **a distant relative** = not a member of the close family; *she's a very distant relative - her grandfather was my grandmother's cousin*; **in the not too distant future** = quite soon; *we expect to move house in the not too distant future*; **in the dim and distant past** = a long time ago; *it all happened in the dim and distant past when I was at university*
(b) not very friendly; *the manager was quite helpful but distant*

③ **distinct**
[dɪ'stɪŋkt] *adjective*
(a) separate; *there are two distinct varieties of this plant*; *they keep their printing works quite distinct from their publishing company*
(b) clear; *I got the distinct impression that he was carrying a gun*; *did you notice the distinct tone of anger in his voice?*

② **distinction**
[dɪ'stɪŋkʃn] *noun*
(a) difference; *there is a distinction between being interested in politics and joining a political party*; **to make a distinction between two things** = to recognize that two things are different; *you must try to make a distinction between the police and the armed forces*
(b) highest mark; *she got a distinction in her exam*
(c) specially excellent quality; *he served in the war with distinction*; *she had the distinction of being the first woman to take a degree at the university*

③ **distinctive**
[dɪs'tɪŋktɪv] *adjective*
very noticeable, which makes one thing different from others; *the zebra has distinctive black and white stripes*; *what is so distinctive about this plant is that it flowers in winter*

③ **distinctly**
[dɪs'tɪŋktlɪ] *adverb*
clearly; *I distinctly heard him say that she was his sister*; *she looked distinctly upset*

③ **distinguish**
[dɪ'stɪŋgwɪʃ] *verb*
(a) to see clearly; to make out details; *with the glasses we could easily distinguish the houses on the other side of the lake*
(b) **to distinguish between two things** = to recognize the difference between two things; *children must be taught to distinguish between right and wrong*; *it's difficult to distinguish by sight between salt and fine sugar*
(c) **to distinguish yourself** = to do something which makes people notice you; *he distinguished himself on the football field*; *she distinguished herself by falling into the river*

③ **distinguished**
[dɪs'tɪŋgwɪʃt] *adjective*
important and well-known (writer, painter, etc.); *a concert by a distinguished Czech musician*

④ **distort**
[dɪ'stɔːt] *verb*
(a) to twist into a different shape; *his face was distorted with pain*; **distorting mirrors** = mirrors made of bent glass, which change your appearance
(b) to give a false impression of; *he distorted the meaning of my speech*

④ **distract**
[dɪ'strækt] *verb*
to attract someone's attention when they should be doing something else; *walking into the exam*

room dressed as a witch was bound to distract the students; **to distract someone's attention** = to make someone look away; *if you distract her attention, I'll try to snatch her handbag*

④ **distress**
[dɪˈstres]
1 *noun*
(a) great sad or painful feeling; *I don't want to cause the family any distress*; *the whole family was in distress at grandmother's death*
(b) difficulty; *we knew the ship was in distress when we saw the rocket signals*; **distress signal** = signal sent when you are in difficulties; *the ship sent out distress signals before she sank*
2 *verb*
to make someone very sad and worried; *the news of her grandmother's death distressed her very much*

③ **distribute**
[dɪˈstrɪbjuːt] *verb*
(a) to share out, to give to several people; *she distributed part of her money to the poor*; *the stewardesses came round, distributing immigration forms to non-EU passengers*; *I'll distribute the list to all the committee members*
(b) to send out goods from a warehouse to retail shops; **we distribute Japanese cars** = we are the agents for Japanese cars

② **distribution**
[dɪstrɪˈbjuːʃn] *noun*
(a) giving to several people; *the newspaper has a wide distribution*; *the staff will organize the distribution of the timetable to the students*
(b) sending of goods from a warehouse to shops; *our distribution centre is in Oxfordshire*

② **distributor**
[dɪsˈtrɪbjʊtɪ] *noun*
(a) company which sells goods for another company which makes them; *who is the local distributor for this make of washing machine?*
(b) *(in a car engine)* mechanism which passes the electric spark to each sparking plug in turn; *the distributor head needs cleaning*

② **district**
[ˈdɪstrɪkt] *noun*
(a) area or region; *it's a district of the town well-known for its Italian restaurants*; **the commercial district** *or* **the business district** = part of a town where offices and shops are located; *the shop is well placed right in the main business district of the town*
(b) official administrative area of a town or country; *US* **district attorney (DA)** = lawyer representing the government in a certain area; **district council** = local council

④ **disturb**
[dɪsˈtɜːb] *verb*
(a) to worry someone; *it disturbed me to see that the plane's wing was shaking*
(b) to interrupt someone; *sorry to disturb you but there's an urgent email message just come in*; *don't disturb your mother - she's resting*;

'do not disturb' = notice placed on a hotel room door, to ask the hotel staff not to come into the room

③ **disturbance**
[dɪsˈtɜːbɪns] *noun*
(a) action of disturbing someone; *I need to work somewhere where there won't be any disturbance*
(b) noisy riot; *the fans caused a disturbance in the hotel bar*; *there are always disturbances after the football match between the two local teams*; *there were several instances of shop windows being broken during the disturbances*

④ **disturbed**
[dɪsˈtɜːbd] *adjective*
(a) worried; *we are disturbed to hear that the company may be forced to close*
(b) ill in the mind; *in her disturbed state, she may do anything*; *highly disturbed children are taught in this special school*

③ **disturbing**
[dɪsˈtɜːbɪŋ] *adjective*
worrying; *a disturbing number of students failed the exam*; *it is a disturbing fact that many children leave school without being able to read*

④ **ditch**
[dɪtʃ]
1 *noun*
long hole in the ground for taking away water; *after the storm, the ditches were full of rainwater*; *he fell into the ditch beside the road*
(NOTE: plural is **ditches**)
2 *verb*
(informal)
(a) to leave something behind; *when we ran out of petrol, we ditched the car and walked to the next town*
(b) to dismiss; *the company decided to ditch its sales director*
(c) to land a plane in the sea; *the pilot ran out of fuel and decided to ditch the plane*

④ **dive**
[daɪv]
1 *noun*
(a) plunge downwards head first into water; *he made a beautiful dive into the pool*
(b) *(informal)* bar or club with a bad reputation; *he met her in some dive in Frankfurt*
2 *verb*
to plunge into water head first; *he dived in and swam across the pool under water* (NOTE: **diving - dived** *US* **dove** [dɪʊv])

③ **diver**
[ˈdaɪvɪ] *noun*
(a) swimmer who plunges head first into water; *an Australian Olympic diver*
(b) person who swims and works under water; *police divers searched the canal*; *the divers carried oxygen cylinders on their backs*

diversion
[daɪˈvɜːʃn] *noun*
(a) temporary road system that sends traffic another way; *all traffic has to take a diversion and join the motorway again 10km further on*
(b) amusement; *fishing is one of the most popular diversions for people at weekends; it's a quiet country town with very few diversions for teenagers*
(c) **to create a diversion** = to distract attention, for example so that some else can commit a crime; *she created a diversion by screaming, while he put the watches into his pocket*

diversity
[daɪˈvɜːsɪti] *noun*
great variety; *various medical journals show a great diversity of opinion among specialists on the subject*

divert
[daɪˈvɜːt] *verb*
(a) to send to another place or in another direction; *because of fog in London, flights have been diverted to Manchester; traffic has been diverted to avoid the town centre*
(b) **to divert someone's attention** = to make someone look away; *try and divert his attention while I steal his keys*

divide
[dɪˈvaɪd] *verb*
(a) to cut into parts; *the cake was divided among the children; how can you divide the cake into thirteen pieces?; the two companies agreed to divide the market between them; our office is one large room divided up with low shelves*
(b) to calculate how many of one number there are in another; *ten divided by two gives five* (NOTE: **divide** is usually shown by the sign ÷ : **10 ÷ 2 = 5**: say 'ten divided by two equals five')
(c) *(in the House of Commons)* to vote; *MPs divided at 10 p.m.*

dividend
[ˈdɪvɪdend] *noun*
part of a company's profits shared out among shareholders; *the company made a loss and there will be no dividend for the shareholders this year;* **to raise** *or* **to increase the dividend** = to pay out a higher dividend than in the previous year

divine
[dɪˈvaɪn] *adjective*
(a) referring to God; *he prayed for divine help*
(b) wonderful, excellent; *her singing was absolutely divine!*

division
[dɪˈvɪʒn] *noun*
(a) important part of a large organization; *the sales division employs twenty people; she is the head of the production division*
(b) splitting into parts; *after his death, the family argued over the division of their father's money* (NOTE: no plural in this meaning)
(c) calculation, where one figure is divided by another; *my little sister is just learning how to do division;* **long division** = complicated division sum, worked out on paper; **division sign** = printed or written sign (÷) showing that one figure is divided by another
(d) difference of opinion between groups of people; *the dispute has widened the divisions between the two sections of the party*
(e) *(in the House of Commons)* voting; *a division will take place in five minutes;* **division bell** = bell which is rung when a vote is going to be taken
(f) large part of an army; *they have three divisions stationed along the border; the general ordered a division to stand by*

divorce
[dɪˈvɔːs]
1 *noun*
legal separation of husband and wife where each is free to marry again; *her parents are getting a divorce; since their divorce, they have both got married again*
2 *verb*
(a) to break off a marriage legally; *they divorced last year*
(b) to separate from your husband or wife; *she divorced her husband and married the man next door; he got divorced after only three years' of marriage*
(c) to separate (two ideas, etc.); *it is difficult to divorce their financial problems from the problems they are having with the house*

divorced
[dɪˈvɔːst] *adjective*
no longer married; *they're both divorced, with children from their previous marriages*

DIY
[diːaɪˈwaɪ] *abbreviation for* DO IT YOURSELF; *he buys a DIY magazine each week; she's very good at DIY;* **a DIY store** = shop which sells paints, tools, etc.

dizzy
[ˈdɪzi] *adjective*
(a) feeling when everything seems to turn round; *can we stop the car, please, I feel dizzy; after standing in the sun, he became dizzy and had to lie down; she has started having dizzy spells*
(b) *(informal)* wild, exciting; *a dizzy round of parties and TV shows* (NOTE: **dizzier - dizziest**)

DJ
[ˈdiːdʒeɪ] *abbreviation for* DISC JOCKEY person who plays recorded music at a night club; *the DJ played another track from the album*

do
[duː]
1 *verb*
(a) *(used with other verbs to make questions)* *does this train go to London?; did the doctor give you any medicine for your cough?; where do they live?; what did you find there?*

(b) *(used with other verbs and 'not' to make the negative)* *they didn't laugh at the film*; *it doesn't matter any more*; *his parents don't live in London*

(c) *(used to make a verb stronger)* *can I sit down? - please do!*; *why don't you work harder? - I do work hard!*; *why didn't you tell me? - I did tell you!*

(d) *(used instead of another verb with* **so**; *and* **neither**)*; *we don't smoke - neither do I*; *he likes jam sandwiches and so does she*

(e) *(used instead of another verb in short answers to questions using the word 'do')* *do you live in London? - yes I do*; *but your parents don't live there, do they? - no they don't*; *does the green colour suit me? - yes it does*; *did you go to the concert after all? - yes I did*

(f) *(used instead of another verb at the end of a question or statement)* *the Russians live here, don't they?*; *it looks very nice, doesn't it?*; *it doesn't rain a lot in Spain, does it?*

(g) *(used instead of another verb)* *can you run as fast as he does?*; *he speaks German better than I do*; *she asked me to close the door but I'd already done so*; *they got to the pub before we did*

(h) *(telling someone not to do something)* *don't throw away that letter!*; *don't put your coffee cups on the computer!*

(i) *(with nouns ending in* -ing; *)* *she's doing the shopping*; *he always does the washing up*; *she was doing the ironing*

(j) *(used when greeting someone)* *how do you do?* (NOTE: this does not normally expect an answer)

(k) *(followed by a noun)* to work at something or to arrange something or to clean something; *she's doing her hair*; *have you done the dishes yet?*; *what have you been doing all day?*; *they're a difficult company to do business with*; **what do you do for a living?** = what is your job?

(l) to succeed, to continue; *she's doing very well in her new job*; *he did badly in the interview*; *how's your business doing?*; **well done!** = congratulations; *I passed my driving test - well done!*

(m) to finish being cooked; *the carrots aren't done yet*; **the chicken is done to a turn** = the chicken is cooked and ready to eat

(n) to be satisfactory; *will this size do?*; **that will do** = that's enough; **that won't do at all** = that's not at all satisfactory

(o) to make do with = to accept something which is not as good as you wanted; *the ordinary plates are all dirty, so we will have to make do with paper ones*

(p) to travel at a certain speed; *the car was doing 100 miles an hour when it hit the tree* (NOTE: **I do; you do; he/she/it does** [dʌz] ; **they do; doing - did** [dɪd] **- has done** [dʌn] ; negative: **do not** usually **don't** [dɪʊnt] ; **does not** usually **doesn't** ['dʌznt] ; **did not** usually **didn't** ['dɪdnt])

2 *noun*
(informal)
(a) party; *we've been invited to a do at the Smiths*

(b) the dos and the don'ts = things you should do and things you should not do; *she told him all the dos and don'ts about working in the office* (NOTE: plural is **dos** [duːz])

③ **do away with**
['duː ə'weɪ wɪθ] *verb*
to get rid of something; *the government did away with customs inspections*

④ **dock**
[dɒk]
1 *noun*
(a) the docks = a harbour where cargo is put on or taken off ships; *cars should arrive at the docks 45 minutes before sailing time*; *we used to go down to the docks to watch the ships come in*; **dry dock** = section of a harbour from which the water can be removed, so that the bottom of a ship can be repaired; **the ship is in dock** = (i) the ship is in the harbour; (ii) the ship is being repaired; *(informal)* **my car is in dock** = my car is being repaired

(b) box in a law court, where the prisoner sits; *she was in the dock, facing charges of theft*

2 *verb*
(a) *(of ship)* to arrive in harbour; *the ship docked at 17.00*; *the cruise liner will dock in Bermuda*

(b) to remove (money from wages); *I will have to dock your pay if you are late for work again*; *they've docked £20 from my pay!*

① **doctor**
['dɒktɪ]
1 *noun*
(a) person who looks after people who are ill; *I have a ten o'clock appointment to see the doctor*; *if you have pains in your chest, you ought to see a doctor*; *he went to the doctor's last Friday*; **doctor's certificate** = document written by a doctor to say that a worker is ill and cannot work; *she has been off sick for ten days and has sent in a doctor's certificate*; **ship's doctor** = doctor who travels on a ship and so is ready to treat passengers who become ill

(b) person with the highest degree from a university; *she has a doctor's degree in physics* (NOTE: **doctor** is written **Dr** with names: **Dr Thorne is our local GP**)

2 *verb*
to change something, so that it is false; *we suspect that he had been doctoring his expenses*; *she was accused of doctoring the test samples*

② **document**
['dɒkjʊmɪnt]
1 *noun*
piece of paper with written text; *file all the*

documents away carefully as we may need them again; please read this document carefully and sign at the bottom of page two

2 *verb*

to note something in official writing; *cases of this disease are well documented in Africa*; *she sent in a fully documented claim for insurance*

④ **documentary**
[dɒkjuˈmentɪrɪ]

1 *noun*

film giving facts about a real subject; *did you see the documentary about elephants last night?*; *the TV documentary had an strong impact on viewers* (NOTE: plural is **documentaries**)

2 *adjective*

referring to documents; **documentary evidence** = evidence in the form of documents; *they are searching in the rubbish for any documentary evidence that the meeting took place*

④ **dodge**
[dɒdʒ]

1 *noun*

(informal) clever trick; *he told me a dodge to avoid paying tax*

2 *verb*

(a) to avoid, to get out of the way; *he ran across the street, dodging the traffic*; *she dodged behind a tree hoping he wouldn't see her*

(b) **to dodge the issue** = to avoid answering questions about a problem or trying to do anything about a problem; *we were very disappointed because the council simply dodged the issue*

① **does, doesn't**
[dʌz or ˈdʌznt]
see DO

① **dog**
[dɒg]

1 *noun*

animal kept as a pet, which barks, and moves its tail from side to side when it is pleased; *can you take the dog out for a walk?*; *police with dogs were hunting the gang of escaped prisoners*; **to let sleeping dogs lie** = not to disturb things; *I wouldn't investigate any further if I were you - better let sleeping dogs lie*; (informal) **to go to the dogs** = to get into a bad condition; *the whole place has gone to the dogs*; **it's a dog's life** = life is difficult, with too much work and no play (NOTE: the young are called **puppies**)

2 *verb*

to follow; *all his life he has been dogged by illness*; **to dog someone's footsteps** = to follow behind someone closely; *failure seems to dog his footsteps* (NOTE: **dogging - dogged**)

③ **doggy**
[ˈdɒgɪ]

(informal) *(children's word)* dog; *she's brought her little doggy with her*; **doggy bag** = bag in which you can put food which you didn't eat in a restaurant to take home, supposedly for your dog

③ **do in**
[ˈduː ˈɪn] *verb*

(informal)

(a) to kill; *what happened to the gang boss? - he was done in and his body was thrown into the river*

(b) to hurt; *I think I did my back in by digging the garden*

③ **do-it-yourself (DIY)**
[duːɪtjɪˈself] *noun*

repairing, building, painting your house by yourself, without employing a professional; *she's good at do-it-yourself jobs*; **do-it-yourself magazine** *or* **DIY magazine** = magazine with articles on work which you can do to repair or paint the house; *he buys a DIY magazine each week*

③ **doll**
[dɒl] *noun*

child's toy which looks like a baby; *Susie is upstairs playing with her dolls and teddy bears*; *we bought little wooden dolls for the children in the market*; **doll's house** = very small house made as a toy

① **dollar**
[ˈdɒlɪ] *noun*

(a) money used in the USA; *a 5-dollar bill*; *the country spends millions of dollars on defence*; *there are two dollars to the pound*

(b) similar currency used in many other countries; *what is the price in Australian dollars?* (NOTE: when used with a figure, usually written $ before the figure: $250. The currencies used in different countries can be shown by the initial letter of the country: **Can$** (Canadian dollar) **Aus$** (Australian dollar), etc. Note also that with the words **bill, money order**, etc., **dollar** is singular: **twenty dollars** but a **twenty-dollar bill**, a **fifty-dollar traveler's check**)

④ **dolphin**
[ˈdɒlfɪn] *noun*

sea animal like a very small whale; *dolphins followed the boat as it crossed the bay* (NOTE: a group of them is a **school of dolphins**)

④ **dome**
[dɪʊm] *noun*

round roof shaped like half of a ball; *you can climb up into the dome of St Paul's Cathedral*

② **domestic**
[dɪˈmestɪk] *adjective*

(a) referring to the home; *she hated having to do all the domestic work while her husband was out at his job*; **domestic animals** = farm animals and pets; **domestic science** = cooking and housework as subject studied at school; **domestic service** = working as a servant in a house

(b) inside a country; *sales in the domestic market have risen*; **domestic flights** = flights between airports inside the same country

dominant 167 doubt

ⓓ **dominant**
['dɒmɪnɪnt] *adjective*
(a) most important; *the dominant colour in the room is dark red; safety will be the dominant theme of the discussion*
(b) very powerful; *he has a very dominant personality and his wife and children have to do what he says; the President's party is the dominant force in the country's political system*

ⓓ **dominate**
['dɒmɪneɪt] *verb*
(a) to rule; *he is dominated by his wife; the Union party dominates the country's political system*
(b) to be very obviously seen; *the volcano dominates the town*

ⓓ **donate**
[dɪʊ'neɪt] *verb*
to give; *he donated a lot of money to charity*

ⓓ **donation**
[dɪʊ'neɪʃn] *noun*
gift, especially of money; *all donations will be gratefully received; I can't afford to make any donations to charity this Christmas*

ⓓ **done**
[dʌn] *verb*
see DO

ⓓ **donor**
['dɪʊnɪ] *noun*
person who gives; *the donor of the kidney lives in Arkansas; the list of the museum's donors is on a board by the entrance;* **blood donor** = person who gives blood regularly for medical use

ⓓ **don't**
[dɪʊnt]
see DO

ⓓ **door**
[dɔː] *noun*
(a) piece of wood, metal, etc., which closes an entrance; *he went into his office and locked the door behind him; she opened the car door and hit a passing cyclist;* **front door** = main door to a building; *she gave him a key to the front door or a front door key;* **back door** = door at the back of a building; *the back door leads out into the garden*
(b) used to show where a building is in a street; *he lives three doors down the street* = he lives three houses further along the street; *they live a few doors away from us*

ⓓ **doorway**
['dɔːweɪ] *noun*
space where there is a door; *she stood in the doorway, sheltering from the rain*

ⓓ **dose**
[dɪʊs]
1 *noun*
quantity of medicine; *normal daily dose: three tablets; it is dangerous to exceed the recommended dose*
2 *verb*

to dose someone with something = to give someone medicine; *he dosed himself with hot lemon juice and aspirin*

ⓓ **dot**
[dɒt] *noun*
(a) small round spot; *a blue tie with white dots*
(b) **on the dot of** = exactly at a time; *the train left on the dot of four;* see also YEAR

ⓓ **dotted line**
['dɒtɪd 'laɪn] *noun*
line made of a series of dots; *please sign on the dotted line; do not write anything below the dotted line*

ⓓ **double**
['dʌbl]
1 *adjective*
(a) twice the size; *she asked for a double portion of ice cream;* **double cream** = thick stiff cream
(b) **in double figures** = with two figures, the numbers from 10 to 99; *inflation is expected to reach double figures next month*
(c) with two parts, for two people; **double bed** = bed for two people; *do you want a double bed or two single beds?;* **double room** = room for two people
2 *adverb*
twice the amount; *it takes double the time; her salary is double mine;* **to see double** = to see two things when there is only one there
3 *noun*
(a) *(in the army)* **at the double** = running; *the soldiers crossed the square at the double*
(b) person who looks exactly like someone else; *it was either him or his double we saw at the cinema*
(c) **doubles** = tennis game for two people on either side; **men's doubles** *or* **women's doubles** = two men against two other men *or* two women against two other women; **mixed doubles** = man and woman against another man and woman
4 *verb*
(a) to multiply by two; *think of a number and then double it*
(b) **to double back** = to turn round and go back along the same way; *the escaped prisoner doubled back towards the village*

ⓓ **double up**
['dʌbl 'ʌp] *verb*
(a) to bend forwards; *she was doubled up in pain*
(b) to do a second job; *the waiter is doubling up as chef because the chef is on holiday*

ⓓ **doubt**
[daʊt]
1 *noun*
(a) not being sure; **to have doubts about** = to say that you are doubtful about; *I have my doubts about how accurate his figures are;* **to cast doubt on** = to be unsure about; *he cast doubt on the whole proposal;* **to give someone the benefit of the doubt** = to allow someone to

continue doing something, because you are not sure that accusations made against him are correct; *the referee gave him the benefit of the doubt*

(b) no doubt = certainly; *no doubt they will be suing for damages*; **there's no doubt about** = it is a certain fact; *there's no doubt about it - France is the best place for a holiday*; *there's no doubt that he is guilty*; **in doubt** = not sure; *the result of the game was in doubt until the last minute*

2 *verb*

not to be sure of something; *I doubt whether he will want to go to the meeting*; *I doubt her honesty*; *did you ever doubt that we would win?*

② **doubtful**
['dautful] *adjective*

not sure; *I am doubtful about whether we should go*; *she had a doubtful expression on her face*; *his future with the company looks increasingly doubtful*; *it is doubtful whether the race will take place because of the snow*

① **do up**
['du: 'ʌp] *verb*

(a) to attach; *he's still a baby and he can't do his buttons up properly*; *can you do up the zip at the back of my dress?*

(b) to repair and make like new; *they bought an old cottage and did it up*; *he's looking for an old sports car to do up*

① **do with**
['du: 'wɪθ] *verb*

(a) to concern; *it has nothing to do with us*; *it is something to do with my new book*

(b) to put somewhere; *what have you done with the newspaper?*

(c) *(informal)* to need; *after that long walk I could do with a cup of tea*; *the car could do with a wash*

① **do without**
['du: wɪð'aut] *verb*

not to have something, to manage without something; *if you live in the country can you do without a car?*; *plants can't do without water*

① **down**
[daun]

1 *preposition*

(a) towards the bottom of; *he fell down the stairs and broke his leg*; *the ball ran down the hill*

(b) away from where the person is speaking; *he went down the road to the Post Office*; *the police station is just down the street*

2 *adverb*

(a) towards the bottom, towards a lower position; *put the box down in the corner*; *he sat down on the carpet*; *she lay down on the bed*; *I looked in the basement, but there's no one down there*

(b) at a lower level; *inflation is down again*

(c) (put) on paper; *did you write down the number of the car?*; *the policeman took down her address*

(d) towards the south; *I'm going down to Brighton tomorrow (from London)* *they live down on the south coast*

(e) *(informal)* **down under** = in Australia and New Zealand

(f) sick; *she is down with flu*

(g) *(informal)* gloomy; *he's feeling a bit down*

(h) *(showing criticism)* **down with the government!**; **down with exams!** (NOTE: **down** is often used with verbs: **to go down; to break down; to fall down,** etc.)

3 *noun*

(a) soft feathers (of a duck); *the duck lined its nest with down* (NOTE: no plural in this meaning)

(b) downs = grass-covered hills with low bushes and very few trees; *we went for a walk over the downs* (NOTE: usually used in names of areas: **the North Downs, The South Downs**)

4 *verb*

(a) to swallow quickly; *he downed three pints of beer*

(b) to down tools = to stop work

④ **Downing Street**
['daunɪŋ 'striːt] *noun*

street in London with the houses of the British Prime Minister (No. 10) and the Chancellor of the Exchequer (No. 11); *the civil rights group protested outside 10 Downing Street*

② **downstairs**
[daun'steɪz]

1 *adverb*

on or to the lower part of a building; *he heard a noise in the kitchen and went downstairs to see what it was*; *I left my cup of coffee downstairs*

2 *adjective*

on the ground floor of a building; *the house has a downstairs bedroom*; *you can use the downstairs loo*

3 *noun*

the ground floor of a building; *the downstairs has three rooms*; *the downstairs of the house is larger than the upstairs*; *compare* UPSTAIRS

② **downtown**
['dauntaun]

1 *adverb*

to the town centre; *you can take the bus to go downtown*

2 *adjective*

in the town centre; *the downtown department stores*; *her office is in downtown New York*

3 *noun*

the central district of a town; *downtown will be very crowded at this time of day*

③ **downward**
['daunwɪd]

1 *adjective*

towards the bottom; *a downward trend in the unemployment figures*

2 *adverb*

US = DOWNWARDS

③ **downwards** US **downward**
['daʊnwɪdz] adverb
towards the bottom; *the path slopes downwards to the stream*; *he went to sleep face downwards on the floor*

③ **doz**
['dʌzɪn] = DOZEN

② **dozen**
['dʌzɪn] noun
(a) twelve; *we ordered two dozen chairs*; **they're cheaper by the dozen** = they are cheaper if you buy twelve at a time; **half a dozen** = six; *half a dozen apples*
(b) **dozens of** = a lot of; *dozens of people visited the exhibition*; *I've been to New York dozens of times* (NOTE: **dozen** does not become plural after a number: **dozens of chairs**, but **two dozen chairs**)

① **Dr**
see DOCTOR

② **draft**
[drɑːft]
1 noun
(a) rough plan of a document; *he quickly wrote out a draft of the agreement*; *it's not the final version, it's just a draft*
(b) US formerly, military service which most young men had to do; *he left the USA to avoid the draft*
(c) order for money to be paid by a bank; *she sent me a draft for one thousand pounds*
(d) US = DRAUGHT
2 adjective
rough (plan, document); *they brought the draft treaty with them*; *she drew up the draft agreement on the back of an envelope*; *the lawyers were working on the draft contract*
3 verb
(a) to draw up a rough plan of; *we drafted the details of the agreement on a piece of paper*
(b) US to call someone for military service; *at the age of eighteen he was drafted into the Marines*
(c) to ask someone to do something; *the police were drafted in to control the crowds*; *compare* DRAUGHT

③ **drag**
[dræg]
1 verb
(a) to pull something heavy along; *she dragged her suitcase across the platform*; *the police dragged the protesters away from the gate*
(b) to hang back, to stay behind; *Tom was dragging along at the end of the line*
(c) to pull a net along the bottom of (a lake) to try to find something; *the police dragged the lake to try to find the body of the missing boy* (NOTE: **dragging - dragged**)
2 noun

(a) boring thing, which stops you doing things you really want to do; *it's a drag, having to write all the Christmas cards*
(b) *(of a man)* **in drag** = wearing women's clothes

④ **dragon**
['drægɪn] noun
large animal in children's stories and old tales, which flies through the air and breathes fire; *the national animal of Wales is a red dragon*; **dragon boat** = long narrow Chinese boat, with a dragon's head on the bow, rowed by a crew of twenty-two to the beat of a drummer; **dragon boat races** = racing dragon boats as a sport

③ **drag on**
['dræg 'ɒn] verb
to go slowly; *the dinner party seemed to drag on for hours*

④ **drain**
[dreɪn]
1 noun
(a) pipe for carrying waste water away; *in the autumn the drains get blocked by leaves*; *we had to phone the council to come and clear the blocked drain*; *(informal)* **it's just like pouring money down the drain** = it's a waste of money; *see also* LAUGH
(b) gradual loss; *the office in Paris is a continual drain on our resources*
2 verb
(a) to remove a liquid; *boil the potatoes for ten minutes, drain and leave to cool*
(b) to drink the contents of (a glass); *he drained his glass and called for another round*

③ **drama**
['drɑːmɪ] noun
(a) serious performance in a theatre; *the 'Globe' has put on an unknown Elizabethan drama*; *I'm reading a book on 19th century French drama*; *a new TV drama series about life in the Lake District*; *she's a drama student or she's studying drama*; **drama department** = department in a college which teaches serious theatre
(b) series of serious and exciting events; *he always makes a drama out of everything*; *a day of high drama in the court*; *the drama of the rescue of the children by helicopter*

③ **dramatic**
[drɪ'mætɪk] adjective
(a) giving a shock; *the door flew open and she made a dramatic entrance*; *the dramatic moment in the film, when the pirates start to attack the children*
(a) referring to drama; *his latest dramatic work for radio*

④ **dramatically**
[drɪ'mætɪkli] adverb
in a very dramatic way; *her appearance has altered dramatically since she was ill*; *the national birth rate rose dramatically in the second half of the 20th century*

③ **drank**
[dræŋk]
see DRINK

③ **draught** *US* **draft**
[drɑːft] *noun*
(a) flow of cool air into a room; *he sat in a draught and got a stiff neck*
(b) draught beer *or* **beer on draught** = beer which is served from a barrel, and not in a bottle or can; *I'll have a pint of draught, please*
(c) draughts = game with black and white pieces; *would you like a game of draughts or to play draughts?*; *draughts is a much simpler game than chess* (NOTE: not plural, and takes a singular verb)
(d) draught animals = animals which are used to pull vehicles or carry heavy loads; *in India cattle are often used as draught animals because they are easy to train*
(e) depth of water which a ship needs to float and not touch the bottom; **shallow-draught boat** = boat which needs only a little water to float

③ **draughty** *US* **drafty**
['drɑːfti] *adjective*
with cool air flowing into it; *sitting in that draughty railway carriage has given me a cold* (NOTE: **draughtier - draughtiest**)

① **draw**
[drɔː]
1 *noun*
(a) selecting the winner in a lottery; *the draw is held on Saturdays*; *we are holding a draw to raise money for the local hospital*
(b) game where there is no winner; *the game ended in a draw, 2 - 2*
(c) attraction; *the zoo is a great draw for children*; *the new Disneyland will be the biggest draw in the area*
2 *verb*
(a) to make a picture with a pen or pencil; *he drew a picture of the house*; *she's drawing a pot of flowers*
(b) not to have a winner in a game; *the teams drew 2 - 2*; **the match was drawn** = neither side won
(c) to pull open or to close; *can you draw the curtains - it's getting dark*; *she drew the curtains and let in the sun*
(d) *(formal)* to pull out; *he drew a gun out of his pocket*; *she was drawing water from a well*; **draw lots** = to take pieces of paper from a box to decide something (the person who has the marked piece wins); *we drew lots to decide who would go first*; *they drew lots for the bottle of wine*
(e) to receive money; *he doesn't draw a salary, but charges us for his expenses*; *in two years' time I'll be drawing my old age pension* (NOTE: **drawing - drew** [druː] - **has drawn** [drɔːn])

③ **drawer**
['drɔːr] *noun*
(a) part of a desk or cupboard like an open box which slides in and out and which you pull with a handle; *I keep my cheque book in the top drawer of my desk*; **a chest of drawers** = piece of bedroom furniture with several drawers for clothes
(b) person who writes a cheque asking for money to be paid to someone; **the bank returned the cheque to drawer** = the bank would not pay the cheque because the person who wrote it did not have enough money in the account to pay it

② **drawing**
['drɔːɪŋ] *noun*
picture done with a pen or pencil; *I've bought an old drawing of the church*; **drawing board** = large board used by designers to work on; *(informal)* **it's back to the drawing board** = we'll have to start planning all over again

④ **drawing pin**
['drɔːɪŋ 'pɪn] *noun*
pin with a large flat head, used for pinning papers to a wall; *give me some drawing pins so that I can pin the poster to the door*; *he put a drawing pin on the teacher's chair* (NOTE: American English is **thumbtack**)

③ **drawn**
[drɔːn] *adjective*
(a) tired and ill; *she looked drawn after spending all night with her sick baby*
(b) *see* DRAW

③ **draw up**
['drɔː 'ʌp] *verb*
(a) to come close and stop; *as I was standing at the bus stop, a car drew up and asked if I wanted a lift*
(b) to write down a plan, etc.; *they have drawn up a plan to save money*; *have you drawn up a list of people you want to invite to the party?*
(c) to move something closer; *draw your chairs up to the table*

④ **dread**
[dred]
1 *noun*
great fear; *the sound of his voice filled her with dread*; *she has a dread of being touched*; **in dread of** = being very afraid of; *they lived in constant dread of being arrested by the secret police*
2 *verb*
to fear greatly; *I'm dreading taking my driving test*; *she dreads her weekly visit to the doctor*

② **dreadful**
['dredful] *adjective*
awful, very bad or unpleasant; *the weather has been dreadful all week*; *what a dreadful colour for a hat!*

② **dreadfully**
['dredfuli] adverb

awfully, extremely; *we're dreadfully busy this morning*; *I'm dreadfully sorry, but we seem to have lost your ticket*

② **dream**
[dri:m]

1 noun

(a) things which you think you see happening when you are asleep; *she had a dream about big pink elephants*

(b) things which you imagine and hope will happen in the future; *all his dreams of wealth collapsed when he lost his job*; *never in your wildest dreams did you imagine you would end up in such an important job*

(c) something you would really like to do or to see happen; *his dream is to appear on Broadway*; *they finally realized their dream of owning a cottage in the country*

(d) *(informal)* something very pleasant or delicious; *that chocolate pudding was a dream*

2 verb

(a) to think you see things happening while you are asleep; *he was dreaming of white sand and a blue tropical sea*; *I dreamt about you last night*; *last night I dreamt I was drowning*

(b) to think about something; **not to dream of doing something** = not to consider doing something; *she wouldn't dream of wearing a big hat like that*

(c) to imagine something which does not exist; *I never said that - you must have been dreaming!*
(NOTE: **he dreamed** or **he dreamt** [dremt])

3 adjective

best possible, what you really want; *their found their dream house in a small town by the sea*; *the game is to select your dream team for the World Cup*

② **dress**
[dres]

1 noun

(a) piece of a woman's or girl's clothing, covering more or less all the body; *she was wearing a blue dress* (NOTE: plural is **dresses**)

(b) special clothes; **evening dress** = formal clothes worn to an evening party (long dresses for women and dinner jacket and bow tie for men); *he was wearing evening dress* (NOTE: no plural in this meaning)

2 verb

(a) to put clothes on; *he got up, dressed and then had breakfast*; *she dressed her little girl all in red*

(b) to clean and put a bandage on a wound; *the nurse will dress the cut on your knee*

(c) to prepare food; *she dressed the salad with slices of cucumber and tomatoes*

③ **dressed**
[drest] adjective

(a) wearing clothes; *I can't come down to see the visitors - I'm not dressed yet*; *he got up, got dressed and then had breakfast*; *she was dressed all in black*

(b) **dressed (up) as** = wearing the costume of; *he went to the party dressed (up) as a policeman*; **dressed up to the nines** = wearing your very best clothes; *I saw her going out all dressed up to the nines*

④ **dressing**
['dresɪŋ] noun

(a) putting on clothes; *dressing the baby takes ages*; **dressing gown** = long light coat worn over night clothes before getting dressed; *the guests ran out of the hotel in their pyjamas and dressing gowns*

(b) sauce (for salad); *a bottle of Italian salad dressing*; **French dressing** = mixture of oil and vinegar

(c) bandage for a wound; *the patient's dressings need to be changed every two hours*

③ **drew**
[dru:]
see DRAW

③ **dried, drier, dries, driest**
[draɪd or 'draɪə or draɪz or 'draɪɪst]
see DRY

④ **drift**
[drɪft]

1 noun

(a) general meaning; *did you follow the drift of the conversation?*; *my Italian isn't very good, but I got the drift of what they were saying*; *I think she got the general drift of my argument*

(b) pile of snow blown by the wind; *snow lay in drifts around the farmhouse*

(c) **North Atlantic Drift** = the current of warm water moving east across the North Atlantic (NOTE: also called the **Gulf Stream**)

2 verb

(a) to move with the flow of water, without steering; *the boat drifted down the river for two miles*

(b) to move in no particular direction; *after the match, the spectators drifted towards the exits*

(c) *(of snow)* to pile up; *the snow began to drift in the high wind*

(d) not to take any decisions; *the government has lost its sense of direction and is starting to drift*

③ **drill**
[drɪl]

1 noun

(a) tool for making holes in wood, metal, etc.; *he used an electric drill to make the holes in the wall*

(b) military practice in marching, etc.; *new recruits spend hours practising their drill*; **boat drill** = practice to escape from a sinking ship by getting into small boats; **fire drill** = practice to

escape from a burning building; *(informal)* ✗ **what's the drill?** = what's the next thing to do now?; *I've never been to a board meeting before so you'll have to tell me what's the drill*
2 *verb*
(a) to make holes; *he drilled two holes for the screws*; *they are drilling for oil*
(b) to do military practice; *recruits were drilling on the parade ground*

① **drink**
[drɪŋk]
1 *noun*
(a) liquid which you swallow; *if you're thirsty, have a drink of water*; *she always has a hot drink before she goes to bed*; **soft drinks** = drinks like orange juice, that have no alcohol in them
(b) alcoholic drink; *would you like a drink?*; *come and have a drink*; *I'll order some drinks from the bar*
2 *verb*
(a) to swallow liquid; *he drank two glasses of water*; *what would you like to drink?*; *do you want something to drink with your meal?*
(b) to drink alcoholic drinks; *she doesn't drink* or *she never drinks*; *he drinks like a fish* = he drinks a lot of alcohol
(c) to drink a toast to someone = to drink and wish someone well; *we all drank a toast to the future success of the company* (NOTE: **drinking - drank** [dræŋk] **- has drunk** [drʌŋk])

④ **drip**
[drɪp]
1 *noun*
(a) small drop of water; *there's a hole in the tent - a drip just fell on my nose*
(b) giving a patient a liquid directly into the body; *she's on a drip*
2 *verb*
to fall in drops; to let a liquid fall in drops; *the tap is dripping*; *his nose is dripping because he has a cold*; *water dripped from the roof* (NOTE: **dripping - dripped**)

① **drive**
[draɪv]
1 *verb*
(a) to make a car, lorry, etc., travel in a certain direction; *he can swim, but he can't drive*; *he was driving a lorry when the accident happened*; *she was driving to work when she heard the news on the car radio*; *I'll drive your aunt to the airport* = I'll take her to the airport in my car
(b) to force; *he drove the nail into the wall*
(c) *(informal)* to **drive someone crazy** or to **drive someone mad** = to have an effect on someone so that they become very annoyed; *the noise is driving me crazy*; *all these telephone calls are driving her mad*
(d) he drives a hard bargain = he is a tough person to negotiate with (NOTE: **driving - drove** [drəʊv] **- has driven** ['drɪvn])

2 *noun*
(a) journey, especially in a car; *let's go for a drive into the country*; *the baby gets sick on long drives*; *it's a four-hour drive to the coast*
(b) the way in which power gets from the engine to a car's wheels; *a car with front-wheel drive*; *a four-wheel-drive car*
(c) place where the driver sits; *car with left-hand drive* (NOTE: British cars are right-hand drive)
(d) part of a computer which works a disk; *the computer has a CD-ROM drive*
(e) energetic way of working; *we need someone with plenty of drive to run the sales department*; **economy drive** = vigorous effort to save money or materials; **sales drive** = vigorous effort to increase sales
(f) little road leading to a house; *visitors can park in the drive*

③ **drive away**
['draɪv ə'weɪ] *verb*
(a) to ride away in a motor vehicle; *the bank robbers leapt into a car and drove away at top speed*
(b) to take someone away in a motor vehicle; *the children were driven away in a police car*
(c) to force something or someone to go away; *the smell of the drains is driving our customers away*

③ **drive back**
['draɪv 'bæk] *verb*
(a) to go back or to come back in a motor vehicle; *we were driving back to London after a weekend in the country*
(b) to force someone or something back; *the police drove the demonstrators back into the High Street*

③ **driven**
['drɪvn]
see DRIVE

③ **drive off**
['draɪv 'ɒf] *verb*
(a) to ride away in a motor vehicle; *the bank robbers leapt into a car and drove off at top speed*
(b) to force someone or something to go away; *they drove off the attackers with sticks and stones*

① **driver**
['draɪvɪ] *noun*
person who drives a car, bus, etc.; *he's got a job as a bus driver*; *the drivers of both cars were injured in the accident*; *US* **driver's license** = DRIVING LICENCE

③ **driving**
['draɪvɪŋ]
1 *noun*
action of driving a motor vehicle; *driving in the centre of London can be very tiring*; *she's taking driving lessons*; **careless driving** = driving in such a way that other people or

vehicles may be harmed; *he was charged with careless driving*; **driving school** = school where you can learn to drive a car, truck, etc.

2 *adjective*

(rain or snow) blown hard by the wind; *they were forced to turn back because of the driving rain*

Ⓐ **driving licence** *US* **driver's license**
['draɪvɪŋ 'laɪsɪns or 'draɪvɪz 'laɪsɪns] *noun*
permit which allows someone to drive a car, truck, etc.; *applicants should hold a valid driving licence*

Ⓐ **driving test**
['draɪvɪŋ 'test] *noun*
test which you have to pass to get a driving licence; *he's taken his driving test three times and still hasn't passed*

Ⓐ **drop**
[drɒp]
1 *noun*
(a) small amount of liquid which falls; *the roof leaks and we placed a bucket to catch the drops*; *drops of rain ran down the windows*
(b) small amount of liquid; *would you like a drop of whisky?* = a small glass of whisky
(c) distance which you might fall; *there is a drop of three metres from the bathroom window to the ground*
(d) decrease; *sales show a drop of 10%*
2 *verb*
(a) to let something fall; *he dropped the glass and it broke*
(b) to decrease; *prices are dropping; take a warm pullover, because at night the temperature can drop quite sharply*; **the wind has dropped** = the wind has stopped blowing
(c) to let someone get off a bus or car at a place; *I'll drop you at your house; the bus dropped her at the school*
(d) *(informal)* **to drop someone a line** = to send someone a note; *drop me a line when you are back from the USA*
(e) to give up; *they have dropped the idea of going to settle in Australia; the whole plan has been dropped because of the cost* (NOTE: **dropping - dropped**)

Ⓐ **drop off**
['drɒp 'ɒf] *verb*
(a) to fall asleep; *she dropped off in front of the TV; it took me ages to drop off*
(b) **to drop someone off** = to let someone who is a passenger in a car get out somewhere; *can you drop me off at the post office?*

Ⓐ **drought**
[draʊt] *noun*
long period when there is no rain and when the land is dry; *relief workers are bringing food to areas affected by drought*

Ⓐ **drove**
[drəʊv]
see DRIVE

Ⓐ **drown**
[draʊn] *verb*
(a) to die by being unable to breathe in water; *he drowned in a shallow pool*
(b) to cover up a sound; *the shouting drowned his speech*

Ⓐ **drug**
[drʌg]
1 *noun*
(a) medicine; *they have found a new drug for people with cancer*
(b) substance which affects the nerves, and which can become a habit; *the customs are looking for such things as drugs or alcohol*; **drug addict** = person who takes drugs as a habit; **drug dealer** = person who sells illegal drugs to other people; **Drug Squad** = section of the police force that investigates crime related to drugs
2 *verb*
to give someone a drug; *they drugged him and took him away in a car* (NOTE: **drugging - drugged**)

Ⓐ **drugstore**
['drʌgstɔː] *noun*
US shop where medicines can be bought, as well as many other goods such as soap, paper, etc.; *you can buy some toothpaste at the drugstore on the corner* (NOTE: the British equivalent is a **chemist's,** though many chemists do not sell the same variety of goods as an American **drugstore**)

Ⓐ **drum**
[drʌm]
1 *noun*
(a) large round musical instrument which is hit with a stick; *he plays the drums in the band*
(b) large barrel or container shaped like a cylinder; *oil drums were piled up in the corner of the yard*
2 *verb*
to hit frequently; *he drummed his fingers on the table*; **to drum something into someone** = to make someone learn something; *my grandfather drummed it into me that I had to be polite to customers* (NOTE: **drumming - drummed**)

Ⓐ **drummer**
['drʌmɪ] *noun*
person who plays the drums; *the band is looking for a new drummer*

Ⓐ **drunk**
[drʌŋk] *adjective*
excited or ill because of drinking too much alcohol; *when he's drunk, he shouts at his children*; *see also* DRINK

Ⓐ **drunken**
['drʌŋkɪn] *adjective*
who has drunk too much alcohol; *nurses had to call the police to help control the drunken patient; people complained about drunken football fans breaking windows in the street*

① **dry**
[draɪ]
1 *adjective*
(a) not wet; *don't touch the door - the paint isn't dry yet*; *the soil is dry because it hasn't rained for weeks*; *this cream will help make your skin less dry*; *at the end of the film there wasn't a dry eye in the house* = the film made all the audience cry
(b) with no rain; *they are forecasting dry sunny periods*; **dry season** = period of the year when it does not rain much (as opposed to the rainy season)
(c) not sweet (wine); *a dry white wine is served with fish*
(e) to have a dry sense of humour = to make jokes without seeming to know they are funny; *he has a wonderfully dry sense of humour* (NOTE: **drier - driest**)
2 *verb*
(a) to stop being wet; *the clothes are drying in the sun*; *leave the dishes by the sink to dry*
(b) to wipe something until it is dry; *if I wash up, can you dry (the dishes)?*

③ **dry up**
['draɪ 'ʌp] *verb*
(a) to stop flowing; *the heat wave has made the rivers dry up*; *the government grants have dried up and it looks as though the theatre will have to close*
(b) to stop talking, because you can't remember what you were going to say; *he dried up in the middle of his speech, and sat down quickly*; *as soon as she got on the stage she dried up*

④ **dual**
['djʊl] *adjective*
double, existing as a pair; *driving school cars have dual controls*; **she has dual nationality** = she is a citizen of two countries

④ **dubious**
['djuːbiːs] *adjective*
(a) suspicious; *there were some dubious characters hanging around outside the shop*; *have you heard about his dubious past in South America?*
(b) doubtful, hesitating; *I'm dubious about getting involved*; *everyone else seems to believe her story, but personally I'm dubious about it*

③ **duck**
[dʌk]
1 *noun*
(a) common water bird; *let's go and feed the ducks in St James' Park*; *see also* WATER
(b) meat of this bird; *we're having roast duck for dinner*
(c) *(in cricket)* score of zero; *he scored a duck in his last two matches*
2 *verb*
to lower your head quickly to avoid hitting something; *she didn't duck in time and the ball hit her on the head*; *he ducked as he went through the low doorway*

① **due**
[djuː] *adjective*
(a) expected; *when is the baby due?*; *we are due to leave London Airport at 5 o'clock*; *the plane is due to arrive at 10.30 or is due at 10.30*
(b) due to = because of; *the trains are late due to fog*
(c) in due course = later; *in due course you will have to pass an exam*
(d) owed; **to fall due** *or* **to become due** = to be ready for payment; **balance due to us** = amount owed to us which should be paid
(e) due for = likely to get; *we're due for a thunderstorm after all this hot weather*; *she must be due for retirement this year*
2 *adverb*
straight; *the plane flew due west*; *go due east for ten miles and you will see the church on your left*

③ **dug**
[dʌg]
see DIG

③ **dull**
[dʌl] *adjective*
(a) not exciting, not interesting; *the story is rather dull*; *what's so interesting about old churches? - I find them dull*
(b) *(weather)* grey and gloomy; *a dull cloudy day*
(c) *(colours)* gloomy, not bright; *they painted the sitting room a dull green* (NOTE: **duller - dullest**)

③ **dumb**
[dʌm] *adjective*
(a) unable to speak; *she was born deaf and dumb or she is deaf and dumb from birth*; **to be struck dumb** = to be so surprised that you cannot say anything; *he was struck dumb by the news*
(b) *(informal)* stupid; *that was dumb thing to do*; *how can anyone be so dumb?*

③ **dump**
[dʌmp]
1 *noun*
(a) place for rubbish; *take your rubbish to the local dump*
(b) what a dump! = what an awful place!; *his house is a dump*
2 *verb*
(a) to put something heavily on the ground; *she just dumped her suitcases in the hall*
(b) to throw away, to get rid of; *someone has dumped an old supermarket trolley in the car park*; *the UK dumps its industrial waste into the North Sea*; **to dump goods on a market** = to sell surplus goods at a very cheap price (usually overseas); *old medicines are being dumped in Africa*
(c) *(informal)* **to dump someone** = to get rid of someone; *she's been dumped by her boyfriend*

④ **duplicate**
1 *adjective*
['dju:plɪkɪt] which is a copy; *put the duplicate invoices in the file*
2 *noun*
['dju:plɪkɪt] copy; *she sent the invoice and filed the duplicate*
3 *verb*
['dju:plɪkeɪt] to make a copy of a letter, etc.; *she duplicated the letter and put a copy into the file*; **you are just duplicating his work** = you are just doing the same work as he did earlier

④ **durable**
['djʊərɪbl]
1 *adjective*
which lasts, which does not wear away; *you need a really durable floor covering in a kitchen*; *they've signed a peace agreement but will it be more durable than the last one?*; **durable effects** = effects which will be felt for a long time; *the strike will have durable effects on the economy*
2 *noun*
consumer durables = goods bought by the public which will be used for a long time (such as washing machines or refrigerators)

③ **duration**
[djʊ'reɪʃn] *noun*
(formal) period of time for which something lasts; *they stayed in the country for the duration of the war*; *luckily the power cut was of short duration*

① **during**
['djʊərɪŋ] *preposition* while something lasts; *he went to sleep during the concert*; *conditions were bad during the war*

③ **dust**
[dʌst]
1 *noun*
thin layer of dry dirt; *the room had never been cleaned - there was dust everywhere*; *a tiny bit of dust got in my eye* (NOTE: no plural)
2 *verb*
(a) to remove dust from something; *don't forget to dust the Chinese bowls carefully*
(b) to sprinkle a powder on something; *she dusted the cake with icing sugar*

③ **dustbin**
['dʌstbɪn] *noun*
large container for household rubbish; *she put the rest of the dinner in the dustbin*; *he threw the letter into the dustbin* (NOTE: American English is **trashcan**)

④ **duster**
['dʌstɪ] *noun*
cloth for removing dust; *rub the surface down with a duster*

③ **dustman**
['dʌstmɪn] *noun*
person employed by a town to remove household rubbish; *the dustmen are supposed to come and empty our dustbins once a week* (NOTE: plural is **dustmen**)

④ **dusty**
['dʌstɪ] *adjective*
covered with dust; *his room is full of dusty old books* (NOTE: **dustier - dustiest**)

① **Dutch**
[dʌtʃ]
1 *adjective*
(a) referring to the Netherlands; *we are going on a tour to visit the Dutch bulb fields*
(b) **to go Dutch** = to share the cost of a meal equally between everyone
2 *noun*
(a) the language spoken in the Netherlands; *you will need to practise your Dutch if you're going to live in Amsterdam*
(b) **the Dutch** = the people living in the Netherlands; *the Dutch are great travellers*

① **duty**
['dju:ti] *noun*
(a) work which you have to do; *one of his duties is to see that the main doors are locked at night*; **to be duty bound to do something** = to be obliged to do something; *if you have any information relating to this case, you are duty bound to pass it to the police*
(b) **on duty** = doing official work which you have to do in a job; *he's on duty from 9.00 to 6.00*; *she's been on duty all day* (NOTE: no plural in this meaning)
(c) tax which has to be paid; **customs duty** = tax which you have to pay to take goods into a country; *you may have to pay customs duty on goods imported from outside the EU*; **estate duty** *US* **death duty** = tax paid on the property left by a dead person

② **dwelling**
['dwelɪŋ] *noun*
(formal) place to live; *they have had permission to build a dwelling on the site*

④ **dye**
[daɪ]
1 *noun*
substance used to change the colour of something; *she used a green dye to change the colour of her hair*; **fast dye** = colour which will not fade when washed
2 *verb*
to stain with a colour; *she dyed her hair green* (NOTE: do not confuse with **die**)

③ **dying**
['daɪɪŋ] *adjective*
dying for *or* **to** = wanting something very much; *we're dying for a cold drink*; *I'm dying to read his book*

④ **dynamic**
[daɪ'næmɪk] *adjective*
very energetic and with a strong personality; *a young and dynamic Prime Minister*

Ee

① **E, e**
[iː]
fifth letter of the alphabet, between D and F; *do you mean 'dependent' spelt with an 'e' or with an 'a'?*; *which is it - 'been' with two e's or 'bean' spelt 'ea'?*

① **each**
[iːtʃ]
1 *adjective*
every person or thing; *each ten-pound note has a number*; *he was holding a towel in each hand*; *each one of us has a separate office*
2 *pronoun*
(a) every person; *they have two houses each* or *each of them has two houses*; *she gave them each five pounds* or *she gave them five pounds each* or *she gave each of them five pounds*
(b) every thing; *each of the books has three hundred pages* or *the books have three hundred pages each*

① **each other**
['iːtʃ 'ʌðɪ] *pronoun* the other one of two people or of two things; *they were shouting at each other*; *we always send each other presents on our birthdays*; *the boxes fit into each other*

④ **eager**
['iːgɪ] *adjective*
wanting to do something very much; *they are eager to see the exhibition*; *I am not very eager for Sam to come to live with us*

④ **eagerly**
['iːgɪli] *adverb*
in a way that shows that you want something very much; *the children were eagerly waiting for the beginning of the holidays*; *he reads the job advertisements eagerly every morning*

① **ear**
[ıı] *noun*
(a) part of your head which you hear with; *rabbits have long ears*; *have you washed behind your ears?*; *(informal)* **to be up to your ears in** = to be very busy with; *he's up to his ears in work*; **to have** or **keep your ear to the ground** = to follow what is happening and know all about something
(b) ability to sense sound; *he has a good ear for music*; **to play an instrument by ear** = to play without reading the printed notes; *she can play the piano by ear*; *(informal)* **to play it by ear** = to do what you think is right at the time; *we won't make a plan, we'll just play it by ear and see how it goes*

① **early**
['ɜːlı]
1 *adverb*
(a) before the usual time; *the plane arrived five minutes early*; *we must get up early tomorrow morning if we want to catch the first boat to France*; *can you come an hour earlier tomorrow?*
(b) at the beginning of a period of time; *we went out early in the evening*; *the snow came early in the year*
2 *adjective*
(a) which happens at the beginning of a period of time or which happens before the proper time; *we picked some early vegetables*; *I caught an early flight to Paris*; *these flowers open in early summer*; **at an early date** = soon; *the meeting must be held at the earliest date possible*; **to take early retirement** = to leave a job with a pension before the usual age for retirement
(b) *(informal)* **an early bird** = someone who likes to get up early and work before breakfast, and who does not stay up late at night; *he's an early bird - he's up at 6.00 every morning*; *compare* NIGHT OWL (NOTE: **earlier - earliest**)

② **earn**
[ɜːn] *verb*
(a) to be paid money for working; *he earns £20,000 a year*; *how much does a bus driver earn?*
(b) to deserve something or to be given something; *you can all take a rest now - you've earned it!*; *his joke earned him a bad mark from the teacher*

④ **earnest**
['ɜːnıst]
1 *adjective*
serious; *they were engaged in some earnest conversation*
2 *noun*
in earnest = seriously; *after lunch the discussions began in earnest*

④ **earnings**
['ɜːnıŋz] *noun*
salary, the money which you earn from work; *his earnings are not enough to pay the rent*

④ **earring**
['ıırıŋ] *noun*
ring worn attached to your ear as an ornament; *he has a gold earring in his left ear*; **a pair of**

earrings = two similar rings, one worn in each ear; *she was wearing a pair of old earrings which belonged to her mother*

② **earth**

[ɜːθ]

1 *noun*

(a) the planet on which we live; *the earth goes round the sun once in twenty-four hours*; *the space shuttle came back to earth safely*; *(informal)* **it costs the earth** = it costs a great deal of money; *it shouldn't cost the earth to have the house painted*

(b) soil, soft material made up of minerals and rotten vegetable matter, which plants grow in; *put some earth in the plant pot and then sow your cucumber seeds*

2 *verb*

to connect an electrical device to the earth; *machines which you use in the home should be properly earthed*; **earth wire** = electric wire which connects with the earth (NOTE: American English is to **ground**)

◊ **on earth**

[ɒn ˈɜːθ] *(used to make questions stronger)* *why on earth did you do that?*; *who on earth is going to pay that much for a bottle of wine?*; *how on earth are we going to afford a holiday in Australia?*; *what on earth are they doing digging up the road?*

④ **earthquake**

[ˈɜːθkweɪk] *noun*

shaking of the surface of the earth caused by movements of the earth's outer crust; *there have been many earthquakes in or near San Francisco*; *only a few houses were still standing after the earthquake*; *the Richter scale is used to measure earthquakes*

③ **earthworm**

[ˈɜːθwɜːm] *noun*

little animal which looks like a very small snake and lives in soil; *the earthworms come to the surface when it rains* (NOTE: usually just called a **worm**)

④ **ease**

[iːz]

1 *noun*

(a) to put someone at their ease = to make someone feel relaxed and confident; *the policeman offered the children sweets to put them at their ease*; **ill at ease** = nervous, uncomfortable; *she was definitely ill at ease during the interview with the manager*

(b) lack of difficulty; *he won the first round with the greatest of ease*; *the bottle has a wide mouth for ease of use*

(c) *(in the army)* **at ease!** = command to stand in a relaxed position, with the feet apart, after standing to attention (NOTE: no plural)

2 *verb*

(a) to make less painful; *a couple of aspirins should ease the pain*

(b) to make easy; *an introduction from his uncle eased his entry into the firm*

③ **easier, easiest**

[ˈiːzɪə or ˈiːzɪɪst]

see EASY

① **easily**

[ˈiːzɪlɪ] *adverb*

(a) without any difficulty; *I passed my driving test easily*; *I can get there easily by 9 o'clock*

(b) *(for emphasis before comparatives or superlatives)* a lot (compared to something else); *he is easily the tallest man in the team*; *our shop is easily the biggest in the high street*

① **east**

[iːst]

1 *noun*

(a) direction of where the sun rises; *the sun rises in the east and sets in the west*; *Germany is to the east of France*; *the wind is blowing from the east*

(b) part of a country which is to the east of the rest; *the east of the country is drier than the west*; *see also* FAR EAST, MIDDLE EAST, NEAR EAST

2 *adjective*

referring to the east; *the east coast is the coldest part of the country*; **East Anglia** = eastern part of England to the north-east of London; **east wind** = wind which blows from the east

3 *adverb*

towards the east; *the kitchen windows face east, so we get the morning sun*; *drive east along the motorway for twenty miles*

③ **Easter**

[ˈiːstə] *noun*

important Christian festival (in March or April) celebrating Christ's death and rising again; *we have two weeks' holiday at Easter*; *what are you doing during the Easter holidays?*; *we plan to go walking in the woods on Easter Monday*; **Easter Day** *or* **Easter Sunday** = Sunday celebrating Christ's rising from the dead; **Easter egg** = chocolate or sugar egg eaten at Easter

② **eastern**

[ˈiːstɪn] *adjective*

from, or in the east; *Bulgaria is part of Eastern Europe*; *the best snow is in the eastern part of the mountains*

① **easy**

[ˈiːzɪ]

1 *adjective*

not difficult, not needing a lot of effort; *the driving test isn't very easy - lots of people fail it*; *it's easy to see why the shop closed - a big supermarket has opened next door*; *the office is within easy reach of the airport*; *my boss is very easy to get on with*; **easy terms** = conditions which mean that you do not have to pay a lot of money; *the shop is let on very easy terms*

2 *adverb*

to take things easy = to rest, not to do any hard work; *the doctor told him to take things easy for a time after his operation*; easy now! *or* easy does it! = be careful!; go easy on *or* with the jam! = don't take too much jam!; it's easier said than done = it's more difficult than you think (NOTE: easier - easiest)

① **eat**
[i:t] *verb*
(a) to chew and swallow food; *I'm hungry - is there anything to eat?*; *we haven't eaten anything since breakfast*; *the children ate all the sandwiches*; *eat as much as you like for £5.95!*; *you'll get thin if you don't eat*; eating apple = sweet apple which you can eat raw (as opposed to a sour apple which has to be cooked)
(b) to have a meal; *he was still eating his breakfast when I arrived*; *we are eating at home tonight*; *have you eaten yet?* (NOTE: eating - ate [et] - has eaten ['i:tn])

④ **eccentric**
[ɪk'sentrɪk]
1 *adjective*
strange, odd; *an eccentric old lady who wears boots all the year round*
2 *noun*
strange or odd person; *in his old age, he became something of an eccentric*

④ **echo**
['ekɪʊ]
1 *noun*
sound which is repeated (as when you shout in a cave, etc.); *we could hear the echo of voices in the tunnel*; *if you go to the Whispering Gallery in the dome of St Paul's Cathedral you can hear the echo very clearly* (NOTE: plural is echoes)
2 *verb*
(a) *(of sound)* to make an echo; *their voices echoed down the tunnel*
(b) to repeat; *the newspaper article echoed the opinions put forward in the minister's speech*

④ **ecological**
[i:kɪ'lɒdʒɪkl] *adjective*
referring to ecology; *the oil installation will affect the area's ecological balance*; ecological disaster = disaster which seriously disturbs the balance of the environment; *the oil from the wrecked tanker caused an ecological disaster*

④ **ecology**
[ɪ'kɒlɪdʒi] *noun*
study of the relationship between plants and animals and their environment; *books on ecology are in the environmental studies section of the library*

① **economic**
[i:kɪ'nɒmɪk] *adjective*
(a) referring to the economy; *I don't agree with the government's economic policy*; *the government has introduced controls to solve the current economic crisis*; *the country enjoyed a period of economic growth in the 1990s*
(b) which provides enough money; *the flat is let at an economic rent*; *it is hardly economic for us to run two cars*

④ **economical**
[i:kɪ'nɒmɪkl] *adjective*
which saves money or resources; *it's more economical to heat water by gas*; economical car = car which does not use much petrol

③ **economics**
[i:kɪ'nɒmɪks] *noun*
(a) scientific study of how money works in trade, society and politics; *she is studying for an economics degree*
(b) the way money is used in a particular activity; *the economics of town planning are very important*; *have you worked out the economics of starting your own business?*

④ **economist**
[ɪ'kɒnɪmɪst] *noun*
person who specializes in the study of money and its uses; *the university has several famous economists in its teaching staff*

① **economy**
[ɪ'kɒnɪmi] *noun*
(a) way in which a country makes and uses money; the financial state of a country; *the country's economy is in ruins*; *when will the economy start to grow again?*; black economy = work which is paid for in cash or goods, but not declared to the tax authorities
(b) something you do to save and not to waste money or materials; *she tried to make a few economies like buying cheaper brands of washing-up liquid*; economy class = air fare which is cheaper than first class or business class; economy drive = vigorous effort to save money or materials; an economy measure = an action to save money or materials; economy pack *or* economy size = pack which is cheaper than the regular size; economies of scale = making a product more profitable by manufacturing it in larger quantities

① **edge**
[edʒ]
1 *noun*
(a) side of something flat; *he put his plate down on the edge of the table*; *she lay down on the roof and looked over the edge*; *you can stand a £1 coin on its edge*; *the knife has a very sharp edge*
(b) line between two quite different things; *he lived in a house at the edge of the forest*; *the factory is built right on the edge of the town by the motorway*
(c) advantage; to have the edge on a rival company = to have a slightly larger share of the market than a rival
2 *verb*

to move in a slow, careful way; *he started edging towards the door*

③ **edible**
['edɪbl] *adjective*
which can be safely eaten; *how do you know which wild mushrooms are edible and which are poisonous?*

④ **edit**
['edɪt] *verb*
(a) to be in charge of a newspaper or magazine; *he edited the 'Sunday Express' for more than twenty years*
(b) to make notes on a text; to change a text to make it better; *the edited text is now ready*; *it took me two hours to edit the first chapter*
(c) to get a text ready for publication; *I am editing a volume of 20th-century poetry*
(d) to cut up a film or tape and stick it together in correct order to make it ready to be shown or played; *once the film has been edited it will run for about 90 minutes*

③ **edition**
[ɪ'dɪʃn] *noun*
(a) number of copies of a book or newspaper printed at the same time; *the book of poems was published in an edition of one thousand copies*
(b) form in which a book is published; *she bought the paperback edition for her father*; **a first edition** = a copy of the first printing of a book

② **editor**
['edɪtɪ] *noun*
(a) journalist in charge of a newspaper or part of a newspaper; *he wrote to the editor of 'The Times' asking for a job*; *she is the sports editor of the local paper*
(b) person who makes notes on a text; person who gets a text, a radio or TV programme, etc., ready for publication; *he worked as a dictionary editor all his life*; *the editor of a TV series on French cooking*
(c) computer program for editing text; *the software contains a basic text editor*

④ **editorial**
[edɪ'tɔːriːl]
1 *adjective*
referring to editors or to editing; *he has general editorial control of the series*; **editorial board** = group of editors (on a newspaper, etc.)
2 *noun*
main article written by the editor of a newspaper; *did you read today's editorial in the 'Times'?* (NOTE: also called a **leading article** or **leader**)

④ **educate**
['edjuːkeɪt] *verb*
to teach someone; *she was educated privately in Switzerland*; *we need to educate young people about the dangers of alcohol*

① **education**
[edjuː'keɪʃn] *noun*
system of teaching, or of being taught; *our children deserve the best education we can give them*; *we spent a lot of money on his education, and he's got a job as a rubbish collector!*; **adult education** = teaching people over the age of 20; **further education** = teaching people who have left school; **higher education** = teaching at colleges and universities; **primary education** = teaching small children; **private education** = teaching in private schools, where the students pay fees; **secondary education** = teaching children from the age of 11 to 16 or 18; **state education** = teaching in schools which belong to the state or local educational authority, where the education is free; **Department for Education and Employment (DfEE)** = British government department which is concerned with education and employment

① **educational**
[edjuː'keɪʃnl] *adjective*
referring to learning and teaching, schools, etc.; *this game for 3 to 5 year-olds is very educational*; *a campaign to improve educational standards*; **educational publisher** = company which publishes school books

④ **eel**
[iːl] *noun*
long thin fish which looks like a snake; *she ordered some smoked eel*

① **effect**
[ɪ'fekt]
1 *noun*
(a) result or influence; *the cuts in spending will have a serious effect on the hospital*; *the cream has had no effect on her rash*; *the effects of the drug took some time to wear off*; **the order takes effect** *or* **comes into effect from January 1st** = the order starts to have to be obeyed on January 1st; **with effect from** = starting from; *prices will be increased by 10% with effect from January 1st*
(b) approximate meaning; *the notice said something to the effect that the shop had closed*; **or words to that effect** = or something with that meaning; *she said she wouldn't pay, or words to that effect*
(c) **sound effects** = artificial sounds in theatre, TV, films; **special effects** = ghosts, cartoon characters appearing with ordinary actors, etc., which are used in films or on stage
(d) *(formal)* **personal effects** = personal belongings
2 *verb*
(formal) to make, to carry out; *she was able to effect a number of changes during her time in charge*; **to effect a payment** = to make a payment

① **effective**

['ɪ'fektɪv] *adjective*

(a) which produces the required result; *it's a very effective remedy against colds*; *his method of keeping the children quiet is very effective*; *advertising on TV is a very effective way of selling*

(b) which takes effect; *an order which is effective from January 1st*

① **effectively**

[ɪ'fektɪvli] *adverb*

in a way which produces a good result; *the stage lighting worked very effectively*

③ **efficiency**

[ɪ'fɪʃnsi] *noun*

being able to produce a good result without wasting time, money or effort; *how can we improve the efficiency of our working methods?*; *she is known for her extreme efficiency*; **business efficiency** = making a business work in an efficient way

② **efficient**

[ɪ'fɪʃnt] *adjective*

able to work well and do what is necessary without wasting time, money or effort; *he needs an efficient assistant to look after him*; *the system of printing invoices is very efficient*; **a fuel-efficient car** = a car which does not use much petrol

④ **efficiently**

[ɪ'fɪʃntli] *adverb*

in an efficient way; *the waitresses served the 250 wedding guests very efficiently*; *the new system of dealing with complaints is working very efficiently*

① **effort**

['efɪt] *noun*

use of the mind or body to do something; *he's made great efforts to learn Spanish*; *thanks to her efforts, we have collected more than £10,000 for the children's home*; *if we make one more effort, we should get all that rubbish cleared away*

③ **eg** or **e.g.**

['i:'dʒi: or fɔ: ig'zɑ:mpl] *abbreviation meaning 'for example'*; *some animals, eg polar bears, live in cold climates* (NOTE: it is short for the Latin phrase **exempli gratia**)

① **egg**

[eg] *noun*

(a) oval object with a hard shell, produced by a female bird or reptile, from which a baby bird or reptile comes; *the owl laid three eggs in the nest*; *snakes lay their eggs in the sand*

(b) a chicken's egg, used as food; *you need three eggs to make this cake*; **boiled egg** = egg which has been cooked by boiling in water; **hard-boiled egg** = egg which has been boiled until it is hard inside; **fried egg** = egg which is fried in fat or butter in a frying pan; **scrambled eggs** = eggs which are mixed up with a fork and

then cooked in butter; *I had fried eggs and bacon for breakfast*; *do you want sausages with your scrambled eggs?*

③ **egg on**

['eg 'ɒn] *verb*

to encourage someone to do something, especially something naughty; *stop egging him on - he's bad enough as it is*

③ **eh**

[eɪ] *interjection used when asking questions*; *what a laugh, eh?*; *what about a drink, eh?*; *eh? what did he say?*

① **eight**

[eɪt]

(a) number 8; *he ate eight chocolates*; *the little girl is eight (years old) I usually have breakfast before eight (o'clock)*

(b) crew of eight people who are rowing in a boat; *our college eight won the race*; *see also* FOUR, PAIR (NOTE: plural in this meaning is **eights**)

① **eighteen**

[eɪ'ti:n]

number 18; *there are eighteen people in our dance class*; *he will be eighteen (years old) next week*; *the train leaves at eighteen twenty (18:20)* **the eighteen hundreds** = the years between 1800 and 1899 (NOTE: compare with **the eighteenth century**)

> COMMENT: eighteen is the age at which young people in Britain become officially adult, independent of their parents and able to vote

① **eighteenth (18th)**

[eɪ'ti:nθ] *adjective & noun*

the eighteenth of April or *April the eighteenth (April 18th) today's the seventeenth, so tomorrow must be the eighteenth*; *that's the eighteenth invoice we've sent out today*; *it's his eighteenth birthday next week*; **the eighteenth century** = the years from 1700 to 1799 (NOTE: compare with **the eighteen hundreds**; note also that with dates **eighteenth** is usually written **18th**: **April 18th, 2001**; **September 18th, 1866** (American style is **September 18, 1866**), say 'the eighteenth of September' or 'September the eighteenth' (American style is 'September eighteenth'); with names of kings and queens, **eighteenth** is usually written **XVIII**: **King Louis XVIII** (say: 'King Louis the Eighteenth')

① **eighth (8th)**

[eɪtθ] *adjective & noun*

the eighth of February or *February the eighth (February 8th) King Henry the Eighth (Henry VIII) had six wives*; *his eighth birthday is next Monday* (NOTE: with dates **eighth** is usually written **8th**: **April 8th, 2000**; **September 8th, 1866** (American style is **September 8, 1866**), say 'the eighth of September' or 'September the eighth'

(American style is 'September eighth'); with names of kings and queens, **eighth** is usually written **VIII**: **King Henry VIII** (say: 'King Henry the Eighth')

ⓘ **eightieth (80th)**
['eɪtiɪθ] *adjective & noun*
four and a half days is about an eightieth of a year; *granny's eightieth birthday is next week*

ⓘ **eighty**
['eɪti]
number 80; *it's about eighty miles from London to Dover*; *she's eighty (years old)* **she's in her eighties** = she is between 80 and 89 years old; **the eighties** *or* **nineteen eighties (1980s)** = the period from 1980 to 1989 (NOTE: **eighty-one** (81), **eighty-two** (82) but **eighty-first** (81st), **eighty-second** (82nd), etc.)

ⓘ **either**
['aɪðɪ or 'iːðɪ]
1 *adjective & pronoun*
(a) one or the other; *you can use either computer - it doesn't matter which*; *I don't like either of them*
(b) each of two; both; *there are trees on either side of the road*; *some people don't take sugar in their coffee, some don't take milk, and some don't take either*; *they sat on either side of him* = one sat on each side of him
2 *conjunction;* *(showing one of two possibilities)* **either ... or;** *either you come here or I'll come to see you*; *what's that awful noise? - it's either a motorbike or a noisy car*; *you must do it either today or tomorrow*
3 *adverb; (with a negative, or to make a statement stronger)* *he isn't Irish and he isn't Scottish either*; *she doesn't want to go, and I don't want to go either*; *the report wasn't on the TV news, and it wasn't on the radio either*

④ **elaborate**
1 *adjective*
[ɪ'læbɪrɪt] very detailed, very complicated; *an elaborate dessert of cream, fruit and cake*
2 *verb*
[ɪ'læbɪreɪt] to go into details; *it's a very complicated plan so I won't elaborate*; *the manager refused to elaborate any further on the salesman's reasons for leaving*

③ **elastic band**
[ɪ'læstɪk 'bænd] *noun*
rubber ring which holds cards, papers, etc., together

③ **elbow**
['elbʊ]
1 *noun*
joint in the middle of your arm; *he sat with his elbows on the table*; *she pushed him with her elbow*; **elbow room** = space to move about; *the seats in tourist class don't give you much elbow room*
2 *verb*
to push with your elbows; *he elbowed his way to the front of the crowd*

④ **elder**
['eldɪ]
1 *adjective*
older than another person; *I have two elder brothers*; *she brought her elder sister*; **elder statesman** = older and wiser politician (NOTE: **elder** is a comparative, used mainly of brothers or sisters, but is never followed by **than**)
2 *noun*
(a) older person; *Mary is the elder of the two*; *which brother is the elder?*; *the village elders met to discuss the plan*
(b) common tree with white flowers and bunches of small purple berries; *there's an elder growing in the hedge by the field*

② **elderly**
['eldɪli]
1 *adjective*
old; *an elderly man sat down beside her*; *my mother is now rather elderly and doesn't drive any more* (NOTE: used as a polite way of saying old)
2 *noun*
the elderly = old people

④ **eldest**
['eldɪst]
1 *adjective*
oldest of a series of people; *this is John, my eldest son*
2 *noun*
oldest person of a series of people; *he is the eldest of the three brothers*

② **elect**
[ɪ'lekt] *verb*
(a) to choose by voting; *she was elected MP for the town*; *the president is elected for a term of four years*; *the chairman is elected by the members of the committee*
(b) **to elect to do something** = to choose to do something; *we all went to the pub, but she elected to stay at home and watch TV*

ⓘ **election**
[ɪ'lekʃɪn] *noun*
process of choosing by voting; *after the election, the crowds were dancing in the streets*; *local elections are being held next week*; *the next item on the agenda is the election of a new secretary for the club*; **general election** = election for Parliament, where everyone in the country over a certain age can vote

COMMENT: in the UK, a general election to choose a new government and parliament must be held every five years, although the Prime Minister may call one sooner. In the USA, a presidential election is held every four years, always in November. The members of Congress are also elected in November elections, each for a two year term, while Senators are elected for six years, one third of the Senate coming up for election every two years

⊕ electoral
[ɪˈlektɪrl] *adjective*
referring to an election; *the party suffered a terrible electoral defeat*; **electoral college** = group who elect someone such as a president; **electoral register** *or* **electoral roll** = REGISTER OF ELECTORS

② electric
[ɪˈlektrɪk] *adjective*
(a) worked by electricity; *he plays an electric guitar*; *he cut the wood with an electric saw*; *she gave me an electric toothbrush for Christmas*
(b) making or carrying electricity; *don't touch those electric wires*; *electric plugs in the USA are different from those in Britain*
(c) full of excitement; *the atmosphere was electric as the votes were being counted*

③ electrical
[ɪˈlektrɪkl] *adjective*
referring to electricity; *the college offers courses in electrical engineering*; *they are trying to repair an electrical fault*

② electricity
[ɪlekˈtrɪsɪti] *noun*
energy used to make light, heat, or power; *we haven't paid the electricity bill this month*; *the electricity was cut off this morning*; *the heating is run by electricity*; *the cottage is in the mountains and doesn't have any electricity* (NOTE: no plural)

④ electron
[ɪˈlektrɒn] *noun*
basic negative particle in an atom

② electronic
[ɪlekˈtrɒnɪk] *adjective*
using devices which affect the electric current which passes through them; **electronic engineer** = engineer who specializes in electronic devices; **electronic mail** = email, the system of sending messages from one computer to another, via telephone lines

④ electronics
[ɪlekˈtrɒnɪks] *noun*
science of the movement of electricity in electronic devices; *he is studying electronics at university*; *she works for a major electronics company*; **the electronics industry** = the industry which makes TV sets, radios, calculators, etc. (NOTE: takes a singular verb)

④ elegant
[ˈelɪgɪnt] *adjective*
very fashionable and stylish; *you look very elegant in that dress*; *who is that elegant woman in black at the back of the church?*; *she led us into her elegant dining room*

① element
[ˈelɪmɪnt] *noun*
(a) **chemical element** = basic chemical substance; *see also* TRACE ELEMENT
(b) basic part of something; *I think we have all the elements of an agreement*
(c) natural environment; *the vicar is in his element when he's talking about cricket*; **the elements** = the weather, usually bad weather; *you don't want to expose your new coat to the elements*
(d) wire which heats in an electric heater, cooker, etc.; *I think the element has burnt out*

④ elephant
[ˈelɪfɪnt] *noun*
very large African or Indian animal, with large ears, a trunk and two long teeth called 'tusks'; *if you go to the zoo, you can have a ride on an elephant*; *in some countries elephants are used for work in the jungle*

COMMENT: there are two types of elephant, the African, which is larger and wilder, and the Indian which is found in India and South-East Asia, and is used as a working animal in forests

④ elevate
[ˈelɪveɪt] *verb*
(formal) to lift up; *he was elevated to the post of chairman*; **elevated railway** = form of local railway system which runs along rails placed high above the street

③ elevator
[ˈelɪveɪtə] *noun*
(a) *US* device for lifting people from floor to floor inside a building; *take the elevator to the 26th floor* (NOTE: British English is **lift**)
(b) **goods elevator** = device for lifting goods from floor to floor inside a building
(c) **grain elevator** = tall building for storing grain

① eleven
[ɪˈlevn]
(a) number 11; *when you're eleven (years old) you will go to secondary school*; *come and see me at eleven (o'clock)* **the eleven hundreds** = the years from 1100 to 1199 (NOTE: compare with **the eleventh century**)
(b) eleven people, as in a football team; *the England eleven* (NOTE: in this meaning, usually written **XI: the England XI**)

① eleventh (11th)
[ɪˈlevɪnθ] *adjective & noun*
the eleventh of June or June the eleventh (June 11th) *his name was eleventh on the list*; *it's her eleventh birthday tomorrow*; **at the eleventh hour** = at the last minute; *the contract was finally signed at the eleventh hour*; *his eleventh-hour decision to stand for election*; **the eleventh century** = the years from 1000 to 1099 (NOTE: compare with **the eleven hundreds**; note also that with dates **eleventh** is usually written

11th: April 11th, 2002; September 11th, 1866 (American style is **September 11, 1866**), say 'the eleventh of September' or 'September the eleventh' (American style is 'September eleventh'); with names of kings and queens, **eleventh** is usually written **XI: King Louis XI** (say: 'King Louis the Eleventh')

④ **eligible**

['elɪdʒɪbl] *adjective*

(a) eligible to do something = able to do something because you are old enough or have the right qualifications; *you aren't eligible to vote until you are eighteen*; *she's not eligible to enter the competition because she works for the company running it*

(b) eligible for something = entitled to do something *or* qualified for something; *the previous president is eligible for reelection*; *she is not eligible for a grant*

④ **eliminate**

[ɪ'lɪmɪneɪt] *verb*

(a) to remove mistakes, waste, etc.; *using a computer should eliminate all possibility of error*; *the disease has been eliminated in most parts of the world*

(b) to remove someone from a competition; *he came last and so was eliminated from the next round of the contest*

④ **elite**

[eɪ'liːt] *noun*

group of the best people; *only the elite can afford private education for their children*

① **else**

[els] *adverb*

(a) *(used after pronouns)* other; *what else can I say?*; *everyone else had already left*; *who else was at the meeting?*; **anyone else** = any other person; *is there anyone else who can't see the screen?*; **anything else** = any other thing; *is there anything else you don't like eating?*; *did you hear anything else?*; **somebody else** *or* **someone else** = some other person, a different person; *she was ill so someone else had to take her place*; **nobody else** *or* **no one else** = no other person; *nobody else's daughter behaved as badly as ours*; **nothing else** = no other thing; *I need one small gold ring - nothing else will do*; **nowhere else** = no other place; *there's nowhere else to go*; **somewhere else** *US* **someplace else** = in some other place, in a different place; *can we go somewhere else?*

(b) or else = or if not; *don't miss the bus, or else you'll have a long wait for the next one*; *put a coat on to go out, or else you'll catch cold*; *we'd better get up early or else we'll miss the train*; *you must have a ticket, or else you will be thrown off the train by the inspector*

(c) *(as informal threat)* **you'd better pay, or else** = if you don't pay, I'll hit you

② **elsewhere**

[els'weɪ] *adverb*

somewhere else, in another place; *this shop doesn't stock maps, so you'll have to try elsewhere*

③ **email** *or* **e-mail**

['iːmeɪl]

1 *noun*

(a) electronic mail, a system of sending messages from one computer to another, using telephone lines; *you can contact me by phone or email if you want*; *I'll give you my email address*

(b) message sent by email; *I had two emails from him this morning*

2 *verb*

to send a message using electronic mail; *I emailed him about the meeting*

④ **embargo**

[ɪm'bɑːgɪʊ]

1 *verb*

to forbid officially the trade in something; *the government has embargoed the sale of arms to Middle Eastern countries*

2 *noun*

official ban on trade; *the oil embargo is still in place*; **to place** *or* **put an embargo on** = to forbid something officially; *they placed an embargo on trade with our country*; **to lift an embargo** = to allow trade to start again; *the government has lifted the embargo on the export of computers*; **to be under an embargo** = to be forbidden (NOTE: plural is **embargoes**)

③ **embarrass**

[ɪm'bærɪs] *verb*

to make someone feel uncomfortable by being rude, etc.; *she wanted to embarrass me in front of my friends*; *it embarrasses me to have to talk about it in public*

③ **embarrassed**

[ɪm'bærɪst] *adjective*

uncomfortable or ashamed, because you have done something wrong; *she gave an embarrassed laugh, and said she had forgotten to bring the present*; *he was so embarrassed that he turned bright red*

④ **embarrassing**

[ɪm'bærɪsɪŋ] *adjective*

that makes you feel embarrassed; *it was very embarrassing to find that the bride's mother was wearing exactly the same dress as me*

④ **embassy**

['embɪsɪ] *noun*

home or offices of an ambassador; *there was a party at the British Embassy in Paris* (NOTE: plural is **embassies**)

④ **embrace**

[ɪm'breɪs]

1 *verb*

to hold and kiss someone to show affection; *they embraced for several minutes before he got on the train*

2 *noun*

(literary) holding someone tightly and kissing them; *she shrank from his embraces*; *they lay on the grass in a close embrace*

④ **embryo**
['embriɪʊ] *noun*

(a) first state of a living organism; *a human embryo*

(b) in embryo = in its early stages; *the plan was presented to us in embryo* (NOTE: plural is **embryos**)

② **emerge**
[ɪ'mɜːdʒ] *verb*

(a) to emerge from inside something = to come out from inside; *they blinked as they emerged into the sunshine from the tunnel*

(b) to appear, to come into existence; *it was only after the election that he emerged as party leader*

(c) to become known; *it soon emerged that the Prime Minister knew nothing about what was happening*

② **emergency**
[ɪ'mɜːdʒɪnsɪ] *noun*

dangerous situation where decisions have to be taken quickly (such as a fire, accident, breakdown of law and order, etc.); *phone for an ambulance - this is an emergency!*; **state of emergency** = time when the police or armed forces are in control of a country; *the government has declared a state of emergency*; **emergency exit** = door in a cinema, etc., used in case of fire; **emergency operation** = operation done immediately on a seriously ill patient; **the emergency services** = the police, fire service and ambulance service; **in case of emergency** *or* **in an emergency** = if a dangerous situation develops; *in an emergency or in case of emergency press the red button* (NOTE: plural is **emergencies**)

④ **emigrant**
['emɪgrɪnt] *noun*

person who emigrates; *Russian emigrants to Israel*; *compare* IMMIGRANT

④ **emigrate**
['emɪgreɪt] *verb*

to leave your country to live in another; *my daughter and her family have emigrated to Australia*

④ **emission**
[ɪ'mɪʃn] *noun*

(a) process of sending out; *we are trying to reduce the emission of toxic gases from the power station* (NOTE: no plural in this meaning)

(b) substance which is sent out; *gas emissions can cause acid rain*

③ **emotion**
[ɪ'mɪʊʃn] *noun*

strong feeling; *jealousy and love are two of the most powerful emotions*; *he tried to hide his emotions when he made his speech*

③ **emotional**
[ɪ'mɪʊʃnl] *adjective*

which shows emotion; *we said an emotional farewell to our son and his family*; *the music made her feel very emotional and she started to cry*

④ **emperor**
['emprɪ] *noun*

ruler of an empire; *Napoleon declared himself emperor*; *the Chinese Emperors lived in the Forbidden City*

② **emphasis**
['emfɪsɪs] *noun*

(a) showing the importance of something, usually in speech; *don't put too much emphasis on his age*; *she banged the table for emphasis as she spoke*

(b) strength of your voice when you pronounce a word or phrase; *everyone noticed the emphasis he put on the word 'peace'* (NOTE: plural is **emphases**)

② **emphasize**
['emfɪsaɪz] *verb*

to show that you feel something is important, by saying it more loudly, slowly, etc.; *please emphasize that the meeting must start on time*; *he emphasized the importance of everyone working together*; *she kept on emphasizing the same point over and over again*

③ **empire**
['empaɪɪ] *noun*

several separate territories ruled by a central government; *we're studying the history of the British Empire*; *the Russian empire covered a huge area from the Pacific Ocean to the middle of Europe*

② **employ**
[ɪm'plɔɪ] *verb*

(a) to give someone regular paid work; *he is employed as a gardener by the town council*; *she is employed in the car industry*

(b) (formal) to use; *if we were to employ more up-to-date methods, would we make more money?*; *how can we best employ our free time on Sunday?*

① **employee**
[emplɔɪ'iː] *noun*

person who is employed; *the company has decided to take on twenty new employees*

① **employer**
[ɪm'plɔɪɪ] *noun*

person or organization that gives work to people and pays them; *her employer was a Hong Kong businessman*; *the car factory is the biggest employer in the area*

① **employment**
[ɪm'plɔɪmɪnt] *noun*

regular paid work; **in employment** = working; *are you still in employment?*; *everyone in paid employment has to pay tax*; **full-time employment** = work for all of a working day; *he is looking for full-time employment*; **part-time** employment = work for part of a working day; *she is in part-time employment*; **seasonal employment** = work which is available at certain times of the year only (such as in a ski resort); **temporary employment** = work which does not last for more than a few months; **contract of employment** *or* **employment contract** = contract between management and an employee showing all the conditions of work; **employment agency** = office which finds jobs for people; **the Department for Education and Employment**; *see* EDUCATION

① **empty**
['emtɪ]
1 *adjective*
with nothing inside; *when we opened it, the box was empty*; *take an empty pot and fill it with soil*; *the fridge is empty - we'll have to go out to eat*; *the ski resorts are empty because there is no snow* (NOTE: **emptier - emptiest**)
2 *noun*
something, usually a bottle, which has nothing in it; *you can take the empties back to the shop* (NOTE: plural is **empties**)
3 *verb*
to make something empty; *she emptied the clothes out of the suitcase*; *he emptied the bottle into the sink*; *they emptied the contents of the cash box into a bag*

① **enable**
[ɪ'neɪbl] *verb*
(formal) to make it possible for someone to do something; *the dictionary should enable you to understand English better*

④ **enact**
[ɪ'nækt] *verb*
(formal) to make a law; *once a Bill has been enacted, it becomes law*

③ **enclose**
[ɪn'kləʊz] *verb*
(a) to put something inside an envelope with a letter; *I am enclosing a copy of our current catalogue*; *please find your tickets enclosed with this letter*
(b) to put a wall or fence round an area of land; *the garden is enclosed with high brick walls*

③ **encounter**
[ɪn'kaʊntɪ]
1 *noun*
(a) meeting; *I had an unexpected encounter with my former boss at the London Book Fair*; *she told him about her encounter with the cows*
(b) short fight; *the encounter only lasted a few minutes, but it seemed longer to the soldiers taking part*
2 *verb*
to meet; *on the journey we encountered several amusing people*; *I have never encountered such jealousy in anyone else*

① **encourage**
[ɪn'kʌrɪdʒ] *verb*
(a) to make it easier for something to happen; *leaving your credit cards on your desk encourages people to steal* or *encourages stealing*
(b) to help someone to do something by giving them confidence; *he encouraged me to apply for the job*; *I always felt encouraged by his interest in what I was doing*

④ **encouragement**
[ɪn'kʌrɪdʒmɪnt] *noun*
giving someone the confidence to do something; *a few words of encouragement and everyone will work better*; *all he needs is a little encouragement and he will do really well*

② **encouraging**
[ɪn'kʌrɪdʒɪŋ] *adjective*
which encourages; *the maths teacher was very encouraging*; *it's an encouraging sign that so many students have applied to take the course*

① **end**
[end]
1 *noun*
(a) last part of something; *she tied the two ends of the ribbon together*; *the telephone rang and I missed the end of the TV programme*; *go down to the end of the road and then turn right*; **in the end** = finally, at last; *in the end the teacher let him go home*; *in the end the shop had to call in the police*; **on end** = with no breaks; *he worked for hours on end*; *(informal)* **no end of** = very many; *the car's caused us no end of problems*; **to come to an end** = to be finished; *the work should come to an end next month*; **to be at a loose end** = to have nothing to do; *I was at a loose end so I decided to go to the cinema*; **to make ends meet** = to have enough money to live on; *after paying tax, we can only just make ends meet*
(b) final part of a period of time; *can you wait until the end of the week?*; **year end accounts** = accounts prepared at the end of a financial year
(c) aim, result intended; **the end justifies the means** = if your final aim is good or honourable, you are right to do anything that is necessary to achieve it; **to this end** *or* **with this end in mind** = in order to do this; *we have decided to sell the house and to this end have put it in the hands of an estate agent*
2 *verb*
to be finished, to come to an end; *the film ends with a wedding*; *the meeting ended with everyone fighting on the floor*; *the concert should end at about 10 o'clock*; *the game ended in a draw*

④ **endanger**
[ɪn'deɪndʒɪ] *verb*
to put in danger; *pollution from the factory is endangering the fish in the lake*; *endangered*

species = any species at risk of becoming extinct; *this little spider is an endangered species*

④ **endless**
['endlıs] *adjective*
with no apparent end; *the afternoon seemed endless, with one boring speech after another; we had an endless string of meetings with our suppliers*

④ **endorse**
[ın'dɔːs] *verb*
(a) to officially mark or sign the back of a document; **to endorse a cheque** = to sign a cheque on the back to show that you accept it; *the bank clerk asked him to endorse the cheque before depositing it; his driving licence was endorsed* = his licence was marked to show that he had committed a traffic offence
(b) to show approval of; *I endorse what has just been said; they asked us to endorse Mrs Martin as the local candidate*

③ **end up**
['end 'ʌp] *verb*
to finish; *we ended up with a bill for £10,000; after the movie we all ended up at my girlfriend's flat; they went to several clubs, and ended up getting arrested by the police in Trafalgar Square*

④ **endure**
[ın'djʊɪ] *verb*
(a) to bear; *the prisoners had to endure great hardship; the pain was more than she could endure*
(b) *(formal)* to last; *the memory of that day will endure for ever in my mind*

② **enemy**
['enɪmɪ] *noun*
(a) person who hates you; *did your husband have many enemies?*
(b) country or people fighting against you in a war; *they attacked enemy targets with bombs; the enemy has or have advanced to three kilometres from the city* (NOTE: plural is **enemies,** but in meaning (b) **enemy** can take a singular or plural verb)

④ **energetic**
[enɪ'dʒetɪk] *adjective*
active and lively; *at 82, my grandmother is still astonishingly energetic; she's an energetic campaigner for animal rights*

① **energy**
['enɪdʒi] *noun*
(a) force or strength of a person; *he used up a lot of energy rushing around doing the Christmas shopping*
(b) power which makes something work; *the use of atomic energy or nuclear energy to make electricity; we try to save energy by switching off the lights when the rooms are empty; if you reduce the room temperature to eighteen degrees, you will save energy; electric buses are an energy-efficient method of public transport;*

energy value = number of calories which a certain amount of a substance, such as a certain food, contains; *a tin of beans has an energy value of 250 calories*

④ **enforce**
[ın'fɔːs] *verb*
to make sure a rule is obeyed; *the police are there to enforce the law; this is a regulation which is very difficult to enforce*

① **engage**
[ın'geɪdʒ] *verb*
(a) to employ a worker; *we have engaged a lawyer to represent us; the company has engaged twenty new salesmen*
(b) to make parts of a machine fit into each other; *the gears aren't properly engaged;* **to engage a low gear** = to put your car into a low gear
(c) **to be engaged in** = to be busy with; *the whole family was engaged in cleaning the car; the general is engaged in important negotiations*

① **engaged**
[ın'geɪdʒd] *adjective*
(a) having officially stated your intention to marry; *she was engaged to Tom and then broke it off; John and Sue are engaged: they got engaged last week*
(b) busy, occupied; *you can't speak to the manager - his line is engaged;* **engaged tone** = ringing sound on a telephone which shows that the line is busy

① **engagement**
[ın'geɪdʒmɪnt] *noun*
(a) statement that you intend to get married; *my son has announced his engagement to Pam; their engagement was announced in the local paper;* **engagement ring** = ring given by a man to a woman at their engagement
(b) appointment; *I have no engagements for the rest of the day; she noted the appointment in her engagements diary; I can't meet you tonight - I have a prior engagement*
(c) agreement to do something; **to break an engagement to do something** = not to do what you have legally agreed to do

① **engine**
['endʒın] *noun*
(a) machine which powers or drives something; *the lift engine has broken down again - we shall just have to walk up to the 4th floor; early industrial equipment was powered by steam engines*
(b) vehicle which pulls a train; *the engine broke down and the train was stuck in the tunnel*

① **engineer**
[endʒɪ'niːɪ]
1 *noun*
(a) person who looks after technical equipment, especially engines; *there are comparatively few*

women telephone engineers; the photocopier's broken down again - we'll have to call the engineer

(b) person whose profession is designing mechanical, electrical or industrial equipment; **civil engineer** = person who specializes in the construction of roads, bridges, etc.

(c) *US* person who drives an engine that pulls a train (NOTE: British English is **engine driver**)

2 *verb*
to arrange something secretly; *she engineered the dismissal of her husband's secretary*

② **engineering**
[endʒɪ'nɪɪrɪŋ] *noun*
science or study of the design of technical equipment; *the college offers courses in electrical engineering;* civil engineering = science of building, especially of roads, bridges, etc. (NOTE: no plural)

① **England**
['ɪŋlɪnd] *noun*
country in the southern part of the island of Great Britain, the largest country in the United Kingdom; *how long does it take to cross from England to France?; a lots of Scottish people live in England* (NOTE: the word **England** is often used instead of Britain, and this is a mistake, as England is only one part of Great Britain; note also the capital: **London;** people: **the English;** language: **English;** currency: **pound sterling**)

① **English**
['ɪŋlɪʃ]
1 *adjective*
(a) referring to England; *the beautiful English countryside; is the English weather really as bad as it is made out to be?; I think she is English although she speaks with an Australian accent*
(b) **English breakfast** = cooked breakfast with bacon, eggs, sausages, etc.; *compare* CONTINENTAL BREAKFAST; **the English Channel** = the sea between England and France; *the boat only takes 50 minutes to cross the English Channel* (NOTE: the word **English** is often used instead of British, and this is a mistake, as England is only one part of Great Britain; do not say **the English Prime Minister** but **the British Prime Minister**)

2 *noun*
(a) language of the United Kingdom, the USA, Australia, and many other countries; *can she speak English?; what's the English for 'Autobahn'?; English is not my first language; we managed to make ourselves understood, even though no one in the hotel spoke English; several of her books have been translated into English*
(b) English language as a subject taught in school or university; *she's good at maths but not so good at English; as well as teaching English, he also teaches drama; Mr Smith is*

our English teacher; she gives English lessons at home in the evenings; there are twenty students in my English class
(c) **the English** = the people of England; *the English on the whole are not a very emotional people*

COMMENT: English is spoken as a first language by 415 million people worldwide, and by a further 800 million people as a second language. It was originally a German type of language, derived from the language of the Angles and Saxons who invaded England in the 4th century AD. However, over the centuries it has borrowed heavily from Latin, French and many other languages, and is nowadays a highly mixed language

③ **Englishman, Englishwoman**
['ɪŋlɪʃmɪn or 'ɪŋlɪʃwʊmɪn] *noun*
person from England; *'an Englishman's home is his castle'; a group of young Englishwomen were helping in the relief effort in Africa* (NOTE: plural is **Englishmen, Englishwomen**)

③ **enhance**
[ɪn'hɑːns] *verb*
(a) to increase the beauty or value of something; *her makeup enhanced the beauty of her dark brown eyes*
(b) to increase the value or power of something; *slot in this new memory board to enhance your computer memory; he took drugs to enhance his performance as a runner*

① **enjoy**
[ɪn'dʒɔɪ] *verb*
to take pleasure in something; *have you enjoyed the holiday so far?; when he asked them if they had enjoyed the film they all answered 'no'; she didn't enjoy the boat trip because she felt sick all the time;* **to enjoy yourself** = to have a good time; *is everyone enjoying themselves?; we enjoyed ourselves so much that we're going to the same place for our holiday next year*

② **enjoyable**
[ɪn'dʒɔɪbl] *adjective*
which pleases; *did you have a good holiday? - yes thank you, it was most enjoyable; we spent an enjoyable evening playing cards*

④ **enlarge**
[ɪn'lɑːdʒ] *verb*
(a) to make a bigger photograph; *I like this photo best: I'll get it enlarged*
(b) to make bigger; *we could enlarge the vegetable plot and grow more potatoes*
(c) *(formal)* **to enlarge on** *or* **upon** = to give details of; *even though we asked him twice, he refused to enlarge upon his meeting with the principal*

② **enormous**
[ɪ'nɔːmɪs] *adjective*
very large; *their dining room is absolutely enormous; he ate an enormous lunch*

③ **enormously**
[ɪˈnɔːmɪsli] *adverb*
very much; *his refusal upset her enormously*;
we were enormously relieved to see her again;
thefts in supermarkets have increased enormously

① **enough**
[ɪˈnʌf]
1 *adjective*
as much as is needed; *have you got enough money for your fare or to pay your fare?*; *there isn't enough light to take photographs*
2 *pronoun* as much of something as is needed; *I had £20 in my purse to pay the taxi, but it wasn't enough*; *have you all had enough to eat?*
3 *adverb*
as much as is needed; *this box isn't big enough for all these books*; *he doesn't work fast enough and so gets behind the others*

③ **enquire** *or* **enquiry**
[ɪnˈkwaɪə *or* ɪnˈkwaɪri]
see INQUIRE, INQUIRY; *see also* DIRECTORY ENQUIRIES

③ **en-suite**
[ˈɒn ˈswiːt] *adjective*
attached to another room; *bedroom with an en-suite shower room*; *is the bathroom en-suite?*

① **ensure**
[ɪnˈʃʊə] *verb*
to make sure of; *when taking a shower, please ensure that the shower curtain is inside the bath* (NOTE: do not confuse with **insure**)

① **enter**
[ˈentə]
1 *verb*
(a) to go in, to come in; *he took off his hat as he entered the church*; *did they stamp your passport when you entered the country?*
(b) to write something in a record; *to enter a name on a list*
(c) to enter for something = to decide to take part in a race or competition; *she has entered for the 2000 metres*
(d) to type information on a keyboard, and put it into a computer system; *we will just enter your name and address on the computer*
(e) to enter into = to begin; *to enter into negotiations with a company*; *to enter into an agreement or a contract*; *see also* ENTRANCE, ENTRY
2 *noun*
key on a keyboard which you press when you have finished keying something, or when you want to start a new line; *to change directory, type cd and press enter*

② **enterprise**
[ˈentəpraɪz] *noun*
(a) business venture, especially something that involves some risk; *his latest enterprise is importing carpets from Turkey*

(b) method of organizing business; *the state should not interfere with free enterprise*; **private enterprise** = all businesses which are not owned by the state
(c) commercial firm, business organization; *they have merged with another huge industrial enterprise*; **a small-scale enterprise** = a small business; **a state enterprise** = a company that is controlled by the state

④ **entertain**
[entəˈteɪn] *verb*
(a) to amuse; *he entertained us with stories of his life in the army*; *we hired a funny man to entertain the children*; *the tourists were entertained by the local dancers*
(b) to offer meals, accommodation, a visit to the theatre, etc., to a visitor; *they're entertaining some Swedish friends this evening*
(c) *(formal)* to be ready to consider a proposal; *they said they would entertain any suggestions we might like to make*

③ **entertaining**
[entəˈteɪnɪŋ] *adjective*
amusing; *he gave a very entertaining talk about his life in Lebanon*

③ **entertainment**
[entəˈteɪnmənt] *noun*
(a) amusement; *she sang for their entertainment*; *there's not much entertainment in the village - the nearest cinema is 25km away*
(b) offering someone meals, visits to the theatre, etc.; *the entertainment of the visiting managing director and his wife cost us a fortune*; **entertainment allowance** = allowance given to a businessman for entertaining guests

③ **enthusiasm**
[ɪnˈθjuːziæzɪm] *noun*
great interest and liking; *we succeeded thanks to the enthusiasm and hard work of a small group of members*; *she showed a lot of enthusiasm for our new project*

③ **enthusiastic**
[ɪnθjuːziˈæstɪk] *adjective*
showing great interest and approval; *the editor was very enthusiastic about my book*; *there were enthusiastic cheers at the end of the performance*

② **entire**
[ɪnˈtaɪə] *adjective*
whole; *we spent the entire day gardening*; *the entire cast came on the stage and bowed to the audience*

② **entirely**
[ɪnˈtaɪli] *adverb*
completely; *I agree with you entirely*; *this is an entirely separate problem*

② **entitle**
[ɪnˈtaɪtl] *verb*
(a) to give the right to; *I am entitled to five weeks' holiday a year*

(b) to give a title to; *Tolstoy wrote a book entitled 'War and Peace'*

③ **entrance**
1 ['entrɪns] *noun*
(a) door for going in; *she was sitting at the entrance to the museum*; *we will meet at the Oxford Street entrance of Selfridges*; **back entrance** = back doorway; **main entrance** = main doorway; *the taxi will drop you at the main entrance*
(b) entrance (charge) *or* **entrance fee** = money which you have to pay to go in; *entrance is £1.50 for adults and £1 for children*
2 [ɪn'trɑːns] *verb*
to make someone very happy; *the audience was entranced by his singing*

④ **entrepreneur**
[ɒntrɪprɪ'nɜː] *noun*
person who directs a company and takes risks commercially; *the company was bought by a couple of young entrepreneurs*

② **entry**
['entri] *noun*
(a) going in; *the sign on the door said 'no entry'*; **entry charge** *or* **entry fee** = price to be paid before going into an exhibition, etc.; *the entry charge is £5* (NOTE: no plural in this sense)
(b) written information in a reference book, an accounting or computer system; *she looked up the entry on 'roses' in the gardening book*; **to make an entry in something** = to write details in a book; *the police looked at the entries in the hotel's register* (NOTE: plural is **entries**)

③ **envelope**
['envɪləʊp] *noun*
folded paper cover for sending letters; *she wrote the address on the envelope and sealed it*; *the shopkeeper wrote down all the information on the back of an envelope*; **airmail envelope** = very light envelope for airmail letters; **a stamped addressed envelope** = an envelope with your own address written on it and a stamp stuck on it to pay for return postage; *please send a stamped addressed envelope for further details and our latest catalogue*

① **environment**
[ɪn'vaɪrɪnmɪnt] *noun*
(a) the earth, its natural features and resources, seen as the place where man lives; *they are trying to protect the environment*; **environment protection** = act of protecting the environment against pollution
(b) surroundings in which any organism lives, but especially where people live; *the environment in the office is not good for concentrated work*; **the working environment** = the general surroundings in which a person works

① **environmental**
[ɪnvaɪrɪn'mentl] *adjective*
referring to the environment; *measures taken to protect against environmental pollution*; *she's*

joined an environmental group; **Environmental Health Officer** = official of a local authority who examines the environment and tests for air pollution, etc.

④ **environmentalist**
[ɪnvaɪrɪn'mentlɪst] *noun*
person who is concerned with protecting the environment; *a group of environmentalists is trying to prevent the trees being cut down*; *environmentalists want to ban the dumping of waste in the sea*

④ **envy**
['envi]
1 *noun*
feeling that you would like to have something which someone else has; *her beautiful long blond hair filled us all with envy*
2 *verb*
to feel you would like to be someone else; *I don't envy him with a job like the one he has*; **to envy someone something** = to want to have something which someone else has; *we all envy him his new car*

④ **epidemic**
[epɪ'demɪk] *noun*
infectious disease which spreads quickly through a large number of people; *the authorities are taking steps to prevent an epidemic of influenza* or *a flu epidemic*; *the disease rapidly reached epidemic proportions*

④ **episode**
['epɪsəʊd] *noun*
(a) short section of a longer story, one part of a TV series; *do you remember the episode where the ghost appears?*; *the hero's father comes out of prison in the third episode*
(b) short period of your life; *it's an episode in his marriage which he would rather forget*

① **equal**
['iːkwɪl]
1 *adjective*
with exactly the same amount as; *his share is equal to mine*; *male and female workers must have equal pay*; *the two sticks are of equal length* or *are equal in length*; **all things being equal** = assuming nothing else has changed; *all things being equal, I'd prefer to go on holiday in June*; **to be equal to the task** = to be strong enough or brave enough to do something; *he was put in charge of the prison, but was quickly found not to be equal to the task*; **equal opportunities** = employing people on their merits, treating them with equal respect, regardless of age, race, sex, etc.
2 *verb*
(a) to be exactly the same as; *his time for the 100 metres equals the existing record*
(b) to give a result; *two plus two equals four*; *ten take away four equals six* (NOTE: **equalling - equalled** but American spelling is **equaling - equaled**)
3 *noun*

person who is on the same level as someone else; *I don't consider him your equal; we're all equals here*

> COMMENT: many business and organizations in the UK and USA operate a policy of **equal opportunities**, that is, they employ people on their merits and treat them with equal respect, regardless of age, race, sex, disability, etc.

④ **equality**
[ɪˈkwɒlɪti] *noun*
situation where you are equal; *the company has policies to ensure equality in the factory*; **equality of opportunity** = situation where everyone, regardless of sex, race, class, etc., has the same opportunity to get a job; *our education policy is designed to promote equality of opportunity* (NOTE: no plural)

① **equally**
[ˈiːkwɪli] *adverb*
in exactly the same way; *they are all equally guilty*; *here men and women are paid equally badly*; *they were both equally responsible for the mistake*

③ **equation**
[ɪˈkweɪʒn] *noun*
(a) formula in mathematics or science showing that two parts are equal; *let me show you how this equation can be solved*; *he drew up the equation for converting mass to energy*
(b) balancing of various factors in a situation; *making a profit is difficult enough, but when higher interest rates are brought into the equation it becomes impossible*

④ **equip**
[ɪˈkwɪp] *verb*
to equip someone or **something with something** = to provide someone *or* something with something; *a holiday flat equipped with a washing machine and dishwasher*; **well-equipped** = with all necessary equipment; *a well-equipped hospital*; *the hotel has a fully-equipped sports centre* (NOTE: equipping - equipped)

② **equipment**
[ɪˈkwɪpmɪnt] *noun*
all the tools, arms, machinery, etc., which are needed; *he brought all his camera equipment with him*; *do you really need all this safety equipment on a ship?* (NOTE: no plural: for one item say **a piece of equipment**)

④ **equity**
[ˈekwɪti] *noun*
(a) fair system of justice; *she complained about the lack of equity in the company's pay structure*; **in equity** = being fair (NOTE: no plural in this meaning)
(b) **equities** = ordinary shares; *the equities market has risen sharply during the last month*

③ **equivalent**
[ɪˈkwɪvɪlɪnt]
1 *noun*
thing which has the same value or the same strength as something else; *what is the American equivalent of the Chancellor of the Exchequer?*; *I gave him $2000 and he paid me the equivalent in French francs*
2 *adjective*
having the same value or the same strength as something else; *two pints and a litre are roughly equivalent*; *she handed me the equivalent amount in Swiss francs*; **to be equivalent to** = to have the same value as, to be the same as; *a litre is roughly equivalent to two pints*

① **er**
[ɜː] *interjection*
showing that you are hesitating; *what time were you, er, thinking of leaving?*

④ **era**
[ˈiːrɪ] *noun*
long period of history; *the Victorian era*

③ **erase**
[ɪˈreɪz] *verb*
to rub out writing or to remove recorded material from a tape or data from a disk; *he erased the pencil marks with a rubber*; *I've erased your recording of the concert by mistake*

③ **eraser**
[ɪˈreɪzɪ] *noun*
US piece of rubber for removing writing in pencil (NOTE: British English is **rubber**)

④ **erect**
[ɪˈrekt]
1 *adjective*
straight upright; *she held herself erect as she walked into the court room*
2 *verb*
to put up something vertical, such as a street light or a building; *they are planning to erect a monument to the princess*; *civilians rushed to hide in hastily-erected bomb shelters*

④ **erode**
[ɪˈrɪʊd] *verb*
to wear away gradually; *the cliffs have been eroded by the sea*

④ **erotic**
[ɪˈrɒtɪk] *adjective*
strongly sexual; *she paints erotic pictures of naked men and women*

② **error**
[ˈerɪ] *noun*
mistake; *the waiter made an error in calculating the total*; *she must have made a typing error*; *there isn't a single error in the whole document*; *I must have made an error because the screen went blank*; **computer error** = mistake made by a computer; **in error** = by mistake; *the parcel was sent to our Edinburgh office in error*

④ **erupt**
[ɪˈrʌpt] *verb*
(a) *(of volcano)* to throw out red hot rocks, ash, etc.; *the volcano last erupted in 1968*
(b) to start to become violent suddenly; *a row erupted over the closing of the railway station*
(c) *(of person)* to become suddenly angry; *he listened to the discussion for a while and then erupted angrily*

④ **eruption**
[ɪˈrʌpʃn] *noun*
(of volcano) throwing out of red hot rocks, ash, etc.; *several villages were destroyed in the volcanic eruption of 1978*

④ **escalate**
[ˈeskɪleɪt] *verb*
(a) to get worse or more violent; *our financial problems have escalated*; *the border conflict escalated into an full-scale war*
(b) to increase steadily; *prices escalated during the year*

④ **escalator**
[ˈeskɪleɪtɪ] *noun*
moving stairs; *they played a game, trying to run down the up escalator*; *one of the escalators at Holborn Station is being repaired*

② **escape**
[ɪˈskeɪp]
1 *noun*
(a) action of getting away from prison or from an awkward situation; *there were three escapes from this jail last year*; *a weekend by the sea was a wonderful escape from the office*; **we had a narrow escape** = we were almost killed
(b) **ESCAPE key (ESC)** = key which stops what is happening on a computer and returns to the main program; *press ESCAPE to get back to the original screen*
2 *verb*
(a) to get away from prison or from an awkward situation; *he escaped from the prison by sawing through the bars*; *the police are looking for the escaped prisoners*; *a lion has escaped from the zoo and is wandering about in the countryside*
(b) to miss; **the name of the restaurant escapes me** = I can't remember the name of the restaurant

④ **escort**
1 *noun*
[ˈeskɔːt]
person or group of people who are accompanying someone; *she wore red silk and her escort wore a dark suit*; *the president had a police escort to the airport*
2 *verb*
[esˈkɔːt] to accompany someone; *the police escorted the group into the hotel*; *I was escorted around by our local MP*

① **especially**
[ɪˈspeʃɪli] *adverb*
particularly, very; *her suitcase is especially heavy*; *do you want to go out? - not especially*

② **essay**
[ˈeseɪ] *noun*
piece of writing on a particular subject; *a collection of the journalist's most famous essays*; *for our homework, we have to write an essay on pollution*

④ **essence**
[ˈesɪns] *noun*
(a) central part of an argument; *the essence of what she had to say was very clear* (NOTE: no plural in this meaning)
(b) pure extract taken from something; *dessert flavoured with coffee essence*

② **essential**
[ɪˈsenʃl]
1 *adjective*
which is very important or which you cannot do without; *the refugees lack essential winter clothing*; *you can survive without food for some time, but water is essential*; *it is essential that we get the delivery on time*
2 *noun*
thing which is very important or which you cannot do without; *sun cream is an essential in the south of France*; *we've got all the basic essentials - food, water and fuel*; **the bare essentials** = the absolute necessities of life

② **essentially**
[ɪˈsenʃɪli] *adverb*
basically, for the most part; *my new job is essentially not so very different from my old one*; *although he's essentially a kind man, he does lose him temper sometimes*

① **establish**
[ɪˈstæblɪʃ] *verb*
(a) to create, to set up; *the business was established in Scotland in 1823*; *we need to establish a good working relationship with our colleagues*
(b) to show something to be true; *the police are trying to establish where the car was parked that evening*; *it's difficult to establish what her reasons are for resigning*

③ **established**
[ɪˈstæblɪʃt] *adjective*
which has been shown to be true; *it is an established fact*

② **establishment**
[ɪˈstæblɪʃmɪnt] *noun*
(a) creation, setting up; *she helped them with the establishment of the local drama society* (NOTE: no plural in this meaning)
(b) business; organization; *it's an establishment which imports radios from China*; *he runs an important teaching establishment*
(c) **the Establishment** = people who occupy influential positions in society or who are in authority; *they appointed several Establishment figures to the board of trustees of the museum*; *see also* GREAT AND THE GOOD

(d) number of people working in a company; **to be on the establishment** = to be a full-time employee

② **estate**
[ɪ'steɪt] *noun*

(a) large area of land belonging to one owner; *he owns a 250-acre estate in Norfolk*; **estate car** = large car with a flat space behind the seats where parcels or suitcases can be put (NOTE: American English for this is **station wagon**)

(b) **real estate** = property (land or buildings); **estate agent** *US* **real estate agent** = person who sells houses, flats, land for customers; **housing estate** *US* **housing project** = development of new flats, houses, etc.; **industrial estate** *or* **trading estate** = area of land near a town specially for factories and warehouses

(c) property owned by a person at the time of death; *the solicitor announced the value of grandfather's estate*; **estate duty** = tax on property left by a dead person

④ **esteem**
[ɪ'stiːm] *noun*

(formal) respect; *the staff seem to have very little esteem for the directors*; **to hold someone in (high) esteem** = to respect someone; *she is someone whose work we hold in the highest esteem* (NOTE: no plural)

② **estimate**
1 *noun*
['estɪmət]

(a) calculation which shows the approximate amount of something, or its worth or cost; *I wasn't in when the man came to read the gas meter, so this bill is only an estimate*; *your estimate of two dozen visitors proved to be correct*; *can you give me an estimate of how much time was spent on the job?*; **rough estimate** = approximate calculation

(b) price quoted by a supplier for work to be done; *three firms put in estimates for the job* (NOTE: often simply called a **quote**)

2 *verb*
['estɪmeɪt]

(a) to calculate approximately the cost or worth, etc., of something; *I estimate that it will cost £100,000*; *he estimated costs at £50,000*

(b) to calculate a price before supplying an item or doing a job; **to estimate for a job** = to state in writing the probable costs of carrying out a job

① **etc.** *or* **etcetera**
[et'setɪrə]

Latin phrase meaning and so on, and other things like this; *fruit such as oranges, bananas, etc.*

④ **eternal**
[ɪ'tɜːnl] *adjective*

which lasts for ever; *she is searching for eternal happiness*; *his eternal complaints really annoy me*

④ **ethic**
['eθɪk] *noun*

good and moral behaviour; **work ethic** = belief that working hard is the best way to live your life

④ **ethical**
['eθɪkl] *adjective*

right, from a moral point of view; *is it ethical for the newspaper to publish the private phone numbers of government ministers?*

④ **ethics**
['eθɪks] *noun*

moral principles; *he doesn't care about the ethics of selling arms, provided he can make some money*

③ **ethnic**
['eθnɪk] *adjective*

relating to race; *the census shows the ethnic makeup of the population*; **ethnic food** = food (such as Chinese or Indian food) from a particular country which is not European; **ethnic minority** = minority of the population which is of different racial origin to the majority

③ **EU**
['iː'juː] = EUROPEAN UNION
EU ministers met today in Brussels; *the USA is increasing its trade with the EU*

① **euro**
['jʊərɪʊ] *noun*

monetary unit of the EU; *many articles are priced in euros*; *what's the exchange rate for the euro?* (NOTE: written € before numbers: **€250**: say: 'two hundred and fifty euros')

① **Europe**
['jʊərɪp] *proper noun*

(a) the continent of Europe, the part of the world to the west of Asia, from Russia to Ireland; *most of the countries of Western Europe are members of the EU*; *Poland is in eastern Europe, and Greece, Spain and Portugal are in southern Europe*

(b) the same area, but not including the UK; *holidays in Europe are less popular than last year*

(c) the European Union (including the UK); *Canadian exports to Europe have risen by 25%*

(d) other EU countries but not including the UK; *UK exports to Europe have increased this year*

① **European**
[jʊərɪ'piːn] *adjective*

referring to Europe; *they do business with several European countries*; *at home we always eat Asian food, not European*; **the European Parliament** = the parliament with members from each country of the EU

③ **European Union (EU)**
[jʊərɪ'piːn 'juːnɪn] *noun*

an organization which links several European countries together based on the four freedoms of movement: movement of goods, of capital, of people and of services

④ **Eurostar**
['jʊərɪʊstɑː] *noun*
train going from England to France and
Belgium, through the Channel Tunnel; *we took
the 8.25 Eurostar to Paris*; *Eurostar is often
used by businessmen who want to go to the
centre of Brussels*

④ **evaluate**
[ɪ'væljʊeɪt] *verb*
(formal) to calculate the value of; *I'm trying to
evaluate how useful our visit was*; *the teacher's
performance in the classroom will be carefully
evaluated*

③ **evaluation**
[ɪvæljʊ'eɪʃn] *noun*
(formal) act of calculating a value; *I agreed with
everything he said in his evaluation of the
problem*; *the inspectors will carry out a careful
evaluation of the teacher's performance*
(NOTE: no plural)

④ **eve**
[iːv] *noun*
(a) the night or day before; *on the eve of the
election the ministers prepared to celebrate*;
Christmas Eve = 24th December; **New Year's
Eve** = 31st December
(b) a short time before; **on the eve of our
departure** = just before we left

① **even**
['iːvn]
1 *adjective*
(a) **even numbers** = numbers which can be
divided by 2; *on the right-hand side of the
street all the houses have even numbers*
(b) equal (in a competition); *at the end of the
competition three teams were even with 96
points*
(c) flat, level; *the road has a smooth even
surface*
(d) which does not change; *they kept up an even
pace for miles*; *the temperature is an even 28°
all through the day*
(e) **to break even** = to make no profit, but no
loss either; *the company is just breaking even*
2 *adverb; (showing surprise or making an
expression stronger)*
he doesn't even like strawberries; *even the
cleverest businessmen can make mistakes*;
she's fat, but her sister is even fatter; **even now**
= at this very moment; *even now, he won't
admit he was wrong*; **even worse** = worse than
before; *that film was bad, but this one is even
worse*

◊ **even if**
['iːvn 'ɪf] *conjunction*
it doesn't matter if; *we'll try and drive there,
even if it's snowing*

◊ **even so**
['iːvn 'sɪʊ] *adverb*
in spite of what has happened; *it was pouring
with rain, but even so they decided to go ahead
with the village fair*

◊ **even though**
['iːvn 'ðɪʊ] *conjunction*
although, in spite of the fact that; *he didn't take
an umbrella, even though it was raining quite
hard*

① **evening**
['iːvnɪŋ] *noun*
(a) late part of the day, when it is getting dark; *I
saw her yesterday evening*; *the accident took
place at 8.30 in the evening*; *we arrived in
London at breakfast time, having left New York
the previous evening*; *we always go to a
restaurant on Sunday evenings*; *they took an
evening flight to Madrid*; *the evening meal is
served from 7.30 to 10.30*; **this evening** = today
in the evening; *we'll all meet this evening after
work*
(b) **evening dress** = clothes worn at formal
occasions in the evening

① **event**
[ɪ'vent] *noun*
(a) thing which happens; *the events leading up
to the war*
(b) **in the event** = as it happened; *in the event,
the party went off very well*; **in the event of** = if
something should happen; *in the event of his
refusing the job then we will advertise it again*;
in any event *or* **at all events** = whatever may
happen; *I don't know exactly what happened -
in any event it doesn't matter*; *even if he doesn't
like the job, at all events he's very well paid*; **in
the normal course of events** = as things usually
happen; *in the normal course of event, the
winner should get a silver cup*
(c) sporting competition; *the last event was the
100 metres hurdles*; **field events** = jumping and
throwing competitions; **track events** = running
races

④ **eventual**
[ɪ'ventjʊl] *adjective*
in the end; *his eventual aim is to become world
champion*

① **eventually**
[ɪ'ventjʊli] *adverb*
in the end; *after weeks of hesitation he
eventually decided to sell the cottage*

③ **even up**
['iːvn 'ʌp] *verb*
to make something balanced; *we've invited
three girls and six boys, so we must invite three
more girls to even things up*

① **ever**
['evɪ] *adverb*
(a) *(used with negatives, questions)* at any time;
nothing ever happens here; *did you ever meet
my brother?*; *have you ever been to Germany?*;
hardly ever = almost never; *I hardly ever go to
the theatre*
(b) *(for emphasis after comparatives)* *she is
singing better than ever*; *he went on playing the
drums louder than ever*

(c) always; *ever the optimist, he suggested we try once again*; **ever since** *or* **ever then** = from that time on; *she was knocked down by a car and ever since has been afraid to go out onto the main road*

(d) *(informal)* **ever so** = extremely; *she's been ever so ill*; *I'm ever so grateful*; *see also* HOWEVER, WHATEVER, WHENEVER, WHEREVER, WHOEVER

◊ **for ever**
[fɪ ˈevɪ] *phrase*

(a) always; *I will love you for ever and ever*; *the good times have gone for ever*

(b) *(exclamation to show support for a team)* *Scotland for ever!*

① **every**
[ˈevrɪ] *adjective*

(a) each; *it rained every day during the holidays*; *we have a party every New Year's Day*; *every Wednesday, he goes for a swim in the local swimming pool*; *every house in the street has a garden*

(b) *(showing regular periods of time)* **every two hours** = with a period of two hours in between; *the medicine is to be taken every four hours*; *have your car checked every 10,000 kilometres*; **every other day** = on one day, not on the next, but on the one after that (e.g. on Monday, Wednesday and Friday, etc.)

① **everybody** *or* **everyone**
[ˈevrɪbɒdi *or* ˈevrɪwʌn] *pronoun* all people, or all people involved in a particular situation; *everyone has to die some day*; *if everybody is here, we can start*; *I sent a Christmas card to everybody at work*; *everyone must show their passport* (NOTE: **everybody** and **everyone** are followed by **they, their, themselves**, etc., but the verb stays singular: **is everybody enjoying themselves? not everybody likes pop music, do they?**)

① **everyone**
[ˈevrɪwʌn] *pronoun*
see EVERYBODY

③ **everyplace**
[ˈevrɪpleɪs] *adverb*
US everywhere, in all places; *we looked everyplace for that key*

① **everything**
[ˈevrɪθɪŋ] *pronoun*

(a) all things; *did you bring everything you need?*; *the burglars stole everything of value*; *everything he says annoys me*

(b) things in general; *everything was dark in the street*; *everything is under control*

① **everywhere**
[ˈevrɪweɪ] *adverb*
in all places; *there were papers lying about everywhere*; *everywhere was white after the first snow fell*; *we've looked everywhere for the key and can't find it* (NOTE: American English is also **everyplace**)

① **evidence**
[ˈevɪdns] *noun*

(a) fact which indicate that something really exists or has happened; *the spots of blood on his coat were evidence of the crime*; *scientists are looking for evidence of life on Mars*; *there is no evidence that he was ever there*; **documentary evidence** = evidence in the form of documents

(b) written or spoken report given by a witness at a trial; *the victim gave evidence in court this morning*; **to give evidence for someone** = to be a witness, and suggest that someone is not guilty; **to give evidence against someone** = to be a witness, and suggest that someone is guilty; **to turn State's evidence** *or* **Queen's evidence** = to give information against criminals who worked with you; *he hoped to get a reduced sentence by turning Queen's evidence*

(c) **in evidence** = very visible; *her love of Italy was nowhere more in evidence than in her kitchen* (NOTE: no plural)

② **evident**
[ˈevɪdnt] *adjective*
obvious; *his disgust was evident in his tone of voice*; *her evident delight at Tom's arrival*; *it was quite evident that they didn't want to sign the agreement*

③ **evil**
[ˈiːvl]

1 *adjective*
very wicked; *she's an evil old woman*; *his evil intentions were evident as soon as he locked the door*; **evil spirit** = wicked thing which harms people

2 *noun*

(a) very wicked acts; *the struggle between the government and the rebels was seen as a fight between good and evil* (NOTE: no plural in this meaning)

(b) bad thing; *we are committed to fighting social evils such as juvenile crime*; *see also* LESSER

③ **evolution**
[iːvɪˈluːʃn] *noun*
gradual development; *by a slow process of evolution, modern railway engines developed from Stephenson's 'Rocket'*; **the theory of evolution** = theory, explained by Charles Darwin, that species develop by a process of natural selection; *see also* SURVIVAL OF THE FITTEST

④ **evolve**
[ɪˈvɒlv] *verb*

(a) to develop gradually; *modern dance evolved from classical ballet*; *birds originally evolved from little dinosaurs*

(b) to work out gradually a scientific theory or a way of working; *the research team has evolved its own methods of testing*

① **exact**
[ɪgˈzækt]
1 *adjective*
completely accurate, not differing at all from what is expected, what has been written, etc.; *what is the exact time of arrival?*; *could you repeat the exact words of the contract?*; *the girl asked me if I had the exact sum, since she had no change*
2 *verb*
(formal) **to exact something from someone** = to force someone to give something; *they stopped all the cars on the road and exacted payment from the drivers*

① **exactly**
[ɪgˈzæktli] *adverb*
(a) not more, not less, not differing at all from an amount; *that comes to exactly ten dollars and fifty cents*; *the time is exactly 16.24*
(b) completely; *he looks exactly like his father*
(c) (*used as an answer*) quite right, I agree; *it's a pity the buses don't run more frequently - exactly!*

◊ **not exactly**
[ˈnɒt ɪgˈzæktli] *phrase*
(a) not really; *was it a disaster? - not exactly a disaster, but it didn't go very well*; *it's not exactly the colour I wanted*
(b) not at all; *he's not exactly pleased at having to pay out so much money*

④ **exaggerate**
[ɪgˈzædʒɪreɪt] *verb*
to make things seem worse, better, bigger, etc., than they really are; *the wide black belt exaggerates her small waist*; *she exaggerated the importance of my mistake*

① **exam**
[ɪgˈzæm] *noun*
see EXAMINATION (b) *the exam was very difficult - half the students failed*; *she passed all her exams*

① **examination**
[ɪgzæmɪˈneɪʃn] *noun*
(a) inspection of something to if it works properly; *he had to have an X-ray examination*; *the examination of the car showed that its brakes were faulty*; **customs examination** = looking at goods or baggage by customs officials; **on examination** = when it was examined; *on further examination, the newspaper report was shown to be full of mistakes*
(b) written or spoken test; *the examination was very difficult - half the students failed*; *he did badly in his English examination*; *she came first in the final examination for the course* (NOTE: often shortened to **exam** in this meaning)

① **examine**
[ɪgˈzæmɪn] *verb*
(a) to inspect something to see if it is correct or healthy, that it works properly, etc.; *the doctor examined her throat*; *we will have to examine the shop's scales to see if they give correct weight*; *customs officials wanted to examine the inside of the car*; *the water samples were examined by chemists*
(b) to test a student; *they examined everyone in mathematics and computer skills*

① **example**
[ɪgˈzɑːmpl] *noun*
(a) something chosen to show something; *this is a good example of French architecture of the eleventh century*; **to set an example** = to do things yourself, so that other people can copy you; *he sets everyone a good example by getting into the office before 8 every morning*; *she sets everyone a bad example by talking for hours to her boyfriend on the phone*; **to make an example of someone** = to punish someone so that others will learn not to do what he did; *the magistrates made an example of him by sending him to prison for two weeks*
(b) **for example** = as a typical case; *she is keen on getting her weight down - for example she's stopped eating bread*; *why don't we sell anything to Eastern Europe, to Poland for example?* (NOTE: **for example** can often be replaced by **e.g.**: *countries in Eastern Europe, e.g. Poland*)

③ **exceed**
[ɪkˈsiːd] *verb*
to go beyond; *the car was exceeding the speed limit*; *our expenses have exceeded our income for the first time*; *did the UN troops exceed their instructions?*

① **excellent**
[ˈeksɪlɪnt] *adjective*
very good; *we had an excellent meal in a Chinese restaurant*; *her handwriting is excellent - it is much clearer than mine*

① **except**
[ɪkˈsept]
1 *preposition*
other than; *she's allowed to eat anything except milk products*; *everyone was sick on the boat, except (for) me*; *in Britain, VAT is levied on all goods except books, newspapers, food and children's clothes* (NOTE: do not confuse with **accept**)
2 *conjunction* other than, apart from; *he doesn't do anything except sit and watch football on the TV*; *everything went well, except that James was sick*; *everyone enjoyed the birthday party, except (that) there wasn't enough to eat*

② **exception**
[ɪkˈsepʃn] *noun*
(a) thing not included; *all the students failed, with one exception*; *are there any exceptions to the rule?*
(b) **to take exception to** = to be annoyed by something; *he took exception to what she said*

④ **exceptional**
[ɪk'sepʃɪnɪl] *adjective*

(a) outstanding, very good; *she's an exceptional runner*

(b) being an exception, not being included; *in exceptional cases, the entrance fee may be reduced*

④ **excerpt**
['eksɜ:pt] *noun*

small part (of a larger piece of music or writing); *they played an except from a Mozart symphony*; *he read excerpts from his latest novel*

④ **excess**
[ɪk'ses]

1 *noun*

(a) too much of something; *he had an excess of alcohol in his blood*; **in excess of** = more than; *quantities in excess of twenty-five kilos*; **to excess** = too much; *he drinks to excess* (NOTE: no plural in this meaning)

(b) **excesses** = bad things that you have done; *on Monday mornings he always feels guilty about the weekend's excesses*

2 ['ekses] *adjective*

too much, not needed; *the factory has excess capacity and may sell off some of its machines*; **excess baggage** = cases which weigh more than you are allowed when travelling by air, and for which you must pay extra

④ **excessive**
[ɪk'sesɪv] *adjective*

more than is usual; *the committee queried the excessive cost of the wallpaper*

④ **excessively**
[ɪk'sesɪvli] *adverb*

too much; *the pattern of the curtains is excessively brilliant*; *she is excessively modest about her achievements*

① **exchange**
[ɪks'tʃeɪndʒ]

1 *noun*

(a) giving one thing for another; *the exchange of rings during the wedding ceremony*; **part exchange** = giving an old machine as part of the payment for a new one; *he took my old car in part exchange*

(b) **foreign exchange** = changing money of different countries; **exchange rate** = rate at which one currency is exchanged for another; *the current rate of exchange is ten francs to the pound*

(c) **telephone exchange** = central telephone switchboard, which organizes phone calls over a wide area; **Stock Exchange** = place where stocks and shares are bought and sold; *he works on the London Stock Exchange*

2 *verb*

(a) to give something and get something similar back; *during the meeting we exchanged ideas on new developments in international law*; **they exchanged addresses** = they each gave the other their address

(b) **to exchange something for something else** = to give one thing and get another in return; *if the trousers are too small you can take them back and exchange them for a larger pair*; *goods can be exchanged only on production of the sales slip*

(c) to change money of one country for money of another; *to exchange francs for pounds*

④ **Exchequer**
[ɪks'tʃekɪ]
see CHANCELLOR

④ **excise**
['eksaɪz]
see CUSTOMS

④ **excite**
[ɪk'saɪt] *verb*

(a) to make someone lively and happy; *his playing during the second half of the match excited the crowd*

(b) to make someone have a particular feeling; *the thought of going to work in Kuala Lumpur excited his imagination*; *the case has excited a lot of interest in the press*

③ **excitement**
[ɪk'saɪtmɪnt] *noun*

being excited; *what's all the excitement about?*; *the children are always in a state of excitement before the holidays*

② **exciting**
[ɪk'saɪtɪŋ] *adjective*

which gives you a particular feeling; *I couldn't sleep after watching an exciting film on TV*; *the news about the house is really exciting*

④ **exclamation mark**
[eksklɪ'meɪʃn 'mɑːk] *noun*

written sign (!) which shows surprise; *she was obviously excited, her letter was full of exclamation marks*

② **exclude**
[ɪk'skluːd] *verb*

(a) not to include; *damage by fire is excluded from the insurance policy*; *don't exclude his name from your list*

(b) **to exclude something** *or* **someone from a place** = to shut something *or* someone out; *women are excluded from the club*

(c) to send a child away from school; *ten children had to be excluded last term*

③ **exclusion**
[ɪk'skluːʒn] *noun*

(a) act of not being included; **social exclusion** = shutting someone out of the rest of society; *the government has drawn up plans to prevent social exclusion*

(b) act of being sent away from school; *the school only considers exclusion as a last resort*; *see also* EXCLUDE

④ **exclusive**
[ɪkˈskluːsɪv] *adjective*
(a) open to selected rich customers, not open to everyone; *an exclusive Caribbean holiday resort; the new health club is very exclusive*
(b) **exclusive right** = right which belongs to one person or organization
(c) **exclusive of** = not including; *the bill was exclusive of service;* **exclusive of tax** = not including tax

② **excuse**
1 *noun*
[ɪkˈskjuːs] reason given for doing something wrong or not as expected; *his excuse for not coming was that he forgot the date*
2 *verb*
[ɪkˈskjuːz] to forgive someone for making a small mistake; *please excuse my arriving late like this*

③ **excuse me**
[ɪkˈskjuːz ˈmiː]
(a) *(to attract someone's attention)* *excuse me, is this the right bus for Oxford Circus?*
(b) please forgive me; *excuse me for arriving so late; excuse me for interrupting, but could you repeat what you have just said?*

④ **execute**
[ˈeksɪkjuːt] *verb*
(a) to carry out instructions or wishes; *press ENTER to execute the program; they did their best to execute his wishes*
(b) to do; *as part of the test, drivers are asked to execute an emergency stop*
(c) to kill someone who has been condemned to death; *murderers are no longer executed in this country*

② **executive**
[ɪgˈzekjʊtɪv]
1 *noun*
(a) businessman who makes decisions; *you can't leave a decision like that to the junior executives; top executives usually earn very high salaries;* **Chief Executive** = main director who runs a company
(b) **the Executive** = the part of Government which runs the state (as opposed to the judges who apply the law, and the Legislature which creates laws); *people are beginning to question the Executive's ability to govern*
2 *adjective*
which carries out plans and puts things into practice; *he has an executive position on the board of directors;* **executive committee** = committee which runs an organization

④ **exempt**
[ɪgˈzempt]
1 *adjective*
not forced to obey tax, laws, etc.; **exempt from tax** *or* **tax-exempt** = not required to pay tax; *children's clothes are exempt from VAT; we all have to pay for medical prescriptions but pensioners are exempt*

2 *verb*
to exempt someone from something or **from doing something** = to free someone from something; *pensioners are exempted from paying for medical prescriptions*

④ **exemption**
[ɪgˈzempʃn] *noun*
act of exempting; **exemption from tax** *or* **tax exemption** = being free from having to pay tax; *you can claim tax exemption in this case*

① **exercise**
[ˈeksɪsaɪz]
1 *noun*
practice in using physical or mental powers; *she does her piano exercises every morning;* **exercise book** = book for writing out school work; **to take exercise** = to do physical things, like walking or jogging, to keep fit; *you should take some exercise every day if you want to lose weight; she ought to take more exercise*
2 *verb*
(a) to use a power or right; *the United Kingdom exercised the right of veto*
(b) to give an animal or person exercise; *she exercised her pony on the race track; you must do something to exercise your stomach muscles*

④ **exhaust**
[ɪgˈzɔːst]
1 *noun*
(a) **exhaust (pipe)** = the tube at the back of a motor vehicle from which gases produced by the engine are sent out into the air; *clouds of white smoke were coming out of the exhaust pipe; fumes from car exhausts pollute the atmosphere*
(b) *US* gas which is produced by a car engine and is released into the air through the exhaust pipe; *we live downtown and the children are breathing car exhausts all day*
2 *verb*
(a) to wear out; *climbing the mountain had exhausted him*
(b) to finish; *we've exhausted our supplies of food*

④ **exhibit**
[ɪgˈzɪbɪt]
1 *verb*
to display; *the company is exhibiting at the Motor Show; she has rows of bowls exhibited on the shelves of her shop; he is exhibiting three paintings in the local art show*
2 *noun*
object displayed in court, at an exhibition, etc.; *Exhibit A is the murder weapon; the museum has several exhibits from relating to local history*

② **exhibition**
[eksɪˈbɪʃn] *noun*
(a) display (of works of art, flowers, etc.); *the exhibition is open from 10 a.m. to 5 p.m.;*

opening time for the exhibition is 10 a.m.; we stood in line for half an hour waiting to get into the Picasso exhibition
(b) show of goods so that buyers can look at them and decide what to buy; *we have a stand at the Ideal Home Exhibition*; **exhibition room** *or* **hall** = place where goods are shown so that buyers can look at them and decide what to buy; **exhibition stand** = separate section of an exhibition where a company shows its products or services

④ **exile**
['egzaɪl]
1 *noun*
(a) state of being sent away from your home country; *the ex-president went into exile in Switzerland* (NOTE: no plural in this meaning)
(b) person who is sent away from his own country; *the former king is now an exile in New York; the coup was mounted by exiles living across the border*
2 *verb*
to send someone away from his home country as a punishment; *the new government exiled the former dictator*

① **exist**
[ɪg'zɪst] *verb*
(a) to be; *when I was a child, colour TV didn't exist; I don't believe the document exists - I think it has been burnt*
(b) to live, to survive; *butterflies have existed on earth for a very long time; they got lost in the jungle and managed to exist on berries and roots*

① **existence**
[ɪg'zɪstɪns] *noun*
(a) life, being; *is there anything which proves the existence of life on Mars?; they lived a miserable existence in a little provincial town*
(b) **in existence** = which exists, which is actually here; *the original painting is no longer in existence; only one version of this car is still in existence in a museum in Geneva*

① **existing**
[ɪg'zɪstɪŋ] *adjective*
actual, which is in operation at this moment; *can we modify the existing structure in some way?; existing regulations do not allow the sale of food in the street*

① **exit**
['egzɪt]
1 *noun*
(a) way out of a building, an aircraft, etc.; *the customers all rushed towards the exits when the fire alarm rang*; **No Exit!** = sign showing that you must not go out this way; **emergency exit** = door used in emergency; **fire exit** = door used in case of fire
(b) **to make your exit** = to go out of a place, a room; *I apologized to my host and made my exit*; **exit visa** = visa allowing someone to leave a country

2 *verb*
(a) to leave a computer system; *press ESC to exit the system*
(b) *(informal)* to leave; *he exited the room as fast as he could*

④ **exotic**
[ɪg'zɒtɪk] *adjective*
unusual, referring to a strange, foreign, often tropical, place; *the silk dresses of the dancers give the show an exotic air; spices make Indian food taste more exotic*

② **expand**
[ɪk'spænd] *verb*
(a) to make something increase in size; *we have had to expand our sales force*
(b) to become larger; *water expands when it freezes; heat caused the metal pipes to expand; his waist is expanding fast*

② **expansion**
[ɪk'spænʃn] *noun*
increase in size; *the heat of the fire caused the expansion of the metal pipes; we are preparing for the company's forthcoming expansion into the North American market* (NOTE: no plural)

① **expect**
[ɪk'spekt] *verb*
(a) to think, to hope that something is going to happen; *I expect you are tired after your long train journey; he expects me to do all the housework; I can't talk for long, we're expecting visitors; we expect him to arrive at any moment* or *he is expected at any moment; the weather proved to be even worse than (they) expected*
(b) to be pregnant with; *my sister's expecting twins*

② **expectation**
[ekspek'teɪʃn] *noun*
hope, feeling that something will happen; *she lived up to all our expectations; we thought our team would do well, but in the end they exceeded all our expectations*

② **expected**
[ɪk'spektɪd] *adjective*
which is thought will happen, or hoped will happen; *the expected tax cuts didn't take place*

④ **expedition**
[ekspɪ'dɪʃn] *noun*
(a) journey to explore; *he set off on an expedition to the South Pole*
(b) short trip; *they went on a shopping expedition to the West End*

④ **expel**
[ɪk'spel] *verb*
to send a child away from school; *he was expelled for taking drugs;* see also EXPULSION (NOTE: **expelling - expelled**)

② **expenditure**
[ɪk'spendɪtʃɪ] *noun*
amount of money spent; *the government's heavy expenditure on arms; the group objects*

to the expenditure of public funds on this project (NOTE: no plural in British English, but American English often uses **expenditures)**

② **expense**
[ɪkˈspens] *noun*

(a) amount of money or cost; *I can't afford the expense of a holiday just now*; *the expense of having a family seems to increase every week*; **he furnished the office regardless of expense** = without thinking how much it cost; **expense account** = money which an employee is allowed to spend on personal expenses and entertaining guests, which will be paid for by his or her firm; **at great expense** = having spent a lot of money; *top designers had been hired at great expense*; *the house has been decorated at great expense*
(b) **at the expense of something** = in preference to something, giving something up; *she brought up her three children at the expense of her career in the bank*

◊ **at someone's expense**
phrase

(a) with someone else paying the cost; *they were flown to Frankfurt at the company's expense*
(b) making fun of someone; *we all had a good laugh at his expense*

① **expenses**
[ɪkˈspensɪz] *noun*

money spent in doing something; *we are making every effort to cut down on expenses*; **the salary offered is £20,000 plus expenses** = the company offers a salary of £20,000 and will repay any money spent by the employee in the course of his or her work; **all expenses paid** = with all costs paid by the company; *the company sent him to San Francisco all expenses paid or he went on an all-expenses-paid trip to San Francisco*; **business expenses** = money spent on running a business, not on stock or assets; **entertainment expenses** = money spent on giving meals, theatre tickets, etc., to business visitors; **legal expenses** = money spent on fees paid to lawyers; **overhead expenses** *or* **general expenses** *or* **running expenses** = money spent on the daily costs of a business; **travelling expenses** = money spent on travelling and hotels for business purposes

① **expensive**
[ɪkˈspensɪv] *adjective*

which costs a lot of money; *don't ask her out - she always orders the most expensive things on the menu*; *fresh vegetables are more expensive in winter*; *send your furniture to Australia by sea - it would be much too expensive by air*

① **experience**
[ɪkˈspɪːriːns]
1 *noun*

(a) knowledge got by working or living in various situations; *I have no experience of travelling in the desert*; *you must write down*

the full details of your past experience on your CV; some experience of selling is required for this job (NOTE: no plural in this meaning)
(b) event, incident that happens to someone; *going to the top of the Eiffel Tower was a wonderful experience*; *you must write a book about your experiences in prison*
2 *verb*

to live through something; *I'm surprised she's so cheerful after all she experienced in prison*; *I have experienced a great deal of pleasure in my career*; *he is experiencing sharp pains in his left arm*

① **experienced**
[ɪkˈspɪːriːnst] *adjective*

wise from plenty of practice; *she's a very experienced doctor*; *he's the most experienced member of our staff*; *the police are experienced in crowd control*

② **experiment**
[ɪkˈsperɪmɪnt]
1 *noun*

scientific test; *to carry out experiments on live animals*; *we're offering our customers free samples as an experiment*
2 *verb*

to carry out a scientific test; *they are experimenting with a new treatment for asthma*; *the laboratory experiments on live animals*

③ **experimental**
[ɪksperɪˈmentl] *adjective*

used in experiments; still being tested, still on trial; *this process is still at the experimental stage*; *the experimental fighter plane crashed*

② **expert**
[ˈekspɜːt]
1 *adjective*

(a) knowing a lot about a subject; *she can give you expert advice on DIY*; **expert system** = computer program which has been devised for a particular purpose
(b) **expert at doing something** = good at doing something; *I'm not very expert at making cakes*
2 *noun*

(a) person who knows a great deal about a subject; *a TV gardening expert*; *he's a leading expert in tropical medicine or on tropical diseases*
(b) person who is very good at doing something; *she's an expert at getting the children to go to bed*; *he's an expert plumber*

③ **expertise**
[ekspɜːˈtiːz] *noun*

specialist knowledge; *we asked Mr Smith to advise us because of his legal expertise*; *her expertise in business administration will be of great use to us* (NOTE: no plural)

④ **expire**
[ɪk'spaɪə] *verb*
to come to an end; *the lease expires in 2010*; **his passport has expired** = his passport is no longer valid

① **explain**
[ɪk'spleɪn] *verb*
(a) to give your reasons for something; *can you explain why the weather is cold in winter and warm in summer?*
(b) to make something clear; *he tried to explain the new pension scheme to the staff*; *she explained what had happened, but the manager still thought she had tried to steal the watch*; *he explained to the customs officials that the drugs were presents for friends*

② **explanation**
[eksplɪ'neɪʃn] *noun*
reason for something; *the policeman asked him for an explanation of why the stolen car was in his garage*; *the government has given no explanation for the change of plan*

④ **explode**
[ɪk'spləʊd] *verb*
(a) *(of bombs, etc.)* to blow up; *a bomb exploded in a crowded train*
(b) to make a bomb go off; *the army cleared the area and then exploded the bomb*

③ **exploit**
1 *verb*
[ɪk'splɔɪt]
(a) to take commercial advantage of something; *we are hoping to exploit the mineral resources of the North Sea*
(b) to make unfair use of someone, usually by paying them very low wages; *the company was accused of exploiting children by employing them in its shoe factories*
2 *noun*
['eksplɔɪt] great or daring achievement; *he told us of his exploits during the war*

② **explore**
[ɪk'splɔː] *verb*
(a) to travel and discover, especially unknown parts of the world; *it is a part of the jungle which has never been explored before*; *we spent our holidays exploring Holland by canal*
(b) to investigate carefully; *we are exploring the possibility of moving the office to London*; *the minister has set up a group to explore this and other issues*

④ **explorer**
[ɪk'splɔːrɪ] *noun*
person who explores unknown parts of the world; *a famous Antarctic explorer*

④ **explosion**
[ɪk'spləʊʒn] *noun*
(a) blowing up of bombs, petrol tanks, etc.; *several explosions were heard during the night as the army occupied the city*

(b) sudden increase; *this summer there has been an explosion in the numbers of mosquitoes*; **population explosion** = rapid increase in population

④ **explosive**
[ɪk'spləʊsɪv]
1 *noun*
material which can blow up; *tests revealed traces of explosive on his hands*; *the box contained explosives*; *police explosives experts made the bomb safe*
2 *adjective*
(a) liable to blow up; *the police found an explosive device in the car*
(b) tense, likely to be embarrassing; *the situation in the office was explosive, with the whole staff demanding to see the manager*; *the paper is running an explosive story about the minister*

② **export**
1 *noun*
['ekspɔːt]
export(s) = goods sent to a foreign country to be sold; *the country's major export is tea*; *exports to Africa have increased by 25%*; **export manager** = person in charge of sales to foreign countries (NOTE: usually used in the plural, but the singular form must be used before a noun)
2 *verb*
[ɪk'spɔːt]
to send goods to a foreign country for sale; *half of our production is exported*; *the company exports half of what it produces*

③ **expose**
[ɪk'spəʊz] *verb*
(a) to show something which was hidden; *he pulled off his shirt, exposing a huge scar across his chest*; *the plastic coating had rubbed off to expose the metal underneath*
(b) to let light go onto a photographic film; *you didn't expose the film for long enough*
(c) to reveal a scandal; *he was exposed as the person who wrote the letters*; *the newspaper has exposed several government scandals*
(d) **to expose something** *or* **someone to** = to place something *or* someone under the influence of something; *don't expose these plants to direct sunlight*; *he had exposed his children to serious danger*

③ **exposed**
[ɪk'spəʊzd] *adjective*
open and not protected; *a stretch of exposed cliff*; *the cottages on the cliff are very exposed*; **a very exposed position** = a position which is not sheltered from the wind

③ **exposure**
[ɪk'spəʊʒɪ] *noun*
(a) placing someone under the influence of something; *the exposure of young children to violence on television*

(b) state of not being sheltered from cold, etc.; *the survivors of the crash were all suffering from exposure after spending a night in the snow*

(c) time and amount of light needed for a picture to be taken on film; *you need a short exposure to photograph a racing car*; **exposure meter** = device for calculating the exposure for a photograph

(d) revealing of corruption, etc.; *the newspaper's exposure of the minister's involvement in the scandal*; *the council was embarrassed by a string of exposures of irregular financial transactions*

① **express**
[ɪkˈspres]
1 *adjective*
(a) rapid (train or postal service); *we have an express delivery service to all parts of the country*
(b) done on purpose; *he did it with the express intention of killing me*
2 *noun*
rapid train; *we took the express from London to Glasgow*
3 *verb*
to put into words or diagrams; *he expressed his thanks in a short speech*; *the chart shows visitors to our stand expressed as a percentage of all visitors to the exhibition*; **I expressed myself badly** = I did not make clear what I wanted to say

① **expression**
[ɪkˈspreʃn] *noun*
(a) word or group of words; *'until the cows come home' is an expression which means 'for a very long time'*
(b) look on a person's face which shows feeling; *his expression showed how miserable he was*; *everyone noticed the expression of surprise on her face*

④ **expulsion**
[ɪkˈspʌlʃn] *noun*
act of being thrown out or sent away (from school, etc.); *the minister ordered the expulsion of the illegal immigrants*; *the school will only consider expulsion as a last resort*; *see also* EXPEL

② **extend**
[ɪkˈstend] *verb*
(a) to stretch out; *she extended both arms in welcome*; *the grounds of the house extend over two hectares*
(b) to make longer or bigger; *we are planning to extend our garden*; *we have asked our landlord to extend the lease for another two years*; **extended family** = family in which relatives outside the central family group, such as aunts and uncles, are included
(c) to give; *I want to extend a warm welcome to our guests from China*

② **extension**
[ɪkˈstenʃn] *noun*
(a) act of extending; *my visa has expired, so I have applied for an extension*
(b) thing added on; *we added an extension at the back of the house*; *I need an extension cable for the electric saw*; *they are planning a further extension of the underground railway*
(c) office telephone; *can you get me extension 21?*; *the manager is on extension 23*

③ **extensive**
[ɪkˈstensɪv] *adjective*
very widespread, vast; *the grounds of the house are very extensive*; *the church roof needs extensive repair work*

① **extent**
[ɪkˈstent] *noun*
degree, size, area; *the extent of the storm damage was only revealed later*; *he opened up the map to its full extent*; **to some extent** *or* **to a certain extent** = partly, in some way; *to some extent, the weather was the cause of the failure of the village fair* (NOTE: no plural)

③ **exterior**
[ɪkˈstɪriɪ]
1 *adjective*
outside; *the exterior walls are of stone*
2 *noun*
the outside parts; *the exterior of the house is painted pink*

② **external**
[ɪkˈstɜːnl] *adjective*
outside; *the external walls of the house are quite solid*; *her injuries were all external*; **external phone** = office phone directly linked to an outside line; **medicine for external use only** = medicine which is used on the skin and must not be drunk or eaten (NOTE: the opposite, referring to the inside, is **internal**)

④ **extinct**
[ɪkˈstɪŋkt] *adjective*
(a) of which all specimens are dead; *several species of birds have become extinct since rats were introduced to the island*
(b) (volcano) which doesn't erupt any more; *this mountain is an extinct volcano*

① **extra**
[ˈekstrɪ]
1 *adjective*
more than normal; additional; *we need an extra four teachers or four extra teachers for this course*; *the charge for delivery is extra*; *there is no extra charge for heating*; *staff get extra pay for working on Sundays*
2 *adverb*
more than normal; in addition; *we need some extra strong string to tie the parcel*; *they charge extra for heavy items*; *if you pay £50 extra you can travel first class*
3 *noun*

(a) something more than usual; *the price covers the hotels and transport but not extras like drinks and special trips*; *air-conditioning is an extra on this car*

(b) actor or actress who appears in a crowd scene in a film or play, but is not a star; *the studio hired thousands of extras to make 'Cleopatra'*

④ **extract**
1 *verb*
[ɪk'strækt]
(a) to pull something out; *the dentist extracted two teeth*; *we managed to extract £10 from him*
(b) to produce something from something else; *it is no longer viable to extract tin from these mines*
2 *noun*
['ekstrækt]
(a) thing reduced from something larger; *he will be reading extracts from his latest novel*
(b) something which is reduced to a concentrated form; *she made a soup from meat extract*

④ **extractor fan**
[ɪk'stræktɪ 'fæn] *noun*
fan which sucks air out (as in a kitchen); *when you switch on the light in the bathroom, the extractor fan comes on automatically*

① **extraordinary**
[ɪk'strɔ:dnrɪ] *adjective*
(a) marvellous, strange and unusual; *seeing her again gave him an extraordinary thrill*; *look at that bird's feathers - they are quite extraordinary*; *it's extraordinary weather for June*
(b) quite different from everything else; *these are extraordinary costs which will not be charged again*; *they called an extraordinary meeting of the club*

③ **extreme**
[ɪk'stri:m]
1 *adjective*
very great; *this engine is made to work well even in extreme cold*; *at the extreme end =* right at the end
2 *noun*
something very unusual, very extraordinary; *you get extremes of temperature here - very hot summers and very cold winters*; *to go to extremes =* to do everything in an extraordinary way; *to go from one extreme to the other =* to change to something completely different; *she can go from one extreme to the other - from being happy and excited one minute to being gloomy and depressed the next*

① **extremely**
[ɪk'stri:mlɪ] *noun*
very; *it was extremely hot in August*; *the film is extremely long, and some people walked out before the end*; *it is extremely difficult to spend less than $50.00 a day on meals in New York*

① **eye**
[aɪ]
1 *noun*
(a) part of your head, used for seeing; *he has brown eyes*; *close your eyes and count to ten while we all hide*; *I've got a bit of dust in my eye*; *as far as the eye can see =* for a very long distance; *the plains stretch as far as the eye can see*; *to catch someone's eye =* to look at someone who is looking at you; *she caught his eye and nodded towards the door*; *keep your eyes open for! =* watch out for!; *keep your eyes open for burglars!*; *to keep an eye on something =* to watch something carefully to see that it is safe; *can you keep an eye on the house while we are away?*; *to keep an eye out for something =* to watch to see if something is near; *I must keep an eye out for Seville oranges to make some marmalade*; *can you keep an eye out for the traffic police while I go into the bank?*; *(informal)* **I'm up to my eyes in work =** I have a lot of work to do; *they don't see eye to eye =* they do not agree; *he doesn't see eye to eye with the boss*; *to have your eye on someone =* to think someone is very good, very attractive, very suspicious; *she's got her eye on her best friend's brother*; *the police have had their eye on him for ages*
(b) *(informal)* **a private eye =** a detective who is not a member of the police force and is employed by an ordinary person
(c) small hole in the end of a needle, through which the thread goes
2 *verb*
to look at something carefully; *she sat in a corner of the café, eyeing the cakes in the window*

③ **eyebrow**
['aɪbraʊ] *noun*
small line of hair above your eye; *she has fine black eyebrows*; *use some eyebrow pencil to make your eyebrows clearer*; *he raised his eyebrows =* he looked surprised

④ **eyelash**
['aɪlæʃ] *noun*
one of the hairs growing round the edge of the eyelids; *one of my eyelashes has got into my eye*; *she wore false eyelashes in the film* (NOTE: plural is **eyelashes**)

③ **eyelid**
['aɪlɪd] *noun*
piece of skin which covers the eye; *her eyelids began to close and soon she was fast asleep*

③ **eyesight**
['aɪsaɪt] *noun*
ability to see; *he has got very good eyesight*; *my eyesight is getting so bad, I can't even thread a needle*; *her eyesight is failing =* she can't see as well as she used to (NOTE: no plural)

Ff

③ **F, f**
[ef]
sixth letter of the alphabet, between E and G; *'raffle' is spelt with a double 'f' or with two 'f's*

③ **fabric**
['fæbrɪk] *noun*
(a) cloth, material; *the curtains are made of some expensive fabric*; *we need a strong fabric for the chairs*
(b) basic structure (of society); *during the revolution, the basic fabric of society collapsed*

④ **fabulous**
['fæbjʊləs] *adjective*
(informal) marvellous, wonderful; *it was a fabulous party*

① **face**
[feɪs]
1 *noun*
(a) front part of your head; *don't forget to wash your face before you go to the party*; **face to face** = looking at each other; *he turned a corner and came face to face with a policeman*; *I don't like doing business on the phone - I prefer to make deals face to face*; **to lose face** = to feel humiliated; *she can't bear being told off in front of the class - it makes her lose face*; **to make a face** = to make a strange expression; *he made funny faces and all the children laughed*; **he tried to keep a straight face** = he tried not to laugh; **to show your face** = to come to a place; *after what he said about my mother he doesn't dare show his face here*
(b) front part of something; *a clock face*; *she put the photograph face down on the desk*; **he has vanished from the face of the earth** = he has disappeared completely
2 *verb*
(a) to have the face or front towards; *can everyone please face the camera?*; *the house faces north*
(b) to meet someone in an unpleasant situation; *the thought of facing all those journalists frightens me*; *she didn't want to face the committee yet again*
(c) **to face something** *or* **be faced with something** = to be likely to have to deal with an unpleasant situation; *she faces a life of poverty*; *will they be able to cope with the problems facing them?*; **not to be able to face something** = not to want to experience something which you expect will be unpleasant; *he couldn't face another meeting*; **to face the facts** = to look at

things in a realistic way; *you really ought to face the facts: you'll never get a job if you don't have any qualifications*; **let's face it** = we must accept it; *let's face it, she's failed her test five times and will probably never pass*; *see also* MUSIC

③ **face up to**
['feɪs ʌp tuː] *verb*
to accept an unpleasant state of affairs and try to deal with it; *he had to face up to the fact that he was never going to be rich*; *the problems won't go away - you must try to face up to them*

④ **facial**
['feɪʃl]
1 *adjective*
referring to a face; *her facial expression reflected her feeling of happiness*
2 *noun*
treatment in which your face is cleaned and made more beautiful; *she went to the beauty salon to have a facial*

① **facility**
[fə'sɪlɪti] *noun*
(a) ability to do something easily; *she has a facility for languages*; *we offer facilities for payment*
(b) **facilities** = equipment which can be used; *the centre provides facilities for a wide range of sports*; *we have free use of all the club facilities*; **the museum has facilities for the disabled** *or* **for the handicapped** = the museum has special sloping paths, lifts, etc., to allow disabled or handicapped people to visit it
(c) large commercial building; *we have opened our new warehouse facility* (NOTE: plural is **facilities**)

① **fact**
[fækt] *noun*
(a) thing that is true; *he faced up to the fact that he wasn't fit enough for the race*; *did you check all the facts before you wrote the article?*; *it's a well-known fact that it rains more often in the west of the country*
(b) **in fact** = really; *he told the police he had seen a man steal a car but in fact he made the whole story up*; *it rained a lot last month, in fact it rained all month*
(c) **the fact of the matter is** = what is true is that; *the fact of the matter is that she is too slow to join the team*; **as a matter of fact** = actually; *have you seen John recently? - as a matter of fact I met him yesterday*

④ **faction**
['fækʃn] *noun*

group of people linked together in opposition to a leader or to a government; *three factions are fighting for control of the political party*; *trying to unite the different factions is an impossible task*

① **factor**
['fæktɪ] *noun*

(a) one of the numbers which produce a certain other number when multiplied; *4 and 2 are factors of 8*; **by a factor of** = multiplied by; *reported cases of the disease have fallen by a factor of 3*

(b) number which indicates the strength of something; **factor 20 sun cream** = cream which gives twenty times protection against the sun's rays

(c) thing which has influence or importance; *the key factor is the price*; *the crucial factor for the success of the village fair is the weather*; **deciding factor** = most important factor which influences a decision

① **factory**
['fæktrɪ] *noun*

building where things are made; *she works in a shoe factory*; *he owns a furniture factory*; *the factory makes computer terminals*; **factory hand** *or* **factory worker** = person who works in a factory (NOTE: plural is **factories**)

④ **faculty**
['fækɪltɪ] *noun*

(a) ability; **mental faculties** = being able to think clearly; *in spite of being over ninety, she is still in possession of all her faculties*

(b) main division of a university; *the Faculty of Arts or the Arts Faculty*

(c) *US* teaching staff (of a school, university, college, etc.); *there is a meeting of the faculty tomorrow* (NOTE: plural is **faculties**)

④ **fade**
[feɪd] *verb*

(a) to lose colour; *the more you wash your jeans, the more they'll fade*; *this T-shirt has faded*

(b) to become less bright or light; *as the light faded, an owl came into the garden*; *the light from the torch began to fade as the batteries ran out*; *the islands faded away into the distance*

④ **Fahrenheit**
['færɪnhaɪt] *noun*

scale of temperatures where the freezing and boiling points of water are 32° and 212°; *what is 75° Fahrenheit in centigrade?*; *do you use Celsius or Fahrenheit in the weather forecasts?*; *compare* CELSIUS, CENTIGRADE (NOTE: used in the USA, but less common in the UK. Normally written as an **F** after the degree sign: **32°F**: say: 'thirty-two degrees Fahrenheit')

COMMENT: to convert Fahrenheit to Celsius, subtract 32 and divide by 1.8. To convert Celsius temperatures to Fahrenheit, multiply by 1.8 and add 32. So 68°F is equal to 20°C.

① **fail**
[feɪl]

1 *noun*

(formal) **without fail** = definitely; *I will be there without fail tomorrow morning*

2 *verb*

(a) not to do something which you were trying to do; *the examination was very difficult - half the students failed*; *he passed in maths, but failed his English exam*; *she failed in her attempt to become an MP*

(b) not to pass a candidate in an examination; *she was failed twice in her driving test*

(c) not to do something; *the car failed to stop at the red light*; *she failed to notify the tax office of her change of address*

(d) not to be able to do something; *I fail to see why she can't come the meeting when everyone else can*

(e) not to work properly; *the brakes failed and he couldn't stop the car*; **if all else fails** = if you can't do anything else; *if all else fails you can always borrow my car*

(f) to become weaker; *her eyesight is beginning to fail*

② **failure**
['feɪljɪ] *noun*

(a) breakdown or stopping; *the accident was caused by brake failure*; *the failure of the plane's engine caused the crash*; **heart failure** = dangerous condition when the heart has stopped beating; **power failure** = breakdown in electricity supplies

(b) person or thing which does not work in a satisfactory way; *his attempts to play the piano were a complete failure*; *I'm no good at anything - I'm a failure*

(c) **failure to do something** = not having done something; *his failure to reach the final disappointed his fans*; *failure to pay the bill will mean we will have to take legal action*

④ **faint**
[feɪnt]

1 *adjective*

difficult to see or hear; *we could just see the faint outline of a man in the fog*; *the rescue team could hear a faint tapping sound coming from the ruins* (NOTE: **fainter- faintest**)

2 *verb*

to become unconscious for a short time; *she fainted when she saw the blood*

① **fair**
[feɪ]

1 *adjective*

(a) light-coloured (hair, skin); *her hair is quite fair*; *she's dark, but her brother is fair*

(b) not very good; *her work is only fair*

(c) right, giving someone what they deserve; *it isn't fair to go on holiday when we have so much work to do*; *that's not fair - you must let other children play with the ball too*

(d) bright and warm (weather); *according to the TV it will be fair tomorrow* (NOTE: do not confuse with **fare**; note also: **fairer - fairest)**

2 *noun*

(a) group of amusements, games, food stalls, etc., set up in one place for a short time; *the fair is coming to the village for the Easter Bank Holiday*; *we went to the fair and won a prize in the shooting competition*

(b) exhibition for selling and advertising goods; *we are going to the car fair tomorrow*

3 *adverb*

in a fair way; *you play fair with me, and I'll play fair with you*

① **fairly**
['feɪli] *adverb*

quite; *I'm fairly certain I have seen this film before*; *she had been working there a fairly short time*; *the hotel is fairly close to the centre of town* (NOTE: the order of words: **he's a fairly good worker** but **he's quite a good worker)**

④ **fairy**
['feɪri] *noun*

little creature who can work magic; *I believed in fairies when I was little*; **fairy godmother** = kind person who gives you magic presents; *Cinderella's fairy godmother helped her go to the ball*; *what we need is a fairy godmother to get us out of trouble*; **fairy lights** = small electric lights for decorating trees, etc.; **fairy story** *or* **fairy tale** = children's story about fairies, princesses, giants, etc.; **a fairy tale castle** = romantic castle like those in fairy stories; **a fairy tale wedding** = romantic wedding (like that of a prince and princess) (NOTE: plural is **fairies)**

② **faith**
[feɪθ] *noun*

(a) belief, trust; **to have faith in someone** = to believe that someone is good and strong, or will protect you; *I have no faith in advice columns in newspapers*; *you must have faith in the leader of the party*; *I don't have any faith in this government*; **blind faith** = absolute trust in someone, however wrong they may seem to be to other people

(b) religious belief; *we must respect people of other faiths*

(c) in good faith = in an honourable way, even though perhaps wrongly; *I sold him the car in good faith - I didn't know it would break down the next day*

④ **faithful**
['feɪθful] *adjective*

(a) *(person)* trusting or loyal; *his faithful old dog sat by his bed*; *we must be faithful to our father's last wishes*

(b) *(of husband, wife)* **to be faithful** = not to have love affairs with someone else

(c) completely correct; *a faithful copy of a document*

③ **faithfully**
['feɪθfili] *adverb*

(a) in a trusting way; *her cleaning lady had worked faithfully for her for years*; *he faithfully did what the instructor told him to do*

(b) Yours faithfully = used as an ending for business letters, when addressed to no specific person (NOTE: not used in American English)

④ **fake**
[feɪk]

1 *noun*

imitation; not the real thing; *that picture isn't by Picasso, it's a fake*

2 *adjective*

not real; *she was wearing a fake fur coat*

3 *verb*

to make an imitation of something, or to imitate something that isn't real; *he faked mental illness to avoid appearing in court*; *they think the laboratory faked the results of the test*

① **fall**
[fɔːl]

1 *noun*

(a) amount of something which has come down; *there was a heavy fall of snow during the night*

(b) going to a lower level; *a welcome fall in the price of oil*; *the fall in the exchange rate*

(c) losing your balance; *he had a fall and hurt his back*; *she had a bad fall while skiing*

(d) *US* **the fall** = autumn, the season of the year between summer and winter; *we go to New England in the fall to see the trees*; *fall colours are at their best in the first week of October*

2 *verb*

(a) to drop down to a lower level; *snow fell all night*; *the pound has fallen against the dollar*; *she fell down the stairs*; *he fell off the ladder*; *did he fall into the river or did someone push him?*; *don't put the bottle of milk on the cushion - it may fall over*

(b) to fall on = to happen or to take place; *my birthday falls on a Tuesday this year* (NOTE: **falling - fell** [fel] **- has fallen)**

③ **fall asleep**
['fɔːl ə'sliːp] *phrase*

to go to sleep; *we all fell asleep after dinner*

③ **fall back on**
['fɔːl 'bæk ɒn] *verb*

to use something which you were keeping as a reserve; *the car broke down, so we had to fall back on public transport*

③ **fall behind**
[fɔːl bɪ'haɪnd] *verb*

to be late in doing something; *he fell behind with his mortgage repayments*

① **fall down**
['fɔːl 'daʊn] *verb*
(a) to drop to the ground; *she fell down and hurt her knee*
(b) to become a ruin; *the house has been empty for so long it's falling down*

③ **fall for**
['fɔːl 'fɔː] *verb*
(a) to fall in love with someone; *she always falls for men twice her age*
(b) to be tricked by something; *don't fall for his sales talk*

③ **fall off**
['fɔːl 'ɒf] *verb*
to become fewer; *the number of visitors to the library has fallen off this year*

③ **fall out**
['fɔːl 'aʊt] *verb*
to have an argument; *they fell out over the bill for drinks*

③ **fall through**
['fɔːl 'θruː] *verb*
not to take place as was planned; *our planned holiday in Spain fell through because we had too much work at the office*

③ **false**
[fɔːls] *adjective*
(a) not true; *the story he told was quite false*
(b) not real; **false teeth** = artificial teeth; **false alarm** = signal for an emergency when there isn't one; *the fire brigade has answered two false alarms today; she was rushed to hospital, but it turned out to be a false alarm*

④ **fame**
[feɪm] *noun*
being famous or well-known; *he walked to London to seek fame and fortune; fame hasn't spoilt her at all*

② **familiar**
[fɪ'mɪljɪ] *adjective*
(a) heard or seen before; *the dog barked as it heard its master's familiar voice at the door; he looked round the room, and saw a couple of familiar faces;* **is he familiar with that type of engine?** = does he know that type of engine well?
(b) very informal, (too) friendly; *don't try to get familiar with me!; she is getting too familiar with the customers*

① **family**
['fæmɪli] *noun*
(a) group of people who are related to each other, especially mother, father and children; *the Jones family are going on holiday to Spain; they have a very big family - three sons and two daughters;* **family pack** *or* **family size** = larger than normal packet of goods which is cheaper to buy; **family room** = hotel room for a family, with a main bed for the parents and small beds for the children

(b) group of animals or plants, etc., which are closely related; *lions are members of the cat family* (NOTE: plural is **families** but family can be used to mean a group and in this case takes the plural: **the family were out**)

④ **famine**
['fæmɪn] *noun*
very serious shortage of food; *famine is widespread in some parts of Africa*

① **famous**
['feɪməs] *adjective*
well-known; *he's a famous footballer; this tea shop is famous for its cakes; he owns a famous department store in the centre of London*

② **fan**
[fæn]
1 *noun*
(a) device for moving air to make things cooler; *we put electric fans in the office to try to keep cool;* **fan belt** = loop of rubber which turns a fan to cool the engine of a car; **extractor fan** = fan which sucks air out; *when you switch on the light in the bathroom, the extractor fan comes on automatically*
(b) enthusiastic supporter of a team, pop group, etc.; *there was a crowd of fans waiting for him outside the theatre;* **a Liverpool fan** = a supporter of Liverpool football team
2 *verb*
to fan yourself = to make yourself cool by making the air move; *he fanned himself with his programme* (NOTE: **fanning - fanned**)

③ **fancy**
['fænsi]
1 *noun*
desire, something you want; **it took his fancy** = he suddenly wanted it; *the watch took her fancy, so she walked into the shop and bought it*
2 *adjective*
(a) pretty, decorated; *he wore a fancy waistcoat to the wedding*
(b) **fancy prices** = high prices (as charged to tourists); *I don't want to pay the fancy prices they ask in London shops*
(c) **fancy dress** = unusual costume worn to a party; **fancy dress party** = party where the guests have to wear costumes; *for the fancy dress party she wore a nurse's outfit*
3 *verb*
(a) to imagine, to believe; *she fancied she saw a dark figure in the garden*
(b) to like, to want to have; *I fancy an ice cream - any one else want one?; do you fancy sharing a taxi to the airport?; (informal)* **I think she fancies you** = I think she is attracted to you
4 *interjection showing surprise*
fancy meeting you here!

③ **fantastic**
[fæn'tæstɪk] *adjective*
(a) strange, like a dream; *his stories are full of fantastic creatures*

(b) *(informal)* wonderful, amazing; *a holiday backpacking in Australia - that sounds fantastic!*; *it's fantastic working in TV!*

④ **fantasy**
['fæntɪsɪ] *noun*

(a) invented story; *her story of meeting a rich man in Paris was just a fantasy*

(b) something you hope for but which cannot come true; *he's living in a fantasy world - one day he'll wake up in the real world and it will be a shock* (NOTE: plural is **fantasies**)

① **far**
[fɑː]
1 *adverb*

(a) a certain distance away; *the railway station is not far from here*; *how far is it from Paris to London?*; *the road was blocked by cars as far as we could see*; **as far as I know** *or* **can tell** = I think, but I'm not absolutely sure; *as far as I know, the train is on time*; *as far as I can tell, the engine is working normally*

(b) a long time ago; *as far back as 1965, he was making a lot of money*

(c) much; *it is far cheaper to go by bus than by train*; *restaurant food is far nicer than the food at college*

2 *adjective*

which is a long way away; *the shop is at the far end of the High Street* (NOTE: **far - farther** *or* **further** ['fɑːðɪ *or* 'fɜːðɪ] - **farthest** *or* **furthest** ['fɑːðɪst *or* 'fɜːðɪst])

◊ **far from**
['fɑː frɒm] *adverb*

not at all; *the food here is far from cheap*

◊ **by far**
['baɪ 'fɑː] *adverb*

very much; *a bike is by far the cheapest way to travel round London*; *of all small cars, this one uses by far the least amount of petrol*

◊ **so far**
['sɪʊ 'fɑː]

up till now; *so far the weather has been very cold*; *so far this winter I have managed not to catch flu*; *have you enjoyed your stay in England so far?*; *see also* IN SO FAR AS

③ **fare**
[feɪ]
1 *noun*

(a) price which you have to pay for a journey; *rail fares have been increased by 10%*; *the tourist class fare is much less than the first class one*; *if you walk to work, you will save £5 a week on bus fares*; **children over 12 must pay the full fare** = they must pay the same price as adults; **single fare** *US* **one-way fare** = fare for a journey from one place to another; **return fare** *US* **round-trip fare** = fare for a journey from one place to another and back again

(b) *(especially in publicity)* food; *the pub serves good country fare*

2 *verb*

to do, to perform; *how did he fare in his driving test?* (NOTE: do not confuse with **fair**)

③ **Far East**
['fɑː 'iːst] *noun*

countries to the east of Pakistan and India; *when he was twenty he sailed to the Far East for the first time to work in Hong Kong*; *our trade with the Far East has suffered because of exchange problems*

④ **farewell**
[feɪ'wel]

1 *interjection & noun; (formal)*

goodbye; *it's time to say farewell*; **to bid someone farewell** = to say goodbye to someone; *he left without bidding us farewell*

2 *adjective*

at which you say farewell; *we gave a farewell party for our neighbours who were going to live in Canada*

② **farm**
[fɑːm]
1 *noun*

land used for growing crops and raising animals; *he runs a pig farm*; *we're going to work on a farm during the holidays*; *you can buy eggs and vegetables at the farm shop*

2 *verb*

to grow crops, raise animals, etc., on a farm; *he farms 250 acres in Devon*

② **farmer**
['fɑːmɪ] *noun*

person who manages or owns a farm; *farmers are worried that the fine weather won't last until harvest time*; *he is one of the biggest pig farmers in the county*

④ **farmhouse**
['fɑːmhaʊs] *noun*

house where a farmer and his family live; *the pig ran out of the barn, straight into the farmhouse*

④ **farming**
['fɑːmɪŋ] *noun*

work of managing a farm, of growing crops, of keeping animals for sale; *sheep farming is important in Wales*

③ **farm out**
['fɑːm 'aʊt] *verb*

to hand over work to another person to do; *we farm out our typing to people working from home*

③ **far off**
['fɑː 'ɒf] *adverb*

(a) a long way away; *we could see the house from far off*

(b) **not far off** = almost correct; *you weren't far off in your estimate*

③ **far out**
['fɑː 'aʊt] *adverb*

(a) a long way away; *we could see the ships far out at sea*

(b) **not far out** = almost correct; *the figure he suggested wasn't very far out*

farther or farthest
['fɑ:ðr or 'fɑ:ðɪst] see FAR

you're too close to the camera - move farther back; how much farther is it to the seaside?; which is farther south - New York or Rome?; Land's End is the farthest west you can go in England

fascinating
['fæsɪneɪtɪŋ] adjective

very interesting; the film gives you a fascinating glimpse of life in a lake; the book gives a fascinating description of London in the 1930s; it was fascinating to hear her talk about her travels in India

fashion
['fæʃn]

1 noun

(a) most admired style at a particular moment; it's the fashion today to wear your hair very short; she always follows the current fashion; in fashion = popular, following the current style; high heels are in fashion this year; out of fashion = unpopular, not the current style; red cars are out of fashion at the moment; fashion victim = person who follows the current fashion all the time

(b) manner or way; she was treated in a most kindly fashion

(c) after a fashion = not very well; he can speak French after a fashion

2 verb

(formal) to make; he fashioned a little boat out of old boxes

fashionable
['fæʃnɪbl] adjective

in fashion; she lives in the fashionable West End of London; it's a fashionable restaurant for film stars and journalists

fast
['fɑ:st]

1 adjective

(a) quick; this is the fast train to London; she was driving in the fast lane of the motorway

(b) (of clock) to show a time which is later than the correct time; your clock is fast; my watch is five minutes fast = is showing a time which is five minutes later than it really is (e.g. 6.15 instead of 6.10)

(c) tightly fixed; fast colours = colours in clothing which do not run when washed; you will have to wash this shirt by hand as the colour isn't fast

2 adverb

(a) quickly; walk faster if you want to catch up with the children in front; don't go so fast - you almost hit that man on the zebra crossing

(b) fast asleep = sleeping so that it is difficult to wake up; she must have been tired - she's fast asleep already (NOTE: faster - fastest)

3 noun

period during which you stop eating for religious or health reasons; he started a 24-hour fast

4 verb

to eat nothing for religious or health reasons; many people fast during the period before Easter

fasten
['fɑ:sɪn] verb

to close or attach securely; please fasten your seatbelts; these shoes fasten with a button

fastener
['fɑ:snɪ] noun

device which fastens; I must have put on weight - I can't do the fastener up; zip fastener = sliding fastener for closing clothes, bags, etc.

fat
[fæt]

1 adjective

(a) (person) round and weighing too much; two fat men got out of the little white car; you'll have to eat less - you're getting too fat; he's fatter than me; (informal) fat cats = businessmen who earn enormous salaries

(b) thick; he pulled a fat bundle of banknotes out of his pocket

(c) (informal) a fat lot of = none at all; he's a fat lot of use on a farm - he can't even drive a tractor!; she wrote complaining letters to the post office, but a fat lot of good it did her! (NOTE: fatter - fattest)

2 noun

(a) part of meat which is yellowish-white; if you don't like fat, cut it off

(b) cooking fat = white substance from animals or plants, used for cooking; fry the onions in hot fat; vegetable fat = fat obtained from nuts, etc., used for cooking

fatal
['feɪtɪl] adjective

(a) which causes death; there were three fatal accidents on this stretch of road last year

(b) which has bad results; it is fatal to ask him to help with the cooking; she made the fatal mistake of asking her grandfather what he thought of French cooking

fate
[feɪt] noun

(a) what is certain to happen to you; they met by chance in a bar in New Zealand, and got married - it must have been fate!; to tempt fate = to do something which could have bad results; it's tempting fate to ask him to look after your girlfriend while you are away; it would be tempting fate to buy that car without having had it checked by a garage

(b) what happens to someone, especially in the end; the people of the country have the right to decide their own fate

① **father**
['fɑːðɪ] *noun*

(a) man who has a son or daughter; *ask your father if he will lend you his car*; *she is coming to tea with her father and mother*

(b) title given to a priest; *Father Thomas is our parish priest*

③ **Father Christmas**
['fɑːðɪ 'krɪsmɪs] *noun*

man in a long red coat, with a big white beard, who is supposed to bring presents to children on Christmas Day

④ **fatigue**
[fɪ'tiːg]

1 *noun*

(a) being tired; *after a long day walking in the mountains, the group were showing signs of fatigue*

(b) **fatigues** = (i) cleaning duty in the army; (ii) overalls worn when doing this; *he was put on fatigues because he had been rude to the officer*

2 *verb*

(formal) to tire someone out; *if you are ill, any physical work is fatiguing*

③ **faucet**
['fɔːsɪt] *noun*

US device with a knob which, when you twist it, lets liquid come out; *the faucet in the bathroom is leaking* (NOTE: British English is always **tap**)

② **fault**
[fɒlt]

1 *noun*

(a) making a mistake; being to blame for something going wrong; *it isn't my fault if there's nothing in the fridge*; *it's all your fault - if you hadn't stayed in bed all morning we would be at the seaside by now*; **at fault** = having made a mistake; *the shop is at fault if they sent you the wrong table*

(b) **to find fault with something** = to criticize something, to find something wrong; *she's always finding fault with my work*

(c) the fact that something is not working properly; *the invoice was wrong because of a computer fault*; *the engineers are trying to mend an electrical fault*

(d) *(in tennis)* mistake in serving; *he served two double faults*

(e) line of a crack in the earth's crust along which movements can take place that lead to major earthquakes; *San Francisco is built near the San Andreas Fault*

2 *verb*

to find something wrong with; *you can't fault her work*

③ **faulty**
['fɔːlti] *adjective*

with mistakes, with something which doesn't work; *the lights keep going on and off - there*

must be a faulty connection somewhere*; *the electrician says that the wiring is faulty*; *the problem was caused by a faulty valve*

① **favour** *US* **favor**
['feɪvɪ]

1 *noun*

(a) friendly act, act of kindness; *can I ask a favour? will you look after my bike while I'm in the post office?*; **to do someone a favour** = to do something to help someone; *he won't charge for it - he did it as a favour*; *will you do me a favour and look after my cat when I'm away?*

(b) approval or popularity; *she tried to win the favour of the committee*; **out of favour** = disliked

(c) preference or liking; **to be in favour of** = to prefer; *the meeting voted in favour of the resolution*; **the score is 4-1 in our favour** = we are leading 4-1

2 *verb*

(a) to like or to prefer; *the managers favour moving to a bigger office*

(b) to make things easier for someone; *the conditions favour the Australian team*

④ **favourable** *US* **favorable**
['feɪvrɪbl] *adjective*

good , which is in your favour; *she made a favourable impression at the interview*

③ **favourite** *US* **favorite**
['feɪvrɪt]

1 *adjective*

which you like best; *which is your favourite TV programme?*

2 *noun*

(a) thing or person which you like best; *which ice cream is your favourite?*; *this chocolate is a favourite with the children*

(b) person, horse, etc., which most people think is likely to win; *he's the favourite to win the election*; *that horse is the favourite in the three o'clock race*

③ **fax**
[fæks]

1 *noun*

copy of a text or picture sent by telephone; *post it to me, or send a fax*; *can you confirm the booking by fax?*; **fax machine** = machine attached to the telephone line which sends faxes; **fax paper** = special paper which is used in fax machines; *we need to order some more fax paper* (NOTE: plural is **faxes**)

2 *verb*

to send a letter or picture by telephone; *I will fax the design to you or I will fax you the design as soon as it is ready*

④ **FBI**
['ef 'biː 'aɪ] = FEDERAL BUREAU OF INVESTIGATION

① fear
['fɪɪ]

1 *noun*

(a) feeling of being afraid; *fear of the dark is common in small children; she has no fear of heights*

(b) *(informal)* **no fear!** = certainly not!; *go on, touch that snake - no fear!*

2 *verb*

(a) to be afraid of something; *what do you fear most?*

(b) to be afraid that something bad will happen; *I fear we are going to get wet - look at those dark clouds; when the little girl had not come back home three days later, everyone began to fear the worst;* **to fear for** = to worry that something might happen; *most parents fear for their children's safety*

④ feast
[fi:st]

1 *noun*

(a) very large meal; *that wasn't an ordinary lunch - it was a feast!*

(b) special religious day; *today is the Feast of St Nicholas*

④ feat
[fi:t] *noun*

action which is difficult to do; *scoring a hat trick is quite a feat;* **no mean feat** = a great achievement; *getting the job done in record time was no mean feat*

③ feather
['feðɪ] *noun*

one of many light soft parts which cover a bird's body; *a bird with green and red feathers in its tail; he stuck a feather in his hat;* **as light as a feather** = very light

① feature
['fi:tʃɪ]

1 *noun*

(a) part of the face, such as the nose or mouth, etc.; *his distinctive features mean that we should find him quite quickly*

(b) important part or aspect; *the main feature of the castle is its huge tower; deep valleys are a feature of Norway*

(c) important item in a TV news programme; important article on a special subject in a newspaper; *did you see the feature on St Petersburg?*

(d) **feature film** = full-length film

2 *verb*

(a) to have as the main performer, especially in a film, on TV, or in a play; *the film featured Charlie Chaplin as a factory worker; the circus features Russian bears*

(b) to show as the most important item; *the tour features a visit to the Valley of the Kings; the next programme will feature a discussion between environmental experts*

(c) to appear as the main actor or subject in a film or on TV; *she has featured in many TV series*

① February
['februɪrɪ] *noun*

second month of the year, between January and March; *my birthday is in February; he died on February 17th US February 17; we are moving to new offices next February* (NOTE: **February 17th:** say 'the seventeenth of February' or 'February the seventeenth'; American English: 'February seventeenth')

③ fed
[fed] *see* FEED

③ federal
['fedɪrl] *adjective*

(a) referring to the central government of the United States; *most federal offices are in Washington; federal law is more important than state law;* **Federal Bureau of Investigation (FBI)** = main police agency for fighting crime in the USA

(b) referring to a system where a group of provinces or states exist under a central government; *the Federal Republic of Germany*

④ federation
[fedɪ'reɪʃn] *noun*

group of states or organizations which have joined together; *the employers' federation*

③ fed up
['fed 'ʌp] *adjective*

(informal) **fed up (with)** = tired of, unhappy because you have had enough of something; *I'm fed up with watching the TV every evening, why can't we go out for a change?; she went back to school last Tuesday and she's already fed up*

② fee
[fi:] *noun*

money paid to doctors, schools and lawyers, etc., for work done; *private school fees are very high; the lawyer's fee for two days' work was more than I earn in a month!;* **entrance fee** *or* **admission fee** = fee paid to go in

① feed
[fi:d]

1 *noun*

(a) food given to animals; *a bag of cattle feed*

(b) meal, especially given to a baby or animal; *the poor little thing - she's crying because she needs a feed*

(c) means of putting material into a machine; **paper feed** *or* **sheet feed** = device on a printer for inserting single sheets of paper; *the paper feed has jammed*

2 *verb*

(a) to give food to someone, to an animal; *let's go to the park and feed the ducks; how can you feed your family when you haven't any money?*

(b) to eat; *the lambs are feeding*

(c) to feed something into a machine = to put something in again and again; *he fed the paper into the printer; the grain is fed into the mill through a special door* (NOTE: feeding - fed [fed] - has fed)

① **feedback**
['fiːdbæk] *noun*
(a) information or comments about something which has been done; *I don't know what the sales are like because we haven't had any feedback from our sales people*
(b) return of a signal in an electronic circuit causing a loud high noise

① **feel**
[fiːl]
1 *noun*
how something seems when touched; *silk has a soft feel; the rough feel of the wooden floor*
2 *verb*
(a) to touch (usually with your fingers); *feel how soft the bed is*; **to feel your way** = (i) to try to find the way forward in the dark by putting out your hands; (ii) to act cautiously until you have more experience; *when the lights went out we had to feel our way out of the cinema; he hasn't made any decisions yet - he's still feeling his way*
(b) to seem soft, cold, etc., when touched; *the bed feels hard; the stone floor felt cold*
(c) to sense something with your body or mind; *did you feel the table move?; I felt the lift go down suddenly; do you feel warmer now that you've had a cup of tea?; they felt happy when they saw that all was well; by twelve o'clock she was feeling hungry*
(d) not to feel yourself = not to feel very well; *she's not coming to the office, she's not feeling herself today*
(e) to think; *he feels it would be wrong to leave the children alone in the house; the police felt that the accident was due to fog* (NOTE: feeling - felt [felt] - has felt)

③ **feel for**
['fiːl 'fɔː] *verb*
to be sympathetic towards; *I feel for him, he's lost his job and now his wife has been taken to hospital*

① **feeling**
['fiːlɪŋ] *noun*
(a) something which you feel; *I had a feeling that this strange man knew who I was; I didn't want to hurt her feelings*
(b) ability to sense something by touching; *my hands were so cold that I lost all feeling in my fingers*

③ **feel like**
['fiːl 'laɪk] *verb*
(a) to want to do something; *I feel like going for a swim; do you feel like a cup of coffee?*
(b) to seem like, when touched; *it feels like plastic, not wood*

(c) *(of weather)* to seem as if it is going to do something; *it feels like snow*

③ **feel up to**
['fiːl 'ʌp tʊ] *verb*
to be strong enough to do something; *do you feel up to walking round the park?*

③ **feet**
[fiːt]
see FOOT

③ **fell**
[fel] *verb*
to cut down a tree; *they felled hundreds of trees to built the new motorway; see also* FALL

③ **fellow**
['felʊ] *noun*
(a) man; *a young fellow came up to me and asked me the time; who's that fellow with a beard who's watching us?*
(b) person who belongs to the same group; *I was OK on the boat, but several of my fellow passengers were sick*; **fellow sufferer** = someone who has the same illness as you; *I get back pains, and I sympathize with all fellow sufferers*
(c) member of a college (at Oxford and Cambridge universities), or of a research institute or academic society; *he's a fellow of Pembroke College, Oxford*

③ **felt**
[felt]
1 *noun*
thick material made of wool fibres pressed together; **felt pen** *or* **felt tipped pen** = pen whose writing end is made of hard felt
2 *verb*
see FEEL

② **female**
['fiːmeɪl]
1 *adjective*
referring to women, girls; referring to the sex which has young; *a female tennis player; a female kitten*
2 *noun*
(a) *(informal)* woman or girl; *three females went into the bar*
(b) animal, insect, bird which gives birth to young or lays eggs; flower which produces seeds; *in some spiders, the female of the species is larger than the male*

③ **feminine**
['femɪnɪn] *adjective*
(a) like a woman, suitable for a woman; *her long white silk dress was very feminine*
(b) *(in grammar)* referring to words which have a particular form or behave in a different way, to show the female gender; *is the French word 'table' masculine or feminine?; 'actress' is the feminine form of 'actor'* (NOTE: the opposite is masculine)

④ **feminist**
['femɪnɪst] *noun*
woman who actively supports the right of women to equal status with men

③ **fence**
[fens]
1 *noun*
barrier of wood or wire, used to keep people or animals in or out of a place; *the fence was blown down*; *the boys looked through the hole in the fence*; *the builders put up a fence round the construction site*; **to sit on the fence** = to avoid giving a definite answer to a question or giving support to one particular side; *he never takes sides - he just sits on the fence*
2 *verb*
(a) to put a fence round something; *the police fenced off the accident site*
(b) to fight with swords as a sport

③ **fender**
['fendɪ] *noun*
US body panel over the wheel of a car, which protects against splashing water and mud; *the front fender was dented in the crash* (NOTE: British English for this is a **wing**)

③ **ferry**
['feri]
1 *noun*
boat which carries cars or trucks or people backwards and forwards across a stretch of water; *the little boat rocked as the ferry passed*; *we are going to take the night ferry to Belgium*; *there's a ferry across the Rhine here*; **car ferry** = ferry which carries cars; **passenger ferry** = ferry which only carries passengers (NOTE: plural is **ferries**)
2 *verb*
to take across by boat; *small boats ferried the refugees across the lake*

④ **fertile**
['fɜːtaɪl *US* 'fɜːtl] *adjective*
(a) *(soil)* rich enough to produce good crops; *the farm has rich black fertile soil*; *along the river valley the soil is very fertile*
(b) *(of female, or egg)* able to produce young; *the zoo hopes the female elephant is fertile, so that she can have young*; *the swans laid several eggs but only two were fertile*
(c) which produces ideas; **he has a fertile imagination** = he imagines things very easily

④ **fertilize**
['fɜːtɪlaɪz] *verb*
to spread fertilizer on land; *the soil is poor and needs to be heavily fertilized*

③ **fertilizer**
['fɜːtɪlaɪzɪ] *noun*
chemical or natural material spread over the soil to make it richer and more able to produce crops; *farmers are being encouraged to use organic fertilizers*; *she spread fertilizer round her carrots*; **liquid fertilizer** = fertilizer in the form of a liquid which is added to water

COMMENT: fertilizers are either 'organic', such as rotted plants, seaweed, powdered fish bones, or made from mixtures of chemicals

③ **festival**
['festɪvl] *noun*
(a) religious celebration which comes at the same time each year and usually is a public holiday; *the tour will visit Hong Kong for the Moon Festival*
(b) artistic celebration or entertainment which is put on at regular intervals; *we saw some excellent plays at the Edinburgh Festival this year*; **arts festival** = competitions in music, drama, painting, etc.; **beer festival** = competition, tasting and exhibition of different types of beer; **cheese festival** = competition, tasting and exhibition of cheeses; **film festival** = competition where different films are shown; *the film won a prize at the Cannes Film Festival*

② **fetch**
[fetʃ] *verb*
(a) to go and bring someone *or* something; *it's your turn to fetch the children from school*; *can you fetch me the dictionary from the library?*
(b) to be sold for a certain price; *that car won't fetch more than £200*; *these CDs fetch very high prices on the black market*

④ **fever**
['fiːvɪ] *noun*
(a) state when the body's temperature is higher than normal; *you must stay in bed until the fever goes down*
(b) excited state; **at fever pitch** = in a great state of excitement; *the crowd waited at fever pitch for the pop group to arrive*

① **few**
[fjuː] *adjective & noun*
(a) not many; *she has very few friends at work*; *we go to fewer concerts than last year*; *I wonder why few of the staff stay with us more than six months*; **few and far between** = not very frequent; *trains are few and far between on Sundays*
(b) **a few** = some, not very many; *I only took a few photographs because it rained all the time*; *I'll call you in a few minutes*; *a few of the wedding guests were sitting playing cards* (NOTE: **fewer - fewest**)

④ **fibre** *US* **fiber**
['faɪbɪ] *noun*
(a) small thread of material; *from the pieces of fibre left at the scene of the murder, the police could work out what the murderer had been wearing*
(b) thin threads in food, which cannot be digested; **high-fibre diet** = diet which contains a large amount of cereals, nuts, fruit and vegetables

④ **fiction**
['fɪkʃn] *noun*
(a) novels; *fiction writers such as Graham Greene*; *to find the latest novels you must look in the fiction section of the library*
(b) story that is not true; *his account of the accident was pure fiction* (NOTE: no plural)

① **field**
[fiːld]
1 *noun*
(a) piece of ground on a farm, with a fence or hedge around it; *the sheep are in the field*; *a field of potatoes*
(b) playing field = piece of ground for playing a game; *the two teams ran onto the field*; **field events** = jumping and throwing competitions; *athletics is made up of both track and field events*
(c) special area of interest or study; *what's your field?*; *his field is English language teaching*
(d) field of vision = area which you can see over clearly
(e) fighting area in a war; *these young soldiers have no experience of combat in the field*
(f) field day = busy and exciting time; *the police had a field day stopping motorists speeding on the motorway*
2 *verb*
(a) to send out a team to play or to negotiate; *England are fielding their strongest side for some years*; *the union fielded a strong negotiating team*
(b) to field questions = to deal with questions; *he fielded questions from the journalists about his private life*

④ **fierce**
['fɪɪs] *adjective*
(a) very angry and likely to attack; *watch out - that dog looks fierce*
(b) violent, very strong; *a fierce storm broke out as they were leaving the harbour*; *the mountains were the scene of fierce fighting*; *he got into a fierce argument about working conditions*

④ **fiercely**
['fɪɪsli] *adverb*
strongly, violently; *she is fiercely independent*; *the shop was blazing fiercely when the fire brigade arrived*

① **fifteen**
[fɪf'tiːn]
(a) number 15; *there are fifteen players in a rugby side*; *she's fifteen (years old) come and see me in fifteen minutes*; *the train leaves at nine fifteen (9.15)* the **fifteen hundreds (1500s)** = the years from 1500 to 1599 (NOTE: compare the fifteenth century)
(b) group of fifteen people (as in a Rugby team); *the England XV* (NOTE: usually written **XV** in this meaning: **the England XV**: say 'the England fifteen')

① **fifteenth (15th)**
[fɪf'tiːnθ] *adjective & noun*
the fifteenth of July or *July the fifteenth (July 15th) that's the fifteenth phone call I've made this morning*; *it will be her fifteenth birthday next week*; **the fifteenth century** = the years from 1400 to 1499 (NOTE: compare **the fifteen hundreds**; Note also that with dates **fifteenth** is usually written **15th**: July 15th, 1935; October 15th, 1991 (American style is **October 15, 1991**), say 'the fifteenth of October' or 'October the fifteenth' (American style is 'October fifteenth'); with names of kings and queens **fifteenth** is usually written **XV**: King Louis XV (say: 'King Louis the Fifteenth')

① **fifth (5th)**
[fɪfθ]
1 *adjective*
the fifth of May or **May the fifth (May 5th)** *it's his fifth birthday tomorrow*; **the fifth century** = period from 400 to 499 AD
2 *noun*
(a) a **fifth** = 20%; *he spends a fifth of the year travelling*
(b) *(in music)* difference in pitch between D and A (NOTE: with dates **fifth** is usually written **5th**: July 5th, 1935; October 5th, 1991 (American style is **October 5, 1991**), say 'the fifth of October' or 'October the fifth' (American style is 'October fifth'); with names of kings and queens **fifth** is usually written **V**: King Henry V (say: 'King Henry the Fifth')

③ **Fifth Amendment**
['fɪfθ ə'mendmənt] *noun*
the Amendment to the Constitution of the USA which allows citizens not to give evidence which might be used against them in court; *he took the Fifth Amendment and refused to answer any questions*

① **fiftieth (50th)**
['fɪftɪɪθ] *adjective & noun*
she came fiftieth and last in the race; *it's her fiftieth birthday on Monday*; **a fiftieth** = 2%

① **fifty**
['fɪfti]
(a) number 50; *my mother made fifty pots of jam*; *she's fifty (years old)* **she's in her fifties** = she's between 50 and 59 years old; **the (nineteen) fifties (1950s)** = the period from 1950 to 1959
(b) fifty-fifty = divided into two equal amounts; **to go fifty-fifty** = with each paying half of the cost; *we'll go fifty-fifty on the bill* (NOTE: **fifty-one** (51), **fifty-two** (52), but **fifty-first** (51st), **fifty-second** (52nd), etc.)

① **fight**
[faɪt]
1 *noun*
(a) struggle against someone *or* something; *he got into a fight with boys who were bigger than*

him; *fights broke out between the demonstrators and the police*; **to pick a fight with someone** = to start a fight with someone

(b) boxing match; *the fight only lasted three rounds*

2 *verb*

(a) to struggle against someone or something using force; *the two boys were fighting over a book*; *rival gangs fought in the street*; *we are committed to fighting crime*; *doctors are fighting to control the disease*

(b) to fight for something = to struggle on behalf of something; *they are fighting for the right to vote* (NOTE: fighting - fought [fɔːt] - has fought)

③ **fighter**
['faɪtɪ] *noun*

(a) person who fights; *the referee stopped the fight when one of the fighters had a cut eye*

(b) fast attacking aircraft; *two fighters went up to attack the enemy bombers*

① **figure**
['fɪgɪ *US* 'fɪgjɪ]

1 *noun*

(a) written number (such as 35); *I can't read the figure on the order - is it 250?*; *he added up the figures on the bill*; *cheques have to be made out in both words and figures*; *see also* DOUBLE, SINGLE

(b) shape such as a square or circle; *a four-sided figure is a square*

(c) drawing or diagram in a book; *see figure 2 on page 23*

(d) shape of a person; *we could see some figures through the mist*; *the figures in the foreground of the painting*

(e) attractive shape of a woman's body; *she still has a great figure*

(f) important person; *he's one of the important figures in the opposition movement*

(g) figure of speech = colourful expression; *a 'storm in a teacup' is a figure of speech meaning a lot of fuss about nothing*

2 *verb*

(a) to figure out = to try to think of an answer or to understand something; *try to figure out the answer yourself instead of asking someone else*

(b) *US (informal)* to consider, to think; *I figure the costs will be high*; *we figured you'd be late because of the show*; *had you figured on being there before two o'clock?*; **that figures** = that makes sense

(c) to appear (in a novel, painting, etc.); *blond girls figure in many of his paintings*

① **file**
[faɪl]

1 *noun*

(a) metal tool used for smoothing rough surfaces; *use a file to round off the edges of the metal*; *see also* NAIL FILE

(b) holder for papers and documents; *when you have finished with the papers, put them back in the file*; *the police have a file on him*

(c) section of data on a computer; *type the name of the file and then press ENTER*

(d) line of people; **in single file** = one behind the other; *the children entered the hall in single file*

2 *verb*

(a) to smooth a surface with a file; *file down the rough edges*

(b) to put papers away in a holder or case; *file that letter under SALES*; **filing cabinet** = piece of office furniture, a tall box with drawers for putting files in; *someone broke open my filing cabinet and removed some documents*

(c) to walk in a line; *they filed past the place where the boy had been killed*

(d) to make an official request; *he filed for divorce*

① **fill**
[fɪl] *verb*

(a) to make something full; *he filled the bottle with water*; *she was filling the boxes with presents*

(b) to fill a tooth = to put metal into a hole in a tooth to stop it going bad; *I hate having my teeth filled but it has to be done*

(c) to fill a gap = to provide something which is needed, but which no one has provided before; *the new range of small cars fills a gap in the market*

(d) to fill a post or a vacancy = to find someone to do a job; *your application arrived too late - the post has already been filled*

③ **fill in**
['fɪl 'ɪn] *verb*

(a) to fill up a hole; *he dug a hole in the garden, put the box inside, and then filled it in*

(b) to write in the empty spaces on a form; *just fill in your name and address*; *to win the prize you have to fill in the missing words*

(c) to fill in for someone = to do something which someone else normally does but cannot do; *I'm filling in for the manager who is on holiday*

④ **filling**
['fɪlɪŋ]

1 *adjective*

which fills (your stomach); *a meal of salad and a glass of water is not very filling*

2 *noun*

(a) metal put into a hole in your tooth by a dentist; *I had to go to the dentist because one of my fillings came out*

(b) food used to put into a sandwich, pie, cake, etc.; *a cake with a jam filling*

(c) filling station = petrol station, place where you can buy petrol; *let's stop at the next filling station to see if we can get a map*

③ **fill out**
['fɪl 'aʊt] *verb*
to write in all the empty spaces on a form; *fill out the form and send it back to this address*

③ **fill up**
['fɪl 'ʌp] *verb*
(a) to make something completely full; *he filled the bottle up with fresh water*; fill her up = please fill the car with petrol
(b) to write in all the empty spaces on a form; *fill up the form and send it back to this address*

① **film**
[fɪlm]
1 *noun*
(a) moving pictures shown at a cinema; *have you seen this old Laurel and Hardy film?*; *we've seen the film already on TV*; film rights = the legal right to make a film from a book (NOTE: American English is **movie**)
(b) roll of material which you put into a camera to take photographs or moving pictures; *I must buy another film before the wedding*; *do you want a colour film or a black and white one?*
(c) thin layer of something; *a film of moisture formed on the cold metal surface*; *everywhere was covered with a film of dust*
2 *verb*
to take pictures of something with a camera; *security cameras filmed him robbing the bank*; *'Star Wars' was filmed in 1977*

③ **film star**
['fɪlm 'stɑː] *noun*
well-known film actor or actress; *there are pictures of famous film stars in entrance to the cinema*

④ **filter**
['fɪltɪ]
1 *noun*
(a) device or material for straining liquids or air, for stopping any solids from passing through; *the filters in the swimming pool have to be cleaned regularly*; filter paper = paper used for filtering liquids; *don't forget to put a filter paper in before you put in the coffee*
(b) glass on a camera which allows only certain colours to pass through; *I use an orange filter to give a warm colour to the picture*
(c) material at the end of a cigarette, used to remove dangerous substances in tobacco
2 *verb*
(a) to remove dirt by passing through a filter; *kidneys filter the blood*
(b) to move gradually; *watch out for traffic filtering in from the left*; filter lane *or* filter light = traffic lane *or* light only for cars which are turning
(c) to go *or* to come slowly through, down, out, etc.; *sunlight filtered through the leaves*; *rumours began to filter out about an attack on the president's plane*

③ **filthy**
['fɪlθi] *adjective*
(a) very dirty; *where have you been playing - you're filthy!*; *don't touch that filthy old carpet*; *filthy children followed the tourists, asking for money wherever they went*
(b) very unpleasant and angry; *watch out - the boss is in a filthy temper* (NOTE: filthier - filthiest)

④ **fin**
[fɪn] *noun*
(a) thin part on the body of a fish which helps it to swim; *from the beach they could see a black fin in the sea*
(b) similar piece on an aircraft; *the tail fin broke off when the plane crashed*

① **final**
['faɪnl]
1 *adjective*
last, coming at the end; *this is your final warning - if you don't work better you will be sacked*; *the competition is in its final stages*; my decision is final = I cannot change my decision; final date for payment = last date by which payment should be made
2 *noun*
(a) last competition in a series between several teams or competitors; *I thought they would win a couple of rounds, but I never imagined they would get to the final*; cup final = last game in a series of football games, where the winner is given a silver cup
(b) finals = last examinations at the end of a university course, after which you get your degree; *after his finals he's planning to travel round Australia*; *everybody's at home studying for their finals*

① **finally**
['faɪnli] *adverb*
at last, in the end; *the police finally cleared up the mystery*; *the little boy finally turned up in Edinburgh*

② **finance**
['faɪnæns]
1 *noun*
money, especially money which belongs to the public or to a company; *how are you going to raise the finance for the expansion plan?*; *my finances are in a poor state at the moment*; Minister of Finance = government minister in charge of a country's finances (NOTE: in Britain this minister is called **the Chancellor of the Exchequer** and in the USA **the Secretary of the Treasury**)
2 *verb*
to provide money for; *how are you going to finance your course at university if you don't have a grant?*; *the development of the city centre is being financed locally*

① **financial**
[fɪ'nænʃl] *adjective*
referring to money; what is our financial position?; the company has got into financial difficulties; **financial year** = 12-month period for which accounts are calculated

④ **financially**
[fɪ'nænʃli] *adverb*
referring to money; with money; *our long-term objective is to make the company financially sound; we try to help our daughter financially while she is at college*

① **find**
[faɪnd]
1 *noun*
thing which you discover; *what a lucky find! a cheap hotel in the centre of Paris*
2 *verb*
(a) to discover (something hidden or lost); *I found a £2 coin behind the sofa; did she find the book she was looking for?*
(b) to discover something which was not known before; *no one has found a cure for the common cold yet*
(c) to have an opinion about something; *I found the book very dull; she finds her work too easy*
(d) to make a legal decision in court; *the tribunal found that both parties were at fault; he was found guilty of murder*; **the judge found for the defendant** = the judge decided that the defendant was right
(e) **to be found** = to exist; *mushrooms are found in fields in the autumn* (NOTE: finding - found [faʊnd])

② **findings**
['faɪndɪŋz] *noun*
(a) facts discovered; *the two companies signed an agreement to share their research findings*
(b) actions which are recommended, recommendations; *the findings of the committee of inquiry will be published next week*

③ **find out**
['faɪnd 'aʊt] *verb*
to discover information; *your job is to find out if the competition is planning a new model; she needs to find out everything she can about Napoleon; the police are trying to find out why she went to Scotland*

③ **find time**
['faɪnd 'taɪm] *phrase*
to do something even though you are short of time; *in the middle of the meeting he still found time to phone his girlfriend; we must find time to visit the new shopping centre*

① **fine**
[faɪn]
1 *adjective*
(a) good (weather); *we'll go for a walk tomorrow if it stays fine; let's hope it's fine for the village fair next week*

(b) well, healthy; *I was in bed with flu yesterday, but today I'm feeling fine*
(c) good; *how are things at home? - fine!; it's fine to wear a short skirt when you're young and slim, but not when you're old and fat*
(d) very thin or very small; *use a sharp pencil if you want to draw fine lines; I can't read the notice - the print is too fine*; **the fine print** = the conditions on a contract, usually printed in very small letters; *don't forget to check the fine print before you sign the contract* (NOTE: finer - finest)
2 *adverb*
in very small pieces; *chop up the orange peel very fine*
3 *noun*
money which you have to pay for having done something wrong; *I had to pay a £25 fine for parking in a no parking area; he was found guilty of theft and got off with a fine*
4 *verb*
to make someone pay money for having done something wrong; *he was fined £25 for parking on double yellow lines*
5 *interjection* all right, agreed; *Fine! We'll all go to the beach tomorrow!*

④ **finely**
['faɪnli] *adverb*
(a) in very small pieces; *cook some finely chopped onions in a little butter*
(b) in a beautiful way; *she bought some finely carved ivory figures*

① **finger**
['fɪŋgɪ]
1 *noun*
(a) one of the parts at the end of your hand, but usually not including the thumb; *he wears a ring on his little finger; he pressed the button with his finger*; **to keep your fingers crossed** = to hope that something will happen as you want it to happen; *have you heard the exam results yet? - no, but I'm keeping my fingers crossed*; **to put your finger on something** = to point something out correctly; *you put your finger on it when you said that he's afraid of appearing to be stupid*; **on the fingers of one hand** = five (or less); *the number of times she's offered to buy me a drink can be counted on the fingers of one hand*; *(informal)* **to pull your finger out** = to work harder; *I told him to pull his finger out*; **not to lift** *or* **raise a (little) finger to help** = not to do anything to help; *we were trying to move the piano and he didn't raise a finger to help; it's unfair to expect her to do all the housework while her sisters don't lift a finger to help*
(b) part of a glove into which a finger goes; *I must mend my glove - there's a hole in one of the fingers*
(c) piece of food shaped like a finger; *a box of chocolate fingers; see also* FISH FINGER
2 *verb*

(a) to touch with your fingers; *don't finger the apples*
(b) *(informal)* to point out a criminal to the police; *he was fingered by someone else in the gang*

④ **fingernail**
['fɪŋɡɪneɪl] *noun*
hard thin part covering the end of each finger; *she painted her fingernails green*; *don't bite your fingernails!*

① **finish**
['fɪnɪʃ]
1 *noun*
(a) final appearance; *the table has an attractive finish*
(b) final appearance which is not real, which is only on the surface; *kitchen cupboards with an oak finish*
(c) end (of a race); *he ran well and came second at the finish*
2 *verb*
to do something completely; to come to an end; *haven't you finished your homework yet?*; *tell me when you've finished reading the paper*; *you can't go out until you've finished doing the washing up*; *the game will finish at about four o'clock*

③ **finish off**
['fɪnɪʃ 'ɒf] *verb*
to do something completely; *finish off your homework and then we can go out*

③ **finish up**
['fɪnɪʃ 'ʌp] *verb*
(a) to be in the end; *we got lost and finished up miles from where we wanted to be*
(b) to eat something completely; *you must finish up all your vegetables*

① **Finland**
['fɪnlənd] *noun*
large country in northern Europe, between Sweden and Russia; *we like to go camping and sailing in Finland in summer* (NOTE: capital: **Helsinki**; people: **the Finns**; language: **Finnish**; currency: **finnmark** or **finnmarkka** or **markka**, **euro**)

① **Finn**
[fɪn] *noun*
person from Finland; *the Finns are a hardy people*

① **Finnish**
['fɪnɪʃ]
1 *adjective*
referring to Finland
2 *noun*
language spoken in Finland; *I bought a Finnish phrase book before going to Helsinki*

① **fire**
['faɪə]
1 *noun*
(a) something which is burning, something which heats; *we have an electric fire in the living room*; *they burnt the dead leaves on a*

fire in the garden; **to catch fire** = to start to burn because of something else which is burning; *the office block caught fire*; *take those papers away - they might catch fire*; **to set fire to** = to make something start burning; *his cigarette set fire to the carpet*; **on fire** = burning; *call the emergency services - the house is on fire!*
(b) shooting with guns; *the soldiers came under fire from the guerrillas*
2 *verb*
(a) to shoot a gun; *the gunmen fired at the police car*; *we could hear guns firing in the distance*
(b) to dismiss someone from a job; *she was fired for being late*
(c) to make excited; *he was fired with the desire to make his fortune*

③ **fire engine**
['faɪə 'endʒɪn] *noun*
large red van used by the fire services, with pumps, ladders, etc., to fight fires; *six fire engines were at the fire*

③ **fireman**
['faɪəmɪn] *noun*
man who tries to put out fires; *the firemen were fighting the fire in the town centre* (NOTE: plural is **firemen**)

④ **fireplace**
['faɪəpleɪs] *noun*
hole in the wall of a room where you can light a fire for heating; *the dog likes to lie on the carpet in front of the fireplace*

③ **fire station**
['faɪə 'steɪʃn] *noun*
centre where fire engines are based; *the fire engines came racing out of the fire station*

④ **firework**
['faɪəwɜːk] *noun*
small cardboard tube holding chemicals which will explode when lit; *there was a big firework display* or *display of fireworks for Bonfire Night*

① **firm**
[fɜːm]
1 *adjective*
(a) solid or fixed; *make sure that the ladder is firm before you climb up*; *my back hurts - I think I need a firmer bed*
(b) not going to change; *there is no firm evidence that he stole the money*; **to stand firm** = not to give in; *in spite of the offers from the motorway construction company he stood firm and refused to leave his house*
(c) which cannot be changed; *to place a firm order for two lorries*; *they are quoting a firm price of £1.22 per unit* (NOTE: **firmer - firmest**)
2 *noun*
business or company; *when he retired, the firm presented him with a watch*; *the firm I work for was taken over last year*

④ **firmly**

['fɜːmli] *adverb*

in a firm way; *he held the rail firmly*

① **first**

[fɜːst]

1 *adjective & noun; (as a number can be written* **1st***)* referring to the thing that comes before all other things; *my birthday is on the first of July or July the first (July 1st) King Charles the First (Charles I) it's our baby's first birthday on Tuesday*; *the bank is the first building on the left past the post office*; **the first century** = the period from the year 1 to 99 AD; **first name** = a person's Christian name or given name, as opposed to the surname or family name (NOTE: with dates **first** is usually written **1st: 1st February 1992; December 1st 1670** (American style is December 1, 1670), say 'the first of December' or 'December the first' (American style is 'December one'); with names of kings and queens **first** is usually written **I: King Charles I** (say 'King Charles the First')

2 *adverb*

(a) at the beginning; *she came first in the exam*; **first come, first served** = dealing with orders, etc., in the order in which they are received; *applications will be dealt with on a first come, first served basis*

(b) before doing anything else; *wash your hands first, and then you can eat*

(c) for the first time; *when did you first meet your girlfriend?*

◊ **at first**

[æt 'fɜːst]

at the beginning; *at first he didn't like the work but later he got used to it*

③ **first aid**

['fɜːst 'eɪd] *noun*

help given to a person who is hurt, before a doctor or ambulance arrives; *the police gave first aid to the accident victims*; **first aid kit** = box with bandages and dressings kept to be used in an emergency; *we keep a first aid kit in the car*

③ **first-class**

['fɜːst'klɑːs] *adjective*

very good; *he is a first-class tennis player*

③ **First Lady**

['fɜːst 'leɪdi] *noun*

wife of a president, especially the wife of the President of the USA; *the President and the First Lady have been invited to lunch at Buckingham Palace*; *the new First Lady is planning to carry out decorations to only a few rooms in the White House*

② **firstly**

['fɜːstli] *adverb*

in the first place, to start with; *why are they getting married? - firstly, they're in love, and secondly, her father has offered to buy them a flat*

④ **first-rate**

['fɜːstreɪt] *adjective*

excellent; *the food here is absolutely first-rate*; *he's a first-rate tennis player*

④ **fiscal**

['fɪskl] *adjective*

referring to tax or to government revenues; *the government's fiscal policy*; **fiscal year** = 12-month period for tax purposes (in Britain from 6th April of one year to 5th April of the next year)

① **fish**

[fɪʃ]

1 *noun*

(a) animal with no legs, which lives in water and which you can usually eat; *I sat by the river all day and only caught two little fish*; **fish tank** = big container of water for keeping fish; *(informal)* **there are plenty more fish in the sea** = there are lots of other people you could be friends with; **I've got other fish to fry** = I have other more important business to deal with (NOTE: plural is usually **fish: some fish, three fish**, but also sometimes **fishes**)

(b) **fish and chips** = traditional British food, obtained from special shops, where portions of fried fish are sold with chips; *we're having fish and chips for supper*

2 *verb*

(a) to try to catch a fish; *we often go fishing in the lake*; *they fished all day but didn't catch anything*

(b) to try to find something; *he fished around in his suitcase and after some delay produced his passport*

③ **fish-and-chip shop**

['fɪʃɪn'tʃɪp 'ʃɒp] *noun*

shop selling cooked fish and chips, and usually other food, such as pies (NOTE: can also be called a **chip shop**)

④ **fisherman**

['fɪʃɪmɪn] *noun*

man who catches fish, either as his job or for sport; *fishermen are complaining that pollution is wiping out fish stocks* (NOTE: plural is **fishermen**)

③ **fish finger** *US* **fish stick**

['fɪʃ 'fɪŋgɪ or 'fɪʃ 'stɪk] *noun*

frozen piece of fish, shaped like a finer and covered in breadcrumbs; *the children don't like fresh fish, but they do like fish fingers*

③ **fishing**

['fɪʃɪŋ] *noun*

sport or business where you try to catch fish; *the sign said 'no fishing'*; **fishing boat** = boat used for fishing; **fishing line** = long string used with a hook to catch fish; **fishing rod** *US* **fishing pole** = long piece of wood to which a line and hook are attached

④ **fist**

[fist] *noun*

tightly closed hand; *he punched her with his fist; she banged on the table with her fist*

① **fit**

[fit]

1 *noun*

sudden sharp attack of illness, etc.; *she had a coughing fit or a fit of coughing; in a fit of anger he threw the plate across the kitchen;* by **fits and starts** = at odd moments, stopping often; *something has gone wrong with the printer - it only prints out by fits and starts*

2 *adjective*

(a) healthy; *he isn't fit enough to go back to work; you'll have to get fit if you're going to run a long-distance race; see also* SURVIVAL OF THE FITTEST

(b) **fit to do something** = in good enough condition to do something; *is he fit to drive?; that car isn't fit to be driven - its brakes don't work and the tyres are worn*

(c) suitable; *is she a fit person to look after small children?* (NOTE: **fitter - fittest**)

3 *verb*

(a) to be the right size or shape; *he's grown so tall that his jackets don't fit him any more; these shoes don't fit me - they're a size too small*

(b) to put in place; *I want to fit a new fridge in the kitchen; fitting the furniture into the new house was quite a problem* (NOTE: **fitting - fitted**)

③ **fit in**

['fit 'ɪn] *verb*

(a) to find room or time for someone *or* something; *we can't fit a holiday in this year as we have too much work; how can you fit six people into that little car?*

(b) to be able to go into a space; *how will the bed fit into that room?*

(c) to be comfortable as part of a group; *he joined the firm two years ago but has never really fitted in*

③ **fitted**

['fitɪd] *adjective*

made to fit into a certain space; **fitted carpet** = carpet cut to the exact size of the room and fixed to the floor; **fitted cupboard** = specially made cupboard which fits into a bedroom, bathroom, etc., and is attached to the wall; **fitted kitchen** = set of kitchen cupboards which are attached to the walls

④ **fitting**

['fitɪŋ]

1 *adjective*

suitable, right; *it's fitting that grandmother should sit at the head of the table - it's her birthday party, after all*

2 *noun*

(a) action of making something fit; action of trying on a new piece of clothing; *she's having the first fitting of her wedding dress this afternoon;* **fitting room** = small room in a shop where you can try on clothes before you buy them

(b) size and shape (of shoe, etc.); *do you take a wide or narrow fitting?*

(c) thing which is fixed in a building but which could be removed; *an electric light fitting; the shop is being sold with all its fixtures and fittings*

① **five**

[faɪv]

number 5; *she drank five cups of tea; he's five (years old) next week; the meeting has been arranged for five (o'clock)*

① **fix**

[fiks]

1 *noun*

difficult position; *he's in a bit of a fix - he's got no cash and can't pay for the taxi; that's a nice fix you've got us into!* (NOTE: plural is **fixes**)

2 *verb*

(a) to fasten or to attach; *fix one end of the rope to the tree and the other to the fence*

(b) to arrange; *we'll try to fix a time for the meeting*

(c) to mend; *the telephone people are coming to fix the telephone; do you know how to fix the printer?*

(d) *US* to make or to prepare a drink, meal, etc.; *let me fix you something to drink; she fixed them some chicken sandwiches*

③ **fixed**

[fikst] *adjective*

(a) attached firmly; *the sign is fixed to the post with big nails*

(b) *(price, etc.)* arranged or agreed upon, which cannot be changed; *we have a fixed scale of charges;* **fixed rate** = charge or interest which cannot be changed; *they chose a fixed-rate mortgage*

④ **fixture**

['fikstʃɪ] *noun*

(a) **fixtures** = objects permanently fixed in a building, like radiators, which are sold with the building; *the shop is for sale with all fixtures and fittings*

(a) sports match; *their next fixture is against Liverpool on Saturday; season ticket holders are sent a list of fixtures at the beginning of the season*

④ **fizzy**

['fizi] *adjective*

full of bubbles; *they all ordered fizzy drinks; I don't like fizzy orange - do you have any squash?* (NOTE: the opposite is **still: still orange.** Drinks which should be fizzy but are not are said to be **flat**)

④ **flag**
[flæg]
1 *noun*

(a) piece of brightly material with the design of a country or club, etc., on it; *the French flag has blue, red and white stripes*; *the ship was flying the British flag*; *the flags were blowing in the wind*; **white flag** = symbol showing that someone is surrendering

(b) small paper badge sold in aid of a charity; *pin the flag to your coat to show that you have given something*

2 *verb*

(a) to grow tired; *we've been travelling all day - no wonder the children are starting to flag*

(b) to flag down = to wave to make a taxi stop; *he stepped out into the street and flagged down a passing taxi*

(c) to put a marker in a computer file; *don't forget to flag the addresses so that we can find them again easily* (NOTE: flagging - flagged)

③ **flag day**
['flæg 'deɪ] *noun*

day on which small paper flags are sold in aid of a particular charity; *tomorrow is a flag day in aid of cancer research*

④ **flame**
[fleɪm]
1 *noun*

bright tongue of fire; *flames could be seen coming out of the upstairs windows*; **in flames** = burning; *the building was already in flames when the fire engine arrived*

2 *verb*

to burn brightly; *they carried flaming torches as they walked through the town*

④ **flap**
[flæp]
1 *noun*

(a) flat part which is attached to a main structure and which can move up and down; *the pilot tested the wing flaps before taking off*; **cat flap** = little door in the door of a house, which allows a cat to go in or out

(b) *(informal)* state of worried excitement; *they got into a flap about the new neighbours' dog*

(c) movement of a bird's wing; *with a flap of its wings, the bird flew off*

2 *verb*

to move up and down like a bird's wing; *flags were flapping in the breeze*; *the swans stood by the edge of the water, flapping their wings* (NOTE: flapping - flapped)

③ **flash**
[flæʃ]
1 *noun*

(a) short sudden burst of light; *flashes of lightning lit up the sky with thunder in the distance*; **in a flash** = very quickly; *in a flash, she said 'yes'*

(b) device for making a bright light, allowing you to take photographs in the dark; *people sometimes have red eyes in photos taken with a flash*

(c) bright light from a camera; *the scene at the entrance to the cinema was lit up with flashes from photographers' cameras*

(d) news flash = short item of news, broadcast at an unexpected time; *there was a news flash about a bomb in central London*; *we interrupt the programme for a news flash* (NOTE: plural is **flashes**)

2 *verb*

(a) to light up quickly and suddenly; *lightning flashed all around us*

(b) to flash by *or* **to flash past** = to move or to pass by quickly; *the champion flashed past to win in record time*

③ **flashlight**
['flæʃlaɪt] *noun*

small portable electric lamp; *take a flashlight if you're going into the cave* (NOTE: British English also uses **torch**)

② **flat**
[flæt]
1 *adjective*

(a) level, not sloping or curved; *a house with a flat roof*; **flat rate** = fixed charge which never changes; *taxi drivers charge a flat rate of £20 for driving you to the airport*; *he is paid a flat rate of £2 per thousand*

(b) a flat tyre = a tyre which has lost all the air in it; *he pulled up at the side of the road to change a flat tyre* (NOTE: American English is simply **a flat**)

(c) flat racing = racing horses over flat ground, without any fences to jump over; **the flat season** = part of the year when flat races are held

(d) *(of drink)* no longer fizzy; *my lemonade's gone flat*

(e) with no electric charge left; *the car wouldn't start because the battery was flat*

(f) *(in music)* playing at a lower pitch than it should be; *that piano sounds flat to me* (NOTE: **flatter - flattest**)

2 *adverb*

(a) level, not sloping or curved; *lay your clothes out flat on the bed*; *he tripped over and fell flat on his face*

(b) completely; in a blunt way; *he turned down the offer flat*; **flat broke** = with no money at all; *I can't pay the rent - I'm flat broke*

(c) exactly; *he ran the mile in four minutes flat*

3 *noun*

(a) set of rooms for one family, on one floor, usually in a building with several similar sets of rooms; *we have bought a flat in London after selling our house in the country*; *the block of flats where they live is next door to the underground station*; *their flat is on the ground floor* (NOTE: American English for this is an **apartment**)

(b) *US* tyre which has lost its air; *I asked the garage to fix the flat* (NOTE: British English is a **flat tyre**)

(c) *(in music)* pitch which is lower; *they played a piece in E flat; he played D sharp instead of D flat*

④ **flatly**
['flætli] *adverb*
in a firm way; *he flatly denied having anything to do with it*

③ **flat out**
['flæt 'aʊt] *adverb*
(a) at full speed; *you'll have to drive flat out to get to the airport in time to catch the plane*
(b) very hard; *he worked flat out to finish his work on time*

④ **flavour** *US* **flavor**
['fleɪvɪ]
1 *noun*
particular taste; *the tomato soup had a strange flavour; (informal)* **the flavour of the month** = the most popular thing at the moment; *girl pop groups are the flavour of the month*
2 *verb*
to add things such as spices and seasoning in cooking something, to give it a special taste; *use pepper to flavour the meat; soup flavoured with herbs*

④ **flea**
[fli:] *noun*
(a) tiny insect that jumps and sucks blood; *if your cat has fleas, buy a special collar which will get rid of them* (NOTE: do not confuse with **flee**)
(b) **flea market** = open-air market for secondhand goods; *I bought this painting in the flea market last Saturday*

③ **fled**
[fled]
see FLEE

④ **flee**
[fli:] *verb*
to flee (from something) = to run away (from something); *as the fighting spread, the village people fled into the jungle; she tried to flee but her foot was caught in the rope* (NOTE: **fleeing - fled** [fled])

④ **fleet**
[fli:t] *noun*
(a) group of ships belonging together; *when the fleet is in port, the pubs are full of sailors*
(b) collection of vehicles; *the company replaces its car fleet* or *fleet of cars every two years; the airline's fleet of Boeing 747s*

③ **flesh**
[fleʃ] *noun*
(a) soft part of the body covering the bones; **a flesh wound** = wound which goes into the flesh but not very deep; **in the flesh** = in real life (not on TV or in photographs); *it was strange to see the TV newsreader in the flesh*

(b) soft part of fruit; *a grapefruit with pink flesh* (NOTE: no plural)

③ **flew**
[flu:]
see FLY (NOTE: do not confuse with **flu**)

④ **flexible**
['fleksɪbl] *adjective*
(a) easy to bend; *shoes with soft rubber soles are flexible*
(b) able to adapt easily; *my timetable is very flexible - we can meet whenever you want*

④ **flick**
[flɪk]
1 *noun*
little sharp blow or movement; *he shook off the bee with a flick of his wrist*
2 *verb*
to hit or move lightly and sharply; *the horse flicked its tail to get rid of flies*

③ **flies**
[flaɪz]
see FLY

② **flight**
[flaɪt] *noun*
(a) travel in a plane; *go to gate 25 for flight AB198; all flights to Paris have been cancelled; she sat next to me on a flight to Montreal; see also* ATTENDANT, CHECK IN
(b) flying, travel through the air; *young birds stay in the nest until they are ready for flight*
(c) **flight of stairs** = set of stairs going in one direction; *go up two flights of stairs and the bathroom is the first door on the left*
(d) *(literary)* **to take flight** = to run away; **to put to flight** = to chase away

④ **fling**
[flɪŋ]
1 *noun*
to have your fling = to relax, letting off your high spirits; *now the students have had their fling, perhaps they can get back to work*
2 *verb*
to throw wildly; *he flung the empty bottle into the sea; she flung herself into an armchair* (NOTE: **flinging - flung** [flʌŋ])

④ **flip**
[flɪp] *verb*
(a) to hit lightly; *she flipped a switch and the lights went off*
(b) **to flip over** = to turn over quickly; *before he could do anything the boat had flipped over*
(c) *(informal)* to get very angry; *he flipped when they told him how much the bill came to* (NOTE: **flipping - flipped**)

③ **float**
[fləʊt]
1 *noun*
(a) piece of cork, etc., attached to a fishing line which floats on the surface of the water, allowing the line and hook to hang down into the water below; *if the float goes up and down in the water it means you have caught a fish*

(b) decorated lorry in a procession; *the long line of carnival floats went down the high street*
(c) milk float = low electric truck for delivering milk; *it is annoying to be stuck behind a milk float when you're in a hurry*
(d) cash float = cash put into the cash box at the beginning of the day to allow business to start; *we start the day with a £20 float in the cash desk*
2 *verb*
(a) to lie or put on the top of a liquid; *dead fish were floating in the river; he floated a paper boat on the lake*
(b) to start selling shares in a new company; *the company is to be floated on the stock exchange next week*
(c) to let a currency find its own exchange rate on the international markets, and not fix it at a certain amount; *the government decided that the best course would be to let the pound float*

④ **flock**
[flɒk]
1 *noun*
group of similar animals together, such as sheep, goats, or birds; *a flock of sheep were grazing on the hillside* (NOTE: flock is usually used with sheep, goats, and birds such as hens or geese; for cattle, the word to use is herd)
2 *verb*
to move in large numbers; *tourists flocked to see the changing of the guard; families with children have been flocking to the beaches on the south coast*

③ **flood**
[flʌd]
1 *noun*
(a) large amount of water over land which is usually dry; *the floods were caused by heavy rain*
(b) large amount of tears, letters, etc.; *the TV station received floods of complaints after the ad was shown; she was in floods of tears when they told her that she had to leave her house*
(c) the Flood = story in the Bible of the time when the earth was covered with water and only Noah and his family and animals were saved
2 *verb*
(a) to cover with water; *they are going to build a dam and flood the valley; fields were flooded after the river burst its banks; he forgot to turn the tap off and flooded the bathroom*
(b) to flow outside the normal area; *the Nile floods each year*
(c) to come in large numbers; *the office was flooded with complaints or complaints came flooding into the office*

① **floor**
[flɔː]
1 *noun*
(a) part of a room on which you walk; *he put the books in a pile on the floor; if there are no empty chairs left, you'll have to sit on the floor*

(b) all the rooms on one level in a building; *the bathroom is on the ground floor; his office is on the fifth floor; there is a good view of the town from the top floor*
2 *verb*
to be floored = not to be able to answer; *he was floored by one of the questions in the exam paper*

> COMMENT: the floors in American buildings are numbered differently from those in Britain: the 'ground floor' in Britain is the 'first floor' in the USA; the 'first floor' in Britain is the 'second floor' in the USA, and so on

④ **flop**
[flɒp]
1 *noun*
(informal) failure; *his new play was a complete flop and closed after only ten performances; the film was a big hit in New York but was a flop in London*
2 *verb*
(a) to fall or sit heavily; *the lions lay flopped out in the shade of the trees; she got back from the sales and flopped down on the sofa*
(b) *(informal)* to be unsuccessful; *the play was a big hit on Broadway but flopped in London* (NOTE: flopping - flopped)

④ **floppy**
['flɒpɪ]
1 *adjective*
(a) which hangs limp; *a white rabbit with long floppy ears*
(b) floppy disk = small disk which can be inserted into a computer and removed; *we sent a floppy disk of the data by post*
2 *noun*
floppy disk; *the data is available on 3.5 inch floppies* (NOTE: plural is floppies)

④ **flounder (about** *or* **around)**
['flaundɪ ə'baut or ə'raund]
1 *verb*
(a) to move with difficulty in water; *he saw her floundering about in the water and realized she couldn't swim*
(b) to be uncertain of an answer to a question; *she started to flounder as soon as they started to ask her more technical questions*
2 *noun*
species of small flat fish

③ **flour**
['flauɪ] *noun*
grain crushed to powder, used for making bread, cakes, etc.; *she made the cake by mixing eggs, sugar and flour*

④ **flourish**
['flʌrɪʃ] *verb*
(a) to grow well; to do well; *palm trees flourish in hot countries; the company is flourishing; there is a flourishing black market in spare parts for cars*

(b) to wave something in the air; *she came in with a big smile, flourishing a cheque*

② **flow**
[fləʊ]
1 *noun*

movement of liquid, air, etc.; *she tried to stop the flow of blood with a tight bandage*; *there was a steady flow of visitors to the exhibition*
2 *verb*

to move along in a smooth way; *the river flows into the sea*; *traffic on the motorway is flowing at 50 miles an hour*

② **flower**
['flaʊə]
1 *noun*

colourful part of a plant which attracts bees and then produces fruit or seeds; *a plant with bright yellow flowers*; **flower shop** = shop which sells flowers; **flower show** = exhibition of flowers; **in flower** = (plant) which is covered with flowers; *you must visit Japan when the cherry trees are in flower*
2 *verb*

to produce flowers; *the cherry trees flowered very late this year*; *I want a plant which flowers in early summer*

③ **flown**
[fləʊn]
see FLY

③ **flu**
[fluː] *noun*

common illness like a bad cold, often with a high temperature; *half of the team are down with flu*; *scores of people have got flu*; *we all caught flu, and so did the teacher* (NOTE: do not confuse with **flew**)

④ **fluid**
['fluːɪd]
1 *noun*

liquid; *you need to drink plenty of fluids in hot weather*
2 *adjective*

which is not settled; *the situation is still fluid - nothing has been agreed yet*

④ **flush**
[flʌʃ]
1 *noun*

red colour on the face; *a flush of anger covered her face* (NOTE: plural is **flushes**)
2 *verb*

(a) to go red in the face; *she flushed with pleasure when she heard the results*
(b) **to flush out** = to drive out of hiding; *the army brought in helicopters to flush the guerillas out of their mountain bases*
(c) **to flush a lavatory** = to wash it out by moving a handle which makes water rush through; *she told the children not to forget to flush the toilet*; **flush lavatory** = lavatory which works by allowing rushing water to clean it
3 *adjective*

(a) **flush with** = level with; *the door must be flush with the wall*
(b) *(informal)* having plenty of money to spend; *I've just been paid, so I'm feeling very flush at the moment*

① **fly**
[flaɪ]
1 *noun*

(a) small insect which lays its eggs on food; *he tried to kill the fly with a newspaper*; *waiter, there's a fly in my soup!* (NOTE: plural is **flies**)
(b) *(also;* **flies**) trouser front fastened by a zip or buttons; *look out - your fly's undone*
2 *verb*

(a) to move through the air (with wings, in a plane, etc.); *when the cat came into the garden, the birds flew away*; *I'm flying to China next week*; *he flies across the Atlantic twice a month*
(b) to make (a plane) move through the air; *the king was flying his own plane*
(c) to move fast; *the door flew open and two men rushed in*; *I must fly if I want to get home by 6 o'clock*; *his daughter is already two - how time flies!*
(d) to have a flag up; *the ship was flying the Russian flag* (NOTE: flying - flew [fluː] - has flown [fləʊn])

③ **FM**
['ef 'em] = FREQUENCY MODULATION; *Radio 4 is on 93.5 FM*

② **focus**
['fəʊkəs]
1 *noun*

(a) point where rays of light from an object meet; *the focus of the beam is a point 20 metres from the spotlight*
(b) *(of a photograph)* point where the details of the photograph are clear and sharp; *adjust the focus so as to get a clear picture*; **in focus** = clear; **out of focus** = not clear
(c) centre of attention; *the director brought the star actress to the front of the stage, so that the focus of the audience's attention would be on her* (NOTE: plural is **foci** ['fəʊsaɪ])
2 *verb*

(a) to adjust so as to be able to see clearly; *he focused his telescope on a ship in the distance*
(b) **to focus on something** = to look particularly at something, to concentrate on something; *the paper is focusing on the problems of the TV star's marriage* (NOTE: focusing - focused)

③ **fog**
[fɒg] *noun*

thick mist made up of millions of drops of water; *all flights out of Heathrow have been delayed by fog*; *the fog is so thick that you can hardly see ten metres in front of you*

④ **foil**

[fɔɪl]

1 *noun*

thin metal sheet; **tin foil** *or* **cooking foil** = foil used for wrapping food before cooking; *wrap the fish in foil before putting it on the barbecue*

2 *verb*

to prevent a plan from being put into effect; *the bank robbery was foiled by the police*

③ **fold**

[fəʊld]

1 *noun*

place where paper, cloth, etc., is bent over on itself; *she wanted the surgeon to remove the folds of skin under her chin*

2 *verb*

(a) to bend something so that one part is on top of another; *fold the piece of paper in half; he folded the newspaper and put it into his pocket*

(b) to fold your arms = to cross your arms in front of your body; *he sat on the stage with his arms folded, looking annoyed*

(c) *(of a business)* to stop trading; *his business folded last December; the company folded with debts of over £1m*

④ **folder**

['fəʊldə] *noun*

cardboard envelope for holding papers; *she took a folder from the drawer*

② **folk**

[fəʊk] *noun*

(a) people; *they took the old folk down to the sea for a picnic* (NOTE: **folk** is plural and takes a plural verb; but the plural form **folks** is also used)

(b) folk dance = traditional country dance; *everyone wears national costume for the folk dances*; **folk song** = traditional country song

① **follow**

['fɒləʊ] *verb*

(a) to come after or behind; *the group followed the guide round the town; what follows B in the alphabet?; the dog followed the man across the field; I had the impression I was being followed*

(b) to do what someone tells you to do; *she followed the instructions on the tin of paint; he made the cake following a recipe in the newspaper*

(c) to be certain because of something; *because I lent you money last week, it doesn't follow that I will lend you some every time you ask; if the owner of the shop is arrested by the police, it follows that his business is likely to close*

(d) to understand; *I don't quite follow you - you want me to drive you all the way to Edinburgh?*

④ **follower**

['fɒləʊə] *noun*

supporter; *the President's followers came into the capital to protest against the decision*

① **following**

['fɒləʊɪŋ] *adjective*

which comes next; *they arrived on Friday and the following day she became ill; look at the following picture*

③ **fond (of)**

[fɒnd 'ɒv] *adjective*

to be fond of something = to like something; *I am fond of music; she's very fond of chocolate*

① **food**

[fuːd] *noun*

things which you eat; *this hotel is famous for its food; do you like German food?; we arrived at the beach and found that we had forgotten to bring the food*; **food poisoning** = poisoning caused by bacteria in food; *the hotel was closed after an outbreak of food poisoning; half the guests at the wedding were ill with food poisoning* (NOTE: **food** is usually used in the singular)

④ **foodstuffs**

['fuːdstʌfs] *noun*

things which can be used as food; *on some islands, most foodstuffs have to be imported*

④ **fool**

[fuːl]

1 *noun*

(a) stupid person; *you fool! why didn't you put the brakes on?; I was a fool to think that I could make her change her mind*

(b) type of cream fruit dessert; *she made some strawberry fool*

2 *verb*

(a) to fool about *or* **fool around** = to play around in a silly way; *stop fooling around with that knife - you're going to have an accident*

(b) to trick someone; *they fooled the old lady into letting them into her house; you can't fool me - I know you're not really ill*; **you could have fooled me** = I find it hard to believe; *she says she did her best - well, you could have fooled me!*

④ **foolish**

['fuːlɪʃ] *adjective*

silly or stupid; *don't be so foolish - you can't go to Paris all alone; playing with matches in a wood store is a foolish thing to do*

① **foot**

[fʊt]

1 *noun*

(a) end part of your leg on which you stand; *she has very small feet; watch out, you trod on my foot!; (informal)* **to find your feet** = to be confident; *she's been with us three months now and has really found her feet*; **to put your foot down** = (i) to say firmly that something is not allowed; (ii) to make a car go faster; *you must put your foot down and stop this habit of everyone arriving late; the taxi driver put his foot down and got us to the airport in time*; **to put your foot in it** = to say something embarrassing; *he really put his foot in it when he said that the boss's wife was fat*; *see also* WRONG

(b) bottom part, end; *there is a door at the foot of the stairs*; *there are traffic lights at the foot of the hill*; *sign your name at the foot of the page*

(c) measurement of how long something is (= 12 inches or approximately 30 cm); *the table is four foot* or *four feet long*; *she's almost six foot tall*; *I'm five foot seven (5' 7")* see also INCH (NOTE: plural is **feet**. Note also that as a measurement **foot** often has no plural: **six foot tall**; **three foot wide**. With numbers **foot** is also often written ' **a 6' ladder; he is 5' 6":** say 'he's five foot six')

2 *verb*

to foot the bill = to pay the bill; *I found I had to foot the bill for the Christmas party*

◊ **on foot**

['ɒn 'fʊt] *phrase*

walking; *we left the car in the car park and went to the church on foot*; *don't wait for the bus - it's quicker to go on foot*

◊ **under foot**

['ʌndɪ 'fʊt] *phrase*

on the ground; *it's very wet under foot after the rain*

① **football**

['fʊtbɔːl] *noun*

(a) ball used for kicking; ball used in the various games of football; *they were kicking a football around in the street*; **a rugby football** = oval-shaped ball used in rugby

(b) game played between two teams of eleven players with a round ball which can be kicked or headed, but not carried; *he's got a new pair of football boots*; *they went to a football match*; *the children were playing football in the street*; *let's have a game of football*; *he spends all his time watching football on TV*

COMMENT: football is a professional sport involving two teams of 11 players who score goals by kicking or heading a ball into their opponents' goal; only the goalkeeper (who usually wears gloves) is allowed to touch the ball with his hands. A game is divided into two 45-minute halves with a 15-minute interval (after which the teams change ends) but in Cup competitions two 15-minute periods of extra time are added if the scores are level at the end of normal time. There is a referee to see that the game is played according to the rules

④ **footballer**

['fʊtbɔːlɪ] *noun*

person who plays football; *Pelé was a famous Brazilian footballer*

④ **footstep**

['fʊtstep] *noun*

(a) sound made by a foot touching the ground; *we heard soft footsteps along the corridor*

(b) to follow in someone's footsteps = to do what someone did before; *he's following in his father's footsteps and is going to become a lawyer*

① **for**

[fɔː] *preposition*

(a) *(showing the purpose or use of something)* *this plastic bag is for old papers*; *what's that key for?*; *what did she say that for?* = why did she say that?

(b) *(showing why something is given)* *what did you get for your birthday?*; *what shall we buy her for Christmas?*

(c) *(showing person who gets something)* *there was no mail for you this morning*; *I'm making a cup of tea for my mother*

(d) *(showing how long something happens)* *he has gone to France for two days*; *we've been waiting here for hours*

(e) *(showing distance)* *you can see for miles from the top of the hill*; *the motorway goes for kilometres without any service stations*

(f) *(showing destination)* *is this the plane for Edinburgh?*; *when is the next bus for Oxford Circus?*

(g) in exchange; *she gave me £10 for the silver spoon*; *that old computer is no use - I wouldn't give you anything for it*

(h) in support of, in order to get; *we're striking for higher pay*

(i) in the place of someone; *can you write this letter for me?*

(j) with the purpose of; *to go for a walk*; *he was running for the bus*; *all these items are for sale*; *see also* AS FOR

◊ **for ever**

[fɪ 'evɪ] *phrase*

(a) always; *I will love you for ever and ever*; *the good times have gone for ever*

(b) *(exclamation to show support for a team)* *Scotland for ever!*

◊ **for example** *or* **for instance**

['fɔː ɪg'zɑːmpl or fɪr 'ɪnstɪns] *phrase*

to mention one thing among many; *some animals, for example polar bears, are not used to hot weather* (NOTE: **for example** can also be written as **e.g.**)

◊ **for good**

[fɔː 'gʊd]

for ever; *she left school for good when she was 16*

④ **forbid**

[fɪ'bɪd] *verb*

to tell someone not to do something; *Parliament has passed a law forbidding the sale of guns*; *she forbade her children to go near the pub*; *smoking has been forbidden on trains*;

swimming in the reservoir is strictly forbidden (NOTE: **forbidding** - **forbade** [fɪ'bæd] - **forbidden** [fɪ'bɪdn])

④ **forbidden**
[fɪ'bɪdn] *adjective*
which is not allowed; *the staff are forbidden to use the front entrance; father's new flower garden is forbidden territory to the children*

① **force**
[fɔːs]
1 *noun*
(a) strength or power; *the force of the wind blew tiles off the roof; the police had to use force to push back the demonstrators*
(b) organized group of people; *he served in the police force for twenty years;* **the armed forces** = the army, navy and air force; **a sales force** = a group of salesmen
2 *verb*
to make someone do something; *he was forced to stop smoking; you can't force me to go if I don't want to*

◊ **in force**
['ɪn 'fɔːs] *phrase*
(a) in large numbers; *the police were there in force*
(b) to be in force = to be operating or working; *the rules have been in force since 1986;* **to come into force** = to start to operate or work; *the new regulations will come into force on January 1st*

④ **forecast**
['fɔːkɑːst]
1 *noun*
description of what you think will happen in the future; *his forecast of sales turned out to be completely accurate;* **economic forecast** = description of how you expect the economy will perform in the future; **population forecast** = calculation of how many people will be living in a country or in a town at some point in the future; **weather forecast** = report on what sort of weather there will be in the next few days
2 *verb*
to say what will happen in the future; *they are forecasting storms for the south coast; they forecast a rise in the number of tourists* (NOTE: **forecasting** - **forecast**)

④ **foreground**
['fɔːgraʊnd] *noun*
part of a picture which seems nearest to the viewer; *there is a boat in the foreground against a background of mountains; compare* BACKGROUND

④ **forehead**
['fɔːhed] *noun*
part of the front of the head between the eyes and the hair; *his hair was falling down over his forehead*

① **foreign**
['fɒrɪn] *adjective*
(a) not from your own country; *there are lots of foreign medical students at our college;* **foreign exchange** = exchanging the money of one country for money of another; *the dollar was firm on the foreign exchange markets;* **foreign language** = language spoken by people in another country; *she speaks several foreign languages, such as German and Chinese;* **Foreign Minister** = government minister in charge of a Foreign Ministry; *the Russian Foreign Minister chaired the meeting* (NOTE: in Britain this is **the Foreign Secretary** and in the USA **the Secretary of State**); **Foreign Ministry** = government department dealing with relations with other countries (NOTE: in other countries this is **the Foreign Ministry** and in the USA **the State Department**); **Foreign Office** = British government department dealing with relations with other countries (NOTE: in other countries this is **the Foreign Ministry** and in the USA **the State Department**); **Foreign Secretary** = British government minister in charge of the Foreign Office (NOTE: in other countries this is **the Foreign Minister** and in the USA **the Secretary of State**)
(b) foreign body = something which should not be there, such as a piece of dust in your eye; *the X-ray showed the presence of a foreign body*
(c) not something which you are used to or can understand; *the concept of grammar is completely foreign to her*

④ **foreigner**
['fɒrɪnə] *noun*
person who does not come from the same country as you; *there are crowds of foreigners in London in the summer; you can tell he's a foreigner when you hear him speak*

② **forest**
['fɒrɪst] *noun*
large area covered with trees; *the country is covered with thick forests; in dry weather there's a danger of forest fires; in winter bears come out of the forest to search for food* (NOTE: in Britain now usually used with names: **Sherwood Forest, the New Forest**)

④ **forever**
[fɔ'evi] always; *I will love you forever; he's forever making a noise; see also* FOR EVER

③ **forgave**
[fɪ'geɪv]
see FORGIVE

④ **forge**
[fɔːdʒ] *verb*
(a) to copy something illegally; *he forged the signature on the cheque; the new design of the banknotes makes them difficult to forge*
(b) to forge ahead = to go forward quickly; *the wind blew harder and the yacht forged ahead; we are forging ahead with our new project*

④ forgery
['fɔːdʒɪri] *noun*
(a) action of making an illegal copy; *he was sent to prison for forgery* (NOTE: no plural in this meaning)
(b) illegal copy; *the signature proved to be a forgery* (NOTE: plural in this meaning is **forgeries**)

① forget
[fɪ'get] *verb*
(a) not to remember; *he's forgotten the name of the restaurant; I've forgotten how to play chess; she forgot all about her doctor's appointment; don't forget we're having lunch together tomorrow; great scenes at home - I forgot my wife's birthday!*
(b) to leave something behind; *when he left the office he forgot his car keys* (NOTE: **forgetting - forgot** [fɪ'gɒt] **- has forgotten** [fɪ'gɒtɪn])

② forgive
[fɪ'gɪv] *verb*
to stop being angry with someone; *don't worry about it - I forgive you!; will she ever forgive me for forgetting her birthday?* (NOTE: **forgiving - forgave** [fɪ'geɪv] **- has forgiven**)

① forgot *or* **forgotten**
[fɪ'gɒt or fɪ'gɒtɪn]
see FORGET

③ fork
[fɔːk]
1 *noun*
(a) object with a handle at one end and several sharp points at the other, used for picking food up when eating; *don't try to eat Chinese food with a knife and fork; it's polite to use a fork to eat cake - don't use your fingers;* **garden fork** = very large fork used for digging
(b) Y-shaped road junction, or one of the roads leading from it; *take the left fork towards the castle and our house is on the right*
2 *verb*
(a) to turn off a road; *fork left at the next road junction*
(b) to split into two parts; *the railway line forks at Crewe and one branch goes to the coast*
(c) *(informal)* **to fork out** = to pay for something, usually without wanting to; *she didn't bring any money, so I had to fork out for the whole meal*
(d) **to fork over** = to turn over with a garden fork; *he was forking over the rose bed*

① form
[fɔːm]
1 *noun*
(a) paper with blank spaces which you have to write in; **application form** = form which has to be filled in to apply for something; *don't forget to fill in the customs form*
(b) state or condition; *their team wasn't in top form and lost;* **in good form** = in a good mood, very amusing; *she's in good form today;* **off form** *or* **out of form** = not performing very well; *he's off form at the moment - he needs more practice*
(c) shape; *a decoration in the form of a ring*
(d) class (in school); *she's in the lowest form; little children go into the first form;* **sixth form** = class for children who are over 16; **sixth form college** = special college for students aged 16 and over, preparing them for exams that allow them to go to university
2 *verb*
(a) to make; *the children formed a circle; form a queue here, please*
(b) **formed of** = made of; *the committee is formed of retired schoolteachers*
(c) to organize; *they got together and formed a club*
(d) to start to exist; *ice formed on the car windows*

② formal
['fɔːml] *adjective*
(a) done according to certain rules; *the formal opening ceremony was performed by the Prime Minister;* **formal dress** = clothes for special occasions, black coats and bow ties for men, long dresses for women; *the guests were all in formal dress*
(b) official (agreement); *we made a formal offer for the house yesterday*

④ formally
['fɔːməli] *adverb*
according to rules, done with ceremony; *the exhibition will be opened formally by the mayor*

③ format
['fɔːmæt]
1 *noun*
(a) measurements of a page or book; *printers can handle all sorts of book formats*
(b) shape or size (in which something is made); *what format do you want your invitations printed in?*
(c) style of a computer disk; *my computer can't read that disk - it's the wrong format*
2 *verb*
(a) to arrange text on a computer, so that it is ready for final printing; *style sheets are used to format documents*
(b) to set a computer disk so that it is ready to receive data; *you have to format the disk before you can save data on it* (NOTE: **formatting - formatted**)

② formation
[fɔː'meɪʃn] *noun*
(a) shape, forming of something; *a beautiful cloud formation; the formation of ice occurs at temperatures below zero*
(b) **in formation** = in a set pattern; *the birds flew past in a V formation*

① **former**
['fɔːmɪ]
1 *adjective*
who was at an earlier time; *a former army officer*; *the former champion came last in the race*
2 *noun*
the former = first person *or* thing mentioned (of two); *Mr Smith and Mr Jones are both directors, but the former has been with the company longer* (NOTE: the second of two is called the **latter**)

④ **formerly**
['fɔːmlɪ] *adverb*
at an earlier time; *her house was formerly a railway station*; *he was formerly head of our department*

③ **formula**
['fɔːmjʊlɪ] *noun*
(a) statement of a scientific fact, often shown by means of symbols; *the chemical formula of water is H_2O; the drug is made to a secret formula*
(b) Formula I race = car race where the cars all have engines of the largest classification
(c) *US* powdered milk food for babies; *don't forget to make up some formula* (NOTE: plural is **formulae** ['fɔːmjʊliː])

④ **fort**
[fɔːt] *noun*
(a) strong army building which can be defended against enemy attacks; *the soldiers rode out of the fort*; *he was posted to a fort in the desert*
(b) to hold the fort = to be in charge while someone is away; *everyone is away on holiday so I've been left holding the fort*

② **forth**
[fɔːθ] *adverb*; *(formal)*
(a) forwards; **back and forth** = backwards and forwards; *I'm fed up with commuting back and forth across town every day*
(b) to go forth *or* **to set forth** = to go out and forward; *the expedition set forth in May*; **to hold forth about something** = to talk without stopping about something; *my father was holding forth about the government* (NOTE: do not confuse with **fourth**)

◊ **and so forth**
[nd ˈsɪʊ ɒn] *adverb*
with other things; *he talked about plants: flowers, vegetables, and so forth*

④ **forthcoming**
[fɔːθ'kʌmɪŋ] *adjective*
(a) soon to come; *his forthcoming novel will be about London*
(b) *(informal)* full of information, talking a lot; *she wasn't very forthcoming about her wedding preparations*

① **fortieth (40th)**
['fɔːtɪɪθ] *adjective & noun*
he came fortieth and last in the race; *it's her fortieth birthday tomorrow*

③ **fortnight**
['fɔːtnaɪt] *noun*
two weeks; *see you in a fortnight!*; *she's taking a fortnight's holiday*; *we visit my mother once a fortnight*; *we will be on holiday during the last fortnight of July* (NOTE: not used in American English)

③ **fortunate**
['fɔːtʃɪnɪt] *adjective*
lucky; *you are very fortunate to have such a lovely family*; *we've been fortunate with the weather this year*

② **fortunately**
['fɔːtʃɪnɪtlɪ] *adverb*
by good luck; *fortunately, he had remembered to take an umbrella*; *he was late getting to the airport, but fortunately his flight had been delayed*

③ **fortune**
['fɔːtjuːn] *noun*
(a) large amount of money; *he won a fortune on the lottery*; *he made a fortune on the stock market*; *she left her fortune to her three children*; **to cost a fortune** = to cost a lot of money; *that shop has shoes that won't cost a fortune*; *see also* SMALL
(b) what will happen in the future; **to tell someone's fortune** = to say what will happen to someone in the future; *she tells fortunes from cards*
(c) luck, chance; *she had the good fortune to be picked for the England team*

① **forty**
['fɔːti]
number 40; *she's forty (years old) he has more than forty pairs of shoes*; *he's in his forties* = between 40 and 49 years old; **the (nineteen) forties (1940s)** = the period from 1940 to 1949 (NOTE: **forty-one** (41), **forty-two** (42), but **forty-first** (41st), **forty-second** (42nd), etc.)

① **forward**
['fɔːwɪd]
1 *adjective*
moving in the direction that someone *or* something is facing; *she made a forward pass across the field to the player on the wing*
2 *adverb*
(a) in the direction that someone *or* something is facing; *she bent forward to hear what he had to say*; *he took two steps forward*; *the policeman made a sign with his hand and the cars began to go forward*
(b) advanced; *thanks to government red tape we're no further forward with our project*
(c) to look forward to something = to think happily about something which is going to happen; *I'm looking forward to my holidays*; *he isn't looking forward to his exams*; *I'm looking forward to seeing her again*
(d) from that day forward = from that time on
3 *verb*

to send on a letter to another address; *the bank forwarded the cheque to his house in the country*; **forwarding address** = address to which mail can be sent; *they moved and forgot to leave a forwarding address so we can't forward their mail*
4 *noun*
player in a team whose job is to attack the other side; *the England defence came under attack from the Brazilian forwards*

④ **fossil**
['fɒsl] *noun*
remains of an ancient animal or plant left in rock; *they found some fossil shells in the cliffs*; **fossil fuels** = fuels such as coal, which are in fact remains of plants

④ **foster**
['fɒstɪ] *verb*
(a) to be paid to bring up a child who is not your own; *they have fostered several children*
(b) to encourage an idea, etc.; *tourism fosters interest in other countries*

③ **fought**
[fɔːt] *see* FIGHT

④ **foul**
[faʊl]
1 *adjective*
(a) bad, unpleasant (taste, language, air, etc.); *what foul weather we're having!*; *the boss has been in a foul temper all day*; *a foul-smelling drain ran down the centre of the street*
(b) **foul play** = murder; *the body was hanging upside down and the police suspected foul play*
(c) **to fall foul of** = to get into trouble with; *the boys fell foul of the police*; *she fell foul of the income tax inspectors* (NOTE: **fouler - foulest**)
2 *noun*
action which is against the rules of a game; *the referee gave a free kick for a foul on the goalkeeper*; *look at the action replay to see if it really was a foul*
3 *verb*
(a) *(in football, etc.)* to do something to another player which is against the rules of a game; *he was fouled inside the penalty box so the referee gave a penalty*
(c) *(informal)* **to foul something up** = to make a mess of something *or* to create problems; *don't ask John to do it - he's sure to foul it up*

① **found**
[faʊnd] *verb*
(a) to establish, to begin something; *the business was founded in 1900*
(b) **to be founded on something** = to be bases on something; *the charges against her are not founded on any definite facts*
(c) *see also* FIND

② **foundation**
[faʊn'deɪʃn] *noun*
(a) **foundations** = stone or concrete base below ground on which a building is built; *the foundations of the building need*

strengthening; **foundation stone** = stone in a wall which records the start of work on a building; *the queen laid the foundation stone of the new library*
(b) establishing, setting up; *ever since its foundation in 1892, the company has been a great success*
(c) charity which provides money for certain projects; *a foundation for educational research*
(d) **foundation course** = basic course at a university, which allows you to go on to a more advanced course

④ **founder**
['faʊndɪ]
1 *noun*
person who establishes or sets up something; *he was one of the founders of the National Trust*; **founder member** = one of the first to establish a club, etc.; *the USA and the UK are both founder members of the United Nations*
2 *verb*
(a) to collapse, to fail; *the project foundered for lack of money*
(b) *(formal)* to sink; *the ship foundered in heavy seas*

④ **fountain**
['faʊntɪn] *noun*
(a) street or garden construction which sends a jet of water into the air; *there is a statue and a fountain in the middle of the lake*; *on New Year's Eve people try to jump into the fountains in Trafalgar Square*
(b) **drinking fountain** = public tap where you can drink water

① **four**
[fɔː]
(a) number 4; *he's four (years old)* *I have an appointment with the doctor at four (o'clock) a square has four corners*; **on all fours** = on hands and knees; *he was creeping around under the desk on all fours*
(b) crew of four people rowing in a boat; *our college four won the race*; *see also* EIGHT, PAIR
(c) *(in cricket)* score of four runs for sending the ball over the boundary; *he scored a century, including seven fours and two sixes*

① **fourteen**
[fɔː'tiːn]
number 14; *there are fourteen houses in our street*; *he's fourteen (years old) next week*; **the fourteen hundreds (1400s)** = the period from 1400 to 1499 (NOTE: compare **the fourteenth century**)

① **fourteenth (14th)**
[fɔː'tiːnθ] *adjective & noun*
she came fourteenth in the race; *the fourteenth of July or July the fourteenth (July 14th) it was her fourteenth birthday yesterday*; **the fourteenth century** = the period from 1300 to 1399 (NOTE: compare **the fourteen hundreds**); (NOTE: that with dates **fourteenth** is usually

written **14th: January 14th, 1985; October 14th 1799** (American style is **October 14, 1991**), say 'the fourteenth of October' or 'October the fourteenth' (American style is 'October fourteenth')

① **fourth, 4th**
[fɔːθ]
1 *adjective*
this is the fourth time he's had to go to hospital this year; *it's her fourth birthday tomorrow*; *the fourth of October or October the fourth (October 4th)* the fourth century = the period from 300 to 399 AD
2 *noun*
one fourth = 25% (NOTE: do not confuse with **forth**; note that instead of **a fourth** or **a fourth part**, you usually say **a quarter**. Note also that with dates **fourth** is usually written **4th: January 4th, 1985; October 4th 1799** (American style is **October 4, 1991**), say 'the fourth of October' or 'October the fourth' (American style is 'October fourth'); with names of kings and queens **fourth** is usually written **IV: King Charles IV** (say 'King Charles the Fourth')

④ **Fourth of July**
[ˈfɔːθ əv dʒʊˈlaɪ] *noun*
the national day of the United States when people celebrate independence; *we're having a Fourth of July party*

③ **fox**
[fɒks]
1 *noun*
clever wild animal with red fur and a thick tail; *foxes attack lambs in this part of the world*; *we traced the fox back to its hole*; *the urban fox has become common in many parts of London*

④ **fraction**
[ˈfrækʃn] *noun*
(a) very small amount; *sales are up a fraction this month*; *if you move a fraction to the right, you'll all get in the picture*
(b) *(in mathematics)* part of a whole number shown in figures; *1/4 and 1/2 are fractions*

④ **fracture**
[ˈfræktʃɪ]
1 *noun*
break (especially in bones); *the X-ray showed up the fracture clearly*
2 *verb*
to break a bone; *he fractured his leg in the accident*; *they put her fractured leg in plaster*

④ **fragile**
[ˈfrædʒaɪl] *adjective*
(a) easily broken, delicate; *be careful when packing the glasses - they're very fragile*
(b) *(informal)* feeling weak and ill after an illness or operation; *she's still very fragile after her recent operation*

③ **fragment**
1 *noun*
[ˈfrægmɪnt] small piece; *when digging on the site of the old house they found fragments of glass*

2 *verb*
[frægˈment] to break into small pieces; *as soon as the founder died the whole organization fragmented*

④ **fragrance**
[ˈfreɪgrɪns] *noun*
pleasant smell; *the fragrance of the roses outside our bedroom windows*

④ **fragrant**
[ˈfreɪgrɪnt] *adjective*
with a sweet smell; *the roses are particularly fragrant when the sun is on them*

③ **frame**
[freɪm]
1 *noun*
(a) border round glasses, a picture, mirror, window, etc.; *he has glasses with gold frames*; *I think the frame is worth more than the painting*
(b) one picture in a film; *the book is illustrated with frames from some of his films*
(c) climbing frame = framework of wooden bars and platforms for children to climb on
2 *verb*
(a) to put a frame round a picture; *the photograph has been framed in red*
(b) to make someone seem to be guilty; *he says he was framed by the police*; *it wasn't me - I've been framed!*
(c) to put words together to make a sentence; *he had some difficulty in framing his reply*; *the note was framed in very formal language*

③ **frame of mind**
[ˈfreɪm əv ˈmaɪnd] *noun*
way of thinking or feeling, general mood; *you must wait until he's in the right frame of mind before you ask the boss for a rise*

③ **framework**
[ˈfreɪmwɜːk] *noun*
(a) structure supporting a building, etc.; *the framework of the shed is sound - it just needs some paint*
(b) basis of a plan; *they are negotiating the framework of the agreement*

① **France**
[frɑːns] *noun*
country in Europe, south of Britain and west of Belgium and Germany; *in 1814 Britain was at war with France*; *last year we went to France on holiday*; *he's visiting friends in France* (NOTE: capital: **Paris**; people: **the French**; language: **French**; currency: **franc** or **French franc, euro**)

④ **frank**
[fræŋk]
1 *adjective*
saying what you think; *he gave her some frank advice*; *to be really frank with you - I think your plan is awful*
2 *verb*

to stamp a letter with a special machine (instead of using a postage stamp); *the letters were all franked before they left the office*

③ **frankly**
['fræŋkli] *adverb*

telling the truth; *frankly, I don't care what you do*; *she spoke frankly about her childhood in Germany*

④ **frantic**
['fræntɪk] *adjective*

wild and very worried; doing things fast; *where have you been? we were getting frantic*; *we had frantic phone calls from your mother*; *it was a frantic race against time to save the children before the tide came in*

④ **fraud**
[frɔːd] *noun*

(a) making money by making people believe something which is not true; *he is facing trial for fraud*; **Serious Fraud Office** = British government department in charge of investigating fraud in large companies; **fraud squad** = special police department which investigates frauds

(b) person pretending to be something he is not; *she's a fraud - she says she's a film star, but she's only been in TV commercials*; *he's an old fraud - he didn't build that car himself*

③ **fray**
[freɪ]

1 *noun*

fight; **to join the fray** = to join the battle or argument; *the government and opposition argued over the problem, and then the unions joined the fray*; **ready for the fray** = ready to fight; *are we all ready for the fray?*

2 *verb*

(of material) to become worn so that threads are loose; *the carpet is fraying at the edges*; *you could see the frayed collar on his shirt*; *she stitched tape along the bottom of his trousers to stop them fraying*

④ **freak**
[friːk]

1 *noun*

(a) unusual type of person, animal or plant; *the white whale is a freak*

(b) person who is mad about something; *my brother's a computer freak*

2 *adjective*

extraordinary (weather); *the walkers were caught out by the freak weather conditions on the mountain*; *the vineyards were hit by a freak snowstorm in June*

① **free**
[friː]

1 *adjective*

(a) not busy, not occupied; *will you be free next Tuesday?*; *there is a table free in the corner of the restaurant*

(b) not costing any money; *send in four tokens from cereal boxes and you can get a free toy*; *I got a free ticket for the exhibition*; *children are admitted free*; **free gift** = present given by a shop to a customer who buys a certain amount of goods; *there is a free gift worth £25 to any customer buying a washing machine*

(c) able to do what you want, not forced to do anything; *he's free to do what he wants*; *it's a free country*; *(in football)* **free kick** = kick which a player is allowed to make without anyone opposing him, to punish the other side for something which they have done; *the referee awarded a free kick*

(d) **to be free from** *or* **of something** = to be without something unpleasant; *the country has been declared free of disease*; **free of charge** = with no payment to be made

(e) not in prison, not in a cage; *after six years in prison he's a free man again*; *lions wander free in the park*; **to set free** = to allow someone to leave prison, to let an animal out of a cage; *the young birds were raised in the zoo and then set free in the wild*; **free-range chickens** = chickens which are allowed to run about freely; *she always buys free-range chickens, even though they are more expensive* (NOTE: **freer - freest**)

2 *verb*

(a) to release someone who is trapped; *it took the fire service some time to free the passengers in the bus*

(b) to let someone out of prison, an animal out of a cage; *the crowd stormed the jail and freed the prisoners*

② **freedom**
['friːdɪm] *noun*

(a) state of being free, not trapped, not in prison; *she felt a sense of freedom being in the country after working all week in the city*; *his lawyer pleaded for his client's freedom*

(b) being free to do what you want; *the four freedoms of movement on which the EU is based are the freedom of movement of goods, of capital, of people and of services*; **freedom of information** = making official information held by government departments available to everyone; **freedom of the press** = being able to write and publish in a newspaper what you want, without fear of prosecution, provided that you do not break the law; **freedom of speech** = being able to say what you like without fear of prosecution, provided that you do not break the law

④ **freelance**
['friːlɑːns]

1 *adjective & noun*

independent (worker), not employed by one particular company; *she is a freelance journalist*; *he works as a freelance*

2 *adverb*

to work freelance = to work for yourself, not being employed by someone else

3 *verb*

to work for yourself; *she freelances for several newspapers*

④ **freely**

['fri:li] *adverb*

in an open manner, without being forced; *he freely admitted he had been in the house where the murder took place*; *he gave himself up to the police and freely confessed to the theft of the car*

② **freeway**

['fri:weɪ] *noun*

US fast motorway with few junctions; *we took the freeway to San Diego*

③ **freeze**

[fri:z]

1 *verb*

(a) to change from liquid to solid because of the cold; *the winter was mild and for the first time ever the river did not freeze over*; *it's so cold that the lake has frozen solid*

(b) to become very cold; *the forecast is that it will freeze tonight*

(c) to make food very cold so that it keeps; *we picked the peas and froze them immediately*

(d) to freeze to death = to die of cold; *she went out into the snow and froze to death*

(e) to keep money or costs, etc., at their present level and not allow them to rise; *we have frozen salaries at last year's level*

(f) to freeze a bank account = to issue a court order stopping anyone from using a bank account, especially preventing them from taking money out

(c) to stay very still; *when they heard the police car coming, they froze* (NOTE: **froze** [frɪʊz] - has **frozen**)

2 *noun*

(a) period when it is very cold; *do you remember the great freeze in the winter of 1980?*

(b) a wages and prices freeze *or* a freeze on wages and prices = period when wages and prices are not allowed to be increased

③ **freezer**

['fri:zɪ] *noun*

refrigerator which freezes food and keeps it frozen; *put the ice cream back into the freezer before it starts to melt*

③ **freezing**

['fri:zɪŋ] *adjective*

very cold; *guests don't appreciate sleeping in freezing bedrooms*; *close the door - it's freezing in here*; **freezing compartment** = part of a refrigerator where food is put to freeze or to be kept frozen; *we've got some frozen pizzas in the freezing compartment in case of emergencies*

④ **freight**

[freɪt]

1 *noun*

(a) action of transporting goods by air, sea or land; *we sent the order (by) air freight*

(b) goods transported; *the government is encouraging firms to send freight by rail*; **freight train** = train used for transporting goods

2 *verb*

to transport goods; *we freight goods to all parts of the world*

① **French**

[frentʃ]

1 *adjective*

(a) referring to France; *the French railways have a system of high speed trains covering the whole country*

(b) to take French leave = to go away without permission

2 *noun*

(a) language spoken in France; *he speaks French very well*; *they are learning French at school*

(b) the French = the people of France; *the French are famous for their wines and their cooking*

④ **French fries**

['frentʃ 'fraɪz] *noun*

thin stick-shaped pieces of potato, fried in deep oil or fat; *she ordered a hamburger and French fries* (NOTE: also called **chips** in British English, but not in American English; often simply called **fries: hamburger and fries**)

③ **frequency**

['fri:kwɪnsɪ] *noun*

(a) rate at which something happens; *the government is becoming alarmed at the frequency of accidents in the construction industry*

(b) number of movements per second made by a radio wave; *what frequency is Radio 3 on?*; **frequency modulation (FM)** = radio system where the number of waves per second varies; *you can pick up Radio 1 on medium wave or FM* (NOTE: plural is **frequencies**)

③ **frequent**

1 *adjective*

['fri:kwɪnt]

happening often; often seen; *he was a frequent visitor to the library*; *skin cancer is becoming more frequent*; *how frequent are the planes to Birmingham?*

2 *verb*

[frɪ'kwent]

(formal) to go somewhere very often; *he frequents the bar at the corner of the street*

② **frequently**

['fri:kwɪntlɪ] *adverb*

often; *the ferries don't run as frequently in the winter*; *she could frequently be seen walking her dog in the park*

② **fresh**
[freʃ] *adjective*
(a) not used or not dirty; *I'll get you a fresh plate*; **fresh air** = open air; *after ten hours, they came out of the coal mine into the fresh air*
(b) made quite recently; *a basket of fresh rolls; let's ask for a fresh pot of coffee*
(c) fresh water = water in rivers and lakes which contains no salt (as opposed to salt water in the sea)
(d) new; *the police produced some fresh evidence*
(e) not tinned or frozen; *you can buy fresh fish at the fish counter; fresh fruit salad is better than tinned; fresh vegetables are difficult to get in winter*
(f) bright and attractive; *she has a fresh complexion; the kitchen is painted a fresh green colour* (NOTE: **fresher - freshest**)

④ **freshly**
['freʃli] *adverb*
newly, recently; *I love the smell of freshly baked bread; I've some freshly made coffee*

① **Friday**
['fraideɪ] *noun*
the fifth day of the week, the day between Thursday and Saturday; *we all had a meal together last Friday; we always go to the cinema on Friday evenings; we normally have our meetings on Fridays; Friday is a day of rest for Muslims; today is Friday, June 20th*; **Good Friday** = the Friday before Easter Day; **Man Friday** *or* **Girl Friday** = general helper in an office

② **fridge**
[fridʒ] *noun*
(informal) refrigerator, kitchen machine for keeping things cold; *the fridge is empty - we must buy some more food; shall I put the milk back in the fridge?*

③ **fried**
[fraid] *adjective*
which is cooked in a little oil or fat; *would you like a fried egg for breakfast?; add the fried onions to the meat; we had fried rice with our sweet and sour pork; see also* FRY

① **friend**
[frend] *noun*
person whom you know well and like; *she's my best friend; we're going on holiday with some friends from work*; **to make friends with someone** = to get to know and like someone; *we made friends with some French people on holiday*

② **friendly**
['frendli]
1 *adjective*
like a friend, wanting to make friends; *don't be frightened of the dog - he's very friendly; we're not on friendly terms with the people who live next door* (NOTE: **friendlier - friendliest**)
2 *noun*

(informal) football match which does not count in a tournament; *England is playing a friendly against Poland*

③ **friendship**
['frendʃip] *noun*
state of being friends; *he formed several lasting friendships at school*

④ **frighten**
['fraitn] *verb*
to make someone afraid; *take off that horrible mask - you'll frighten the children; the cat has frightened all the birds away*

② **frightened**
['fraitnd] *adjective*
full of fear, scared; *the frightened children ran out of the building*; **frightened of something** *or* **someone** = afraid of someone *or* something; *don't be frightened of the dog - he won't hurt you*

③ **frightening**
['fraitniŋ] *adjective*
which causes fear; *a frightening sound of footsteps in the corridor; he had a frightening thought - what if no one heard his cries for help?*

④ **fringe**
[frindʒ] *noun*
(a) hair hanging down over your forehead; *she has her hair cut in a fringe*
(b) edging of a scarf, carpet, etc., consisting of loose threads hanging down; *a lampshade with a yellow fringe*
(c) outer edge of an area; *round the fringe of the crowd people were selling souvenirs*; **fringe benefits** = extra benefits on top of a salary (such as a free car, etc.); **fringe theatre** = experimental theatre, often not using a traditional theatre building

③ **frog**
[frɒg] *noun*
(a) small animal with long legs, which lives on both land and water; *can you hear the frogs calling round the pond?; the wicked queen turned the prince into a frog*
(b) *(informal)* **to have a frog in your throat** = to have something in your throat which stops you speaking clearly; *he said 'excuse me, I've a frog in my throat' and coughed several times*

① **from**
[frɒm] *preposition*
(a) away; *take three from four and you get one*
(b) *(showing the place where something starts or started)* *he comes from Germany; the bees went from flower to flower; we've had a letter from the bank; he read the book from beginning to end or from cover to cover*
(c) *(showing the time when something starts or started)* *I'll be at home from 8 o'clock for the rest of the evening; the hours of work are 9.30 to 5.30, from Monday to Friday; from now on I'm going to get up early*

(d) *(showing distance) it is more than 3km from here to the railway station*
(e) *(showing difference) can you tell butter from margarine?*; *his job is totally different from mine*
(f) *(showing a cause) he died from the injuries he received in the accident*; *she suffers from coughs every winter*

① **front**
[frʌnt]
1 *noun*
(a) part of something which is furthest forward; *the front of the house is on London Road*; *there is a picture of the Houses of Parliament on the front of the book*; *she spilt coffee down the front of her dress*
(b) road or pedestrian walk along the edge of the sea; *we went for a walk along the front*; *a hotel on the sea front* or *a sea front hotel*
(c) line marking the point where two masses of air meet; **cold front** = edge of a mass of cold air, bringing clouds and rain; **warm front** = moving mass of warm air which pushes away a mass of cold air and also brings rain
2 *adjective*
which is in front; *she sat in the front seat, next to the driver*
◊ **in front of**
[ɪn ˈfrʌnt ɒv] *phrase*
before something; *don't stand in front of the car - it may start suddenly*; *there are six people in front of me in the queue*; *you can park your car in front of the shop*

③ **front door**
[ˈfrʌnt ˈdɔː] *noun*
main door to a house or building; *he came to the front door and rang the bell*

④ **frontier**
[ˈfrʌntɪə] *noun*
border between two countries; *the customs men at the frontier didn't even bother to look at our passports*; *she was stopped at the frontier because her passport was invalid*

④ **frost**
[frɒst] *noun*
(a) white covering on the ground, trees, etc., when the temperature is below freezing; *the garden was white with frost*
(b) cold weather, when the temperature is below freezing; *there was a hard frost last night*; *a late frost can damage young plants*

④ **frown**
[fraʊn]
1 *noun*
pulling your eyebrows together as a sign that you are angry, disapprove of something, or are worried; *take that frown off your face - everything's going to be all right*
2 *verb*
to pull your eyebrows together because you are concentrating or worried; *he frowned as he tried to do the calculation*; **to frown on** *or* **upon**

something = to disapprove of something; *the teachers frown on singing in the corridors*; *the company frowns on people who bring food into the office*; *this type of behaviour is frowned upon by the municipal authorities*

③ **froze**
[frəʊz]
see FREEZE

③ **frozen**
[ˈfrəʊzn] *adjective*
(a) very cold; *come inside - you must be frozen out there*
(b) at a temperature below freezing point; *we went skating on the frozen lake*; **frozen food** = food stored at a temperature below freezing point; *use frozen peas if you can't get fresh ones*
(c) not allowed to be changed or used; **frozen account** = bank account where the money cannot be taken out or used because of a court order; *see also* FREEZE

② **fruit**
[fruːt]
1 *noun*
part of a plant which has seeds and which is often eaten raw and is usually sweet; *I must remember to buy some fruit at the market before we go on our picnic*; *he has six fruit trees in his garden*; **fruit salad** = pieces of different fruit, cut up and mixed together; *for pudding we had fruit salad and ice cream* (NOTE: no plural: **some fruit, a piece of fruit**)
2 *verb*
to produce fruit; *the strawberries have finished fruiting*; *some pears fruit quite late in the season*

③ **fruit juice**
[ˈfruːt dʒuːs] *noun*
juice from fruit; *she started breakfast with a glass of fruit juice*

④ **frustrate**
[frʌˈstreɪt] *verb*
to prevent someone doing what he wants to do; *the weather frustrated the efforts of the rescue team*

③ **fry**
[fraɪ] *verb*
to cook in oil or fat in a shallow pan; *fry the onions on a low heat so that they don't burn*; *fry the eggs in some fat* (NOTE: **fries** [fraɪz] - **frying - fried** [fraɪd])

③ **frying pan**
[ˈfraɪɪŋ pæn] *noun*
shallow, open pan used for frying; *she burnt her hand on the hot frying pan*; *put some butter in the frying pan and fry the mushrooms*

③ **ft**
= FOOT, FEET

② **fuel**
[ˈfjʊəl]
1 *noun*

substance (coal, gas, oil, petrol, wood, etc.) which can be burnt to give heat or power; *what fuel do you use to heat the house?*; *what's the fuel consumption of your car?*; *we ran out of fuel on the motorway*

2 *verb*

(a) to provide fuel for; *the power station is fuelled by coal*

(b) to increase; *our money worries were fuelled by news of an increase in the mortgage rate* (NOTE: **fuelling - fuelled** but American spelling is **fueling - fueled**)

Ⓐ **fulfil** *US* **fulfill**
[fʊlˈfɪl] *verb*

to complete something in a satisfactory way; *did he fulfil his promise and take you to the theatre?*; *he died before he could fulfil his ambition to climb Everest*; *we are so busy that we cannot fulfil any more orders before Christmas* (NOTE: **fulfilling - fulfilled**)

Ⓞ **full**
[fʊl] *adjective*

(a) with as much inside as is possible; *is the box full?*; *the bag is full of potatoes*; *we couldn't get on the first bus because it was full*; *all the hotels were full*; *I'm full up* = I've eaten so much that I can't eat any more

(b) complete; *you must give the police full details of the accident*; *write your full name and address at the top of the paper*; *he got full marks* = he got 100 out of 100; *full fare* = price of a ticket for an adult, without any reduction; *children over 12 must pay full fare*; *full moon* = time when the moon appears as a complete circle (NOTE: **fuller - fullest**)

Ⓐ **full English breakfast**
[ˈfʊl ˈɪŋglɪʃ ˈbrekfəst] *noun*

cooked breakfast, with eggs, bacon, sausages, etc., as opposed to a continental breakfast; *see also the note at* BREAKFAST

Ⓐ **full-scale**
[fʊlˈskeɪl] *adjective*

(a) the same size as in real life; *a full-scale model of a Roman house*

(b) complete; *it started as a dispute over a few islands and soon developed into a full-scale war*

Ⓐ **full stop**
[ˈfʊl ˈstɒp] *noun*

(a) printed mark like a small dot, showing the end of a sentence or an abbreviation; *when reading, you can take a breath when you come to a full stop*

(b) (meaning 'there's nothing more to say') *she doesn't like German food, full stop* (NOTE: American English for meanings (a) and (b) is **period**)

(c) complete stop; *the car slid across the road and came to a full stop when it hit a wall*

Ⓐ **full-time**
[fʊlˈtaɪm] *adjective & adverb*

working all the normal working time (i.e. about seven hours a day, five days a week); *she is in full-time work or she works full-time*; *we have 8 full-time and two part-time teachers at our school*; *compare* PART-TIME

Ⓐ **fully**
[ˈfʊli] *adverb*

completely or entirely; *he was fully aware that he had made a mistake*; *she still hasn't fully recovered from her accident*; *the hotel is fully booked for the Christmas week*; *when fully grown, an elephant can weigh several tons*

Ⓐ **fume**
[fjuːm]

1 *noun*

fumes = smoke or gas; *the children died from breathing in the fumes from the gas cooker*

2 *verb*

to be angry; *after he had read the report he was absolutely fuming*

Ⓐ **fun**
[fʌn]

1 *noun*

amusement; *having to stay in bed on my birthday is not much fun*; *to have fun* = to enjoy yourself; *we had a lot of fun on the river*; *to make fun of someone* = to laugh at someone; *don't make fun of her - she's trying her best*; *he made fun of the Prime Minister*; *for fun* = as a joke; *she poured water down his neck for fun*; *just for fun, he drove the car through town dressed as a monkey*; *why did you do that? - just for the fun of it!*

2 *adjective*

amusing; *sitting on the grass in St James's Park is a fun way of passing a Sunday afternoon*

Ⓞ **function**
[ˈfʌŋkʃn]

1 *noun*

(a) party, gathering of people; *we have two wedding functions in the main restaurant this weekend*; *the Prime Minister is tied up with official functions all week*; *function room* = room in a restaurant or hotel where private parties are held

(b) work done by something; *what's the function of that red switch?*

2 *verb*

(a) to work; *the computer is still functioning well after months of constant use*

(b) *to function as* = to serve as; *the sofa functions as a bed if we have visitors*

Ⓞ **fund**
[fʌnd]

1 *noun*

(a) sum of money set aside for a special purpose; *she contributes to a pension fund*

(b) collection; *he has a fund of stories about his time at sea*

2 *verb*

to provide money for a special purpose; *we have asked the government to fund the building of the new library*; *the company is funding her manager's course*

② **fundamental**

[fʌndɪ'mentl] *adjective*

basic, essential; *the fundamental difference between us is that I apologize for my mistakes and you don't*; *good air quality is fundamental for children's health*

③ **funding**

['fʌndɪŋ] *noun*

money for something; *who is providing the funding for the relief mission?*; *where is the funding for the new library coming from?*

① **funds**

[fʌndz] *noun*

money which is available for spending; *he started a course at college and then ran out of funds*; *the company has the funds to set up the research programme*; *funds are available to get the project off the ground*

③ **funeral**

['fjuːnɪrəl] *noun*

(a) ceremony when a dead person is buried; *the church was packed for her funeral*; *the funeral will take place on Friday morning*

(b) *(informal)* **it's your funeral** = it something that only you are responsible for; *if he insists on riding his motorbike without a helmet, then that's his funeral*

① **funny**

['fʌnɪ] *adjective*

(a) which makes you laugh; *we watched a funny programme on children's TV*; *he made funny faces and all the children laughed*; **funny bone** = part of the elbow which gives a painful sensation when you hit it by accident

(b) strange or odd; *she's been behaving in a funny way recently*; *there's a funny smell in the bathroom*

(c) a little bit ill; *I'm feeling funny* (NOTE: **funnier - funniest**)

④ **fur**

[fɜː] *noun*

soft coat of an animal; *this type of cat has very short fur*; *she was wearing a fur coat*

④ **furious**

['fjuːrɪəs] *adjective*

very angry; *he's furious because someone has scratched his new car*; *the passengers were furious at having to wait four hours*; *she had a furious row with her brother*

④ **furnish**

['fɜːnɪʃ] *verb*

(a) to put furniture into a house, office, etc.; *we rented a furnished flat for a year*; *his house is furnished with antiques*

(b) *(formal)* to provide; *he furnished the police with a complete list of addresses*; *the town council furnished details of the improvement plan*

② **furniture**

['fɜːnɪtʃɪ] *noun*

tables, chairs, beds, cupboards, etc.; *the burglars stole all our office furniture*; *you should cover up all the furniture before you start painting the ceiling* (NOTE: there is no plural: **some furniture; a lot of furniture; a piece of furniture**)

① **further**

['fɜːðɪ]

1 *adverb*

a greater distance; *can you all move further back, I can't get you in the picture*; *the police station is quite close, but the post office is further away*; *Edinburgh is further from London than Paris*

2 *adjective*

(a) more; *the bank needs further information about your salary*; *please send me further details of holidays in Greece*; **further education** = teaching for people who have left school; *she goes to evening classes at the local College of Further Education*

(b) **further to** = referring to something; **further to our letter of the 21st** = in addition to what we said in our letter; **further to your letter of the 21st** = here is information which you asked for in your letter

③ **furthermore**

[fɜːðɪ'mɔː] *adverb*

also, in addition; *the party was good fun, and furthermore it didn't end too early*

③ **furthest**

['fɜːðɪst] *adverb & adjective*

the greatest distance; *some of the staff live quite close to the office, but James lives furthest away*; *the furthest distance I have ever flown is to Hong Kong*

④ **fury**

['fjuːrɪ] *noun*

fierce anger; *he turned to us in fury and shouted at us to get out*; *in a fit of fury he threw the plate across the kitchen*

③ **fuss**

[fʌs]

1 *noun*

unnecessary excitement or complaints; **to make a fuss** *or* **to kick up a fuss about something** = to complain at length about something which is not important; *what's all the fuss about?*; *don't make such a fuss - it's only a little scratch*; **to make a fuss of someone** = to pay great attention to someone; *the children made a fuss of their mother on her birthday* (NOTE: no plural)

2 *verb*

to fuss over something = to worry about something, or to pay too much attention to something; *don't fuss - it will be all right*; *stop fussing over your hair, you look fine*

① **future**
['fju:tʃɪ]
2 *noun*
(a) time which has not yet happened; *what are his plans for the future?*; *you never know what the future will bring*; *can you imagine what London will be like in the future?*

(b) in future = from now on; *try to get to the office on time in future*
(c) future (tense) = form of a verb which shows that something will happen; *'he will eat' and 'he is going to eat' are future forms of the verb 'to eat'*
2 *adjective*
which is coming, which has not happened yet; *they are spending all their time preparing for their future retirement*; *I try to save something each week for future expenses*

Gg

③ **G, g**
[dʒi:]
seventh letter of the alphabet, between F and H; *'jogging' is spelt with two g's*

③ **g**
= GRAM

② **gain**
[geɪn]
1 *noun*
(a) profit; **capital gains** = profit made by selling assets
(b) increase in weight, quantity, size; *there was no gain in weight*; **gain in experience** = getting more experience
2 *verb*
(a) to get; *the army gained control of the country*; *she gained some useful experience working on a farm*
(b) to increase in value; *the pound gained six cents on the foreign exchange markets*
(c) *(of a clock, watch)* to move ahead of the correct time; *my watch gains five minutes a day*
(d) to gain on someone *or* **something** = to get closer to a person or thing you are chasing; *with each lap he was gaining on the race leader*

④ **galaxy**
['gæləksi] *noun*
(a) huge group of stars; *there are vast numbers of galaxies*; *the speed of stars near the centre of a galaxy may indicate the presence of black holes*
(b) mass of film stars, etc.; *there is a galaxy of singers on our show tonight* (NOTE: plural is **galaxies**)

③ **gallery**
['gæləri] *noun*
(a) (art) gallery = place where pictures and sculptures are shown to the public; *the National Gallery is in Trafalgar Square*; *the Tate Gallery has a collection of modern paintings*

(b) (art) gallery = shop selling pictures, antiques; *she runs an art gallery selling pictures by local artists*
(c) balcony inside a church, hall or theatre; *a group of musicians played in the gallery*; **public gallery** = place in a court, council chamber, etc., where the public can sit to listen to what is being said (NOTE: plural is **galleries**)

④ **gallon**
['gælən] *noun*
measure of quantity of liquid; *the car was empty and I had to put in seven gallons of petrol*; *an economical car does 40 miles to the gallon* (NOTE: **gallon** is written **gal(l)** with figures: **80 gal(l)**

> COMMENT: in Britain one gallon equals 4.55 litres, but in the USA only 3.78 litres

④ **gamble**
['gæmbl]
1 *noun*
risk; *this investment is a bit of a gamble*; *he took a gamble with the weather in planning his picnic for the beginning of March*
2 *verb*
to bet money on cards, horses, etc.; *he lost all his money gambling on dog races*; **to gamble on something happening** = to do something, hoping that something will happen; *we're gambling on fine weather for the school sports day*

① **game**
[geɪm]
1 *noun*
(a) sport which can be won with skill, strength or luck; *she's not very good at games*

(b) single match between two opponents or two opposing teams; *everyone wanted to watch the game of football*; *do you want a game of snooker?*; *our team have won all their games this year*

(c) to give the game away = to reveal a secret plan; **so that's his little game!** = now we know what his plans are; **the game's up** = you've been found out

(d) single round in tennis, bridge, etc.; *game, set and match to Becker*; *she's winning by six games to three*

(e) Games = large organized sports competition; *the Olympic Games*; *the Commonwealth Games*

(f) wild animals and birds (deer, rabbits, etc.) which are killed for sport or food; *our cookery book has several recipes for game*; **big game** = large wild animals, such as lions, elephants, etc.; **game reserve** *or* **game park** = park where wild animals are preserved (NOTE: no plural in this meaning)

2 *adjective*

ready and willing; *I'm game to have a go*; *she's always game for anything*

③ **gang**
[gæŋ]

1 *noun*

(a) band of criminals, youths, etc.; *an important South American drugs gang*; *gangs of football fans wandered round the streets breaking shop windows*

(b) group of workers; *gangs of men worked all night to repair the railway track*

2 *verb*

to gang up (with someone) = to join up with someone to do something; *the different unions are ganging up to put in a joint pay claim*; **to gang up on someone** = to form a group to attack one person; *she felt as if the rest of office staff were ganging up on her*

④ **gangster**
['gæŋstə] *noun*

member of a gang of criminals; *gangsters have taken over all the bars in the town*

③ **gaol**
[dʒeɪl]

see JAIL (NOTE: the American spelling is always jail)

② **gap**
[gæp] *noun*

(a) space between two things; *the sheep all rushed through the gap in the hedge*; *his retirement will leave a gap in the committee*; *we need someone to fill a gap in our sales force*; **gap in the market** = place where you may be able to sell; *we think we've found a gap in the market*; **gap year** = year which a student takes off from his or her studies, between finishing school and starting at university

(b) difference; *the gap is widening between rich and poor*; **age gap** = difference between people of different age groups; **generation gap** = difference between people of different generations; **trade gap** = difference between the value of a country's exports and the value of its imports

② **garage**
['gærɪdʒ or 'gærɑːʒ]

1 *noun*

(a) small building where you can keep a car; *he put the car into the garage overnight*; *she drove the car out of the garage*; *don't forget to lock the garage door*; *the hotel has garage space for thirty cars*; **garage sale** = private sale of household goods which you don't want, held in you garage

(b) business where petrol is sold and cars, etc., are repaired or sold; *where's the nearest garage? - I need some petrol*; *I can't drive you to the station - my car is in the garage*; *you can hire cars from the garage near the post office* (NOTE: this type of garage is also called a **service station**)

2 *verb*

to keep a vehicle in a garage; *the car was garaged overnight in the hotel's underground car park*

③ **garbage**
['gɑːbɪdʒ] *noun*

(a) *(informal)* rubbish; *I don't believe a word of what he said - it's just garbage*

(b) *(mainly US)* household waste; *don't forget to put the garbage out* (NOTE: no plural; note also that British English is usually **rubbish**)

③ **garbage can**
['gɑːbɪdʒ 'kæn] *noun*

US large plastic or metal container for household rubbish; *they come to empty the garbage cans once a week*; *she put the rest of the dinner in the garbage can* (NOTE: also called a **trashcan**; British English for this is **dustbin**)

① **garden**
['gɑːdɪn] *noun*

(a) piece of ground near a house, used for growing vegetables, flowers, etc.; *we grow all the vegetables we need in the back garden*; *your sister's outside, sitting in the garden*; *he hurt his foot with a garden fork*; *we keep the tools in the garden shed* (NOTE: American English for this is **yard**)

(b) gardens = large area of garden, usually in several sections; *the hotel is surrounded by flower gardens*; *when you're in London you must visit Kew Gardens*; **public gardens** = place in a town where there are flowers, trees and grass, where people can go to walk around and enjoy themselves

④ **gardener**
['gɑːdnɪ] *noun*
person who looks after a garden; *she's a keen gardener*; *I was just looking through the small ads when I saw that they wanted a gardener*

④ **gardening**
['gɑːdnɪŋ] *noun*
looking after a garden; *he reads his gardening magazine every week*; *she does some gardening every Saturday*

③ **garlic**
['gɑːlɪk] *noun*
bulb of a plant with a strong smell, a little like an onion; *his breath smelled of garlic*; **garlic bread** = French bread heated with butter and garlic

④ **garment**
['gɑːmɪnt] *noun*
piece of clothing; *she was dressed in a long loose garment with wide sleeves*

① **gas**
[gæs]
1 *noun*
(a) chemical substance which has no form and which becomes liquid if it is cooled; *air is formed of several gases, mainly nitrogen and oxygen*; **gas attack** = attack on the enemy using poison gas (NOTE: plural in this meaning is **gases**)
(b) chemical substance used for cooking or heating; *there is a smell of gas or it smells of gas in the kitchen*; *turn down the gas or turn the gas down - it's too hot*; *turn up the gas or turn the gas up - the kettle hasn't boiled yet*; *the hotel is heated by gas*; **gas fire** = fire which heats with gas; *we sat in front of the gas fire, trying to keep warm*
(c) *US* = GASOLINE; *we ran out of gas on the freeway*; *(informal)* **to step on the gas** = to drive faster; *step on the gas - we'll miss the train!* (NOTE: no plural in meanings (b) and (c))
2 *verb*
to poison or kill someone using gas; *thousands of people were gassed during the war* (NOTE: **gassing - gassed**)

④ **gasoline**
['gæsɪliːn] *noun*
US liquid used to drive a car engine (NOTE: usually shortened to **gas**; British English is **petrol**)

④ **gasp**
[gɑːsp]
1 *noun*
(a) taking in your breath suddenly, showing surprise or pain; *she gave a gasp when she saw the face at the window*
(b) **last gasp** = final action, which marks the end of something; *the killings were the last gasp of the army regime*; *he's at his last gasp* = it is almost the end of his life, reign, etc.; *the poor car is at its last gasp - we really must get a new one*
2 *verb*

(a) to take a short deep breath; *he gasped when he saw the bill*
(b) to have difficulty in breathing; *after the race he lay on the ground gasping for breath*

④ **gas station**
['gæs 'steɪʃn] *noun*
US place where you can buy gasoline; *where's the nearest gas station?* (NOTE: British English is **petrol station**)

② **gate**
[geɪt] *noun*
(a) low door made of bars of wood or metal, in a wall or fence, not in a building; *shut the gate - if you leave it open the sheep will get out of the field*; *there is a white gate leading into the garden*
(b) door which leads to an aircraft at an airport; *flight AZ270 is now boarding at Gate 23*
(c) number of people attending a sports match; *there was a gate of 50,000 at the football final*

② **gather**
['gæðɪ] *verb*
(a) to bring together; *he gathered his papers together after the meeting*; *she has been gathering information on the history of the local school*
(b) to come together; *groups of people gathered outside the Parliament Building*
(c) to understand; *I gather that his father is in hospital*; *we gather he has left the office*
(d) to pick plants, flowers, fruit, etc.; *the children were gathering blackberries*; *the grape harvest has been gathered*
(e) **to gather speed** = to go faster; *the bus gathered speed as it ran down the hill*

② **gathering**
['gæðɪrɪŋ]
1 *noun*
group of people who have come together; *a speaker from another association will address the gathering*
2 *adjective*
which is coming together; *the gathering crowds did not realize that the president had already left the country*; **the gathering storm** = the storm which is coming

② **gauge**
[geɪdʒ]
1 *noun*
instrument to measure depth, pressure, etc.; **petrol gauge** *or* **fuel gauge** = instrument which shows how much petrol there is in a petrol tank; *I don't know how much petrol I have left, because the gauge has stuck*; **tyre gauge** *or* **pressure gauge** = instrument for measuring the amount of air in a tyre
2 *verb*
to measure or to calculate; *this is an instrument which gauges the speed of the wind*; *the chairman tried to gauge the feeling of the meeting*

③ **gave**
[geɪv]
see GIVE

③ **gay**
[geɪ]
1 *adjective*
(a) homosexual; *did you know her brother is gay?*; *it's a club where gay men and women meet*; *they met in a gay bar in Soho*
(b) *(old)* bright, lively colours; *the houses along the street are all painted in gay colours* (NOTE: gayer - gayest)
2 *noun*
homosexual man (or woman); *a club for gays*

④ **gaze**
[geɪz]
1 *noun*
steady look; *she refused to meet his gaze*
2 *verb*
to look in a steady way; *she gazed into his eyes*; *he stood on the cliff, gazing out to sea*

③ **GB**
[ˈdʒiː ˈbiː] = GREAT BRITAIN
he must be going to France in the car - he has his GB stickers on

④ **GDP**
[dʒiːdiːˈpiː] = GROSS DOMESTIC PRODUCT

③ **gear**
[gɪə]
1 *noun*
(a) equipment; *he took all his climbing gear with him*; *she was carrying her painting gear in a bag*; **landing gear** = wheels of an aircraft and their supports
(b) *(informal)* clothes; *she was putting on her tennis gear*
(c) *(of car, bicycle, etc.)* **gears** = arrangement of wheels of different sizes with teeth which link together, controlling the rate at which the machine moves; **to change gear** = to move from one gear into another; *there was a loud noise as he tried to change gear*; **bottom gear** *or* **first gear** *or* **low gear** = the lowest gear, used when going slowly, or when climbing hills; **top gear** *or* **high gear** = the highest gear, used for fast speeds; *the car is most economical in top gear*; *always use a low gear when going down steep hills*; **in gear** = with the gears engaged (as opposed to 'in neutral')
2 *verb*
to gear something to = to fit something to; *the ferry services are geared to the tourist season*; *lessons must be geared to the students' ability*

③ **geese**
[giːs] *see* GOOSE

④ **gel**
[dʒel]
1 *noun*
thick substance, especially one spread on your hair to keep it tidy; *he smoothed the gel over his hair*

2 *verb*
to become more certain or more clear; *the details of the plan began to gel* (NOTE: gelling - gelled)

④ **gender**
[ˈdʒendɪ] *noun*
(a) being male or female; *everyone has the same rights, regardless of race, religion or gender*
(b) *(in grammar)* system where nouns and adjectives have different forms to indicate if they are masculine or feminine; *what's the gender of 'Tisch' in German?*

② **gene**
[dʒiːn] *noun*
element in the body which carries characteristics from parent to children; *all the children have red hair like their mother - it must be in their genes*

① **general**
[ˈdʒenɪrɪl]
1 *adjective*
(a) ordinary, not special; *he had a good general education, but didn't specialize in any particular field*; **in general** = normally; *in general, the weather is warmer in the south*
(b) referring to everything, everybody; *they issued a general instruction to all the staff*; **the General Assembly of the United Nations** = meeting of the representatives of all countries that are members of the UN; **general election** = election where all voters can vote for a government; *which party won the 1997 general election?*; **general store** = small country shop which sells a large range of goods; **general strike** = strike of all workers in a country
(c) **general anaesthetic** = substance given to make a patient lose consciousness so that a major operation can be carried out; *you will have to be given a general anaesthetic for this operation*; *this operation can be carried out under local rather than general anaesthetic* (NOTE: an anaesthetic for part of the body is a local anaesthetic)
2 *noun*
army officer of high rank; *he has only recently been promoted to general*

① **generally**
[ˈdʒenɪrɪlɪ] *adverb*
normally; *the office is generally closed between Christmas and the New Year*

③ **general practitioner (GP)**
[ˈdʒenɪrɪl prækˈtɪʃɪnɪ] *noun*
family doctor who does not work in a hospital, and treats all patients, all illnesses, without specializing in any particular branch of medicine; *see your GP first, and he or she will refer you to a specialist*

② **generate**
[ˈdʒenɪreɪt] *verb*
to produce power, etc.; *we use wind to generate electricity*

② **generation**
['dʒenɪ'reɪʃn] *noun*
(a) production of power, etc.; *the generation of electricity from waves*
(b) all people born at about the same time; *the 1960s generation had an easier life than we did*; *people of my father's generation cannot understand computer technology*; **generation gap** = lack of understanding between generations
(c) members of a family born about the same time; **the younger generation** = the younger members of a family; **the older generation** = the older members of a family
(d) series of machines made at about the same time; *they are developing a new type of engine for the next generation of aircraft*

② **generator**
['dʒenɪreɪtɪ] *noun*
machine which makes electricity; *the hospital had to use the generator because there was a power cut*

④ **generous**
['dʒenɪrɪs] *adjective*
(a) giving money or presents gladly; *a generous birthday present*
(b) very willing to give your time, etc., to help someone; *he's been very generous with his time*
(c) large; *a generous helping of pudding*

② **genetic**
[dʒɪ'netɪk] *adjective*
referring to genes; **genetic code** = information which makes up a cell, and which is passed on as the cell divides

③ **genetically**
[dʒɪ'netɪkli] *adverb*
in a way which involves changes to genes; **genetically modified crops** = plants where the genes have been changed to make them resist diseases

④ **genetics**
[dʒɪ'netɪks] *noun*
the science and study of genes; *he wrote an article on the latest advances in genetics*

② **genius**
['dʒiːnɪs] *noun*
(a) very intelligent person; person who has great ability; *she's a chess genius*; *Napoleon was a military genius*; *she came top of the class - she's a real genius* (NOTE: plural in this meaning is **geniuses**)
(b) **evil genius** = wicked person who influences others; *Rasputin was the evil genius of the Russian court*
(c) great ability; *he has a genius for keeping people amused*

④ **genre**
['ʒɑːnrɪ] *noun*
type of art, writing, etc.; *he is one of best writers in this genre*; **genre painting** = painting of scenes of everyday life; *Pieter de Hoogh is a master of Dutch genre painting*

③ **gentle**
['dʒentl] *adjective*
(a) soft and kind; *the nurse has gentle hands*
(b) not very strong; *with a little gentle persuading she agreed to the plan*; *he gave the door a gentle push*
(c) not very steep; *there is a gentle slope down to the lake* (NOTE: **gentler - gentlest**)

② **gentleman**
noun
(a) man, especially an educated man from a good family; *he's such a gentleman, he always opens the door for me*
(b) *(polite way of referring to a man)* *this gentleman is waiting to be served*; *well, gentlemen, if everyone is here, the meeting can start*; **'ladies and gentlemen'** = way of starting to talk to a group of men and women (NOTE: plural is **gentlemen**)

③ **gently**
['dʒentli] *adverb*
(a) softly; *he gently put the blanket over her*; *she rocked the baby gently*; **gently does it!** = be careful!
(b) not strongly; *the wind blew gently through the bushes*
(c) not very steep; *the path rises gently to the top of the hill*

③ **genuine**
['dʒenjuɪn] *adjective*
real, true; *the painting was not a genuine Picasso*; *a genuine leather purse will cost a lot more than that*

③ **geographic** *or* **geographical**
[dʒiːɪ'græfɪk or dʒiːɪ'græfɪkl] *adjective*
referring to geography

③ **geography**
[dʒiː'ɒgrɪfɪ] *noun*
study of the earth's surface; *we're studying the geography of the Thames Valley*; *I'm worse at English than at geography*

③ **germ**
[dʒɜːm] *noun*
(a) something which causes disease; *wash your hands after emptying the dustbin so you don't spread any germs*
(b) the beginning of something; *he had the germ of an idea*

① **German**
['dʒɜːmɪn]
1 *adjective*
referring to Germany; *there are three German players in the team*; *do you like German food?*; *see also* MEASLES
2 *noun*
(a) language spoken in Germany, Austria and parts of Switzerland and Italy; *do you know the German for 'one - two - three'?*; *you must brush up your German if you are going to work in Germany*; *he took a crash course in German*; *he works all day in the office, and then goes to German classes in the evening*

(b) person from Germany; *our next-door neighbours are Germans*

① **Germany**

['dʒɜːmɪnɪ] *proper noun*

large west European country, to the east of France, and west of Poland; *they used to live in Germany; Germany is an important member of the EU* (NOTE: capital: **Berlin**; people: **Germans**; language: **German**; currency: **Deutschmark** or **D-mark, euro**)

③ **gesture**

['dʒestʃɪ]

1 *noun*

(a) movement of hands, etc., to show feeling; *she made an impatient gesture with her hand*

(b) action which shows feeling; *the gift of fruit was a kind gesture on her part; as a gesture to the staff, the management has had the toilets decorated*; **token gesture** = small action done to show that you intend to deal with a problem; *the motion criticizing the government was simply a token gesture by the opposition parties*

2 *verb*

to make a movement with your hands; *he gestured to the audience to sit down*

① **get**

[get] *verb*

(a) to receive; *we got a letter from the bank this morning; he will get £10 for washing the car; she gets more money than I do*

(b) to become; *I'm getting too old for rugby; she's getting deaf; he's got much fatter over the last year or so; the sun got hotter and hotter; the carpet's getting dirty*

(c) to have something done; *I must get my suit cleaned; we got the car mended in time to go on holiday*

(d) to persuade someone to do something; *can you get the garage to mend the brakes?; I'll try and get her to bring some CDs*

(e) to catch (an illness); *I think I'm getting a cold; he got measles just before the holiday started*

(f) to make something become; *he always gets his clothes dirty; she's busy getting the meal ready*

(g) to understand; *do you think he got my meaning?*; **got it!** = I've solved the problem! (NOTE: **getting - got** [gɒt] - **has got** *US* **gotten**)

② **get across**

['get ə'krɒs] *verb*

(a) to manage to cross; *they got across the river in little boats*

(b) to make someone understand; *I'm trying to get across to the people in the office that they all have to work harder; we just can't seem to get our message across*

② **get along**

['get ə'lɒŋ] *verb*

(a) to manage; *she got along quite well when her mother was away on holiday; we seem to get along very happily without the telephone; how are you getting along?*

(b) to get along (with someone) = to be friendly with someone, to work well with someone; *I don't think they get along*

③ **get at**

['get 'æt] *verb*

(a) to reach; *you'll need to stand on a chair to get at the box on the top shelf*

(b) *(informal)* **to get at someone** = to criticize someone all the time; *she thinks she's being got at*

(c) to mean; *what was he really getting at when he said that some people were not working hard enough?*

② **get away**

['get ə'weɪ] *verb*

(a) to escape; *the robbers got away in a stolen car*

(b) to get away with something = not to be punished for having done something; *he was rude to the magistrate, but got away with it somehow*; *(formal)* **to get away with murder** = to do something really bad and still not be punished for it; *he's the teacher's favourite and she lets him get away with murder*

(c) *(informal)* **get away with you!** = don't try to make me believe that!

① **get back**

['get 'bæk] *verb*

(a) to return; *they got back home very late; when did they get back from the cinema?*

(b) to get something again which you had before; *I got my money back after I had complained to the manager*; **to get your breath back** = to breathe normally after having been out of breath; *at my age, I can't walk uphill very far without stopping to get my breath back*

(c) to phone back or reply by post; *I'll find out what the situation is and get back to you as soon as I can*

③ **get by**

['get 'baɪ] *verb*

(informal)

(a) to manage to do something with difficulty; *I can just get by in German; how are you going to get by without a car?*

(b) to manage to live; *it is difficult for them to get by in New York on only $30 a day; they get by somehow on only £50 a week*

② **get down**

['get 'daun] *verb*

(a) to go back down onto the ground; *the cat climbed up the tree and couldn't get down; he got down off the ladder*

(b) to bring down; *can you get my suitcase down for me?*

(c) to make someone sad; *rainy weather always gets me down*

② **get down to**
['get 'daun tu:] *verb*
to get down to some hard work = to start working hard; *he will have to get down to work if he wants to pass the test*

② **get going**
['get 'gıuıŋ] *verb*
(informal) to start; *come on, let's get going!*

① **get in**
['get 'ın] *verb*
(a) to go inside (a car, etc.); *get in! - the train's going to leave; the burglars must have got in through the bathroom window*
(b) to arrive at home, at the office, etc.; *what time did you get in last night?; because of the train strike, we didn't get in until eleven o'clock*
(c) to ask someone to come to do a job; *we'll get a builder in to mend the wall*

① **get into**
['get 'ıntu:] *verb*
(a) to go inside (a car, etc.); *they got into the back of the car; I was just getting into bed when the phone rang; the burglars got into the building through a window on the ground floor*
(b) to get into the habit = to start to do something regularly; *he got into the habit of calling his father 'Boss'*; **to get into trouble** *or* **into difficulties** = to start to have problems; *he got into trouble with the police*

③ **get lost**
['get 'lɒst] *verb*
(a) not to know where you are; *he's hopeless, he got lost walking from Oxford Circus to Piccadilly; they should be back by now - do you think they've got lost?*
(b) *(slang)* **get lost!** = go away!; *when she asked him for money he told her to get lost*

① **get off**
['get 'ɒf] *verb*
(a) to come down from *or* out of (a vehicle, etc.); *she got off her bicycle at the red light; if you want the post office, you should get off at the next stop; to go to the Science Museum, you have to get off the Underground at South Kensington*
(b) not to be punished, or only receive a light punishment; *she was lucky to get off so lightly; he was found guilty of theft and got off with a fine*
(c) *(informal)* **to get off someone's back** = to stop being a nuisance to someone; *how can I get him off my back?*

① **get on**
['get 'ɒn] *verb*
(a) to go inside or onto (a vehicle, etc.); *they got on the bus at the bank; the policeman got on his bike and rode away*
(b) *(informal)* to become old; *he's getting on and can't work as hard as he used to*

(c) **to get on (well)** = to do well; *she's getting on well at university; my son is getting on well in his new job - he has just been promoted*
(d) to manage; *how is the new secretary getting on?*
(e) to be friendly with someone; *they don't get on at all well*

① **get on with**
['get ɒn 'wıð]
(a) to be friendly with someone; *he gets on very well with everyone; she doesn't get on with her new boss; they don't get on with one another*
(b) to continue to do some work; *he got on with his work and finished the job early*

① **get out**
['get 'aut] *verb*
(a) to take out; *I'll get the book out of the library; she was getting the car out of the garage and backed into a man on the pavement*
(b) to go out of something; *the bus stopped and the driver got out; the burglars got in through a window, but got out through the front door*
(c) **to get out of the habit of doing something** = not to do something any more; *I've got out of the habit of eating chocolates*
(d) **to get out of (doing) something** = to avoid doing something; *I want an excuse to get out of going to the office party*

② **get over**
['get 'ıuvı] *verb*
(a) to climb over; *they got over the wall into the garden*
(b) to become better; *he's got over his flu*
(c) to recover from a shock; *she never got over the death of her father*

② **get ready**
['get 'redı] *phrase*
(a) to prepare yourself for something; *how long will it take you to get ready for the wedding?*
(b) to get something prepared; *we need to get the dinner ready - the guests will be arriving in 30 minutes*

③ **get through**
['get 'θru:] *verb*
(a) to go through; *the cows got through the hole in the fence*
(b) to be successful; *he got through his exams, so he is now a qualified engineer*

③ **get through to**
['get 'θru: tu:] *verb*
(a) to make someone understand; *I could not get through to her that I had to be at the airport by 2.15*
(b) to manage to speak to someone on the phone; *I tried to get through to the complaints department but the line was always engaged*

③ **get to**
['get 'tu:] *verb*
(a) to arrive, to reach (a place); *we only got to the hotel at midnight; when does your train get*

to London?; the plane gets to New York at 4 p.m.; when you get to my age you'll see why I'm suggesting you should plan for the future

(b) to have got to = must or to be obliged to; you've got to come = you must come; he's got to be at the station at 8 o'clock; have you really got to work all night?

① **get up**
['get 'ʌp] verb

(a) to get out of bed; he went to bed so late that he didn't get up until 11 o'clock; it is 9.30 and John still hasn't got up

(b) to make someone get out of bed; you must get everyone up by 7.30 if we are going to leave on time

(c) to stand up; when he had finished his meal, he got up from the table and walked out of the room

③ **get up to**
['get 'ʌp tu:] verb

(a) to reach; stop reading when you get up to page 23

(b) to get up to something = to do something naughty; look at the mess in here - whatever did you get up to last night?

④ **ghost**
[gɪʊst] noun

(a) image of a dead person which appears; they say the Tower of London is haunted by the ghost of Anne Boleyn, who was executed there; his face is white - he looks as if he has seen a ghost; ghost story = frightening story about ghosts

(b) not to have a ghost of a chance = to have no chance at all; she's gone in for the competition, but she doesn't have a ghost of a chance of winning

④ **giant**
['dʒaɪnt]
1 noun

(a) (in children's stories) very large man; a story about a giant who lived in a castle at the top of a mountain

(b) any very large person, company, plant or building; he's a giant of a man; shares in the computer giant have soared
2 adjective

very large; he's grown a giant cabbage; they are planning a giant car factory in South Wales

② **gift**
[gɪft] noun

(a) present, something given to someone; the wedding gifts were displayed on a table; she was wrapping up gifts to put under the Christmas tree; gift shop = shop which sells things which are often given as presents; gift token = card given as a present, which you can exchange for goods to a certain value; I couldn't think of what to buy her, so I gave her a gift token for her birthday; gift voucher = card bought in a store, which you give as a present and which must be exchanged in that store for

goods; it will be simpler to give her a gift voucher since we can't decide on a present; see also LOOK

(b) special ability for something; he has a gift for maths; she has a gift for saying things which annoy her father

② **giggle**
['gɪgl]
1 noun

(a) little laugh, often showing you are embarrassed; fit of the giggles = attack of laughter which you cannot stop; when the singer came onto the stage, I had a fit of the giggles

(b) (informal) for a giggle = for fun, as a joke; we did it for a giggle
2 verb

to make a little laugh; when she saw her mother's hat she started giggling; the class giggled at his way of walking

④ **ginger**
['dʒɪndʒɪ]
1 noun

(a) plant whose root has a sharp taste and is used in cooking; fry the meat with onions and slices of ginger; add a pinch of powdered ginger to the cake mixture; ginger biscuits = hard biscuits, flavoured with ginger

(b) (informal) name given to someone with orange hair; hey, Ginger! come and help with these boxes

(c) ginger beer or dry ginger = fizzy non-alcoholic drink flavoured with ginger
2 adjective

(of hair) bright orange in colour; she has ginger hair and green eyes; a ginger cat sat on the doorstep in the sun
3 verb

to ginger something up = to make something more lively; we need something to ginger up the party conference

① **girl**
[gɜːl] noun

(a) female child; they have four children - two boys and two girls; a crowd of girls waiting at the bus stop; my sister goes to the local girls' school

(b) young woman; career girl = woman who is working in business and does not plan to stop working to look after the house or children (NOTE: it is sometimes better to use the word **career woman** in this meaning)

③ **girlfriend**
['gɜːlfrend] noun

girl or woman, usually young, that someone is very friendly with; he's broken up with his girlfriend; on Saturdays she always has lunch with a group of girlfriends; see also BOYFRIEND

① **give**
['gɪv]
1 *verb*
(a) to send or pass something to someone as a present; *we gave her flowers for her birthday*; *what are you going to give him when he gets married?*; *we gave ten pounds to the Red Cross*
(b) to pass something to someone; *give me another piece of cake*; *can you give me some information about holidays in Greece*
(c) to do something (to someone); *she gave a deep sigh*; *he gave me a broad smile*; *he gave her a kiss*; *she gave the ball a kick*
(d) to organize; *they gave a dinner for the visiting Foreign Minister*; *we gave a party to celebrate her twenty-first birthday*
(e) to do something in public; *she gave a concert in aid of the Red Cross*; *he will be giving the opening speech at the conference*; *she has been asked to give a lecture on Shakespeare*
(f) to bend; *the piece of wood gave as he stepped on it* (NOTE: **giving - gave** [geɪv] - **has given** ['gɪvn])
2 *noun*
give and take = agreement between two people to make concessions; *what we need is a little give and take on both sides*

① **give away**
['gɪv ə'weɪ] *verb*
(a) to give as a present; *we are giving away a pocket calculator with each £10 of purchases*
(b) to reveal something which you are trying to keep secret; *his accent gave him away*; *she gave herself away by saying that she had never been to France*
(c) to lead the bride to the bridegroom at a wedding; *she was given away by her father*

① **give back**
['gɪv 'bæk] *verb*
to hand something back to someone; *give me back my watch* or *give me my watch back*; *the burglars gave back everything they had taken*; *she borrowed my book and hasn't given it back*

③ **give in**
['gɪv 'ɪn] *verb*
to agree to do something even if you didn't want to do it; *the children kept on asking him if they could go to the cinema and in the end he gave in*

② **given**
['gɪvn]
1 *adjective*
(a) having the habit of; *he is given to sitting at home drinking all by himself*
(b) particular; **at a given point in time** = at a particular moment
(c) **given name** = first name *or* Christian name of a person, as opposed to the surname or family name
2 *conjunction*

given that = because; *given that it's his birthday, it's a shame he couldn't have the day off*

③ **give out**
['gɪv 'aut] *verb*
(a) to give to everyone; *she gave out presents to all the children*
(b) to come to an end; *the battery has given out so I can't use my watch*

① **give up**
['gɪv 'ʌp] *verb*
(a) to stop doing something; *she's trying to give up smoking*
(b) **I give up** = I don't know the answer
(c) **to give yourself up** = to surrender to an enemy, the police, etc.; *he gave himself up to the police*; *they shouted to the gang to come out of the bank and give themselves up*

③ **give way**
['gɪv 'weɪ] *phrase*
(a) to let someone go first; *give way to traffic coming from the right*
(b) to collapse; *the chair gave way when he sat on it*

② **glad**
[glæd] *adjective*
pleased; *Aunt Jane was glad to get your postcard*; *the bank manager is glad you paid*; *after shopping all day, she was glad to find somewhere to sit down*; *(informal)* **glad rags** = party clothes

④ **gladly**
['glædli] *adverb*
in a pleased way, with great pleasure; *I'll gladly look after your dog while you're away*

④ **glamorous**
['glæmɪrɪs] *adjective*
attractive; *your grandmother looks very glamorous for her age*; *he came to dinner with a glamorous blonde*; *she wants to lead the glamorous life of a film star*

③ **glance**
[glɑːns]
1 *noun*
quick look; *she gave him an admiring glance*; *she took a quick glance over her shoulder*
2 *verb*
(a) to look quickly; *he glanced over his shoulder to see who was following him*; *she glanced round to attract the waiter's attention*
(b) **to glance off something** = to slide off something instead of hitting it straight on; *the ball glanced off the edge of the table*

④ **gland**
[glænd] *noun*
organ in the body which produces a chemical substance; *sweat comes from the sweat glands*; *hormones are produced by glands*

④ glare
['gleɪ]

1 *noun*

(a) very bright light; *the glare of the sun on the wet road blinded me*; *pop stars live their lives in the glare of publicity*

(b) fierce look; *he gave her a glare and walked on*

2 *verb*

(a) to shine very brightly; *the sun was glaring down on the square*

(b) to look angrily; *she glared at me and went on reading her book*

① glass
[glɑːs] *noun*

(a) material which you can see through, used to make windows, etc.; *a bowl made of glass* or *a glass bowl*; *the roof of the house is made of glass* or *the house has a glass roof*; *a car with black glass windows* (NOTE: no plural: *some glass, a piece of glass*)

(b) thing to drink out of, usually made of glass; *we took plastic wine glasses on the picnic*; *she put the dirty glasses in the sink*

(c) liquid contained in a glass; *she asked for a glass of water*; *he was so thirsty he drank three glasses of lemonade*; *add a glass of red wine to the sauce* (NOTE: plural is **glasses** for meanings (b) and (c))

② glasses
['glɑːsɪz] *noun*

two pieces of plastic or glass in a frame which you wear in front of your eyes to help you see better; *have you seen my glasses anywhere?*; *she has to wear glasses to read*; **dark glasses** = glasses made of dark glass, for wearing in sunshine; *he noticed he was being followed by two men wearing dark glasses* (NOTE: **glasses** are also called **spectacles**. Dark glasses are also called **sunglasses**)

④ gleam
[gliːm]

1 *noun*

(a) small light; *he saw the gleam of a flashlight in the distance*

(b) slight sign of feeling shown by your eyes; *he saw a gleam of recognition in the boy's eyes*; *there was a wild gleam in her eyes*

2 *verb*

to shine as if polished; *a line of gleaming black cars*

④ glimpse
[glɪmps]

1 *noun*

brief sight; *we caught a glimpse of the princess as she drove past*; *there was a brief glimpse of the sun during the afternoon*

2 *verb*

to catch sight of; *we only glimpsed the back of her head as she was leaving*

④ glitter
['glɪtɪ]

1 *noun*

bright sparkle of light; *the glitter of the sun on the sea*; *she was attracted by the glitter of the West End theatres*

2 *verb*

to sparkle; *the jewels in the king's crown were glittering in the light of the candles*; *her eyes glittered hopefully as she spoke*; **all that glitters is not gold** = things which look very attractive on the surface often turn out not to be attractive really

③ global
['gloʊbl] *adjective*

(a) referring to the whole world; *we offer a global parcel delivery service*; **global warming** = warming of the earth's atmosphere, caused by pollution

(b) referring to the whole of something; *we are carrying out a global review of salaries*

④ globe
[gloʊb] *noun*

(a) **the globe** = the earth; *he is trying to be the first person to fly round the globe in a balloon*

(b) map of the world on a ball; *he spun the globe round and pointed to Canada*

(c) **the Globe (Theatre)** = one of the original London theatres where Shakespeare's plays were performed, now built again; *have you seen the production of 'Henry V' at the Globe?*

④ gloom
[gluːm] *noun*

(a) darkness; *it was difficult to see anything in the gloom of the old church*

(b) deep despair; *a feeling of deep gloom came down on the family*; *when the exam results came out everyone was filled with gloom*

③ gloomy
['gluːmɪ] *adjective*

(a) miserable, unhappy; *she was gloomy about her chances of passing the exam*; *he's very gloomy about his job prospects*

(b) dark; *a gloomy Sunday afternoon in November* (NOTE: **gloomier - gloomiest**)

④ glorious
['glɔːrɪɪs] *adjective*

splendid; *a glorious June afternoon*

④ glory
['glɔːrɪ]

1 *noun*

(a) fame; *I did it for the glory of the school, not for myself*; **the team covered themselves with glory** = the team had a marvellous win

(b) wonderful sight; *it is one of the glories of ancient Rome*

2 *verb*

to glory in = to take great pride in; *she glories in beating her brother at chess*

glove
[glʌv] *noun*

piece of clothing worn on your hand; *she gave him a pair of gloves for his birthday*; *you might have left one of your gloves on the train*; **oven gloves** = thick gloves which you wear to take hot dishes out of an oven; *see also* HAND

glow
[gləʊ]

1 *noun*

(a) soft bright light; *the warm glow of the fire*
(b) bright red colour of your cheeks; *the glow of the children's cheeks as they came back into the house*

2 *verb*

to shine red; *the logs glowed in the fireplace*; *her face glowed with pride*

glue
[gluː]

1 *noun*

substance which sticks; *she spread the glue carefully onto the back of the poster*; *the glue on the envelope doesn't stick very well*; **glue sniffing** = form of drug abuse where addicts breathe in the gas from a strong glue

2 *verb*

(a) to stick things together; *he glued the label to the box*
(b) **to be glued to** = to sit in front of without moving; *the children sat glued to the TV set*

GNP
[dʒiːenˈpiː] = GROSS NATIONAL PRODUCT

go
[gəʊ]

1 *verb*

(a) to move from one place to another; *the plane goes to Frankfurt, then to Rome*; *she is going to London for the weekend*; *he has gone to work in Washington*; *they are going on a tour of the south of Spain*; *she was going downstairs when she fell*; *the car was carrying so much luggage that it had difficulty going up hills*; *they went on board at 8 o'clock*; *how do you go to school - by bike or by bus?*; *she has gone shopping*
(b) to work; *can you phone the garage? - the car won't go*; *he's trying to get his motorbike to go*
(c) to leave; *get your coat, it's time to go*; *the last bus goes at half past two*
(d) to fit; *it's too big to go into the box*; *this case won't go into the back of the car*
(e) to be placed; *the date should go at the top of the letter*; *that book goes on the top shelf*
(f) to become; *her face went red from sitting in the sun*; *he went pale and rushed out of the room*; *you have to shout, my father's going deaf*; *she's going grey, but it suits her*
(g) to happen (successfully or not); *the party went very well*; *things are not going badly at the office*
(h) to make a sound; *the balloon landed on a candle and went 'pop'*; *do you remember the song that goes: 'there's no place like home'?*
(i) *(informal)* to fail to work; *as we were going down the hill, the brakes went* (NOTE: **going - went** [went] **- has gone** [gɒn])

2 *noun*

(a) **on the go** = always busy; *the shop is so busy before Christmas that we're on the go from morning till night*; **to make a go of something** = to make something work successfully; *they're struggling to make a go of their business*; **she's always full of go** = she always has plenty of energy
(b) try, attempt; *he won the lottery at the first go*; *she had three goes at the test and still didn't pass*; *we'll give it one more go, and if the car doesn't start I'll call the garage*

◊ to be going to
[biː ˈgəʊɪŋ tuː] *phrase*

(a) *(showing future)* *we're going to win*; *I hope it's going to be fine tomorrow*; *when are you going to wash your hair?*; *he's going to be a great tennis player when he's older*; *is she going to sing at the concert?*
(b) **to be going to do something** = to be about to do something; *I'm going to be late for the meeting*; *watch out - that tree is going to fall down!*; *I am going to sit in bed and read my newspaper*

go about
[ˈgəʊ əˈbaʊt] *verb*

to arrange to do something; *how do you go about getting a new passport?*; *we'd like to set up a company but I'm not sure how to go about ti*

go ahead
[ˈgəʊ əˈhed] *verb*

to start; *the project went ahead even though there were not enough staff*

go-ahead
[ˈgəʊhed]

1 *noun*

to give something the go-ahead = to give permission for something to start; *we got the council's go-ahead to build the new supermarket*

2 *adjective*

(person) who works hard; *a go-ahead publicity firm*; *the company needs a go-ahead managing director*

goal
[gəʊl] *noun*

(a) *(in games)* two posts between which you have to send the ball to score a point; *he was unlucky to miss the goal with that shot*
(b) *(in games)* point scored by sending the ball between the posts; *he scored a goal before being sent off*; *our team scored three goals*
(c) aim; *our goal is to open a new pizza restaurant every month*; *he achieved his goal of becoming a millionaire before he was thirty*

③ **goalkeeper**
['gəʊlkiːpə] *noun*
player who stands in front of the goal to stop the
ball going in; *the goalkeeper dropped the ball
and the other team scored*

④ **goat**
[gəʊt] *noun*
small farm animal with horns and a beard,
giving milk and wool; *they keep a herd of goats*;
goat's cheese = cheese made from goat's milk;
to separate the sheep from the goats = to
divide the good from the bad (NOTE: males are
called **billy goats,** and females are called **nanny
goats,** and the young are **kids**)

① **go away**
['gəʊ ə'weɪ] *verb*
to leave; *he went away and we never saw him
again*

① **go back**
['gəʊ 'bæk] *verb*
to return; *she went back to the shop and asked if
she could change the gloves; she worked for
two years and then went back to college*

③ **go back on**
['gəʊ 'bæk ɒn] *verb*
not to do what has been promised; *he promised
faithfully to lend me his car, and then went
back on his promise*

① **God**
[gɒd]
1 *noun*
(a) **God** = the most important being, the being to
whom people pray; *do you believe in God?; we
pray to God that the children will be found
alive*
(b) superior being, not a human being; *Bacchus
was the Roman god of wine*
2 *interjection*
(a) *(showing surprise, etc.)* **God, what awful
weather!; my God, have you seen how late it
is?; Good God, that's John from accounts
department over there!**
(b) *(showing thanks)* **Thank God no one was
hurt in the crash!; Thank God the ambulance
arrived in time!**

④ **goddess**
['gɒdes] *noun*
female god; *Diana was the goddess of hunting*
(NOTE: plural is **goddesses**)

① **go down**
['gəʊ daʊn] *verb*
(a) to go to a lower level; *there are thirty-nine
steps which go down to the beach; be careful
when going down the hill; after having a rest in
her bedroom, she went down to the hotel bar*
(b) *(informal)* to catch a disease; *half the crew
went down with flu*

① **go in**
['gəʊ 'ɪn] *verb*
to enter; *she opened the door and went in; did
you see anyone go in?*

① **go in for**
['gəʊ 'ɪn fɔː] *verb*
(a) to take (an examination); *she went in for her
swimming test*
(b) to take up as a career; *he's going in for
medicine*

① **going**
['gəʊɪŋ]
1 *adjective*
(a) working well; *the business is being sold as a
going concern*
(b) normal, usual; **the going rate** = the usual
rate, the current rate of payment; *what is the
current going rate for a 1996 model?; he was
happy to pay the going rate; the going rate for
secretaries is £15.00 per hour*
2 *noun*
(a) surface of a race track; *the going is soft after
last night's rain*; **do it while the going is good** =
do it while it is still possible
(b) **goings-on** = strange things that happen; *you
would never believe the goings-on in the flat
upstairs*

① **go into**
['gəʊ 'ɪntuː] *verb*
(a) to enter; *she went into the bedroom*
(b) to examine, to look at something carefully;
*the bank wants to go into the details of his
account*
(c) to explain in detail; *she said she had a job
offer but wouldn't go into any details*
(d) *(in maths)* to be able to divide a number to
give a figure; *seven into three won't go*

② **gold**
[gəʊld] *noun*
(a) very valuable yellow-coloured metal; *that
ring isn't made of gold; gold is worth more
than silver; he wears a gold ring on his little
finger*; see also GOOD (NOTE: no plural: **some
gold, a bar of gold.** Note also that gold is a
chemical element: chemical symbol: **Au**; atomic
number: **79**)
(b) **gold (medal)** = medal given to someone
who finishes first in a race or competition;
England won three golds at the Olympics; see
also BRONZE, SILVER

③ **gold card**
['gəʊld 'kɑːd] *noun*
special credit card for people with high salaries;
*after I was promoted, the bank offered me a
gold card*

③ **golden**
['gəʊldɪn] *adjective*
coloured like gold; *she has beautiful golden
hair*; **golden boy** = young man who is popular
and a great success; *he's the golden boy of
English football*; *(in World Cup football)*
golden goal = the first goal to be scored in extra
time which decides the winner of a match;
golden opportunity = marvellous chance which
will not happen again; *he had a golden
opportunity to make his fortune and he didn't*

take it; **golden wedding (anniversary)** = celebration when two people have been married for fifty years

② **golf**
[gɒlf] *noun*
a game played on a large open course, by hitting a small ball into 18 separate holes with a variety of clubs, using as few strokes as possible; *he plays golf every Saturday; do you want a game of golf?*

COMMENT: the game is for two people, or two couples; a small hard ball is struck with a thin club with a long handle, into a series of little holes (either 9 or 18), the object being to use as few strokes as possible

---

③ **golf club**
['gɒlf 'klʌb] *noun*
(a) stick used to hit the ball in golf; *she put her golf clubs into the back of the car*
(b) organization for people who play golf together; *he's joined his local golf club*

④ **golfer**
['gɒlfɪ] *noun*
person who plays golf

③ **gone**
[gɒn] *see* GO

① **good**
[gʊd]
1 *adjective*
(a) not bad; *we had a good breakfast and then started work; did you have a good time at the party?; it would be a good idea to invest in these shares; her Spanish is better than his*
(b) clever; *he's good at making things out of wood; she's good with her hands; he is good at football*
(c) who behaves well; *be a good girl and I'll give you a sweet; have you been good while we've been away?;* **as good as gold** = not at all naughty; *the children were as good as gold*
(d) **a good deal of** *or* **a good many** = a lot of; *he won a good deal of money on the lottery; a good many people saw the accident*
(e) **good for** = making better or healthy; *running a mile before breakfast is good for you; they say that eating carrots is good for your sight* (NOTE: **good - better** ['betɪ] **- best** [best])
2 *noun*
(a) advantage, making better; *the medicine didn't do me any good; he decided to give up smoking for the good of his health; what's the good of having a big garden if you don't like gardening?; governments should work for the good of the people*
(b) **for good** = for ever; *he's left the town for good*
(c) **no good** = useless, not working; *this computer's no good*

① **good afternoon**
['gʊd ɑːftɪ'nuːn] *interjection; (used when meeting or leaving someone in the afternoon)* **I just want to say good afternoon to the head teacher**

① **goodbye**
[gʊd'baɪ] *noun & interjection; (used when leaving someone)* **say goodbye to your teacher; goodbye! we'll see you again on Thursday** (NOTE: often shortened to **bye**)

① **good evening**
['gʊd 'iːvnɪŋ] *interjection; (used when meeting or leaving someone in the evening)* **good evening, Mrs Smith!**

③ **Good Friday**
['gʊd 'fraɪdeɪ] *noun*
the Friday before Easter Day

COMMENT: traditionally, hot cross buns (little round loaves, with spices inside and a sugar cross on top) are eaten on Good Friday

---

④ **good-looking**
['gʊd'lʊkɪŋ] *adjective*
(of a person) pleasant to look at; *she's a very good-looking girl; he's very good-looking, with lots of girlfriends; he's far better-looking than his brother*

① **good morning**
['gʊd 'mɔːnɪŋ] *interjection; (used when meeting or leaving someone in the morning)* **good morning, Mr Smith!**

④ **goodness**
['gʊdnɪs] *noun*
(a) being good; *she did it out of pure goodness of heart*
(b) **thank goodness!** = phrase which shows relief; *thank goodness the ambulance arrived quickly!*
(c) **for goodness' sake** = expression showing you are annoyed, or that something is important; *what are you screaming for? - it's only a little mouse, for goodness' sake; for goodness' sake try to be quiet, we don't want the guards to hear us!*

① **goodnight**
[gʊd'naɪt] *interjection; (used when leaving someone late in the evening)* **goodnight, everyone! sleep well!**

② **goods**
[gʊdz] *noun*
(a) things that are produced for sale; *the company sells goods from various European countries;* **goods train** = train for carrying goods, not passengers
(b) possessions, things which you own; *she carried all the goods she possessed in a bag*

④ **goodwill**
[gʊd'wɪl] *noun*
(a) kind feeling; *the charity relies on the goodwill of people who give money regularly*

(b) *(of a business)* value of the customers, reputation, site, etc.; *he paid £10,000 for the goodwill of the restaurant and £40,000 for the fittings*

> COMMENT: goodwill can include the reputation of the business, the trade names it uses, the value of a 'good site', etc.; all this is very difficult to calculate accurately

ⓘ **go off**
['gɪʊ 'ɒf] *verb*
(a) to go to another place; *he went off to look for a parking space; she went off saying something about buying cheese*
(b) to start working suddenly; *the burglar alarm went off in the middle of the night*
(c) to explode; *the bomb went off when there were still lots of people in the building*
(d) to become rotten; *throw that meat away - it's gone off; fish goes off quickly in hot weather*
(e) *(informal)* not to like something any more; *I've gone off modern music; she went off her new boyfriend quite quickly*

ⓘ **go on**
['gɪʊ 'ɒn] *verb*
(a) to continue; *please go on, I like hearing you sing; they went on working in spite of the fire; she went on speaking for two hours; don't ask questions, just go on with your work;* to go on about something = to talk all the time about something; *she keeps going on about how poor she is*
(b) to happen; *what's been going on here?*
(c) to base your opinion and actions on; *the police investigating the murder don't have much to go on; we have to go on the assumption that the concert will start on time*
(d) *(informal)* *(showing you don't believe someone)* *Go on! She's not as old as that!*

ⓘ **goose**
[guːs] *noun*
large bird, living near water, both wild and bred on farms; *a flock of wild geese landed on the runway; they keep a flock of geese in the warehouse to ward off thieves* (NOTE: plural is **geese** [giːs])

ⓘ **go out**
['gɪʊ 'aʊt] *verb*
(a) to leave a building; *I don't go out often at night; he forgot to lock the door when he went out*
(b) not to be burning any more; *the fire went out and the room got cold; all the lights in the building suddenly went out*
(c) to go out of business = to stop trading; *the firm went out of business last week*

ⓘ **gorgeous**
['gɔːdʒɪs] *adjective*
magnificent; *the bird spread out its gorgeous tail; he came to the party with a gorgeous blonde*

ⓘ **go round**
['gɪʊ 'raʊnd] *verb*
(a) to turn; *the wheels went round and round*
(b) to turn round something; *we went round the roundabout and took the third road on the left*
(c) to visit; *you'll need at least two hours to go round the museum*
(d) to be enough; *there wasn't enough ice cream to go round*
(e) to go to somewhere near; *let's go round to your sister's; we all went round to the pub for a drink*

④ **gospel**
['gɒspl] *noun*
(a) part of the Bible which tells the life of Jesus Christ; it's the gospel truth = it's absolutely true
(b) gospel music = religious music which first became popular in the USA during the Depression

② **gossip**
['gɒsɪp]
1 *noun*
(a) stories or news about someone, which may or may not be true; *have you heard the latest gossip about Sue?;* to spread gossip about someone = to tell stories about someone (which may or may not be true); gossip column = column in a newspaper which tells stories about famous people; gossip columnist = person who writes a gossip column
(b) person who spreads gossip; *be careful what you say to him - he's a great gossip*
2 *verb*
to talk about people; *they spent hours gossiping about the people working in the office*

③ **got**
[gɒt]
see GET

③ **go through**
['gɪʊ 'θruː] *verb*
to go through with something = to continue with something; *they decided not to go through with their planned pig farm because of the objections from their neighbours*

③ **gotten**
['gɒtn] *US see* GET

③ **go under**
['gɪʊ 'ʌndɪ] *verb*
to fail, to go bankrupt; *the company went under during the recession*

ⓘ **go up**
['gɪʊ 'ʌp] *verb*
(a) to go to a higher place; *take the lift and go up to the fourth floor*
(b) to increase, to rise to a higher level; *the price of bread has gone up*

③ **govern**
['gʌvɪn] *verb*
(a) to rule a country; *the country is governed by three generals*

(b) to influence, to have an effect on; *inflation is governed by interest rates and exchange rates*

① **government**
['gʌvimint] *noun*
(a) system of ruling a country; *the country is aiming to achieve democratic government* (NOTE: no plural in this meaning)
(b) central government = main organization, dealing with the affairs of the whole country; **local government** = organizations dealing with the affairs of small areas of the country, such as towns and counties; **provincial government** *or* **state government** = government of a province or state
(c) people or political party which governs; *the president asked the leader of the largest party in parliament to form a new government*; *everything was working very well until the government stepped in*; *the government controls the price of bread*; *he has an important job in the government*; **the Thatcher government** = the ministers who formed the cabinet when Mrs Thatcher was Prime Minister; **a government department** = a section of the government with a particular responsibility

③ **governor**
['gʌvni] *noun*
person who runs a state, institution, etc.; *the Governor of Alabama*; **a prison governor** = person in charge of a prison; **the Governor of the Bank of England** = person (nominated by the British government) who is in charge of the Bank of England

① **go with**
['gɪʊ 'wɪθ] *verb*
(a) to match; *blue shoes won't go with a green dress*; *red wine goes best with meat*
(b) to be linked to; *that remote control goes with the TV*; *he has a big house that goes with his job*

① **go without**
['gɪʊ wɪ'ðaʊt] *verb*
not to have something which you usually have; *after getting lost in the mountains, they went without food for three days*; *she got up late and had to go without breakfast*; *we have too much work, so we'll have to go without a holiday this year*

④ **gown**
[gaʊn] *noun*
(a) long black coat worn by a judge, person with degree, etc., over normal clothes; *she wore her new gown to the degree ceremony*; *see also* DRESSING GOWN
(b) *(formal)* woman's long formal dress; *a ball gown*

③ **go wrong**
['gɪʊ 'rɒŋ] *phrase*
to stop working properly; *the station clock's gone wrong*; *something has gone wrong with the central heating*

③ **GP**
['dʒiː 'piː] *noun*
= GENERAL PRACTITIONER
family doctor who does not specialize in any particular branch of medicine; *our son wants to be a GP*; *see your GP first, and he will refer you to a specialist*

③ **grab**
[græb]
1 *noun*
to make a grab for something = to try to seize something; *he made a grab for her wallet*; *(informal)* **up for grabs** = available to anyone who wants to get it; *the company is up for grabs*; *now the champion has retired the world title is up for grabs*
2 *verb*
(a) to pick something up suddenly; *he grabbed his suitcase and ran to the train*
(b) to get something quickly; *let's grab some lunch before the meeting starts*
(c) *(informal)* **how does it grab you?** = what do you think of it?; *a weekend in Paris - how does that grab you?* (NOTE: **grabbing - grabbed**)

④ **grace**
[greɪs] *noun*
(a) being elegant and attractive; *the grace of the deer as they ran off into the woods*; **with good grace** = quite cheerfully; *he accepted the criticisms with good grace*
(b) prayer before a meal; *father always says grace before dinner*
(c) extra time to pay; *to give a creditor two weeks' grace to pay*

③ **grade**
[greɪd]
1 *noun*
(a) level of quality; *I always buy grade I eggs*; *what grade of vegetables do you sell most of?*; **to make the grade** = to succeed, to do well; **high-grade** *or* **top-grade** = best quality; **low-grade** = worst quality
(b) exam mark; *she got top grades in maths*
(c) *US* class in school; *students in fifth grade*; *she's a fifth grade student*
2 *verb*
to sort according to size or quality; *a machine for grading fruit*; *hotels are graded with two, three, four or five stars*

③ **grade crossing**
['greɪd 'krɒsɪŋ] *noun*
US place where a road crosses a railroad line; *the bus was held up at a grade crossing while a train passed* (NOTE: British English is **level crossing**)

③ **gradual**
['grædjʊɪl] *adjective*
which changes a little at a time; *we're forecasting a gradual improvement in the weather*

gradually

['grædjʋili] *adverb*

little by little; *his condition improved gradually day by day*; *she gradually learnt how to deal with customers' complaints*

graduate

1 *noun*

['grædjʋit]

person with a degree from a university *US* person with a degree from a college; *he's a graduate of London University*; *she's a physics graduate*; **graduate training scheme** = scheme which trains graduates for work in business

2 *verb*

['grædjʋeit] to get a degree; *she graduated from Edinburgh university last year*

grain

[grein] *noun*

(a) cereal crop; *a field of grain*; *the grain harvest*; *see also* ELEVATOR

(b) a very small piece; *a grain of sand*

(c) patterns of lines in wood; *this old oak table has a beautiful grain*; **to go against the grain** = to go against your natural feelings; *it goes against the grain to throw away all that good food*

gram *or* gramme

[græm] *noun*

weight equal to one thousandth of a kilogram; *you will need 250g of sugar*; *this piece of fish weighs 500 grams* (NOTE: when used with numbers, **gram** is usually written **g** *or* **gm: 50g**)

grammar

['græmi] *noun*

(a) rules of a language; *Russian grammar is very difficult*; *he's been learning English for years, and still makes grammar mistakes*

(b) book of rules of a language; *I'll look it up in my new German grammar*

grand

[grænd]

1 *adjective*

(a) big and important; *his grand plan for making a lot of money*

(b) imposing; *we went to a very grand wedding*; *for the grand final scene everyone wore gold dresses*

(c) final; **grand total** = the total of all the figures (NOTE: **grander - grandest**)

2 *noun*

(informal) one thousand pounds *or* dollars; *they offered him fifty grand for the information*

grandchild

['græntʃaild] *noun*

child of a son or daughter; *all her grandchildren came to the old lady's eightieth birthday party* (NOTE: plural is **grandchildren** ['græntʃɪldrɪn])

granddaughter

['grændɔːti] *noun*

daughter of a son or daughter; *my granddaughter is nineteen now, and at university*; *our little granddaughter is just starting to talk*

grandfather

['grænfaːði] *noun*

father of your mother or father; *tomorrow is grandfather's hundredth birthday*; *my grandfather can remember seeing the first planes flying*; **a grandfather clock** = a tall clock (NOTE: often called **grandad** *or* **grandpa** by children)

grandmother

['grænmʌði] *noun*

mother of your mother or father; *it will be grandmother's ninetieth birthday next month*; *grandmother showed me how to make bread* (NOTE: often called **gran** *or* **granny** *or* **grandma** *or* **nan** by children)

grandparents

['grændpeirints] *noun*

parents of your mother or father; *my grandparents are all dead*

grandson

['grænsʌn] *noun*

son of a son or daughter; *her grandson is nearly eighteen, and will be leaving school soon*; *our grandson is called Nicholas*

grant

[graːnt]

1 *noun*

sum of money to help; *not many students get a full grant*; *my grant only pays for a few books*; *we have applied for a grant to plant trees by the side of the road*

2 *verb*

(a) to agree to give something; *the government has granted them a loan at very low interest*; **to take something for granted** = to assume that you will get something, or will keep something, and so not to appreciate it; *the children seem to take it for granted that I will give them big presents every birthday*

(b) *(formal)* to admit; *I grant you it's going to be difficult, but I'm sure you'll do it well*

grape

[greip] *noun*

fruit of the vine, eaten as dessert or used to make wine; *he bought a bunch of grapes*; *see also* SOUR

grapefruit

['greipfruːt] *noun*

large yellow fruit, like an orange but not as sweet; *a glass of grapefruit juice*; *I'll start my breakfast with half a grapefruit, please* (NOTE: plural is **grapefruit**)

graph

[graːf] *noun*

chart showing figures in the form of a line; *the sales graph is going up*; *he drew a graph to show the fall in the number of fatal accidents over the last ten years*; *he plotted the rise in house prices on a graph*; **graph paper** = paper with little squares, for drawing graphs

④ **graphic**
['græfik] *adjective*
(a) drawn; *the results are shown in graphic form*
(b) vivid; *he gave a graphic description of the accident*

③ **graphics**
['græfiks] *noun*
pictures on a computer screen or designed on a computer; *the graphics on this game are brilliant*

④ **grasp**
[grɑːsp]
1 *noun*
(a) tight hold; *she pulled his hair, and forced him to loosen his grasp on her arm*
(b) understanding; *she has a good grasp of physics*
2 *verb*
(a) to hold tightly; *she grasped the branch of the tree with both hands*
(b) to understand; *they didn't seem to grasp my meaning*

② **grass**
[grɑːs]
1 *noun*
(a) low green plant, which is eaten by sheep and cows in fields, or used in gardens to make lawns; *the grass is getting too long - it needs cutting*; *the cows are eating the fresh green grass*
(b) lawn; *keep off the grass!*; *we'll sit on the grass and have our picnic*; *(informal)* **not to let the grass grow under your feet** = to waste no time in doing something; *they don't let the grass grow under their feet - they phoned immediately they saw the ad*
(c) *(informal)* person who gives information to the police; *the police gave the grass special protection*
2 *verb*
(informal) **to grass on someone** = to give information about someone to the police; *he grassed on his friends*

④ **grate**
[greit]
1 *noun*
metal frame for holding coal or logs in a fireplace; *he put some more coal into the grate*
2 *verb*
(a) to make into small pieces by rubbing against a rough surface; *sprinkle grated cheese over your pasta*; *we made a salad of grated carrots and spring onions*
(b) to make a rough irritating noise; *the sound of metal grating on stone makes my teeth hurt*
(c) to make someone annoyed; *the way he sings while he works is beginning to grate on my nerves* (NOTE: do not confuse with **great**)

③ **grateful**
['greitfʊl] *adjective*
showing thanks for something that someone has done for you; *we are most grateful to you for your help*

④ **gratefully**
['greitfʊli] *adverb*
in a grateful way; *she took the money gratefully*

④ **grave**
[greiv]
1 *noun*
hole in the ground where a dead person is buried; *the whole family put flowers on the grave*; *(informal)* **to have one foot in the grave** = to be old; *(of dead person)* **would turn in their grave** = would be annoyed; *Father would turn in his grave if he saw what they have done to his house*
2 *adjective*
(a) important, worrying; *it is a very grave offence*; *he is in court facing grave charges*
(b) quietly serious; *she looked at him with a grave expression* (NOTE: **graver - gravest**)

③ **gravity**
['græviti] *noun*
(a) force which pulls things towards the ground; *apples fall to the ground because of the earth's gravity*; **centre of gravity** = the point in an object at which it will balance; *a bus has a very low centre of gravity*
(b) *(formal)* being very serious; *no one seems to realize the gravity of the situation*

② **gray**
[grei] *US* = GREY

④ **graze**
[greiz]
1 *noun*
slight wound; *he had a graze on his knee*
2 *verb*
(a) to hurt the skin slightly; *he fell off his bicycle and grazed his knee*
(b) to feed on grass; *the sheep were grazing on the hillside*

① **great**
[greit] *adjective*
(a) large; *we visited the Great Wall of China*; *she was carrying a great big pile of sandwiches*; **a great deal of** *or* **a great many** = a lot of; *there's a great deal of work to be done*; *she earns a great deal of money*; *a great many people will lose their jobs*
(b) important or famous; *New York is a great city*; *Picasso was a great artist*; *the greatest tennis player of all time*
(c) *(informal)* wonderful, very good; *we had a great time at the party*; *what did you think of the film? - it was great!*; *it was great of you to help*; *it was great that they could all get to the picnic*
(d) *(humorous)* **the great and the good** = people who occupy influential positions in society; *the government looked through the*

ranks of the great and the good to find someone to be chairman of the board of the museum (NOTE: do not confuse with **grate**. Note also: **greater - greatest**)

② **Great Britain (GB)**
[greɪt 'brɪtɪn] *noun*
country formed of England, Scotland and Wales (which with Northern Ireland makes up the United Kingdom); *they came to live in Great Britain some time ago; in Great Britain cars drive on the left hand side of the road* (NOTE: capital: **London**; people: **British**; language: **English**; currency: **pound sterling (£)**)

③ **greatly**
['greɪtli] *adverb*
very much; *they greatly enjoyed the birthday party*

① **Greece**
[griːs] *noun*
country in southern Europe; *we go to Greece on holiday every year; Greece exports olive oil and wine* (NOTE: capital: **Athens**; people: **Greeks**; language: **Greek**; currency: **drachma**)

① **Greek**
[griːk]
1 *adjective*
referring to Greece; *she married the son of a Greek ship owner; he's opened a Greek restaurant near us; the letters of the Greek alphabet are used in science*
2 *noun*
(a) person from Greece; *the ancient Greeks lived many years before the Romans*
(b) language spoken in Greece; *he reads Plato in the original Greek; she bought a Greek phrase book before going on holiday*

① **green**
[griːn]
1 *adjective*
(a) of a colour like the colour of grass; *he was wearing a bright green shirt; they painted the door dark green; go on - the traffic lights are green*
(b) **to give the green light to** = to give permission to; *the government gave the project the green light*
(c) relating to, interested in, or concerned about the environment; *she's very worried about green issues; he's a leading figure in the green movement* (NOTE: **greener - greenest**)
2 *noun*
(a) colour like grass; *the door was painted a very dark green; have you any paint of a darker green than this?*
(b) piece of public land covered with grass in the middle of a village; *they were playing cricket on the village green*
(c) piece of smooth short grass for playing golf; *the grass on the greens is cut very short; his ball landed about two feet from the hole on the tenth green*

(d) **greens** = green vegetables, especially cabbage; *eat up your greens - they're good for you*

③ **greenhouse**
['griːnhaʊs] *noun*
glass building for growing plants; *we grow tomatoes in our greenhouse in winter*; **greenhouse effect** = effect of gases in the earth's atmosphere which prevent loss of heat and so make the climate hotter; **greenhouse gases** = gases which are produced by burning oil, gas and coal, and which rise into the atmosphere, forming a barrier which prevents loss of heat and creates the greenhouse effect (NOTE: plural is **greenhouses** ['griːnhaʊzɪz])

② **greet**
[griːt] *verb*
to meet someone and say hello; *she greeted him with a kiss*

④ **greeting**
['griːtɪŋ] *noun*
(a) words said when meeting or welcoming someone; *he said a few words of greeting to the guests and disappeared into the kitchen*
(b) **greetings** = good wishes; *we send you birthday greetings; Christmas greetings from all our family!*

③ **grew**
[gruː] *see* GROW

② **grey** *US* **gray**
[greɪ]
1 *noun*
colour like a mixture of black and white; *he was dressed all in grey*
2 *adjective*
of a colour like a mixture of black and white; *her hair has turned quite grey; a grey-haired old lady; she was wearing a light grey suit; look at the grey clouds - I think it is going to rain* (NOTE: **greyer - greyest**)

② **grief**
[griːf] *noun*
very sad feeling; *she couldn't hide her grief as she watched the pictures on TV*; **to come to grief** = to meet with a disaster; *his horse came to grief at the first fence; the project came to grief when the council refused to renew their grant; (informal)* **to give someone grief** = to make someone want to criticize you

③ **grill**
[grɪl]
1 *noun*
(a) part of a cooker where food is cooked under the heat; *cook the chops under the grill*
(b) restaurant serving grilled food; *we'll meet up at the Mexican Grill*
(c) **mixed grill** = dish of different sorts of food grilled together, usually chops, sausages, bacon and mushrooms
2 *verb*
(a) to cook under a grill; *we're having grilled sardines for dinner*

(b) *(informal)* to ask someone questions; *the police grilled him about the missing money*

② **grim**
[grɪm] *adjective*
(a) stern and not smiling; *his expression was grim; he gave a grim laugh and went on working*
(b) unpleasant, worrying; *there is some grim news about the war*
(c) grey and unpleasant; *the town centre is really grim*; *(informal)* **like grim death** = in a determined way; *she held on to the railings like grim death* (NOTE: **grimmer - grimmest**)

② **grin**
[grɪn]
1 *noun*
broad smile; *she gave me a big grin*
2 *verb*
to give a broad smile; *he grinned when we asked him if he liked his job;* **to grin and bear it** = to accept a difficult situation; *no one likes doing all these rehearsals, but we've just got to grin and bear it* (NOTE: **grinning - grinned**)

② **grind**
[graɪnd]
1 *noun*
the daily grind = dull work done every day
2 *verb*
(a) to crush to powder; *to grind corn or coffee; a cup of freshly ground coffee*
(b) to rub surfaces together; **to grind your teeth** = to rub your teeth together and make a noise (usually because you are annoyed); **to grind to a halt** = to stop working gradually; *the men went on strike, and the production line ground to a halt; the driver put on the brakes and the train ground to a halt* (NOTE: **grinding - ground** [graʊnd])

④ **grip**
[grɪp]
1 *noun*
(a) firm hold; *he has a strong firm grip; these new tyres give a better grip on the road surface;* **to lose your grip** = not to be as much in control as before; *she simply doesn't make any decisions - I think she's losing her grip*
(b) *(informal)* **to get** *or* **to come to grips with something** = to start to deal with something; *the president is having to come to grips with the failing economy;* **to get a grip on yourself** = to try to control yourself, to try to be less worried about everything; *get a grip on yourself - you've got an interview in half an hour*
(c) big soft bag for carrying clothes; *he rolled up some T-shirts and underwear and put them into his grip*
2 *verb*
to hold tight; *she gripped the rail with both hands* (NOTE: **gripping - gripped**)

④ **groan**
[grəʊn]
1 *noun*

deep moan; *he uttered a groan and closed his eyes*
2 *verb*
(a) to moan deeply; *she groaned when she saw how much work had to be done*
(b) to groan under a weight = to carry a heavy weight; *the floor groaned under the weight of the gold bars*

④ **groove**
[gruːv] *noun*
wide line cut into a surface; *the door slides along a groove in the floor; the ridges on the nut have to fit into the grooves on the screw;* **to be stuck in a groove** = to be in a routine job, leading a dull life with no excitement

③ **gross**
[grʊs]
1 *adjective*
(a) total, with nothing taken away; **gross domestic product (GDP)** = value of goods and services paid for inside a country; **gross income** *or* **gross salary** = salary which is paid without taking away any tax, insurance, etc.; **gross national product (GNP)** = value of goods and services paid for in a country, including income earned in other countries; **gross profit** = profit before overheads, tax, etc., are taken away; **gross weight** = full weight, including the container and packing material (NOTE: the opposite in this meaning is **net**)
(b) very great and bad; *it was a gross error on the part of the referee* (NOTE: **grosser - grossest**)
2 *adverb*
with nothing taken away; *his salary is paid gross*
3 *verb*
to make a gross turnover; *the film grossed $25m in its first week*
4 *noun*
twelve dozen (i.e. 144); *we ordered two gross of the bars of chocolate* (NOTE: plural is **gross**)

① **ground**
[graʊnd]
1 *noun*
(a) soil or earth; *you should dig the ground in the autumn; the house is built on wet ground; it has been so dry that the ground is hard*
(b) surface of the earth; *the factory was burnt to the ground; there were no seats, so we had to sit on the ground; she lay down on the ground and went to sleep;* **to get a project off the ground** = to get a project started; *he played an important role in getting the project off the ground; see also* EAR
(c) land used for a special purpose; *a football ground; a sports ground; a cricket ground; a show ground*
(d) space between competitors in a race; **to lose ground to someone** = to fall behind someone; **to gain ground** = to catch up on someone
2 *verb*

(a) to put or keep on the ground; *after the mechanical failure was discovered, the fleet of aircraft was grounded*
(b) to base; *our teaching system is grounded on years of practice*
(c) *US* to connect an electrical device to the earth; *machines you use in the home should be properly grounded* (NOTE: British English is to **earth**)
(d) *see also* GRIND

① **ground floor**
['graʊnd 'flɔː] *noun*
floor (in a shop, block of flats, etc.) which is level with the street; *the men's department is on the ground floor; he has a ground-floor office;* **lower ground floor** = BASEMENT (NOTE: in America the **ground floor** is called the **first floor**)

① **group**
[gruːp] *noun*
(a) a number of people or things taken together; *a group of houses in the valley; groups of people gathered in the street; she is leading a group of businessmen on a tour of Italian factories; there are reduced entrance prices for groups of 30 and over*
(b) way of classifying things; *these drugs belong to the same group;* **age group** = people of the same age; *children in the 5 to 10 age group;* **blood group** = people with the same type of blood
(c) people playing music together; *he plays in a jazz group; she's the lead singer in a pop group*
(d) several different companies linked together; *the Shell group of companies; a major travel group*

④ **grouping**
['gruːpɪŋ] *noun*
putting together in a group; **blood grouping** = classifying patients according to their blood groups

④ **grove**
[grəʊv] *noun*
small group of trees; *a birch grove or a grove of birch trees*

① **grow**
[grəʊ] *verb*
(a) to live (as a plant); *there was grass growing in the middle of the road; roses grow well in our garden*
(b) to make plants grow; *he grows all his vegetables in his garden; we are going to grow some carrots this year*
(c) to become taller *or* bigger; *he's grown a lot taller since I last saw him; rubbing with oil will encourage your hair to grow; the profit has grown to £1m; the town's population is growing very fast*
(d) to become gradually; *she grew weak with lack of food; the nights are growing colder now; all the time he grew richer and richer* (NOTE: **growing - grew** [gruː] **- grown** [grəʊn])

④ **grower**
['grəʊə] *noun*
farmer who grows a certain type of plant; *an apple grower; a tomato grower*

③ **grown**
[grəʊn] *adjective*
(person) full size; *a grown man like you shouldn't be afraid of a little spider* (NOTE: do not confuse with **groan**)

③ **grown-up**
['grəʊn 'ʌp] *noun*
adult; *the family consists of three grown-ups and ten children; she has a grown-up daughter; the grown-ups had wine with their meal*

② **growth**
[grəʊθ] *noun*
increase in size; *the rapid growth of the population since 1980; they measured the tree's growth over the last fifty years;* **the country's economic growth** = rate at which a country's national income grows

③ **grow up**
['grəʊ 'ʌp] *verb*
to become an adult; *what does your son want to do when he grows up?*

④ **grumble**
['grʌmbl]
1 *noun*
complaint about something; *do you have any grumbles about the food?;* **she's full of grumbles** = she is always complaining
2 *verb*
to grumble about something = to complain about something; *he's always grumbling about the noise from the flat above*

② **guarantee**
[gærɪn'tiː]
1 *noun*
(a) legal document in which someone states that something is going to happen; *the travel agent could not give a guarantee that the accommodation would be in the hotel shown in the catalogue*
(b) legal document which promises that a machine is in good condition and will work without problems for a certain length of time; *the fridge is sold with a twelve-month guarantee;* **under guarantee** = covered by a guarantee; *the car is still under guarantee, so the manufacturers will pay for the repairs* (NOTE: also called a **warranty**)
(c) firm promise that something will happen; *we can't give you a guarantee that the weather will be fine; there is no guarantee that he will get a job even if he gets through the training course successfully*
2 *verb*
(a) to give a legal assurance that something will work, that something will be done; *the product is guaranteed for twelve months*

(b) to make a firm promise that something will happen; *I can guarantee that the car will give you no trouble*; *we can almost guarantee good weather in the Caribbean at this time of year*

② **guaranteed**
[gærɪn'tiːd] *adjective*
which has been promised legally; *guaranteed delivery within 24 hours*; **guaranteed minimum wage** = minimum wage which all employers must pay

③ **guard**
[gɑːd]
1 *noun*
(a) **to be on guard** *or* **to keep guard** = to be looking out for danger; *you must be on your guard against burglars at all times*
(b) person who protects, often a soldier; *security guards patrol the factory at night*; *our squad is on guard duty tonight*; **changing of the guard** = military ceremony, where one group of soldiers is replaced by another on guard duty at a palace, etc.; *at 10.30 we're going to watch the changing of the guard at Buckingham Palace*; **guard dog** = dog used to guard a house or other buildings; *Alsatians are often used as guard dogs*; *when we arrived at the hotel we were welcomed by a couple of barking guard dogs*
(c) man in charge of a train; *the guard helped my put my bike into his van* (NOTE: American English is **conductor**); **guard's van** = wagon in a train, where the guard is
2 *verb*
to protect; *the prison is guarded at all times*

② **guardian**
['gɑːdiin] *noun*
person who protects, especially someone who has been legally appointed to look after a child; *when his parents died, his uncle became his guardian*

④ **guerrilla** *or* **guerilla**
[gɪ'rɪlɪ] *noun*
soldier who is not part of a regular national army; *the guerrillas fought their way to the capital*; **guerrilla warfare** = type of warfare fought by guerrillas, who attack in small groups in unexpected places

① **guess**
[ges]
1 *noun*
trying to give the right answer or figure; *go on - make a guess!*; *at a guess, I'd say it weighs about 10 kilos*; **it is anyone's guess** = no one really knows what is the right answer (NOTE: plural is **guesses)**
2 *verb*
(a) to try to give the right answer or figure; *I would guess it's about six o'clock*; *neither of them guessed the right answer*; *he guessed right*; *I've bought you a present - shut your eyes and guess what it is*
(b) *US* to think; *I guess the plane's going to be late*

② **guest**
[gest] *noun*
(a) person who is asked to your home or to an event; *we had a very lively party with dozens of guests*; *none of the guests left the party early*; **be my guest** = help yourself, I'm paying
(b) person staying in a hotel; **guests' lounge** = special lounge for guests in a hotel

③ **guidance**
['gaɪdɪns] *noun*
advice; *an instructor will be on hand to give you guidance*; *he asked the bank manager for guidance about how to fill in his tax form*; **moral guidance** = advice as to what is right or wrong behaviour; *part of a teacher's job is to give the students moral guidance*

② **guide**
[gaɪd]
1 *noun*
(a) person who shows the way; *they used local farmers as guides through the forest*; **guide dog** = dog which has been trained to lead a blind person; *the only dogs allowed into the restaurant are guide dogs*
(b) person who shows tourists round a place; *the guide showed us over the castle or showed us round the castle*; *the museum guide spoke so fast that we couldn't understand what she was saying*
(c) book which gives information; *a guide to Athens*; *a guide to the butterflies of Europe*
2 *verb*
to show the way; to show tourists round a place; *she guided us up the steps in the dark*; *he guided us round the castle*

③ **guidebook**
['gaɪdbʊk] *noun*
book with information about a place; *the guidebook lists three hotels by the beach*

④ **guidelines**
['gaɪdlaɪnz] *noun*
general advice on what to do; *if you follow the government guidelines, you should not have any trouble*; *the minister has issued a new set of guidelines about city planning*

④ **guilt**
[gɪlt] *noun*
(a) state of having committed a crime; *the prisoner admitted his guilt*
(b) being or feeling responsible for wrong which has happened; *the whole group bears the guilt for his tragic death*

② **guilty**
['gɪltɪ] *adjective*
(a) who has committed a crime; *he was found guilty of murder*; *the jury decided she was not guilty*
(b) feeling unhappy because you have done something wrong; *I feel very guilty about not having written to you* (NOTE: **guiltier - guiltiest**)

③ **guitar**
[gɪ'tɑ:] *noun*
musical instrument with six strings, played with the fingers; *he plays the guitar in a pop group*

④ **guitarist**
[gɪ'tɑ:rɪst] *noun*
person who plays a guitar; *he's the lead guitarist with a pop group*

③ **gulf**
[gʌlf] *noun*
(a) area of sea partly surrounded by land; *the Gulf of Mexico*
(b) *(especially)* **the Gulf** = the Persian Gulf (the sea near Iran, Iraq, Saudi Arabia, etc.); *the tanker was carrying crude oil from the Gulf*
(c) *(formal)* great distance between two points of view; *the gulf that separates the two parties will be difficult to bridge*

③ **Gulf Stream**
['gʌlf 'stri:m] *noun*
warm current which crosses the North Atlantic from west to east (NOTE: also called the **North Atlantic Drift**)

③ **gum**
[gʌm]
1 *noun*
(a) glue; *she spread gum on the back of the photo and stuck it onto a sheet of paper*
(b) flesh around the base of your teeth; *brushing your teeth every day is good for your gums*
(c) **(chewing) gum** = sweet substance which you chew but do not swallow; *he slowly took a piece of gum out of his mouth and put it in the ashtray; I've got some gum stuck to my shoe*
(d) small fruit sweet which can be sucked until it melts away; *a packet of fruit gums*
2 *verb*
to stick with glue; *she gummed the pictures onto a sheet of paper* (NOTE: **gumming - gummed**)

② **gun**
[gʌn]
1 *noun*
(a) weapon which shoots bullets; *the robber pulled out a gun; she grabbed his gun and shot him dead;* **starting gun** = gun fired to start a race; *(informal)* **to jump the gun** = to start too quickly; *the law on Sunday opening starts in a month's time, but some shops have already jumped the gun;* **to stick to your guns** = to keep to your point of view even if everyone says you are wrong
(b) large weapon which shoots shells; *we heard the guns firing all night; the ship trained its guns on the town*
(c) small device which you hold in your hand to spray paint, glue, etc.; *a spray gun gives an even coat of paint*
2 *verb*
(a) **to gun someone down** = to shoot and kill someone; *the policeman was gunned down in the street*

(b) *(informal)* **to be gunning for someone** = to try to find a reason to criticize someone; *the papers are gunning for the minister* (NOTE: **gunning - gunned**)

③ **gunman**
['gʌnmɪn] *noun*
armed robber; *the gunman pulled out his gun and started shooting* (NOTE: plural is **gunmen**)

③ **gut**
[gʌt] ·
1 *noun*
(a) *(informal)* **gut** *or* **guts** = the tube inside your body which passes down from the stomach and in which food is digested as it passes through; *he complained of pain in the gut;* **gut reaction** = instinctive reaction; *my gut reaction is to vote for the woman candidate;* **I hate his guts** = I dislike him a lot
(b) *(informal)* **guts** = courage; *he had the guts to tell the boss what he should do*
2 *verb*
(a) to remove the insides of an animal or fish before cooking; *the pigeons have not been gutted; women stood in the market gutting fish; (informal)* **to feel gutted** = to feel extremely upset; *when he missed the penalty kick we all felt gutted*
(b) to destroy the inside of a building totally; *the house was gutted by fire* (NOTE: **gutting - gutted**)

① **guy**
[gaɪ]
1 *noun*
(a) *(informal)* man; *she married a guy from Texas; the boss is a very friendly guy; hey, you guys, come and look at this!* (NOTE: in American English, **you guys** can be used when speaking to men, women or children); *(in a story or film)* **bad guy** = wicked character; *the bad guy is the one with the black hat and the five o'clock shadow;* **good guy** = hero; *the good guys always win*
(b) rope which holds a tent; *make sure the guys are tight before the storm comes*
(c) figure of a man burnt on 5th November; *the children are collecting clothes to make a guy; penny for the guy!*

③ **gym** *or* **gymnasium**
[dʒɪm *or* dʒɪm'neɪziːm] *noun*
hall for indoor sports; *because it rained, we had to hold the village fair in the gym; the room in the basement has been fitted out as a gymnasium*

④ **gypsy**
['dʒɪpsɪ] *noun*
member of a people who wander from place to place, perhaps originally coming from India; *gypsies have camped at the bottom of our field* (NOTE: plural is **gypsies**)

Hh

H, h
[eɪtʃ]

eighth letter of the alphabet, between G and I; *the sign for a hospital is a white H on a blue background*

ha
[hɑː] *interjection showing surprise*
ha! there's a mistake on page one of the book!

habit
['hæbɪt] *noun*

regular way of doing things; *he has the habit of going to bed at 9 o'clock and reading until midnight*; **to develop the habit** *or* **to get into the habit of doing something** = to start to do something regularly; *he's getting into the habit of playing football every week*; **to break the habit** = to stop doing something which you used to do regularly; *I haven't had a cigarette for six months - I think I've broken the habit!*; **bad habit** *or* **nasty habit** = regular way of doing something which is not nice; *she has the bad habit of biting her nails*; **from force of habit** = because this is what you do normally; *he switched off all the lights from force of habit*

habitat
['hæbɪtæt] *noun*

place where an animal or plant lives; *this is an ideal habitat for butterflies*

hack
[hæk] *verb*

(a) to chop roughly; *he hacked off the branches of the tree*

(b) to enter a computer system illegally; *he hacked into the bank's computer*

had, hadn't
[hæd or 'hædnt]
see HAVE

hail
[heɪl]

1 *noun*

frozen rain; *I thought the hail was going to break the windscreen*

2 *verb*

(a) to fall as frozen rain; *it hailed for ten minutes and then the sun came out*

(b) to wave, call, etc., to make a taxi stop; *he whistled to hail a taxi*

(c) to hail from = to come from; *he hails from Montana*

hair
[heə] *noun*

(a) mass of long threads growing on your head; *she has long brown hair or her hair is long and brown*; *she always brushes her hair before washing it*; *you must get your hair cut*; *he's had his hair cut short*; *use some hair spray to keep your hair in place*; *(informal)* **keep your hair on!** = don't get annoyed; **to let your hair down** = to relax and enjoy yourself; *when the exams are finished we're all going to let our hair down* (NOTE: no plural in this meaning)

(b) one of the long threads growing on the body of a human or animal; *waiter, there's a hair in my soup!*; *the cat has left hairs all over the cushion*; *he's beginning to get some grey hairs*; **to split hairs** = to try to find minute differences between things when arguing; *stop splitting hairs, you know you're in the wrong* (NOTE: the plural in this meaning is **hairs)**

haircut
['heəkʌt] *noun*

cutting of the hair on your head; *you need a haircut*; *he went to get a haircut*

hairdresser
['heədresɪ] *noun*

person who cuts and washes your hair; *ask the hairdresser to trim your beard*; **hairdresser's** = shop where you have your hair cut, washed, etc.; *I must go to the hairdresser's*

hairstyle
['heəstaɪl] *noun*

way of cutting and styling hair; *she's decided to change her hairstyle*; *what do you think of my new hairstyle?*

half
[hɑːf]

1 *noun*

(a) one of two parts which are the same in size; *she cut the orange in half*; *one half of the apple fell on the carpet*; *half of six is three*

(b) *(in sport)* one of two parts of a match; *our team scored a goal in the first half*; *we thought we were going to win, and then they scored in the final minutes of the second half*

(c) part of a financial year; *the sales in the first half were down on last year*

(d) *(informal)* half a pint (of beer); *an orange juice and two halves of bitter, please* (NOTE: plural is **halves** [hɑːvz])

2 *adjective*

divided into two equal parts; **half a bottle of wine** = half of a bottle of wine; *we drank half a bottle of wine each*; **a half bottle of wine** = a small bottle of wine, containing half the amount of a normal bottle; *he ordered his meal and a half bottle of Bordeaux*; **half an hour** *or* **a half hour** = 30 minutes; *I'll be back in half an hour*; *the journey takes two and a half hours or two hours and a half*

3 *adverb*

(a) **half as big** = only 50 per cent of the size; *this book is half as big or half the size of that one*; **half as big again** = 50 per cent bigger

(b) *(informal)* **not half** = certainly, of course; *this cheese doesn't half smell!*; *did you have a good time at the pub? - not half!*

② **half-dozen** *or* **half a dozen**
[ha:f'dʌzn or 'ha:f ə 'dʌzn] *noun*
six; *I bought half a dozen eggs*

② **half-hour**
['ha:f'auɪ] *noun*
period of thirty minutes; *there's a bus to town every half-hour*

② **half past**
['ha:f 'pa:st] *phrase* 30 minutes after an hour; *I have an appointment with the doctor at half past five (= 5.30)*

② **half price**
['ha:f 'praɪs] *noun & adjective*
50 per cent of the price; *tours at half price or half-price tours*; *to sell goods off at half price*; **half-price sale** = sale of all goods at 50% of the usual price; *the shop is holding a half-price sale*

② **half-term**
['ha:f 'tɜ:m] *noun*
short holiday in the middle of a school term; *we took a few days' holiday at half-term*; *there are masses of children in the museums at half-term*; *we took a few days' holiday at half-term*

③ **halfway**
[ha:f'weɪ] *adverb*
in the middle; *come on, we're more than halfway there!*; *the post office is about halfway between the station and our house*; **to meet someone halfway** *or* **to go halfway to meet someone** = to compromise; *I'll meet you halfway: I write the report and you present it at the meeting*

① **hall**
[hɔ:l] *noun*
(a) passage at the entrance to a house, where you can leave your coat; *don't wait in the hall, come straight into the dining room*; *she left her umbrella in the hall*

(b) large room for meetings; *the children have their dinner in the school hall*; **concert hall** = large building where concerts are given; **sports hall** = large building for playing indoor sports (like basketball); **town hall** = building where the town council meets and from where the town is

governed; **village hall** = building in a village where meetings, shows, etc., can take place; *the flower show will be held in the village hall*

(c) **hall of residence** = building where students live at university or college; *how many students live in halls of residence?*

③ **hallo**
[hɪ'lɪʊ]
see HELLO

④ **Halloween**
[hælɪʊ'i:n] *noun*
31st October, when witches and ghosts are said to be seen

COMMENT: traditionally, there are parties with apples hung on strings, and pumpkins hollowed out with faces cut into them and candles put inside them; children go from house to house to ask for sweets or fruit. *See also* TRICK OR TREAT

③ **halt**
[hɔ:lt]
1 *noun*
complete stop; **to come to a halt** = to come to a dead stop; *the lorry came to a halt just before the wall*; **to call a halt to something** = to make something stop; *he tried to call a halt to arguments inside the party*; **to grind to a halt** = to stop working gradually; *the whole plan ground to a halt for lack of funds*
2 *verb*
to stop; *the car halted when the traffic lights went red*; *we are trying to halt experiments on live animals*

④ **halve**
[ha:v] *verb*
(a) to cut into two equal parts; *she halved the cake*
(b) to reduce by half; *because we have been on holiday, our telephone bill has been halved*

③ **halves**
[ha:vz]
see HALF

④ **ham**
[hæm]
1 *noun*
(a) salted or smoked pork; *she cut three slices of ham*; *we had a ham and tomato salad*; *she had a ham sandwich for lunch*; **ham and eggs** = fried ham with fried eggs; **ham roll** = bread roll with ham in it

(b) **(radio) ham** = person who sends and receives radio messages unofficially; *a radio ham picked up the signals*

(c) *(old)* bad actor who uses too many gestures and speaks too loudly
2 *verb*
(informal) **to ham it up** = to act badly on purpose

③ **hamburger**
['hæmbɜːgɪ] *noun*
chopped beef grilled and served in a toasted roll;
*the children want hamburgers and French
fries for lunch*; **hamburger bar** = restaurant
selling hamburgers; *we stopped for a meal at a
hamburger bar*

③ **hammer**
['hæmɪ]
1 *noun*
tool with a heavy head for knocking nails; *she
hit the nail hard with the hammer*; **to go under
the hammer** = to be sold by auction; *all his
furniture went under the hammer last week*
2 *verb*
(a) to knock something into something with a
hammer; *it took him a few minutes to hammer
the tent pegs into the ground*
(b) to hit hard, as with a hammer; *he hammered
the table with his fist*; *she hammered on the
door with her stick*
(c) to hammer it into someone = to try to make
someone understand by repeating; *they're
trying to hammer it into schoolchildren that
drugs are dangerous*

④ **hamper**
['hæmpɪ]
1 *noun*
large basket; *we packed the hamper with food
for the picnic*
2 *verb*
to get in the way; *lack of funds is hampering
our development project*

① **hand**
[hænd]
1 *noun*
(a) part of the body at the end of each arm,
which you use for holding things; *she was
carrying a cup of tea in each hand*; *she held out
her hand, asking for money*; **to shake hands** =
to hold someone's hand to show you are pleased
to meet them or to show that an agreement has
been reached; *the visitors shook hands and the
meeting started*; **to shake hands on a deal** = to
shake hands to show that a deal has been agreed;
to give someone a hand *or* **lend a hand with
something** = to help with something; *can you
lend a hand with moving the furniture?*; *he
gave me a hand with the washing up*; **the shop
has changed hands** = the shop has a new
owner; **they walked along hand in hand** =
holding each other by the hand
(b) to be hand in glove with someone = to be
working closely with someone; *we discovered
he was hand in glove with our main rivals*; **to
have your hands full** = to be very busy, totally
occupied; *with three little children to look after
she has her hands full*; **hand over fist** = in large
quantities; *they were making money hand over
fist*; *see also* WASH

(c) one of the two pieces on a clock (the minute
hand and the hour hand) which turn round and
show the time; *the minute hand is longer than
the hour hand*
(d) at hand = near; *the emergency exit is close
at hand*; **by hand** = using your hands and tools
but not using large machines; *he made the table
by hand*; **in hand** = supply kept ready; *we have
a supply of extra paper in hand for
emergencies*; **on hand** = ready; *there's a doctor
on hand if accidents occur*; **on the one hand** =
showing the first part of a comparison; **on the
other hand** = as the second part of a
comparison; but; *on the one hand he's a good
salesman, on the other hand he can't work out
discounts correctly*; **out of hand** = not
controlled; *our expenses have got out of hand*
(e) worker; *to take on ten more hands*; **factory
hand** = worker in a factory; **old China hand** =
someone who has had a lot of experience in
doing business in China
(f) action of beating your hands together; *he did
very well - give him a big hand, everyone*
2 *verb*
to pass something to someone; *can you hand me
that box?*; *she handed me all her money*;
(informal) **you've got to hand it to him** = he has
to be admired for; *you've got to hand it to her,
she's a great cook!*

① **hand back**
['hænd 'bæk] *verb*
to give something back; *the customs officer
handed me back my passport*

③ **handbag**
['hænbæg] *noun*
small bag which a woman carries to hold her
money, pens, handkerchief, etc.; *a robber
snatched her handbag in the street* (NOTE:
American English is **purse**)

④ **handbook**
['hænbʊk] *noun*
book which gives instructions on how to use or
repair something; *look in the handbook to see if
it tells you how to clean the photocopier*;
service handbook = book which shows how a
machine should be serviced

③ **handful**
['hænfʊl] *noun*
(a) as much as you can hold in your hand; *she
paid with a handful of loose change*
(b) very few; *only a handful of people came to
the wedding*
(c) difficult child; *their son is a bit of a handful*

③ **handicap**
['hændɪkæp]
1 *noun*
(a) physical or mental disability; *she was born
with a physical handicap*
(b) something which puts you at a disadvantage;
not being able to drive is a handicap in this job

(c) penalty imposed on a player to make it harder for him to win; *he has a golf handicap of 7*

2 *verb*

to put someone at a disadvantage; *she was handicapped by not being able to speak Russian* (NOTE: handicapping - handicapped)

③ **handicapped**
['hændɪkæpt]

1 *adjective*

with a mental or physical disability; *a school for handicapped children*

2 *noun*

the handicapped = people with disabilities; *the cinema has facilities for the handicapped; there is a toilet for the handicapped on the ground floor*

① **hand in**
['hænd 'ɪn] *verb*

to give in something by hand; *please have the completed form ready to hand in at the reception desk; he handed in his notice or his resignation* = he resigned

③ **handkerchief**
['hæŋkɪtʃiːf] *noun*

piece of cloth or thin paper for wiping your nose; *she carries a pack of paper handkerchiefs in her bag; he wiped his eyes on his handkerchief* (NOTE: often called a **hanky**, especially by children)

② **handle**
['hændl]

1 *noun*

(a) part of something which you hold in your hand to carry or use the object held; *I turned the handle but the door didn't open; be careful, the handle of the frying pan may be hot; the handle has come off my suitcase; he broke the handle off the cup*

(b) *(informal)* to fly off the handle = to lose your temper; *stop telling him what to do or he'll fly off the handle*

2 *verb*

(a) to move by hand; *be careful when you handle the bottles of acid*

(b) to deal with something; *his company handles most of the traffic through the port; leave it to me - I'll handle it;* handling charge = charge made for dealing with something

(c) to sell or to trade in (a sort of service or product); *we do not handle washing machines*

① **hand over**
['hænd 'əʊvə] *verb*

to give something to someone; *she handed over all the documents to the lawyers*

④ **handsome**
['hænsɪm] *adjective*

(a) good-looking; *her boyfriend is very handsome - I'm jealous!* (NOTE: used of men, rather than women)

(b) large; *we made a handsome profit on the deal*

③ **handwriting**
['hændraɪtɪŋ] *noun*

way of writing by hand; *his handwriting's so bad I can't read it; I can't read her handwriting*

④ **handwritten**
[hænd'rɪtn] *adjective*

written by hand, not typed or printed; *send a handwritten letter of application to the personnel manager*

③ **handy**
['hændi] *adjective*

practical and useful; *this small case is handy when travelling; it's handy having the post office next door;* to come in handy = to be useful; *the knife will come in handy when we are camping* (NOTE: handier - handiest)

① **hang**
[hæŋ]

1 *verb*

(a) to attach something to something so that it does not touch the ground; *hang your coat on the hook behind the door; he hung his umbrella over the back of his chair; he hung the painting in the hall; the boys were hanging upside down from a tree* (NOTE: hanging - hung [hʌŋ])

(b) to kill someone by tying a rope round his neck and hanging him off the ground; *he was sentenced to be hanged for murder;* to hang yourself = to commit suicide by hanging; *he hanged himself in his prison cell* (NOTE: in this meaning, hanging - hanged)

2 *noun*

to get the hang of something = to understand how something works; *I don't think I'll ever get the hang of this software package*

③ **hang around**
['hæŋ ə'raʊnd] *verb*

(informal) to wait in a certain place without doing anything much; *groups of teenagers were hanging around the bar*

③ **hang back**
['hæŋ 'bæk] *verb*

to stay behind when others go on; *they all ran forward but she hung back; they want him to put money into their scheme, but he's hanging back to see if it works properly*

③ **hang down**
['hæŋ 'daʊn] *verb*

to hang in a long piece; *her hair hung down to her waist; plants were hanging down from the rocks*

④ **hanger**
['hæŋə] *noun*

coat hanger = piece of wood, wire or plastic on which you can hang a coat, a shirt, etc.; *keep your clothes on coat hangers - they won't need ironing*

③ **hang on**
['hæŋ 'ɒn] *verb*

(a) to wait; *if you hang on a few minutes you will be able to see her*

(b) *(while phoning)* to wait; *if you hang on a moment, Mr Smith will be off the other line soon*

(c) *(when thinking again)* hang on! do you mean you're not coming with us?

(d) to hang on to something = to hold something tight; *hang on to the ladder and don't look down*

(e) to keep; *I've decided to hang on to my shares until the price goes up*

③ **hang out**
['hæŋ 'aʊt] *verb*

(a) to hang things outside on a string; *they hung out flags all around the square*; *mother's hanging out her washing to dry*

(b) *(informal)* to wait in a certain place without doing anything much; *teenagers like to hang out round the internet café*

③ **hang up**
['hæŋ 'ʌp] *verb*

(a) to put something on a hanger or on a hook; *don't leave your jacket on the back of your chair, hang it up!*

(b) to stop a telephone conversation by putting the telephone back on its hook; *when I asked him when he was going to pay, he hung up*; *see also* HUNG UP

③ **hankie** *or* **hanky**
['hæŋki] *noun*

(informal) = HANDKERCHIEF; *don't sniff, use your hanky*

① **happen**
['hæpɪn] *verb*

(a) to take place; *the accident happened at the traffic lights*; *how did the accident happen?*; *something happened to make all the buses late*; *he's late - something must have happened to him*

(b) what's happened to his brother? = what is his brother doing now?

(c) to be somewhere by chance; *the fire engine happened to be there when the fire started*; *the shop happened to be empty at the time*; *we happened to meet at the library*; *do you happen to have change for £10?*; it so happens that *or* it so happened that *or* as it happens *or* as it happened = quite by chance; *as it happens I have the car today and can give you a lift*; *it so happened that my wife bumped into her sister at the supermarket*

② **happening**
['hæpnɪŋ] *noun*

event, something that happens; *tell me about all the happenings in the village while I've been away*

④ **happily**
['hæpɪli] *adverb*

in a happy way; *the children played happily in the sand for hours*; *we waited for her for hours in the rain, and in the meantime, she was happily sitting at home watching TV*; *they seem to get along very happily without the telephone*

④ **happiness**
['hæpɪnɪs] *noun*

feeling of being happy; *her expression reflected her feeling of happiness*

① **happy**
['hæpɪ] *adjective*

(a) *(of people)* very pleased; *I'm happy to say we're getting married next month*; *I'm so happy to hear that you are better*; *she's very happy in her job*

(b) *(of event)* pleasant; *it was the happiest day of my life*; *by a happy coincidence, we both like Dutch painters and met at the exhibition*; **happy hour** = period when drinks are cheaper in a bar; *there's a happy hour every day from 6 to 7*

(c) to be happy to do something = to do something very willingly; *I'd be happy to lend you my car*; **to be happy with something** = to be satisfied with something; *are you happy with your new car?*; *no one is happy with the plans for the new town centre*

(d) *(greetings)* **Happy Birthday** *or* **many Happy Returns of the Day** = greeting said to someone on their birthday; **Happy Christmas** = greeting said to someone at Christmas; **Happy Easter** = greeting said to someone at Easter; **Happy New Year** = greeting said to someone at the New Year (NOTE: **happier - happiest**)

④ **harass**
['hærɪs *US* hɪ'ræs] *verb*

to keep on talking to someone and worrying them; *she was harassed by a man at work*; *they harassed him by phoning every day until he finally paid the bill*

④ **harassment**
['hærɪsmɪnt *US* hɪ'ræsmɪnt] *noun*

action of keeping on talking to someone and worrying them; *he complained of police harassment*; **sexual harassment** = worrying someone by making sexual approaches which they do not want; *she complained of sexual harassment by her manager*

④ **harbour** *US* **harbor**
['hɑːbɪ]

1 *noun*

port, place where boats can come and tie up; *the yacht moved away from the harbour*; *the ship came into harbour last night*; **fishing harbour** = harbour which is used by fishing boats

2 *verb*

to protect a criminal; *he was arrested and charged with harbouring illegal immigrants*

① **hard**
[hɑːd]

1 *adjective*

(a) not soft; *if you have back trouble, you ought to get a hard bed*; *the ice cream is rock hard or hard as a rock*; *the cake she made is so hard I can't bite it*

(b) difficult; *the test is too hard - I can't even begin to do it*; *the exam was very hard, and most students failed*; *she finds it hard to cope without any money*; *(informal)* it's hard to say = it's difficult to know; *it's hard to say if it's going to rain or not*
(c) severe; *there was a hard winter in 1962*; *(informal)* **hard lines!** *or* **hard luck!** = I'm sorry you didn't win
(d) *he's rather hard of hearing* = he's quite deaf
(e) *(of water)* containing calcium, which makes it difficult to wash with; *the water in this area is very hard* (NOTE: **harder - hardest**)
2 *adverb*
strongly; *he hit the nail hard*; *it's snowing very hard*; *they worked hard to finish the order on time*; *they tried hard, but couldn't score enough goals*

④ **harden**
['hɑːdn] *verb*
(a) to become hard; *leave the cement for a couple of days to harden*
(b) to make harder; *we use specially hardened steel in the building of the boat*
(c) to make more experienced; *he's a hardened criminal*

② **hardly**
['hɑːdli] *adverb*
(a) almost not; *do you know her? - hardly at all*; *we hardly slept last night*; *she hardly eats anything at all*
(b) **hardly ever** = almost never; *I hardly ever see her these days*; *it hardly ever rains in September*
(c) **hardly anyone** = almost no one; *hardly anyone came to the party*

④ **hardship**
['hɑːdʃɪp] *noun*
difficult conditions, suffering; *she faced hardship when her husband died and left her in debt*

③ **hard up**
['hɑːd 'ʌp] *adjective*
with very little money; *I can't lend you anything because I'm rather hard up at the moment*

④ **hardware**
['hɑːdweɪ] *noun*
(a) tools and pans used in the home; *I bought the paint in a hardware shop*
(b) **military hardware** = guns, shells, tanks, etc.; **computer hardware** = computers, printers, keyboards, etc.; *if I had the money I would buy the latest computer hardware*; *compare* SOFTWARE (NOTE: no plural)

④ **hardy**
['hɑːdi] *adjective*
able to survive in cold weather; *plants need to be hardy to grow high up on the Scottish mountains*; *the Finns are a hardy people* (NOTE: **hardier - hardiest**)

① **harm**
[hɑːm]
1 *noun*
damage; *he didn't mean to do any harm* or *he meant no harm*; *there's no harm in having a little drink before you go to bed*; **to do more harm than good** = not to be helpful at all; *talking to him now about the project will do more harm than good* (NOTE: no plural)
2 *verb*
to damage; *luckily, the little girl was not harmed*; *the bad publicity has harmed our reputation*

③ **harmful**
['hɑːmful] *adjective*
which causes damage; *harmful sprays are banned on our farm*; *smoking is harmful to the health*

③ **harmless**
['hɑːmlɪs] *adjective*
which does not hurt; *are you sure this spray is harmless to animals?*; *our dog barks a lot, but really he's quite harmless*; **harmless fun** = jokes, etc., which are not supposed to harm anyone; *we were just having a bit of harmless fun*

④ **harmony**
['hɑːmɪnɪ] *noun*
(a) pleasant musical sounds; *the group sang in harmony*
(b) general peace; *they want to live in harmony with their neighbours*

④ **harsh**
[hɑːʃ] *adjective*
(a) severe, cruel; *the prosecutor asked for a harsh sentence to fit the crime*
(b) rough; *he shouted in a harsh voice* (NOTE: **harsher - harshest**)

④ **harvest**
['hɑːvɪst]
1 *noun*
(a) picking ripe crops; *the corn harvest is in August*
(b) ripe crops which have been picked; *the best corn harvest for years*
2 *verb*
to pick ripe crops; *the corn will be ready to harvest next week*; *they have started harvesting the grapes in the vineyard*

③ **has, hasn't**
[hæz or 'hæzɪnt]
see HAVE

④ **hash**
[hæʃ] *noun*
(a) dish prepared from chopped meat and vegetables; *US* **corned beef hash** = dish made of corned beef, onions and mashed potatoes, cooked in the oven; **hash brown potatoes** *or* **hash browns** = boiled potatoes, diced or mashed and fried till crisp and brown

(b) *(informal)* **to make a hash of something** = to make a bad job of something; *he was supposed to be the expert, and then he made a hash of it*

(c) hash sign = printed sign (# which indicates something

COMMENT: in American usage, # is used to mean 'number': so # means apartment number 32, etc. In computer usage, the pound sign (£) is sometimes used in the United States instead of the hash, to avoid confusion

④ **hastily**
['heɪstɪli] *adverb*
carelessly and rapidly; *he hastily jotted down the car's number*

④ **hasty**
['heɪsti] *adjective*
careless and too fast; *it was a hasty decision, which he regretted afterwards*; *he went into the ladies' toilet by mistake and had to beat a hasty retreat* (NOTE: **hastier - hastiest**)

② **hat**
[hæt] *noun*
(a) piece of clothing which you wear on your head; *take your hat off when you go into a church*; *he's bought a Russian hat for the winter*; **hard hat** = solid hat worn by building workers, etc.; *visitors to the building site must wear hard hats*
(b) *(informal)* **keep it under your hat** = keep it secret; **to take your hat off to someone** = (i) to greet someone, by lifting your hat up a little; (ii) to say that you admire someone; *those helicopter pilots were very brave - I take my hat off to them*; *she's made a great success of her business - I take my hat off to her*; **to be talking through your hat** = to be talking nonsense; *that's rubbish - you're talking through your hat*; *see also* PASS ROUND
(c) hat trick = score of three goals, etc., by the same person in football, three wickets taken by the same bowler in cricket, etc.; *out of the five goals, Jones scored a hat trick and the other two were by Leonard and Williams*

④ **hatch**
[hætʃ]
1 *noun*
(a) opening in the deck of a ship; cover for this opening; *he opened the hatch and went down into the cabin*
(b) serving hatch *or* **service hatch** = small opening in a wall between a kitchen and a dining room (NOTE: plural is **hatches**)
2 *verb*
(a) *(of a baby bird)* to break out of the egg; *all the chicks hatched on the same day*; *(informal)* **don't count your chickens before they're hatched** = don't be too sure that everything will be all right; *he's a very cautious man, he never counts his chickens before they're hatched*

(b) to plan; *they hatched a plot to kidnap the Prime Minister's daughter*

① **hate**
[heɪt]
1 *verb*
to dislike very strongly; *I think she hates me, but I don't know why*; *I hate going to the dentist*; **hate mail** = letters showing that the writer hates someone; *he received a lot of hate mail after his speech*
2 *noun*
intense dislike; *cucumber sandwiches are one of my pet hates*

④ **hatred**
['heɪtrɪd] *noun*
feelings of great dislike; *he has a hatred of exams*; **racial hatred** = dislike of people of other races

④ **haul**
[hɔːl]
1 *verb*
to pull with difficulty; *they hauled the boat up onto the beach*; *the police hauled the body out of the water*
2 *noun*
(a) large quantity of things which have been stolen; *the burglars made off with their haul*
(b) distance travelled with difficulty; *it's a long haul up the hill*; **long-haul flight** = long-distance flight (for example, across the Atlantic)

④ **haunt**
[hɔːnt]
1 *noun*
place which you visit frequently; *I went back to some of my old haunts*; *the pub is a favourite haunt of actors*
2 *verb*
(of ghosts) to visit frequently; *the castle is supposed to be haunted by the ghost of a soldier*; *they say the Tower of London is haunted by the ghost of Anne Boleyn, who was executed there*

① **have**
[hæv] *verb*
(a) *(also* **to have got)** to own or possess; *she has a lot of money*; *they have a new green car*; *she has long dark hair*; *the house has no telephone*; *do you have a table for three, please?*
(b) to take, to eat, to play, etc.; *have you had any tea?*; *she has sugar in her coffee*; *they had a meal of bread and cheese*; *she had her breakfast in bed*; *they had a game of tennis*; *I had a long walk*
(c) to pay someone to do something for you; *I must have my hair cut*; *she's having the house painted*

(d) *(used to form the past of verbs)* **have they finished their work?**; *she has never been to Paris*; *they had finished supper when we arrived*; *I haven't seen him for two days*; *if she had asked me I would have said no*

(e) *(greetings)* **have a nice day!**; *have a good trip!*

(f) had better = it would be a good thing if; *you had better stay here instead of going to the hotel*; *hadn't you better answer the phone?* (NOTE: have *or* has - having - had - has had)

① **have got**
['hæv 'gɒt] *verb*

(a) to have; *she's got dark hair*; *have you got a table for three, please?*; *half the people in the office have got flu*

(b) to own or possess; *she's got a lot of money*; *they've got a new green car*; *the house hasn't got a telephone*; *they haven't got enough to eat*

(c) *(used to mean* must*)*; *she's got to learn to drive*; *why have you got to go so early?*

③ **have (got) to do with**
[hæv gɒt tɪ 'duː 'wɪθ] *verb*

to concern; *it's got nothing to do with you*

③ **haven't**
['hævɪnt]
see HAVE

③ **have on**
['hæv 'ɒn] *verb*

(a) to wear; *what did she have on when she left the party?*; *I can't answer the door - I've got nothing on*

(b) to have something on = to be busy with visits, meetings, etc.; *I haven't anything on tonight so I'll be able to finish painting the bathroom*

(c) *(informal)* **to have someone on** = to trick someone; *I think he's having you on*

① **have to**
['hæv 'tuː] *verb*

used with other verbs to mean 'must'; *in England everyone has to drive on the left*; *he had to walk to work because he missed the bus*; *do we have to get up early?*; *you have to go through customs*; *the car has to have its 10,000km service*

④ **hawk**
[hɔːk]
1 *noun*

large bird that catches and eats other birds or small animals; *the hawk was hovering over the motorway*; **she has eyes like a hawk** = she notices everything

2 *verb*

to sell goods from door to door or in the street; **to hawk something round** = to take an idea or a project to various companies to see if anyone will accept it; *he hawked his idea for a film round all the studios but no one wanted it*

④ **hayfever**
['heɪfiːvɪ] *noun*

running nose and eyes caused by an allergy to flowers, scent or dust; *when I have hayfever I prefer to stay indoors*; *the hayfever season starts in May*

④ **hazard**
['hæzɪd]
1 *noun*

dangerous situation; *don't leave those cardboard boxes in the passage - they're a fire hazard*; **at hazard** = at risk; **hazard warning lights** = warning lights on a car; *he stopped the car and switched on his hazard warning lights*

2 *verb*

to risk; **to hazard a guess** = to risk making a guess; *I wouldn't hazard a guess at how many people will come to the concert*

① **he**
[hiː] *pronoun referring to a man or boy, and some animals*; *he's my brother*; *he and I met in Oxford Circus*; *he's eaten all my pudding*; *don't be frightened of the dog - he won't hurt you*; *(see also* HIM, HIS*)* (NOTE: when it is the object he becomes him: he hit the ball *or* the ball hit him; when it follows the verb to be, he usually becomes him: who's that? - it's him, the man who borrowed my knife)

① **head**
[hed]
1 *noun*

(a) top part of the body, which contains the eyes, nose, mouth, brain, etc.; *he says he can relax by standing on his head*; *she hit her head on the cupboard door*; **head over heels** = over and over; *she rolled head over heels down the hill*; **to be head over heels in love** = to be madly in love; *he's head over heels in love with my sister*; **to shake your head** = to move your head from side to side to mean 'no'; *she asked him if he wanted any more coffee and he shook his head*; *(informal)* **head and shoulders above** = much better than; *she's head and shoulders above all the others in the class*

(b) brain, intelligence; *she has a good head for figures*; *he tried to do the sum in his head*; *if we all put our heads together we might come up with a solution*; **to take it into your head to do something** = to decide to do something suddenly; *he took it into his head to join the army*

(c) first place, top part; *an old lady was standing at the head of the queue*; *his name comes at the head of the list*

(d) most important person; *she's the head of the sales department*; *the head waiter showed us to our table*

(e) top side of a coin, usually with the head of a person on it; **to play heads or tails** = to spin a coin to see which side comes down on top, and so decide something; **heads I win** = if the coin falls with the top side up, then I will win (NOTE: the opposite side is **tails**)

(f) one person, when counting; *she counted heads as the party got onto the coach*; **a head** *or* **per head** = for each person; *the trip costs £25.00 a head or per head*

(g) to come to a head = to reach a crisis point; *things came to a head when all the family met to discuss grandfather's will*

(h) *(informal)* head teacher; *he went into the head's study*; *the head was very annoyed by the boys' behaviour*

2 *verb*

(a) to be the first, to lead; *he heads the list of champions*

(b) to go towards; *she headed immediately for the manager's office*; *the car headed east along the motorway*; *he's heading towards the Channel ports*; *she's heading for trouble*

(c) to be the manager, the most important person; *he heads our research department*

(d) *(in football)* to hit the a ball with your head; *he headed the ball into the goal*

④ **headache**
['hedeɪk] *noun*

(a) pain in your head, caused by changes in pressure in the blood vessels; *I must lie down, I've got a dreadful headache*; *take an aspirin if you have a headache*

(b) problem; *the lack of resources in the education system is one of the government's biggest headaches*

④ **head-first**
['hed'fɜːst] *adverb*

(a) with your head first; *he tripped and fell head-first down the stairs*

(b) hastily; *don't rush head-first into a deal with someone you hardly know*

④ **heading**
['hedɪŋ] *noun*

words at the top of a piece of text; *items are listed under several headings*; *look under the heading 'Hotels and Restaurants'*

② **headlights**
['hedlaɪts] *noun*

main white lights on the front of a vehicle; *dip your headlights when coming to the crossroads*; **dipped headlights** = headlights with the beam set low so as not to hurt the eyes of other drivers

③ **headline**
['hedlaɪn] *noun*

(a) words in large letters on the front page of a newspaper; *did you see the headlines about the accident?*; *the newspaper headline says TAXES TO GO UP*

(b) news headlines = summary of the news on TV or radio; *we will have an interview with the minister following the headlines*

② **head-on**
['hedɒn] *adjective & adverb*

(a) with the front first, direct; *we had a head-on battle with the police*; **a head-on collision** = collision where two vehicles run into each other front to front

(b) directly; *he decided to meet objections head-on*

④ **headphones**
['hedfɪʊnz] *noun*

devices which you put on your ears to listen to music tapes, etc.; *please use your headphones if you want to listen to the music programme or watch the film*

③ **headquarters (HQ)**
['hed'kwɔːtɪz] *noun*

main offices; *several people were arrested and taken to the police headquarters*; **the headquarters staff** = the staff working in a headquarters

④ **heal**
[hiːl] *verb*

to mend, to become healthy again; *after six weeks, his wound has still not healed* (NOTE: do not confuse with **heel**)

① **health**
[helθ] *noun*

(a) being well, being free from any mental or physical illness; *he has enjoyed the best of health for years*; *smoking is bad for your health*; **health club** = club for people who want to improve their health by taking exercise, dieting, etc.; **health farm** = clinic in the country for people who want to improve their health and appearance by taking exercise, dieting, etc.; **health risk** = something which may be bad for people's health; *waste thrown into the river poses a health risk to the population*; **health service** = service in charge of doctors, hospitals, etc.; **health warning** = warning that something may be bad for your health; *each pack of cigarettes carries a government health warning*

(b) your health! *or* **good health!** = greeting said to someone when drinking

③ **healthy**
['helθi] *adjective*

(a) not ill; *he's healthier than he has ever been*

(b) which makes you well; *she's keeping to a healthy diet*; *East Anglia is the healthiest place in England*; *jacket potatoes are healthier than chips*

(c) good, strong; *he has a healthy dislike of politicians*; *the company's bank account is looking very healthy* (NOTE: **healthier - healthiest**)

④ **heap**
[hiːp]

1 *noun*

(a) pile; *heaps of coal lay in the yard*; *step over that heap of rubbish*

(b) *(informal)* **heaps of** = lots of; *apple pie with heaps of cream*; *don't rush - we've heaps of time*

2 *verb*

to pile up; *a pile of presents were heaped under the Christmas tree*; *boxes were heaped up on the station platform*

① **hear**
[hɪɪ] *verb*

(a) to catch sounds with your ears; *he heard footsteps behind him*; *you could hear the sound of church bells in the distance*; *I heard her drive up in the car*; *can you hear him singing in the bath?*

(b) to listen to something; *did you hear the talk on the radio?*; *I heard it on the BBC news*

(c) to get information; *I hear he's got a new job*; *have you heard that the Minister has resigned?*; *we have not heard from them for some time* (NOTE: hearing - heard [hɜːd])

② **hearing**
['hɪɪrɪŋ] *noun*

(a) being able to hear; *bats have a very sharp sense of hearing*; *she has hearing difficulties* (NOTE: no plural in this meaning)

(b) hearing aid = electric device put in the ear to improve hearing; *she wears a little hearing aid which you can hardly see*

(c) session of a tribunal or court; *the hearing is expected to last three days*

③ **hear of**
['hɪɪ 'ɒv] *verb*

(a) to know about something; *I've heard of a new restaurant in the High Street*; *she's never heard of the Rolling Stones*

(b) *(formal)* **not to hear of it** = not to accept an offer; *I said I would pay for the glass I broke, but she wouldn't hear of it*

① **heart**
[hɑːt] *noun*

(a) main organ in the body, which pumps blood around the body; *she isn't dead - her heart's still beating*; *the doctor listened to his heart*; *he has had heart trouble for years*

(b) centre of feelings; *my heart sank when I realized that he hadn't read my letter*; **with all my heart** = with all my love; **to know something by heart** = to know and remember something; *I don't know his phone number by heart, so I'll just look it up for you*; **to learn something by heart** = to learn and remember something; *she learnt the poem by heart*; **to lose heart** = to stop being interested in something; *after all the delays she lost heart in the project*; **don't take it to heart** = don't be too sad about it; **his heart isn't in it** = he has lost interest in it; **to set your heart on something** = to want something very much; *he has set his heart on buying a little sailing boat*

(c) centre, middle; *the restaurant is in the heart of the old town*

(d) one of the red suits in a game of cards, shaped like a heart; *my last two cards were the ten and the queen of hearts* (NOTE: the other red suit is **diamonds; clubs** and **spades** are the black suits)

① **heart attack**
['hɑːt ə'tæk] *noun*

condition where the heart suffers because of bad blood supply; *she had a heart attack but is recovering well*

② **heat**
[hiːt]

1 *noun*

(a) being hot; *the heat of the sun made the ice cream melt*; *cook the vegetables over a low heat*; **heat wave** = sudden period of high temperature; *the heat wave has made rivers dry up* (NOTE: no plural)

(b) one part of a sports competition; *there are two heats before the final race*; **dead heat** = race where two competitors finish equal; *the race finished in a dead heat*

2 *verb*

to make hot; *can you heat the soup while I'm getting the table ready?*; *the room was heated by a small electric fire*; *heat the milk to room temperature*

② **heated**
['hiːtɪd] *adjective*

(a) made warm; *the car has a heated rear window*; **a heated swimming pool** = pool where the water is kept warm; *the school has a heated swimming pool*

(b) angry; *there was a heated discussion after the meeting*; *MPs became very heated during the debate*

② **heater**
['hiːtɪ] *noun*

device for heating; *there is an electric heater in the bathroom*; *I'm cold - I'll to put the heater on*; **water heater** = device for heating water in a house; **electric heater** = heating device which runs on electricity; *the island can be cool in the winter, so the flat has several portable electric heaters*; **gas heater** = heating device which runs on gas

② **heating**
['hiːtɪŋ] *noun*

way of warming a house, an office, etc.; *we switch the heating off on May 1st*; *I'm cold - I'm going to switch the heating on*; **central heating** = heating of a whole house from one main heater and several radiators; *our central heating comes on at 6.30*; *the central heating has broken down again*

③ **heaven**
['hevn] *noun*

(a) paradise, place where good people are believed to go after they die; *she believes that when she dies she will go to heaven*

(b) the heavens = the sky above; **the heavens opened** = it poured with rain

(c) *(phrase showing surprise)* **good heavens!** *it's almost ten o'clock!*; **for heaven's sake =** expression showing you are annoyed, or that something is important; *what are you screaming for? - it's only a little mouse, for heaven's sake*; *for heaven's sake try to be quiet, we don't want the guards to hear us!*

③ **heavily**
['hevɪlɪ] *adverb*
(a) as if you are heavy; *he sat down heavily on the little chair*
(b) to a great extent, very much; *the company was heavily criticized in the press*; *she is heavily in debt*; *it rained heavily during the night*
(c) to sleep heavily = to sleep without waking

① **heavy**
['hevɪ] *adjective*
(a) which weighs a lot; *this suitcase is so heavy I can hardly lift it*; *she's heavier than I am*; **heavy goods vehicle (HGV) =** very large truck
(b) a heavy meal = a meal which is filling and uncomfortable in your stomach; *don't go to bed just after you've had a heavy meal*
(c) in large amounts; *there has been a heavy demand for the book*; *there was a heavy fall of snow during the night*; *the radio says there is heavy traffic in the centre of town*; **to make heavy weather of something =** to make something you are doing more difficult and complicated than it should be; *we asked him to sort out the invoices but he's really making heavy weather of it*; **heavy smoker =** person who smokes a lot of cigarettes; *he was a heavy smoker and died of lung cancer* (NOTE: **heavier - heaviest**)

③ **hectare**
['hektɑː] *noun*
area of land measuring 100 metres by 100 metres, i.e. 10,000 square metres or 2.47 acres; *what is the normal yield per hectare?*; *the farm buildings and 20 hectares of land are for sale by auction* (NOTE: usually written **ha** after figures: **2,500 ha**)

④ **hedge**
[hedʒ]
1 *noun*
(a) row of bushes planted and kept trimmed to form a screen around a field or garden; *there is a thick hedge round the churchyard*
(b) financial protection; *a hedge against inflation*
2 *verb*
to hedge your bets = to invest in several areas so as to be protected against loss in one of them

④ **heel**
[hiːl]
1 *noun*
(a) the back part of the foot; *after walking all day in the mountains, her heel hurt*; **she rolled head over heels down the hill =** she rolled over and over like a ball; **to take to your heels =** to

run away; *when they heard the police car, they took to their heels and disappeared round the corner*; **on the heels of someone** *or* **something =** following immediately behind someone *or* something; *with the police hot on his heels he fled to Argentina*; **to turn on your heel =** to turn suddenly and go in the opposite direction; *she turned on her heel and walked out of the room*
(b) back part of a sock, stocking or shoe; *he's got a hole in the heel of his sock*; *she always wear shoes with high heels* or *high-heeled shoes*
2 *verb*
to put a new heel on a shoe; *I want these shoes soled and heeled, please* (NOTE: do not confuse with **heal**)

② **height**
[haɪt] *noun*
(a) measurement of how high something is; *the height of the bridge is only 3m*; **he is of above average height =** he is taller than most men
(b) highest point; *looking down on the city from the heights around*; *it is difficult to find hotel rooms at the height of the tourist season*; **I don't like heights** *or* **I haven't got a head for heights =** my head goes round and round when I am high up on a building

④ **heighten**
['haɪtn] *verb*
to increase; *the TV programme has helped to heighten public awareness of the drug problem*

④ **heir, heiress**
['eɪ or eɪ'res] *noun*
(a) man or woman who will receive property from someone after they die; *he's the heir to the banking fortune*; *you've heard of Barbara, the tobacco heiress?*; *his heirs divided the estate between them* (NOTE: the plural of **heiress** is **heiresses**)
(b) the heir to the throne = the man or woman who will be king or queen when the present king or queen dies (NOTE: do not confuse with **hair, air**)

③ **held**
[held]
see HOLD

④ **helicopter**
['helɪkɒptɪ] *noun*
aircraft which can rise straight up in the air; *you can take a helicopter from the airport to the centre of the town*; *it is only a short helicopter flight from the centre of town to the factory site*

③ **he'll**
[hiːl] = HE WILL

① **hell**
[hel] *noun*
(a) bad place where wicked people are sent after they die; *old pictures show hell as a burning place where wicked people are pushed into the fires* (NOTE: does not take the articles **a** *or* **the**)
(b) *(informal)* miserable place; *it's hell working in the office these days*; **to give someone hell =** to treat someone very badly

(c) a hell of a or **one hell of a** = (i) a dreadful thing; (ii) a marvellous thing; *the car's making a hell of a noise*; *that was one hell of a party last night!*
(d) *(informal word used to make a phrase stronger)* *what the hell's been going on here?*; *am I going to lend you £50? Am I hell!*

① **hello**
[hɪ'ləʊ] *interjection showing a greeting*
hello! Mary, I'm glad to see you; *when you see her, say hello to her from me*; *she called hello from the other side of the street* (NOTE: also spelt **hallo, hullo**; in American English, use **hi**)

④ **helmet**
['helmɪt] *noun*
solid hat used as a protection; *soldiers wear helmets when they are on patrol*; *you must wear a helmet when riding a motorbike*; **crash helmet** = solid hat worn by motorcyclists, etc.; *many cyclists now wear crash helmets*; **safety helmet** = solid hat worn by building workers, etc.; *visitors to the building site must wear safety helmets* (NOTE: also called **hard hats**)

① **help**
[help]
1 *noun*
(a) something which makes it easier for you to do something; *she was washing the floor with the help of a big brush*; *do you need any help with moving the furniture?*; *she finds the computer a great help in writing her book*; *her assistant is not much help in the office - he can't type or drive*
(b) providing aid and assistance to someone; *people were calling for help from the ruins of the house*; *the nurses offered help to people injured in the accident*; **to go to someone's help** = to try to rescue someone; *the rescue teams went to the help of the flood victims*
(c) financial assistance; *the government provides help to areas with high unemployment*
(d) person who helps; *she has a home help who comes in twice a week to do the housework*
2 *verb*
(a) to make it easier for someone to do something; *he helped the old lady up the steps*; *the government wants to help small businesses*; *your father can help you with your homework*; *one of my friends helped me move the piano into the bedroom*
(b) *(with* **cannot***)* not to be able to stop doing something; *he couldn't help laughing*; *she can't help stealing clothes from shops*; **it can't be helped** = nothing can be done to improve the situation; **he can't help it** = it's not his fault; *she can't help it if she has a bad back*
(c) to help yourself = to serve yourself with food, etc.; *she helped herself to some cake*; *if you feel thirsty just help yourself*; *(informal)* **to help yourself to** = to steal; *she helped herself to my wallet*

3 *interjection meaning that you are in difficulties*; *help! help! call the police!*; *help! I can't stop the car!*

④ **helper**
['helpə] *noun*
person who helps; *she works two mornings a week as a helper in a playgroup*; *I need two willing helpers to wash the car*

② **helpful**
['helpfʊl] *adjective*
which helps; *she made some helpful suggestions*; *they were very helpful when we moved house*

③ **helping**
['helpɪŋ] *noun*
1 amount of food given to someone; *the helpings are very small in this restaurant*; *children's helpings are not as large as those for adults*; **second helping** = more of the same food; *can I have a second helping of pudding, please?*
2 *adjective*
which helps; **to give someone a helping hand** = to help someone with work; *he gave me a helping hand with the cleaning*

② **helpless**
['helpləs] *adjective*
not able to do anything; *the house was burning and I couldn't do anything - I felt so helpless!*; *he's helpless when his car breaks down*

④ **hen**
[hen] *noun*
adult female chicken; *the hens were scared by the neighbour's dog*; *look, one of the hens has laid an egg!*

② **hence**
[hens] *adverb*
(a) this is why; *he's got flu, hence his not coming to work*
(b) *(formal)* from now; *five months hence, the situation should be better*

① **her**
[hɜː]
1 *object pronoun referring to a female*
did you see her?; *he told her to go away*; *there's a parcel for her in reception*
2 *adjective*
(belonging to a female, a ship, a country) *someone has stolen all her luggage*; *have you seen her father?*; *the dog doesn't want to eat her food*; *France is helping her businesses to sell more abroad*

④ **herb**
[hɜːb *US* ɜːb] *noun*
plant used to give flavour to food, or as a medicine; *add some herbs to the sauce*

④ **herd**
[hɜːd] *noun*
a group of animals, especially cows; *herds of cows were grazing on the hillside* (NOTE: do not

confuse with **heard**; the word **herd** is usually used with cows; for sheep, goats, and birds such as hens or geese, the word to use is **flock**)

① **here**
[hɪɪ] *adverb*
(a) in this place; *I'll sit here in the shade and wait for you; here are the keys you lost; I'll put the book down here next to your computer; they have been living here in England for a long time; here you are* = take this; *here you are, today's newspaper!*
(b) to this place; *come here at once!; can you bring the chairs here, please?; here comes the bus!* (NOTE: when **here** comes at the beginning of a sentence, the following subject comes after the verb if the subject is a noun and not a pronoun: **here comes the bus** but **here it comes**)

④ **heritage**
['herɪtɪdʒ] *noun*
important national treasures passed from one generation to the next; *the castle is part of our national heritage*; **heritage attraction** *or* **heritage museum** *or* **heritage park** = tourist facility which is based on the area's historical or cultural background

③ **hero**
['hɪɪrɪʊ] *noun*
(a) brave man; *the hero of the fire was the fireman who managed to rescue the children from an upstairs room*; **hero worship** = excessive praise and love for someone who is considered a hero
(b) main male character in a book, play, film, etc.; *the hero of the story is a little boy* (NOTE: plural is **heroes**)

④ **heroine**
['herɪʊɪn] *noun*
(a) brave woman; *the heroine of the accident was a passing cyclist who pulled the children out of the burning car*
(b) main female character in a book, play, film, etc.; *the heroine of the film is a school teacher*

① **hers**
[hɜːz] *pronoun*
belonging to her; *that watch is hers, not mine*; **she introduced me to a friend of hers** = to one of her friends

① **herself**
[hɜːˈself] *pronoun referring to a female subject; the boss' wife wrote to me herself; did your sister enjoy herself?; she's too young to be able to dress herself*; **she lives all by herself** = she lives all alone; **she did it all by herself** = she did it with no one to help her; *now she's eight, we let her go to the shops all by herself*

③ **he's**
[hiːz] = HE HAS, HE IS

④ **hesitate**
['hezɪteɪt] *verb*
to be slow to act, because you can't decide; *she's hesitating about whether to accept the job; he hesitated for a moment and then said 'no'*

④ **hesitation**
[hezɪˈteɪʃn] *noun*
waiting and not deciding; *after a moment's hesitation he jumped into the water; I have no hesitation in recommending him for the job*

③ **hey!**
[heɪ] *interjection showing a greeting or surprise; hey! you!, what are you doing there?; hey! that's my chair!*

③ **HGV**
= HEAVY GOODS VEHICLE

① **hi!**
[haɪ] *interjection showing a greeting*
Hi! I'm your tour leader; Hi! Mary, how are you today?; say hi to her from me (NOTE: **hallo**, **hullo** are more usual in British English, **hi** in American English)

① **hid**
[hɪd]
see HIDE

① **hidden**
['hɪdn] *adjective*
which cannot be seen; *there's a hidden safe in the wall behind his desk; they're digging in the castle, looking for hidden treasure*; *see also* HIDE

① **hide**
[haɪd]
1 *verb*
(a) to put something where no one can see or find it; *she hid the presents in the kitchen; they kept some gold coins hidden under the bed; someone has hidden my car keys*
(b) to put yourself where no one can see or find you; *they hid in the bushes until the police car had gone past; quick! hide behind the door!* (NOTE: **hiding - hid** [hɪd] **- has hidden** ['hɪdn])
2 *noun*
(a) thick skin of a large animal, treated to make leather; *how many hides are needed to make that leather sofa?; a real hide wallet*
(b) place where people can sit to watch birds without being seen by them; *they set up hides all round the lake*

② **hiding**
['haɪdɪŋ] *noun*
(a) action of putting yourself where no one can find you; *he stayed in hiding for three days until the soldiers left the village; they decided to go into hiding for a time until the police called off their search*; **hiding place** = place where you can hide
(b) *(informal)* beating; *he'll get a hiding from his father when he's caught*

① **high**
[haɪ]
1 *adjective*
(a) reaching far above other things; *Everest is the highest mountain in the world; the new building is 20 storeys high; they are planning a 10-storey-high hotel next to the royal palace; the kitchen has a high ceiling; the door is not*

high enough to let us get the tall pieces of furniture into the room (NOTE: it is used with figures: **the mountain is 1000 metres high; high** also refers to things that are a long way above the ground: **a high mountain, high clouds**; for people and thin things like trees use **tall: a tall man**)

(b) large in quantity; *he earns a high income; the high level of unemployment in the country; high prices put customers off; the car shakes when going at high speeds; the price of petrol is higher every year*

(c) important; *she occupies a high post in the ministry; he was quite high up in the police force when he retired*

(d) *(meat, especially game)* which has been kept until it is beginning to rot and has a strong flavour

(e) *(informal)* **high on drugs** = influenced by drugs; *some of the teenagers were high on drugs when they were arrested*

2 *adverb*

above; up in the air; *the sun rose high in the sky; the bird flew higher and higher* (NOTE: **higher - highest**)

3 *noun*

high point; **sales have reached an all-time high** = sales are higher than they have ever been before

③ **higher education**
['haɪər edjuːˈkeɪʃn] *noun*
education in universities and colleges; *if you pass your A Levels, you can go on to higher education*

COMMENT: the British higher education system is formed of universities and colleges, where students can take degrees in various specialized subjects. Students need a certain number of passes at 'A' levels to enter a university, and most universities ask students to come for special entrance exams and interviews. Fees in higher education are in some cases met by grants, but many students are required to pay for their own fees and have to take out loans to do this

③ **highlight**
['haɪlaɪt]
1 *noun*

(a) most important or interesting event; *the highlight of our tour of Greece was our visit to the Parthenon*

(b) **highlights** = characters which stand out from the text on a screen by being brighter than the rest

2 *verb*

(a) to draw attention to; *the report highlights the problems of inner city housing*

(b) to make part of the text stand out from the rest; *the headings are highlighted in bold*

③ **highlighter**
['haɪlaɪtər] *noun*
marker pen, a coloured felt pen used to highlight text; *use a highlighter to show where corrections need to be made*

② **highly**
['haɪlɪ] *adverb*
greatly; *the restaurant has been highly recommended; their employees are not very highly paid*; **highly-priced** = with a very high price; **he thinks highly of her** = he admires her very much

④ **high-pitched**
[haɪˈpɪtʃt] *adjective*
making a shrill sound; *he speaks in a very high-pitched voice*

④ **high school**
['haɪ skuːl] *noun*

(a) secondary school; *she moves from primary school to the high school in the autumn*

(b) *US* secondary school, from grade 9 to grade 12; *he's in grade 10 or tenth grade at high school*

④ **high-speed**
['haɪspiːd] *adjective*
which runs or operates at a very high speed; *we took the high-speed train to Paris*

① **High Street**
['haɪ striːt] *noun*
most important street in a village or town, where shops and banks are; *he is the manager of a high street bookshop; there are two fish and chip shops in the High Street* (NOTE: often written **High St.**; the American equivalent is **Main Street**)

③ **high tech**
['haɪ tek] *adjective*
referring to high technology; *high tech industries*

② **highway**
['haɪweɪ] *noun*
main public road; *a little bridge crosses the highway*

③ **the Highway Code**
[ðɪ 'haɪweɪ 'kəʊd] *noun*
British government publication containing the rules for people travelling on roads; *you need to know the Highway Code if you're taking your driving test*

④ **hike**
[haɪk]
1 *noun*

(a) long vigorous walk in the country; *we went for a 10-mile hike in the mountains*

(b) increase; *the gas company has announced another price hike*

2 *verb*

(a) to go for a long vigorous walk; *they were hiking in the Pyrenees when the accident happened*

(b) to increase prices, etc.; *petrol companies have hiked up their prices*

② **hill**

[hɪl] *noun*

piece of high land, but lower than a mountain; *the hills are covered with spring flowers; their house is on top of a hill; if you climb to the top of the hill you will get a good view of the valley*

④ **hillside**

['hɪlsaɪd] *noun*

sloping side of a hill; *their house is halfway up the hillside; a flock of sheep were grazing on the hillside*

① **him**

[hɪm] *object pronoun referring to a male*
have you spoken to him today?; tell him there's a letter waiting for him; that's him! - the man with the beard

① **himself**

[hɪm'self] *pronoun referring to a male subject*
I was served by the manager himself; the doctor has got flu himself; did your brother enjoy himself?; **he lives all by himself** = he lives all alone; **he did it all by himself** = he did it with no one to help him; *now he's eight, we let him go to the shops all by himself*

④ **hint**

[hɪnt]

1 *noun*

(a) hidden suggestion, clue; *he didn't give a hint as to where he was going on holiday; I don't know what to give her for her birthday - have you any hints?;* **to drop a hint** = to make a suggestion; *she's been dropping hints about what she wants for her birthday;* **to take a hint** = to accept a suggestion; *he took the hint and offered to pay for the lamp he broke*

(b) very small quantity; *there's just a hint of garlic in the soup*

(c) piece of advice; *she gave me some useful hints about painting furniture*

2 *verb*

to say something in a way that makes people guess what you mean; *she hinted that her sister was pregnant*

④ **hip**

[hɪp]

1 *noun*

(a) part of the body at the top of your legs; *the tailor measured him round the hips*

(b) joint at the top of the leg bone; **hip replacement** = operation to replace the whole hip joint with an artificial one; *old people sometimes need to have hip replacements*

2 *adjective*

very up-to-date; *that's a very hip shirt she's wearing*

③ **hire**

['haɪ]

1 *noun*

(a) paying money to rent a car, boat, piece of equipment, etc., for a period of time; **boat hire** *or* **cycle hire** *or* **car hire** = lending of boats, cycles, cars to people for money; **car hire firm** *or* **coach hire firm** = company which owns cars *or* coaches and lends them to people for money; **hire car** = car which has been hired; *he was driving a hire car when the accident happened*

(b) **'for hire'** = sign on a taxi showing it is empty and available for hire

2 *verb*

(a) *(of owner)* **to hire out** = to allow other people to take something and use it, against payment of a fee; *he hires out boats on the river*

(b) *(of borrower)* to pay money to use a car, boat, piece of equipment, etc., for a time; *she hired a car for the weekend; he was driving a hired car when the accident happened*

(c) to engage someone to work for you; *we've hired three more sales assistants; they hired a small company to paint their offices*

③ **hire purchase (HP)**

['haɪ 'pɜːtʃɪs] *noun*

system of buying something by paying a sum of money regularly each month; *we've planning to buy our new refrigerator on hire purchase; she had to sign a hire-purchase agreement* (NOTE: American English uses **to buy on the installment plan**)

① **his**

[hɪz]

1 *adjective*

belonging to him; *he's lost all his money; have you met his mother?; our dog wants his food*

2 *pronoun* belonging to him; *that watch is his, not mine;* **he introduced me to a friend of his** = to one of his friends

③ **Hispanic**

[hɪs'pænɪk]

1 *adjective*

referring to countries where Spanish is spoken, especially South American countries; *Hispanic communities in the southern United States*

2 *noun*

person whose native language is Spanish, especially one living in the United States; *Hispanics form an important community in Florida*

③ **historian**

[hɪ'stɔːriːn] *noun*

person who studies or writes history; *a historian who specializes in the Chinese Empire; the book was written by a French historian*

③ **historic**

[hɪ'stɒrɪk] *adjective*

famous in history; *a historic agreement has been signed* (NOTE: can be preceded by **an** in formal style: **it is an historic day for the town**)

② **historical**

[hɪ'stɒrɪkl] *adjective*

referring to history; *he likes books of historical interest;* **historical novel** = story set in a particular period in the past

① **history**
['hɪstɪri] *noun*
(a) study of the past, of past events; *he is studying Greek history*; *she failed her history exam*; *she teaches history at London University*
(b) book which tells the story of what happened in the past; *he wrote a history of the French Revolution*
(c) natural history = the study of plants and animals

① **hit**
[hɪt]
1 *noun*
(a) very popular song, film, performer, etc.; *the song rapidly became a hit*; *the play was a West End hit*; *she was a hit with the old people's club*; **the hit parade** = a list of hit songs
(b) blow or knock; *just one more hit on the nail and that will be enough*
(c) action of visiting a site on the Internet; *how many hits did we have on our site last week?*
2 *verb*
(a) to knock; *the car hit the tree*; *she hit him on the head with a bottle*; *she hit the ball so hard that we can't find it*; *I hit my head on the cupboard door*; *(informal)* **to hit the town** = to go and have a night out; *come on, let's hit the town*
(b) to damage, to affect badly; *the company has been hit by falling sales*
(c) to realize; *it suddenly hit her that now she was divorced she would have to live alone*
(d) to reach a figure or target; *our sales hit a record high last month*; *new cases of flu hit two thousand last week* (NOTE: **hitting - hit**)

③ **hit back**
['hɪt 'bæk] *verb*
(a) to hit someone who has hit you; *the muggers hit him so hard that he collapsed before he could hit them back*
(b) to do something as a reaction to something; *when the supermarket chain lowered their prices, the other chains hit back by lowering prices too*; *he hit back at the inspectors, saying that their report was unfair*

④ **hitch**
[hɪtʃ]
1 *noun*
unexpected temporary problem; *there's a hitch, and the wedding has been postponed*; **without a hitch** = with no trouble or problems; *the party went off without a hitch*
2 *verb*
(a) to hitch up = to pull up; *he hitched up his trousers*
(b) to hitch (a lift) = to ask a driver to take you as a passenger, usually by signalling with the thumb or by holding a sign with your destination written on it; *he hitched a lift to Birmingham*; *her car broke down and she hitched a lift from a passing motorist*

(c) to attach; *the trailer was hitched to the back of the car*

③ **hit on**
['hɪt 'ɒn] *verb*
to discover, to get a good idea; *we hit on the idea of taking him to a concert as a birthday present*

③ **hobby**
['hɒbi] *noun*
favourite thing which you do in your spare time; *his hobby is making model planes* (NOTE: plural is **hobbies)**

④ **hockey**
['hɒki] *noun*
(a) team game played on grass, where you try to hit a small ball into your opponents' goal using a long stick which is curved at the end; *he played in the hockey team at school* (NOTE: called **field hockey** in American English)
(b) ice hockey = form of hockey played on ice using a hard rubber disk instead of a ball; *the ice hockey gold medal will be fought out between Canada and Russia* (NOTE: called simply **hockey** in American English)

> COMMENT: hockey is played between two teams of 11 players, each game having two 35-minute halves; ice hockey is played between two teams of six players, each game being made up of three 20-minute periods

③ **Hogmanay**
['hɒgmɪneɪ] *noun*
festival in Scotland on 31st December, celebrating the New Year

> COMMENT: it is a tradition that the first person who comes through the door on New Year's Day (i.e. after midnight on New Year's Eve) should bring luck. If possible the person should be a dark stranger, and should carry a piece of coal for the fire, as well as food and drink, usually whisky. This tradition also exists in the north of England

① **hold**
[hɪʊld]
1 *verb*
(a) to keep tight, especially in your hand; *she was holding the baby in her arms*; *she held her ticket between her teeth as she was carrying suitcases in both hands*; *hold tight - the machine is going to start*; *he held the bag close to his chest*
(b) to contain, to be large enough for something to fit inside; *the bottle holds two litres*; *the box will hold four pairs of shoes*; *will the car hold eight people?*; *the plane holds 250 passengers*
(c) to make something happen; *they are holding a party for their wedding anniversary*; *the meeting will be held next Tuesday in the town hall*; *we are holding the village flower show next week*

(d) to stay the same; *will the fine weather hold until Saturday?*

(e) to possess; *she holds a valid driving licence*; *he holds the record for the 2000 metres*

(f) *(on telephone)* hold the line please = please wait; *the chairman is on the other line - will you hold?*

(g) to keep inside; *the prisoners were held in police cells overnight*; to hold water = to be valid, to be true; *his argument doesn't hold water*; to hold your breath = to keep air in your lungs to go under water, as a test or because you are afraid that something will happen; *she held her breath under water for a minute*; *we're all holding our breath to see if he wins a gold medal*

(h) to capture and control a place; *the rebels are holding the airport*; *government forces still hold about half the country* (NOTE: holding - held [held])

2 *noun*

(a) bottom part of a ship or an aircraft, in which cargo is stored; *you can't take all that luggage with you, it has to go in the hold*

(b) action of gripping something; *he lost his hold on the ladder*; *keep tight hold of the bag, we don't want it stolen*; to get hold of someone = to find someone you need by telephone; *I tried to get hold of the doctor but he was out*; to get hold of something = to find something which you want to use; *do you know where I can get hold of a ladder?*; to take hold of something = to grip something, to take control of something; *the fire took hold rapidly*

(c) action of having a strong influence over someone; *she has some sort of hold over her husband*

③ **hold back**

['hɪʊld 'bæk] *verb*

(a) not to tell; *she held back important information from the police*

(b) not to go forward; *most of the crowd held back until they saw it was safe*

③ **hold down**

['hɪʊld 'daʊn] *verb*

(a) to keep at a low level; *we are holding our prices down*

(b) to hold down a job = to manage to do a difficult job

② **holder**

['hɪʊldɪ] *noun*

(a) thing which holds; *put the pen back into its holder*

(b) person who holds; *she is a British passport holder or she is the holder of a British passport*; *he is the world record holder in the 1000 metres*

③ **holding**

['hɪʊldɪŋ] *noun*

investments owned; *she has holdings in several British companies*; holding company = company which owns shares in other companies

① **hold on**

['hɪʊld 'ɒn] *verb*

(a) to hold something tightly; *she held on to the rope with both hands*; *hold on to your purse in the crowd*; *hold on tight, we're turning!*

(b) to wait; *hold on a moment, I'll get my umbrella*; *do you want to speak to the manager? - hold on, I'll find him for you*

③ **hold out**

['hɪʊld 'aʊt] *verb*

(a) to move something towards someone; *hold out your plate to be served*; *he held out his hand but she refused to shake it*

(b) to resist against; *the castle held out for ten weeks against a huge enemy army*

③ **hold out for**

['hɪʊld 'aʊt fɔ:] *verb*

to wait and ask for more; *you should hold out for a 10% pay rise*

① **hold up**

['hɪʊld 'ʌp] *verb*

(a) to lift; *he held up his hand*; *he held the little boy up so that he could see the procession*; *the roof is held up by those pillars*

(b) to make late; *the planes were held up by fog*; *government red tape is holding up the deal*; *the strike will hold up deliveries*

(c) to attack and rob; *six gunmen held up the security van*

③ **hold-up**

['hɪʊldʌp] *noun*

(a) delay, time when something is later than planned; *long hold-ups are expected because of road works on the motorway*; *there's been a hold-up and the shipment won't arrive till next week*

(b) armed attack; *the gang carried out three hold-ups in the same day*

① **hole**

[hɪʊl] *noun*

opening, space in something; *you've got a hole in your shoe*; *we all looked through the hole in the fence*; *rabbits live in holes in the ground*

① **holiday**

['hɒlɪdeɪ] *noun*

(a) day on which no work is done because of laws or religious rules; *the office is closed for the Christmas holiday*; bank holiday = special day when most people do not go to work and the banks are closed; *New Year's Day is a bank holiday*; public holiday = day when all workers rest and enjoy themselves instead of working; statutory holiday = holiday which is fixed by law

(b) period when you don't work, but rest, go away and enjoy yourself; *when are you taking your holiday or when are you planning to go on holiday?*; *he's going to Spain on holiday*; *we always spend our holidays in the mountains*; *how many days' holiday do you have each year?*; *the manager isn't in the office - he's on holiday*; *the job carries five weeks' holiday =*

one of the conditions of the job is that you have five weeks' holiday each year; **the summer holidays** = period during the summer when children do not go to school, and when many families go away; *our summer holidays last from July to September*; *the weather was awful during the summer holidays*; *see also* BANK HOLIDAY (NOTE: **holiday** is often used without **the**; Note also that the American English is usually **vacation**)

③ **Holland**
['hɒlɪnd] *noun*

another name for the Netherlands (NOTE: strictly speaking, **Holland** is only one of the provinces of the Netherlands (the province to the north of Amsterdam), but the word is very frequently used in English to mean the whole country)

④ **hollow**
['hɒlɪʊ]

1 *noun*

lower part on a flat surface; *they made a hollow in the ground for a camp fire*

2 *adjective*

with a hole inside; *a hollow log*; *if you tap the box it sounds hollow*

④ **holly**
['hɒlɪ] *noun*

small evergreen tree with shiny dark green leaves with sharp spines, and bright red berries; *for the Christmas party, we decorate the house with holly and balloons*

③ **holy**
['hɪʊlɪ] *adjective*

(a) sacred; *they went to ask a holy man his advice* (NOTE: do not confuse with **wholly**; note: **holier - holiest**)

(b) the Holy Father = the Pope; **the Holy See** = the office of Pope

① **home**
[hɪʊm]

1 *noun*

(a) place where you live; *their home is a flat in the centre of London*; *will you be at home tomorrow morning?*; *when do you leave home for work in the morning?*; **make yourself at home** = do as if you were in your own home; *he lay down on the sofa, opened a bottle of beer, and made himself at home*; **home from home** = comfortable and welcoming place, just like your home; *the hotel is a real home from home*; *(informal)* **nothing to write home about** = nothing very exciting or special; *his new job is nothing to write home about*

(b) area where you come from; *she lives in London but her home is in the mountains of Wales*; *his home is in the West Country*

(c) house; *they are building fifty new homes on the outskirts of the village*

(d) house where people are looked after; *my aunt has moved to an old people's home*; **a children's home** = a home for children who have no parents or who come from broken homes

(e) *(in sports)* **at home** = on the local sports ground; *our team is playing at home next Saturday* (NOTE: the opposite is **away**)

(f) family, household; *she comes from a broken home*

2 *adverb*

towards the place where you usually live; *we've got to go home now*; *he usually gets home by 7 o'clock*; *don't send it - I'll take it home with me*; *if you don't want to walk, you can always take the bus home* (NOTE: used without a preposition: **he went home, she's coming home,** etc.)

3 *adjective*

(a) referring to where you live or where you were born; *my home town is Birmingham*; *send the letter to my home address, not to my office*; **home cooking** = style of food as cooked at home, not in restaurants; *I like good home cooking*

(b) *(in sports)* local; *the home side won*; *our team beat the home team 3 - 0*; *we have a home game next Saturday*

(c) in this country, not abroad; *home sales were better than exports last month*; *they find it difficult selling into the home market*

④ **homeland**
['hɪʊmlænd] *noun*

home of a people; *the refugees tried to return to their homeland after the war*

④ **homeless**
['hɪʊmlɪs]

1 *adjective*

with nowhere to live; *the council has a duty to house homeless families*

2 *noun*

the homeless = people with nowhere to live; *the homeless sleep in parks or doorways*

④ **Home Office**
['hɪʊm 'ɒfɪs] *noun*

British Government department dealing with internal affairs, such as the police and prisons (NOTE: the department is run by the **Home Secretary**. In other countries this department is usually called the **Ministry of the Interior**; in the USA it is called the **Department of the Interior**)

④ **Home Secretary**
['hɪʊm 'sekrɪtɪrɪ] *noun*

British government minister in charge of the Home Office (NOTE: in other countries, this minister is usually called the **Minister of the Interior**; in the USA, he is the **Secretary of the Interior**)

② **homework**
['hɪʊmwɜːk] *noun*

work which you take home from school to do in the evening; **have you finished your maths homework?**; **I haven't any homework today, so I can watch TV** (NOTE: no plural)

④ **homosexual**
[hɪʊmɪʊˈseksjʊɪl] *adjective & noun* (person) who is attracted to people of the same sex; **did you know her brother is homosexual?**

① **honest**
['ɒnɪst] *adjective*
(a) who tells the truth; **he was honest with the police and told them what he had done**
(b) (person) who can be trusted; **I wouldn't buy a car from that garage - I'm not sure they're completely honest**

① **honestly**
['ɒnɪstli] *adverb*
telling the truth; **honestly, it was John who took the money, not me**; **I honestly don't think she will ever come back to live here**

④ **honesty**
['ɒnɪsti] *noun*
(a) telling the truth; **I admire him for his honesty in saying the job was too difficult for him**; **in all honesty** = saying what is true; **in all honesty I don't think we'll be able to finish the job on time**
(b) garden plant with purple flowers, and silver seed cases

③ **honey**
['hʌni] *noun*
(a) sweet substance produced by bees; **I like honey on toast**; **Greek cakes are often made with honey**
(b) (calling a person you love) **hey, honey, come and look at this!**; **honey, don't get mad at me!**

③ **honeymoon**
['hʌnimuːn]
1 *noun*
(a) holiday taken immediately after a wedding; **they went on honeymoon to Corsica**; **honeymoon couple** = two people on honeymoon
(b) period after an election when the new government is popular; **the president's honeymoon period has come to an end**
2 *verb*
to go on a honeymoon; **they plan to honeymoon in Florida**

③ **honour** *US* **honor**
['ɒnɪ]
1 *noun*
(a) acting according to what you think is right; **he's a man of honour**; **code of honour** = rules of right and wrong which are applied to what people do
(b) mark of respect; **it is an honour for me to be invited here today**
(c) **honours degree** = university degree, showing a high level of study
(d) **Your Honour** = way of addressing a judge

(e) (informal) **to do the honours** = to act as host at a party; **we all need some drinks, will you do the honours, John?**
2 *verb*
(a) to respect, to pay respect to; **to honour the dead**
(b) to give an award as a mark of respect; **he was honoured by the university**
(c) to do what you promised; **he honoured the agreement and gave the staff a pay rise**
(d) (of a bank) **to honour a cheque** = to pay the sum written on the cheque

④ **honourable** *US* **honorable**
['ɒnrɪbl] *adjective*
who or which can be respected; **he lived the rest of his life in honourable retirement**

③ **hook**
[huk]
1 *noun*
(a) bent piece of metal for hanging things on; **hang your coat on the hook behind the door**
(b) very small piece of bent metal, attached to a line for catching fish; **the fish ate the worm but didn't swallow the hook**; **to get someone off the hook** = to get someone out of a difficult situation; **she got him off the hook by lying to his boss**
2 *verb*
to hang on a hook; to attach with a hook; **she hooked the curtains back to let in more light**

③ **hop**
[hɒp]
1 *noun*
(a) little jump; **some birds walk in a series of little hops**; (informal) **to catch someone on the hop** = to catch unexpectedly
(b) short flight; **it's only a short hop from London to Paris**
(c) bitter fruit of a climbing plant, used in making beer; **hops are used to give the bitter flavour to British beer**
2 *verb*
(a) to jump on one leg; **he hurt his toe and had to hop around on one foot**; **hopping mad** = very angry; **he was hopping mad when they told him his car had been stolen**
(b) (of birds, animals, etc.) to jump with both feet together; **the bird hopped across the grass**; **the frog hopped onto the lily leaf**; (informal) **hop it!** = go away!
(c) (informal) **to hop in** = to get in; **I stopped the car and told him to hop in**; **to hop on** *or* **to hop off** = to get on *or* off; **with the old London buses, you can hop on and off anywhere along the street, although it can be dangerous** (NOTE: **hopping - hopped**)

① **hope**
[hɪʊp]
1 *noun*
wanting and expecting something to happen; **our only hope is that she will get better soon**; **they have given up all hope of rescuing any**

more victims from the floods; **in the hope that** = wanting something to happen; *I rang in the hope that you might have a table free for tonight*

2 *verb*

(a) to want and expect something to happen; *we all hope our team wins*; *she's hoping she will soon be able to drive a car*; *I hope it doesn't rain*; **I hope so** = I want it to happen; *are you coming to the party? - yes, I hope so*; **I hope not** = I don't want it to happen; *it's going to rain tomorrow, isn't it? - I hope not!*; **to hope for something** = to want something to happen; *we are hoping for a change in the weather, it's rained every day this week so far*

(b) to expect to do something; *the chairman hopes to be at the meeting tomorrow*; *they said they hoped to be back home by 6 o'clock*; *I had hoped to go to the party but in the end I couldn't*

② **hopeful**
['hɪʊpfʊl]

1 *adjective*

confident that something will happen; *we are hopeful that the company will accept our offer*

2 *noun*

(informal) person who hopes to get a job, a place in a team, etc.; *we are looking at six young hopefuls for the England team*

① **hopefully**
['hɪʊpfʊli] *adverb*

(a) confidently; *he looked hopefully at the list of lottery winners*

(b) let us hope; *hopefully the rain will stop*

② **hopeless**
['hɪʊplɪs] *adjective*

(a) with no hope; *the invoices are in a hopeless mess*; **he's a hopeless case** = he will never get any better

(b) no good; *she's hopeless at tennis*; *he's hopeless when it comes to mending cars*

③ **horizon**
[hɪ'raɪzn] *noun*

line where the earth and the sky meet; *two ships could be seen on the horizon*

③ **horizontal**
[hɒrɪ'zɒntl] *adjective*

flat, level with the ground; *he drew a horizontal line under the text*

④ **hormone**
['hɔːmɪʊn] *noun*

substance produced by glands in the body and carried to other parts of the body by the bloodstream to stimulate certain cells into action; **growth hormone** = hormone which stimulates the growth of the long bones in the body; **hormone replacement therapy** = treatment for women to relieve the symptoms of growing old

③ **horn**
[hɔːn] *noun*

(a) sharp pointed bone growing out of an animal's head; *that bull's horns look very dangerous*

(b) warning device on a car; **to sound a horn** = to make a warning noise with a horn; *sound your horn when you come to the corner*

(c) metal musical instrument which is blown into to make a note; *they played a piece for horn and orchestra*

② **horrible**
['hɒrɪbl] *adjective*

awful, terrible; *the victims of the fire had horrible injuries*; *he's a horrible little boy*; *we had a horrible meal at the restaurant*

③ **horrific**
[hɪ'rɪfɪk] *adjective*

which makes you shocked; *the victims of the crash suffered horrific injuries*; *the police discovered a horrific murder*

③ **horrified**
['hɒrɪfaɪd] *adjective*

frightened or shocked; *when she saw the pictures she was horrified*; *the horrified spectators watched the two planes collide*

④ **horrify**
['hɒrɪfaɪ] *verb*

to frighten, to shock; *the pictures of accident victims are meant to horrify*; *he was horrified by the bill from the builders*

④ **horrifying**
['hɒrɪfaɪɪŋ] *adjective*

frightening, shocking; *they told horrifying tales of their escape from the burning town*

③ **horror**
['hɒrɪ] *noun*

(a) feeling of being very frightened; *he couldn't hide his horror at hearing the news*; *she has a horror of spiders*; *everyone watched in horror as the planes collided*; **horror film** *or* **horror movie** = frightening film, with ghosts, dead bodies, etc.

(b) *(informal)* naughty child; *that boy is a little horror!*

① **horse**
[hɔːs] *noun*

(a) large animal used for riding or pulling; *she was riding a black horse*; *the coach was pulled by six white horses*; *he's out on his horse every morning*; **dark horse** = person you know nothing about and who may win; *the third candidate is something of a dark horse*; *(informal)* **straight from the horse's mouth** = from a very reliable source; *it's straight from the horse's mouth - the manager told me so himself*; *see also* LOOK

(b) **clothes horse** = wooden frame used for drying clothes

① **hospital**
['hɒspɪtl] *noun*

place where sick or hurt people are looked after; *she was taken ill at work and sent to hospital*; *when is she due to go into hospital?*; *he was in hospital for several days after the accident*; **general hospital** = hospital which deals with all types of injuries and illnesses

ⓞ **host**
[hɪʊst]
1 *noun*
(a) person who has invited guests; *the host asked his guests what they wanted to drink*
(b) landlord of a hotel or pub, also sometimes of a restaurant; *the host of the 'King's Head'*
(c) *(on a TV, radio show)* the person who introduces and talks to the guests; *she's the host of a popular chat show*; *the best hosts on Saturday night TV are those that make jokes*
(d) a host of = large number of; *we face a host of problems*
2 *verb*
(a) to act as host; *the company hosted a party for two hundred guests*; *she hosted a dinner for the visiting diplomats*
(b) to be the centre where something takes place; *Barcelona hosted the Olympic games in 1992*

④ **hostage**
['hɒstɪdʒ] *noun*
person who is captured and held by someone or an organization, which threatens to kill him unless certain demands are met; *three of the hostages will be freed tomorrow*; *he was held hostage for more than a year by the rebels*

④ **hostile**
['hɒstaɪl *US* 'hɒstl] *adjective*
(a) referring to an enemy; *hostile forces are moving towards the airport*
(b) showing a dislike of someone; *the crowd seemed hostile, so the president decided not to make his speech*; **hostile questioning** = asking questions which attack the person being asked; **hostile takeover** = takeover where the board of the company being bought do not recommend the sale and try to fight it

ⓞ **hot**
[hɒt] *adjective*
(a) very warm; with a high temperature; *the weather is very hot in June but August is the hottest month*; *if you're too hot, take your coat off*; *plates should be kept hot before serving the meal* (NOTE: the opposite is **cold**)
(b) very highly spiced (food); *this curry is particularly hot*; *he chose the hottest dish on the menu* (NOTE: the opposite is **mild**)
(c) to make things hot for someone = to make difficulties for someone; **to be hot and bothered** = to be annoyed and nervous about something; *(informal)* **to sell like hot cakes** = to sell very fast; *this new toy is selling like hot cakes*; **to get into hot water** = to get into trouble; *he got into hot water with the local authority after he built a garage without permission*; **in the hot seat** = having to take decisions; *I pity the club chairman - he's really in the hot seat*

(d) vigorous and energetic; **in hot pursuit** = chasing someone actively; *the rebels retreated into the mountains with the government forces in hot pursuit* (NOTE: **hotter - hottest**)

③ **hot dog**
['hɒt 'dɒg] *noun*
snack made of a hot German sausage eaten in a roll of bread; *you can buy hot dogs at the food stall by the station*

ⓞ **hotel**
[hɪʊ'tel] *noun*
building where travellers can rent a room for the night, eat in a restaurant, drink in a bar, etc.; *they are staying at the Grand Hotel, which is the only five-star hotel in town*; *I'll meet you in the hotel lobby*; *all the hotel rooms in the town are booked*; *see also* CHECK IN, CHECK OUT

ⓞ **hour**
['aʊɪ] *noun*
(a) period of time which lasts sixty minutes; *the train journey takes two hours*; *it's a three-hour flight to Greece*; *the train travels at over 150 miles an hour*; **he is paid by the hour** = he is paid for each hour he works; *the pay is £10 an hour*; *the hours of work are from 9.30 to 5.30*; *the lunch hour is from 12.30 to 1.30*; *she works a thirty-five hour week*; **a quarter of an hour** = 15 minutes; **half an hour** = 30 minutes; *I'll be ready in a quarter of an hour*; *the next train will be in half an hour's time*; **hour hand** = short hand on a clock or watch which shows the hours
(b) *(informal)* **hours** = a very long time; *they took hours to serve us*; *we waited hours for the bus*
(c) on the hour = at an exact hour, and not before or after that hour; *trains for London leave every hour on the hour*
(d) banking hours = time when a bank is open for its customers; *you cannot get money from a bank outside banking hours*; **office hours** = time when an office is open; *staff are not allowed to make private calls during office hours*; **outside hours** *or* **out of hours** = when the office is not open; *there is a special number you can ring outside office hours*; *see also* SMALL

④ **hourly**
['aʊli] *adjective*
happening every hour; *he's paid on an hourly basis*; **hourly-paid workers** = workers paid at a fixed rate for each hour worked; **hourly rate** = amount of money paid for an hour worked; *the minimum hourly rate is £3.60*

ⓞ **house**
1 *noun*
[haʊs]
(a) building in which someone lives; *he has bought a house in London*; *he has a small flat in town and a large house in the country*; *all the houses in our street look the same*

(b) *(informal)* they get on like a house on fire = they're very friendly

(c) business; *she runs a publishing house*; *an important finance house has financed the deal*; **house magazine** *or* **house journal** = magazine produced for the workers or shareholders in a company to give them news about the company

(d) part of a Parliament; *the British Parliament is formed of the House of Commons and the House of Lords*; *the American Congress is formed of the House of Representatives and the Senate*

(e) bar or pub, etc.; *drinks are on the house* = drinks are free to customers; **house wine** = special cheap wine selected by a restaurant; *we'll have a bottle of your house red, please*; *see also* PUBLIC HOUSE

(f) showing of a film, play, etc.; **full house** *or* **house full** = notice showing that a cinema or theatre is full; *the play has played to full houses all week* (NOTE: plural is **houses** ['hauzɪz])

2 *verb*

[hauz] to provide accommodation for someone or something; *his collection of old cars is housed in a barn*; *we have been asked if we can house three students for the summer term*

② **household**
['haushəʊld] *noun*

people living together in a house; *this free newspaper is distributed to every household in the town*; **household goods** = goods which are used in a house; *the household goods department is on the ground floor*; **a household name** = a well-known brand

④ **House of Commons**
['haus əv 'kɒmənz] *noun*

lower house of the British Parliament; *the Bill will come before the House of Commons* (NOTE: members of the House of Commons are called **Members of Parliament** *or* **MPs**)

④ **House of Lords**
['haus əv 'lɔːdz] *noun*

upper house of the British Parliament; *the House of Lords made several amendments to the Bill*

④ **House of Representatives**
['haus əv reprɪ'zentətɪvz] *noun*

lower house of the US Congress; *he's been elected to the House of Representatives* (NOTE: members of the House of Representatives are called **Congressmen**)

③ **Houses of Parliament**
['hauzɪz əv 'pɑːləmənt] *noun*

building in London where Parliament meets; *he took a picture of the Houses of Parliament*; *you can go on a tour of the Houses of Parliament*

④ **housework**
['hauswɜːk] *noun*

cleaning work in a house or flat; *his wife does all the housework* (NOTE: no plural)

② **housing**
['hauzɪŋ] *noun*

providing places where people can live; *the local council is responsible for housing homeless people*; **housing benefit** = money paid by the government to unemployed people to help them pay their rent; **housing estate** = group of houses and flats belonging to a local authority, and let to tenants at cheap rents

④ **hover**
['hɒvɪ] *verb*

(a) to hang in the air without moving forward; *flies hovering over the surface of a pool*

(b) to hover around = to stay near; *he hovered around her for the whole evening*; *he was hovering round the bar, hoping that someone would offer him a drink*

① **how**
[hau] *adverb*

(a) *(showing or asking the way in which something is done)* *how do you switch off the fridge?*; *can you tell me how to get to the railway station from here?*; *I don't know how he does it*

(b) *(showing or asking to what extent)* *how big is their house?*; *how many people are there in your family?*; *she showed us how good she was at skiing*; *how old is your little boy?*; *how far is it to the church?*

(c) *(showing surprise)* *how cold it is outside!*; *how different it is from what I remember!*

(d) *(informal)* **how about?** = would you like?; *how about a swim before breakfast?*; *how about a cup of coffee?*; **how do you mean?** = what do you mean?; *how do you mean, the payment won't be made until next week?*

① **how are you** *or* **how do you do**
[hau 'ɑː juː or 'hau djɪ 'duː]

(a) *(showing a general greeting)* *how do you do, sir?*; *hi Robert! how are you?* (NOTE: in this meaning a detailed reply is not expected)

(b) *(asking the state of your health)* *how are you today?*; *the doctor asked me how I was*

④ **how come**
['hau 'kʌm]

(informal) why; *how come you're late?*; *how come the front door was left open?*; NOTE: the word order: **how come you're late?** but **why are you late?**)

① **however**
[hau'evɪ]

1 *adverb*

(a) to whatever extent; *however many times she tried, she couldn't pass the driving test*; *I must have the house painted, however expensive it's going to be*; *however hard he tried, he still couldn't swim*

(b) *(form of 'how' which emphasizes)* *however did you manage to get in?*

(c) in this case; *we never go out on Saturdays - however, this Saturday we're going to a wedding*

2 *conjunction* in whatever way; *do it however you like*

④ **howl**
[haʊl]
1 *verb*
to make a long loud cry; *the wild dogs howled outside the cabin*; *the wind howled in the chimney*
2 *noun*
long loud cry; *howls of disappointment came from the fans*

③ **HP**
['haɪ 'pɜːtʃɪs]
= HIRE PURCHASE; *I'm buying the fridge on HP*

④ **HQ**
['eɪtʃ 'kjuː]
= HEADQUARTERS; *we had a call from HQ asking for more details*

④ **hug**
[hʌɡ]
1 *noun*
throwing your arms round someone; *she ran to the little girl and gave her a hug*
2 *verb*
(a) to throw your arms around someone; *the players hugged each other when the goal was scored*
(b) to hold something very tightly; *the little girl was hugging a blue blanket*
(c) to keep very close to something; *the road hugs the foot of the mountain*; *she drove along slowly, hugging the pavement* (NOTE: hugging - hugged)

② **huge**
[hjuːdʒ] *adjective*
very large; *huge waves hit the ship*; *the concert was a huge success*; *failing the test was a huge disappointment for him*

③ **hullo**
[hʌ'ləʊ]
see HALLO, HELLO

④ **hum**
[hʌm]
1 *verb*
(a) to make a low buzz; *bees were humming around the pots of jam*
(b) to sing without words; *if you don't know the words of the song, you can always hum the tune* (NOTE: humming - hummed)
2 *noun*
low buzz; *a loud hum came out of the loudspeaker*

① **human**
['hjuːmɪn]
1 *adjective*
referring to people; **human error** = mistake made by a person, and not by a machine; *they concluded that the accident was due to human error*; **he's only human** = he can make mistakes like anyone else; *I know there's a mistake in the exam question, teachers are only human, after*

all!; **human resources** = the workers in a company, seen as a group; **human resources manager** = manager who deals with pay, sick leave, administration, etc., for all the staff (NOTE: also called a **personnel manager**)
2 *noun*
person, a human being; *the animals in the park don't seem to be afraid of humans*; *humans have only existed on earth for a short time compared to fish*

① **human being**
['hjuːmɪn 'biːɪŋ] *noun*
a person; *the first human beings lived many thousands of years ago*; *I've been walking all day in the forest and you're the first human being I've met*

④ **humanity**
[hjuːˈmænɪti] *noun*
(a) all people; *a crime against humanity*
(b) *(formal)* great kindness; *she showed great humanity to the refugees*
(c) **the humanities** = the arts subjects at university, such as English, History, Philosophy, as opposed to the sciences; *the Dean of the Faculty of Humanities*

① **human rights**
['hjuːmɪn 'raɪts] *noun*
rights which each member of society should enjoy, such as freedom of speech, freedom of movement, etc.; *demonstrators are protesting against abuses of human rights in various parts of the world*

④ **humble**
['hʌmbl] *adjective*
(a) modest, feeling you are not important; *seeing how much work she does for charity makes me feel very humble*
(b) poor, ordinary; *he comes from a humble family*; *they live in a humble little house in the mountains* (NOTE: humbler - humblest)

④ **humid**
['hjuːmɪd] *adjective*
damp, (air) which contains moisture; *I don't like humid weather - I much prefer a hot dry climate*

③ **humidity**
[hjuːˈmɪdɪti] *noun*
measurement of how much moisture is contained in the air; *the temperature is 32° with 90% humidity*; *flowers are sensitive to changes in temperature and humidity*

④ **humiliate**
[hjuːˈmɪlieɪt] *verb*
to make someone feel unimportant or stupid; *our team was completely humiliated - they lost 10 - 2!*; *she is supposed to be his best friend but she humiliated him in front of everyone*

④ **humiliation**
[hjuːmɪlɪˈeɪʃn] *noun*
making someone feel stupid or not important; *the humiliation of failing his exams once again*

④ **humorous**
['hju:mırıs] *adjective*
(formal) funny; *our host made some humorous remarks to try to make everyone relax*

④ **humour** US **humor**
['hju:mı]
1 *noun*
(a) seeing what is funny; *he has a good sense of humour; she has absolutely no sense of humour; 'female wants to meet male, aged 30 - 35, with a good sense of humour'*
(b) *(formal)* general feeling; *I am in no humour to talk about holidays just now; he was not in a humour to discuss what happened during their holiday in Greece; his good humour lasted until the end of the party*
2 *verb*
to humour someone = to say you agree with what someone wants; *when he starts shouting and cursing, you to have to try to humour him*

④ **hump**
[hʌmp]
1 *noun*
(a) raised part on the back of a person or animal; *Arabian camels have only one hump, while Bactrian camels have two*
(b) small raised part in the ground; *they have built humps in the road to slow down the traffic*
2 *verb*
(informal) to carry on your shoulder; *we spent all morning humping sacks of sand*

① **hundred**
['hʌndrıd]
(a) number 100; *the church is over a hundred years old; my grandfather will be 100 next month; they came in their hundreds to visit the grave; do I have to tell you a hundred times to stop that noise?*
(b) **one hundred per cent** = 100%; **one hundred per cent happy with** = totally satisfied with; *I'm not one hundred per cent happy with his work*
(c) **hundreds of** = very many; *hundreds of birds were killed by the cold weather; hundreds of people caught flu last winter* (NOTE: in numbers **hundred** does not change and is followed by **and** when reading: **491** = four hundred and ninety-one; **102** = a hundred and two. Note also: **a hundred and one** (101), **three hundred and six** (306) but **the hundred and first** (101st), **the three hundred and sixth** (306th), etc.)

③ **hundredth (100th)**
['hʌndrıdθ] *adjective & noun*
the clock is correct to one hundredth of a second (100th of a second) tomorrow is his hundredth birthday; a penny is one hundredth of a pound

① **hung**
[hʌŋ]
see HANG

① **Hungary**
['hʌŋgırı] *noun*
country in central Europe, east of Austria and west of Romania; *the river Danube flows north-south through the centre of Hungary* (NOTE: capital: **Budapest;** people: **the Hungarians;** language: **Hungarian;** currency: **forint**)

① **Hungarian**
[hʌn'geırıın]
1 *adjective*
referring to Hungary; *Franz Liszt was a famous Hungarian composer*
2 *noun*
(a) person from Hungary; *it has been 3 years since a Hungarian last won a gold medal*
(b) language spoken in Hungary; *I am being transferred to Budapest and want to take a course in Hungarian*

④ **hunger**
['hʌŋgı] *noun*
state of wanting to eat, of needing to eat; **to die of hunger** = to die because you do not have enough to eat; *there are children dying of hunger in some countries in Africa;* **hunger strike** = refusing to eat, as a form of protest; *the prisoners went on hunger strike*

② **hungry**
['hʌŋgrı] *adjective*
wanting to eat; *you must be hungry after that game of football; I'm not very hungry - I had a big lunch; hurry up with the food - we're getting hungry;* **to go hungry** = not to have enough to eat; *students had to go hungry when their grants were not paid* (NOTE: **hungrier - hungriest**)

③ **hung up**
['hʌŋ 'ʌp] *adjective*
(informal) worried or bothered about something; *he's really hung up about his promotion prospects*

④ **hunt**
[hʌnt]
1 *verb*
(a) **to hunt for something** = to search for something; *we're hunting for a cheap flat; they came to London in the week after Christmas, hunting for bargains*
(b) to chase wild animals for food or sport; *we took the dogs out hunting rabbits; our cat is not very good at hunting mice; they go to Scotland to hunt deer* (NOTE: you hunt animals, but you hunt **for** things)
2 *noun*
search; *the hunt for new offices has just started*

④ **hunter**
['hʌntı] *noun*
person who hunts; *a deer hunter;* **bargain hunter** = person who looks for bargains; *bargain hunters were queuing outside the shop on the first day of the sales*

④ **hurdle**
['hɜːdl] *noun*
(a) small fence which you have to jump over in a race; *she fell at the first hurdle*
(b) hurdles = race where you jump over fences; *the last event was the 100 metres hurdles*
(c) obstacle in the way of something; *only one more hurdle to clear and then we will have bought the shop*

④ **hurricane**
['hʌrɪkən] *noun*
tropical storm with strong winds and rain; *the hurricane damaged properties all along the coast* (NOTE: used in the Caribbean or Eastern Pacific; in the Far East this is called a **typhoon**; in the Indian Ocean it is called a **cyclone**)

③ **hurried**
['hʌrɪd] *adjective*
done in a rush, too quickly; *we just had time to snatch a hurried lunch before catching the train*

③ **hurry**
['hʌrɪ]
1 *noun*
in a hurry = doing things fast; *the waiters are always in a hurry; can't you drive any faster? - we're in a hurry to catch our plane!; he wants the report in a hurry;* **what's the hurry?** = why are you going so fast?; *what's the hurry? it's only two o'clock and the plane doesn't leave until nine;* **there's no hurry** = you need not do it fast; *there's no hurry for the figures, we do not need them until next week* (NOTE: no plural)
2 *verb*
(a) to go, do or make something fast; *she hurried across the room; you'll have to hurry if you want to catch the last post; there's no need to hurry - we've got plenty of time*
(b) to make someone go faster; *don't hurry me, I like to take my time*

③ **hurry up**
['hʌrɪ 'ʌp] *verb*
(a) to go or do something faster; *hurry up - we'll be late for the film; can't you get the cook to hurry up, I'm getting hungry?*
(b) to make someone do something faster; *can you hurry up that order, the customer wants it tomorrow?*

② **hurt**
[hɜːt]
1 *verb*

(a) to have pain; to give pain; *my tooth hurts; no one was badly hurt in the accident; where did you hurt yourself?; is he badly hurt?; two players got hurt in the game*
(b) to harm, to damage; *the bad publicity did not hurt our sales; the news report will certainly hurt his reputation;* it won't hurt to *or* it never hurts to = it would be a good thing to; *it wouldn't hurt to complain to the local council; it never hurts to be polite to customers* (NOTE: hurting - hurt)
2 *noun*
(a) *(informal) (children's language)* place where you have a pain; *he has a hurt on his toe*
(b) feeling of sadness because you have been badly treated; *she feels upset because of the hurt to her pride*

① **husband**
['hʌzbənd]
1 *noun*
man to whom a woman is married; *her husband is Scottish; he's the doctor's husband;* to live as husband and wife = to live together as if you were married without being married; *they lived together as husband and wife for twenty years;* compare WIFE
2 *verb*
(formal) not to waste money, supplies, etc.; *we must learn to husband our resources*

③ **hut**
[hʌt] *noun*
small rough wooden house; *they found a shepherd's hut where they spent the night*

④ **hybrid**
['haɪbrɪd] *adjective & noun*
cross between two varieties of plant or animal; *she is well known for growing hybrid roses*

④ **hydrogen**
['haɪdrɪdʒɪn] *noun*
a common gas which combines with oxygen to form water (NOTE: Chemical element: chemical symbol: **H**; atomic number: **1**)

③ **hyphen**
['haɪfn] *noun*
printing sign (-) used to show that two words are joined or that a word has been split; *'cooperate' doesn't take a hyphen but 'first-class' does*

Ii

③ **I, i**
[aɪ]
ninth letter of the alphabet, between H and J; *she said 'I' for 'Italian'*; **to dot one's i's and cross one's t's** = to be very careful to get the final details right

① **I**
[aɪ] *pronoun used by a speaker when talking about himself or herself; she said, 'I can do it', and she did it; she and I come from the same town; he told me that I could go home early; I said I was going to be late* (NOTE: when it is the object of a verb, **I** becomes **me: I gave it to him - he gave it to me; I hit him - he hit me;** when it follows the verb **be, I** usually becomes **me: who is it? - it's me!**)

② **ice**
[aɪs]
1 *noun*
(a) water which is frozen and has become solid; *when water freezes, it turns into ice; the ice on the lake is dangerous, it isn't thick enough to walk on; would you like ice in your drink?*; **her hands are like ice** = her hands are very cold
(b) to break the ice = to start to talk when everyone has been silent; *the party started quietly, but the drinks soon broke the ice;* **to keep something on ice** = not to do anything about something for the moment; **to put something on ice** = to file a plan or document as the best way of forgetting about it; *we can't afford the expense at the moment, so we'll put the project on ice until next year*
(c) ice bucket = bucket of ice in which a wine bottle is placed to keep cool
(d) ice cream; *we had ices during the interval; two coffee ices, please* (NOTE: no plural for meaning (a): **some ice, a lump of ice**; the plural **ices** means **ice creams**)
2 *verb*
(a) to add ice to a drink; *she asked for a glass of iced water*
(b) to put icing on a cake; *a cake iced with chocolate*

② **ice cream**
['aɪs 'kriːm] *noun*
frozen sweet made from cream and flavoured with fruit juice or other sweet substance; *a lemon ice cream; what sort of ice cream do you want - strawberry or chocolate?; can you help me - I can't carry six ice creams at the same time?*

③ **ice up**
['aɪs 'ʌp] *verb*
to become covered with ice; *the wings of the plane had iced up*

③ **icing**
['aɪsɪŋ] *noun*
covering of sugar and flavours, spread over a cake or biscuits; *she made some chocolate icing for the cake;* **icing sugar** = fine powdered white sugar, mixed with water or egg white and flavoured with fruit or other sweet substance, used to cover cakes or biscuits; *mix the icing sugar with water to make hard white icing*

③ **I'd**
[aɪd] *short for* I HAD, I SHOULD, I WOULD

③ **ID (card)**
['aɪ 'diː kɑːd] *noun*
identity card, a card which shows a photograph of the holder, with the name, date of birth and other details, carried by citizens of a country or members of a group to prove who they are; *show your ID card when entering the Ministry; in some European countries you are legally required to carry an ID card around with you; have you got any ID on you?*

> COMMENT: British citizens are not required to have ID cards, but many firms have them for their employees, and some football clubs have them for their supporters, all for security purposes

① **idea**
[aɪ'dɪə] *noun*
(a) something which you think of; **to have an idea that** = to think that; *I have an idea that the buses don't run on Sundays;* **to have no idea** *or* **not to have the faintest idea** = not to know; *where's your brother? - I've no idea or I haven't the faintest idea; I had no idea it was as late as that*
(b) plan which you make in your mind; *some of his ideas were really original; I've had an idea - let's all go for a picnic!; that's a good idea!;* **a bright idea** = a good plan; *he had the bright idea of painting the bathroom red*

② **ideal**
[aɪ'dɪəl]
1 *noun*
highest point of good life which people try to reach; *my ideal would be to work hard and get rich;* **man of ideals** = person who has high moral standards

2 *adjective*

perfect, extremely suitable; *this is the ideal site for a factory*; *the cottage is an ideal place for watching birds*

③ **ideally**

[aɪ'dɪːlɪ] *adverb*

if everything were perfect; *ideally, I'd take three weeks off, but there's too much work at the office*

④ **identical**

[aɪ'dentɪkl] *adjective*

exactly the same; *the twins wore identical clothes for the party*; *their political opinions are identical*; **identical to** = exactly the same as; *her political opinions are identical to mine*; **identical twins** = twins who look exactly alike

④ **identification**

[aɪdentɪfɪ'keɪʃn] *noun*

(a) saying who someone is, giving his or her name, personal details, etc.; *the identification of the body was made by the victim's sister*; **identification parade** = line of people at a police station from whom a witness is asked to identify a suspected criminal; *she was asked to pick out the mugger at an identification parade*
(b) document which shows who someone is; *the bank manager asked him for identification*; *see also* PIN NUMBER

① **identify**

[aɪ'dentɪfaɪ] *verb*

(a) to say who someone is or what something is; *can you identify what sort of rock this is?*; *she was able to identify her attacker*
(b) to state that something belongs to you; *each person was asked to identify his or her baggage*
(c) to identify with = to feel you have the same feelings as someone or to have a feeling of sympathy for someone *or* something; *I can identify with the hero who spends his life trapped in a small provincial town*

② **identity**

[aɪ'dentɪtɪ] *noun*

someone's name, personal details, etc.; *he changed his identity when he went to work for the secret services*; **identity card (ID card)** = a card which shows a photograph of the holder, with the name, date of birth and other details, carried by citizens of a country or members of a group to prove who they are; *show your identity card when entering the Ministry*; *in some European countries you are legally required to carry an identity card with you at all times*; **proof of identity** = proof in the form of a document, such as a driving licence, that a person is who he or she claims to be; *the police asked her for proof of identity*

③ **ideology**

[aɪdɪ'ɒlɪdʒi] *noun*

theory of life based not on religious belief, but on political or economic philosophy; *her socialist ideology led her to join the party*; *he wrote a study of Chinese ideology*

④ **idle**

['aɪdl]

1 *adjective*

(a) lazy (person); *he's the idlest man I know - he never does any work at all*; **he's bone idle** = he never does any work
(b) not working; *the machines stood idle during the strike*; *2,000 employees were made idle by the recession* (NOTE: **idler - idlest**)
2 *verb*

(of machine) to run at a low speed; *he waited for her in the car with the engine idling*

③ **ie** *or* **i.e.**

['aɪ 'iː] *abbreviation meaning 'that is'*

it's best to study Russian in a country where they speak it - i.e. Russia; *the import restrictions apply to expensive items, i.e. items costing more than £2,500* (NOTE: it is short for the Latin phrase **id est**)

① **if**

[ɪf]

1 *conjunction*

(a) *(showing what might happen)* *if it freezes tonight, the pavements will be dangerous tomorrow*; *if I'm in London, I'll come and see you*; *if he had told me you were ill, I'd have come to see you in hospital*; *if I won the lottery, I would take a long holiday*; *if he's going to be late, he'll phone to tell me*
(b) *(asking questions)* *do you know if the plane is late?*; *I was wondering if you would like to have some tea*
(c) although; *he is nice, if rather lazy*
2 *noun*

question which is not certain; *he'll catch the plane if he gets up in time, and that's a very big if*

◊ **if only**

['ɪf 'əʊnlɪ] *(exclamation showing regret)*

if only I had some money!; *if only she'd told me, I could have advised her what to do*

④ **ignorance**

['ɪɡnɪrɪns] *noun*

not knowing; *ignorance of the law is no excuse*; **to keep someone in ignorance of something** = not to tell someone about something; *the soldiers were deliberately kept in ignorance of the dangers facing them* (NOTE: no plural)

② **ignore**

[ɪɡ'nɔː] *verb*

not to notice someone *or* something on purpose; *she ignored the red light and just drove straight through*; *when we met he just ignored me*

③ **ill**

[ɪl] *adjective*

(a) sick, not well; *stress can make you ill*; *if you're feeling ill you ought to see a doctor*; **to fall ill** = to become ill; *she fell seriously ill and we thought she was going to die*; **to be taken ill** = to become ill suddenly; *he was taken ill while on holiday in Greece*

(b) ill at ease = embarrassed, not comfortable; *she seemed ill at ease when we started talking about the missing money; he felt ill at ease in his new suit at a party where he knew nobody* (NOTE: ill - **worse** [wɜːs] - **worst** [wɜːst])

③ **I'll**
[aɪl]
short for I WILL, I SHALL

④ **illegal**
[ɪˈliːgl] *adjective*
against the law; *it is illegal to serve alcohol to people under 16; illegal immigrants will be deported*

④ **illegally**
[ɪˈliːgli] *adverb*
against the law; *he was accused of entering the country illegally; the car was illegally parked*

② **illness**
[ˈɪlnɪs] *noun*
not being well; *she developed a serious illness; a lot of the staff are absent because of illness* (NOTE: plural is **illnesses**)

④ **illusion**
[ɪˈluːʒn] *noun*
impression which is not true; **an optical illusion** = thing which seems real when you see it, but which is not; *the sword seemed to go right through his body, but it was just an optical illusion; the lines are not different lengths - it's just an optical illusion;* **to have no illusions about something** = to know the real unpleasant facts about something; *she has no illusions about her husband being faithful*

② **illustrate**
[ˈɪlʌstreɪt] *verb*
(a) to put pictures into a book; *the book is illustrated with colour photographs of birds*
(b) to show as an example; *the article illustrates his views on the way the company should develop*
(c) to be an example of; *this poem illustrates the sort of style I prefer*

③ **illustration**
[ɪlʌˈstreɪʃn] *noun*
(a) picture in a book; *the book has 25 colour illustrations*
(b) example; *his daughter's birthday party is a good illustration of the way he likes to spend money*

③ **I'm**
[aɪm]
short for I AM

① **image**
[ˈɪmɪdʒ] *noun*
(a) portrait; *I want the portrait to be a faithful image of my mother;* (*informal*) **he's the spitting image of his father** = he looks exactly like his father
(b) idea which other people have of a person or of an organization; *the children are so badly behaved that it gives quite a wrong image of the*

family; in an attempt to change his image he bought a lot of new clothes; they are spending a lot of money to improve the company's image
(c) picture produced by a lens, mirror or computer; *the mirror throws an image onto the paper; can this software handle images in that format?; can you adjust the camera, the image on the screen is out of focus?*

④ **imaginary**
[ɪˈmædʒɪnɪri] *adjective*
not real, which is imagined; *all his novels are set in an imaginary town in Central Europe*

③ **imagination**
[ɪmædʒɪˈneɪʃn] *noun*
ability to picture things in your mind; *she let her imagination run riot in her stories for children;* **to use your imagination** = to imagine what is possible; *try and use your imagination - think of the money we could make;* **to let your imagination get the better of you** *or* **run away with you** = to think things are possible when they are not; *he let his imagination get the better of him and saw himself as a future Prime Minister*

② **imagine**
[ɪˈmædʒɪn] *verb*
to picture something in your mind; *imagine yourself sitting on a beach in the hot sun; she thought she had heard footsteps, and then decided she had imagined it*

④ **imitate**
[ˈɪmɪteɪt] *verb*
to copy something *or* someone; to do as someone does; *he made us all laugh by imitating the head teacher*

④ **imitation**
[ɪmɪˈteɪʃn] *noun*
(a) act of imitating; *he does a very good imitation of the Prime Minister*
(b) copy made of something; *it's not real leather, just imitation; the bag is made of imitation leather;* **beware of imitations** = be careful not to buy low quality goods which are made to look like other more expensive items

② **immediate**
[ɪˈmiːdjɪt] *adjective*
(a) very soon; *he wrote an immediate letter of complaint; you didn't expect an immediate reply, did you?; your order will receive immediate attention*
(b) closest, (sitting) next to you; *he had to share his programme with his immediate neighbour*

① **immediately**
[ɪˈmiːdɪtli] *adverb*
straight away; *he got my letter, and wrote back immediately; as soon as he heard the news he immediately phoned his wife*

④ **immense**
[ɪ'mens] *adjective*
huge; very big; enormous; *he has an immense black beard; the bill was immense, and we all complained; the president decided to build an immense palace in the mountains*

④ **immigrant**
['ɪmɪgrɪnt] *noun*
person who comes to a country to settle; *many immigrants came to Britain during the 1930s; immigrants are rushing to Germany because the economy is booming;* **illegal immigrant** = person who has entered a country illegally and wants to settle there; *compare* EMIGRANT

④ **immigration**
[ɪmɪ'greɪʃn] *noun*
(a) settling in a new country; *the government is encouraging immigration because of the shortage of workers in key industries;* **immigration controls** = restrictions placed by a country on the numbers of immigrants who can come into the country; *many countries have imposed immigration controls*
(b) **Immigration** = section of an airport where new arrivals have to show their passports; *he was stopped at Immigration; you will need to show all these documents when you go through Immigration*

④ **immune**
[ɪ'mjuːn] *adjective*
(a) *(person)* protected against infection; *I seem to be immune to colds - I just never have any; this injection should make you immune to yellow fever;* **immune system** = complex network of cells which protects the body from disease; *in people with this disease, the immune system gradually fails to work*
(b) legally protected against, not liable to; *she believed she would be immune from prosecution* (NOTE: you are immune **to** a disease, and **from** prosecution)

③ **immunity**
[ɪ'mjuːnɪtɪ] *noun*
(a) **immunity to a disease** = being able to resist attacks of a disease; *the injection will give immunity to the disease for six months*
(b) **immunity from** *or* **against arrest** = protection against being arrested; *when he offered to give information to the police, he was granted immunity from prosecution;* **diplomatic immunity** = freedom from the control of the laws of the country you are living in because of being a diplomat; *the ambassador refused to pay his parking fines and claimed diplomatic immunity;* **parliamentary immunity** = protection of Members of Parliament against being arrested

② **impact**
['ɪmpækt]
1 *noun*
(a) strong effect; *the TV documentary had an strong impact on the viewers*

(b) shock; *the car was totally crushed by the impact of the collision;* **on impact** = as soon as it hit; *the plane burst into flames on impact with the ground*
2 *verb*
to impact on something = to have a strong effect on something; *the fall in the value of the currency will impact strongly on the stock market*

④ **impatient**
[ɪm'peɪʃnt] *adjective*
unable to wait for something, always in a hurry to do something; *we were all impatient for the film to start; he's very impatient with anyone who works slowly*

④ **impatiently**
[ɪm'peɪʃntlɪ] *adverb*
in a hurried way, not patiently; *'can't you go any faster,' she said impatiently; we are all waiting impatiently for the new book to come out; she looked at her watch impatiently*

③ **implement**
1 *noun*
['ɪmplɪmɪnt] tool or instrument; *the builder brought an implement for bending pipes;* **garden implements** = tools such as forks and spades which are used in the garden
2 *verb*
['ɪmplɪment] to put into effect; *the changes must be implemented immediately*

② **implication**
[ɪmplɪ'keɪʃn] *noun*
(a) suggestion that someone is connected with a crime; *the newspaper revealed his implication in the affair of the stolen diamonds*
(b) **implications** = possible effects of an action; *what will be the implications of the election results for public spending?*

② **imply**
[ɪm'plaɪ] *verb*
to suggest; *he implied that he knew where the papers had been hidden; the lawyer implied that the witness had not in fact seen the accident take place*

④ **import**
1 *noun*
['ɪmpɔːt]
imports = goods which are brought into a country for sale; *the volume of imports from Poland has risen by 20% this year; all imports must be declared to customs;* **import controls** = rules limiting goods which can be brought into a country; *import controls on foreign makes of cars have been lifted;* **import duty** = tax paid on goods brought into a country; *the government charges an import duty on some items coming into the country;* **import licence** *or* **import permit** = official document which allows goods to be imported; *don't try to import guns if you don't have an import licence;* **import quota** = fixed quantity of a particular type of goods which the government allows to be imported;

the government has imposed an import quota on cars (NOTE: usually in the plural, **imports,** but always **import** before another noun)

2 *verb*
[ɪmˈpɔːt]

to bring goods into a country; *the company imports television sets from Japan; this car was imported from France*

① **importance**
[ɪmˈpɔːtɪns] *noun*

serious effect or influence; *do not attach too much importance to what he says; the bank attaches great importance to the deal*

① **important**
[ɪmˈpɔːtɪnt] *adjective*

(a) which matters a great deal; *it's important to be in time for the meeting; I have to go to London for an important meeting; he left a file containing important papers in the taxi*

(b) (person) in a high position; *he has an important government job; she's an important government official; he was promoted to a more important position*

② **impose**
[ɪmˈpɪuz] *verb*

(a) to ask someone to pay a fine, a tax; *the judge imposed a fine on the bus driver; the government imposed a 10% tax increase on electrical items*

(b) to put something into action; *they have tried to impose a ban on smoking*

(c) to impose on someone = to cause someone trouble; *I hope it's not imposing on you too much, but I need to have the report today*

③ **imposing**
[ɪmˈpɪuzɪŋ] *adjective*

grand or solemn; *the cathedral is an imposing brick building in the centre of the city*

② **impossible**
[ɪmˈpɒsɪbl] *adjective*

(a) which cannot be done; *it's impossible to do all this work in two hours; getting skilled staff is becoming impossible*

(b) (person or situation) awkward and difficult; *the new secretary is completely impossible*

③ **impress**
[ɪmˈpres] *verb*

(a) to make someone admire or respect someone *or* something; *her rapid response to the request impressed her boss; she was impressed by his skill with oil paints; the military government organized the display to impress the neighbouring states*

(b) to impress something on someone = to make someone understand; *I must impress on you just how urgent this is*

③ **impressed**
[ɪmˈprest] *adjective*

admiring the effect; *what a beautiful garden - I'm really impressed!*

② **impression**
[ɪmˈpreʃn] *noun*

(a) effect on someone's mind; *blue walls create an impression of cold; the exhibition made a strong impression on her*

(b) to be under *or* **to labour under an impression** = to have a wrong impression, to assume something which is quite wrong; *he was labouring under the impression that air fares were cheaper in Europe than in the USA;* **to get the impression that** = to sense that, to have a feeling that; *I got the impression that she wanted us to leave*

③ **impressive**
[ɪmˈpresɪv] *adjective*

which impresses; *he had a series of impressive wins in the chess tournament; the government staged an impressive display of military hardware*

④ **imprison**
[ɪmˈprɪzn] *verb*

to put or to keep someone in prison; *he was imprisoned by the secret police for six months*

④ **imprisonment**
[ɪmˈprɪzɪnmɪnt] *noun*

putting or keeping someone in prison; *the maximum penalty for this offence is two years imprisonment;* **a term of imprisonment** = time which a prisoner has to spend in prison; *he was sentenced to the maximum term of imprisonment;* **life imprisonment** = being put in prison for a long time (the penalty for murder); *the murderer was sentenced to life imprisonment*

> COMMENT: life imprisonment is a term of many years, but in the UK does not necessarily mean for the rest of the prisoner's life; in the USA it means what it says

① **improve**
[ɪmˈpruːv] *verb*

(a) to make something better; *we are trying to improve our image with a series of TV commercials;* **to improve on something** = to try to do better than something; *she tried to improve on her previous best time*

(b) to get better; *the general manager has promised that the bus service will improve; it poured down all morning, but in the afternoon the weather improved a little*

① **improvement**
[ɪmˈpruːvmɪnt] *noun*

(a) making or becoming better; *there has been no improvement in the train service since we complained; the new software is a great improvement on the old version*

(b) thing which is better; *they carried out some improvements to the house; we are planning some home improvements such as a new kitchen*

④ **impulse**

['ɪmpʌls] *noun*

sudden feeling or decision; *he had a sudden impulse to take the car and drive to France*; **to do something on impulse** = to do something because you have just thought of it, not because it was planned; **impulse buying** = buying goods which you have just seen, not because you had planned to buy them

① **in**

[ɪn]

1 *preposition & adverb*

(a) *(showing place) he lives in the country; in Japan it snows a lot during the winter; she's in the kitchen; he's still in bed; don't stand outside in the pouring rain*

(b) at home, in an office, at a station; *is the boss in?; he isn't in yet; my husband usually gets in from work about now; the train from Birmingham is due in at 6.30*

(c) *(showing time) in autumn the leaves turn brown; on holiday there was nothing to do in the evenings; she was born in 1996; he ate his meal in five minutes; we went for a skiing holiday in January*

(d) *(showing time in the future) I'll be back home in about two hours; she should arrive in twenty minutes' time*

(e) in fashion; *this year, short skirts are in*

(f) *(showing a state or appearance) he was dressed in black; she ran outside in her dressing gown; we're in a hurry; the words in a dictionary are set out in order of their first letters*

(g) *(showing a proportion or ratio) one in ten of the children wears glasses*

2 *noun*

the ins and outs of something = the complicated details; *he knows all the ins and outs of trading on the Internet*

3 *adjective*

(informal) fashionable; *round dark glasses are the in thing this summer*

◊ **in for**

['ɪn 'fɔː] *adverb*

to be in for something = to be about to get something; *I think we're in for some bad weather; she's in for a nasty shock*

◊ **in front**

['ɪn 'frʌnt]

1 *adverb*

further forwards; *my mother sat in the back seat and I sat in front*

2 *preposition*

in front of = placed further forwards than something; *a tall man came and sat in front of me and I couldn't see the screen*

◊ **in on**

['ɪn 'ɒn] *adverb*

to be in on a secret = to know a secret; *who else was in on the secret?*; **to let someone in on a secret** = to tell someone a secret; *the gang let the driver in on the secret*

◊ **in so far as**

['ɪn sɪʊ 'fɑː 'æz] *adverb; (formal)*

to the extent that; *we found the assembly instructions, in so far as they applied to our model, quite easy to understand*

④ **inability**

[ɪnɪ'bɪlɪtɪ] *noun*

not being able to do something; *his inability to write English correctly is a handicap*

④ **inadequate**

[ɪn'ædɪkwɪt] *adjective*

(a) not enough; *the island has inadequate supplies of water in the summer months*

(b) not competent, not good enough for a job; *being compared to his brother the MP, made him feel quite inadequate*

④ **inappropriate**

[ɪnɪ'prɪʊprɪɪt] *adjective*

not suitable, not fitting the circumstances; *jeans are quite inappropriate clothes for a wedding*

③ **Inc**

[ɪn'kɔːpɪreɪtɪd]   US   *abbreviation   for* INCORPORATED; *we're dealing with a company called John Doe, Inc*

③ **incentive**

[ɪn'sentɪv] *noun*

thing which encourages; *the possibility of extra pay is an incentive to the sales force*; **incentive bonus** = extra money paid when production is increased; **incentive scheme** = plan to encourage better work by paying higher commissions or bonuses; *we are setting up an incentive scheme which we hope will increase sales*

② **inch**

[ɪnʃ]

1 *noun*

measure of length (= 2.54cm); *snow lay six inches deep on the ground; she is five foot six inches tall (5' 6"); a three and a half inch floppy disk; see also* FOOT (NOTE: plural is **inches**. Note also that with numbers **inch** is usually written "; a 3½"disk; he is 5' 9": say: 'a three and a half inch disk, he's five foot nine')

2 *verb*

to inch forward = to go forward little by little; *the queue inched forward slowly; the project is inching forward, but it's hard work getting things moving*

② **incident**

['ɪnsɪdɪnt] *noun*

(a) something which happens; *last year six hundred incidents of oil pollution were reported*

(b) usually violent action or disturbance; *there were several incidents during the demonstration*; **incident room** = special room in a police station to deal with a particular crime

② **incidentally**
[ɪnsɪ'dentɪli] *adverb*
by the way; *incidentally, you didn't see my watch anywhere in the office, did you?*

③ **inclined**
[ɪn'klaɪnd] *adjective*
(a) sloping; *an inclined path gives easy access to the warehouse*
(b) likely to do something; *she is inclined to get very annoyed when anyone criticizes her golf*

① **include**
[ɪn'kluːd] *verb*
to count someone *or* something along with others; *the waiter did not include service in the bill*; *the total is £140, not including insurance and handling charges*; *there were 120 people at the wedding if you include the children*

① **included**
[ɪn'kluːdɪd] *adjective*
taken together with something else; *the holiday costs £500, everything included*; *the service is not included in the bill*

① **including**
[ɪn'kluːdɪŋ] *preposition*
taking something together with something else; *the total comes to £25.00 including VAT*; **not including** = not counting; *there were thirty people at the lunch, not including the children*

④ **inclusive**
[ɪn'kluːsɪv] *adjective*
(a) which counts something in with other things; **inclusive of tax** = including tax; *all prices are shown inclusive of VAT*; **inclusive charge** = charge which includes all costs; *the charge is not inclusive, you will have to pay extra for car parking*
(b) *(giving figures or dates)* **the conference runs from the 12th to the 16th inclusive** = it starts on the morning of the 12th and ends on the evening of the 16th; *for the next lesson, you need to study pages 23 to 31 inclusive*

① **income**
['ɪŋkʌm] *noun*
money which you receive, especially as pay for your work, or as interest on savings; *their weekly income is not really enough to live on*; **income tax** = tax on money earned as wages or salary; *income tax is deducted from his salary each month*; *she pays income tax at the lowest rate*

③ **incorporate**
[ɪn'kɔːpɪreɪt] *verb*
(a) to bring something into something else to make one main whole; *we are trying to incorporate the suggestions from the committees into the main proposal*

(b) to form an official body or a registered company; *the company was incorporated three years ago*

① **increase**
1 *noun*
['ɪŋkriːs]
(a) growth, process of becoming larger; *an increase in tax or a tax increase*; *an increase in the cost of living*
(b) rise in salary; *she went to her boss and asked for an increase*; **cost-of-living increase** = increase in salary to allow it to keep up with higher cost of living
(c) **on the increase** = becoming more frequent; *stealing from shops is on the increase*
2 *verb*
[ɪŋ'kriːs]
(a) to rise, to grow, to expand; *the price of oil has increased twice in the past year*; **to increase in price** = to become more expensive; **to increase in size** *or* **in value** = to become larger *or* more valuable
(b) to make something become bigger; *the boss increased her salary*; *rail fares have been increased by 10%*

① **increased**
[ɪŋ'kriːst] *adjective*
which has become bigger; *these increased rail fares mean that we cannot afford to travel so much*

② **increasingly**
[ɪŋ'kriːsɪŋli] *adverb*
more and more; *he found it increasingly difficult to keep up with all the work he had to do at the office*; *his future with the company looks increasingly doubtful*

④ **incredible**
[ɪn'kredɪbl] *adjective*
(a) which you find difficult to believe; *it is absolutely incredible that anyone as rich as he is can avoid paying tax*
(b) of remarkable size, quantity, etc.; *over the years he has made an incredible fortune from selling old cars*; *you should go to see 'Jaws' - it's an incredible film*

③ **incredibly**
[ɪn'kredɪbli] *adverb*
(a) difficult to believe; *incredibly, he passed his driving test first time*
(b) very, extremely; *she's incredibly tall*; *it is incredibly difficult to find a parking space near my office in the middle of the day*

① **indeed**
[ɪn'diːd]
1 *adverb*
(a) *(for emphasis)* greatly, really; *thank you very much indeed for inviting me to stay*; *they have been very kind indeed to their daughter*
(b) in fact; *they are very poor - indeed they have no money at all*

2 *interjection showing indignation; she called me stupid - indeed! what cheek!; it wasn't you who scratched my car was it? - indeed not!*

③ **indefinite**
[ɪnˈdefɪnɪt] *adjective*
(a) without a definite end; *he has been suspended for an indefinite period, pending an inquiry*
(b) **the indefinite article** = 'a' or 'an' (as opposed to the definite article 'the')

② **independence**
[ɪndɪˈpendəns] *noun*
(a) freedom; *the country achieved independence in 1994; Scotland is aiming for independence in the next few years*; **the American War of Independence** = war by the Americans against Britain (1775-1786) by which the United States of America was formed; **Declaration of Independence** = document written by Thomas Jefferson (1776) by which the American states declared their independence from Britain
(b) not needing or not relying on anyone else; *she's eighteen and is looking forward to a life of independence from her family*

② **independent**
[ɪndɪˈpendɪnt]
1 *adjective*
(a) free, not ruled by anyone else; *Slovenia has been independent since 1991*
(b) not owned by a group, not run by the state; *the big chains are squeezing the independent bookshops out of the market*; **independent school** = private school, not run by the state
(c) **of independent means** = with enough income from investments, etc., to be able to live without working; *a man of independent means*
(d) not needing or not relying on anyone else; *she's eighteen and wants to be independent of her family*
2 *noun*
(a) candidate who does not belong to a political party; *he stood in the general election as an independent*
(b) shop which is owned by a person and is not part of a chain; *supermarkets have a bad effect on the small independents*

③ **index**
[ˈɪndeks]
1 *noun*
(a) list showing the references in a book; *look up the references to London in the index* (NOTE: plural in this meaning is **indexes**)
(b) regular report which shows rises and falls in prices, unemployment, etc.; *the economic indices look very promising at the moment*; **cost-of-living index** = way of measuring the cost of living, shown as a percentage increase on the figure for the previous year; *some pensions are linked to the cost-of-living index* (NOTE: plural in this meaning is **indexes** or **indices** [ˈɪndɪsiːz])

2 *verb*
to relate pensions, wages, etc., to the cost-of-living index; *the government is considering indexing pensions*

③ **India**
[ˈɪndjə] *noun*
large country in southern Asia, south of China and east of Pakistan; *India is bounded to the north by the Himalayas; India is the largest democracy in the world* (NOTE: capital: **New Delhi**; people: **Indians**; official languages: **Hindi, English, Gujerati, Tamil, etc.**; currency: **rupee**)

③ **Indian**
[ˈɪndjən]
1 *adjective*
(a) referring to India; *Indian cooking is famous for its curries*; **Indian elephant** = elephant found in India and South-East Asia, slightly smaller than the African elephant, and used as a working animal in forests; **Indian ink** = very black ink which cannot be removed by washing; *Indian ink is used for drawing maps*
(b) referring to one of the original peoples of America; *the traditional Indian skills of hunting and tracking*; **in Indian file** = in line, one behind the other; *the children walked into the assembly in Indian file*; **Indian summer** = period of hot weather in autumn; *why not take advantage of the Indian summer and visit Scotland for a weekend break?*
2 *noun*
(a) person from India; *many Indians came to live in Britain in the 1960s*
(b) person from one of the original American peoples; *the train of pioneers' wagons was attacked by Indians* (NOTE: now usually called **Native Americans**)
(c) *(informal)* ordinary worker, as opposed to a manager; **the company suffers from having too many chiefs and not enough Indians** = the situation in the company is that there are too many managers, but not enough people to do the actual work

① **indicate**
[ˈɪndɪkeɪt] *verb*
to show; *can you indicate the position of the enemy camp on this map?*; *the latest figures indicate a fall in the number of unemployed men*

③ **indication**
[ɪndɪˈkeɪʃn] *noun*
sign; *he gave absolutely no indication that he was thinking of leaving the company*

④ **indicator**
[ˈɪndɪkeɪtɪ] *noun*
(a) something which indicates; *the inflation rate is a good indicator of the strength of the economy*
(b) flashing light on a car which shows which way the driver is going to turn; *his left indicator was flashing and then he turned right!*

(c) indicator (panel) = large board which shows details of plane or train departures and arrivals; *we're much too early, the flight isn't even on the indicator panel yet; look on the indicator to see if the train has been delayed*

④ **indignant**
[ɪnˈdɪgnɪnt] *adjective*
feeling offended or angry; *he was very indignant when the inspector asked him for his ticket; the manager came out to speak to the indignant shoppers who had been queuing for hours in the rain*

④ **indignation**
[ɪndɪgˈneɪʃn] *noun*
being indignant; *much to her indignation, she was asked to come for a medical test; the crowd showed their indignation at the referee's decision by throwing bottles*

④ **indirect**
[ɪndɪˈrekt or ɪndaɪˈrekt] *adjective*
(a) not direct; *the taxi took us to the airport by a very indirect route*
(b) indirect tax = tax, such as VAT or a sales tax, that is added to the price of goods and not paid directly to the government

① **individual**
[ɪndɪˈvɪdjuːl]
1 *noun*
(a) one single person; *we cater for private individuals as well as for groups*
(b) *(informal)* person; *the police would like to talk to the individual who was responsible for this*
2 *adjective*
(a) single, for a particular person; *we treat each individual case on its merits; we provide each member of the tour group with an individual map of the town*
(b) enough for one person; *I want three individual portions of ice cream, please*

④ **indoor**
[ˈɪndɔː] *adjective*
inside a building; *if it's raining we can play indoor games; our school has an indoor swimming pool*

③ **indoors**
[ɪnˈdɔːz] *adverb*
inside a building; *if it's cold and wet, you should stay indoors; in view of the weather, we had the party indoors; everyone ran indoors when it started to rain*

④ **indulge**
[ɪnˈdʌldʒ] *verb*
(a) to indulge in = to enjoy yourself doing something; *I like to indulge in a hot bath and massage once in a while*
(b) to give someone little luxuries; *she always indulges her little grandson with sweets and presents;* **to indulge yourself** = to give yourself a little luxury; *I love Greek cakes, but I don't often get the chance to indulge myself*

① **industrial**
[ɪnˈdʌstrɪl] *adjective*
referring to manufacturing work; *the Midlands is the main industrial region in Britain;* **industrial action** = strike or protest by workers; *the union members have voted in favour of industrial action;* **industrial estate** = group of factories built together; *we are moving to a new industrial estate near the motorway*

④ **industrialize**
[ɪnˈdʌstrɪlaɪz] *verb*
to set up industries in a country where there were none before; *the government set out to industrialize the agricultural region in the north of the country; South-East Asian countries industrialized very rapidly*

① **industry**
[ˈɪndʌstrɪ] *noun*
manufacturing companies, or other types of commercial activity; *oil is a key industry; the car industry has had a good year; the government is helping industry to sell more products abroad; the tourist industry brings in a lot of foreign currency* (NOTE: plural is **industries**)

④ **inefficient**
[ɪnɪˈfɪʃnt] *adjective*
not efficient; *this model is very inefficient - its petrol consumption is much higher than it should be*

③ **inevitable**
[ɪnˈevɪtɪbl] *adjective*
which must happen, which cannot be avoided; *it was inevitable that the younger children would want to leave home*

③ **inevitably**
[ɪnˈevɪtɪblɪ] *adverb*
naturally, of course; *inevitably after walking all day in the mountains they came back hungry and tired*

③ **infant**
[ˈɪnfənt] *noun*
(formal) very young child; *infants need feeding every few hours;* **infant school** = school for little children from 4 years old

④ **infantry**
[ˈɪnfəntrɪ] *noun*
soldiers who fight on foot, not in tanks, or on horses, etc.; *the infantry was advancing to the front line* (NOTE: no plural)

④ **infect**
[ɪnˈfekt] *verb*
to pass a disease on to someone, or to a part of the body; *she claimed she had been infected by her boyfriend; the disease infected his liver; his whole arm soon became infected*

③ **infection**
[ɪnˈfekʃn] *noun*
disease which spreads from one person to another; *her throat infection keeps coming*

back; *he was sneezing and spreading infection to other people in the office; she seems to catch every little infection there is*

③ **infectious**

[ɪnˈfekʃɪs] *adjective*

(a) (disease) which can be passed from one person to another; *this strain of flu is highly infectious; German measles is infectious, so children who have it must be kept away from others* (NOTE: compare **contagious**).

(b) which can be passed on to someone else; *he's a great music teacher and his enthusiasm for church music is very infectious*

④ **inferior**

[ɪnˈfɪəriɪ]

1 *adjective*

(a) not as large as; *the enemy's inferior numbers meant they could not attack the castle*

(b) inferior to = not as good as something *or* someone else; *this camera is inferior to that one, although they are both the same price; the shop was accused of selling cheap inferior goods at high prices*

2 *noun*

person of a lower rank; *he always speaks to his inferiors in a very superior way* (NOTE: the opposite is **superior**)

④ **infinite**

[ˈɪnfɪnɪt] *adjective*

with no end, which will never end; *she has infinite patience with little children*

② **inflation**

[ɪnˈfleɪʃn] *noun*

state of the economy where prices and wages are rising to keep pace with each other; *the government is trying to keep inflation down below 3%; we have 15% inflation or inflation is running at 15%;* **rate of inflation** *or* **inflation rate** = percentage increase in prices over a twelve-month period

③ **inflict**

[ɪnˈflɪkt] *verb*

to inflict pain or damage on someone = to cause pain or damage to someone; *drugs can inflict serious harm on young people; the bombs inflicted heavy damage on the capital*

① **influence**

[ˈɪnfluɪns]

1 *noun*

being able to change someone *or* something; *he has had a good influence on the other staff in the department; the influence of the moon on the tides; he was charged with driving under the influence of alcohol*

2 *verb*

to make someone *or* something change; *she was deeply influenced by her old teacher; the moon influences the tides; the price of oil has influenced the price of industrial goods*

③ **influential**

[ɪnfluˈenʃl] *adjective*

(a) which causes change; *her speech was influential in changing the opinion of the other members of the committee*

(b) powerful; *she has influential friends who got the police to drop the charges*

③ **influenza**

[ɪnfluˈenzɪ] *noun*

infectious disease like a bad cold, with fever and pains in the muscles, transmitted by a virus; *she is in bed with influenza; half the staff in the office are off with influenza* (NOTE: usually shortened to **flu**)

> COMMENT: influenza is spread by little drops of moisture in the air, transmitted by coughs or sneezes. It can be quite mild, but there are violent strains like Hong Kong flu, which weaken patients a lot

② **inform**

[ɪnˈfɔːm] *verb*

(a) to tell someone officially; *have you informed the police that your watch has been stolen?; I regret to inform you that your father has died; we are pleased to inform you that your offer has been accepted*

(b) to inform on someone = to tell the authorities that someone has done something wrong; *he met the police secretly and informed on his colleagues*

② **informal**

[ɪnˈfɔːml] *adjective*

relaxed, not formal; *dress casually - the party will be informal; the guide gave us an informal talk on the history of the castle*

① **information**

[ɪnfɪˈmeɪʃn] *noun*

facts about something; *can you send me information about holidays in Greece?; she couldn't give the police any information about how the accident happened; she gave me a very useful piece or bit of information; for further information, please write to Department 27;* **information office** = office which gives information to tourists and visitors (NOTE: no plural: **some information;** for one item say **a piece of information)**

③ **information technology (IT)**

[ɪnfɪˈmeɪʃn tekˈnɒlɪdʒi] *noun*

computers, and forms of technology that depend on computers; *the government is determined to increase the resources for information technology in schools*

> COMMENT: information technology covers everything involved in the acquiring, storing, processing and distributing of information by electronic means, including email, the Internet, radio, television, telephone as well as computers

④ **ingredient**
[ɪnˈgriːdiːnt] *noun*
material which goes to make something; *the ingredients are listed on the packet*; *all the ingredients for the cake can be bought at the local supermarket*

④ **inhabit**
[ɪnˈhæbɪt] *verb*
to live in a place; *nobody inhabits the island*; *the area is mainly inhabited by wild goats*

④ **inhabitant**
[ɪnˈhæbɪtɪnt] *noun*
person who lives in a place; *the local inhabitants do not like noisy tourists in summer*; *London has over seven million inhabitants*; *the local council warned the inhabitants of the island that they should boil their drinking water*

④ **inherit**
[ɪnˈherɪt] *verb*
(a) to receive money, etc., from a person who has died; *she inherited a small fortune from her father*; *when her grandfather died she inherited the shop*
(b) to have characteristics passed on from a parent; *I think she has inherited her father's gloomy character*
(c) to take over a client or a problem from a someone who had the job before you; *when they bought the shop they inherited a lot of ancient equipment*; *the new manager had inherited a lot of financial problems*

② **initial**
[ɪˈnɪʃl]
1 *adjective*
first; *the initial stage of the project went off very well*; *my initial reaction was to say 'no'*; *he started the business with an initial investment of £500*
2 *noun*
initials = the first letters of a person's names; *John Smith has a bag with his initials JS on it*
3 *verb*
to write your initials on a document to show you have read and approved it; *can you initial each page of the contract to show that you have approved it?*; *please initial the agreement at the place marked with an X* (NOTE: initialling - initialled but American spelling initialing - initialed)

③ **initially**
[ɪˈnɪʃɪli] *adverb*
at the beginning; *initially we didn't like our new flat, but we have got used to it now*

④ **initiate**
[ɪˈnɪʃɪeɪt] *verb*
(a) to start something; *he initiated the new project last year*
(b) to introduce someone into something secret, to show someone the basic information about something; *she was initiated into the club*

② **initiative**
[ɪˈnɪʃɪtɪv] *noun*
decision which you hope will get something moving; *the government has proposed various initiatives to get the negotiations moving again*; **to take the initiative** = to decide to do something which other people don't want to do; *the manager decided to take the initiative and ask for a meeting with the boss*; *the president took the initiative in asking the rebel leader to come for talks*

④ **inject**
[ɪnˈdʒekt] *verb*
(a) to force a liquid into something under pressure; *the nurse injected the drug using a needle*; *he injected himself with a drug*
(b) to put something new into something; *come on, let's try to inject some life into these rehearsals!*

③ **injection**
[ɪnˈdʒekʃn] *noun*
(a) act of injecting a liquid into the body; *the doctor gave him injections against tropical diseases*
(b) liquid which is to be injected; *the clinic has ordered another batch of flu injections*

④ **injure**
[ˈɪndʒə] *verb*
to hurt; *he injured his spine playing rugby*; *two people were injured in the bank hold-up*; *when the goalkeeper was injured they sent on a substitute*; *he was badly injured in a motorway accident*

③ **injured**
[ˈɪndʒɪd] *noun*
the injured = people who have been wounded; *the badly injured were taken to hospital by helicopter* (NOTE: plural; for one person say **the injured man, the injured girl, etc.**)

② **injury**
[ˈɪndʒɪri] *noun*
hurt, wound; *he never really recovered from his football injury*; *she received severe back injuries in the accident* (NOTE: plural is **injuries**)

④ **injustice**
[ɪnˈdʒʌstɪs] *noun*
lack of justice; *the injustice of the court's decision caused a storm of protest in the newspapers*; *we all believe that an injustice has been done*

④ **ink**
[ɪŋk]
1 *noun*
liquid for writing with a pen; *he has ink marks on his shirt*; *the ink won't come off the tablecloth*; *she wrote comments on his work in red ink*
2 *verb*
to ink in = to write or draw using ink on top of something which was written or drawn in pencil

④ **inland**
['ınlænd] *adverb*
towards the interior of a country; *if you go inland from the port, you soon get into the forest*

④ **Inland Revenue**
['ınlænd 'revınjuː] *noun*
the British government department dealing with tax; *the Inland Revenue wrote claiming we owe some tax from last year* (NOTE: the American equivalent is the **Internal Revenue Service** *or* **IRS**)

④ **in-line skates**
['ınlaın 'skeıts] *noun*
type of roller skates, with a series of little wheels in line; *two girls on in-line skates zoomed past us at great speed*

④ **inmate**
['ınmeıt] *noun*
person living in a home or in a prison; *five inmates escaped last week*

④ **inn**
[ın] *noun*
small hotel; *we stayed in a little inn in the mountains*

② **inner**
['ını] *adjective*
inside; *go through that arch and you will come to the inner garden; heat is conducted from the inner to the outer layer of the material; the area code for inner London is 0207;* **inner tube** = thin rubber tube containing air inside a tyre (NOTE: the opposite is **outer**)

③ **inner city**
['ını 'sıti] *noun*
the central part of a city; *inner-city problems or problems of the inner city; there are always traffic jams in the inner city at rush hour; inner-city hotels are most convenient, but can be noisy*

④ **innocence**
['ınısıns] *noun*
(a) not being guilty; *the lawyers tried to prove his innocence*
(b) not having any experience or particular knowledge; *in my innocence, I believed them when they said they were police officers*

④ **innocent**
['ınısınt]
1 *adjective*
(a) not guilty; *he was found to be innocent of the crime; in English law, the accused is always presumed to be innocent until he is proved to be guilty*
(b) not having any experience or knowledge; *she's quite innocent when dealing with TV reporters*
2 *noun*
person who has no experience or knowledge; *he's a total innocent when it comes to dealing with car salesmen*

③ **innovation**
[ını'veıʃn] *noun*
new invention, new way of doing something; *the computer is an innovation which has changed everyone's lives; it was something of an innovation to have a wedding in the local fire station*

③ **input**
['ınput] *noun*
(a) electric current which goes into an apparatus; *plug the input cable into the computer*
(b) data fed into a computer; *the input from the various branches is fed automatically into the head office computer*
(c) contribution to a discussion; *that you very much for your useful input during the meeting*
(d) **inputs** = goods or services bought on which you pay VAT (NOTE: the opposite, i.e. goods and services sold on which VAT is charged, are **outputs**)

③ **inquire**
[ın'kwaıı] *verb*
(a) to ask questions about something; *the cook inquired if anything was wrong with the meal; she phoned the travel agent to inquire about air fares to Australia; she inquired about my mother's health;* 'inquire within' = ask for more details inside the office or shop
(b) to conduct an official investigation into a problem; to investigate, to try to find out about something; *the police are inquiring into his background; the social services are inquiring about the missing girl* (NOTE: also spelt **enquire**)

③ **inquiry**
[ın'kwaıri] *noun*
(a) formal investigation into a problem; *a government inquiry into corruption in the police force; a public inquiry will be held about plans to build another airport*
(b) question about something; *I refer to your inquiry of May 25th; all inquiries should be addressed to this department; he made an inquiry about trains to Edinburgh; see also* DIRECTORY ENQUIRIES (NOTE: plural is **inquiries**; also spelt **enquiry**)

④ **insect**
['ınsekt] *noun*
small animal with six legs and a body in three parts; *a butterfly is a kind of insect; insects have eaten the leaves of the cabbages; she was stung by an insect;* **insect bite** = sting caused by an insect which goes through the skin and hurts

④ **insecure**
[ınsı'kjuı] *adjective*
(a) not safe; *she felt insecure when walking down the High Street alone at night*
(b) not firmly fixed; *be careful! that ladder looks insecure*

insert

1 *verb*

[ɪnˈsɜːt] to put something inside; *he inserted each leaflet into an envelope*; *insert a coin into the slot and press the button to select the drink you want*

2 *noun*

[ˈɪnsɜːt] paper which is put inside something; *the wedding invitation card had an insert with a map showing how to get to the church*

inside

[ɪnˈsaɪd]

1 *adverb*

indoors; *come on inside - it's cold in the street*; *it rained all afternoon, so we just sat inside and watched TV*; *is there anyone there? - the house seems quite dark inside*

2 *preposition*

(a) in; *there was nothing inside the bottle*; *she was sitting inside the car, reading a book*; *I've never been inside his office*

(b) within; **inside two hours** = in less than two hours

3 *noun*

part which is in something; *I know their office from the outside, but what is the inside like?*; *the meat isn't cooked - the inside is still quite red*

4 *adjective*

(a) which is indoors; *the office has an inside garage*

(b) inside information = information which is only known by people working in a certain organization; *she said she had inside information about the company's plans*

◊ **inside out**

[ˈɪnsaɪd ˈaʊt] *phrase*

(a) turned with the inner part facing out; *he put his pyjamas on inside out*

(b) to know something inside out = to know something very well; *she knows Central London inside out*

insides

[ɪnˈsaɪdz] *noun*

(informal) the interior of something, especially your stomach; *my insides are upset after last night's Indian meal*

insight

[ˈɪnsaɪt] *noun*

clear ideas or knowledge; *we appreciated the insight into the workings of the Foreign Office he was able to bring us*

insist

[ɪnˈsɪst] *verb*

to state in a firm way; *he insisted that he had never touched the car*; *she insisted that she should be paid compensation for the delay*; **to insist on something** = to state in a firm way that something must be done or given; *she insisted on being given a refund*; *I insist on an immediate explanation*

in so far as *or* insofar as

[ɪn ˈsɪʊ ˈfɑː ˈæz] *(formal)*

to a certain extent, partly; *we found the assembly instructions, insofar as they applied to our model, quite easy to understand*

inspect

[ɪnˈspekt] *verb*

to look at something closely; *the kitchens are regularly inspected by health inspectors*; *she inspected the room to see if it had been cleaned properly*; *the customs officers were inspecting the luggage of all travellers coming from Amsterdam*

inspection

[ɪnˈspekʃn] *noun*

examining something closely; *they carried out an inspection of the kitchen*

inspector

[ɪnˈspektɪ] *noun*

senior official who examines something closely; *inspectors come onto the trains to check that everyone has a ticket*; **health inspector** = official who inspects buildings to see if they are clean; **police inspector** = officer in the police force above a sergeant and below a chief inspector; *the police inspector made a statement on TV*; **schools inspector** = official of the department of education who examines the teaching in schools; *a team of inspectors visited the school last week*; **inspector of taxes** *or* **tax inspector** = government official who examines tax returns and decides how much tax someone should pay

inspiration

[ɪnspɪˈreɪʃn] *noun*

(a) sudden urge to write poems, to compose music, etc.; *her inspiration comes from the countryside of her native Cornwall*

(b) sudden good idea; *we had run out of sugar and all the shops were closed, but she had an inspiration and tried the railway station snack bar*

install

[ɪnˈstɔːl] *verb*

to put a person into a job, a machine into a workshop, etc.; *it took the builder a week to install the new central heating system*

installation

[ɪnstɪˈleɪʃn] *noun*

(a) putting a machine in place; *the installation of the central heating took six days*

(b) group of machines which have been put in place; *the harbour installations are very modern*; *the fire seriously damaged the oil installations*

instalment US installment

[ɪnˈstɔːlmɪnt] *noun*

(a) payment of part of a total sum which is made regularly; *they are paying for the kitchen by monthly instalments*; *you pay £25 down and twelve monthly instalments of £20*; US **installment plan** = system of buying something by paying a sum regularly each month until the purchase is completed; *they bought the car on the installment plan* (NOTE: the British equivalent is **hire purchase**)

(b) part of something which is being shown or delivered in parts; *the next instalment of the series will be shown on Monday evening*

② **instance**
['ɪnstəns] *noun*

case, example; *there have been several instances of theft in our local school*; *in this instance, we will pay for the damage*; **for instance** = as an example; *why don't you take up a new sport - golf, for instance?*

② **instant**
['ɪnstənt]

1 *noun*

moment or second; *for an instant, he stood still and watched the policemen*

2 *adjective*

immediate; *a savings account can give you instant access to your money*; **instant coffee** = coffee powder to which you add hot water to make a fast cup of coffee; *she made a cup of instant coffee; do you mind if it's instant coffee, we've run out of fresh?*

④ **instantly**
['ɪnstəntlɪ] *adverb*

immediately, at once; *he got my letter, and instantly wrote to the bank*; *all the passengers must have died instantly*

① **instead (of)**
[ɪn'sted] *adverb*

in place of; *since he's ill, I'm going instead of him*; *instead of stopping when the policeman shouted, he ran away*; *why don't you help me with the housework, instead of sitting and watching TV all day?*; *we haven't any coffee - would you like some tea instead?*; *if you can't go, can I go instead?*

④ **instinct**
['ɪnstɪŋkt] *noun*

something which you have from birth and have not learnt; *many animals have an instinct to hunt*; **by instinct** = from a feeling which you have inside you; *our little daughter seems to know by instinct if we have bought any chocolates*; *he seemed to feel by instinct that the plane was dangerous*

④ **instinctive**
[ɪn'stɪŋktɪv] *adjective*

natural (reaction); *my instinctive reaction was to call the police*

② **institute**
['ɪnstɪtjuːt]

1 *noun*

organization set up for a special purpose; *they are proposing to set up a new institute of education*; *she goes to the research institute's library every week*

2 *verb*

to set up or to start; *to institute a lawsuit against someone*

① **institution**
[ɪnstɪ'tjuːʃn] *noun*

(a) organization, a society set up for a special purpose; *a prison is an institution which houses criminals*; **financial institution** = bank or other company whose work involves lending or investing large sums of money

(b) permanent custom; *the lottery has rapidly become a national institution*; *British institutions such as cream teas and the royal family*

(c) *(formal)* setting up, starting; *the institution of legal proceedings against the president*

③ **instruct**
[ɪn'strʌkt] *verb*

(a) **to instruct someone to do something** = to tell someone officially to do something; *the inspectors instructed the restaurant to replace its kitchen equipment*; *the firemen instructed us to leave the building*

(b) to show someone how to do something; *my assistant will instruct you in various ways of coping with a fire*

(c) **to instruct a solicitor** = to give information to a solicitor and to ask him to start an action on your behalf; *(of a solicitor)* **to instruct a barrister** = to give a barrister all the details of a case which he will plead in court

② **instruction**
[ɪn'strʌkʃn] *noun*

(a) orders; *he gave instructions to the driver*; **shipping instructions** = details of how goods are to be shipped and delivered; **to await instructions** = to wait for someone to tell you what to do; **according to instructions** = as the instructions show; *we assembled the machine according to the manufacturer's instructions*; **failing instructions to the contrary** = unless someone tells you to do the opposite; *failing instructions to the contrary, everyone should meet at the bus station at 9.00*

(b) indication of how something is to be done or used; *I can't read the instructions on the medicine bottle - the letters are too small*; *she gave us detailed instructions how to get to the church*; **instruction manual** = booklet which tells you how something should be used

④ **instructor**
[ɪn'strʌktɪ] *noun*

teacher, especially of a sport; **driving instructor** = person who teaches people how to drive; **ski instructor** = person who teaches people how to ski; **swimming instructor** = person who teaches people how to swim

② **instrument**
['ɪnstrʊmənt] *noun*

piece of equipment; *the technical staff have instruments which measure the output of electricity*; **musical instrument** = device which is blown or hit, etc., to make a musical note; *he* *doesn't play the piano, the drums or any other musical instrument*; **wind instruments** = musical instruments which you have to blow to make a note; *she plays several wind instruments*; *see also* STRING INSTRUMENTS

④ **insult**

1 *noun*

['ɪnsʌlt] rude word said to or about a person; *that is an insult to the government*; *the crowd shouted insults at the police*; **an insult to someone's intelligence** = something which is so obvious or easy that anyone could understand it; *that TV quiz is an insult to the intelligence of the viewers*

2 *verb*

[ɪn'sʌlt] to say rude things about someone; *he was accused of insulting the president's wife*

③ **insulting**

[ɪn'sʌltɪŋ] *adjective*

rude; *he made some insulting remarks about the teachers*; *don't be insulting - it's a very beautiful hat*

② **insurance**

[ɪn'ʃuːrɪns] *noun*

agreement with a company by which you are paid compensation for loss or damage in return for regular payments of money; *do you have insurance for your travel?*; **to take out an insurance against fire** = to pay money, so that if a fire happens, compensation will be paid to you; **insurance company** = company which provides insurance; *we contacted the insurance company as soon as the theft was discovered*; **insurance policy** = document with the details of an insurance; *the insurance policy will be sent to you by post*; **car insurance** *or* **motor insurance** = insuring a car, the driver and passengers in case of accident; *my car insurance only covers drivers named in the policy*; **general insurance** = insurance covering theft, loss, damage, etc. (but not life insurance); **home insurance** *or* **house insurance** = insuring a house and its contents against damage; *house insurance can be arranged by your bank*; **life insurance** = insurance paying a sum of money when someone dies; *the mortgage company requires you to take out a life insurance policy*; *see also* ASSURANCE; **National Insurance** = government-run insurance which provides for state medical care, unemployment payments, etc.; *National Insurance contributions are deducted from your salary by your employer*

④ **insure**

[ɪn'ʃuː] *verb*

to agree with a company that if you pay them a regular sum, they will pay you compensation for loss or damage to property or persons; *she insured her watch for £10,000*; *they forgot to insure the building against fire*; *have you insured the contents of the house?* (NOTE: do not confuse with **ensure**)

④ **insurer**

[ɪn'ʃuːrɪ] *noun*

person or company which insures; *we contacted the insurer as soon as we discovered the burglary*

④ **intact**

[ɪn'tækt] *adjective*

in one piece, not broken; *the cups arrived intact, but several plates were broken during the move*

④ **intake**

['ɪnteɪk] *noun*

(a) thing or things which are absorbed or taken in; *she is trying to reduce her calorie intake or her intake of calories*

(b) group of new students, soldiers, etc.; *we are increasing our intake of mature students again this year*; *this year's intake of recruits has more potential officers than usual*

④ **integrate**

['ɪntɪɡreɪt] *verb*

to link up to form a whole; *to integrate immigrants into the community*

③ **integration**

[ɪntɪ'ɡreɪʃn] *noun*

act of integrating; *the integration of the two schools will allow for better use of our resources*

④ **integrity**

[ɪn'teɡrɪti] *noun*

(a) honesty, strong moral principles; *his integrity is in doubt since the report on the company loan scandal*

(b) existence as a single thing or group; *we must try to maintain the integrity of the association by avoiding a split among the members*

③ **intellectual**

[ɪntɪ'lektʃuːl]

1 *adjective*

(a) referring to the way you use your brain; *the puzzle requires considerable intellectual effort*; *she has great intellectual capacity*

(b) *(person)* who is good at using their brain; *she is more intellectual than her husband*

2 *noun*

person who believes that the brain is very important, who uses his or her brain to make a living; *left-wing intellectuals have criticized the Prime Minister*

③ **intelligence**

[ɪn'telɪdʒɪns] *noun*

(a) ability to think and understand; *his intelligence is well above average*; **intelligence quotient (IQ)** = number believed to show how intelligent a person is compared to others; *she has an IQ of 110*

(b) information provided by the secret services; *intelligence gathered by our network of agents is very useful to us in planning future attacks*; **the intelligence services** = the government departments involved in spying

③ **intelligent**
[ɪn'telɪdʒɪnt] *adjective*
(a) clever, able to understand things very well;
she is more intelligent than her brother; *he's
the most intelligent child in his class*
(b) able to think and reason; *is there intelligent
life on Mars?*; *an intelligent computer terminal*

① **intend**
[ɪn'tend] *verb*
to intend to do something = to plan to do
something; *I intended to get up early but I
didn't wake up till 9*; *the company intends to
sue for damages*; **I intended no insult** = I did
not mean my words to be taken as an insult

③ **intended**
[ɪn'tendɪd] *adjective*
(a) which is aimed at; *they never reached their
intended destination*; *the murderer followed
his intended victim*
(b) provided for a special purpose; *the big plate
is intended to be used for serving meat*

③ **intense**
[ɪn'tens] *adjective*
(a) very strong or vigorous; *there was a period
of intense diplomatic activity to try to get the
hostages released*; *he had an intense period of
study before the exams*
(b) extremely serious (person); *she is a very
intense young woman*

④ **intensify**
[ɪn'tensɪfaɪ] *verb*
(a) to become stronger; *the rain intensified and
continued all night*
(b) to make something stronger; *he intensified
his attacks on the government*

④ **intensive**
[ɪn'tensɪv] *adjective*
(a) with a lot of effort; *he took a two-week
intensive course in German*
(b) intensive care (unit) = section of a hospital
dealing with seriously ill patients who need a lot
of attention; *two of the accident victims are still
in intensive care*

④ **intent**
[ɪn'tent]
1 *adjective*
determined; *she's intent on becoming a
manager*
2 *noun*
aim, intention; **to all intents and purposes** =
virtually, in almost every way; *he is to all
intents and purposes the boss of the business*

② **intention**
[ɪn'tenʃn] *noun*
aim or plan to do something; *I can assure you
that I have no intention of going to the party*;
*the fans came with the deliberate intention of
stirring up trouble*

④ **interact**
[ɪntɪ'rækt] *verb*
to interact with someone or **something** = to
have a sympathetic effect on someone or
something; *the students are interacting well
with the teachers*

④ **intercourse**
['ɪntɪkɔːs] *noun*
sex act between a man and a woman; *they had
intercourse on the first night they met*

① **interest**
['ɪntrɪst]
1 *noun*
(a) special attention to something; *she takes a
lot of interest in politics*; *he has no interest in
what his sister is doing*; *why doesn't he take
more interest in local affairs?*
(b) thing which you pay attention to; *her main
interest is sailing*; *list your special interests on
your CV*
(c) percentage which is paid to someone who
lends money; *if you put your money in a
building society you should get 6% interest on
it*; *deposit accounts pay more interest*; *how
much interest do I have to pay if I borrow
£1000?*; **simple interest** = interest calculated on
the capital only, and not added to it; **compound
interest** = interest which is added to the capital
and then itself earns interest; **interest rate** *or*
rate of interest = percentage charged for
borrowing money; *the Bank of England has
raised interest rates*; *savings accounts offer a
good interest rate* or *a good rate of interest*
(d) financial share in something; **he has a
controlling interest in the company** = he owns
more than 50% of the shares and so can direct
how the company is run; **majority interest** =
situation where someone owns a majority of the
shares in a company; *he has a majority interest
in a supermarket chain*; **minority interest** =
situation where someone owns less than 50% of
the shares in a company; **conflict of interest(s)**
= situation where a person may profit personally
from decisions which he takes in his official
capacity
2 *verb*
to attract someone; *he's particularly interested
in old cars*; *nothing seems to interest him very
much*; *the book didn't interest me at all*; *he
tried to interest several companies in his new
invention*

① **interested**
['ɪntrɪstɪd] *adjective*
with a personal interest in something; *he's
interested in old churches*; *she's interested in
crime fiction*

① **interesting**
['ɪntrɪstɪŋ] *adjective*
which attracts your attention; *there's an
interesting article in the newspaper on*

European football; she didn't find the TV programme very interesting; what's so interesting about old cars? - I find them dull

④ **interfere**
[ɪntɪˈfɪɪ] *verb*
to interfere in or **with something** = to get in the way of something, to be involved in something in such a way that it doesn't work well; *her mother is always interfering in her life; stop interfering with the TV controls*

④ **interim**
[ˈɪntɪrɪm]
1 *adjective*
(report) given halfway through a period, before the final result is known; *please send us an interim report on the first year of your research project*; **interim dividend** = dividend paid at the end of six months
2 *noun*
in the interim = meanwhile; *we are still painting the offices: in the interim you will have to share an office with your boss*

④ **interior**
[ɪnˈtiːɪrɪɪ]
1 *adjective*
inside; **interior decorating** = arranging and decorating the inside of a house (curtains, paint, wallpaper, carpets, etc.)
2 *noun*
(a) inner part (of a building, car, etc.); *she climbed down into the interior of the cave; the interior of the building is fine, but the exterior needs painting*
(b) **minister of the interior** or **interior minister** = government minister who deals with affairs inside a country, such as police, law and order, etc.; **ministry of the interior** = ministry dealing with affairs inside a country (NOTE: in the UK these are called the **Home Office** and the **Home Secretary**) *US* **Department of the Interior** = government department dealing with the conservation and development of natural resources

③ **interior designer**
[ɪnˈtiːrɪɪ dɪˈzaɪnɪ] *noun*
person who designs the inside of a building, including wallpaper, paint colours, furniture, curtains, carpets, etc.; *we have asked an interior designer to advise us on the design of the restaurant*

③ **interjection**
[ɪntɪˈdʒekʃn] *noun*
exclamation, a word used to show surprise; *interjections like 'ooh' are usually followed by an exclamation mark*

② **internal**
[ɪnˈtɜːnl] *adjective*
inside; **internal flight** = flight inside a country; **internal telephone** = private telephone inside a building (NOTE: the opposite, referring to the outside, is **external**)

① **international**
[ɪntɪˈnæʃɪnɪl] *adjective*
1 *adjective*
between countries; *an international conference on the environment*; *an important international company*; **international call** = telephone call to another country
2 *noun*
(a) sportsman who has played for his country's team against another country; *there are three England internationals in our local team*
(b) game between two countries; *the Rugby international will be held next Saturday at Twickenham*

② **Internet**
[ˈɪntɪnet] *noun*
international network linking thousands of computers using telephone links; *we send messages over the Internet to hundreds of users of our products*; *he searched the Internet for information on cheap tickets to Alaska* (NOTE: also called simply **the Net**)

COMMENT: Internet addresses of companies and other organizations are made up of two or three parts. The first part is the name of the organization (often written in a short form); the second can be .co (for a company), .com (for companies based in the USA), .edu (for educational establishments), .net (for Internet suppliers), .gov for government organizations and .mil (for military). With the exception of the USA, all countries add a further two-character country of origin name, such as .au for Australia, .cn for China, .uk for the United Kingdom, or .de for Germany

---

③ **interpret**
[ɪnˈtɜːprɪt] *verb*
(a) to translate aloud what is spoken in one language into another; *the guide knows Greek, so he will interpret for us*
(b) to explain the meaning of something; *his letter was interpreted as meaning that he refused the offer; her fit of giggles was interpreted as 'yes'*

② **interpretation**
[ɪntɜːprɪˈteɪʃn] *noun*
(a) meaning; *a poem can have many interpretations; the book puts quite a different interpretation on the meaning of the rule*
(b) translating aloud what is being said in one language into another; *she is taking a course in German interpretation*
(c) way of playing a piece of music; *two of the young musicians were praised for their interpretations of Bach*

③ **interpreter**
[ɪnˈtɜːprɪtɪ] *noun*
person who translates aloud from one language to another; *the hotel secretary will act as interpreter; we need an Italian interpreter*

④ **interrupt**

[ɪntɪˈrʌpt] *verb*

to start talking when someone else is talking; to do something to stop something working; *excuse me for interrupting, but have you seen the office keys anywhere?*; *the strike interrupted the flow of spare parts to our factory*

③ **interval**

[ˈɪntɪvl] *noun*

(a) period of time between two points; *there will be bright intervals during the morning, but it will rain in the afternoon*; *there will be a short interval during which the table will be cleared*

(b) period of time between two acts in a play; *anyone arriving late won't be allowed in until the first interval*

(c) **at intervals** = from time to time; *at intervals, he almost seems normal*; **at regular intervals** = quite often; *at regular intervals during my interview, the phone would ring and the man interviewing me would take down messages*

(d) *(in music)* difference in pitch; *the interval between D and A is a fifth*

③ **intervention**

[ɪntɪˈvenʃn] *noun*

coming between two things; acting to make a change in a system; *the central bank's intervention in the banking crisis*; *the intervention of the army ended the fighting between the two political parties*

② **interview**

[ˈɪntɪvjuː]

1 *noun*

(a) questioning by one or more people of a person applying for a job; *we asked six candidates for interview*; *he's had six interviews, but still no job offers*; *when will you attend your first interview?*

(b) discussion (on radio, TV, in a newspaper) between an important or interesting person and a journalist; *she gave an interview to the Sunday magazine*

2 *verb*

(a) to talk to a person applying for a job to see if he or she is suitable; *we interviewed ten candidates, but did not find anyone we liked*

(b) to ask a famous or interesting person questions and publish them afterwards; *the journalist interviewed the Prime Minister*

④ **intimate**

1 *adjective*

[ˈɪntɪmɪt]

(a) very close; *she is an intimate friend from my time at school*

(b) sexual; *they have had an intimate relationship for some months*

(c) very detailed; *the burglars must have had intimate knowledge of the layout of the house*

2 *verb*

[ˈɪntɪmeɪt] to announce or to suggest, but not very clearly; *he intimated that he was going to resign and go to work in Australia*

④ **intimidate**

[ɪnˈtɪmɪdeɪt] *verb*

to frighten someone by threatening them or appearing to threaten them; *witnesses had been intimidated by local criminals*; *the teacher did not realize how much he intimidated his students*

① **into**

[ˈɪntuː] *preposition*

(a) *(showing movement towards the inside)* *she went into the shop*; *he fell into the lake*; *put the cards back into their box*; *you can't get ten people into a taxi*; *we all stopped talking when he came into the room*; *the bus is going into the town centre*

(b) against, colliding with; *the bus drove into a tree*

(c) *(showing a change)* *water turns into steam when it is heated*; *she changed into an evening dress for the party*; **to burst into tears** = to start crying suddenly; *when she opened the box she burst into tears*

(d) *(showing that you are dividing)* *try to cut the cake into ten equal pieces*; **six into four won't go** = you can't divide four by six

(e) *(informal)* liking something very much; *he's into ethnic music*

① **introduce**

[ɪntrɪˈdjuːs] *verb*

(a) to present someone to another person or to people who did not know him or her previously; *he introduced me to a friend of his called Anne*; *she introduced me to her new teacher*

(b) to announce a TV or radio programme, etc.; *he introduced the start of the cricket special*

(c) to bring something to a new place; *several species of plant now common in Britain were introduced by the Romans*

① **introduction**

[ɪntrɪˈdʌkʃn] *noun*

(a) letter making someone known to other people who did not know him previously; *I'm going to Moscow next week - can you give me an introduction to anyone there?*; *I'll give you an introduction to Mike Smith - he is an old friend of mine*

(b) act of presenting something for the first time; *the World Fair in Chicago was his introduction to the American business scene*

(c) piece at the beginning of a book which explains the rest of the book; *read the introduction which gives details of how the book should be used in class*

(d) basic book about a subject; *he's the author of an introduction to mathematics*

(e) bringing into use; **the introduction of new technology** = putting new computers into a business or industry

④ **invade**

[ɪnˈveɪd] *verb*

(a) to attack and enter a country with an army; *William the Conqueror invaded England in 1066*

(b) *(of the press, official inspectors, etc.)* to **invade someone's privacy** = to disturb someone's private life; *she claimed that the photographers had invaded her privacy by climbing over the garden wall*

③ **invalid**

1 *adjective*

(a) [ˈɪnvɪlɪd]

sick or disabled; *her invalid mother lives in a nursing home*; **invalid carriage** = small vehicle for one disabled person

(b) [ɪnˈvælɪd]

not valid, not legal; *she was stopped at the frontier because her passport was invalid*; *your library card is invalid, so you need to renew it*

2 *noun*

[ˈɪnvɪlɪd] sick or disabled person; *she's been an invalid since her operation*

3 *verb*

[ˈɪnvɪliːd]

to invalid someone out = to make someone retire because of ill health; *he was invalided out of the navy*

④ **invasion**

[ɪnˈveɪʒn] *noun*

(a) entering a country by force with an army; *the invasion took place in early June*

(b) **invasion of privacy** = behaviour of the press, official inspectors, etc., which disturbs someone's private life; *the photographers climbing over the wall was an invasion of my privacy*

③ **invent**

[ɪnˈvent] *verb*

(a) to create a new process or a new machine; *she invented a new type of computer terminal*; *who invented the electric car?*

(b) to think up an excuse; *when she asked him why he was late he invented some excuse*

③ **invention**

[ɪnˈvenʃn] *noun*

(a) act of creating a new process or a new machine; *the invention of computers was made possible by developments in electronics*

(b) new device; *he tried to sell his latest invention to a US car manufacturer*

③ **inventory**

[ˈɪnvɪntri] *noun*

(a) list of contents (of a house, etc.); *the landlord checked the inventory when the tenants left* (NOTE: plural in this meaning is **inventories**)

(b) *(mainly US)* stock of goods held in a warehouse; *the whole inventory was destroyed by fire*; **inventory control** = system of checking that there is not too much stock in a warehouse, but just enough to satisfy orders (NOTE: the word

'inventory' is used in American English where British English uses the word 'stock'. So, the American 'inventory control' is 'stock control' in British English)

④ **inverted**

[ɪnˈvɜːtɪd] *adjective*

upside down; **inverted commas** = printed or written marks (« «) showing that a quotation starts or finishes; *that part of the sentence should be in inverted commas*

③ **invest**

[ɪnˈvest] *verb*

(a) to put (money) into savings, property, etc., so that it will increase in value; *she was advised to invest in electricity companies*; *he invested all his money in a fish-and-chip restaurant*

(b) to spend money on something which you believe will be useful; *we have invested in a new fridge*

② **investigate**

[ɪnˈvestɪɡeɪt] *verb*

to study or to examine something closely; *the detective is investigating the details of the case*; *we are investigating the possibility of going to live in Costa Rica*

② **investigation**

[ɪnvestɪˈɡeɪʃn] *noun*

close examination; *a police investigation into the causes of the crash*; **on investigation** = when it was examined; *on further investigation, the newspaper report was shown to be quite false*

① **investment**

[ɪnˈvesmɪnt] *noun*

(a) money in the form of shares or deposits that are expected to increase in value; *he has been very successful with his investments*; **long-term investments** *or* **short-term investments** = shares, etc., which are likely to increase in value over a long or short period; *buying a house is considered a good long-term investment*

(b) money spent by a government or a company to improve its resources; *the economy is suffering from a lack of investment in training*; *investment always falls during a recession*

③ **investor**

[ɪnˈvestɪ] *noun*

person who puts money into savings or property; *a wise investor has to be cautious sometimes*

④ **invisible**

[ɪnˈvɪzɪbl] *adjective*

(a) which cannot be seen; *the message was written in invisible ink and hidden inside the pages of the telephone directory*

(b) **invisible earnings** = foreign currency earned by a country by providing services, (such as banking, insurance or tourism) but not selling goods; *compare* VISIBLE

③ **invitation**
[ɪnvɪ'teɪʃn] *noun*
letter or card, asking someone to do something; *he received an invitation to his sister's wedding*; *she had an invitation to dinner*; **at someone's invitation** = invited by someone; *she spoke to the meeting at the invitation of the committee*

② **invite**
[ɪn'vaɪt] *verb*
to ask someone to do something, especially to come to a party, etc.; *we invited two hundred people to the party*; *she invited us to come in*; *she's been invited to talk to the club*

③ **inviting**
[ɪn'vaɪtɪŋ] *adjective*
which looks attractive; *the empty restaurant didn't look very inviting*; *after the long, hot, dusty walk the water of the lake looked inviting*

② **invoice**
['ɪnvɔɪs]
1 *noun*
note sent to ask for payment for services or goods; *our invoice dated November 10th has still not been paid*; *they sent in their invoice six weeks late*; *ask the salesman to make out an invoice for £250*; **VAT invoice** = invoice which shows VAT separately
2 *verb*
to send a note asking for payment for services or goods; **we invoiced you on November 10th** = we sent you an invoice on November 10th

① **involve**
[ɪn'vɒlv] *verb*
(a) to bring someone *or* something into an activity, situation, dispute or crime, etc.; *we want to involve the local community in the decision about the new airport*; *a competition involving teams from ten different countries*; *members of the local council are involved in the company which has won the contract for the new road*
(b) to make necessary; *going to Oxford Circus from here involves taking a bus and then the Underground*

② **involved**
[ɪn'vɒlvd] *adjective*
complicated; *the new tax forms are very involved*; *the whole process of getting a visa was terribly involved*

③ **involvement**
[ɪn'vɒlvmɪnt] *noun*
contact with someone, taking part in something; *did she have any involvement with the music festival?*; *the police were unable to prove his involvement in the crime*

③ **IQ**
['aɪ 'kjuː] = INTELLIGENCE QUOTIENT
she has an IQ of 110

③ **Ireland**
['aɪlɪnd] *noun*
large island forming the western part of the British Isles, containing the Republic of Ireland and Northern Ireland; *these birds are found all over Ireland*; **Northern Ireland** = the northern part of the island of Ireland, which is part of the United Kingdom

① **Ireland (the Republic of Ireland)**
['aɪlɪnd] *noun*
country to the west of the United Kingdom, forming the largest part of the island of Ireland, a member of the EU; *Ireland was declared a republic in 1949* (NOTE: capital: **Dublin**; people: **the Irish**; languages: **Irish, English**; currency: **Irish pound** *or* **punt, euro**)

① **Irish**
['aɪrɪʃ]
1 *adjective*
referring to Ireland; *the Irish Sea lies between Ireland and Britain*; **Irish coffee** = hot coffee, served in a glass, with Irish whiskey added to it and whipped cream poured on top
2 *noun*
(a) Celtic language still spoken in parts of Ireland; *Eire is the Irish name for the Republic of Ireland*
(b) the Irish = people who live in Ireland; *the Irish are famous for their folk music*

② **iron**
['aɪn]
1 *noun*
(a) common grey metal; *the old gates are made of iron* (NOTE: Chemical element: chemical symbol: **Fe**; atomic number: **26**; note also, no plural in this meaning: **some iron, lumps of iron, pieces of iron**)
(b) electric device that is heated to make clothes smooth after washing; *don't leave the iron plugged in, it will burn the clothes*; *if your iron is not hot enough it won't make the shirts smooth*
(c) golf club with a metal head
2 *verb*
(a) to make cloth smooth, using an iron; *she was ironing shirts when the telephone rang*; *her skirt doesn't look as though it has been ironed*
(b) to iron out = to sort out, to solve a problem; *we had a very productive meeting - all the remaining problems were ironed out*

③ **ironing**
['aɪnɪŋ] *noun*
clothes which have been washed and are ready to be ironed; *she was doing the ironing*; *there's a lot of ironing waiting to be done*

③ **ironing board**
['aɪnɪŋ 'bɔːd] *noun*
special narrow table used when ironing clothes

irony
['aɪrɪni] *noun*
(a) way of referring to something where you say the opposite of what you mean; *do I detect a note of irony in his letter?*
(b) situation when something happens at the wrong moment, as if on purpose; *the irony of it was that the rain finally stopped on the last day of our holiday*

irregular
[ɪ'regjʊlɪ] *adjective*
(a) not regular; *an irregular pattern of lines and circles*; *his heart had an irregular beat*
(b) not level; *an irregular stone path leads across the garden*
(c) not happening always at the same time; *his payments are very irregular*; *he makes irregular visits to his mother in hospital*
(d) not according to the rules; *this procedure is highly irregular*

irrelevant
[ɪ'relɪvɪnt] *adjective*
not relevant, with no connection to the subject; *his comments about the weather were quite irrelevant to the subject being discussed*; *whether he's rich or not is irrelevant - I love him!*

irritate
['ɪrɪteɪt] *verb*
(a) to annoy; *it irritates me when the trains run late*
(b) to make a burning feeling; *some plants irritate the skin*

irritated
['ɪrɪteɪtɪd] *adjective*
annoyed; *'leave me alone,' she said in an irritated voice*

irritating
['ɪrɪteɪtɪŋ] *adjective*
which annoys; *it's irritating to see how badly the work has been done*; *he has the irritating habit of scratching the top of his head*

is
[ɪz]
see BE

Islam
['ɪzlɑːm] *noun*
the religion of the Muslims, founded by Muhammad

island
['aɪlɪnd] *noun*
(a) piece of land with water all round it; *they live on a little island in the middle of the river*; *the Greek islands are favourite holiday destinations*
(b) **traffic island** = small piece of pavement in the centre of the road where people walking across can safely stand

isn't
['ɪznt]
see BE

isolated
['aɪsɪleɪtɪd] *adjective*
(a) separated from others; *they live in an isolated village in the hills*
(b) one only; **isolated attack** = single attack, which has not been repeated; *an isolated case of mugging*

issue
['ɪʃuː]
1 *noun*
(a) problem; *the main issues will be discussed at the meeting*; **to make an issue of something** = to have a big discussion about something; *she's apologized so don't try to make an issue of it*; **the point at issue** = the question which is being discussed; *the point at issue is whether the government is prepared to compromise*; **to take issue with someone** = to disagree with someone
(b) publication of a book; putting new stamps on sale; putting new coins or notes into circulation; *there will be a new issue of stamps this month*
(c) giving out of permits, licences, uniforms, etc.; *the issue of TV licences has been delayed*
(d) one copy of a newspaper or magazine; *we bought the January issue of the magazine*
(e) giving out new shares; **rights issue** = giving shareholders the right to buy more shares more cheaply
2 *verb*
(a) to put (new stamps) on sale; to publish (books); to put (new coins or notes) into circulation; *the new set of stamps will be issued next week*; *initially the euro will be issued alongside national currencies*
(b) to give out or to hand out permits, licences, uniforms, etc.; *the government issued a report on London's traffic*; *the Secretary of State issued guidelines for expenditure*
(c) to come out; *smoke began to issue from the hole in the ground*

it
[ɪt] *pronoun referring to a thing*
(a) *(used to show something which has just been mentioned)* *what do you want me to do with the box? - put it down*; *where's the box? - it's here*; *she picked up a potato and then dropped it on the ground*; *I put my book down somewhere and now I can't find it*; *where's the newspaper? - it's on the chair*; *the dog's thirsty, give it something to drink*
(b) *(referring to no particular thing)* *look! - it's snowing*; *it's miles from here to the railway station*; *is it the 30th today?*; *it's almost impossible to get a ticket at this time of year*; *what time is it? - it's ten o'clock*; *it's dangerous to use an electric saw when it's wet* (NOTE: **it's** = **it is** or **it has**; do not confuse with **its**)

IT
['aɪ 'tiː]
= INFORMATION TECHNOLOGY

① **Italian**
[ɪ'tæljɪn]
1 *adjective*
referring to Italy; *my wife loves Italian food; we bought some Italian wine last week*
2 *noun*
(a) person from Italy; *the Italians have a passion for football*
(b) language spoken in Italy; *Italian is one of the languages that come from Latin; we go to Italy on holiday every year, and the children speak quite good Italian*

④ **italic**
[ɪ'tælɪk]
1 *adjective*
sloping (of letters); *the text under the illustrations is printed in italic type*
2 *noun*
italics = sloping letters; *this example is printed in italics* (NOTE: the other two main styles of print are **roman** and **bold**)

COMMENT: as the word suggests, italics were invented in Italy (in the fifteenth century). Italics are used to show words which you want to highlight in some way, but are not used for whole paragraphs

① **Italy**
['ɪtɪli] *noun*
country in southern Europe, south of France, Switzerland and Austria; *Italy is the home of great sixteenth century painters like Michaelangelo and Raphael* (NOTE: capital: **Rome**; people: **Italians**; language: **Italian**; currency: **lira, euro**)

① **item**
['aɪtɪm] *noun*
(a) thing (in a list); *we are discussing item four on the agenda; do you have any items of*

jewellery in your luggage?; *please find enclosed an order for the following items from your catalogue*

(b) piece of information, for example on a news programme; *here is a summary of the main items of news* or the main news items

③ **it'll**
[ɪtl] *short for* IT WILL

① **its**
[ɪts] *adjective referring to 'it'; I can't use the car - one of its tyres is flat; the company pays its staff very badly* (NOTE: do not confuse with **it's**)

① **it's**
[ɪts] *short for* IT IS, IT HAS

① **itself**
[ɪt'self] *pronoun referring to a thing*
(a) *(referring to an object) the dog seems to have hurt itself; the screw had worked itself loose;* **all by itself** = alone, with no one helping; *the church stands all by itself in the middle of the street; the bus started to move all by itself*
(b) *(for emphasis) if the plug is all right there must be something wrong with the computer itself*

③ **I've**
[aɪv] = I HAVE

④ **ivory**
['aɪvɪri] *noun*
(a) hard white substance from an elephant's tooth; *she bought some finely carved ivory figures; trade in ivory has been banned*
(b) **ivory tower** = imaginary place where an intellectual can live, isolated from the ordinary world; *just because I'm a university lecturer doesn't mean I live in an ivory tower*

Jj

② **J, j**
[dʒeɪ]
tenth letter of the alphabet, between I and K

④ **jack**
[dʒæk]
1 *noun*
(a) device for raising something heavy, especially a car; *I used the jack to lift up the car and take the wheel off*
(b) *(in playing cards)* the card with the face of a young man, with a value between the queen and the ten; *I won because I had the jack of hearts*

(c) *(at bowls)* small white or black ball for players to aim at
(d) electric or telephone plug with a single pin; *when he had plugged the jack in he could use the modem; see also* UNION JACK

② **jacket**
['dʒækɪt] *noun*
(a) short coat worn with trousers; *he was wearing a blue jacket and brown trousers; this orange jacket shows up in the dark when I ride my bike;* **dinner jacket** = man's formal black jacket, worn with a black bow tie; *see also* LIFE JACKET

(b) paper cover wrapped round a book; *the design of a book jacket has to be very attractive to make people want to buy the book*

(c) jacket potatoes *or* **potatoes in their jackets** = potatoes cooked in an oven with their skins on; *she had a jacket potato and salad for lunch*; *jacket potatoes are healthier than chips*

ⓘ **jail**
[dʒeɪl]
1 *noun*
prison; *she was sent to jail for three months*
2 *verb*
to put someone in prison; *he was jailed for six years* (NOTE: in British English also spelled **gaol**)

ⓘ **jam**
[dʒæm]
1 *noun*
(a) sweet food made by boiling fruit and sugar together; *a pot of blackcurrant jam*; *do you want jam or honey on your bread?*; *we made jam with the fruit in the garden*; *have you any more jam - the jar is empty?*; *(informal)* **it's money for jam** = it's a profit which is easy to make (NOTE: no plural in this meaning: **some jam, a pot of jam**; note also the difference with **marmalade** which is made from sour fruit like oranges and lemons)
(b) block which happens when there are too many things in too small a space; *there is a paper jam in the printer*; **traffic jam** = too much traffic on the roads, so that cars and trucks can't move; *the accident on Waterloo Bridge caused traffic jams all over London*; *there are rush hour jams every evening between 5.00 and 6.30*
(c) *(informal)* awkward situation; *he's got himself into a jam*
2 *verb*
(a) *(of machine)* to stick and not to be able to move; *hold on - the paper has jammed in the printer*
(b) to force things into a small space; *don't try to jam all those boxes into the back of the car*; *the telephone system was jammed with calls*
(c) *(informal)* **to jam on the brakes** = to brake suddenly; *he jammed on the brakes and the car went into a spin* (NOTE: **jamming - jammed**)

ⓘ **January**
['dʒænjuːri] *noun*
first month of the year, followed by February; *he was born on January 26th US on January 26*; *we never go on holiday in January because it's too cold*; *we all went skiing last January* (NOTE: **January 26th** *or* **January 26**: say 'the twenty-sixth of January' or 'January the twenty-sixth'; American English: 'January twenty-sixth')

ⓘ **Japan**
[dʒɪ'pæn] *noun*
large country in the Far East, formed of several islands to the east of China and south of Korea;

Japan hosted the 1998 Winter Olympics (NOTE: capital: **Tokyo**; people: **the Japanese**; language: **Japanese**; currency: **yen**)

ⓘ **Japanese**
[dʒæpɪ'niːz]
1 *adjective*
referring to Japan; *a typical Japanese meal can include rice and raw fish*
2 *noun*
(a) the Japanese = people from Japan; *the Japanese are very formal*
(b) language spoken in Japan; *he has lived in Japan for some time and speaks quite good Japanese*; *we bought a Japanese phrase book before we went to Japan*

ⓘ **jar**
[dʒɑː]
1 *noun*
container for jam, etc., usually made of glass; *there was some honey left in the bottom of the jar*; *open another jar of jam - this one is empty*; **jam jar** = special jar for putting jam in; *he kept the money in an empty jam jar*
2 *verb*
to produce an unpleasant effect; *the sound of the drill jarred on my ears*; *those orange curtains jar with the purple cushions* (NOTE: **jarring - jarred**)

ⓘ **jaw**
[dʒɔː] *noun*
bones in the face which hold the teeth and form the mouth; **upper jaw** = part of the skull holding the top set of teeth; **bottom jaw** *or* **lower jaw** = bone holding the lower teeth, which moves to make the mouth open or shut; *she hit him so hard that she broke his lower jaw*

ⓘ **jazz**
[dʒæz] *noun*
type of music with a strong rhythm, first played in the southern United States; *I'm a real jazz fan*; *Louis Armstrong was one of the kings of jazz*

ⓘ **jealous**
['dʒeləs] *adjective*
feeling annoyed because you want something which belongs to someone else; *John was jealous of Mark because all the girls crowded round him*; *she was jealous of his new car*; *her new boyfriend is very handsome - I'm jealous!*

ⓘ **jealousy**
['dʒeləsi] *noun*
feeling of being annoyed because someone has something which you don't have; *his jealousy of his wife's success ended their marriage*

ⓘ **jeans**
[dʒiːnz] *noun*
trousers made of a type of strong cotton, often blue; *I like wearing jeans better than wearing a skirt*; *she came into the restaurant in her jeans*; **designer jeans** = fashionable jeans designed by a famous designer (NOTE: sometimes also called **blue jeans**)

③ **Jell-O™**
['dʒeləʊ]
see JELLY

③ **jelly**
['dʒeli] *noun*
(a) type of sweet food which shakes, flavoured with fruit; *the children had fish fingers and chips followed by jelly and ice-cream* (NOTE: plural is **jellies**; note also, in the USA this is often called by a trademark, **Jell-O**)
(b) type of jam made of fruit juice boiled with sugar; *she loves peanut butter and jelly sandwiches*; *see also* ROLL
(c) to turn to jelly = to tremble and become soft; *when he heard the sound of the bell his legs turned to jelly*

③ **jelly baby**
['dʒeli 'beibi] *noun*
children's sweet made of coloured jelly, shaped like a little baby; *she gave the little girl a bag of jelly babies*

④ **jelly bean**
['dʒeli 'biːn] *noun*
sweet of coloured jelly, shaped like a bean

④ **jerk**
[dʒɜːk]
1 *noun*
(a) sudden sharp pull; *he felt a jerk on the fishing line*
(b) *(slang)* stupid person; *don't ask that jerk anything!*
2 *verb*
to pull something sharply; *he jerked the rope*

④ **jersey**
['dʒɜːzi] *noun*
(a) woollen pullover which fits close to the body; *she was knitting a pink jersey for the new baby*
(b) special shirt worn by a member of a football team, etc.; *after the game the players swapped jerseys with the other team*; **yellow jersey** = the yellow shirt worn by the leader of the Tour de France cycle race

④ **jet**
[dʒet]
1 *noun*
(a) long narrow stream of liquid or gas; *a jet of water put out the flames*
(b) aircraft with jet engines; *jets flew low overhead*; **jet lag** = being tired after flying by jet aircraft across several time zones; *she suffered dreadful jet lag after the flight from New York*
(c) jet black = very black and shiny; *a new jet black car*
2 *verb*
(informal) to travel by jet aircraft; *she jetted off to Los Angeles for a short holiday*; *Nice airport was busy with stars jetting in for the Cannes Film Festival* (NOTE: **jetting - jetted**)

③ **jet engine**
['dʒet 'endʒɪn] *noun*
engine which is worked by a jet of gas; *the two jet engines are located on either side of the plane*

④ **jewel**
['dʒuɪl] *noun*
precious stone, such as a diamond; *I'll just lock up these jewels in the safe*; *she admitted having stolen the jewels*

② **jewellery** *US* **jewelry**
['dʒuːlri] *noun*
pretty decorations to be worn, made from precious stones, gold, silver, etc.; *the burglar stole all her jewellery* (NOTE: no plural)

④ **jingle**
['dʒɪŋgl]
1 *noun*
(a) sound made when little pieces of metal knock together; *the jingle of tiny bells*
(b) song with a simple rhythm; **advertising jingle** = tune which advertises a product
2 *verb*
to make a sound like little pieces of metal knocking together; *the bell jingled as he went into the shop*

③ **Jnr** *US* **Jr**
['dʒuːniɪ] = JUNIOR

① **job**
[dʒɒb] *noun*
(a) regular work which you get paid for; *she's got a job in the supermarket*; *he's finding it difficult getting a job because he can't drive*; *when the factory closed, hundreds of people lost their jobs*; **to be out of a job** = to lose your regular paid work; *if they introduce that new computer system, the secretary will be out of her job*; *(informal)* **jobs for the boys** = the practice of giving work to your friends or supporters; *there'll be plenty of jobs for the boys when the new government comes in*
(b) piece of work; *don't sit down, there are a couple of jobs I want you to do*; *he does all sorts of little electrical jobs around the house*; **to make a good job of something** = to do something well; *they made a very good job of mending the table*; **odd jobs** = small items of work, especially repairs, done in the house; *he does odd jobs for us around the house*; **odd job man** = person who does small items of work; *our odd job man will mend the leaking pipe for you*
(c) *(informal)* **it's a good job that** = it's lucky that; *it's a good job he can drive*; *what a good job you brought your umbrella!*; *it's a good job you're not hungry, as there's nothing in the fridge*; **to give something up as a bad job** = to stop trying to do something; *he tried to get the car to go, and in the end had to give it up as a bad job*; **just the job** = just the right thing, exactly what we need; *that heavy hammer is just the job for breaking up concrete*

(d) *(informal)* difficulty; *I had a job trying to find your house*; *what a job it was getting a hotel room at the time of the music festival!*

① **jobcentre**
['dʒɒb'sentɪ] *noun*
official office which displays vacant jobs in the district; *every week he went to the local jobcentre to see if there was anything available*

① **jobless**
['dʒɒblɪs]
1 *adjective*
with no job; *jobless teenagers pose a problem for the government*
2 *noun*
the jobless = people who have no jobs (NOTE: takes a plural verb)

④ **jockey**
['dʒɒkɪ] *noun*
(a) person who rides horses in races; *he's the youngest jockey to ride in the race*
(b) disc jockey (DJ) = person who plays music discs at a disco or on radio; *who's your favourite DJ on Radio One?*

③ **jog**
[dʒɒg]
1 *noun*
(a) rather slow run, especially when taken for exercise; *she goes for a jog every morning*
(b) quite slow running pace; *he ran at a jog round the park*
2 *verb*
(a) to run at an easy pace, especially for exercise; *he jogged along the river bank for two miles*; *she was listening to her personal stereo as she was jogging*
(b) to move at a steady, but rather slow pace; *the train jogged along, stopping at every station*
(c) to push lightly; *someone jogged my elbow and I spilt my drink*; *it jogged his memory* = it made him remember; *the police are hoping that the film from the security camera will jog people's memories* (NOTE: jogging - jogged)

③ **jogging**
['dʒɒgɪŋ] *noun*
running at an easy pace for exercise; *jogging every morning is good for you*; *to go jogging* = to run at an easy pace for exercise; *they went jogging in the streets near their home*

① **join**
[dʒɔɪn]
1 *verb*
(a) to put things together; *you have to join the two pieces of wood together*; *the rooms were joined together by making a door in the wall*
(b) to come together; *go on for about two hundred metres, until a road joins this one*; *the two rivers join about four kilometres beyond the town*
(c) to become a member of a club, group, etc.; *after university, he is going to join the police*; *she joined the army because she wanted to travel*

(d) to join a firm = to start work with a company; *he joined on January 1st* = he started work on the January 1st
(e) to do something with someone; *we're going to have a cup of coffee - would you like to join us?*; *won't you join me for a game of golf?*
2 *noun*
place where pieces are joined; *can you see the join where I added an extra piece of cloth?*

③ **join in**
['dʒɔɪn 'ɪn] *verb*
to take part in something done as a group; *he started to sing and everyone else joined in*

① **joint**
[dʒɔɪnt]
1 *noun*
(a) place where several pieces are attached, especially in building; *the joints of the drawer have worked loose*
(b) place where bones come together and can move, such as the knee or elbow; *her elbow joint hurt after the game of tennis*
(c) large piece of meat, especially for roasting; *the joint of lamb was very tender*; *we all sat round the table while Father carved the Sunday joint*
(d) *(informal)* club or restaurant; *let's go to Rick's joint*
(e) *(slang)* cigarette with drugs; *he smoked a couple of joints during the evening*
2 *adjective*
combined, with two or more things linked together; **joint account** = bank account for two people, such as husband and wife; **joint authors** = two authors who have written a book together; **joint ownership** = owning of a property by several owners

④ **jointly**
['dʒɔɪntlɪ] *adverb*
together with one or more other people; *this law applies when two or more people own a property jointly*; *the prize was awarded jointly to the British and Russian teams*

③ **join up**
['dʒɔɪn 'ʌp] *verb*
(a) to link things together; *she's getting better at writing, and can do joined-up letters*
(b) to join the army, navy or air force; *he joined up when he was 18 and soon rose to become an officer*

② **joke**
[dʒɪʊk]
1 *noun*
thing said or done to make people laugh; *she poured water down his neck as a joke*; *they all laughed at his jokes*; *he told jokes all evening*; **practical joke** = trick played on someone to make other people laugh; *he's fond of practical jokes - once he tied a tin to the back of his father's car*
2 *verb*

to tell jokes; to say or do something to make people laugh; *he used to joke about always being late for the office*; *he was only joking* = he did not mean it seriously; *you're joking!* or *you must be joking!* = you are not being serious, are you?; *he's just bought a new Rolls Royce - you must be joking, he's only the office boy!*

③ **jolly**

['dʒɒli]

1 *adjective*

happy, pleasant, enjoyable; *it was marvellous to see all the jolly faces of the children*; *her birthday party was a very jolly affair* (NOTE: jollier - jolliest)

2 *adverb (informal)*

(a) very; *it's jolly hard work carrying all those boxes upstairs*

(b) *(used to emphasize) if you don't want to pay the proper rate for the job, then you can jolly well do it yourself*

④ **journal**

['dʒɜːnl] *noun*

(a) diary; *he kept a journal during his visit to China*; *she wrote a journal of the gradual progress of her illness*

(b) magazine which comes out every month or three months, especially one on a learned subject; *she edits the journal of the Historical Society*

(c) book for recording each day's business; *she wrote the day's sales in the sales journal*

③ **journalism**

['dʒɜːnəlɪzm] *noun*

profession of writing for newspapers or reporting on events for radio or TV; *she took a journalism course to help her chances of getting a job on a newspaper*

③ **journalist**

['dʒɜːnəlɪst] *noun*

person who writes for newspapers or reports on events for radio or TV; *journalists asked the policeman some very awkward questions*; *film stars were greeted by journalists from around the world at the first night of the new film*

② **journey**

['dʒɜːni]

1 *noun*

travelling, usually a long distance; *it's at least two days' journey from here*; *they went on a train journey across China*; *she has a difficult journey to work every day - she has to change buses twice*

2 *verb*

(formal) to travel; *they journeyed many miles to find the treasure*; *the book tells the story of a man who journeyed from Italy to China in the 13th century*

③ **joy**

[dʒɔɪ] *noun*

state of being very happy; *we all wished them great joy on their wedding day*; *they were full of joy at seeing their son again*

④ **JP**

['dʒeɪ'piː] *abbreviation for* JUSTICE OF THE PEACE; *JPs try cases in the magistrate's court*

③ **Jr**

['dʒuːniɪ] *abbreviation for* JUNIOR

② **judge**

[dʒʌdʒ]

1 *noun*

(a) person appointed to make legal decisions in a court of law; *he was convicted for stealing, but the judge let him off with a small fine*

(b) person who decides which is the best entry in a competition; *the three judges of the beauty contest couldn't agree*

(c) person with good sense; *he's a good judge of character*

2 *verb*

(a) to make decisions in a court of law or competition, etc.; *he was judged guilty*; *her painting was judged the best and she won first prize*

(b) to estimate a value, to decide on the quality of a situation; *to be a good driver you need to be able to judge distances well*; *the Senator judged it would be impossible for him to win the election so he dropped out of the race*

② **judgement** *or* **judgment**

['dʒʌdʒmɪnt] *noun*

(a) legal decision by a judge or court; *the judgement of the tribunal was fair*; *the defendant will appeal against the judgement*

(b) ability to see things clearly and to make good decisions; *he trusted his wife's judgement in everything*; **against your better judgement** = although you feel it is not the right thing to do; *he accepted the money against his better judgement*; *against her better judgement, she reported her son to the police*

④ **juice**

[dʒuːs] *noun*

liquid from fruit, vegetables, meat, etc.; *they charged me £1 for two glasses of orange juice*; *she had a glass of grapefruit juice for breakfast*

④ **juicy**

['dʒuːsi] *adjective*

full of juice; *juicy peaches taste wonderful*; *these are the juiciest oranges we've had this year* (NOTE: juicier - juiciest)

① **July**

[dʒuˈlaɪ] *noun*

seventh month of the year, between June and August; *she was born in July - her birthday is July 23rd US July 23*; *we went to Spain last July*; *July is always one of the busiest months for holidays* (NOTE: July 23rd or July 23: say 'July the twenty-third' or 'the twenty-third of July'; American English: 'July twenty-third')

① **jump**
[dʒʌmp]
1 *noun*
sudden movement into the air; *the jump was higher than she thought and she hurt her leg*; *(in sports)* **long jump** *or* **high jump** = sport where you see who can jump the furthest or highest; *she won a gold medal in the high jump*
2 *verb*
(a) to go suddenly into the air off the ground; *quick, jump on that bus - it's going to Oxford Circus!*; *the horse jumped over the fence*; *she jumped down from the chair*
(b) to jump the gun = to start before it is your turn, before it is the right time; **to jump the queue** = to go in front of someone who has been waiting longer than you have
(c) to move upwards suddenly; *the price of oil has jumped from $15.50 to $30.00*
(d) to make a sudden movement because you are frightened; *she jumped when I came up behind her quietly and said 'Boo!'*; *when they fired the gun, it made me jump*
(e) to miss something; *the typewriter jumped a line*; *I think I jumped a page in my book*

③ **jump at**
['dʒʌmp 'æt] *verb*
to accept eagerly; *she jumped at the chance to work in Australia*

③ **jumper**
['dʒʌmpɪ] *noun*
warm woollen knitted pullover; *I bought a pink jumper in the sales*

③ **junction**
['dʒʌŋkʃn] *noun*
(a) place where railway lines or roads meet; *go as far as the next junction and you will see the library on your right*; *leave the motorway at Junction 5*; **T-junction** = junction where one road joins another at right angles; *go down the road and turn right at the T-junction*
(b) junction box = box where several electric wires are joined

① **June**
[dʒuːn] *noun*
sixth month of the year, between May and July; *she was born in June: her birthday is June 17th US June 17*; *last June we had a holiday in Canada* (NOTE: **June 17th** *or* **June 17:** say 'June the seventeenth' or 'the seventeenth of June'; American English: 'June seventeenth')

④ **jungle**
['dʒʌŋgl] *noun*
thick tropical forest which is difficult to travel through; *they explored the jungle, hoping to find rare birds*

③ **junior**
['dʒuːnɪɪ]
1 *adjective*
(a) younger, less important; *he was the junior member of the team*

(b) for younger children; *she plays for the junior hockey team*; **junior school** = school for children from 7 to 11 years old
2 *noun*
(a) office junior = young man or woman who does all types of work in an office
(b) *US* student in his or her third year at college
(c) son in a family who has the same name as his father; *John Smith, Junior*

③ **junk**
[dʒʌŋk] *noun*
(a) useless articles, rubbish; *don't keep that - it's junk*; *you should throw away all that junk under your bed*; **junk food** = bad commercially prepared food which is less nutritious than food made at home; *they just watch TV and live off junk food* (NOTE: no plural in this meaning)
(b) large Chinese sailing boat; *Hong Kong harbour was full of junks*

③ **junk shop**
['dʒʌŋk 'ʃɒp] *noun*
shop selling useless old articles; *I bought this old clock for £10 in a junk shop*

④ **jurisdiction**
[dʒʊrɪs'dɪkʃn] *noun*
legal power over someone *or* something; *the tribunal has no jurisdiction over the case*; **within the jurisdiction of the court** = in the legal power of the court; **outside the jurisdiction of the court** = not covered by the legal power of the court; *the matter is outside the jurisdiction of the court*

④ **jury**
['dʒʊrɪ] *noun*
(a) group of twelve citizens who are sworn to decide whether someone is guilty or innocent on the basis of the evidence given in a court of law; *the jury brought in a verdict of not guilty*; **jury service** = service which all citizens may be asked to perform, to sit on a jury
(b) the jury is still out on this = no one is sure what the result will be
(c) group of judges in a competition; *he's been chosen to serve on the jury for the literary prize*

① **just**
[dʒʌst]
1 *adverb*
(a) exactly; *is that too much sugar? - no, it's just right*; *thank you, that's just what I was looking for*; *just how many of students have got computers?*; *what time is it? - it's just seven o'clock*; *he's just fifteen - his birthday was yesterday*
(b) just enough = scarcely, almost not enough; *she had just enough money to pay the bill*; *he had just enough time to get dressed before the police arrived*
(c) *(showing a very small quantity in space or time)* *your umbrella is just by the door*; *don't come in just yet - we're not ready*; *can you wait just a minute?*

(d) *(showing the immediate past or future) the train has just arrived from Paris; she had just got into her bath when the phone rang; I don't want any coffee, thank you, I'm just going out; thanks for calling - I was just going to phone you*

(e) only; *we're just good friends, nothing more; I've been to Berlin just once*

2 *adjective*

fair, without favouring anyone; *the decision of the court was just*

◊ **just about**

['dʒʌst ə'baut]

(a) nearly, more or less; *I've just about finished my homework; the meal's just about ready*

(b) just about to do something = going to do something very soon; *we were just about to leave; they were just about to go to bed when someone knocked on the door*

◊ **just as**

['dʒʌst 'æz]

(a) at the same time; *just as I got into the car there was a loud bang*

(b) in exactly the same way; *the film is just as good as the book; it is just as hot inside the house as it is outside; she loves her cats just as other people love their children*

◊ **just now**

['dʒʌst 'nau]

(a) at the present time; *we're very busy in the office just now*

(b) a short time ago; *I saw her just now in the post office*

② **justice**

['dʒʌstɪs] *noun*

(a) fair treatment in law; *justice must always be seen to be done*

(b) to bring someone to justice = to start legal action against someone; **rough justice** = judging someone in a rough and unfair way

(c) to do justice to = to treat something as it deserves; *I wasn't very hungry so I couldn't do justice to your marvellous meal; his rather dull description doesn't do justice to the garden*

(d) magistrate; **Justice of the Peace (JP)** = magistrate or local judge

② **justification**

[dʒʌstɪfɪ'keɪʃn] *noun*

(a) reason which shows that something has been done correctly; *what was his justification for doing that?; they tried to find some justification for what they had done*

(b) *(in typing and printing)* spacing out the words in the lines so that the right margin is straight; *we use an automatic justification program*

② **justify**

['dʒʌstɪfaɪ] *verb*

(a) to show that something is fair, to prove that something is right; *how can you justify your behaviour?*

(b) the end justifies the means = if your final aim is good or honourable, you are right to do anything that is necessary to achieve it

(c) *(in printing)* to space letters and figures on the page so that the ends of lines are neat and straight; *the text should be fully justified*

③ **juvenile**

['dʒuːvɪnaɪl]

1 *adjective*

(a) referring to young people; *young offenders are tried before a juvenile court*

(b) silly, like a young person; *the new comedy series on TV is really juvenile*

2 *noun*

(formal) young person (officially, someone under seventeen years of age); *the police entered the club and arrested four people, two of them juveniles*

Kk

③ **K, k**

[keɪ]

eleventh letter of the alphabet, between J and L; *K is the eleventh letter of the alphabet*

③ **K**

[keɪ] *abbreviation*

one thousand; **£20K** = twenty thousand pounds (NOTE: say 'twenty K': 'the salary is around twenty K')

③ **keen**

[kiːn] *adjective*

(a) keen on something *or* **someone** = liking something *or* someone, enthusiastic about something; *he's keen on keeping fit - he goes running every morning; I am not very keen on classical music; I don't think she's very keen on her new maths teacher*

(b) keen competition = strong competition; *we are facing some keen competition from European manufacturers*

(c) very sensitive; *bats have a keen sense of hearing* (NOTE: **keener - keenest**)

① **keep**
[ki:p] *verb*
(a) to have for a long time or for ever; *can I keep the newspaper I borrowed from you?; I don't want that hat any more, you can keep it; the police kept my gun and won't give it back*
(b) to continue to do something; *the clock kept going even after I dropped it on the floor; he had to keep smiling so that people would think he was pleased; keep quiet or they'll hear you; luckily the weather kept fine for the fair; the food will keep warm in the oven*
(c) to have or put something in a particular place; *I keep my car keys in my pocket; where do you keep the paper for the laser printer?*
(d) to make someone stay in a place or state; *it's cruel to keep animals in cages; I was kept late at the office; they kept us waiting for half an hour; we put the plates in the oven to keep them warm*
(e) to prevent someone from doing something or from going somewhere; *she kept him from going out and playing football; he kept her from seeing her friends; (informal) what kept you?* = why are you so late?
(f) to stay; *let's keep in touch* = we mustn't lose contact with each other; **she kept him company** = she stayed with him; **to keep an eye on** = to watch carefully; *he's keeping an eye on the shop while I'm away;* **to keep your ear to the ground** = to follow what is happening and know all about something
(g) **to keep a diary** = to write notes every day about what has happened; *she kept a diary of her holiday in Spain*
(h) to stay in good condition and not to go rotten; *strawberries don't keep* (NOTE: **keeps - keeping - kept** [kept])

③ **keep back**
['ki:p 'bæk] *verb*
(a) to hold on to something which you should give to someone; *they kept back £20 from the deposit to cover damage to the carpet*
(b) **to keep something back from someone** = not to tell someone information which you could give to them; *I have the feeling that she's keeping something back from us*

③ **keep down**
['ki:p 'daun] *verb*
(a) to keep at a low level; *keep your voice down, the police will hear us!*
(b) to stay bent down and hidden; *keep down behind the wall so that they won't see us*

④ **keeper**
['ki:pɪ] *noun*
(a) person in charge of a certain type of animal in a zoo; *an elephant keeper*
(b) person in charge of a section of a museum; *the keeper of Roman coins in the British Museum*

(c) *(sport)* goalkeeper, the player who stands in front of the goal to stop the ball going in; *the goalkeeper dropped the ball and the other team scored*
(d) fruit which can be kept in good condition for a long time; *you should eat those pears immediately as they are not good keepers*

③ **keep off**
['ki:p 'ɒf] *verb*
(a) not to walk on; *keep off the grass!*
(b) not to use; *if he can keep off drink, his health will improve*

① **keep on**
['ki:p 'ɒn] *verb*
to continue to do something; *my computer keeps on breaking down; the cars kept on moving even though the road was covered with snow*

③ **keep on at**
['ki:p 'ɒn ət] *verb*
(informal) to criticize someone constantly; **she keeps on at me about getting a job** = she tells me all the time that I should get a job

① **keep out**
['ki:p 'aut] *verb*
(a) to stop someone going in; *there were 'Keep Out!' notices round the building site; we have put up notices telling people to keep their dogs out of the field where the lambs are*
(b) not to get involved; *he kept out of the quarrel; try to keep out of trouble with the police*

③ **keep to**
['ki:p 'tu:] *verb*
(a) to stay in a position; *when you drive in France, remember to keep to the right*
(b) not to move away from a subject; *let's keep to the subject of the new motorway*
(c) **to keep something to yourself** = to keep something secret, not to talk about something; *he doesn't want to talk about his illness, he'd rather keep it to himself*

① **keep up**
['ki:p 'ʌp] *verb*
to make something stay at the same high level; *he finds it very difficult to keep up his German; they won't be able to keep up that speed for very long;* **keep it up!** = continue doing what you doing!; *you're doing very well - keep it up!*

① **keep up with**
['ki:p 'ʌp wɪð] *verb*
(a) to go at the same speed as; *my foot hurts, that's why I can't keep up with the others; his salary hasn't kept up with the cost of living;* **to keep up with the Joneses** = to try to do the same things as your neighbours or friends to show that you have as much money as they have
(b) to keep yourself informed about; *have you kept up with the news from Russia?*

③ **kept**
[kept]
see KEEP

④ **kerb**
[kɜːb] *noun*
stone edge to a pavement; *try not to hit the kerb when you park*; *she slipped on the edge of the kerb and twisted her ankle* (NOTE: American English is **curb**)

④ **kettle**
['ketl] *noun*
container with a lid, used for boiling water; *turn the gas up, the kettle hasn't boiled yet*; *each bedroom has an electric kettle, tea bags and packs of instant coffee*; **to put the kettle on** = to start heating the water in a kettle; *I've just put the kettle on so we can all have a cup of tea*; **the kettle's boiling** = the water in the kettle is boiling

① **key**
[kiː]
1 *noun*
(a) piece of metal used to open a lock; *I can't start the car, I've lost the key*; *where did you put the front door key?*; **key ring** = ring on which you can put several keys to keep them together; *the garage gave me a key ring with their telephone number on it*
(b) part of a computer, piano, etc., which you push down with your fingers; *the 'F' key always sticks*; *there are sixty-four keys on the keyboard*; **control key** = key on a computer which works part of a program; **shift key** = key on a typewriter or computer keyboard which makes capital letters or switches to another function; *hold down the shift key while you click on 'help'*
(c) explanation of a problem; *the key to the signs is written under the diagram*
(d) system of musical tones; *the symphony is written in the key of F major*
2 *adjective*
most important; *the key person in the company is the sales manager*; *oil is a key industry*
3 *verb*
to type letters or figures on a keyboard; *she keyed in the data*

③ **keyboard**
['kiːbɔːd]
1 *noun*
set of keys on a computer, piano, etc.; *she spilled her coffee on the computer keyboard*; *he practises on the keyboard every day*
2 *verb*
to put data into a computer, using a keyboard; *she was keyboarding the figures*

③ **kg**
= KILOGRAM

② **kick**
[kɪk]
1 *noun*
(a) hitting with your foot; *the goalkeeper gave the ball a kick*; **free kick** = kick which a player is allowed to make without anyone opposing

him, to punish the other side for something which they have done; *the referee awarded a free kick*
(b) *(informal)* thrill, feeling of excitement; *he gets a kick out of watching a football match on TV*; **he did it for kicks** = he did it to give himself some excitement
(c) *(informal)* strong effect; *my! this drink has a kick in it!*
2 *verb*
(a) to hit something with your foot; *he kicked the ball into the net*; *she kicked her little brother*
(b) *(informal)* **to kick the habit** = the get rid of a bad habit; *I wish he's kick the habit of whistling while he works*; *he doesn't smoke any more - he kicked the habit a couple of months ago*; *see also* BUCKET
(c) **to kick yourself** = to be annoyed with yourself because of doing something silly, forgetting something, etc.; *I could have kicked myself as soon as I said it*; *they must be kicking themselves now for not having bought the house when they had the chance*

③ **kick off**
['kɪk 'ɒf] *verb*
(a) to start a game of football; *they kicked off at 3.00 and after 30 minutes there was still no score*
(b) to start; *let's kick off with a discussion about modern painters*

③ **kick out**
['kɪk 'aʊt] *verb*
to get rid of someone; *he was kicked out of the club for not paying his subscription*; *they kicked him out of the team because he had started to take drugs*

③ **kick up**
['kɪk 'ʌp] *verb*
(informal) **to kick up a fuss** = to make a fuss, a row; *the kids are only messing about - there's no need to kick up a fuss by calling the police*

① **kid**
[kɪd]
1 *noun*
(a) *(informal)* child; *there were a few school kids on their bicycles*; *I saw your kids going off on the bus this morning*; *they've been married a few years, and have got a couple of kids*; **kid brother** = younger brother; *I have to stay in to baby-sit my kid brother*
(b) young goat
2 *verb*
(informal) to make someone believe something which is not true; **I was only kidding** = I didn't mean it; **no kidding?** = is it really true? (NOTE: **kidding - kidded**)

③ **kidnap**
['kɪdnæp] *verb*
to steal a child or an adult and take them away; *the millionaire's son was kidnapped and held for two weeks* (NOTE: **kidnapping - kidnapped**)

③ **kidney**

['kɪdni] *noun*

(a) one of a pair of organs in animals that clean the blood; **kidney machine** = apparatus through which a patient's blood is passed to be cleaned when his kidneys have failed; *he has to be linked to the kidney machine for several hours each week*; **kidney stone** = hard mass like a little piece of stone, which forms inside a kidney; **kidney transplant** = operation to transplant a kidney; *the kidney transplant was a success*

(b) this organ from a lamb, pig, etc., used as food; *steak and kidney pie*

① **kill**

[kɪl] *verb*

(a) to make someone *or* something die; *he was sentenced to death for killing his wife*; *the drought has killed all the crops*; *the car hit a cat and killed it*; *six people were killed in the plane crash*

(b) to kill time = to spend time while waiting for something important; *I killed some time waiting for the train by having a coffee*; **to kill two birds with one stone** = to get two successful results from one action; *while I'm in London for the conference I could kill two birds with one stone and visit my parents*; *(informal)* **my feet are killing me** = my feet are hurting; *(informal)* **he was killing himself laughing** = he was laughing a lot

④ **killer**

['kɪlɪ] *noun*

(a) person who kills; *the police are still hunting for the killer*; **serial killer** = person who has committed several murders, one after the other; *because there are similarities between the murders, the police think they are dealing with a serial killer*

(b) which kills; *a killer flu virus*; **killer whale** = black and white whale which eats fish and seals

④ **killing**

['kɪlɪŋ]

1 *noun*

(a) murder, putting a person or animal to death; *the police are investigating the killing of the tourists*; *there have been reports of killings in the villages*; *the killing of elephants has been banned*

(b) to make a killing = to make a very large profit; *he made a killing on the stock market*

2 *adjective*

(informal) very funny; *I thought it was killing, but no one else laughed at all*

③ **kilo**

['kiːləʊ] *noun*

= KILOGRAM; *he weighs 78 kilos*; *I want to buy two kilos of sugar*; *these oranges cost 75p a kilo* (NOTE: plural is **kilos**)

③ **kilogram**

['kɪligræm] *noun*

measure of weight (= one thousand grams) (NOTE: written **kg** after figures: **20kg**)

③ **kilometre** *US* **kilometer**

[kɪ'lɒmɪtɪ] *noun*

one thousand metres; *the car was only doing 80 kilometres an hour when the accident occurred*; *the two roads join about three kilometres from here*; *the town is about ten kilometres from the sea*; **the car has just had its 100,000 kilometre service** = it has been checked by the garage after having travelled 100,000 kilometres (NOTE: written **km** after figures: **70km**)

① **kind**

[kaɪnd]

1 *adjective*

friendly, helpful, thinking about other people; *it's very kind of you to offer to help*; *how kind of you to invite him to your party!*; *you should always be kind to little children*; *he's a kind old gentleman* (NOTE: **kinder - kindest**)

2 *noun*

(a) sort, type; *a butterfly is a kind of insect*; *we have several kinds of apples in our garden*; *we discussed all kinds of things*

(b) *(informal)* **kind of** = in a certain way; *I was kind of annoyed when she told me that*

(c) of a kind = similar; *the three sisters are three of a kind*; **it's nothing of the kind** = that's not correct at all

④ **kindly**

['kaɪndli]

1 *adjective*

thoughtful and pleasant; *a kindly neighbour brought him soup when he was ill*

2 *adverb*

(a) in a thoughtful or pleasant way; *he behaved very kindly towards me*; **not to take kindly to** = not to like; *she doesn't take kindly to being told she's fat*

(b) *(formal)* please, if you don't mind; *kindly shut the door*; *customers are kindly requested to pay at the cash desk*

③ **kindness**

['kaɪndnɪs] *noun*

being kind; *she was touched by his kindness*

① **king**

[kɪŋ] *noun*

(a) man who reigns over a country by right of his birth; *the king and queen came to visit the town* (NOTE: **king** is spelt with a capital letter when used with a name or when referring to a particular person: **King Henry VIII**)

(b) main piece in chess; *she moved her knight to place his king in check*

(c) *(in cards)* the card with the face of a man with a beard; *he knew he could win when he drew the king of spades*

(d) champion, top person; *he's king of the pop music scene*; *the lion is king of the jungle*

COMMENT: there have been thirty-five kings of England since William the Conqueror invaded in 1066. The most common names have been Henry and Edward (eight kings each) followed by George (six kings). The first king of England and Scotland was James I (he was previously James VI of Scotland). The most recent English king was George VI, father of the present queen

③ **kingdom**
['kɪŋdʌm] *noun*
(a) land ruled over by a king or queen; *England is part of the United Kingdom; he gave her a book of old stories about a magic kingdom*
(b) part of the world of nature; *the animal kingdom*
(c) *(informal)* till kingdom come = for ever, for a very long time; *on Saturday mornings you can wait till kingdom come to be served*

③ **kiss**
[kɪs]
1 *noun*
(a) touching someone with your lips to show love; *she gave the baby a kiss;* to blow someone a kiss = to show your love for someone by touching your lips with your hands and making a gesture to the person at a distance; *as the train left, she blew him a kiss*
(b) kiss of life = bringing someone back to life by breathing into his or her mouth; kiss of death = something which ruins a business, etc.; *the new supermarket is the kiss of death to small businesses in the town* (NOTE: plural is **kisses**)
2 *verb*
to touch someone with your lips to show that you love them; *she kissed her daughter and walked away; they kissed each other goodbye; the politicians are in town, shaking hands with voters and kissing babies*

③ **kit**
[kɪt] *noun*
(a) clothes and personal equipment, usually packed for carrying; *did you bring your tennis kit?*
(b) first aid kit = box with bandages kept to be used in an emergency; *the doctor rushed to the scene with his first aid kit;* repair kit = box with tools for repairing a machine, especially for repairing a car; *there is a repair kit provided in the boot of each car*
(c) box containing pieces which can be put together to make a piece of furniture, a model, etc.; *he spent the afternoon building a model aircraft from a kit; the new garden furniture arrived as a kit and we had to put it together ourselves*

① **kitchen**
['kɪtʃɪn] *noun*
room where you cook food; *she put the meat down on the kitchen table; if you're hungry, have a look in the kitchen to see if there's anything to eat; don't come in with dirty shoes on - I've just washed the kitchen floor; see also* FITTED

③ **kitten**
['kɪtn] *noun*
(a) young cat; *the kittens are playing in their basket; the cat carefully picked up her kitten by the back of its neck*
(b) *(informal)* to have kittens = to be very nervous; *she was having kittens, waiting for her interview*

③ **km**
[kɪ'lɒmɪti] = KILOMETRE; *it is 2km from here to the Post Office; the furthest distance I have travelled by train is 800km; the road crosses the railway line about 2km from here*

② **knee**
[niː] *noun*
(a) joint in the middle of your leg, where it bends; *she sat the child on her knee; he went down on one knee and asked her to marry him;* knee socks = long socks which go up to your knees
(b) part of a pair of trousers that covers the knee; *my jeans have holes in both knees*

② **kneel**
[niːl] *verb*
to go down on your knees; *everyone knelt down and the priest said a prayer; she knelt beside his bed and listened to his breathing* (NOTE: kneeling - kneeled *or* knelt [nelt])

① **knew**
[njuː]
see KNOW

③ **knife**
[naɪf]
1 *noun*
instrument used for cutting, with a sharp metal blade fixed in a handle; *put out a knife, fork and spoon for each person; you need a sharp knife to cut meat;* bread knife = special large knife for cutting bread (NOTE: plural is **knives** [naɪvz])
2 *verb*
to stab someone with a knife; *he was knifed in the back during the fight* (NOTE: knifes - knifing - knifed)

③ **knight**
[naɪt] *noun*
(a) man honoured by a king for services to his country (and taking the title 'Sir'); *he was made a knight*
(b) *(in medieval times)* brave soldier; *King Arthur and the Knights of the Round Table; many knights were killed in the Wars of the Roses*
(c) one of two pieces in a chess set with a horse's head; *with a clever move she took his knight*

① knit

[nɪt] *verb*

(a) to make a piece of clothing out of wool by linking threads together with the aid of two long needles; *my mother is knitting me a pullover; she was wearing a blue knitted hat* (NOTE: knitting - knitted)

(b) to knit your brow = to make folds of skin on your forehead as you try to do something difficult; *she knit her brow as she tried to understand the guidebook* (NOTE: knitting - knit)

③ knives

[naɪvz]

see KNIFE

④ knob

[nɒb] *noun*

(a) round handle on a door, a chest of drawers, etc.; *to open the door, just the knob*

(b) round button which you turn on a radio, TV, etc.; *turn the knob to increase the volume*

(c) round lump; *put a knob of butter in the frying pan*

① knock

[nɒk]

1 *noun*

(a) sound made by hitting something; *suddenly, there was a knock at the door*

(b) hitting something; *she received a knock on the head with a brick*

2 *verb*

(a) to hit something; *knock twice before going in; you'll need a heavy hammer to knock that nail in*

(b) to criticize; *she wrote an article knocking the Prime Minister*

③ knock about

['nɒk ə'baʊt] *verb*

(a) to wander about doing nothing; *he spent several years knocking about the back streets of New Orleans*

(b) to knock someone about = to beat someone; *he was badly knocked about in the fight*; **to knock something about** = to damage something; *the town was badly knocked about in the war*

(c) *(informal)* to be in a place; *can you see my hammer knocking about anywhere?*

③ knock back

['nɒk 'bæk] *verb*

(a) to drink a drink quickly; *he knocked back his drink and ran outside*

(b) to knock someone back a sum = to cost someone a sum; *it will knock me back a few hundred pounds*

③ knock down

['nɒk 'daʊn] *verb*

(a) to make something fall down; *they are going to knock down the old house to build a factory*

(b) to hit; *she was knocked down by a car*

(c) to reduce a price; *they knocked the price down to £50*

(d) to sell something to someone at an auction; *it was knocked down to a German buyer for £250*

③ knock off

['nɒk 'ɒf] *verb*

(a) to make something fall off by hitting it; *the cat knocked the glass off the shelf*

(b) *(informal)* to stop work; *the workmen all knocked off at 4.30*

(c) to reduce the price of something (by an amount); *he knocked £1000 off the price of the car*

③ knock out

['nɒk 'aʊt] *verb*

(a) to hit someone so hard that he is no longer conscious; *she was knocked out by a blow on the head; the boxer was knocked out in the third round*

(b) to make someone go to sleep; *the doctor gave her something which knocked her out*

③ knot

[nɒt]

1 *noun*

(a) the ends of a piece of string, rope, etc., fastened together; *he's too small to be able to tie knots properly; is the knot of my tie straight?*; **to tie the knot** = to get married

(b) small group; *knots of people stood and watched the firemen*

(c) measure of speed used to show the speed of a ship or of the wind; *the ship was doing 22 knots when she hit the rocks; there's a wind speed of 60 knots*

(d) round place on a piece of wood where a branch was originally growing; *this piece of wood is no good - it is full of knots*

2 *verb*

(a) to tie a knot in something; *he knotted the end of the rope*

(b) *(slang) (rejecting someone in a way that shows you are annoyed)* **get knotted!** = go away, don't bother me; *if they ask for money again, tell them to get knotted* (NOTE: knotting - knotted)

① know

[nəʊ]

1 *verb*

(a) to have learned something, to have information about something; *do you know how to start the computer?; he didn't know she had died; how was I to know she wasn't his wife?; you knew it would be expensive; do you know the Spanish for 'one - two - three'?; his secretary doesn't know where he is; he is known to have right-wing views; is she in trouble? - not that I know of*

(b) to have met someone; *I know your sister - we were at school together; I used to know a man called Jones who worked in your company*; **to know someone by sight** = to know who someone is, even though you have never spoken to him or her

(c) to have been to a place often; *I know Paris very well*; *she doesn't know Germany at all*
(d) to experience; *she knew years of poverty before she became famous*; *he knows what it is like to be out of work*
(e) you never know = perhaps; *you never know, she may still turn up*; **as far as I know** = all I know is that; *as far as I know, he left by car at 6 p.m.*; *is she in trouble? - not as far as I know*
(f) to know better than = to have the experience which allows you to avoid making a mistake; *you should know better than to wake grandfather up when he's having his afternoon sleep* (NOTE: **knowing - knew [njuː] - has known**)
2 *noun*
(informal) **in the know** = knowing something that most people do not know; *those in the know say that's the best restaurant in town*; *someone in the know gave me the tip*

④ **know-how**
['nɪʊhaʊ] *noun*
(informal) knowledge about how something is made or is done; *this book gives you all the know-how you'll need about fixing a sink*

① **knowledge**
['nɒlɪdʒ] *noun*
(a) what a particular person knows about something; *to my knowledge, he left the house at 10 p.m.*; *the police have no knowledge of the accident*; **to the best of my knowledge** = as far as I know; *to the best of my knowledge, no one else has seen this document*; **it is common knowledge that** = everyone knows that; *it is common knowledge that his wife wants to go to live in France*
(b) general facts or information that people know; *this book is supposed to list all human knowledge*

③ **known**
[nɪʊn] *adjective*
which is known; **a known quantity** = something, a fact or a situation, which you know about; *when trading with American companies, at least you are dealing with a known quantity* (NOTE: the opposite is an **unknown quantity**)

Ll

① **L, l**
[el]
twelfth letter of the alphabet, between K and M; *Louise wrote her initial 'L' on the back of the letter*; *see also* L-PLATES

③ **l**
= LITRE

③ **lab**
[læb] *noun*
short for LABORATORY

③ **label**
['leɪbl]
1 *noun*
(a) piece of paper, plastic, etc., attached to something to show price, contents, someone's name and address, etc.; **address label** = label with an address on it; **tie-on label** = label with a piece of string attached so that it can be tied on to an item; *put a luggage label on your bag if you don't want it to get lost*; *she stuck a label on the parcel*; *the price on the label is £25.00*
(b) especially, the name of a recording company on a record or CD; *the group have made their first single on the Virgin label*
2 *verb*

to put a label on something; *all the goods are labelled with the correct price* (NOTE: **labelling - labelled** but American spelling is **labeling - labeled**)

③ **laboratory**
[lɪ'bɒrɪtri *US* 'læbrɪtɔːri] *noun*
place where scientific experiments, testing and research are carried out; *she's a chemist working in the university laboratories*; *all products are tested in our own laboratories* (NOTE: plural is **laboratories**)

③ **labor union**
['leɪbɪ 'juːnɪn] *noun*
US organization which represents workers who are its members in discussions with employers about wages and conditions of employment; *the staff are all members of a labor union* (NOTE: British English is **trade union**)

① **labour** *US* **labor**
['leɪbɪ]
1 *noun*
(a) (hard) work; *after digging the garden, it is good to lie on the grass and rest from your labours*; **to charge for materials and labour** = to charge for both the materials used in a job and also the hours of work involved; **hard labour** =

prison sentence where the prisoner has to do hard work with his hands (NOTE: plural can be **labours** in this meaning)

(b) all workers; *cheap labour is difficult to find*; **sweated labour** = workers who work hard for little money; **labour dispute** = argument between management and workers

(c) the Labour Party = political party, one of the main political parties in Britain, which is in favour of state involvement in industry and welfare; *the polls showed a strong swing to Labour or to the Labour Party; Labour Party officials denied the reports*

(d) the process of giving birth to a baby; *she went into labour at home, and her husband drove her to the hospital; she was in labour for 12 hours*

2 *verb*

(a) to work very hard; *they laboured night and day to finish the project in time*

(b) to labour under an impression = to have a wrong impression, to assume something which is quite wrong; *he was labouring under the impression that air fares were cheaper in Europe than in the USA*; **to labour the point** = to discuss something too long; *I don't want to labour the point, but may I raise the question for the third time?*

④ **lace**
[leɪs]
1 *noun*

(a) thin strip of leather, cord, etc., for tying up a shoe, etc.; *his laces kept coming undone; she's too little to be able to do up her laces herself*

(b) decorative fabric with open patterns of threads like a net; *a lace tablecloth; her wedding dress was trimmed with lace* (NOTE: no plural in this meaning)

2 *verb*

to fasten with laces; *he laced up his boots*

② **lack**
[læk]
1 *noun*

not having enough of something; *the children are suffering from a lack of food; the project was cancelled because of lack of funds* (NOTE: no plural)

2 *verb*

not to have enough of something; *the sales staff lack interest; he doesn't lack style - he puts on his sunglasses the moment the sun comes out*

③ **lacking**
['lækɪŋ] *adjective*

lacking in = without any; *she's completely lacking in business sense*

③ **lad**
[læd] *noun*

boy or young man; *don't expect too much - he's just a young lad*

③ **ladder**
['lædɪ] *noun*

(a) device made of horizontal bars between two uprights, used for climbing; *the ladder was leaning against the wall; he was climbing up a ladder; she got down off the ladder*

(b) the promotion ladder = series of steps by which people can be promoted; *by being appointed sales manager, he moved several steps up the promotion ladder*

(c) series of little holes in stockings or tights; *bother, I can't wear these tights because they've got a ladder* (NOTE: American English for this is a **run**)

③ **ladies**
['leɪdɪz] *noun*

(informal) women's toilet; *can you tell me where the ladies is, please?; the ladies is down the corridor on the right* (NOTE: is singular, and takes a singular verb)

② **lady**
['leɪdi] *noun*

(a) *(polite way of referring to a woman)* *there are two ladies waiting to see you*; *US* **the First Lady** = the wife of the President (NOTE: plural is **ladies**)

(b) name given to a female worker; *she was tried by a lady judge; she has a job as a school dinner lady*

(c) title given to a woman (NOTE: as a title **Lady** is followed by the family name: **Lord and Lady Forbes; Sir Peter and Lady Ross**)

④ **lag**
[læg]
1 *noun*

interval of time between two things that happen; *there's often a long time lag between setting up in business and seeing any results*; *see also* JET LAG

2 *verb*

(a) to be behind, to fall behind; *she was lagging 10m behind the leaders in the race*

(b) to cover water pipes, etc., to prevent them losing heat or freezing; *make sure your pipes are lagged before the winter* (NOTE: **lagging - lagged**)

③ **lager**
['lɑːgɪ] *noun*

(a) type of light beer; *he came to the bar and ordered six pints of lager*

(b) a glass of this beer; *he came to the bar and ordered six lagers*

COMMENT: lager was originally German beer, but is now made widely in the UK. It is served cold, while British 'bitter' is served at a higher temperature

③ **laid**
[leɪd]
see LAY

③ **laid up**
['leɪd ˈʌp] *adjective*
unable to work because of illness; *half the staff
are laid up with flu*

③ **lain**
[leɪn]
see LIE

③ **lake**
[leɪk] *noun*
area of fresh water surrounded by land; *let's take
a boat out on the lake; we can sail across the
lake; the hotel stands on the shores of Lake
Windermere;* **the Lake District** = area of
north-west England where there are several
large lakes

③ **lamb**
[læm] *noun*
(a) young sheep; *in spring, the fields are full of
sheep and their tiny lambs*
(b) meat from a lamb or sheep; *a leg of lamb;
roast lamb and mint sauce* (NOTE: no plural in
this meaning)

> COMMENT: The commonest forms of lamb
> in British cooking are lamb chops and roast
> lamb; traditionally, lamb is served with mint
> sauce

③ **lamp**
[læmp] *noun*
device which makes light; *the camp site is lit by
large electric lamps;* **street lamp** = large light in
a street; **table lamp** = lamp on a table; **standard
lamp** = room lamp on a tall pole standing on the
floor (NOTE: American English is **floor lamp**)

③ **lampshade**
['læmpʃeɪd] *noun*
decorative cover put over a lamp; *I don't like
the bright orange lampshade you bought*

① **land**
[lænd]
1 *noun*
(a) earth (as opposed to water); *they were glad
to be back on (dry) land again after two weeks
at sea*
(b) piece of ground; *she owns some land in the
north of the country; we bought a piece of land
to build a house*
(c) country; *people from many lands visited the
exhibition; he wants to see his native land
again before he is too old to travel* (NOTE:
usually no plural in meanings (a) and (b): **some
land; a piece of land**)
2 *verb*
(a) to arrive on the ground, or on another
surface; *the flight from Amsterdam has landed;
we will be landing at London Airport in five
minutes; the ducks tried to land on the ice;
(informal)* **to land on one's feet** = to be
successful; *after being made redundant he
joined the police force and has really landed on
his feet*

(b) to be successful in hitting someone; *he
landed several punches on his opponent's head*
(c) to put goods or passengers on to land after a
voyage by sea or by air; *the ship was landing
goods at the port; we landed several passengers
at Heathrow Airport*
(d) to catch a big fish; *we landed three salmon*
(e) to manage to get something; *he landed a
contract with a Chinese company*

④ **landing**
['lændɪŋ] *noun*
(a) *(especially of aircraft)* arriving on the
ground or on a surface; *the plane made a
smooth landing; strong winds meant that
landing on the aircraft carrier was difficult*
(b) flat place at the top of stairs; *she was waiting
for me on the landing*

③ **landlord**
['lændlɔːd] *noun*
(a) man or company from whom you rent a
house, room, office, etc.; *tell the landlord if
your roof leaks; the landlord refused to make
any repairs to the roof*
(b) man who is in charge of a hotel or pub, etc.;
there's a new landlord at the 'Half Moon'

④ **landmark**
['lændmɑːk] *noun*
(a) building or large object on land which you
can see easily; *the Statue of Liberty is a famous
New York landmark*
(b) outstanding or important event, etc.; *the day
when power was handed over to China was a
landmark in the history of Hong Kong*

③ **landscape**
['lændskeɪp]
1 *noun*
(a) scenery, appearance of the country; *go to the
West Country if you want to see beautiful
landscapes;* **landscape gardening** = making a
garden more beautiful by making artificial lakes,
planting trees, etc.
(b) painting of a country scene; *he collects 18th
century English landscapes*
2 *verb*
to improve the appearance of a garden by
making artificial lakes, planting trees, etc.; *he
spent years landscaping his garden*

③ **land up**
['lænd ˈʌp] *verb*
to end (in a place); *we were trying to go to the
city and landed up on the opposite side of the
river; he tried to break into a school and landed
up in prison*

③ **lane**
[leɪn] *noun*
(a) narrow road, often in the country; *a lane
with hedges on both sides*
(b) way for traffic going in a particular direction
or at a certain speed; *motorways usually have
three lanes on either side; one lane of the
motorway has been closed for repairs;* **bus lane**
= part of a road where only buses may go; **inside**

lane *or* **slow lane** = track nearest the side of the road, used by vehicles which are moving slowly, or those which are planning to turn off the road; **centre lane** *or* **middle lane** = track in the centre of the three lanes on a motorway; **outside lane** *or* **fast lane** = track nearest the centre of a road, used by vehicles which are moving fast

(c) way for one runner in a race; *she is coming up fast on the inside lane*

① **language**

['læŋgwɪdʒ] *noun*

(a) way of speaking or writing used in a country or by a group of people; *Chinese is a very difficult language to learn, but it is the language spoken by most people in the world; we go to English language classes twice a week; I don't like travelling in places where I don't know the language; his first language is German, but he speaks several other languages very well;* **sign language** = way of communicating with deaf people, making signs with your fingers

(b) **bad language** = swearing and rude words; *you should have heard the bad language when he ran into her new car*

(c) **programming language** = system of signs and words used to program a computer

④ **lap**

[læp]

1 *noun*

(a) your body from your waist to your knees, when you are sitting; *she listened to the story, sitting in her father's lap*

(b) circuit, one trip round a racetrack; *he's finished lap 23 - only two laps to go!*

(c) part of a long journey; *the last lap of the tour was from Bangkok to Singapore*

(d) **it's in the lap of the gods** = no one knows what will happen; *I can't predict the result of the election - it's all in the lap of the gods;* **in the lap of luxury** = in great luxury; *they live in the lap of luxury*

2 *verb*

(a) *(of animal)* to drink with its tongue; *the dog lapped the water in the pond*

(b) *(of waves)* to wash against something; *little waves lapped against rocks; the water was lapping round his ankles*

(c) to go so fast that you are one whole lap ahead of another competitor in a race; *the winner had lapped three other runners* (NOTE: **lapping - lapped**)

③ **laptop**

['læptɒp] *noun*

small computer which can be held on your knees; *I take my laptop with me into the plane so that I can write my reports*

③ **lap up**

['læp ˈʌp] *verb*

(a) *(of animals)* to drink fast with the tongue; *the cat was lapping up the milk*

(b) *(informal)* to accept something in an eager way; *she told him how good his book was, and he just sat there lapping it up*

① **large**

[lɑːdʒ] *adjective*

(a) big; *she ordered a large cup of coffee; our house has one large bedroom and two very small ones; how large is your garden?; why has she got an office which is larger than mine?*

(b) **by and large** = generally speaking; *by and large, it is cheaper living in Madrid than in London* (NOTE: **larger - largest**)

◊ **at large**

['æt 'lɑːdʒ] *phrase*

(a) not in prison; *two prisoners escaped and one is still at large*

(b) in general; *the advertising campaign is aimed at the public at large*

② **largely**

['lɑːdʒli] *adverb*

mainly, mostly; *the strange weather is largely due to El Niño; his farm is largely fields of grass*

③ **large-scale**

['lɑːdʒskeɪl] *adjective*

involving large numbers of people or large sums of money; *the police are launching a large-scale campaign against car thefts;* compare SMALL-SCALE

④ **laser**

['leɪzɪ] *noun*

instrument which produces a concentrated beam of light; **laser printer** = office printing machine which prints using a laser beam

④ **lash**

[læʃ]

1 *verb*

(a) to hit something with a whip; *she lashed at the horse to make it go faster*

(b) to hit against something, as if with a whip; *the rain was lashing against the windows*

(c) to fasten or tie down tightly with rope; *containers carried on the deck of a ship must be securely lashed down*

2 *noun*

(a) stroke with a whip; *he was sentenced to six lashes*

(b) flexible part of a whip; *he hit the horse with the tip of his lash*

(c) eyelash; *she has lovely long lashes* (NOTE: plural is **lashes**)

① **last**

[lɑːst]

1 *adjective*

(a) which comes at the end of a list, line or period of time; *the post office is the last building on the right; the invoice must be paid by the last day of the month; she's the last person I would want to take to a smart restaurant* = I would never go to a smart restaurant with her; **last thing at night** = at the very end of the day; *we always have a drink of* *hot milk last thing at night*; **last but not least** = the last in a list, but by no means the least important; *last but not least, mother topped the cake with chocolate icing*; **the last straw** = the final problem which makes everything seem hopeless; *there was one problem after another with our move, and the last straw was when the new house caught fire*

(b) most recent; *she's been ill for the last ten days*; *the last three books I read were rubbish*; **last but one** = the one before the last one; *my last car but one was a Rolls Royce*

(c) *(time)* **last night** = the evening and night of yesterday; *we had dinner together last night*; **last Tuesday** = the Tuesday before today; *I saw her last Tuesday*; *have you still got last Tuesday's newspaper?*; **last week** = the week before this one; *the fair was in town last week - you've missed it!*; **last month** = the month before this one; *last month it rained almost every day*; **last year** = the year before this one; *where did you go on holiday last year?*

2 *noun*

(a) thing or person coming at the end; *she was the last to arrive*; **that's the last of the apples** = we have finished all the apples

(b) final words; *that's not the last they've heard from me*

(c) *(time)* **before last** = the one before the most recent; **the Tuesday before last** = two Tuesdays ago; **the week before last** = two weeks ago; **the year before last** = two years ago; *he changed his car the year before last*

3 *adverb*

(a) at the end; *she came last in the competition*; *out of a queue of twenty people, I was served last*

(b) most recently; *when did you see her last?*; *she was looking ill when I saw her last or when I last saw her*

4 *verb*

to stay; to go on; *the fine weather won't last*; *our holidays never seem to last very long*; *the storm lasted all night*; *the meeting lasted for three hours*

◊ **at last** *or* **at long last**
[æt 'lɑːst or æt 'lɒŋ lɑːst]
in the end, after a long time; *we walked for hours and got home at last at six o'clock*; *I waited for half an hour, and at long last two buses came together*

④ **lasting**
['lɑːstɪŋ] *adjective*
which lasts for a long time; *his visit to China made a lasting impression on him*; *I've had these batteries for months - they're very long lasting*

③ **last-minute**
['lɑːst 'mɪnɪt] *adjective*
very late; *she made some last-minute changes to the wedding dress*; *people making last-minute bookings can get tours at half price*

① **late**
[leɪt]

1 *adjective*

(a) after the usual time; after the time when it was expected; *the plane is thirty minutes late*; *it's too late to change your ticket, hurry or you'll be late for the show*; *we apologize for the late arrival of the plane from Amsterdam*; **at the latest** = no later than; *I'll ring back before 7 o'clock at the latest*

(b) at the end of a period of time; *the traffic was bad in the late afternoon*; *he moved to London in the late 1980s*

(c) towards the end of the day; *it's late - I'm going to bed*

(d) **latest** = most recent; *have you seen his latest film?*; *he always drives the latest model car*; *the latest snow reports are published each day in the papers*

(e) dead; *his late father was a director of the company*; *the late president was working on this book when he died* (NOTE: only used before a noun in this meaning)

2 *adverb*

(a) after the usual time; *the plane arrived late*; *I went to bed later than usual last night*; *our visitors got up late this morning*

(b) **later** = at a time after the present; after a time which has been mentioned; *the family came to live in England and she was born a month later*; *can we meet later this evening?*; **see you later!** = I hope to see you again later today; **later (on)** = afterwards, at a later time; *I'll do it later on*; *we were only told later that she was very ill* (NOTE: later - latest)

④ **lately**
['leɪtli] *adverb*
during recent days or weeks; *have you seen her father lately?*; *we've been very busy at the office lately*

④ **Latin America**
['lætɪn ə'merɪkə] *noun*
countries in South and Central America where Spanish and Portuguese are spoken

② **latter**
['lætɪ]

1 *adjective*

(formal) coming at the end of a list; *I'm busy on Monday and Tuesday, but I'll be free during the latter part of the week*

2 *noun*

the latter = second person *or* thing mentioned of two things; *which do you prefer, apples or pears? - I prefer the latter* (NOTE: the first of two is called the **former**)

② **laugh**
[lɑːf]

1 *noun*

(a) sound you make when you think something is funny; *he's got a lovely deep laugh*; *'that's right,' she said with a laugh*; **to do something for a laugh** = to do something as a joke or for fun; *don't be angry - they only did it for a laugh*

(b) to have the last laugh = to be successful in the end, after people have laughed at you earlier on; *everyone told him that his new type of vacuum cleaner wouldn't work, but he had the last laugh when it sold in millions*

2 *verb*

(a) to make a sound to show you think something is funny; *he was very good last night - he had everyone laughing at his jokes*; *he fell off the ladder and everyone laughed*; **to laugh like a drain** = to laugh a lot; *he laughed like a drain when he was told the story*; *see also* SLEEVE

(b) to laugh at someone = to make fun of someone; *don't laugh at her because she's so fat*; *you mustn't laugh at his hat - he's very proud of it*

④ **laughter**
['lɑːftɪ] *noun*

sound or act of laughing; *laughter greeted his appearance on the stage*; *as soon as he opened his mouth, the audience burst into laughter* (NOTE: no plural)

② **launch**
[lɔːntʃ]
1 *noun*

(a) act of starting off a boat, a rocket, a new product, etc.; *the launch of the new car went off successfully*; *the rocket launch has been delayed by two weeks*; **launch party** = party held to advertise the launching of a new product

(b) type of small motor boat; *he took the launch out on the lake* (NOTE: plural is **launches**)

2 *verb*

(a) to put a boat into the water, especially for the first time and with a lot of ceremony; *the Queen launched the new ship*

(b) to put a new product on the market; *they are launching their new car at the motor show*

(c) to give something *or* someone a start; *the TV ad helped to launch her film career*

(d) to begin; *the enemy launched an attack on our headquarters*

④ **lavatory**
['lævɪtrɪ] *noun*

(a) toilet, a small room for getting rid of waste matter or water from the body; *the men's lavatory is to the right*; *the lavatories are situated at the rear of the plane*; **lavatory paper** = toilet paper, soft paper to use in a lavatory

(b) bowl with a seat and water system, for getting rid of waste matter from the body; *the drink was so awful that I poured it down the lavatory* (NOTE: plural is **lavatories**)

① **law**
[lɔː] *noun*

(a) the law = the set of rules by which a country is governed; *everyone is supposed to do what the law says*; **within the law** = according to the laws of a country; **against the law** = not according to the laws of a country; *it is against the law to drive at night without lights*; **to break the law** = to do something which is not allowed by law; *he is breaking the law by selling cigarettes to little children*

(b) to lay down the law = to tell someone to do something; *he insists on laying down the law, which makes the office staff unhappy*; **to take the law into your own hands** = to do things which are illegal, because you want to punish someone; *they took the law into their own hands and burnt down his house*; **law and order** = situation where the laws of the country are followed by most people; *the government reacted quickly to impose law and order again*

(c) one single part of the rules governing a country, usually in the form of an act of parliament; *Parliament has passed a law against the ownership of guns*

(d) all the laws of a country taken together; **civil law** = laws relating to people's rights and agreements between individuals; **commercial law** = laws regarding business; **company law** = laws which refer to the way companies work; **contract law** *or* **the law of contract** = laws relating to private agreements; **criminal law** = laws which deal with crimes against the law of the land, which are punished by the state; **international law** = laws referring to the way countries deal with each other; **the law of the sea** = laws referring to ships, ports, etc. (NOTE: no plural in this meaning)

(e) general scientific rule; *the law of gravity can be demonstrated by showing how an apple falls to the ground and not up into the air*; **the law of supply and demand** = general rule that the amount of a product which is available is related to what possible customers need

④ **lawn**
[lɔːn] *noun*

part of a garden covered with short grass; *he lay on his back on the lawn*; *your lawn needs cutting*; *we need to water the lawn every day during the summer*

④ **lawsuit**
['lɔːsuːt] *noun*

legal case brought to a court; **to bring a lawsuit against someone** = to tell someone to appear in court because you think they have acted wrongly towards you; *the parents of the victims brought a lawsuit against the bus company*

② **lawyer**
['lɔːjɪ] *noun*

person who has studied law and can advise you on legal matters; *if you are arrested you have the right to speak to your lawyer*

① **lay**
[leɪ]
1 *verb*
(a) to put something down flat; *he laid the papers on the table; a new carpet has been laid in the dining room*
(b) to lay the table = to put knives, forks, spoons, etc., on the table ready for a meal; *the table is laid for four people*
(c) to produce an egg; *the hens laid three eggs*
(d) *see also* LIE (NOTE: **laying - laid**)
2 *adjective*
not trained for a profession or to be a member of a religious group; *lay people often cannot understand doctors' language; lay members of the church helped the priest to organize the Christmas party*

③ **layer**
['leɪə] *noun*
flat, usually horizontal, covering of something; *she put a layer of chocolate on the cake, then one of cream*

④ **layout**
['leɪaʊt] *noun*
design, especially of a building, a garden, a book, etc.; *they have altered the layout of the offices; the burglars must have had a plan of the layout of the house*

② **lazy**
['leɪzi] *adjective*
not wanting to do any work; *she's just lazy - that's why the work never gets done on time; he is so lazy he does not even bother to open his mail* (NOTE: **lazier - laziest**)

③ **lb**
[paʊndz]
= POUND(S); *it weighs 26lb; take 6lb of sugar*

① **lead**
1 [led] *noun*
(a) very heavy soft metal; *tie a piece of lead to your fishing line to make it sink* (NOTE: Chemical element: chemical symbol: Pb; atomic number: 82)
(b) black part in the middle of a pencil; *you can't draw if your lead's broken*
2 [liːd] *noun*
(a) electric wire, etc., which joins a machine to the electricity supply; *the lead is too short to go across the room*
(b) first place (in a race); *he went into the lead or he took the lead; who's in the lead at the halfway stage?; she has a lead of 20m over her nearest rival*
(c) string or thin piece of leather to hold a dog; *all dogs must be kept on a lead in the park*
(d) main part in a play, opera, ballet, etc.; *the male lead fell and broke his arm*
3 [liːd] *verb*
(a) to be in first place, to have the most important place; *our side was leading at half time; they were leading by three metres*

(b) to go in front to show the way; *she led us to the secret box; the road leads you to the top of the hill*
(c) to be in charge of; to be the main person in a group; *she is leading a group of businesswomen on a tour of Chinese factories*
(d) to lead to = to make something happen; *the discussions led to an international treaty; it led me to think she was lying* = it made me think she was lying (NOTE: **leading - led** [led])
4 [liːd] *adjective*
(person) who sings or plays the main tunes in a pop group; *she's the lead singer of the group*

① **leader**
['liːdə] *noun*
(a) person who leads; *he is the leader of the Labour Party; the leader of the construction workers' union;* **leader of a council** *or* **council leader** = head of the majority party on a local council
(b) leading article, one of the main articles in a newspaper, giving the newspaper's views on a topic of current interest; *the rail disaster was featured in the leader*

② **leadership**
['liːdəʃɪp] *noun*
(a) ability to be the person who manages or directs others; *we think he has certain leadership qualities*
(b) position of a leader; *under his leadership the party went from strength to strength*
(c) group of leaders of an organization; *the leadership was weaker after the president's resignation;* **collective leadership** = group of leaders who take decisions together (NOTE: no plural)

② **leading**
['liːdɪŋ] *adjective*
most important; **leading article** = leader, one of the main articles in a newspaper, giving the newspaper's views on a topic of current interest; **leading lady** = actress who plays the main part in a play or film; **leading light** = person who plays an important part in a group; *she's one of the leading lights of the women's movement;* **leading question** = question which is put in such a way as to get a particular answer; *he prepared a few leading questions to use in the interview*

③ **lead on**
['liːd 'ɒn] *verb*
(a) to go first; *lead on, we will all follow you!*
(b) to lead someone on = to promise someone something, and then not do it; *they promised him a new car, but they were just leading him on*

③ **lead up to**
['liːd 'ʌp tuː] *verb*
to prepare the way for something to happen; *the events which led up to the war*

② **leaf**
[liːf]
1 *noun*

(a) one of many flat green parts of a plant; *the leaves of the trees turn brown or red in autumn*; *insects have eaten the leaves of the roses*

(b) sheet of paper, especially a page of a book; **to turn over a new leaf** = to make a new start; *after years of wild living he decided to turn over a new leaf and join the family firm*

(c) very thin sheet of metal, etc.; *the ceiling is covered in gold leaf* (NOTE: plural is **leaves** [liːvz])

2 *verb*

to leaf through = to turn the pages of a book rapidly without reading properly; *he leafed through the book, looking at the illustrations*

② **leaflet**
[ˈliːflɪt] *noun*

sheet of paper, often folded, giving information; *opposition groups handed out leaflets at the beginning of the rally*; *they did a leaflet mailing to 20,000 addresses*

② **league**
[liːg]
1 *noun*

(a) association of sports clubs which play against each other; *he plays for one of the clubs in the local football league*; **not in the same league as** = not as good or as successful as; *you can't compare our little corner shop to the supermarket, they're not in the same league*

(b) **league table** = list of things placed in order of merit, efficiency, etc.; *the newspapers published the government's annual league table of schools*

(c) group joined together for a particular purpose; **to be in league with someone** = to work with someone against someone else

2 *verb*

(formal) to join together; *the opposition parties all leagued together to vote against the government*

③ **leak**
[liːk]
1 *noun*

(a) escape of liquid or gas, etc., through a hole; *I can smell gas - there must be a gas leak in the kitchen*

(b) escape of secret information; *the leak of the report led to the minister's resignation*

2 *verb*

(a) *(of liquid or gas, etc.)* to flow away, to escape; *water must have been leaking through the ceiling for days*

(b) to pass on secret information; *governments don't like their plans to be leaked to the press*; *we found that the sales director was leaking information to a rival company*

③ **lean**
[liːn]
1 *adjective*

(a) *(of person)* thin; *he's a tall lean man, with a beard*

(b) *(of meat)* with little fat; *a slice of lean ham* (NOTE: **leaner - leanest**)

2 *verb*

to be in or to put into a sloping position; *the ladder was leaning against the shed*; *she leant her bike against the wall*; *he leaned over and picked up the cushion*; *it's dangerous to lean out of car windows* (NOTE: **leaning - leaned** or **leant** [lent])

③ **lean on**
[ˈliːn ˈɒn] *verb*

(a) to try to influence someone; *someone must have leant on the committee to get them to agree*

(b) to depend on someone; *if things get difficult she always has her father to lean on*

④ **leap**
[liːp]
1 *noun*

(a) jump; *she took a leap forwards and fell into the water*

(b) great improvement or progress; **by leaps and bounds** = making rapid progress; *his German has improved by leaps and bounds*

(c) **a leap in the dark** = an action where you are not sure of what the result will be; *the deal is something of a leap in the dark, but we hope it will pay off*

2 *verb*

(a) to jump; *she leapt with joy when she heard the news*

(b) to go up suddenly; *sales leapt during March* (NOTE: **leaping - leaped** or **leapt** [lept])

③ **leap at**
[ˈliːp ˈæt] *verb*

to accept eagerly something which is suggested; *she leapt at the offer of a part in the play*

③ **leap year**
[ˈliːp ˈjɜː] *noun*

every fourth year, in which February has 29 days; *the years 2004 and 2008 are both leap years*

① **learn**
[lɜːn] *verb*

(a) to find out about something, or how to do something; *he's learning to ride a bicycle*; *we learn French and German at school*; **to learn something by heart** = to learn and remember something; *she learnt the poem by heart*; **to learn from your mistakes** = to make mistakes and because of them learn how something should be done; *he doesn't want to ask advice, so I only hope he learns from his mistakes*

(b) to hear (news); *her boss learned that she was planning to leave the company*; *how did you come to learn about the product?* (NOTE: **learning - learnt** [lɜːnt] or **learned**)

③ **learner**
['lɜːnə] *noun*
person who is learning; *she's in the learners' class at the swimming pool*; **a learner driver** = someone who is learning to drive

② **learning**
['lɜːnɪŋ] *noun*
getting knowledge about something or of how to do something; *learning how to run the machine will take up most of his first week at work*; **learning curve** = gradual process of learning; **a steep learning curve** = having to learn new skills fast; *being promoted from being a secretary to sales director involved a steep learning curve*

① **lease**
[liːs]
1 *noun*
(a) written contract, allowing someone to use a building, piece of land, etc., for a specified period; *we're renting our offices on a twenty-year lease*; **the lease expires** *or* **runs out in 2020** = the lease comes to an end in 2020
(b) **to give someone a new lease of life** = to make someone want to make a fresh start or to live life in a better way; *Alan's retirement has given him a new lease of life*
2 *verb*
(a) **to lease (out)** = to give on a lease; *he leased the shop to an Australian company*; *my landlord leases out six other flats*
(b) to take or hold on a lease; *we're leasing our offices at a good rent*; *we lease our printer as it's cheaper than buying one*

① **least**
[liːst]
1 *adjective*
smallest; *this car uses by far the least amount of petrol*
2 *pronoun*; **the least** = the smallest amount; *she was the one who spent the least during their trip round Holland*; **to say the least** = which was worse that I expected; *I thought he was in the office so when I saw him in the supermarket I was surprised to say the least*; **not in the least** = not at all; *it doesn't bother me in the least to have to work on Sundays*
3 *adverb*
less than everyone or everything else; *I liked that part of the book least*; *he was the least proud man she had ever met*; **least of all** = absolutely less than everyone else; *no one was interested in what I said, least of all my son*; *see also* AT LEAST

③ **leather**
['leðə] *noun*
skin of certain animals used to make shoes, bags, etc.; *a leather bag*; *my shoes have leather soles*

① **leave**
[liːv]
1 *noun*

permission to be away from work; *he has six weeks' annual leave*; **leave of absence** = being allowed to be away from work; **sick leave** = period when a worker is away from work because of illness; **to go on leave** *or* **to be on leave** = to go or be away from work; *she is away on two months' sick leave*
2 *verb*
(a) to go away from somewhere; *when they couldn't find what they wanted, they left the shop*; *Eurostar leaves Waterloo for Brussels every day at 8.25*; *when does the next bus leave for Oxford?*
(b) to forget to do something; to forget to take something with you; *I packed in a rush and left my toothbrush at home*
(c) to allow something to stay in a certain condition; *did you leave the light on when you locked up?*; *yesterday she left the iron on, and burnt a hole in the ironing board*; *someone left the door open and the dog got out*; *the coffee left a stain on the cloth*
(d) not to take something; *leave some pizza for your brother*
(e) to go away from someone; *she's left her husband*; **leave me alone** = don't bother me
(f) not to do something, so that someone else has to do it; *she went out leaving me all the washing up to do*
(g) to give (something) to someone in your will; *he left all his property to his grandson*
(h) **leave it to me** = let me do it; *leave it to me, I'll find out the address for you*; **I leave it to you to decide** = you are the one who has to decide, not me (NOTE: **leaving - left** [left])

③ **leave behind**
['liːv bɪ'haɪnd] *verb*
to forget to take something with you; not to take something with you; *he left his car keys behind in the post office*; *the car was too full, so we had to leave Aunt Maud behind at home*

④ **leave off**
['liːv 'ɒf] *verb*
(a) to stop doing something; **leave off!** = stop doing that
(b) to forget to include; *she left the postcode off the address*; *the waitress left the drinks off the bill*

① **leave out**
['liːv 'aʊt] *verb*
to forget something; not to put something in; *she left out the date on the cheque*; *she described the accident, but left out the most important detail*; *he was left out of the football team because he had hurt his leg*

③ **leaves**
[liːvz]
see LEAF, LEAVE

③ **lecture**
['lektʃɪ]
1 *noun*

talk to students or any other group of people on a particular subject; *she gave a lecture on Chinese art*; *are you going to the lecture this evening?*; *the lecture lasted thirty minutes, and then there was time for questions*; **lecture tour** = tour with lectures on the places visited, paintings or other objects seen, etc.; *the museum has a programme of lecture tours on 20th-century art*

2 *verb*

(a) to give a lecture on something; *he will lecture on Roman history next Thursday*

(b) to teach a subject, by giving lectures; *she lectures on history at Birmingham University*

④ **lecturer**
['lektʃɪrɪ] *noun*

(a) person who gives a talk on a particular subject; *this week's lecturer is from Sweden*

(b) ordinary teacher in a university or college; *he has been a lecturer for five years*; *many of the students knew the lecturer when he was a student himself*

③ **led**
[led]
see LEAD

④ **ledge**
[ledʒ] *noun*

narrow flat part which sticks out from a cliff or building; *every little ledge on the cliff is occupied by a nesting bird*; *he climbed up 50 metres and stopped on a narrow ledge just wide enough to stand on*; **window ledge** = flat part which sticks out under a window; *the cat was sunning herself on the window ledge*

④ **lee**
[li:] *noun*

side of a building, hill, ship, etc., sheltered from the wind; *they picnicked on the lee of the hill, so as to be out of the wind*

① **left**
[left]

1 *adjective*

(a) not right, referring to the side of the body which usually has the hand you use less often; *I can't write with my left hand*; *the post office is on the left side of the street as you go towards the church*

(b) *(in politics)* referring to the socialists; *his politics are left of centre*; *compare* RIGHT

(c) **left** *or* **left over** = still there, not used up; *after paying for the food and drink, I've still got £3 left*; *if you eat three of the sweets, there will be only two left for everyone else*; *there was nobody left in the building*; *see also* LEAVE

2 *noun*

(a) the side towards the left; *remember to drive on the left when you are in Britain*; *the school is on the left as you go towards the town centre*; *she was sitting at the chairman's left*

(b) *(in politics)* **the left** = the socialists, the group supporting the rights of the workers; *we support the left by campaigning for our local*

Labour candidate; **swing to the left** = movement of votes towards the left-wing candidates

3 *adverb*

towards the left; *go straight ahead and turn left at the traffic lights*

④ **left-hand**
['left'hænd] *adjective*

on the left side; *the cheque book is in the left-hand drawer of his desk*; *the post office is on the left-hand side as you go towards the station*; *in England cars drive on the left-hand side of the road*; **left-hand drive car** = car where the driver sits on the left side of the car

COMMENT: most cars are left-hand drive: British and Japanese cars are right-hand drive

④ **left-handed**
['left'hændɪd] *adjective*

using the left hand more often than the right for doing things; *she's left-handed, so we got her a left-handed cup for her birthday*

④ **left luggage office**
['left 'lʌgɪdʒ 'ɒfɪs] *noun*

place where suitcases, etc., can be left and collected later; *don't forget that the left luggage office closes at 11.00 p.m.*; *the station doesn't have any left luggage facilities* (NOTE: American English is **baggage room**)

③ **left-wing**
['leftwɪŋ] *adjective*

in politics, on the left; *his views are very left-wing*; *a left-wing government was formed*; *left-wing intellectuals have criticized the Prime Minister*

① **leg**
[leg]

1 *noun*

(a) part of the body with which a person or animal walks; *the bird was standing on one leg, asleep*; *some animals can't stand on their back legs*; *she fell down the steps and broke her leg*; *see also* ARM

(b) **to pull someone's leg** = to tease someone, to try to make someone believe something that isn't true; *don't worry, she will get here on time - I was only pulling your leg*; **on its last legs** = almost worn out; *the poor old car is on its last legs*; **not to have a leg to stand on** = to be in an awkward situation because you cannot prove what you say; *the children produced a later will, so the claimants to the estate didn't have a leg to stand on*

(c) one of the parts of a chair, etc., which touch the floor; *the table has four legs*

(d) leg of an animal used for food; *roast leg of lamb*; *would you like a chicken leg?*

(e) stage (of a journey, tour, bicycle race, etc.); *the last leg of the trip goes from Paris to Amsterdam*; *the first leg of the tour takes in London, Hampton Court and Windsor*

2 *verb*

(informal) **to leg it** = to run away; *they legged it round the corner when they saw the police coming*

④ **legacy**

['legɪsɪ] *noun*

(a) what is left to a person according to the instructions in someone's will; *he received a large legacy from his uncle; the legacy can be paid only to a claimant who can prove his or her right to it*

(b) what is left behind by someone; *the company's overdraft is a legacy of the previous finance director* (NOTE: plural is **legacies**)

① **legal**

['liːgl] *adjective*

(a) according to the law, allowed by the law; *it's legal to drive at 17 if you have a provisional driving licence*; **legal tender** = money which must legally be accepted if you give it in payment; *foreign currency isn't legal tender, but some shops accept it*

(b) referring to the law; **to take legal action** = to sue someone, to take someone to court; **to take legal advice** = to ask a lawyer to advise about a legal problem; **legal aid** = free legal work done for people without enough money to pay lawyers' fees; *you can apply for legal aid if you want to take the case further*

④ **legally**

['liːgɪlɪ] *adverb*

in accordance with the law; *you must be over 18 to drink in a pub legally; in some European countries you are legally required to carry an identity card with you at all times*

④ **legend**

['ledʒɪnd] *noun*

story from the past which may not be based on fact; *the legend of Jason and the Golden Fleece*

④ **legendary**

['ledʒɪndrɪ] *adjective*

(a) famous, often talked about; *his liking for money is legendary; her legendary dislike of men with beards*

(b) referring to legends; *a legendary tale of witches and good fairies*

② **legislation**

[ledʒɪ'sleɪʃn] *noun*

laws, written rules which are passed by Parliament and applied in the courts; *the new legislation was passed in the Commons yesterday; Congress has voted on the new legislation;* **labour legislation** = laws concerning the employment of workers (NOTE: no plural)

③ **legislative**

['ledʒɪslɪtɪv] *adjective*

referring to laws or to the making of laws; *the legislative system in England and Wales is different from that in Scotland*

③ **legislature**

['ledʒɪslɪtʃɪ] *noun*

(a) body which makes laws; *members of the legislature voted against the proposal*

(b) building where a parliament body meets; *the protesters marched towards the State Legislature*

COMMENT: the Legislature in the UK is Parliament and in the USA, Congress. The Legislature is one of the three arms of Government, the others being the Executive and the judges

④ **legitimate**

[lɪ'dʒɪtɪmɪt] *adjective*

(a) according to the law; *he acted in legitimate defence of his rights*

(b) born to married parents; *the old king had no legitimate children, so the title passed to his brother*

(c) **legitimate concern** = reasonable concern which is justified; *if you think it's a subject of legitimate concern you should tell your manager*

③ **leisure**

['leʒɪ *US* 'liːʒɪ] *noun*

(a) **leisure (time)** = free time when you can do what you want; **leisure centre** = building where people can play sports, put on plays, dance, act, etc.; *she goes to the dance class at the local leisure centre*

(b) **do it at your leisure** = do it when there is an opportunity, without any hurry; *please send in your report at your leisure* (NOTE: no plural)

④ **lemon**

['lemɪn] *noun*

(a) pale yellow fruit with a sour taste; *oranges are much sweeter than lemons*; **lemon squash** = drink made of concentrated lemon juice and water; **lemon tea** = tea served with a slice of lemon and sugar, and not with milk

(b) tree which produces these fruit; *lemons grow best in hot dry climates*

③ **lemonade**

[lemɪ'neɪd] *noun*

drink flavoured with lemons; *can I have a glass of lemonade with ice, please?*

③ **lend**

[lend] *verb*

(a) to let someone use something for a certain period of time; *he asked me if I would lend him £5 till Monday; I lent her my dictionary and now she won't give it back; compare* BORROW

(b) **to lend a hand** = to help; *can you lend a hand with the cooking?;* **to lend an ear to someone** = to listen to what someone has to say; **to lend itself to** = to be able to be used for something special; *the garden lends itself to landscaping; the room lends itself to playing chamber music*

(c) to make a certain effect; *the Christmas decorations lend a seasonal air to the shopping centre*; *her new hairstyle lends her an air of authority* (NOTE: **lending - lent** [lent])

④ **lender**
['lendɪ] *noun*
person who lends money; *the interest on the loan must be paid to the lender every month*

② **length**
[leŋθ] *noun*
(a) measurement of how long something is from end to end; *the table is at least twelve feet in length*
(b) length of time = amount of time something takes or lasts; *can you estimate the length of time you need to do this?*; *she was a bit vague about the length of her visit* = she was not certain how long she was going to stay
(c) long piece of something; *she bought a length of curtain material in the sale*; *we need two 3m lengths of copper pipe for the new central heating system*
(d) distance from one end to the other of a swimming pool; *he swam two lengths of the swimming pool*
(e) to go to great lengths to get something = to do anything (even commit a crime) to get something; *he went to considerable lengths to get a photograph of the queen*; *see also* AT LENGTH

③ **lengthy**
['leŋθi] *adjective*
(very) long; *she wrote a lengthy note, detailing all the problems involved* (NOTE: **lengthier - lengthiest**)

④ **lens**
[lenz] *noun*
piece of curved glass or plastic, etc., used in spectacles, cameras, etc.; *my eyesight is not very good, and I have to have glasses with strong lenses*; *if the sun is strong enough you can set fire to a piece of paper using a lens*; **contact lenses** = tiny lenses worn directly on the eye

③ **lent**
[lent]
see LEND

① **less**
[les]
1 *adjective & pronoun*
a smaller amount (of); *you will get thinner if you eat less bread*; *the total bill came to less than £10*; *she finished her homework in less than an hour*; *he sold it for less than he had paid for it*
2 *adverb*
(a) not as much; *I like that one less than this one*; *the second film was less interesting than the first*; *I want a car which is less difficult to drive*; **less and less** = getting smaller all the time; *I enjoy my work less and less*; *he's less and less able to look after his garden*; **more or**

less = almost, not completely; *the rain has more or less stopped*; *I've more or less finished painting the kitchen*
(b) in less than no time = very quickly; *they repaired the car in less than no time*; **nothing less than** = absolutely no less than; *she'll be satisfied with nothing less than a husband who is a millionaire*
3 *preposition*
minus, with a certain amount taken away; *we pay £10 an hour, less 50p for insurance*

④ **lesser**
['lesɪ] *adjective*
smaller, not as large or important; *the pieces of pot found on the site were of lesser importance than the sword found with them*; **the lesser of two evils** = one of two things which is not quite as bad as the other; *faced with the choice of taking a taxi or waiting in the rain for a bus, we chose the lesser of two evils and decided to take the taxi*

② **lesson**
['lesɪn] *noun*
(a) period of time in school, etc., when you are taught something; *he went to sleep during the French lesson*; *we have six lessons of history a week*; *she's taking or having driving lessons*; *he gives Spanish lessons at home in the evenings*
(b) something which you learn from experience and which makes you wiser; *he's learnt his lesson, he knows you shouldn't be rude to policemen*; **to teach someone a lesson** = to punish someone for doing something wrong; *I locked up her bike - that will teach her a lesson*

① **let**
[let]
1 *verb*
(a) to allow someone to do something; *he let her borrow his car*; *will you let me see the papers?*; *let me see what I can do for you*
(b) to let someone know something = to tell someone about something, to give someone information about something; *please let me know the result as soon as you can*; *can you let me know when the parcel arrives?*
(c) to allow someone to borrow a house or office for a while and pay for it; *we're letting our cottage to some friends for the weekend*; **the flat is to let at £1000 a month** = the flat can be rented for £1000 per month; *see also* LET'S (NOTE: **letting - has let**)
2 *noun*
period of the lease of a property; *they took the house on a short let*

③ **let down**
['let 'daʊn] *verb*
(a) not to help when someone expects you to help; *I asked three people to speak at the meeting but they all let me down*
(b) to lower something *or* someone; *they let him down into the old mine on a rope*

(c) to make the air go out of a tyre, etc.; *someone had let down my front tyre*

③ **let go**
['let 'gɪʊ] *verb*
to stop holding on to something; *don't let go of the driving wheel; she was holding on to a branch, but then had to let go*

④ **lethal**
['li:θl] *adjective*
which kills; *she took a lethal dose of the tablets*

③ **let in**
['let 'ɪn] *verb*
to allow to come in; *don't let the dog in if she's wet; my boots let in water*

③ **let yourself in for**
['let jɪ'self 'ɪn fɔ:] *verb*
to allow yourself to get involved in something difficult or unpleasant; *you're letting yourself in for all sorts of problems; she didn't realize what she was letting herself in for when she said she would look after the children*

③ **let off**
['let 'ɒf] *verb*
(a) not to punish someone severely; *he was charged with stealing, but the judge let him off with a fine*
(b) to agree that someone need not do something; *she let the class off their homework*

③ **let on**
['let 'ɒn] *verb*
to tell a secret; *they didn't let on to the police that I was there*

① **let out**
['let 'aʊt] *verb*
(a) to allow to go out; *the boys let the pigs out of the field; we let the dogs out into the garden in the evening; she let the air out of my front tyre*
(b) to make a piece of clothing bigger; *can you let out these trousers, they're getting too tight?* (NOTE: in this meaning the opposite is to **take in**)

① **let's**
[lets] *(making a suggestion that you and someone else should do something together) let's go to the cinema; don't let's leave yet or let's not leave yet*

① **letter**
['letɪ] *noun*
(a) piece of writing sent from one person or organization to another to pass on information; *there were two letters for you in the post; don't forget to write a letter to your mother to tell her how we all are; we've had a letter from the bank manager*
(b) one of the signs which make up the alphabet, a sign used in writing which means a certain sound; *Z is the last letter of the alphabet; I'm trying to think of a word with ten letters beginning with A and ending with R; to the letter = exactly as written; they followed his*

instructions to the letter; *the referee makes sure that the rules of the game are followed to the letter; see also* CAPITAL

④ **lettuce**
['letɪs] *noun*
plant with large green leaves which are used in salads; *he made a salad with lettuce, tomatoes, and cucumber with an oil dressing* (NOTE: no plural except when referring to several plants: **a row of lettuces**)

③ **let up**
['let 'ʌp] *verb*
to do less, to become less; *the rain didn't let up all day; she's working too hard - she ought to let up a bit*

① **level**
['levl]
1 *noun*
(a) position relating to height or amount; *I want to lower the level of our borrowings; the floods had reached a level of 5m above normal;* **decisions taken at top level** = decisions taken by the head of an organization
(b) floor in a building; *go up to the next level; the toilets are at street level*
(c) *(informal)* **on the level** = honest, not trying to deceive; *I don't think the salesman is being on the level with us*
2 *adjective*
(a) flat, even; *are these shelves level, or do they slope to the left?*
(b) **level with** = at the same level as; *the floor which is level with the street is the ground floor*
3 *verb*
(a) to make level; *they levelled the house to the ground* = they destroyed the house completely
(b) **to level off** *or* **to level out** = to stop going up or down; *price increases are starting to level off; the road climbs for about two kilometres and then levels out* (NOTE: **levelling - levelled** but American spelling is **leveling - leveled**)

③ **level crossing**
['levl 'krɒsɪŋ] *noun*
place where a road crosses a railway line without a bridge or tunnel; *the level crossing gates opened when the train had passed* (NOTE: American English is **grade crossing**)

③ **lever**
['li:vɪ] *noun*
instrument like a metal rod, which helps to lift a heavy object, or to move part of a machine, etc.; *we used a pole as a lever to lift up the block of stone;* **gear lever** = handle in a car which changes the gears; *you push the gear lever down and towards you to get into reverse*

④ **levy**
['levi]
1 *noun*
tax or other payment demanded and collected; *I think the import levies on luxury goods are too high; we paid the levy on time* (NOTE: plural is **levies**)

2 *verb*

to demand or to collect a tax or other payment; *customs levied a large fine on the company*

② **liability**
[laɪˈbɪlɪti] *noun*

(a) legal responsibility; *make sure you understand your legal liabilities before you sign the contract*; **to accept liability for something** = to agree that you are responsible for something; **to refuse liability for something** = to refuse to agree that you are responsible for something; **they couldn't meet their liabilities** = they couldn't pay their debts; *see also* LIMITED (NOTE: plural in this meaning is **liabilities**)

(b) tendency to do something; *he has an unfortunate liability to burst into tears when anyone criticizes him*

(c) disadvantage; *bad eyesight is a liability if you want to be a pilot*

(d) person who causes problems; *he has been arrested several times and is something of a liability to his parents*

④ **liable**
[ˈlaɪbl] *adjective*

(a) **liable for** = legally responsible for something; *you will be liable for the payment of the fine; parents can be made liable for their children's debts*

(b) **liable to** = likely to do something; *the trains are liable to be late; she is liable to burst into tears at the slightest criticism*

③ **libel**
[ˈlaɪbl]

1 *noun*

written statement which is not true and which can damage someone's reputation; *I will sue you for libel*

2 *verb*

to libel someone = to damage someone's reputation in writing; *he accused the newspaper of libelling him*; *compare* SLANDER (NOTE: **libelling - libelled** but American spelling is **libeling - libeled**)

② **liberal**
[ˈlɪbrəl]

1 *adjective*

(a) not strict, happy to accept other people's views; *the liberal view would be to let the teenagers run the club themselves*

(b) generous; *he left a very liberal tip*

(c) *(in politics)* **Liberal** = referring to or supporting the Liberal Party

2 *noun*

(in politics) **a Liberal** = member or supporter of a Liberal Party; *the Liberals voted against the government*

④ **liberate**
[ˈlɪbəreɪt] *verb*

(formal) to set someone *or* something free from something; *the hostages were finally liberated by the security forces; the capital was liberated by government troops*

④ **liberty**
[ˈlɪbɪti] *noun*

(a) freedom; *when he was in prison he wrote poems about his lost liberty; the new legislation is a restriction of the liberty of the individual*

(b) **at liberty** = free; not in prison; *two of the escaped prisoners are still at liberty*; **to be at liberty to do something** = to be free to do something; *you are at liberty to go now*

(c) **to take liberties** = to do something without permission; **to take liberties with something** *or* **someone** = to treat something *or* someone as if they belong to you; *she borrowed my mobile without asking - she's always taking liberties with other people's property; the boss felt she was taking liberties by using the office phone to ask about getting another job*; **civil liberties** = freedom of people to act within the law (liberty of the press, liberty of the individual, etc.); *outside security cameras can be seen as a restriction on civil liberties*

④ **librarian**
[laɪˈbreɪrɪn] *noun*

trained person who works in a library; *the librarian helped us find what we wanted in the catalogue; she is starting her career as a librarian*

① **library**
[ˈlaɪbrɪ] *noun*

(a) place where books are kept which can be borrowed; *he forgot to take his books back to the library; you can't sell it, it's a library book*; **reference library** = library with reference books, where readers can search for information but not take the books away from the library

(b) collection of books, records, etc.; *he has a big record library* (NOTE: plural is **libraries**)

① **licence** *US* **license**
[ˈlaɪsɪns] *noun*

(a) document which gives official permission to own something or to do something; *she has applied for an export licence for these paintings*; **driving licence** *US* **driver's license** = permit which allows someone to drive a car, truck, etc.; *applicants should hold a valid driving licence; you must apply for a provisional driving licence before taking your first driving lesson*; *US* **license plate** = plate (one on the front and one on the back of a car) which shows a number that identifies the vehicle (NOTE: British English is **number plate**)

(b) **under licence** = with a permit from someone who has a right to something; *the cars are made in South America under licence from the British firm*

① **license**
['laɪsɪns]
1 *verb*
to give someone official permission to do something; *the restaurant is licensed to serve beer, wines and spirits; she is licensed to run an employment agency*
2 *noun*
US *see* LICENCE

③ **lick**
[lɪk]
1 *noun*
(a) a stroke with the tongue; *the dog gave him a friendly lick; can I have a lick of your ice cream?*
(b) *(informal)* quick coat of paint; *the door could do with a lick of paint*
2 *verb*
(a) to stroke with your tongue; *you shouldn't lick the plate when you've finished your pudding; they licked their lips when they saw the cakes*
(b) to beat, to hit; **to lick someone into shape** = to train someone to do something properly; *a few weeks with the army and he'll soon be licked into shape*

③ **lid**
[lɪd] *noun*
covering for a container, sometimes with a handle; *where's the lid of the black saucepan?; he managed to get the lid off the jam jar*

① **lie**
[laɪ]
1 *verb*
(a) to say something which is not true; *she was lying when she said she had been at home all evening; he lied to the police about the accident* (NOTE: in this meaning: **lying - lied**)
(b) to be in a flat position; to be situated; *six soldiers lay dead on the ground; the dog spends the evening lying in front of the fire; there were bits of paper and cigarette packets lying all over the pavement; the capital lies near the centre of the country;* **to lie in wait for someone** = to hide and wait for someone to come so as to attack him (NOTE: in this meaning: **lying - lay** [leɪ] **- has lain** [leɪn])
2 *noun*
something which is not true; *that's a lie! - don't believe what he says; someone has been telling lies about her*

③ **lie down**
['laɪ 'daʊn] *verb*
to put yourself in a flat position, especially on a bed; *I'll just go and lie down for five minutes; the burglars told him to lie down on the floor*

③ **lie in**
['laɪ 'ɪn] *verb*
to stay in bed late in the morning; *I think I'll lie in this morning*

③ **lie-in**
['laɪɪn] *noun*
(informal) **to have a lie-in** = to stay in bed longer than usual; *I can't wait until Saturday comes, then I can have a lie-in*

③ **lie low**
['laɪ 'ləʊ] *verb*
to keep hidden and quiet; *you'd better lie low until the police go away; after the robbery, they lay low for a few months*

③ **lieutenant**
[lef'tenɪnt US luː'tenɪnt] *noun*
(a) rank in the armed forces below a captain; *the lieutenant has to report to his captain;* **lieutenant-colonel** = rank in the armed forces above major and below colonel
(b) main helper; *the Prime Minister came into the room with two of his lieutenants*

① **life**
[laɪf] *noun*
(a) time when you are alive; *he spent his whole life working on the farm;* **in early life** = when you are a child; *in early life he lived in the country;* **for life** = for as long as someone is alive; *his pension gives him a comfortable income for life; (informal)* **not on your life!** = certainly not!; *don't you want to go camping? - not on your life!*
(b) being a living person; **to lose your life** = to die; *several lives were lost when the ship sank; she saved my life* = she saved me from dying; **to take your (own) life** = to commit suicide; *in a fit of despair she took her life* (NOTE: plural is **lives** in meanings (a) and (b))
(c) experience; *life can be hard when you don't have much money; being a miner is a hard life;* **it's a matter of life and death** = it's a very serious matter; *call the hospital immediately - it's a matter of life and death*
(d) living things; *is there life on Mars?;* **there's no sign of life in the house** = it looks as though there is no one in it; **pond life** = animals and plants which live in ponds
(e) being lively and energetic; *the young actors injected some life into the old play; the film comes to life when she appears on the screen*
(f) biography, the written story of someone's life; *she has written a life of Henry VIII*

④ **lifebelt**
['laɪfbelt] *noun*
large ring which helps you to float in water; *they threw lifebelts to the passengers from the sinking ferry* (NOTE: American English is also **life preserver**)

④ **life jacket**
['laɪf 'dʒækɪt] *noun*
light coat filled with air or cork, to keep you from drowning; *children must all wear life jackets on the river; instructions for putting on the life jacket are in the pocket in front of your seat* (NOTE: American English is also **life preserver**)

④ **life preserver**
['laɪf prɪ'zɜːvɪ] *noun*
US = LIFEBELT, LIFE JACKET

③ **life-span**
['laɪfspæn] *noun*
length of time something exists; *some artificial elements have a life-span of a few millionths of a second*

③ **lifestyle**
['laɪfstaɪl] *noun*
way in which someone or a group of people live their daily lives; *I don't want to be a film star, I don't envy their lifestyle at all*; *we live in the centre of London and enjoy an urban lifestyle*

④ **lifetime**
['laɪftaɪm] *noun*
time when you are alive; *I hope to see men on Mars in my lifetime*; *he finally won the lottery after a lifetime of poverty*; **the chance of a lifetime** = the best chance you are ever likely to get; *take the offer - it's the chance of a lifetime*

② **lift**
[lɪft]
1 *noun*
(a) machine which takes people up or down from one floor to another in a building; *take the lift to the tenth floor*; *push the button to call the lift*; *your room is on the fifteenth floor, so you had better use the lift* (NOTE: American English for this is **elevator**)
(b) ride in a car offered to someone; *she gave me a lift to the station*; **to hitch a lift** = to ask a driver to take you as a passenger, usually by signalling with the thumb or by holding a sign with your destination written on it; *he hitched a lift to Birmingham*; *her car broke down and she hitched a lift from a passing motorist*
(c) **chair lift** *or* **ski lift** = chairs which take people up to the top of a mountain slope; *the chair lift takes about ten minutes to reach the top*
2 *verb*
(a) to pick something up or move it to a higher position; *my briefcase is so heavy I can hardly lift it off the floor*; *he lifted the little girl up so that she could see the soldiers*; *he hurt his back lifting the box down from the shelf*
(b) to remove; *the government has lifted the ban on selling guns*
(c) to go away; *the fog had lifted by lunchtime*
(d) *(informal)* to copy; *whole sections of his book were lifted from one I wrote two years ago*

① **light**
[laɪt]
1 *noun*
(a) being bright, the opposite of darkness; *I can't read the map by the light of the moon*; *there's not enough light to take a photo*; **to stand in someone's light** = to stand between someone and a source of light

(b) electric bulb which gives light; *turn the light on - I can't see to read*; *it's dangerous to ride a bicycle with no lights*; *in the fog, I could just see the red lights of the car in front of me*; *(informal)* **there's light at the end of the tunnel** = there is some hope that everything will be all right in the end
(c) way of making a cigarette, etc., catch fire; *can you give me a light? or do you have a light?*
(d) **to cast light** *or* **to throw light on something** = to make something easier to understand; *the papers throw light on how the minister reached his decision*; **to come to light** = to be discovered; *documents have come to light which could help the police in their investigations*; **in the light of something** = when something is considered; *in the light of the reports in the press, can the minister explain his decision?*
2 *verb*
(a) to start to burn, to make something start to burn; *can you light the oven for me?*; *he couldn't get the fire to light*; *light a candle - it's dark in the shed*
(b) to give light to something; *the full moon lit the village, so we could see the church clearly*; *the police used torches to light the accident site* (NOTE: **lighting - lit** [lɪt])
3 *adjective*
(a) not heavy; *I can lift this box easily - it's quite light or it's as light as a feather*; *you need light clothing for tropical countries*; *she's just been ill, and can only do light work*
(b) *(colour)* pale; *he was wearing a light green shirt*; *I prefer a light carpet to a dark one*
(c) having a lot of light so that you can see well; *the big windows make the kitchen very light*; *it was six o'clock in the morning and just getting light*
(d) not very serious; *I like to listen to light music when I am doing the cooking*; *she took some detective novels as light reading on the train* (NOTE: **lighter - lightest**)
4 *adverb*; **to travel light** = to travel with very little luggage; *if you're hitching across Australia, it's best to travel light*

① **light bulb**
['laɪt 'bʌlb] *noun*
glass ball which gives electric light; *you'll need a ladder to change the light bulb*

① **lighting**
['laɪtɪŋ] *noun*
the light in a place; *the lighting is very bad in this restaurant - I can't see what I'm eating*

④ **lightly**
['laɪtli] *adverb*
(a) not heavily; *she touched my arm lightly*; *I always sleep lightly and wake up several times each night*
(b) not severely; **she was lucky to get off so lightly** = she was lucky not to be punished

(c) not very much; *some lightly cooked vegetables*

② **lightning**
['laɪtnɪŋ] *noun*
(a) flash of electricity in the sky, followed by thunder; *the storm approached with thunder and lightning*
(b) like lightning = very fast; *deer can run like lightning*

③ **lights**
[laɪts] *noun*
red, green and orange lights for making traffic stop and start; *turn left at the next set of lights; he drove straight across the junction when the lights were red* (NOTE: short for **traffic lights**)

③ **light up**
['laɪt 'ʌp] *verb*
(a) to make something bright; *the flames from the burning petrol store lit up the night sky*
(b) to become bright and cheerful; *her face lit up when she saw the presents under the Christmas tree*
(c) lighting up time = official time when you have to switch your car lights on as it gets dark

③ **light year**
['laɪt 'jɜː] *noun*
(a) distance travelled by light during one year (about 9.3 billion kilometres); *stars are light years from earth*
(b) light years apart = very different; *the new model is light years in advance of its competitors*

① **like**
[laɪk]
1 *preposition*
(a) similar to, in the same way as; *he's like his mother in many ways, but he has his father's nose; like you, I don't get on with the new boss; the picture doesn't look like him at all; he can swim like a fish; it tastes like strawberries; what's that record? - it sounds like Elgar; it feels like snow* = it feels as if it is going to snow; *do you feel like a cup of coffee?* = do you want a cup of coffee?
(b) *(asking someone to describe something) what was the weather like when you were on holiday?; what's he like, her new boyfriend?*
2 *adverb;* as like as not = probably; *as like as not, Dan will arrive late*
3 *conjunction* in the same way as; *she looks just like I did at her age*
4 *verb*
(a) to have pleasant feelings about something *or* someone; *do you like the new manager?; she doesn't like eating meat; how does he like his new job?; no one likes driving in rush hour traffic; in the evening, I like to sit quietly and read the newspaper*
(b) to want; *I'd like you to meet one of our sales executives; I'd like to go to Paris next week; take as many apples as you like*
5 *noun*

(a) thing which you like; *we try to take account of the likes and dislikes of individual customers*
(b) the likes of = someone like; *the likes of him should not be allowed in*

④ **likelihood**
['laɪlihud] *noun*
being likely to happen; *there's every likelihood that he will be late; it's cloudy so the likelihood of rain is high; the likelihood is that no party will be the outright winner in the elections*

① **likely**
['laɪkli]
1 *adjective*
which you think is going to happen; *it's likely to snow this weekend; he's not likely to come to the party; is that at all likely?* (NOTE: likelier - likeliest)
2 *adverb*
probably; *most likely he's gone home;* not likely! = certainly not; *Are you going to the office party? - Not likely!*

④ **likewise**
['laɪkwaɪz] *adverb*
in the same way, similarly; *John got an 'A' in the maths exam - likewise his sister Penny*

③ **liking**
['laɪkɪŋ] *noun*
pleasant feeling towards someone *or* something; *she has a liking for chocolate; this drink is too sweet for my liking;* to take a liking to someone = to start to like someone; *the manager has taken a liking to her*

④ **lily**
['lɪli] *noun*
type of flower shaped like a trumpet, which grows from a bulb; *the church was decorated with arrangements of white lilies* (NOTE: plural is **lilies**)

④ **lily-of-the-valley**
['lɪli əv ðə 'væli] *noun*
spring plant with small white flowers and a strong scent; *we picked some lily-of-the-valley on May 1st* (NOTE: plural is **lilies-of-the-valley** or **lily-of-the-valley**)

③ **limb**
[lɪm] *noun*
(a) leg or arm; *he was lucky not to break a limb in the accident;* danger to life and limb = danger that someone may be hurt; *when he's on his motorbike he's a danger to life and limb*
(b) branch of a tree; out on a limb = in a difficult or exposed situation; *he feels out on a limb, with no one to share responsibility for running the company*

④ **lime**
[laɪm] *noun*
(a) white substance containing calcium, used in making cement; *the builder ordered some bags of lime* (NOTE: no plural in this meaning)
(b) small green tropical fruit, similar to a lemon; tree which bears such fruit; *you need the juice of two limes to make this recipe*

(c) lime (tree) = large northern tree with smooth leaves; *an avenue of limes*

② **limit**
['lɪmɪt]
1 *noun*
furthest point beyond which you cannot go; **age limit** = youngest or oldest age at which you are allowed to do something; *we put an age limit of thirty-five on new employees*; **speed limit** = highest speed at which you are allowed to drive; *the speed limit in towns is 30 miles per hour*; *the police hope that the new speed limits will cut down the number of accidents*; **weight limit** = heaviest weight which something can stand; *the bridge has a weight limit of 3 tonnes*; **over the limit** = with more alcohol in your blood than is allowed by law; *the breath test showed he was way over the limit*; **within limits** = in a modest way, not excessively; *we're prepared to help you within limits*
2 *verb*
not to allow something to go beyond a certain point; *her parents limited the number of evenings she could go out*; *the boss wants to limit expenditure on entertainment*

③ **limitation**
[lɪmɪ'teɪʃn] *noun*
(a) act of limiting; **damage limitation** = limiting the amount of damage which will occur; **damage limitation exercise** = using the media in response to some bad publicity, so as to make it less harmful; *the minister's press secretary put out photographs of the minister with his family, as part of a damage limitation exercise*
(b) thing which stops you going further; **to know your limitations** = to know what you are capable of doing; *I'd love to go skiing but I know my limitations*

② **limited**
['lɪmɪtɪd] *adjective*
which has been limited; **limited (liability) company** = private company in which the shareholders are only responsible for the company's debts up to the amount of capital they have put in (NOTE: written **Ltd** in a company name: **Jones & Black Ltd**)

④ **limp**
[lɪmp]
1 *noun*
way of walking, when one leg hurts or is shorter than the other; *his limp has improved since his operation*
2 *verb*
to walk with a limp; *after the accident she limped badly*
3 *adjective*
soft, not stiff; *all we had as a salad was two limp lettuce leaves*; *he gave me a limp wave of the hand*

① **line**
[laɪn]
1 *noun*

(a) long thin mark; *she drew a straight line across the sheet of paper*; *parking isn't allowed on the yellow lines*; *the tennis ball went over the line*; **to draw the line at** = to refuse to do; *I don't mind having a cup of coffee with the boss, but I draw the line at having to invite him for a meal at home*

(b) long string; *she hung her washing on the (washing) line*; *he sat with his fishing line in the river, waiting for a fish*

(c) wire along which telephone messages are sent; *the snow brought down the telephone lines*; *can you speak louder - the line is bad*; **crossed line** = when two telephone conversations are mixed together; **to be on the line** = to be talking to someone on the telephone; *don't interrupt - I'm on the line to New York*; *do you want to speak to Charles while he's on the line?*

(d) row of people, etc.; *we had to stand in line for half an hour to get into the exhibition*; *the line of trucks and buses stretched for miles at the border*

(e) row of written or printed words; *he printed the first two lines and showed them to me*; *can you read the bottom line on the chart?*; *(informal)* **to drop someone a line** = to send someone a short letter; *I'll drop you a line when I get to New York*

(f) lines = words learnt and then spoken by an actor; *he forgot his lines and had to be prompted*

(g) railway line = rails on which trains run; *don't cross the line when a train might be coming*; **to be on the right lines** = to be doing things the right way

(h) way of doing things; **in line with** = according to, following (a decision); *we acted in line with the decision taken at the meeting*; **to take a hard line** = not to be weak; *the teacher takes a hard line with boys who sell drugs in school*

(i) type of work; *what's his line of business?*

(j) series of different products, all sold or made by the same company; *we sell several lines of refrigerators*; *I'm afraid we don't stock that line any more*
2 *verb*

(a) to stand side by side in a line; *soldiers were lining the streets*

(b) to put a lining inside something, especially a piece of clothing; *his jacket is lined with red silk*; *you'll need thick lined boots in Canada*

③ **lined**
[laɪnd] *adjective*
(a) with lines on it; **lined paper** = paper with lines printed on it; *a pad of A4 lined paper*
(b) with people or things standing side by side; **an avenue lined with trees** *or* **a tree-lined avenue** = an avenue with trees along both sides

④ **linen**
['lɪnɪn] *noun*
(a) cloth made from fibres from a plant; *he bought a white linen suit*
(b) (household) linen = sheets, pillowcases, tablecloths, etc.; *put clean linen on the bed for the visitors*
(c) underwear; *you should change your linen more often in hot weather*; **to wash your dirty linen in public** = to tell dreadful personal secrets about yourself and your family; *politicians try to be careful not to wash their dirty linen in public* (NOTE: no plural in meanings (a) and (c))

④ **liner**
['laɪnə] *noun*
(a) large passenger ship; *they went on a cruise round the Caribbean on an American liner*
(b) thing used for lining; **bin liner** = plastic bag for putting inside a dustbin
(c) eye liner = makeup for putting round your eyes

③ **line up**
['laɪn ˈʌp] *verb*
to stand in a line; *line up over there if you want to take the next boat*

③ **linguistic**
[lɪŋˈgwɪstɪk] *adjective*
referring to language(s); *translating this letter into Slovenian is going to test her linguistic skills*

④ **lining**
['laɪnɪŋ] *noun*
(a) material put on the inside of something, especially of a piece of clothing; *you'll need a coat with a warm lining if you're going to Canada in winter*; **every cloud has a silver lining** = however gloomy things may seem, there is always something which is good
(b) brake lining = curved strip round the inside of the brake round a wheel of a car

② **link**
[lɪŋk]
1 *noun*
(a) thing which connects two things or places; *the Channel Tunnel provides a fast rail link between England and France*; **telephone link** = direct line from one telephone to another
(b) one of the rings in a chain; *a chain with solid gold links*
2 *verb*
to join together; *they linked arms and walked down the street*; *his salary is linked to the cost of living*; *all the departments are linked to the main computer*; *Eurostar links London and Paris or Brussels*

③ **link up**
['lɪŋk ˈʌp] *verb*
to join two or more things together; *we have been able to link up all our computers to form a network*

④ **lion**
['laɪən] *noun*
(a) large wild animal of the cat family; *lions can be seen in African nature reserves*; **mountain lion** = large brown wild cat of North and South America
(b) the lion's share = the biggest part; *Pat took £750, the lion's share of the £1000 prize*

② **lip**
[lɪp] *noun*
(a) one of the two parts forming the outside of the mouth; *put some cream on your lips to stop them getting cracked*; **to lick your lips** = to show that you expect you are going to enjoy something; *they licked their lips when they saw the cakes*; **my lips are sealed** = I have promised not to say anything
(b) edge of something round and deep, such as a cup, bowl, etc.; *there's a chip on the lip of that cup*

② **lipstick**
['lɪpstɪk] *noun*
substance for colouring the lips; *she was wearing red lipstick*; *she bought a stick of pink lipstick*

④ **liquid**
['lɪkwɪd]
1 *noun*
substance like water, which flows easily and which is neither a gas nor a solid; *you will need to drink more liquids in hot weather*; **washing-up liquid** = liquid soap used for washing dirty dishes
2 *adjective*
(a) which is neither gas nor solid, and which flows easily; *a bottle of liquid soap*
(b) liquid assets = cash, or items which can easily be changed into cash

① **list**
[lɪst]
1 *noun*
(a) number of items, names, addresses, etc., written or said one after another; *we've drawn up a list of people to invite to the party*; *he was ill, so we crossed his name off the list*; *the things on the list are in order of importance*; **address list** *or* **mailing list** = list of names and addresses of people and companies; **black list** = list of people, companies or countries which are banned or disapproved of; **shopping list** = list of things which you need to buy; **to be on the sick list** = to be reported sick; **to be on the danger list** *or* **on the critical list** = to be dangerously ill; *after the accident, she was on the critical list for some hours*
(b) catalogue; **list price** = price of something as shown in a catalogue; *he asked for a discount on the list price*; **wine list** = list of wines available in a restaurant; *he asked to see the wine list*

(c) situation where a boat leans to one side; *the ship had taken in water and had developed a 5° list*

2 *verb*

(a) to say or to write a number of items one after the other; *she listed the ingredients on the back of an envelope*; *the catalogue lists twenty-three models of washing machine*

(b) *(of a ship)* to lean to one side; *the ship was listing badly and the crew had to be taken off by helicopter*

① **listen**
['lɪsɪn] *verb*

to pay attention to someone who is talking or to something which you can hear; *don't make a noise - I'm trying to listen to a music programme*; *why don't you listen to what I tell you?*; **to listen out for** = to wait to see if something makes a noise; *can you listen out for the telephone while I'm in the garden?*

④ **listener**
['lɪsnɪ] *noun*

person who listens; *the BBC has millions of listeners all over the world*; *Cathy is a good listener - I often go to talk over my problems with her*

④ **listing**
['lɪstɪŋ] *noun*

published list of information; *cinema listings are found on the back page of the local paper*; **computer listing** = printout of a list of items taken from the data stored in a computer; **listing paper** = paper made as a long sheet, used in computer printers

③ **lit**
[lɪt]
see LIGHT

③ **liter**
['liːtɪ] *US* = LITRE

③ **literal**
['lɪtrɪl] *adjective*

keeping to the exact meaning of the original words; *a literal translation usually sounds odd*

② **literally**
['lɪtɪli] *adverb*

(a) word for word, in a literal way; *she translated the text literally*

(b) *(to emphasize)* *she was literally horrified by the question*

② **literary**
['lɪtɪrɪ] *adjective*

referring to literature; *her style of writing is very literary*; **literary critic** = person who writes reviews of books; **literary prize** = prize given to the writer of a novel, poems, etc.

② **literature**
['lɪtrɪtʃɪ] *noun*

(a) books or writing, especially novels, poetry, drama, etc.; *she's studying English and American literature*

(b) what has been written on a particular subject; *he knows the literature on the Roman Empire very well*

(c) written publicity material about something; *do you have any literature on holidays in Greece?* (NOTE: no plural)

① **litre** *US* **liter**
['liːtɪ] *noun*

measurement for liquids (almost 2 pints); *I need a 2 litre tin of blue paint*; *this bottle holds two litres* (NOTE: usually written l after figures: **25 l** say 'twenty-five litres')

④ **litter**
['lɪtɪ]

1 *noun*

(a) rubbish left on streets or in public places; *the council tries to keep the main street clear of litter* (NOTE: no plural in this meaning)

(b) group of young animals born at one time; *she had a litter of eight puppies*

2 *verb*

to drop rubbish about; *the street was littered with bits of paper*

① **little**
['lɪtl]

1 *adjective*

(a) small, not big; *they have two children - a baby boy and a little girl* (NOTE: no comparative or superlative forms in this sense)

(b) not much; *we drink very little milk*; *a TV uses very little electricity* (NOTE: **little - less - least** [liːst])

2 *pronoun*

a little = a small quantity; *I'm not hungry - just give me a little of that soup*; *can I have a little more coffee please?*

3 *adverb*

not much; not often; *it's little more than two miles from the sea*; *we go to the cinema very little these days*

◊ **little by little**
['lɪtlbaɪ'lɪtl] *adverb*

gradually, not all at once; *they planted trees here and there, until little by little the garden became like a jungle*; *she's getting better little by little*

① **live**
1 *adjective* [laɪv]

(a) living, not dead; *there are strict rules about transporting live animals*; *guess who's moved to the house next door? - a real live TV star*

(b) not recorded; *a live radio show*

(c) carrying electricity; *don't touch the live wires*; *the boys were killed trying to jump over the live rail*

2 *adverb* [laɪv]

not recorded; *the show was broadcast live*

3 *verb* [lɪv]

(a) to have your home in a place; *they have gone to live in France*; *do you prefer living in the country to the town?*; *he lives next door to a film star*; *where does your daughter live?*; *see also* SUITCASE

(b) to be alive; *King Henry VIII lived in the 16th century*; *the doctor doesn't think mother will live much longer*

③ **live in**
['lɪv 'ɪn] *verb*
to live in the building where you work; *we want a nurse to live in*

④ **live-in**
['lɪv'ɪn] *adjective*
who lives in the place of work; *we have a live-in nurse who looks after the children*

③ **lively**
['laɪvli] *adjective*
very active; *the boss is still a lively old man*; *it was a very lively party with a dance band and dozens of young people*; *it's the liveliest nightclub in town* (NOTE: livelier - liveliest)

③ **live off**
['lɪv 'ɒf] *verb*
to earn money from; *the whole population of the village lives off tourism*

③ **live on**
['lɪv 'ɒn] *verb*
to use food or money to stay alive; *they seem to live on tins of fish*; *a family can't live on £50 a week*; *our son is staying with us until he earns enough to live on*

④ **liver**
['lɪvɪ] *noun*
(a) large organ in the body which helps to digest food and cleans the blood; *her liver was damaged in the car crash*
(b) animal's liver used as food; *I'll start with chicken livers and salad*; *he looked at the menu and ordered liver and bacon*

③ **lives**
[lɪvz]
see LIVE

③ **lives**
[laɪvz]
see LIFE

③ **live through**
['lɪv 'θruː] *verb*
to experience something dangerous; *we lived through two world wars*

③ **live together**
['lɪv tɪ'geðɪ] *verb*
(of two people) to live in the same house and have a sexual relationship; *they lived together for two years before they got married*

③ **live up**
['lɪv 'ʌp] *verb*
(a) to live up to expectations = to succeed as was expected; *the film didn't live up to the publicity that preceded it*

(b) *(informal)* **to live it up** = to lead a life when you spend a lot of money on wild parties, etc.; *she won the lottery and immediately started to live it up*

③ **live with**
['lɪv 'wɪθ] *verb*
(a) to put up with something; *we can't do anything about the noise of the aircraft - you'll just have to live with it*
(b) to live with someone = to live in the same house and have a sexual relationship with someone; *he lives with a writer of children's books*

② **living**
['lɪvɪŋ]
1 *adjective*
alive; *does she have any living relatives?*
2 *noun*
(a) money that you need for your daily life; *he earns his living by selling postcards to tourists*; *what do you do for a living?* = what job do you do?; *he doesn't earn a living wage* = he does not earn enough to pay for food, heating, rent, etc.
(b) cost of living = money which a person has to pay for food, heating, rent, etc.; *higher interest rates increase the cost of living*; *see also* COST OF LIVING

② **living room**
['lɪvɪŋ 'ruːm] *noun*
(in a house or flat) comfortable room for sitting in; *they were sitting in the living room watching TV*; *why is the living room door shut?*; *she does her homework on the sofa in the living room*

② **load**
[lɪʊd]
1 *noun*
(a) heavy objects which are carried in a truck, wagon, etc.; *the lorry delivered a load of bricks*; **lorry-load** *or* **truck-load** *or* **van-load** = amount of goods carried on a truck or van; *they delivered six lorry-loads of coal*; *when we moved we had three van-loads of books*
(b) responsibility, thing which is difficult to live with; **that's a load off my mind** = I feel much less worried; *I've finished my exams - that's a load off my mind*
(c) *(informal)* **loads of** = plenty, lots of; *it was a wonderful party - there was loads to eat*; *you don't need to rush - there's loads of time before the train leaves*; *John always has loads of good ideas*
2 *verb*
(a) to put something, especially something heavy, into or on to a truck, van, etc.; *they loaded the furniture into the van*
(b) to put a film into a camera
(c) to put a program into a computer; *load the program before you start keyboarding*

④ **loaf**
[lıuf]
1 *noun*

large single piece of bread made separately, which you cut into slices before eating it; *he bought a loaf of bread at the corner shop*; *we eat about 10 loaves of bread per week*; **sliced loaf** = loaf of bread which has already been sliced in a machine before it is sold (NOTE: plural is **loaves** [lıuvz])

2 *verb*

to loaf around = to hang around, doing nothing; *he hasn't any proper job and just loafs around Leicester Square all day*

② **loan**
[lıun]
1 *noun*

(a) act of lending; *I had the loan of his car for three weeks*; **on loan** = being lent; *the picture is on loan to the National Gallery*

(b) thing lent, especially a sum of money; *he bought the house with a £100,000 loan from the bank*; **bridging loan** *US* **bridge loan** = short-term loan to help someone buy a new house when he has not yet sold his old one (NOTE: do not confuse with **lone**)

2 *verb*

to lend; *the furniture for the exhibition has been loaned by the museum*

④ **lobby**
['lɒbi]
1 *noun*

(a) entrance hall; *I'll meet you in the hotel lobby in half an hour*

(b) group of people who try to influence important people, especially members of parliament; *the MPs met members of the green lobby*

(c) hall in the House of Commons used especially for interviews with members of the public; **lobby correspondent** = journalist who reports on parliamentary matters; **division lobby** = corridor where MPs go to vote (NOTE: plural is **lobbies**)

2 *verb*

to try to influence someone (especially in order to get a bill through Parliament); *she lobbied her MP with a detailed letter and other documents* (NOTE: **lobbying - lobbied**)

① **local**
['lıukıl]
1 *adjective*

(a) referring to a place or district near where you are; *she works as a nurse in the local hospital*; *the local paper comes out on Fridays*; *she was formerly the head of the local school*; **local authority** = section of elected government which runs a town or district; *we complained to the local authority about the bus service*; **local call** = telephone call to a number in the same

area as the person making the call; **local time** = time of day in a particular place; *it will be 1 a.m. local time when we arrive in Tokyo*

(b) **local anaesthetic** = substance which removes the feeling in a certain part of the body only; *she had the operation under local anaesthetic*; *this operation can be carried out under local rather than general anaesthetic* (NOTE: an anaesthetic for the whole of the body is a **general anaesthetic**)

2 *noun*

(a) **locals** = people who live in the area; *the locals don't like all the rich people who have weekend cottages in the village*; *the restaurant caters for the tourist trade rather than for the locals*

(b) *(informal)* pub near where you live; *you can find him in his local every evening*

② **locally**
['lıukıli] *adverb*

in the district near where you are; *when we go camping we usually try to buy everything locally*

③ **locate**
[lıu'keıt] *verb*

(a) to find the position of something; *divers are trying to locate the old Spanish ship*

(b) **to be located** = to be in a particular position; *the heart is located in the left side of the body*; *the warehouse is located near to the motorway*

② **location**
[lıu'keıʃn] *noun*

(a) place or position; *the hotel is in a very central location*

(b) *(filming)* **on location** = in a real setting, not in a studio; *the film was shot on location in North Africa*

(c) finding the position of something; **echo location** = finding objects in the sea by using echoes

② **lock**
[lɒk]
1 *noun*

(a) device which closes a door, safe, box, etc., so that you can only open it with a key; *she left the key in the lock, so the burglars got in easily*; *we changed the locks on the doors after a set of keys were stolen*

(b) amount by which the wheels of a car can turn left or right; *the car has an excellent lock - it turns easily in a narrow road*

(c) section of a river with gates which can be opened or closed to control the flow of water, and so allow boats to move up or down to different levels; *they passed through dozens of locks on their trip down the Thames*

2 *verb*

(a) to close a door, safe, box, etc., so that it has to be opened with a key; *I forgot to lock the safe*; *we always lock the front door before we go to bed*

(b) to fix or to become fixed in a certain position; *the wheels suddenly locked as he went round the corner*

② **locked**
['lɒkt] *adjective*
which has been shut with a key; *the burglars managed to break into a locked safe*; *the cash box wasn't locked*

③ **lock in**
['lɒk 'ɪn] *verb*
to make someone stay inside a place by locking the door; *I think we've been locked in*

③ **lock out**
['lɒk 'aʊt] *verb*
to make someone stay outside a place by locking the door; *she took the key and locked her husband out*; *he came back late at night and found he was locked out of the hotel*; *I've left the keys inside the car and locked myself out*

③ **lock up**
['lɒk 'ʌp] *verb*
(a) to close a building by locking the doors; *he always locks up before he goes home*; *she was locking up the shop when a man walked in*
(b) to keep a person or thing inside a place or container by locking the door or lid; *lock up the jewels in the safe* or *lock the jewels up in the safe*
(c) to put someone in prison; *they locked him up for a week*

④ **locomotive**
[lɪʊkɪ'mɪʊtɪv] *noun*
engine of a train; *the line became electric and they got rid of the old steam locomotives*

④ **lodge**
[lɒdʒ] *verb*
(a) to rent a room in a house; *he lodges with Mrs Bishop in London Road*
(b) *(formal)* to lodge a complaint against someone = to make an official complaint about someone; *they lodged a complaint with the local electricity company*; to lodge something with someone = to deposit something with someone to look after for you; *they lodged all the documents with the solicitor*
(c) to become stuck; *a piece of bread was lodged in her throat*; *the bullet was lodged in his spine*

③ **log**
[lɒg]
1 *noun*
(a) thick piece of a tree; *he brought in a load of logs for the fire*; to sleep like a log = to sleep very deeply; *after his 12-mile walk he slept like a log*
(b) daily detailed record of speed, position, etc., especially on a ship or plane; *the ship's log gave details of their position when the fire broke out*
2 *verb*
(a) to write down details of something which has happened in a book as a record; *have you logged your day's activities into the journal?*

(b) *(computing)* to log in or log on = to enter a special code and start to access a computer system; to log off or log out = to exit a computer system by entering an instruction (NOTE: logging - logged)

④ **logic**
['lɒdʒɪk] *noun*
(a) power of formal reasoning; *your logic is faulty - just because she has an MA doesn't mean she's a good teacher*
(b) sense, good reason; *I don't see the logic of owning two cars and not being able to drive*

③ **logical**
['lɒdʒɪkl] *adjective*
(a) clearly reasoned; *a logical conclusion*
(b) *(of person)* able to reason clearly; *she's a very logical person and thinks everything through carefully*

① **London**
['lʌndɪn] *proper noun* capital of England and the United Kingdom; *the plane arrives in London at 4 o'clock*; *she went to the railway station to ask about cheap tickets to London*; *most London buses are red*; *London has changed a lot in the past few years*; *London is on the river Thames*; *Charles II was king at the time of the Fire of London*; *there is a picture of the Tower of London on the front of the book*

④ **lone**
[lɪʊn] *adjective*
single, one alone; *she was the lone Englishwoman in a crowd of Germans*; *a lone house on the edge of the forest*; *a lone rider on the beach* (NOTE: do not confuse with **loan**)

③ **lonely**
['lɪʊnlɪ] *adjective*
(a) feeling sad because of being alone; *it's odd how lonely you can be in a big city full of people*; lonely hearts ad = advertisement in a newspaper to try to find a girlfriend or boyfriend; *she answered a lonely hearts ad in her local paper*
(b) (place) with few or no people; *the top of the mountain is a lonely place at night*; *we spent the weekend in a lonely cottage in the Welsh hills* (NOTE: lonelier - loneliest)

① **long**
[lɒŋ]
1 *adjective*
(a) not short in length; *a long piece of string*; *the Nile is the longest river in the world*; *my hair needs cutting - it's getting too long*
(b) not short in time; *what a long programme - it lasted almost three hours*; *they've been waiting for the bus for a long time*; *we don't approve of long holidays in this job*
(c) *(indicating measurement in time)* how long is it before your holiday starts?; *(said when meeting someone)* long time no see! = I haven't seen you for a long time (NOTE: the use with figures: the road is six miles long; a piece of string a metre long)

2 *adverb*

(a) for a long time; *have you been waiting long?*; *I didn't want to wait any longer*; *long ago, before the war, this was a wealthy farming area*

(b) as long as *or* so long as = provided that; *I like going on picnics as long as it doesn't rain*

(c) no longer = not any more; *I no longer have it* = I had it at some time in the past, but not any more (NOTE: **longer - longest**)

3 *verb*

to want something very much; *I'm longing for a cup of tea*; *everyone was longing to be back home*

④ **long-distance**
[lɒŋ'dɪstɪns] *adjective*

(a) *(in sport)* (race) between two places which are far apart; *she was over fifty when she took up long-distance running*; *you'll have to get fit if you're going to run a long-distance race*

(b) made over a long distance; *we spent three days walking along one of the long-distance paths in the hills*; *long-distance telephone calls cost less after 6 p.m.*

③ **longing**
['lɒŋɪŋ] *noun*

great desire for something; *after three months travelling in South America, he had a longing to be back home in Scotland*

③ **long-lasting**
['lɒŋ'lɑːstɪŋ] *adjective*

which lasts a long time; *long-lasting batteries can run for a much longer time than ordinary batteries*; *the effects of exposure to sunlight can be very long-lasting*

③ **long-range**
[lɒŋ'reɪndʒ] *adjective*

which covers a long distance or a long time; *the long-range weather forecast is not very reliable*; *they stationed long-range missiles along the border*

② **long-term**
[lɒŋ'tɜːm] *adjective*

planned to last for a long time; *he asked the bank for a long-term loan*; *they never make any long-term plans*; *see also* SHORT-TERM

④ **long-time**
['lɒŋtaɪm] *adjective*

who has existed for a long time; *his long-time partner*

③ **long wave**
['lɒŋ'weɪv] *noun*

radio wave longer than 1000 metres; *we listened to the BBC on long wave*; *see also* MEDIUM WAVE, SHORT WAVE

③ **loo**
[luː] *noun*

(informal) lavatory, toilet; *where's the ladies' loo?*; *he's in the loo, but will be back in a minute* (NOTE: this is the term which is used most often in the UK)

① **look**
[lʊk]

1 *noun*

(a) seeing something with your eyes; *have a good look at this photograph and tell me if you recognize anyone in it*; *we only had time for a quick look round the town*

(b) searching for something; *we had a good look for the ring and couldn't find it anywhere*

(c) the way someone *or* something appears; *there is a French look about her clothes*; **good looks** = pleasing and beautiful appearance; *his good looks and charm attracted many women*

2 *verb*

(a) to turn your eyes towards something; *I want you to look carefully at this photograph*; *look in the restaurant and see if there are any tables free*; *if you look out of the office window you can see our house*; *he opened the lid of the box and looked inside*

(b) **to look someone in the eye** = to look straight at someone in a confident way; *he didn't dare look me in the eye*; **don't look a gift horse in the mouth** = don't criticize something which someone has given you for free

(c) to appear to be; *I went to see her in hospital and she looks worse*; *is he only forty? - he looks much older than that*; *those pies look good*; *it looks as if it may snow*

① **look after**
['lʊk ɑ'ftɪ] *verb*

to take care of; *nurses look after patients in hospital*; *who's going to look after your dog when you're away?*

③ **look ahead**
['lʊk ə'hed] *verb*

to make plans for the future; *I'm looking ahead to the summer and hoping to get a casual job*

③ **look back**
['lʊk 'bæk] *verb*

(a) to turn your head to see what is behind you; *he looked back and saw a police car was following him*

(b) **he never looked back** = he was very successful; *the first year after starting the business was difficult, but after that they never looked back*

③ **look back on**
['lʊk 'bæk ɒn] *verb*

to think about something which happened in the past; *he looked back on his time with the company with satisfaction*; *looking back on the events of last week, I think we could have handled the problems better*

① **look down**
['lʊk 'daʊn] *verb*

to look down on someone = to think you are better than someone; *he looks down on anyone who hasn't been to university*

① **look for**
['lʊk 'fɔ:] *verb*
to search for, to try to find; *we looked for the watch everywhere but couldn't find it*; *the police are looking for three escaped prisoners*

① **look forward to**
['lʊk 'fɔ:wɪd 'tu:] *phrase*
to think happily about something which is going to happen; *the whole family is looking forward to going on holiday*; *she isn't looking forward to taking her driving test*; *I'm looking forward to seeing my parents again*

③ **look in (on)**
['lʊk 'ɪn ɒn] *verb*
to pay a short visit; *I'll look in on my aunt to see how she is*; *they didn't stay long - they just looked in*

① **look into**
['lʊk 'ɪntʊ] *verb*
to try to find out about a matter or problem; *I've asked the manager to look into the question of staff holidays*

① **look like**
['lʊk 'laɪk] *phrase*
(a) to be similar to; *he looks just like his father*
(b) *(asking someone to describe something)* *what's he look like, her new boyfriend?*; *tell me what she looks like so that I can recognize her when she gets off the train*
(c) to seem to be going to happen; *take an umbrella, it looks like rain*; *the sky is dark, it looks like snow*

① **look out**
['lʊk 'aʊt] *verb*
(a) to be careful; *look out! - the car is going backwards!*
(b) to look out on *or* over = to have a view towards; *the windows of the office look out over a park*

③ **lookout**
['lʊkaʊt] *noun*
(a) careful watch; *keep a sharp lookout for pickpockets*; *from their lookout post they could see across the square*; to be on the lookout for = to watch carefully for; *she's always on the lookout for bargains*; *the police are on the lookout for car thieves*; *the club is always on the lookout for fresh talent*
(b) business, affair; *that's his lookout* = that is something he must deal with himself

③ **look out for**
['lʊk 'aʊt fɔ:] *verb*
(a) to keep looking to try to find; *we're looking out for new offices because ours are too small*; *I'll look out for his sister at the party*
(b) to be careful about; *look out for ice on the pavement*
(c) *US* to look out for someone = to protect someone; *the falling rock missed us by inches - someone was obviously looking out for us!*

③ **look over**
['lʊk 'əʊvɪ] *verb*
(a) to examine briefly; *she looked over the figures and said they seemed to be OK*
(b) to have a view over something; *the office looks over an old railway line*

③ **look round**
['lʊk 'raʊnd] *verb*
(a) to turn to see what is behind you; *she heard footsteps behind her and quickly looked round*
(b) to go round looking at something; *did you have time to look round the town?*; *can I help you? - no, I'm just looking round to see what is available*

① **look up**
['lʊk 'ʌp] *verb*
(a) to turn your eyes upwards; *she looked up and saw clouds in the sky*
(b) to try to find some information in a book; *I'll look up his address in the telephone book*; *look up the word in the dictionary if you don't know what it means*
(c) to get in contact with; *look me up when you're next in London*
(d) to get better; *things are looking up*

③ **look up to**
['lʊk 'ʌp tu:] *verb*
to admire, to respect someone; *she looks up to her professor and copies everything he does*

④ **loom**
[lu:m]
1 *verb*
to appear in a threatening way; *a storm loomed on the horizon*; *a bus suddenly loomed out of the fog*
2 *noun*
machine on which cloth is woven; *she weaves cloth on a hand loom at home*

④ **loop**
[lu:p]
1 *noun*
circle made by a piece of thread or ribbon, etc., which crosses over itself; *to tie your laces, start by making a loop*
2 *verb*
to attach with a loop; *she looped the cord over the tent pole*

③ **loose**
[lu:s]
1 *adjective*
(a) not attached; *watch out! - the sail is loose and swinging towards you!*; *the front wheel is loose and needs to be tightened*; *the boat came loose and started to drift away*
(b) to be at a loose end = to have nothing special to do; *we're at a loose end this weekend*
(c) loose change = money in coins only; *can you spare some loose change for the charity?*
(NOTE: **looser - loosest**)
2 *verb*

to start something happening; *the government's proposals loosed off demonstrations in all parts of the country*

④ **loosely**

['luːsli] *adverb*

not tightly; *the skirt fits loosely round her waist; he tied the boat loosely to the post*

④ **loosen**

['luːsɪn] *verb*

(a) to make something less tight; *he loosened his belt and relaxed*

(b) **to loosen your grip on something** = to hold something less tightly than before; *the parliament forced the president to loosen his grip on the civil service*

④ **loot**

[luːt]

1 *verb*

to steal, especially from shops and houses, during a riot or other emergency; *some houses were looted after the floods*

2 *noun*

(a) things which have been stolen; *the police discovered the rest of the loot under his bed*

(b) *(slang)* money; *he's got plenty of loot* (NOTE: no plural)

② **lord**

[lɔːd]

1 *noun*

(a) person who rules or is above other people in society; *powerful lords forced King John to sign the Magna Carta*

(b) title for peers; *Lord Smith;* **the House of Lords** = the upper house of the British Parliament

(c) **the Lord** = God or Jesus Christ; *praise the Lord for his mercy*

(d) *(expression of surprise or shock)* **good lord!** *I didn't realize it was so late!*

2 *verb*

to lord it over someone = to treat someone like a servant; *she lords it over the junior staff in the office*

④ **lore**

[lɔː] *noun*

traditional beliefs and knowledge; *it's part of children's lore that it is unlucky to walk under a ladder* (NOTE: no plural)

③ **lorry**

[lɒri] *noun*

GB large motor vehicle for carrying goods; *they put the bricks onto his lorry; big lorries make the house shake when they go past; he drives a five-ton lorry;* **lorry-load** = amount of goods carried on a lorry; *they delivered six lorry-loads of coal; see also* TRUCK (NOTE: plural is **lorries**)

① **lose**

[luːz] *verb*

(a) to put or drop something somewhere and not to know where it is; *I can't find my purse - I think I lost it on the train; if you lose your ticket you'll have to buy another one*

(b) not to have something any longer; *we lost money on the lottery;* **to lose weight** = to get thinner; *she doesn't eat potatoes as she's trying to lose weight;* **the clock loses 10 minutes every day** = it falls 10 minutes behind the correct time every day; **to lose sight of** = not to see something any longer; *we lost sight of her in the crowd;* **to lose your temper** = to become angry; *he lost his temper when they told him there were no tables free;* **to lose time** = to waste time, not to do something quickly enough; *don't lose any time in posting the letter;* **to lose your way** = to end up not knowing where you are; *they lost their way in the fog on the mountain; see also* HEART

(c) not to win; *we lost the match 10 - 0; did you win? - no, we lost* (NOTE: **losing - lost** [lɒst])

① **loss**

[lɒs] *noun*

(a) no longer having something; *he was very sad at the loss of his house;* **it's no great loss** = it doesn't matter now that we no longer have it; *the map's no great loss - I brought two along, just in case*

(b) money which you have spent and have not got back; *companies often make losses in their first year of operations;* **they sold it at a loss** = they sold it for less than they paid for it

(c) *(informal)* **it's a dead loss** = it's no use at all; *the plan was a dead loss*

(d) **to be at a loss what to do** = not to know what to do; *we are at a loss to know what to do next; I'm at a loss for something to do now that the party has been cancelled* (NOTE: plural is **losses**)

② **lost**

[lɒst] *adjective*

to be lost = to end up not knowing where you are; *did you bring a map? I think we're lost!;* **lost property office** = place where articles which people have left on trains, buses, etc., are kept, and where they can be claimed by their owners; *go to the lost property office tomorrow and ask if anyone has found the hat; have you asked the lost property office if they've got your bag?; we found an umbrella on the train and handed it in at the lost property office; see also* GET LOST

① **lot**

[lɒt] *noun*

(a) **a lot of** *or* **lots of** = a large number *or* a large quantity; *there's lots of time before the train leaves; what a lot of cars there are in the car park!; I've been to the cinema quite a lot recently; she's feeling a lot better now; lots of* *people are looking for jobs; (informal)* **a fat lot of** = not much; **a fat lot of help you are!** = you are no help at all

(b) the lot = everything; *that's the lot - there's nothing left; there were old pots and books and newspapers - we sold the lot for £50; we picked pounds of beans and ate the lot for dinner*

(c) *US* piece of land, especially one to be used for development; **parking lot** = place where you can park cars (NOTE: British English is **car park**)

(d) item or group of items sold at an auction; *lot 23 is a collection of books and pictures*

(e) to draw lots = to take pieces of paper from a box to decide something (the person who has the marked piece wins); *we drew lots to decide who would go first; they drew lots for the bottle of whisky*

③ **lottery**
['lɒtri] *noun*

(a) game of chance in which numbered tickets are sold with prizes given for certain numbers; **the National Lottery** = British lottery which takes place twice a week, where you try to forecast a series of numbers; *she won over £2m on the lottery; there were three winners on this week's lottery; he buys a lottery ticket every week*

(b) situation where anyone may win; *getting a government contract is something of a lottery* (NOTE: plural is **lotteries**)

③ **loud**
[laʊd]
1 *adjective*

(a) which is very easily heard; *can't you stop your watch making such a loud noise?; turn down the radio - it's too loud*

(b) *(of colours)* too bright; *he was wearing a particularly loud tie which didn't go with his jacket at all*

2 *adverb*
loudly; *I can't sing any louder; she laughed out loud in church* (NOTE: **louder - loudest**)

④ **loudspeaker**
[laʊd'spiːkɪ] *noun*

part of a radio, TV, public address system, etc., which allows sound to be heard; *he set up two loudspeakers in opposite corners of the room; the captain called the passengers over the loudspeaker and asked them to go on deck*

④ **lounge**
[laʊnʒ]
1 *noun*

(a) comfortable room for sitting in; *let's go and watch TV in the lounge;* **lounge bar** = bar in a pub or hotel which has comfortable chairs

(b) departure lounge = room at an airport where passengers wait to board their planes; *as more flights were delayed, the departure lounge filled up with angry travellers*

2 *verb*

to lounge about = to sit or lie doing nothing or very little; *he doesn't do anything on Saturdays, he just lounges about waiting for the pubs to open; it rained all the time, so we had to spend the day lounging about in the hotel*

① **love**
[lʌv]
1 *noun*

(a) great liking for someone *or* something; *give my love to your wife; her great love is opera;* **to be in love** = to love each other; *they seem to be very much in love;* **to fall in love with someone** = to start to like them very much; *they fell in love at first sight*

(b) to make love (to someone) = to have sex with someone; *she swore that he had never made love to her or that they had never made love*

(c) there's no love lost between them = they hate each other; *the partners got on well to begin with, but now there's no love lost between them*

(d) *(in games such as tennis)* score of zero points; *she lost the first set six - love (6-0)*

(e) person whom you love; *she's the love of his life*

(f) *(informal) (way of addressing, especially to a woman or child)* hallo, love, what can I do for you this morning?

2 *verb*

(a) to have strong feelings for someone *or* something; *she loves little children; the children love their teacher; his wife thinks he loves someone else*

(b) to like something very much; *we love going on holiday by the seaside; I'd love to come with you, but I've got too much work to do*

② **lovely**
['lʌvlɪ] *adjective*

very pleasant; *it's a lovely warm day; she was wearing a lovely pink hat* (NOTE: **lovelier - loveliest**)

③ **lover**
['lʌvɪ] *noun*

(a) person, especially a man, who is having a sexual relationship with someone; *her lover was arrested when the woman's body was found on the beach*

(b) person who loves something; *a lover of French food*

① **low**
[lɪʊ]
1 *adjective*

(a) not high; *she hit her head on the low branch; the town is surrounded by low hills; we shop around to find the lowest prices; the engine works best at low speeds; the temperature here is too low for oranges to grow; sales were lower in December than in November*

(b) sad and depressed; *she was very low when I saw her last* (NOTE: **lower - lowest**)

2 *adverb*

towards the bottom; not high up; *the plane was flying too low - it hit the trees*; **supplies are running low** = supplies are becoming scarce; *see also* LIE LOW

3 *noun*

point where something is very small; *the exchange rate has reached a new low*

4 *prefix meaning* 'with not much of'; **low-fat** = containing very little fat; *do you have any low-fat yoghurt?*

③ **lower**

['ləʊə]

1 *adjective*

which is below something else of the same sort; **lower deck** = bottom deck on a ship or bus; *they booked a cabin on the lower deck*; **lower jaw** = bottom jaw, the bone holding the lower teeth, which moves to make the mouth open or shut; *she hit him so hard that she broke his lower jaw* (NOTE: the opposite is **upper**)

2 *verb*

(a) to make something go down; *they lowered the boats into the water*; *the crane lowered the machine into the building*

(b) to make smaller; *all the shops have lowered their prices to attract customers*; **to lower your voice** = to speak more quietly

④ **loyal**

['lɔɪl] *adjective*

faithful, who supports someone *or* something; *dogs are usually very loyal to their owners*; *she's a loyal member of the Conservative Party*

④ **loyalty**

['lɔɪltɪ] *noun*

being loyal; *all the staff should show their loyalty by coming to the meeting*

③ **L-plates**

['el'pleɪts] *noun*

two white plastic squares, each with a large red L on it, attached to a car driven by a learner driver; *he took off his L-plates as soon as he passed his test*

① **Ltd**

['lɪmɪtɪd] *short for* LIMITED COMPANY (NOTE: used for private companies. Public companies, that is companies on the Stock Exchange, are called **Plc**)

② **luck**

[lʌk] *noun*

something, usually good, which happens to you; *the bus is empty - that's a bit of luck!*; **good luck with your driving test!** = I hope you do well in your driving test; **I wear this ring for luck** = because I hope it will bring me luck; **bad luck** = something bad which happens to you; *it was just my bad luck to have homework when everyone else went swimming*; **bad luck!** *or* **hard luck!** = I am sorry you didn't do well; *you failed the driving test again? - bad luck!*; **tough**

luck! = I'm sorry you have a problem, that you didn't win, that you didn't do well, etc., but there's nothing I can do to help you; *you've missed the last bus? - tough luck, you'll just have to walk*; **to be down on your luck** = to be going through a period of bad luck; *he was down on his luck and thought of trying to find work in Scotland*

③ **luckily**

['lʌkɪlɪ] *adverb*

which is a good thing; *it started to rain but luckily I had taken my umbrella*; *luckily I was at home when the telephone engineer called*

② **lucky**

['lʌkɪ] *adjective*

(a) having good things happening to you; *he's lucky not to have been sent to prison*; *how lucky you are to be going to Spain!*; *(informal)* **you'll be lucky!** = it will never happen; *she's hoping to get an extra day off this week - she'll be lucky!*

(b) which brings luck; *15 is my lucky number* (NOTE: **luckier - luckiest**)

④ **ludicrous**

['luːdɪkrəs] *adjective*

ridiculous, which makes you laugh; *it's ludicrous that we have to carry our bags from the train up three flights of stairs*

② **luggage**

['lʌgɪdʒ] *noun*

suitcases, bags, etc., for carrying your belongings when travelling; *check that you haven't left any luggage behind on the coach*; **luggage rack** = space for bags, etc., above the seats in a plane, train, etc.; *she put her suitcase in the luggage rack*; *please place all hand luggage in the overhead luggage racks*; **luggage trolley** = metal holder on wheels, on which luggage can be moved easily in an airport, station, etc.) (NOTE: **luggage** has no plural; to show one suitcase, etc., say **an item of luggage, a piece of luggage.** Note also that American English prefers to use the word **baggage; luggage trolley** is **baggage cart** in American English)

② **lump**

[lʌmp]

1 *noun*

(a) piece of something, often with no particular shape; *a lump of coal*; *a lump of sugar*

(b) **lump sum** = money paid in one amount; *he received a lump sum from an insurance policy*

(c) hard or swollen part on the body; *she went to the doctor because she had found a lump on her breast*

2 *verb*

(a) **to lump together** = to bring several different things together; *we lump all the cash purchases together under 'other items' in the account book*

(b) *(informal)* **to lump it** = to put up with something; *if he doesn't like it he can lump it!*

① **lunch**
[lʌnʃ]
1 *noun*
meal eaten in the middle of the day; *come on - lunch will be ready soon*; *we always have lunch at 12.30*; *we are having fish and chips for lunch*; *I'm not hungry so I don't want a big lunch*; *the restaurant serves 150 lunches a day*; **business lunch** *or* **working lunch** = lunch where you discuss business; *see also the note at* DINNER (NOTE: plural is **lunches**)
2 *verb*
to have lunch; *I'm lunching with my sister today*; *don't forget we're lunching with the agents tomorrow*

① **lunchtime**
['lʌnʃtaɪm] *noun*
time when you usually have lunch; *it's half past twelve - almost lunchtime*; *the office is closed at lunchtimes*

④ **lung**
[lʌŋ] *noun*
one of two organs in the chest with which you breathe; *the doctor listened to his chest to see if his lungs were all right*

> COMMENT: the two lungs are situated in the chest, with the heart between them. Air goes down into the lungs and the oxygen in it is deposited in the blood

④ **luxurious**
[lʌk'ʒʊəriːs] *adjective*
very comfortable; *the flat is furnished with luxurious carpets and fittings*; *business class is not as luxurious as first class*

④ **luxury**
['lʌkʃəri] *noun*
(a) great comfort; *he lived a life of great luxury*; *a hot bath is a real luxury after two weeks camping in the mountains*; **luxury hotel** = a five-star hotel, a very good hotel, with luxurious rooms and higher prices

(b) thing which is pleasant to have but not necessary; *she often buys little luxuries for dessert on Friday nights* (NOTE: plural in this meaning is **luxuries**)

③ **lying**
['laɪɪŋ] *see* LIE

④ **lynch**
[lɪnʃ] *verb*
(of a mob) to catch an accused person and kill him, especially by hanging, without a trial; *the crowd lynched one man, but the actual murderer escaped*

③ **lyrical**
['lɪrɪkl] *adjective*
(poem, etc.) concerned with feeling; *a lyrical description of the countryside in spring*; *(informal)* **to wax lyrical about something** = to be full of enthusiasm about something; *the reviewer waxed lyrical about the young painter*

④ **lyrics**
['lɪrɪks] *noun*
words of a song; *he wrote the lyrics for the musical*

Mm

① **M, m**
[em]

thirteenth letter of the alphabet, between L and N; *'accommodation' is spelt with two Ms*

① **machine**
[mɪ'ʃiːn] *noun*

(a) thing which works with a motor; *we have bought a machine for putting leaflets in envelopes*; *there is a message on my answering machine*; *she made her dress on her sewing machine*; *the washing machine has broken and flooded the kitchen*

(b) organization; *the party machine moved into action to prepare for the general election*

④ **machine gun**
[mɪ'ʃiːn 'gʌn] *noun*
gun which automatically fires many bullets rapidly, one after the other; *the rapid fire of a machine gun could be heard in the distance*; *from their lookout post they were able to cover the whole square with machine-gun fire*

③ **machinery**
[mɪ'ʃiːnɪri] *noun*

(a) many machines, taken as a group; *the factory has got rid of a lot of old machinery*

(b) way of organizing; *a review of local government machinery*; *the machinery for awarding government contracts* (NOTE: no plural: **some machinery, a piece of machinery**)

② **mad**
[mæd] *adjective*
(a) having a serious mental disorder; *he's quite mad; she became mad and had to be put in a special hospital*
(b) silly, crazy; *everyone thought he was mad to try to cross the Atlantic in a rowing boat; (informal)* **mad about** = very keen on; *he's mad about doing puzzles in newspapers*; **mad as a hatter** = totally crazy; *don't ask him for advice - he's as mad as a hatter*
(c) wildly frantic; *the noise is driving her mad; (informal)* **like mad** = very fast; with a lot of enthusiasm; *he drove like mad and managed to get to the station in time to catch the train; they worked like mad to finish the job on time*
(d) very angry; *she's mad at or with him for borrowing her car; he was hopping mad when they told him his car had been stolen* (NOTE: **madder - maddest**)

④ **madam**
['mædɪm] *noun*
(a) *(way of referring to a lady, often used by waiters or servants) after you, madam; would madam like some more tea?*
(b) *(writing a letter to a lady whom you do not know)* **Dear Madam**

① **made**
[meɪd]
see MAKE

③ **made-up**
['meɪdʌp] *adjective*
(a) wearing makeup; *she was heavily made-up to try to hide the mark on her cheek*
(b) invented; *it was a made-up story - none of the report was true*

④ **madly**
['mædli] *adverb*
in a wild way; *they were madly in love; as soon as we came through the gate, the dogs rushed across the yard, barking madly*

④ **mafia**
['mæfɪə] *noun*
secret Italian organization dealing in crime; *many mafia leaders have been arrested*

② **magazine**
[mægɪ'ziːn] *noun*
(a) illustrated paper which comes out regularly; *the gardening magazine comes out on Fridays*
(b) radio or TV programme made up from various items on the same theme, broadcast regularly; *following the news, this week's science magazine has features on space telescopes and global warming*
(c) container for bullets which can be attached to a gun; *he clipped the magazine to the gun*

④ **magic**
['mædʒɪk] *noun*
spells, tricks, etc., which do not appear to follow normal scientific rules; *he made a rabbit appear in his hat, and the children all thought it was magic*; **as if by magic** = suddenly, without any possible explanation; *he pushed a button and, as if by magic, lights came on all over the garden*

③ **magistrate**
['mædʒɪstreɪt] *noun*
judge who hears cases in a minor court; *she appeared before the magistrates; the magistrate sent him for trial to London court; he was fined £500 by the magistrates;* **magistrates' court** = (i) building where magistrates try cases; (ii) court presided over by magistrates; *the magistrates' court is just opposite the police station; he appeared before the magistrates' court on a charge of theft* (NOTE: magistrates who do not receive a salary are also called **Justices of the Peace** or **JPs**)

③ **magnet**
['mægnɪt] *noun*
(a) piece of metal which attracts iron and steel and will point roughly north and south when balanced on a point; *you can move little pieces of iron around on a piece of paper by holding a magnet underneath; she has a Mickey Mouse which sticks to the fridge door with a magnet*
(b) anything which attracts; *butterflies were attracted to the flowers like a magnet; the big city is a magnet for teenagers running away from home*

④ **magnetic**
[mæg'netɪk] *adjective*
(a) which attracts metal; *iron and steel can be made magnetic, but wood and paper cannot;* **magnetic field** = area around a magnet which is under its influence; **magnetic north** = the point near the North Pole to which a floating magnet will point; *see also* STRIP, TAPE
(b) having a power of attraction; *she has a magnetic personality - everyone looks at her when she enters a room*

④ **magnificent**
[mæg'nɪfɪsɪnt] *adjective*
very fine, very splendid, very luxurious; *he lives in a magnificent 20-bedroom castle by the lake; she gave a magnificent performance as Cleopatra*

④ **maid**
[meɪd] *noun*
female servant; *the maid forgot to change the towels* (NOTE: do not confuse with **made**)

③ **mail**
[meɪl] *noun*
1 *noun*
(a) letters which are delivered; *the mail hasn't come yet; my secretary opens my mail as soon as it arrives; the receipt was in this morning's mail*
(b) service provided by the post office; *the cheque was lost in the mail; we sent the parcel by sea mail; it's cheaper to send the order by surface mail than by air;* **mail merge** =

computer program which allows the same letter to be written to many different addresses; *see also* AIRMAIL, EMAIL

2 *verb*
to send something by the postal services; *we mailed the catalogue to addresses all over Europe*; *he mailed the order last Wednesday* (NOTE: **mail** is used in both British and American English; British English also uses **post**, while American English does not)

③ **mailing list**
['meɪlɪŋ 'lɪst] *noun*
list of names and addresses of people to whom information can be sent; *his name is on our mailing list*; *we are building up a mailing list of possible customers*

⓪ **mail order**
[meɪl 'ɔːdɪ] *noun*
ordering and buying by post; *I bought the sofa by mail order or from a mail-order catalogue*

① **main**
[meɪn]
1 *adjective*
most important; *the main thing is to get to work on time*; *their main factory is in Scotland*; *January is the main month for skiing holidays*; *a car will meet you at the main entrance*; *US* **Main Street** = most important street in a town, where the shops and banks are (NOTE: in British English, this is the **High Street**)
2 *noun*
(a) large pipe for water, gas, etc.; *a water main burst and flooded the street*; *workmen hit a gas main when they were digging a hole in the road*
(b) **the mains** = electricity brought into a building; *that computer is plugged into the mains*; *our radio can run either on a battery or the mains*
(c) **in the main** = generally speaking; *in the main, English speakers have difficulty in learning other languages*

④ **mainland**
['meɪnlənd] *noun*
large solid mass of land, as opposed to an island; *the ferry from the Isle of Wight takes 15 minutes to reach the mainland*; **mainland Europe** = Europe, not counting the British Isles

② **mainly**
['meɪnli] *adverb*
(a) most often; *we sell mainly to businesses*; *people mainly go on holiday in the summer*
(b) chiefly; *she is mainly interested in old churches*

④ **mainstream**
['meɪnstriːm]
1 *adjective*
(group, trend, etc.) most important; *it took him more than ten years to become a mainstream Hollywood director*; *she wants to get into mainstream politics*
2 *noun*

the most important part of a group, etc.; *the opinion of the mainstream of the party is very important*

② **maintain**
[meɪn'teɪn] *verb*
(a) to keep something going; *we like to maintain good relations with our customers*
(b) to keep something in good working order; *the boiler needs to be regularly maintained*
(c) to state as a fact; *throughout the trial he maintained that the car was not his*

② **maintenance**
['meɪntɪnɪns] *noun*
(a) keeping in working order; *we offer a full maintenance service*
(b) keeping things going or working; *the maintenance of contacts with government officials*
(c) money for upkeep, especially paid by a divorced or separated person to help pay for living expenses for children; *he refused to pay maintenance for their children*

④ **majesty**
['mædʒɪsti] *noun*
(a) beautiful or impressive sight; *the majesty of the range of white mountains took his breath away*
(b) *(formal)* *(used as a form of address to a king or queen)* **Her Majesty, Queen Elizabeth II** (NOTE: the plural **majesties** is used to refer to several kings and queens: **Their Majesties, the King and Queen of Norway**; when speaking formally to a king or queen, say **Your Majesty**)

② **major**
['meɪdʒə]
1 *adjective*
(a) important; *cigarettes are a major cause of lung cancer*; *computers are a major influence on modern industrial society*; *many small roads are blocked by snow, but the major roads are open*; **the major part of** = most of; *the major part of the film takes place in Scotland*
(b) musical key; *she played a piece by Bach in B major*; *compare* MINOR
2 *noun*
rank of an officer in the army below colonel; *a major came up in a truck with six soldiers* (NOTE: used as a title with a surname: **Major Smith**)
3 *verb*
US to specialize in a subject at university; *she majored in English literature*

② **majority**
[mɪ'dʒɒrɪti] *noun*
(a) larger part of a group; *the majority of the members of the club don't want to change the rules*; **in the majority** = being more than half of the members; *women are in a majority on the committee*; *see also* SILENT
(b) number of voters which is larger than half; *she was elected with a majority of 10,000*; **the government has a majority of one** = the

government has one MP more than the opposition; **two-thirds majority** = more than 66%; *you need a two-thirds majority to get the approval of the shareholders* (NOTE: plural is **majorities**)

① **make**
['meɪk]
1 *noun*
the country or the company which makes something; *Japanese makes of cars*; *what is the make of your refrigerator?*
2 *verb*
(a) to put together, to build; *he made a boat out of old pieces of wood*; *these knives are made of steel*; *she is making a Christmas cake*
(b) to get ready; *do you want me to make some tea?*; **to make a bed** = to make a bed tidy after someone has slept in it; *when we got to the hotel, the beds hadn't been made*
(c) to add up to a total; *six and four makes ten*
(d) to earn (money); *he made millions of pounds by buying and selling property*
(e) to give someone a feeling; *the smell of coffee makes me hungry*; *the rough sea made him feel sick*; *looking at old photographs made her sad*; *he made himself comfortable in the armchair*
(f) to force someone to do something; *his mother made him clean his room*; *the teacher made us all stay in after school*; *I can't make the car go any faster*; *what on earth made you do that?* (NOTE: **making - made** [meɪd])

③ **make do with**
['meɪk 'du: 'wɪθ] *verb*
to use something because there is nothing else available; *she forgot her pyjamas, and had to make do with a T-shirt*; *the shop has no brown bread left so we'll have to make do with white*; *all the glasses are broken, so we'll have to make do with plastic cups*

③ **make for**
['meɪk 'fɔ:] *verb*
(a) to go towards; *the army was making for the capital*; *as soon as the film started, she made straight for the exit*
(b) to help something to happen; *frozen food makes for easier meals*

③ **make of**
['meɪk ɒv] *verb*
to have an impression or opinion about something; *what did you make of the news on TV?*; *I don't know what to make of this letter*

③ **make off with**
['meɪk 'ɒf wɪð] *verb*
to steal something; *the burglar made off with all their silver*

① **make out**
['meɪk 'aʊt] *verb*
(a) to be able to see clearly; *can you make out the house in the dark?*
(b) to be able to understand; *I can't make out why he doesn't want to come*

(c) to claim something which is probably not true; *the English weather isn't really as bad as it is made out to be*; *she tries to make out that she's very poor*
(d) to write something, such as a name; *the cheque is made out to Mr Smith*
(e) *(informal) US* to be successful; *he tried opening a fish restaurant but it didn't make out*; *how is Bobby making out at school?*

④ **maker**
['meɪkɪ] *noun*
person who makes something; *the makers of the Mini must have made a lot of money over the years*; *the company is the world's biggest maker of ice-cream*

① **make up**
['meɪk 'ʌp] *verb*
(a) to invent a story; *he said he had seen a man climbing into the house, but in fact he made the whole story up*
(b) **to make yourself up** = to put on powder, lipstick, etc.
(c) to form; *the staff is made up of secretaries and drivers*
(d) **to make up your mind** = to decide; *they can't make up their minds on where to go for their holiday*; *his mind is made up* = nothing will make him change his mind; *it's no use talking to him - his mind is made up*
(e) **to make up for lost time** = to act quickly because you did not act earlier; *it's June already - we'll have to plant our beans now to make up for lost time*

③ **makeup**
['meɪkʌp] *noun*
(a) face powder, lipstick, etc., which are put on your face to make it more beautiful or to change its appearance; *she wears no makeup apart from a little lipstick*; *he spent hours over his makeup for the part of the old grandfather*
(b) way in which something is formed or arranged; *by bringing in ministers from another party, the Prime Minister has altered the whole makeup of the Cabinet*; *the census shows the ethnic makeup of the population*

② **male**
[meɪl]
1 *adjective*
(a) referring to the sex which does not produce young; *a male deer crossed the road in front of out car*
(b) referring to men or boys; *the male population is more likely to get flu than the female*
2 *noun*
(a) man or boy; *the wreckage contained the bodies of two males and two females*
(b) animal or insect of the sex which does not give birth to young or lay eggs; *with spiders, the female is usually bigger than the male* (NOTE: do not confuse with **mail**)

④ **mall**
noun
(a) [mɔːl]
shopping mall = enclosed covered shopping area with shops, restaurants, banks and other facilities; *the new shopping mall is taking customers away from the stores in the town centre*
(b) [mæl]
the Mall = street in London leading from Trafalgar Square to Buckingham Palace; *the soldiers paraded down the Mall to Buckingham Palace*

① **man**
[mæn]
1 noun
(a) male human being; *that tall man is my brother; there's a young man at reception asking for Mr Smith*
(b) any human being; *Stone Age men existed several thousand years ago*
(c) **the man in the street** = an ordinary person; *the man in the street isn't interested in a united Europe* (NOTE: plural is **men** [men])
2 verb
to provide staff to work something; *the switchboard is manned all day; the exhibition stand was manned by three salesgirls; he sometimes mans the front desk when everyone else is at lunch* (NOTE: **mans - manning - manned**)

① **manage**
['mænɪdʒ] verb
(a) to be in charge of something; *she manages all our offices in Europe; we want to appoint someone to manage the new shop*
(b) **to manage to do something** = to do something successfully; *did you manage to phone the office?; the burglars managed to open the door of the safe*
(c) to be able to work properly or cope with a situation; *can you manage all by yourself?; how are we going to manage without a driver?*

① **management**
['mænɪdʒmɪnt] noun
(a) group of people who direct workers; *the management has decided to move to new offices*; **under new management** = with a new owner or manager; *the shop is under new management*; **senior management** = senior managers or directors; **middle management** = managers of departments who are not as important as directors; *there have been redundancies, even at middle management level*
(b) directing and control of work; *he's taking a course in management; if anything goes wrong now it's just a case of bad management*

① **manager**
['mænɪdʒɪ] noun
(a) person in charge of a department in a shop or in a business; *the bank manager wants to talk about your account; the sales manager organized a publicity campaign; she's the manager of the shoe department*
(b) organizer of a sports team; *the club have just sacked their manager*
(c) person who is employed to organize the work of a singer, sportsman, actor, etc.; *her manager is organizing her tour of North America*

④ **manageress**
[mænɪdʒɪ'res] noun
woman who manages a shop or department; *the assistant called the manageress to help her sort out the problem; the manageress of our accounts department is an extremely capable person* (NOTE: plural is **manageresses**)

② **managing director (MD)**
['mænɪdʒɪŋ daɪ'rektɪ] noun
director who runs everything in a company; *she was made managing director of a textile firm; the MD is in Australia on business*

④ **maneuver**
[mɪ'nuːvɪ] US see MANOEUVRE

④ **manipulate**
[mɪ'nɪpjuleɪt] verb
(a) to handle; *she found it difficult to manipulate the steering wheel while wearing gloves*
(b) to influence people or situations so that you get what you want; *by manipulating the media the government made sure its message got across to the people*
(c) to produce false accounts to make a company seem more profitable than it really is; *he was accused of manipulating the sales figures to protect the share price*

② **manner**
['mænɪ] noun
(a) way of behaving; *she has a very unpleasant manner; the staff don't like the new assistant's manner*
(b) **manners** = way of behaving in public; *it's bad manners to speak with your mouth full; those boys need to be taught some manners*
(c) sort; **in a manner of speaking** = in some sort of way; *in a manner of speaking, I'm glad to have got the sack, as I won't have to work in that dreadful office again*

④ **manoeuvre** US **maneuver**
[mɪ'nuːvɪ]
1 noun
(a) **manoeuvres** = military exercises; *the fleet is on manoeuvres in the Mediterranean*
(b) planned action to avoid something; *the captain had to make a sudden manoeuvre to avoid hitting the smaller ship; the company has carried out various manoeuvres to avoid bankruptcy*
2 verb
(a) to move something heavy or difficult to handle; *we manoeuvred the piano into position on the stage*

(b) to work to put yourself in a good position; *she managed to manoeuvre herself onto the board of the company*

④ **manslaughter**
['mænslɔːtɪ] *noun*
offence of killing someone without having intended to do so; *he was acquitted of murder but found guilty of manslaughter*; compare MURDER

④ **manual**
['mænjʊɪl]
1 *adjective*
(a) done by hand; **manual work** = work done with your hands; *he has no qualifications, so he does some manual work while studying*; **manual worker** = worker who works with his hands
(b) (car) where the gears are changed by hand; *I prefer a manual model to an automatic*
2 *noun*
book of instructions; *look in the manual to see if it tells you how to clean the printer*

④ **manufacture**
[mænjʊˈfæktʃɪ]
1 *noun*
making of a commercially produced product; *most of the cars are of foreign manufacture*
2 *verb*
to make products commercially; *we no longer manufacture buses here*

② **manufacturer**
[mænjʊˈfæktʃɪrɪ] *noun*
person or company producing industrial products; *an aircraft manufacturer*; *a shoe manufacturer*

③ **manufacturing**
[mænjʊˈfæktʃɪrɪŋ]
1 *noun*
the business of making things in large quantities for sale; *only 25% of the nation's workforce is now engaged in manufacturing*
2 *adjective*
that manufactures things; **manufacturing industries** = industries which take raw materials and make them into finished products; **a manufacturing town** = a town which has many industries based in it; *this used to be a prosperous manufacturing town before the factories closed*

④ **manuscript**
['mænjʊskrɪpt] *noun*
(a) document, letter, poem, etc., which has been written by hand; *one of the original manuscripts of the book is on display in the British Library*; *the sale of several manuscript letters by King Charles II*
(b) handwritten or typed version of a book which has not been printed or published; *he sent his manuscript to several publishers, but no one wanted to publish it* (NOTE: often written **MS**, plural **MSS**, say 'manuscripts')

① **many**
['menɪ]
1 *adjective*
(a) a large number of things or people; *many old people live on the south coast*; *so many people wanted rooms that the hotel was booked up*; *she ate twice as many cakes as her sister did*
(b) (asking a question) how many times have you been to France?; *how many passengers were there on the plane?*
(c) **a great many** or **a good many** = quite a lot; *a good many people think we should build a ring road round the town*; **too many** = more than necessary; *there were too many people waiting and not enough room on the bus for all of them*; **one too many** = one more than enough (NOTE: **many - more** [mɔː] **- most** [mɪʊst]. Note also that **many** is used with nouns which you can count: **not many apples** but **not much bread**)
2 *pronoun* a large number of people; *many of the students knew the lecturer when he was a student himself*; *many would say that smoking should be banned in all public places*

② **map**
[mæp]
1 *noun*
drawing which shows a place, such as a town, a country or the world as if it is seen from the air; *here's a map of Europe*; *the village where they live is so small I can't find it on the map*; *show me on the map where the mountains are*; *they lost their way because they'd forgotten to take a map*; **street map** = plan showing streets with their names; *if you're going to Paris, you'll need a street map*
2 *verb*
(a) to make a map of a country, etc.; *the explorers mapped the whole of the south of the country*
(b) **to map out** = to plan in advance; *we met yesterday to map out our publicity programme*; *he mapped out a plan to buy the company* (NOTE: **mapping - mapped**)

④ **marathon**
['mærɪθɪn] *noun*
(a) long distance race; *a marathon is run over 26 miles*; *she's training for the New York marathon*
(b) anything which lasts a long time and is very tiring; *the marathon meeting of club members lasted for over five hours*; *after a marathon negotiating session, we finally reached agreement*

④ **marble**
['mɑːbl] *noun*
(a) very hard type of stone which can be polished so that it shines brilliantly; *the entrance hall has a marble floor*; *the table top is made from a single piece of green marble*

(b) marbles = set of small glass balls for playing with; *children were playing marbles in the school playground*; *I found a marble under the sofa*

④ **march**
[mɑːtʃ]
1 *noun*
(a) walking in step by soldiers, sailors, etc.; *the soldiers were tired after their long march through the mountains*; **march past** = ceremony where soldiers march in step in front of someone important; *all sections of the armed forces took part in the march past at which the Queen took the salute*; **route march** = long training march; **quick march** = rapid walking pace; **slow march** = slow walking pace
(b) protest march = mass of people walking to protest about something; *the police estimate that around 5000 people took part in the protest march*
(c) music with a regular beat for marching; *at the end of the ceremony the band played a slow march*; **wedding march** = music which is played after a wedding; *as the bride and bridegroom came out of the church the organ played the wedding march* (NOTE: plural is **marches**)
2 *verb*
(a) to walk in step; *the guards marched after the band*; *we were just in time to see the soldiers march past*; **quick march!** = order to soldiers to march at a rapid pace
(b) the police marched him off to prison = they took him away quickly to prison
(c) to walk quickly and with a particular purpose; *she marched into the shop and asked to speak to the manager*
(d) to walk in a protest march; *thousands of workers marched to the parliament building*

① **March**
[mɑːtʃ] *noun*
third month of the year, between February and April; *her birthday is in March*; *today is March 6th US March 6*; *we moved house last March*; *we often have storms in March* (NOTE: **March 6th** or **March 6**: say 'March the sixth' or 'the sixth of March'; American English: 'March sixth')

④ **mare**
['meɪ] *noun*
female horse; *the mares were running in the field*

④ **margarine**
['mɑːdʒɪ'riːn] *noun*
mixture of animal or vegetable oil which is used instead of butter; *can you tell the difference between butter and margarine?*; *I prefer butter to margarine*

③ **margin**
['mɑːdʒɪn] *noun*
(a) white space at the edge of a page of writing; *write your comments in the margin*; *we left a wide margin so that you can write notes in it*

(b) extra space, time, etc.; **leave a margin for error** = allow extra space or time in case you have made a mistake; **safety margin** = space or time left to allow for safety; **by a wide margin** = by a big distance, by a large number of votes, etc.; *the Labour candidate won by a wide margin*
(c) money received which is more than money paid; *small businesses operate on very narrow margins*; *we have to cut our margins to remain competitive*; **gross margin** = difference between the price received and the cost of manufacture; **net margin** = difference between the price received and all costs, including overheads

④ **marine**
[mɪ'riːn]
1 *adjective*
referring to the sea; *she studied marine biology*
2 *noun*
(a) the merchant marine = the merchant navy
(b) soldier serving in the navy; *he decided not to join the Marines, but to become a pilot instead*; *the Marines attacked the enemy air base*

① **mark**
[mɑːk]
1 *noun*
(a) small spot of a different colour; *the red wine has made a mark on the tablecloth*; *she has a mark on her forehead where she hit her head*
(b) points given to a student; *she got top marks in English*; *what sort of mark did you get for your homework?*; *no one got full marks - the top mark was 8 out of 10*
(c) line showing a certain point; *his income has reached the £100,000 mark*; **high-water mark** = line showing where the high tide reaches
(d) target; **wide of the mark** = not at all correct; *his estimate of the costs was wide of the mark*
(e) printed sign; **exclamation mark** = written sign (!) which shows surprise; **question mark** = written sign (?) which shows that a question is being asked
(e) *(order given to runners at the beginning of a race)* **on your marks, get set, go!**
2 *verb*
(a) to make a mark; **the box is marked 'dangerous'** = it has the word 'dangerous' written on it
(b) to correct and give points to work; *the teacher hasn't finished marking our homework*; *has the English exam been marked yet?*
(c) *(in games)* **to mark an opponent** = to follow an opposing player closely, so as to prevent him getting the ball
(d) to mark time = to stay on one spot, not to move forward; *sales are simply marking time*

③ **mark down**
['mɑːk 'daʊn] *verb*
to reduce the price of something; *we have marked all prices down by 30% for the sale*

① **marked**

[mɑːkt] *adjective*

(a) very obvious, definite; *this month's sales showed a marked improvement; his performance was first class - in marked contrast to his game last week*

(b) a marked man = man who has been selected by an enemy as a probable target; *he informed on the leader of the gang, and since has become a marked man*

③ **marker**

['mɑːkɪ] *noun*

(a) thing which marks; **marker pen** = coloured felt pen which makes a wide mark

(b) person who gives a mark to a piece of work, an examination, an entry in a competition, etc.; *our teacher is a very hard marker - nobody gets more than seven out of ten*

① **market**

['mɑːkɪt]

1 *noun*

(a) place where fruit and vegetables, etc., are sold from small tables, often in the open air; *we buy all our vegetables and fish at the market; market day is Saturday, so parking will be difficult;* **covered market** = building in which a market is held

(b) sale; **on the market** = for sale; *their house has been on the market for three months;* **to put on the market** = to offer for sale; *we put our house on the market three months ago and no one has even been to look at it*

(c) place where a product is required, where a product could be sold; *the market for Russian cars has almost disappeared; the potential global market for this product is enormous;* **market research** = examining the possible sales of a product and the possible customers before it is put on the market; *if we had done proper market research we would have discovered that there were several products that are cheaper than ours; before you launch the product, you must do thorough market research;* **market share** *or* **share of the market** = percentage of possible sales which a company or product has; *they started an advertising campaign aimed at increasing their market share;* **domestic market** *or* **home market** = the market in the country where you live; *sales in the domestic market have not increased;* **export markets** *or* **overseas markets** = markets outside the country where you live

(d) black market = illegal selling at high prices; *there is a flourishing black market in spare parts for cars; we had to pay black market prices; you can buy whisky on the black market*

2 *verb*

to sell products using marketing techniques; *this product is being marketed in all European countries*

③ **marketing**

['mɑːkɪtɪŋ] *noun*

techniques of publicity, design, etc., used to sell a product; *our marketing strategy needs to be revised totally; they used aggressive marketing to boost sales;* **marketing department** = department in a company which specializes in ways of selling a product; **marketing director** = director in charge of marketing

③ **mark up**

['mɑːk 'ʌp] *verb*

to increase the price of something; *these prices have been marked up by 10%; if retailers find the discount too low they mark the prices up to make a better margin*

③ **marmalade**

['mɑːmɪleɪd] *noun*

jam made from oranges, lemons, grapefruit, etc.; *I've made fifty pots of lemon marmalade;* **Seville orange marmalade** = marmalade made with bitter oranges; **marmalade cat** = orange and white coloured cat

> COMMENT: marmalade is eaten with toast at breakfast, and not at any other time of day. Compare JAM

② **marriage**

['mærɪdʒ] *noun*

(a) being legally joined as husband and wife; *a large number of marriages end in divorce; she has two sons by her first marriage*

(b) wedding, the ceremony of being married; *they had a simple marriage, with just ten guests; the marriage took place in the town hall*

② **married**

['mærɪd] *adjective*

joined as husband and wife; *are you married or single?; married life must suit him - he's put on weight;* **married name** = name taken by a woman when she gets married; *after the divorce she stopped using her married name*

> COMMENT: in Britain, the USA and many other countries, it is usual for a woman to drop her family name when she gets married and to replace it by her husband's family name. However, many women, especially professional women, now prefer to keep their original family name

① **marry**

['mæri] *verb*

(a) to make two people husband and wife; *they were married in the village church*

(b) to become the husband or wife of someone; *she married the boy next door; how long have you been married?; she's married to a policeman; they're getting married next Saturday*

④ **marsh**

[mɑːʃ] *noun*

area of wet land; *ducks and geese come to the marshes during winter; the developers want to drain the marsh and build on it*; **salt marsh** = wet land covered by the sea at high tide (NOTE: plural is **marshes**)

④ **marshal**
['mɑːʃl]
1 *noun*
(a) military officer of the highest rank; **Marshal of the Royal Air Force** = highest rank in the Royal Air Force
(b) organizer of a race or a show; *marshals directed the crowds to the stands*; *some marshals rushed to the scene of the crash and others waved flags to try to stop the race*
(c) *US* officer of a court; *federal marshals raided several houses looking for a prisoner who had escaped from jail*
(d) *US* chief of police or chief of the fire brigade in an area
2 *verb*
to organize people, things, etc., into order; *extra police were brought in to marshal the crowds of fans*; *he tried to marshal the facts but was too sleepy to think clearly* (NOTE: **marshalling - marshalled** but American spelling is **marshaling - marshaled**)

② **marvellous** *US* **marvelous**
['mɑːvɪlɪs] *adjective*
wonderful; *the children had a marvellous time at the circus*; *I've got some marvellous news - Mary is pregnant!*; *soft music is marvellous for getting babies to sleep*

③ **masculine**
['mæskjʊlɪn] *adjective*
(a) male, referring to men; *she had a very masculine hair style*
(b) with qualities that are typical of men; *the boy answered in a deep masculine voice*
(c) *(in grammar)* referring to words which have a particular form to show the male gender; *is the French word 'table' masculine or feminine?* (NOTE: the opposite is **feminine**)

③ **mashed potatoes**
['mæʃd pɪ'teɪtɪuz] *noun*
potatoes which have been boiled until they are soft and then crushed smooth and mixed with butter and milk; *our children prefer chips to mashed potatoes*; *see also* BANGER

④ **mask**
[mɑːsk]
1 *noun*
something which covers or protects your face; *the burglars wore black masks*; *he wore a mask to go diving*; **gas mask** = mask which covers the face and allows you to breathe when there is poisonous gas about; *the soldiers were told to put on their gas masks*; **oxygen mask** = mask which appears from a panel above your head if there is a drop in pressure in a plane; *if there is an emergency an oxygen mask will automatically drop down in front of you*
2 *verb*

to cover up or to hide; *she masked her face with her scarf*; *too much curry will mask the flavour of the other spices*

② **mass**
[mæs]
1 *noun*
(a) large number or large quantity of things; *masses of people went to the exhibition*; *a mass of leaves blew onto the pavement*; *I have a mass of letters or masses of letters to write*
(b) main Catholic religious service; *she's a strict Catholic and goes to mass every week*; **high mass** = mass with full ceremony; **low mass** = mass without much ceremony (NOTE: plural is **masses**)
2 *verb*
to gather in large numbers; *the rebel army is massing on the border*
3 *adjective*
involving a large number of people; *they found a mass grave on the hillside*; *the group is organizing a mass protest to parliament*; **mass media** = communications such as TV, radio or newspapers, which reach a large number of people; *politicians use the mass media to try to influence the way people think*; **mass meeting** = meeting attended by a lot of people; *the union has called a mass meeting of all workers*; **mass murderer** = killer of a large number of people at one time

④ **massacre**
['mæsɪkɪ]
1 *noun*
killing of a large number of people or animals; *witnesses to the massacre led reporters to a mass grave in the hillside*
2 *verb*
to kill many people or animals; *the soldiers massacred hundreds of innocent civilians*

④ **massage**
['mæsɑːʒ]
1 *noun*
rubbing of the body to relieve pain or to get someone to relax; *she gave me a massage*; *I like to indulge in a hot bath and massage once in a while*
2 *verb*
to rub someone's body to relieve pain or to get them to relax; *he asked the nurse to massage his back*

② **massive**
['mæsɪv] *adjective*
very large; *he had a massive heart attack*; *the company has massive losses*; *a massive rock came rolling down the mountain towards the climbers*

④ **master**
['mɑːstɪ]
1 *noun*
(a) man who teaches in a school; *Mr Smith is the maths master*

(b) person in control of a ship; *the ship's doctor asked the master to radio for a helicopter*
(c) skilled person; *a master potter*; *he's a master of disguise*; **an old master** = painting by a great painter of the past; *the collection of old masters in the National Gallery is priceless*
2 *adjective*
(a) controlling; *details of the master plan are known to only a few people*; **master disk** = main disk from which copies are made; *keep the master disk in a safe place*; **master key** = main key; *the director has a master key which opens all the doors in the building*; **master switch** = switch which controls all other switches; *the burglars turned off the master switch and all the lights went out*
(b) master bedroom = main bedroom in a house; *the master bedroom has a bathroom attached*
3 *verb*
to become skilled at something; *she has mastered the art of reading the news on TV*; *although he passed his driving test some time ago, he still hasn't mastered motorway driving*

④ **masterpiece**
['mɑːstpiːs] *noun*
very fine painting, book, piece of music, etc.; *some people think that 'War and Peace' is a masterpiece, but others think it's much too long*; *the 'Mona Lisa' is a masterpiece, but what about Warhol's picture of Marilyn Monroe?*

④ **mat**
[mæt] *noun*
(a) small piece of carpet, etc., used as a floor covering; *wipe your shoes on the mat before you come in*; **bath mat** = small carpet to step on to when getting out of a bath
(b) place mat = small piece of cloth, wood, etc., put under a plate on a table; *the table was laid with glasses, knives and forks, and place mats*; *she placed little cork mats on the table to stop the wine glasses marking it*

② **match**
[mætʃ]
1 *noun*
(a) game between two teams, etc.; *we watched the football match on TV*; *he won the last two table tennis matches he played*; *see also* TEST MATCH
(b) small piece of wood or cardboard with a tip which catches fire when you rub it against a rough surface; *he bought a packet of cigarettes and a box of matches*; *she struck a match and lit a candle*
(c) thing or person which is equal; *she's met her match* = she has met someone who is as strong, powerful, etc., as she is
(d) thing which goes together with another; **they make a good match** = they go well together
(NOTE: plural is **matches**)
2 *verb*
(a) to be equal to; *our sales match those of our rivals in the export market*

(b) to fit or to go with; *the yellow wallpaper doesn't match the bright green carpet*

① **matching**
['mætʃɪŋ] *adjective*
which fits or goes with something; *she wore a long bright yellow coat with matching hat and shoes*

① **mate**
[meɪt]
1 *noun*
(a) one of a pair of people or animals, male or female, husband or wife; *some birds sing and others show off their feathers to attract a mate*
(b) *(informal)* friend, companion; *he's gone down to the pub with his mates*; **running mate** = person who stands for election as number two to the main candidate; *if the candidate for president wins, then his running mate becomes vice-president*
(c) *(informal) (way of addressing someone)* hey mate, come and look at this!; *sorry, mate, I can't help you!*
(d) *(in the merchant navy)* **first mate** = second officer after the captain
(e) *(in chess)* position where the king cannot move, and the game ends; *mate in three moves!*
2 *verb*
(a) *(of animals)* to breed; *the zoo staff are hoping the old bear will mate with the new female*
(b) *(in chess)* to put your opponent's king in a position where he cannot move

① **material**
[mɪ'tɪərɪəl]
1 *noun*
(a) substance which can be used to make something; *you can buy all the materials you need in the DIY shop*; **building materials** = cement, wood, bricks, etc.; *the bill for building materials alone came to over £2000*; **raw materials** = materials like wool or iron which have not been made into anything; *the country exports raw materials such as copper, and imports finished products*
(b) cloth; *I bought three metres of material to make a curtain*; *what material is your coat made of?*
(c) facts, information; *she's gathering material for a TV programme on drugs* (NOTE: no plural in meanings (b) and (c))
2 *adjective*
(a) referring to physical things or to money; *the explosion caused a lot of material damage*; *his success on TV has improved his material life*
(b) important or relevant; *if you have any material evidence please contact the police*

① **math**
['mæθ] *US see* MATHS

① **mathematics** *or* **maths** *US* **math**
[mæθɪˈmætɪks *or* mæθs *or* mæθ] *noun*
science of numbers and measurements; *I'm taking a course in mathematics*; *he passed in maths, but failed in English*

① **matter**
[ˈmætɪ]
1 *noun*
(a) problem, difficulty; *what's the matter?*; **there's something the matter with the engine** = there is something which makes the engine not work properly
(b) concern, business; **it's a matter for the police** = it is something which we should tell the police about
(c) as a matter of fact = to tell you the truth; *I know Paris quite well, as a matter of fact I go there every month on business*; **as a matter of course** = in the usual way; *the police checked his driving licence as a matter of course*
(d) material; *we put rotting vegetable matter on the garden as fertilizer*
(e) no matter what = whatever; *no matter what time it is, call the doctor immediately the symptoms appear*; **no matter how** = however; *no matter how hard he tried he couldn't ride a bike*
2 *verb*
to be important; *it doesn't matter if you're late*; *his job matters a lot to him*; *does it matter if we sit by the window?*

④ **mattress**
[ˈmætrɪs] *noun*
thick pad forming the part of a bed that you lie on; *those who didn't have beds slept on mattresses on the floor*; *the children jumped up and down on our mattress and ruined it*; **sprung mattress** = mattress with springs inside (NOTE: plural is **mattresses**)

④ **mature**
[mɪˈtjʊɪ]
1 *adjective*
(a) older, adult; *the park has many mature trees*; **mature student** = student who is older than the usual age for students; *the college is trying to encourage more mature students to take courses*
(b) ripe; *mature cheese is normally quite strong*
(c) which is reasonable, like an adult; *she's very mature for her age*; *that's not a very mature way to behave*
2 *verb*
(a) to become mature; *whisky is left to mature for years*; *he matured a lot during his year in Germany*; *girls are supposed to mature faster than boys*
(b) to become due for payment; *the policy will mature in 20 years' time*

④ **maturity**
[mɪˈtjʊrɪti] *noun*
(a) state of being an adult, or of doing things like an adult; *he's only twelve, yet his painting already shows signs of considerable maturity*

(b) time when a bond becomes due to be paid; *the bonds have reached maturity*; **maturity date** = date when an insurance policy matures (NOTE: no plural)

② **maximum**
[ˈmæksɪmɪm]
1 *adjective*
largest possible; *what is the maximum number of guests the hotel can take?*
2 *noun*
the greatest possible number or amount; *the management is aiming to increase profits to the maximum*; **fifteen at the maximum** = at most fifteen, not more than fifteen (NOTE: plural is **maximums** *or* **maxima**)

① **May**
[meɪ] *noun*
fifth month of the year, after April and before June; *her birthday's in May*; *today is May 15th US May 15*; *we went on holiday last May* (NOTE: **May 15th** *or* **May 15**: say 'the fifteenth of May' or 'May the fifteenth'; American English: 'May fifteenth')

① **may**
[meɪ] *verb used with other verbs*
(a) *(to mean it is possible)* *if you don't hurry you may miss the train*; *take your umbrella, they say it may rain this afternoon*; *here we are sitting in the bar, and he may be waiting for us outside*
(b) *(to mean 'can', 'it is allowed')* *guests may park in the hotel car park free of charge*; *you may sit down if you want*
(c) *(asking questions politely)* *may I ask you a question?*; *may we have breakfast early tomorrow as we need to leave the hotel before 8 o'clock?* (NOTE: present: **I may, you may, he may, we may, they may.** Note also that **may** is always used with other verbs and is not followed by **to**)

① **maybe**
[ˈmeɪbiː] *adverb*
possibly, perhaps; *maybe the next bus will be the one we want*; *maybe you should ask a policeman*; *maybe the weather forecast was right after all*; **maybe not** = possibly not; *are you coming? - maybe not*

④ **mayor**
[ˈmeɪ] *noun*
person who is chosen as the official head of a town, city or local council; *the new leisure centre was opened by the mayor*; *after his election, the mayor led the procession to a reception in the town hall*; **Lord Mayor** = Mayor of a very large town (such as London, Liverpool); *the Lord Mayor of London*

COMMENT: previously, a mayor was the head of the elected government of a town, and the head of the majority party. His responsibilities have now been taken over by the leader of the council, and the office of mayor is largely ceremonial. It is an honour often given to a distinguished councillor. However, in the case of London, the mayor is elected by popular vote. In the USA, mayors are all elected by popular vote, and appoint their team to run the various departments in a city. Note also that 'Mayor' is used in English to apply to persons holding similar positions in other countries: **the Mayor of Berlin; the Mayor of Paris**

③ **MD**
['em 'di:]
= MANAGING DIRECTOR director who is in charge of a whole company; *the MD's office is on the first floor*; *she was appointed MD of a property company*

① **me**
[mi:] *object pronoun used by the person who is speaking to talk about himself or herself*; *give me that book*; *I'm shouting as loud as I can - can't you hear me?*; *she's much taller than me*; *who is it? - it's me!*

② **meal**
[mi:l] *noun*
(a) occasion when people eat food at a special time; *most people have three meals a day - breakfast, lunch and dinner*; *you sleep better if you only eat a light meal in the evening*; *when they had finished their evening meal they watched TV*; *you can have your meals in your room at a small extra charge*; *(informal)* to **make a meal of something** = to spend a lot of time and effort doing something without really doing it well; *she made a meal of painting the kitchen*
(b) **meals on wheels** = municipal service providing hot meals for old or disabled people in their own homes

① **mean**
[mi:n]
1 *adjective*
(a) nasty or unpleasant; *he played a mean trick on his mother*; *that was a mean thing to say*
(b) not liking to spend money or to give something; *don't be mean - let me borrow your car*; *she's very mean with her money*
(c) average; *the mean temperature in summer is 20°*
(d) *(informal)* good; *he cooks a mean chicken curry*; *that motorbike's a mean machine!* (NOTE: **meaner - meanest**)
2 *noun*
middle or average figure; *sales are higher than the mean for the first quarter*
3 *verb*
(a) to talk about, to refer to; *did he mean me when he was talking about fat old men?*; *what do you mean when you when you say she's old-fashioned?*

(b) to show, to represent; *when a red light comes on it means that you have to stop*; *'Zimmer' means 'room' in German*; *what does that sign mean with two people with sticks? - it means that old people may be crossing the road*
(c) to be meant to; *see* MEANT (NOTE: meaning - meant [ment])

① **meaning**
['mi:nɪŋ] *noun*
what something represents; *if you want to find the meaning of the word, look it up in a dictionary*; *the meaning of a red light is pretty clear to me*

② **means**
[mi:nz] *noun*
(a) way of doing something; *is there any means of sending the message to London this afternoon?*; *do we have any means of copying all these documents quickly?*; *the bus is the cheapest means of getting round the town*
(b) **by all means** = of course; *by all means use my phone if you want to*; **by no means** = not at all; *she's by no means sure of getting the job*
(c) money; *they don't have the means to buy another shop*; **it is beyond my means** = I don't have enough money to buy it; **means test** = inquiry to find out how much money someone has, to see whether he or she should qualify for a benefit or grant

③ **meant**
[ment] *verb*
to be meant to = should, ought to; *we're meant to be at the station at 11 o'clock*; *this medicine is not meant to be used by children*; *trains are meant to leave every half hour*; *see also* MEAN

② **meantime**
['mi:ntaɪm]
1 *noun*
in the meantime = meanwhile, during this time; *we waited for her for hours in the rain, and in the meantime, she was happily sitting at home watching TV*; *the new stadium will be finished by Easter but in the meantime matches are still being played in the old one*
2 *adverb*
during this time; *the little girl hid under the table - meantime, we were all looking for her in the garden*

② **meanwhile**
['mi:nwaɪl] *adverb*
during this time; *she hid under the table - meanwhile, the sound of boots on the stairs was coming nearer*

④ **measles**
['mi:zlz] *noun*
children's disease which gives a red rash and a high temperature; *one of our children has got measles*; *children can have injections against measles*; **German measles** = usually mild disease which gives a red rash but which can affect the baby if caught by a pregnant woman

measure
['meʒ1]

1 *noun*

(a) certain amount or size; *there was a measure of truth in what she said*; *we have no accurate measure of the pressure inside the volcano*; **made to measure** = made specially to fit; *he only wears made-to-measure suits*; **short measure** = less than the correct amount; *the pub was fined for serving short measures*

(b) thing which shows the size or quantity of something; **tape measure** = long strip of plastic marked in centimetres or inches, etc., used for measuring; *he took out a tape measure and measured the length of the table*

(c) action; *the government has taken measures to reform the welfare system*; *what measures are you planning to fight air pollution?*

(d) type of action, especially a law passed by Parliament; *a new government measure to combat crime*

2 *verb*

(a) to be of a certain size, length, quantity, etc.; *how much do you measure round your waist?*; *the table measures four foot long by three foot wide*; *a package which measures or a package measuring 10cm by 25cm*

(b) to find out the length or quantity of something; *she measured the window for curtains*; *he measured the size of the garden*; **measuring tape** = TAPE MEASURE

(c) **to measure your length on the floor** = to fall flat on your face

measurement
['meʒ1mint] *noun*

(a) quantity or size, etc., found out when you measure; *he took the measurements of the room*; *the piano won't go through the door - are you sure you took the right measurements?*; *the measurements of the box are 25cm x 20cm x 5cm*

(b) the action of measuring; *the measurement of pollution levels is being carried out by satellites*

meat
[mi:t] *noun*

food from an animal; *can I have some more meat, please?*; *would you like meat or fish for your main course?*; *I like my meat very well cooked* (NOTE: no plural: **some meat, a piece** *or* **a slice of meat**)

COMMENT: the names of different types of meat are different from the names of the animal from which they come. Fully grown cows give 'beef'; young cows give 'veal'; pigs give 'pork', or if salted, 'bacon' and 'ham'. Only lambs and birds (chicken, duck, turkey, etc.), give meat with the same name as the animal

mechanic
[mɪ'kænɪk] *noun*

person who works on engines; *the mechanics managed to repair the engine and we went on with the race*

mechanical
[me'kænɪkl] *adjective*

referring to a machine; *engineers are trying to fix a mechanical fault*

mechanism
['mekɪnɪzm] *noun*

(a) working parts of a machine; *if you take the back off the watch you can see the delicate mechanism inside*

(b) way in which something works; *the mechanism for awarding government contracts*

medal
['medl] *noun*

metal disc, usually attached to a ribbon, made to remember an important occasion or battle, and given to people who have performed well; *the old soldiers put on all their medals for the parade*; **gold medal** *or* **silver medal** *or* **bronze medal** = medal for first, second, third place in sporting competitions; *she won a silver medal at the 96 Olympics*

media
['mi:dɪ1] *noun*

(a) **the (mass) media** = means of passing information to a large number of people, such as newspapers, TV, radio; *the book attracted a lot of interest in the media or a lot of media interest*

(b) *see also* MEDIUM

mediate
['mi:dɪeɪt] *verb*

to intervene to try to make two opponents agree; *he was asked to mediate between the two sides*; *I don't want to get involved in mediating between the manager and his staff*

medical
['medɪkl]

1 *adjective*

referring to medicine; *she's a medical student*; *the Red Cross provided medical help*; **medical certificate** = document signed by a doctor to show that a worker has been ill; **medical insurance** = insurance which pays the cost of treatment by a doctor, surgeon, etc.

2 *noun*

(informal) examination of someone by a doctor; *you need to pass a medical to join the army*; *after a routine medical, the new forward will be ready to play on Saturday*

medication
[meɪ'keɪʃn] *noun*

(a) drugs taken by a patient; *are you taking any medication?*

(b) treatment by giving drugs; *the doctor prescribed a course of medication*

② **medicine**
['medsɪn] *noun*
(a) drug taken to treat a disease; *if you have a cough you should take some cough medicine*; *the chemist told me to take the medicine four times a day*; *some cough medicines make you feel sleepy*; *(informal)* **to have a taste of your own medicine** = to be treated in the same way as you have treated others; *he made us fill in all those forms, let's give him a taste of his own medicine*
(b) study of diseases and how to cure or prevent them; *he went to university to study medicine* (NOTE: no plural in this meaning)

③ **medieval**
[medɪ'iːvl] *adjective*
referring to the Middle Ages; *the ruins of a medieval castle stand high above the town*

④ **Mediterranean**
[medɪtɪ'reɪniɪn]
1 *noun*
the Mediterranean (Sea) = the sea between Europe and Africa; *we went for a cruise round the Mediterranean*
2 *adjective*
referring to the Mediterranean Sea; *the Mediterranean climate is good for olives*; *she has bought a villa on one of the Mediterranean islands*

③ **medium**
['miːdiɪm]
1 *adjective*
(a) middle, average; *he is of medium height*
(b) **medium wave** = radio frequency range between 200 and 1000 metres; *the BBC's medium wave broadcasts*
2 *noun*
(a) middle point; **happy medium** = compromise; *finding a happy medium between the demands of work and the family is not easy*
(b) type of paint or other materials used by an artist; *he started to experiment with different mediums, such as poster paints*
(c) means of doing something, of communicating something; *television is the most popular medium of communication*; *deaf people can communicate through the medium of sign language* (NOTE: plural is **media** or **mediums)**

① **meet**
[miːt] *verb*
(a) to come together with someone; *he met her at the railway station*; *we'll meet for lunch before we go to the cinema*; *if you don't know how to get to our office, I'll meet you at the bus stop*
(b) to come together; *several streets meet at Piccadilly Circus*; *if you draw a line from each corner of a square to the opposite corner, the two lines will meet in the centre*
(c) to get to know someone; *I've never met your sister - come and meet her then!*; *have you met our sales manager?*; *yes, we have already met*

(d) to pay for; *the company will meet your expenses*; *he was unable to meet his mortgage repayments*
(e) to be suitable for; *does the car now meet the standards set by the motor racing authorities?* (NOTE: **meeting - met** [met])

① **meeting**
['miːtɪŋ] *noun*
(a) action of coming together in a group; *the next meeting of the club will be on Tuesday*; *there were only four people at the committee meeting*; **to address a meeting** = to speak to a meeting; **to conduct a meeting** = to be chairman of a meeting; *as he was going away on business, he asked his deputy to conduct the meeting*; **to close a meeting** = to end a meeting; **to hold a meeting** = to organize a meeting of a group of people; *the meeting will be held in the committee room*; **to open a meeting** = to start a meeting
(b) sports competition or series of horse races held over several days; *Britain won a gold and three bronzes at the sports meeting*

③ **meet up**
['miːt 'ʌp] *verb*
(of several people) to come together; *we all met up in the local restaurant*

③ **meet with**
['miːt 'wɪθ] *verb*
(a) to find, to come up against (a problem); to have (an accident); *the advancing soldiers met with stiff resistance*; *she met with an accident in the lift*
(b) *(usually US)* to meet someone; *he met with the sales people in New York*

④ **melody**
['melɪdɪ] *noun*
tune; *the melody of the song is easy to remember*; *according to grandfather the old Victorian melodies are still the best* (NOTE: plural is **melodies)**

③ **melon**
['melɪn] *noun*
large round fruit which grows on a low plant; *we had melon and ham as a starter*; **water melon** = very large type of melon with red flesh and black seeds; *she cut the water melon into slices*; *they sat in the shade eating slices of water melon*

③ **melt**
[melt] *verb*
to change from solid to liquid by heating; *if the sun comes out the ice will start to melt*; *the heat of the sun made the road melt*; *at very high temperatures glass will melt*

① **member**
['membɪ] *noun*
(a) person who belongs to a group; *the two boys went swimming while the other members of the family sat on the beach*; *three members of staff are away sick*

(b) organization which belongs to a society; *the member states of the EU; the members of the United Nations*

② **membership**
['membɪʃɪp] *noun*
(a) belonging to a group; *I must remember to renew my membership; membership costs £50 a year;* **membership card** = card which shows you belong to a club or to a political party; *bring your membership card with you*
(b) all the members of a group; *the membership voted to reject the proposal; the club has a membership of five hundred*

③ **memo**
['memɪʊ] *noun*
note or short message between people working in the same organization; *did you see the memo from head office?; he sent a memo to all heads of department;* **memo pad** = pad of paper for writing short notes; *he wrote the number down on a memo pad* (NOTE: plural is **memos**)

④ **memorable**
['memrɪbl] *adjective*
which you cannot forget easily; *we didn't have a very memorable holiday as it rained all the time; I can still remember that memorable afternoon in 1977 when his horse won the gold cup*

④ **memorial**
[mɪ'mɔːrɪil]
1 *adjective*
which reminds you of something *or* someone; **memorial service** = church service to remember someone who has died
2 *noun*
monument to remind you of something *or* someone; *the mayor unveiled the memorial to the dead poet;* **war memorial** = monument to soldiers who died in a war; *on 11th November a ceremony is held at the local war memorial*

① **memory**
['memri] *noun*
(a) *(in people)* being able to remember; *he repeated the poem from memory;* **if my memory serves me right** = if I can remember it correctly; *see also* PHOTOGRAPHIC
(b) *(in computers)* capacity for storing information; *this computer has a much larger memory than the old one*
(c) **memories** = things which you remember; *we have many happy memories of our holidays in Greece;* **in memory of** = to remind you of; *we are holding this church service in memory of the sailors who died* (NOTE: the plural, only in this meaning, is **memories**)

③ **men**
[men]
see MAN; **men's toilet** *(especially US)* **men's room** = public lavatory for men

③ **mend**
[mend]
1 *verb*

to make something which has a fault work again; to repair something which is broken or damaged; *I dropped my watch on the pavement, and I don't think it can be mended; she's trying to mend the washing machine; I tore my coat on the fence - can you mend it for me?*
2 *noun*
on the mend = getting better; *she has been quite ill, but I'm glad to say she's on the mend now*

① **menswear**
['menzweɪ] *noun*
clothes for men; *the menswear department is on the first floor* (NOTE: no plural)

② **mental**
['mentl] *adjective*
(a) referring to the mind; **mental age** = method of showing a person's mental development by giving the age when such a stage of development is normally reached; *she is 19 with a mental age of 8;* **mental cruelty** = being cruel to someone by what you say, rather than by what you do; **mental illness** = illness which affects the mind
(b) **mental hospital** = hospital for patients with mental illnesses

④ **mentality**
[men'tælɪti] *noun*
way of thinking which is typical of someone or of a group; *I don't understand the mentality of people who are cruel to animals; see also* SIEGE

① **mention**
['mentʃɪn]
1 *noun*
act of referring to something; *there was no mention of the explosion in the morning papers; just the mention of his name made her furious*
2 *verb*
(a) to refer to something; *the press has not mentioned the accident; can you mention to the secretary that the date of the next meeting has been changed?*
(b) **not to mention** = as well as, not forgetting; *it cost us £20 just to get into the exhibition, not to mention the expensive meal we had in the museum restaurant*

③ **menu**
['menjuː] *noun*
(a) list of food available in a restaurant; *what's on the menu today?; the lunch menu changes every week; some dishes are not on the menu, but are written on a blackboard*
(b) list of options available on a computer program; **menu bar** = series of little pictures on a computer screen which are the options you can choose; **pull-down menu** = menu which appears as a list on part of the screen; *the pull-down menu is displayed by clicking on the menu bar at the top of the screen*

③ **merchandise**
['mɜːtʃɪndaɪs] *noun*
goods for sale; *we have a wide range of merchandise for sale* (NOTE: no plural)

③ **merchandize**
['mɜːtʃɪndaɪz] *verb*
to sell goods by a wide variety of means; *her children's books make more money through merchandizing than through sales in bookshops*

④ **merchant**
['mɜːtʃɪnt] *noun*
(a) businessman; person who buys and sells a particular product; *a tobacco merchant; a wine merchant*
(b) merchant bank = bank which lends money to companies, not to people; **merchant navy** *or* **merchant marine** = a country's commercial ships; *at sixteen he ran away from school to join the merchant navy;* **merchant seaman** = seaman on a commercial ship; **merchant ship** = commercial ship; *he's serving on a merchant ship running between the Caribbean and Europe*

④ **mercy**
['mɜːsɪ] *noun*
(a) kindness towards unfortunate people; *the parents of the little boy pleaded for mercy with the gang who had kidnapped him;* **to have mercy on** = not to want to punish or harm someone; **mercy killing** = killing of someone who is very ill, in pain, and not likely to get better
(b) gift of fate; **at the mercy of** = which depends entirely on; *the success of the flower show is very much at the mercy of the weather;* **we must be thankful for small mercies** = we must be grateful that everything has turned out relatively well so far; *despite lots of things going wrong, at least it didn't rain - we must be thankful for small mercies;* **left to the tender mercies of someone** = left to someone to deal with as he likes; *the tour guide went back to the hotel, leaving us to the tender mercies of the local taxi drivers*

③ **mere**
['mɪɪ] *adjective*
simply, only; *the merest hint of garlic makes her ill; she could feel the merest breath of wind on her face;* **he's a mere boy** = he's only a boy; **the mere sight of grass makes me sneeze** = simply seeing grass makes me sneeze (NOTE: superlative is **merest**)

② **merely**
['mɪɪlɪ] *adverb*
simply, only; *I'm not criticizing you - I merely said I would have done it in a different way*

④ **merge**
[mɜːdʒ] *verb*
to join together with something; *the two motorways merge here; the firm has merged with its main competitor*

④ **merger**
['mɜːdʒɪ] *noun*
joining together of two companies; *he has a proposed a merger between his manufacturing company and our retail company; as a result of the merger, the company is the largest in the field*

③ **merit**
['merɪt]
1 *noun*
being good, or excellent; *there is some merit in what he says, but I can't agree with all of it; this film has no merit whatsoever;* **to go into the merits of** = to examine the good and bad points of; *the committee spent hours going into the merits of the various development plans;* **merit bonus** = extra pay given because of good work
2 *verb*
to be worthy of or to deserve something; *the plan merits further discussion; her essay only merited a 'B+'*

④ **merry**
['merɪ] *adjective*
happy and cheerful; *to wish somebody a Merry Christmas;* **the more the merrier** = the more there are the happier everyone is; *invite anyone you like, the more the merrier!* (NOTE: **merrier - merriest**)

③ **mess**
[mes] *noun*
(a) dirt or disorder; *the milk boiled over and made a mess on the floor; we had to clear up the mess after the party*
(b) to make a mess of something = to do something badly; *they made a mess of the repair job*
2 *verb*
see MESS ABOUT, MESS UP

③ **mess about**
['mes ə'baʊt] *verb*
(a) *(informal)* to spend your spare time doing something without having planned what to do; *he spends his weekends messing about in the garden*
(b) *(informal)* **to mess someone about** = to treat someone badly; *if you start messing me about, there'll be trouble; the garage has messed me about so much I'm going to take my car somewhere else for servicing*

① **message**
['mesɪdʒ] *noun*
(a) information which is sent; *I will leave a message with his secretary; can you give the director a message from his wife?; we got his message by email;* **message board** = board on which messages can be left for anyone to see (such as at a conference, or in a hotel lobby)
(b) political or religious idea which a group is trying to pass on to the public; *their message is one of universal peace; his message of hard work and simple living did not always attract the voters*

(c) *(informal)* to get the message = to understand; *she finally got the message when he stood up and handed her her coat*; to get the message across to someone = to make someone understand something; *we managed to get the message across, even though no one spoke English*

③ **mess around**
['mes ə'raʊnd] = MESS ABOUT

③ **mess up**
['mes ʌp] *verb*
(informal)
(a) to make dirty; *you've messed up your brand new shoes!*
(b) to ruin or to spoil; *I'm sorry we can't come - I hope it doesn't mess up your arrangements*

③ **messy**
['mesi] *adjective*
(a) dirty; *painting a ceiling is a messy business*; *little children are always messy*
(b) unpleasant and full of problems; *it was a long messy divorce case* (NOTE: **messier - messiest**)

③ **met**
[met] *see* MEET

④ **Met**
[ði 'met] *see* METROPOLITAN POLICE

② **metal**
['metl] *noun*
material, such as iron, copper, etc., which can carry heat and electricity and is used for making things; *a metal frying pan*; *these spoons are plastic but the knives are metal*; *these chairs are very heavy - they must be made of metal*

④ **metaphor**
['metɪfɪ] *noun*
way of describing something by giving it the qualities of something else, as in 'our hawk-eyed readers soon spotted the mistake'; *he uses an ant's nest as a metaphor for the centre of town on a busy market day*

③ **meter**
['miːtɪ]
1 *noun*
(a) device for counting how much time, water, gas, etc., has been used; *he came to read the gas meter*; **parking meter** = device into which you put money to pay for parking for a certain time
(b) *US* = METRE
2 *verb*
to measure with a meter; *the quantity of water used is metered by the water company*

① **method**
['meθɪd] *noun*
way of doing something; *we use the most up-to-date manufacturing methods*; *what is the best method of payment?*

② **metre** *US* **meter**
['miːtɪ] *noun*
(a) standard measurement of length (approximately 39.4 inches); *the room is about three metres square*; *the river is 50 metres across*; *the table is more than two metres long*; *the walls are two metres thick*; **ten square metres** = area of 5 metres x 2 metres (NOTE: **ten square metres** is usually written **10 msup2**)
(b) race over a certain distance; *he holds the world record for the 1000 metres*

④ **metric**
['metrɪk] *adjective*
using the metre as a basic measurement; **the metric system** = system of measuring, using metres, litres and grams

> COMMENT: the metric system is a decimal system, using various basic units multiplied or divided by hundreds, thousands, etc. The basic measurements are: **length:** metre; **weight:** gram; **area:** are (= 10 square metres); **capacity:** litre. Each of these basic units can be divided into hundredths (prefix centi-) or thousandths (prefix milli-), or can be multiplied by one thousand (prefix kilo-). So the basic measurements of length are: millimetre, centimetre, metre and kilometre, and of weight: milligram, gram, kilogram

④ **metropolitan**
[metrɪ'pɒlɪtɪn] *adjective*
(a) referring to a large capital city; *she spent her childhood in a little village and found it difficult to get used to the metropolitan crowds of central London*
(b) the **Metropolitan Police** = the police force of Greater London (NOTE: also in informal speech called **the Met**)

④ **Mexican**
['meksɪkɪn]
1 *adjective*
referring to Mexico; *Mexican cooking is hot and spicy*; *the Mexican football team looks like winning*; *have you seen the photos from our Mexican holiday?*; **Mexican wave** = action at a football game or big meeting, when spectators stand up in turn, wave their arms, and then sit down again, giving the impression that a wave is running through the crowd
2 *noun*
person from Mexico; *many Mexicans have emigrated to California*

④ **Mexico**
['meksɪkʊ] *noun*
large country in Latin America, south of the United States; *there is a long border between the USA and Mexico* (NOTE: capital: **Mexico City**; people: **Mexicans**; language: **Spanish**; currency: **Mexican peso**)

③ **mice**
[maɪs] *see* MOUSE

④ **microchip**
['maɪkrɪʊtʃɪp] *noun*
very small piece of a chemical substance with printed circuits on it; *smart cards have microchips on them*

① **microphone**

['maɪkrɪfɪʊn] *noun*

(a) device which you speak into to send sound through the radio or TV, or to record on disk or tape; *he had difficulty in making himself heard without a microphone*

(b) device for capturing sound and passing it to a secret listening device; *there was a microphone hidden in the bedside light*

④ **microscope**

['maɪkrɪskɪʊp] *noun*

instrument with lenses which makes things which are very small appear much larger; *he examined the blood sample under the microscope*

④ **microwave**

['maɪkrɪweɪv]

1 *noun*

small oven which cooks very rapidly using very short electric waves; *put the dish in the microwave for three minutes*

2 *verb*

to cook something in a microwave; *you can microwave those potatoes*

① **middle**

['mɪdl]

1 *adjective*

in the centre; halfway between two ends; *they live in the middle house of the row, the one with the green door*

2 *noun*

(a) centre; *she was standing in the middle of the road, trying to cross*; *Chad is a country in the middle of Africa*

(b) *(referring to time)* halfway through a period; *we were woken in the middle of the night by a dog barking*; *we were just in the middle of eating our supper when they called*; *his mobile rang in the middle of the meeting*; *the house was built in the middle of the eighteenth century*

(c) waist; *it's quite deep - the water comes up to my middle*; *how much does he measure round his middle?*

③ **middle-aged**

[mɪdl'eɪdʒd] *adjective*

no longer very young, but not very old (between 40 and 60 years old); *her brother is much older than she is, he's quite middle-aged*; *there were two middle-aged women in the seats next to ours*

③ **the Middle Ages**

[ðɪ 'mɪdl 'eɪdʒɪz] *noun*

historical period from about 1000 to 1500 AD; *parts of the castle date back to the Middle Ages* (NOTE: the adjective from **Middle Ages** is **medieval**)

① **middle class**

['mɪdl 'klɑːs] *noun*

professional class between the upper class and the lower or working class; *as people become more wealthy, so the middle class expands*; *they live in a middle-class suburb*

① **Middle East**

['mɪdl 'iːst] *noun*

area between Egypt and Pakistan; *tensions are running high in the Middle East*; *the USA has made peace in the Middle East one of its top priorities*

③ **midnight**

['mɪdnaɪt] *noun*

twelve o'clock at night; *I must go to bed - it's after midnight*; *we only reached the hotel at midnight*

① **might**

[maɪt]

1 *noun*

(formal) force; *she pulled at it with all her might, and still could not move it*; *all the might of the armed forces is displayed during the National Day parade*

2 *verb used with other verbs*

(a) *(to mean it is possible)* take an umbrella, it might rain; *if he isn't here, he might be waiting outside*; *I might call in to see you tomorrow if I have time*; *that was a stupid thing to do - you might have been killed!*; *they might win, but I wouldn't bet on it*

(b) *(to mean something should have been)* you might try and stay awake next time; he might have done something to help = it would have been better if he had done something to help; you might have told me = I wish you had told me; *you might have told me you'd invited her as well*

(c) *(asking a question politely)* might I have another cup of tea? (NOTE: negative: **might not** is usually **mightn't**. Note also that **might** is always used with other verbs and is not followed by **to**)

④ **mighty**

['maɪti]

1 *adjective*

strong, powerful; *with one mighty swing he lifted the sack onto the lorry*; *all she could remember was getting a mighty blow on the head, and then everything went black* (NOTE: **mightier - mightiest**)

2 *adverb*

great; *that's mighty kind of you*; *(informal)* he's in a mighty hurry = he's very impatient

④ **migrant**

['maɪgrɪnt]

1 *noun*

(a) worker who moves from one job to another or from one country to another to look for work; *the government is trying to prevent migrants coming into the country*; economic migrant = person who moves to live in another country where living conditions are better

(b) bird which moves from one place to another with the seasons; *the marshes are an ideal place to see the winter migrants*
2 *adjective*
who moves from one job to another or from one country to another; *migrant workers often do the jobs no one wants to do*; *migrant farm workers are exploited by rich land owners*

④ **migrate**
[maɪˈɡreɪt] *verb*
to move from one place to another with the seasons; *herds of animals migrate across the desert in search of water*; *the marshes are an ideal place to see migrating geese*

④ **migration**
[maɪˈɡreɪʃn] *noun*
movement of animals and birds from one country to another; *the swallows are starting to gather in groups, ready for their long migration south for the winter*; *we tag birds so that we can study their migration routes*

③ **mild**
[maɪld] *adjective*
(a) not harsh, not too bad; *there was some mild criticism, but generally the plan was welcomed*; *he had a mild heart attack and was soon back to work again*
(b) not severe (weather); *winters in the south of the country are usually milder than in the north*
(c) not strong-tasting; *we'll choose the mildest curry on the menu* (NOTE: in this meaning the opposite is **hot**. Note also: **milder - mildest**)

① **mile**
[maɪl] *noun*
(a) measure of length (= 1,760 yards or 1.61 kilometres); *he thinks nothing of cycling ten miles to work every day*; *the car can't go any faster than sixty miles per hour*; *the line of cars stretched for three miles from the road works*; **the car was doing 100 miles an hour** = was travelling at 100 miles an hour
(b) miles = long distance; *there are no shops for miles around*; *we walked for miles and came back to the point where we started from*
(c) *(informal)* **miles** = a lot of; *she's miles better at swimming now than she was six months ago*; **miles of string** = very long piece of string; **it's miles too big** = it's much too big

④ **militant**
[ˈmɪlɪtnt]
1 *adjective*
very active in supporting a cause or political party; *he is on the militant wing of the party*
2 *noun*
(a) person who is very active in supporting a cause or a political party; *the party must keep its militants under control*
(b) person who supports a policy of using violence to achieve aims; *a few militants in the march started throwing stones at the police*

① **military**
[ˈmɪlɪtri]
1 *adjective*
referring to the armed forces; *the two leaders discussed the possibility of military intervention*; *military spending has fallen over the past three years*; **military service** = period of time served in the armed forces; *in some countries there is still compulsory military service for all young men*
2 *noun*
the military = the army; *faced with riots all over the country, the government called in the military*

① **milk**
[mɪlk]
1 *noun*
white liquid produced by female animals to feed their young, especially the liquid produced by cows; *do you want milk with your coffee?*; *can we have two glasses of milk, please?*; *don't forget to buy some milk, there's none in the fridge*; **milk chocolate** = pale brown chocolate made with milk; *see also* CRY (NOTE: no plural: **some milk, a bottle of milk, a glass of milk**)
2 *verb*
(a) to take milk from an animal; *the cows are waiting to be milked*
(b) *(informal)* to get as much advantage as possible from a situation; *the newspapers milked the story for all it was worth*

③ **mill**
[mɪl] *noun*
(a) small machine for grinding seeds into powder; *there is a pepper mill on the table*
(b) large machine for grinding corn into flour; *corn is fed into the mill through a little door*
(c) building which contains such a machine; *after lunch the visitors were shown round the mill*
(d) *(informal)* **to go through the mill** *or* **to be put through the mill** = (i) to be fully trained; (ii) to suffer a great deal; *her divorce has really put her through the mill*
(e) run-of-the-mill = ordinary; *it's a run-of-the-mill operation which any doctor can do*
(f) large factory; **paper mill** = factory producing paper; **steel mill** = factory producing steel

③ **millimetre** *US* **millimeter**
[ˈmɪlɪmiːtə] *noun*
one thousandth of a metre; *one inch equals roughly 25 millimetres* (NOTE: usually written **mm** after figures: **35mm**)

① **million**
[ˈmɪljən]
(a) number 1,000,000; *the population of Great Britain is just over 58 million*
(b) millions of = a very large number of; *millions of trees are chopped down for paper*; *the country spends millions of dollars on imports of oil*; *millions of people spend their*

holidays in Italy (NOTE: no plural with figures: **sixty million**. With figures, **million** can be written **m**: £2m, $2m: say 'two million pounds, two million dollars')

③ **millionaire**
[mɪljɪ'neɪ] *noun*
person who has more than a million pounds or a million dollars; *if you win the lottery you will become an instant millionaire*; *only a millionaire could afford a yacht like his* (NOTE: to show the currency in which a person is a millionaire, say **a dollar millionaire, a sterling millionaire**, etc.)

① **millionth (1,000,000th)**
['mɪljɪnθ] *adjective & noun*
referring to a million; *a millionth of a second*; *the museum gave a prize to their millionth visitor*

③ **mince**
[mɪns]
1 *noun*
meat which has been ground into very small pieces; *she bought a pound of mince*; *add the mince to the onions and fry till it is brown*
2 *verb*
(a) to grind up meat or vegetables until they are in very small pieces; *a pound of minced beef or of minced lamb*; *hamburgers are made of minced beef* (NOTE: American English for **minced beef** and **mince** is **ground beef**)
(b) he didn't mince his words = he said exactly what he thought; *I didn't mince my words - I told them exactly what I thought of their plan*

① **mind**
[maɪnd]
1 *noun*
part of the body which controls memory and thought; *his mind always seems to be on other things*; *I've forgotten her name - it just slipped my mind*; *I think of her night and day - I just can't get her out of my mind*; *my mind went blank as soon as I saw the exam paper*; **what do you have in mind?** = what are you thinking of?; *let's do something unusual this weekend - what do you have in mind?*; **she's got something on her mind** = she's worrying about something; *she's not her usual happy self today - I think she's got something on her mind*; **let's try to take his mind off his exams** = let's try to stop him worrying about the exams; **state of mind** = general feeling; *she was in a very gloomy state of mind*; **to make up your mind (to do something)** = to decide (to do something); *I can't make up my mind whether to take the afternoon off to do some shopping or stay in the office and work*; *she couldn't make up her mind what clothes to wear to the wedding*; **to change your mind** = to decide to do something different; *he was going to go by car but then changed his mind and went by bus*; *he has decided to go on holiday next week and nothing will make him change his mind*; **to**

be in two minds about something = not to be sure about something, not to have decided yet about something; *I'm in two minds about his proposal*
2 *verb*
(a) to be careful, to watch out; *mind the steps - they're very steep!*; *mind you get back early*; *mind the plate - it's hot!*
(b) to worry about; *don't mind me, I'm used to working with children*; **never mind** = don't worry; *never mind - you'll get another chance to enter the competition next year*
(c) to look after something for someone, or while the owner is away; *who will be minding the house while you're on holiday?*; **mind your own business!** = don't interfere with other people's problems
(d) to be bothered or annoyed by; *nobody will mind if you're late*; *there aren't enough chairs, but I don't mind standing up*
(e) *(asking politely)* *do you mind if I open the window?*
(f) wouldn't mind = would rather like; *I wouldn't mind a cup of coffee*

① **mine**
[maɪn]
1 *pronoun* belonging to me; *that book is mine*; *can I borrow your bike, mine's been stolen*; *she's a great friend of mine*
2 *noun*
(a) deep hole in the ground from which coal, etc., is taken out; *the coal mine has stopped working after fifty years*; *he has shares in an African gold mine*
(b) sort of bomb which is hidden under the ground or under water; *the tank went over a mine and two soldiers were killed*; *it will take years to clear all the mines left by the rebel army*
3 *verb*
(a) to dig coal, etc., out of the ground; *they mine gold in the south of the country*
(b) to place mines in land or water; *the entrance to the harbour has been mined*

④ **miner**
['maɪnɪ] *noun*
person who works in a mine; *twelve miners were trapped when the roof of a coal mine collapsed yesterday* (NOTE: do not confuse with **minor**)

④ **mineral**
['mɪnɪrɪl] *noun*
(a) substance, such as rock, which is dug out of the earth, or which is found in food, etc.; *what is the mineral content of cabbage?*; *the company hopes to discover valuable minerals in the mountains*
(b) mineral water = water from a spring; *pure mineral water was bubbling up out of the ground*; *do you want orange juice or mineral water?*

④ **miniature**
['mɪnɪtʃɪ]
1 *noun*
(a) very small model, portrait, painting, bottle of alcohol, etc.; *we went to an exhibition of Elizabethan miniatures*
(b) in miniature = reproduced on a very small scale; *the Parliament in the colony is like Westminster in miniature*; *in the model village, everything is in miniature*
2 *adjective*
very small; *he has a miniature camera*

④ **minimal**
['mɪnɪmɪl] *adjective*
very low or small, the smallest possible; *there is a minimal charge to cover some of our expenses*; *the cars were moving very slowly when they hit each other, so damage was minimal*

② **minimum**
['mɪnɪmɪm]
1 *adjective*
smallest possible; *the minimum amount you can save is £25 per month*; *the minimum age for drivers is 18*
2 *noun*
smallest possible amount; *we try to keep expenditure to a minimum*; *she does the bare minimum of work, just enough to pass her exams*

④ **mining**
['maɪnɪŋ] *noun*
action of taking coal and other minerals out of the land; *we used a Welsh mining village as a base for climbing in the mountains*; *the company is engaged in mining for diamonds or in diamond mining*

① **minister**
['mɪnɪstɪ]
1 *noun*
member of a government in charge of a department; *the inquiry is to be headed by a former government minister*; *he was the Minister of Defence in the previous government*; **cabinet minister** = minister who is also a member of the cabinet; *see also* PRIME MINISTER (NOTE: in the UK and USA, Ministers are also called **secretaries: the Foreign Secretary, Secretary for Commerce**)
2 *verb*
to minister to someone's needs = to take care of someone; *nurses went to the country to minister to the needs of the refugees*

① **ministry**
['mɪnɪstri] *noun*
(a) government department; offices of a government department; *he works in the Ministry of Defence* (NOTE: plural is **ministries**; in the UK and USA, important ministries are also called **departments: the Department of Trade and Industry; the Commerce Department)**

(b) government; *the Conservative Ministry of 1951* (NOTE: you can also say **administration** in this sense: **the Conservative Administration of 1951**)

② **minor**
['maɪnɪ]
1 *adjective*
(a) not very important; *it was just a minor injury*; *she has a minor role in the film*; *he played a minor part in the revolution*
(b) Asia Minor = Turkey
(c) musical key; *she played a Mozart piece in B minor*; *compare* MAJOR
2 *noun*
young person under the age of 18; *we are forbidden to serve alcohol to minors* (NOTE: do not confuse with **miner**)

② **minority**
[maɪ'nɒrɪti] *noun*
number or quantity which is less than half of a total; *although the proposal was carried, a large minority of members voted against it*; **the men are in the minority** = there are more women than men; **minority government** = government with fewer members of parliament than the opposition; *a minority government can be defeated if all the opposition parties vote together*

④ **mint**
[mɪnt]
1 *noun*
(a) factory where coins are made; *the mint is preparing to make the new coins*; **in mint condition** = perfect, in exactly the same condition as when it was made; *he is offering a camera for sale in mint condition*; *(informal)* **a mint of money** = a great deal of money; *the person who invented the zip must have made a mint of money*
(b) common herb used as flavouring; **mint sauce** = sauce made of chopped mint, served with lamb
(c) small white sweet, tasting of peppermint; *he always keeps a packet of mints in his pocket to suck when travelling*
2 *verb*
to make coins; *British coins are minted by the Royal Mint*

② **minus**
['maɪnɪs]
1 *preposition*
(a) less, take away; *ten minus eight equals two (10 - 8 = 2) net salary is gross salary minus tax and National Insurance deductions*
(b) *(informal)* not with; **luckily they came minus children** = luckily they came without their children
2 *noun*
sign (-) meaning less; *minus 10 degrees (-10°)*

① **minute**

1 ['mɪnɪt] *noun*

(a) one sixtieth part of an hour; *there are sixty minutes in an hour, and sixty seconds in a minute*; *the doctor can see you for ten minutes only*; *if you don't mind waiting, Mr Smith will be free in about twenty minutes' time*; *the house is about ten minutes' walk or is a ten-minute walk from the office*; **six minutes to four** = 3.54; **eight minutes past three** = 3.08; **minute hand** = long hand on a clock or watch which shows the minutes

(b) very short space of time; *I'll be ready in a minute*; *why don't you wait for a minute and see if the dentist is free?*; **I won't be a minute** = I'll be very quick; *I'm just going to pop into the bank - I won't be a minute*; **at any minute** *or* **any minute now** = very soon; *I expect the train to arrive at any minute*

(c) **minutes** = notes taken of what has been said at a meeting; *the secretary will take the minutes of the meeting*; *copies of the minutes of the last meeting will be sent to all members of the committee*

2 ['mɪnɪt] *verb*

to write the record of a meeting; *my objection to the proposal has been minuted*

3 [maɪ'njuːt] *adjective*

very small; *a minute piece of dust must have got into the watch*; **in minute detail** = with all details carefully drawn or explained; *I explained it all to you in the minutest detail, and you still got it wrong* (NOTE: superlative is **minutest**)

④ **miracle**

['mɪrɪkl] *noun*

(a) very lucky happening; *it was a miracle she was not killed in the accident*

(b) marvellous event which happens apparently by the power of God; *she went to the church and was cured - it must have been a miracle*

③ **mirror**

['mɪrɪ]

1 *noun*

piece of glass with a metal backing which reflects an image; *they looked at themselves in the mirror*; **bathroom mirror** = mirror in a bathroom; **driving mirror** *or* **rear-view mirror** = mirror inside a car which allows the driver to see what is behind without turning his head

2 *verb*

to be very similar to; to be the same as; *the report mirrors the information given to the committee by local doctors*; *her astonishment at the news mirrored mine*

④ **miscarriage**

['mɪskærɪdʒ] *noun*

(a) **miscarriage of justice** = wrong decision by a court, which can be changed on appeal; *the papers think there has been a gross miscarriage of justice*

(b) loss of a baby during pregnancy; *she had two miscarriages before having her first child*

④ **miserable**

['mɪzrɪbl] *adjective*

(a) sad, unhappy; *he's in a very miserable state of mind*; *can't you do something to cheer her up? - she's very miserable since her boyfriend left her*

(b) bad or unpleasant (weather); *what miserable weather! will it ever stop raining?*

(c) very low (salary); *she earns a miserable wage as a library assistant*

③ **misery**

['mɪzɪri] *noun*

being very unhappy; *there were terrible scenes of human misery in the refugee camps*; *his life in the home was sheer misery*; **to put someone out of his misery** = not to keep someone waiting any longer, but tell them the result of the exam, etc.; *let's go and put the candidates out of their misery*

④ **misleading**

[mɪs'liːdɪŋ] *adjective*

quite wrong; likely to cause a mistake; *the map he gave us was very misleading*; *she gave misleading information to the press*

① **Miss**

[mɪs] *noun*

(a) title given to a girl or woman who is not married; *have you met Miss Jones, our new sales manager?*; *the letter is addressed to Miss Anne Smith*

(b) way of addressing a teacher; *Miss! John keeps hitting me* (NOTE: with a name, **Miss** can be followed by the surname, or by the Christian name and surname; without a name, **Miss** is used to call a school teacher)

① **miss**

[mɪs]

1 *noun*

not having hit something; *he hit the target twice and then had two misses*; **let's give it a miss** = let's not go to see it; **a near miss** = situation where you almost hit something; *that was a near miss - we missed the other car by inches* (NOTE: plural is **misses**)

2 *verb*

(a) not to hit; *he missed the target*; *she tried to shoot the rabbit but missed*

(b) not to see, hear, notice, etc.; *we missed the road in the dark*; *I missed the article about books in yesterday's evening paper*; *I arrived late, so missed most of the discussion*; **you didn't miss much** = there wasn't much to see, the film, etc., wasn't very good; **he just missed being knocked down** = he was almost knocked down

(c) not to catch; *he tried to catch the ball but he missed it*; *she missed the last bus and had to walk home*

(d) to be sad because you don't do something any more, because someone is not there any more; *do you miss living by the sea?*; *I miss going on those long country walks*; *you'll be missed if you go to work in another office*; *we'll all miss Jack when he retires*

④ **missile**
['mɪsaɪl *US* 'mɪsl] *noun*
(a) rocket with a bomb inside, which can be guided to its target; *they think the plane was brought down by an enemy missile*
(b) thing which is thrown to try to hit someone; *the students threw missiles at the police*

③ **missing**
['mɪsɪŋ] *adjective*
lost, which is not there; *I'm looking for my missing car keys*; *they found there was a lot of money missing*; *the police searched everywhere for the missing children*

③ **mission**
['mɪʃn] *noun*
(a) aim or purpose for which someone is sent; *the students were sent on a mission to find the best place for a picnic*; **her mission in life is to help refugee children** = her chosen task is to help refugee children; **mission statement** = statement which gives the aims of an organization
(b) group of people sent somewhere with a particular aim; *several firms took part in a business mission to Japan*; *a United Nations peace mission*; *a rescue mission was sent out into the mountains*
(c) place where diplomats work, an embassy; *there were riots outside several diplomatic missions in the capital*

③ **miss out**
['mɪs 'aʊt] *verb*
to leave out, to forget to put in; *remember not to miss out the news about the wedding when you're writing to your family*

③ **miss out on**
['mɪs 'aʊt ɒn] *verb*
(informal) not to enjoy something because you are not there; *I missed out on the skiing trip because I had measles*

④ **mist**
[mɪst]
1 *noun*
thin fog; *early morning mist covered the fields*
2 *verb*
to mist up = to become covered with a fine layer of drops of water; *the steam in the bathroom had misted up the mirror*; *switch on the heating for the rear window to stop it misting up*

② **mistake**
[mɪs'teɪk]
1 *noun*
act or thought which is wrong; *she made a mistake in typing the address*; *there are lots of mistakes in this book*; **by mistake** = wrongly; *they sent the wrong items by mistake*; *by*

mistake she put my letter into an envelope for the chairman; *we took the wrong bus by mistake*
2 *verb*
to think wrongly; **I mistook him for his brother** = I thought he was his brother; *he is mistaken in thinking I am your brother*; *there's no mistaking him, with his red hair and purple tie* (NOTE: **mistakes - mistaking - mistook** [mɪs'tʊk] **- has mistaken** [mɪs'teɪkɪn])

② **mistaken**
[mɪs'teɪkɪn] *adjective*
wrong; *I am afraid you are mistaken - I was in Edinburgh on that date*; *it must be a case of mistaken identity - it can't have been me she saw because I wasn't there*; *unless I am very much mistaken, that's an owl up there on top of the tree*; *if I'm not mistaken, Dr James is your brother*

③ **mistook**
[mɪs'tʊk] *see* MISTAKE

④ **mistress**
['mɪstrɪs] *noun*
(a) woman who has a sexual relationship with a man without being married to him; *she had engaged a detective to follow her husband and photograph him with his mistress*
(b) woman teacher; *the geography mistress*
(c) woman in charge; *the dog chased after a rabbit but came back when his mistress whistled*; **she's her own mistress** = she is independent (NOTE: plural is **mistresses**)

④ **misunderstand**
[mɪsʌndɪ'stænd] *verb*
not to understand correctly; *sorry, I misunderstood the question* (NOTE: **misunderstanding - misunderstood** [mɪsʌndɪ'stʊd])

④ **misunderstanding**
[mɪsʌndɪ'stændɪŋ] *noun*
not understanding something correctly; *there was a misunderstanding over my tickets*

② **mix**
[mɪks]
1 *noun*
mixture of things together; *there was an odd mix of people at the party*; **cake mix** = main ingredients for a cake which are bought ready mixed in a packet
2 *verb*
(a) to blend different things together; *she made the cake by mixing eggs and flour*; *oil and water do not mix*
(b) to get along with other people; *he finds it hard to mix with the other staff in the office*

② **mixed**
[mɪkst] *adjective*
made up of different things put together; *the reaction to the proposal has been rather mixed - some people like it, but others don't*; **I have very mixed feelings about the project** = I like some things about the project but not others; *in*

mixed company = when both men and women are together; *that's not the sort of joke you can tell in mixed company*; *(in tennis)* **mixed doubles** = doubles match where a man and woman play against another man and woman; **a mixed marriage** = marriage between two people of different races; **a mixed school** = school with both boys and girls

③ **mixture**
['mɪkstʃɪ] *noun*
different things mixed together; *if the mixture is too thick, add some more water*; *his latest paintings are a strange mixture of shapes and colours*; **cough mixture** = liquid medicine to cure a cough

③ **mix up**
['mɪks 'ʌp] *verb*
(a) to think someone or something is someone or something else; *I always mix her up with her sister*; *she must have got the addresses mixed up*; *his papers got all mixed up* = the papers were out of order, upside down, etc.
(b) **to be mixed up in** *or* **with** = to be part of, involved in; *he was mixed up in the bank scandal*; *how did she get mixed up with those awful people*

③ **mm**
abbreviation for MILLIMETRE

④ **moan**
[məʊn]
1 *noun*
(a) low sound from someone who is hurt; *the rescue team could hear moans from inside the wrecked aircraft*; *when she read the news she gave a loud moan*
(b) *(informal)* complaining about various things; *the staff are having a moan about their pay*
2 *verb*
(a) to make a low sound as if you are hurt; *they could hear someone moaning in the locked room*
(b) to complain about something; *they are moaning about working conditions*; *stop moaning, it will be your turn soon*

④ **mob**
[mɒb]
1 *noun*
crowd of people who are out of control; *mobs of football fans ran through the streets*; *an angry mob surged towards the palace gates*
2 *verb*
to surround with a wild crowd; *as the stars arrived they were mobbed by teenage fans* (NOTE: **mobbing - mobbed**)

② **mobile**
['məʊbaɪl *US* 'məʊbl]
1 *adjective*
which can move; *she is not very mobile* = she can't walk easily; **mobile library** = library in a van which travels around from place to place; *US* **mobile home** = van with beds, table,

washing facilities, etc., which can be towed by a car (NOTE: also called a **trailer**; British English is **caravan**); **mobile shop** = van fitted out like a small shop which travels round selling meat, fish, etc.
2 *noun*
(a) mobile phone; *I'll call him on his mobile*; *he gave me the number of his mobile*
(b) artistic construction using small pieces of metal, card, etc. which when hung up move in the slightest draught; *they bought a mobile of coloured fish to hang over the baby's bed*

② **mobile phone**
['məʊbaɪl 'fəʊn] *noun*
small telephone which you can carry around; *the sound is bad because I'm calling on my mobile phone*; *mobile phones won't work in the London Underground*

③ **mode**
[məʊd] *noun*
way of doing something; *she will have to change her mode of life when she goes to university*; **mode of payment** = way in which payment is made (such as cash or cheque)

① **model**
['mɒdl]
1 *noun*
(a) small version of something larger; *the exhibition has a model of the new town hall*; *he spends his time making model planes*
(b) person who wears new clothes to show them to customers; *he used only top models to show his designs during the London Fashion Week*
(c) particular type of car, etc., produced at a particular time; *this is this year's model*; *he bought a 1979 model Mini*; **demonstration model** = car, or other piece of equipment, which has been used by a shop to show how it works, and is then sold at a lower price
2 *verb*
(a) to make shapes in a soft material; *he modelled a statue of the little girl*
(b) to copy; **she modelled her way of working on that of her father** = she imitated her father's way of working
(c) to wear newly designed clothes to show to customers; *she is modelling the autumn collection by Dior* (NOTE: **modelling - modelled** but American spelling is **modeling - modeled**)

② **modem**
['məʊdem] *noun*
device which links a computer to the telephone lines, so as to send data; *you'll need a modem to connect to the Internet*

④ **moderate**
1 *adjective*
['mɒdɪrt] not excessive; *she had moderate success in her exams*; *the economy has ended a period of steady moderate growth*; *the union's wage demands are really quite moderate*
2 *noun*

['mɒdɪrɪt] person whose political ideas are not very violent; *after years of struggle the moderates have gained control of the party*

3 *verb*

['mɒdɪreɪt] to make or become less strong; *they moderated their demands; as the wind moderated, the waves became smaller;* **to moderate your language** = to be less rude or violent in what you say; *she asked him to moderate his language because there were children present*

① **modern**

['mɒdɪn] *adjective*

referring to the present time; *it is a fairly modern invention - it dates back to the 1980s; her parents have a very modern attitude to boyfriends; you expect really modern offices to have automatic windows and central heating systems;* **modern languages** = languages which are spoken today; *she's studying German and Italian in the modern languages department*

③ **modernize**

['mɒdɪnaɪz] *verb*

to make something up to date; *it took a lot of effort to modernize the party; if we want to modernize the factory, we'll have to throw out all the old equipment*

④ **modest**

['mɒdɪst] *adjective*

(a) not boasting; *he was very modest about his gold medal*

(b) not very expensive; *the union's demands were really quite modest; we had a modest meal in a local restaurant;* **a modest flat** = a flat which does not look expensive

④ **modify**

['mɒdɪfaɪ] *verb*

to change or to alter something to fit a different use; *the management modified its wage proposals in the light of the tribunal's ruling; the car will have to be modified if we want to sell it here*

② **module**

['mɒdjuːl] *noun*

part of a larger thing made up of various sections; *the science course is made up of a series of modules*

③ **moist**

[mɔɪst] *adjective*

slightly wet; *mushrooms grow well in moist soil; to clean the oven, just wipe with a moist cloth* (NOTE: moister - moistest)

③ **moisture**

['mɔɪstʃɪ] *noun*

small drops of water in the air or on a surface; *there's a lot of moisture in the air; this soil is too dry - it lacks moisture* (NOTE: no plural)

③ **mold**

[mɪʊld] *US* = MOULD

④ **molecule**

['mɒlɪkjuːl] *noun*

smallest unit in a substance that can exist by itself; *a molecule of water has one oxygen atom and two hydrogen atoms*

③ **mom**

[mɒm] *noun*

US child's name for mother; *his mom always waits for him outside school* (NOTE: British English is **mum, mummy**)

① **moment**

['mɪʊmɪnt] *noun*

(a) very short time; *can you please wait a moment - the doctor is on the phone?; I only saw her for a moment;* **a moment ago** = just now; *we only heard of it a moment ago*

(b) **at any moment** = very soon; *I expect it to rain at any moment;* **at the moment** = now; *I'm rather busy at the moment;* **at this moment in time** = at this particular point; *at this moment in time, it is not possible for me to answer reporters' questions;* **for the moment** = for a little while; *we won't take any action for the moment*

④ **momentum**

[mɪ'mentɪm] *noun*

forward movement; *he stopped rowing a few metres from the end of the race but his momentum carried him over the finishing line;* **to gain momentum** *or* **to gather momentum** = to go forward faster; *the protest movement is gathering momentum;* **to lose momentum** = to go more slowly; *when a spinning top loses momentum it falls over*

④ **monarch**

['mɒnɪk] *noun*

king or queen; *France used to have a monarch but is now a republic*

④ **monarchy**

['mɒnɪki] *noun*

system of government with a ruler such as a king or queen; *there's a big debate about whether we should get rid of the monarchy and become a republic;* **constitutional monarchy** = system of government where a king or queen is the head of state, but the country is ruled by an elected government; *all European countries with kings or queens are constitutional monarchies* (NOTE: plural is **monarchies**)

① **Monday**

['mʌndeɪ] *noun*

first day of the week, the day between Sunday and Tuesday; *some supermarkets are shut on Mondays; she had to go to the doctor last Monday; next Monday is a bank holiday; the 15th is a Sunday, so the 16th must be a Monday*

③ **monetary**

['mʌnɪtɪri] *adjective*

referring to money or currency; *the government's monetary policy is in ruins;* **monetary union** = joining various national currencies together to form one single currency

money
['mʌnɪ] noun

(a) coins or notes which are used for buying things; *how much money have you got in the bank?*; *he doesn't earn very much money*; *we spent more money last week than in the previous month*; *we ran out of money in Spain and had to come home early*; *(informal)* to have money to burn = to have more money than you know what to do with; *they spent thousands on their house - they simply have money to burn*; *see also* SENSE

(b) currency used in a country; *I want to change my British pounds into German money*

(c) to make money = to make a profit; *(informal)* it's money for old rope *or* it's money for jam = it's a profit which is easy to make (NOTE: no plural)

monitor
['mɒnɪtɪ]

1 *noun*

screen of a computer or a small television screen used for checking what is happening; *the larger the monitor, the less strain it will be on your eyes*; *my computer has a colour monitor*; *a bank of monitors allows the police to see everything which happens in the shopping centre*; *details of flight arrivals and departures are displayed on monitors around the airport*

2 *verb*

to check, to watch over (the progress of something); *doctors are monitoring her heart condition*; *how do you monitor the performance of the sales staff?*

monk
[mʌŋk] *noun*

man who is a member of a religious group; *the monks lived on a little island off the north coast* (NOTE: the equivalent women are nuns)

monkey
['mʌŋkɪ]

1 *noun*

(a) a tropical animal which lives in trees and normally has a long tail; *monkeys ran up the trees looking for fruit*

(b) *(informal)* little monkey = naughty little child

2 *verb*

to monkey around with something = to play with something; *stop monkeying around with that saw!*

monopoly
[mɪ'nɒpɪlɪ] *noun*

system where one person or company supplies all of a product in one area without any competition; *the state has a monopoly of the tobacco trade*; *the company has a monopoly of French wine imports* (NOTE: plural is monopolies)

monster
['mɒnstɪ]

1 *noun*

(a) large, horrible, strange and frightening animal; *the Loch Ness Monster is said to be a dinosaur living in the bottom of Loch Ness in Scotland*; *she drew a picture of a green monster with purple horns and huge teeth*

(b) cruel or wicked person; *her father was a monster who used to beat her with his belt*

2 *adjective*

(informal) very large; *look at the monster cabbage Dad's grown in the garden*; *what a monster sandwich!*

month
[mʌnθ] *noun*

(a) one of the twelve parts that a year is divided into; *December is the last month of the year*; *what day of the month is it today?*; *there was a lot of hot weather last month, in fact it was hot all month (long)* *she's taken a month's holiday to visit her parents in Australia*

(b) months = a long time; *it's months since we went to the cinema*; for months = for a very long time; *we haven't had any homework for months*

monthly
['mʌnθlɪ]

1 *adjective & adverb* happening every month; *he is paying for his car by monthly instalments*; *my monthly salary cheque is late*; *she gets paid monthly*

2 *noun*

magazine which is published each month; *I buy all the computer monthlies* (NOTE: plural is monthlies)

monument
['mɒnjʊmɪnt] *noun*

(a) building, statue, etc., erected in memory of someone who is dead; *they put up a monument to the people from the village who died in the war*; the Monument = tall column built in the City of London in memory of the Great Fire of 1666

(b) ancient monument = building which is officially listed as being very old and is protected by the state; *the chapel is an ancient monument and is protected*

mood
[muːd] *noun*

(a) feeling in general; *wait until she's in a good mood and then ask her*; *he's in a terrible mood this morning*; *her mood changed as soon as she opened the letter*; *a mood of gloom fell over the office*

(b) fit of bad temper; *don't talk to the boss - he's in one of his moods*

moon
[muːn] *noun*

thing in the sky which goes round the earth and shines at night; *the first man walked on the moon in 1969*; *the moon is shining very brightly tonight*; *there's no moon because it's cloudy*; full moon = time when the moon is a full circle; *by the light of the full moon they could clearly make out people moving on the hills*; **new moon** = time when the moon is visible as only a thin curved line; *the guerillas waited for the new moon to make their attack*; *(informal)* **once in a blue moon** = very rarely; *we only go to the theatre once in a blue moon*; **to be over the moon about something** = to be very happy and excited; *she's over the moon about her exam results*; *they're absolutely over the moon with their first baby*

③ **mop up**
['mɒp 'ʌp] *verb*
(a) to clear up spilt liquid; *use a cloth to mop up the water on the floor*; *we spent days mopping up after the floods*
(b) to overcome small groups of enemy fighters; *it took our soldiers several days to mop up the last pockets of enemy resistance in the mountains*

② **moral**
['mɒrɪl]
1 *adjective*
(a) referring to right and wrong behaviour; *judges have a moral obligation to be fair*; *he refused to join the army on moral grounds*
(b) referring to good behaviour; *she's a very moral person*; **to give someone moral support** = to encourage someone without active help; *motorists showed their moral support for the striking nurses by sounding their horns as they drove past the hospital*
2 *noun*
(a) lesson which you can find in a story; *there must be a moral in this somewhere*; *the moral of the story is that if you always tell lies, no one will believe you when you tell the truth*
(b) **morals** = way of behaving of society as a whole or of each individual; *some people blame TV for the corruption of public morals*

③ **morale**
[mɪˈrɑːl] *noun*
feeling of confidence; *the manager gave us a little talk to try to raise staff morale*; *low morale has made everyone gloomy*; *after his interview, his morale was low*

④ **morality**
[mɪˈrælɪti] *noun*
sense of moral standards; *where is the morality in spending millions on celebrating the president's wedding and not doing anything to help the poor and disabled?* (NOTE: no plural)

① **more**
[mɔː]
1 *adjective*
extra, which is added; *do you want any more tea?*; *there are many more trains on weekdays than on Sundays*
2 *pronoun* extra thing; *is there any more of that soup?*; *£300 for that suit - that's more than I can afford!*; *we've only got nine men, we need two more to make a football team*
3 *adverb*

(a) *(used with adjectives to make the comparative)* *the dog was more frightened than I was*; *she is much more intelligent than her sister*; *the dinner was even more unpleasant than I had thought it would be*
(b) **more or less** = not completely; *the rain has more or less stopped*; *I've more or less finished my homework*
(c) **not...any more** = no longer; *she doesn't write to me any more*; *we don't go to France on holiday any more*
(d) **once more** = one more time; *he played the song once more before the show ended* (NOTE: **more** is used to make the comparative of adjectives which do not take the ending **-er**)

② **moreover**
[mɔːˈruvi] *adverb; (formal)*
in addition; *we all felt cold, wet and hungry, and moreover, we were lost*; *if you do that again I will report you to the head teacher and moreover tell your parents*

① **morning**
['mɔːnɪŋ] *noun*
(a) first part of the day before 12 o'clock; *every morning he took his packed lunch and went to the office*; *tomorrow morning we will be meeting our Japanese agents*; *have you read the morning paper?*; *if we want to be in Paris for lunch you have to get the early morning train*; **morning coffee** = coffee served with biscuits as a snack in the middle of the morning; **morning dress** *or* **morning suit** = clothes for men consisting of a long black coat, light grey waistcoat and black and grey trousers, worn by men at weddings; **early morning tea** = tea brought to a hotel guest's bedroom early in the morning, often with the day's newspaper
(b) *(showing times)* **I woke up at four in the morning** = at 04.00 (NOTE: **in the morning** is often written and said as **a.m.**: **we were woken at four a.m.**)

④ **mortal**
['mɔːtl]
1 *adjective*
(a) which causes death; *he suffered a mortal blow in the fight*; **mortal enemy** = enemy who wants to kill you
(b) referring to death; **we are all mortal** = we are all going to die eventually
2 *noun*
an ordinary mortal = an ordinary human being; *Olympic runners can run at speeds which we ordinary mortals have no chance of reaching*

④ **mortar**
['mɔːtɪ] *noun*
cement mixture for holding together the bricks or stones used in building; *the wall is dangerous - you can see how the mortar is falling away*; *after the wall was built they pointed it with grey mortar*

① **mortgage**
['mɔːgɪdʒ]
1 *noun*
(a) agreement by which someone lends money on the security of a property; *he took out a mortgage on the house; she bought a house with a £200,000 mortgage*
(b) money lent on the security of a property; *she is behind with her mortgage repayments*; **second mortgage** = second loan obtained using a property which is already mortgaged as a security
2 *verb*
to give a property as security for a loan; *he mortgaged his house to set up his business; because his house was already mortgaged, he had to take out a second mortgage to pay for his car*

③ **Moslem**
['mɒzlɪm] *see* MUSLIM

② **mosque**
[mɒsk] *noun*
building where Muslims meet for prayer; *everyone must take off their shoes before entering a mosque; Muslims are called to prayer from the tower of the mosque*

③ **mosquito**
[mɪsˈkiːtɪʊ] *noun*
small flying insect which sucks blood and stings; *her arms were covered with mosquito bites; I was woken up by a mosquito buzzing round my head*; **mosquito net** = thin net spread over a bed to prevent mosquitoes biting at night; *your mosquito net won't do much good - it's got a big hole in it* (NOTE: plural is **mosquitoes**)

① **most**
[mɪʊst]
1 *adjective*
the largest number of; *most people go on holiday in the summer; he spends most evenings watching TV; most apples are sweet*
2 *pronoun* very large number or amount; *most of the work was done by my wife; she spent most of the evening on the phone to her sister; it rained for most of our holiday; most of the children in the group can ride bikes*
3 *adverb*
(a) *(making the superlative)* *she's the most intelligent child in the class; the most important thing if you are a salesman is to be able to drive a car*
(b) very; *I find it most frustrating that the train service is so slow; most probably the plane will be held up by the fog; thank you, you are most kind* (NOTE: **most** is used to form the superlative of adjectives which do not take the ending **-est**)

② **mostly**
['mɪʊstli] *adverb*
usually, most often; *we sometimes go to France for our holidays, but mostly we stay in Britain; the staff are mostly women of about twenty*

④ **moth**
[mɒθ] *noun*
flying insect with large wings like a butterfly, but which flies mainly at night; *moths were flying round the street light; she screamed as a moth flew into her face*

COMMENT: a moth's wings fold flat covering its back when it is not flying, while a butterfly's wings stand upright, or open out on each side of its body

① **mother**
['mʌðɪ]
1 *noun*
(a) woman who has children; *he's twenty-two but still lives with his mother; her mother's a dentist; Mother! there's someone asking for you on the telephone!*
(b) *(informal)* **shall I be mother?** = shall I pour the tea?; *who's going to be mother?; John, will you be mother?*
(c) **mother tongue** = language which you spoke when you were a little child; *she speaks English very well, but German is her mother tongue* (NOTE: **Mother** is sometimes used as a name for a **mother**, but in British English **Mum** or **Mummy**, and in American English **Mom** or **Mommy** are more usual)
2 *verb*
to look after someone *or* something very carefully; *the new recruits will have to be mothered along until they get some experience*

③ **motion**
['mɪʊʃn]
1 *noun*
(a) act of moving; *the motion of the ship made him feel ill*; **in motion** = moving; *do not try to get on or off while the train is in motion; now that we have planning permission for the new sports hall, we can set things in motion to get the foundations laid*
(b) movement of part of the body; *a slight motion of his head indicated that he was making a bid at the auction; she made a motion as if to get up, but in the end stayed in her seat*
(c) **to go through the motions** = to do something for the sake of appearances without believing in it; *he's lost all interest in his job - he's just going through the motions*
(d) proposal which is to be put to the vote at a meeting; *the motion was carried by 220 votes to 196*; **to second a motion** = to support the person who proposed the motion; **to table a motion** = to put forward a proposal for discussion by putting details of it on the table at a meeting
(e) *(formal)* **motions** = passing of solid waste matter out of the body; *the doctor asked her if her motions were regular*
2 *verb*
to make a movement with your hands which means something; *he motioned us to our chairs; she motioned to me to open the window*

④ **motivate**
['mıʊtıveıt] *verb*

to encourage someone to do something; *it's the job of the coach to motivate his team*; *we need some extra incentives to motivate the sales force*; **highly motivated** = eager; *the staff are all highly motivated and eager to tackle the new job*; *she's a hard-working, highly-motivated individual*; **racially motivated** = done because of racial hatred; *the attack on the house was racially motivated*

④ **motivation**
[mıʊtı'veıʃn] *noun*

encouragement to do something; *the staff lack motivation - hence the poor sales*; *his only motivation is money*

④ **motive**
['mıʊtıv]
1 *noun*

reason for doing something; *the police are trying to find a motive for the murder*
2 *adjective*

motive force = force which makes something move; *wind is the motive force which makes a yacht move forward*

② **motor**
['mıʊtı]
1 *noun*

(a) the part of a machine which makes it work; *the model plane has a tiny electric motor*

(b) car; **motor insurance** = insuring a car, the driver and passengers in case of accident

(c) **motor nerve** = nerve which makes part of the body move
2 *verb*

(old) to travel in a car for pleasure; *we motored down to Brighton*

④ **motorbike**
['mıʊtıbaık] *noun*

(informal) motorcycle, a two-wheeled cycle driven by a motor; *motorbike accidents are quite common*; *my brother let me sit on his new motorbike*; *I'm learning to ride a motorbike*

④ **motorcycle**
['mıʊtısaıkl] *noun*

two-wheeled cycle driven by a motor; *he fell off his motorcycle as he went round the corner*; *he learnt to ride a motorcycle when he was 65*

④ **motorcyclist**
['mıʊtısaıklıst] *noun*

person who rides a motorcycle; *all motorcyclists have to wear crash helmets*; *the police watched as the motorcyclist raced away up the hill*

② **motorist**
['mıʊtırıst] *noun*

person who drives a car; *the government is trying to persuade motorists to use their cars less*; *motorists are warned of long delays on all roads leading to the coast*

② **motorway**
['mıʊtıweı] *noun*

road with several lanes and very few junctions, on which traffic can travel at high speeds; *we drove south along the new motorway*; *you will get there faster if you take the motorway*; *there is a lot of traffic on the motorway on bank holidays* (NOTE: the American equivalent is **freeway**)

COMMENT: in Britain, motorways are given numbers, following the letter M: *take the M3 if you want to go to Wales; the M25 goes right round London*

③ **mould** *US* **mold**
[mıʊld]
1 *noun*

(a) soft earth; **leaf mould** = soft earth formed from dead leaves; *plant the bulbs in pots of leaf mould*

(b) hollow shape into which a liquid is poured, so that when the liquid becomes hard it takes that shape; *gold bars are made by pouring liquid gold into moulds*; **jelly mould** = shape for making jelly; *pour the jelly into the mould and put it in the fridge to set*

(c) grey plant growth which looks like powder; *throw that bread away - it's got mould on it*
2 *verb*

to shape something; *she moulded a little dog out of wax*

④ **mount**
[maʊnt]
1 *noun*

(a) frame for a picture; *he stuck the photograph into a mount and put it on his desk*

(b) (formal) horse, etc., on which a rider sits; *he tried to make his mount jump the fence*

(c) (usually in names) mountain; *Mount Kilimanjaro*; *Mount St Helens*
2 *verb*

(a) to climb on to something; to climb up something; *they mounted their horses and rode off*; *he mounted the stairs two at a time*; *the car turned, mounted the pavement, and hit a wall*

(b) to increase; *tension is mounting as the time for the football final approaches*

(c) **to mount guard over** = to stand on guard to protect something; *soldiers are mounting guard over the parliament building to prevent attacks*; *there were ten security men mounting guard over the president as he went for a walk in the town*

(d) to set something in a frame or in a metal holder, etc.; *mount the photograph in a black frame*; *the diamonds were mounted in silver*

(e) to organize something; *the unions are mounting a campaign to get the government to back down*; *our forces mounted a surprise attack on the enemy*; *the British Museum is mounting an exhibition of drawings*; *the coup was mounted by exiles living across the border*

② **mountain**
['maʊntɪn] *noun*

(a) very high piece of land, rising much higher than the land which surrounds it; *Everest is the highest mountain in the world*; *every weekend we go climbing in the Scottish mountains*; *how far is it to the top of the mountain?*; **mountain railway** = special railway which climbs steep mountains

(b) large amount; *there is a mountain of letters on the manager's desk*; **mountains of** = a large quantity of; *I have mountains of work to do*

③ **mounting**
['maʊntɪŋ] *adjective*

increasing; *the crowd waited with mounting excitement*; *the committee was horrified at the mounting cost of the exhibition*

③ **mount up**
['maʊnt 'ʌp] *verb*

to increase; *during his absence the bills mounted up*

② **mouse**
[maʊs]
1 *noun*

(a) small animal with a long tail, often living in holes in the walls of houses; *I saw a mouse sitting in the middle of the kitchen floor*; *our cat is good at catching mice* (NOTE: plural is **mice** [maɪs])

(b) device which is held in the hand and moved across a flat surface, used to control a computer; *you can copy text to another file using the mouse*; *click twice on the mouse to start the program*

① **mouth**
1 [maʊθ] *noun*

(a) opening in your face through which you take in food and drink, and which has your teeth and tongue inside; *it's not polite to talk with your mouth full*; *he sleeps with his mouth open*; *the cat was carrying a mouse in its mouth*; **to make your mouth water** = to look so good that you want to eat it or own it; *those cakes make my mouth water*; *his new car made her mouth water*

(b) wide or round entrance; *the mouth of the cave is hidden by bushes*; *the train came out of the mouth of the tunnel*; *New York is built on the mouth of the Hudson river* (NOTE: plural is **mouths** [maʊðz])

2 [maʊð] *verb*

to speak without making any sound; *I could see her mouthing something on the other side of the window*

④ **mouthful**
['maʊθfʊl] *noun*

(a) amount which you can hold in your mouth; *he took a mouthful of meat and chewed hard*; *the baby took a mouthful and immediately spat it out*; *she dived into the waves and got a mouthful of salt water*

(b) *(informal)* complicated word or phrase; *I'll spell the name of the Welsh village for you - it's a bit of a mouthful*

① **move**
[muːv]
1 *noun*

(a) change from one place to another; *the police were watching every move he made*; **it's time to make a move** = we must leave; **on the move** = moving; *after I've been on the move all day I just want to get home and go to bed*; **get a move on!** = hurry up!

(b) action done to achieve something; *it was a clever move to get here early before the crowds arrive*; **what's the next move?** = what do we have to do next?; **who will make the first move?** = who will act first?

(c) change of house or office; *luckily, nothing got broken during our move*

(d) changing the place of a piece in chess, etc.; *it's your move - I've just moved my queen*

2 *verb*

(a) to change the place of something; *move the chairs to the side of the room*; *who's moved my drink? - I left it on the table*; *he moved his hand to show he had heard*

(b) to change your position; *I could hear some animal moving about outside the tent*; *the only thing moving was the tip of the cat's tail*; **don't move!** = stand still

(c) to leave one house, flat or office to go to another; *he got a new job and they had to move from Scotland to London*; *they didn't like living in the country, so they moved back to London*; *the company is moving office, from London Road to the centre of town*

(d) to propose formally that a motion be accepted by a meeting; *I move that the committee should meet again next week*

(e) to make someone feel sad; *the sad Irish songs moved her to tears*; *we were all deeply moved by the ceremony*

③ **move about**
['muːv ə'baʊt] *verb*

(a) to change the place of something often; *he keeps on moving the chairs about*

(b) to change position often; *I can hear someone moving about downstairs*; *crowds of people were moving about in the square*

③ **move away**
['muːv ə'weɪ] *verb*

to change place to somewhere further away; *the ship gradually moved away from the dock*; **we're moving away from Oxford** = we are going to live in another town away from Oxford

③ **move back**
['muːv 'bæk] *verb*

(a) to go back; *after the meeting, please move the chairs back to where they were before*

(b) to change house or office to where you were before; *after three years in Central London they decided to move back to the country*

③ **move in**
['mu:v 'ɪn] *verb*
(a) to put your furniture into a new house and start to live there; *they only moved in last week*; *they got married and moved in with her parents*
(b) to come together as a group; *when everything is ready the police will move in on the gang*

① **movement**
['mu:vmɪnt] *noun*
(a) moving, not being still; *there was hardly any movement in the trees*; *all you could see was a slight movement of the cat's tail*
(b) group of people who are working towards the same aims; *the movement for equal pay for women*; *he's a leading figure in the green movement*
(c) mechanism; *a clock movement*

③ **move off**
['mu:v 'ɒf] *verb*
to start moving; *the car moved off when the lights changed to green*; *she tried to get on the train as it was moving off*

③ **move on**
['mu:v 'ɒn] *verb*
(a) to go forward; *we stopped for a quick visit to the cathedral and then moved on to the next town*
(b) to make people move; *the police moved the crowd on*
(c) to deal with the next item; *we will now move on to item 10 on the agenda*

② **movie**
['mu:vi] *noun*
(usually US) cinema film; *we go to the movies most weekends*; **movie theater** = place where films are shown (NOTE: British English is usually **cinema**)

② **moving**
['mu:vɪŋ] *adjective*
(a) which is changing position; *make sure all the moving parts are clean*
(b) which makes you feel sad; *a moving ceremony*; *his final speech was very moving*

① **MP**
['em 'pi:] *noun*
= MEMBER OF PARLIAMENT; *I saw our local MP speak in Parliament last night*; *you should write to your MP to complain about the government's plans* (NOTE: plural is **MPs** ['em 'pi:z])

① **Mr**
['mɪstɪ] *noun*
title given to a man; *Mr Jones is our new sales manager*; *here are Mr and Mrs Smith*; *(at the beginning of a letter) Dear Mr Smith* (NOTE: **Mr** is always used with a surname, sometimes with both the Christian name and surname)

① **Mrs**
['mɪsɪz] *noun*
title given to a married woman; *Mrs Jones is our manager*; *(at the beginning of a letter) Dear*

Mrs Jones (NOTE: **Mrs** is always used with a surname, sometimes with both the Christian name and surname)

① **Ms**
[mʌz or mɪz] *noun*
way of referring to a woman (without showing if she is married or not); *(at the beginning of a letter) Dear Ms Jones* (NOTE: **Ms** is always used with a surname, sometimes with both the Christian name and surname)

① **much**
[mʌtʃ]
1 *adjective*
(a) a lot of; *with much love from Aunt Mary*; *how much sugar do you need?*; *I never take much money with me when I go on holiday*; *she eats too much meat*; **as much as** = the same quantity; *you haven't eaten as much fruit as she has*; *he spends twice as much money as I do*
(b) *(asking the price)* how much does it cost to go to Edinburgh?; *how much is that book?* (NOTE: **much** is used with nouns you cannot count: **not much money** but **not many boys**)
2 *adverb*
very; a lot; *he's feeling much better today*; *it's much less cold in the south of the country*; *does it matter very much?*; *much as I like her, I don't want to share an office with her*; *much to my surprise, he arrived on time*; **much the most** = by far the most; *it's much the best restaurant in town*; **as much as** = the same amount as; *you haven't eaten as much as she has* (NOTE: **much - more** [mɔ:] - **most** [mɪʊst])
3 *pronoun*
a lot; *he didn't write much in his exam*; *much of the work has already been done*; **do you see much of him?** = do you see him often?; *(informal)* **not up to much** = not very good; *his latest film isn't up to much*

③ **mud**
[mʌd] *noun*
very wet earth; *you need a stiff brush to get the mud off your shoes*; *the pigs were lying in the mud*; *the boat got stuck in the mud as the tide went out*

④ **muddle**
['mʌdl]
1 *noun*
confused mess; *the papers were lying all over the floor in a muddle*; *she tried to put up the tent on her own but she got into a muddle*; *there was some muddle over the tickets*
2 *verb*
to muddle (up) = to confuse, to mix up; *don't muddle the papers - I've just put them in order*; *granny is 96 so she often muddles up our names*; *I always muddle him up with his brother - they are very alike*

① **muddy**

['mʌdɪ] *adjective*

full of mud; covered with mud; *don't come into the kitchen with your muddy boots on*; *the car stopped in the middle of a muddy field* (NOTE: muddier - muddiest)

③ **mug**

[mʌg]

1 *noun*

(a) large china cup with a handle; *she passed round mugs of coffee*

(b) *(informal)* stupid person, person who is easily taken in; *some poor mugs actually lent him money*

2 *verb*

(a) to attack and rob someone in the street; *she was mugged as she was looking for her car keys*; *she's afraid of going out at night for fear of being mugged*; *the gang specializes in mugging tourists*

(b) *(informal)* **to mug up on** = to study something very hard at the last minute; *I'm mugging up on my maths - the exams tomorrow morning* (NOTE: mugging - mugged)

③ **mugger**

['mʌgɪ] *noun*

person who attacks and robs someone in the street; *the muggers were caught in the next street*

③ **multiple**

['mʌltɪpl]

1 *adjective*

involving many people or things; *she was taken to hospital suffering from multiple injuries*; **multiple crash** = crash involving several cars or lorries; **multiple ownership** = situation where something is owned by several people jointly; **multiple store** = chain of stores belonging to the same company

2 *noun*

(a) number which contains another number several times exactly; *nine is a multiple of three*

(b) repeated groups of the same number of something; **sold in multiples of five** = you can buy five, ten, fifteen, etc.; *Premium Bonds are available in multiples of £100*

③ **multiply**

['mʌltɪplaɪ] *verb*

to calculate the result when several numbers are added together a certain number of times; *square measurements are calculated by multiplying length by width*; *ten multiplied by five gives fifty* (NOTE: multiply is usually shown by the sign x : **10 x 4 = 40**: say 'ten multiplied by four equals forty' or 'ten times four is forty')

① **mum**

[mʌm] *see* MUMMY

① **mummy**

['mʌmɪ] *noun*

(a) child's name for mother; *tell your mum I want to see her*; *hello, John, is your mummy at home?*; *Mummy! can I have a biscuit?* (NOTE: also often shortened to **Mum**; the American equivalent is **Mom, Mommy**)

(b) ancient dead body which has been treated with chemicals to stop it from going rotten; *we went to see the Egyptian mummies in the British Museum* (NOTE: plural is **mummies**)

② **municipal**

[mju:'nɪsɪpl] *adjective*

referring to a town which has its own local government; *we're going to play on the municipal golf course*; *municipal elections will be held on June 14th*; *take your household rubbish to the municipal refuse dump*; **municipal gardens** = park which belongs to a town; **municipal buildings** = offices where a town council works

② **murder**

['mɜ:dɪ]

1 *noun*

(a) act of deliberately killing someone; *the murder was committed during the night*; *she was accused of murder*; *they denied the murder charge*; *compare* MANSLAUGHTER

(b) *(informal)* difficult situation; *it was sheer murder getting to work this morning*

2 *verb*

(a) to kill someone deliberately; *he was accused of murdering a policeman*

(b) *(informal)* to want something to eat or drink very badly; *I could murder a pint of beer!*

② **murderer**

['mɜ:dɪrɪ] *noun*

person who has committed a murder; *the murderer was sentenced to life imprisonment*; **mass murderer** = killer of a large number of people at one time; *see also* SERIAL

④ **murmur**

['mɜ:mɪ]

1 *noun*

low sound of people talking, of water flowing, etc.; *there was a murmur of voices in the hall*

2 *verb*

to speak very quietly; *she murmured something and closed her eyes*

② **muscle**

['mʌsl]

1 *noun*

part of the body which makes other parts move; *he has very powerful arm muscles*; **to strain a muscle** *or* **to pull a muscle** = to injure a muscle by using it too much; *she strained a muscle in her back*

2 *verb*

(informal) **to muscle in on something** = to try to interfere with something; *he's always trying to muscle in on our projects and get all the credit for them*

④ **muscular**
['mʌskjʊlɪ] *adjective*
referring to muscles; *she suffered from muscular pain after working in the garden*; *he has very muscular arms*

② **museum**
[mju:'zi:ɪm] *noun*
building which you can visit to see a collection of valuable or rare objects; *the museum has a rich collection of Italian paintings*; *the Natural History Museum is always very popular with school parties*

③ **mushroom**
['mʌʃru:m] *noun*
round white plant which can be eaten; *do you want fried mushrooms with your steak?*

① **music**
['mju:zɪk] *noun*
(a) sound made when you sing or play an instrument; *do you like Russian music?*; *she's taking music lessons*; *her music teacher says she plays the piano very well*
(b) written signs which you read to play an instrument; *here's some music, see if you can play it on the piano*; *he can play the piano by ear - he doesn't need any music*
(c) *(informal)* **to face the music** = to receive punishment; *the manager went abroad when the bank collapsed, but came back to face the music* (NOTE: no plural: **some music; a piece of music**)

③ **musical**
['mju:zɪkl]
1 *adjective*
(a) referring to music; *do you play any musical instrument?*
(b) loving music, being able to play musical instruments; *his whole family is very musical - they all either sing or play in orchestras*
2 *noun*
play with songs and popular music; *musicals such as 'Cats' and 'Evita' have been playing for years*

④ **musician**
[mju:'zɪʃn] *noun*
person who plays music as a profession; *a group of young musicians playing the street*; *the actors applauded the group of musicians who had played during 'Twelfth Night'*

② **Muslim**
['mɒzlɪm]
1 *adjective*
following the religion of Muhammad; *he comes from a strict Muslim family*
2 *noun*
person who follows the religion of Muhammad; *Islam is the religion of Muslims or the Muslim religion*; *he comes from a family of strict Muslims*

① **must**
[mʌst]
1 *verb used with other verbs*

(a) *(meaning it is necessary)* *you must go to bed before eleven*; *we mustn't be late or we'll miss the last bus*; *you must hurry up if you want to see the TV programme*; *must you really go so soon?* (NOTE: the negative: **mustn't, needn't** Note also the meanings: **mustn't** = not allowed; **needn't** = not necessary: **we mustn't be late; you needn't hurry**)
(b) *(meaning it is very likely)* *I must have left my umbrella on the train*; *there is someone knocking at the door - it must be the postman*; *you must be wet through after walking in the rain* (NOTE: negative is **can't; it can't be the doctor**; past is **had to; I must go to the dentist: yesterday I had to go to the dentist**; negative: is **didn't have to**; perfect: **must have; I must have left it on the train**; negative: **can't have; I can't have left it on the train**. Note also that **must** is only used with other verbs and is not followed by **to**)
2 *noun*
something important; *when in Florida, a trip to the Everglades is a must*

③ **mustard**
['mʌstɪd] *noun*
yellow paste with a hot taste, made from mixing powdered seeds and water, eaten with meat, especially ham and beef; *would you like some mustard on your beef sandwich?*; *English mustard is yellow and quite strong*; **mustard powder** = sharp-tasting yellow powder made from crushed mustard seeds; **mustard yellow** = dull yellow colour

④ **mutual**
['mju:tʃʊɪl] *adjective*
referring to what is done by two people, countries, companies, etc., to each other; *they have a lot of mutual respect*; *if we work together, it could prove to be to our mutual advantage*; *she doesn't like him and the feeling is entirely mutual*; **our mutual friend** = the friend of both of us; **by mutual agreement** *or* **by mutual consent** = with the agreement of both parties; *by mutual agreement they have decided to sell the flat and split the money between them*

① **my**
[maɪ] *adjective*
belonging to me; *is that my pen you're using?*; *have you seen my glasses anywhere?*; *we went skiing and I broke my leg*

① **myself**
[maɪ'self] *pronoun*
referring to me; *I hurt myself climbing down the ladder*; *it's true - I saw it myself*; *I enjoyed myself a lot at the party*; **all by myself** = all alone, with no one else; *I built the house all by myself*; *I don't like being all by myself in the house at night*

③ **mysterious**
[mɪˈstɪɪrɪs] *adjective*
which cannot be explained; *who is the mysterious stranger at the back of the hall?*; *she died in mysterious circumstances, but the police are not sure it was murder*

③ **mystery**
[ˈmɪstrɪ] *noun*
thing which cannot be explained; *the police finally cleared up the mystery of the missing body*; *it's a mystery how the box came to be hidden under her bed* (NOTE: plural is **mysteries**)

④ **myth**
[mɪθ] *noun*
(a) ancient story about gods; *poems based on the myths of Greece and Rome*
(b) idea which is not true, but which many people believe; *it was many years before people stopped believing the myth that the earth was flat*; *the sales figures showed up the myth of their so-called super sales force*

Nn

③ **N, n**
[en]
fourteenth letter of the alphabet, between M and O; *can you think of a five-letter word beginning with N and ending in R?*

③ **nail**
[neɪl]
1 *noun*
(a) little metal rod use to hold two things together; *hit the nail hard with the hammer*; *you need a hammer to knock that nail in*; *(informal)* **to hit the nail on the head** = to judge something accurately
(b) **as hard as nails** = very hard; *she's as hard as nails - she'll never agree to what you want*
(c) hard part at the end of your fingers and toes; *she painted her nails red*; *he was cutting his nails*; **nail file** = flat stick covered with rough paper, used to smooth your nails; *have you got a nail file? - I've broken a nail*; **nail scissors** = special small scissors for cutting nails
2 *verb*
to attach with nails; *he nailed the notice to the door*

④ **naive**
[naɪˈiːv] *adjective*
innocent, lacking experience; *he is very naive for his age*; *it was naive of her to think he was offering her money just because he admired her work*

④ **naked**
[ˈneɪkɪd] *adjective*
(a) with no clothes on; *crowds of naked children were playing around in the river*; *a naked man stood on the balcony*
(b) without any covering; *a naked electric bulb hung from the ceiling*; **naked flame** = flame which is burning without any protection round it

① **name**
[neɪm]

1 *noun*
(a) special way of calling someone or something; *hello! my name's James*; *what's the name of the shop next to the post office?*; **I know him by name** = I have never met him, but I know who he is; **in the name of someone** = using someone's name; *the table is booked in the name of 'Green'*; **to put your name down for** = to apply for; *she put her name down to join the club*; **under the name of** = using the name of; *he wrote his novels under the name 'Saki'*; *they checked into the hotel under the name of 'Smith'*; **to make a name for yourself** = to do something which makes you famous; *he made a name for himself as a criminal lawyer*

(b) **Christian name** *or* **first name** = a person's first name, the special name given to someone as a child; *I know his surname's Smith, but what's his Christian name?*; *her Christian name or her first name is Natasha, but I don't know her surname*; **family name** = surname, the name of someone's family, shared by all people in the family; *Smith is the commonest name in the London telephone directory*

(c) **to call someone names** = to be rude to someone; *don't call the teacher names*; **to give something a bad name** = to give something a bad reputation; *employing waiters who are rude to customers is going to give the restaurant a bad name*

2 *verb*
to call someone or something by a name; *can you name three British Prime Ministers?*; *the Queen named the ship 'Britannia'*; *they have a black cat named Jonah*; **to name someone**

after someone = to give someone the same name as someone else; *they named their son Peter after his grandfather*

④ **namely**
['neɪmlɪ] *adverb*
that is to say; *only one student failed the exam, namely poor Bruce*

④ **nanny**
['nænɪ] *noun*
(a) girl who looks after small children in a family; *she's training to be a nanny*; *our new nanny starts tomorrow*; **the nanny state** = a state where the government looks after everyone and tells them what to do; *telling people at what time their children should go to bed is another example of the nanny state* (NOTE: plural is **nannies**)
(b) *(children's word)* **nanny goat** = female goat; *a nanny goat and her two kids* (NOTE: a male goat is a **billy goat**)

③ **nappy**
['næpɪ] *noun*
cloth which is wrapped round a baby's bottom to keep it clean; *she changed the baby's nappy*; *they bought a a pack of nappies* (NOTE: plural is **nappies**; American English for this is **diaper**)

④ **narrative**
['nærɪtɪv]
1 *noun*
written story; *he's writing a narrative about their journeys in South America*
2 *adjective*
describing an action; *he wrote a narrative poem about the war against Troy*

② **narrow**
['nærɪʊ] *adjective*
(a) not wide; *why is your bicycle seat so narrow?*; *we went down a narrow passage to the shop*
(b) **narrow escape** = near miss, situation where you almost hit something; *she had a narrow escape when her bike was hit by a truck*; **narrow majority** = majority of only a few votes; *the government had a narrow majority in the vote on the European Union* (NOTE: **narrower - narrowest**)
2 *verb*
(a) to make less wide; *he narrowed his eyes*
(b) to become less wide; *the road narrows suddenly, and there is hardly enough room for two cars to pass*
(c) **to narrow something down to** = to reduce something to; *we have narrowed down our choice of candidates to two*

② **nasty**
['nɑːstɪ] *adjective*
unpleasant; *what a nasty smell!*; *he's in for a nasty shock*; *it was nasty of her to report you to the teacher*; **to turn nasty** = to become unpleasant suddenly; *when she couldn't pay, the manager turned quite nasty* (NOTE: **nastier - nastiest**)

② **nation**
['neɪʃɪn] *noun*
(a) country; *a great nation such as the USA has a duty to protect smaller countries from attack*; *the member nations of the EU*; *see also* UNITED NATIONS
(b) people living in a country; *the Prime Minister spoke to the nation about the declaration of war*

① **national**
['næʃɪnl]
1 *adjective*
(a) belonging to a country; *this is in our national interest*; *the story even appeared in the national newspapers*; *we're going to see a new play at the National Theatre*
(b) **National Health Service (NHS)** = system of free doctors, nurses, hospitals, etc., run by the government; **National Insurance** = insurance run by the government which provides for state medical care, unemployment payments, etc.; **national park** = area of land protected by the government for people to enjoy; **National Savings** = scheme for saving money by lending it to the government
2 *noun*
person from a certain country; *two German nationals were arrested at the scene of the crime*

④ **nationalism**
['næʃnlɪzm] *noun*
feeling of great pride in your country, feeling that your country is better than others; *Danish nationalism as shown by their football supporters*

④ **nationalist**
['næʃnlɪst]
1 *noun*
person who wants his country to be independent; *a Welsh nationalist*; *the nationalists have not been invited to the negotiations*
2 *adjective*
wanting your country to be independent; *there is a lot of nationalist feeling in the country*

④ **nationality**
[næʃɪ'nælɪtɪ] *noun*
being a citizen of a state; *he is of United Kingdom nationality*; **she has dual nationality** = she is a citizen of two countries at the same time (NOTE: plural is **nationalities**)

③ **native**
['neɪtɪv]
1 *noun*
(a) person born in a place; *he's a native of Cornwall*
(b) flower, bird, etc., which has always existed in a place; *the oak is a native of the British Isles*
(c) original inhabitant; *the sailors were killed by natives as they came onto the beach*
2 *adjective*

belonging to a country; *the elephant is native to Africa*; **native language** *or* **native tongue** = language which you spoke when you were a little child; *she speaks English very well, but German is her native language*; *her native language is Italian*

① **natural**
['nætʃɪrɪl] *adjective*
(a) ordinary, not unusual; *her behaviour at the meeting was quite natural*; *it's only natural if you can't sleep the night before your exams*; *it's natural to worry about your first baby*; *it was natural for small shopkeepers to feel annoyed when the supermarket opened*
(b) coming from nature, and not made by man; *do you think the colour of her hair is natural?*; *yes, she's a natural blonde*; *the inquest decided that he died from natural causes*; **natural gas** = gas which is found in the earth and not made by men; **natural history** = study of plants, animals, etc.

① **naturally**
['nætʃɪrɪli] *adverb*
(a) of course; *naturally the top team beat the bottom team*; *do you want to watch the game? - naturally!*
(b) because of nature, not made by man; *she has naturally fair hair*
(c) in a normal way; *he behaved quite naturally at the office, so we were surprised when he was arrested for murder*

① **nature**
['neɪtʃɪ] *noun*
(a) plants and animals; *we must try to protect nature and the environment*; **nature study** = school lessons where you learn about plants and animals
(b) character of a person, thing, animal; *he has a very violent nature*; **human nature** = the general character of people; *it's only human nature to want to get on and do better than others*; **better nature** = feelings of kindness which you have inside you; *they appealed to the president's better nature to release the prisoners*

③ **naughty**
['nɔːti] *adjective*
(usually of a child) behaving badly, not doing what you are told to do; *the children are very quiet - they must be doing something naughty*; *that boy is very naughty - but his sister is worse*; *it was very naughty of you to put glue on your daddy's chair* (NOTE: **naughtier - naughtiest**)

④ **naval**
['neɪvl] *adjective*
referring to the navy; *he comes from a naval family*; *we are very interested in naval history*; **naval base** = base for ships of the navy; **naval college** = college where students study before entering the navy

③ **navy**
['neɪvɪ]
1 *noun*
(a) military force which fights battles at sea; *he left school and joined the navy*; *the navy has many ships*; **the Royal Navy** = British naval ships and the men who serve in them
(b) dark blue colour; *she was dressed in navy*
2 *adjective*
navy (blue) = of a dark blue colour; *she was wearing a navy skirt*; *he's bought a navy blue pullover*

① **near**
[nɪɪ] *adverb, preposition & adjective*
(a) close to, not far away from; *our house is near the post office*; *bring your chair nearer to the table*; *he lives quite near or quite near here*; *which is the nearest chemist's?*; **a near miss** = situation where you almost hit something; *that was a near miss - we missed the other car by inches!*; *(in a car)* **the near side** = the side closer to the side of the road; *someone has scratched the near-side door* (NOTE: the other side, the side where the driver sits, is the **off side**)
(b) soon, not far off in time; *her birthday is on December 21st - it's quite near to Christmas*; *can you phone again nearer the day and I'll see if I can find a few minutes to see you?* (NOTE: **nearer - nearest**)

④ **nearby**
[nɪɪ'baɪ] *adverb & adjective*
not far away; *he lives just nearby*; *they met in a nearby restaurant*

③ **Near East**
['nɪɪ 'iːst] *noun*
countries at the eastern end of the Mediterranean; *flights to the Near East have been stopped because of fighting in the area*

① **nearly**
['nɪɪli] *adverb*
almost; *he's nearly 18 - he'll be going to university next year*; *the film lasted nearly three hours*; *the book isn't nearly as good as the last one I read*; *hurry up, it's nearly time for breakfast*

② **neat**
[niːt] *adjective*
(a) tidy, without any mess; *leave your bedroom neat and tidy*; *a shirt with a neat white collar*
(b) alcohol without any water added; *I prefer my whisky neat* (NOTE: American English only uses **straight** in this meaning)
(c) *(mainly US)* **a neat idea** = a good idea (NOTE: **neater - neatest**)

① **necessarily**
[nesɪ'serɪli] *adverb*
which cannot be avoided; *going to Newcastle from here necessarily means changing trains twice*; **not necessarily** = possibly sometimes but not always; *taking the train isn't necessarily slower than going by plane*

① **necessary**

['nesesrɪ] *adjective*

which has to be done; *it's absolutely necessary for taxes to be paid on time*; *it is necessary to have a current passport if you are going abroad*; *are you sure all this equipment is really necessary?*; *does she have the necessary qualifications for the job?*

④ **necessity**

[nɪ'sesɪtɪ] *noun*

what is needed; essential thing; *a car is a necessity if you live in the country*; *can they afford the simple necessities of life?* (NOTE: plural is **necessities**)

② **neck**

[nek] *noun*

(a) part which joins your head to your body; *she was sitting in a draught and got a stiff neck*; *he wore a gold chain round his neck*

(b) *(informal)* **a pain in the neck** = an annoying person; *he's a real pain in the neck*; **to breathe down someone's neck** = to watch what someone is doing and be ready to criticize; *I wish he would stop breathing down my neck all the time*; **to stick your neck out** = to do something risky; *I'll stick my neck out and say that the government will lose the next election*

(c) **neck and neck** = equal (in a race, in an election); *the two boats finished neck and neck*; *the result is still not clear - the two parties are neck and neck*

(d) part of a piece of clothing which goes round your neck; *he takes size 16 neck in shirts*

(e) narrow part; *the neck of a bottle*; **a neck of land** = narrow piece of land between two pieces of water; *(informal)* **in this neck of the woods** = in this part of the country; *not many people live in this neck of the woods*

③ **necktie**

['nektaɪ] *noun*

(especially US) long piece of coloured cloth which men wear round their necks under the collar of their shirts; *is it the sort of party for which you have to wear a necktie?* (NOTE: British English only uses **tie**)

① **need**

[niːd]

1 *noun*

what is necessary or wanted; *there's no need for you to wait - I can find my own way home*; **in need** = requiring food and help; *the Red Cross is bringing supplies to families in need*; **to be in need of** = to want something; *they're in urgent need of medical supplies*

2 *verb*

(a) *(meaning to be necessary)* *we shall need Spanish pesetas for our holiday*; *painting needs a lot of skill*; *I need someone to help me with the cooking*

(b) *(meaning to want to use)* *does anyone need any more coffee?*; *we don't need all these chairs*; *will you be needing this hammer any more or can I use it?*; *do you need any help?*

(c) *(used with other verbs meaning to be necessary)* *need you make so much noise in the bath?*; *need you go now?*; *the living room needs painting* or *needs to be painted*; *you don't need to come if you have a cold*; *the police need to know who saw the accident*

④ **needle**

['niːdl] *noun*

(a) metal tool for sewing, like a long pin, with a hole at one end for the thread to go through; *this needle hasn't got a very sharp point*; *you must try to pull the piece of wool through the hole in the needle*; **knitting needle** = thin pointed plastic or metal stick used for knitting

(b) hollow metal tool used for injections; *it is a serious disease transmitted by infected blood or needles*

(c) hand on a dial; *he looked at the dial and saw the needle was pointing to zero*

(d) thin leaf of a pine tree

③ **needn't**

['niːdnt] *verb (used with other verbs to mean 'it isn't necessary')*; *she needn't come if she has a cold*; *you needn't have made a cake - I'm not hungry*; *she needn't make such a fuss about a little spider* (NOTE: **needn't** is only used with other verbs and is not followed by **to**. Note also the difference in meanings: **mustn't** = not allowed; **needn't** = not necessary: **we mustn't be late; you needn't hurry**)

② **negative**

['negɪtɪv]

1 *noun*

(a) meaning 'no'; *the answer was in the negative*

(b) developed film with an image where the light parts are dark and dark parts light; *don't touch the negatives with your dirty fingers*

2 *adjective*

(a) showing the absence of something; *her blood test was negative*; **a negative response** = saying 'no'

(b) **negative pole** = the end of a magnet which points to the south

(c) **negative film** = film where the light parts are dark and the dark parts are light (as opposed to positive film)

(d) **negative terminal** = one of the terminals in a battery, shown by a minus (-) sign; *the brown wire should be attached to the negative terminal* (NOTE: the opposite is **positive**)

④ **neglect**

[nɪ'glekt]

1 *noun*

lack of care; *the building has suffered from years of neglect* (NOTE: no plural)

2 *verb*

(a) to fail to look after someone *or* something properly; *he neglected his three children; the building had been neglected by its owners*

(b) *(formal)* not to do something; *she neglected to return her income tax form; he neglected to tell the police that he had been involved in an accident*

③ **negotiate**
[nɪˈɡɪʊsɪeɪt] *verb*

(a) to discuss with someone; *we are negotiating with the travel agent about a refund*

(b) to make a commercial arrangement; *the two parties negotiated the terms of the contract*

(c) to go round something which is in the way; *we had to negotiate several large rocks in the road; the burglars managed to negotiate the alarm system successfully*

② **negotiation**
[nɪɡɪʊsɪˈeɪʃn] *noun*

(a) discussing; *the only answer to this conflict is peaceful negotiation*; **it is open to negotiation** = the terms can be negotiated (NOTE: no plural in this meaning)

(b) **negotiations** = discussions; *we have started negotiations with the management over new contracts of employment*

④ **negotiator**
[nɪˈɡɪʊsɪeɪtɪ] *noun*

person who discusses; *union negotiators discussed terms with the directors; the negotiators shook hands and sat down at the conference table*

② **neighbour** *US* **neighbor**
[ˈneɪbɪ] *noun*

(a) person who lives near you, who is sitting next to you, etc.; *help yourself and then pass the plate on to your neighbour; he doesn't get on with his neighbours*; **next-door neighbours** = people who live in the house next to yours; **the Swedes and the Norwegians are neighbours** = their countries are close together

(b) *(old)* another person; *love of your neighbour is one of the essentials of Christian beliefs*

④ **neighbourhood** *US* **neighborhood**
[ˈneɪbɪhʊd] *noun*

(a) small area and the people who live in it; *this is a quiet neighbourhood, we don't like noisy parties; the doctor knows everyone in the neighbourhood*

(b) **in the neighbourhood of** = (i) near; (ii) approximately; *there are three hotels in the neighbourhood of the Conference Centre; the sum involved is in the neighbourhood of £100,000*

④ **neighbouring** *US* **neighboring**
[ˈneɪbɪrɪŋ] *adjective*

which is close to you; *there are no shops where we live, so we go to the neighbouring village to do our shopping; Sweden and Denmark are neighbouring countries*

② **neither**
[ˈneɪðɪ or ˈniːðɪ]

1 *adjective & pronoun*

not either of two (people, etc.); *neither car or neither of the cars passed the test; neither sister is dark or neither of the sisters is dark*

2 *adverb*

not either; *he doesn't eat meat and neither does his wife; she isn't fat but neither is she really very thin*

3 *conjunction*

(a) **neither...nor** = not one...and not the other; *the water is neither too hot nor too cold - it's just right; she's neither Chinese nor Japanese - she comes from Korea; neither his mother nor his father is coming to the wedding*

(b) **neither here nor there** = not important; *whether you go by bus or tube is neither here nor there, provided you get to the meeting on time*

③ **nerve**
[nɜːv]

1 *noun*

(a) thread in the body which takes messages to and from the brain; *nerves are very delicate and easily damaged*

(b) **to be in a state of nerves** = to be tense and worried; **to get on someone's nerves** = to annoy someone; *that buzzing noise is really getting on my nerves*

(c) *(informal)* being too confident; *he's got a nerve to ask for a day off, when he was away all last week*

2 *verb*

to nerve yourself = to get all your strength together; *he nerved himself against the meeting with the police; she nerved herself to take her driving test*

③ **nervous**
[ˈnɜːvɪs] *adjective*

(a) referring to the nerves; *the nervous system*; **nervous energy** = excited tense energy; *see also* BREAKDOWN

(b) worried; *she gets nervous if she is alone in the house at night; he's nervous about driving in London*

④ **nervously**
[ˈnɜːvɪsli] *adverb*

in a nervous way; *the bridegroom and best man waited nervously in the church*

③ **nest**
[nest]

1 *noun*

construction built by birds to lay their eggs in; *the birds built their nests among the trees; the owls have laid three eggs in their nest*

2 *verb*

(of birds) to build a nest and lay eggs; *the ducks are nesting by the river bank*; **nesting site** = place where a bird may build a nest

③ **nest egg**
['nest 'eg] *noun*
money which you have saved; *we've saved up a nice little nest egg for our retirement*

② **net**
[net]
1 *noun*
(a) woven material with large holes; **net curtains** = light curtains made of thin material
(b) piece of this material used for a special purpose; **a butterfly net** = bag of very light net with which you can catch butterflies; **a fishing net** = a large net used by fishermen to catch fish; **a tennis net** = a net stretched across the middle of a tennis court; *he hit the ball into the net*
(c) the Net = INTERNET
2 *verb*
to make a profit; *we netted £3,000 on the deal* (NOTE: **netting - netted**)
3 *adjective*
after deductions; *that figure is net, not gross*; **net earnings** *or* **net income** *or* **net salary** = money earned after tax has been deducted; **net price** = final price which is paid by the buyer; **net profit** = profit calculated after deducting all expenses; **net weight** = weight after deducting the weight of packaging material (NOTE: also spelt **nett weight** in this meaning; the opposite is **gross**)

③ **Netherlands**
['neðɪləndz] *noun*
European country, to the west of Germany and north of Belgium; *Amsterdam is the largest city in the Netherlands*; *see also* DUTCH, HOLLAND (NOTE: capital: **Amsterdam**; people: **the Dutch**; language: **Dutch**; currency: **guilder, euro**)

③ **nett**
[net] *see* NET

③ **nettle**
['netl] *noun*
(stinging) nettle = type of common weed which stings when you touch it; *he walked with bare legs through the wood and got stung by nettles*; **to grasp the nettle** = to deal with a problem quickly and firmly to settle it before it causes you any more trouble; *no politician has dared grasp the nettle of corruption in sport*

③ **network**
['netwɜːk]
1 *noun*
(a) system of linked roads, railways, etc.; *there is a network of tunnels under the castle*; *the British rail network*; *a satellite TV network*
(b) linked computer system; *how does this network operate?*; *you can book at any of our hotels throughout the country using our computer network*
(c) group of people linked together; *his rapidly developing network of contacts in government*; *see also* OLD BOY NETWORK
2 *verb*

to link up two or more computers to allow them to exchange information; *desk PCs are usually networked and share resources*

④ **neutral**
['njuːtrl]
1 *adjective*
(a) not in favour of one side or the other in a dispute; *the UN sent in neutral observers*; *the referee has to stay neutral*
(b) refusing to take part in a war; *during the war, Switzerland remained neutral*
(c) with a light colour, such as pale brown or pale grey; *red walls, green furniture and a neutral carpet*
2 *noun*
(a) country which does not take part in a war
(b) citizen of a neutral country; *only neutrals were admitted to the talks*
(c) *(cars, trucks, etc.)* not in gear; *the car is in neutral*

① **never**
['nevɪ] *adverb*
not at any time; not ever; *we'll never forget that restaurant*; *I've never bought anything in that shop although I've often been inside it*; *he never eats meat*; **never mind!** = don't worry, don't bother about it; **well I never!** = how surprising!; *well I never - it's James!*

② **nevertheless**
[nevɪðɪ'les] *adverb*
in spite of all that; *I know it is raining, but nevertheless I'd like to go for a walk along the beach*; *she had a cold, but went to the meeting nevertheless*

① **new**
[njuː] *adjective*
(a) made quite recently, never used before; *this is the new model - it's just come out*; *are your shoes new?*
(b) which arrived recently, fresh; *there are two new secretaries in the office*; **new potatoes** = first young potatoes of a year's harvest
(c) which has just been bought; *she bought herself a new motorbike*; *he's trying to get his new computer to work*
(d) quite different from what was before; *we need someone with new ideas*; *they put some new wallpaper in the bedroom* (NOTE: **newer - newest**)

④ **newcomer**
['njuːkʌmɪ] *noun*
person who has just come to a place; *the family are newcomers to the village*; *could all newcomers to the meeting please sign the register?*

③ **newly**
['njuːli] *adverb*
recently; *he was showing off his newly purchased car*; *the house has been bought by a newly married couple*

① **news**

[njuːz] *noun*

spoken or written information about what has happened; *what's the news of your sister?*; *she told me all the latest news about the office*; *he was watching the 10 o'clock news on TV*; *I don't want to hear any bad news*; **have you heard the news?** = have you heard what has happened?; *have you had any news about your pay rise?*; **to break the news to someone** = to tell someone the bad news; *he broke the news to his daughters*; **no news is good news** = if there is nothing new to mention, things must be going well (NOTE: **news** is singular, not plural)

④ **news agency**

['njuːz 'eɪdʒɪnsi] *noun*

office which distributes information to newspapers and TV; *he works for an international news agency*

④ **newsagent**

['njuːzeɪdʒɪnt] *noun*

person who sells newspapers; *some newsagents sell groceries as well as newspapers*; **a newsagent's** = shop selling newspapers, sweets, cigarettes, etc.; *he went to the newsagent's to buy some cigarettes*; *there's a newsagent's next door to the pub*; *can you stop at the newsagent's on your way home and buy the local paper?* (NOTE: **newsagent** has no connection with a **news agency**)

④ **newscaster**

['njuːzkɑːstɪ] *noun*

person who reads the news on radio or TV; *a highly-respected BBC newscaster*

③ **news conference**

['njuːz 'kɒnfɪrɪns] *noun*

meeting with journalists to give information about something and answer questions; *the climbers held a news conference at the airport on their return from Everest*

① **newspaper**

['njuːzpeɪpɪ] *noun*

publication consisting of loose folded sheets of paper, which usually comes out each day, with news of what has happened; *he was so absorbed in his newspaper that he didn't notice that the toast had burnt*; *we saw your picture in the local newspaper*; *the newspapers are full of news of the election*; *there's an interesting article on fishing in the newspaper*; **a daily newspaper** = newspaper which is published every day except Sunday (NOTE: **a newspaper** is often simply called a **paper**)

③ **newsreader**

['njuːzriːdɪ] *noun*

person who reads the news on radio or TV; *you don't often hear newsreaders pronouncing names wrongly* (NOTE: also called a **newscaster**)

② **New Year**

['njuː 'jɜː] *noun*

first few days of the year; *I started my new job in the New Year*; **Happy New Year!** = good wishes for the New Year; **New Year's resolution** = plan to improve your way of living, decided on at the New Year, and usually abandoned shortly afterwards; *each New Year I make the same resolutions, but never manage to keep them*; **to stay up to see the New Year in** = to stay up until after midnight on 31st December to celebrate the beginning of the New Year

③ **New Year's Day**

[njuː jɜːz 'deɪ] *noun*

1st January; *it's a shame you have to work on New Year's Day*

③ **New Year's Eve**

[njuː jɜːz 'iːv] *noun*

31st December; *the only time we drink champagne is on New Year's Eve*

① **New York**

['njuː 'jɔːk] *noun*

large town on the Eastern coast of the USA; *we are due to arrive in New York at 5 o'clock*; *she's the manager of our New York office*; *New York seems to get busier and busier each time I visit*; *yesterday New York had three inches of snow*

① **New Zealand**

['njuː 'ziːlɪnd] *noun*

country in the Pacific Ocean, to the east of Australia; *the sheep trade is important to the New Zealand economy* (NOTE: capital: **Wellington**; people: **New Zealanders**; language: **English**; currency: **New Zealand dollar**)

① **New Zealander**

['njuː 'ziːlɪndɪ] *noun*

person from New Zealand; *my sister recently married a New Zealander*

① **next**

[nekst]

1 *adjective & adverb*

(a) coming after in time; *on Wednesday we go to Paris, and the next day we travel to Italy*; *first you put the eggs into a bowl and next you add some sugar*; *don't forget to give me a call when you're next in town*; *next week is the start of our holiday*; *the next time you go to the supermarket, can you get some coffee?*

(b) nearest in place; *the ball went over the fence into the next garden*; *she took the seat next to mine*; **it costs next to nothing** = it doesn't cost very much

2 *pronoun*

the thing or person following; *after two buses went past full, the next was almost empty*; *I'll be back from holiday the week after next*; *(asking the next person in the queue to come) next, please!*

○ **next door**
['nekst 'dɔ:] *adjective & adverb*
in the house next to this one; *who lives next door to your mother?*; *the shop is next door to a bank*; *our next-door neighbours have gone on holiday, and we are looking after their cat*

④ **NHS**
['en 'eɪtʃ 'es] = NATIONAL HEALTH SERVICE

④ **NIC**
= NATIONAL INSURANCE CONTRIBUTIONS

① **nice**
[naɪs] *adjective*
(a) pleasant, fine; *we had a nice time at the seaside*; *if the weather's nice let's have a picnic*; *the nicest thing about the town is that it is on the sea*
(b) pleasant, polite; *that wasn't a very nice thing to say*; *try and be nice to your grandfather* (NOTE: **nicer - nicest**)

① **nicely**
['naɪsli] *adverb*
(a) very well; *that will do nicely, thank you*
(b) politely; *you can have a biscuit if you ask for it nicely*

④ **nickname**
['nɪkneɪm]
1 *noun*
short or informal name given to someone; *her real name's Henrietta, but everyone calls her by her nickname 'Bobbles'*
2 *verb*
to give a nickname to; *he was nicknamed 'Camel' because of his big nose*

① **night**
[naɪt] *noun*
(a) part of the day when it is dark; *it's dangerous to walk alone in the streets at night*; *burglars got into the office during the night*; *he is on night duty three days a week*; *they're planning to have a night out tomorrow*
(b) *(informal)* **a night owl** = someone who likes to work, eat, etc., until late at night, and does not get up early in the morning; *she's a night owl and finds it difficult to get up in time for work*; *compare* EARLY BIRD (NOTE: do not confuse with **knight**)

④ **nightclub**
['naɪtklʌb] *noun*
club which is only open at night; *our daughter will only come with us on holiday if we go to a resort with lots of nightclubs*

④ **nightmare**
['naɪtmeɪ] *noun*
(a) very frightening dream; *I had a nightmare that I was drowning*
(b) horrible experience; *the dinner party was a nightmare*; *a nightmare journey across the desert*

○ **nil**
[nɪl] *noun*
nothing; *our advertising budget has been cut to nil*

① **nine**
[naɪn]
(a) number 9; *she's nine (years old) tomorrow*; *the shop opens at 9 o'clock*; **nine times out of ten** = very often; *see also* DRESSED
(b) **999** ['naɪn 'naɪn 'naɪn] telephone number to call the emergency services in Britain; *the firemen came quickly when we called 999*; *the ambulance drove through the snow to answer the 999 call*

① **nineteen**
[naɪn'ti:n]
number 19; *he's nineteen (years old) tomorrow*; **the nineteen fifteen train** = the train leaving at 19.15; **in the 1950s** = during the years 1950 to 1959; **the nineteen hundreds (1900s)** = the years from 1900 to 1999 (NOTE: compare with **the nineteenth century**)

① **nineteenth (19th)**
[naɪn'ti:nθ] *adjective & noun*
referring to nineteen; *it's his nineteenth birthday tomorrow*; **the nineteenth of August** or **August the nineteenth (August 19th)** **the nineteenth century** = the period from 1800 to 1899 (NOTE: compare with **the nineteen hundreds**; note also that with dates **nineteenth** is usually written **19th**: July 19th, 1935; October 19th, 1991 (American style is **October 19, 1991**), say 'the nineteenth of October' or 'October the nineteenth' (American style is 'October nineteenth'))

① **ninetieth (90th)**
['naɪntiɪθ] *adjective & noun*
referring to ninety; *a ninetieth of a second*; *it will be grandfather's ninetieth birthday next month*

① **ninety**
['naɪnti]
number 90; *my old aunt will be ninety (years old) next week and her husband is ninety-two: they are both in their nineties*; **the nineteen nineties (1990s)** = the years from 1990 to 1999 (NOTE: **ninety-one** (91), **ninety-two** (92), etc., but **ninety-first** (91st), **ninety-second** (92nd), etc.)

① **ninth (9th)**
[naɪnθ] *adjective & noun*
referring to nine; *tomorrow is his ninth birthday*; *today is the ninth of June* or *June the ninth (June 9th)* *he missed the record by a ninth of a second*; **the ninth century** = the period from 800 to 899 AD (NOTE: with dates **ninth** is usually written **9th**: July 9th, 1935; October 9th, 1991 (American style is **October 9, 1991**) say 'the ninth of October' or 'October the ninth' (American style is 'October ninth'); with names of kings and queens **ninth** is usually written **IX: King Charles IX** (say: 'King Charles the Ninth'))

④ **nip**
[nɪp]
1 *noun*
short sharp bite; *the little dog gave him a nasty nip*
2 *verb*
(a) *(informal)* to go very quickly; *I'll just nip round to the newsagent's and get the evening paper; we'll nip down to the pub for a drink*
(b) to pinch sharply; *he nipped off the end of the stalk to stop the plant growing any taller*; *see also* BUD
(c) to bite sharply; *the dog nipped the postman in the leg* (NOTE: nipping - nipped)

③ **nitrogen**
['naɪtrɪdʒɪn] *noun*
important gas which is essential for life, and which forms most of the atmosphere; *nitrogen is absorbed into the body from protein* (NOTE: Chemical element: chemical symbol: **N**; atomic number: 7)

① **no**
[nɪʊ] *adjective & adverb*
(a) *(showing the opposite of 'yes')* I asked my mother if we could borrow her car but she said 'no'; *do you want another cup of coffee? - no, thank you*
(b) not any; *there's no milk left in the fridge; we live in a little village, and there's no post office for miles around; we had no reply to our fax*
(c) *(signs)* **no entry** = do not go in this way; **no exit** = do not go out this way; **no parking** = do not park; **no smoking** = do not smoke
(d) *(informal)* **no way** = certainly not; *will you lend me £2000? - no way!*
(e) not at all; *my new kitchen knife is no sharper than the old one; she no longer works here; I'm no good at maths*

③ **no.**
['nʌmbɪ] *abbreviation for* NUMBER

④ **noble**
['nɪʊbl]
1 *noun*
person of high rank; *the nobles forced the king to sign the treaty*
2 *adjective*
(a) with a fine character; *it was very noble of him to lend her his umbrella; she did it for the noblest of reasons*
(b) of high rank in society; *she comes from a noble family - her father is in the House of Lords* (NOTE: nobler - noblest)

① **nobody**
['nɪʊbɪdi] *pronoun*
no one *or* no person; *there was nobody in the café; we met nobody on our way here; nobody wants to do her job; you'll have to drive the bus - nobody else has a driving licence*

② **nod**
[nɒd]
1 *noun*

little movement of the head up and down, meaning 'yes'; *he gave me a nod as I came in*; *(informal)* **it went through on the nod** = it was accepted without any discussion
2 *verb*
(a) to move the head slightly up and down, meaning 'yes'; *when he asked her if she understood the question, she nodded or nodded her head; he nodded to show his agreement* (NOTE: the opposite is to **shake** your head, meaning 'no')
(b) to move the head slightly up and down, to mean 'hello' or 'goodbye'; *she nodded at me as I went past*
(c) **to nod off** = to go to sleep; *she was nodding off in front of the television* (NOTE: nodding - nodded)

② **noise**
[nɔɪz] *noun*
(a) loud or unpleasant sound; *don't make any noise - the guards might hear you; the workmen are making such a lot of noise that we can't use the telephone*
(b) sound in general; *the baby made a little sucking noise; is there anything the matter with the washing machine - it's making a funny noise; there was a noise of running water in the bathroom; he woke up when he heard a noise in the kitchen*

④ **noisily**
['nɔɪzɪli] *adverb*
making a lot of noise; *he drank his tea noisily*

③ **noisy**
['nɔɪzi] *adjective*
which makes a lot of noise; *a crowd of noisy little boys; unfortunately, the hotel overlooks a noisy road junction; the new electric drill is even noisier than our old one* (NOTE: noisier - noisiest)

④ **nominate**
['nɒmɪneɪt] *verb*
to propose someone for a post; *he's been nominated to the committee; she was nominated as Labour candidate in the next election*

② **nomination**
[nɒmɪ'neɪʃn] *noun*
(a) action of nominating; *her nomination to the board of directors*; **nomination papers** = official forms by which someone is nominated as a candidate in an election
(b) name which has been proposed; *there are three nominations for the post of secretary*

① **none**
[nʌn] *pronoun*
(a) not any; *how many dogs have you got? - none; can you buy some milk, we've none left in the fridge?; a little money is better than none at all*; **her health is none too good** = it is not very good
(b) not one; *none of my friends smokes; none of the group can speak Chinese*

2 *adverb; (used with 'the' and comparative)*
not at all; *she seems none the better for her holiday*; **he was none the worse for his accident** = he was not at all hurt in the accident; **to be none the wiser** = to know no more about it than you did before; *I read his report, and I'm still none the wiser*; *his lengthy explanation left us none the wiser about how the system would work*

④ **nonetheless**
[nʌnθɪˈles] *adverb*
in spite of all that; *I know it is raining, but nonetheless I'd like to go for a swim before breakfast*; *he had a cold, but went to the meeting nonetheless*

③ **nonsense**
[ˈnɒnsɪns] *noun*
silly ideas; *I'm too fat - nonsense, you're a nice shape!*; *he talked a lot of nonsense*; *it's nonsense to expect people to pay money for that* (NOTE: no plural)

④ **noon**
[nuːn] *noun*
twelve o'clock in the middle of the day; *we'll stop for lunch at noon*

① **no one**
[ˈnɪuwʌn] *pronoun* nobody *or* no person; *you can go to the bathroom - there's no one there*; *we met no one we knew*; *no one here takes sugar in their tea*; *no one else has a driving licence so you'll have to be the driver*

① **nor**
[nɔː] *conjunction*
and not; *I did not meet him that year nor in subsequent years*; *I never went there again, nor did my wife*; *I don't want to go - nor me!*; *see also* NEITHER

① **normal**
[ˈnɔːmɪl] *adjective*
usual, what usually happens; *we hope to resume normal service as soon as possible*; *look at the rain - it's just a normal British summer*; *what's the size of a normal swimming pool?*; *at her age, it's only normal for her to want to go to parties*

① **normally**
[ˈnɔːmɪli] *adverb*
usually; *the bus is normally late*; *she doesn't normally drink wine*

① **north**
[nɔːθ]
1 *noun*
direction to your left when you are facing the direction where the sun rises; *there will be snow in the north of the country*; *it's cold when the wind blows from the north*
2 *adjective*
referring to the north; *we went on holiday to the north coast of Scotland*; *the north side of our house never gets any sun*; *when the north wind blows, you can expect snow*
3 *adverb*

towards the north; *they were travelling north at the time*; *go north for three miles and then you'll see the road to London*; *our office windows face north*

③ **North America**
[ˈnɔːθ əˈmerɪkə] *noun*
part of the American continent to the north of Mexico, formed of the USA and Canada; *he has travelled widely in North America from Alaska to Florida*

③ **north-east**
[nɔːˈθiːst]
1 *adverb*
direction between north and east; *they were travelling north-east at the time*; *go north-east for three miles and then you'll come to our village*; *our office windows face north-east*
2 *noun*
part of country to the north and east; *the North-East of England will have snow showers*; *it's cold when the wind blows from the north-east*

② **northern**
[ˈnɔːðɪn] *adjective*
referring the north; *northern countries have more rain*; *they live in the northern part of the country*

③ **North Pole**
[ˈnɔːθ ˈpɪul] *noun*
furthest point at the north of the earth; *an explorer who has been to the North Pole*

③ **north-west**
[nɔːˈθwest]
1 *adverb*
direction between west and north; *they were travelling north-west at the time*; *go north-west for a few miles and then you'll come to our house*
2 *noun*
part of the country to the north and west; *the North-West of England is wetter than the east coast*; *we can expect rain when the wind blows from the north-west*; *the old castle stood to the north-west of the cathedral*

① **Norway**
[ˈnɔːweɪ] *noun*
country in northern Europe, to the west of Sweden; *in northern Norway it is light almost all day long in summer* (NOTE: capital: **Oslo**; people: **Norwegians**; language: **Norwegian**; currency: **Norwegian krone**)

① **Norwegian**
[nɔːˈwiːdʒɪn]
1 *adjective*
referring to Norway; *Ibsen is the most famous Norwegian author*
2 *noun*
(a) person from Norway; *the Norwegians have a very large fishing fleet*
(b) language spoken in Norway; *Norwegian is similar in many ways to Swedish*

① nose

[nɪʊz]

1 *noun*

part of the head which you breathe through and smell with; *he has a cold, and his nose is red*; *dogs have wet noses*; *she's got flu - her nose is running*; *don't wipe your nose on your sleeve, use a tissue*; **to blow your nose** = to blow air through your nose into a handkerchief to remove liquid from your nose; **to speak through your nose** = to talk as if your nose is blocked, so that you say 'b' instead of 'm' and 'd' instead of 'n'; **to look down your nose at something** = to look at something as if you don't think it is very good; *she's got a degree and looks down her nose at the other secretaries*; **to do something under someone's nose** = to do something right in front of someone who doesn't notice; *the prisoners walked out of the prison under the noses of the guards*; **to pay through the nose for something** = to pay far more for something than you should; *he paid through the nose for his ticket to New York because it was the only seat left*; **to turn your nose up at something** = to show that you don't feel something is good enough for you; *it's a marvellous deal, I don't see why you should turn your nose up at it*

2 *verb*

(informal) **to nose about** *or* **to nose around** = to look or to search in a place; *what are you doing nosing around in my papers?*; *I don't like people nosing about in the office safe*

① not

[nɒt] *adverb; (often shortened to* **n't**)

(a) *(used with verbs to show the negative)* *she can't come*; *it isn't there*; *he didn't want any meat*; *we couldn't go home because of the fog*; *don't you like coffee?*; *a service charge is not included*

(b) not...either = and not...also; *she doesn't eat meat, and she doesn't eat fish either*; *it wasn't hot, but it wasn't very cold either*

(c) not only...but also = not just this...but this as well; *she isn't only blind, but she's deaf also*; *the film wasn't only very long, but it was also very bad*

(d) *(used to make a strong negative - not shortened in this sense)* *is it going to rain? - I hope not*; *I don't like bananas - why on earth not?*; *he begged her not to leave him alone*; *there was not one single shop open*; *everyone was invited, not forgetting the bus driver*; **not a few** = many; **not very well** = quite ill

④ notable

[ˈnɪʊtɪbl] *adjective*

which is worth noticing; *it was a notable achievement*; *she was notable by her absence*; *the town is notable for its ginger cakes*

③ notably

[ˈnɪʊtɪbli] *adverb*

(a) especially; *some Western countries, notably Canada and the United States, have a very high standard of living*

(b) in a way that is easily noticed; *the food was notably better than the last time we ate there*

① note

[nɪʊt]

1 *noun*

(a) a few words in writing to remind yourself of something; *she made a few notes before she gave her speech*; *she made a note of what she needed to buy before she went to the supermarket*; **to take note of** = to pay attention to; *we have to take note of public opinion*

(b) short message; *she left a note for the managing director with his secretary*; *he wrote me a note to say he couldn't come*

(c) piece of paper money; *I tried to pay with a ten-pound note* (NOTE: American English for this is **bill**)

(d) musical sound or a written sign meaning a musical sound; *he can't sing high notes*

(e) key on a piano; *she played a tune, using only the black notes on the piano*

(f) further explanations about a text; *the notes are at the back of the book*

2 *verb*

(a) to write down something in a few words; *the policeman noted in his notebook all the details of the accident*

(b) to take notice of; *please note that our prices were raised on January 1st*

④ notebook

[ˈnɪʊtbʊk] *noun*

(a) small book for making notes; *the policeman wrote down the details in his notebook*

(b) very small computer which you can carry around with you

③ noted

[ˈnɪʊtɪd] *adjective*

famous; *the town is noted for its public gardens*; *Mr Smith, the noted local artist*

① nothing

[ˈnʌθɪŋ] *pronoun*

(a) not anything; *there's nothing interesting on TV*; *she said nothing about what she had seen*; *there's nothing more we can do*; **nothing much happened** = not very much happened; **he has nothing left in the bank** = no money left; **for nothing** = free, without having to pay; *we're friends of the organizer and she got us into the exhibition for nothing*

(b) to think nothing of doing something = to do something easily; *he thinks nothing of cycling ten miles to work*; **it's nothing to do with you** = it doesn't concern you

① notice

[ˈnɪʊtɪs]

1 *noun*

(a) piece of writing giving information, usually put in a place where everyone can see it; *he pinned up a notice about the staff tennis match*

(b) official warning that something has to be done, that something is going to happen; *they gave us five minutes' notice to leave the office*; *if you want to resign, you have to give a month's notice*; *the train times were changed without notice*; **until further notice** = until different instructions are given; *you must pay £200 on the 30th of each month until further notice*; **at short notice** = with very little warning; *it had to be done at short notice*; *the bank manager will not see anyone at such short notice*

(c) attention; *it has been brought to my notice that students have been going into town at lunchtime*; **take no notice of what the policeman says** = pay no attention to what he says, don't worry about what he says

2 *verb*

to see; to take note of; *I wore one blue and one white sock all day and nobody noticed*; *I didn't notice you had come in*; *did you notice if John was sitting next to Sarah?*

③ **noticeable**
['nɪʊtɪsɪbl] *adjective*

which is easily noticed; *the mark on your tie is hardly noticeable*; *I can't see any noticeable difference between them*

④ **noticeboard**
['nɪʊtɪsbɔːd] *noun*

flat piece of wood, etc., on a wall, on which notices can be pinned; *did you see the list of films on the club noticeboard?*; *the students clustered round the noticeboard to read their exam results* (NOTE: American English is **bulletin board**)

④ **notification**
[nɪʊtɪfɪ'keɪʃn] *noun*

(formal) act of informing someone; *have they received any notification of the date of the court case?*; *we have had no notification that the sale has taken place*; *on receipt of the notification, they decided to appeal*

④ **notify**
['nɪʊtɪfaɪ] *verb*

to notify someone of something = to tell someone something formally; *customs were notified that the shipment had arrived*; *the local doctor notified the Health Service of the case of tropical fever*

③ **notion**
['nɪʊʃn] *noun*

(a) idea; *she has this strange notion that she ought to be a TV star*

(b) *US* **notions** = small articles used in sewing, like needles, ribbon, etc.

④ **notorious**
[nɪʊ'tɔːrɪɪs] *adjective*

well known for something bad; *he comes from a notorious gangster family*; *this road junction is notorious for accidents*

③ **noun**
[naʊn] *noun*

(in grammar) word which can be the subject of a verb and is used to refer to a person or thing; *nouns are words such as 'brick' and 'elephant'*; **proper noun** = word which is the name of a place, a person, a building, etc.; *proper nouns such as 'The Tower of London', 'the Mona Lisa', etc.* (NOTE: proper nouns are almost always written with a capital letter)

③ **novel**
['nɒvl]

1 *noun*

long story with invented characters and plot; *'Pickwick Papers' was Dickens' first major novel*

2 *adjective*

new; *being in New York is a novel experience for me*

④ **novelist**
['nɒvɪlɪst] *noun*

person who writes novels; *Jane Austen is one of the most important English women novelists*

① **November**
[nɪ'vembɪ] *noun*

eleventh month of the year, the month after October and before December; *today is November 5th US November 5*; *she was born in November*; *we never go on holiday in November* (NOTE: **November 5th** or **November 5**: say 'November the fifth' or 'the fifth of November'; American English: 'November fifth')

> COMMENT: November 5th is the date when people celebrate the Gunpowder Plot with bonfires and fireworks

① **now**
[naʊ]

1 *adverb*

at this point in time; *I can hear a train coming now*; *please can we go home now?*; *the flight is only two hours - he ought to be in Berlin by now*; *now's the best time for going skiing*; *a week from now we'll be sitting on the beach*; **until now** *or* **up to now** = until this point in time; *until now, I've never had to see a doctor*

2 *conjunction*

now that = since, because; *now that I know how to drive I can take more holidays by myself*; *now you've mentioned it, I do remember having a phone call from him last week*

3 *interjection*

(a) *(showing a warning)* now then, *don't be rude to the teacher!*; *come on now, work hard!*; *now, now! nobody wants to hear you crying*

(b) *(attracting someone's attention)* now, *everyone, let's begin the meeting*

② **nowadays**
['naʊɪdeɪz] *adverb*

at the present time; *nowadays lots of people go to Spain on holiday*; *the traffic is so bad nowadays that it takes us an hour to drive to Piccadilly Circus*

① **nowhere**
['nɪʊweɪ] *adverb*

(a) not in *or* to any place; *my purse was nowhere to be found*; *where are you going? - nowhere*; *there is nowhere else for them to live*; to get nowhere = to be unsuccessful; *I rang six shops to try and find a part for the washing machine, but got nowhere*; to be getting nowhere = not to have any success; *I'm getting nowhere with my research*

(b) nowhere near = not at all; *the work is nowhere near finished*; *he has nowhere near done all his homework*

③ **nuclear**
['nju:klɪɪ] *adjective*

(a) referring to energy from atoms; *a nuclear power station*; nuclear power = electricity produced by a nuclear power station; nuclear weapons = weapons made from energy from atoms, as opposed to conventional weapons such as guns

(b) nuclear family = family consisting simply of parents and children; *see also* EXTENDED FAMILY

③ **nuisance**
['nju:sɪns] *noun*

thing which annoys; *the dog's a nuisance because she always wants attention*; *it's a nuisance the bus doesn't run on Sundays*

① **number**
['nʌmbɪ]

1 *noun*

(a) figure; *13 is not a lucky number*; *they live on the opposite side of road at number 49*; *can you give me your telephone number?*; *a number 6 bus goes to Oxford Street*; *please quote your account number*; box number = reference number used when asking for mail to be sent to a post office or to a newspaper's offices; *please reply to Box No. 209*

(b) quantity of people or things; *the number of tickets sold was disappointing*; *a large number of children or large numbers of children will be sitting the exam*; *there were only a small number of people at the meeting*; a number of times = often; *I've seen that film a number of times*; any number of times = very often; *I've been to France any number of times*; *she could take her driving test any number of times but she still wouldn't pass it* (NOTE: when **a number** refers to a plural noun it is followed by a plural verb: **a number of houses were damaged**)

(c) issue of a magazine, newspaper, etc.; *we keep back numbers of magazines for six months and then throw them away*

(d) piece of music, song; *she played a selection of numbers by Noel Coward*

2 *verb*

(a) to give something a number; *the raffle tickets are numbered 1 to 1000*; *I refer to our invoices numbered 234 and 235*; *all the seats are clearly numbered*

(b) to count; *visitors to the exhibition numbered several thousand*; *he numbers among the most important writers of the 20th century*

③ **number plate**
['nʌmbɪ 'pleɪt] *noun*

one of two plates on a car (one on the front and one on the back) which shows a number that identifies the vehicle; *the thieves had changed the van's number plates* (NOTE: American English is **license plate**)

④ **Number Ten**
['nʌmbɪ 'ten] *noun*

No. 10 Downing Street, London, the house of the British Prime Minister; *sources close to Number Ten say the plan has not been agreed*; *the plan was turned down by Number Ten*; *it is rumoured that Number Ten was annoyed at the story* (NOTE: used to refer to the Prime Minister or to the government in general)

④ **numeral**
['nju:mɪrɪl] *noun*

written sign representing a number; *a computer file name can be made up of letters or numerals*; Arabic numerals = figures such as 3, 4 and 20; Roman numerals = figures such as III, IV and XX

③ **numerous**
['nju:mɪrɪs] *adjective*

very many; *he has been fined for speeding on numerous occasions*

④ **nun**
[nʌn] *noun*

woman member of a religious order; *a Tibetan nun*; *nuns served hot soup to the refugees* (NOTE: do not confuse with **none**; note: the equivalent men are **monks**)

③ **nurse**
[nɜːs]

1 *noun*

(woman or man) person who looks after sick people; *she has a job as a nurse in the local hospital*; *he's training to be a nurse*

2 *verb*

(a) to look after people who are ill; *when she fell ill her daughter nursed her until she was better*

(b) to be ill with something; *he's sitting in bed nursing his cold*; *she came back from her holiday nursing a broken arm*

(c) to nurse a feeling = to have a secret feeling against someone; *he has been nursing feelings of jealousy about his brother for years*

④ **nursery**
['nɜːsɪri] *noun*
(a) place where babies or young children are looked after; *my sister went to a nursery every day from the age of 18 months*; **day nursery** = nursery which is open during the day; **nursery school** = first school for very small children; **nursery rhyme** = children's traditional song

(b) nursery slopes = easy slope on a mountain where you learn to ski

(c) place where young plants are grown and sold; *buy some plants from the nursery* (NOTE: plural is **nurseries**)

④ **nursing**
['nɜːsɪŋ]
1 *noun*
profession of being a nurse; *she decided to go in for nursing*; *have you considered nursing as a career?*
2 *adjective*
referring to the job of looking after sick people; **nursing home** = small private hospital, especially one looking after old people

③ **nut**
[nʌt] *noun*
(a) fruit of a tree, with a hard shell; **to crack nuts** = to break the shells of nuts to get at the fruit inside; *he cracked the nuts with his teeth*

(b) metal ring which screws onto a metal rod to hold it tight; *screw the nut on tightly*; *(informal)* **the nuts and bolts of something** = the main details of something; *you'll need to master the nuts and bolts of the stock market before going to work in the city*; *see also* NUTS

④ **nutrient**
['njuːtriːnt] *noun*
(formal) substance in food which encourages the growth of living things; *plants take nutrients from rain*

> COMMENT: proteins, fats, vitamins are all nutrients needed to make animals grow; carbon, hydrogen, etc., are nutrients needed by plants

④ **nutrition**
[njuːˈtrɪʃn] *noun*
(a) study of food; *we are studying nutrition as part of the food science course*
(b) receiving food; *a scheme to improve nutrition in the poorer areas*

④ **nutritious**
[njuːˈtrɪʃəs] *adjective*
valuable as food because it provides nutrients which are needed by the body; *ice cream is not a very nutritious food*

③ **nuts**
[nʌts] *adjective*
(informal) mad; **nuts about someone** *or* **something** = very keen on someone *or* something; *he's nuts about old cars*; **to drive someone nuts** = to make someone crazy; *I wish they'd turn the music down - it's driving me nuts*

Oo

③ **O, o**
[əʊ]
fifteenth letter of the alphabet, between N and P; *'cooperate' can be spelt with a hyphen between the Os*

③ **oak**
[əʊk] *noun*
(a) type of large tree which loses its leaves in winter; *oaks grow to be very old*; *a forest of oak trees*
(b) wood from this tree; *an oak table*

③ **oath**
[əʊθ] *noun*
(a) solemn legal promise that someone will say or write only what is true; *all the members of the jury have to take an oath*; *the lords swore an oath to serve the king*; *he was on oath or*
under oath = he had promised in court to say what was true; *he was accused of lying to the court when he was under or on oath*
(b) swear word; *as the police grabbed him, he let out a long string of oaths* (NOTE: plural is **oaths** [əʊðz])

③ **oats**
[əʊts] *noun*
(a) cereal plant of which the grain is used as food; *the farmer has decided to grow oats in this field this year*
(b) to sow your wild oats = to behave in a wild way when young

③ **obey**
[əʊˈbeɪ] *verb*
to do what someone tells you to do; *if you can't obey orders you shouldn't be a policeman*; *everyone must obey the law*

② **object**

1 *noun*

['ɒbdʒekt]

(a) thing; *they thought they saw a strange object in the sky*

(b) aim; *their object is to take control of the radio station*

(c) *(in grammar)* noun or pronoun, etc., which follows directly from a verb or preposition; *in the phrase 'the cat caught the mouse', the word 'mouse' is the object of the verb 'caught'*

(d) money is no object = money is not a problem; *money is no object to them - they're very wealthy*

2 *verb*

[əb'dʒekt]

(a) to object (to) = to refuse to agree to; *she objected to the council's plans to widen the road; I object most strongly to paying extra for my little suitcase*

(b) to say why you refuse to agree; *he objected that the pay was too low*

③ **objection**

[əb'dʒekʃn] *noun*

reason for refusing to agree to something; *do you have any objection to me smoking?; any objections to the plan?; to raise an objection to something* = to object to something; *she raised several objections to the proposal*

③ **objective**

[əb'dʒektɪv]

1 *adjective*

considering things from a general point of view and not from your own; *you must be objective when planning the future of your business* (NOTE: the opposite is **subjective**)

2 *noun*

aim, object which you are aiming at; *our long-term objective is to make the company financially sound; the company has achieved its main objectives*

③ **obligation**

[ɒblɪ'geɪʃn] *noun*

(a) duty; legal debt; **to meet your obligations** = to pay your debts; *he cannot meet his obligations*

(b) duty to do something; *you have an obligation to attend the meeting*; **to be under an obligation to someone** = it is your duty to help someone; *she felt under an obligation to look after her friend's cat*; **two weeks' free trial without obligation** = the customer can try the item at home for two weeks without having to buy it at the end of the trial

③ **oblige**

[ə'blaɪdʒ] *verb*

(a) to force someone to do something; *he was obliged to hand the money back*

(b) to feel obliged to do something = to feel it is your duty to do something; *he felt obliged to study medicine at university because his father was a doctor*

(c) to do something useful or helpful; *he wanted to oblige you by weeding your garden for you*

(d) *(formal)* **to be obliged to someone** = to be grateful to someone for having done something; *thank you - I'm much obliged to you for your help; I'd be obliged if you could shut the window*

④ **obscure**

[əb'skjʊə]

1 *adjective*

(a) not clear; *there are several obscure points in his letter*

(b) not well-known; *they always stay in some obscure village in the Alps which no one has ever heard of*

2 *verb*

to hide, especially by covering; *the view from the top of the mountain was obscured by low clouds*

③ **observation**

[ɒbzɪ'veɪʃn] *noun*

(a) action of observing; *by careful observation, the police found out where the thieves had hidden the money*; **under observation** = being carefully watched; *the patient will be kept under observation for a few days*

(b) remark; *he made several observations about the government*

② **observe**

[əb'zɜːv] *verb*

(a) to follow or to obey (a law, rule, custom, etc.); *his family observes all the Jewish festivals; the local laws must be observed*

(b) to watch or to look at; *they observed the sunset from the top of the mountain*

(c) to notice; *the police observed the car coming out of the garage*

(d) to make a remark; *I merely observed that the bus was late as usual*

④ **observer**

[əb'zɜːvə] *noun*

person who attends an event and watches (especially without taking part); *the UN sent observers to the elections*

④ **obsess**

[əb'ses] *verb*

to occupy someone's mind all the time; *he is obsessed by wanting to make money; she is obsessed with wanting everything to be tidy*

④ **obsession**

[əb'seʃn] *noun*

(a) fixed idea which occupies your mind all the time; *making money is an obsession with him*

(b) idea or problem which worries you all the time, often associated with mental illness; *she has an obsession with washing her hair*

④ **obstacle**

['ɒbstɪkl] *noun*

thing which is in the way, which prevents someone going forward; *the truck had to negotiate rocks and other obstacles to cross the mountain pass*; *their computer system is not compatible with ours, which is an obstacle to any joint projects*

② **obtain**
[əb'teɪn] *verb*

(a) to get; *she obtained a copy of the will*; *he obtained control of the business*

(b) *(formal)* to be in existence, to have the force of law; *this rule still obtains in cases involving the Inland Revenue*

② **obvious**
['ɒbviːs] *adjective*

clear; easily seen; *it's obvious that we will have to pay for the damage*; *it was obvious to everyone that the shop was not making any money*

① **obviously**
['ɒbviːsli] *adverb*

clearly; *obviously we will need to borrow various pieces of equipment*

① **occasion**
[ə'keɪʒən] *noun*

(a) **a special occasion** = a special event (such as a wedding, etc.); *the baby's first birthday was a special occasion*; *it's an extra-special occasion - she's one hundred years old today!*

(b) happening, time when something happens; *it is an occasion for celebrations*; **on occasion** = from time to time; *on occasion, we spend a weekend in the country*

③ **occasional**
[ə'keɪʒnəl] *adjective*

happening now and then, not very often; *he was an occasional visitor to my parents' house*; *we make the occasional trip to London*; **occasional table** = small table used from time to time

② **occasionally**
[ə'keɪʒnəli] *adverb*

sometimes, not very often; *occasionally he has to work late*; *we occasionally go to the cinema*

③ **occupation**
[ɒkju'peɪʃn] *noun*

(a) act of occupying, of being occupied; *the occupation of the country by enemy soldiers*; *the occupation of the TV station by protesters*

(b) job, position, employment; *what is her occupation?*; *his main occupation is running a small engineering works*; *my Sunday afternoon occupation is washing the car*

③ **occupational**
[ɒkju'peɪʃnl] *adjective*

referring to a job; *stress is an occupational hazard, I'm afraid*; **occupational therapist** = person who treats patients by making them do certain activities and exercises; **occupational therapy** = treating patients by using activities to help them deal with problems or disabilities, used especially for handicapped patients or patients suffering from mental illness

③ **occupied**
['ɒkjupaɪd] *adjective*

(a) being used; *all the rooms in the hotel are occupied*; *all the toilets are occupied, so you'll have to wait*

(b) **occupied with** = busy with; *she is always occupied with her family*; *he is occupied with sorting out the mail*

② **occupy**
['ɒkjuːpaɪ] *verb*

(a) to live in or work in; *they occupy the flat on the first floor*; *the firm occupies offices in the centre of town*

(b) to be busy with; *dealing with the office occupies most of my time*

(c) to take control of a place by being inside it; *protesters occupied the TV station*

① **occur**
[ə'kɜː] *verb*

(a) to happen; *when did the accident occur?*

(b) to come to your mind; *it has just occurred to me* = I have just thought that; *did it never occur to you that she was lying?*

(c) to exist; *coal deposits occur in several parts of the country* (NOTE: **occurring - occurred**)

② **ocean**
['əʊʃn] *noun*

very large area of sea surrounding the continents; *ocean currents can be very dangerous*; *ocean liners used to dock here*

> COMMENT: the oceans are: the Atlantic, the Pacific, the Indian, the Antarctic (or Southern) and the Arctic

① **o'clock**
[ə'klɒk] *phrase; (used with numbers to show the time)* *get up - it's 7 o'clock*; *we never open the shop before 10 o'clock*; *by 2 o'clock in the morning everyone was asleep* (NOTE: **o'clock** is only used for the exact hour, not for times which include minutes. It can also be omitted: **we got home before eight** *or* **we got home before eight o'clock**)

① **October**
[ɒk'təʊbə] *noun*

tenth month of the year, between September and November; *do you ever go on holiday in October?*; *today is October 18th US October 18*; *last October we moved to London* (NOTE: **October 18th** *or* **October 18**: say 'October the eighteenth' or 'the eighteenth of October'; in American English: 'October eighteenth')

① **odd**
[ɒd] *adjective*

(a) strange, peculiar; *it's odd that she can never remember how to get to their house*; *he doesn't like chocolate - really, how odd!*

(b) **odd numbers** = numbers (like 17 or 33) which cannot be divided by two; *the odd-numbered buildings or the buildings with odd numbers are on the opposite side of the street*

(c) roughly, approximately; *she had twenty odd pairs of shoes in cardboard boxes*

(d) one forming part of a group; **an odd shoe** = one shoe of a pair; **we have a few odd boxes left** = we have a few boxes left out of all the boxes we had (NOTE: **odder - oddest**)

① **odds**
[ɒdz] *noun*

(a) difference between the amount which can be won and the amount which has been bet; *odds of 10 to 1*

(b) the possibility that something will happen; *the odds are against it*; *the odds are that she'll get the job*

(c) it makes no odds = it makes no difference; **to be at odds with someone** = to quarrel with someone all the time

(d) odds and ends = group of various things that have no connection with each other; *he used odds and ends found on the beach to make a sculpture*; *we made a meal from various odds and ends we found in the fridge*

① **of**
[ɒv] *preposition*

(a) *(showing a connection)* *she's the sister of the girl who you met at the party*; *where's the top of the jam jar?*; *what are the names of Henry VIII's wives?*

(b) *(showing a part or a quantity)* *how much of the cloth do you need?*; *today is the sixth of March*; *there are four boys and two girls - six of them altogether*; *half of the staff are on holiday*; *a litre of orange juice*

(c) *(making a description)* *the school takes children of ten and over*; *the town of Edinburgh is important for its festival*

(d) *(showing position, material, cause)* *he lives in the north of the town*; *the jumper is made of cotton*; *she died of cancer* (NOTE: of is often used after verbs or adjectives **to think of, to be fond of, to be tired of, to smell of, to be afraid of,** etc.)

① **of course**
['ɒv 'kɔːs]

(a) *(used to make 'yes' or 'no' stronger)* *are you coming with us? - of course I am!*; *do you want to lose all your money? - of course not!*

(b) naturally; *he is rich, so of course he lives in a big house*

① **off**
[ɒf]
1 *adverb & preposition*

(a) *(showing movement or position away from a place)* *we're off to the shops*; *the office is just off the main road*; *they spent their holiday on an island off the coast of Wales*; *the children got off the bus*; *take your boots off before you come into the house*

(b) away from work; *she took the week off*; *it's my secretary's day off today*; *half the staff are off with flu*

(c) not switched on; *switch the light off before you leave the office*; *is the TV off?* (NOTE: **off** is often used after verbs **to keep off, to break off, to fall off, to take off,** etc.)

2 *adjective*

(a) switched off; *make sure the switch is in the OFF position*

(b) not good to eat; *I think this meat's a bit off*

(c) *(in a restaurant)* not available; *chicken is off today*

(d) cancelled; *she phoned to say the deal was off*

(e) not liking food; not taking food or drink; *I'm off alcohol for six months*; *she's off shellfish because it gives her a rash*

◊ **off and on**
['ɒf ənd 'ɒn] *adverb*

not all the time, with breaks in between; *it's been raining off and on all afternoon*

③ **off-colour** *US* **off-color**
[ɒf'kʌlɪ] *adjective*

to be off-colour = to feel unwell, not very well; *John's feeling a bit off-colour today*; *she's a bit off-colour today, so she won't be coming to the party*

③ **offence** *US* **offense**
[ə'fens] *noun*

(a) state of being offended; **to take offence at** = to be offended by; *he took offence at being called lazy*; *don't take offence - I didn't really mean it*

(b) crime, act which is against the law; *he was charged with committing an offence*; *since it was his first offence, he was let off with a fine*

④ **offend**
[ə'fend] *verb*

(a) to be or to go against public opinion, someone's feelings; *he offended the whole village by the article he wrote in the local paper*

(b) to commit a crime; *he was released from prison and immediately offended again*

④ **offender**
[ə'fendə] *noun*

person who commits an offence against the law; *the job of the police is to bring offenders to justice*; **first offender** = someone who commits an offence for the first time; *since he was a first offender, he was let off with a warning*; **young offender** = young person who commits a crime

④ **offensive**
[ə'fensɪv]
1 *adjective*

(a) unpleasant, which offends; *what an offensive smell!*; *the waiter was quite offensive*

(b) *(in army)* **offensive weapons** = weapons which are used in an attack; *it is against the law to carry offensive weapons*

2 *noun*

(a) *(military)* attack; *the offensive was successful, and the enemy retreated*

(b) to take the offensive *or* **to go on the offensive** = to start to do something against someone; *he took the offensive and demanded an explanation*

① **offer**
['ɒfɪ] *verb*
1 *noun*
(a) thing which is proposed; *she accepted his offer of a job in Paris*; **on offer** = which has been offered; *there are several good holiday bargains on offer*
(b) bargain offer *or* **special offer** = goods which are put on sale at a reduced price; *this week's bargain offer - 30% off all holidays in Egypt*; *oranges are on special offer today*; *this supermarket always has special offers*
2 *verb*
to say that you will give something or do something; *she offered to drive him to the station*; **to offer someone a job** = to tell someone that he can have a job in your company; *if they offer you the job, take it*; *he was offered a job, but he turned it down*

④ **offering**
['ɒfrɪŋ] *noun*
thing which is offered; a present; *it's only a small offering, I'm afraid*; *all offerings will be gratefully received!*

① **office**
['ɒfɪs] *noun*
(a) room or building where you carry on a business or where you organize something; *I'll be working late at the office this evening*; *why is Miss Jones's office bigger than mine?*; *we bought some new office furniture*; *US* **doctor's office** = room where a doctor sees his patients (NOTE: British English for this is a **surgery**)
(b) position, job; *she holds the office of secretary*; **term of office** = period of time when someone has a position; *during his term of office as President*
(c) government department; **the Foreign Office** = British government department dealing with relations with other countries; **the Home Office** = British Government department dealing with internal affairs, such as the police and prisons; **Serious Fraud Office** = government department in charge of investigating fraud in large companies; *see also* POST OFFICE

① **officer**
['ɒfɪsɪ] *noun*
(a) person who holds an official position; *the customs officer asked me to open my suitcase*
(b) person who is in charge of others in the army, navy, air force, etc.; *ordinary soldiers must always salute officers*
(c) police officer = policeman; *there are two police officers at the door*

② **official**
[ə'fɪʃl]
1 *adjective*

(a) referring to any organization, especially one which is recognized as part of a government, etc.; *he left official papers in his car*; *we had an official order from the local authority*; *he represents an official body*
(b) done or approved by someone in authority; *she received an official letter of explanation*; *the strike was made official by the union headquarters*
2 *noun*
person holding a recognized position; *they were met by an official from the embassy*; *I'll ask an official of the social services department to help you*; **customs official** = person working for customs

④ **offshore**
[ɒf'ʃɔː] *adjective*
(a) at a distance from the shore; *we went to visit an offshore oil installation*
(b) offshore wind = wind which blows from the coast towards the sea
(c) on an island which is a tax haven; *offshore investments have produced a good rate of return*

③ **off side** *or* **offside**
['ɒf 'saɪd]
1 *noun*
(in a car) side nearest the middle of the road; *you usually overtake on the off side of another vehicle*
2 *adjective*
referring to the side of a car nearest to the middle of the road; *your offside rear light isn't working* (NOTE: the other side, where the passenger sits, is the **near side**)
3 *adverb; (in football)* between the ball and the opposing team's goal; *he was offside, so the goal did not count*

① **often**
['ɒfn] *adverb*
many times, frequently; *I often have to go to town on business*; *do you eat beef often?*; *how often is there a bus to Richmond?*; **every so often** = from time to time; *we go to the cinema every so often*

① **oh**
[əʊ] *interjection; (showing surprise, interest, excitement)* *Oh look, there's an elephant!*; *Oh can't you stop making that noise?*; *Oh, Mr Smith, someone phoned for you while you were out*; *you must write to the bank manager - oh no I won't*

② **oil**
[ɔɪl]
1 *noun*
(a) thick mineral liquid found mainly underground and used as a fuel or to make something move easily; *the door squeaks - it need some oil*; *some of the beaches are covered with oil*; *the company is drilling for oil in the desert*

(a) liquid of various kinds which flows easily, produced from plants and used in cooking; *cook the vegetables in hot oil*; olive oil = oil made from olives

(c) oil (paint) = paint made with colours and oil; *I used to paint in oils but now I prefer water colours*; oil painting = picture painted in oils, not in water colour

2 *verb*

to put oil on *or* in (especially to make a machine run more easily); *you should oil your bicycle chain; that door needs oiling*

④ **oily**
['ɔɪli] *adjective*

(a) containing oil; *oily food makes me feel sick; the tank was full of some oily liquid*

(b) covered with oil; *he used an old oily rag to clean his motorbike* (NOTE: oilier - oiliest)

④ **ointment**
['ɔɪntmɪnt] *noun*

smooth healing cream which you spread on the skin; *rub the ointment onto your knee*

① **OK** *or* **okay**
['ɪʊ'keɪ]

1 *interjection*

all right, yes; *would you like a coffee? - OK!; it's ten o'clock - OK, let's get going*

2 *adjective*

all right; *he was off ill yesterday, but he seems to be OK now; it is OK for me to bring the dogs?*

3 *noun*

to give something the OK = to approve something; *the committee gave our plan the OK*

4 *verb*

to approve something; *the committee OK'd or okayed our plan* (NOTE: OK'd ['ɪʊ'keɪd])

① **old**
[əʊld] *adjective*

(a) not young; *my uncle is an old man - he's eighty-four; she lives in an old people's home*

(b) having existed for a long time; *he collects old cars; play some old music, I don't like this modern stuff*

(c) not new; which has been used for a long time; *put on an old shirt if you're going to wash the car; he got rid of his old car and bought a new one*

(d) with a certain age; *he's six years old today; how old are you?*

(e) (used as a pleasant way of talking about someone) *he's a sweet old man; come on, old thing, it's time to go home* (NOTE: older - oldest)

③ **old boy**
['ʊld 'bɔɪ] *noun*

(a) (informal) old man; *you'll have to shout - the old boy's gone quite deaf*

(b) former pupil of a school; *did you know that the bank manager is an old boy of this school?; the old boy network = system where men who were at school together help each other get

ahead in later life; *thanks to the old boy network he got a good job in the bank; he got himself a job in insurance through the old boy network*

④ **old-fashioned**
[əʊld'fæʃənd] *adjective*

not in fashion; out of date; *she wore old-fashioned clothes; call me old-fashioned, but I don't approve of the way young people behave*

④ **olive**
['ɒlɪv] *noun*

(a) small black or green fruit from which oil is made for use in cooking; *olives are grown in Mediterranean countries like Spain, Greece and Italy*; black olives = ripe olives; green olives = olives which are eaten before they are ripe; *which do you prefer - green or black olives?*; olive oil = oil made from olives; *add a little olive oil to the pan*

(b) tree which produces this fruit; olive branch = sign of peace; *the negotiators held out the olive branch*

(c) olive (green) = dull green colour like that of olives which are not yet ripe; *he wore an olive green coat*

④ **Olympics** *or* **Olympic Games**
[ə'lɪmpɪks or ə'lɪmpɪk 'geɪmz] *noun*

international athletic competition held every four years; *he's an Olympic sportsman; she broke the world record or she set up a new world record in the last Olympics; the Olympic Games were held in Sydney in 2000*

④ **omit**
[ə'mɪt] *verb*

(a) to leave something out; *she omitted the date when typing the contract*

(b) to omit to do something = not to do something; *he omitted to tell the police that he had lost the documents* (NOTE: omitting - omitted)

① **on**
[ɒn]

1 *preposition*

(a) on the top or surface of something; *put the box down on the floor; flies can walk on the ceiling*

(b) hanging from; *hang your coat on the hook*

(c) (showing movement or place) *a crowd of children got on the train; the picture's on page three; the post office is on the left-hand side of the street*

(d) part of; *she's on the staff of the bank; he's been on the committee for six years*

(e) doing something; *I have to go to Germany on business; we're off on holiday tomorrow*

(f) (showing time, date, day) *the shop is open on Sundays; we went to see my mother on her birthday*; on his arrival = when he arrived

(g) (means of travel) *you can go there on foot - it only takes five minutes; she came on her new bike*

(h) about; *the committee produced a report on German industry; she wrote a book on wild flowers*

(i) *(showing an instrument or machine)* he *played some music on the piano; the song is available on CD; he was on the telephone for most of the morning; the film was on TV last night*

(j) *(informal)* paid by someone; *the drinks are on me*

2 *adverb*

(a) being worn; *have you all got your wellingtons on?; the central heating was off, so he kept his coat on in the house*

(b) working; *have you put the kettle on?; the heating is on; she left all the lights on; she turned the engine on; he switched the TV on*

(c) being shown or played; *what's on at the cinema this week?*

(d) continuing, not stopping; *he didn't stop to say hello, but just walked on; he went on playing the drums even though we asked him to stop; go on - I like to hear you play the piano*

(e) *(showing time has passed)* later on that evening, the phone rang; he almost drowned, and from that time on refused to go near water (NOTE: on is often used after verbs: to sit on, to jump on, to put on, to lie on, etc.)

◊ **on and off**
['ɒn ənd 'ɒf] *adverb*
not continuously, with breaks in between; *it's been raining on and off all afternoon*

◊ **on and on**
['ɒn ənd 'ɒn] *adverb*
without stopping; *we drove on and on through the night*

① **once**
[wʌns]
1 *adverb*

(a) one time; *take the tablets once a day; the magazine comes out once a month; how many times did you go to the cinema last year? - only once; once in a while* = from time to time, but not often; *it's nice to go to have an Indian meal once in a while*

(b) formerly, at a time in the past; *once, when it was snowing, the car slid off the road; he's a man I knew once when I worked in London; (beginning children's stories)* once upon a time = at a certain time in the past; *once upon a time, there was a wicked old woman; see also* AT ONCE

2 *conjunction* as soon as (in the future); *once he starts talking you can't get him to stop; once we've moved house I'll give you a phone call*

① **one**
[wʌn]
1 number 1; *one plus one makes two; our grandson is one year old today; his grandmother is a hundred and one*
2 *noun*

(a) single item; *have a chocolate - oh dear, there's only one left!;* last but one = the one before the last; *this is the last weekend but one before Christmas;* one by one = one after another; *he ate all the chocolates one by one; they came in one by one and sat in a row at the back of the hall*

(b) *(informal)* a quick one = a quick drink; *let's have a quick one before the meeting starts;* one for the road = a last drink before leaving the bar; *let's have one for the road*

(c) *(informal)* she hit him one with the bottle = she hit him with the bottle

2 *adjective & pronoun*

(a) single (thing); *which hat do you like best - the black one or the red one?; one of the staff will help you carry the box to your car; I've lost my map - have you got one?; small cars use less petrol than big ones; all the china plates were dirty so we made do with paper ones*

(b) *(formal)* you; *one can't spend all the morning waiting to see the doctor, can one?; at his age, one isn't allowed to drive a car*

(c) one another = each other; *we write to one another every week* (NOTE: one (1) but first (1st))

③ **oneself**
[wʌn'self] *pronoun*
referring to the person speaking as an indefinite subject; *it's important to be able to look after oneself; it's not easy to do it oneself*

③ **one-way**
['wʌn 'weɪ]
going in one direction only; *US* one-way ticket = ticket for one journey from one place to another (NOTE: British English is a single); one-way street = street where the traffic only goes in one direction; *don't turn left here - it's a one-way street*

③ **onion**
['ʌnjɪn] *noun*
strong-smelling vegetable with a round white bulb; *fry the onions in butter; I don't like onion soup;* spring onion = young onion eaten raw in salad

④ **online**
['ɒnlaɪn] *adjective & adverb*
directly connected to a computer; *you need to have the right software to access the data online*

① **only**
['ʊnli]
1 *adjective*
one single (thing or person), when there are no more; *don't break it - it's the only one I've got;* only child = son or daughter who has no other brothers or sisters; *she's an only child*
2 *adverb*

(a) with no one or nothing else; *we've only got ten pounds between us; only an accountant can deal with this problem; this lift is for staff only*

(b) as recently as; *we saw her only last week*; *only yesterday the bank phoned for information*

3 *conjunction*

(a) but, except; *I like my mother-in-law very much, only I don't want to see her every day of the week*

(b) *(phrase showing a strong wish)* if only we had known you were in town!; *she's late - if only she'd phone to let us know where she is!*

◊ **only just**
['ıunli 'dʒʌst]
almost not; *we only just had enough money to pay the bill*; *he had to run and only just caught the last bus*

◊ **only too**
['ınli 'tuː]
very much; *we would be only too glad to help you if we can*

① **onto**
['ɒntuː] *preposition*
on to; *the speaker went up onto the platform*; *the door opens directly onto the garden*; *turn the box onto its side* (NOTE: also spelt **on to**)

④ **ooh!**
[uː] *interjection; (showing surprise or shock) ooh you are awful!*; *ooh look at that spider!*

④ **oops!**
[uːps] *interjection; (showing surprise or that you are sorry) oops! I didn't mean to tread on your toe*

① **open**
['ıupın]
1 *adjective*

(a) not shut; *the safe door is open*; *leave the window open - it's very hot in here*

(b) working, which you can go into; *is the supermarket open on Sundays?*; *the show is open from 9 a.m. to 6 p.m.*; *the competition is open to anyone over the age of fifteen*

(c) without anything to protect you; *we like walking in the open air*; **the garden is open on three sides** = there is a fence or wall on one side of the garden only; **open space** = area of land which has no buildings or trees on it; *the parks provide welcome open space in the centre of the city*

(d) **with an open mind** = with no particular opinions; *I'd like to keep an open mind until the investigation is completed*

2 *noun*

(a) place outside which is not covered or hidden; *keep the plants in the greenhouse during the winter, but bring them out into the open in the summer*; *the police investigation brought all sorts of offences out into the open*

(b) competition which anyone can enter provided he or she is good enough; *he has qualified for the British Open*

3 *verb*

(a) to make something open; *can you open the door for me, I'm trying to carry these heavy boxes?*; *don't open the envelope until I tell you to*

(b) to start doing something, to start a business; *a new restaurant is going to open next door to us*; *most shops open early in the morning*

(c) to make something begin officially; *the new hotel was opened by the Minister of Tourism*; *the exhibition will be formally opened by the queen*; *the chairman opened the meeting at 10.30*

③ **opener**
['ıupnı] *noun*
device which opens; *see also* CAN OPENER, TIN OPENER

③ **opening**
['ıupnıŋ] *noun*

(a) action of becoming open; *the opening of the exhibition has been postponed*; *the office opening times are 9.30 to 5.30*

(b) hole or space; *the cows got out through an opening in the wall*

(c) opportunity, such as a job vacancy; *we have openings for telephone sales staff*

④ **openly**
['ıupnli] *adverb*
in a frank and open way; *they discussed the plan quite openly*; *can I talk openly to you about my sister?*

③ **open on to**
['ıupın 'ɒn tuː] *verb*
to lead out on to or to look out on to; *the door opens straight onto the street*; *the windows open onto the garden*

④ **opera**
['ɒprı] *noun*
performance on the stage with music, in which the words are sung and not spoken; *'the Marriage of Figaro' is one of Mozart's best-known operas*; *we have tickets for the opera tomorrow*; *we are going to see the new production of an opera by Britten*

② **operate**
['ɒpıreıt] *verb*

(a) to make something work; *he knows how to operate the machine*; *she is learning how to operate the new telephone switchboard*

(b) to function, to work; *small businesses operate on very narrow margins*; *how does this network operate?*

(c) **to operate on a patient** = to treat a patient by cutting open the body; *she was operated on by Mr Jones*; **operating theatre** = special room in a hospital where surgeons carry out operations; *they rushed him straight into the operating theatre* (NOTE: American English is **operating room**)

① **operation**
['ɒpɪ'reɪʃn] *noun*
(a) action of operating; *the rescue operation was successful*; **to come into operation** = to begin to be applied; *the new schedules came into operation on June 1st*
(b) treatment when a surgeon cuts open the body; *she's had three operations on her leg*; *the operation lasted almost two hours*

③ **operator**
['ɒpɪreɪtɪ] *noun*
(a) person who works instruments, etc.; *he's a computer operator*; *she's a machine operator*
(b) person who works a central telephone system; *dial 0 for the operator*; *you can place a call through or via the operator*
(c) person who organizes things; **tour operator** = travel agent who organizes package holidays or tours; *(informal)* **a smart operator** = a clever businessman

① **opinion**
[ə'pɪnjən] *noun*
(a) what someone thinks about something; *ask the lawyer for his opinion about the letter*; **he has a very high** *or* **very low opinion of his assistant** = he thinks his assistant is very good *or* very bad
(b) **in my opinion** = as I think; *in my opinion, we should wait until the weather gets warmer before we go on holiday*; *tell me what in your opinion we should do*

③ **opinion poll**
[ə'pɪnjən 'pɪʊl] *noun*
asking a sample group of people questions, so as to get the probable opinion of the whole population; *the opinion poll taken before the election did not reflect the final result*; *opinion polls showed that people preferred butter to margarine*

③ **opponent**
[ə'pəʊnɪnt] *noun*
(a) person or group which is against something; *opponents of the planned motorway have occupied the site*
(b) *(in boxing, an election, etc.)* person who fights someone else; *his opponent in the election is a local councillor*; *he knocked out his last three opponents*

① **opportunity**
[ɒpɪ'tjuːnɪti] *noun*
chance or circumstances which allow you to do something; *when you were in London, did you have an opportunity to visit St Paul's Cathedral?*; *I'd like to take this opportunity to thank all members of staff for the work they have done over the past year*; **a good opportunity for doing something** = a good time for doing something; *it is an excellent opportunity to buy the business*; **equal opportunities** = employing people on their merits, treating them with equal respect, regardless of age, race, sex, etc.; *see also* WINDOW

③ **oppose**
[ə'pəʊz] *verb*
(a) to put yourself against someone in an election; *she is opposing him in the election*
(b) to try to prevent something happening; *several groups oppose the new law*

① **opposed to**
[ə'pəʊzd 'tuː] *adjective*
(a) not in favour of; *he is opposed to the government's policy on education*
(b) in contrast to; *if you paint the kitchen a light colour as opposed to dark red, you will find it will look bigger*

② **opposite**
['ɒpɪzɪt]
1 *preposition* on the other side of, facing; *I work in the offices opposite the railway station*; *she sat down opposite me*
2 *adjective*
which is on the other side; *the shop's not on this side of the street - it's on the opposite side*; *her van was hit by a lorry going in the opposite direction*
3 *noun*
something which is completely different; *'black' is the opposite of 'white'*; *she's just the opposite of her brother - he's tall and thin, she's short and fat*; *he likes to say one thing, and then do the opposite*

① **opposition**
[ɒpɪ'zɪʃn] *noun*
(a) action of opposing; *there was a lot of opposition to the company's plans to knock down the town hall and build a supermarket*
(b) *(in politics)* the party or group which opposes the government; *the leader of the opposition rose to speak*; *the party lost the election and is now in opposition*

④ **opt**
[ɒpt] *verb*
to choose; **to opt for something** = to choose something, to decide in favour of something; *in the end, she opted for a little black dress*; *we couldn't decide where to go on holiday, and in the end opted for Greece*; *see also* OPT OUT

③ **optical**
['ɒptɪkl] *adjective*
(a) referring to the eyes or to eyesight; **an optical illusion** = thing which seems real when you see it, but is not; *the sword seemed to go right through his body, but it was just an optical illusion*; **optical telescope** = telescope which uses mirrors and lenses to make the image and light coming from stars very much larger (as opposed to a radio telescope)
(b) referring to the science of light; **optical fibres** = fine threads of glass used for transmitting light signals; *metal telephone cables are being replaced by optical fibres*

③ **optician**
['ɒp'tɪʃn] *noun*
person who tests your eyesight, prescribes and
sells glasses or contact lenses, etc.; *the optician
prescribed some reading glasses*; **the optician's**
= the shop and offices of an optician; *I must go
to the optician's to have my eyes tested*

④ **optimism**
['ɒptɪmɪzm] *noun*
belief that everything is as good as it can be or
will work out for the best in the future; cheerful
attitude; *he showed considerable optimism for
the future of the company*; *I like your brother -
he's always full of optimism*

④ **optimist**
['ɒptɪmɪst] *noun*
person who believes everything will work out
for the best in the end; *he's an optimist - he
always thinks everything will turn out fine*

④ **optimistic**
[ɒptɪ'mɪstɪk] *adjective*
feeling that everything will work out for the
best; *we are optimistic about the plan* or *that
the plan will succeed*

① **option**
['ɒpʃn] *noun*
(a) choice, other possible action; *one option
would be to sell the house*; *the tour offers
several options as visits to churches and
museums*
(b) **to hold an option on something** = to have
the opportunity to buy or sell something within a
certain time or at a certain price

③ **opt out**
['ɒpt 'aʊt] *verb*
to opt out of something = to decide not to take
part in something; *he opted out of the trip
because he couldn't afford the price of a ticket*

① **or**
[ɔː] *conjunction*
(a) *(linking alternatives, showing other things
that can be done)* *you can come with us in the
car or just take the bus*; *do you prefer tea or
coffee?*; *was he killed in an accident or was he
murdered?*; *the film starts at 6.30 or 6.45, I
can't remember which*
(b) *(approximately)* *five or six people came into
the shop*; *it costs three or four dollars*

◊ **or else**
[ɔː 'els]
(a) or if not; *don't miss the bus, or else you'll
have a long wait for the next one*; *put a coat on
to go out, or else you'll catch cold*; *we'd better
get up early or else we'll miss the train*; *you
must have a ticket, or else you will be thrown
off the train by the inspector*
(b) *(as informal threat)* **you'd better pay, or
else** = if you don't pay, I'll hit you

④ **oral**
['ɔːrɪl]
1 *adjective*

(a) spoken, by speaking; *there is an oral test as
well as a written one*
(b) **oral medicine** = medicine taken by the
mouth
2 *noun*
examination where you answer questions by
speaking, not writing; *he passed the written
examination but failed the oral*

③ **orange**
['ɒrɪnʒ]
1 *noun*
(a) sweet tropical fruit, coloured between red
and yellow; *she had a glass of orange juice and
a cup of coffee for breakfast*; *we had roast duck
and orange sauce for dinner*; **orange
marmalade** = marmalade made from oranges
(usually bitter oranges); **orange squash** = drink
made of concentrated orange juice and water; *do
you want some orange squash?*
(b) **orange (tree)** = tree which bears this fruit; *a
grove of oranges and lemons*; *the orange farms
of Spain*; *we have a little orange tree in a pot*
(c) the colour of an orange, a colour between
yellow and red; *he painted the bathroom a very
bright orange*
2 *adjective*
of the colour of an orange; *that orange tie is
awful*

④ **orbit**
['ɔːbɪt]
1 *noun*
curved path of something moving through
space; *the rocket will put the satellite into orbit
round the earth*
2 *verb*
to move in an orbit round something; *the
satellite orbits the earth once every five hours*

④ **orchestra**
['ɔːkɪstrɪ] *noun*
(a) large group of musicians who play together;
the London Symphony Orchestra
(b) **orchestra pit** = part of a theatre, usually
next to the stage and just below it, where the
musicians sit; *you can see into the orchestra pit
from where we're sitting*; **orchestra stalls** =
seats on the ground floor of a theatre nearest the
orchestra and the stage

① **order**
['ɔːdɪ]
1 *noun*
(a) instruction to someone to do something; *he
shouted orders to the workmen*; *if you can't
obey orders you can't be a soldier*
(b) *(from a customer)* asking for something to be
served or to be sent; *we've had a large order for
books from Russia*; *she gave the waitress her
order*
(c) things ordered in a restaurant; goods ordered
by a customer; *the waiter brought him the
wrong order*; *our order has been lost in the post*

(d) special way of putting things; *put the invoices in order of their dates*; **the stock in the warehouse is all in the wrong order** *or* **all out of order** = it is not in the right place

(e) functioning correctly; **out of order** = not working; *you'll have to use the stairs, the lift is out of order*; **in order** = correct; *are his papers in order?*

(f) **in order that** = so that; *cyclists should wear orange coats in order that drivers can see them in the dark*; **in order to** = so as to; *she ran as fast as she could in order to catch the bus*; *he looked under the car in order to see if there was an oil leak*

2 *verb*

(a) to tell someone to do something; *they ordered the protesters out of the building*; *the doctor ordered him to take four weeks' holiday*

(b) *(of a customer)* to ask for something to be served or to be sent; *they ordered chicken and chips and some wine*; *I've ordered a new computer for the office*; *they ordered a Rolls Royce for the managing director*

③ **order about**
['ɔːdɪ ə'baʊt] *verb*
(informal) to tell someone what to do all the time; *I don't like being ordered about*

① **ordinary**
['ɔːdɪnri] *adjective*
not special; *I'll wear my ordinary suit to the wedding*; *they lead a very ordinary life*; **out of the ordinary** = not usual, very different; *their flat is quite out of the ordinary*; **nothing out of the ordinary** = normal; *the weather in June was nothing out of the ordinary*

③ **organ**
['ɔːgɪn] *noun*
(a) part of the body with a special function, such as the heart, liver, etc.; *he was very ill and some of his organs had stopped functioning*

(b) musical instrument with a keyboard and many pipes through which air is pumped to make a sound; *she played the organ at our wedding*; *the organ played the 'Wedding March' as the bride and bridegroom walked out of the church*

(c) *(formal)* official newspaper; *it is the organ of the book trade*; *the appointments will be published in the official organs*

④ **organic**
[ɔːˈgænɪk] *adjective*
(a) referring to living things; **organic chemistry** = chemistry of carbon compounds

(b) gown using natural fertilizers without any chemicals; *organic vegetables are more expensive but are better for you*; **organic farming** = farming using only natural fertilizers

③ **organism**
['ɔːgɪnɪzm] *noun*
living thing; *with a microscope you can see millions of tiny organisms in ordinary tap water*

① **organization**
[ɔːgɪnaɪ'zeɪʃn] *noun*
(a) action of arranging something; *the organization of the meeting was done by the secretary*

(b) organized group or institution; *he's chairman of an organization which looks after blind people*; *international relief organizations are sending supplies*

① **organize**
['ɔːgɪnaɪz] *verb*
(a) to arrange; *she is responsible for organizing the meeting*; *we organized ourselves into two groups*; *the company is organized in three sections*

(b) to put into good order; *we have put her in charge of organizing the historical documents relating to the town*

③ **organizer**
['ɔːgɪnaɪzɪ] *noun*
(a) person who arranges things; **tour organizer** = company or person who arranges a tour

(b) **personal organizer** = little computer or book in which you enter your appointments, addresses, etc.; *I'll put the dates in my personal organizer*; *he was lost when someone stole his organizer*

② **origin**
['ɒrɪdʒɪn] *noun*
beginning, where something *or* someone comes from; *his family has French origins*; **country of origin** = country where a product is manufactured or where food comes from; *there should be a label saying which is the country of origin*

① **original**
[əˈrɪdʒɪnl]
1 *adjective*
(a) from the beginning; *the original ideas for his paintings came from his own garden*

(b) new and different, made for the first time; with ideas not based on those of other people; *they solved the problem by using a very original method*; *the planners have produced some very original ideas for the new town centre*

(c) not a copy; *they sent a copy of the original invoice*; *he kept the original receipt for reference*

2 *noun*
thing from which other things are copied, translated, etc.; *the original was lost in the post but luckily I kept a copy*; *she found that the old painting she had bought in a sale was an original and not a copy*

② **originally**
[əˈrɪdʒnəli] *adverb*
in the beginning; *originally it was mine, but I gave it to my brother*; *the family originally came from France in the 18th century*

④ **originate**
[ə'rɪdʒɪneɪt] *verb*
(a) to begin, to start from, to have a beginning; *this strain of flu originated in Hong Kong; his problems at work originated in his home life*
(b) to make for the first time; *we have originated a new style of computer keyboard*

④ **orthodox**
['ɔːθɪdɒks] *adjective*
(a) holding the generally accepted beliefs of a religion, a philosophy, etc.; *the finance minister is following orthodox financial principles*
(b) (people) who observe traditional religious practices very strictly; *he was brought up in an orthodox Jewish family*
(c) the Orthodox Church = the Christian Church of Eastern Europe

① **other**
['ʌðɪ] *adjective & pronoun*
(a) different (person or thing), not the same; *we went swimming while the other members of the group sat and watched; I don't like chocolate cakes - can I have one of the other ones or one of the others?; I'm fed up with Spain - can't we go to some other place next year?*
(b) second one of two; *he has two cars - one is red, and the other (one) is blue; one of their daughters is fat, but the other (one) is quite thin*
(c) *(showing something which is not clear)* she *went to stay in some hotel or other in London; he met some girl or other at the party*
(d) the other day *or* **the other week** = a day or two ago *or* a week or two ago; *I'm surprised to hear he's in hospital - I saw him only the other day and he looked perfectly well*; **every other** = every second one; *he wrote home every other day* = on Monday, Wednesday, Friday, etc.
(e) one after the other = following in line; *the trees were cut down one after the other; all the family got colds one after the other*

① **otherwise**
['ʌðɪwaɪz] *adverb*
(a) in other ways; *your little boy can be noisy sometimes, but otherwise he's an excellent pupil*
(b) if not, or else; *are you sure you can't come on Tuesday? - otherwise I'll have to cancel my visit to the doctor*

① **ought**
[ɔːt] *verb used with other verbs*
(a) *(to mean it would be a good thing to)* you *ought to go swimming more often; you ought to see the doctor if your cough doesn't get better; he oughtn't to eat so much - he'll get fat; the travel agent ought to have told you the hotel was full before you went on holiday*
(b) *(to mean it is probable that)* she *ought to pass her driving test easily; he left his office at six, so he ought to be home by now* (NOTE:

negative is **ought not,** shortened to **oughtn't.** Note also that **ought** is always followed by **to** and a verb)

③ **ounce**
[aʊns] *noun*
measure of weight (= 28 grams); *the baby weighed 6lb 3oz (six pounds three ounces) mix four ounces of sugar with two eggs* (NOTE: usually written **oz** after figures: **3oz of butter:** say 'three ounces of butter')

① **our**
[aʊɪ] *adjective*
which belongs to us; *our office is near the station; our cat is missing again; two of our children caught flu* (NOTE: do not confuse with **hour**)

① **ours**
[aʊɪz] *pronoun*
thing or person that belongs to us; *that house over there is ours; friends of ours told us that the restaurant was good; can we borrow your car, because ours is being serviced?* (NOTE: do not confuse with **hours**)

① **ourselves**
[aʊɪ'selvz] *pronoun*
(a) referring to us; *we all organized ourselves into two teams; we were enjoying ourselves when the police came*
(b) all by ourselves = with no one else; *we built the house all by ourselves; we don't like being all by ourselves in the dark house*

① **out**
[aʊt] *adverb*
(a) away from inside; *how did the rabbit get out of its cage?; she pulled out a box of matches; take the computer out of its packing case; see also* OUT OF
(b) not at home; *no one answered the phone - they must all be out*
(c) away from here; *the tide is out; the fishing boats left the harbour and are now out at sea*
(d) wrong (in calculating); *the cash in the till was £10 out*
(e) not in fashion; *long hair is out this year*
(f) just appeared; **the roses are all out** = the roses are all in flower; **her book is just out** = her book has just been published (NOTE: **out** is often used with verbs: **to jump out, to come out, to get out,** etc.)

④ **outbreak**
['aʊtbreɪk] *noun*
sudden series of cases of an illness or disturbance; *there has been an outbreak of measles at the school; there was an outbreak of violence at the prison yesterday*

③ **outcome**
['aʊtkʌm] *noun*
result; *the outcome of the match was in doubt until the final few minutes; what was the outcome of the appeal?*

③ **outdoor**
[aʊt'dɔ:] *adjective*
in the open air; *the club has an outdoor swimming pool; the hotel offers all sorts of outdoor activities* (NOTE: the opposite is **indoor**)

③ **outdoors**
[aʊt'dɔ:z]
1 *adverb*
in the open air, not inside a building; *the ceremony is usually held outdoors; why don't we take our coffee outdoors and sit in the sun?; the concert will be held outdoors if the weather is good;* NOTE: you can also say **out of doors**. The opposite is **indoors**)
2 *noun*
the open air, the open countryside; *the pictures of the Rocky Mountains covered in snow are a typical scene of the great American outdoors*

③ **outer**
['aʊtə] *adjective*
on the outside; *though the outer surface of the pie was hot, the inside was still cold;* **outer space** = space beyond the earth's atmosphere

③ **outfit**
['aʊtfɪt] *noun*
(a) set of clothes needed for a particular purpose; *she bought a new outfit for the wedding; for the fancy dress party she wore a nurse's outfit*
(b) *(informal)* organization; *I want some really professional builders, not an outfit like my brother's; she works for some local government outfit*

④ **outgoing**
['aʊtgəʊɪŋ] *adjective*
(a) outgoing call = phone call going out of a building to someone outside; **outgoing mail** = mail which is sent out
(b) lively, who likes to be with others; *he has a very outgoing personality*
(c) (person) who is leaving a job; *she proposed a vote of thanks to the outgoing chairman*

④ **outing**
['aʊtɪŋ] *noun*
short trip; *the children went on an outing to the seaside*

④ **outlet**
['aʊtlɪt] *noun*
(a) place where something can be sold or distributed; *he owns a small number of clothing outlets in south-east London;* **retail outlets** = retail shops
(b) means by which an idea or feeling can get out; *he ran the marathon as a outlet for his stress at work*
(c) outlet (pipe) = pipe through which a liquid goes out; *the outlet pipe takes excess water out of the boiler; the waste water outlet goes directly into the sea*

④ **outline**
['aʊtlaɪn]
1 *noun*
(a) line showing the outer edge of something; *he drew the outline of a car on the paper*
(b) broad description without giving much detail; *she gave the meeting an outline of her proposals; I don't have much time - just give me the outline of the story*
2 *verb*
to make a broad description of a plan, etc.; *he outlined the plan to the bank manager; she outlined her proposals to the meeting*
3 *adjective*
as a broad description, without any details; *the outline proposal was rejected; the council gave outline planning permission for a new house*

④ **outlook**
['aʊtlʊk] *noun*
(a) view of the world in general; *his gloomy outlook can be seen in his novels*
(b) view of what will happen in the future; *we think the outlook for the company is excellent; the economic outlook is not good; the outlook for tomorrow's weather is mainly sunny with some rain*

① **out of**
['aʊt 'ɒv] *preposition*
(a) outside of, away from; *get out of my way!; they went out of the room;* **out of your mind** = mad; *are you out of your mind?*
(b) from among a total; *she got 60 marks out of 100 for her exam; the report states that one out of ten policemen takes bribes;* **nine times out of ten** = nearly all the time; *nine times out of ten it's the other driver who is wrong*
(c) from; *her dress is made out of a piece of old silk; he made a fortune out of buying and selling antiques*
(d) no longer available; *we're out of carrots today; I'm out of change - can I borrow £5?;* **out of print** = with no printed copies left; *all his books are now out of print*

① **out of date**
['aʊt əv 'deɪt] *adjective*
(a) no longer in fashion; *wide trousers are rather out of date*
(b) no longer valid; *I'm afraid your bus pass is out-of-date; she tried to travel with an out-of-date ticket*

③ **out of touch**
['aʊt əv 'tʌtʃ] *adjective*
(a) not having the most recent information about something; *he seems out of touch with what's been happening in his department*
(b) not communicating with somebody by letter, telephone, etc.; *we've been out of touch with our relations in Canada for several years* (NOTE: the opposite is **in touch**)

③ **out of work**
['aʊt əv 'wɜ:k]
1 *adverb*
with no job, unemployed; *the recession has put millions out of work*
2 *adjective*

with no job, unemployed; *the company was set up by three out-of-work engineers*

② **output**
['aʊtpʌt] *noun*
(a) amount which a firm, machine or person produces; *the factory has doubled its output in the last six months*
(b) outputs = goods or services sold on which VAT is charged (NOTE: the opposite, i.e. goods and services bought on which VAT is paid, are **inputs**)

④ **outrage**
['aʊtreɪdʒ]
1 *noun*
offence; vigorous attack against moral standards; *the terrorist attack on the market is an outrage*; *I think the new tax on food is an outrage*
2 *verb*
to shock, to be a cause of great indignation; *his behaviour outraged his parents*

④ **outrageous**
[aʊt'reɪdʒɪs] *adjective*
annoying and shocking; *it is outrageous that they can charge these prices*

④ **outright**
['aʊtraɪt]
1 *adjective*
complete; *she's the outright winner of the competition*
2 *adverb*
straight out, openly; *he told me outright that he didn't like me*

① **outside**
['aʊtsaɪd]
1 *noun*
part which is not inside; *he polished the outside of his car*; *the apple was red and shiny on the outside, but rotten inside*
2 *adjective*
which is on the outer surface; *the outside walls of the house are brick*; outside line = line from an internal telephone to the main telephone system; *you dial 9 to get an outside line*; *see also* BROADCAST
3 *adverb*
not inside a building; *it's beautiful and warm outside in the garden*; *the dog's all wet - it must be raining outside*
4 *preposition* in a position not inside; *I left my umbrella outside the front door*

③ **outsider**
[aʊt'saɪdə] *noun*
(a) person who does not belong to a group, etc.; *she has always been a bit of an outsider*
(b) horse which is not expected to win a race; *the outsider won the race by a neck*

④ **outskirts**
['aʊtskɜːts] *noun*
outer edges of a town, etc.; *most of the workers live in blocks of flats round the outskirts of the city*

③ **outstanding**
[aʊt'stændɪŋ] *adjective*
(a) excellent; of very high quality, of a very high standard; *her performance was outstanding*; *an antique Chinese bowl of outstanding quality*
(b) not yet paid; *the invoice from the solicitor is still outstanding*; *I have some outstanding bills to settle*

④ **oval**
['əʊvl]
1 *noun*
long rounded shape like an egg; *he drew an oval on the paper*
2 *adjective*
with a long rounded shape like an egg; *the pie was cooked in an oval bowl*; *a rugby ball isn't round but oval*

③ **oven**
['ʌvn] *noun*
metal box with a door, which is heated for cooking; *don't put that plate in the oven - it's made of plastic*; *supper is cooking in the oven*; *can you look in the oven and see if the meat is cooked?*

① **over**
['əʊvə]
1 *preposition*
(a) above or higher than; *he put a blanket over the bed*; *planes fly over our house every minute*; *the river rose over its banks*
(b) on the other side, to the other side; *our office is just over the road from the bank*; *he threw the ball over the wall*; *the children ran over the road*
(c) from the top of; *he fell over the cliff*; *she looked over the edge of the root*
(d) during; *over the last few weeks the government has taken several measures*; *let's discuss the problem over lunch*
(e) more than; *children over 16 years old have to pay full price*; *the car costs over £40,000*; *we had to wait for over two hours*
2 *adverb*
(a) several times; *he plays the same CD over and over again*; *she did it ten times over*
(b) down from being upright; *the bottle fell over and all the contents poured out*; *she knocked over the plant pot*; *he leaned over and picked up a pin from the floor*; *see also* ALL OVER
(c) more than; *children of 16 and over pay full price*; *there are special prices for groups of 30 and over*
(d) not used, left behind; *any food left over after the meal can be given to the dog* (NOTE: over is used after many verbs: to run over, to fall over, to come over, to look over, etc.)
3 *adjective*
finished; *is the match over yet?*; *when the war was over everyone had more food to eat*

overall

1 [əʊvə'ɔːl] *adjective*

covering or taking in everything; *the overall outlook for the country is good*; *the overall impression was favourable*; **overall majority** = majority over all other parties in Parliament taken together

2 [əʊvə'ɔːl] *adverb*

taking in everything; *overall, her work has improved considerably*

3 ['ɪʊvɪɔːl] *noun*

(a) light coat worn at work; *he was wearing a white overall as he had just come out of the laboratory*; *put an overall over your clothes before you start painting*

(b) overalls = suit of working clothes (trousers and top) worn over normal clothes to keep them clean when you are working; *all the workers wear white overalls*

overboard

['ɪʊvɪbɔːd] *adverb*

into the water from the edge of a ship, etc.; *he fell overboard and was drowned*; **man overboard!** = someone has fallen into the water!; **to be washed overboard** = to be pulled off a boat by waves; *he was washed overboard during the night*

overcome

[əʊvə'kʌm] *verb*

to gain victory over an enemy, a problem, etc.; *the army quickly overcame the rebels*; *do you think the drugs problem can ever be overcome?* (NOTE: **overcame** [əʊvə'keɪm] - **has overcome**)

overdraft

['ɪʊvɪdrɑːft] *noun*

amount of money which you can withdraw from your bank account with the bank's permission, which is more than there is in the account, i.e. you are borrowing money from the bank; *he has an overdraft of £500*; *she arranged an overdraft with her bank manager*; *he had to have an overdraft to buy the car*

overhead

1 [əʊvə'hed] *adverb*

above you, above your head; *look at that plane overhead*

2 [əʊvə'hed] *adjective*

(a) above (your head); *please put your hand luggage in the overhead racks*; **an overhead reading light** = a small light directly over your head

(b) overhead expenses = general expenses involved in a business as a whole, such as salaries, heating, rent, etc.; *the accounts department is calculating the overhead expenses for next year's budget*

3 ['ɪʊvɪhed] *noun*

US overhead expenses; *by cutting back on the overhead we should make a profit* (NOTE: British English in this meaning is **overheads**)

overheads

['ɪʊvɪhedz] *noun*

overhead expenses; *by cutting back on overheads we should make a profit* (NOTE: American English is **overhead**)

overlap

[əʊvə'læp] *verb*

to cover part of something else; *try not to let the pieces of wallpaper overlap*; *the two meetings are likely to overlap, so I will ask for one to be put back* (NOTE: **overlapping - overlapped**)

overlook

[əʊvə'lʊk] *verb*

(a) not to notice; *she overlooked several mistakes when she was correcting the exam papers*

(b) to pretend not to notice; *in this instance we will overlook the delay in making payment*

(c) to look out on to; *my office overlooks the factory*; *I want a room overlooking the hotel gardens, not the car park*

overnight

[əʊvə'naɪt]

1 *adverb*

for the whole night; *we will stay overnight in France on our way to Italy*; *will the food stay fresh overnight?*

2 *adjective*

lasting all night; *they took an overnight flight back from China*; *there are three sleeping cars on the overnight express*

overseas

[əʊvə'siːz]

1 *adverb*

in a foreign country, across the sea; *he went to work overseas for some years*

2 *adjective*

referring to foreign countries, across the sea; *overseas sales are important for our company*

overtake

[əʊvə'teɪk] *verb*

to go past someone travelling in front of you; *she overtook three trucks on the motorway*; *we were going so slowly that we were overtaken by cyclists* (NOTE: **overtaking - overtook - has overtaken**)

overthrow

1 ['ɪʊvɪθrɪʊ] *noun*

removal of a government or ruler from power; *the revolution led to the overthrow of the military ruler*

2 [əʊvə'θrɪʊ] *verb*

to defeat; *do you think the rebels can overthrow the military government?*; *the former régime was overthrown and the President fled* (NOTE: **overthrew** [əʊvə'θruː] - **overthrown**)

overtime

['ɪʊvɪtaɪm]

1 *noun*

hours worked more than normal working time; *he worked six hours' overtime*; *the overtime rate is one and a half times normal pay*; *the basic wage is £110 a week, but you can expect to earn more than that with overtime*; **overtime pay** = money paid for working beyond normal hours; *overtime pay is calculated at one and a half times the standard rate*; *I'm owed lots of overtime pay*

2 *adverb*

more than normal hours of work; *the staff had to work overtime when the hotel was full*; *how much extra do I get for working overtime?*

④ **overturn**
[əʊvəˈtɜːn] *verb*

(a) to make something fall over; to turn upside down; *the baby accidentally overturned the bowl of fish*; *the fishing boat overturned in the storm*

(b) to vote against a previous decision; *the verdict was overturned on appeal*; *the decision to raise subscriptions was overturned by the council*

④ **overwhelming**
[əʊvəˈwelmɪŋ] *adjective*

enormous; *there was an overwhelming response to their appeal for money*; *they got an overwhelming 'yes' vote*

② **owe**
[əʊ] *verb*

(a) to owe money to someone = to be due to pay someone money; *he still owes me the £50 he borrowed last month*

(b) to owe something to something = to have something because of something else; *he owes his good health to taking a lot of exercise*

③ **owing to**
[ˈəʊɪŋ ˈtuː] *preposition*

because of; *the plane was late owing to fog*; *I am sorry that owing to staff shortages, we cannot supply your order on time*

④ **owl**
[aʊl] *noun*

bird which is mainly active at night; *owls hunt mice and other small animals*; *(informal)* a **night owl** = someone who likes to work, eat, etc., until late at night, and does not get up early in the morning; *she's a night owl and finds it difficult to get up in time for work*; *compare* EARLY BIRD

① **own**
[əʊn]

1 *adjective*

belonging to you alone; *I don't need to borrow a car - I have my own car*; *he has his own hairdressing shop*

2 *noun*

(a) of my own *or* **of his own, etc.** = belonging to me *or* to him alone; *he has an office of his own*; *I have a car of my own*; *they got married and now have a house of their own*

(b) on my own *or* **on his own, etc.** = alone; *I'm on my own this evening - my wife's playing bridge*; *he built the house all on his own*

3 *verb*

to have, to possess; *there's no sense in owning two cars, since my wife doesn't drive*; *who owns this shop?*

② **owner**
[ˈəʊnə] *noun*

person who owns something; *the police are trying to find the owner of the stolen car*; *insurance is necessary for all house owners*

③ **ownership**
[ˈəʊnəʃɪp] *noun*

situation where someone owns something; *the ownership of the land is in dispute*; *the hairdresser's shop has been sold and is under new ownership*; **private ownership** = situation where a company is owned by private shareholders; *the company is being sold into private ownership*; **public ownership** = situation where an industry is owned by the state

③ **own up (to)**
[ˈəʊn ˈʌp tuː] *verb*

to say that you have done something wrong; *she owned up to having tried to steal the jewels*; *the teacher asked who had thrown ink bombs but no one would own up*

④ **oxygen**
[ˈɒksɪdʒɪn] *noun*

common gas which is present in the air and is essential for plant and animal life; *hydrogen combines with oxygen to form water*; *the divers ran out of oxygen and had to end their dive early*; **oxygen mask** = mask which appears from a panel above your head if there is a drop in pressure in a plane; *if there is an emergency an oxygen mask will automatically drop down in front of you* (NOTE: Chemical element: chemical symbol: **O**; atomic number: **8**)

③ **oz**
[ˈaʊnsɪz] *abbreviation for* OUNCE *or* OUNCES; *according to the recipe I need 12oz flour and 5oz butter* (NOTE: say 'twelve ounces of flour', 'five ounces of butter')

④ **ozone**
[ˈəʊzəʊn] *noun*

harmful form of oxygen, which is found in the atmosphere and which is poisonous to humans; **ozone hole** = gap which forms in the ozone layer, allowing harmful radiation from the sun to reach the earth; *the ozone hole is getting larger every year*; **ozone layer** = layer of ozone in the upper atmosphere, formed by the action of sunlight on oxygen, which protects the earth from harmful rays from the sun

Pp

P, p
[pi:]
(a) sixteenth letter of the alphabet, between O and Q; *you spell 'photo' with a PH and not an F*
(b) letter used to show a price in pence; *this book costs 99p*; *you should get a 60p ticket from the machine*; *I bought the children 50p ice creams each*; *see also* PENNY

pace
[peɪs]
1 *noun*
(a) distance covered by one step; *walk thirty paces to the north of the stone*; *step three paces back*
(b) speed; **to keep pace with** = to keep up with; *she kept pace with the leaders for the first three laps*; *wages haven't kept pace with inflation*; *(of a runner, driver, horse, etc.)* **to set the pace** = to go fast, showing how fast a race should be run; *the German driver set the pace in his Ferrari*
2 *verb*
(a) to walk; *he paced backwards and forwards in front of the door*
(b) to measure by walking; *he paced out the distance between the tree and the house*
(c) to set the pace for a runner, etc.; *to help him train for the marathon she paced him on her bicycle*

pacific
[pɪ'sɪfɪk] *adjective*
preferring peace and calm; **the Pacific Ocean** *or* **the Pacific** = huge ocean between North America and Asia and South America and New Zealand; *they set out to cross the Pacific in a small boat*; **the Pacific Rim** = the countries round the edge of the Pacific Ocean, including South-East Asia, Japan, the Western States of the USA, South America, Australia and New Zealand

pack
[pæk]
1 *noun*
(a) set of things put together in a box; *he bought a pack of chewing gum*; **a pack of cards** = set of playing cards (NOTE: American English is a **deck of cards**)
(b) group of wild animals together; *a pack of wild dogs*

(c) bag which you can carry on your back; *he carried his pack over his shoulder*
(d) **face pack** = thick substance which you put on your face to improve your skin; *don't come in, I've still got my face pack on*
(e) *(in Rugby)* the group of forward players who push together against the forwards of the other team
2 *verb*
(a) to put things into a suitcase ready for travelling; *the taxi's arrived and she hasn't packed her suitcase yet*; *I've finished packing, so we can start*; *he packed his toothbrush at the bottom of the bag*; *(informal)* **to tell someone to pack their bags** = to tell someone to leave, to sack someone; *when he got home, she told him to pack his bags*; **to send someone packing** = to send someone away; *when the boys started to throw stones at her cat she soon sent them packing*
(b) to put things in containers ready for sending; *the books are packed in boxes of twenty*; *fish are packed in ice*
(c) to put a lot of people or things into something; *how can you pack ten adults into one tent?*; *the streets are packed with Christmas shoppers*; *the supermarket shelves are packed with fruit and vegetables*

package
['pækɪdʒ]
1 *noun*
(a) parcel which has been wrapped up for sending; *there was a package for you in the post*; *we mailed the package to you yesterday*
(b) box or bag in which goods are sold; *instructions for use are printed on the package*
(c) **package holiday** *or* **package tour** = holiday where everything (hotel, food, travel, etc.) is arranged and paid for before you leave; *they went on a package holiday to Greece*
(d) **salary package** = salary and other benefits offered with a job
2 *verb*
to put into packages; *the chocolates are attractively packaged in silver paper*

packed
[pækt] *adjective*
(a) full of people; *the restaurant was packed and there were no free tables*

(b) put in a container; **packed lunch** = sandwiches, etc., put ready in a box

② **packet**
['pækɪt] *noun*
(a) small bag, parcel or box; *a packet of cigarettes*; *a packet of soup*
(b) *(informal)* large amount of money; *he made a packet on the deal*

③ **packing**
['pækɪŋ] *noun*
(a) putting things into suitcases, etc.; *my wife's in the hotel room doing our packing*
(b) packing case = special wooden box for sending goods; **packing list** *or* **packing slip** = list of goods which have been packed, sent with the goods to show they have been checked
(c) material used to protect goods which are being packed; *the goods are sealed in clear plastic packing*

③ **pack off**
['pæk 'ɒf] *verb*
to send someone away; *as soon as they were old enough, she packed her children off to France to learn French*; *we've packed the children off to their grandparents for the summer holidays*

③ **pack up**
['pæk 'ʌp] *verb*
(a) to put things into a box before going away; *they packed up all their equipment and left*
(b) to stop working; *I'll pack up now and finish the job tomorrow morning*
(c) to break down; *one of the plane's engines packed up when we were taking off*

④ **pact**
[pækt] *noun*
agreement, treaty; *the two countries signed a defence pact*

③ **pad**
[pæd]
1 *noun*
(a) soft cushion which protects; *put a pad of cotton on your knee*; **shoulder pads** = thick pads put inside the shoulders of a coat, to make it look bigger
(b) set of sheets of paper attached together; **desk pad** = pad of paper kept on a desk for writing notes; **memo pad** *or* **note pad** = pad of paper for writing memos or notes; **phone pad** = pad of paper kept by a telephone for noting messages; *I wrote down his address on the phone pad*
2 *verb*
(a) to walk with heavy soft feet; *the lion was padding up and down in its cage*
(b) to soften something hard by using soft material; *the chairs should be padded to make them more comfortable*; *see also* PAD OUT
(NOTE: **padding - padded**)

③ **pad out**
['pæd 'aʊt] *verb*
to add text to a speech or article, just to make it longer; *he padded out his talk to last half an hour*

① **page**
[peɪdʒ]
1 *noun*
(a) a side of a sheet of paper used in a book, newspaper, etc.; *it's a short book, it only has 64 pages*; *the photograph of the author is on the back page*; *start reading at page 34* (NOTE: with numbers the word **the** is left out: **on the next page** but **on page 50**)
(b) boy who is one of the bride's attendants at a wedding; *two little pages boys followed the bride into the church* (NOTE: a girl who does the same is a **bridesmaid**)
2 *verb*
to call someone by radio, over a loudspeaker, etc.; *Mr Smith isn't in his office at the moment - I'll page him for you*

① **paid**
[peɪd] *see* PAY

② **pain**
[peɪn]
1 *noun*
(a) feeling of being hurt; *if you have a pain in your chest, you ought to see a doctor*; *she had to take drugs because she could not stand the pain*; *I get pains in my teeth when I eat ice cream*
(b) to take pains over something *or* **to do something** = to take care to do something well; *they took great pains over the organization of the conference*; *she took pains to make everyone feel at home*
(c) *(informal)* **a pain (in the neck)** = annoying person; *he's a real pain in the neck*; *she's a pain - she's always gets top marks*
2 *verb*
(formal) to hurt; *it pains me to have to do this, but we must report you to the police*

③ **painful**
['peɪnfʊl] *adjective*
which hurts, which causes pain; *she got a painful blow on the back of the head*; *I have very painful memories of my first school*

② **paint**
[peɪnt]
1 *noun*
coloured liquid which you use to give something a colour or to make a picture; *we gave the ceiling two coats of paint*; *I need a two-litre tin of green paint*; *the paint's coming off the front door*; *see also* PAINTS (NOTE: no plural in this meaning)
2 *verb*
(a) to cover something with paint; *we got a man in to paint the house*; *they painted their front door blue*; *she painted her nails bright red*
(b) *(informal)* **to paint yourself into a corner** = to get yourself into a situation that you cannot get out of; **to paint the town red** = to have a wild party in the town; *after the exam results come out we are all going up to London to paint the town red*

(c) to cover with a liquid; *the nurse painted his knee with antiseptic*
(d) to make a picture of something using paint; *she painted a picture of the village; he's painting his mother; the sky is not easy to paint*

④ **painter**
['peɪntə] *noun*
(a) person who paints (a house, etc.); *the painters are coming next week to paint the kitchen*
(b) artist, a person who paints pictures; *he collects pictures by 19th century French painters*

② **painting**
['peɪntɪŋ] *noun*
(a) action of putting on paint; *painting the kitchen always takes a long time*
(b) picture done with paints; *do you like this painting of the old church?*

③ **paints**
[peɪnts] *noun*
set of tubes of paint or cubes of watercolour paint, in a box; *she bought me a box of paints for my birthday*

② **pair**
[peɪ]
1 *noun*
(a) two things taken together; *a pair of socks; a pair of gloves; she's bought a new pair of boots;* **these socks are a pair** = they go together
(b) two things joined together to make a single one; *I'm looking for a clean pair of trousers; where's my pair of green shorts?; this pair of scissors is blunt*
(c) two people rowing in a boat; *the British pair won the silver medal; see also* EIGHT, FOUR
2 *verb*
to pair up = to join with another person to do something; *everyone paired up for the treasure hunt*

③ **pajamas**
[pɪˈdʒɑːmɪz] *US see* PYJAMAS

③ **palace**
['pælɪs] *noun*
large building where a king, queen, president, etc., lives; *the presidential palace is in the centre of the city; the Queen lives in Buckingham Palace*

③ **pale**
[peɪl] *adjective*
(a) with a light colour; *what colour is your hat? - it's a pale blue colour*
(b) not looking healthy, with a white face; *she's always pale and that worries me; when she read the letter she went pale* (NOTE: **paler - palest**)

④ **palm**
[pɑːm] *noun*
(a) soft inside surface of your hand; *she held out some bits of bread in the palm of her hand and the birds came and ate them*

(b) tall tropical tree with long leaves; *date palms grow in the desert; the boy climbed a coconut palm a brought down a nut*

③ **pan**
[pæn]
1 *noun*
metal container with a handle, used for cooking; *boil the potatoes in a pan of water; she burnt her hand on the hot frying pan; see also* FRYING PAN
2 *verb*
(a) *(informal)* to criticize; *his latest film has been panned by the critics*
(b) **to pan for gold** = to wash mud in a stream hoping to find gold in it (NOTE: **panning - panned**)

① **panel**
['pænl]
1 *noun*
(a) flat piece which forms part of something; *take off the panel at the back of the washing machine;* **instrument panel** = flat part of a car in front of the driver, with dials which show speed, etc.
(b) group of people who answer questions or who judge a competition; *she's on the panel that will interview candidates for the post;* **panel of experts** = group of people who give advice on a problem
2 *verb*
to cover with sheets of wood; *he decided to panel the study in oak; the room is panelled in oak* (NOTE: **panelling - panelled**) but American spelling is **paneling - paneled**)

③ **panic**
['pænɪk]
1 *noun*
terror, great fear; *the forecast of flooding caused panic in towns near the river;* **panic buying** = rush to buy something at any price because stocks may run out or because the price may rise
2 *verb*
to become frightened; *don't panic, the fire engine is its way* (NOTE: **panicking - panicked**)

③ **pants**
[pænts] *noun*
(a) *GB (informal)* shorts worn on the lower part of the body under other clothes; *I put on clean pants and socks every morning*
(b) *US (informal)* trousers, clothes which cover your body from the waist down, split in two parts, one for each leg; *the waiter was wearing a black jacket and a pair of striped pants; I need a belt to keep my pants up*

① **paper**
['peɪpə]
1 *noun*
(a) piece of thin material which you write on, and which is used for wrapping or to make books, newspapers, etc.; *he got a letter written on pink paper; I need another piece of paper or*

another sheet of paper to finish my letter; there was a box of paper handkerchiefs by the bed (NOTE: no plural for this meaning: **some paper, a piece of paper, a sheet of paper**)

(b) newspaper; *I buy the paper to read on the train every morning; my photo was on the front page of today's paper; our local paper comes out on Fridays; the Sunday papers are so big that it takes me all day to read them*

(c) papers = documents; *she sent me the relevant papers; he has lost the customs papers; the office is asking for the VAT papers*

(d) on paper = in theory; *on paper the system is ideal, but no one has ever seen it working*

(e) exam; *the English paper was very difficult; she wrote a good history paper*

(f) scientific essay; *he wrote a paper on economics which was published in one of the learned journals*

2 *verb*

to cover the walls of a room with wallpaper; *they papered the room in a pattern of red and blue flowers*

④ **paperback**
['peɪpɪbæk] *noun*

cheap book with a paper cover; *I took a couple of paperbacks to read on the plane; the novel will come out in paperback in the spring*

④ **par**
[pɑː] *noun*

(a) being equal; **to be on a par with** = to be equal to; *it isn't really on a par with their previous performances*

(b) to buy shares at par = to buy shares at their face value; **the shares are below par** = they are less than their face value

(c) below par = not very well; *he's feeling a bit below par after his illness*

(d) *(in golf)* number of strokes usually needed by a good player to hit the ball into the hole; *he went round in five under par*

③ **paracetamol**
[pærɪˈsiːtɪmɒl] *noun*

common drug, used to stop the symptoms of flu, colds, headaches, etc.; *she always keeps a bottle of paracetamol (tablets) in her bag* (NOTE: no plural: **take two paracetamol before breakfast**)

④ **parade**
[pɪˈreɪd] *noun*

1 *noun*

(a) display of soldiers; *an officer inspects the men before they go on parade*; **parade ground** = square area on a military camp where parades are held

(b) series of bands, decorated cars, etc., passing in a street; *the parade was led by a children's band; Independence Day is always celebrated with a military parade through the centre of the capital*; **fashion parade** = display of new clothes by models

(c) wide street where people can walk up and down; **a parade of shops** = series of shops side by side

2 *verb*

to march past in rows; *the soldiers paraded down the Mall to Buckingham Palace; the winning horse paraded round the ring*

④ **paradise**
['pærɪdaɪs] *noun*

(a) wonderful place where good people are supposed to live after death; *for a moment, I thought I must have died and gone to paradise*

(b) any beautiful place or a place where you feel very happy; *their grandparents' farm was a paradise for the children*

③ **paragraph**
['pærɪɡrɑːf] *noun*

section of several lines of writing, which can be made up of several sentences; *to answer the first paragraph of your letter or paragraph one of your letter; please refer to the paragraph headed 'shipping instructions'*

> COMMENT: a paragraph always starts a new line, often with a small blank space at the beginning. A blank line is usually left between paragraphs

③ **parallel**
['pærɪlɪl]

1 *adjective*

(lines) which are side by side and remain the same distance apart without ever touching; *draw two parallel lines three millimetres apart; the road runs parallel to or with the railway*

2 *noun*

line running round the earth at a certain distance from the poles; *the 49th parallel forms the border between the United States and Canada*

③ **parcel**
['pɑːsɪl]

1 *noun*

package (to be sent by post, etc.); *the postman has brought a parcel for you; the parcel was wrapped up in brown paper; if you're going to the post office, can you post this parcel for me?*

2 *verb*

to wrap and tie something up to send by post; *I parcelled the books up yesterday but I haven't posted them yet* (NOTE: **parcelling - parcelled** but American spelling is **parceling - parceled**)

② **pardon**
['pɑːdɪn]

1 *noun*

(a) forgiving someone; **I beg your pardon!** = excuse me, forgive me; *I beg your pardon, I didn't hear what you said; I do beg your pardon - I didn't know you were busy*

(b) act of legally forgiving an offence which someone has committed; *the prisoners received a free pardon from the president*

2 *verb*

(a) to forgive someone for having done something wrong; *pardon me for interrupting, but you're wanted on the phone*; *please pardon my late reply to your letter*

(b) to forgive an offence which someone has committed, and allow him or her to leave prison; *some political prisoners were pardoned and set free*

3 *interjection*

pardon! = excuse me, forgive me

ⓘ **parent**
['peırınt] *noun*

(a) **parents** = mother and father; *his parents live in Manchester*; *did your parents tell you I had met them in London?*

(b) father or mother; **single parent** = one parent (mother or father) who is bringing up a child or children alone; *single parent families are more and more common*

④ **parish**
['pærıʃ] *noun*

(a) area served by a church; *he's the vicar of a country parish*; *they worship regularly in their local parish church*; *Father Thomas is our parish priest*

(b) administrative district in a county with a church as its centre; *he's going through the local parish records to try to establish when his family first came to the village*; **parish council** = elected committee which runs a parish; **parish councillor** = elected member of a parish council; *he's been a parish councillor for the last four years* (NOTE: plural is **parishes**)

ⓘ **park**
[pɑːk]
1 *noun*

(a) open space with grass and trees; *Hyde Park and Regents Park are in the middle of London*; *you can ride a bicycle across the park but cars are not allowed in*

(b) **national park** = area of land protected by the government for people to enjoy; *the Peak District in Derbyshire is a national park*; *we went camping in the national park*

(c) **car park** = area where you can leave a car when you are not using it; *he left his car in the hotel car park*; *the office car park is full* (NOTE: American English is **parking lot**)

2 *verb*

(a) to leave your car in a place while you are not using it; *you can park your car in the street next to the hotel*; *you mustn't park on a yellow line*

(b) *(informal)* **to park yourself** = to put yourself in a place, especially where you are not wanted; *he came and parked himself next to me*

③ **parked**
[pɑːkt] *adjective*

(of vehicle) left in a car park, standing at the side of the road, etc.; *the bus crashed into two parked cars*

② **parking**
['pɑːkıŋ] *noun*

action of leaving a car in a place; *parking is difficult in the centre of the city*; **no parking** = sign showing that you must not park your car in a certain place; **parking meter** = device into which you put money to pay for parking; *US* **parking lot** = area where you can leave a car when you are not using it (NOTE: British English is **car park**)

② **parliament**
['pɑːlımınt] *noun*

group of elected representatives who vote the laws of a country; *Parliament has passed a law forbidding the sale of dangerous drugs*; **Act of Parliament** = law which has been passed by parliament; **Houses of Parliament** = building in London where Parliament meets; *he took a picture of the Houses of Parliament*

③ **parliamentary**
[pɑːlıˈmentırı] *adjective*

referring to parliament; *parliamentary procedure*; **parliamentary elections** = elections to parliament (as opposed to local elections)

④ **parsley**
['pɑːslı] *noun*

green herb used in cooking; *sprinkle some chopped parsley on top of the fish*

ⓘ **part**
[pɑːt]
1 *noun*

(a) piece; *parts of the film were very good*; *they live in the downstairs part of a large house*; *they spend part of the year in France*; **spare parts** = pieces used to put in place of broken parts of a machine, car, etc.; *see also* PARTS OF SPEECH

(b) **in part** = not completely; *to contribute in part to the costs* or *to pay the costs in part*

(c) character in a play, film, etc.; *he played the part of Hamlet*; **to play a part** = to be one of several people or things which do something; *the guests played an important part in putting out the hotel fire*; **to take part in** = to join in; *they all took part in the game*; *did he take part in the concert?*

2 *verb*

(a) to divide into sections; *he parts his hair on the right side*

(b) **to part company** = to leave, to split up; *we all set off together, but we parted company when we got to Italy*; *see also* PART WITH

③ **partial**
['pɑːʃl] *adjective*

(a) not complete; *he got partial compensation for the damage to his house*; *the treatment was only a partial success*

(b) **partial to** = with a liking for; *everyone knows he is partial to chocolate*

(c) in a way which is not fair; *the judge was accused of being partial*

④ partially
['pɑːʃɪli] *adverb*
not completely; *he is partially deaf*; *I partially agree with what they are proposing*

③ participant
[pɑːˈtɪsɪpɪnt] *noun*
person who takes part; *all participants should register with the organizers before the race starts*; *conference participants are asked to meet in the entrance hall*

③ participate
[pɑːˈtɪsɪpeɪt] *verb*
to take part in something; *he refused to participate in the TV discussion*

③ participation
[pɑːtɪsɪˈpeɪʃn] *noun*
taking part in something; *their participation is vital to the success of the talks*; *his participation in the show will ensure that we get a good audience*

④ particle
['pɑːtɪkl] *noun*
very small piece; *they found tiny particles of glass in the yoghurt*; *an electron is a basic negative particle in an atom*

① particular
[pɪˈtɪkjuːlɪ]
1 *adjective*
(a) special, referring to one thing or person and to no one else; *the printer works best with one particular type of paper*
(b) in particular = especially; *fragile goods, in particular glasses, need careful packing*
(c) having special likes and dislikes; *she's very particular about her food*; *give me any room you have available - I'm not particular*
2 *noun*
particulars = details; *the sheet which gives particulars of the house for sale*; *the inspector asked for particulars of the missing car*

① particularly
[pɪˈtɪkjuːlɪli] *adverb*
especially; *I particularly asked them not to walk on the lawn*; *it's a particularly difficult problem*; *he isn't particularly worried about the result*

② partly
['pɑːtli] *adverb*
not completely; *the house is partly built, but still needs to be decorated*; *I'm only partly satisfied with the result*; *we're selling our house in London, partly because we need the money, but also because we want to move nearer to the sea*

② partner
['pɑːtnɪ]
1 *noun*
(a) person who works in a business and has a share in it with others; *he became a partner in a firm of solicitors*; **sleeping partner** = partner who has a share in a business but does not work in it

(b) person you live with, without necessarily being married; *we invited him and his partner for drinks*
(c) person who plays games or dances with someone; *take your partners for the next dance*; *Sally is my usual tennis partner*
2 *verb*
to be the partner of someone; *she was partnered by her sister in the doubles*

③ partnership
['pɑːtnɪʃɪp] *noun*
business association between two or more people where the risks and profits are shared according to an agreement between the partners; **to go into partnership with someone** = to join with someone to form a partnership; *they went into partnership to market his new invention*

③ parts of speech
['pɑːts əv 'spiːtʃ] *noun*
different types of words, such as nouns, verbs, etc., which are classified according to their use in grammar; *nouns, adjectives and verbs are different parts of speech*; *what part of speech is 'this'?*

③ part-time
[pɑːtˈtaɪm] *adjective & adverb*
not for the whole working day; *he is trying to find part-time work when the children are in school*; *we are looking for part-time staff to keyboard data*; *she works part-time in the local supermarket*

③ part with
['pɑːt 'wɪθ] *verb*
to give or sell something to someone; *he refused to part with his old bicycle*; *I'm reluctant to part with the keys to the house*

① party
['pɑːti] *noun*
(a) special occasion when several people meet, usually in someone's house; *we're having a party on New Year's Eve*; *our family Christmas party was a disaster as usual*; *she invited twenty friends to her birthday party*
(b) group of people doing something together; *parties of tourists walking round the gardens*; *see also* WORKING PARTY
(c) **political party** = organization of people with similar political opinions and aims; *which party does he belong to?*; *she's a member of the Labour Party*
(d) person or organization which is involved in a legal dispute, a contract, or a crime; **third party** = any third person, in addition to the two main parties involved in a contract (NOTE: plural is **parties**)

① pass
[pɑːs]
1 *noun*
(a) *(in football, etc.)* sending the ball to another player; *he sent a long pass across the field and Smith headed it into goal*

(b) low area where a road can cross between two mountain peaks; *the Brenner Pass is closed by snow*; *the road winds up a steep pass to the border*
(c) season ticket on a bus or train; *I left my bus pass at home, so I had to pay for a ticket*
(d) permit to go in or out regularly; *you need a pass to enter the ministry offices*; *all members of staff must show a pass* (NOTE: plural is **passes**)
2 *verb*
(a) to go past; *if you walk towards the bank you will pass the office on your right*; *I passed her on the stairs*; *if you're passing the bookshop, can you pick up the book I ordered?*
(b) to move something towards someone; *can you pass me the salt, please?*; *he passed the ball to one of the backs*
(c) to be successful in a test or examination; *he passed in English, but failed in French*; *she passed her driving test first time!*
(d) to vote to approve something; *Parliament has passed a law against the ownership of guns*; *the proposal was passed by 10 votes to 3*

② **passage**
['pæsɪdʒ] *noun*
(a) corridor; *she hurried along the passage*; *there's an underground passage between the two railway stations*
(b) section of a text; *she quoted passages from the Bible*; *I photocopied a particularly interesting passage from the book*
(c) *(formal)* action of moving from one place to another; *the attackers promised the soldiers safe passage if they surrendered* (NOTE: no plural in this meaning)

③ **pass away**
['pɑːs ə'weɪ] *verb*
to die; *mother passed away during the night* (NOTE: also **pass on**)

② **passenger**
['pæsɪndʒɪ] *noun*
person who is travelling in a car, bus, train, plane, etc. but who is not the driver or one of the crew; *his car's quite big - it can take three passengers on the back seat*; *the plane was carrying 104 passengers and a crew of ten*; **foot passenger** = passenger on a ferry who is not travelling with a car; **passenger side** = the side of the car nearest to the kerb; **passenger train** = train which carries passengers but not goods

④ **passer-by**
[pɑːsɪ'baɪ] *noun*
person who is walking past; *a passer-by saw what happened and called the police*; *she was looked after by passers-by until the ambulance came* (NOTE: plural is **passers-by**)

③ **passing**
['pɑːsɪŋ] *adjective*
(a) which is going past; *the driver of a passing car saw the accident and called the police on his mobile phone*

(b) not permanent; *it's just a passing fashion*

③ **passion**
['pæʃn] *noun*
very strong emotion or enthusiasm; *she has a passion for motor racing*; *he didn't put enough passion into the love scene*

④ **passionate**
['pæʃɪnɪt] *adjective*
strongly emotional; *he's passionate about promoting honesty in the police force*; *she has a passionate love for Italian art*

④ **passive**
['pæsɪv]
1 *adjective*
allowing things to happen to you and not taking any action yourself; **passive resistance** = protesting against something by refusing to do it, but not by using violence; *the protesters organized a programme of passive resistance*; **passive smoking** = breathing in smoke from other people's cigarettes, when you do not smoke yourself; *passive smoking is believed to be one of the causes of lung cancer*
2 *noun*
form of a verb which shows that the subject is being acted upon (NOTE: if you say 'the car hit him' the verb is active, but 'he was hit by the car' is passive)

③ **pass off**
[pɑːs 'ɒf] *verb*
(a) to take place; *the meeting passed off without any problems*
(b) to pass something off as something else = to pretend that it is another thing in order to cheat; *he passed the wine off as French*; **to pass yourself off as** = to pretend to be; *he passed himself off as a rich banker from South America*

③ **pass on**
['pɑːs 'ɒn] *verb*
(a) to move something on to someone else; *she passed on the information to her boss*
(b) to die; *my father passed on two years ago* (NOTE: also **pass away** in the same meaning)

③ **pass out**
['pɑːs 'aut] *verb*
to become unconscious for a short time; *he passed out when he saw the blood*; *when he told her that her mother was seriously ill in hospital, she passed out*

③ **passport**
['pɑːspɔːt] *noun*
official document allowing you to pass from one country to another; *if you are going abroad you need to have a valid passport*; *we had to show our passports at customs*; *his passport is out of date*

③ **pass round**
['pɑːs raund] *verb*
(a) to hand something to various people; *she passed the box of chocolates round the table*; *the steward passed round immigration forms*

(b) *(informal)* **to pass the hat round** = to ask for money; *we don't have the funds to put on the school play this year, so we'll have to pass the hat round*

③ **pass up**
['pɑːs 'ʌp] *verb*

(informal) not to make use of a chance or opportunity which is offered; *he passed up the chance of going to work in our office in Australia*

① **past**
[pɑːst]

1 *preposition*

(a) later than, after; *it's past lunchtime, and mother's still not come back from the shops; it's ten past nine (9.10) - we've missed the TV news*

(b) from one side to the other in front of something; *if you go past the bank, you'll see the shop on your left; she walked past me without saying anything; the car went past at at least 60 miles an hour* (NOTE: **past** is used for times between o'clock and the half hour: **3.05** = five past three; **3.15** = a quarter past three; **3.25** = twenty-five past three; **3.30** = half past three. For times after **half past** see **to**. **Past** is also used with many verbs: **to go past, to drive past, to fly past,** etc.)

2 *adjective*

which has passed; *he has spent the past year working in France; the time for talking is past - what we need is action*

3 *noun*

(a) time before now; *in the past we always had an office party just before Christmas*

(b) past (tense) = form of a verb which shows that it happened before the present time; *'sang' is the past (tense) of the verb 'to sing'*

④ **pasta**
['pæstɪ] *noun*

Italian food made of flour and water, cooked by boiling and eaten with oil or sauce; *spaghetti is a type of pasta; I'll just have some pasta and a glass of wine* (NOTE: no plural: **some pasta, a bowl of pasta**; note that **pasta** takes a singular verb: **the pasta is very good here**)

④ **paste**
[peɪst]

1 *noun*

(a) thin liquid glue; *spread the paste evenly over the back of the wallpaper*

(b) soft food; *mix the flour, eggs and milk to a smooth paste; add tomato paste to the soup;* **curry paste** = hot spicy paste, used to make Indian dishes; *see also* TOOTHPASTE

2 *verb*

to glue paper, etc.; *she pasted a sheet of coloured paper over the front of the box; he pasted the newspaper cuttings into a big book; see also* CUT

③ **pastry**
['peɪstrɪ] *noun*

(a) mixture of flour, fat and water, used to make pies; *she was in the kitchen making pastry*

(b) pastries = sweet cakes made of pastry filled with cream or fruit, etc.; **Danish pastries** = sweet pastry cakes with jam or fruit folded inside

④ **pat**
[pæt]

1 *noun*

(a) little tap with the hand; *I didn't hit her - I just gave her a little pat;* **a pat on the back** = praise; *the committee got a pat on the back for having organized the show so well*

(b) a pat of butter = small round piece of butter

2 *verb*

to give someone *or* something a pat; *he patted his pocket to make sure that his money was still there;* **to pat someone on the back** = to praise someone (NOTE: **patting - patted**)

③ **patch**
[pætʃ]

1 *noun*

(a) small piece of material used for covering up a hole; *his mother sewed a patch over the hole in his trousers; (informal)* **not a patch on** = not nearly as good as; *this year's model isn't a patch on the old one*

(b) small area; *they built a shed on a patch of ground by the railway line;* **a cabbage patch** = small piece of ground where you grow cabbages (NOTE: plural is **patches**)

2 *verb*

to repair by attaching a piece of material over a hole; *her jeans are all mended and patched; we patched the curtains with some material we had left over*

③ **patch up**
['pætʃ 'ʌp] *verb*

(a) to mend with difficulty; *the garage managed to patch up the engine; the surgeon patched him up but warned him not to fight with knives again*

(b) to patch up a quarrel = to become more friendly again after quarrelling; *they had a bitter argument, but patched up their quarrel in time for the party*

④ **patent**
['peɪtɪnt or 'pætɪnt]

1 *noun*

(only ['pætɪnt]) official confirmation that you have the sole right to make or sell a new invention; *to take out a patent for a new type of light bulb; they have applied for a patent for their new invention*

2 *adjective*

(a) covered by an official patent; **patent medicine** = medicine made under a trade name by one company

(b) patent leather = leather with an extremely shiny surface

3 *verb*

to patent an invention = to register an invention with a government department to prevent other people from copying it

② **path**

[pɑːθ] *noun*

(a) narrow track for walking; *there's a path across the field; follow the path until you get to the sea*

(b) bicycle path = narrow lane for bicycles by the side of a road

(c) direction in which something is moving or coming; *people in villages in the path of the tropical storm were advised to get away as fast as possible; the school stands right in the path of the new motorway*

③ **pathetic**

[pɪ'θetɪk] *adjective*

(a) which makes you feel pity; *he made a pathetic attempt at a joke; she looked so pathetic I hadn't the heart to tell her off*

(b) *(informal)* extremely bad; *their performance in the final game was absolutely pathetic*

③ **patience**

['peɪʃns] *noun*

(a) being patient; *with a little patience, you'll soon learn how to ride a bike; I don't have the patience to wait that long;* **to try someone's patience** = to make someone impatient; *looking after a class of thirty little children would try anyone's patience*

(b) card game for one person; *she sat by herself in her hotel room, playing patience*

COMMENT: the simplest form of patience is when you lay out nine cards, face upwards, and cover with other cards any pairs of cards which add up to eleven (9 and 2, or 8 and 3, for example). You also cover up the king, queen and jack if all three are there. You continue to do this until you only have two cards left, and can calculate from the cards on the table in front of you which cards you are holding in your hand

---

① **patient**

['peɪʃɪnt]

1 *adjective*

(a) being able to wait a long time without getting annoyed; *you must be patient - you will get served in time*

(b) careful and thorough; *weeks of patient investigation by the police resulted in his arrest*

2 *noun*

sick person who is in hospital or who is being treated by a doctor, dentist, etc.; *there are three other patients in the ward; the nurse is trying to take the patient's temperature*

① **patiently**

['peɪʃɪntlɪ] *adverb*

without getting annoyed; *they waited patiently for the bus to arrive*

④ **patriot**

['peɪtrɪɪt] *noun*

person who is proud of his country and is willing to defend it; *he's a real patriot; all true patriots must fight to save their country*

④ **patriotic**

[pætrɪ'ɒtɪk] *adjective*

proud of your country and willing to defend it; *they sang patriotic songs before the football match; I'm not ashamed of being patriotic - I think this is a wonderful country*

④ **patrol**

[pɪ'trɒʊl]

1 *noun*

(a) keeping guard by walking or driving up and down; *they make regular patrols round the walls of the prison; he was on patrol in the centre of town when he saw some men wearing masks running away from a bank*

(b) group of people keeping guard; *each time a patrol went past we hid behind a wall*

2 *verb*

to keep guard by walking or driving up and down; *armed security guards are patrolling the warehouse* (NOTE: **patrolling - patrolled**)

⓪ **pattern**

['pætɪn] *noun*

(a) instructions which you follow to make something; *she followed a pattern from a magazine to knit her son a pullover*

(b) design of lines, flowers, etc., repeated again and again on cloth, wallpaper, etc.; *she was wearing a coat with a pattern of black and white spots; do you like the pattern on our new carpet?*

(c) general way in which something usually happens; *a change in the usual weather pattern*

③ **pause**

[pɔːz]

1 *noun*

short stop during a period of work, etc.; *the exercise consists of running on the spot for ten minutes, with a short pause after each 100 steps; he read his speech slowly, with plenty of pauses*

2 *verb*

to rest for a short time; to stop doing something for a short time; *she ran along the road, only pausing for a second to look at her watch*

④ **pave**

[peɪv] *verb*

(a) to cover a road or path, etc., with a hard surface; *in the old town, the streets are paved with round stones; there is a paved yard behind the restaurant*

(b) to pave the way for something = to prepare the way for something to happen; *the election of the new president paves the way for a change of government*

③ **pavement**
['peɪvmɪnt] *noun*
(a) hard path for walkers at the side of a road; *walk on the pavement, not in the road; look out! - the pavement is covered with ice* (NOTE: in American English this is **sidewalk**)
(b) *US* hard road surface

③ **pawn**
[pɔːn]
1 *noun*
(a) smallest piece in chess; *he took two of my pawns*
(b) **in pawn** = left in exchange for money which has been borrowed; *he left his watch in pawn for twenty pounds*
2 *verb*
to leave an object in exchange for borrowing money: you claim back the object when you pay back the money; *I was so desperate that I pawned my mobile phone; he was in a bad state, even his shoes had been pawned*

① **pay**
[peɪ]
1 *noun*
wages or salary; *they're on strike for more pay; I can't afford luxuries on my miserable pay;* **basic pay** = normal salary without extra payments; **take-home pay** = pay left after tax and insurance have been deducted; **holidays with pay** = holiday which a worker can take by contract and for which he or she is paid; **unemployment pay** = money given by the government to someone who is unemployed; *see also* RISE
2 *verb*
(a) to give money for something; *how much did you pay for your car?; how much rent do you pay?; please pay the waiter for your drinks; she paid him £10 for his old bike*
(b) to give money to someone for doing something; *we pay secretaries £10 an hour; I paid them one pound each for washing the car; I'll pay you a pound to wash my car* (NOTE: you **pay someone to wash the car** before he washes it, but you **pay someone for washing the car** after he has washed it)
(c) **to pay attention to** = to note and think about something carefully; *pay attention to the following instructions;* **to pay a visit** = to visit; *we'll pay my mother a visit when we're in town* (NOTE: **paying - paid** [peɪd])

④ **payable**
['peɪɪbl] *adjective*
which must be paid; *this invoice is payable at 30 days; no tax is payable on these items; the first quarter's rent is payable in advance*

③ **pay back**
['peɪ 'bæk] *verb*
(a) to give someone money which you owe; *he borrowed ten pounds last week and hasn't paid me back*

(b) **to pay someone back for** = to take revenge on someone for having done something; *'that will pay them back for ruining our party,' he said as he smashed their car window*

③ **pay in**
['peɪ 'ɪn] *verb*
to put money into a bank account; *I've got several cheques and some cash to pay in*

① **payment**
['peɪmɪnt] *noun*
(a) giving money for something; *I make regular monthly payments into her account; she made a payment of £10,000 to the solicitor*
(b) money paid; *did you receive any payment for the work?; if you fall behind with your payments, they will take the car back*

③ **pay off**
['peɪ 'ɒf] *verb*
(a) to finish paying money which is owed; *he's aiming to pay off his mortgage in ten years; she said she couldn't pay off the loan*
(b) to pay all the money owed to someone and terminate his or her employment; *when the company was taken over the factory was closed and all the workers were paid off*
(c) *(informal)* to be successful; *their more cautious approach paid off in the end; all that hard work paid off when she came top of her class*

③ **pay out**
['peɪ 'aʊt] *verb*
(a) to give money to someone; *the insurance company paid out thousands of pounds after the storm; we have paid out half our profits in dividends*
(b) to let a rope go out bit by bit; *they paid out the rope as I climbed down the cliff*

③ **pay up**
['peɪ 'ʌp] *verb*
to pay all the money which you owe; *the tourist paid up quickly when the taxi driver called the police*

③ **PC**
['piː'siː] = PERSONAL COMPUTER, POLICE CONSTABLE

③ **pea**
[piː] *noun*
climbing plant of which the round green seeds are eaten as vegetables; *what vegetables do you want with your meat? - peas and carrots, please;* **pea soup** = green soup, made with peas; **sweet peas** = plant of the pea family with scented flowers

② **peace**
[piːs] *noun*
(a) state of not being at war; *the UN troops are trying to keep the peace in the area; both sides are hoping to reach a peace settlement;* **peace process** = negotiations, concessions, discussions, etc., which take place over a long time, with the aim of ending a war

(b) calm, quiet state; *noisy motorcycles ruin the peace and quiet of the village*

③ **peaceful**
['pi:sful] *adjective*
(a) calm; *we spent a peaceful afternoon by the river*
(b) liking peace; *the Swiss seem to be a very peaceful nation*

④ **peacekeeping**
['pi:ski:pɪŋ] *adjective & noun*
trying to keep peace in a region where there is a war; *the army is mainly involved in peacekeeping rather than in fighting; UN peacekeeping forces are in the area*

③ **peach**
[pi:tʃ] *noun*
(a) sweet fruit, with a large stone and soft skin; *we had peaches and cream for dessert*
(b) peach (tree) = tree which bears peaches; *he's planted two peaches in his back garden; the peach trees were all in flower* (NOTE: plural is **peaches**)
(c) pink and yellow colour; *they painted the bathroom a light peach colour*

③ **peak**
[pi:k]
1 *noun*
(a) top of a mountain; *can you see that white peak in the distance? - it's Everest*
(b) highest point; *the team reached a peak during training and have fallen back since; the graph shows the peaks of pollution over the last month*; peak period = period of the day when most electricity is used, when most traffic is on the roads, etc.
(c) front part of a cap which sticks out; *he wore a white cap with a dark blue peak*
2 *verb*
to reach the highest point; *sales peaked in January*

④ **peanut**
['pi:nʌt] *noun*
(a) nut which grows in the ground in seed cases like a pea; *I bought a packet of peanuts to eat with my beer*; peanut butter = paste made from crushed peanuts; *she made peanut butter sandwiches for the children*
(b) *(informal)* very small amount of money; *why does he stay in that job, when he only earns peanuts?; she worked for peanuts in the family shop*

③ **pear**
[peɪ] *noun*
(a) fruit like a long apple, with one end fatter than the other; *when are pears in season?*
(b) pear (tree) = tree which bears pears; *we've planted a pear and an apple in the garden* (NOTE: do not confuse with **pair**)
(c) *(informal)* to go pear-shaped = to go wrong, not to work properly; *since the shop opened, everything seems to be going pear-shaped*

③ **pearl**
[pɜ:l] *noun*
(a) precious little round white ball; *she wore a string of pearls which her grandmother had given her*
(b) pearl bulb = light bulb which is not clear, but covered with a pale white coating (NOTE: a bulb without this coating is a **clear bulb**)

④ **peasant**
['pezɪnt] *noun*
farm worker or farmer living in a backward region; *the peasants still use traditional farming methods*

③ **peculiar**
[pɪ'kju:lɪɪ] *adjective*
(a) odd, strange; *it's peculiar that she refuses to have a TV in the house; there's a peculiar smell coming from the kitchen*
(b) *(formal)* peculiar to = only found in one particular place or person; *fish and chips is a dish which is peculiar to Britain*

③ **pedal**
['pedɪl]
1 *noun*
(a) lever worked by the foot; *if you want to stop the car put your foot down on the brake pedal*; pedal bin = rubbish bin with a lid worked by a pedal
(b) flat part which you press down on with your foot to make a bicycle go forwards; *he stood up on his pedals to make the bike go up the hill*
2 *verb*
to make a bicycle go by pushing on the pedals; *he had to pedal hard to get up the hill* (NOTE: **pedalling - pedalled** but American spelling is **pedaling - pedaled**)

③ **pedestrian**
[pɪ'destrɪn]
1 *noun*
person who walks on a pavement, along a road; *two pedestrians were also injured in the accident*
2 *adjective*
(a) referring to pedestrians; *the street is open to pedestrian traffic only*; pedestrian crossing = place where pedestrians can cross a road; pedestrian precinct *or* pedestrian zone = street or group of streets closed to traffic, where people can walk about freely; *the town centre has been made into a pedestrian zone*
(b) heavy, done without any imagination; *she gave a terribly pedestrian performance as Juliet*

④ **peel**
[pi:l]
1 *noun*
outer skin of a fruit, etc.; *throw the banana peel into the rubbish bin; this orange has got very thick peel* (NOTE: no plural)
2 *verb*

(a) to take the outer skin off a fruit or a vegetable; *he was peeling a banana*; *if the potatoes are very small you can boil them without peeling them*
(b) to come off in layers; *I went into the sun yesterday and now my back is peeling*

④ **peer**
['pɪɪ]
1 *noun*
(a) lord; *peers sit in the House of Lords*
(b) person of the same rank or class as another; *he's always trying to compete with his peers*; **peer group** = group of people of equal status
2 *verb*
to look at something hard when you cannot see very well; *she peered at the screen to see if she could read the figures*

④ **peg**
[peg]
1 *noun*
(a) small wooden or metal stake or pin; *the children hang their coats on pegs in the hall*; *they used no nails in building the roof - it is all held together with wooden pegs*; **tent peg** = metal peg driven into the ground, to which ropes are attached to keep a tent firm; *the ground was so hard that we had to bang the tent pegs in with a hammer*
(b) **clothes peg** = little wooden clip, used to attach wet clothes to a washing line (NOTE: American English is **clothes pin**)
2 *verb*
(a) to attach with a peg; *she pegged the washing out on the line*
(b) to hold prices, etc., stable; *prices will be pegged at the current rate for another year* (NOTE: **pegging - pegged**)

② **pen**
[pen]
1 *noun*
(a) object for writing with, using ink; *I've lost my red pen - can I borrow yours?*; *if you haven't got a pen you can always write in pencil*; **felt pen** = pen with a point made of hard cloth; **marker pen** = pen which makes a wide coloured mark
(b) place with a fence round it where animals, such as sheep, can be kept; *they put the sheep in a pen overnight*; *somehow the lambs managed to get out of their pen*
2 *verb*
(a) to put in a pen; *the sheep were penned while waiting to be taken to the market*
(b) **to be penned in** = to be in a small space, closely surrounded by other things; *she felt penned in, living in the same house as her husband's parents* (NOTE: **penning - penned**)

③ **penalty**
['penɪltɪ] *noun*
(a) punishment; *the maximum penalty for this offence is two years imprisonment*; **to pay the penalty** = to be punished for something; *the*

coup failed and the leaders had to pay the penalty; **death penalty** = punishment by death; *the judge passed the death penalty on the murderer*
(b) punishment in sport, especially a kick at goal awarded to the opposite side in football; *he was awarded a penalty kick*; *they scored from a penalty*
(c) disadvantage; *being chased by photographers is one of the penalties of being rich and famous* (NOTE: plural is **penalties**)

③ **penalty area**
['penɪltɪ 'eɪrɪɪ] *noun*
(in football) the area in front of the goal where if a player breaks the rules the other team is given a free shot at the goal from a short distance away; *a free kick from just outside the penalty area*

③ **pence**
[pens] *see* PENNY

② **pencil**
['pensɪl]
1 *noun*
object for writing with, made of a tube of wood, with a strip of coloured material in the middle; *examination answers must be written in ink, not in pencil*
2 *verb*
to write with a pencil; **to pencil in** = to write something with a pencil, which you rub out later if it isn't correct; *I'll pencil in the meeting for next Wednesday* (NOTE: **pencilling - pencilled** but American spelling is **penciling - penciled**)

④ **pending**
['pendɪŋ]
1 *adjective*
which has not happened or been dealt with; which will happen or be dealt with soon; *an official announcement is pending*; **pending tray** = tray for papers and letters waiting to be dealt with
2 *preposition; pending advice from our lawyers* = while waiting for advice from our lawyers; *he has been suspended on full pay, pending an inquiry*

④ **penetrate**
['penɪtreɪt] *verb*
to go into *or* through something; *the knife penetrated his lung*; *a bullet which can penetrate three centimetres of solid wood*

④ **penguin**
['peŋgwɪn] *noun*
black and white bird found in the regions near the South Pole, which swims well but cannot fly

④ **peninsula**
[pɪ'nɪnsjʊlɪ] *noun*
large piece of land which goes out into the sea; *Singapore is situated at the tip of the Malay Peninsula*; *Cornwall is a peninsula sticking out into the Atlantic Ocean*

① **penny**
['peni] *noun*

(a) smallest British coin, one hundredth of a pound; *it cost £4.99, so I paid with a five-pound note and got a penny change*; *I came out without my purse and I haven't got a penny on me*; *a cup of tea is cheap - it only costs 50 pence* (NOTE: plural is **pennies** or **pence**; **pennies** is used to refer to several coins, but **pence** refers to the price. In prices, **pence** is always written **p** and often said as [piː] **this book only costs 60p:** say 'sixty p' or 'sixty pence')

(b) *(informal)* **the penny's dropped** = he's understood at last; *it took ages for the penny to drop*; **to spend a penny** = to go to the toilet; *wait a moment, I want to spend a penny*

② **pension**
['penʃn]

1 *noun*

money paid regularly to someone who has retired from work, to a widow, etc.; *he has a good pension from his firm*; *she finds a teacher's pension quite enough to live on*; **old age pension** = money paid regularly by the state to people over a certain age

2 *verb*

to pension someone off = to make someone stop working and live on a pension; *they pensioned him off at the age of 55*

② **pensioner**
['penʃnɪ] *noun*

person who gets a pension; *we offer special discounts for pensioners*; *he's a pensioner, so he has to be careful with his money*; **old age pensioner** = person who has retired and lives on a pension

① **people**
['piːpl]

1 *noun*

(a) men, women or children taken as a group; *there were at least twenty people waiting to see the doctor*; *so many people wanted to see the film that there were queues every night*; *a group of people from our office went to Paris by train*

(b) inhabitants of a country; *the people of China work very hard*; *government by the people, for the people*

2 *verb*

peopled with = filled with inhabitants; *the island was peopled with natives who had sailed across the Pacific*

③ **pepper**
['pepɪ] *noun*

(a) sharp spice used in cooking, made from the seeds of a tropical climbing plant; *add salt and pepper to taste* (NOTE: no plural in this meaning)

(b) green or red fruit used as a vegetable; *we had stuffed green peppers for lunch* (NOTE: these are called **bell peppers** in American English)

> COMMENT: there are basically two types of the spice: black pepper from whole seeds, and white pepper from seeds which have had their outer layer removed. You can buy pepper in the form of seeds or already ground. There is no connection between the spice and the plants which give green and red peppers

③ **peppermint**
['pepɪmɪnt] *noun*

(a) herb which produces an oil used in sweets, drinks and toothpaste; *I always use peppermint-flavoured toothpaste*

(b) a sweet flavoured with peppermint; *a bag of peppermints*

① **per**
[pɜː] *preposition*

(a) out of each; **twenty per thousand** = twenty out of every thousand; *there are about six mistakes per thousand words*; *see also* PER CENT

(b) for each; *I can't cycle any faster than fifteen miles per hour*; *potatoes cost 10p per kilo*; *we paid our secretaries £7 per hour*

③ **perceive**
[pɪ'siːv] *verb*

to notice through the senses; to become aware of something; *the changes are so slight that they're almost impossible to perceive with the naked eye*; *doctors perceived an improvement in his condition during the night*; *some drugs are perceived as being a danger to health*

③ **per cent** *or* **percent**
[pɪ 'sent]

1 *noun*

out of each hundred; **twenty-five per cent (25%)** = one quarter, twenty-five parts out of a total of one hundred; **fifty per cent (50%)** = half, fifty parts out of a total of one hundred; *sixty two per cent (62%) of the people voted*; *eighty per cent (80%) of the cars on the road are less than five years old*

2 *adjective*

showing a quantity out of a hundred; *they are proposing a 5% increase in fares*

3 *adverb;* **one hundred per cent happy with** = totally satisfied with; *I'm not one hundred percent happy with his work* (NOTE: **per cent** is written **%** when used with figures: **30%** (say 'thirty per cent')

③ **percentage**
[pɪ'sentɪdʒ] *noun*

figure shown as a proportion of a hundred; *a low percentage of the population voted*; *what percentage of businesses are likely to be affected?*; **percentage point** = 1 per cent; **half a percentage point** = 0.5 per cent

③ **perception**
['pɪ'sepʃn] *noun*
ability to notice or realize; *he doesn't have a very clear perception of what he is supposed to do*

④ **perch**
[pɜːtʃ]
1 *noun*
branch or ledge on which a bird can sit; *the pigeon flew down from his perch and landed on the back of my chair* (NOTE: plural is **perches**)
2 *verb*
(a) *(of bird)* to sit; *the pigeon was perched on a high branch*
(b) *(of person, building)* to be placed high up; *she was sitting perched on a high seat at the bar; a castle perched high on the side of a mountain*

② **perfect**
1 ['pɜːfɪkt] *adjective*
(a) which is good in every way; *your coat is a perfect fit; don't change anything - the room is perfect as it is*
(b) ideal; *she's the perfect secretary; George would be perfect for the job of salesman; I was in a perfect position to see what happened*
(c) **perfect (tense)** = past tense of a verb which shows that the action has been completed; *in English the perfect is formed using the verb 'to have'*
2 [pɪ'fekt] *verb*
to make something new and perfect; *she perfected a process for speeding up the invoicing system*

④ **perfection**
[pɪ'fekʃn] *noun*
state of being perfect; *perfection is not always easy to achieve*; **to perfection** = perfectly; *he timed his kick to perfection*

② **perfectly**
['pɜːfɪktli] *adverb*
extremely well; *she typed the letter perfectly; the suit fits you perfectly; I'm perfectly capable of finding my own way home; she's perfectly willing to take the test*

② **perform**
[pɪ'fɔːm] *verb*
(a) to carry out an action; *she performed a perfect dive; it's the sort of task that can be performed by any computer*
(b) to act in public; *the group will perform at the outdoor theatre next week; the play will be performed in the village hall*

① **performance**
[pɪ'fɔːməns] *noun*
(a) how well a machine works, a sportsman runs, etc.; *we're looking for ways to improve our performance; after last night's miserable performance I don't think the team is likely to reach the final*

(b) public show; *the next performance will start at 8 o'clock; there are three performances a day during the summer*

③ **performer**
[pɪ'fɔːmɪ] *noun*
person who gives a public show; *in Covent Garden, street performers entertain the tourists*

④ **perfume**
['pɜːfjuːm] *noun*
scent, a liquid which smells nice, and which is put on the skin; *do you like my new perfume?*

① **perhaps**
[pɪ'hæps] *adverb*
possibly; *perhaps the train is late; they're late - perhaps the snow's very deep; is it going to be fine? - perhaps not, I can see clouds over there*

① **period**
['pɪriɪd] *noun*
(a) length of time; *she swam under water for a short period; the offer is open for a limited period only; it was an unhappy period in her life*
(b) time during which a lesson is given in school; *we have three periods of English on Thursdays*
(c) *US* printed mark like a small dot, showing the end of a sentence or an abbreviation; *when reading, you can take a breath at a period* (NOTE: British English is **full stop**)
(d) *meaning* 'and that's all'; *she doesn't like German food, period* (NOTE: also used in British English as well as American in this sense)

② **permanent**
['pɜːmənɪnt] *adjective*
lasting for ever; supposed to last for ever; *he has found a permanent job; she is in permanent employment; they are living with her parents for a few weeks - it's not a permanent arrangement*

④ **permanently**
['pɜːmənɪntli] *adverb*
for ever; always; *the shop seems to be permanently closed; you can never speak to him on the phone - he's permanently in meetings; the car crash left him permanently disabled*

② **permission**
[pɪ'mɪʃn] *noun*
freedom which you are given to do something; *you need permission from the boss to go into the warehouse; he asked the manager's permission to take a day off*

③ **permit**
1 ['pɜːmɪt] *noun*
paper which allows you to do something; *you have to have a permit to sell ice cream from a van;* **parking permit** = paper which allows you to park a car
2 [pɪ'mɪt] *verb*

to allow; *this ticket permits three people to go into the exhibition*; *smoking is not permitted in underground stations* (NOTE: permitting - permitted)

④ **persist**
[pɪˈsɪst] *verb*

to continue to exist; *the fog persisted all day*; **to persist in doing something** = to continue doing something, in spite of problems; *he will persist in singing while he works although we've told him many times to stop*; *she persists in refusing to see a doctor*

③ **persistent**
[pɪˈsɪstɪnt] *adjective*

continuing to do something, even though people want you to stop; *he can be very persistent if he wants something badly enough*; *she broke down under persistent questioning by the police*

① **person**
[ˈpɜːsɪn] *noun*

man or woman; *the police say a person or persons entered the house by the window*; *his father's a very interesting person*; **the manager was there in person** = he was there himself; **missing person** = someone who has disappeared, and no one knows where he is; *her name is on the police Missing Persons list*

① **personal**
[ˈpɜːsnɪl] *adjective*

(a) belonging or referring to a particular person or people; *they lost all their personal property in the fire*; **personal best** = best time, speed, etc., which a sportsman has achieved, though not necessarily a record; **personal computer (PC)** = small computer used by a person at home; **personal organizer** = little computer or book in which you enter your appointments, addresses, etc.; *I'll put the dates in my personal organizer*; **personal stereo** = small stereo set which you can carry around and listen to as you walk

(b) referring to someone's private life in an offensive way; *the attacks on the minister became increasingly personal*

③ **personality**
[pɜːsɪˈnælɪti] *noun*

(a) character; *he has a strange personality*; *she's got lots of personality* = she's a lively and interesting person; *see also* SPLIT

(b) famous person, especially a TV or radio star; *the new supermarket is going to be opened by a famous sporting personality*; **personality cult** = publicity given to a political leader, making him into a kind of god

② **personally**
[ˈpɜːsnɪli] *adverb*

(a) from your own point of view; *personally, I think you're making a mistake*

(b) in person; *he is sorry that he can't be here to accept the prize personally*

(c) **don't take it personally** = don't think it was meant to criticize you

③ **personnel**
[pɜːsɪˈnel] *noun*

staff, the people employed by a company; *we've made some changes to the personnel in the last few weeks*; **personnel manager** = manager who deals with pay, sick leave, administration, etc., for all the staff (NOTE: now often called a **human resources manager**)

③ **perspective**
[pɪˈspektɪv] *noun*

(a) *(in art)* way of drawing objects or scenes, so that they appear to have depth or distance; *he's got the perspective wrong - that's why the picture looks so odd*

(b) way of looking at something; *a French politician's perspective on the problem will be completely different from mine*; *she was looking at the situation from the perspective of a parent with two young children*; **to put things in perspective** = to show things in an objective way; *you must put the sales figures in perspective - they look bad, but they're much better than last year*

② **persuade**
[pɪˈsweɪd] *verb*

to get someone to do what you want by explaining or asking; *she managed to persuade the bank manager to give her a loan*; *after hours of discussion, they persuaded him to hand over his gun*

④ **pessimism**
[ˈpesɪmɪzm] *noun*

state of believing that only bad things will happen; *he sits alone in his bedroom all day, full of pessimism at his prospects of finding another job*; *her pessimism is starting to affect the other members of the team*

④ **pessimist**
[ˈpesɪmɪst] *noun*

person who thinks only bad things will happen; *pessimists thought the policy was bound to fail*

④ **pessimistic**
[pesɪˈmɪstɪk] *adjective*

believing that only bad things will happen; *I'm pessimistic about our chances of success*

④ **pest**
[pest] *noun*

(a) plant, animal, or insect that harms other plants or animals; *many farmers look on rabbits as a pest*

(b) *(informal)* person who annoys; *that little boy is an absolute pest - he won't stop whistling*

④ **pet**
[pet]
1 *noun*

(a) animal kept in the home to give pleasure; *the family has several pets - two cats, a dog and a white rabbit*

(b) teacher's pet = school child who is the favourite of the teacher and so is disliked by the other children

2 *adjective*

(a) favourite; *the weather is his pet topic of conversation*; **pet hate** = something which you dislike very much; *cucumber sandwiches are one of my pet hates*; **pet name** = special name given to someone you are fond of; *ever since he was a baby he's been called by his pet name 'Bootsie'*

(b) (animal) kept at home; *you can't keep your pet snake in the bath!*

④ **petition**
[pɪ'tɪʃn]
1 *noun*

(a) official request, signed by many people; *she wanted me to sign a petition against the building of the new road*; *we went to the town hall to hand the petition to the mayor*

(b) legal request; *a divorce petition*

2 *verb*
to ask someone for something officially, to make an official request; *they petitioned the town council for a new library*; *he petitioned the government to provide a special pension*; *she is petitioning for divorce*

③ **petrol**
['petrɪl] *noun*
liquid used as a fuel for engines; *this car doesn't use very much petrol*; *the bus ran out of petrol on the motorway*; *petrol prices are lower at supermarkets*; **petrol pump** = machine which supplies petrol at a petrol station (NOTE: no plural: **some petrol, a litre of petrol** Note also that American English is **gas** *or* **gasoline**)

③ **petrol station**
['petrɪl 'steɪʃn] *noun*
place where you can buy petrol for your car; *I'll have to stop at the next petrol station - the tank is almost empty* (NOTE: American English is **gas station**)

③ **petrol tank**
['petrɪl 'tæŋk] *noun*
tank in a vehicle in which the fuel is stored; *I put water into my petrol tank by mistake*; *the reason your car won't start is that the petrol tank is empty*

④ **pharmacist**
['fɑːmɪsɪst] *noun*
person who prepares and sells medicines; *ask the pharmacist for advice on which sun cream to use* (NOTE: also called a **chemist**)

④ **pharmacy**
['fɑːmɪsi] *noun*

(a) shop which makes and sells medicines; *he runs the pharmacy in the High Street* (NOTE: plural in this meaning is **pharmacies**; also called a **chemist's**)

(b) study of medicines; *she's studying pharmacy*; *he has a diploma in pharmacy* (NOTE: no plural in this meaning)

② **phase**
[feɪz]
1 *noun*
period or stage in the development of something; *the project is now in its final phase*; *it's a phase she's going through and hopefully she will grow out of it*; *I'm sure dyeing his hair green is just a phase*; **critical phase** = important point where things may go wrong; *negotiations have reached a critical phase*

2 *verb*
to phase something in or **to phase something out** = to introduce *or* to remove something gradually; *the new telephone system will be phased in over the next two months*

③ **phenomenon**
[fe'nɒmɪnɪn] *noun*
very remarkable thing which happens; *a strange phenomenon which only occurs on the highest mountains*; *scientists have not yet found an explanation for this phenomenon*; **natural phenomenon** *or* **phenomenon of nature** = remarkable thing which happens naturally; *volcanoes are natural phenomena* (NOTE: plural is **phenomena**)

④ **philosopher**
[fɪ'lɒsɪfɪ] *noun*
person who studies the meaning of human existence; person who teaches philosophy; *as a famous philosopher once said: 'I think, therefore I am'*

④ **philosophical**
[fɪlɪ'sɒfɪkl] *adjective*

(a) thoughtful; calm in the face of problems; *to take a philosophical attitude*; *it's best to be philosophical about it and not get too upset*

(b) referring to philosophy; *she was involved in a philosophical argument*

③ **philosophy**
[fɪ'lɒsɪfɪ] *noun*

(a) study of the meaning of human existence; *he's studying philosophy*

(b) general way of thinking; *my philosophy is that you should treat people as you want them to treat you*

① **phone**
[fəʊn]
1 *noun*
telephone, a machine which you use to speak to someone who is some distance away; *can't someone answer the phone - it's been ringing and ringing*; *I was in the garden when you called, but by the time I got to the house the phone had stopped ringing*; *if someone rings, can you answer the phone for me?*; *she lifted the phone and called the ambulance*; **by phone** *or* **over the phone** = using the telephone; *she reserved a table by phone*; *he placed the order over the phone*

2 *verb*

to call someone using a telephone; *your wife phoned when you were out*; *can you phone me at ten o'clock tomorrow evening?*; *I need to phone our office in New York*; **to phone for something** = to make a phone call to ask for something; *he phoned for a taxi*; **to phone about something** = to make a phone call to speak about something; *he phoned about the message he had received* (NOTE: **phone** is often used in place of **telephone: phone call, phone book**, etc., but not in the expressions **telephone switchboard, telephone operator, telephone exchange**)

◊ **on the phone**

['ɒn ðɪ 'fɪʊn]

(a) speaking by telephone; *don't make such a noise - the boss is on the phone*; *she has been on the phone all morning*

(b) with a telephone in the house; *don't look for their address in the phone book - they're not on the phone*

③ **phone back**

['fɪʊn 'bæk] *verb*

to reply by telephone; *the manager is out - can you phone back in about fifteen minutes?*

③ **phone book**

['fɪʊn 'bʊk] *noun*

book which gives the names of people and businesses in a town, with their addresses and phone numbers; *the restaurant must be new - it isn't in the phone book*

③ **phone booth** *or* **phone box**

['fɪʊn 'buːð or 'bɒks] *noun*

small glass shelter in a public place, containing a public telephone; *call me from the phone box outside the station, and I'll come and pick you up*; *there was a queue of people waiting to use the phone box*

③ **phone call**

['fɪʊn 'kɔːl] *noun*

telephone call, speaking to someone by telephone; *I had a phone call from an old friend today*; *I need to make a quick phone call before we leave*

③ **phonecard**

['fɪʊnkɑːd] *noun*

plastic card which you use in a telephone; *you can buy phonecards at post offices and newsagents*

③ **phone number**

['fɪʊn 'nʌmbɪ] *noun*

number of one particular phone; *what's the phone number of the garage?*; *if I give you my phone number promise you won't forget it*; *his phone number's Birmingham 878 1405*

COMMENT: British phone numbers are formed of a town or area code followed by the number of the actual telephone. Area codes always start with 0, and may have three further figures for large towns (Central

London is 020 7, Liverpool is 0151) or several figures for smaller towns (Oxford is 01865). The number for the actual telephone usually has eight figures. These are spoken as area code + four + four: so 020 8943 1673 is spoken as 'oh two oh, eight nine four three, one six seven three'

② **photo**

['fɪʊtɪʊ] *noun*

photograph, a picture taken with a camera; *here's a photo of the village in the snow*; *I've brought some holiday photos to show you* (NOTE: plural is **photos**)

③ **photocopier**

['fɪʊtɪʊkɒpɪɪ] *noun*

machine which makes photocopies; *I'll just take this down to the photocopier and make some copies*; *the paper has jammed in the photocopier*; *you can make colour photocopies on a colour photocopier*

③ **photocopy**

['fɪʊtɪʊkɒpɪ]

1 *noun*

copy of a document made by photographing it; *she made six photocopies of the contract*

2 *verb*

to copy something and make a print of it; *can you photocopy this letter, please?*

② **photograph**

['fɪʊtɪɡrɑːf]

1 *noun*

picture taken with a camera; *I've found an old black and white photograph of my parents' wedding*; *she's trying to take a photograph of the cat*; *he kept her photograph on his desk*; *you'll need two passport photographs to get your visa*

2 *verb*

to take a picture with a camera; *she was photographing the flowers in the public gardens*

④ **photographer**

[fɪ'tɒɡrɪfɪ] *noun*

person who takes photographs; *the photographer asked us to stand closer together*; *she's a photographer for a local newspaper*; *a photographer was at the scene to record the ceremony*

④ **photographic**

[fɪʊtɪʊ'græfɪk] *adjective*

(a) referring to photography; *all your photographic kit is still in the back of my car*

(b) **photographic memory** = being able to remember things in exact detail, as if you were still seeing them

③ **photography**

[fɪ'tɒɡrɪfɪ] *noun*

taking pictures on sensitive film with a camera; *she bought a camera and took up photography*;

an exhibition of 19th-century photography; photography is part of the art and design course; photography is one of the visual arts

③ **phrase**
[fraɪz]
1 noun
short sentence or group of words; *try to translate the whole phrase, not just one word at a time; I'm trying to remember a phrase from 'Hamlet'*; **phrase book** = book of translations of common expressions; *we bought a Japanese phrase book before we went to Japan; (informal)* **to coin a phrase** = to emphasize that you are saying something which everyone says; *'it never rains but it pours' - to coin a phrase*
2 verb
to put into words; *I try and phrase my letter as politely as I can*

① **physical**
['fɪzɪkl] adjective
(a) referring to the human body; *the illness is mental rather than physical; he has a strong physical attraction for her*; **physical exercise** = exercise of the body; *you should do some physical exercise every day*
(b) referring to matter, energy, etc.; **physical geography** = study of rocks and earth, etc.; **physical chemistry** = study of chemical substances

③ **physically**
['fɪzɪkli] adverb
(a) referring to the body; *she is physically handicapped, but manages to look after herself; I find him physically very attractive*
(b) referring to the laws of nature; *it is physically impossible for a lump of lead to float*

④ **physician**
[fɪ'zɪʃn] noun
US (formal) doctor; *consult your physician before taking this medicine*

④ **physicist**
['fɪzɪsɪst] noun
person who studies physics; *an atomic physicist*

③ **physics**
['fɪzɪks] noun
study of matter, energy, etc.; *she teaches physics at the local college; it's a law of physics that things fall down to the ground and not up into the sky*

③ **piano**
['pjænɪʊ] noun
large musical instrument with black and white keys which you press to make music; *she's taking piano lessons; she played the piano while her brother sang*; **grand piano** = large horizontal piano; **upright piano** = smaller piano with a vertical body

① **pick**
[pɪk]
1 noun

(a) something which you choose; **take your pick** = choose which one you want; *we've got green, red and blue balloons - just take your pick!*
(b) a large heavy tool with a curved metal head with a sharp end that you lift up and bring down to break things; *they started breaking up the concrete path with picks and spades*
2 verb
(a) to choose; *the captain picks the football team; she was picked to play the part of Hamlet's mother; the Association has picked Paris for its next meeting*
(b) to take fruit or flowers from plants; *they've picked all the strawberries; don't pick the flowers in the public gardens*
(c) to take away small pieces of something; *she picked the bits of grass off her skirt*; **to pick your teeth** = to push something between your teeth to remove little bits of food; *he was picking his teeth with a match*; **to pick at your food** = to eat little bits as if you have no appetite; *she's lost her appetite - she just picks at her food*
(d) **to pick someone's brains** = to ask someone for advice or information; **to pick someone's pocket** = to take something from someone's pocket without them noticing; *I lost my purse - someone picked my pocket on the train!*; **to pick a lock** = to open a lock with a piece of wire; *he picked the look of the car and drove off before I could stop him*

① **pick on**
['pɪk 'ɒn] verb
to choose someone to attack or criticize; *why do you always pick on children who are younger than you?; the manager is picking on me all the time*

① **pick out**
['pɪk 'aʊt] verb
to choose; *he picked out all the best fruit*

③ **pickpocket**
['pɪkpɒkɪt] noun
person who steals things from people's pockets; *'Watch out! Pickpockets are operating in this area!'*; *visitors should be on the watch for pickpockets*

① **pick up**
['pɪk 'ʌp] verb
(a) to lift something up which is lying on the surface of something; *she dropped her handkerchief and he picked it up; he bent down to pick up a pound coin which he saw on the pavement*
(b) to learn something easily without being taught; *she never took any piano lessons, she just picked it up; he picked up some German when he was working in Germany*
(c) to give someone a lift in a vehicle; *the car will pick you up from the hotel; can you send a taxi to pick us up at seven o'clock?*

(d) to meet someone by chance and start a relationship with them; *she's a girl he picked up in a bar*

(e) to arrest; *he was picked up by the police at the airport*

(f) to improve, to get better; *she's been in bed for weeks, but is beginning to pick up*; *business is picking up after the Christmas holiday*

(g) to pick up speed = to go faster; *the truck began to pick up speed as it went down the hill*

(h) *(informal)* **to pick up the bill** = to pay the bill; *don't worry about the hotel expenses - the company will pick up the bill*

① **pick-up**
['pɪkʌp] *noun*

(a) light van with an open back; *they loaded all their gear into the back of a pick-up*

(b) act of collecting someone or something; *the customer pick-up point is behind the store*; *I've got several pick-ups to do before I can go home*

③ **picnic**
['pɪknɪk]

1 *noun*

meal eaten in the open air; *if it's fine, let's go for a picnic*; *they stopped by a wood, and had a picnic lunch*

2 *verb*

to eat a picnic; *people were picnicking on the bank of the river* (NOTE: picnicking - picnicked)

① **picture**
['pɪktʃɪ]

1 *noun*

(a) drawing, painting, photo, etc.; *she drew a picture of the house*; *the book has pages of pictures of wild animals*; *she cut out the picture of the President from the magazine*

(b) *(informal)* **to put someone in the picture** = to give someone all the information about a problem; *let me put you in the picture*; **to get the picture** = to understand the problem; *I get the picture - you want me to arrange to get rid of her*

(c) the pictures = the cinema; *we went to the pictures twice last week*

2 *verb*

to imagine; *it takes quite an effort to picture him in a skirt*

② **pie**
[paɪ] *noun*

(a) meat or fruit cooked in a pastry case; *for pudding, there's apple pie and ice cream*; *if we're going on a picnic, I'll buy a big pork pie*; *(informal)* **pie in the sky** = ideal situation which you can never reach

(b) cottage pie *or* **shepherd's pie** = cooked meat in a dish with potatoes on top; **fisherman's pie** = cooked fish in a dish with potatoes on top

① **piece**
[piːs]

1 *noun*

(a) (small) bit of something; *would you like another piece of cake?*; *I need two pieces of black cloth*; *she played a piece of music by Chopin*

(b) *(informal)* **to be a piece of cake** = to be very easy; *that test was simple - a piece of cake!*

(c) pieces = broken bits of something; *the watch came to pieces in my hand*; *the plate was in pieces on the floor*; *you will have to take the clock to pieces to mend it* (NOTE: piece is often used to show one item of something which has no plural: **equipment: a piece of equipment; concrete: a piece of concrete; cheese: a piece of cheese; news: a piece of news; advice: a piece of advice**)

2 *verb*

to piece together = to put things together to form a whole; *the police are trying to piece together the events which took place during the evening of the murder*

④ **pierce**
['pɪɪs] *verb*

to make a hole in something; *she decided to have her ears pierced*; *he pierced the metal cap on the jar with the point of a kitchen knife*

② **pig**
[pɪg] *noun*

pink or black farm animal with short legs, which gives meat; *the farmer next door keeps pigs* (NOTE: fresh meat from a **pig** is called **pork**; **bacon** and **ham** are types of smoked or cured meat from a pig)

③ **pigeon**
['pɪdʒn] *noun*

fat greyish bird which is common in towns; *let's go and feed the pigeons in Trafalgar Square*

② **pile**
[paɪl]

1 *noun*

(a) heap; *look at that pile of washing*; *the pile of plates crashed onto the floor*; *the wind blew piles of dead leaves into the road*; *he was carrying a great pile of books*

(b) *(informal)* **piles of** = a lot of; *they brought piles of food with them*; *there's no need to hurry, we've got piles of time*

(c) thick wooden or concrete post, driven into the ground; *they drove piles into the bed of the river to support the bridge*

(d) soft surface of cloth; *just feel the pile on these cushions*; *we have put a thick pile carpet in the sitting room*

2 *verb*

to pile (up) = to heap up; *all the Christmas presents are piled (up) under the tree*; *complaints are piling up about the service*

④ **pilgrim**
['pɪlgrɪm] *noun*

person who goes to visit a holy place; *pilgrims came to Rome from all over the world*; **the Pilgrims** *or* **Pilgrim Fathers** = emigrants who left England to settle in America in 1620

① pill
[pɪl] *noun*
(a) small round tablet of medicine; *take two pills before breakfast*
(b) *(informal)* on the pill = taking a course of contraceptive tablets; *she went on the pill when she was seventeen*

④ pillar
['pɪlə] *noun*
column which supports part of a building; *the roof is supported by a row of wooden pillars; one of the pillars supporting the bridge collapsed*

③ pillar box
['pɪlə 'bɒks] *noun*
round red metal container into which you can post letters; *there's a pillar box at the corner of the street; the postman was emptying the pillar box when I came with my letter; pillar-box red = bright red; she has a pillar-box red coat, so she's easy to see in a crowd*

③ pillow
['pɪləʊ] *noun*
bag full of soft material which you put your head on in bed; *I like to sleep with two pillows; she sat up in bed, surrounded by pillows*

④ pillowcase *or* **pillowslip**
['pɪləʊkeɪs *or* 'pɪləʊslɪp] *noun*
cloth bag to cover a pillow with; *the maids change the room and put clean sheets and pillowcases on the beds every morning*

③ pilot
['paɪlət]
1 *noun*
(a) person who flies a plane; *he's training to be an airline pilot; he's a helicopter pilot for an oil company*
(b) person who guides boats into or out of a harbour; *ships are not allowed into the harbour without a pilot*
(c) made or used as a test; *a pilot for a new TV series; pilot scheme = small scheme used as a test before starting a full-scale scheme; he is running a pilot scheme for training unemployed young people*
(d) pilot light = little gas flame, which burns all the time, and which lights the main gas jets automatically when a heater or oven is switched on; *there's a smell of gas in the kitchen - the pilot light has gone out*
2 *verb*
(a) to guide a boat, aircraft, etc.; *he safely piloted the ship into harbour*
(b) to guide someone; *he piloted her through a series of underground passages to the meeting room*

③ pin
[pɪn]
1 *noun*
(a) small thin sharp metal stick with a round head, used for attaching clothes, papers, etc., together; *she fastened the ribbons to her dress with a pin; drawing pin = pin with a large flat head, used for pinning papers to a wall; give me some drawing pins so that I can pin the poster to the door; safety pin = pin whose point fits into a cover when it is fastened, and so can't hurt anyone*
(b) *US* clothes pin = little wooden clip, used to attach wet clothes to a washing line (NOTE: British English is clothes peg)
(c) pins and needles = sharp tickling feeling in your hand or foot after it has lost feeling for a time; *wait a bit - I've got pins and needles in my foot*
2 *verb*
(a) to attach with a pin; *she pinned up a notice about the meeting; he pinned her photograph on the wall; he pinned the calendar to the wall by his desk*
(b) to trap someone so that they cannot move; *several people were pinned under the fallen roof; the car pinned her against the wall* (NOTE: pinning - pinned)

④ pinch
[pɪntʃ]
1 *noun*
(a) squeezing tightly between finger and thumb; *he gave her arm a pinch*
(b) small quantity of something held between finger and thumb; *add a pinch of salt to the boiling water*
(c) at a pinch = if really necessary; *at a pinch, we can manage with only one sales assistant; to feel the pinch = to find you have less money than you need; we really started to feel the pinch when my father lost his job* (NOTE: plural is pinches)
2 *verb*
(a) to squeeze tightly, using the finger and thumb; *Ow! you're pinching me!*
(b) *(informal)* to steal; *someone's pinched my pen!*

③ pin down
['pɪn 'daʊn] *verb*
to pin someone down = to get someone to say what he or she really thinks, to get someone to make his or her mind up; *I'm trying to pin the chairman down to make a decision; she's very vague about dates - it's difficult to pin her down*

④ pine
[paɪn]
1 *noun*
(a) pine (tree) = type of tree with needle-shaped leaves which stay on the tree all year round; *they planted a row of pines along the edge of the field*
(b) wood from a pine tree; *we've bought a pine table for the kitchen; there are pine cupboards in the children's bedroom*
2 *verb*
to pine for something = to feel sad because you do not have something any more; *she's pining for her cat*

④ **pineapple**
['paɪnæpl] *noun*
large sweet tropical fruit, with stiff leaves on top; *she cut up a pineapple to add to the fruit salad*

④ **ping pong**
['pɪŋpɒŋ] *noun*
(informal) table tennis; *let's have a game of ping pong*; *he was playing ping pong with the children*

② **pink**
[pɪŋk]
1 *adjective*
(a) pale red or flesh colour; *she uses pink paper when she writes to her friends*; **shocking pink** = very bright pink, which seems to glow; *he wore a pair of shocking pink socks*
(b) *(informal)* **tickled pink** = very much amused; *we were tickled pink to get our first letter from our little granddaughter*
2 *noun*
(a) pale red colour; *the bright pink of the flowers shows clearly across the garden*
(b) small scented garden flower; *there was bunch of pinks on the table*

③ **pin money**
['pɪn 'mʌnɪ] *noun*
(informal) money earned by a woman for part-time work; *she earns some pin money typing at home*

③ **PIN number**
['pɪn 'nʌmbɪ] *noun*
(= PERSONAL IDENTIFICATION NUMBER) special number which is allocated to the holder of a credit card or cash card; *I can never remember my PIN number*

② **pint**
[paɪnt] *noun*
liquid measure (= .568 of a litre); *he drinks a pint of milk a day*; *two pints of bitter, please*

④ **pioneer**
[paɪ'nɪɪ]
1 *noun*
(a) person who is among the first to try to do something; *he was one of the pioneers of radar*; *the pioneers in the field of laser surgery*
(b) person who is among the first to explore or settle in a new land; *the first pioneers settled in this valley in about 1860*
2 *verb*
to be first to do something; *the company pioneered developments in the field of electronics*; *she pioneered a new route across the Andes*

② **pipe**
[paɪp] *noun*
(a) tube; *he's clearing a blocked pipe in the kitchen*; *the water came out of the hole in the pipe*
(b) tube for smoking tobacco, with a bowl at one end in which the tobacco burns; *he only smokes a pipe, never cigarettes*

④ **pipeline**
['paɪplaɪn] *noun*
(a) very large tube for carrying oil, natural gas, water, etc., over long distances; *an oil pipeline crosses the desert*
(b) **in the pipeline** = being worked on, coming; *the company has a series of new products in the pipeline*; *she has two new novels in the pipeline*

④ **pirate**
['paɪrɪt] *noun*
(a) sailor who attacks and robs ships; *pirates buried treasure on the island hundreds of years ago*
(b) person who copies a patented invention or a copyright work; **pirate radio** = illegal radio station; **video pirates** = people who organize the copying of videos to make a profit
2 *verb*
to copy a book, disk, design, etc., which is copyright; *the designs for the new dress collection were pirated in the Far East*; *I found a pirated copy of my book on sale in a street market*

④ **pistol**
['pɪstl] *noun*
small gun which is held in the hand; *he pointed a pistol at the shopkeeper and asked for money*; **starting pistol** = small gun which you fire to start a race

④ **pit**
[pɪt]
1 *noun*
(a) deep, dark hole in the ground; *they dug a pit to bury the rubbish*
(b) mine where coal is dug; *my grandfather spent his whole life working down a pit*
(c) *US* hard stone inside a fruit; *a date pit*
2 *verb*
to pit your strength against someone = to try to fight someone; *the little country pitted her strength against her much larger neighbour* (NOTE: **pitting - pitted**)

③ **pitch**
[pɪtʃ]
1 *noun*
(a) ground on which a game is played; *I'll time you, if you run round the football pitch*; *the pitch is too wet to play on*; *he ran the whole length of the pitch and scored* (NOTE: plural is **pitches**)
(b) *(music)* being able to sing or play notes correctly; *he's got perfect pitch*
(c) high point (of anger or excitement); *excitement was at fever pitch*
(d) **sales pitch** = smooth talking, aimed at selling something; *she was completely taken in by his sales pitch*
2 *verb*
(a) to put up a tent; *they pitched their tent in a field by the beach*; **pitched battle** = battle where the opposing sides stand and face each other

(b) to throw a ball; *I pitched him a high ball to see if he could catch it*

(c) *(of boat)* to rock with the front and back going up and down; *the little boat was pitching up and down on the waves* (NOTE: the other movement of a boat, from side to side, is to **roll**)

③ **pity**
['pɪti]
1 *noun*

(a) feeling of sympathy for someone who is in an unfortunate situation; *have you no pity for the homeless?*; **to take pity on someone** = to feel sorry for someone; *at last someone took pity on her and showed her how to work the machine*

(b) it's a pity that = it is sad that; *it's a pity you weren't there to see it*; *it's such a pity that the rain spoiled the picnic*; **it would be a pity to** = it would be unfortunate to; *it would be a pity not to eat all this beautiful food*

2 *verb*

to feel sympathy for someone; *I pity his children*

② **pizza**
['piːtsɪ] *noun*

Italian dish, consisting of a flat round pie base cooked with tomatoes, onions, etc., on top; *we can pick up a pizza for supper tonight*

① **place**
[pleɪs]
1 *noun*

(a) where something is, or where something happens; *here's the place where we saw the cows*; *make sure you put the file back in the right place*; **all over the place** = everywhere; *there were dead leaves lying all over the place*

(b) *(informal)* home; *would you like to come back to my place for a cup of coffee?*; *he has a flat in London and a little place in the country*

(c) seat; *I'm keeping this place for my sister*; *I'm sorry, but this place has been taken*; **to change places with someone** = to take each other's seat; *if you can't see the screen, change places with me*

(d) space for one person at a table; *please set two places for lunch*; **place setting** = set of knife, fork and spoon, etc., for one person; *we need an extra place setting - Frank's bringing his girlfriend*

(e) position (in a race); *the British runners are in the first three places*

(f) page where you have stopped reading a book; *I left a piece of paper in the book to mark my place*; *I've lost my place and can't remember where I got to*

(g) to take place = to happen; *the fight took place outside the football ground*; *the film takes place in China*

(h) name given to a smart street in a town; *they live in Regent Place*

2 *verb*

to put; *the waitress placed the bottle on the table*; *please place the envelope in the box*

④ **plague**
[pleɪg]
1 *noun*

(a) fatal infectious disease transmitted by fleas from rats; *thousands of people died in the Great Plague of London in 1665*; **to avoid someone like the plague** = to try not to meet someone; *I avoid him like the plague because he's always asking if he can borrow money*

(b) great quantity of pests; *we've had a plague of ants in the garden*

2 *verb*

to annoy or to bother someone; *we were plagued with wasps last summer*; *she keeps plaguing me with silly questions*

① **plain**
[pleɪn]
1 *adjective*

(a) easy to understand; *the instructions are written in plain English*

(b) obvious; *it's perfectly plain what he wants*; *we made it plain to them that this was our final offer*

(c) simple, not decorated; *we put plain wallpaper in the dining room*; *the outside is covered with leaves and flowers, but the inside is quite plain*; **plain cover** = envelope without any company name on it

(d) not pretty; *his two daughters are rather plain*

(e) plain chocolate = dark bitter chocolate; **plain flour** = ordinary white flour; **plain yoghurt** = yoghurt without any flavouring (NOTE: do not confuse with **plane**; note: **plainer - plainest**)

2 *noun*

flat area of country; *a broad plain bordered by mountains*

③ **plaintiff**
['pleɪntɪf] *noun*

person who starts a legal action against someone in the civil courts; *she's the plaintiff in a libel action*; *the court decided in favour of the plaintiff* (NOTE: this is an old term; it has now been replaced by **claimant**; the other party in an action is the **defendant**)

① **plan**
[plæn]
1 *noun*

(a) organized way of doing things; *he made a plan to get up earlier in future*; *she drew up plans for the school trip to Germany*; **according to plan** = in the way it was arranged; *the party went off according to plan*

(b) drawing of the way something is arranged; *here are the plans for the kitchen*; *the fire exits are shown on the plan of the office*; **town plan** *or* **street plan** = map of a town; *can you find London Road on the town plan?*

2 *verb*

(a) to arrange how you are going to do something; *she's busy planning her holiday in Greece*

(c) to intend to do something; *they are planning to move to London next month; we weren't planning to go on holiday this year; I plan to take the 5 o'clock flight to New York*

(c) to arrange how to build something; *she planned the bathroom herself; a new town is being planned next to the airport* (NOTE: planning - planned)

② **plane**
[pleɪn]
1 *noun*

(a) aircraft, machine which flies; *when is the next plane for Glasgow?; how are you getting to Paris? - we're going by plane; don't panic, you've got plenty of time to catch your plane; he was stuck in a traffic jam and missed his plane*

(b) tool with a sharp blade for making wood smooth; *he smoothed off the rough edges with a plane*

(c) **plane (tree)** = large tree with broad leaves, often grown in towns; *the bark of plane trees comes off in large pieces; many London squares are planted with planes* (NOTE: do not confuse with **plain**)

2 *verb*

to make wood smooth with a plane; *he planed the top of the table*

④ **planet**
['plænɪt] *noun*

(a) one of the bodies which turn round the sun; *is there life on any of the planets?; Earth is the third planet from the Sun*

(b) the planet Earth; *an environmental disaster which could affect the whole planet*

> COMMENT: the planets in our system are in order of their distance from the Sun: Mercury, Venus, Earth, Mars, Jupiter, Saturn, Uranus, Neptune, and Pluto

③ **planner**
['plænə] *noun*

(a) person who draws up plans; *the planners made the car park too small*; **town planner** = person who designs the layout of a town

(b) **wall planner** = chart which is pinned on a wall, showing days and weeks for the whole year, allowing work to be planned

① **planning**
['plænɪŋ] *noun*

making plans; *the trip will need very careful planning; the project is still in the planning stage*; **family planning** = decision by parents on how many children to have; *a family planning clinic; the clinic gives advice on family planning*; **planning permission** = official document which allows a person or company to build new buildings on empty land or adapt an old building; *you need planning permission to*

build an extension to your house; **town planning** = designing how a town should develop

① **plant**
[plɑːnt]
1 *noun*

(a) living thing which grows in the ground and has leaves, a stem and roots; *he have several rows of cabbage plants in his garden; some plants grow very tall*; **house plants** *or* **pot plants** = plants which you grow in pots in the house; *will you water my house plants for me while I'm on holiday?*; **plant pot** = special pot for growing plants in

(b) machinery; *investment in buildings and plant accounts for 90% of our costs*; **plant-hire firm** = company which lends large machines (such as cranes) to building companies (NOTE: no plural in this meaning)

(c) large factory; *they are planning to build a car plant near the river*

2 *verb*

(a) to put a plant in the ground; *we've planted two pear trees and a peach tree in the garden*

(b) to put in a place; *someone phoned to say that a bomb had been planted in the High Street*

(c) to put goods secretly in a place in order to make it look as if they were placed there illegally; *the police were accused of planting the drugs in her car*

④ **plantation**
[plɑːn'teɪʃn] *noun*

(a) area of trees specially planted; *the Scottish mountains are covered with plantations of young trees*

(b) tropical estate growing a particular crop; *a coffee plantation; a rubber plantation*

④ **plaster**
['plɑːstə]
1 *noun*

(a) mixture of fine sand and lime which is mixed with water and is used for covering the walls of houses; *the flat hasn't been decorated yet and there is still bare plaster in most of the rooms*

(b) white paste used to make coverings to hold broken arms and legs in place; *he had an accident skiing and now has his leg in plaster*

(c) **sticking plaster** = sticky tape used for covering small wounds; *she put a piece of sticking plaster on my cut*

2 *verb*

(a) to cover with plaster; *they had to take off the old plaster and plaster the walls again*

(b) to cover with a thick layer, as if with plaster; *she plastered her face with makeup*

② **plastic**
['plæstɪk]
1 *noun*

(a) material made in factories, used to make all sorts of things; *we take plastic plates when we go to the beach; the supermarket gives you*

plastic bags to put your shopping in; *we cover our garden furniture with plastic sheets when it rains* (NOTE: no plural: **a bowl made of plastic**)
(b) *(informal)* **plastic (money)** = credit cards and charge cards; *I don't have any cash with me, do you take plastic?*
2 *adjective*
plastic surgery = surgery to repair parts of the body which do not look as they should

> COMMENT: plastic surgery is used especially to treat accident victims or people who have suffered burns

② **plate**
[pleɪt]
1 *noun*
(a) flat round dish for putting food on; *put one pie on each plate*; *pass all the plates down to the end of the table*; **dinner plate** = large plate for serving a main course on; **tea plate** = smaller plate for serving cakes and sandwiches, etc.
(b) food which is served on a plate; *they passed round plates of sandwiches*; *she ate two plates of cold meat*
(c) flat piece of metal, glass, etc.; *the dentist has a shiny plate on his door*; *see also* LICENSE PLATE, NUMBER PLATE
(d) picture in a book; *the book is illustrated with twenty colour plates*
(e) objects made of copper covered with a thin layer of gold or silver; *the spoons aren't sterling silver - they're just plate*
2 *verb*
to cover a metal object with a thin layer of gold or silver; *the metal cross is plated with gold*

③ **platform**
[ˈplætfɔːm] *noun*
(a) high flat structure by the side of the railway lines at a station, to help passengers get on or off the trains easily; *crowds of people were waiting on the platform*; *the train for Liverpool will leave from platform 10*; *the next train at this platform is the Circle Line to Paddington*
(b) high wooden floor for speakers to speak from; *the main speakers sat in a row on the platform*
(c) **platform shoes** = shoes with very thick soles; *I can't imagine how she can walk in those platform shoes*
(d) programme of action outlined by a political party at an election

① **play**
[pleɪ]
1 *noun*
(a) written text which is acted in a theatre or on TV; *did you see the play on TV last night?*; *we went to the National Theatre to see the new play*; *two of Shakespeare's plays are on the list for the English exam*
(b) taking part in a game; *play will start at 3 o'clock*; **out of play** = not on the field; *the ball was kicked out of play*

(c) way of amusing yourself; *they watched the children at play*; *all right, you children, it's time for play*
(d) **it's child's play** = it is very easy; *it's child's play if you've got the right tools for the job*
2 *verb*
(a) to take part in a game; *he plays rugby for the university*; *do you play tennis?*
(b) *(of a game)* to be held; *the tennis match was played on the Centre Court*; *cricket isn't played in the winter*
(c) to amuse yourself; *the boys were playing in the garden*; *when you've finished your lesson you can go out to play*; *he doesn't like playing with other children*
(d) to make music on a musical instrument or to put on a disk; *he can't play the piano very well*; *let me play you my new Bach CD*
(e) to act the part of a person in a film or play; *Orson Welles played Harry Lime in 'The Third Man'*

③ **play back**
[ˈpleɪ ˈbæk] *verb*
to listen to something which you have just recorded on tape; *he played back the messages left on his answerphone*

① **player**
[ˈpleɪə] *noun*
(a) person who plays a game; *you only need two players for chess*; *rugby players have to be fit*; *four of the players in the opposing team are ill*
(b) person who plays a musical instrument; *a famous horn player*

④ **playground**
[ˈpleɪɡraʊnd] *noun*
place, at a school or in a public area, where children can play; *the little girls were playing quietly in a corner of the playground*

③ **playing cards**
[ˈpleɪɪŋ ˈkɑːdz] *noun*
set of 52 pieces of card with pictures or patterns on them, used for playing various games; *a pack of playing cards* US *a deck of cards*; *he can do tricks with playing cards*; *see also* CARD

③ **PLC** *or* **Plc**
[ˈpiːelˈsiː] = PUBLIC LIMITED COMPANY

④ **plea**
[pliː] *noun*
(a) answer to a charge in court; *he entered a plea of 'not guilty'*
(b) *(formal)* request; *her pleas for help were rejected*

④ **plead**
[pliːd] *verb*
(a) to answer a charge in a law court; *he pleaded guilty to the charge of murder*
(b) to give an excuse; *she said she couldn't come, pleading pressure of work*
(c) **to plead with someone** = to try to change someone's mind by asking again and again; *I pleaded with her not to go*

③ **pleasant**
['plezɪnt] *adjective*
which pleases; *what a pleasant garden!*; *how pleasant it is to sit here under the trees!*; he didn't bring the pleasantest of news = he brought bad news (NOTE: **pleasanter - pleasantest**)

④ **pleasantly**
['plezɪntli] *adverb*
in a pleasant way; *he smiled at me pleasantly*; *I was pleasantly surprised that she had remembered my birthday*

① **please**
[pliːz]
1 *interjection; (used to ask politely)* *can you close the window, please?*; *please sit down*; *can I have a ham sandwich, please?*; *do you want some more tea? - yes, please!*; *compare* THANK YOU
2 *verb*
to make someone happy or satisfied; *she's not difficult to please*; **please yourself** = do as you like; *shall I take the red one or the green one? - please yourself*

② **pleased**
[pliːzd] *adjective*
happy; *we're very pleased with our new house*; *I'm pleased to hear you're feeling better*; *he wasn't pleased when he heard his exam results*

③ **pleasing**
['pliːzɪŋ] *adjective*
which pleases; *she's made very pleasing progress this year*; *the whole design of the garden is very pleasing*

② **pleasure**
['pleʒɪ] *noun*
pleasant feeling; *his greatest pleasure is sitting by the river*; *it gives me great pleasure to be able to visit you today*; **with pleasure** = gladly; *I'll do the job with pleasure*; **pleasure cruise** = cruise taken just to enjoy it

④ **pledge**
[pledʒ]
1 *noun*
(a) promise; *they made a pledge to meet again next year, same time, same place*; *the government never fulfilled its pledge to cut taxes*
(b) to take the pledge = to swear never to drink alcohol again
(c) object given to a lender when borrowing money, and which will be returned to the borrower when the money is paid back; *any pledges which have not been claimed after six months will be sold*
2 *verb*
(a) to promise formally; *she pledged £50 to the charity*; *thousands of people have pledged their support for the scheme*
(b) to give something as a pledge when borrowing money; *she had to pledge her wedding ring to buy food for the children*

① **plenty**
['plenti] *noun*
large quantity; *you've got plenty of time to catch the train*; *plenty of people complain about the bus service*; *have you got enough bread? - yes, we've got plenty* (NOTE: no plural)

④ **plot**
[plɒt]
1 *noun*
(a) small area of land for building, for growing vegetables, etc.; *they own a plot of land next to the river*; *the plot isn't big enough to build a house on*
(b) basic story of a book, play, film; *the novel has a complicated plot*; *I won't tell you the plot of the film so as not to spoil it for you*
(c) wicked plan; *they discussed a plot to hold up the security van*
2 *verb*
(a) to mark on a map; *we plotted a course to take us to the island*
(b) to draw a graph; *they plotted the rise in house prices on a graph*
(c) to draw up a wicked plan; *they plotted to assassinate the Prime Minister* (NOTE: **plotting - plotted**)

④ **plough** *US* **plow**
[plaʊ]
1 *noun*
(a) farm machine for turning over soil; *the plough is pulled by a tractor*
(b) snow plough = powerful machine with a large blade in front, used for clearing snow from streets, railway lines, etc.; *the snow ploughs were out all night clearing the main roads*
2 *verb*
to turn over the soil; *some farmers still use horses to plough the fields*

④ **plough on** *US* **plow on**
['plaʊ 'ɒn] *verb*
to continue with something difficult; *in spite of the shouting from the audience, the minister ploughed on with his speech*; *it's a difficult job, but we'll just have to plough on until it's finished*

④ **plow**
[plaʊ] *US see* PLOUGH

③ **plug**
[plʌg]
1 *noun*
(a) device with pins which go into holes and allow electric current to pass through; *the vacuum cleaner is supplied with a plug*
(b) flat rubber disc which covers the hole for waste water in a bath or sink; *can you call reception and tell them there's no bath plug in the bath*; *she pulled out the plug and let the dirty water drain away*; **ear plugs** = pieces of soft wax which you put in your ears to stop you hearing loud sounds

(c) *(in a car)* **(sparking) plug** *US* **spark plug** = device which passes the electric spark through the petrol; *if the plugs are dirty, the engine won't start; the garage put in a new set of sparking plugs*
(d) *(informal)* piece of publicity; **to give a plug to a new product** = to publicize a new product; *during the radio interview, she got in a plug for her new film*
2 *verb*
(a) to block up (a hole); *we plugged the leak in the bathroom; he plugged his ears with cotton wool because he couldn't stand the noise*
(b) *(informal)* to publicize; *they ran six commercials plugging holidays in Spain; they paid the radio station to plug their new album* (NOTE: **plugging - plugged**)

③ **plug in**
['plʌg 'ɪn] *verb*
to push an electric plug into holes and so attach a device to the electricity supply; *the computer wasn't plugged in - that's why it wouldn't work*

④ **plumber**
['plʌmɪ] *noun*
person who installs or mends water pipes, radiators, etc.; *there's water dripping through the kitchen ceiling, we'll have to call a plumber*

④ **plunge**
[plʌnʒ]
1 *noun*
to take the plunge = to decide suddenly to do something; *I've decided to take the plunge and buy a satellite dish*
2 *verb*
(a) to throw yourself into water; *he plunged into the river to rescue the little boy*
(b) to fall sharply; *share prices plunged on the news of the change of government*

④ **plural**
['pluːrɪl] *adjective & noun; (in grammar)*
form of a word showing that there are more than one; *does 'government' take a singular or plural verb?; what's the plural of 'mouse'?; the verb should be in the plural after 'programs'*

① **plus**
[plʌs]
1 *preposition*
(a) added to; *his salary plus commission comes to more than £25,000* (NOTE: in calculations **plus** is usually shown by the sign + : **10 + 4 = 14**: say 'ten plus four equals fourteen')
(b) more than; **houses valued at £200,000 plus** = houses valued at over £200,000
2 *adjective*
favourable, good and profitable; *being able to drive is certainly a plus factor; on the plus side* = this is a favourable point; *the weather wasn't very good, but on the plus side, it didn't actually rain*
3 *noun*
(a) plus (sign) = sign (+) meaning more than; *she put in a plus instead of a minus*

(b) *(informal)* favourable sign, a good or favourable point; *it's a definite plus that the hotel has room service*

④ **PM**
['piː 'em] = PRIME MINISTER

① **p.m.** *US* **P.M.**
['piː 'em] *adverb*
in the afternoon, after 12.00; *the exhibition is open from 10 a.m. to 5.30 p.m.; if you phone New York after 6 p.m. the calls are at a cheaper rate*

③ **PO**
['piː'ʊ] = POST OFFICE
PO Box number = reference number given for delivering mail to a post office, so as not to give the actual address of the person who will receive it

② **pocket**
['pɒkɪt]
1 *noun*
(a) one of several little bags sewn into the inside of a coat, etc., in which you can keep your money, handkerchief, keys, etc.; *she looked in all her pockets but couldn't find her keys; he was leaning against a fence with his hands in his pockets*; **breast pocket** = pocket on the inside of a jacket; **hip pocket** *or* **back pocket** = pocket at the back of a pair of trousers; **pocket calculator** = small calculator which you can put in your pocket; **pocket dictionary** = small dictionary which you can put in your pocket

(b) to be £25 in pocket = to have made a profit of £25; *when we counted the takings we found we were over £100 in pocket*; **to be out of pocket** = having lost money which you paid personally; **to be £25 out of pocket** = to have lost £25; *the lunch left him £25 out of pocket; if you are out of pocket you can always get some cash from the accounts department; nobody paid my expenses, so I was £100 out of pocket at the end of the day*

(c) hole with a small bag at each corner and side of a billiard table; *the black ball stopped at the edge of the pocket*
2 *verb*
to put in your pocket, to keep; *at the end of the sale, she pocketed all the money*

③ **pocket money**
['pɒkɪt 'mʌni] *noun*
money which parents give to their children each week; *she gets more pocket money than I do*

③ **poem**
['pʊɪm] *noun*
piece of writing, with words carefully chosen to sound attractive, set out in lines usually of a regular length; *he wrote a long poem about an old sailor; the poem about the First World War was set to music by Britten*

③ **poet**
['pʊɪt] *noun*
person who writes poems; *Lord Byron, the famous English poet; the poet gives a wonderful description of a summer morning*

③ **poetry**
['pʊɪtri] *noun*
poems taken as a type of literature; *reading poetry makes me cry; this is a good example of German poetry* (NOTE: no plural)

① **point**
[pɔɪnt]
1 *noun*
(a) sharp end of something long; *the point of my pencil has broken; the stick has a very sharp point*
(b) decimal point = dot used to show the division between whole numbers and parts of numbers (NOTE: three and a half is written: **3.5** (say 'three point five'). Note also that in many other languages, this is a comma)
(c) particular place; *the path led us for miles through the woods and in the end we came back to the point where we started from; we had reached a point 2000m above sea level;* **starting point** = place where something starts
(d) particular moment in time; *from that point on, things began to change; at what point did you decide to resign?;* **at that point** = at that moment; *all the lights went off at that point;* **at this point in time** = at this particular moment; *at this point in time, it is not possible for me to answer reporters' questions;* **on the point of doing something** = just about to do something; *I was on the point of phoning you*
(e) meaning or reason; *there's no point in asking them to pay - they haven't any money; the main point of the meeting is to see how we can continue to run the centre without a grant; what's the point of doing the same thing all over again?;* **I see your point** = I see what you mean; *I see your point, but there are other factors to be considered; I can't see the point of doing that*
(f) score in a game; *their team scored three points; in rugby, a try counts as five points*
(g) temperature; *what's the boiling point of water?*
(h) points = movable rails which allow trains to cross from one line to another; *the accident occurred as the train was crossing the points*
2 *verb*
(a) to aim a gun or your finger at something; to show with your finger; *the teacher is pointing at you; it's rude to point at people; don't point that gun at me - it might go off; the guide pointed to the map to show where we were*
(b) to put mortar between bricks in a completed wall, so as to make the surface smooth; *after the wall was built they pointed it with grey mortar*

② **pointed**
['pɔɪntɪd] *adjective*
(a) with a sharp point at one end; *a pointed stick*
(b) sharp and critical; *he made some very pointed remarks about the waitress*

① **point of view**
['pɔɪnt əv 'vjuː] *noun*
particular way of thinking about something; *from our point of view, it's been a great success; try to see things from your parents' point of view*

③ **point out**
['pɔɪnt 'aʊt] *verb*
(a) to show; *the tour guide will point out the main things to see in the town; the report points out the mistakes made by the agency over the last few years*
(b) to give a point of view; *she pointed out that the children in her class were better behaved than in previous years*

③ **poison**
['pɔɪzn]
1 *noun*
substance which kills or makes you ill if it is swallowed or if it gets into the blood; *there's enough poison in this bottle to kill the whole town; don't drink that - it's poison*
2 *verb*
(a) to kill with poison; *she was accused of poisoning her husband*
(b) to put poison in; *he didn't know the wine was poisoned; chemicals from the factory are poisoning the river*

③ **poisoning**
['pɔɪznɪŋ] *noun*
(a) taking poison into your system; **blood poisoning** = condition caused by bacteria in the blood; *wash the wound carefully or you might get blood poisoning;* **food poisoning** = poisoning caused by bacteria in food; *the hotel was closed after an outbreak of food poisoning; half the guests at the wedding were ill with food poisoning*
(b) using poison to kill or harm people; *he was accused of the poisoning of several old ladies*

③ **poisonous**
['pɔɪsɪnɪs] *adjective*
which can kill or harm with poison; *it is dangerous to try to catch poisonous snakes; these plants are deadly poisonous*

① **Poland**
['pʊlɪnd] *noun*
large country in Eastern Europe, between Germany and Russia; *Poland is an important industrial country* (NOTE: capital: **Warsaw;** people: **the Poles;** language: **Polish;** currency: **zloty)**

③ **polar**
['pʊlɪ] *adjective*
referring to the North Pole or South Pole; *he went to explore the polar regions;* **polar bear** = big white bear found in areas near the North Pole

① **pole**

[pəʊl] *noun*

(a) long rod of wood or metal; **tent pole** = pole which holds up a tent; *one of the tent poles snapped in the wind*

(b) one of the points at each end of the line around which the earth turns; **magnetic pole** = one of the two poles which are the centres of the earth's magnetic field; **North Pole** = furthest point at the north of the earth; **South Pole** = furthest point at the south of the earth

① **Pole**

[pəʊl] *noun*

person from Poland; *Pope John Paul II is a Pole*

③ **pole position**

['pəʊl pɪ'zɪʃn] *noun*

position of the first car in a race; *he was in pole position at the start of the Grand Prix*

① **police**

[pə'liːs]

1 *noun*

organization which controls traffic, tries to stop crime and tries to catch criminals; *the police are looking for the driver of the car*; *the police emergency number is 999*; *call the police - I've just seen someone drive off in my car*; **military police** = police force which is part of the army; *a military police van arrived as the fight between the soldiers and sailors developed into a riot*; **secret police** = part of the police force which spies on people; **traffic police** = branch of the police force dealing with traffic on roads (NOTE: takes a plural verb: **the police are looking for him**)

2 *verb*

to make sure that rules or laws are obeyed; *we need more constables to police the area*; *the problem is how to police the UN resolutions*

③ **police constable**

['pliːs 'kʌnstɪbl] *noun*

ordinary member of the police; *the inspector was accompanied by a sergeant and three police constables* (NOTE: used as a title, followed by a name: **Police Constable John Smith** or **PC John Smith**; usually written **PC** and **WPC**)

④ **police force**

['pliːs 'fɔːs] *noun*

group of police in a certain area; *he joined the police force after leaving university*; *the local police force is trying to cope with drug dealers coming from London*

② **policeman, policewoman**

['pliːsmɪn or 'pliːswʊmɪn] *noun*

ordinary member of the police; *three armed policemen went into the building*; *if you don't know the way, ask a policeman* (NOTE: plurals are **policemen, policewomen**)

③ **police officer**

['pliːs 'ɒfɪsɪ] *noun*

member of the police force; *I'm a police officer, madam, please get out of the car*; *a passing police officer chased the robbers as they tried to escape from the bank*

③ **police station**

['pliːs 'steɪʃn] *noun*

building with the offices of a particular local police force; *three men were arrested and taken to the police station*

① **policy**

['pɒlɪsi] *noun*

(a) decisions on the general way of doing something; *the government's policy on wages* or *the government's wages policy*; *it is not our policy to give details of employees over the phone*; *people voted Labour because they liked their policies*

(b) **insurance policy** = document which shows the conditions of an insurance contract; **an accident policy** = an insurance contract against accidents; **a comprehensive** or **an all-in policy** = an insurance which covers all risks; **to take out a policy** = to sign the contract for an insurance and start paying the premiums; *she took out a house insurance policy* (NOTE: plural is **policies**)

③ **polish**

['pɒlɪʃ]

1 *noun*

substance used to make things shiny; *give the car a good wash before you put the polish on*; **floor polish** = polish used to make wooden floors shiny; **furniture polish** = wax used to make furniture shiny; **shoe polish** = wax used to make shoes shiny (NOTE: plural is **polishes**)

2 *verb*

to rub something to make it shiny; *he polished his shoes until they shone*

① **Polish**

['pəʊlɪʃ]

1 *adjective*

referring to Poland; *the Polish Army joined in the military exercises*

2 *noun*

language spoken in Poland; *I know three words of Polish*; *you will need an English-Polish dictionary if you're visiting Warsaw*

③ **polish off**

['pɒlɪʃ 'ɒf] *verb*

(a) to finish off a job quickly; *he polished off his essay in half an hour*

(b) to eat a meal quickly; *they polished off a plate of fried eggs and potatoes and then asked for baked beans*

③ **polish up**

['pɒlɪʃ 'ʌp] *verb*

to improve a skill; *she spent a term in Spain polishing up her Spanish*

③ **polite**

[pɪ'laɪt] *adjective*

not rude; *sales staff should always be polite to customers* (NOTE: politer - politest)

④ **politely**

[pɪ'laɪtli] *adverb*

in a polite way; *she politely answered the tourists' questions*

① **political**

[pɪ'lɪtɪkl] *adjective*

referring to government or to party politics; *I don't want to get involved in a political argument*; *she gave up her political career when she had the children*; political refugee = person who has left his country because he is afraid of being put in prison for his political beliefs; *these political refugees are afraid that they will be jailed if they go back to their country*

② **politician**

[pɒlɪ'tɪʃn] *noun*

person who works in politics, especially a Member of Parliament; *politicians from all parties have welcomed the report*; local politician = member of a local political party, especially one who is a member of the town council

② **politics**

['pɒlɪtɪks] *noun*

(a) ideas and methods used in governing a country

(b) study of how countries are governed; *he studied politics and economics at university*

③ **poll**

[pɒʊl]

1 *noun*

(a) vote, voting; *we are still waiting for the results of yesterday's poll*; *a poll of factory workers showed that more than 50% supported the union's demands*

(b) number of votes cast in an election; *the poll was lower than usual - only 35% of the voters bothered to vote*

(c) the polls = places where people vote in an election; *the polls close at 9 o'clock*; to go to the polls = to vote in an election; *the people of France go to the polls next Sunday to elect a new President*; *see also* OPINION POLL

2 *verb*

(a) to get a number of votes in an election; *she polled more than ten thousand votes*

(b) to poll a sample of the population = to ask a sample group of people what they feel about something

③ **pollute**

[pɪ'luːt] *verb*

to make the environment dirty by putting harmful substances into it; *the company was fined for polluting the lake with chemicals*

② **pollution**

[pɪ'luːʃn] *noun*

(a) action of making the environment dirty; *pollution of the atmosphere has increased over the last 50 years*

(b) dirty or harmful materials that are put into the environment; *it took six months to clean up the oil pollution on the beaches*; *the pollution in the centre of town is so bad that people have started wearing face masks*; air pollution = dirt and gas in the air; noise pollution = spoiling people's pleasure by making a lot of noise

③ **pond**

[pɒnd] *noun*

small lake; *there's a duck pond in the middle of the village*; *children sail their boats on the pond in the park*

④ **pony**

['pɪʊni] *noun*

small horse; *my best friend lets me ride her pony sometimes* (NOTE: plural is ponies)

④ **ponytail**

['pɪʊniteɪl] *noun*

hairstyle where your hair is tied at the back and falls loosely; *she usually wears her hair in a ponytail*; *our new postman has a ponytail*

② **pool**

[puːl]

1 *noun*

(a) (swimming) pool = large bath of water for swimming in; *we have a little swimming pool in the garden*; *he swam two lengths of the pool*; an indoor pool = swimming pool inside a building; *our school has an indoor swimming pool*; an outdoor pool = swimming pool in the open air; a heated pool = pool where the water is kept warm

(b) small lake; *he dived in and swam across the mountain pool*

(c) group where people share facilities; *we belong to a pool of people who baby-sit for one another*; car pool = arrangement where several people travel to work in one car

(d) supply of something ready to be used; *we can draw on a pool of unemployed teenagers*

(e) football pools = system of gambling where you bet on the results of football matches; *she won £1500 on the pools*

(f) game rather like snooker, where you hit balls into pockets using a cue; *we were playing pool in the bar*

2 *verb*

to pool resources = to group resources together; *the only way we can afford it will be to pool our resources*

① **poor**

[pɔː] *adjective*

(a) with little or no money; *the family is very poor now that the father has no work*; *the poorer students find it difficult to get through university without grants*; *this is one of the poorest countries in Africa*

(b) poor in = with very little of something; *the soil in my garden is very poor in vegetable matter*

(c) not very good; *vines can grow even in poor soil; they were selling off poor quality vegetables at a cheap price; she's been in poor health for some months*

(d) *(showing you are sorry) poor old you! - having to stay at home and finish your homework while we go to the cinema; my poor legs - after climbing up the mountain!* (NOTE: poorer - poorest)

④ **poorly**
['pɔːli]
1 *adverb*
not in a very good way; *the offices are poorly laid out; the job is very poorly paid*
2 *adjective*
ill; *she felt quite poorly and had to go home; he was very poorly on Monday, but by the end of the week he was a little better*

③ **pop**
[pɒp]
1 *noun*
(a) noise like a cork coming out of a bottle; *there was a pop as she lit the gas;* **to go pop** = to make a noise like a cork; *the car engine went pop and we stopped suddenly; the balloon landed on the candles and went pop*

(b) *(informal)* **pop (music)** = modern popular music; *she prefers jazz to pop; he spends all day listening to pop records; we went to a pop concert last night;* **pop chart** = list showing the most popular songs at a certain time; *the record is at number ten in the pop charts;* **pop group** = group of singers and musicians who play pop songs; *he was lead singer in a 1980s pop group*

(c) *US (informal)* name for a father; *I'll ask my Pop if we can borrow his ladder*
2 *verb*
(a) *(informal)* to go quickly; *I'll just pop down to the town; he popped into the chemist's; I'm just popping round to Jane's; I'd only popped out for a moment*

(b) to put quickly; *pop the pie in the oven for ten minutes*

(c) to make a noise like 'pop'; *champagne corks were popping as the result was announced* (NOTE: popping - popped)

④ **Pope**
[pəup] *noun*
the head of the Roman Catholic Church; *the Pope said mass in a stadium before 50,000 people; security was very tight for the Pope's visit*

③ **popper**
['pɒpɪ] *noun*
(informal) little metal fastener for clothes, in two parts which you press to attach together; *the coat fastens with poppers down the front* (NOTE: American English is **snap**)

① **popular**
['pɒpjuli] *adjective*
(a) liked by a lot of people; *the department store is popular with young mothers; the South Coast is the most popular area for holidays*

(b) referring to the mass of ordinary people; *he was elected by popular vote; it is a popular belief that walking under a ladder brings bad luck*

④ **popularity**
[pɒpju'læriti] *noun*
being liked by a lot of people; *the scandal doesn't seem to have affected the President's popularity*

① **population**
[pɒpju'leɪʃn] *noun*
number of people who live in a place; *the population of the country is 60 million; Paris has a population of over three million*

④ **pork**
[pɔːk] *noun*
fresh meat from a pig, eaten cooked; *we're having pork for dinner tonight;* **pork pie** = pie with pork filling; *let's buy a pork pie to eat on the picnic* (NOTE: no plural; note also that salted or smoked meat from a pig is **ham** or **bacon**)

> COMMENT: roast pork is traditionally stuffed with herbs and onions, and served with apple sauce

② **port**
[pɔːt] *noun*
(a) harbour, or town with a harbour; *the ship is due in port on Tuesday; we left port at 12.00;* **to call at a port** = to stop at a port to pick up or drop off cargo; **port of call** = port at which a ship stops; *our next port of call is Hamburg;* **fishing port** = port which is used mainly by fishing boats

(b) left side (when looking forward on board a ship or aircraft); *passengers sitting on the port side of the plane can see Tower Bridge; the ship turned to port to avoid the yacht*

(c) opening in a computer for plugging in a piece of equipment; *a mouse port*

(d) strong sweet wine from Portugal; *at the end of the meal the port was passed round*

③ **portable**
['pɔːtɪbl]
1 *adjective*
which can be carried; *he used his portable computer on the plane*
2 *noun*
small computer which can be carried; *I keyboard all my orders on my portable*

④ **porter**
['pɔːtɪ] *noun*
(a) person who carries luggage for travellers at railway stations; *find a porter to help us with all this luggage*

(b) person who does general work in a hospital, including moving the patients around; *the nurse asked a porter to fetch a wheelchair*

④ **portion**
['pɔːʃn]
1 *noun*
(a) small part of something larger; *this is only a small portion of the material we collected; our carriage was in the rear portion of the train*
(b) serving of food, usually for one person; *the portions in that French restaurant are tiny; ask the waitress if they serve children's portions*
2 *verb*
to portion out = to share out; *we portioned out the money between the four of us*

④ **portrait**
['pɔːtreɪt] *noun*
painting or photograph of a person's face; *he has painted a portrait of the Queen; old portraits of members of the family lined the walls of the dining room*

④ **portray**
[pɔː'treɪ] *verb*
(formal) to paint or to describe a scene or a person; *in the biography he is portrayed as gloomy and miserable, while in real life he was nothing like that at all*

① **Portugal**
['pɔːtjʊgɪl] *noun*
country is Southern Europe, to the west of Spain; *Portugal is a country of great travellers* (NOTE: capital: **Lisbon**; people: **the Portuguese**; language: **Portuguese**; currency: **Portuguese escudo, euro**)

① **Portuguese**
[pɔːtjʊ'giːz]
1 *adjective*
referring to Portugal; *a Portuguese sailor*
2 *noun*
(a) person from Portugal; *she married a Portuguese*; **the Portuguese** = people from Portugal
(b) language spoken in Portugal, Brazil, etc.; *I don't know the word for it in Portuguese*

③ **pose**
[pɪʊz]
1 *noun*
(a) way of standing, sitting, etc.; *she is painted standing in an elegant pose; he struck a funny pose as I was taking the photo*
(b) way of behaving which is just pretending; *he'd like you to think he's an expert but it's just a pose*
2 *verb*
(a) to pose for someone = to stand or sit still while someone paints or photographs you; *he posed for her in his uniform*
(b) to pretend to be; *he got into the prison by posing as a doctor*
(c) to set a problem; to put a question; *what to do with illegal immigrants poses a problem for the immigration services*

① **position**
[pɪ'zɪʃɪn]
1 *noun*
(a) place where someone or something is; *from his position on the roof he can see the whole of the street; the ship's last known position was 200 miles east of Bermuda*
(b) job; *the sales manager has a key position in the firm; he's going to apply for a position as manager; we have several positions vacant*
(c) situation or state of affairs; *what is the company's cash position?*
(d) to be in a position to do something = to be able to do something; *I am not in a position to answer your question at this point in time*
2 *verb*
to put, to place in a position; *she positioned herself near the exit*

② **positive**
['pɒzɪtɪv]
1 *adjective*
(a) meaning 'yes'; *she gave a positive answer*
(b) certain, sure; *I'm positive I put the key in my pocket; are you positive he said six o'clock?*
(c) plus, more than zero; *a positive quantity*
(d) *(in a test)* showing that something is there; *the cancer test was positive*
(e) positive film = film where the light parts are light and the dark are dark (as opposed to negative film)
(f) positive terminal = one of the terminals in a battery, shown by a plus (+) sign; *the wire should be attached to the positive terminal*
2 *noun*
photograph printed from a negative, where the light and dark appear as they are in real life (NOTE: the opposite is **negative**)

③ **possess**
[pɪ'zes] *verb*
(a) to own; *he possesses several farms in the south of the country; he lost all he possessed in the fire*
(b) to occupy someone's mind and influence their behaviour; *terror possessed her as she saw the door slowly open*; **what possessed him to do it?** = why on earth did he do it?
(c) *(of an evil spirit)* to control someone in mind and body

③ **possession**
[pɪ'zeʃn] *noun*
(a) ownership; **in someone's possession** = being held by someone; *the jewellery came into my possession when my mother died; when he couldn't keep up the mortgage payments the bank took possession of the house*
(b) possessions = things which you own; *they lost all their possessions in the flood*

② **possibility**
[pɒsɪ'bɪlɪti] *noun*
being likely to happen; *is there any possibility of getting a ticket to the show?; there is always*

the possibility that the plane will be early; there is no possibility of the bank lending us any more money

① **possible**
['pɒsɪbl] *adjective*

which can be; *that field is a possible site for the factory; it is possible that the plane has been delayed; a bicycle is the cheapest possible way of getting round the town*

◊ **as possible**
[æz 'pɒsɪbl]

(used to make a superlative) I want to go as far away as possible for my holiday; please do it as quickly as possible; they will need as much time as possible to finish the job*

① **possibly**
['pɒsɪbli] *adverb*

(a) perhaps; *the meeting will possibly finish late; January had possibly the most snow we have ever seen*

(b) *(used with 'can' or 'can't' to make a phrase stronger) you can't possibly eat twenty-two cakes!; how can you possibly expect me to do all that work in one day?*

① **post**
[pəʊst]

1 *noun*

(a) long piece of wood, metal, etc., put in the ground; *the fence is attached to concrete posts; his shot hit the post*

(b) job; *he applied for a post in the sales department; we have three posts vacant; they advertised the post in 'The Times'*

(c) letters, etc., sent; *the morning post comes around nine o'clock; there were no cheques in this morning's post; has the post arrived yet?;* **to open the post** = to open the envelopes and parcels which have arrived; *she usually opens the post before the rest of the staff arrive*

(d) system of sending letters, parcels, etc.; *it is easier to send the parcel by post than to deliver it by hand;* **letter post** *or* **parcel post** = service for sending letters or parcels

2 *verb*

(a) to send a letter, parcel, etc.; *don't forget to post your Christmas cards; the letter should have arrived by now - we posted it ten days ago;* **to keep someone posted** = to keep someone informed; *please keep us posted about your holiday arrangements*

(b) to send someone to another place, often overseas, to work; *he was posted to an air base in East Anglia; she has been posted overseas* (NOTE: referring to the postal services, American English only uses **mail** where British English uses both **mail** and **post**)

③ **postage**
['pəʊstɪdʒ] *noun*

money which you pay to send something by post; *what is the postage for an airmail letter to India?;* **postage stamp** = piece of paper which you buy and stick on a letter, etc., to pay for it to be sent on by the postal service

③ **postal**
['pəʊstl] *adjective*

referring to the post; *postal charges are going up by 10% in September;* **postal ballot** = ballot where the votes are sent by post; **postal order** = order to pay money, which can be bought and cashed at a post office; *you can pay by cheque or postal order; she enclosed a postal order for £10*

③ **postbox**
['pəʊstbɒks] *noun*

box into which you can put letters, which will then be collected and sent on by the post office; *if you're going out, could you put this letter in the postbox for me?*

> COMMENT: in Britain, postboxes are red, and can be square or set into a wall. Round boxes are called 'pillar boxes'

③ **postcard**
['pəʊstkɑːd] *noun*

flat piece of card (often with a picture on one side) which you send to someone with a short message on it; *send us a postcard when you arrive in China; they sent me a postcard of the village where they were staying*

③ **postcode**
['pəʊstkəʊd] *noun*

system of letters or numbers to indicate a town or street in an address, to help with the sorting of mail; *my postcode is BA2 5NT; don't forget the postcode when addressing the envelope* (NOTE: the American equivalent is **zip code**)

③ **poster**
['pəʊstə] *noun*

large notice, picture or advertisement stuck on a wall; *they put up posters advertising the concert; the wall was covered with election posters;* **poster paints** = water paints in bright colours, often used by children

④ **postman**
['pəʊstmən] *noun*

person who delivers letters to houses; *the postman comes very early - before eight o'clock; can you give this parcel back to the postman - it's not for us* (NOTE: plural is **postmen**)

② **post office (PO)**
['pəʊst 'ɒfɪs] *noun*

(a) building where you can buy stamps, send letters and parcels, pay bills, collect your pension, pay your car tax, etc.; *the main post office is in the High Street; there are two parcels to be taken to the post office; post offices are shut on Sundays;* **Post Office box number** *or* **PO box number** = reference number given for delivering mail to a post office, so as not to give the actual address of the person who will receive it

(b) organization which runs the postal services; *the government are planning to sell off the Post Office to a private company*; *he worked for the Post Office for 50 years*

④ **postpone**
[pɪs'pɪʊn] *verb*
to put back to a later date or time; *the meeting has been postponed until next week*; *he asked if the meeting could be postponed to tomorrow*

④ **posture**
['pɒstʃɪ] *noun*
way of sitting, standing, etc.; *she does exercises to improve her posture*

② **pot**
[pɒt]
1 *noun*
(a) glass or china container, usually without a handle; *the plant is too big - it needs a bigger pot*; *she made ten pots of strawberry jam*; *can we have a pot of tea for two, please?*
(b) *(informal)* **pots of money** = lots of money; *ask him to pay - he's got pots of money*
(c) *(informal)* **to go to pot** = to become ruined, useless; *my service has gone to pot since I stopped playing tennis regularly*
2 *verb*
(a) to put a plant into a pot; *she potted her tomatoes*
(b) *(in billiards)* to send a ball into one of the pockets; *he potted the black to win the match* (NOTE: **potting - potted**)

② **potato**
[pɪ'teɪtɪʊ] *noun*
(a) common white root vegetable which grows under the ground; *do you want any more potatoes?*; *we're having roast lamb and potatoes for Sunday lunch*; *(informal)* **to look like a sack of potatoes** = to be badly dressed; *this dress makes me look like a sack of potatoes*; **baked potatoes** = POTATOES IN THEIR JACKETS; **boiled potatoes** = potatoes cooked in boiling water; **mashed potatoes** = potatoes which have been boiled until they are soft and then mashed and mixed with butter and milk; **roast potatoes** = potatoes cooked in the oven with fat; **jacket potatoes** *or* **potatoes in their jackets** = potatoes cooked in the oven with their skins on; **potato crisps** = thin slices of potato fried until they are hard, served as a snack with drinks (NOTE: American English is **chips**); **potato skins** = skins of potatoes, cooked until crisp and filled with cream cheese or other fillings
(b) **sweet potato** = a tropical vegetable like a long red potato with sweet yellow flesh inside (NOTE: plural is **potatoes)**

② **potential**
[pɪ'tenʃl]
1 *adjective*

possible; *he's a potential world champion*; *the potential profits from the deal are enormous*; **potential customers** = people who could be customers; **potential market** = market which could be exploited

2 *noun*

possibility of developing into something useful or valuable; *the discovery has enormous potential*; *she doesn't have much experience, but she has a lot of potential*; *the whole area has great potential for economic growth*

④ **potter**
['pɒtɪ]

1 *noun*

person who makes pots; *the potter makes cups and bowls to sell to tourists*

2 *verb*

to potter about = not to do anything in particular, to do little jobs here and there; *he spent Saturday morning pottering about in the garden*

① **pound**
[paʊnd]

1 *noun*

(a) measure of weight (about 450 grams); *she bought a pound of onions and five pounds of carrots*; *the baby was tiny - she only weighed three pounds when she was born*; *how much is tea? - it's 50p a pound* (NOTE: with numbers the word **pound** is usually written **lb** after the figure: **it weighs 26lb; take 6lb of sugar:** say 'twenty-six pounds, six pounds')

(b) money used in Britain and several other countries; *the cheapest lunch will cost you £25 (twenty-five pounds) at that restaurant*; *he earns more than a six pounds an hour*; *the price of the car is over £50,000 (fifty thousand pounds)*; *he tried to pay for his bus ticket with a £20 note (twenty pound note)* (NOTE: with numbers **pound** is usually written **£** before figures: **£20, £6,000,** etc. (say 'twenty pounds, six thousand pounds'). Note also that with the words **note, money order,** etc., **pound** is singular: **twenty pounds** but **a twenty pound note, a fifty-pound traveller's cheque)**

(c) place where cars are taken when they have been parked in places where parking is forbidden; *he had to go to the police pound to get his car back*

2 *verb*

(a) to hit hard; *he pounded the table with his fist*

(b) to smash into little pieces; *the ship was pounded to pieces by heavy waves*

(c) to run or walk heavily; *the policeman pounded along after the bank robbers*; *he pounded up the stairs*

(d) *(of heart)* to beat fast; *her heart was pounding as she opened the door*

② pour
['pɔ:] *verb*

(a) to make a liquid flow; *the waiter poured water all over the table*; *he poured the wine into the glasses*; *she poured water down his neck as a joke*

(b) to flow out or down; *clouds of smoke poured out of the house*; *there was a sudden bang and smoke poured out of the engine*

(c) **pouring with rain** = raining very hard; *it poured with rain all afternoon*; *(informal)* **it never rains but it pours** = troubles, problems, etc., never come one at a time, but several together

③ pour down
['pɔ: 'daun] *verb*

to rain very hard; *don't go out without an umbrella - it's pouring down*

③ poverty
['pɒvɪti] *noun*

(a) being poor; *he lost all his money and died in poverty*; *poverty can drive people to crime*; **the poverty line** = amount of money which you need to buy the basic things to live on; *thousands of families are living below the poverty line*

(b) *(formal)* **the poverty of** = the very small amount of; *the poverty of our resources means that we are dependent on outside funds* (NOTE: no plural)

④ POW
['pi:ɪəʊ'dʌblju:] = PRISONER OF WAR

④ powder
['paʊdɪ] *noun*

1 very fine dry grains (like flour); *to grind something to powder*; *the drug is available in the form of a white powder*; **face powder** = scented powder for putting on your face; **washing powder** *or* **soap powder** = soap in powder form, used in washing machines; *we've run out of soap powder*; *can you buy some washing powder next time you go to the supermarket?*

2 *verb*

to put powder on something; *she was powdering her cheeks*; *(informal) (of a woman)* **to powder your nose** = to go to the toilet; *can you wait a minute, I'm just going to powder my nose*

① power
['paʊwɪ]

1 *noun*

(a) being able to control people or happenings; *he is the official leader of the party, but his wife has all the real power*; *I haven't the power or it isn't in my power to ban the demonstration*; **the full power of the law** = the full force of the law

(b) driving force; *they use the power of the waves to generate electricity*; *the engine is driven by steam power*; **wind power** = force of the wind (used to make sails go round, make a yacht go forward, etc.)

(c) **(electric) power** = electricity used to drive machines or devices; *turn off the power before you try to repair the TV set*; **power station** *or* **power plant** = factory where electricity is produced; *this power station burns coal*; *they are planning to scrap their nuclear power stations*

(d) political control; *the socialists came to power in 1997*; *during the period when he was in power the country's economy was ruined*

(e) important, powerful country; *China is one of the great world powers*

(f) *(in mathematics)* number of times one number is multiplied by another; *3 to the power 4* (NOTE: written 3^4)

2 *verb*

(a) **to be powered by** = to be driven by; *powered by two Olympic champions, the boat raced across the lake*; *the aircraft is powered by four jet engines*

(b) to move fast; *with its huge engine the boat powered through the water*

② powerful
['paʊwɪfʊl] *adjective*

very strong; *this model has a more powerful engine*; *the chairman is the most powerful person in the organization*; *she was swept away by the powerful current*; *this is the most powerful personal computer on the market*

③ PR
[pi:'ɑ:] *noun*

= PUBLIC RELATIONS

② practical
['præktɪkl]

1 *adjective*

(a) referring to practice and action rather than ideas; *she needs some practical experience*; *he passed the practical exam but failed the written part*; *I need some practical advice on how to build a wall*

(b) **practical joke** = trick played on someone to make other people laugh; *he's fond of practical jokes - once he tied a tin to the back of his father's car*

(c) possible or sensible; *it isn't practical to attach two computers to the same lead*; *has anyone got a more practical suggestion to make?*; *we must be practical and not try anything too difficult*

2 *noun*

examination or test to show how well someone can work in practice; *she passed the written test but failed the practical*

② practically
['præktɪkli] *adverb*

(a) almost; *practically all the students passed the test*; *the summer is practically over*; *his suit is such a dark grey it is practically black*

(b) in a practical way; *we must try to solve the problem practically*

① practice
['præktɪs]

1 *noun*

(a) actually applying something; **to put something into practice** = to apply something, to use something; *I hope soon to be able to put some of my ideas into practice*; **in practice** = when actually done; *the plan seems very interesting, but what will it cost in practice?*

(b) repeated exercise; *you need more practice before you're ready to enter the competition*; *he's at football practice this evening*; *the cars make several practice runs before the race*; **out of practice** = not able to do something because of not having done it recently; *I used to be able to play quite well, but I'm a bit out of practice*

(c) **medical practice, dental practice, legal practice** = business of a doctor, dentist, lawyer, etc.; *there are three doctors in this practice*; **private practice** = doctor's or dentist's practice where the clients pay, as opposed to one which is part of the National Health Service

(d) **practices** = ways of doing things; *he has written a study of marriage practices on the Pacific islands*; **code of practice** = rules drawn up which people must follow when doing business

2 *verb*

US see PRACTISE

① **practise** *US* **practice**
['præktɪs] *verb*

(a) to do repeated exercises; *he's practising catching and throwing*

(b) to carry on a job as a doctor or lawyer; *he's officially retired but still practises part-time*

③ **practitioner**
[præk'tɪʃɪnɪ] *noun*

person who does a skilled job; *she's a practitioner of the ancient Japanese art of flower arranging*; *see also* GENERAL PRACTITIONER

④ **praise**
[preɪz]

1 *noun*

admiration, showing approval; *the rescue team earned the praise of the people they had saved*; **to sing the praises of someone** = to praise someone all the time; *she's always singing the praises of the new doctor*

2 *verb*

to express strong approval of something; *the mayor praised the firemen for their efforts to put out the fire*

③ **pray**
[preɪ] *verb*

(a) to speak to God, asking God for something; *farmers prayed for rain*; **to pray for someone** = to ask God to protect someone; *we pray for the children from the village, missing in the mountains*

(b) *(old)* please; **pray be seated** = please sit down

③ **prayer**
[preɪ] *noun*

speaking to God; *she says her prayers every night before going to bed*; *they said prayers for the sick*

④ **preach**
[priːtʃ] *verb*

to speak in church about religious matters; *she preached to a crowded church about the need for tolerance*; **to preach to the converted** = to try to convince people of something when they already know about it; *it's a waste of time telling us about the advantages of using computers - you're just preaching to the converted*

④ **precautions**
[prɪ'kɔːʃnz] *noun*

care taken in advance to avoid something unpleasant; *the company has taken precautions to avoid fire in the warehouse*; *the restaurant did not take proper fire precautions*; *what safety precautions must be taken before we can open the swimming pool to the public?*

③ **precede**
[prɪ'siːd] *verb*

to take place before something; *a period of calm often precedes a storm*; *the concert was preceded by a short talk given by the musician*

③ **preceding**
[prɪ'siːdɪŋ] *adjective*

which comes before; *the three weeks preceding the school play were taken up with constant rehearsals*; *they spent the preceding two weeks interviewing candidates*

③ **precinct**
['priːsɪŋkt] *noun*

(a) **pedestrian precinct** *or* **shopping precinct** = part of a town which is closed to traffic so that people can walk about and shop; *the council plans to turn the main shopping area into a pedestrian precinct*

(b) *US* administrative district in a town; *they live in the 16th precinct* (NOTE: British English for this is **ward**)

④ **precious**
['preʃɪs] *adjective*

(a) worth a lot of money; **precious metal** = metal, such as gold, which is worth a lot of money; **precious stones** = stones, such as diamonds, which are rare and very valuable

(b) of great value to someone; *all her precious photographs were saved from the fire*; *the memories of that holiday are very precious to me*

(c) *(informal)* which you don't think is valuable; *she can't talk about anything except her precious boyfriend*; *do you really think I'm interested in you and your precious car?*

① precise
[prɪ'saɪs] *adjective*

exact; *we need to know the precise measurements of the box; at that precise moment my father walked in; can you be more precise about what the men looked like?*

② precisely
[prɪ'saɪsli] *adverb*

exactly; *the train arrived at 12.00 precisely; I don't know precisely when it was, but it was about three months ago; how, precisely, do you expect me to cope with all this work?*

④ precision
[prɪ'sɪʒn] *noun*

accuracy; *her instructions were carried out with the greatest precision;* precision drawing = very accurate drawing; precision instrument = instrument for very accurate work

③ predict
[prɪ'dɪkt] *verb*

to tell what you think will happen in the future; *the weather forecast predicted rain; he predicted correctly that the deal would not last; everything happened exactly as I had predicted*

④ predictable
[prɪ'dɪktɪbl] *adjective*

which could be predicted; *his reaction was totally predictable*

④ prediction
[prɪ'dɪkʃn] *noun*

telling what you think will happen in the future; *here are my predictions for the year 2010; most of her predictions turned out to be correct*

② prefer
[prɪ'fɜ:] *verb*

to prefer something to something = to like (to do) something better than something else; *I prefer butter to margarine; she prefers walking to going on the underground; we went to the pub, but she preferred to stay at home and watch TV; I'd prefer not to go to Germany this summer* (NOTE: preferring - preferred)

④ preferable
['prefrɪbl] *adjective*

which you would prefer; *any exercise is preferable to sitting around doing nothing*

③ preference
['prefrɪns] *noun*

liking for one thing more than another; *the girl at the reception desk asked him if he had any preference for a room with a view; the children all showed a marked preference for ice cream as dessert*

③ prefix
['pri:fɪks] *noun*

part of a word put in front of another to form a new word; *the prefix 'anti-' is very common* (NOTE: plural is prefixes; the opposite, letters which are added at the end of a word, is a suffix)

④ pregnancy
['pregnɪnsi] *noun*

state of being pregnant; *smoking during pregnancy can harm your child; her second pregnancy was easier than the first;* pregnancy test = test to see if a woman is pregnant

③ pregnant
['pregnɪnt] *adjective*

(a) carrying a child inside your body before it is born; *don't carry heavy weights when you're pregnant; she hasn't told her family yet that she's pregnant; we have a pregnant girl in our class*

(b) pregnant pause = pause while everyone waits for someone to say something; *Martha's extraordinary announcement was followed by a pregnant pause*

④ prejudice
['predʒɪdɪs]
1 *noun*

feeling against someone or preference for one person or thing over another; *the committee seems to have a prejudice against women candidates;* colour prejudice = prejudice against someone whose skin is not white; racial prejudice = prejudice against someone because of race; *he accused his former boss of racial prejudice; she was a victim of racial prejudice*
2 *verb*

to make someone have less friendly feelings towards someone *or* something; *the newspaper reports prejudiced the jury against the accused*

④ preliminary
[prɪ'lɪmɪnɪri] *adjective*

which goes before something; *the committee will hold a preliminary meeting the day before the conference opens; this is only the preliminary report - the main report will be published later*

④ premier
['premiɪ]
1 *noun*

Prime Minister; *the French premier is visiting London*
2 *adjective*

first, most important; *the town advertises itself as Britain's premier holiday resort;* premier league = group of top football clubs who play against each other; *the team is in the premier league*

③ premise
['premɪs] *noun*

(formal) assumption, thing which you assume to be true; *her argument is based on false premises; he argued from the premise that all wars are evil*

③ premises
['premɪsɪz] *noun*

building and the land it stands on; *smoking is not allowed on the premises; there is a doctor on the premises at all times;* business premises *or* commercial premises = building used for commercial use; **office premises** *or* **shop premises** = building which houses an office or shop (NOTE: the word is plural, even if it only applies to one building)

④ **premium**
['priːmiəm] *noun*
(a) amount paid for an insurance policy; *the house insurance premium has to be paid this month*; *we pay a monthly premium of £5*
(b) **at a premium** = scarce, and therefore valuable; *fresh vegetables were at a premium during the winter months*; **to put a premium on something** = to show that something is useful or valuable; *employers put a premium on staff who can speak good English*
(c) bonus; *they pay a premium for work completed ahead of schedule*; **premium offer** = offer for sale at a specially attractive price

③ **premium bond**
['priːmiəm 'bɒnd] *noun*
British government bond which pays no interest but gives you the chance of winning a monthly prize; *I won £100 with my Premium Bonds*

② **preparation**
[prepɪ'reɪʃn] *noun*
(a) action of getting ready; *the preparations for the wedding went on for months*; *we've completed our preparations and now we're ready to start*; **in preparation for** = to get ready for; *she bought a hat in preparation for the wedding*
(b) substance which has been mixed; *a chemical preparation*

① **prepare**
[prɪ'peə] *verb*
to get something ready; *he is preparing for his exam*; *you'd better prepare yourself for some bad news*; *I have some friends coming to dinner and I haven't prepared the meal*

① **prepared**
[prɪ'peəd] *adjective*
(a) ready; *be prepared, you may get quite a shock*; *six people are coming to dinner and I've got nothing prepared*
(b) **prepared to do something** = willing to do something; *they are prepared to sell the house if necessary*; **prepared for something** = ready for something; *she wasn't really prepared for her exam*; *the country is prepared for an attack*

③ **preposition**
[prepɪ'zɪʃn] *noun*
word used with a noun or pronoun as its object to show place or time; *prepositions like 'by' and 'near' are very common, as in 'he was knocked down by a motorbike' or 'she was sitting near me'*

④ **prescribe**
[prɪ'skraɪb] *verb*
(of a doctor) to tell someone to use something; *he prescribed a course of injections*; *she prescribed some antibiotics*

③ **prescription**
[prɪ'skrɪpʃn] *noun*
order written by a doctor to a chemist asking for a drug to be prepared and sold to a patient; *she took the prescription to the chemist*; **available on prescription** = available from a chemist only when prescribed by a doctor; *this medicine is only available on prescription*

② **presence**
['prezns] *noun*
(a) being present; *the presence of both his wives in court was noted*; *your presence is requested at a meeting of the committee on June 23rd*; **in someone's presence** = when someone is near; *she actually said that in my presence*; *he slapped her face in the presence of witnesses*
(b) **presence of mind** = being calm and sensible, and able to act quickly; *the hotel staff showed great presence of mind in getting the guests out quickly*
(c) effect you have on other people; *the general has a commanding presence*

① **present**
1 *noun*
['preznt]
(a) thing which you give to someone as a gift; *I got a watch as a Christmas present*; *how many birthday presents did you get?*; *the office gave her a present when she got married*
(b) the time we are in now; *the novel is set in the present*; **at present** = now; *the hotel still has some vacancies at present*; **for the present** = for now; *that will be enough for the present*
(c) form of a verb showing that the action is happening now; *the present of the verb 'to go' is 'he goes' or 'he is going'*
2 *adjective*
['preznt]
(a) being there when something happens; *how many people were present at the meeting?*
(b) at the time we are in now; *what is his present address?*; **present tense** = form of a verb showing that the action is happening now; *the present tense of 'to stand' is 'he stands' or 'he is standing'*
3 *verb*
[prɪ'zent]
(a) to give formally (as a present); *when he retired after thirty years, the firm presented him with a large clock*
(b) to introduce a show on TV, etc.; *she's presenting a programme on gardening*
(c) **to present yourself** = to go to a place; *he was asked to present himself at the police station the next morning*

② **presentation**
[prezɪn'teɪʃn] *noun*
(a) act of giving a present; *the chairman will make the presentation to the retiring sales manager*

(b) demonstration of a proposed plan; *the distribution company made a presentation of the services they could offer*

③ **present-day**
[prezɪntˈdeɪ] *adjective*
modern; *by present-day standards his old car uses far too much petrol*

③ **preserve**
[prɪˈzɜːv]
1 *verb*
(a) *(formal)* to look after and keep in the same state; *our committee aims to preserve the wild flowers in our area; the doctors' aim is to preserve the life of the child*
(b) to treat food so that it keeps for a long time; *freezing is a common method of preserving meat*
2 *noun*
preserves = jams, fruit cooked for keeping, etc.; *she has a stall in the market where she sells her preserves*

③ **preside (over)**
[prɪˈzaɪd ˈɪʊv] *verb*
(a) to be president or chairman of something; *she presided over the university appointments committee for several years*
(b) to be in charge when something happens; *he presided over a radical reorganization of the party's structure*

④ **presidency**
[ˈprezɪdnsi] *noun*
(a) job of being president; *he has been proposed as a candidate for the presidency*
(b) time when someone is president; *during Britain's presidency of the European Union; the Second World War ended during the Truman presidency*

① **president**
[ˈprezɪdnt] *noun*
(a) head of a republic; *during his term of office as President* (NOTE: usually used as a title followed by the surname: **President Wilson**)
(b) chief member of a club; *we're wondering who'll be the next president of the cricket club; A. B. Smith was elected president of the sports club*

④ **presidential**
[prezɪˈdenʃl] *adjective*
referring to a president; *the presidential palace is in the centre of the city*

① **press**
[pres]
1 *noun*
(a) newspapers taken as a group; *the election wasn't reported in the British press; there has been no mention of the problem in the press*; **freedom of the press** = being able to write and publish in a newspaper what you want, without being afraid of prosecution unless you break the law

(b) journalists and other people who work for newspapers, or on radio and TV; *everywhere she went she was followed by the press; press photographers were standing outside Number 10* (NOTE: no plural in meanings (a) and (b))
(c) machine which presses; *the car body is formed from a metal sheet in a press*; **printing press** = machine for printing books, newspapers, etc. (NOTE: plural is **presses**)
2 *verb*
(a) to push, to squeeze, to get very close to someone; *everyone pressed round the film stars*
(b) to push a button to call something; *press 12 for room service; press the top button for the sixth floor*
(c) to iron; *his jacket needs pressing*
(d) **to press on** *or* **to press forward** = to continue, to go ahead; *in spite of the weather they pressed on with the preparations for the village fair*

③ **press conference**
[ˈpres ˈkɒnfɪrɪns] *noun*
meeting where newspaper, radio and TV reporters are invited to hear news of a new product, a takeover bid or to talk to a famous person; *he gave a press conference on the steps of Number Ten*

③ **pressed**
[prest] *adjective*
we're pressed for time = we are in a hurry; **I'd be hard pressed to do it** = it would be difficult for me to find time to do it

③ **pressing**
[ˈpresɪŋ] *adjective*
urgent, which needs to be done quickly; *he had to leave because of a pressing engagement in London*

③ **press release**
[ˈpres rɪˈliːs] *noun*
sheet giving news about something which is sent to newspapers and TV and radio stations; *the company sent out a press release about the launch of the new car*

① **pressure**
[ˈpreʃɪ] *noun*
(a) something which forces you to do something; *pressure from farmers forced the minister to change his mind*; **to put pressure on someone to do something** = to try to force someone to do something; *they put pressure on the government to build a new motorway*; **under pressure** = being forced (to do something); *he did it under pressure; we're under pressure to agree to changes to the contract*
(b) force of something which is pushing or squeezing; *there is not enough pressure in your tyres*; **blood pressure** = pressure at which the heart pumps blood; *he has to take pills for his high blood pressure*
(c) stress caused by having a lot of responsibility; *he gave up his job in the bank because he couldn't stand the pressure*

③ **pressure group**
['preʃɪ 'gruːp] *noun*

group of people who try to influence the government, the local town council, etc.; *they formed a pressure group to fight for animal welfare*

③ **prestige**
[pre'stiːʒ] *noun*

importance because of high quality, high value, etc.; *there's a lot of prestige attached to working for the royal family*; **prestige offices** = expensive offices in a good area of the town

④ **prestigious**
[pre'stɪdʒɪs] *adjective*

which makes you seem very important; *they are based at a prestigious address in Park Lane*

① **presumably**
[prɪ'zjuːmɪblɪ] *adverb*

probably; as you think is true; *presumably this is what she wanted us to do*; *they've presumably forgotten the date of the meeting*

③ **presume**
[prɪ'zjuːm] *verb*

(a) to suppose, to assume; *I presume this little bridge is safe for cars?*; *the jury has to presume he is innocent until he is proved guilty*; *she is presumed to have fled to South America*

(b) *(formal)* not to presume to do something = not to do something because it would be rude to do it; *I wouldn't presume to contradict her - she's the expert*

② **pretend**
[prɪ'tend] *verb*

to make someone believe you are something else, so as to deceive them; *he got into the house by pretending to be a telephone engineer*; *she pretended she had flu and phoned to say she was having the day off*

② **pretty**
['prɪtɪ]

1 *adjective*

pleasant to look at; *her daughters are very pretty*; *she is prettier than her mother*; *what a pretty little house!* (NOTE: **prettier - prettiest.** Note also that **pretty** is used of things or girls, but not of boys or men)

2 *adverb*; *(informal)* quite; *the patient's condition is pretty much the same as it was yesterday*; *I'm pretty sure I'm right*; *you did pretty well, considering it's was the first time you had played billiards*

① **prevent**
[prɪ'vent] *verb*

(a) to stop something happening; *we must try to prevent any more flooding*

(b) to prevent someone from doing something = to stop someone doing something; *we can't do much to prevent the river from flooding*; *the police prevented anyone from leaving the building*

① **previous**
['priːvɪs]

1 *adjective*

former, earlier; *the letter was sent to my previous address*; *the gang of workers arrived the previous night and started work first thing in the morning*; *I had spent the previous day getting to know my way round the town*; *he could not accept the invitation because he had a previous engagement* = because he had earlier accepted another invitation to go somewhere

2 *adverb*

previous to = before; *what job were you in, previous to this one?*

① **previously**
['priːvɪslɪ] *adverb*

before; *this is my first visit to Paris by train - previously I've always gone by plane*; *the arrangements had been made six weeks previously*; *at that time they were living in New York, and previously had lived in London*

④ **prey**
[preɪ]

1 *noun*

animal eaten by another animal; *mice and small birds are the favourite prey of owls*; **birds of prey** = birds which eat other birds or small animals (NOTE: no plural)

2 *verb*

(a) to prey on *or* upon = to attack animals and eat them; *lions mainly prey on deer and zebra*

(b) something is preying on her *or* on her mind = something is worrying her (NOTE: do not confuse with **pray**)

① **price**
[praɪs]

1 *noun*

money which you have to pay to buy something; *the price of petrol is going up*; *I don't want to pay such a high price for a hotel room*; *there has been a sharp increase in house prices during the first six months of the year*; **cut price** = very cheap price; **net price** = price which cannot be reduced by a discount; **retail price** = price at which the shopkeeper sells to a customer; **price list** = sheet giving prices of goods for sale; **price war** = sales battle between companies, where each lowers prices to get more customers; **to increase in price** = to become more expensive

2 *verb*

to give something a price; *the book is priced at £25*; *that house won't sell - it is too highly priced*; **the company has priced itself out of the market** = the company has raised its prices so high that its products do not sell

④ **priceless**
['praɪslɪs] *adjective*

extremely valuable; *his priceless collection of paintings was destroyed in the fire*

③ **price tag**
['prais 'tæg] *noun*
(a) ticket with a price written on it; *how much is this shirt? - the price tag has come off it*
(b) price at which something is for sale; *car with a £50,000 price tag*

③ **pride**
[praid]
1 *noun*
(a) pleasure in your own ability or possessions; *he takes great pride in his garden*
(b) very high opinion of yourself; *his pride would not let him admit that he had made a mistake; (saying)* 'pride goes before a fall' = if you are very proud of yourself, you are likely to find yourself in trouble
2 *verb*
to pride yourself on = to be extremely proud of; *she prides herself on her cakes*

③ **priest**
[priːst] *noun*
person who has been blessed to serve God, to carry out formal religious duties, etc.; *they were married by the local priest*

③ **primarily**
['praimrili] *adverb*
mainly, mostly; *this is primarily a business trip; we're examining primarily the financial aspects of the case*

② **primary**
['praimiri]
1 *adjective*
main, basic; *our primary concern is the safety of our passengers;* **primary colours** = basic colours (red, yellow and blue) which can combine to make up all the other colours; **primary education** = teaching small children; *US* **primary election** = first election to choose a candidate to represent a political party in a main election; *a candidate who does not win the primary election in his own state is certain to fail in the national vote*
2 *noun*
US primary election; *he won the New Hampshire primary* (NOTE: plural is **primaries**)

② **primary school**
['praimiri 'skuːl] *noun*
school for children up to the age of eleven; *John is still at primary school; she's a primary school teacher; children concentrate on reading, writing and maths in primary school*

④ **prime**
[praim]
1 *adjective*
(a) most important; *the prime suspect in the case is the dead woman's husband; she is a prime target for any kidnap gang; this is a prime example of what is wrong with this country;* **prime position** *or* **prime site** = good position for a commercial property; *the restaurant is in a prime position in the High Street;* **prime time television** = TV programmes shown at the time when most people watch television; *the interview is being shown on prime time TV*
(b) of best quality; *prime Scottish beef*
(c) **prime number** = number (such as 2, 5, 11, etc.) which can only be divided by itself or by 1
2 *noun*
period when you are at your best; *he was at his prime when he won the championship;* **past your prime** = no longer at your best; *at 35, as a tennis player, she's past her prime*
3 *verb*
(a) to give wood or metal a first coat of special paint, before giving the top coat; *the paint is coming off because the wood hadn't been primed properly*
(b) to get something prepared; *the bomb had been primed and would have exploded in ten minutes*
(c) to put water into a water pump or oil into a machine, so as to start it working
(d) **to prime someone to do something** = to prepare someone in advance by giving information, advice, etc.; *she came primed with questions which would embarrass the speaker*

③ **Prime Minister (PM)**
['praim 'ministi] *noun*
head of the government in Britain and other countries; *the Australian Prime Minister or the Prime Minister of Australia; she cut out the picture of the Prime Minister from the newspaper; the Prime Minister will address the nation at 6 o'clock tonight*

④ **primitive**
['primitiv] *adjective*
(a) referring to very early times; *a primitive people who flourished in the Stone Age*
(b) rough, crude; *they live in a primitive hut in the woods; our accounts system is a bit primitive but it works*

③ **prince**
[prins] *noun*
son of a king or queen; **Prince of Wales** = title given to the eldest son of a British king or queen, the heir to the throne (NOTE: used as a title with a name: **Prince Edward**)

③ **princess**
[prin'ses] *noun*
(a) daughter of a king or queen; *once upon a time a beautiful princess lived in a castle by the edge of the forest*
(b) wife of a prince (NOTE: used as a title with a name: **Princess Sophia**; note also that the plural is **princesses**)

② **principal**
['prinsipl]
1 *adjective*
main, most important; *the country's principal products are paper and wood; she played a principal role in setting up the organization*
2 *noun*

(a) head (of a school, a college); *the principal wants to see you in her office*

(b) main performer (actor, dancer, singer, etc.); *the principals were quite good but the rest of the dancers were awful*

(c) money on which interest is paid, capital which has been invested; *up to now you've been paying interest, but now you can start repaying some of the principal* (NOTE: do not confuse with **principle**)

① **principle**
['prɪnsɪpl] *noun*

(a) law; general rule; *the principles of nuclear physics*; *it is a principle in our system of justice that a person is innocent until he is proved guilty*; **in principle** = in agreement with the general rule; *I agree in principle, but we need to discuss some of the details very carefully*; *in principle, the results should be the same every time you do the experiment*

(b) personal sense of what is right; *she's a woman of very strong principles*; *it's against my principles to work on a Sunday*; **on principle** = because of what you believe; *she refuses to eat meat on principle* (NOTE: do not confuse with **principal**)

② **print**
[prɪnt]
1 *noun*

(a) letters printed on a page; *I can't read this book - the print is too small*; **the small print** *or* **the fine print** = the conditions on a contract, usually printed in very small letters; *always check the small print before you sign a contract*

(b) mark made on something; *the print of an animal's foot has been preserved in this rock*; *the police examined the tyre prints left by the vehicle*

(c) picture or photograph which has been printed; *the print is very blurred*; *I'm going to have some more prints made of this photo*

2 *verb*

(a) to mark letters or pictures on paper by a machine, and so produce a book, poster, newspaper, etc.; *the book is printed directly from a computer disk*; *we had five hundred copies of the leaflet printed*

(b) to write capital letters or letters which are not joined together; *print your name in the space below*

③ **printed**
['prɪntɪd] *adjective*

produced on paper using a printing press; **printed matter** = paper with printing on it, such as posters, books, newspapers, magazines, etc.; *printed matter can be sent through the post at a lower rate*; **the printed word** = information in a printed form; *people rely more on television and radio for news and less on the printed word*

③ **printer**
['prɪntə] *noun*

(a) person or company that prints books, newspapers, etc.; *the book has gone to the printer, and we should have copies next week*

(b) machine which prints; **laser printer** = printing machine which prints using a laser beam

③ **print out**
['prɪnt 'aut] *verb*

to print information from a computer through a printer; *she printed out three copies of the letter*

③ **printout**
['prɪntaut] *noun*

printed information from a computer; *the travel agent gave me a printout of flight details and hotel reservations*

③ **prior**
['praɪə] *adjective*

(a) before; previous; *the house can be visited by prior arrangement with the owner*; *I had to refuse her invitation because I had a prior engagement in London*; **without prior agreement** = without any agreement in advance

(b) *(formal)* **prior to** = before; *they had left prior to my arrival*

② **priority**
[praɪˈɒrɪti] *noun*

(a) right to be first; **to have priority over** *or* **to take priority over something** = to be more important than something, to need to be done first; *people with serious injuries have priority over those with only minor cuts*; **to give something top priority** = to make something the most important item; *we should give top priority to solving our financial problems*; *the President want us to give the problem top priority*

(b) thing which has to be done first; *finding somewhere to stay the night was our main priority*

② **prison**
['prɪzn] *noun*

building where people are kept when they are being punished for a crime; *the judge sent him to prison for five years*; *his father's in prison for theft*; *the prisoners managed to escape from prison by digging a tunnel* (NOTE: **prison** is often used without the article **the**)

② **prisoner**
['prɪznə] *noun*

person who is in prison; *the prisoners were taken away in a police van*; **prisoner of war (POW)** = soldier, sailor, etc., who has been captured by the enemy

④ **privacy**
['prɪvɪsɪ] *noun*

not being disturbed by other people; *she read the letter in the privacy of her bedroom*

① **private**
['praɪvɪt]
1 *adjective*

(a) which belongs to one person, not to everyone; *he flew there in his private jet; (informal)* **private eye** = a detective who is not a member of the police force and is employed by an ordinary person; **private property** = property which belongs to a private person, not to the public; *you can't park here - this is private property*; the **private sector** = companies which are listed on the stock exchange or owned by individuals, and not by the government; *the research is financed by money from the private sector*; **private view** = showing of an exhibition, etc., to specially invited guests, before it is open to the public; *we've been invited to a private view of her latest exhibition*

(b) which refers to one particular person and should kept secret from others; *you have no right to interfere in my private affairs*; *this is a private discussion between me and my son*; in **private** = away from other people; *she asked to see the teacher in private*

2 *noun*

ordinary soldier of the lowest rank (NOTE: can be used with the surname: **Private Jones**)

③ **privilege**
['prɪvɪlɪdʒ] *noun*

favour or right granted to some people but not to everyone; *it is a great privilege being asked to speak to you tonight*; *I once had the privilege of meeting the Pope*

④ **privileged**
['prɪvɪlɪdʒd] *adjective*

who has a special advantage; *you must think yourselves privileged to have her as your colleague*; *only a privileged few will be able to see the exhibition*

④ **prize**
[praɪz]

1 *noun*

something given to a winner; *he won first prize in the music competition*; *he answered all the questions correctly and claimed the prize*; *the prize was awarded jointly to the young British and Russian competitors*; **prize money** = money given to the person who wins a competition; *there is £10,000 in prize money at stake*

2 *adjective*

which has won a prize because of being of good quality; *he showed a prize sheep at the agricultural show*

3 *verb*

to value something highly; *I prize his friendship particularly*

④ **probable**
['prɒbɪbl] *adjective*

likely; *it's probable that she left her bag on the train*; *the police think it is probable that she knew her murderer*

① **probably**
['prɒbɪblɪ] *adverb*

likely to happen; *we're probably going to France for our holidays*; *are you going to Spain as usual this year? - very probably*

① **problem**
['prɒblɪm] *noun*

(a) something which is difficult to answer; *half the students couldn't do all the problems in the maths test*; **to pose a problem** = to be a difficult question; *what to do with illegal immigrants poses a problem for the immigration services*; **to solve a problem** = to find an answer to a problem; *the police are trying to solve the problem of how the thieves got into the house*; *we have called in an expert to solve our computer problem*

(b) no problem! = don't worry, it isn't difficult

② **procedure**
[prɪ'siːdʒɪ] *noun*

(a) way in which something ought to be carried out; *to obtain permission to build a new house you need to follow the correct procedure*

(b) medical treatment; *a new procedure for treating cases of drug addiction*

③ **proceed**
[prɪ'siːd] *verb*

(a) to go further; *he proceeded down the High Street towards the river*

(b) to do something after something else; *the students then proceeded to shout and throw bottles at passing cars*

(c) to proceed with something = to go on doing something; *shall we proceed with the committee meeting?*

③ **proceed against**
[prɪ'siːd ə'geɪnst] *verb*

to start a lawsuit against someone; *the police can't proceed against her without more evidence*

② **proceedings**
[prɪ'siːdɪŋz] *noun*

(a) legal proceedings = lawsuit or legal action; *if payment is not made within two days, we shall start proceedings against you*; *the proceedings are expected to last three days*

(b) report of what takes place at a meeting; *the proceedings of the Historical Society*

③ **proceeds**
['prəʊsiːdz] *noun*

money which you receive when you sell something; *she sold her house and invested the proceeds in a little shop*; *all the proceeds of the village fair go to charity*

① **process**
['prəʊsɪs]

1 *noun*

(a) method of making something; *a new process for extracting oil from coal*; see also PEACE (NOTE: plural is **processes**)

(b) in the process of doing something = while doing something; *she interrupted me while I was in the process of writing my report*; *we were in the process of moving to London when I had the offer of a job in Australia*

2 *verb*

(a) to manufacture goods from raw materials; *the iron is processed to make steel*; **processed cheese** = cheese which has been treated so that it will keep for a long time

(b) to deal with a claim, bill, etc., in the usual routine way; *to process an insurance claim*; *orders are processed in our warehouse*

(c) to sort out information, especially using a computer; *the computer processes the data and then prints it out*

④ **processing**
['prəʊsesɪŋ] *noun*

data processing or **information processing** = selecting and examining data in a computer to produce information in a special form; **word processing** *or* **text processing** = working with words, using a computer to produce, check and print letters, texts, reports, etc.; *she did a course in word processing before taking a job as a secretary*; *what word-processing software do you use?*; *the word-processing package is bundled with the computer*

④ **procession**
[prɪ'seʃn] *noun*

group of people (with a band, etc.) walking in line; *the procession will march down Whitehall to the Houses of Parliament*; *he carried the little boy on his shoulders so that he could see the procession*; *the funeral procession will arrive at the cathedral at 11.00*; **in procession** = in a line as part of a ceremony; *the people who have received their degrees will walk in procession through the university grounds*

④ **processor**
['prəʊsesə] *noun*

(a) machine that processes; *mix the ingredients in a food processor*

(b) computer that processes information; **word processor** = computer which is used for working with words, to produce texts, reports, letters, etc.; *she offered to write the letter for me on her word processor*

① **produce**
1 *noun*
['prɒdjuːs] things grown on the land; *vegetables and other garden produce* (NOTE: do not confuse with **product**)

2 *verb*
[prɪ'djuːs]
(a) to show or bring out; *the tax office asked him to produce the relevant documents*; *he produced a bundle of notes from his inside pocket*

(b) to make; *the factory produces cars and trucks*

(c) to put on a play, a film, etc.; *she is producing 'Hamlet' for the local drama club*

(d) to grow crops, to give birth to young, etc.; *the region produces enough rice to supply the needs of the whole country*; *our cat has produced six kittens*

③ **producer**
[prɪ'djuːsɪ] *noun*

(a) company or country which makes or grows something; *an important producer of steel*; *the company is a major car producer*

(b) person who puts on a play or a film; *the producers weren't happy with the director's choice of cast*

> COMMENT: a producer of a film is the person who has general control of the making of the film, especially of its finances, but does not deal with the technical details. The director organizes the actual making of the film, giving instructions to the actors, dealing with the lighting, sound, etc.

① **product**
['prɒdʌkt] *noun*

(a) thing which is manufactured; *Germany is helping her industry to sell more products abroad*; *how did you come to learn about our product?* (NOTE: do not confuse with **produce**)

(b) **gross domestic product (GDP)** = annual value of goods sold and services paid for inside a country; **gross national product (GNP)** = annual value of goods and services in a country, including income from other countries

(c) *(in mathematics)* number which is the result when numbers are multiplied; *the product of 4 times 10 is 40*

① **production**
[prɪ'dʌkʃn] *noun*

(a) manufacturing; *we are trying to step up production*; *production will probably be held up by the strike*

(b) putting on a play or film; *the film is currently in production at Teddington Studios*

(c) particular version of a play; *have you seen the production of 'Henry V' at the Globe Theatre?*

(d) showing something; **on production of** = when something is shown; *goods bought can be exchanged only on production of the sales slip*

④ **productive**
[prɪ'dʌktɪv] *adjective*

which produces; *the 1590s were a very productive period for the English theatre*; *how can we make our workforce more productive?*; **a productive meeting** = a useful meeting which should lead to an agreement; *we had a very productive morning - all the remaining problems were ironed out*

④ **productivity**
[prɒdʌk'tɪvɪti] *noun*

rate of output, rate of production in a factory; *bonus payments are linked to productivity*; *productivity has fallen since the company was taken over*; **productivity bonus** = bonus paid for increased rate of production

③ **profession**
[prɪˈfeʃn] *noun*
(a) work which needs special training, skill or knowledge; *the legal profession*; *the medical profession*; *the teaching profession*; *she is an accountant by profession*
(b) declaration of belief in something; *a profession of faith*

① **professional**
[prɪˈfeʃnl]
1 *adjective*
(a) referring to a profession; *he keeps his professional life and his private life completely separate*; professional qualifications = documents showing that someone has successfully finished a course of study which allows him to work in one of the professions; *he got a job as an accountant even though he had no professional qualifications*
(b) expert or skilled; *they did a very professional job in designing the new office*
(c) *(sportsman)* who is paid to play; *a professional footballer*
2 *noun*
(a) expert; *don't try to deal with the problem yourself - get a professional in*
(b) sportsman who is paid to play; *for many years, professionals were not allowed to compete in the Olympics*; *he ran as an amateur for several years, then turned professional*
(c) sportsman who coaches others; *a golf professional*

④ **professor**
[prɪˈfesɪ] *noun*
(a) most senior teacher in a subject at a university; *a professor of English*; *an economics professor*
(b) title taken by some teachers of music, art, etc.; *she goes to Professor Smith for piano lessons* (NOTE: **professor** is written with a capital letter when used as a title: **Professor Smith**)

③ **profile**
[ˈprəʊfaɪl] *noun*
(a) view of someone's head, seen from the side; *a photograph showing her in profile*
(b) to keep a low profile = to be quiet, not to be obvious; *it would be better if you kept a low profile until all the fuss has died down*; to keep *or* maintain a high profile = to keep yourself in the view of the public; *a politician needs to keep a high profile*; *advertising helps to maintain the company's profile*
(c) short biography of a famous person in a newspaper; *there's a profile of the MP in the Sunday paper*

① **profit**
[ˈprɒfɪt]
1 *noun*
money you gain from selling something which is more than the money you paid for it; *the sale produced a good profit or a handsome profit*; **gross profit** = profit calculated as income from

sales less the cost of the goods sold (i.e., without deducting any other expenses); **net profit** = profit calculated as income from sales less all expenditure; **profit and loss account** = statement of company expenditure and income over a period of time, showing whether the company has made a profit or loss; **profit margin** = percentage of money gained against money paid out; **to make a profit** = to have more money as a result of a deal; *we aim to make a quick profit*; *we made a large profit when we sold our house*; *it you don't make a profit you will soon be out of business*; **to show a profit** = to make a profit and put it in the company accounts; *we are showing a small profit for the first quarter*; **to take your profit** = to sell shares at a higher price than you paid for them, rather than to keep them as an investment
2 *verb*
to profit from = to gain from; *I profited from her advice*

④ **profitable**
[ˈprɒfɪtɪbl] *adjective*
likely to produce a profit; *he signed a profitable deal with a Polish company*; *I am sure he will find a profitable use for his talents as a salesman*

④ **profound**
[prɪˈfaʊnd] *adjective*
very serious, very deep; *he showed a profound understanding of the problems of the unemployed*; *we gave profound thanks for our rescue*

① **program**
[ˈprəʊɡræm]
1 *noun*
instructions given to a computer; *to load a program*; *to run a program*; *a graphics program*; *a text editing program*
2 *verb*
to give instructions to a computer; *the computer is programmed to print labels*; **programming language** = system of signs and words used to program a computer (NOTE: **programming - programmed**)

① **programme** *US* **program**
[ˈprəʊɡræm *US* ˈprəʊɡrɪm]
1 *noun*
(a) TV or radio show; *we watched a programme on life in the 17th century*; *there's a football programme after the news*; *I want to listen to the programme at 9.15*; *there are no good television programmes tonight*
(b) paper in a theatre or at a football match, etc., which gives information about the show; *the programme gives a list of the actors*; *the match programme costs £5*
2 *verb*
to arrange programmes on TV or radio; *the new chat show is programmed to compete with the news on the other channel*

② **progress**
  1 *noun*
['prɪʊgres]
(a) movement forwards; *we are making good progress towards finishing the house* (NOTE: no plural)
(b) in progress = which is happening or being done; *the meeting is still in progress*; *we still have a lot of work in progress*
  2 *verb*
[prɪ'gres] to advance; *work on the new road is progressing slowly*

④ **progressive**
[prɪ'gresɪv] *adjective*
(a) (movement) in stages; *I have noticed a progressive improvement in your work*
(b) advanced (ideas); *they elected a leader with progressive views on education*

④ **prohibit**
[prɪ'hɪbɪt] *verb*
to say that something must not be done; *the rules prohibit singing in the dining room*

① **project**
  1 ['prɒdʒekt] *noun*
(a) plan, scheme; *we are working on a building project*
(b) work planned by students on their own; *her project is to write the history of her village*; *she asked her teacher for some help with her project*
  2 [prɪ'dʒekt] *verb*
(a) to plan something, to expect to do something; *they are projecting to build a new science park near the university*
(b) to send a picture onto a screen; *the lecturer projected slides of his visit to Africa*

③ **projection**
[prɪ'dʒekʃn] *noun*
(a) calculation of something which is forecast for the future; *we have made a projection of the additional housing needed in this area by the year 2010*; *computer projections forecast an easy win for the government*
(b) *(formal)* thing which sticks out; *she cut her arm on a sharp projection of rock*
(c) action of sending a picture onto a screen; **the projection room** = room in a cinema, with the projector, where the film is sent onto the screen

④ **projector**
[prɪ'dʒektɪ] *noun*
machine which sends pictures onto a screen; *the projector broke down so we couldn't see the end of the film*

④ **prolonged**
[prɪ'lɒŋd] *adjective*
lasting for a long time; *his prolonged absence worried his family*; *she died after a prolonged illness*

④ **prominent**
['prɒmɪnɪnt] *adjective*
(a) standing out, easily seen; *she has a very prominent nose*
(b) famous or important; *a prominent trade union leader*; *terrorists shot a prominent member of the ruling party*

② **promise**
['prɒmɪs]
  1 *noun*
(a) act of saying that you will definitely do something; *but you made a promise not to tell anyone else and now you've told my mother!*; *I'll pay you back on Friday - that's a promise*; **to go back on a promise** *or* **to break a promise** = not to do what you said you would do; *the management went back on its promise to increase salaries*; *he broke his promise to take her to Mexico on holiday*; **to keep a promise** = to do what you said you would do; *he says he will pay next week, but he never keeps his promises*; *she kept her promise to write to him every day*
(b) to show promise = to make people feel that you will do well in the future; *this year's students certainly show promise*
  2 *verb*
(a) to give your word that you will definitely do something; *they promised to be back for supper*; *you must promise to bring the computer back when you have finished with it*; *he promised he would look into the problem*; *she promised the staff an extra week's holiday but they never got it*
(b) to look as if something will happen; *the meeting promises to be very interesting*

② **promising**
['prɒmɪsɪŋ] *adjective*
(a) who is likely to succeed; *she's the most promising candidate we have interviewed so far*
(b) good, and likely to become much better; *the results of the antibiotic have been very promising*; *the economic situation looks much more promising than it did a year ago*

② **promote**
[prɪ'mɪʊt] *verb*
(a) to give someone a better job; *he was promoted from salesman to sales manager*
(b) to make sure that people know about a product or service, by advertising it; *there are posters all over the place promoting the new supermarket*
(c) to encourage; *the club's aim is to promote gardening*

③ **promotion**
[prɪ'mɪʊʃn] *noun*
(a) move to a better job; *he ruined his chances of promotion when he argued with the boss*
(b) advertising of a new product; *we're giving away small bottles of shampoo as a promotion*

④ **prompt**
['prɒmpt]
  1 *adjective*
done immediately; *thank you for your prompt reply* (NOTE: **prompter - promptest**)

2 *verb*

(a) to suggest to someone that he should do something; *it prompted him to write to the local paper*

(b) to tell an actor words which he has forgotten; *he had to be prompted in the middle of a long speech*

3 *noun*

message to a computer user, telling him to do something; *the prompt came up on the screen telling me to insert the disk in drive A*

③ **promptly**
['prɒmptli] *adverb*

immediately; rapidly; *he replied to my letter very promptly*

④ **prone**
[prəʊn] *adjective*

(a) prone to = likely to do something, likely to suffer from something; *when you're tired you are prone to make mistakes*; *he's prone to chest infections*; accident-prone = likely to have accidents often; *the new waitress seems to be accident-prone*

(b) (lying) flat; *they found her lying prone on the floor*

③ **pronoun**
['prəʊnaʊn] *noun*

word used instead of a noun, such as 'I', 'you', 'he', 'she' and 'it'; *there are three pronouns in the sentence 'she gave it to me'*

④ **pronounce**
[prə'naʊns] *verb*

(a) to speak sounds which form a word; *how do you pronounce 'Paris' in French?*

(b) to state officially; *he was pronounced dead on arrival at hospital*; *the priest pronounced them man and wife*

④ **pronunciation**
[prənʌnsi'eɪʃn] *noun*

way of speaking words; *what's the correct pronunciation of 'controversy'?*; *you should try to improve your pronunciation by taking lessons from native speakers*

② **proof**
[pruːf]

1 *noun*

(a) thing which proves or which shows that something is true; *the police have no proof that he committed the murder*; proof of identity = proof in the form of a document, such as a driving licence, that a person is who he or she claims to be; *the police asked her for proof of identity*

(b) sheet with text or pictures printed on it, for the publisher, author or designer to look at and make corrections; *she has a pile of proofs to check*; *he was looking at the first proofs of his latest cartoon*

2 *adjective*

proof against = safe from, not affected by; *after it has been treated, the wood is proof against insects and rot*; *no one was proof against her charms*

④ **propaganda**
[prɒpɪ'gændɪ] *noun*

spreading of (usually false) information about something which you want the public to believe; *they conducted a propaganda campaign against the minister*

① **proper**
['prɒpɪ] *adjective*

right and correct; *she didn't put the sugar back into its proper place in the cupboard*; *this is the proper way to use a knife and fork*; *the parcel wasn't delivered because it didn't have the proper address*

① **properly**
['prɒpɪli] *adverb*

correctly; *the accident happened because the garage hadn't fitted the wheel properly*; *the parcel wasn't properly addressed*

③ **proper noun**
['prɒpɪ 'naʊn] *noun*

noun which is the name of a person, a country, the title of a book, film, etc.; *most proper nouns begin with a capital letter*

① **property**
['prɒpɪti] *noun*

(a) thing that belongs to someone; *the furniture is the property of the landlord*; *the hotel guests lost all their property in the fire*; *the management is not responsible for property left in the restaurant*; see also LOST PROPERTY OFFICE

(b) buildings and land; *the family owns property in West London*; *a lot of industrial property was damaged in the war*; commercial property = buildings used as offices or shops

(c) a building; *we have several properties for sale in the centre of town* (NOTE: no plural for meanings (a) and (b); plural for (c) is **properties**)

② **proportion**
[prə'pɔːʃn] *noun*

(a) part of a whole; *only a small proportion of his income comes from his TV appearances*

(b) relationship between the amount of something and the amount of something else; *mix equal proportions of sugar and flour*; *what is the proportion of men to women on the committee?*

(c) in proportion to = showing how something is related to something else; *our sales in Europe are tiny in proportion to those in the USA*; *the payment is very high in proportion to the time worked*; out of proportion = not in a proper relationship; *his salary is totally out of proportion to the work he does*

(d) proportions = the relative height, length of a building, picture, etc.; *they proposed building a library of huge proportions*; *the picture looks odd, the artist seems to have got the proportions of the people wrong*

① **proposal**
[prɪ'pɪʊzl] *noun*
(a) suggestion, plan which has been suggested; *the committee made a proposal to rebuild the club house*; *his proposal was accepted by the committee*; *she put forward a proposal but it was rejected*
(b) proposal (of marriage) = asking someone to marry you; *she thought he liked her, but she didn't expect a proposal*

① **propose**
[prɪ'pɪʊz] *verb*
(a) to suggest, to make a suggestion; *I propose that we all go for a swim*
(b) to propose to do something = to say that you intend to do something; *they propose to repay the loan at £20 a month*
(c) to propose to someone = to ask someone to marry you; *he proposed to me in a restaurant*

② **proposed**
[prɪ'pɪʊzd] *adjective*
which has been suggested; *the proposed route of the motorway*

④ **proposition**
[prɒpɪ'zɪʃn] *noun*
(a) thing which has been proposed; *their proposition is not very attractive*; **it will never be a commercial proposition** = it is not likely to make a profit
(b) tough proposition = problem which is difficult to solve

④ **prose**
[prɪʊz] *noun*
writing which is not poetry; *his letters are examples of classical English prose*

④ **prosecute**
['prɒsɪkjuːt] *verb*
to bring someone to court to answer a criminal charge; *he was prosecuted for a traffic offence*; *people found stealing from the shop will be prosecuted*

③ **prosecution**
[prɒsɪ'kjuːʃn] *noun*
(a) bringing someone to court to answer a charge; *he faces prosecution for fraud*
(b) lawyers who represent the party who brings a charge against someone; *the costs of the case will be borne by the prosecution*; *the prosecution argued that the money had been stolen*; **prosecution counsel** *or* **counsel for the prosecution** = lawyer acting for the prosecution (NOTE: the opposing side in a court is the **defence**)

④ **prosecutor**
['prɒsɪkjuːtɪ] *noun*
lawyer who prosecutes; *it was the prosecutor's turn to question the witness*; **public prosecutor**

= government lawyer who brings charges against a criminal in a law court on behalf of the state

② **prospect**
1 *noun*
['prɒspekt]
(a) future possibility; *there is no prospect of getting her to change her mind*; *faced with the grim prospect of two weeks at home he decided to go on holiday*; **to have something in prospect** = to expect something to happen
(b) prospects = future possibilities in a job; *his prospects are very good*; *what are her job prospects?*; *he's very gloomy about his job prospects*
2 *verb*
[prɪ'spekt] to search for minerals; *the team went into the desert to prospect for oil*

④ **prospective**
[prɪ'spektɪv] *adjective*
who may do something in the future; *he's been nominated as prospective candidate for parliament*; **a prospective buyer** = someone who may buy in the future; *there is no shortage of prospective buyers for the house - I'm sure we'll sell it easily*

④ **prosperity**
[prɒs'perɪti] *noun*
being rich; *they owe their prosperity to the discovery of oil on their land*; **in times of prosperity** = when people are rich (NOTE: no plural)

④ **prosperous**
['prɒspɪrɪs] *adjective*
wealthy, rich; *Salisbury is a very prosperous town*

② **protect**
[prɪ'tekt] *verb*
to keep someone or something safe from dirt, germs, etc.; *the cover protects the machine against dust*; *the injection is supposed to protect you against flu*

② **protection**
[prɪ'tekʃn] *noun*
shelter, being protected; *the trees give some protection from the rain*; *the legislation offers no protection to part-time workers*; *the injection gives some protection against flu*

③ **protective**
[prɪ'tektɪv] *adjective*
who or which protects; *visitors to the factory must wear protective clothing*; *she's very protective towards her little brother*; *he put a protective arm around her*

② **protein**
['prɪʊtiːn] *noun*
compound which is an essential part of living cells, one of the elements in food which you need to keep the human body working properly; *the doctor told her she needed more protein in her diet*

COMMENT: meat, eggs, soya beans and fish contain a lot of protein. Compare with carbohydrates, which provide the body with energy

③ **protest**
1 *noun*
['prɪʊtest]
(a) statement that you object or disapprove of something; *the new motorway went ahead despite the protests of the local people*; *she resigned as a protest against the change in government policy*; **protest march** = march through streets to show that you protest against something; *we're organizing a protest march to the town hall*
(b) **in protest at** = showing that you do not approve of something; *the staff occupied the offices in protest at their low pay*; **to do something under protest** = to do something, but say that you do not approve of it
2 *verb*
[prɪ'test]
(a) **to protest against something** = to say that you do not approve of something, to raise a violent objection to; *everyone has protested against the increase in bus fares* (NOTE: British English is **to protest against something**, but American English is **to protest something**)
(b) to insist that something is true, when others think it isn't; *she went to prison still protesting her innocence*

③ **Protestant**
['prɒtestɪnt]
1 *adjective*
referring to the Christian Church which separated from the Catholic Church in the 16th century; *the Church of England is a Protestant Church*
2 *noun*
member of a Christian Church which separated from the Catholic Church in the 16th century

③ **protester**
[prɪ'testɪ] *noun*
person who protests; *several protesters lay down in the street and were arrested*

② **proud**
[praʊd] *adjective*
(a) **proud of something** = full of pride about something; *you must be very proud of your children*; *he is proud to have served in the navy*
(b) *(informal)* **to do someone proud** = to give someone plenty to eat and drink; *the restaurant did us proud*; **to do yourself proud** = to give yourself an expensive treat; *he did himself proud and bought himself a bottle of wine* (NOTE: **prouder - proudest**)

④ **proudly**
['praʊdli] *adverb*
with pride; *she proudly showed me her new car*

① **prove**
[pru:v] *verb*
(a) to show that something is true; *the police think he stole the car but they can't prove it*; *I was determined to prove him wrong or to prove that he was wrong*
(b) **to prove to be something** = to actually be something when it happens; *the weather for the holiday weekend proved to be even hotter than was expected*; *it's proving very difficult to persuade him to sell his house*

① **provide**
[prɪ'vaɪd] *verb*
to supply; *medical help was provided by the Red Cross*; *our hosts provided us with a car and driver*

① **provided (that)** *or* **providing**
[prɪ'vaɪdɪd ðæt *or* prɪ'vaɪdɪŋ] *conjunction* on condition that; as long as, so long as; *it's nice to go on a picnic provided it doesn't rain*; *you can all come to watch the rehearsal providing you don't interrupt*

③ **provide for**
[prɪ'vaɪd 'fɔ:] *verb*
(a) **to provide for someone** = to give enough money to buy food and clothes for someone; *he earns very little and finds it difficult to provide for a family of six children*; *will your family be provided for when you die?*
(b) **to provide for something** = to allow for something which may happen in the future; *the lease provides for an annual increase in the rent*

② **province**
['prɒvɪns] *noun*
(a) large administrative division of a country; *the provinces of Canada*
(b) **the provinces** = parts of a country away from the capital; *there are fewer shops in the provinces than in the capital*
(c) area of knowledge or of responsibility; *that's not my province - you'll have to ask the finance manager*

② **provincial**
[prɪ'vɪnʃl]
1 *adjective*
(a) referring to a province, to the provinces; *a provincial government*
(b) not very sophisticated; *they're very provincial down in that part of the world*; *he's too provincial to appreciate this kind of music*
2 *noun*
person from the provinces; *you provincials are out of touch with London fashion*

① **provision**
[prɪ'vɪʒn] *noun*
(a) providing something; *the provision of medical services is the responsibility of local government*; **to make provision for** = to see that something is allowed for in the future; *we've made provision for the computer*

network to be expanded; there is no provision for or no provision has been made for car parking in the plans for the office block
(b) provisions = food; *people in remote areas need to stock up with provisions for the winter*
(c) condition in a contract; *it's a provision of the contract that the goods should be sent by air*

③ **provisional**
[prɪˈvɪʒnɪl] *adjective*
(a) temporary; *a provisional government was set up by the army*
(b) not final; *they faxed their provisional acceptance*; *we made a provisional booking over the phone*; **provisional licence** = temporary driving licence held by someone who is learning to drive

④ **provoke**
[prɪˈvʊk] *verb*
(a) to make someone angry, so that he does something violent; *she provoked him into throwing a brick through her front window*
(b) to make a reaction take place; *his reply provoked an angry response from the crowd*

④ **prune**
[pruːn]
1 *noun*
dried plum; *he had a bowl of cooked prunes for breakfast*
2 *verb*
to cut back a tree or bush, to keep it in good shape; *that bush is blocking the window - it needs pruning*

④ **psychiatrist**
[saɪˈkaɪɪtrɪst] *noun*
person who studies and treats mental disease; *I think she should see a psychiatrist not a doctor*

④ **psychiatry**
[saɪˈkaɪɪtri] *noun*
study of mental disease; *when he finished his basic medical training he chose to specialize in psychiatry*

③ **psychological**
[saɪkɪˈlɒdʒɪkl] *adjective*
referring to psychology; *her problems are mainly psychological*; *this could have a very bad effect on the child's psychological development*

③ **psychologist**
[saɪˈkɒlɪdʒɪst] *noun*
person who studies the human mind; *psychologists have developed a new theory to explain why some people get depressed*

③ **psychology**
[saɪˈkɒlɪdʒi] *noun*
study of the human mind; *she's taking a psychology course*; *the psychology department in the university*

③ **pt**
[paɪnt] = PINT

③ **PTO**
[piːtiːˈʊ]
short for 'please turn over', letters written at the bottom of a page, showing that there is something written on the other side

③ **pub**
[pʌb] *noun*
(informal) public house, place where you can buy beer and other alcoholic drinks, as well as snacks, meals, etc.; *I happened to meet him at the pub*; *we had a sandwich and some beer in the pub*; *don't tell your mother you've been to the pub*

① **public**
[ˈpʌblɪk]
1 *adjective*
(a) referring to the people in general; *the crown jewels are on public display in the Tower of London*; *it's in the public interest that the facts should be known*; **public gardens** = place in a town where there are flowers and trees and grass, where people can walk around and enjoy themselves; **public holiday** = holiday for everyone, when everyone can rest and enjoy themselves instead of working; *most of the shops are shut today because it's a public holiday*; **Public Limited Company (Plc)** = company in which the general public can invest and whose shares can be bought and sold on the Stock Exchange; **public opinion** = general feeling held by most of the public; **public sector** = state-owned companies; **public telephone** = telephone which can be used by anyone; **public transport** = transport (such as buses, trains) which can be used by anyone; *its quicker to go by public transport into central London than by car*
(b) to go public = (i) to tell something to everyone; (ii) to sell shares in a company on the stock exchange; *after the leaks to the press, the government finally went public on the proposal*; *the plan is for the company to go public next year*
2 *noun*
(a) people in general; *the public have the right to know what is going on*; **the travelling public** = people who travel frequently; *(humorous)* **the great British public** = the British people (NOTE: public can take either a singular or plural verb)
(b) in public = in the open; in front of everyone; *this is the first time he has appeared in public since his accident*; *I dared him to repeat his remarks in public*

② **publication**
[pʌblɪˈkeɪʃn] *noun*
(a) action of making public, publishing; *the publication of the official figures has been delayed*
(b) book or newspaper which has been published; *he asked the library for a list of gardening publications*

③ **public conveniences**
['pʌblɪk kɪn'viːniːnsɪz] *noun*
toilets for the general public; *why are there are no public conveniences in the centre of town?*

③ **public house**
['pʌblɪk 'haʊs] *noun*
(formal) place where you can buy beer and other alcoholic drinks, as well as snacks, meals, etc.; *the village has the usual church, post office and public house* (NOTE: usually shortened to **pub**)

② **publicity**
[pʌb'lɪsɪti] *noun*
advertising, attracting people's attention to a product; *we're trying to get publicity for our school play; the failure of the show was blamed on bad publicity;* **publicity campaign** = period when planned publicity takes place

④ **publicize**
['pʌblɪsaɪz] *verb*
to attract people's attention to something; to make publicity for something; *the advertising campaign is intended to publicize the services of the tourist board*

② **public relations (PR)**
['pʌblɪk rɪ'leɪʃnz] *noun*
maintaining good connections with the public, especially to put across a point of view or to publicize a product; *the company does not have a public relations department; the council needs better public relations to improve its image; our public relations department organized the launch of the new model*

④ **public school**
['pʌblɪk 'skuːl] *noun*
(a) *(in Britain)* private secondary school which is not part of the state education system, and for which the parents pay; *Eton and Winchester are two famous British public schools*
(b) *(in the USA)* school which is funded by public taxes; *the state has decided to spend more money on its public school system* (NOTE: British English is **state school**)

① **publish**
['pʌblɪʃ] *verb*
to make known to the public; to bring out a book, a newspaper for sale; *the government has not published the figures yet; the company publishes six magazines for the business market; we publish dictionaries for students*

③ **publisher**
['pʌblɪʃɪ] *noun*
person who produces books or newspapers for sale; *I'm trying to find a publisher for my novel; he's a publisher who specializes in reference works*

③ **publishing**
['pʌblɪʃɪŋ] *noun*
producing books or newspapers for sale; *she works in publishing or she has a job in publishing; if you're interested in books, have you thought of publishing as a career?;* **publishing house** = firm which publishes books

③ **pudding**
['pʊdɪŋ] *noun*
(a) dessert, the sweet course at the end of the meal; *I'll have some ice cream for my pudding*
(b) sweet food which has been cooked or boiled; *there's too much sugar in this pudding; he helped himself to some more pudding;* **Christmas pudding** = special pudding eaten on Christmas Day; *see also* RICE
(c) *(not sweet)* **steak and kidney pudding** = dish of steak and kidney cooked in soft pastry, boiled or steamed; **black pudding** = type of dark sausage made with blood

① **pull**
[pʊl]
1 *verb*
(a) to move something towards you or after you; *pull the door to open it, don't push; the truck was pulling a trailer; she pulled some envelopes out of her bag; these little boys spend their time pulling girls' hair;* **to pull someone's leg** = to make someone believe something as a joke; *don't believe anything he says - he's just pulling your leg*
(b) **to pull a muscle** = to injure a muscle by using it too much; *she's pulled a muscle in her back*
2 *noun*
(informal) influence; *she must have some pull over him*

① **pull down**
['pʊl 'daʊn] *verb*
to knock down (a building); *they pulled down the old railway station to build a new supermarket*

① **pull in(to)**
['pʊl 'ɪn] *verb*
to drive close to the side of the road and stop; *all the cars pulled into the side of the road when they heard the fire engine coming*

① **pull off**
['pʊl 'ɒf] *verb*
(a) to take off a piece of clothing by pulling; *he sat down and pulled off his dirty boots*
(b) to do something successfully; *he pulled off a big financial deal; it will be marvellous if we can pull it off*

① **pull out**
['pʊl 'aʊt] *verb*
(a) to pull something out of something; *they used a rope to pull the car out of the river; see also* FINGER
(b) to drive a car away from the side of the road; *he forgot to signal as he was pulling out; don't pull out into the main road until you can see that there is nothing coming*
(c) to stop being part of a deal or agreement; *our Australian partners pulled out at the last moment*

① **pull over**
['pʊl 'ɪʊvɪ] *verb*
to drive a car towards the side of the road; *the police car signalled to him to pull over*

① **pullover**
['pʊlɪʊvɪ] *noun*
piece of clothing made of wool, which covers the top part of your body, and which you pull over your head to put it on; *he's wearing a new red pullover*; *my girlfriend's knitting me another pullover, this time with a V neck*

① **pull round** *or* **pull through**
['pʊl 'raʊnd or 'pʊl 'θruː] *verb*
to recover from an illness; *she pulled through, thanks to the expert work of the specialists*

① **pull together**
['pʊl tɪ'geðɪ] *verb*
to pull yourself together = to become more calm; *although he was shocked by the news he soon pulled himself together*

① **pull up**
['pʊl 'ʌp] *verb*
(a) to bring something closer; *pull your chair up to the window*
(b) to stop a car, etc.; *a car pulled up and the driver asked me if I wanted a lift*; *he didn't manage to pull up in time and ran into the back of the car in front*
(c) *(informal)* **to pull your socks up** = to try to do better; *he'll have to pull his socks up or he'll lose his job*

③ **pulse**
[pʌls] *noun*
(a) regular beat of the heart; *the doctor took his pulse*; *her pulse is very weak*
(b) dried seed of peas or beans; *pulses are used a lot in Mexican cooking*

③ **pump**
[pʌmp]
1 *noun*
machine for forcing liquid or air; **bicycle pump** = small hand pump for blowing up bicycle tyres; **petrol pump** = machine which supplies petrol at a petrol station
2 *verb*
(a) to force in something, such as liquid or air, with a pump; *your back tyre needs pumping up*; *the banks have been pumping money into the company*; *the heart pumps blood round the body*
(b) *(informal)* **to pump someone** = to ask someone a lot of questions to try to get information; *we pumped her after the interview to find out the sort of questions she had been asked*

③ **punch**
[pʌnʃ]
1 *noun*
(a) blow with the fist; *she landed two punches on his head*

(b) metal tool for making holes; *the holes in the belt are made with a punch* (NOTE: plural is **punches**)
2 *verb*
(a) to hit someone with your fist; *he punched me on the nose*
(b) to make holes in something with a punch; *the conductor punched my ticket*

④ **puncture**
['pʌŋktʃɪ]
1 *noun*
hole in a tyre; *I've got a puncture in my back tyre* (NOTE: American English is also a **flat**)
2 *verb*
to make a small hole in something; *the tyre had been punctured by a nail*

④ **punish**
['pʌnɪʃ] *verb*
to make someone suffer because of something he has done; *the children must be punished for stealing apples*; *the simplest way to punish them will be to make them pay for the damage they caused*

③ **punishment**
['pʌnɪʃmɪnt] *noun*
treatment given to punish someone; *as a punishment, you'll wash the kitchen floor*

① **pupil**
['pjuːpl] *noun*
(a) child at a school; *there are twenty-five pupils in the class*; *the piano teacher thinks he is her best pupil*
(b) black hole in the central part of the eye, through which the light passes; *the pupil of the eye grows larger when there is less light*

③ **puppy**
['pʌpɪ] *noun*
(a) baby dog; *our dog has had six puppies* (NOTE: plural is **puppies**)
(b) *(informal)* **puppy fat** = fat on the bodies of young children; *she's nine, and is beginning to lose her puppy fat*

③ **purchase**
['pɜːtʃɪs]
1 *noun*
(formal)
(a) thing bought; *she had difficulty getting all her purchases into the car*; **to make a purchase** = to buy something; *we didn't make many purchases on our trip to Oxford Street*; **purchase price** = price paid for something; *we offer a discount of 10% off the normal purchase price*; **purchase tax** = tax paid on things which are bought; *see also* HIRE PURCHASE
(b) ability to get a grip on something; *I couldn't get any purchase on the smooth face of the rock*; *it's difficult to get a purchase on a box as large as this one* (NOTE: no plural in this meaning)
2 *verb*

(formal) to buy; *they purchased their car in France and brought it back to the UK*; **purchasing power** = quantity that can be bought with a certain amount of money; *the fall in the purchasing power of the pound*

④ **purchaser**
['pɜːtʃɪsɪ] *noun*
(formal) person who buys something; *he has found a purchaser for his house*

③ **pure**
['pjʊɪ] *adjective*
(a) very clean; not mixed with other things; *a bottle of pure water*; *a pure silk shirt*; *a pure mountain stream*
(b) innocent; with no faults; *she led a pure life*
(c) total, complete; *this is pure nonsense*; *it is pure spite on his part*; *it was by pure good luck that I happened to find it* (NOTE: purer - purest)

② **purely**
['pjʊɪlɪ] *adverb*
only, solely; *he's doing it purely for the money*; *this is a purely educational visit*

④ **purple**
['pɜːpl]
1 *adjective*
(colour) mixing red and blue; *the sky turned purple as night approached*
2 *noun*
colour like a mixture of red and blue; *they painted their living room a deep purple*

① **purpose**
['pɜːpɪs] *noun*
(a) aim or plan; *the purpose of the meeting is to plan the village fair*; **I need the invoice for tax purposes** = I need the invoice so that I can declare it to the tax
(b) **on purpose** = in a way which was planned; *don't be cross - he didn't do it on purpose*; *she pushed him off the chair on purpose*

③ **purse**
[pɜːs]
1 *noun*
(a) small bag for carrying money; *I know I had my purse in my pocket when I left home*; *she put her ticket in her purse so that she wouldn't forget where it was*; **to control** *or* **hold the purse strings** = to control the money; *as she's the only person in the family earning any money, she holds the purse strings*
(b) *US* small bag which a woman carries to hold her money, pens, handkerchief, etc.; *a robber snatched her purse in the street* (NOTE: British English is **handbag**)
2 *verb*
to purse your lips = to press your lips together to show you are annoyed

② **pursue**
[pɪˈsjuː] *verb*
(a) to chase someone *or* something; *the police pursued the stolen car across London*; *the guerrillas fled, pursued by government troops*

(b) to carry on a career, an activity; *he pursued his career in the Foreign Office*; *we intend to pursue a policy of reducing taxation*

④ **pursuit**
[pɪˈsjuːt] *noun*
(a) chase after someone; *the pursuit lasted until the thieves were caught*; **in pursuit of** = looking for; *we set off in pursuit of our friends who had just left the hotel*; *the robbers left in a stolen car with the police in pursuit*; **in hot pursuit** = chasing someone actively; *the rebels retreated into the mountains with the government forces in hot pursuit*
(b) trying to find something, to do something; *her aim in life is the pursuit of pleasure*
(c) *(old)* occupation; *he spends his time in country pursuits like gardening and hunting*

① **push**
[pʊʃ]
1 *noun*
(a) action of making something move forward; *he gave the trolley a little push and sent it out into the road*; *can you give the car a push? - it won't start*
(b) action of attacking, of moving forward against someone; *our troops made a sudden push into enemy territory*; *the company made a big push to get into European markets*
(c) *(informal)* **at a push** = with some difficulty; *the cottage will sleep ten people at a push*
(d) *(informal)* **to give someone the push** = to sack someone; *he kept making mistakes with his discounts, so in the end we had to give him the push*
2 *verb*
(a) to make something move away from you or in front of you; *we'll have to push the car to get it to start*; *the piano is too heavy to lift, so we'll have to push it into the next room*; *did she fall down the stairs or was she pushed?*
(b) to press with your finger; *push the right-hand button to start the computer*; *(in a lift) he pushed fourth floor*
(c) *(informal)* **I am pushed for time** = I haven't much time to spare; *let's have a snack because I'm pushed for time*

③ **push off**
['pʊʃ 'ɒf] *verb*
(informal) to start (on a journey); **we really ought to push off now** = it's time for us to go; **push off!** = go away!

③ **puss** *or* **pussy** *or* **pussycat**
[pʊs *or* 'pʊsɪ *or* 'pʊsɪkæt] *noun*
children's names for a cat; *a big black pussy came to meet us*; *you mustn't pull pussy's tail* (NOTE: plural is **pussies**)

① **put**
[pʊt] *verb*
(a) to place; *did you remember to put the milk in the fridge?*; *where do you want me to put this book?*

(b) to say in words; *if you put it like that, the proposal seems attractive; can I put a question to the speaker?*

(c) **to put the shot** = to throw a heavy ball as a sport; *he has put the shot further than anyone else in our team* (NOTE: putting - put - has put)

③ **put away**
['pʊt ə'weɪ] *verb*

to clear things away; *put your football things away before you go to bed*

① **put back**
['pʊt 'bæk] *verb*

to put something where it was before; *go and put that tin of beans back on the shelf; did you put the milk back in the fridge?*; **to put the clocks back** = to change the time on clocks back to one hour earlier at the beginning of summer; *did you remember to put the clocks back last night?*

① **put by**
['pʊt 'baɪ] *verb*

to save (money); *she has some money put by to live on when she retires*

① **put down**
['pʊt 'daʊn] *verb*

(a) to place something lower down onto a surface; *he put his suitcase down on the floor beside him*

(b) to charge, to note; *put that book down on my account; we put it down to her nerves*

(c) to let passengers get off; *the taxi driver put me down outside the hotel*

(d) **to put your foot down** = (i) to insist that something is done; (ii) to make a car go faster; *she put her foot down and told them to stop playing music all night; he put his foot down and we soon left the police car behind*

(e) to make a deposit; *to put down money on a house*

(f) to kill a sick animal; *the cat is very old, she'll have to be put down*

① **put forward**
['pʊt 'fɔːwɪd] *verb*

(a) to suggest; *I put forward several suggestions for plays we might go to see*

(b) to change an appointment to a earlier time; *can we put forward the meeting from Thursday to Wednesday?*

(c) to change the time on a clock to a later one; *you have to put the clocks forward by one hour in October; remember to put your watch forward one hour when you go to Germany*

① **put in**
['pʊt 'ɪn] *verb*

(a) to place inside; *I forgot to put in my pyjamas when I packed the case*

(b) to install; *the first thing we have to do with the cottage is to put in central heating*

(c) to do work; *she put in three hour's extra work yesterday evening*

(d) **to put in for** = to apply; *she put in for a job in the accounts department; he has put in for a grant to study in Italy*

① **put off**
['pʊt 'ɒf] *verb*

(a) to arrange for something to take place later; *we have put the meeting off until next month*

(b) to bother someone so that he can't do things properly; *stop making that strange noise, it's putting me off my work*

(c) to say something to make someone decide not to do something; *he told a story about cows that put me off my food; I was going to see the film, but my brother said something which put me off*

① **put on**
['pʊt 'ɒn] *verb*

(a) to place something on top of something, on a surface; *put the lid on the saucepan; he put his hand on my arm; put the suitcases down on the floor*

(b) to dress yourself in a certain piece of clothing; *I put a clean shirt on before I went to the party; put your gloves on, it's cold outside; put on your boots if you're going out in the rain*

(c) to switch on; *can you put the light on, it's getting dark?; put on the kettle and we'll have some tea*

(d) to add; *she has put on a lot of weight since I saw her last*

① **put out**
['pʊt 'aʊt] *verb*

(a) to place outside; *did you remember to put the cat out?*

(b) to stretch out your hand, etc.; *she put out her hand to stop herself from falling*

(c) to switch off; *he put the light out and went to bed*

(d) *(informal)* **to be put out** = to be annoyed; *he was very put out because you didn't ask him to stay for dinner*

① **put up**
['pʊt 'ʌp] *verb*

(a) to attach to a wall, to attach high up; *I've put up the photos of my family over my desk; they are putting up Christmas decorations all along Regent Street*

(b) to build something so that it is upright; *they put up a wooden shed in their garden*

(c) to lift up; *the gunman told us to put our hands up*

(d) to increase, to make higher; *the shop has put up all its prices by 5%*

(e) to give someone a place to sleep in your house; *they've missed the last train, can you put them up for the night?*

① **put up with**
['pʊt 'ʌp wɪθ] *verb*

to tolerate someone *or* something unpleasant; *living near London Airport means that you have to put up with a lot of aircraft noise; how can you put up with the noise of all those barking dogs?*

④ **puzzle**
['pɪzl]

1 *noun*

(a) game where you have to find the answer to a problem; *I can't do the puzzle in today's paper*
(b) something you can't understand; *it's a puzzle to me why they don't go to live in the country*

2 *verb*

(a) to be difficult to understand; *it puzzles me how the robbers managed to get away*
(b) to find something difficult to understand; *she puzzled over the problem for hours*

③ **pyjamas** *US* **pajamas**
[pɪ'dʒɑːmɪz] *noun*

light shirt and trousers which you wear in bed; *I bought two pairs of pyjamas in the sale; when fire broke out in the hotel, the guests ran into the street in their pyjamas* (NOTE: **a pair of pyjamas** means one shirt and one pair of trousers)

Qq

③ **Q, q**
[kjuː]

seventeenth letter of the alphabet, between P and R; *a 'q' is always followed by the letter 'u'*

④ **QC**
['kjuːsiː] = QUEEN'S COUNSEL

GB senior British lawyer; *she was represented by a leading QC* (NOTE: plural is **QCs**)

② **qualification**
[kwɒlɪfɪ'keɪʃn] *noun*

(a) proof that you have completed a specialized course of study; *does she have the right qualifications for the job?*; **professional qualifications** = proof that you have studied for and obtained a diploma for a particular type of skilled work; **what are his qualifications?** = what sort of degree or certificate does he have?

(b) something which limits the meaning of a statement, or shows that you do not agree with something entirely; *I want to add one qualification to the agreement: if the goods are not delivered by the 30th of June, then the order will be cancelled*

(c) being successful in a test or competition which takes you on to the next stage; *she didn't reach the necessary standard for qualification*

③ **qualified**
['kwɒlɪfaɪd] *adjective*

(a) with the right qualifications; *she's a qualified doctor*; **highly qualified** = with very good results in examinations; *all our staff are highly qualified*

(b) not complete, with conditions attached; *the committee gave its qualified approval*; *the school fair was only a qualified success*

④ **qualifier**
['kwɒlɪfaɪə] *noun*

(a) person who qualifies in a sporting competition; *how many qualifiers were there from the first round?*

(b) round of a sporting competition which qualifies a team to go to the next round; *they won their qualifier and went through to the second round*

② **qualify**
['kwɒlɪfaɪ] *verb*

(a) **to qualify as** = to study for and obtain a certificate which allows you to do a certain type of work; *he has qualified as an engineer; when I first qualified I worked as a solicitor*

(b) **to qualify for** = (i) to be in the right position for, to be entitled to; (ii) to pass a test or one section of a competition and so go on to the next stage; *the project does not qualify for a government grant; she qualified for round two of the competition*

(c) to attach conditions to; *I must qualify the offer by saying that your proposals still have to be approved by the chairman*; **the auditors have qualified the accounts** = the auditors have found something in the accounts of the company which they do not agree with

① **quality**
['kwɒlɪti]

1 *noun*

(a) how good something is; *we want to measure the air quality in the centre of town; there are several high-quality restaurants in the West End*; **quality control** = checking a product to make sure that it is of the right standard; *quality control is important for making sure all goods leaving the factory are of the right standard*; **quality of life** = how good it is to live in a certain town or country, including low pollution and crime levels, good shops, restaurants, schools, etc.

(b) of quality = of good quality; *they served a meal of real quality*; *the carpet is expensive because it is of very good quality*

(c) something characteristic of a person; *she has many qualities, but unfortunately is extremely lazy*; *what qualities do you expect in a good salesman?* (NOTE: plural is **qualities**)

2 *adjective*

of good quality; *we aim to provide a quality service at low cost*

② **quantity**
['kwɒntɪti] *noun*

(a) amount; **a quantity of** = (i) a lot of; (ii) a certain amount of; *the police found a quantity of stolen jewels*; *a small quantity of illegal drugs was found in the car*; **quantities of** = a large amount of; *quantities of stolen goods were found in the garage*

(b) an unknown quantity = person or thing you know nothing about; *the new boss is something of an unknown quantity* (NOTE: plural is **quantities**)

④ **quantum**
['kwɒntɪm] *noun*

(formal) small amount; **quantum leap** = great movement forwards; *his discovery was a quantum leap forwards in the fight against cancer*; **quantum theory** = theory in physics that energy exists in amounts which cannot be divided

④ **quarrel**
['kwɒrɪl]

1 *noun*

argument; *they have had a quarrel and aren't speaking to each other*; *I think the quarrel was over who was in charge of the cash desk*; **to pick a quarrel with someone** = to start an argument with someone; *it was very embarrassing when my father picked a quarrel with the waiter over the bill*; **to patch up a quarrel** = to settle an argument; *after several months of arguing they finally patched up their quarrel*; **to have no quarrel with someone** or **something** = not to have any reason to complain about someone or something; *I have no quarrel with the idea of women priests*

2 *verb*

to quarrel about or **over something** = to argue about something; *they're always quarrelling over money* (NOTE: **quarrelling - quarrelled** but American spelling is **quarreling - quarreled**)

① **quarter**
['kwɔːtɪ] *noun*

(a) one of four parts, a fourth, 25%; *she cut the pear into quarters*; *the jar is only a quarter empty*; *he paid only a quarter of the normal fare because he works for the airline*

(b) three quarters = three out of four parts, 75%; *three quarters of the offices are empty*; *the bus was three quarters full* (NOTE: **a quarter** and **three quarters** are often written **1/4** and **3/4**)

(c) a quarter of an hour = 15 minutes; **it's (a) quarter to three** = it's 2.45; **at a quarter past eight** = at 8.15

(d) *US* 25 cent coin; *do you have a quarter for the machine?*

(e) period of three months; *the repayments are due at the end of each quarter*; *the first quarter's rent is payable in advance*; **first quarter** = period of three months from January to the end of March; **second quarter** = period of three months from April to the end of June; **third quarter** = period of three months from July to the end of September; **fourth quarter** or **last quarter** = period of three months from October to the end of the year; **quarter day** = day at the end of a quarter, when rents, fees, etc., should be paid

> COMMENT: in England, the quarter days are 25th March (Lady Day), 24th June (Midsummer Day), 29th September (Michaelmas Day) and 25th December (Christmas Day)

③ **quarter-final**
['kwɔːtɪ'faɪnɪl] *noun*

(in sport) one of four matches in a competition, the winners of which go into the semi-finals; *Ireland got through to the quarter-finals of the World Cup*

③ **quarterly**
['kwɔːtɪli]

1 *adjective & adverb*

which happens every three months; *a quarterly payment*; *there is a quarterly charge for electricity*; *we pay the rent quarterly* or *on a quarterly basis*

2 *noun*

magazine which appears every three months; *he writes for one of the political quarterlies* (NOTE: plural is **quarterlies**)

③ **quarters**
['kwɔːtɪz] *noun*

(a) accommodation for people in the armed forces or for servants; *when they come off duty the staff go back to their quarters*; **married quarters** = accommodation for families in the armed forces

(b) at close quarters = close to, very near; *I had seen her often on TV, but this was the first time I had seen her at close quarters*

④ **quartet**
[kwɔː'tet] *noun*

(a) four musicians playing together; *she plays the cello in a string quartet*

(b) piece of music for four musicians; *a Beethoven string quartet*

(c) four people or four things; *a quartet of British scientists discovered the cancer cure*; *have you read his quartet of novels about Egypt?*

② **queen**
[kwi:n] *noun*
(a) wife of a king; *King Charles I's queen was the daughter of the King of France*
(b) woman ruler of a country; *the Queen sometimes lives in Windsor Castle*; *Queen Victoria was queen for many years*
(c) queen bee = the main bee in a group, which can lay eggs
(d) second most important piece in chess, after the king; *in three moves he had captured my queen*
(e) *(in playing cards)* the card with the face of a woman; *he had the queen of spades* (NOTE: queen is spelt with a capital letter when used with a name or when referring to a particular person: **Queen Elizabeth I**)

COMMENT: there have been six queens of England in their own right since William the Conqueror invaded in 1066. The first was Mary I, daughter of Henry VIII; she was followed by her sister Elizabeth I. Queen Mary II was queen jointly with her husband, William III: this was the only time there has been a king and queen who reigned jointly in England. Queen Anne was the last of the Stuart monarchs, and was followed by a series of German kings. The longest reigning English monarch was Queen Victoria, who was queen for sixty-four years. The present queen, Elizabeth II, came to the throne in 1952

④ **query**
['kwɪɪri]
1 *noun*
question; *she had to answer a mass of queries about the tax form* (NOTE: plural is **queries**)
2 *verb*
to doubt whether something is true; to ask a question about something; *I would query whether these figures are correct*; *the committee members queried the payments to the chairman's son*

① **question**
['kweʃtʃɪn]
1 *noun*
(a) sentence which needs an answer; *the teacher couldn't answer the children's questions*; *some of the questions in the exam were too difficult*; *the manager refused to answer questions from journalists about the fire*
(b) problem or matter; *the question is, who do we appoint to run the shop when we're on holiday?*; *the main question is that of cost*; *he raised the question of moving to a less expensive part of town*; *it is out of the question = it cannot possibly be done*; *you cannot borrow*

any more money - it's out of the question; *it's out of the question for her to have any more time off*
2 *verb*
(a) to ask questions; *the police questioned the driver for four hours*
(b) to query, to suggest that something may be wrong; *we all question how accurate the computer printout is*

② **question mark**
['kweʃtʃɪn 'mɑːk] *noun*
sign (?) used in writing to show that a question is being asked; *there should be a question mark at the end of that sentence*; *there's a question mark over something = it is doubtful if something will happen or will be good enough*; *there's still a question mark over whether or not he can come*; *there's a big question mark over the England captain*

③ **queue**
[kjuː]
1 *noun*
(a) line of people, cars, etc., waiting one behind the other for something; *there was a queue of people waiting to get into the exhibition*; *we joined the queue at the entrance to the stadium*; *to form a queue = to stand in line*; *please form a queue to the left of the door*; *queues formed at ticket offices when the news of cheap fares became known*; *to jump the queue = to go in front of other people standing in a queue*; *are you trying to jump the queue? - go to the back!*
(b) series of documents (such as orders, application forms) or telephone calls which are dealt with in order; *your call is being held in a queue and will be dealt with as soon as a member of staff is free*; *his order went to the end of the queue = his order was dealt with last* (NOTE: do not confuse with **cue**)
2 *verb*
to queue (up) = to stand in a line waiting for something; *we queued for hours to get the theatre tickets*; *queue here for the London tourist bus*; *queuing system = system where telephone calls are held and answered in turn*; *your call is in a queuing system* (NOTE: **queuing - queued**)

① **quick**
[kwɪk] *adjective*
rapid or fast; *I'm trying to work out the quickest way to get to the Tower of London*; *we had a quick lunch and then went off for a walk*; *he is much quicker at calculating than I am*; *I am not sure that going by air to Paris is quicker than taking the train*; *quick as a flash = very quickly*; *I dropped my purse and quick as a flash a little boy picked it up* (NOTE: **quicker - quickest**)

① **quickly**
['kwɪklɪ] *adverb*
rapidly, without taking much time; *he ate his supper very quickly because he wanted to watch the match on TV*; *the firemen came quickly when we called 999*

② **quid**
[kwɪd] *noun*
(slang) pound (in money); *it only costs ten quid*; *give me a couple of quid and I'll wash your car* (NOTE: no plural form)

② **quiet**
['kwaɪt]
1 *adjective*
(a) without any noise; *can't you make the children keep quiet - I'm trying to work?*; *the hotel leaflet said that the rooms were quiet, but ours looked out over a busy main road*; **quiet as a mouse** = very quiet; *she sat in the corner, as quiet as a mouse, watching what was going on*
(b) with no great excitement; *we had a quiet holiday by the sea*; *it's a quiet little village*; *the hotel is in the quietest part of the town* (NOTE: quieter - quietest)
2 *noun*
(a) calm and peace; *all I want is a bit of peace and quiet and then he starts playing drums*; *the quiet of the Sunday afternoon was spoilt by aircraft noise*
(b) **on the quiet** = in secret; *they got married last weekend on the quiet*
3 *verb*
to make calm; *she tried to quiet the screaming child*

③ **quietly**
['kwaɪtlɪ] *adverb*
without making any noise; *the burglar climbed quietly up to the window*; *she shut the door quietly behind her*

③ **quit**
[kwɪt] *verb*
(a) *(informal)* to leave a job, a house, etc.; *when the boss criticized her, she quit*; *I'm fed up with the office, I'm thinking of quitting*
(b) US *(informal)* to stop doing something; *will you quit bothering me!*; *he quit smoking*; *see also* QUITS (NOTE: quitting - quit *or* quitted)

① **quite**
[kwaɪt] *adverb*
(a) more or less; *it's quite a long play*; *she's quite a good secretary*; *the book is quite amusing but I liked the TV play better*
(b) completely; *you're quite mad to go walking in that snow*; *he's quite right*; *I don't quite understand why you want to go China*; *not quite* = not completely; *the work is not quite finished yet*; *have you eaten all the bread? - not quite*
(c) **quite a few** *or* **quite a lot** = several *or* many; *quite a few people on the boat were sick*; *quite a lot of staff come to work by car*

③ **quits**
[kwɪts] *adjective*
even; *if you pay the bill and I pay you half, then we'll be quits*; *(informal)* **to call it quits** = (i) to say that you are even; (ii) to decide to stop doing something; *give me £2.50 and we'll call it quits*; *it's getting late, let's call it quits and start again tomorrow morning*

④ **quota**
['kwɪʊtə] *noun*
fixed amount of goods which can be supplied; *the government has set quotas for milk production*; **import quota** = fixed quantity of a particular type of goods which the government allows to be imported; *the government has set an import quota on cars*

④ **quotation**
[kwɪʊ'teɪʃn] *noun*
(a) words quoted; *the article ended with a quotation from one of Churchill's speeches*
(b) estimate of the cost of work to be done; *we asked for quotations for painting the shop*; *his quotation was much lower than all the others*
(c) **quotation marks** = inverted commas (« «), printed or written marks showing that a quotation starts or finishes; *that part of the sentence should be in quotation marks*

② **quote**
[kwɪʊt]
1 *noun*
(a) *(informal)* estimate of the cost of work to be done; *we asked for quotes for painting the kitchen*; *in the end, we accepted the lowest quote*
(b) quotation, words quoted; *I need some good quotes from his speech to put into my report*
(c) *(informal)* **quotes** = inverted commas (« «); *that part of the sentence should be in quotes*
2 *verb*
(a) to repeat a number as a reference; *in reply please quote this number*; *he replied, quoting the number of the invoice*
(b) to repeat what someone has said or written; *he started his speech by quoting lines from Shakespeare's 'Hamlet'*; **can I quote you on that?** = can I repeat what you have just said?; *I think the fee will be £15,000, but don't quote me on that*
(c) to give an estimate for work to be done; *he quoted £10,000 for the job*; *their prices are always quoted in dollars*

Rr

③ **R, r**
['ɑː]

eighteenth letter of the alphabet, between Q and S; **the three Rs** = basic skills which should be taught to children in primary school

> COMMENT: the three Rs are Reading, Riting and Rithmetic (note the spellings! - they should of course be Reading, Writing and Arithmetic (= doing sums)

③ **rabbit**
['ræbɪt]

1 *noun*

common wild animal with grey fur, long ears and a short white tail; *the rabbit ran down its hole*; *he tried to shoot the rabbit but missed*; *she keeps a pet rabbit in a cage*

2 *verb*

(informal) **to rabbit on about something** = to talk for a long time about something; *he was rabbitting on about his collection of toy soldiers*

② **race**
[reɪs]

1 *noun*

(a) contest to see which person, horse, car, etc., is the fastest; *she was second in the 200 metres race*; *the bicycle race goes round the whole country*; **race against time** = struggle to get something finished on time; *they tried to block the hole in the sea wall but with the high tide rising it was a race against time*; *see also* BOAT RACE

(b) large group of people with similar skin colour, hair, etc.,; *the government is trying to stamp out discrimination on grounds of race*; *they are prejudiced against people of mixed race*; **race relations** = relations between different groups of races in the same country; *race relations officers have been appointed in some police forces*

2 *verb*

(a) to run, ride, etc., to see who is the fastest; *I'll race you to see who gets to school first*

(b) to run fast; *they saw the bus coming and raced to the bus stop*; *he snatched some watches from the shop window and then raced away down the street*

③ **racecourse**
['reɪskɔːs] *noun*

track where horse races are run

③ **races**
['reɪsɪz] *noun*

series of horse races held during one single day, or over several days; *we go to the races on Saturday afternoons*; *the races had to be cancelled because the ground was too wet*

③ **racetrack**
['reɪstræk] *noun*

(b) track where races are run; *we're also going to the races - we'll meet you at the racetrack at 2.00 pm*; *his car ran off the racetrack into the crowd*

④ **racial**
['reɪʃl] *adjective*

referring to different races; *the election was fought on racial issues*; **racial discrimination** = bad treatment of someone because of his or her race; **racial prejudice** = prejudice against someone because of race; *he accused his ex-boss of racial discrimination or of racial prejudice*

④ **racially**
['reɪʃɪli] *adverb*

in a racial way; **racially motivated** = done because of racial hatred; *the attack on the house was racially motivated*

③ **racing**
['reɪsɪŋ] *noun*

contests to see who is fastest; *we enjoy watching the racing at weekends*; *he was a famous motor racing driver*; *horse-racing is a favourite sport with people living in London*; **flat racing** = horse-racing over flat ground, without any fences to jump

④ **racism**
['reɪsɪzm] *noun*

believing that a group of people are not as good as others because they are of a different race, and treating them differently; *there was no question of racism in this instance, it was more just bad temper on the part of the manager*

④ **racist**
['reɪsɪst]

1 *adjective*

believing that some people are not as good as others because of race and treating them differently; *the family live in constant terror of racist attacks*; *the murder was thought to have been a racist attack*

2 *noun*

person who treats someone differently because of race; *the manager's a racist and you won't change his views*

③ **rack**
['ræk]
1 *noun*
frame which holds things such as luggage, or letters; *he put the envelope in the letter rack on his desk*; **luggage rack** = space for bags above the seats in a plane, train, etc.; *the luggage rack was full so she kept her bag on her lap*; *please place all hand luggage in the overhead luggage racks*; **wine rack** = frame in which bottles of wine can be kept flat; *see also* ROOF RACK
2 *verb*
(a) **to rack your brains** = to think very hard; *I'm racking my brains, trying to remember the name of the shop*
(b) **racked with** = suffering continuously from; *she was racked with pain*

③ **racket**
['rækɪt] *noun*
(a) light frame with a handle and tight strings, used for hitting the ball in games; **tennis racket** = racket used to play tennis; *she bought a new tennis racket at the start of the summer season*; *she asked if she could borrow his racket for the tournament*
(b) (*informal*) loud noise; *stop that racket at once!*; *the people next door make a terrible racket when they're having a party*
(c) (*informal*) illegal deal which makes a lot of money; *don't get involved in that racket, you'll go to prison if you get caught*; *he runs a cut-price ticket racket*

④ **radar**
['reɪdɑ:] *noun*
(a) system for finding objects such as ships or aircraft, and judging their position, from radio signals which are reflected back from them as dots on a monitor; *the plane's radar picked up another plane coming too close*
(b) **radar trap** = small radar device by the side of a road which senses and notes details of cars which are travelling too fast (NOTE: also called a **speed trap)**

④ **radiation**
[reɪdɪ'eɪʃn] *noun*
sending out rays or heat; *local residents were concerned about the effects of radiation from the nearby nuclear power station*; *any person exposed to radiation is more likely to develop certain types of cancer*

④ **radiator**
['reɪdɪeɪtɪ] *noun*
(a) metal panel filled with hot water for heating; *turn the radiator down - it's boiling in here*; *when we arrived at the hotel our room was cold, so we switched the radiators on*
(b) metal panel filled with cold water for cooling a car engine; *the radiator froze causing the car to break down*

③ **radical**
['rædɪkl]
1 *adjective*
(a) complete; basic (difference); *the government has had a radical change of mind about press freedom*; *he pointed out the radical difference between the two parties' policies on education*
(b) new and totally different; *his more radical proposals were turned down by the committee*; **radical party** = a party which is in favour of great and rapid change in the way a country is governed; *he's not a radical and doesn't belong to the radical party*
2 *noun*
member of a radical party; *two Radicals voted against the government*

④ **radically**
['rædɪklɪ] *adverb*
in a completely different, radical way; *the British political scene has changed radically over the last twelve months*

① **radio**
['reɪdɪʊ]
1 *noun*
(a) method of sending out and receiving messages using air waves; *they got the news by radio*; *we always listen to BBC radio when we're on holiday*; **radio cab** *or* **radio taxi** = taxi which is in contact with its base by radio, and so can be called quickly to pick up a client; *it will be quicker to phone for a radio cab*; **radio telescope** = telescope which uses radio waves to find or see stars and other objects in the sky; *astronomers used a new advanced radio telescope to observe the planet*; **radio waves** = way in which radio signals move through the atmosphere; *the transmission and reception of sound and data by radio waves is called radio communications*
(b) device which sends out and receives messages using air waves; *turn on the radio - it's time for the weather forecast*; *I heard the news on the car radio*; *please, turn the radio down - I'm on the phone*
2 *verb*
to send a message using a radio; *they radioed for assistance*

③ **radioactive**
[reɪdɪʊ'æktɪv] *adjective*
(substance) which gives off energy in the form of radiation which can pass through other substances; *after the accident, part of the nuclear plant remained radioactive for 20 years*; *the problems of disposal of radioactive waste*

③ **raffle**
['ræfl]
1 *noun*
lottery where you buy a ticket with a number on it, in the hope of winning a prize; *she won a bottle of perfume in a raffle*

2 *verb*

to give a prize in a lottery; *they raffled a car for charity*

④ **rag**

[ræg]

1 *noun*

(a) piece of torn cloth; *he used an old oily rag to clean his motorbike*; *(informal)* **like a red rag to a bull** = making someone very annoyed; *any mention of socialists is like a red rag to a bull to him*

(b) rags = old torn clothes; *the children were dressed in rags*; *(informal)* **the rag trade** = the trade of making women's clothes; *the heart of London's rag trade is to be found in the East End*

(c) *(informal)* newspaper; *I read about it in the local rag*

(d) *(informal)* **rag day** *or* **rag week** = day or week when students dress up and collect money for charity

2 *verb*

to play jokes on someone; *he was ragged a lot at school*; *the other girls ragged her about her rich boyfriend*

④ **rage**

[reɪdʒ]

1 *noun*

(a) violent anger; *he rushed up to the driver of the other car in a terrible rage*; **to fly into a rage** = to get very angry suddenly; *when he phoned her she flew into a rage*; *see also* ROAD RAGE

(b) *(informal)* **it's all the rage** *or* **it's the latest rage** = it follows the current fashion; *it's all the rage to wear wide trousers again*

2 *verb*

to be violent; *the storm raged all night*

④ **raid**

[reɪd]

1 *noun*

sudden attack; *robbers carried out six raids on post offices during the night*; *police carried out a series of raids on addresses in London*; **air raid** = sudden attack by planes

2 *verb*

to make a sudden attack on a place; *the police raided the club*; *we caught the boys raiding the fridge*

② **rail**

[reɪl]

1 *noun*

(a) straight metal or wooden bar; *the pictures all hang from a picture rail*; *hold on to the rail as you go down the stairs*; *there is a heated towel rail in the bathroom*

(b) one of two parallel metal bars on which trains run; *don't try to cross the rails - it's dangerous*; *in the autumn, trains can be delayed by leaves on the rails*

(c) the railway, a system of travel using trains; *six million commuters travel to work by rail each day*; *we ship all our goods by rail*; *rail travellers are complaining about rising fares*; *rail travel is cheaper than air travel*

2 *verb*

(a) to rail off = to close an area with fences; *police railed off the entrance to the court*

(b) to rail against = to speak violently against; *he railed against the actions of the authorities*

④ **railings**

['reɪlɪŋz] *noun*

metal bars used as a fence; *don't put your hand through the railings round the lion's cage*; *he leant over the railings and looked down at the street below*

② **railroad**

['reɪlrɪʊd] *noun*

US see RAILWAY

② **railway** *US* **railroad**

['reɪlweɪ *or* 'reɪlrɪʊd] *noun*

way of travelling which uses trains to carry passengers and goods; *the railway station is in the centre of town*; *the French railway system has high-speed trains to all major cities*; *by the end of the 19th century, the railroad stretched from the east to the west coast of America*

① **rain**

[reɪn]

1 *noun*

(a) drops of water which fall from the clouds; *the ground is very dry - we've had no rain for days*; *yesterday we had 3cm of rain or 3cm of rain fell here yesterday*; *if you have to go out in the rain take an umbrella*; *all this rain will help the plants grow*; **driving rain** = rain which is blown by the wind; *they were forced to turn back because of the driving rain* (NOTE: no plural in this meaning: **some rain, a drop of rain**)

(b) *(in tropical countries)* **the rains** = the season when it rains a lot; *the rains came late last year*

2 *verb*

to fall as drops of water from the clouds; *as soon as we sat down and took out the sandwiches it started to rain*; *it rained all day, so we couldn't visit the gardens*; **to rain hard**; *(informal)* **to be raining cats and dogs** = to rain a lot; *it rained hard all morning, but had cleared up by early afternoon* (NOTE: **rain** is only used with the subject **it**; do not confuse with **reign, rein**)

④ **rainbow**

['reɪnbɪʊ] *noun*

arch of colour which shines in the sky when it is sunny and raining at the same time; *a rainbow shone across the valley when the sun came out*

> COMMENT: the colours of the rainbow are: red, orange, yellow, green, blue, indigo (dark blue) and violet

④ **raincoat**
['reinkɒt] *noun*
coat which keeps off water, which you wear when it is raining; *take a raincoat with you if you think it's going to rain*; *she took off her raincoat in the hall*

③ **rainy**
['reini] *adjective*
when it rains; *our holiday was spoilt by the rainy weather*; **rainy season** = period of the year when it rains a lot (as opposed to the dry season); *the rainy season lasts from April to August*; *don't go there in October - that's the beginning of the rainy season* (NOTE: **rainier - rainiest**)

> COMMENT: the phrase 'rainy season' is only used of areas where there is a very marked difference between the seasons. It is not used of Britain or any other European country

① **raise**
[reiz]
1 *noun*
US increase in salary; *she asked the boss for a raise* (NOTE: British English is **rise**)
2 *verb*
(a) to make something higher; *he picked up the flag and raised it over his head*; *the newspaper headline says TAXES TO BE RAISED*; *air fares will be raised on June 1st*; *when the shop raised its prices, it lost half of its customers*; **he raised his eyebrows** = he looked surprised
(b) to mention a subject which could be discussed; *no one raised the subject of politics*; *the chairman tried to prevent the question of redundancies being raised*
(c) to obtain money; *the hospital is trying to raise £2m to finance its expansion programme*; *where will he raise the money from to start up his business?*
(d) to grow plants from seed; *the new varieties are raised in controlled conditions*

④ **rake**
[reik]
1 *noun*
garden tool with a long handle and metal teeth, used for smoothing earth or for pulling dead leaves together; **as thin as a rake** = very thin; *she's a model and is as thin as a rake*
2 *verb*
(a) to smooth loose soil; *she raked the vegetable bed before sowing her carrots*
(b) to pull dead leaves together with a rake; *he raked the leaves from under the trees*
(c) to move a camera or gun slowly sideways so that it covers a wide area; *from their lookout post they were able to rake the whole square with their machine gun*

④ **rally**
['ræli]
1 *noun*

(a) large meeting of members of an association or political party; *we are holding a rally to protest against the job cuts*
(b) competition where cars have to go through difficult country in a certain time; *he won the Monte Carlo rally by 55 minutes*; *the passenger has to deal with the maps, signs and timing for a rally driver*
(c) series of shots in tennis; *it was a great final - full of powerful serves and exciting rallies*
(d) rise in price when the trend has been downwards; *shares staged a rally on the Stock Exchange* (NOTE: plural is **rallies**)
2 *verb*
(a) to gather together; **to rally round** = to group together to support someone; *when her husband was sent to prison her friends rallied round*
(b) to recover for a time from an illness, or from a setback; *he was very poorly on Monday, but by the end of the week he had rallied a little*
(c) to rise in price, when the trend has been downwards; *shares rallied on the news of the latest government figures*

③ **ran**
[ræn] *see* RUN

④ **random**
['rændim]
1 *adjective*
done without any planning; **random check** = check on items taken from a group without choosing them in any particular order; *the customs officer carried out a random check for drugs*; **random sample** = sample for testing which has not been specially selected; *a random blood sample proved that he had been taking drugs*
2 *noun*
done without any planning; **at random** = without choosing; *pick any card at random*

③ **rang**
[ræŋ] *see* RING

① **range**
[reindʒ]
1 *noun*
(a) series of buildings or mountains in line; *there is a range of small buildings next to the farm which can be converted into holiday cottages*; *they looked out at the vast mountain range from the plane window*
(b) *(especially US)* wide open fields for animals to graze; *the cattle were left to feed on the range during the summer*
(c) choice or series of colours, etc., available; *we offer a wide range of sizes*; *we have a range of holidays at all prices*; *I am looking for something in the £20 - £30 price range*
(d) distance which you can go; distance over which you can see or hear; *the missile only has a range of 100km*; *the police said the man had been shot at close range*; *the optician told her that her range of vision would be limited*

2 *verb*

to range from = to spread; *the sizes range from small to extra large; holidays range in price from £150 to £350 per person; the quality of this year's examination papers ranged from excellent to very poor*

③ **rank**

[ræŋk]

1 *noun*

(a) position in society, in the army; *what rank does he hold in the police force?; after ten years he had reached the rank of sergeant;* **other ranks** = ordinary soldiers; **he rose from the ranks** = from being an ordinary soldier he became an officer; *General Smith rose from the ranks*

(b) the rank and file = ordinary people; *rank-and-file union members voted against the proposal*

(c) row of soldiers; *the soldiers kept rank as they advanced towards the enemy*

(d) taxi rank = place where taxis wait in line; *they queued at the taxi rank for half an hour; there's a taxi rank is just outside the station*

2 *verb*

to be classified in order of importance; *Shakespeare ranks among the greatest world authors; as an artist he doesn't rank as highly as his sister*

④ **ranking**

[ˈræŋkɪŋ] *noun*

place in order of importance; *she moved several places up the tennis rankings; the commissioner of police is the highest ranking police officer*

④ **rap**

[ræp]

1 *noun*

(a) sharp tap; *there was a rap on the door*

(b) *(informal)* **to take the rap** = to accept responsibility, to take the blame; *he had to take the rap for the team's bad results*

(c) form of music where the singer speaks words rapidly over a regular beat, making up the words as he or she does so; **a rap artist** = person who speaks words to rap music; *he's the greatest rap artist playing today*

2 *verb*

to give a sharp tap; *he rapped on the door with a stick, but no one came to open it* (NOTE: **rapping - rapped**)

④ **rape**

[reɪp]

1 *noun*

(a) offence of forcing a person to have sexual intercourse without consent; *there's been a dramatic increase in the number of rapes in this area over the past year; he was in court, charged with rape*

(b) plant with yellow flowers, whose seeds are used to produce oil; *market prices for rape soared last autumn*

2 *verb*

to force someone to have sexual intercourse without consent; *the girl was raped at the bus stop; he was in court, charged with raping the student*

③ **rapid**

[ˈræpɪd]

1 *adjective*

fast; *there has been a rapid rise in property prices this year; the rapid change in the weather forced the yachts to return to the harbour*

2 *noun*

rapids = place where a river runs fast over rocks; *he took her down the rapids in a small boat;* **to shoot rapids** = to sail over rapids in a boat

③ **rapidly**

[ˈræpɪdli] *adverb*

quickly; *the new shop rapidly increased sales; she read the letter rapidly and threw it away*

② **rare**

[reɪ] *adjective*

(a) not usual, not common; *it's very rare to meet a foreigner who speaks perfect Chinese; experienced salesmen are rare these days; this wood is the breeding ground of a rare species of frog*

(b) (meat) which is very lightly cooked; *how would you like your steak? - rare, please!* (NOTE: **rarer - rarest**)

② **rarely**

[ˈreɪli] *adverb*

not often, hardly ever; *I rarely buy a Sunday newspaper; he is rarely in his office on Friday afternoons*

④ **rash**

[ræʃ]

1 *noun*

mass of red spots on the skin, which stays for a time and then disappears; *he showed the rash to the doctor; she had a rash on her arms;* **to break out in a rash** = to suddenly get a rash; **heat rash** = spots caused by hot weather; *he suffers from heat rash every summer;* **nappy rash** *US* **diaper rash** = rash on a baby's bottom, caused by the baby having a wet nappy; *she puts cream on the baby's bottom to prevent nappy rash* (NOTE: plural is **rashes**)

2 *adjective*

not cautious, not careful; done without thinking; *it was a bit rash of him to suggest that he would pay for everyone* (NOTE: **rasher - rashest**)

③ **rasher**

[ˈræʃi] *noun*

slice of bacon; *'two rashers of bacon and a sausage, please!'*

④ **rat**

[ræt] *noun*

common small grey animal with a long tail, living in basements, refuse dumps, on ships, etc.; *rats live in the drains in the city; plague is* a disease which is transmitted to people by fleas from rats; **like rats leaving a sinking ship** = when large numbers of people leave a company or an organization which they think is going to collapse; *ministers are leaving the government like rats leaving a sinking ship*

① **rate**
[reɪt]

1 *noun*

(a) number shown as a proportion of another; **birth rate** = number of children born per 1000 of the population; *the national birth rate rose dramatically in the second half of the 20th century*; **death rate** = number of deaths per 1000 of population; *the death rate from flu soared during the winter*

(b) how frequently something is done; *his heart was beating at a rate of only 59 per minute*

(c) level of payment; *he immediately accepted the rate offered*; *before we discuss the position further, I would like to talk about the rates of pay*; *their rate of pay is lower than ours*; **all-in rate** = price which covers everything; *the hotel offers an all-in rate of £350 a week*; **fixed rate** = charge or interest which cannot be changed; *they chose a fixed-rate mortgage*; **flat rate** = fixed charge which never changes; *we charge a flat rate of £10.00 per visit*; *taxi drivers charge a flat rate of £20 for driving you to the airport*; **the going rate** = the usual rate, the current rate of payment; *what is the going rate for a 1996 model Porsche?*; *we are happy to pay you the going rate*; **interest rate** *or* **rate of interest** = percentage charged for borrowing money; *the bank has raised interest rates again*; *savings accounts offer a good interest rate or a good rate of interest*

(d) **exchange rate** *or* **rate of exchange** = rate at which one currency is exchanged for another; *the current rate of exchange is 9.60 francs to the pound*; *what is today's rate for the dollar?*

(e) speed; *at the rate he's going, he'll be there before us*; *if you type at a steady rate of 70 words per minute you'll finish copying the text today*

(f) **first-rate** = very good; *he's a first-rate tennis player*; *the food here is absolutely first-rate*; **second-rate** = not very good; *I don't want any second-rate actor, I want the best you can find*

(g) **at any rate** = whatever happens; *I don't think he really wants to come, at any rate he won't be able to since he's ill*; *the taxi cost more than I expected, but at any rate we got to the airport on time*

2 *verb*

to give a value to something; *she's rated in the top 20 players*; *I don't rate his chances of winning very highly*

① **rather**
[ˈrɑːðə] *adverb*

(a) quite; *their house is rather on the small side*; *her dress is a rather pretty shade of blue*

(b) *(used with* **would***; to mean* **prefer***)*; *we'd rather stay in the office than go to the party*; *is your company going to pay for everybody? - we'd rather not*; *I'd rather we stayed with her*; *they'd rather she went with them*

(c) *(showing that something is done instead of something else)* *rather than wait for hours for a bus, we decided to walk home*; *he tried to use his credit card rather than pay cash*

(d) **or rather** = or to be more precise; *his father is a doctor, or rather a surgeon*

④ **rating**
[ˈreɪtɪŋ] *noun*

(a) assessment, giving a score; *what rating would you give that film?*; **credit rating** = amount of money which someone feels a customer can afford to borrow; *his credit rating was excellent so he was able to open a charge account with the store*

(b) **TV ratings** = estimated number of people who watch TV programmes; *the show is high in the ratings, which means it will attract good publicity*

(c) *(Navy)* ordinary sailor; *the new captain joined the navy 20 years ago as a rating*

③ **ratio**
[ˈreɪʃɪʊ] *noun*

proportion; *the ratio of successes to failures*; *our runners beat theirs by a ratio of two to one* (NOTE: plural is **ratios**)

④ **ration**
[ˈræʃn]

1 *noun*

amount of food or supplies allowed; *the rations allowed for the expedition were more than enough*

2 *verb*

to allow only a certain amount of food or supplies; *petrol may be rationed this winter*; *during the war we were rationed to one ounce of cheese per person per week*

④ **rational**
[ˈræʃɪnl] *adjective*

sensible, based on reason; *she had made a rational decision*; *it's not being rational when you say you're going to build a house all by yourself*

③ **raw**
[rɔː] *adjective*

(a) not cooked; *don't be silly - you can't eat raw potatoes!*; *we had a salad of raw cabbage and tomatoes*; *sushi is a Japanese dish of raw fish*; *they served the meat almost raw*

(b) **raw materials** = substances in their natural state which have not yet been made into manufactured goods (such as wool, wood, sand, etc.); *what raw materials are needed for*

making soap?; *a Malaysian company provides the raw materials used by the tyre manufacturer*
(c) cold and damp (weather); *a very raw winter's morning*; *the driving wind was cold and raw*
(d) *(skin)* sensitive because the surface has been rubbed off; *her new shoes left her heel red and raw*; *(informal)* **to touch a raw nerve** = to mention something which someone is sensitive about; *his mention of the money they owed touched a raw nerve*
(e) *(informal)* **a raw deal** = unfair treatment; *he got a raw deal from the government when they refused to pay him a pension*

④ **ray**
[reɪ] *noun*
(a) beam of light or heat; *a ray of sunshine lit up the gloomy room*; **a ray of hope** = small hopeful sign; *see also* X-RAYS
(b) type of large flat sea fish; *we had ray cooked in butter*

③ **Rd**
[rʊd] *short for* ROAD; *our address is 1 Cambridge Rd*

① **reach**
[riːtʃ]
1 *noun*
(a) how far you can stretch out your hand; *keep the medicine bottle out of the reach of the children*
(b) how far you can travel easily; *the office is within easy reach of the railway station*
(c) **reaches** = section of a river; *the upper reaches of the Thames*
2 *verb*
(a) to stretch out your hand to; *she reached across the table and took some meat from my plate*; *he's quite tall enough to reach the tool cupboard*; *can you reach me down the suitcase from the top shelf?*
(b) to arrive at a place; *we were held up by fog and only reached home at midnight*; *the plane reaches Hong Kong at 16.00*; *we wrote to tell her we were coming to visit, but the letter never reached her*
(c) to get to a certain level; *the amount we owe the bank has reached £100,000*
(d) to do something successfully; **to reach an agreement** = to agree; *the two parties reached an agreement over the terms of the sale*; **to reach a decision** = to decide; *the board has still not reached a decision about closing the factory*

③ **react**
[riˈækt] *verb*
(a) to do or to say something in response to words or an action; *how will he react when we tell him the news?*; *when she heard the rumour she didn't react at all*; **to react against something** = to show opposition to something; *the farmers reacted against the new law by*

blocking the roads with their tractors; **to react to something** = to have a particular response to something; *how did he react to news of her death?*; *he didn't react at all well to the injection*
(b) *(of a chemical)* **to react with something** = to change chemical composition because of a substance; *acids react with metals*

② **reaction**
[riˈækʃn] *noun*
(a) thing done or said in response; *his immediate reaction to the news was to burst into laughter*; *there was a very negative reaction to the proposed building development*; **a natural reaction** = a normal way of responding; *bursting into tears is a natural reaction when you pass your exams*; **what was his reaction to the news?** = what did he say? what did he do?; *what was his reaction when you told him you were leaving him?*
(b) act of reacting; *a chemical reaction takes place when acid is added*

③ **reactor**
[riˈæktɪ] *noun*
nuclear reactor = plant which creates heat and energy by starting and controlling atomic processes; *a nuclear disaster could have happened if the reactor had exploded*

① **read**
[riːd]
1 *verb*
(a) to look at and understand written words; *she was reading a book when I saw her*; *what are you reading at the moment?*; *we're reading about the general election*
(b) to speak aloud from something which is written; *the chairman read a message from the president during the meeting*; *she read a story to the children last night*; *can you read the instructions on the medicine bottle - the print is too small for me?*
(c) to look at and understand written music; *she can play the piano by ear, but can't read music*
(d) *(computers)* to take in and understand data from a disk or sent via a modem, etc.; *our PCs cannot read these disks because they are not from our system*; *the reader at the cash desk reads the bar code on each product*
(e) **to read between the lines** = to understand a hidden meaning which is not immediately obvious; *if you read between the lines of his letter you can tell that he is deeply unhappy*
(f) to study a subject at university; *he read mathematics at Cambridge* (NOTE: **reading - read** [red])
2 *noun*
(a) action of looking at and understanding the words in a book, etc.; *I like to have a read in the train on my way to work*
(b) good book for reading; *his latest novel will be a good holiday read*; *you can't beat that book for a fantastic read*

③ **read aloud** or **read out**
['ri:d ə'laud or 'ri:d 'aut] *verb*
to speak the words you are reading; *she read the letter aloud to the family*; *the teacher read out all the students' marks to the whole class*

② **reader**
['ri:dɪ] *noun*
(a) person who reads books, newspapers, etc.; *a message from the editor to all our readers*; *she's a great reader of detective stories*
(b) school book to help children to learn to read; *the teacher handed out the new readers to the class*; *I remember one of my first readers - it was about two children and their dog*
(c) electronic device which understands data or symbols; *a bar code reader*

③ **readily**
['redɪli] *adverb*
(a) easily and quickly; *this product is readily available in most shops*
(b) willingly, without any hesitation; *is there anyone readily available to help me this weekend?*; *she came readily when I asked her to help me*

② **reading**
['ri:dɪŋ] *noun*
(a) act of looking at and understanding written words; *reading and writing should be taught early*; **reading glasses** = glasses that help you to read things which are close; **reading lamp** = small lamp on a desk or beside a bed, for use when reading or writing; *make sure that the reading lamp on your desk is switched off*; *I can't read in bed at night, I haven't got a reading lamp*; **reading room** = room in a library where people can read books or newspapers without taking them away from the library; *there are people who don't like the reading room of the new British Library*
(b) material (such as books, etc.) which is read; *this book is too difficult, it's not suitable reading for a child her age*
(c) speaking aloud from something which is written; *they gave a poetry reading in the bookshop*
(d) way of understanding a text; *a new reading of 'Hamlet'*
(e) one of the stages of the discussion of a Bill in Parliament; *the bill had its second reading in Parliament last night*

① **ready**
['redi] *adjective*
(a) prepared for something; *hold on - I'll be ready in two minutes*; *are all the children ready to go to school?*; *why isn't the coach here? - the group are all ready and waiting to go*; **ready for anything** = prepared to do anything; *now that I've had some food, I'm ready for anything!*
(b) fit to be used or eaten; *don't sit down yet - the meal isn't ready*; *is the coat I brought to be cleaned ready yet?*

(c) *(informal)* **ready cash** or **ready money** = cash which is immediately available; *I won't be able to come out tonight as I'm a bit short of ready cash*; *I always keep some ready cash handy in case of emergencies* (NOTE: **readier - readiest**)

① **real**
['rɪl] *adjective*
(a) not a copy, not artificial; *is that watch real gold?*; *that plastic apple looks very real or looks just like the real thing*; *he has a real leather case*
(b) *(used to emphasize)* *that car is a real bargain at £300*; *their little girl is going to be a real beauty*; *insects can be a real problem on picnics*; *getting all the staff to agree to move to Scotland is a real problem*
(c) which exists; *have you ever seen a real live tiger?*; *there's a real danger that the shop will be closed*; **real life** = everyday existence, as opposed to life in a film or novel, etc.; *he dreams of being a pilot, but in real life he's an insurance salesman*; *winning the lottery is the sort of thing you read about in the newspapers, but it never happens to you in real life*; **real world** = the world as it actually exists, with all its faults, not the world of novels or TV; *it's back to the real world now after our holiday*
(d) **real estate** = land or buildings which are bought or sold; *he made his money from real estate deals in the 1990s*; US **real estate agent** = person who sells property for customers (NOTE: British English is simply **estate agent**)

③ **realistic**
[rɪ'lɪstɪk] *adjective*
(a) which looks as if it is real; *these flowers look so realistic, I can't believe they're made of plastic*
(b) accepting life as it really is; *let's be realistic - you'll never earn enough money to buy this house*; *I'm just being realistic when I say that you should think again about the offer*

② **reality**
[rɪ'ælɪti] *noun*
what is real and not imaginary; *the grim realities of life in an industrial town*; *he worked hard, and his dreams of wealth soon became a reality*

① **realize**
['rɪːlaɪz] *verb*
(a) to get to a point where you understand clearly; *she didn't realize what she was letting herself in for when she said she would look after the children*; *we soon realized we were on the wrong road*; *when she went into the manager's office she did not realize she was going to be sacked*
(b) to get money by selling something; *the sale of his stamp collection realized £100,000*
(c) to make something become real; *after four years of hard work, the motor racing team realized their dream of winning the Grand*

Prix; *by buying a house by the sea he realized his greatest ambition*; **to realize a project** *or* **a plan** = to make a project *or* a plan happen; *the plan took five years to realize*

① **really**
['rɪəli] *adverb*
(a) in fact; *she's not really French, is she?*; *the building really belongs to my father*
(b) *(used to show surprise)* *it's really time you had your hair cut*; *she doesn't like apples - really, how strange!*; *did you really mean what you said?*; *asking all the staff to move house is a really tall order*

④ **rear**
['rɪə]
1 *noun*
part at the back; *the rear of the car was damaged in the accident*; *they sat towards the rear of the bus*; **to bring up the rear** = to walk behind the others; *the military band brought up the rear of the parade*
2 *adjective*
at the back; *the children sat in the rear seats in the car*; *he wound down the rear window*; **rear-view mirror** = mirror in the centre of the front of a car, so that the driver can see what is behind him without turning round; *he checked in his rear-view mirror before turning into the side road*
3 *verb*
(a) to breed animals; *they rear horses on their farm*; *they stopped rearing pigs because of the smell*
(b) to rise up, to lift up; *an elephant suddenly reared up out of the long grass*; *the walls of the castle reared up before them*
(c) *(of horse, etc.)* to rise on its back legs; *the terrified horse reared (up) and threw its rider*

① **reason**
['riːsn]
1 *noun*
(a) thing which explains why something has happened; *the airline gave no reason for the plane's late arrival*; *the boss asked him for the reason why he was late with his work*; **for some reason** = in a way which you cannot explain; *for some reason (or other) the builders sent us two invoices*
(b) the power of thought; *use reason to solve a problem in mathematics*
(c) ability to make sensible judgements; *she wouldn't listen to reason*; **it stands to reason** = it makes sense; *it stands to reason that he wants to join his father's firm*; **to see reason** = to see the wisdom of someone's argument; *she was going to report her neighbours to the police, but in the end we got her to see reason*; **within reason** = to a sensible degree, in a sensible way; *the children get £5 pocket money each week, and we let them spend it as they like, within reason*
2 *verb*

(a) to think or to plan carefully and in a logical way; *he reasoned that any work is better than no work, so he took the job*; *if you take the time to reason it out, you'll find a solution to the problem*
(b) **to reason with someone** = to try to calm someone, to try to make someone change his mind; *the policewoman tried to reason with the man who was holding a knife*

① **reasonable**
['riːznəbl] *adjective*
(a) not expensive; *the hotel's charges are quite reasonable*; *the restaurant offers good food at reasonable prices*
(b) sensible, showing sense; *the manager of the shop was very reasonable when she tried to explain that she had left her credit cards at home*

② **reasonably**
['riːznəbli] *adverb*
in a reasonable way; *the meals are very reasonably priced*; *very reasonably, he asked to have the brakes of the car checked before buying it*

④ **reassure**
[riːə'ʃɔː] *verb*
to make someone less afraid or less worried; *he tried to reassure everyone that the bus service would not be cut*; *the manager wanted to reassure her that she would not lose her job*

④ **rebel**
1 *noun*
['rebl] person who fights against a government or against those who are in authority; *the rebels fled to the mountains after the army captured their headquarters*; *he considers himself something of a rebel because he wears his hair long*
2 *verb*
[rɪ'bel] to fight against someone *or* something; *the peasants are rebelling against the king's men*; *the class rebelled at the idea of doing extra homework* (NOTE: **rebelling - rebelled**)

④ **rebellion**
[rɪ'beljən] *noun*
revolt, fight against the government; *the rebellion began when some people refused to pay taxes*; *government troops crushed the student rebellion*

④ **rebuild**
[riː'bɪld] *verb*
to build again; *the original house was knocked down and rebuilt*; *how long will it take to rebuild the wall?*; *rebuilding the house took longer than we expected* (NOTE: **rebuilding - rebuilt** [riː'bɪlt])

② **recall**
[rɪ'kɔːl]
1 *verb*
(a) to remember; *I don't recall having met her before*; *she couldn't recall any details of the accident*

(b) *(of a manufacturer)* to ask for products to be returned because of possible faults; *they recalled 10,000 washing machines because of a faulty electrical connection*; *they have recalled all their 1999 models as there is a fault in the steering*

(c) to tell an ambassador to come home from a foreign country; *the United States recalled their ambassador after the military coup*

(d) to ask Parliament to meet during a vacation period; *in the light of the current crisis, the Prime Minister has asked for Parliament to be recalled or has recalled Parliament*

2 *noun*

calling to come back or to be brought back; *the recall of the washing machine because of an electrical fault caused the manufacturers some serious problems*; *the recall of the ambassador is expected anytime now*; **recall of Parliament** = bringing MPs back to Parliament when they are on holiday, to discuss an important matter; **beyond recall** = gone and will never come back; *those days beyond recall when we were young!*

② **receipt**
['rɪ'siːt] *noun*

(a) act of receiving; **to acknowledge receipt of a letter** = to write to say that you have received a letter; *we acknowledge receipt of your letter of the 15th*; *we would like you to confirm receipt of the goods*; *invoices are payable within 30 days of receipt*; **on receipt of** = when you receive; *on receipt of the notification, they decided to appeal*

(b) paper showing that you have paid, that you have received something; *goods cannot be exchanged unless a sales receipt is shown*; *would you like a receipt for that shirt?*

(c) **receipts** = money taken in sales; *our receipts are down against the same period last year*

① **receive**
[rɪ'siːv] *verb*

(a) to get something which has been sent; *we received a parcel from the supplier this morning*; *we only received our tickets the day before we were due to leave*; *the staff have not received any wages for six months*; **'received with thanks'** = words put on an invoice to show that a sum has been paid; *(informal)* **to be on the receiving end of** = to have to suffer; *he was on the receiving end of a lot of criticism*

(b) to greet or to welcome a visitor; *the group was received by the minister*

① **recent**
['riːsɪnt] *adjective*

new, which took place not very long ago; *we will mail you our most recent catalogue*; *the building is very recent - it was finished only last year*

① **recently**
['riːsɪntlɪ] *adverb*

only a short time ago; *I've seen him quite a lot recently*; *they recently decided to move to Australia*

③ **reception**
[rɪ'sepʃn] *noun*

(a) welcome; *the committee gave the proposal a favourable reception*; *the critics gave the play a warm reception*; *the minister had a rowdy reception at the meeting*

(b) *(at a hotel)* place where guests register; *let's meet at reception at 9.00 am tomorrow*; **reception clerk** = person who works at the reception desk; **reception desk** = desk where visitors check in; *please leave your key at the reception desk when you go out*

(c) *(at an office)* place where visitors register and say who they have come to see; *there's a parcel waiting for you in reception*

(d) big party held to welcome special guests; *he hosted a reception for the prince*; **wedding reception** = party held after a wedding, including the wedding breakfast, drinks, toasts, etc.; *only the members of the two families will be at the church, but we've been invited to the reception afterwards*; *will you be attending Anne and John's wedding reception?*

(e) quality of the sound on a radio or the sound and picture on a TV broadcast; *perhaps you'd get better reception if you moved the TV to another room*

② **recession**
[rɪ'seʃn] *noun*

situation when a country's economy is doing badly; *many businesses failed during the recession*

COMMENT: the general way of deciding if a recession is taking place is when the country's GNP falls for three quarters running

③ **recipe**
['resɪpi] *noun*

(a) instructions for cooking food; *I copied the recipe for onion soup from the newspaper*; *you can buy postcards with recipes of local dishes*; **recipe book** = book of recipes; *I gave her an Indian recipe book for her birthday*; *if you're not sure how long to cook turkey, look it up in the recipe book*

(b) effective way to do something; *there is no single recipe for success*; **it's a recipe for disaster** = it's certain to lead to disaster; *the way the management is approaching the problem is a recipe for disaster*

② **reckon**
['rekn] *verb*

(a) to calculate, to estimate; *we reckon the costs to be about £25,000*

(b) to think; *we reckon we'll be there before lunch*

(c) to reckon on = to count on or to depend on; *we can reckon on the support of the Prime Minister; don't reckon on good weather for your holidays*

(d) to reckon with = to have to deal with; *he didn't realize that he still had to reckon with the bank manager; leave early, don't forget you'll have to reckon with the rush hour traffic*

② **recognition**
[rekɪg'nɪʃn] *noun*
recognizing or acknowledging; *in recognition for his services he was given a watch; he's changed beyond all recognition* = he has changed so much that I didn't recognize him

① **recognize**
['rekɪgnaɪz] *verb*
(a) to know someone or something because you have seen him or it before; *he'd changed so much since I last saw him that I hardly recognized him; he didn't recognize his father's voice over the phone; do you recognize the handwriting on the letter?*
(b) to recognize a mistake *or* that you have made a mistake = to admit that you have made a mistake; *she should have recognized her mistake and said she was sorry; I recognize that we should have acted earlier*
(c) to approve of something or someone officially; *the language school has been recognized by the Ministry of Education; she is recognized as an expert in the field of genetics; to recognize a government* = to say that a new government which has taken power in a country is the legal government of that country; *Germany was one of the first countries to recognize Croatia as a new independent country*

③ **recognized**
['rekɪgnaɪzd] *adjective*
which has been approved officially; *he has a certificate from a recognized language school; she's a recognized expert on kidney disease*

② **recommend**
[rekɪ'mend] *verb*
(a) to suggest that someone should do something; *I would recommend you to talk to the bank manager; the doctor recommended seeing an eye specialist*
(b) to praise something *or* someone; *she was highly recommended by her boss; I certainly would not recommend Miss Smith for the job; can you recommend a good hotel in Amsterdam?*

③ **recommendation**
[rekɪmen'deɪʃn] *noun*
(a) advice; *my recommendation is that you shouldn't sign the contract; he's staying in bed at the doctor's recommendation*
(b) praise; *we appointed her on the recommendation of her boss*

① **record**
1 *noun*
['rekɔːd]
(a) success in sport which is better than any other; *she holds the world record for the 100 metres; he broke the world record or he set up a new world record at the last Olympics; the college team is trying to set a new record for eating pizzas;* **at record speed** *or* **in record time** = very fast; *he finished the book in record time*
(b) success which is better than anything before; **record sales** = sales which are higher than ever before; *we're looking forward to record sales this month; last year was a record year for our shop; sales for 1999 equalled our previous record of 1996;* **we broke our record for June** = we sold more than we have ever sold before in June
(c) written evidence of something which has happened; *we have no record of the sale;* **for the record** *or* **to keep the record straight** = so as to note something which has been done; *for the record, we will not deal with this company again;* **he is on record as saying** = he is accurately reported as saying; **off the record** = in private, not to be made public; *she spoke off the record about her marriage*
(d) description of what someone has done in the past; *he has a record of dishonest business deals;* **track record** = success or failure of someone or a business in the past; *he has a good track record as a salesman*
(e) flat, round piece of black plastic on which sound is stored; *she bought me an old Elvis Presley record for Christmas; burglars broke into his flat and stole his record collection*
2 *verb*
[rɪ'kɔːd]
(a) to report; to make a note; *first, I have to record the sales, then I'll post the parcels;* **recorded delivery** = postal service where the person receiving the parcel, letter, etc., must sign a receipt to show that it has been delivered; *it is safer to send the parcel by recorded delivery*
(b) to fix sounds on a film or tape; *the police recorded the whole conversation through a hidden microphone; this song has been badly recorded*

④ **recorder**
[rɪ'kɔːdɪ] *noun*
(a) instrument which records sound; *my tape recorder doesn't work, so I can't record the concert*
(b) small wooden musical instrument which you play by blowing; *like most children, I learnt to play the recorder at school*

③ **recording**
[rɪ'kɔːdɪŋ] *noun*
(a) action of fixing sounds on tape or on disc; *be on time - the recording session starts at 3pm*

(b) music or speech which has been recorded; *did you know there was a new recording of the piece?*

② **recover**
[rɪˈkʌvɪ] *verb*
(a) to recover from an illness = to get well again after an illness; *she is still recovering from flu*
(b) to recover from a shock = to get over a shock; *it took him weeks to recover from the shock of seeing his son in court*
(c) to get back something which has been lost, stolen, invested, etc.; *she's trying to recover damages from the driver of the car; you must work much harder if you want to recover the money you invested in your business*
(d) [riːˈkʌvɪ] to put a new cover on a piece of furniture; *instead of buying a new chair, I had the old one recovered*

③ **recovery**
[rɪˈkʌvrɪ] *noun*
(a) getting well again; *she made a quick recovery and is now back at work*
(b) getting back something which has been lost, stolen, invested, etc.; *the TV programme led to the recovery of all the stolen goods; we are aiming for the complete recovery of the money invested*
(c) recovery vehicle = truck that goes to find vehicles which have broken down and brings them back to the garage for repair
(d) upwards movement of the economy, of a company's shares; *the British economy staged a rapid recovery*

④ **recreation**
[rekrɪˈeɪʃn] *noun*
pleasant activity for your spare time; *what is your favourite recreation?; doesn't he have any recreations other than sitting watching TV?;* **recreation ground** = public area with playgrounds for children and sports fields for adults

④ **recruit**
[rɪˈkruːt]
1 *noun*
new soldier, new member of staff, etc.; *recruits are not allowed in the officers' mess; the club needs new recruits*
2 *verb*
to encourage someone to join the army, a company, etc.; *they have sent teams to universities to recruit new graduates;* **to recruit new staff** = to get new staff to join a company; *we are recruiting staff for our new store*

④ **recycle**
[riːˈsaɪkl] *verb*
to process waste material so that it can be used again; *glass and newspapers are the main items for recycling; the council is encouraging us to recycle more household rubbish;* **recycled paper** = paper made from waste paper; *she always writes to me on recycled paper*

① **red**
[red]
1 *adjective*
(a) coloured like the colour of blood; *she turned bright red when we asked her what had happened to the money; don't start yet - the traffic lights are still red*
(b) red hair = hair which is a red or orange colour; *all their children have red hair; red-haired girls often wear green clothes*
(NOTE: **redder - reddest**)
2 *noun*
(a) colour, like the colour of blood; *I would like a darker red for the door; don't start yet - the traffic lights are still on red*
(b) in the red = showing a loss; *my bank account is in the red; the company went into the red*
(c) a red ball in billiards or snooker; *he's potted a red*
(d) *(informal)* red wine; *a glass of the house red, please*

③ **red carpet**
[ˈred ˈkɑːpɪt] *noun*
carpet put down when an important visitor comes, hence an official welcome; *they rolled out the red carpet for the president's visit; he got the red-carpet treatment*

② **Red Cross**
[ˈred ˈkrɒs] *noun*
international organization which provides emergency medical help, and also relief to victims of floods, etc.; *Red Cross officials have been sent to the refugee camps; we met a representative of the Red Cross*

③ **red hot**
[redˈhɒt] *adjective*
(a) *(of metal)* so hot that it is red; *the bar of steel is red hot when it comes out of the mill*
(b) *(informal)* very hot; *watch out - that pan is red hot!*

③ **red tape**
[ˈred ˈteɪp] *noun*
official forms which take a long time to complete; *the project has been held up by government red tape*

① **reduce**
[rɪˈdjuːs] *verb*
to make smaller or less; *the police are fighting to reduce traffic accidents; prices have been reduced by 15%; I'd like to reduce the size of the photograph so that we can use it as a Christmas card;* **reduced prices** = lower prices; *there are reduced prices for groups of 30 and over;* **to reduce staff** = to sack employees in order to have a smaller number of staff; *unfortunately, the best way to save money is to reduce staff;* **to reduce (weight)** = to get thinner; *she started a new diet in order to reduce weight*

② reduction

[rɪ'dʌkʃn] *noun*

making smaller (price, speed, standards, etc.); *price reductions start on 1st August*; *the company was forced to make job reductions*

② redundancy

[rɪ'dʌndənsi] *noun*

being no longer employed, because the job is no longer needed; *there were fifty redundancies this month alone*; redundancy payment = payment made to a worker to compensate for losing his job; *he received £10,000 redundancy payment when he left his job*; voluntary redundancy = situation where the worker asks to be made redundant, usually in return for a large payment; *so many nurses have taken voluntary redundancy that now the hospitals are short of staff*

② redundant

[rɪ'dʌndɪnt] *adjective*

no longer needed, more than necessary; *two of the offices are redundant - we should let them*; *redundant workers are being offered a good benefits package*; to be made redundant = to lose your job because you are not needed any more; *five employees were made redundant this week*; *my son thinks he'll be made redundant, so he's already looking for another job*

④ reel

[ri:l]

1 *noun*

(a) round object used for winding thread, wire or film round; *she put a new reel of cotton on the sewing machine*

(b) wild Scottish dance; *after the wedding breakfast, some of the guests started to dance reels*

2 *verb*

to stagger; *two men came out of the pub and went reeling down the street*; *the punch on the face sent the boxer reeling*; *the company is still reeling from its losses in the Far East*

④ reelect

[ri:'lekt] *verb*

to elect again; *she was reelected with a large majority*

④ reelection

[ri:ɪ'lekʃn] *noun*

being reelected; *her reelection was unexpected*; *the previous president is eligible for reelection*

③ reel off

['ri:l 'ɒf] *verb*

to give a list of names or figures rapidly; *he reeled off a list of hotels and their prices*; *she reeled off a series of dates and invoice numbers*

② ref

[ref] *noun*

(informal)

(a) *(in sports)* = REFEREE; *come on ref - that was foul!*

(b) = REFERENCE; your ref: = way of referring to the number of the letter which you have received, when replying to it; our ref: = giving a reference number to a letter you are writing

① refer to

[rɪ'fɜ: tʊ] *verb*

(a) to mention something; *do you think he was referring to me when he talked about clever managers?*; *the note refers you to page 24*

(b) to look into something for information; *he referred to his diary to see if he had a free afternoon*

(c) to pass a problem to someone to decide; *we have referred your complaint to our head office*; *he was referred to an ear specialist by his GP*; *see your GP first, and he or she will refer you to a specialist* (NOTE: referring - referred)

② referee

[refɪ'ri:]

1 *noun*

(a) *(in sports)* person who supervises a game, making sure that it is played according to the rules; *when fighting broke out between the players, the referee stopped the match*; *the referee sent several players off* (NOTE: referees are in charge of most sports, such as football, rugby or boxing, but not for tennis and cricket, where the person in charge is an **umpire**)

(b) person who gives a report on your character, ability, etc.; *she gave the name of her former boss as a referee*; *when applying please give the names of three referees*

2 *verb*

to act as a referee in a sports match; *there's no one to referee the match this afternoon*

① reference

['refrɪns] *noun*

(a) reference to something = mention of something; *she made a reference to her brother-in-law*; *the report made no reference to the bank*; with reference to = concerning, about; *with reference to your letter of May 25th*

(b) direction for further information; *there are references to various documents at the back of the book*; reference book = book, such as a dictionary or directory, where you can look for information; *we sell far more novels than reference books*; reference library = library with reference books, where readers can search for information but not take the books away from the library

(c) report on someone's character, ability, etc.; *we ask all applicants to supply references*; to take up references = to get in touch with referees to see what they think of the person applying for a job; *when she applied for the job we took up her references and found they were not as good as we had expected*

(d) person who gives a report on your character; *he gave my name as a reference; please use me as a reference if you wish*

(e) terms of reference = areas which a committee has to examine or discuss; *the terms of reference of the committee do not extend to EU policy; under the committee's terms of reference, it cannot investigate complaints from the public*

④ **referendum**
[refɪˈrendɪm] *noun*
vote where all the people of a country are asked to vote on a single question; *they will hold a referendum on the issue of joining the European Union* (NOTE: plural is **referenda** or **referendums**)

① **reflect**
[rɪˈflekt] *verb*
(a) to send back light, heat, an image, etc.; *the light reflected on the top of the car; white surfaces reflect light better than dark ones; a photograph of white mountains reflected in a clear blue lake*

(b) to reflect (on something) = to think carefully about something; *he reflected that this was the sixth time he had been arrested for speeding; when you reflect on the events of the past few days, you realize the truth of the saying that 'pride goes before a fall'*; **to reflect badly on someone** = to show someone in a bad way; *the story reflects badly on the way the manager runs his department*

③ **reflection** *or* **reflexion**
[rɪˈflekʃn] *noun*
(a) sending back of light or heat; *you should wear dark glasses because of the reflection of the sun on the snow*

(b) reflected image in a mirror, in water, etc.; *she saw her reflection in the mirror and smiled*

(c) thought; *a few moments' reflection convinced her that she had done the right thing*; **on reflection** = on thinking more; *on reflection, I think I'd better leave today rather than tomorrow*

(d) to be a reflection on someone = to show someone in a bad way; *it's no reflection on you if your father is in prison*

② **reform**
[rɪˈfɔːm]
1 *noun*
act of changing something to make it better; *the government is planning a series of reforms to the benefit system*

2 *verb*
(a) to change to make better, to improve; *they want to reform the educational system*

(b) to stop committing crimes, to change your habits to become good; *after his time in prison he became a reformed character; he used to drink a lot, but since he got married he has reformed*

④ **refreshing**
[rɪˈfreʃɪŋ] *adjective*
(a) which makes you clean and fresh again; *I had a refreshing drink of cold water; a refreshing shower of rain cooled the air*

(b) exciting and new; *our new offices are a refreshing change from the old building*

④ **refreshments**
[rɪˈfreʃmɪnts] *noun*
food and drink; *light refreshments will be served after the meeting; refreshments are being offered in a tent on the lawn*

③ **refrigerator**
[rɪˈfrɪdʒɪreɪtɪ] *noun*
electric kitchen cabinet for keeping food and drink cold; *there's some cold orange juice in the refrigerator; milk will keep for several days in a refrigerator; each hotel bedroom has a small refrigerator with cold drinks* (NOTE: often called a **fridge**)

③ **refuge**
[ˈrefjuːdʒ] *noun*
place of refuge = place to shelter; **to seek refuge** = to try to find shelter; *during the fighting, they sought refuge in the British embassy*; **to take refuge** = to shelter; *when the hurricane approached, they took refuge in the cellar*

③ **refugee**
[refjuːˈdʒiː] *noun*
person who has left his country because of war, religious differences, etc.; *at the beginning of the war, thousands of refugees fled over the border*; **economic refugee** = person who has left his country because the economic situation is bad, and it is difficult to find work; **political refugee** = person who has left his country because he is afraid of being put in prison for his political beliefs; *these political refugees are afraid that they will be jailed if they go back to their country*

③ **refund**
1 *noun*
[ˈriːfʌnd] money paid back; *she got a refund after she complained to the manager*; **full refund** *or* **refund in full** = paying back all the money paid; *he got a full refund when he complained about the service*

2 *verb*
[riːˈfʌnd] to pay money back; *we will refund the cost of postage; the tour company only refunded £100 of the £400 I had paid*

④ **refusal**
[rɪˈfjuːzl] *noun*
(a) saying that you do not accept something, saying no; *did you accept? - no! I sent a letter of refusal*; **to meet with a flat refusal** = to be refused completely; *his request met with a flat refusal*

(b) to give someone first refusal of something
= to let someone have first choice when doing
something; *I asked him if I could have first
refusal of his flat if ever he decided to sell it*

① **refuse**
1 *noun*
['refju:s]
rubbish, things which are not wanted; *please put
all refuse in the bin*; *refuse collection on our
road is on Thursdays* (NOTE: no plural)
2 *verb*
[rɪ'fju:z]
(a) to say that you will not do something; *his
father refused to lend him any more money*; *he
asked for permission to see his family, but it
was refused*
(b) the car refused to start = the car would not
start; *once again this morning the car refused
to start* (NOTE: you refuse **to do something** or
refuse **something**)

④ **regain**
[rɪ'geɪn] *verb*
to get something back which was lost; *she soon
regained her strength and was able to walk*;
*what can I do to regain any of the money I've
lost?*; **to regain consciousness** = to become
conscious again; *she never regained
consciousness after the accident*

① **regard**
[rɪ'gɑːd]
1 *noun*
(a) concern for something; **with regard to** =
relating to, concerning; *with regard to your
request for extra funds*
(b) opinion of someone; *he is held in high
regard by his staff*
(c) regards = best wishes; *she sends her (kind)
regards*; *please give my regards to your mother*
2 *verb*
(a) to regard someone *or* **something as** = to
consider someone *or* something to be; *the police
are regarding the case as attempted murder*
(b) to have an opinion about someone; *she is
highly regarded by the manager*
(c) as regards = relating to, concerning; *as
regards the cost of the trip, I'll let you know
soon what the final figure is*

③ **regarding**
[rɪ'gɑːdɪŋ] *preposition*
relating to, concerning; *he left instructions
regarding his possessions*; *regarding your
offer, I think we will have to say no*

③ **regardless**
[rɪ'gɑːdlɪs] *adverb*
without paying any attention to; **regardless of** =
in spite of; *they drove through the war zone
regardless of the danger*; *they furnished their
house regardless of expense* = without thinking
of how much it would cost; **to carry on
regardless** = to continue in spite of everything;
*although the temperature was well over 40°,
they carried on working regardless*

② **regime** *or* **régime**
[reɪ'ʒiːm] *noun*
(a) usually strict type of government or
administration; *under a military régime, civil
liberties may be restricted*
(b) government of a country; *the former régime
was overthrown and the President fled*

④ **regiment**
['redʒɪmənt] *noun*
group of soldiers, usually commanded by a
colonel; *an infantry regiment was sent to the
war zone*

① **region**
['riːdʒɪn] *noun*
(a) large administrative area; *the South-West
region is well known for its apples*; **the London
region** = the area around London
(b) in the region of = about or approximately;
he is earning a salary in the region of £25,000;
*the house was sold for a price in the region of
£200,000*

① **regional**
['riːdʒɪnl] *adjective*
referring to a region; *the recession has not
affected the whole country - it is only regional*;
*after the national news, here is the regional
news for the South West*

③ **register**
['redʒɪstɪ]
1 *noun*
(a) list of names; *I can't find your name in the
register*; *his name was struck off the register*;
the register of electors = list of the names of
people who can vote in an election
(b) book in which you sign your name; *after the
wedding, the bride and bridegroom and
witnesses all signed the register*; *please sign the
hotel register when you check in*
(c) cash register = machine which shows and
adds the prices of items bought in a shop, with a
drawer for keeping the money received; *she
opened the cash register to put in the money
given by the customer*
2 *verb*
(a) to write a name officially in a list; *if you
don't register, we won't be able to get in touch
with you*; *babies have to be registered as soon
as they are born*; **to register at a hotel** = to
write your name and address when you arrive at
the hotel; *they registered at the hotel under the
name of Macdonald*
(b) to put a letter into the special care of the post
office; *she registered the letter, but it still got
lost*
(c) to record, to show a feeling, a figure;
*temperatures of over 50° were registered in the
desert*; *the amount of pollution was so small it
didn't register on our monitor*; *his face
registered anger and pain*
(d) *(informal)* to notice, to pay attention; *I told
him he was getting a big pay rise, but it didn't
seem to register*

③ **registered**
['redʒɪstɪd] *adjective*

(a) which has been noted on an official list; *a registered trademark*

(b) registered post *or* **registered mail** = system where details of a letter or parcel are noted by the post office before it is sent, so that compensation can be claimed if it is lost; *to send documents by registered mail or registered post*; **registered letter** = letter which has been officially recorded at the post office; *the registered letter which arrived this morning was not important*

③ **registrar**
['redʒɪstrɑ:] *noun*

person who keeps official records; *all births have to be registered with the registrar of births, marriages and deaths*; *they were married by the registrar*

③ **registration**
[redʒɪ'streɪʃn] *noun*

act of registering; *registration of new students will start at 1pm*; **registration number** = official number of a car; *we are trying to buy him a car registration number which forms his initials*

③ **registry**
['redʒɪstri] *noun*

place where official records are kept; **registry office** = office where records of births, marriages and deaths are kept and where you can be married in a civil ceremony; *they didn't want a church wedding so they got married in the registry office*; *to get a copy of your birth certificate you have to apply to the registry office*; **a registry wedding** = wedding held in a registry office or other place, but not a church, which is performed by a registrar

④ **regret**
[rɪ'gret]

1 *noun*

being sorry; *I have absolutely no regrets about what we did*; *she showed no regret for having made so much mess*; **much to someone's regret** = making someone very sorry; *much to my regret I will not be able to go to Chicago*; *much to the children's regret* or *much to the regret of the children, the ice cream van drove away*

2 *verb*

to be sorry that something has happened; *I regret to say that you were not successful*; *I regret the trouble this has caused you*; *we regret the delay in the arrival of our flight from Amsterdam*; *we regret to inform you that the tour has been cancelled* (NOTE: **regretting - regretted**)

② **regular**
['regju:lɪ]

1 *adjective*

(a) done at the same time each day; *his regular train is the 12.45*; *the regular flight to Athens leaves at 06.00*; **regular customer** = customer who always buys from the same shop; *he's a regular customer, you don't need to ask for proof of identity*; **regular income** = income which comes in every week or month; *it is difficult to budget if you don't have a regular income*

(b) ordinary, standard; *the regular price is $1.25, but we are offering them at 99c*; **regular size** = ordinary size of goods (smaller than economy size, family size, etc.); *just buy a regular size packet, it will be enough for the two of us*

2 *noun*

(informal) customer who always goes to the same shop, who drinks in the same pub, etc.; *the regulars were very sorry when the old landlord retired*

③ **regularly**
['regju:lɪli] *adverb*

in a regular way; *she is regularly the first person to arrive at the office each morning*

④ **regulate**
['regjuleɪt] *verb*

(a) to adjust a machine so that it works in a certain way; *the heater needs to be regulated to keep the temperature steady*; *turn this button regulate the volume*; *her heart is regulated by a tiny device in her chest*

(b) to maintain something by law; *speed on the motorway is strictly regulated*

② **regulation**
[regju'leɪʃn] *noun*

(a) act of regulating; *the greenhouse is fitted with an automatic heat regulation system*; *the regulation of the body's temperature by sweating*

(b) regulations = laws, rules; *the restaurant broke the fire regulations*; *safety regulations were not being properly followed*; *the new government regulations on housing standards*

④ **regulator**
['regjuleɪtɪ] *noun*

(a) person whose job it is to see that regulations are followed in an industry; *the industry regulator makes sure that the rules are followed to the letter*

(b) instrument which regulates a machine; *this lorry is fitted with a speed regulator*

④ **rehearsal**
[rɪ'hɜ:sɪl] *noun*

practice of a play or concert, etc., before the first public performance; *the director insisted on extra rehearsals because some of the cast didn't know their lines*; *see also* DRESS REHEARSAL

④ **rehearse**
[rɪ'hɜːs] *verb*
to practise a play, a concert, etc., before a public performance; *we're rehearsing the concert in the village hall*

④ **reign**
[reɪn]
1 *noun*
(a) period when a king or queen rules; *during the reign of Elizabeth I*
(b) **reign of terror** = period when law and order have broken down and people live in a continual state of fear
2
(a) *verb*
to rule; *Queen Victoria reigned between 1837 and 1901; she reigned during a period of great economic development*
(b) to be in existence; *chaos reigned when the town's electricity supply broke down* (NOTE: do not confuse with **rain, rein**)

④ **rein**
[reɪn]
1 *noun*
(a) leather strap which the rider holds to control a horse; *she walked beside the horse holding the reins; the rider pulled hard on the reins to try to make the horse stop*
(b) **to keep something on a tight rein** = to control something strictly; *unless you keep your expenses on a tight rein, you'll have problems*
2 *verb*
to rein back or **rein in** = to keep under control; *the leader of the opposition tried to rein in his supporters who wanted to attack the President's palace* (NOTE: do not confuse with **rain, reign**)

③ **reinforce**
[riːɪn'fɔːs] *verb*
to make stronger or more solid; *you must reinforce that wall before it collapses; this event has reinforced my decision to leave*; **reinforced concrete** = concrete strengthened with metal rods; *the new bridge was built with reinforced concrete*

② **reject**
1 *noun*
['riːdʒekt]
thing which has been thrown away as not satisfactory; **rejects** = goods which are not up to standard and are sold at a reduced price; **reject shop** = shop which specializes in the sale of rejects; *I bought these plates in the reject shop - they were seconds and very cheap*
2 *verb*
[rɪ'dʒekt]
(a) to refuse to accept something; *she flatly rejected his proposal; we rejected his offer for the house because it was too low; she rejected three different wallpaper designs because they were too bright*
(b) to throw something away as not satisfactory; *half the batch was rejected and sold off cheaply as seconds*
(c) *(medical)* not to accept a transplanted organ; *his body rejected the new heart*

① **relate**
[rɪ'leɪt] *verb*
(a) to be concerned with; *the regulations which relate to landing passengers at the harbour*
(b) **to relate to someone** = to understand someone and be able to communicate with them; *do you find it difficult to relate to him?*
(c) to tell a story; *it took him half an hour to relate what had happened*

① **related (to)**
[rɪ'leɪtɪd tʊ] *adjective*
(a) belonging to the same family; *are you related to the Smith family in London Road?*
(b) linked; *a disease which is related to the weakness of the heart muscle; he has a drug-related illness; there are several related items on the agenda*

③ **relating to**
[rɪ'leɪtɪŋ tʊ] *adverb*
referring to, connected with; *documents relating to the sale*

① **relation**
[rɪ'leɪʃn] *noun*
(a) member of a family; *all my relations live in Canada; Laura's no relation of mine, she's just a friend*
(b) link between two things; *is there any relation between his appointment as MD and the fact that his uncle owns the business?*; **in relation to** = referring to, connected with; *documents in relation to the sale*
(c) **relations** = links (with other people); *we try to maintain good relations with our customers; relations between the two countries have become tense; see also* PUBLIC RELATIONS

① **relationship**
[rɪ'leɪʃnʃɪp] *noun*
(a) link or connection; *there is a relationship between smoking and lung cancer; we try to have a good working relationship with our staff*; **love-hate relationship** = situation where two people get on well together and then dislike each other in turn
(b) close (sexual) friendship; *she decided to end the relationship when she found he had been seeing other women*

② **relative**
['relɪtɪv]
1 *noun*
person who is related to someone; member of a family; *we have several relatives living in Canada; he has no living relatives*
2 *adjective*
(a) compared to something else; *everything is relative - if you have ten cows you are rich in some African countries*; **their relative poverty**

= their poverty compared with really wealthy people or with the wealth they used to have; *my old uncle lives in relative poverty*

(b) *(in grammar)* relative pronoun = pronoun, such as 'who' or 'which', which connects two clauses

② **relatively**
['relɪtɪvli] *adverb*
more or less; *the children have been relatively free from colds this winter*; *we are dealing with a relatively new company*

③ **relax**
[rɪ'læks] *verb*
(a) to rest from work; to be less tense; *they spent the first week of their holiday relaxing on the beach*; *guests can relax in the bar before going to eat in the restaurant*; *just lie back and relax - the injection won't hurt*
(b) to make less strict; *the club has voted to relax the rules about the admission of women members*

④ **relaxation**
[ri:læk'seɪʃn] *noun*
rest from work; *do you consider gardening a form of relaxation?*; *he plays tennis for relaxation or as a relaxation*

③ **relaxed**
[rɪ'lækst] *adjective*
(informal) calm, not upset; *even if he failed his test, he's still very relaxed about the whole thing*

③ **relaxing**
[rɪ'læksɪŋ] *adjective*
which makes you less tense; *I always enjoy a relaxing hot bath after a game of rugby*; *if you feel stressed, just close your eyes and listen to relaxing music*

④ **relay**
1 *noun*
['ri:leɪ]
(a) group of people working in turn with other groups; *a shift is usually composed of groups of workers who work in relays*; *all the work had been done by the time the next relay arrived*
(b) relay race = running race by teams in which one runner passes a stick to another who then runs on; *they won the 400m relay*
2 *verb*
[rɪ'leɪ]
(a) to pass on a message; *she relayed the news to the other members of her family*; *all messages are relayed through this office*
(b) to pass on a TV or radio broadcast through a secondary station; *the programmes are received in the capital and then relayed to TV stations round the country*

② **release**
[rɪ'li:s]
1 *noun*
(a) setting free; *the release of prisoners from jail*; *the release of hormones into the blood*; day release = arrangement where a company

allows a worker to go to college to study for one day each week; *she is attending a day release course*
(b) press release = sheet giving news about something which is sent to newspapers and TV and radio stations so that they can use the information in it; *we issued a press release about the opening of the new shop*
(c) new releases = new records or CDs which are put on the market
(d) setting free from pain; *his death was a release*
2 *verb*
(a) to set free; *six prisoners were released from prison*; *the customs released the goods after we paid a fine*; *we nursed the injured rabbit for a week and then released it in the field*; *the glands release hormones into the blood*
(b) to make public; *the government has released figures about the number of people out of work*

② **relevant**
['relɪvɪnt] *adjective*
which has to do with something being mentioned; *which is the relevant government department?*; *he gave me all the relevant papers*; *is this information at all relevant?*

④ **reliable**
[rɪ'laɪbl] *adjective*
which can be relied on, which can be trusted; *it is a very reliable car*; *the sales manager is completely reliable*

② **relief**
[rɪ'li:f] *noun*
(a) reducing pain or stress; *an aspirin should bring relief*; *he breathed a sigh of relief when the police car went past without stopping*; *what a relief to have finished my exams!*
(b) help; *international aid agencies are trying to bring relief to the starving population*; relief road = road built to help reduce traffic; *if the relief road is not built, the traffic will make life in the village impossible*
(c) person who takes over from another; *a relief nurse will take over from you at one o'clock*; *your relief will be here in half an hour*; relief shift = shift which comes to take the place of another shift; *the relief shift is due in ten minutes*
(d) carving in which the details of design stand out; in relief = standing out, prominent; relief map = map where height is shown by colour, so mountains are brown and plains are green

③ **relieve**
[rɪ'li:v] *verb*
(a) to make better, easier; *he took aspirins to relieve the pain*
(b) *(formal)* to relieve oneself = to pass waste matter out of the body; *he stopped by the side of the road to relieve himself*; *people complained about drunken football fans relieving themselves in the street*

(c) to help; *an agency which tries to relieve stress after divorce*
(d) to take over from someone; *you can go and have something to eat - I'm here to relieve you*
(e) to remove a problem from someone; *let me relieve you of some of these parcels*; *this piece of equipment will relieve you of some of your work*

③ **relieved**
[rɪ'liːvd] *adjective*
glad to be rid of a problem; *everyone is relieved that she has passed her driving test; she was relieved to find that she did not owe him any money after all; how relieved I am to hear the news!*

② **religion**
[rɪ'lɪdʒɪn] *noun*
belief in gods or in one God; *does their religion help them to lead a good life?; it is against my religion to eat meat on Fridays*

② **religious**
[rɪ'lɪdʒɪs] *adjective*
(a) referring to religion; *there is a period of religious study every morning*
(b) having strong belief in God; *she's very religious - she goes to church every day*

④ **reluctant**
[rɪ'lʌktɪnt] *adjective*
reluctant to = not eager to, not willing to; *he was reluctant to go into the water because it looked cold*

② **rely (on)**
[rɪ'laɪ ɒn] *verb*
to depend on; *I'm relying on you to read the map; we rely on part-time staff to help out during the Christmas rush*

① **remain**
[rɪ'meɪn] *verb*
(a) to stay; *we expect it will remain fine for the rest of the week; she remained behind at the office to finish her work*
(b) to be left; *half the food remained on the guests' plates and had to be thrown away; after the accident not much remained of the car*
(c) it remains to be seen = we will find out later; *how many people have survived the crash remains to be seen; it remains to be seen whether she's ever going to be able to walk again*

③ **remainder**
[rɪ'meɪndɪ]
1 *noun*
(a) what is left after everything else has gone; *what shall we do for the remainder of the holidays?; after the bride and bridegroom left, the remainder of the party stayed in the hotel to have supper*
(b) remainders = new books which are sold off cheaply because they are not selling well; *remainders are sold through special bookshops*
2 *verb*

to sell off new books cheaply; *a shop full of piles of remaindered books*

① **remaining**
[rɪ'meɪnɪŋ] *adjective*
which is left; *the only remaining house in the village was damaged; she's not the only remaining member of her family - her sister is still alive*

③ **remains**
[rɪ'meɪnz] *noun*
(a) things left over or left behind; *the remains of the evening meal were left on the table until the next morning; we're trying to save the Roman remains from destruction by the construction company*
(b) *(formal)* body of a dead person; *the emperor's remains were buried in the cathedral*

③ **remark**
[rɪ'maːk]
1 *noun*
comment; *I heard his remark even if he spoke in a low voice*; **to make** *or* **pass remarks about** = to make sharp or rude comments about; *she made some remarks about the dirt in the restaurant*
2 *verb*
to notice, to comment on; *she remarked on the dirty cloth on the table*

③ **remarkable**
[rɪ'maːkɪbl] *adjective*
very unusual, which you might notice; *she's a remarkable woman; it's remarkable that the bank has not asked us to pay back the money*

④ **remarkably**
[rɪ'maːkɪblɪ] *adverb*
unusually; *remarkably, the bank didn't ask for the money to be paid back; he did remarkably well in his exams; apart from a minor infection, his health has been remarkably good*

③ **remedy**
['remɪdɪ]
1 *noun*
thing which may cure; *it's an old remedy for colds* (NOTE: plural is **remedies**)
2 *verb*
to correct something, to make something better; *tell me what's wrong and I'll try to remedy it right away*

① **remember**
[rɪ'membɪ] *verb*
(a) to bring back into your mind something which you have seen or heard before; *do you remember when we got lost in the fog?; my grandmother can remember seeing the first television programmes; she remembered seeing it on the dining room table; she can't remember where she put her umbrella; I don't remember having been in this hotel before; I remember my grandmother very well; it's strange that I can never remember my father's birthday; did you remember to switch off the kitchen light?*

(NOTE: you **remember doing something** which you did in the past; you **remember to do something** in the future)

(b) to ask someone to pass your good wishes to someone; *please remember me to your father when you see him next*

① **remind**
[rɪ'maɪnd] *verb*
(a) to make someone remember something; *now that you've reminded me, I do remember seeing him last week; remind me to book the tickets for New York; she reminded him that the meeting had to finish at 6.30*
(b) **to remind someone of** = to make someone think of something; *do you know what this reminds me of?; she reminds me of her mother*

④ **reminder**
[rɪ'maɪndɪ] *noun*
(a) thing which reminds you of something; *keep this picture as a reminder of happier days*
(b) letter to remind a customer to do something; *we had a reminder from the gas company that we hadn't paid the bill*

④ **reminiscent**
[remɪ'nɪsɪnt] *adjective*
which reminds you of the past; *this landscape is reminiscent of paintings by Constable; his whole attitude is reminiscent of that of his father*

③ **remote**
[rɪ'məʊt] *adjective*
(a) far away; *the hotel is situated in a remote mountain village*; **remote control** = device which controls a model plane, TV, etc., by radio signals; *has anyone seen the remote control for the TV or the TV remote control?*
(b) slight, not very strong; *there's a remote chance of finding a cure for his illness; the possibility of him arriving on time is remote; look at the fog - there is not the remotest possibility of the plane taking off*
(c) *(person)* who does not communicate very much; *their daughter is difficult to get to know, she seems so remote* (NOTE: **remoter - remotest**)

③ **removal**
[rɪ'muːvl] *noun*
(a) taking something away; *the removal of the ban on importing computers; refuse collectors are responsible for the removal of household waste; the opposition called for the removal of the Foreign Secretary*
(b) moving to a new home, new office, etc.; **removal men** = workers who move furniture from one house to another; **removal van** = van which takes your furniture from one house to another; *today's the day we move - the removal van is already here*

① **remove**
[rɪ'muːv] *verb*
to take away; *you can remove his name from the mailing list; the waitress removed the dirty plates and brought us some tea*

④ **renew**
[rɪ'njuː] *verb*
(a) to start again; *renew your efforts and don't lose hope*
(b) to replace something old with something new; *we need to renew the electric wires in the kitchen*
(c) to continue something for a further period of time; *don't forget to renew your insurance policy*; **to renew a subscription** = to pay a subscription for another year; *I don't think I'll renew my subscription to the magazine - I hardly ever read it*

④ **renewable**
[rɪ'njuːɪbl] *adjective*
(a) which can be renewed; *the season ticket is renewable for a further year*
(b) which can be replaced, which can renew itself; *renewable sources of energy such as solar power, and power from wind or water*

④ **renewal**
[rɪ'njuːl] *noun*
act of renewing; *we noticed a renewal of interest in old paintings*; **the subscription is up for renewal** = the subscription needs to be renewed

④ **renowned**
[rɪ'naʊnd] *adjective*
(a) *(formal)* very famous; *Florence is renowned as the centre of Italian art*
(b) **renowned for** = famous for something; *she's renowned for being late; a shop which is renowned for the quality of its products*

② **rent**
[rent]
1 *noun*
money paid to live in a flat, house, to use an office, etc.; *rents are high in the centre of the town; the landlord asked me to pay three months' rent in advance*; **rent control** = government regulation of rents
2 *verb*
(a) to pay money to use a house, flat, car, etc.; *he rents an office in the centre of town; they were driving a rented car when they were stopped by the police; he rented a cottage by the beach for three weeks*
(b) **to rent (out)** = to let someone use a house, office, flat, etc., for money; *we rented (out) one floor of our building to an American company*

④ **rental**
['rentl] *noun*
rent, money paid to use a room, flat, office, car, etc.; *the telephone rental has gone up this quarter*; **car rental firm** = company which specializes in offering cars for rent; *there are no reliable car rental firms around here*

④ **reorganization**
[rɪɔːɡɪnaɪ'zeɪʃn] *noun*
act of reorganizing; *the reorganization of the company will take a long time*

④ **reorganize**
[rɪˈɔːgɪnaɪz] *verb*

to organize in a new way; *do you plan to reorganize the club and accept more members?*; *she reorganized the library and we can't find anything any more*

③ **rep**
[rep] *(informal)* = REPRESENTATIVE
salesman who visits clients, trying to sell them something; *they have vacancies for reps in the north of the country*; *we have a reps' meeting every three months*

③ **repaid**
[rɪˈpeɪd] *see* REPAY

③ **repair**
[rɪˈpeə]

1 *noun*

(a) mending something which is broken or has been damaged; *his car is in the garage for repair*; *the hotel is closed while they are carrying out repairs to the heating system*; **repair kit** = box with tools for repairing a machine, especially for repairing a car; *there is a repair kit provided in the boot of each car*

(b) to be in a good state of repair *or* **in good repair** = to be in good condition; *this car is still in a very good state of repair, I won't change it yet*

2 *verb*

to mend, to make something work which is broken or damaged; *I dropped my watch on the pavement, and I don't think it can be repaired*; *she's trying to repair the washing machine*; *the photocopier is being repaired*

④ **repay**
[rɪˈpeɪ] *verb*

(a) to pay back; *I'll try to repay what I owe you next month*; *thank you for your help - I hope to be able to repay you one day*; **he repaid me in full** = he paid me back all the money he owed me

(b) to be worth; **it will repay close analysis** = it would be worth looking at it carefully (NOTE: **repaying - repaid** [riːˈpeɪd])

④ **repayment**
[ˈriːpeɪmɪnt] *noun*

paying back; *repayment of the loan is by monthly instalments*; **mortgage repayments** = the instalments paid back on a mortgage; *he fell behind with his mortgage repayments*; *my mortgage repayments have increased this month*

② **repeat**
[rɪˈpiːt]

1 *verb*

to say something again; *could you repeat what you just said?*; *he repeated the address so that the policeman could write it down*; *she kept on repeating that she wanted to go home*; **to repeat yourself** = to say the same thing over and over again; *he's getting old - he keeps repeating himself*

2 *adjective*

repeat performance = performance which is done a second time; *the play is being performed on Friday, and there will be a repeat performance on Saturday*

3 *noun*

performance (of a play, TV show) which is done a second time; *during the summer the TV seems to be showing only repeats*

① **replace**
[rɪˈpleɪs] *verb*

(a) to put something back where it was before; *please replace the books correctly on the shelves*

(b) to replace something with something else = to put something in the place of something else; *the washing machine needs replacing*; *we are replacing all our permanent staff with part-time people*; *see also* SEARCH

③ **replacement**
[rɪˈpleɪsmɪnt] *noun*

(a) replacing something with something else; *the garage recommended the replacement of the hand pump with an electric model*; *the republican movement would like to see the replacement of the king by a president*; **hip replacement** = operation to replace the whole hip joint with an artificial one; *old people sometimes need to have hip replacements*; *see also* HORMONE

(b) thing which is used to replace something; *an electric motor was bought as a replacement for the old one*; **replacement parts** = spare parts of an engine used to replace parts which have worn out

(c) person who replaces someone; *my secretary leaves us next week, so we are advertising for a replacement*

④ **replay**

1 *noun*

[ˈriːpleɪ]

(a) match which is played again because the first match was a draw; *they drew 2-2 so there will be a replay next week*

(b) action replay = section of a sporting event which is shown again on TV at a slower speed, so that the action can be examined carefully; *look at the action replay to see if it really was a foul*

2 *verb*

[riːˈpleɪ] to play again; *he replayed the message on the answerphone several times, but still couldn't understand it*; *the match will be replayed next week*

② **reply**
[rɪˈplaɪ]

1 *noun*

(a) answer; *I asked him what he was doing but got no reply*; *we wrote last week, but haven't had a reply yet*; *send a stamped addressed envelope for a reply*; *we had six replies to our advertisement*

(b) in reply = as an answer; *in reply to my letter, I received a fax two days later*; *she just shook her head in reply and turned away* (NOTE: plural is **replies**)

2 *verb*

to answer; *he never replies to my letters*; *we wrote last week, but he hasn't replied yet*; *he refused to reply to questions until his lawyer arrived*

① **report**

[rɪˈpɔːt]

1 *noun*

(a) description of what has happened or what will happen; *we read the reports of the accident in the newspaper*; *can you confirm the report that the council is planning to sell the old town hall?*

(b) school report = document from a school, telling how a student has done over a period; *we discussed little Jane's report with her teacher*

2 *verb*

(a) to write a description of what happened; *you must report the burglary to the police*; *she reported that her purse had been stolen from her bedroom*; *the British press reported a plane crash in Africa*; *she reported seeing the missing man in her shop*; **to report back** = to send a report back to the office, etc., on what has happened; *you must report back as soon as you find out what happened*; *go and visit our suppliers and report back to me on the situation*

(b) to present yourself officially; *to report for work*; *candidates should report to the personnel office at 9.00*

(c) to report to someone = to be responsible to someone, to be under someone; *she reports directly to the managing director himself*

③ **reporter**

[rɪˈpɔːtɪ] *noun*

journalist who writes reports of events for a newspaper or for a TV news programme; *the BBC sent reporters to cover the floods*; *all the reporters gathered in a room to interview the president*; *he works as a reporter for a regional newspaper*

③ **reporting**

[rɪˈpɔːtɪŋ] *noun*

action of reporting something in the press; *any reporting of the details of the trial has been forbidden*; *the BBC is famous for its reporting of world events*

① **represent**

[reprɪˈzent] *verb*

(a) to speak or act on behalf of someone or of a group of people; *he asked his solicitor to represent him at the meeting*

(b) to work for a company, showing goods or services to possible buyers; *he represents an American car firm in Europe*

(c) to indicate, to be a symbol of; *the dark green on the map represents woods*

② **representation**

[reprɪzenˈteɪʃn] *noun*

(a) act of selling goods for a company; *we can provide representation throughout Europe*

(b) having someone to act on your behalf; *the residents' association wants representation on the committee*

(c) way of showing; *the design on the Canadian flag is a representation of a red leaf*

(d) representations = complaints or protests; *we made representations to the manager on behalf of the junior members of staff*

② **representative**

[reprɪˈzentɪtɪv]

1 *adjective*

typical; *the sample isn't representative of the whole batch*

2 *noun*

(a) person who represents, who speaks on behalf of someone else; *he asked his solicitor to act as his representative*; *representatives of the workers have asked to meet the management*

(b) travelling salesman; *they have vacancies for representatives in the north of the country* (NOTE: often called simply a **rep**)

(c) *(in the United States)* **the House of Representatives** = the lower house of Congress (NOTE: the upper house of Congress is the **Senate**)

④ **reproduce**

[riːprɪˈdjuːs] *verb*

(a) to copy; *some of his letters have been reproduced in the book of his poems*; *it is very difficult to reproduce the sound of an owl accurately*

(b) to produce young; *some animals will not reproduce when kept in zoos*

④ **reptile**

[ˈreptaɪl] *noun*

cold-blooded animal with a skin covered with scales, which lays eggs; *snakes are reptiles*

② **republic**

[rɪˈpʌblɪk] *noun*

system of government which is governed by elected representatives headed by an elected or nominated president; *France and Germany are republics, but Spain and the UK are not*

④ **republican**

[rɪˈpʌblɪkɪn]

1 *adjective*

referring to a republic; *the republican movement would like to see the replacement of the king by a president*

2 *noun*

person who believes that a republic is the best form of government; *some republicans made speeches against the emperor*

③ **Republican**

[rɪˈpʌblɪkɪn]

1 *adjective*

US referring to the Republican Party, one of the two main political parties in the USA

2 *noun*
US member of the Republican Party, one of the two main political parties in the USA

③ **Republican Party**
[rɪˈpʌblɪkɪn ˈpɑːti] *noun*
one of the two main political parties in the USA, which supports business and is against too much state intervention in industry and welfare; *the Republican Party's candidate for the presidency*; *compare* DEMOCRATIC PARTY

③ **reputation**
[repjʊˈteɪʃn] *noun*
opinion that people have of someone; *he has a reputation for being difficult to deal with*; *the cook has a reputation for having a sharp temper*; *his bad reputation won't help him find a suitable job*

② **request**
[rɪˈkwest]
1 *noun*
asking for something; *your request will be dealt with as soon as possible*; **on request** = if asked for; *'catalogue available on request'*; **request stop** = bus stop where buses stop only if you signal to them
2 *verb*
to ask for something politely; *I am enclosing the leaflets you requested*; *guests are requested to leave their keys at reception*

① **require**
[rɪˈkwaɪɪ] *verb*
(a) to demand that someone should do something; *we were required to go to the local police station*; *you are required to fill in the forms when you register*
(b) to need; *the disease requires careful treatment*; *writing the program requires a computer specialist*

② **requirement**
[rɪˈkwaɪɪmɪnt] *noun*
(a) what is necessary; *it is a requirement of the job that you should be able to drive*
(b) **requirements** = things which are needed; *we try to meet our customers' requirements*; *if you send us a list of your requirements, we shall see if we can supply them*

④ **rescue**
[ˈreskjuː]
1 *noun*
action of saving; *mountain rescue requires teams of specially trained people*; *no one could swim well enough to go to her rescue*; **rescue party** *or* **rescue team** *or* **rescue squad** = group of people who are going to save someone; *rescue parties were sent out immediately after the plane came down in the jungle*
2 *verb*
to save someone from a dangerous situation; *the helicopter rescued the crew of the sinking ship*; *the company nearly collapsed, but was rescued by the bank*; *when the river flooded, the party of tourists had to be rescued by boat*

① **research**
[rɪˈsɜːtʃ]
1 *noun*
(a) scientific study, which tries to find out facts; *the company is carrying out research to find a cure for colds*; *the research laboratory has come up with encouraging results*; *our researches proved that the letter was a forgery*
(b) **market research** = examining the possible sales of a product and the possible customers before it is put on the market; *if we had done proper market research we would have discovered that there were several products that are cheaper than ours*; *before you launch the product, you must do thorough market research*
2 *verb*
to study, to try to find out facts; *research your subject thoroughly before you start writing your article*

④ **resent**
[rɪˈzent] *verb*
to feel annoyed because of a real or imaginary hurt; *she resents having to look after her father-in-law*; *we bitterly resent the suggestion that the company has tricked its customers*

③ **reservation**
[rezɪˈveɪʃn] *noun*
(a) booking of a seat, table, etc.; *I want to make a reservation on the train to Plymouth tomorrow evening*; **(room) reservations** = department in a hotel which deals with bookings for rooms; *can you put me through to reservations?*
(b) doubt; *I have no reservations whatsoever that I have made the right decision*; *if you have any reservations about the contract, please let me know as soon as possible*
(c) area kept separate from other areas; **central reservation** = section of road or grass, bushes, etc., between the two sections of a major road; *the car had crossed the central reservation and hit a vehicle travelling in the opposite direction*

③ **reserve**
[rɪˈzɜːv]
1 *noun*
(a) amount kept back in case it is needed in the future; *our reserves of coal were used up during the winter*; **in reserve** = waiting to be used; *we're keeping the can of petrol in reserve*
(b) *(in sport)* extra player who can play if someone drops out of the team; *one of the players was hurt so a reserve was called up*; **the reserves** = second football team made up of reserve players; *he's playing in the reserves today*
(c) **nature reserve** = area of land where animals and plants are protected; *we often go to a nature reserve in Suffolk to watch birds and walk by the sea*

(d) being shy, not being open about your feelings; *he had to break down her reserve before he could get her to talk about her illness*
2 *verb*
(a) to book a seat or a table; *I want to reserve a table for four people; have you reserved? - if not, we have only two tables free; can you reserve two seats for me for the evening performance?*
(b) to keep back for a special use, or for use at a later date; *put half the cherries into the cake mixture and reserve the rest for decoration; don't read this book now, reserve it for your holidays; I'm reserving my right to change my mind*
(c) to reserve judgement = not to make up your mind about something until later; *I'll reserve judgement until I've heard all the facts*

③ **reserved**
[rɪ'zɜːvd] *adjective*
(a) booked; *there are two reserved tables and one free one; is this seat reserved?*
(b) who does not reveal his or her thoughts and feelings; *Clare is very reserved and doesn't talk much; he's a very reserved man and does not mix with other members of staff*

④ **reservoir**
['rezɪvwɑː] *noun*
(a) large, usually artificial, lake where drinking water is kept for pumping to a city; *there has been very little rain this year and the reservoirs are only half full*
(b) large collection of something kept ready; *there is a huge reservoir of skilled labour waiting to be employed*

③ **residence**
['rezɪdɪns] *noun*
(a) *(formal, especially US)* place where you live; *this is Mrs Smith's residence; they have a country residence where they spend their weekends*
(b) act of living in a place; **hall of residence** = building where students live at university or college; *how many students live in halls of residence?*; **in residence** = living in a place; *when the Queen is in residence, the royal flag flies over Buckingham Palace*

② **resident**
['rezɪdɪnt]
1 *adjective*
who lives permanently in a place; *there is a resident caretaker*
2 *noun*
person who lives in a place, a country, a hotel, etc.; *you need an entry permit if you're not a resident of the country; only residents are allowed to park their cars here*

③ **residential**
[rezɪ'denʃl] *adjective*
residential area = part of a town with houses rather than shops or factories; *the flat is not in a residential area, it's above a shoe shop;*

residential street = street with houses, and no shops or factories; *he lives in a quiet residential street*

③ **resign**
[rɪ'zaɪn] *verb*
(a) to give up a job; *he resigned with effect from July 1st; she has resigned (her position) as finance director*
(b) to resign yourself to something = to accept something; *I have to resign myself to never being rich; he was still 20 metres behind his rival and resigned himself to coming in second*

③ **resignation**
[rezɪg'neɪʃn] *noun*
(a) act of giving up a job; *his resignation was accepted by the Prime Minister; have you written your letter of resignation?*; **he tendered** *or* **he handed in his resignation** = he resigned
(b) accepting an unpleasant situation; *he looked at his exam results with resignation*

③ **resigned**
[rɪ'zaɪnd] *adjective*
accepting something unpleasant; *a resigned look appeared on his face*; **resigned to** = accepting that something unpleasant will happen; *I'm resigned to living by myself for the rest of my life*

③ **resist**
[rɪ'zɪst] *verb*
to fight against something, not to give in to something; *he resisted all attempts to make him sell the house; bands of guerrillas resisted in the mountains; they resisted the enemy attacks for two weeks*

② **resistance**
[rɪ'zɪstns] *noun*
opposition to something, fighting against something; *bands of guerrillas put up a fierce resistance in the mountains; the refugees had no resistance to disease; there was a lot of resistance to the new plan from the local residents*; **resistance movement** = movement of ordinary people against an enemy occupying their country; *the resistance movement was very strong in their area during the war*; **passive resistance** = resisting the police by refusing to do something, but without using violence; *the protesters organized a programme of passive resistance to the new presidential decree*; **he took the line of least resistance** = he did the easiest thing

④ **resistant**
[rɪ'zɪstnt] *adjective*
which resists; *this plate is not heat resistant and shouldn't be used in an oven*

③ **resolution**
[rezɪ'luːʃn] *noun*
(a) decision to be decided at a meeting; **to put a resolution to a meeting** = to ask a meeting to vote on a proposal; *the meeting passed or*

carried or adopted the resolution; the meeting rejected the resolution or the resolution was defeated by ten votes to twenty

(b) being determined to do something; *her resolution to succeed is strong, and I am sure she will get through*; **New Year's Resolution** = plan to improve your way of living, decided on at the New Year, and usually abandoned shortly afterwards; *each New Year I make the same resolutions, but never manage to keep them; my New Year's resolution was to take more exercise, but it didn't last long*

(c) *(of a TV or computer image)* being clear; *a high resolution screen*

③ **resolve**
[rɪˈzɒlv]

1 *noun*

determination, what you have firmly decided to do; *the head teacher encouraged him in his resolve to go to university*

2 *verb*

to firmly decide to do something; *we all resolved to work harder*

③ **resort**
[rɪˈzɔːt]

1 *noun*

(a) place where people go on holiday; *a famous Swiss ski resort; crowds have been flocking to the resorts on the south coast*

(b) as a last resort *or* **in the last resort** = when everything else fails; *he accepted her offer of a lift as a last resort*

2 *verb*

to resort to = to use something in a difficult situation, when everything else has failed; *in the end the police had to resort to using tear gas*

① **resource**
[rɪˈsɔːs] *noun*

source of supply for what is needed or used; *we have enough resources - financial or otherwise - to build a rocket*; **financial resources** = supply of money for something; **natural resources** = raw materials which come from nature, such as minerals, oil, wood; *the country is rich in natural resources*; **resource centre** = section of a school where reference books and equipment are kept for the use of students; *the school does not have enough funds to buy CD-ROMs for the resource centre*; *see also* HUMAN RESOURCES

① **respect**
[rɪˈspekt]

1 *noun*

(a) admiration or regard for someone; *he showed very little respect for his teacher; no one deserves more respect than her mother*; **to command respect** = to be admired; *her TV programmes about the war commanded much respect*

(b) with respect to = concerning; *I have nothing to say with respect to the new treatment*; **in some respects** = in some ways; *in some respects, she doesn't act like a mature person*

(c) respects = polite good wishes; *my father sends you his respects*; **to pay your respects to someone** = to go to visit someone important; **to pay your last respects to someone** = to go to someone's funeral

2 *verb*

(a) to admire or to honour someone; *everyone respected her decision to quit her job*

(b) to show you care about something; *farmers have been accused of not respecting the environment*

(c) to do what is required by something; *the landlord has not respected the terms of the contract*

④ **respectable**
[rɪˈspektɪbl] *adjective*

(a) considered by people to be good, proper, and worthy of respect; *she's marrying a very respectable young engineer; I don't want to bring up my children here, it is not a respectable area*

(b) fairly large; *he made quite a respectable score*

③ **respected**
[rɪˈspektɪd] *adjective*

admired by many people; *he's a highly-respected professor of physics; the book is a very respected work of reference*

③ **respectively**
[rɪˈspektɪvli] *adverb*

in the order just mentioned; *Mr Smith and Mr Jones are respectively owner and manager of the shop*

② **respond**
[rɪˈspɒnd] *verb*

(a) to give a reply; *she shouted at him, but he didn't respond*

(b) to show a favourable reaction to; *I hope the public will respond to our new advertisement; the government has responded to pressure from industry*; **he is responding to treatment** = he is beginning to get better

① **response**
[rɪˈspɒns] *noun*

(a) answer; *there was no response to our call for help*; **in response to** = as an answer to; *in response to the United Nations' request for aid, the government has sent blankets and tents*

(b) answers given by the people attending a service in church; *a series of prayers with repeated responses*

① **responsibility**
[rɪspɒnsɪˈbɪlɪti] *noun*

(a) being in a position where you look after or deal with something; *the management accepts no responsibility for customers' property; there is no responsibility on his part for the poor*

results; *who should take responsibility for the students' welfare?*; **he has taken on a lot of responsibility** = he has agreed to be responsible for many things; **position of responsibility** = job where important decisions have to be taken
(b) thing which you are responsible for; **responsibilities** = duties; *he finds the responsibilities of being chairman of the club too demanding*

① **responsible**
[rɪ'spɒnsɪbl] *adjective*
(a) responsible for = causing; *the fog was responsible for the accident*
(b) looking after something, and so open to blame if it gets lost, damaged, etc.; *he is not responsible for the restaurant next door to his hotel*; *we hold customers responsible for any items which are broken*
(c) responsible to someone = being under the authority of someone; *she's directly responsible to the head nurse*
(d) (person) who can be trsuted; *you can rely on him, he's very responsible*; **responsible position** *or* **responsible job** = job where decisions have to be taken; *he is looking for a responsible position in the Post Office*

① **rest**
[rest]
1 *noun*
(a) being quiet and peaceful, being asleep, doing nothing; *all you need is a good night's rest and you'll be fine again tomorrow*; *we took a few minute's rest and started running again*; *I'm having a well-earned rest after working hard all week*
(b) not moving; *the ball finally came to rest two inches from the hole*
(c) what is left; *here are the twins, but where are the rest of the children?*; *I drank most of the milk and the cat drank the rest*; *throw the rest of the food away - it will go bad* (NOTE: rest takes a singular verb when it refers to a singular: here's the rest of the milk; where's the rest of the string? the rest of the money has been lost; it takes a plural verb when it refers to a plural: here are the rest of the children; where are the rest of the chairs? the rest of the books have been lost)
(d) thing which supports; *she pulled up another chair as a rest for her foot*; **head rest** = cushion on top of a car seat against which you can lean your head
2 *verb*
(a) to be quiet and peaceful; *don't disturb your father - he's resting*; *they ran for ten miles, rested for a few minutes, and then ran on again*
(b) to lean something against something; *she rested her bike against the wall*
(c) *(formal)* **to let something rest** = to stop discussing something; *after advice from our solicitor, we decided to let the matter rest*

② **restaurant**
['restɪrɒnt] *noun*
place where you can buy and eat a meal; *I don't want to stay at home tonight - let's go out to the Italian restaurant in the High Street*; *she's was waiting for me at the restaurant*; **restaurant car** = wagon on a train where you can eat a full meal

④ **restless**
['restlɪs] *adjective*
always moving about; *after five days of rain, the children were restless and really needed to go out to play*; *she's becoming restless, she's hardly been here two months and she wants to go abroad again*

③ **restore**
[rɪ'stɔː] *verb*
(a) to repair, to make something like new again; *the old house has been restored and is now open to the public*
(b) to give back; *after the war the castle was not restored to its former owners*
(c) to make something exist again; *to everyone's delight, the management decided to restore the bonus system*

④ **restrain**
[rɪ'streɪn] *verb*
to try and stop someone doing something; *it took six policemen to restrain him*; **to restrain yourself** = to keep your temper under control; *next time, I won't restrain myself: I'll tell him exactly what I think of him*

④ **restraint**
[rɪ'streɪnt] *noun*
control; *she showed remarkable restraint when he criticized her work so rudely*; **with great restraint** = without losing your temper; *with great restraint, he quietly wiped the tomato sauce off his trousers and said nothing to the waitress*; **lack of restraint** = giving people too much freedom; *the lack of restraint in the school doesn't go down well with the parents*; **wage restraint** *or* **pay restraint** = keeping wage increases under control; *the government is planning to impose pay restraints*

③ **restrict**
[rɪ'strɪkt] *verb*
to limit; *you are restricted to two bottles per person*; *the government is trying to restrict the flow of foreign workers coming into the country*

③ **restricted**
[rɪ'strɪktɪd] *adjective*
limited; *there will be a restricted train service next Sunday*; *these seats are cheaper because you only have a restricted view of the stage*; **restricted area** = (i) area where cars must obey a speed limit; (ii) place where only certain people are allowed

② **restriction**
[rɪ'strɪkʃn] *noun*
limitation; *the police have placed restrictions on his movements*; *restrictions have been imposed on certain imports*; *there is no general speed restriction on German motorways*

① **result**
[rɪ'zʌlt]
1 *noun*
(a) something which happens because of something else; *what was the result of the police investigation?*; **as a result (of)** = because of; *there was a traffic jam and as a result, she missed her plane*
(b) final score in a game, final marks in an exam, etc.; *she isn't pleased with her exam results*; *I enjoyed making the carpet but I'm only partly happy with the result*; *he listened to the football results in the radio*
2 *verb*
to result from = to happen because of something which has been done; *the increase in the company's debts resulted from the expansion programme*; **to result in** = to produce as an effect; *adding new staff to the sales force resulted in increased sales*

④ **resume**
[rɪ'zju:m] *verb*
to start again after stopping; *the meeting resumed after a short break*; *normal train services will resume after the track has been repaired*; *after the fire, the staff resumed work as normal*

③ **résumé**
['rezu:meɪ] *noun*
(a) short piece which sums up the main points of a discussion, of a book; *a brief résumé of the book is all I need*
(b) *US* summary of the details of a person's life, especially details of education and previous jobs; *attach a résumé to your application form*
(NOTE: British English is **curriculum vitae** *or* **CV**)

④ **retail**
['ri:teɪl]
1 *noun*
selling small quantities of goods direct to the public; *the goods in stock have a retail value of £10,000*; **retail outlet** *or* **retail shop** = shop which sells goods direct to the customer; *he buys wholesale and then sells to various retail outlets*; **retail park** = specially built area of shops outside a town; *compare* WHOLESALE
2 *verb*
(a) to sell goods direct to customers who do not sell them again; **to retail at** *or* **for** = to sell for a certain price; *these glasses retail at £5.95 for two*
(b) *(formal)* to pass on gossip; *she immediately retailed the story to her friends*
3 *adverb*

he sells retail and buys wholesale = he buys goods in bulk at a wholesale discount and sells in small quantities at full price to the public

④ **retailer**
['ri:teɪlɪ] *noun*
shopkeeper who sells goods directly to the public; *as a retailer, I buy either from a wholesaler or direct from the factory*; *retailers buy goods from wholesalers and then sell them on to the public*; *compare* WHOLESALER

② **retain**
[rɪ'teɪn] *verb*
(formal)
(a) to keep; *please retain this invoice for tax purposes*; *one news item especially retained my attention*; *he managed to retain his calm in spite of constant shouting from the audience*; **retaining wall** = wall which holds back earth or the water in a reservoir
(b) **to retain a lawyer to act for you** = to agree with a lawyer that he will act for you, and to pay him a fee in advance

② **retire**
[rɪ'taɪɪ] *verb*
(a) to stop work and take a pension; *he will retire from his job as manager next April*; *when he retired, the firm presented him with a watch*; *she's retiring this year*
(b) to make a worker stop work and take a pension; *they decided to retire all staff over 50*
(c) to come to the end of an elected term of office; *the secretary retires from the committee after six years*
(d) *(literary)* **to retire for the night** = to go to bed; *it was two o'clock in the morning and all the hotel guests had retired to their bedrooms*

② **retired**
[rɪ'taɪd] *adjective*
who has stopped work and draws a pension; *the club is run by a retired teacher*

② **retirement**
[rɪ'taɪɪmɪnt] *noun*
(a) act of retiring from work; *he was given a watch as a retirement present*; *he says that the pension he'll get on his retirement won't be enough to live on*; **to take early retirement** = to retire from work before the usual age; *I enjoy my work and I don't want to take early retirement*; **retirement age** = age at which people retire (in the UK usually 65 for men and 60 for women); *she reached retirement age last week*
(b) period of life when you are retired; *he spent his retirement in his house in France*; *most people look forward to their retirement*

④ **retreat**
[rɪ'tri:t]
1 *noun*
(a) pulling back an army from a battle; *the army's retreat was swift and unexpected*; **in retreat** = going back from a battle; **in full retreat** = going back fast; *the army is in full*

retreat; *(informal)* **to beat a retreat** = to go backwards; *he went into the ladies' toilet by mistake and had to beat a hasty retreat*
(b) quiet place; *they spent the weekend at their retreat in the Scottish hills*
2 *verb*
(a) to pull back from a battle; *Napoleon retreated from Moscow in 1812*
(b) to go to a quiet place; *our dog retreats to his basket if we shout at him*

① **return**
[rɪ'tɜːn]
1 *noun*
(a) going back, coming back to a place; *it snowed on the day of her return from Canada*; *I'll come and see you on my return*; **return ticket** *or* **a return** = ticket which allows you to go to one place and come back; *I want two returns to Edinburgh*
(b) sending back; *he asked for the immediate return of the borrowed tools*; **she replied by return of post** = she replied by the next postal service back; **to sell something on sale or return** = to sell something and give the purchaser the right to send it back it if he doesn't sell it
(c) action of going back to a former condition; *the government wants to encourage a return to old family traditions*
(d) key on a keyboard which you press when you have finished keying something, or when you want to start a new line; *to change directory, type C: and press return*; **carriage return** = key on a typewriter which you press to start a new line
(e) **many happy returns of the day** = greetings said to someone on their birthday
(f) income from money invested; *this account should bring in a quick return on your investment*
(g) **official return** = official report; **to make an income tax return** = to send a statement of income to the tax office; *your income tax return should be sent no later than 1st July*; **to fill in a VAT return** = to complete the form showing VAT receipts and expenditure
(h) **returns** = goods which a shop hasn't sold and which are sent back to the supplier
2 *verb*
(a) to come back or to go back; *when she returned from lunch she found two messages waiting for her*; *when do you plan to return to Paris?*
(b) to give back or to send back; *the letter was returned to the sender*
3 *adjective*
return address = address to send something back; *there was no return address on the letter so we couldn't send it back*; **return fare** = fare for a journey from one place to another and back again; *a return fare is cheaper than two one-way fares*; **return match** = match played between the same two teams again

① **reveal**
[rɪ'viːl] *verb*
to show something which was hidden; *he revealed his total lack of knowledge of car engines*; *an unexpected fault was revealed during the test*; *the X-ray revealed a broken bone*

④ **revealing**
[rɪ'viːlɪŋ] *adjective*
which shows something which is usually hidden; *he made a very revealing remark*; **a revealing dress** = dress which shows parts of the body which are normally kept hidden

④ **revenge**
[rɪ'vendʒ]
1 *noun*
punishing someone in return for harm he has caused you; *they broke the windows of the judge's house in revenge for the fines he had imposed*; *all the time he spent in prison, his only thought was of revenge*; *he had his revenge in the end, when her car broke down and she had to phone for help*; **to get** *or* **take your revenge on someone** = to punish someone for something he has done to you
2 *verb*
to revenge yourself on someone = to punish someone for something he has done to you; *she planned to revenge herself on the people who had treated her so badly*

② **revenue**
['revɪnjuː] *noun*
(a) money which is received; *his only source of revenue is his shop*
(b) money received by a government in tax; **Inland Revenue** *US* **Internal Revenue Service** = government department which deals with tax; *the Inland Revenue wrote again claiming we owe some tax from last year*

③ **reverse**
[rɪ'vɜːs]
1 *adjective*
opposite; *the reverse side of the carpet is made of rubber*; *the conditions are printed on the reverse side of the invoice*; **in reverse order** = backwards; *they called out the names of the winners in reverse order*; **reverse charge call** = telephone call where the person receiving the call agrees to pay for it; *since I had no money I made a reverse charge call to my mother* (NOTE: American English is **collect call**)
2 *noun*
(a) opposite side; *didn't you read what was on the reverse of the letter?*
(b) the opposite; *you're mistaken, the reverse is true*
(c) side of a coin which does not bear the head of a king, a queen, etc.; *there is a flower on the reverse of this coin* (NOTE: also called 'tails'; the opposite is **heads**)

(d) car gear which makes you go backwards; *put the car into reverse and back very slowly into the garage*; *the car's stuck in reverse!*

(e) defeat in battle or in an election; *the army suffered a disastrous reverse*; *the Conservatives suffered a series of reverses*

3 *verb*

(a) to make something do the opposite; *the page order was reversed by mistake*; *just follow the trend, don't try to reverse it*

(b) to make a car go backwards; *reverse as far as you can, then go forward*; *be careful not to reverse into that tree*

(c) *(on the phone)* **to reverse the charges** = to ask the person you are calling to pay for the call; *my father told me to reverse the charges when I call him* (NOTE: American English is to **call collect**)

(d) to change a legal decision to another, opposite, one; *the judge's decision was reversed by the appeal court*

② **review**
[rɪ'vjuː]

1 *noun*

(a) written comments on a book, play, film, etc., published in a newspaper or magazine; *did you read the review of her latest film in today's paper?*; *his book got some very good reviews*

(b) examination of several things together; *the company's annual review of each department's performance*; **salary review** = examination of salaries in a company to see if the workers should earn more; *let's hope we all get an increase at the next salary review*

(c) monthly or weekly magazine which contains articles of general interest; *his first short story appeared in a Scottish literary review*

(d) *(formal)* general inspection of the army, navy, etc.; *a naval review will be held on the king's birthday*

2 *verb*

(a) to read a book, see a film, etc., and write comments about it in a newspaper or magazine; *her exhibition was reviewed in today's paper*; *whoever reviewed her latest book, obviously didn't like it*; **review copy** = copy of new book sent to a newspaper or magazine, asking them to review it

(b) to examine in a general way; *the bank will review our overdraft position at the end of the month*; *let's review the situation in the light of the new developments*

(c) *US* to study a lesson again; *you must review your geography before the test* (NOTE: British English in this meaning is to **revise**)

(d) *(formal)* to inspect soldiers, sailors, ships, etc.; *the general rode on his white horse to review the troops*

④ **reviewer**
[rɪ'vjuːɪ] *noun*

person who writes comments on books, plays, films, etc.; *there's a new film reviewer on the Sunday paper and he didn't like this film*; *she's the book reviewer for our local newspaper*

② **revise**
[rɪ'vaɪz] *verb*

(a) to study a lesson again; *there isn't enough time to revise before the exam*; *I'm revising for my history test* (NOTE: American English is **to review**)

(b) to change, to make something correct; *he is revising the speech he is due to give this evening*; *these figures will have to be revised, there seems to be a mistake*

④ **revive**
[rɪ'vaɪv] *verb*

(a) to recover, to get well again; *after drinking some water he had revived enough to go on with the marathon*

(b) to bring someone back to life again; *the ambulance crew managed to revive her on the way to the hospital*

(c) to make something popular again; *it won't be easy to revive people's interest in old country crafts*

④ **revolt**
[rɪ'vɪʊlt]

1 *noun*

mass protest against an authority; *the government faces a revolt from its main supporters*

2 *verb*

(a) to rise up against authority; *the prisoners revolted against the harsh treatment in the jail*

(b) to disgust; *it revolted me to see all that food being thrown away*

④ **revolting**
[rɪ'vɪʊltɪŋ] *adjective*

disgusting, which makes you feel ill; *don't ask me to eat that revolting food again*; *look at the state of the kitchen - it's revolting!*

② **revolution**
[revɪ'luːʃn] *noun*

(a) armed rising against a government; *the government soldiers shot the leaders of the revolution*; *he led an unsuccessful revolution against the last president*; *during the French Revolution many innocent people were executed*

(b) turning around a central point; *the engine turns at 5000 revolutions a minute*

(c) change in the way things are done; *a revolution in data processing*; **the Industrial Revolution** = the development of industry during the 19th century in western Europe and the United States; **the technological revolution** = the change to computers and other developments in information technology; *the twentieth century was the century of the technological revolution*

④ revolutionary
[revɪ'luːʃɪnɪri]
1 *adjective*
(a) aiming to change things completely; very new; *there is a new revolutionary treatment for cancer*
(b) referring to a political revolution; *his revolutionary ideas upset the establishment*
2 *noun*
person who takes part in an uprising against a government; *the captured revolutionaries were shot when the army took control*

③ reward
[rɪ'wɔːd]
1 *noun*
money given to someone as a prize for finding something, or for information about something; *she got a £25 reward when she took the purse she had found to the police station; he is not interested in money - the Olympic gold medal will be reward enough*
2 *verb*
to give someone money as a prize for finding something, or for doing something; *he was rewarded for finding the box of papers; all her efforts were rewarded when she won first prize*

③ rheumatism
['ruːmɪtɪzm] *noun*
disease which gives painful or stiff joints or muscles; *I get rheumatism in the winter; she has rheumatism in her knees; she is being treated for rheumatism*

④ rhyme
[raɪm]
1 *noun*
(a) way in which some words end in the same sound; *can you think of a rhyme for 'taught'?*
(b) little piece of poetry; **nursery rhyme** = little piece of poetry for children; *the children sang nursery rhymes and danced in a ring*
2 *verb*
to rhyme with = to end with the same sound as another word; *'Mr' rhymes with 'sister'*

④ rhythm
['rɪðɪm] *noun*
strong regular beat in music, poetry, etc.; *they stamped their feet to the rhythm of the music*

④ rib
[rɪb] *noun*
(a) one of twenty-four curved bones which protect your chest; *he fell down while skiing and broke two ribs*
(b) the same bones of an animal, cooked and eaten; **spare ribs** = pork ribs cooked in a savoury sauce

④ ribbon
['rɪbn] *noun*
long thin strip of material for tying things or used as decoration; *she had a red ribbon in her hair*; **printer ribbon** *or* **typewriter ribbon** = thin strip of material or plastic, with ink or carbon on it, used in a printer or typewriter

④ rice
[raɪs] *noun*
(a) very common food, the seeds of a tropical plant; *she only had a bowl of rice for her evening meal*; **rice pudding** = a pudding made of rice, milk and sugar, cooked together (NOTE: no plural: **some rice, a bowl of rice, a spoonful of rice**)
(b) common food plant, grown mainly in Asian countries; *women were planting rice in the fields*

COMMENT: rice with long grains is grown in tropical countries, such as India; rice with short grains is grown in colder countries such as Japan. There are thousands of varieties of rice, and the world's leading rice exporting countries are the USA and Thailand. Wild rice is not rice at all, but a form of North American grass

② rich
[rɪtʃ]
1 *adjective*
(a) who has a lot of money; *they're so rich that they can afford to go on holiday for six months; if only we were rich, then we could buy a bigger house; he never spends anything, and so he gets richer and richer*
(b) thick and dark (colour); *she painted the kitchen a rich chocolate colour*
(c) with many treasures; *our local museum has an unusually rich collection of paintings by local artists*; **rich in** = containing a lot of; *the area is rich in old churches; the south of the country is rich in coal; these tablets are rich in vitamin B*
(d) made with a lot of cream, butter, etc.; *this cream cake is too rich for me* (NOTE: **richer - richest**)
2 *noun*
the rich = rich people; *at that price, the car is only for the really rich*

① rid
[rɪd] *phrase*
to get rid of something = to dispose of something or to throw something away; *do you want to get rid of that old chair?; we have been told to get rid of twenty staff; she doesn't seem able to get rid of her cold* (NOTE: **getting rid - got rid**)

① ride
[raɪd]
1 *noun*
(a) pleasant trip on a horse, on a bike, in a car, etc.; *does anyone want to come for a bike ride?; he took us all for a ride in his new car; the station is only a short bus ride from the office*
(b) *(informal)* **to take someone for a ride** = to trick someone; *free beer? - there's no free beer, someone's been taking you for a ride!; the*

recruit was really taken for a ride when the others told him that there was a party at the colonel's house and he believed them

(c) action of travelling; *you will enjoy the smooth ride of the new four-wheel drive model*

2 *verb*

to go on a horse, on a bike, etc.; *he rode his bike across the road without looking; she's never ridden (on) an elephant; my little sister is learning to ride, but she's frightened of big horses* (NOTE: **rides - riding - rode** [rʊd] **- has ridden** [ˈrɪdɪn])

④ **rider**
[ˈraɪdɪ] *noun*
(a) person who rides; *the rider of the black horse fell at the first fence; motorcycle riders must wear helmets*
(b) additional clause; *to add a rider to a contract*

④ **ridge**
[rɪdʒ] *noun*
long narrow raised part; *the mountain ridge stretches for miles*

② **ridiculous**
[rɪˈdɪkjʊlɪs] *adjective*
silly, which everyone should laugh at; *it's ridiculous to tell everyone to wear suits when it's so hot in the office*

④ **rifle**
[ˈraɪfl]
1 *noun*
gun with a long barrel; *gunmen with rifles were on the roofs surrounding the ministry*; **rifle range** = place where you practise shooting with rifles; *she goes to the rifle range every Saturday to practise*
2 *verb*
to search for something, usually to steal it; *the burglars rifled through the drawers of her desk*

④ **rig**
[rɪg]
1 *noun*
(a) **oil rig** = construction for drilling for oil; *how many oil rigs are there in the North Sea?*
(b) *(informal)* large truck; *he drives a 16-wheel rig*
2 *verb*
to arrange a dishonest result; *they were accused of rigging the election*; *see also* RIG UP (NOTE: **rigging - rigged**)

① **right**
[raɪt]
1 *adjective*
(a) not wrong, correct; *you're right - the number 8 bus doesn't go to Marble Arch; she gave the right answer every time; he says the answer is 285 - quite right!; is the station clock right?; is this the right train for Manchester?; she didn't put the bottles back in the right place; if you don't stand the jar the right way up it will leak; see also* ALL RIGHT, SIDE

(b) not left, referring to the hand which most people use to write with; *outside Britain, cars drive on the right side of the road; the keys are in the top right drawer of my desk; he was holding the suitcase in his right hand*
(c) *(in politics)* referring to the conservatives; *he's on the right wing of the party; his politics are right of centre*
(d) *(informal)* **Mr Right** = the man who would be the right man to be someone's husband; *she's still waiting for Mr Right to come along*
2 *noun*
(a) what is correct, not wrong; **in the right** = correct, which should not be criticized; *she was proved to be in the right*
(b) the side opposite to the left; *when driving in France remember to keep to the right; when you get to the next crossroads, turn to the right; who was that girl sitting on the right of your father?; go straight ahead, and take the second road on the right*
(c) being legally entitled to do or to have something; *the accused has the right to remain silent; the manager has no right to read my letters; the staff have a right to know why the shop is closing down; see also* RIGHTS
(d) *(in politics)* **the right** = the political group supporting traditional values and rights; *we support the right by campaigning for our local Conservative candidate*; **swing to the right** = movement of votes towards the right-wing candidates
3 *adverb*
(a) straight; *to get to the police station, keep right on to the end of the road, and then turn left; go right along to the end of the corridor, you'll see my office in front of you; instead of stopping at the crossroads, he drove right on across the main road and into a tree*
(b) **right (away)** = immediately; *they called the ambulance right after the accident; the ambulance came right away*; **right now** = at this particular point in time; *right now, it is not possible for me to answer reporters' questions*
(c) exactly; *the pub is right at the end of the road; the phone rang right in the middle of the TV programme; she stood right in front of the TV and no one could see the screen*
(d) correctly; *she guessed the answer right; everything is going right for her*; *(informal)* **it serves you right** = you deserve what has happened to you
(e) towards the right-hand side; *to get to the station, turn right at the traffic lights; children should be taught to look right and left before crossing the road*
4 *verb*
(a) **to right a wrong** = to correct something which is wrong; *she campaigned to right the wrongs done to single mothers*
(b) **to right itself** = to turn the right way up again; *the yacht turned over and then righted itself*

5 *interjection* agreed, OK; *right, so we all meet again at 7 o'clock?*

③ **right angle**
['raɪt 'æŋgl] *noun*
angle of 90°; *the two streets meet at a right angle*

④ **right-hand**
['raɪt 'hænd] *adjective*
on the right side; *look in the right-hand drawer of my desk; the pub is on the right-hand side of the street;* **right-hand man** = main assistant; *he's my right-hand man, I couldn't do without him;* **right-hand drive car** = car where the driver sits on the right side of the car

> COMMENT: most cars have left-hand drives; British, New Zealand and Japanese cars have right-hand drives

③ **rights**
[raɪts] *noun*
(a) what you should be allowed to do or to have; *they are working for women's rights or for the rights of women; the rights of ordinary working people are being ignored;* **human rights** = rights which each ordinary member of society should enjoy, such as freedom of speech, freedom of movement, etc.; *demonstrators are protesting against abuses of human rights in various parts of the world*
(b) legal right to have something; *he has the British rights to the invention; she sold the American rights to an American publisher;* **film rights** = the legal right to make a film from a book; **foreign rights** = legal right to sell something in another country
(c) rights issue = issue of new shares in a company which are offered to existing shareholders at a cheap price

④ **right-wing**
[raɪt'wɪŋ] *adjective*
belonging to the conservative political parties; *the defeat was a blow to the right-wing candidate*

④ **rigid**
['rɪdʒɪd] *adjective*
stiff, which doesn't bend; *this pole is too rigid, you will need something more flexible; the club's rules are so rigid that a lot of members are leaving*

④ **rigorous**
['rɪgɪrɪs] *adjective*
very thorough; *the customs inspection is rigorous, they open every single case; these tests are too rigorous for small children*

③ **rig up**
['rɪg 'ʌp] *verb*
to arrange, to construct something quickly; *they rigged up a telescope in the garden*

① **ring**
[rɪŋ]
1 *noun*
(a) round shape of metal, etc.; *she has a gold ring in her nose; he wears a ring on his little finger;* **wedding ring** = ring which is put on the finger during the wedding ceremony
(b) circle of people or things; *the teacher asked the children to sit in a ring round her*
(c) noise of an electric bell; *there was a ring at the door*
(d) phone call; *give me a ring tomorrow*
(e) space where a show takes place, where a boxing match is held, etc.; *everyone shouted when the lions ran into the ring;* **boxing ring** = square area, surrounded with a rope fence, in which boxing matches take place; *the two boxers climbed into the ring*
2 *verb*
(a) to make a sound with a bell; *the delivery man rang the bell; at Easter, all the church bells were ringing; if you ring your bicycle bell people will get out of the way; is that your mobile ringing?*
(b) to telephone; *he rang me to say he would be late; don't ring tomorrow afternoon - the office will be closed; don't ring me, I'll ring you*
(c) to ring a bell = to remind someone of something; *does the name Arbuthnot ring any bells?; yes, the name does ring a bell* (NOTE: ringing - rang [ræŋ] - has rung [rʌŋ])
3 *verb*
(a) to draw a ring round something; *I have ringed the mistakes in red*
(b) to surround; *rebel troops ringed the president's palace* (NOTE: ringing - ringed)

③ **ring back**
['rɪŋ 'bæk] *verb*
to telephone to answer someone; *Mr Smith isn't in - can you ring back in half an hour?; she said she would ring back but she didn't*

③ **ring off**
['rɪŋ 'ɒf] *verb*
to put down the phone; *when I answered the phone, the caller rang off*

③ **ring road**
['rɪŋ 'rəʊd] *noun*
road which goes right round a town; *instead of driving through the town centre, it will be quicker to take the ring road*

③ **ring up**
['rɪŋ 'ʌp] *verb*
to make a telephone call; *I rang up his office to say I was going to be late; a Mr Smith rang you up while you were out; he rang up the police to say that his car had been stolen*

③ **rink**
[rɪŋk] *noun*
skating rink = large enclosed area for ice skating, playing ice hockey, etc.; *in the evening we all went to the skating rink; there used to be an indoor skating rink in Richmond*

③ **riot**
['raɪt]
1 *noun*

(a) wild disorder by a crowd of people; *the riot was started by some university students*; **to run riot** = to get out of control; *after the match, the supporters ran riot and the police had to be called in*; *in her stories for children she lets her imagination run riot*; **to read someone the riot act** = to warn someone to stop doing something; *I read her the riot act when I found she had been using the office telephone to call her mother in Australia*

(b) mass of colours; *the colour scheme is a riot of reds and greens*

(c) very amusing film, play, etc.; *the whole show was a riot, I never laughed so much*

2 *verb*

to take part in a riot; to get out of control; *furious farmers rioted when they heard the decision of the Minister of Agriculture*

④ **rip**

[rɪp] *verb*

(a) to tear, to pull roughly; *I ripped my sleeve on a nail*; *she ripped open the parcel to see what he had given her*; *the old bathroom is being ripped out and new units put in*

(b) to go through something violently; *the tropical storm ripped through the town*

(c) *(informal)* **to let rip** = to start to complain, protest, etc., without any restraint; *when he saw the bill for the meal he really let rip*; *see also* RIP OFF (NOTE: **ripping - ripped**)

③ **ripe**

[raɪp] *adjective*

(a) ready to eat or to be harvested; *don't eat that apple - it isn't ripe yet*

(b) **the time is ripe** = it is the right time to do something; *the time is ripe to take steps to stop imports of the drug* (NOTE: **riper - ripest**)

④ **rip off**

['rɪp 'ɒf] *verb*

(a) to tear off; *it's the last day of the month so you can rip the page off the calendar*; *someone has ripped off the book's cover*

(b) *(slang)* **to rip someone off** = to cheat someone, to make someone pay too much; *they were ripped off by the taxi driver*

④ **rip-off**

['rɪpɒf] *noun*

(slang) bad deal, something which costs too much; *what a rip-off! - it's not worth half the price*; *that car was a rip-off - it had been involved in an accident*

① **rise**

[raɪz]

1 *noun*

(a) movement or slope upwards; *there is a gentle rise until you get to the top of the hill*; *salaries are increasing to keep up with the rise in the cost of living*; *the recent rise in interest rates has made mortgages more expensive*

(b) **pay rise** = increase in salary; *she asked the manager for a pay rise*; *he's had two rises this year*; *if I don't get a rise soon I'll start looking for another job* (NOTE: American English for this is **raise**)

(c) *(formal)* **to give rise to something** = to make something happen; *the news gave rise to rumours about a coup*

2 *verb*

(a) to go up; *the sun always rises in the east*; *the road rises gently for a few miles*; *prices have been rising steadily all year*; *if you open the oven door, the cake won't rise properly*

(b) *(formal)* to get up, to get out of bed or out of a chair; *he always rises early*

(c) *(formal)* to stop being in session; *the court rose at one o'clock* (NOTE: **rising - rose** [rʊz] - **has risen** ['rɪzn])

① **risk**

[rɪsk]

1 *noun*

(a) possible harm; *the risk of becoming blind is very remote*; *there is a financial risk attached to this deal*; *at the risk of looking silly, I'm going to ask her out for a meal*

(b) **to run the risk of** = to be in danger of; *they run the risk of being caught by the customs*; *if you ask for a pay rise now, you run the risk of losing your job*; **to take a risk** = to do something which may make you lose money or suffer harm; *he's so careful, he never takes any risks*; *drive slowly, we're in no hurry and there's no need to take any risks*

(c) **at owner's risk** = the owner is responsible if something happens to his property; *cars are parked at owners' risk*; *goods left in the left luggage office are at owners' risk*; **fire risk** = situation or materials which could start a fire; *that room full of waste paper is a fire risk*

2 *verb*

to do something which may possibly harm; *the fireman risked his life to save her*; *he risked all his savings on buying the bookshop*

④ **risky**

['rɪski] *adjective*

which is dangerous; *he lost all his money in some risky ventures in South America*; *there is ice on the road, driving would be very risky* (NOTE: **riskier - riskiest**)

④ **ritual**

['rɪtjuɪl]

1 *adjective*

referring to a religious ceremony; *the people of the village performed a ritual rain dance*

2 *noun*

(a) regular ceremony; *the ritual of the mass*

(b) something which you do regularly in the same way; *every evening it's the same ritual: he puts the cat out and locks the door*

④ **rival**

['raɪvl]

1 *adjective*

competing, who competes; *two rival companies are trying to win the contract; is this the rival product you were talking about?*; *Simon and I are friends but we play for rival teams*

2 *noun*

person who competes; company which competes; *do you know if he has any rivals?*; *we keep our prices low to be cheaper than our biggest rival*

3 *verb*

to compete with someone; to be of similar quality to someone; *it will not be easy to rival such a good product; our local pub rivals any London pub of the same size* (NOTE: rivalling - rivalled but American spelling is rivaling - rivaled)

② **river**
['rɪvɪ] *noun*

large mass of fresh water which runs across the land and goes into the sea or into a lake; *London is on the River Thames; the river is very deep here, so it's dangerous to swim in it* (NOTE: with names of rivers, you usually say the River: the River Thames; the River Amazon; the River Nile)

④ **roach**
[rəʊtʃ] *noun*

US (informal) cockroach, big black or brown insect, a common household pest; *in hot damp climates, roaches are often found in kitchens* (NOTE: plural is roaches)

① **road**
[rəʊd] *noun*

(a) hard way used by cars, trucks, etc., to travel along; *the road to York goes directly north from London; drivers must be careful because roads are covered with ice; children are taught to look both ways before crossing the road; what is your office address? - 26 London Road* (NOTE: often used in names: London Road, York Road, etc., and usually written Rd: London Rd, etc.)

(b) road signs = signs put at the side of the road giving information to drivers; *if you come to a road sign saying 'Kingston', turn back because you will have gone too far; there are no road signs at that junction, but that is where you have to turn left*

(c) on the road = travelling; *as a salesman, he's on the road thirty weeks a year; we were on the road for thirteen hours before we finally reached the hotel*

③ **road rage**
['rəʊd 'reɪdʒ] *noun*

violent attack by a driver on another car or its driver, caused by anger at the way the other driver has been driving; *there have been several incidents of road rage lately; in the latest road rage attack, the driver jumped out of his car and knocked a cyclist to the ground*

③ **road tax**
['rəʊd 'tæks] *noun*

tax paid by owners of cars, trucks, etc., to the government for permission to drive their vehicle on the road; *a tax disk shows that you have paid your road tax*

④ **roar**
[rɔː]
1 *noun*

loud noise of shouting, of an engine, etc.; *you could hear the roar of the crowd at the football match several miles away; the roar of the jet engines made it impossible for me to hear what she said*

2 *verb*

to make a loud noise; *he roared with laughter at the film; the lion roared and then ran towards us*

③ **roaring**
['rɔːrɪŋ] *adjective*

wild; roaring fire = big fire, with flames going up the chimney; *we sat in front of a roaring fire and ate mince pies*; to do a roaring trade = to sell something very fast; *the ice cream sellers have been doing a roaring trade during the hot weather*

③ **roast**
[rəʊst]
1 *verb*

to cook over a fire or in an oven; *if you want the meat well cooked, roast it for a longer period at a lower temperature; you can either roast pigeons or cook them in red wine*

2 *adjective*

which has been roasted; *what a lovely smell of roast meat!; we had roast chicken for dinner*; roast potato = potato baked in fat in an oven; *serve the meat with roast potatoes and green vegetables* (NOTE: although the verb has the forms roasting - roasted, when referring to meat, the adjective roast is used: roast meat, roast turkey, but roasted peanuts)

3 *noun*

meal with meat cooked in an oven; *we always have a roast on Sundays*

③ **rob**
[rɒb] *verb*

to attack and steal from someone; *a gang robbed our local bank last night; the old lady was robbed of all her savings* (NOTE: robbing - robbed)

③ **robber**
['rɒbɪ] *noun*

person who attacks and steals from someone; *the robbers attacked the bank in broad daylight; three of the robbers were caught*

④ **robbery**
['rɒbrɪ] *noun*

attacking and stealing; *there was a robbery in our street yesterday; did they ever find out who committed the bank robbery?* (NOTE: plural is robberies)

④ **robust**

[rɪˈbʌst] *adjective*

(a) strong, vigorous; *this young tree is very robust and should survive the winter*; *my grandmother is not very robust but she still manages to look after herself*

(b) vigorous and determined; *he gave some robust answers to the journalists' questions*; *our troops will give a robust response to any enemy attack*

② **rock**

[rɒk]

1 *noun*

(a) large stone, large piece of stone; *the ship was breaking up on the rocks*

(b) hard pink sweet shaped like a rod, often with the name of a town printed in it, bought mainly by tourists; *a stick of Brighton rock*

(c) music with a strong rhythm; *rock (music) is the only music he listens to*

2 *verb*

(a) to sway from side to side; to make something sway from side to side; *the little boat rocked in the wake of the ferry*; *the explosion rocked the town*; *(informal)* **don't rock the boat** = don't do anything to disturb what has been arranged; *everything has been organized, so please don't rock the boat with any new suggestions*

(b) to move from side to side, holding something; *the baby is crying, I'll try to rock him to sleep*

◊ **on the rocks**

phrase

(a) in great difficulties; *the company is on the rocks*; *their marriage is on the rocks*

(b) served with ice; *a whisky on the rocks*

③ **rock bottom**

[ˈrɒk ˈbɒtɪm] *noun*

the lowest point; *sales have reached rock bottom*; **rock-bottom prices** = the lowest prices possible; *we can't give you a bigger discount - the prices quoted are rock-bottom prices*

④ **rocket**

[ˈrɒkɪt]

1 *noun*

(a) type of firework which flies up into the sky; *we stood in the square and watched the rockets lighting up the sky*

(b) type of bomb which is shot through space at an enemy; *they fired a rocket into the police station*

(c) **space rocket** = large device which is fired into space, carrying satellites, etc.; *the Americans are sending a rocket to Jupiter*

(d) *(slang)* **to give someone a rocket** = to criticize someone sharply; *the manager gave him a rocket when he was late back from lunch*; *she'll get a rocket from the boss if he catches her on the phone to her boyfriend again*

(e) type of green vegetable eaten in salads

2 *verb*

to shoot upwards very fast; *prices have rocketed this summer*

④ **rocky**

[ˈrɒkɪ] *adjective*

(a) full of rocks and large stones; *they followed a rocky path up the mountain*

(b) *(informal)* difficult; *the company has had a rocky year*

(c) **the Rocky Mountains** *or* **the Rockies** = range of high mountains, running south from western Canada into the western United States; *the pictures of the Rocky Mountains covered in snow are a typical postcard scene*; *we picked up two backpackers who were hitching a lift into the Rockies*

④ **rod**

[rɒd] *noun*

(a) long stick; *you need something like a metal rod to hold the tent upright*; **fishing rod** = long stick with a line attached, used for fishing

(b) *(informal)* **with an iron rod** *or* **with a rod of iron** = very strictly, without allowing any weakness; *the secretary rules the office with an iron rod*; *she's a tiny little woman but she rules the office with a rod of iron*

③ **rode**

[rəʊd] *see* RIDE

③ **role**

[rəʊl] *noun*

(a) part played by someone, in a play or film; *he plays the role of the king*; **title role** = part after which a play is named; *who's playing the title role in 'Hamlet'?*

(b) part played by someone in real life; *he played an important role in getting the project off the ground* (NOTE: do not confuse with **roll**)

① **roll**

[rəʊl]

1 *noun*

(a) tube of something which has been turned over and over on itself; *a roll of fax paper*; *a roll of toilet paper* *or* *a toilet roll*

(b) list of names; **to call the roll** = to read out the list of names to see if everyone is there; **roll of honour** = list of people who have done something special, such as students who have won prizes, or soldiers killed in battle

(c) very small loaf of bread for one person, sometimes cut in half and used to make a sandwich; *will an egg salad and a bread roll be enough for you?*; *the airline's continental breakfast was just a roll and a cup of coffee*; **cheese roll** *or* **ham roll** = roll with cheese or ham in it

(d) **sausage roll** = small pastry with sausage meat inside; **Swiss roll** *US* **jelly roll** = cake made by rolling up a thin sheet of cake covered with jam

(e) action of rolling; *it takes time to get used to the roll of the ship*; *with a roll of her eyes and a shake of her head, she left the room* (NOTE: do not confuse with **role**)

2 *verb*

(a) to make something go forward by turning it over and over; *he rolled the ball to the other player*

(b) to go forward by turning over and over; *the ball rolled down the hill; my pound coin has rolled under the piano*

(c) to make something move on wheels; *the table is fitted with wheels, just roll it into the room; the patient was rolled into the operating theatre ten minutes ago*

(d) to turn something flat over and over; *he rolled the poster into a tube*

(e) to move from side to side; *the ship rolled in the heavy seas; she rolled her eyes and pointed at the door* (NOTE: the other movement of a boat, where the front and back go up and down, is to **pitch**)

(e) *US (informal)* to attack and rob someone

③ **roll up**
['rʊl 'ʌp] *verb*

(a) to turn something flat over and over until it is like a tube; *he rolled up the carpet or he rolled the carpet up*

(b) *(informal)* to arrive; *they just rolled up and asked if we could put them up for the night; the bridegroom finally rolled up an hour late and said he'd had a flat tyre*

④ **Roman**
['rʊmɪn]

1 *adjective*

referring to Rome, the capital of Italy and of the ancient Roman Empire; *a book about Roman emperors*; **Roman alphabet** = the alphabet used in many European languages (A, B, C, D, etc.), as opposed to the Greek or Russian alphabets; *the Inuit would like to preserve their own alphabet rather than use the Roman one*; **Roman numerals** = numbers written as by the Romans (I, II, III, IV, etc.) (NOTE: Roman numerals are still used for names of kings and queens, and in copyright dates on some films and TV programmes)

2 *noun*

(a) person who lives or lived in Rome; *the Romans invaded Britain in AD 43*

(b) printing type with straight letters; *the book is set in Times Roman* (NOTE: the other two styles of print are **italic** and **bold**)

④ **romance**
[rɪ'mæns]

1 *noun*

love affair; *she told us all about her holiday romance; their romance didn't last*

2 *adjective*

romance language = language which is based on Latin; *French is a romance language, can you name any others?*

④ **romantic**
[rɪ'mæntɪk] *adjective*

(a) full of mystery and love; *we had a romantic dinner by the beach which I'll never forget; the atmosphere on the ship was very romantic*; **romantic novel** = novel which is a love story

(b) *(literary or artistic style)* which is very imaginative; which is based on personal emotions; *his style is too romantic for my liking; the romantic period is not my favourite literary period*

② **roof**
[ruːf] *noun*

(a) part of a building, etc., which covers it and protects it; *the cat walked across the roof of the greenhouse; she lives in a little cottage with a red roof*

(b) top of the inside of the mouth; *I burnt the roof of my mouth drinking hot soup*

(c) top of a car, bus, lorry, etc.; *we had to put the cases on the roof of the car*; **roof rack** = frame fixed to the roof of a car for carrying luggage; *our car doesn't have a roof rack, so all the luggage had to go in the boot*

① **room**
[ruːm] *noun*

(a) part of a building, divided from other parts by walls; *the flat has six rooms, plus kitchen and bathroom; we want an office with at least four rooms*; **dining room** = room where you eat; *see also* BATHROOM, BEDROOM, LIVING ROOM, etc.

(b) bedroom in a hotel; *your room is 316 - here's your key; his room is just opposite mine*; **double room** = room for two people; *do you have a double room for three nights?*; **single room** = room for one person; *I would like to book a single room for tomorrow night*; **room service** = arrangement in a hotel where food or drink can be served in a guest's bedroom; *if we call room service, we can have food sent up to our room*

(c) space for something; *the table is too big - it takes up a lot of room; there isn't enough room in the car for six people; we can't have a piano in our flat - there just isn't enough room*; **to make room for** = to squeeze together to make space for; *there is no way we can make room for another passenger*; **there's room for improvement** = things could be improved; *the system is better than it was, but there is still room for improvement* (NOTE: no plural in this meaning: **some room, no room, too much room**)

④ **roost**
[ruːst]

1 *noun*

perch where a bird sleeps; **to rule the roost** = be in charge, to the boss; *he's the MD, but it's his secretary who rules the roost in the firm*

2 *verb*

(a) to perch asleep; *six chickens were roosting in the shed*

(b) to come home to roost = to come back to have a bad effect on the person who actually did it; *his mistakes in investing on the stock market have come home to roost*

④ **rooster**

['ruːstɪ] *noun*

(mainly US) male domestic chicken; *we were woken by the rooster on our neighbour's farm* (NOTE: British English is **cock**)

② **root**

[ruːt] *noun*

(a) part of a plant which goes down into the ground, and which takes energy from the soil; *I'm not surprised the plant died, it has hardly any roots*; *(of a cutting)* **to take root** = to make roots; *the cuttings died, none of them took root*; **to put down roots** = to begin to feel at home in a place; *we have been living in Berlin for three months and are beginning to put down roots*; **root crops** *or* **root vegetables** = vegetables which are grown for their roots which are eaten, such as carrots, etc.; *it is impossible to grow root vegetables in this kind of soil*

(b) part of a hair or a tooth which goes down into the skin; *he pulled her hair out by the roots* (NOTE: do not confuse with **route**)

③ **root up** *or* **root out**

['ruːt 'ʌp *or* 'ruːt 'aʊt] *verb*

(a) to pull up a plant with its roots; *I spent the morning rooting up weeds in the garden*

(b) to remove something completely; *the police are trying to root out corruption*

③ **rope**

[rəʊp]

1 *noun*

(a) very thick string; *you'll need a rope to pull the car out of the ditch*; *the burglar climbed down from the balcony on a rope*

(b) to learn the ropes = to learn how to do something; *we send new salesmen out with an experienced rep to learn the ropes*; *(informal)* **it's money for old rope** = it's money which is easy to make

2 *verb*

(a) to tie together with a rope; *the climbers roped themselves together*; *we roped the sofa onto the roof of the car*

(b) to rope someone in = to get someone to help or to join in; *rope in as many people as you can, we need all the help we can get*; *she was roped in to deal with the children's tea*

(c) to rope off = to stop people going into a place by putting a rope around it; *the VIP area has been roped off - you need a special ticket to get in*

③ **rose**

[rəʊz]

1 *noun*

(a) common garden flower with a strong scent; *he gave her a bunch of red roses*; *these roses have a beautiful scent*

(b) common wild shrub with these strongly scented flowers; *wild roses were growing along the path*

2 *verb*

see RISE

④ **rot**

[rɒt]

1 *noun*

decay; *once rot infects the roots, it will kill the plant quickly*; **dry rot** = decay in the wooden parts of a house caused by a type of mushroom; *get rid of the dry rot before you do any other repairs to the house*; *(informal)* **the rot has set in** = things have begun to go badly wrong; *we thought things were going well, but then the rot set in and the shop had to close*

2 *verb*

to decay, to go bad; *the wooden fence is not very old but it has already started to rot*; *see also* ROTTEN (NOTE: **rotting - rotted**)

④ **rotate**

[rəʊ'teɪt] *verb*

to turn round like a wheel; *rotate the knob to the right to increase the volume*

④ **rotation**

[rəʊ'teɪʃn] *noun*

turning; *the rotation of the Earth round the sun*

③ **rotten**

['rɒtɪn] *adjective*

(a) decayed; *the apple looked nice on the outside, but inside it was rotten*; *don't walk across that little bridge, I think it is rotten*

(b) *(informal)* miserable; *I had a rotten time at the party - no one would dance with me*; *we had rotten weather on holiday*; **to feel rotten** = (i) to feel ill; (ii) to feel ashamed; *yesterday I felt slightly unwell, but today I feel really rotten*; *I feel so rotten for having spoiled your birthday party*

② **rough**

[rʌf]

1 *adjective*

(a) not smooth; *the sea's rough today - I hope I won't be sick*; *we had a rough crossing from England to France*

(b) with a sharp, unpleasant taste; *this wine's a bit rough - but what can you expect for £2.99?*

(c) approximate, not very accurate; *I made some rough calculations on the back of an envelope*

(d) not finished; *he made a rough draft of the new design*

(e) not gentle; *don't be rough when you're playing with the puppy* (NOTE: **rougher - roughest**)

2 *noun*

(a) design which has not been finished; *she showed me some roughs for the new gardening magazine*

(b) *(informal)* **to take the rough with the smooth** = to accept that there are bad times as well as good times

(c) part of a golf course where the grass is not cut; *his ball went into the rough*

3 *verb*

(a) *(informal)* **to rough it** = to live in uncomfortable conditions; *the four-star hotels are all full, so we'll just have to rough it in a bed and breakfast*

(b) to rough something out = to make a rough design for something; *he roughed out the plan of the house on the back of an envelope*

(c) *(informal)* **to rough someone up** = to attack someone; *when he refused to pay, the landlord sent some people round to rough him up*

4 *adverb;* **to sleep rough** = to sleep in the open, on the pavement; *hundreds of young people were sleeping rough in doorways*

③ **rough and ready**
['rʌf n 'redi] *adjective*

approximate; not beautifully finished; *the plan is a bit rough and ready, but it will give you a general idea of what we want; I'm not too pleased with the work he did - it is a bit too rough and ready*

② **roughly**
['rʌfli] *adverb*

(a) approximately, more or less; *there are roughly ten francs to the pound; the cost of building the new kitchen will be roughly £25,000*

(b) in a rough way; *don't play so roughly with the children; the removal men threw the boxes of china roughly into the back of their van*

① **round**
[raʊnd]

1 *adjective*

(a) with a shape like a circle; *in Chinese restaurants, you usually sit at round tables*

(b) with a shape like a globe; *soccer is played with a round ball, while a Rugby ball is oval; people used to believe that the Earth was flat, not round*

(c) in round figures = not totally accurate, but correct to the nearest 10 or 100; *expect to pay £5000 in round figures*

2 *adverb & preposition*

(a) in a circular way; *the wheels of the lorry went round and round; the Earth goes round the Sun; he was the first person to sail round the world single-handed; we all sat round the table chatting*

(b) towards the back; *she turned round when he tapped her on the shoulder; don't look round when you're driving on the motorway; he ran down the street and disappeared round a corner*

(c) from one person to another; *they passed round some papers for everyone to sign; can you pass the plate of cakes round, please?;* **enough to go round** = enough for everyone; *there aren't enough glasses to go round*

(d) in various places, here and there; *they spent the afternoon going round the town* (NOTE: **round** is used with many verbs: **go round, come round,** etc.)

3 *noun*

(a) regular route for delivering; **the postman's round** = the streets where a postman delivers mail every day; **a newspaper round** = the houses which a newspaper boy or girl delivers newspapers to every day; *our son started doing a newspaper round last week*

(b) round (of drinks) = drinks bought by one person for a group of people; *it's my turn to buy the next round*

(c) slice of bread; **a round of toast** = piece or pieces of toast made from one slice of bread; **a round of sandwiches** = two or four sandwiches made from two slices of bread

(d) part of a competition; *those who answer all the questions correctly, go on to the next round; he was knocked out in the first round*

(e) playing all the holes on a golf course; *I think we have time for one more round before it gets dark*

(f) series of meetings; *a round of pay negotiations*

(g) one bullet; *the police fired several rounds into the crowd of students*

4 *verb*

to go round; *he rounded the corner and saw a crowd in front of him; the boat sank as it was rounding the little island*

③ **roundabout**
['raʊndɪbaʊt]

1 *noun*

(a) place where several roads meet, and traffic has to move in a circle; *when you get to the next roundabout, turn right* (NOTE: in American English, this is called a **traffic circle**)

(b) *(in a children's playground)* heavy wheel which turns, and which children ride on; *the children all ran to get on the roundabout*

(c) *(in a fair)* large amusement machine, which turns round and plays music, usually with horses to sit on which move up and down

2 *adjective*

not direct; *the taxi took a very roundabout route to get to Trafalgar Square*

③ **round down**
['raʊnd daʊn] *verb*

to decrease to the nearest full figure; *the figures have been rounded down to the nearest dollar*

③ **rounds**
[raʊndz] *noun*

regular visits; *the doctor made his rounds of the patients*

③ **round-the-world**
['raʊndðɪ'wɜːld] *adjective*

which goes round the world, returning to the original departure point; *a round-the-world ticket allows you to stop in several places; twenty yachts are taking part in the round-the-world yacht race*

③ **round trip**
['raund 'trɪp] *noun*

journey from one place to another and back again; *by train, the round trip will cost £15;* **round-trip ticket** = ticket for a journey from one place to another and back again; *a round-trip ticket is cheaper than two one-way tickets* (NOTE: also called a **return ticket**)

③ **round up**
['raund 'ʌp] *verb*

(a) to gather people or animals together; *the secret police rounded up about fifty suspects and took them off in vans; she rounded up the children and took them into the museum; the farmer is out in the fields rounding up his sheep*

(b) to increase to the nearest full figure; *the figures have been rounded up to the nearest dollar; I owed him £4.98 so I rounded it up to £5.00*

② **route**
[ru:t *US also* raut]

1 *noun*

(a) way to be followed to get to a destination; *we still have to decide which route we will take;* **bus route** = normal way which a bus follows; *the cinema is not on the bus route, we'll have to go there by car*

(b) **en route** = on the way; *the tanker sank when she was en route to the Gulf*

(c) **route march** = training march by soldiers (NOTE: do not confuse with **root**)

2 *verb*

to send someone along a route; *the demonstration was routed along Piccadilly to St James' Park*

③ **routine**
[ru:'ti:n]

1 *noun*

(a) normal, regular way of doing things; *children don't like their routine to be changed; a change of routine might do you good; having a cup of coffee while reading the newspaper is part of his morning routine;* **daily routine** = things which you do every day; *buying a newspaper on his way to work and a bar of chocolate on his way home is all part of his daily routine*

(b) instructions which carry out a task as part of a computer program; *the routine copies the screen display onto a printer*

(c) sequence of dance steps; *the dancers were practising a very complicated routine*

2 *adjective*

normal or everyday; *he went to the doctor for a routine checkup; we're making a routine check of the central heating system*

② **row**

1 *noun*

(a) [rʊ] line of things, side by side or one after the other; *he has a row of cabbages in the garden; they pulled down an old house to build a row of shops; I want two seats in the front row*

(b) [rau] loud noise; *stop making that dreadful row!*

(c) [rau] serious argument; *they had a row about who was responsible for the accident*

2 *verb*

(a) [rʊ] to make a boat go forward by using long blades; *she rowed across the lake to fetch a doctor*

(b) [rau] *(informal)* to argue; *they were rowing about who would pay the bill*

③ **rowboat**
['rʊbɪʊt] *US* = ROWING BOAT

④ **rowdy**
['raudi] *adjective*

making a great deal of noise; *a rowdy party in the flat next door kept us all awake; the minister had a rowdy reception at the meeting* (NOTE: **rowdier - rowdiest**)

③ **rowing**
['rɪʊɪŋ] *noun*

making a boat move by the use of long wooden blades; *I'm not good at rowing; the boys' school has a rowing club;* **rowing boat** = small boat for rowing; *we hired a rowing boat and went down the river* (NOTE: American English is **rowboat**)

① **royal**
['rɔɪl] *adjective*

referring to a king or queen; **the Royal Family** = family of a king or queen; **royal blue** = dark blue

④ **royalty**
['rɔɪlti] *noun*

(a) members of a king's or queen's family; *please dress formally, there will be royalty present* (NOTE: no plural in this meaning)

(b) money paid to the author of a book or an actor in a film, or the owner of land where oil is found, etc., as a percentage of sales; *do you receive royalties on the sales of your book?; all royalty cheques are paid direct to my account in Switzerland* (NOTE: plural is **royalties**)

③ **RSVP**
['ɑ: es vi: 'pi:] *abbreviation for the French phrase répondez s'il vous plaît, meaning 'please answer'*

letters printed on an invitation asking the person invited to reply

① **rub**
[rʌb]

1 *verb*

to move something across the surface of something else; *he rubbed his hands together to get them warm*; *these new shoes have rubbed against my heel*; *the cat rubbed herself against my legs* (NOTE: **rubbing - rubbed**)

2 *noun*

action of rubbing; *she gave her shoes a quick rub to remove the dust*; *he hit his head on the low ceiling, and gave it a rub*

④ **rubber**
['rʌbɪ] *noun*

(a) elastic material made from juice from a tropical tree; *car tyres are made of rubber*; *many years ago, we visited a rubber plantation in Malaysia*; **rubber band**; *see* ELASTIC BAND

(b) piece of rubber used for removing pencil marks; *he used a rubber to try to rub out what he had written* (NOTE: the American equivalent is an **eraser**)

③ **rubbish**
['rʌbɪʃ] *noun*

(a) waste, things which are no use and are thrown away; *we had to step over heaps of rubbish to get to the restaurant*; **rubbish bin** = container for putting rubbish; *throw all those old cans into the rubbish bin*

(b) nonsense, something which has no value; *have you read the new bestseller? - it's rubbish!*; *he's talking rubbish, don't listen to him* (NOTE: no plural; note also American English is **garbage** *or* **trash**)

③ **rub in**
['rʌb 'ɪn] *verb*

(a) to make a cream enter the skin by rubbing; *she rubbed sun cream into her skin*

(b) *(informal)* **don't rub it in** = don't go on talking about my mistake; *yes, I know I made a mistake, but please, don't rub it in*

③ **rub out**
['rʌb 'aʊt] *verb*

to remove a pencil mark with a rubber; *it's written in pencil so you can rub it out easily*

③ **rub up**
['rʌb 'ʌp] *verb*

(informal) **to rub someone up the wrong way** = to make someone annoyed; *she's in a bad mood, someone must have rubbed her up the wrong way*

④ **rucksack**
['rʌksæk] *noun*

bag carried on the back of a walker; *he put extra clothes and a bottle of water in his rucksack*; *a group of walkers with muddy boots and rucksacks came into the pub* (NOTE: larger bags are called **backpacks**)

④ **rude**
[ruːd] *adjective*

not polite, likely to offend, trying to offend; *don't point at people - it's rude*; *the teacher*

asked who had written rude words on the board; *he was rude to the teacher and has had bad marks ever since* (NOTE: **ruder - rudest**)

④ **rudely**
['ruːdlɪ] *adverb*

in a rude way; *she told him rudely what he could do with his offer*

④ **rudeness**
['ruːdnɪs] *noun*

being rude; *he was sacked for his rudeness to the customers*

④ **rug**
[rʌg] *noun*

(a) small carpet; *this beautiful rug comes from the Middle East*

(b) thick blanket, especially one used when travelling; *put a rug over your knees if you're cold*; *we spread rugs on the grass to have our picnic*

③ **rugby**
['rʌgbɪ] *noun*

rugby football = type of football played with an oval ball which is thrown as well as kicked; *when and where is the next rugby match?*; **rugby ball** = type of oval ball used in rugby

COMMENT: the game developed from football when, in 1823, a pupil at Rugby School picked up the ball and started to run with it. After that, rules of play were developed, and an oval ball introduced. There are two forms of rugby: Rugby Union, which was until 1996 the amateur game, and is also the international game, and Rugby League, which has always been a professional game, played mainly in the north of England. There are fifteen players in a Rugby Union team and thirteen in a Rugby League team. Each match is divided into two 40-minute halves separated by a 10-minute interval. Players can pick up the ball and run with it but are not allowed to pass forward, and players with the ball can be tackled and brought to the ground. Points are scored by touching the ground with the ball behind the opponents' goal line (a try) and by kicking the ball over a bar between two posts (a conversion). A try counts as 5 points in Rugby Union and 4 points in Rugby League; a conversion counts as 3 points in Rugby Union and 2 points in Rugby League

③ **ruin**
['ruːɪn]

1 *noun*

(a) complete loss of all your money; *he faces complete ruin*

(b) remains of an old building with no roof, fallen walls, etc.; *the house was a total ruin when I bought it*; **to fall into ruin** = to become a ruin; *the house was empty for many years and gradually fell into ruin*

2 *verb*

(a) to wreck or to spoil completely; *our holiday was ruined by the weather*
(b) to bring to financial collapse; *the failure of the bank ruined a lot of businesses*

③ **ruined**
['ruːɪnd] *adjective*
(a) in ruins; *smoke rose from the ruined houses*
(b) not able to pay your debts; *a ruined company director*

③ **ruins**
['ruːɪnz] *noun*
remains of old buildings with no roofs, fallen walls, etc.; *the ruins of the house are still smoking*; **in ruins** = wrecked; *the town was in ruins after the war*; *after being arrested at the night club, his career was in ruins*

② **rule**
[ruːl]
1 *noun*
(a) strict order of the way to behave; *there are no rules that forbid parking here at night*; *according to the rules, your ticket must be paid for two weeks in advance*; **against the rules** = not as the rules say; *you can't hold the football in your hands - it's against the rules*
(b) **as a rule** = usually; *as a rule, we go to bed early during the week*
(c) **rule of thumb** = easily remembered way of doing a simple calculation; *as a rule of thumb you can calculate that a pound is half a kilo*
(d) government; *the country became prosperous under the rule of the generals*
2 *verb*
(a) to govern or to control; *the president rules the country according to military principles*; *who rules here, the MD or his wife?*
(b) to give an official or legal decision; *the judge ruled that the documents had to be brought to the court*
(c) to draw a straight line using a ruler; **ruled paper** = paper with lines on it

② **rule out**
[ruːl 'aʊt] *verb*
to leave something out, not to consider something; *you can rule out the possibility of leaving tomorrow*; *you can rule me out - I'm much too tired to go dancing*; *only graduates should apply, so that rules me out*; *I wouldn't rule out the possibility of the voters staying at home on polling day*

③ **ruler**
['ruːlə] *noun*
(a) strip of wood or plastic with measurements marked on it, used for measuring and drawing straight lines; *you need a ruler to draw straight lines*
(b) person who governs; *he's the ruler of a small African state*

③ **ruling**
['ruːlɪŋ]
1 *adjective*

(a) in power, governing; **ruling party** = party which forms the government; *the ruling party is not very popular and will not succeed in winning enough votes*
(b) in operation at the moment; *we will invoice at ruling prices*
2 *noun*
legal decision made by a judge, etc.; *the judge will give a ruling on the case next week*; *according to the ruling of the court, the contract was illegal*

④ **rumour** *US* **rumor**
['ruːmɪ]
1 *noun*
story spread from one person to another but which may not be true; *there's a rumour going around that John's finally getting married*
2 *verb*
to spread a story; *it was rumoured in the press that they were about to get divorced*

① **run**
[rʌn]
1 *noun*
(a) going quickly on foot as a sport; *she entered for the 10-mile run*; *I always go for a run before breakfast*; *you must be tired out after that long run*
(b) short trip in a car; *let's go for a run down to the seaside*
(c) making a machine work; **test run** = trial made on a machine; *a test run will help you to see if the machine is working properly*
(d) rush to buy something; *the Post Office reported a run on the new stamps*
(e) regular route of a plane, bus, etc.; *on this run, the bus does not go as far as the Post Office*; *she's a stewardess on the London - New York run*
(f) score of 1 in cricket; *he made 45 runs before he was out*
(g) *US* series of little holes in stockings or tights; *I can't wear these stockings because there's a run in them* (NOTE: British English for this is a **ladder**)
2 *verb*
(a) to go quickly on foot; *when she heard the telephone, she ran upstairs*; *children must be taught not to run across the road*; *she's running in the 200 metre race*
(b) *(of buses, trains, etc.)* to be working; *all underground trains are running late because of the accident*; *this bus doesn't run on Sundays*
(c) *(of machines)* to work; *he left his car in the street with the engine running*; *my car's not running very well at the moment*
(d) to go; *the main street of the town runs north and south*; *the film runs for three hours*

(e) to direct, to organize a business, a club, etc.; *he runs a chain of shoe shops; I want someone to run the sales department for me when I'm away on holiday; he runs the local youth club; the country is run by the army*

(f) to use a car regularly; *we can't afford to run two cars*

(g) to drive by car; *let me run you to the station*

(h) to be in force; *the lease has only six months more to run*

(i) to amount to; *the costs ran into thousands of pounds*

(j) *(of liquid)* to flow, to move along easily; *the river runs past our house; this colour won't run* = the colour will not stain other clothes if they are all washed together

(k) to run in a family = to be an inherited feature; *red hair runs in their family*

(l) to publish a story in several editions of a newspaper; *the paper is running a shocking story about the minister's wife* (NOTE: running - ran [ræn] - has run)

① **run across**
['rʌn ə'krɒs] *verb*

(a) to cross quickly on foot; *the little boy ran across the road after his ball*

(b) to find or to meet by accident; *I ran across it in a secondhand bookshop*

① **run after**
['rʌn 'ɑːftɪ] *verb*

to follow someone fast; *he ran after the postman to give back the letter which was wrongly addressed; the dog never runs after cats, only birds*

① **run away**
['rʌn ə'weɪ] *verb*

(a) to escape, to go away fast; *they were running away from the police; she ran away from school when she was 16; the youngsters ran away to Paris*

(b) to run away with someone = to go away from your family to live with someone or to marry someone; *she ran away with her German teacher*

(c) to let your imagination run away with you = to think things are possible when they are not; *don't let your imagination run away with you!*

① **run down**
['rʌn 'daʊn] *verb*

(a) to go down quickly on foot; *she ran down the stairs two at a time; can you run down to the village and buy me some bread?*

(b) *(of clock, machine)* to stop working or go slower because of lack of power; *the clock has stopped - the battery must have run down*

(c) to criticize someone; *it's not fair to run him down when he's not there to defend himself*

(d) to reduce the quantity of something; *we're running down our stocks of coal before the summer*

(e) to knock down with a vehicle; *she was run down by a car which did not stop*

② **run for**
['rʌn 'fɔː] *verb*

(a) to go fast to try to catch; *he ran for the bus but it left before he got to the stop*

(b) to be a candidate for an office; *he's running for president*

② **rung**
[rʌŋ]

1 *noun*

one of the bars on a ladder; *if you stand on the top rung you can climb onto the roof; put your foot on the bottom rung to hold the ladder steady*

2 *verb*

see RING

② **run into**
['rʌn 'ɪntʊ] *verb*

(a) to go into a place fast; *she ran into the street, shouting 'Fire!'*

(b) to go fast and hit something (usually in a vehicle); *he didn't look where he was going and ran into an old lady; the bus turned the corner too fast and ran into a parked van*

(c) to amount to; *costs have run into thousands of pounds; her income runs into five figures*

(d) to find someone by chance; *I ran into him again in a café on the South Bank*

③ **runner**
['rʌnɪ] *noun*

(a) person or horse running in a race; *my horse came in last of seven runners; there are 40,000 runners in the London Marathon*

(b) runner bean = type of climbing bean

③ **runner-up**
['rʌnɪ'ʌp] *noun*

person who comes after the winner in a race or competition; *Natasha won the competition and her younger brother was runner-up; France won the World Cup and Brazil were runners-up* (NOTE: plural is **runners-up**)

③ **running**
['rʌnɪŋ]

1 *adjective*

(a) which runs; **running battle** = battle which moves around from place to place; *the police were engaged in running battles with the protesters*; **running commentary** = commentary on an action while the action is taking place; *the BBC reporter gave a running commentary on the riots from his hotel window*; **running total** = total which is carried from one column of figures to the next; *the running total appears at the bottom of the first column and at the top of the next one*; **running water** = water which is available in a house through water pipes and taps; *I'm not sure that all the houses in the village have running water; there is hot and cold running water in all the rooms*

(b) used when running a race; *running shorts; running shoes*

(c) for three days running = one day after another for three days; *the company have made a profit for the sixth year running*

(d) running mate = person who stands for election as number two to the main candidate; *if the candidate for president wins, then his running mate becomes vice-president*

2 *noun*

(a) race; **to be in the running for** = to be a candidate for; *three candidates are in the running for the post of chairman*; **out of the running** = with no chance of doing something; *she's out of the running for the job in the bookshop*

(b) action of managing; *I now leave the running of the firm to my son*

① **run off**
['rʌn 'ɒf] *verb*

(a) to go away fast; *he grabbed the watch and ran off down the street*

(b) to print using a machine; *she ran off a few copies of the leaflet*

① **run off with**
['rʌn 'ɒf 'wɪð] *verb*

(a) to go away with someone; *he ran off with the girl next door and phoned his parents to say they had gone to Paris*

(b) to steal something and go away; *the secretary ran off with our cash box*

① **run on**
['rʌn 'ɒn] *verb*

(a) to use something as a fuel; *the machine runs on electricity*

(b) to continue; *the text runs on to the next page*; *does the play run on until very late?*

① **run out**
['rʌn 'aʊt] *verb*

to run out of something = to have nothing left of something; *the car ran out of petrol on the motorway*; *I must go to the supermarket - we're running out of butter*

① **run over**
['rʌn 'əʊvɪ] *verb*

(a) to knock someone down by hitting them with a vehicle; *she was run over by a taxi*; *the car ran over a dog*

(b) to continue; *the description of the accident runs over two pages*

① **run through**
['rʌn 'θruː] *verb*

(a) to read a list rapidly; *let's run through the agenda before the meeting starts to see if there are any problem areas*; *she ran through the paragraph again to make sure she understood what it meant*; *we must run through the list of guests to see if we have forgotten anyone*

(b) to use up; *we have run through our entire stock of wine in one weekend*

(c) to repeat; *just run through that scene again to see if you all know your lines*

① **run up**
['rʌn 'ʌp] *verb*

(a) to go up quickly on foot; *she ran up the stairs carrying a thermometer*; *the runners have to run up the mountain and back again*

(b) to run up to = to come closer quickly on foot; *he ran up to the policeman and asked him to call an ambulance*

(c) to make debts go up quickly; *the business was running up debts of thousands of pounds each week*

(d) to sew something quickly; *I can run up a dress in less than an hour*

① **run up against**
['rʌn 'ʌp ə'genst] *verb*

to find your way blocked by something; *whatever we try to do, we seem to run up against local regulations*; *we ran up against unexpected difficulties*

① **runway**
['rʌnweɪ] *noun*

track on which planes land and take off at an airport; *the plane went out onto the runway and then stopped for half an hour*

② **rural**
['rʊərɪl] *adjective*

referring to the countryside; *rural roads are usually quite narrow*; *we live quite close to a town but the country round us still looks very rural*

② **rush**
[rʌʃ]

1 *noun*

(a) fast movement; *there was a rush of hot air when they opened the door*; *there has been a rush to change pounds to francs*; *when the film ended there was a rush for the loos*; **rush job** = job which has to be done fast; *it is a rush job that needs to be dealt with immediately* (NOTE: no plural in this meaning)

(b) type of wild grass growing in water; *rushes grow along the shores of lakes and rivers* (NOTE: plural in this meaning is **rushes**)

(c) rushes = first prints of a film which are shown before being edited

2 *verb*

to hurry, to go forward fast; *the ambulance rushed to the accident*; *crowds of shoppers rushed to the shops on the first day of the sales*; **don't rush me** = don't keep on making me hurry; *I need time to do this work, please don't rush me*

① **rush hour**
['rʌʃ 'aʊɪ] *noun*

time of day when traffic is bad, when trains are full, etc.; *don't travel during the rush hour if you want to avoid the traffic*; *his taxi was stuck in the rush-hour traffic*

① **Russia**
['rʌʃɪ] *proper noun*

large country in Eastern Europe, covering also a large part of Asia up to the Pacific Ocean; *have you ever been to Russia?*; *he went on a journey across Russia* (NOTE: capital: **Moscow**; people: **Russians**; language: **Russian**; currency: **rouble**)

① **Russian**
['rʌʃn]
1 *adjective*
referring to Russia; *she speaks English with a Russian accent*; *Russian winters can be extremely cold*
2 *noun*
(a) person from Russia; *are there any Russians in the group?*
(b) language spoken in Russia; *we'll start the Russian lesson by learning the alphabet*; *he can speak Russian quite well*; *I can read Russian but I can't speak it*

④ **rust**
[rʌst]
1 *noun*
orange layer which forms on metal left in damp air; *there is a bit of rust on the bonnet of the car*; *the underneath of the car is showing signs of rust*

2 *verb*
to form rust; *don't leave the hammer and screwdriver outside in the rain - they'll rust*

④ **rusty**
['rʌsti] *adjective*
(a) covered with rust; *she tried to cut the string with a pair of rusty old scissors*; *he has a rusty old fridge in his front garden*
(b) out of practice; *my German used to be good, but it is very rusty now* (NOTE: **rustier - rustiest**)

④ **ruthless**
['ruːθlɪs] *adjective*
cruel, with no pity for anyone; *the new ruler is just as ruthless as the man he replaced*; *the manager has the reputation for being ruthless with employees who don't pull their weight*; *be ruthless, throw all those old letters away*

Ss

③ **S, s**
[es]
nineteenth letter of the alphabet, between R and T; *'she sells sea shells on the sea shore' - how many S's are there in that?*

④ **sack**
[sæk]
1 *noun*
(a) large bag made of strong cloth or paper, used for carrying heavy things; *he hurt his back lifting up the sack of potatoes*
(b) *(informal)* to get *or* to be given the sack = to be dismissed from a job; *you'll get the sack if you talk to the boss like that*
(c) complete destruction of a town; *the sack of Rome*
2 *verb*
(a) *(informal)* to dismiss someone from a job; *he was sacked because he was always late for work*
(b) to destroy a town completely; *the town was captured and sacked by the advancing enemy forces*

④ **sacred**
['seɪkrɪd] *adjective*
(a) associated with religion; *the sacred texts were kept locked away*; **sacred art** = paintings

of Christian religious scenes; **sacred music** = music to be played at Christian religious ceremonies
(b) holy; *Hindus believe that cattle are sacred*
(c) respected; *nothing is sacred to a reporter chasing a good story*; *she believed it was her sacred duty to look after his garden while he was away*

④ **sacrifice**
['sækrɪfaɪs]
1 *noun*
(a) things which you give up to achieve something more important; *he finally won the competition, but at great personal sacrifice*; *she made many financial sacrifices to get her children through university*
(b) making an offering to a god by killing an animal or person; *he ordered the sacrifice of two lambs to please the gods*
(c) animal offered to a god; *chickens, sheep and lambs were all offered as sacrifices to their gods*
2 *verb*
(a) to give up; *I have sacrificed my career to be able to stay at home and bring up my children*; *she has sacrificed herself for the cause of animal welfare*

(b) to offer something as a sacrifice; *the priests sacrificed a sheep to the god*

② **sad**
[sæd] *adjective*

(a) not happy, miserable; *he's sad because the holidays have come to an end; what a sad film! - everyone was crying; reading his poems makes me sad; it was sad to leave the house for the last time; he felt sad watching the boat sail away; it's sad that he can't come to see her; isn't it sad about her little boy being in hospital?*

(b) *(slang)* boring, not in fashion; *only sad people collect stamps* (NOTE: **sadder - saddest**)

④ **saddle**
['sædl]
1 *noun*

(a) rider's seat on a bicycle or motorbike; *she threw her leg across the saddle and settled herself behind him; my old saddle was very comfortable but this new one is harder*

(b) rider's seat on a horse; *he leapt into the saddle and rode away*; **in the saddle** = in command; *she's in the saddle now - you have to do what she says*

(c) cut of meat from the back of an animal; *saddle of lamb*

2 *verb*

(a) to put a saddle on a horse; *she quickly saddled her horse and rode off*

(b) to saddle someone with = to give someone a difficult job or heavy responsibility; *he got saddled with the job of sorting out the rubbish; don't saddle me with all your problems!*

④ **sadly**
[sædli] *adverb*

in a sad way; *after the funeral we walked sadly back to the empty house; she stared sadly out of the window at the rain; sadly, John couldn't join us for lunch that day*

④ **sadness**
['sædnɪs] *noun*

feeling of being very unhappy; *her sadness at finding her cat dead*

② **safe**
[seɪf]
1 *adjective*

(a) not in danger, not likely to be hurt; *in this cave, we should be safe from the storm; all the children are safe, but the school was burnt down; a building society account is a safe place for your money; is it safe to touch this snake?; it isn't safe for women to go into the centre of town alone at night*

(b) in safe hands = in no danger; *the guide is very experienced, so we are in safe hands*; **safe and sound** = without being hurt or damaged; *we all arrived at our destination, safe and sound; the present reached me safe and sound, thanks to the efficiency of the post office*

(c) to be on the safe side = just in case, to be certain; *it should only take an hour to get to the airport, but let's give ourselves an hour and a half, just to be on the safe side* (NOTE: **safer - safest**)

2 *noun*

strong box for keeping documents, money, jewels, etc., in; *put your valuables in the hotel safe; the burglars managed to open the safe*; **wall safe** = safe installed in a wall

② **safely**
['seɪfli] *adverb*

(a) without being hurt; *the rescue services succeeded in getting all the passengers safely off the burning train; we were shown how to handle bombs safely; 'drive safely!' she said as she waved goodbye*

(b) without being damaged; *the cargo was safely taken off the sinking ship*

(c) without making a mistake or having problems; *can we safely say that this is a genuine Picasso?; she got safely through the first part of her exams*

② **safety**
['seɪfti] *noun*

(a) being safe; *the police tried to ensure the safety of the public; I am worried about the safety of air bags in cars*; **fire safety** = measures taken to keep a place safe for workers and visitors in case of fire; **road safety** = care taken by drivers on the roads to make sure that accidents don't happen; **safety belt** = belt which you wear in a plane to stop you being hurt if there is an accident; **safety curtain** = special curtain in front of the stage in a theatre, to protect against fire; *the safety curtain is lowered and raised at the beginning of each performance*; **safety helmet** = solid hat worn by construction workers, etc.; *visitors to the building site must wear safety helmets* (NOTE: also called **hard hats**); **safety pin** = pin whose point fits into a little cover when it is fastened, and so can't hurt anyone; **to take safety precautions** *or* **safety measures** = to act to make sure something is safe; *be sure to take proper safety precautions when handling gas cylinders*; **safety regulations** = rules to make a place of work safe for the workers

(b) for safety = to make something safe, to be safe; *put the money in the office safe for safety; keep a note of the numbers of your traveller's cheques for safety* (NOTE: no plural)

③ **said**
[sed] *see* SAY

③ **sail**
[seɪl]
1 *noun*

(a) piece of cloth which catches the wind and drives a boat along; *the wind dropped so they lowered the sail and started to row; they pulled up the sail and set out across the Channel*

(b) to set sail = to leave by boat; *they set sail for France*

(c) trip in a boat; *they went for a sail down the Thames* (NOTE: do not confuse with **sale**)

2 *verb*

(a) to travel on water; *the ship was sailing towards the rocks*; *we were sailing east*

(b) to travel in a sailing boat; *he was the first person to sail alone across the Atlantic*; *she's planning to sail round the world*

(c) to leave harbour; *the ferry sails at 12.00*

(d) to go without difficulty; *the car just sailed along the motorway*; *it's annoying to see a bus sail past just when you're getting to the bus stop*; **to sail through** = to pass easily; *he sailed through his driving test*

③ **sailboat**
['seɪlbɪʊt] *US* = SAILING BOAT

③ **sailing**
['seɪlɪŋ] *noun*

(a) travel in a ship; **sailing boat** *or* **sailing ship** *US* **sailboat** = boat (such as a yacht) which uses mainly sails to travel

(b) sport of going in a sailing boat; *I plan to take up sailing when I retire*; *we have booked to go on a sailing holiday in the Mediterranean*

(c) departure (of a ship); *there are no sailings to France because of the strike*; *there are three sailings every day to Dieppe*; **sailing time** = time when a boat leaves the harbour

(d) plain sailing = easy progress; *once he had passed the first year exams, it was just plain sailing until he got his degree*

④ **sailor**
['seɪlɪ] *noun*

(a) person who works on a ship; *the sailors were washing down the deck of the ship*

(b) good sailor *or* bad sailor = person who is liable or not liable to be sick on a boat; *he doesn't worry about the water being rough - he's a good sailor*

④ **saint**
[seɪnt] *noun*

(a) person who led a very holy life, and is recognized by the Christian church; *there are more than 50 statues of saints on the west front of the cathedral*; *St Peter was a fisherman*; *will Mother Teresa be made a saint?*

(b) very good or devoted person; *she has the patience of a saint and never shouts at the children*; *he may be no saint in his personal life but he has the support of the voters* (NOTE: written **St** [snt] with names: **St Cecilia, St Christopher**)

② **sake**
[seɪk] *noun*

(a) for the sake of something *or* for something's sake = for certain reasons, because of something; *he's not really hungry, he's just eating for eating's sake*; *the president decided to resign for the sake of the country*; *they gave the children sweets, just for the sake of a little*

peace and quiet; *the muggers killed the old lady, just for the sake a few pounds*; **for the sake of someone** *or* **for someone's sake** = because you want to help someone, because you think someone needs something; *will you come to the party for my sake?*; **for old times' sake** = to remember how good the old times were; *let's have a meal together for old times' sake*

(b) *(exclamation)* **for heaven's sake** *or* **for goodness' sake** = expressions showing you are annoyed, or that something is important; *what are you screaming for? - it's only a little mouse, for heaven's sake*; *for goodness' sake try to be quiet, we don't want the guards to hear us!*

④ **salad**
['sæləd] *noun*

cold food, such as vegetables, often served raw; cold fish or meat served with cold vegetables; *we found some ham, tomatoes and lettuce in the fridge, and made ourselves a salad*; *a chicken salad sandwich*; **salad bar** = bar where customers help themselves to a wide variety of meat, fish or vegetable salads; **salad dressing** = mixture of oil, etc., used on salad; **fruit salad** = pieces of fresh fruit, mixed and served cold

③ **salaried**
['sælɪrɪd] *adjective*

paid a salary; *the company has 250 salaried staff*

③ **salary**
['sælɪri] *noun*

payment for work, made to an employee with a contract of employment, especially in a professional or office job; *she started work at a low salary, but soon went up the salary scale*; *the company froze all salaries for a period of six months*; *I expect a salary increase as from next month*; **basic salary** = normal salary without extra payments; **gross salary** = salary before tax is deducted; **net salary** = salary which is left after deducting tax and national insurance contributions; **starting salary** = amount of payment for an employee when starting work with a company; *he was appointed at a starting salary of £20,000*; **salary cheque** = monthly cheque by which an employee is paid (NOTE: plural is **salaries**)

COMMENT: in Britain and the USA, salaries are usually paid monthly but are quoted in annual terms. So you say 'her salary is £20,000', 'the job carries a salary of $50,000'. Although bonuses are paid, a regular extra month's salary at Christmas (the 'thirteenth month' in some European countries) is not common in Britain or the USA

① **sale**
[seɪl] *noun*

(a) act of selling, act of giving an item or doing a service in exchange for money, or for the promise that money will be paid; *the sale of the* house produced £200,000; the shop only opened this morning and we've just made our first sale; **cash sale** = transaction paid for in cash; **credit card sale** = transaction paid for by credit card

(b) occasion when things are sold at cheaper prices; there's a sale this week in the department store along the High Street; I bought these plates for £1 in a sale; the sale price is 50% of the normal price; **half-price sale** = sale of all goods at 50% of the usual price

(c) **for sale** = ready to be sold; **to offer something for sale** or **to put something up for sale** = to announce that something is ready to be sold; they put the factory up for sale; these items are not for sale to the general public; the office building is for sale at £1m; I noticed there was a 'for sale' sign outside her house

(d) **on sale** = ready to be sold in a shop; his latest novel is on sale in all good bookshops; local cheeses are on sale in the market (NOTE: do not confuse with **sail**)

① **sales**
[seɪlz] noun

(a) money which a business receives from selling things; the business has annual sales of over £250,000; sales have risen over the first quarter; **sales forecast** = estimate of future sales; **sales manager** = person in charge of a sales department; **sales representative** = person who works for a company, showing goods or services for sale

(b) time when many shops sell goods at low prices; the sales start on Saturday; I bought these shirts in the January sales; she bought the cups in the sales or at the sales

③ **sales assistant**
[seɪlz ə'sɪstənt] noun

person who sells goods to customers in a shop; the sales assistant will help you

③ **salesgirl**
[seɪlzgɜːl] noun

girl who sells goods to customers in a shop; this purse hasn't got a price on it - I'll just go and ask a salesgirl how much it is

③ **saleslady**
[seɪlzleɪdɪ] noun

woman who sells goods to customers in a shop; ask the saleslady if they have that skirt in your size (NOTE: plural is **salesladies**)

③ **salesman**
[seɪlzmɪn] noun

(a) man who sells goods to customers in a shop; the salesman is going to show us the latest model

(b) person who represents a company, selling its products or services to other companies; we have six salesmen calling on accounts in central London (NOTE: plural is **salesmen**)

③ **saleswoman**
[seɪlzwʊmɪn] noun

woman in a shop who sells goods to customers; our saleswomen are all dressed in pale blue dresses (NOTE: plural is **saleswomen** [seɪlzwɪmɪn])

④ **salmon**
[sæmɪn]
1 noun

large fish with silver skin and pink flesh; in Alaska the bears love to catch salmon as they swim up the rivers; we had grilled salmon and new potatoes; **salmon steak** = thick slice of salmon; **smoked salmon** = salmon which has been cured by smoking, and is served in very thin slices, usually with brown bread and lemon (NOTE: plural is **salmon**)

2 adjective

with a pink colour like salmon; we put a salmon-pink wallpaper in the bathroom

COMMENT: salmon live in the sea, but swim up rivers in the winter. Nowadays, salmon are also farmed in fish farms

④ **salon**
[sælɒn] noun

shop where people can have their hair cut or styled, or have beauty treatments; the hairdressing salon is on the fifth floor; she went to the beauty salon for a facial

② **salt**
[sɒlt]
1 noun

(a) white substance used to make food taste better (used especially with meat, fish and vegetables); there's too much salt in this soup; you don't need to put any salt on your fish; **to take something with a pinch of salt** = not to believe something entirely; you have to take everything she says with a pinch of salt (NOTE: no plural: **some salt, a spoonful** or **a pinch of salt**)

(b) large pieces of a chemical compound used to put on frozen streets to melt ice or snow; lorries were out all night spreading salt on the streets

(c) **the salt of the earth** = ordinary good honest person; he's a wonderful man - the salt of the earth!

2 adjective

containing salt; the sea is made up only of salt water

3 verb

(a) to spread salt on; they were salting the streets during the night

(b) to add salt to; you forgot to salt the soup

③ **salt water**
[sɒlt 'wɔːtɪ] noun

water which contains salt, such as sea water (as opposed to fresh water in rivers and lakes); she dived into the waves and got a mouthful of salt water; you can float more easily in salt water than in a lake

④ **salute**

[sɪˈluːt]

1 *noun*

(a) movement to express respect, recognition, etc., especially putting your right hand up to touch the peak of your cap; *the officer returned the soldier's salute*; **to take the salute** = to be the person whom soldiers on parade salute; *the general took the salute at the march past*

(b) firing guns to mark an important occasion; *the birthday of the Queen was marked with a 21-gun salute*

2 *verb*

(a) to give a salute to someone; *ordinary soldiers must salute their officers*

(b) to praise someone; *we salute the brave firemen who saved the children*

④ **salvage**

[ˈsælvɪdʒ]

1 *noun*

(a) saving a ship or cargo from being destroyed; **salvage money** = payment made by the owner of a ship or cargo to the person who saved it; *were you paid any salvage money for the goods rescued from the boat?*; **salvage vessel** = ship which specializes in saving other ships and their cargoes

(b) goods saved from a wreck, fire, etc.; *a sale of flood salvage items*

(c) saving rubbish for use; *a company specializing in the salvage of plastics from household waste*

2 *verb*

(a) to save from a wreck, fire, etc.; *we are selling off a warehouse full of salvaged goods*; *we managed to salvage the computer discs from the fire*

(b) to save something from loss; *the company is trying to salvage its reputation after the managing director was sent to prison for fraud*; *the banks managed to salvage something from the collapse of the company*

③ **salvation**

[sælˈveɪʃn] *noun*

action of saving a person's soul from sin; *he sought his salvation in working for the homeless*

③ **Salvation Army**

[sælˈveɪʃn ˈɑːmi] *noun*

Christian organization run on military lines, which does welfare work; *my sister has joined the Salvation Army*; *we tracked him down to a Salvation Army home in the city centre*

① **same**

[seɪm] *adjective & pronoun*

(a) being, looking, sounding, etc., exactly alike; *these two beers taste the same*; *you must get very bored doing the same work every day*; *she was wearing the same dress as me*; *this book is not the same size as that one*; **to stay the same** = not to change; *the weather is expect to stay the*

same for the next few days; *(informal)* **same again, please!** = please serve us the same drinks or food, etc., as before

(b) showing that two or more things are in fact one; *they all live in the same street*; *should we all leave at the same time?*; *our children go to the same school as theirs*; *see also* ALL THE SAME

② **sample**

[ˈsɑːmpl]

1 *noun*

specimen, a small part which is used to show what the whole is like; *a sample of the cloth or a cloth sample*; *try a sample of the local cheese*; *we interviewed a sample of potential customers*; **free sample** = sample given free to advertise a product

2 *verb*

(a) to test, to try by taking a small amount; *why don't you sample the wine before placing your order?*

(b) to ask a group of people questions to find out a general reaction; *they sampled 2,000 people at random to test the new soap*

④ **sanction**

[ˈsæŋkʃn]

1 *noun*

(a) approval, permission; *you will need the sanction of the local authorities before you can knock the house down*

(b) **economic sanctions** = restrictions on trade with a country in order to try to influence its political development; *to impose sanctions on a country or to lift sanctions from a country*

2 *verb*

to approve; *the committee sanctioned the expenditure of £1.2m on the development project*

③ **sand**

[sænd]

1 *noun*

mass of tiny bits of rock, found on beaches, in the desert, etc.; *a beach of fine white sand*; *the black sand beaches of the Northern coast of New Zealand*; *he kicked sand in my face*; **sand castle** = little castle of sand made by children on a beach; *the children built sand castles on the beach with their buckets*

2 *verb*

(a) *(also;* **sand down)** to rub smooth; *they sanded the floor before polishing it*

(b) to spread sand on; *trucks have been out all night sanding the motorways*

④ **sands**

[sændz] *noun*

area of sandy beach; *the sands stretch for miles along the coast*

② **sandwich**

[ˈsændwɪtʃ]

1 *noun*

(a) snack made with two slices of bread with meat, salad, etc., between them; *she ordered a cheese sandwich and a cup of coffee*; *what sort of sandwiches do you want to take for your lunch?*; *I didn't have a big meal - just a sandwich with some beer in the pub*; **club sandwich** = sandwich made of three slices of bread, with a filling of meat, salad, fish, etc., between them; **sandwich bar** = small shop which mainly sells sandwiches (NOTE: plural is **sandwiches**)

(b) **sandwich boards** = boards carried in front of and behind a person with advertisements on them; **sandwich man** = man who carries sandwich boards

2 *verb*

to insert something between two others; *I stood all the way home on the Underground, sandwiched between two fat men*

③ **sandy**
['sændi] *adjective*
covered with sand; *the resort has miles of safe sandy beaches* (NOTE: **sandier - sandiest**)

③ **sang**
[sæŋ] *see* SING

③ **sank**
[sæŋk] *see* SINK

④ **sardine**
[saː'diːn] *noun*
small fish which can be eaten fresh, or is commonly bought in tins; *we had grilled sardines in a little restaurant overlooking the harbour*; **packed (together) like sardines** = packed very close together; *in the rush hour we were packed like sardines on the Underground*

③ **sat**
[sæt] *see* SIT

④ **SAT**
[sæt] *US* = SCHOLASTIC APTITUDE TEST; *(trademark of the College Entrance Examination Board)* tests taken before entry to college

④ **SATs**
[sæts] *GB* = STANDARD ASSESSMENT TASKS national tests taken at various ages during secondary school

④ **satellite**
['sætɪlaɪt] *noun*
(a) device that orbits the earth, receiving and transmitting signals, pictures and data; *the signals are transmitted by satellite all round the world*; **communications satellite** = satellite that relays radio or TV signals from one part of the earth to another; **satellite broadcasting** = sending radio or TV signals from one part of the earth to another using a communications satellite; **satellite dish** =device, shaped like a large saucer, used to capture satellite broadcasts; **satellite TV** = television system, where pictures are sent via a space satellite; *we watched the programme on satellite TV*

(b) body in space which goes round a planet; *the Moon is the only satellite of the Earth*

③ **satisfaction**
[sætɪs'fækʃn] *noun*
(a) good feeling; sense of comfort or happiness; *after finishing his meal he gave a deep sigh of satisfaction*; *I get no satisfaction from telling you this - you're fired*; **job satisfaction** = feeling which you have that you are happy in your work and pleased with the work you do

(b) *(formal)* payment of money or goods to someone, who then agrees to stop a claim against you; *they demanded satisfaction from the driver of the other car*

④ **satisfactory**
[sætɪs'fæktrɪ] *adjective*
quite good, which satisfies; *the result of the election was very satisfactory for big business*; *a satisfactory outcome to the discussions*

③ **satisfied**
['sætɪsfaɪd] *adjective*
contented; *I've finished painting the kitchen, and I hope you're satisfied with the result*; *she gave a satisfied smile*; **satisfied customer** = customer who has got what he wanted

② **satisfy**
['sætɪsfaɪ] *verb*
(a) to make someone pleased with what he has bought, with the service he has received; *the council's decision should satisfy most people*; *our aim is to satisfy our customers*

(b) **to satisfy a demand** = to fill a demand; *we cannot produce enough to satisfy the demand for the product*; **to satisfy yourself** = to make sure; *the buyer must satisfy himself that the car is in good condition*

(c) to comply with conditions; *the payments received so far do not satisfy the conditions attached to the contract*

③ **satisfying**
['sætɪsfaɪɪŋ] *adjective*
which satisfies; *it was very satisfying to see the two of them getting on so well*; *to grow all our own fruit and vegetables is very satisfying*

① **Saturday**
['sætɪdeɪ] *noun*
sixth day of the week, the day between Friday and Sunday; *he works in a shop, so Saturday is a normal working day for him*; *we go shopping in London most Saturdays*; *Saturday is the Jewish day of rest*; *today is Saturday, November 15th*; *the 15th is a Saturday, so the 16th must be a Sunday*; *we arranged to meet up at the cinema next Saturday evening*

④ **sauce**
[sɔːs] *noun*
liquid with a particular taste, poured over food; *ice cream with chocolate sauce*; *we had chicken with a curry sauce*; *the waitress put a bottle of tomato sauce on the table*; *we had roast duck and orange sauce for dinner*

③ **saucepan**
['sɔːspæn] noun
deep metal cooking pan with a lid and a long handle; *where's the lid of the saucepan?*; *watch the saucepan - I don't want the milk to boil over*; *put the mixture in a saucepan and cook over a low heat*; *I never put the saucepans in the dishwasher*

③ **saucer**
['sɔːsɪ] noun
shallow dish which a cup stands in; *where are the cups and saucers? - they're in the cupboard*; **a saucer of milk** = milk put in a saucer, usually for a cat to drink

③ **sausage**
['sɒsɪdʒ] noun
tube full of minced and seasoned meat, eaten hot; *you can't possibly eat all those sausages!*; *I'll have sausages and eggs for breakfast*

④ **savage**
['sævɪdʒ]
1 adjective
fierce, likely to hurt; *hunger had made the dogs really savage*; *she suffered a savage beating and had to have stitches in her head*
2 noun
wild human being; *how could he turn into such a savage and attack her like that?*
3 verb
to attack with teeth; *he was savaged by an Alsatian*

① **save**
[seɪv]
1 verb
(a) to stop someone from being hurt or killed; *the firemen saved six people from the burning house*; *how many passengers were saved when the ferry sank?*; **the policeman saved my life** = the policeman helped me and prevented me from being killed
(b) to stop something from being damaged; *we managed to save most of the paintings from the fire*
(c) to put things such as money to one side so that you can use them later; *I'm saving to buy a car*; *if you save £10 a week, you'll have £520 at the end of a year*; *they save old pieces of bread to give to the ducks in the park*; *he saves bits of string in case he may need them later*
(d) not to waste (time, money, etc.); *by walking to work, he saves £25 a week in bus fares*; *she took the parcel herself so as to save the cost of postage*; *if you have your car serviced regularly it will save you a lot of expense in the future*; *going to Scotland by air saves a lot of time*
(e) to store data on a computer disk; *don't forget to save your files when you have finished keyboarding them*
(f) *(in football)* to stop an opponent from scoring; *the goalkeeper saved two goals*
2 noun
(in football) action of stopping the ball from going into the net; *the goalkeeper made a brilliant save, and the result was that the match was drawn*
3 preposition & conjunction; (formal)
except for; *everyone was there, save Richard, who was ill*

① **save on**
['seɪv 'ɒn] verb
not to waste, to use less; *by introducing shift work we find we can save on fuel*; *by walking to work, you will find that you can save on bus fares*

① **save up**
['seɪv 'ʌp] verb
not to spend the money you get because you are keeping it for a special purpose; *I'm saving up to buy a motorbike*; *they are saving up for a holiday in the USA*

③ **saving**
['seɪvɪŋ]
1 noun
using less; *we are aiming for a 10% saving in fuel*
2 suffix
which uses less; **an energy-saving** *or* **labour-saving device** = machine which saves energy *or* labour

① **savings**
['seɪvɪŋz] noun
(a) money which you can save; *he put all his savings into a building society account*; *she spent all her savings on a round the world trip*; **savings account** = bank account where you can put money in regularly and which pays interest, often at a higher rate than a deposit account; **savings bank** = bank where you can deposit money and receive interest on it
(b) money which you do not need to spend; *there are incredible savings on flights to Florida*

④ **saw**
[sɔː]
1 noun
tool with a long metal blade with teeth along its edge, used for cutting; *he was cutting logs with a saw*; *my old saw doesn't cut very well*; **chain saw** = saw made of a chain with teeth in it, which turns very fast when driven by a motor
2 verb
(a) to cut with a saw; *she was sawing wood*; *they sawed the old tree into pieces*; *you will need to saw that piece of wood in half* (NOTE: **sawing - sawed - has sawn** [sɔːn])
(b) *see also* SEE

① **say**
[seɪ]
1 verb
(a) to speak words; *what's she saying? - I don't know, I don't understand Dutch*; *she says the fee is £3 per person*; *don't forget to say 'thank you' after the party*; *the weather forecast said it*

was going to rain and it did; I was just saying that we never hear from my brother, when he phoned

(b) to give information in writing; *the letter says that we owe the bank £200; the notice says that you are not allowed to walk on the grass*

(c) to suggest; *choose any number - (let's) say eighteen; let's have another meeting next week - shall we say Thursday?* (NOTE: **says** [sez] - **saying** - **said** [sed] - **has said**)

2 *noun*

right to speak about something; *the children have no say in the matter; she always wants to have the final say in an argument; they will all expect to have their say in choosing the new leader*

3 *interjection US (to show surprise)*

say! haven't we met someplace before?

① **saying**
['seɪɪŋ] *noun*

phrase which is often used; *it's an old north country saying; my mother was fond of old sayings like 'red sky at night - sailor's delight';* **as the saying goes** = according to the old saying; *'more haste, less speed' as the saying goes*

② **scale**
[skeɪl]

1 *noun*

(a) proportion used to show a large object in a smaller form; *map with a scale of 1 to 100,000; the architect's design is drawn to scale; a scale model of the new town centre development*

(b) measuring system which is graded into various levels; *the Richter scale is used to measure earthquakes;* **scale of charges** *or* **scale of prices** = list showing prices for different goods or services; **scale of salaries** *or* **salary scale** = list showing the range and system of salaries in a company; *he was appointed at the top end of the salary scale*

(c) large scale *or* **small scale** = working with large or small amounts of investment, staff, etc.; **to start in business on a small scale** = to start in business with a small staff, few products, little capital

(d) thin plate protecting the skin of fish and snakes; *don't forget to scrape the scales off the fish before you cook it*

(e) series of musical notes arranged in a rising or falling order; *she practises her scales every morning*

2 *verb*

(a) *(formal)* to climb up; *six climbers tried to scale the north face of the mountain*

(b) to scale up *or* **to scale down** = to increase *or* to reduce in proportion; *not enough students have passed the exam, so the marks will have to be scaled up; the company is scaling down its operations in Thailand*

③ **scales**
[skeɪlz] *noun*

small machine for weighing; *she put two bananas on the scales; the bathroom scales must be wrong - I'm heavier than I was yesterday;* **to tip the scales at** = to weigh; *he tipped the scales at 210lb* (NOTE: no singular: for one say **a pair of scales**)

④ **scan**
[skæn]

1 *verb*

(a) to look very carefully at something all over; *we scanned the horizon but no ships were to be seen; he scanned the map to try to find Cambridge Road*

(b) to pass a radar beam over (an area); to pass X-rays through part of the body; *first they scanned the right side of the brain; the hospital has decided to see again all patients who have been scanned over the last year*

(c) to examine a drawing or text and produce computer data from it; *they scanned the text of the book*

(d) to analyze a line of poetry to identify the rhythm; *some modern poetry is impossible to scan*

(e) *(of poetry)* to fit a regular rhythm; *the second line of the poem doesn't scan* (NOTE: **scanning - scanned**)

2 *noun*

(a) examination of part of the body by passing X-rays through the body and analyzing the result in a computer; *she went to have a scan after ten weeks of pregnancy;* **brain scan** = examining the inside of the brain by passing X-rays through the head

(b) picture of part of the body shown on a screen, derived by computers from X-rays

(c) examination of an image or an object to obtain data; *a heat scan will quickly show which of the components is getting too hot*

④ **scandal**
['skændl] *noun*

(a) talking about wrong things someone is supposed to have done; *have you heard the latest scandal about him?*

(b) wrong action that produces a general feeling of public anger; *the government was brought down by the scandal of the president's wife's diamonds; the government should do something about the scandal of unemployed teenagers; it's a scandal that her father never allowed her to go to university*

④ **scar**
[skɑː]

1 *noun*

mark left on the skin after a wound has healed; *he still has the scars of his operation*

2 *verb*

(a) to leave a mark on the skin; *he was scarred for life as a result of the accident*

(b) to leave a mark on the mind of someone; *the abuse she suffered at school has scarred for ever* (NOTE: scarring - scarred)

④ **scarce**
['skeɪs] *adjective*

(a) not enough for the amount needed; *this happened at a period when food was scarce*; *good designers are getting scarce*
(b) *(informal)* to make oneself scarce = to hide, to keep out of someone's way (NOTE: scarcer - scarcest)

③ **scarcely**
['skeɪsli] *adverb*

almost not; *he can scarcely walk because of his bad back*; *I can scarcely believe it!*; scarcely anyone = almost no one; *scarcely anyone bought tickets for the show*

④ **scare**
[skeɪ]
1 *noun*

making someone frightened; *what a scare you gave me - jumping out at me in the dark like that!*; bomb scare = frightening rumour or announcement that there might be a hidden bomb somewhere
2 *verb*

to frighten; *the thought of travelling alone scares me*; *she was scared by the spider in the bathroom*; *(informal)* to scare the life out of someone = to frighten someone completely; to scare away = to frighten something so that it goes away; *the cat has scared all the birds away from the garden*

③ **scared**
[skeɪd] *adjective*

frightened; *don't be scared - the snake is harmless*; *she was too scared to answer the door*; *I'm scared at the idea of driving in London's rush hour traffic*; *she looked round with a scared expression*; scared stiff = so frightened that you cannot move; *I was scared stiff when I saw the children playing with the gun*

④ **scarf**
[skɑːf] *noun*

(a) long piece of cloth which is worn round your neck to keep you warm; *take your scarf - it's snowing*; *the students were wearing college scarves*; *it's cold - wrap your scarf round your neck*
(b) square piece of cloth which a woman can wear over her head; *put a scarf over your head - it's windy outside* (NOTE: plural is scarves [skɑːvz])

④ **scatter**
['skætɪ] *verb*

(a) to throw in various places; *the crowd scattered flowers all over the path*
(b) to run in different directions; *when the police arrived, the children scattered*

③ **scattered**
['skætɪd] *adjective*

spread out over a wide area; *there are scattered farms in the hills*; *I found the photos scattered all over the floor*

③ **scattering**
['skætɪrɪŋ] *noun*

a small quantity or number of things; *only a scattering of people turned up to the meeting*; *there was a scattering of snow during the night*

④ **scenario**
[sɪˈnɑːriʊ] *noun*

(a) written draft of a film with details of plot, characters, scenes, etc.; *he wrote the scenario for 'Gone with the Wind'*
(b) general way in which you think something may happen; *the worst scenario would be if my wife's mother came on holiday with us* (NOTE: plural is scenarios)

② **scene**
[siːn] *noun*

(a) short part of a play or film; *did you like the scene where he is trying to climb up the skyscraper?*; *it was one of the funniest scenes I have ever seen*
(b) behind the scenes = without being obvious, without many people knowing; *she helped her mother a lot behind the scenes*
(c) place where something has happened; *the fire brigade were on the scene very quickly*; *it took the ambulance ten minutes to get to the scene of the accident*; *a photographer was at the scene to record the ceremony*
(d) *(informal)* general area in which something happens; *the British political scene has changed radically over the last twelve months*; *he's king of the pop music scene*; it's not my scene = it's not the sort of thing I usually do or like
(e) view; *he took a photo of the scene from the hotel window*
(f) display of angry emotion; *she made a terrible scene when she discovered her husband with a girl*; *I can't stand it when people make scenes*

④ **scenery**
['siːnri] *noun*

(a) features of the countryside, such as mountains, lakes, rivers, etc.; *the beautiful scenery of the Lake District*
(b) painted cloth background used to imitate real buildings, rooms, landscapes, etc., on the stage in a theatre; *they lowered the scenery onto the stage*; *in between the acts all the scenery has to be changed* (NOTE: no plural)

④ **scent**
[sent]
1 *noun*

(a) pleasant smell of something which you can recognize; *the scent of roses in the cottage garden*

(b) perfume, a liquid which smells nice, and which is put on the skin; *that new scent of yours makes me sneeze*

(c) smell; **on the scent of** = following a trail left by; *the dogs followed the scent of the robbers*; **to put someone off the scent** = to give someone misleading information; *she tried to put the reporters off the scent by saying that her husband had gone into hospital*

2 *verb*

(a) to give something a pleasant smell; *the lavatory cleaner is scented with pine*

(b) to discover something by smelling; *dogs can scent rabbits in holes in the ground*

(c) to begin to feel that something exists; *the team raced forward, scenting victory* (NOTE: do not confuse with **cent, sent**)

④ **scented**
['sentɪd] *adjective*
with a pleasant scent; *strongly scented roses*; *a slightly scented soap*

③ **sceptical** *US* **skeptical**
['skeptɪkl] *adjective*
doubtful, who doubts; *you seem sceptical about his new plan*; *I'm sceptical of the success of the experiment*; *he listened to her with a sceptical look on his face*

③ **schedule**
['ʃedjuːl *US* 'skedʒuːl]
1 *noun*

(a) timetable, plan of times drawn up in advance; *he has a busy schedule of appointments*; *his secretary tried to fit me into his schedule*; **to be ahead of schedule** = to be early; *the building of the hotel was completed ahead of schedule*; **to be on schedule** = to be on time; *the flight is on schedule*; **to be behind schedule** = to be late; *I am sorry to say that we are three months behind schedule*

(b) list of times of departure and arrival of trains, planes, coaches, etc.; *the summer schedules have been published*

(c) programme or list of events; *the schedule of events for the music festival*

(d) list, especially of documents attached to a contract; *please find enclosed our schedule of charges*; *the schedule of territories to which an insurance policy applies*

2 *verb*

(a) to put something on an official list; *see the list of scheduled prices*; *the house has been scheduled as an ancient monument*

(b) to arrange the times for something; *the building is scheduled for completion in May*; *the flight is scheduled to arrive at six o'clock*; *we have scheduled the meeting for Tuesday morning*; **scheduled flight** = flight which is in the airline timetable (as opposed to a chartered flight); *he left for Helsinki on a scheduled flight*; **scheduled service** = regular bus or train service

① **scheme**
[skiːm]
1 *noun*
plan or arrangement for making something work; *she joined the company pension scheme*; *he has thought up some scheme for making money very quickly*; *I think the opposition parties have some scheme to embarrass the government*

2 *verb*
to plan something in secret; *she spent most of her time in the office scheming against the finance department*; *they have been scheming to buy the shop cheaply*

④ **scholar**
['skɒlɪ] *noun*

(a) person who has great learning; *he is a well-known scholar of French history*

(b) student at school or university who has a scholarship; *because I was a scholar my parents didn't have to pay any fees*

④ **scholarship**
['skɒlɪʃɪp] *noun*

(a) money given to someone to help pay for the cost of his or her study; *the college offers scholarships to attract the best students*; *she got or won a scholarship to carry out research into causes of cancer*

(b) deep learning; *the article shows sound scholarship* (NOTE: no plural in this meaning)

④ **Scholastic Aptitude Test**
[skɒ'læstɪk 'æptɪtjuːd 'test] *see* SAT

① **school**
[skuːl]
1 *noun*

(a) place where students, usually children, are taught; *our little boy is four, so he'll be going to school this year*; *some children start school younger than that*; *what did the children do at school today?*; *when he was sixteen, he left school and joined the army*; *which school did you go to?*; *we moved here because there are good schools nearby*; **school year** = period which starts in September and finishes in August; **nursery school** = school for very small children, for children under five years old; **primary school** = school for small children; **secondary school** = school for children after the age of eleven or twelve

(b) section of a college or university; *the school of medicine is one of the largest in the country*; *she's studying at law school*

(c) **art school** = college where students learn to draw, paint, etc.; **music school** = college where students learn to play or write music; *he's been teaching at the London School of Music for two years*

(d) group of similar artists; *these painters belong to the abstract school*

2 *verb*
(formal) to train; *he was schooled in the art of tapping telephones*

③ **schoolbook**
['sku:lbʊk] *noun*
book used when learning a subject at school; *schools need more funds to purchase schoolbooks*

③ **school bus**
['sku:l 'bʌs] *noun*
bus which collects children from home in the morning, takes them to school and brings them back home in the afternoon; *the school bus leaves her in front of the house every afternoon*; *the school bus collects our children every morning*

④ **schoolchildren**
['sku:ltʃɪldrɪn] *nouns*
children who go to school; *the village schoolchildren are collected by bus every morning*; *she took a group of schoolchildren to visit the museum*

③ **school kid**
['sku:l 'kɪd] *noun*
(informal) child who is at school; *at half past three the shop was full of school kids trying to buy sweets*

③ **schoolteacher**
['sku:ltiːtʃɪ] *noun*
person who teaches in a school; *she has taken her degree in history and is now training to be a schoolteacher*

① **science**
['saɪns] *noun*
(a) study of natural physical things, based on observation and experiment; *she took a science course or she studied science*; *we have a new science teacher this term*; *he has a master's degree in marine science*; *see also* SOCIAL SCIENCE
(b) **the sciences** = the science subjects at university, such as physics, chemistry, as opposed to the arts

③ **science park**
['saɪns 'pɑːk] *noun*
area outside a town which is set aside for scientific companies

② **scientific**
[saɪən'tɪfɪk] *adjective*
referring to science; *we employ hundreds of people in scientific research*; *he's the director of a scientific institute*; *she loved art and music and was never very scientific*

④ **scientifically**
[saɪən'tɪfɪkli] *adverb*
by using scientific experiments; *we must try to prove our theory scientifically*

② **scientist**
['saɪntɪst] *noun*
person who specializes in a science, often doing research; *scientists have not yet found a cure for the common cold*; *space scientists are examining the photographs of Mars*

④ **scissors**
['sɪzɪz] *noun*
tool for cutting paper, cloth, etc., made of two blades attached in the middle, with handles with holes for the thumb and fingers; *these scissors aren't very sharp*; *have you got a pair of scissors I can borrow?*; **nail scissors** = special small curved scissors for cutting your nails; *she cut the story out of the paper with her nail scissors* (NOTE: no singular form: for one, say **a pair of scissors**)

④ **scoop**
[sku:p]
1 *noun*
(a) deep round spoon with a short handle, for serving ice cream, etc.; *you must wash the scoop each time you use it*
(b) portion of ice cream, etc.; *I'll have one scoop of strawberry and one scoop of chocolate, please*
(c) exciting news story which a reporter is the first to find, or which no other newspaper has reported; *he came back from the visit to the footballer's girlfriend with a scoop*
2 *verb*
(a) to cut out with a scoop; *he scooped out a helping of mashed potato*; **to scoop out the inside of something** = to remove the inside of something with a spoon, etc.; *take a melon, and scoop out the seeds*
(b) to lift up, as with a scoop; *she scooped up the babies into her arms and ran upstairs*; *he scooped all the newspapers off the floor*
(c) **to scoop a newspaper** = to report a news item before another paper does; *they scooped their rivals with the story of the minister's girlfriend*

③ **scope**
[skəʊp] *noun*
(a) furthest area covered by observation or action; *these matters are beyond the scope of our investigation*
(b) opportunity or possibility; *we keep the children busy so there is no scope for them to get bored*; **there is scope for improvement** = it could be improved; *there is considerable scope for expansion into the export market*

② **score**
[skɔː]
1 *noun*
(a) number of goals or points made in a match; *the final score in the rugby match was 22 - 10*; *I didn't see the beginning of the match - what's the score?*; (informal) **what's the score?** = what is the news?; **I know the score** = I know all the problems involved
(b) **scores of** = many; *scores of people stayed at home during the train strike*; *I must have seen that film scores of times*
(d) written music; *he composed the score for the musical*

(e) to settle old scores = to take revenge for things that happened a long time ago

(f) on that score = as far as that is concerned; *he will eat any sort of food, so you won't have any trouble on that score*

2 *verb*

(a) to make a goal or point in a match; *they scored three goals in the first twenty minutes; she scored sixty-five!*

(b) *(music)* to arrange music for certain instruments; *a piece scored for piano and three drums*

(c) to scratch a flat surface; *score the surface of the wood with a sharp knife so that glue will hold better*

④ **Scot**
[skɒt] *noun*
person from Scotland; *is she English? - no, she's a Scot; the Scots have voted 'yes' in the referendum*

③ **Scotch**
[skɒtʃ]
1 *adjective*
referring to Scotland (NOTE: 'Scottish' is the usual adjective, but 'Scotch' is always used in the following phrases); **Scotch broth** = thick soup with grain, vegetables and lamb; *a hot bowl of Scotch broth will be very welcome;* **Scotch eggs** = hard boiled eggs covered with minced meat and breadcrumbs; **Scotch whisky** = whisky made in Scotland

2 *noun*

(a) Scotch whisky; *a bottle of scotch*

(b) a glass of this drink; *a large scotch, please* (NOTE: plural is **scotches**)

(c) Scotch tape = trademark for a type of transparent sticky tape; *can you pass me the reel of Scotch tape, please?; he sealed the parcel with some Scotch tape*

3 *verb*
to prove something wrong, to put a stop to something; *by appearing in public, the president scotched rumours of his death*

① **Scotland**
['skɒtlənd] *noun*
country to the north of England, forming part of the United Kingdom; *he was brought up in Scotland; Scotland's most famous export is whisky* (NOTE: capital: **Edinburgh**; people: **the Scots**)

① **Scottish**
['skɒtɪʃ] *adjective*
referring to Scotland; *is she English? - no, she's Scottish; the beautiful Scottish mountains*

④ **scramble**
['skræmbl]
1 *noun*

(a) rush; *there was a last-minute scramble for tickets*

(b) motorcycle race across rough country; *we went to watch the scramble and got very cold and wet*

2 *verb*

(a) to hurry, using your hands and knees if necessary; *he scrambled over the wall*

(b) to rush; *everyone was scrambling to get food*

(c) scrambled eggs = eggs mixed together and stirred as they are cooked in butter; *we had a starter of scrambled eggs with smoked salmon*

(d) to mix up a radio signal or telephone link so that it cannot be understood without a device for making it clear; *calls from the army chief of staff to the president are scrambled*

④ **scrap**
[skræp]
1 *noun*

(a) little piece; *a scrap of paper; there isn't a scrap of evidence against him; she is collecting scraps of cloth to make a blanket*

(b) waste materials; *to sell a car for scrap; the scrap value of the car is £200;* **scrap dealer** *or* **scrap merchant** = person who deals in scrap; **scrap heap** = heap of rubbish; *that car's good for the scrap heap;* **scrap metal** *or* **scrap paper** = waste metal *or* waste paper

(c) scraps = bits of waste food; *they keep the scraps to feed to their pigs*

(d) *(informal)* fight; *the football fans got into a scrap with local youths*

2 *verb*

(a) to throw away as useless; *they had to scrap 10,000 faulty spare parts; they are planning to scrap their nuclear power stations*

(b) to give up, to stop working on a plan; *we've scrapped our plans to go to Greece*

(c) to fight; *they were scrapping over who should get the best bit of the chicken* (NOTE: **scrapping - scrapped**)

④ **scrape**
[skreɪp]
1 *verb*
to scratch with a hard object which is pulled across a surface; *she scraped the paint off the door; he fell off his bike and scraped his knee on the pavement*

2 *noun*
(informal) awkward situation which is you get into by mistake; *he's always getting into scrapes*

③ **scrape through**
['skreɪp 'θruː] *verb*
to pass an examination with difficulty; *he thought he was going to fail, but in the end he just scraped through*

① **scratch**
[skrætʃ]
1 *noun*

(a) long wound on the skin; *put some antiseptic on the scratches on your arms;* **without a scratch** = with no injuries; *he came out of the car crash without a scratch*

(b) long mark made by a sharp point; *I will never be able to cover up the scratches on the car door*

(c) to start from scratch = to start something new without any preparation; **up to scratch** = of the right quality; *the recording was not up to scratch* (NOTE: plural is **scratches**)

2 *verb*

(a) to make a long wound on the skin; *his legs were scratched by the bushes along the path*

(b) to make a mark with a sharp point; *I must touch up the car where it has been scratched*

(c) to rub a part of the body with your fingernails; *he scratched his head as he wondered what to do next; stop scratching - it will make your rash worse!*

(d) to remove your name from the list of competitors; *one of the players scratched at the last minute*

3 *adjective*

collected together at the last minute; *our opponents were a scratch side from the next village*

④ **scream**
[skri:m]

1 *noun*

(a) loud cry of pain; *he let out a scream of pain; the screams of the victims of the fire*

(b) screams of laughter = loud laughter

(c) *(informal)* funny person; *she's an absolute scream when she starts talking about the office*

2 *verb*

(a) to make loud cries; *people on the third floor were screaming for help; they screamed with pain*

(b) to shout in a high voice; *she screamed at the class to stop singing*

(c) to scream with laughter = to laugh very loudly

② **screen**
[skri:n]

1 *noun*

(a) flat panel which acts as protection against draughts, fire, noise, etc.; *a screen decorated with flowers and birds; the hedge acts as a screen against the noise from the motorway*

(b) flat glass surface on which a picture is shown; *a computer screen; I'll call the information up on the screen; our new TV has a very large screen*

(c) flat white surface for projecting films or pictures; *we'll put up the screen on the stage; a cinema complex with four screens; the small screen* = television

2 *verb*

(a) to protect from draught, fire, noise, etc.; *they planted a row of trees to screen the farm buildings; part of the room was screened off; put the umbrella up to screen us from the sun*

(b) to show a film in a cinema *or* on TV; *tonight's film will be screened half an hour later than advertised*

(c) to consider or investigate people, such as candidates for a job, before making a final choice; *applicants will be screened before being invited to an interview*

(d) to screen people for a disease = to examine a lot of people to see if they have a disease; *all women over 40 should be screened for breast cancer*

④ **screw**
[skru:]

1 *noun*

metal pin with a groove winding round it, which you twist to make it go into a hard surface; *I need some longer screws to go through this thick piece of wood; the plate was fixed to the door with brass screws; (informal)* **to have a screw loose** = to be slightly mad

2 *verb*

(a) to attach with screws; *the picture was screwed to the wall*

(b) to attach by twisting; *he filled up the bottle and screwed on the top; screw the lid on tightly; (informal)* **he's got his head screwed on the right way** = he's very sensible

④ **screwdriver**
['skru:draɪvɪ] *noun*

tool with a long handle and special end which is used for turning screws; *she tightened up the screws with a screwdriver*

④ **script**
[skrɪpt] *noun*

(a) written text of a film or play; *the actors settled down with their scripts for the first reading*

(b) written examination answer; *at the end of the exam the teacher gathered up all the scripts*

(c) style or system of handwriting; *the Germans used to write in medieval script*

④ **scrub**
[skrʌb]

1 *noun*

(a) area of land with a few small bushes; *they walked for miles through the scrub until they came to a river*

(b) action of scrubbing; *after a game of rugby you will need a good scrub*

2 *verb*

(a) to clean by rubbing with soap and a brush; *scrub your fingernails to get rid of the dirt; a well-scrubbed kitchen table*

(b) *(informal)* to remove something that has been recorded on tape; *can you scrub the last five minutes of the recording?;* **scrub that** = you can forget about that (NOTE: **scrubbing - scrubbed**)

③ **sculpture**
['skʌlptʃɪ] *noun*

figure carved out of stone or wood, etc., or made out of metal; *there is a sculpture of King Charles in the centre of the square*

① **sea**
[si:] *noun*

(a) area of salt water between continents or islands, but not as large as an ocean; *swimming in the sea is more exciting than swimming in a river*; *the sea's too rough for the ferries to operate*; *his friends own a house by the sea*; *the North Sea separates Britain from Denmark and Germany*; **at sea** = travelling by ship; *we were at sea for only five days*; **by sea** = using ships as a means of transport; *when we moved to Australia we sent our furniture by sea*; **sea crossing** = journey across the sea; *the sea crossing between Denmark and Sweden can be quite rough*; **by sea mail** = sent by post abroad, using a ship, not by air; **to run away to sea** = to leave home to work as a sailor; *when he was sixteen he ran away to sea* (NOTE: in names **Sea** is written with a capital letter: **the North Sea,** etc.)

(b) mass of things; *standing on the platform looking at the crowd, all I could see was a sea of faces*

③ **seafood**
['si:fud] *noun*

fish or shellfish which can be eaten; *I never eat seafood - it doesn't agree with me*; **a seafood restaurant** = a restaurant which specializes in seafood (NOTE: no plural)

③ **seal**
[si:l]

1 *noun*

(a) large animal with short fur, which eats fish, living mainly near to or in the sea; *seals lay sunning themselves on the rocks*

(b) piece of paper, metal, or wax which is used to attach something to close it so that it cannot be opened; *the customs officials attached their seal to the box*

(c) way in which something is closed; *the screw top gives a tight seal*

2 *verb*

(a) to close something tightly; *a box carefully sealed with sticky tape*; **sealed envelope** = envelope where the flap has been stuck down to close it; *the information was sent in a sealed envelope* (NOTE: an envelope left open is an **unsealed envelope**)

(b) to attach a seal; to stamp something with a seal; *the customs sealed the shipment*

④ **seaman**
['si:mɪn] *noun*

man who works on a ship; *he works as an ordinary seaman on an oil tanker* (NOTE: plural is **seamen**)

② **search**
[sɜ:tʃ]

1 *noun*

(a) action of trying to find something; *our search of the flat revealed nothing*; *they carried out a search for the missing children*; *I did a quick search on the Internet for references to Penang*; **search party** = group of people sent to look for someone; *the children haven't come back from the beach - we'll have to send out a search party*; **search warrant** = official document signed by a magistrate which allows police to go into a building and look for criminals, weapons or stolen goods

(b) examination of records to make sure that a property belongs to the person who is trying to sell it; *the solicitor's searches revealed that part of the land belonged to the neighbouring farm* (NOTE: plural is **searches**)

2 *verb*

(a) to examine very carefully; *the police searched the house from top to bottom but still couldn't find any weapons*; *she was stopped and searched by the customs*

(b) **to search for** = to try to find; *the police searched for the missing children*; *I searched the Internet for references to Ireland*; **to search through** = to look for something carefully; *she searched through her papers, trying to find the document*

(c) *(computing)* **search and replace** = looking for words or phrases and replacing them automatically with other words or phrases

③ **seasick**
['si:sɪk] *adjective*

ill because of the movement of a ship; *he gets seasick every time he crosses the Channel*; *she didn't enjoy the cruise because she was seasick all the time*; *I'll stay on deck because I feel seasick when I go down to my cabin*

③ **seaside**
['si:dsaɪd] *noun*

area at the edge of the sea; *we always take the children to the seaside in August*; *they'd like a seaside holiday instead of a holiday in the mountains*; *seaside towns are empty in the winter*

① **season**
['si:zɪn]

1 *noun*

(a) one of four parts of a year; *the four seasons are spring, summer, autumn, and winter*; *spring is the season when the garden is full of flowers*

(b) part of the year when something usually happens; *the tourist season is very long here - from March to September*; *the football season lasts from September to May*; *London is very crowded during the school holiday season*; **high season** = period when there are lots of travellers, and when fares and hotels are more expensive; **low season** = time of year (often during the winter) when there are fewer travellers, and so fares and hotels are cheaper; *tour operators urge more people to travel in the low season*; **dry season** = period of the year when it does not rain much (as opposed to the rainy season); **rainy season** = period of year when it rains a lot (as opposed to the dry season); *don't go there in October - that's the* *beginning of the rainy season*; **shooting season** = period of the year when you can shoot game; *the shooting season starts in August*

(c) *(of fruit, etc.)* **in season** = which is fresh, easily available and ready to buy; *strawberries are cheaper in season*; *pears are in season just now*; **out of season** = more expensive because the growing season is over

2 *verb*

(a) to add flavouring, spices, etc., to a dish; *the meat is seasoned with mint*

(b) to dry wood until it is ready to be used; *they made the windows with wood which had not been seasoned properly*

③ **seasonal**

['si:znil] *adjective*

(a) which only lasts for a season, usually the holiday season; *work on the island is only seasonal*; **seasonal demand** = demand which exists only during the high season; **seasonal employment** = job which is available at certain times of the year only (such as in a ski resort); **seasonal labour** = workers who work for a season (usually the summer) only

(b) characteristic of a particular time of year; *in December the supermarket shelves are stocked with Christmas decorations and other seasonal goods*; *we can expect seasonal weather, with temperatures about average for the time of year*

② **season ticket**

['si:zn 'tikit] *noun*

railway or bus ticket or theatre ticket, which you can use for a whole year or a month at a time; *his employer gives him a loan free of interest, to buy his annual season ticket*; *season-ticket holders will receive a refund if their train is cancelled*

① **seat**

[si:t]

1 *noun*

chair, something which you sit on; *he was sitting in the driver's seat*; *can we have two seats in the front row?*; *please take your seats, the play is about the begin*; *all the seats on the bus were taken so I had to stand*; *our kitchen chairs have wooden seats*; *bicycle seats are narrow and not very comfortable*; **to take a seat** = to sit down; *please take a seat, the dentist will see you in a few minutes*

2 *verb*

to have room for people to sit down; *the restaurant seats 75*

③ **seat belt**

['si:t 'belt] *noun*

belt which you wear in a car or plane to stop you being hurt if there is an accident; *the sole survivor of the crash had been wearing a seat belt*; *the 'fasten seat belts' sign came on*

COMMENT: in Britain, the driver and front-seat passenger in a car are obliged by law to wear seat belts. Rear seat passengers must also wear seat belts if the car has them. All new cars are fitted with rear seat belts

③ **seated**

['si:tid] *adjective*

sitting down; *everyone stood up when the chairman came in, except John who remained seated*

③ **seaweed**

['si:wi:d] *noun*

plant which grows in the sea; *the rocks are covered with seaweed* (NOTE: no plural: **some seaweed, a piece of seaweed**)

① **second**

['sekind]

1 *noun*

(a) one of sixty parts which make up a minute; *I'll give you ten seconds to get out of my room*; *they say the bomb will go off in twenty seconds*

(b) very short time; *please wait a second*; *wait here - I'll be back in a second*

(c) something *or* someone that comes after the first thing or person; *today is the second of March or March the second (March 2nd) the Great Fire of London took place when Charles the Second (Charles II) was king* (NOTE: in dates **second** is usually written **2nd: August 2nd, 1932, July 2nd, 1666** (American style is **July 2, 1666**), say 'the second of July' or 'July the second' (American style is 'July second'); with names of kings and queens **second** is usually written **II: Queen Elizabeth II** (say 'Queen Elizabeth the Second')

(d) person who helps a boxer during a fight; **seconds out** = instruction to the seconds to leave the ring before a round begins

2 *adjective*

(a) coming after the first and before the third; *February is the second month of the year*; *he came second in the race*; *it's his second birthday next week*; *B is the second letter in the alphabet*; *women's clothes are on the second floor*; *that's the second time the telephone has rung while we're having dinner*; **the second century** = the period from 100AD to 199; **second helping** = another helping of the same dish; *after we had finished, the waiter came round with a second helping of fish*

(b) *(followed by a superlative)* only one other is more; *this is the second longest bridge in the world*; *he's the second highest paid member of staff*

3 *verb*

(a) ['sekind] **to second a motion** = to be the first person to formally support a proposal put forward by someone else in a meeting; *the motion was seconded by Mrs Smith*

(b) [si'kɒnd] to lend a member of staff to another company, to a government department, etc., for a fixed period of time; *he was seconded to the Department of Trade for two years*

② **secondary**
['sekɪndri] *adjective*

(a) which comes after the first (or primary); **secondary education** = teaching children from the age of 11 to 16 or 18; **secondary school** = school for children after the age of 11 or 12

(b) **of secondary importance** = not so very important; *the colour of the car is of secondary importance*

③ **second-class**
['sekɪnd 'klɑːs] *adjective & adverb*

(a) *(of travel, hotels, etc.)* less expensive and less comfortable than first-class; *I find second-class hotels are perfectly adequate; we always travel second-class because it is cheaper*

(b) *(of postal service)* less expensive and slower than first-class; *a second-class letter is cheaper than a first-class; send it second-class if it is not urgent*

(c) **second-class citizens** = people who have fewer rights, opportunities, etc., than others; *unemployed people are in danger of becoming second-class citizens*

③ **secondhand**
[sekɪnd'hænd]
1 *adjective*

not new; which someone else has owned before; *we've just bought a secondhand car; we bought this sofa from a secondhand dealer; the car is worth £6,000 on the secondhand market*
2 *adverb*

to buy something secondhand = to buy something which someone else has owned before; *we bought this car secondhand*

③ **second-in-command**
['sekɪnd ɪn kɪ'mɑːnd] *noun*

chief officer who is under a commanding officer; *after he was wounded he handed over to his second-in-command*

③ **secondly**
['sekɪndli] *adverb*

in second place; *I'm not going to his party: firstly it's my mother's birthday, and secondly, I don't really like his family*

③ **seconds**
['sekɪndz] *noun*

(a) *(informal)* another helping of the same dish; *can I have seconds of pudding, please?*

(b) items which have been turned down as not being of top quality; *the shop has a sale of seconds; we bought our dinner service from a shop selling seconds*

④ **secrecy**
['siːkrɪsi] *noun*

being secret; keeping something secret; *you will see that secrecy is extremely important when we're discussing the new project; why is there so much secrecy about the candidate's age?*

③ **secret**
['siːkrɪt]
1 *adjective*

hidden, not known by other people; *there is a secret door into the tower*; **to keep something secret** = to make sure that no one knows about it; *she kept his birth secret for twenty years*
2 *noun*

(a) thing which is not known or which is kept hidden; *if I tell you a secret will you promise not to repeat it to anyone?*; **is he in on the secret?** = does he know the secret?; **to keep a secret** = not to tell someone something which you know and no one else does; *can he keep a secret?*

(b) **in secret** = without anyone knowing; *they met in secret by the lake in the park*; **he makes no secret of where the money came from** = everyone knows where the money came from; **what's the secret of?** = how do you do something successfully; *what's the secret of making marmalade?*

① **secretary**
['sekrɪtri] *noun*

(a) person who writes letters, answers the phone, files documents, etc., for someone; *both my daughters are training to be secretaries; his secretary phoned to say he would be late*

(b) official who keeps the minutes and official documents of a committee or club; *he was elected secretary of the committee or committee secretary*

(c) **company secretary** = person who is responsible for a company's legal and financial affairs

(d) a Secretary of State, a member of the government in charge of a department; **the Secretary for Education** *or* **the Education Secretary** = the head of the Department for Education (NOTE: plural is **secretaries**)

① **Secretary General**
['sekrɪtri 'dʒenrɪl] *noun*

chief administrative officer of an international organization; *the United Nations Secretary General has called a meeting of the Security Council* (NOTE: plural is **Secretaries General**)

① **Secretary of State**
['sekrɪtri əv 'steɪt] *noun*

(a) *GB* member of the government in charge of a department; *the Secretary of State for Northern Ireland is one of the few women members of the cabinet*

(b) *US* senior member of the government in charge of foreign affairs; *the US Secretary of State is having talks with the Israeli Prime Minister* (NOTE: the British equivalent is the **Foreign Secretary**)

③ **secretly**
['siːkrɪtli] *adverb*

without anyone knowing; *they used to meet secretly in the park; he secretly photocopied the plans and took them home*

① section

['sekʃn] *noun*

(a) part of something which, when joined to other parts, goes to make up a whole; *the wind section of an orchestra*; *the financial section of a newspaper*; *he works in a completely different section of the organization*

(b) the cutting of tissue in a surgical operation

(c) diagram showing the inside of something as if cut open; *the drawing shows a section through the main part of the engine*

(d) part of a legal document or Act of Parliament; *we qualify for a grant under Section 23 of the Act*

① sector

['sektɪ] *noun*

(a) part of the economy or of the business organization of a country; *all sectors of industry suffered from the rise in the exchange rate*; *computer technology is a booming sector of the economy*; **private sector** = part of industry which is privately owned; *the leisure centre is funded completely by the private sector*; **public sector** = the civil service and industries which belong to the state; *salaries in the private sector have increased faster than in the public sector*

(b) part of a circle between two lines drawn from the centre to the outside edge; *the circle had been divided into five sectors*

② secure

[sɪ'kjuːɪ]

1 *adjective*

(a) safe against attack, robbers, etc.; *you need to keep your jewels secure against theft*; *he made all the doors secure by fitting bolts to them*

(b) firmly fixed; *don't step on that ladder, it's not secure*; **secure job** = job which you are sure to keep for a long time

(c) secure institution = mental hospital in which dangerous prisoners can be kept

2 *verb*

(a) to make safe, to attach firmly; *secure all the doors before the storm comes*; *she secured herself to the rock with a strong rope*

(b) to get something safely so that it cannot be taken away; *he secured the backing of a big bank*; *they secured a new lease on very favourable terms*

④ securely

[sɪ'kjuːɪlɪ] *adverb*

in a secure way; *don't worry, all the silver is securely locked away*; *she tied the dog securely to a fence*

③ securities

[sɪ'kjuːɪɪtɪz] *noun*

investments in stocks and shares; certificates to show that someone owns stocks or shares; **government securities** = investments in British government stock; *she invested her redundancy money in government securities*

① security

[sɪ'kjuːɪɪtɪ] *noun*

(a) safety, protection against criminals; *there were worries about security during the prince's visit*; *security in this office is nil*; *security guards patrol the factory at night*; **airport security** = measures to protect aircraft against terrorists or bombs; **hotel security** = measures taken to protect a hotel against theft or fire; **security check** = check to see that no one is carrying a bomb, etc.; **security van** = specially protected van for delivering cash and other valuable items; *six gunmen held up the security van*

(b) thing given to someone who has lent you money and which is returned when the loan is repaid; *he uses his house as security for a loan*; *the bank lent him £20,000 without security*; **to stand security for someone** = to guarantee that if the person does not repay a loan, you will repay it for him

(c) **job security** *or* **security of employment** = feeling which a worker has that he has a right to keep his job, that he can stay in his job until he retires

(d) **social security** = money or help provided by the government to people who need it; *he lives on social security payments* (NOTE: no plural in these meanings; but compare **securities**)

① Security Council

['sɪ'kjuːɪɪtɪ 'kaʊnsɪl] *noun*

ruling body of the United Nations; *France is a permanent member of the Security Council*

> COMMENT: the Security Council has fifteen members, five of which are permanent: these are the United States, Russia, China, France and the United Kingdom. The other ten members are elected for periods of two years. The five permanent members each have a veto over the decisions of the Security Council

④ seduce

[sɪ'djuːs] *verb*

(a) to persuade someone to have sex; *she was seduced by her French teacher*

(b) to persuade someone to do something which is perhaps wrong; *he was seduced by the idea of earning a vast salary*

① see

[siː]

1 *verb*

(a) to use your eyes to notice; *can you see that tree in the distance?*; *they say eating carrots helps you to see in the dark*; *we ran because we could see the bus coming*; *I have never seen an elephant before*

(b) to watch a film, etc.; *I don't want to go to the cinema this week, I've seen that film twice already*; *we saw the football match on TV*

(c) to go with someone to a place; *the little boy saw the old lady across the road*; *I'll see her home*; *my secretary will see you out*

(d) to understand; *I can't see why they need to borrow so much money*; *you must see that it's very important for everything to be ready on time*; *don't you see that they're trying to trick you?*; *I see - you want me to lend you some money*

(e) to check to make sure that something happens; *the baby-sitter will see that the children are in bed by nine o'clock*; *can you see if a cheque has arrived in the post?*

(f) to meet; *we see her quite often*; *she doesn't see much of him*; *see you next week!*; *see you again soon!*

(g) to visit a lawyer, doctor, etc.; *if your tooth hurts you should see a dentist*; *he went to see his bank manager to arrange a mortgage*

(h) *(showing a possibility)* *will you be able to take a holiday this year? - we'll see!* (NOTE: **sees - seeing - saw** [sɔ:] **- has seen** [si:n])

2 *noun*

administrative area run by a bishop; **he was appointed to the see of Durham** = he was made bishop of Durham; **the Holy See** = the Vatican, the office of the Pope

③ **seed**
[si:d]

1 *noun*

(a) part of a plant which is formed after the flowers die and from which a new plant will grow; *sow the seed(s) in fine earth*; *a packet of parsley seed*; *can you eat melon seeds?*

(b) *(of plant)* **to go to seed** = to become tall and produce flowers and seeds; *the lettuces have gone to seed*; **he's gone to seed** = he doesn't look after himself properly, he doesn't look as well as he did before (NOTE: **seed** can be plural when it refers to a group: **a packet of lettuce seed; sow the celery seed in sand**)

(c) *(in tennis)* player selected as one of the best players in a tournament; *she's the top women's seed*; *the number one seed was beaten in the first round of the tournament*

2 *verb*

(a) **to seed itself** = to produce seed which falls onto the ground and grows; *flowers have seeded themselves all along the side of the motorway*

(b) to choose the seeds in a tennis competition; *he was seeded No. 5*

③ **see in**
['si: 'ɪn] *verb*

(a) to have a midnight party to celebrate; *we stayed up late to see the New Year in*

(b) **to see something in someone** = to be attracted by someone; *I can't understand what she sees in him*

③ **seeing**
['si:ɪŋ]

1 *noun*

action of sensing with the eyes; *seeing is believing*

2 *conjunction*

seeing that = since; *seeing that everyone's here, why don't we open a bottle of wine?*

① **seek**
[si:k] *verb*

(a) to look for; *the police are seeking a group of teenagers who were in the area when the attack took place*; **to seek refuge** = to try to find shelter; *during the fighting, they sought refuge in the British embassy*

(b) to ask for; *they are seeking damages from the driver of the car*; *she sought an interview with the minister* (NOTE: **seeking - sought** [sɔ:t] **- has sought**)

① **seem**
[si:m] *verb*

to look as if; *she seems to like her new job* or *it seems that she likes her new job*; *everyone seemed to be having a good time at the party*; *the new boss seems very nice*; *it seems to me that the parcel has gone to the wrong house*; *it seemed strange to us that no one answered the phone*

④ **seemingly**
['si:mɪŋlɪ] *adjective & adverb*

apparently; *the seemingly endless flow of refugees*; *he had seemingly lost his way*

③ **seen**
[si:n] *see* SEE

③ **see off**
['si: 'ɒf] *verb*

to go to the airport or station with someone who is leaving on a journey; *the whole family went to see her off at the airport*

③ **see through**
['si: 'θru:] *verb*

(a) to see from one side of something to the other; *I can't see through the windscreen - it's so dirty*

(b) to understand everything, not to be tricked by something; *we quickly saw through their plan*

③ **see to**
['si: 'tu:] *verb*

to arrange, to make sure that something is done; *can you see to it that the children are in bed by nine o'clock?*; *my wife will see to the Christmas cards*

④ **segment**
['segmɪnt] *noun*

(a) part of a circle or sphere when a line is drawn across it; **grapefruit segments** = pieces of grapefruit

(b) part of something which seems to form a natural division; *30 to 40 year-olds are the richest segment of the population*

③ **seize**

[si:z] *verb*

(a) to grab something and hold it tight; *she seized the bag of sweets in both hands and would not let go*; **to seize the opportunity** = to take advantage of the situation to do something; *when the President's car slowed down, he seized the opportunity and threw his bomb*

(b) to take possession of something by force; *the customs seized the shipment of books*

③ **seize on** *or* **seize upon**

['si:z ə'pɒn] *verb*

to take and use; *she immediately seized upon his suggestion*; *my idea was seized on and developed by a rival company*

③ **seize up**

['si:z 'ʌp] *verb*

to stop working properly; *the car seized up on the hill and we had to call a garage*; *my back seized up after my game of tennis and I couldn't move*

③ **seldom**

['seldɪm] *adverb*

not often; *I seldom get invited to parties*; *seldom do you hear such a beautiful voice* (NOTE: the word order when **seldom** is at the beginning of a phrase: **you seldom hear** *or* **seldom do you hear**)

② **select**

[sɪ'lekt]

1 *verb*

to choose carefully; *she looked carefully at the shelves before selecting a book*; *he was selected for the England squad*; *selected items are reduced by 25%*

2 *adjective*

the best, chosen by or for the best people; *she went to a very select school in Switzerland*; *they live in a very select area*; *a select group of players who have scored more than 100 goals in international football*

② **selection**

[sɪ'lekʃn] *noun*

(a) range; *there is a huge selection of hats to choose from*

(b) thing which has (or things which have) been chosen; *a selection of our product line*; *a selection of French cheeses*; **selection board** *or* **selection committee** = committee which chooses a candidate for a job; **selection procedure** = general method of choosing a candidate for a job

③ **selective**

[sɪ'lektɪv] *adjective*

(a) which chooses (carefully); *I'm very selective about the invitations I accept*; **selective school** = school which chooses pupils by asking them to take an entrance exam

(b) which only kills certain plants; *use a selective spray on the rose bushes*

② **self**

[self] *noun*

your own person or character; *she was ill for some time, but now she's her old self again*; *she's not her usual happy self today - I think she's got something on her mind* (NOTE: plural is **selves**)

② **self-**

[self] *prefix referring to yourself*
a self-taught scientist

③ **selfish**

['selfɪʃ] *adjective*

doing things only for yourself and not for other people; *don't be so selfish - pass the box of chocolates round*

① **sell**

[sel]

1 *verb*

(a) to give something to someone for money; *he sold his house to my father*; *she sold him her bicycle for a few pounds*; *we managed to sell the car for £500*; *the shop sells vegetables but not meat*

(b) to be sold; *those packs sell for £25 a dozen*; *his latest book is selling very well* (NOTE: **selling - sold** [sɪʊld])

2 *noun*

the act of selling something; **to give a product the hard sell** = to make great efforts to persuade customers to buy it; **to give a product the soft sell** = to persuade people to buy something, by encouraging and not forcing them to do so (NOTE: do not confuse with **cell**)

④ **seller**

['selɪ] *noun*

(a) person who sells something; *there were a few postcard sellers by the cathedral*; **seller's market** = market where a person selling goods or a service can ask high prices because there is a large demand for the product; *prices are high in a seller's market*; *compare* BUYER'S MARKET

(b) thing which sells; *this book is a steady seller*; **good seller** = thing that sells well; *we've dropped that item from our catalogue - it was never a very good seller*

① **sell off**

['sel 'ɒf] *verb*

to sell goods quickly and cheaply to get rid of them; *at the end of the day the market traders sell off their fruit and vegetables very cheaply*

① **sell out**

['sel 'aʊt] *verb*

(a) to sell your business; *he sold out to his partner and retired to the seaside*

(b) to sell all the stock of an item; *this item has sold out*; *have you got it in a size 12? - no, I'm afraid we're sold out*

(c) *(informal)* to give in to a group of influential people; *the environmental group has accused the government of selling out to the oil companies*; *see also* SELL OUT OF

① **sell out of**
['sel 'aʊt 'ɒv] *verb*

to sell out of an item = to sell all the stock of an item; *the shop has sold out of bread; have you got it in a size 12? - no, I'm afraid we're sold out of all the small sizes*

④ **semester**
[sɪ'mestɪ] *noun*

US one of two terms in a school or college year; *they arrived at college for the fall semester; after the spring semester we look for summer jobs*

③ **semi-final**
['semi'faɪnɪl] *noun*

one of the last two matches in a competition, the winners of which go into the final game; *the two semi-finals will be held on the same day*

④ **seminar**
['semɪnɑː] *noun*

meeting of a small group of university students to discuss a subject with a teacher; *the French seminar is being held in the conference room*

④ **senate**
['senɪt] *noun*

(a) upper house of the legislative body in some countries; *she was first elected to the Senate in 1990*

(b) body which rules a university; *does Senate concern itself solely with administrative matters?*

④ **senator**
['senɪtɪ] *noun*

member of a senate (in parliament); *she was first elected a senator in 1980* (NOTE: written with a capital letter when used as a title: **Senator Jackson**)

① **send**
[send] *verb*

(a) to make someone *or* something go from one place to another; *my mother sent me to the shops to buy some bread; I was sent home from school because I had a headache; he sent the ball into the net; the firm is sending him out to Australia for six months*

(b) to use the postal services; *the office sends 200 Christmas cards every year; send me a postcard when you get to Russia; send the letter airmail if you want it to arrive next week; send your gifts to the following address*

(c) *(informal)* to make someone act or feel in a certain way; **to send someone crazy** *or* **round the bend** *or* **up the wall** = to make someone extremely annoyed; *the noise of drilling in the road outside the office is sending me up the wall* (NOTE: **sending - sent** [sent])

① **send away for** *or* **send off for**
['send ə'weɪ 'fɔː or 'ɒf 'fɔː] *verb*

to write and ask someone to send you something, usually something which you have seen in an advertisement; *we sent away for the new catalogue; I sent away for a book which was advertised in the Sunday paper*

③ **send back**
['send 'bæk] *verb*

to return something by post; *if you don't like the shirt, send it back and I'll get you something different*

④ **sender**
['sendɪ] *noun*

person who sends; *the sender of the package did not put enough stamps, so we had to pay extra*; **'return to sender'** = words on an envelope or parcel to show that it is to be sent back to the person who sent it; *the letter was returned to the sender*

③ **send for**
['send 'fɔː] *verb*

to ask someone to come; *he collapsed and we sent for the doctor; the restaurant had to send for the police*

③ **send in**
['send 'ɪn] *verb*

to send a letter to an organization; *he sent in his resignation; she sent in an application for the job*

③ **send off**
['send 'ɒf] *verb*

(a) *(in games)* to tell someone to go off the field; *the referee sent both players off*

(b) to post; *he sent the postcard off without a stamp*

③ **send off for**
['send 'ɒf 'fɔː] *see* SEND AWAY FOR

② **senior**
['siːnjɪ]

1 *adjective*

(a) older; *the senior members of the family sat at the head table*; **senior citizen** = old retired person; **senior school** = school for older children

(b) more important in rank, etc.; *a sergeant is senior to a corporal; my senior colleagues do not agree with me*; **senior manager** = manager who has a higher rank than others

2 *noun*

(a) older person; *he must be at least ten years your senior*; **the seniors** = the older children in a school; *when she's eleven, she'll move up into the seniors*

(b) *US* student in his or her fourth year or last year at school or college

(c) the father in a family where the son has the same name; *Harry Markovitz Senior*

① **sensation**
[sen'seɪʃn] *noun*

(a) general feeling; *I felt a curious sensation as if I had been in the room before*

(b) physical feeling; *she had a burning sensation in her arm*

(c) thing *or* person that causes great excitement; *the new ballet was the sensation of the season*

④ **sensational**
[sen'seɪʃnl] *adjective*
(a) which causes great excitement; *his sensational discovery shocked the world of pharmacy*
(b) *(informal)* very good; *a sensational new film - don't miss it!*; *she looks sensational in that outfit*

① **sense**
[sens]
1 *noun*
(a) one of the five ways in which you notice something (sight, hearing, smell, taste, touch); *he may be 93, but he still has all his senses*; *his senses had been affected by the drugs he was taking*; *dogs have a good sense of smell*
(b) general feeling about something; *staying in the Grand Hotel, she had a sense of being cut off from the real world*; *the police seemed to have no sense of urgency*
(c) meaning; *he was using 'bear' in the sense of 'to carry'*; **to make sense** = to have a meaning; *the message doesn't make sense*; **to make sense of something** = to understand something; *I can't make any sense of what she's trying to say*
(d) being sensible; *at least someone showed some sense and tried to calm the situation*; *she didn't have the sense to refuse*; *I thought Patrick would have had more sense than that*; *(informal)* **to have more money than sense** = to have too much money and not know how to spend it carefully; *did you see what she bought? - she's got more money than sense!*
(e) **in one sense** *or* **in a sense** = up to a point, partly; *in a sense, he was right*; **in no sense** = in no way, not at all; *she's in no sense to blame for what happened*
2 *verb*
to be aware of, to feel; *I could sense the feeling of anger in the room*

③ **sense of direction**
['sens əv daɪ'rekʃn] *noun*
ability to know which way to go in a place which you do not know well; *she has a very good sense of direction: she managed to find her way round London with no difficulty at all*

③ **sense of humour**
['sens əv 'hjuːmə] *noun*
ability to see the funny side of things; *he has a good sense of humour*; *she has no sense of humour at all*

③ **sensible**
['sensɪbl] *adjective*
showing good judgement and wisdom; *staying indoors was the sensible thing to do*; *try and be sensible for once!*; **sensible shoes** = shoes that are strong and comfortable for walking, rather than fashionable

③ **sensitive**
['sensɪtɪv] *adjective*
(a) with keen feelings, easily upset; *she's a very sensitive young woman*; *some actors are extremely sensitive to criticism*; **price-sensitive** = selling better or worse depending on the price
(b) controversial, which may provoke an argument; *human rights is a very sensitive issue at the moment*
(c) which measures very accurately; *we need a more sensitive thermometer*; *a very sensitive light meter*
(d) which reacts to light, etc.; *if you have very sensitive skin use plenty of sun cream*; *flowers are sensitive to changes in temperature and humidity*

③ **sent**
[sent] *see* SEND

① **sentence**
['sentɪns]
1 *noun*
(a) words put together to make a complete statement, usually ending in a full stop; *I don't understand the second sentence in your letter*; *begin each sentence with a capital letter*
(b) judgement of a court; *he was given a six-month prison sentence*; *the judge passed sentence on the accused*
2 *verb*
to give someone an official legal punishment; *she was sentenced to three weeks in prison*; *he was sentenced to death for murder*

④ **sentiment**
['sentɪmɪnt] *noun*
(a) general feeling; *the government had to take public sentiment into account*
(b) **sentiments** = opinions; *I think it's all a waste of time - my sentiments exactly!*

③ **sentimental**
[sentɪ'mentl] *adjective*
showing emotions of love or pity, not reason; *she gets all sentimental on her son's birthday*; *her father sang a sentimental old love song*; **sentimental value** = being valuable because of the memories attached to it, not because of its actual money value; *the stolen watch was of great sentimental value*

② **separate**
1 *adjective*
['sepɪrɪt] not together, not attached; *they are in separate rooms*; *the house has one bathroom with a separate toilet*; *the dogs were kept separate from the other pets*; *can you give us two separate invoices?*; **to send something under separate cover** = to send something in a different envelope or parcel
2 *verb*
['sepɪreɪt]
(a) to divide; *the personnel are separated into part-time and full-time staff*; *the teacher separated the class into two groups*

(b) to keep apart; *the police tried to separate the two gangs*; *is it possible to separate religion and politics?*

(c) to break away from a partner and become independent; *they are arguing all the time - it wouldn't surprise me if they were to separate*; *the Baltic states separated from Russia*

② **separately**
['sepɪrɪtli] *adverb*
in a separate way, each alone; *each of us will pay separately*

④ **separation**
[sepɪ'reɪʃn] *noun*
(a) dividing; *he favours the separation of the students into smaller groups*; *the separation of the house into two flats will require planning permission*
(b) living apart; *a six-month separation of mother and child may have long-term effects*; *after my parents' separation I lived with my father*

① **September**
[sep'tembɪ] *noun*
ninth month of the year, between August and October; *the weather is usually good in September*; *her birthday is in September*; *today is September 3rd US September 3*; *we always try to take a short holiday in September* (NOTE: **September 3rd** or **September 3**: say 'September the third' or 'the third of September'; American English: 'September third')

② **sequence**
['siːkwɪns] *noun*
(a) series of things which happen or follow one after the other; *the sequence of events which led to the accident*
(b) **in sequence** = in order of numbers; *make sure that the invoices are all in sequence according to their dates*
(c) scene in a film; *they showed some sequences from her latest film*

③ **sergeant**
['saːdʒɪnt] *noun*
rank in the army or the police, above a corporal; *Sergeant Jones drilled the new recruits*; *a police sergeant arrested him* (NOTE: used as a title with a surname: **Sergeant Jones**)

④ **serial**
['sɪrɪl]
1 *adjective*
in a series; *place the cards in serial order*; **serial murderer** or **serial killer** = person who has committed several murders, one after the other; *because there are similarities between the murders, the police think they are dealing with a serial killer*; **serial number** = number in a series; *this batch of shoes has the serial number 25-02*
2 *noun*
radio or TV play which is presented in several instalments; *an Australian police serial* (NOTE: do not confuse with **cereal**)

① **series**
['sɪːrɪz] *noun*
(a) group of things which come one after the other in order; *we had a series of phone calls from the bank*
(b) TV or radio programmes which are broadcast at the same time each week; *there's a new wildlife series starting this week* (NOTE: plural is **series**)

① **serious**
['sɪːrɪɪs] *adjective*
(a) not funny; not joking; *we watched a very serious programme on drugs*; *he's such a serious little boy*; *stop laughing - it's very serious*; *he's very serious about the proposal*; *the doctor's expression was very serious*
(b) important and possibly dangerous; *there was a serious accident on the motorway*; *the storm caused serious damage*; *there's no need to worry - it's nothing serious*
(c) carefully planned; *the management is making serious attempts to improve working conditions*

① **seriously**
['sɪːrɪɪsli] *adverb*
(a) in a serious way; *she should laugh more - she mustn't always take things so seriously*
(b) badly; *the cargo was seriously damaged by water*; *her mother is seriously ill*
(c) with a lot of thought; *they seriously considered going to live in Australia*; *we are taking the threat from our competitors very seriously*

② **servant**
['saːvɪnt] *noun*
(a) person who is paid to work for a family; *they employ two servants in their London home*; *get it yourself - I'm not your servant!*
(b) **civil servant** = person who works in a government department; *as a government translator I was considered a civil servant*; *the civil servants who advise ministers have a tremendous influence on government policy*

① **serve**
[saːv]
1 *verb*
(a) to give food or drink to someone; *she served the soup in small bowls*; *I'll serve the potatoes*; *take a plate and serve yourself from the dishes on the table*; *has everyone been served?*
(b) to bring food or drink to someone at table; *which waitress is serving this table?*; *I can't serve six tables at once*
(c) to go with a dish, etc.; *fish is served with a white sauce*; *you should serve red wine with meat*
(d) to work as an official; *he served in the army for ten years*
(e) to help a customer in a shop, etc.; *are you being served?*; *the manager served me himself*; *will you serve this lady next, please?*; *I waited ten minutes before being served*

(f) to provide a service; *the local bus serves the villages in the hills*; *the aim of our organization is to serve the local community*; *this hospital serves the western side of the city*

(g) to serve as = to be useful as; *the tall hedge serves as a screen to cut out the noise from the motorway*

(h) *(in games like tennis)* to start the game by hitting the ball; *she is serving to win the match*; *he served first*

(i) *(informal)* **it serves you right** = you deserve what has happened to you; *it serves them right if they missed the train, they shouldn't have taken so long to get ready*

2 *noun*

(in tennis) action of hitting the ball first; *she has a very powerful serve*; *three of his serves hit the net*

① **service**
['sɜːvɪs]
1 *noun*

(a) time when you work for a company, or organization, or in the armed forces; *did he enjoy his service in the army?*; *she did six years' service in the police*; *he was awarded a gold watch for his long service to the company*; *he saw service in Africa*; **length of service** = number of years someone has worked

(b) serving or helping someone in a shop or restaurant; *the food is good here, but the service is very slow*; *the bill includes an extra 10% for service*; *is the service included?*; *the bill does not include service*; *to add on 10% for service*; **service charge** = money which you pay for service in a restaurant; *a 10% service charge is added*; **room service** = arrangement in a hotel for food or drink to be served in your bedroom

(c) regular check of a machine; *the car has had its 20,000-kilometre service*; **after-sales service** = maintenance of a machine carried out by the seller for the buyer; **service centre** = office or workshop which specializes in keeping machines in good working order; **service handbook** *or* **service manual** = book which shows how to keep a machine in good working order

(d) group of people working together; **the civil service** = organization and personnel which administer a country; *you have to pass an examination to get a job in the civil service or to get a civil service job*; **the health service** = doctors, nurses, hospitals, etc., all taken as a group; *we have the best health service in the world*; *I don't want to rely on the National Health Service*; **the (armed) services** = the army, the navy and the air force; *have you thought about a career in the services?*; *service families often have to travel abroad*

(e) provision of a facility which the public needs; *our train service to London is very bad*; *the postal service is efficient*; *the bus service is very irregular*; *the hotel provides a shoe cleaning service*; **the rent includes services** = the rent includes the cost of water, gas and electricity

(f) favour, something done for someone; *you would do me a great service if you could carry my suitcases for me*; *(formal)* **to be of service to someone** = to help someone; *can I be of service to anyone?*

(g) religious ceremony; *my mother never misses the nine o'clock service on Sundays*

(h) *(in tennis)* action of hitting the ball first; *she has a very powerful service*

(i) set of china for a meal; **dinner service** = big and small plates, serving dishes, etc.; *a complete dinner service costs a lot, so I'll buy it for you bit by bit*; **tea service** = plates, cups, saucers, teapot, etc.,

2 *verb*

to keep (a machine) in good working order; *the car needs to be serviced every six months*; *the photocopier has gone back to the manufacturer for servicing*

③ **services**
['sɜːvɪsɪz] *noun*

area with a service station, restaurants and sometimes hotel, on a motorway; *there are no services for 50 miles*; *we'll stop at the next services and have a cup of coffee*

③ **service station**
['sɜːvɪssteɪʃn] *noun*

garage where you can buy petrol and have small repairs done to a car; *we need petrol - I'll stop at the next service station*

② **session**
['seʃn] *noun*

(a) time when an activity is taking place; *all these long sessions in front of the computer screen are ruining my eyesight*; **practice session** = time when a tennis player, etc., practises; **recording session** = time when music is being recorded

(b) meeting of a committee, parliament, etc.; *the first session of the talks will be held on Monday*; **closing session** = last part of a conference; **opening session** = last part of a conference; **in session** = in the process of meeting; *the committee has been in session for two hours*

① **set**
[set]
1 *noun*

(a) group of things which go together, which are used together, which are sold together; *he carries a set of tools in the back of his car*; *the six chairs are sold as a set*; **a tea set** = cups, saucers, plates, teapot, etc.,

(b) TV set = piece of electrical equipment which shows TV pictures; *they have bought a new 20-inch colour set*

(c) *(in films)* place where a film is shot; *she has to be on set at 7.00 a.m.*; *we went on a tour of the studios and watched a set being built*

(d) *(in tennis)* one part of a tennis match, consisting of several games; *she won the set 7-5*; *he lost the first two sets*

2 *verb*

(a) to put in a special place; *she set the plate of biscuits down on the table next to her chair*; **to set the table** = to put the knives, forks, plates, glasses, cups, etc., in their right places on the table

(b) to fix; *when we go to France we have to set our watches to French time*; *the price of the new computer has been set at £500*

(c) *(surgery)* to fix a broken limb; *the doctor set his broken arm*; *(of a limb)* to heal; *the broken wrist is setting very well*

(d) to give work to someone; *the teacher has set us some homework for the weekend*; *who set this exam? - it is very difficult*; **this book has been set for the exam** = this book is on the list of books which have to be studied before the exam; **to set someone to work** = to give someone work to do; *the children were set to work washing the dishes*

(e) to make something happen; *he went to sleep smoking a cigarette and set the house on fire*; *all the prisoners were set free*; *I had been worried about her, but her letter set my mind at rest*

(f) to go down; *the sun rises in the east and sets in the west*

(g) to write music to go with words; *the poem about cats was set to music*

(h) *(printing)* to put a text into printed characters; *the phrases in this dictionary have been set in bold* (NOTE: **sets - setting - has set**)

3 *adjective*

(a) fixed, which cannot be changed; *visits are only allowed at set times*; **set book** = book which is on the list of books which have to be studied for an exam; **set menu** = menu which cannot be changed

(b) ready; *we're all set for a swim*; *my bags are packed and I'm all set to leave*; *the government is set to introduce new regulations against smoking*; *her latest novel is set to become the best-selling book of the year*; **'on your marks, get set, go!'** = orders given to runners at the beginning of a race

① **set about**
['set ə'baut] *verb*

to start to do something; *they set about making a camp fire*; *we haven't started building the wall yet because we don't know how to set about it*

① **set aside**
['set ə'said] *verb*

(a) to dismiss, to reject; *the proposal was set aside by the committee*

(b) to save and keep for future use; *we set money aside every month for the children's holidays*

① **set back**
['set 'bæk] *verb*

(a) to delay, to make something late; *the bad weather has set the harvest back by two weeks*

(b) to place further back; *the house is set back from the road*

(c) *(informal)* **to set someone back** = to be a cost to someone; *the meal set me back £100*

① **setback**
['setbæk] *noun*

problem which makes something late or stops something going ahead; *the company suffered a series of setbacks in 1999*; *just when we thought he was better, he had a setback and had to go back to hospital*

① **set down**
['set 'daun] *verb*

(a) to let passengers get off; *the bus set down several passengers and two others got on*

(b) *(formal)* to put something in writing; *the rules are set down in this book*

① **set in**
['set 'in] *verb*

to start and become permanent; *then the bad weather set in and we couldn't climb any more*; *winter has set in early this year*

① **set off**
['set 'ɒf] *verb*

(a) to begin a trip; *we're setting off for Germany tomorrow*; *they all set off on a long walk after lunch*

(b) to start something working; *they set off a bomb in the shopping centre*; *if you touch the wire it will set off the alarm*; *being in the same room as a cat will set off my cough*

① **set out**
['set 'aut] *verb*

(a) to begin a journey; *the walkers set out to cross the mountains*; *we have to set out early tomorrow*

(b) to explain clearly; *we asked her to set out the details in her report*

(c) to aim to do something; *he set out to ruin the party*

② **setting**
['setɪŋ] *noun*

(a) background for a story; *the setting for the story is Hong Kong in 1935*

(b) **place setting** = set of knives, forks, spoons, etc., for one person; *we only need two place settings on table 6*

(c) silver or gold frame in which a precious stone is fixed; *a diamond in a silver setting*

② **settle**
['setl] *verb*

(a) to arrange, to agree; to end (a dispute); *well, I'm glad everything's settled at last*; *have you settled the title for the new film yet?*; *it took six months of negotiation for the union and management to settle their differences*

(b) to settle a bill = to pay the bill; *please settle this invoice without delay*; *the insurance company refused to settle his claim for damages*

(c) to go to live in a new country; *they sold everything and settled in Canada*; *the first pioneers settled in this valley in about 1860*

(d) to place yourself in a comfortable position; *she switched on the television and settled in her favourite armchair*

(e) to settle money on someone = to arrange for money to be passed to trustees to hold for someone in the future; *they settled £2,000 a year on their new grandson*

(f) to fall to the ground, to the bottom; *wait for the dust to settle*; *a layer of mud settled at the bottom of the pond*

③ **settle down**
['setl 'daʊn] *verb*

(a) to place yourself in a comfortable position; *after dinner, she likes to settle down in a comfortable chair with a good book*

(b) to change to a calmer way of life without many changes of house or much travelling; *he has worked all over the world, and doesn't seem ready to settle down*; *she had lots of boyfriends, and then got married and settled down in Surrey*

③ **settle for**
['setl 'fɔː] *verb*

to choose or to decide on something which is not quite what you want; *they didn't have any white sofas, so we settled for a brown one*

③ **settle in**
['setl 'ɪn] *verb*

to become used to a new house, job, etc.; *she's enjoying her job, though she took some time to settle in*; *the children have all settled into their new school*

② **settlement**
['setlmɪnt] *noun*

(a) payment of a bill; *this invoice has not been paid - can you arrange for immediate settlement?*

(b) agreement in a dispute; *in the end a settlement was reached between management and workers*

(c) place where a group of people come to live; *a mining settlement in the hills*

② **settle on**
['setl 'ɒn] *verb*

(a) to decide on, to choose; *after a lot of hesitation we finally settled on the red one*

(b) *(of insect, etc.)* to sit on; *if only the butterfly would settle on that flower I'd be able to take a picture of it*

③ **settle up**
['setl 'ʌp] *verb*

to pay a bill, to pay the total of what is owed; *you pay the bill and I'll settle up with you later*

① **set up**
['set 'ʌp] *verb*

(a) to establish; *to set up a committee or a working party*; *a fund has been set up to receive donations from the public*; *he set himself up as an estate agent*; **to set up a company** = to start a company legally; **to set up home** *or* **to set up house** = to go somewhere to live in your own flat, house, etc.; *they don't intend to set up house yet*

(b) *(informal)* to deceive someone on purpose; *we were set up by the police*

② **setup**
['setʌp] *noun*

(informal) organization; *he works for some public relations setup*

① **seven**
['sevɪn]

number 7; *there are only seven children in his class*; *she's seven (years old) next week*; *the train is supposed to leave at seven (o'clock)*; **seven hundreds** = the years from 700 to 799 AD (NOTE: compare **the seventh century**)

① **seventeen**
[sevɪn'tiːn]

number 17; *he will be seventeen (years old) next month*; *the train leaves at seventeen sixteen (17.16)* **the seventeen hundreds (1700s)** = the years from 1700 to 1799 (NOTE: compare **the seventeenth century**)

① **seventeenth (17th)**
[sevɪn'tiːnθ] *adjective & noun*

today is October the seventeenth or the seventeenth of October (October 17th) Q is the seventeenth letter of the alphabet; *it's his seventeenth birthday next week*; *he came seventeenth out of thirty*; **the seventeenth century** = the years from 1600 to 1699 (NOTE: compare **the seventeen hundreds**; Note also that with dates **seventeenth** is usually written **17th**: **July 17th, 1935**; **October 17th, 1991** (American style is **October 17, 1991**), say 'the seventeenth of October' or 'October the seventeenth' (American style is 'October seventeenth'); with names of kings and queens **seventeenth** is usually written **XVII**: **King Louis XVII** (say: 'King Louis the Seventeenth')

① **seventh (7th)**
['sevɪnθ] *adjective & noun*

his office is on the seventh floor; *it's her seventh birthday on Saturday*; *what is the seventh letter of the alphabet?*; *the seventh of July or July the seventh (July 7th) Henry the Seventh (Henry VII)* **the seventh century** = the period from 600 to 699 AD (NOTE: in dates **seventh** is usually written **7th**: **January 7th 1959, April 7th 1797 (American style is April 7, 1797)** say 'the seventh of April' or 'April the seventh' (American style is 'April seventh'); with names of kings and queens **seventh** is usually written **VII**: **King Henry VII**: say 'King Henry the seventh')

① seventieth (70th)
['sevɪntiɪθ] *adjective & noun*
don't forget tomorrow is your grandmother's seventieth birthday

① seventy
['sevɪntɪ]
number 70; *she will be seventy (years old) on Tuesday; that shirt cost him more than seventy dollars;* **she's in her seventies** = she is between 70 and 79 years old; **the (nineteen) seventies (1970s)** = the years from 1970 to 1979 (NOTE: **seventy-one (71), seventy-two (72)** etc., but **seventy-first (71st), seventy-second (72nd)** etc.)

① several
['sevrɪl] *adjective & pronoun* more than a few, but not a lot; *several buildings were damaged in the storm; we've met several times; several of the students are going to Italy; most of the guests left early but several stayed on till midnight*

② severe
[sɪ'vɪɪ] *adjective*
(a) very strict; *he was very severe with any child who did not behave; discipline in the school was severe*
(b) *(illness, weather, etc.)* very bad; *the government imposed severe limits on capital spending; the severe weather has closed several main roads; she had a severe attack of flu* (NOTE: **severer - severest**)

③ severely
[sɪ'vɪɪli] *adverb*
(a) strictly; *she was severely punished for being late*
(b) badly; *train services have been severely affected by snow; a severely handicapped child*

④ severity
[sɪ'verɪti] *noun*
being severe; *he attacked the government with increasing severity; the severity of the cold has killed many small birds*

③ sew
[sɪʊ] *verb*
to attach, make or mend by using a needle and thread; *I've taught both my sons how to sew; the button's come off my shirt - can you sew it back on?* (NOTE: do not confuse with **sow**; note also: **sewing - sewed - sewn** [sɪʊn])

① sex
[seks] *noun*
(a) one of two groups (male and female) into which animals and plants can be divided; *they've had a baby, but I don't know what sex it is; there is no discrimination on the grounds of sex, race and religion;* **the opposite sex** = people of the other sex to yours (ie, men to women, women to men); *he's very attractive to the opposite sex*
(b) sexual relations; *a film full of sex and violence; sex was the last thing on her mind;* **to have sex with someone** = to have sexual

relations with someone; **safe sex** = having sex in a way that avoids transmission of a sexual disease

② sexual
['sekʃʊɪl] *adjective*
referring to sex; *their relationship was never sexual;* **sexual partner** = person you have sex with; *see also* DISCRIMINATION

④ sexually
['sekʃʊɪli] *adverb*
in a sexual way; *do find her sexually attractive?;* **sexually transmitted disease** = disease transmitted by having sexual intercourse

② sexy
['seksi] *adjective*
(informal) attractive in a sexual way; *she was wearing a very sexy dress; you look very sexy in that suit; he's the sexiest actor in the movies today* (NOTE: **sexier - sexiest**)

④ shade
[ʃeɪd]
1 *noun*
(a) variation of a colour; *her hat is a rather pretty shade of green*
(b) dark place which is not in the sunlight; *let's try and find some shade - it's too hot in the sun; the sun's so hot that we'll have to sit in the shade*
(c) **to put someone in the shade** = to make someone seem less impressive; *his acting puts the rest of the cast in the shade*
(d) *(informal)* **shades** = sunglasses; *you can take off your shades now we're indoors*
(e) lampshade, a decorative cover put over a lamp; *I don't like the bright orange shade you bought; a brass table lamp with a red silk shade*
2 *verb*
to protect something from sunlight; *she shaded her eyes against the sun; the old birch tree shades that corner of the garden*

② shadow
['ʃædɪʊ]
1 *noun*
(a) dark place behind an object where light is cut off by the object; *in the evening, the trees cast long shadows across the lawn; she saw his shadow move down the hall; they rested for a while, in the shadow of a large tree*
(b) **the shadow cabinet** = senior members of the Opposition in parliament who cover the same areas of responsibility as the ministers in the government and will form the next government if they are elected to power; *the Leader of the Opposition has appointed his shadow cabinet; the shadow Foreign Secretary*
(c) *(informal)* **five o'clock shadow** = dark chin, where the beard is starting to grow again after it was shaved in the morning; *the bad guy is the one with the black hat and the five o'clock shadow*
2 *verb*

(a) to follow someone closely, but without being seen; *the drugs dealer was shadowed by two policemen*

(b) to be the Opposition spokesman covering a government department; *she is shadowing the Health Secretary*

③ **shaft**

[ʃɑːft] *noun*

(a) long handle of a spade, etc.; *the shaft of the spade was so old it snapped in two*

(b) thin beam of light; *tiny particles of dust dancing in a shaft of sunlight*

(c) rod which connects parts of an engine; *the shaft transmits power from the engine to the wheels*

(d) deep hole or big tube; *the air shaft had become blocked*; **lift shaft** = tube inside a building in which a lift moves up and down; **mine shaft** = hole in the ground leading down to a mine

② **shake**

[ʃeɪk]

1 *verb*

(a) to move something from side to side or up and down; *shake the bottle before pouring*; *the house shakes every time a train goes past*; *his hand shook as he opened the envelope*; **to shake your head** = to move your head from side to side to mean 'no'; *when I asked my dad if I could borrow the car he just shook his head* (NOTE: the opposite, meaning 'yes', is to **nod**)

(b) to surprise, to shock; *his family was shaken by the news that he had been arrested*; *the sight of it really shook me* (NOTE: **shaking - shook** [ʃʊk] **- has shaken**)

2 *noun*

(a) action of moving rapidly up and down; *if the tomato sauce won't come out, give the bottle a shake*

(b) **milk shake** = drink made by mixing milk and sweet flavouring; *he drank two chocolate milk shakes*

(c) moving from side to side; *he indicated 'no' with a shake of his head*

② **shake hands**

[ʃeɪk 'hændz] *verb*

to shake hands or **to shake someone's hand** = to greet someone by holding their right hand; *he shook hands with me*; *she refused to shake my hand*; *the negotiators shook hands and sat down at the conference table*; **to shake hands on a deal** = to shake hands to show that a deal has been agreed

COMMENT: in Britain and the USA you shake hands with someone mainly in quite formal circumstances, for example when you meet them for the first time or when you are saying goodbye to someone and do not expect to see them again soon. You do not normally shake hands with people you see every day

③ **shake off**

[ʃeɪk 'ɒf] *verb*

to get rid of something, usually something unpleasant; *before you leave the beach, remember to shake the sand off your towel*; *they drove at top speed but couldn't shake off the police car*; *I don't seem able to shake off this cold*

① **shall**

[ʃæl] *verb used with other verbs*

(a) *(to make the future)* *we shall be out on Saturday evening*; *I shan't say anything - I shall keep my mouth shut!*; *tomorrow we shan't be home until after 10 o'clock*

(b) *(to show a suggestion)* *shall we open the windows?*; *shall I give them a ring?* (NOTE: negative: **shan't** [ʃɑːnt] ; past: **should, should not** usually **shouldn't** Note also that **shall** is mainly used with **I** and **we**)

③ **shallow**

[ˈʃæliʊ]

1 *adjective*

(a) not deep, not far from top to bottom; *children were playing in the shallow end of the pool*; *the river is so shallow in summer that you can walk across it*

(b) without any serious meaning; *it's a very shallow treatment of a serious subject* (NOTE: **shallower - shallowest**)

2 *noun*

shallows = parts of a river or the sea where the water is shallow; *the children walked into the shallows looking for little fish*

② **shame**

[ʃeɪm]

1 *noun*

(a) feeling caused by having done something which you should not have done; *she went bright red with shame*; *to my shame, I did nothing to help*; **to die of shame** = to feel very ashamed; *I could have died of shame!*

(b) **what a shame!** = how sad; *what a shame you couldn't come to the party!*; *it's a shame your father isn't well - I'm sure he would have enjoyed the play*; *it's a shame to have to go to the office on such a beautiful sunny day*; **shame on you!** = you should be ashamed of yourself

2 *verb*

to make someone feel ashamed; *we hope to shame her into contributing to the party*; **naming and shaming** = publishing the name of someone or an organization that is not working correctly, in the hope that this will make them change their ways; *the government hopes that naming and shaming the councils will lead to a reduction in town hall corruption*; *see also* ASHAMED

③ **shampoo**

[ʃæmˈpuː]

1 *noun*

(a) liquid soap for washing hair, carpets, cars, etc.; *there are bottles of shampoo in the bathroom*
(b) action of washing the hair; *she went to the hairdresser's for a shampoo*
2 *verb*
to wash your hair, a carpet, a car, etc., with liquid soap; *the hairdresser shampooed her hair, and then cut it*; *they have a machine for shampooing carpets* (NOTE: shampooing - shampooed)

③ **shan't**
[ʃɑːnt] = SHALL NOT

② **shape**
[ʃeɪp]
1 *noun*
(a) form of how something looks; *she's got a ring in the shape of a letter S*; *the old table was a funny shape*; *this pullover's beginning to lose its shape* = it is beginning to stretch
(b) in good shape = in good physical form; *he's in good shape for the race*; *she's in a very bad shape*; **to take shape** = to begin to look as it will do when finished; *after all his hard work, the new garden in beginning to take shape*; **in any shape or form** = of any type; *the boss does not tolerate criticism in any shape or form*
2 *verb*
(a) to make into a certain form; *he shaped the pastry into the form of a little boat*
(b) to shape up = to result, to end up; *things are shaping up as we expected*; *it's shaping up to be a fine day*

② **shaped**
[ʃeɪpt] *adjective*
with a certain shape; *the new art gallery is shaped like an enormous tube*; *a square-shaped hole in the floor*

① **share**
[ʃeɪ]
1 *noun*
(a) part of something that is divided between two or more people; *take your share of the cake and leave me the rest*; *she should have paid her share of the food bill*; *there's a lot of work to do, so everyone must do their share*; **to have a share in** = to take part in, to have a part of; *all the staff should have a share in decisions about the company's future*; *she has her share of the responsibility for the accident*; **market share** or **share of the market** = percentage of a total market which the sales of a company cover; *their share of the market has gone up by 10%*
(b) one of the many equal parts into which a company's capital is divided; *the owners of shares are called 'shareholders'*; *he bought 2000 shares in Marks and Spencer*; *shares fell on the London Stock Exchange* (NOTE: American English often used the word **stock** where British English uses **share**. See the note at STOCK)
2 *verb*

(a) to share (out) = to divide up something among several people; *let's share the bill*; *in her will, her money was shared (out) among her sons*; *they shared the pencils out amongst them*
(b) to share something with someone = to allow someone to use something which you also use; *we offered to share our information with them*; *he doesn't like sharing his toys with other children*
(c) to use something which someone else also uses; *we share an office*; *we shared a taxi to the airport*

④ **shareholder**
[ˈʃeɪhɪʊldɪ] *noun*
person who owns shares in a company; *our first duty is to our shareholders*; *he called a shareholders' meeting*; **majority** or **minority shareholder** = person who owns more or less than half the shares in a company; *the solicitor acting on behalf of the minority shareholders* (NOTE: American English is **stockholder**)

③ **share index**
[ˈʃeɪ ˈɪndeks] *noun*
figure based on the current market price of certain shares on a stock exchange; *all the European share indexes rose following the rise in the Dow Jones Index*

> COMMENT: all the stock exchanges publish share indexes. The best known are the Footsie in London, the Dow Jones and Nasdaq in New York and the Nikkei in Tokyo

② **sharp**
[ʃɑːp]
1 *adjective*
(a) with a good edge for cutting or pushing in; *for injections, a needle has to have a very sharp point*; *the beach is covered with sharp stones*; *this knife is useless - it isn't sharp enough*
(b) sudden, great or severe; *there was a sharp drop in interest rates*; *the road makes a sharp right-hand bend*; *he received a sharp blow on the back of his head*; *we had a sharp frost last night*; *it's cold, there's a sharp north wind*
(c) bitter, unpleasant; *these onions have a very sharp taste*
(d) sharp practice = way of doing business which is not honest, but not illegal; *we suspect the lawyers of sharp practice but we can't prove anything*
(e) very keen and sensitive; *he has a sharp sense of justice*; *she has a sharp eye for a bargain*; *he's pretty sharp at spotting mistakes*
(f) showing criticism; *he got a very sharp reply to his fax*; **a sharp tongue** = a tendency to criticize people openly; *her sharp tongue has landed her in trouble once again*
(g) *(in music)* playing at a higher pitch than it should be; *that piano sounds sharp* (NOTE: sharper - sharpest)
2 *adverb*

(a) exactly; *the coach will leave the hotel at 7.30 sharp*

(b) suddenly, making a tight turn; *the road turned sharp right*

3 *noun*

(in music) pitch which is higher; *they played Bach's Sonata in F sharp major; he played D sharp instead of D flat*

④ **sharpen**
['ʃɑːpɪn] *verb*

to make something sharp; *I must sharpen my pencil; my old saw doesn't cut very well - it needs sharpening*

③ **sharply**
['ʃɑːpli] *adverb*

(a) strongly; *he felt his mother's death very sharply*

(b) completely; *the two groups are sharply divided on this issue*

(c) in a way that criticizes; *she spoke quite sharply to the poor old lady*

(d) suddenly; *the temperature fell sharply during the night; the road turns sharply to the right*

③ **shave**
[ʃeɪv]

1 *noun*

act of cutting off the hair on your face; *he went to have a shave at the men's hairdresser's next to the hotel;* a close shave = situation where you almost hit something; *it was a close shave - we missed the other car by inches*

2 *verb*

(a) to cut off the hair on your face; *he cut himself shaving*

(b) to cut the hair on your head or legs, etc., very short; *I didn't recognize him with his head shaved*

(c) to cut a thin piece off something; *you need to shave a bit more off to make the door fit the frame*

① **she**
[ʃiː] *pronoun referring to a female person, a female animal, and sometimes to cars, ships and countries; she's my sister; she and I are going on holiday to France together; I'm angry with her - she's taken my motorbike; she's a sweet little cat, but she's no good at catching mice; the customs officers boarded the ship when she docked* (NOTE: when it is the object **she** becomes **her: she hit the ball** *or* **the ball hit her;** when it follows the verb to **be, she** usually becomes **her: who's that? - it's her, the girl we met yesterday)**

③ **shed**
[ʃed]

1 *noun*

small wooden building; *they kept the garden tools in a shed at the bottom of the garden; she's in the garden shed putting flowers into pots*

2 *verb*

(a) to lose something which you are carrying or wearing; *in autumn, the trees shed their leaves as soon as the weather turns cold; a lorry has shed its load of wood at the roundabout; we shed our clothes and dived into the cool water*

(b) to let blood, tears, light, etc., flow; *she shed tears of anger as she listened to the speech; not one drop of blood was shed*

(c) to shed light on = to make clearer; *can anyone shed any light on what actually happened?; the finds in the cave shed light on the history of this region*

(d) *(formal)* to lose weight, to become lighter; *he goes on a run every morning to try to shed some weight; by stopping eating potatoes, she managed to shed three pounds* (NOTE: **shedding - shed**)

① **she'd**
[ʃiːd] = SHE WOULD

② **sheep**
[ʃiːp] *noun*

common farm animal, which gives wool and meat; *a flock of sheep; the sheep are in the field; see also* BLACK SHEEP (NOTE: no plural: **one sheep, ten sheep.** The young are **lambs.** Note also that the meat from a **sheep** is also called **lamb**)

④ **sheer**
['ʃɪr]

1 *adjective*

(a) complete; *it was sheer heaven to get into a hot bath after the marathon; it was sheer jealousy that made him write that letter*

(b) very steep; *it was a sheer ten-metre drop to the beach below*

2 *adverb*

straight up or down; *the cliff drops sheer to the beach below*

3 *verb*

to sheer off = to move to the side at an angle; *the car was speeding towards the tunnel but sheered off into the crowd instead*

② **sheet**
[ʃiːt] *noun*

(a) large piece of thin cloth which is put over a bed (you put two of them on a bed, one to lie on, and one to cover you); *she changed the sheets on the bed; guests are asked to bring their own towels and sheets*

(b) large flat piece of paper, cardboard, metal, ice, etc.; *can you give me another sheet of paper?;* **sheet lightning** = lightning where you cannot see the flash, but the clouds are lit up by it; *see also* BALANCE SHEET

③ **shelf**
[ʃelf] *noun*

flat piece of wood attached to a wall or in a cupboard on which things can be put; *he put up or built some shelves in the kitchen; the shelves were packed with books; put that book back on the shelf; can you reach me down the box from the top shelf?; the plates are on the top shelf in the kitchen cupboard*; **shelf life** = number of days or weeks when a product can be kept in a shop and still be good to use; *(informal)* **on the shelf** = still not married; *she thought she was on the shelf at thirty-five, and then Mr Right came along* (NOTE: plural is **shelves** [ʃelvz])

③ **shell**
[ʃel]
1 *noun*
(a) hard outside part covering some animals; *the children spent hours collecting shells on the beach*
(b) hard outside part of an egg or a nut; *I found a big piece of shell in my scrambled eggs*
(c) hard outside part of a building; *only the shell of the building remained after the fire*
(d) metal tube like a small bomb, which is fired from a gun; *a shell landed on the president's palace*
2 *verb*
to attack with shells; *anti-government forces shelled the capital*

③ **she'll**
[ʃiːl] = SHE WILL

③ **shellfish**
[ˈʃelfɪʃ] *noun*
sea animals with shells; *I never eat shellfish - they don't agree with me* (NOTE: no singular: **a plate of shellfish, a shellfish restaurant**)

④ **shelter**
[ˈʃeltɪ]
1 *noun*
(a) protection; *we stood in the shelter of a tree waiting for the rain to stop; on the mountain there was no shelter from the pouring rain;* **to take shelter** = to go somewhere for protection; *when the gunmen started to shoot we all took shelter behind a wall*
(b) construction where you can go for protection; *people ran to the bomb shelters as soon as they heard the planes*; **bus shelter** = construction with a roof where you can wait for a bus
2 *verb*
(a) to give someone protection; *the school sheltered several families of refugees*
(b) to go somewhere for protection; *sheep were sheltering from the snow beside the hedge*

④ **shelve**
[ʃelv] *verb*
(a) to put back to a later date which is not certain; *the project was shelved for lack of money; discussion of the problem has been shelved*
(b) to slope down; *the beach shelves gently so it is safe for little children*

③ **shelves**
[ʃelvz] *noun*
see SHELF

④ **shepherd**
[ˈʃepɪd]
1 *noun*

man who looks after sheep; *do shepherds still carry a stick with a hooked end?*; **shepherd's pie** = minced meat cooked in a dish with a layer of mashed potatoes on top (NOTE: also called **cottage pie**)
2 *verb*
to guide; *the children were shepherded into the building; the police were shepherding the crowds away from the scene of the accident*

④ **shield**
[ʃiːld]
1 *noun*
(a) large plate held in one hand, carried by riot police, etc., as protection; *the policemen bent down behind their plastic shields*
(b) thing which protects from danger; *you need a shield over your face when working with this equipment*
2 *verb*
(a) to protect from danger; *he tried to shield her from the wind*
(b) to protect someone who has done something wrong; *she's just shielding her father*

③ **shift**
[ʃɪft]
1 *noun*
(a) change of position, of direction, etc.; *the company is taking advantage of a shift in the market towards higher priced goods; there has been a shift of emphasis from competition to partnership; I don't understand this shift in attitude*
(b) period of time during which one group of workers works before being replaced by another group; *which shift are you working today?; we work an eight-hour shift*; **day shift** = shift worked during the day; **night shift** = shift worked during the night; *there are 150 men on the day shift; he works the night shift*
(c) loose dress; *as it was so hot she wore only a light cotton shift*
2 *verb*
(a) to move; to change position or direction; *we've shifted the television from the kitchen into the dining room; the centre of attention shifted to Downing Street*
(b) *US* **to shift gears** = to change from one gear to the next when driving a car; **to shift up** = to move to a higher gear when driving a car; *shift up to top gear when you get onto the freeway*; **to shift down** = to move to a lower gear when driving a car; *shift down when you come to the hill* (NOTE: British English is **to change gear, to change up, to change down**)
(c) *(informal)* **to shift for yourself** = to look after yourself; *you'll have to shift for yourselves while your mother's in hospital*
(d) *(informal)* to sell; *we shifted 20,000 Christmas trees in one week*

③ **shift key**

['ʃɪft 'kiː] *noun*

key on a typewriter or computer keyboard which makes capital letters or switches to another function; *hold down the shift key while you click on 'help'*

③ **shine**

[ʃaɪn]

1 *noun*

(a) reflection of light; *the shine of polished tables*

(b) action of polishing; *give the brass bowl a shine*

2 *verb*

(a) to be bright with light; *the sun is shining and they say it'll be hot today; she polished the table until it shone; the wine glasses shone in the light of the candles; why do cats' eyes shine in the dark?; the moon shone down on the waiting crowd*

(b) to make light fall on something; *he shone his torch into the well* (NOTE: in these meanings **shining - shone** [ʃɒn])

(c) to polish something to make it bright; *she was shining the silver; don't forget to shine your shoes* (NOTE: in this meaning **shining - shined**)

③ **shiny**

['ʃaɪni] *adjective*

which shines; *the book has a shiny cover; he drove up in his new and very shiny car* (NOTE: **shinier - shiniest**)

② **ship**

[ʃɪp]

1 *noun*

large boat for carrying passengers and cargo on the sea; *she's a fine ship; how many ships does the Royal Navy have?; the first time we went to the United States, we went by ship;* **cargo ship** = ship which carries only goods and not passengers; **to jump ship** = (i) to leave the ship on which you are working and not come back; (ii) to leave a project or team to go to work for a rival (NOTE: a **ship** is often referred to as **she** or **her**)

2 *verb*

(a) to send goods (or people) but not always on a ship; *we ship goods all over the country; the container of spare parts was shipped abroad last week; we've shipped the children off to my sister's for two weeks*

(b) to take on board a ship; *we shipped a lot of water during the storm* (NOTE: **shipping - shipped**)

③ **shipment**

['ʃɪpmɪnt] *noun*

(a) sending of goods; *we make two shipments a week to France*

(b) goods which are shipped; *two shipments were lost in the fire; a shipment of computers was damaged*

③ **shipping**

['ʃɪpɪŋ] *noun*

(a) sending of goods; *shipping by rail can often work out cheaper;* **shipping company** = company which specializes in the sending of goods; **shipping instructions** = details of how goods are to be shipped and delivered (NOTE: in this meaning, **shipping** does not always mean using a ship)

(b) cost of transporting goods; *shipping is not included in the invoice*

(c) ships; *they attacked enemy shipping in the Channel;* **shipping lanes** = routes across the sea which are regularly used by ships; **shipping line** = company which owns ships (NOTE: no plural)

② **shirt**

[ʃɜːt] *noun*

light piece of clothing which you wear on the top part of the body under a pullover or jacket; *the teacher wore a blue suit and a blue shirt; when he came back from the trip he had a suitcase full of dirty shirts; it's so hot that the workers in the fields have taken their shirts off, (informal)* **keep your shirt on!** = don't lose your temper

④ **shiver**

['ʃɪvɪ]

1 *noun*

action of trembling because of cold, fear, etc.; **to send shivers down someone's spine** = to make someone very afraid; *the mere thought of grandfather driving along the motorway at his age sends shivers down my spine*

2 *verb*

to tremble with cold, fear, etc.; *she shivered in the cold night air; he was coughing and shivering, so the doctor told him to stay in bed*

② **shock**

[ʃɒk]

1 *noun*

(a) sudden unpleasant surprise; *it gave me quite a shock when you walked in; he's in for a nasty shock*

(b) weakness caused by low blood pressure, after an illness or injury or having a sudden surprise; *several of the passengers were treated for shock; she was in a state of shock after hearing that her son had drowned*

(c) **electric shock** = sudden painful passing of electric current through the body; *I got a shock when I touched the back of the TV set*

2 *verb*

to give someone a sudden unpleasant surprise; *the conditions in the hospital shocked the inspectors*

③ **shocked**

[ʃɒkt] *adjective*

having an unpleasant surprise; *we were all shocked to hear that he had been arrested; she said 'How could you do it?' in a shocked voice*

③ **shocking**

['ʃɒkɪŋ] *adjective*

very unpleasant, which gives a sudden surprise; *it is a very shocking film*; *the shocking news of the plane crash*; *it is shocking that no one offered to help*

② **shoe**

[ʃuː] *noun*

(a) piece of clothing which is worn on the foot; *she's bought a new pair of shoes*; *he put his shoes on and went out*; *take your shoes off if your feet hurt*; **tennis shoes** = special shoes worn to play tennis (NOTE: two shoes are called **a pair of shoes**)

(b) in his shoes = in his place, in the situation he is in; *what would you do if you were in his shoes?*; *I wouldn't like to be in her shoes*

③ **shone**

[ʃɒn] *see* SHINE

③ **shook**

[ʃʊk] *see* SHAKE

② **shoot**

[ʃuːt]

1 *noun*

little new growth of a plant, growing from a seed or from a branch; *one or two green shoots are already showing where I sowed my lettuces*; *the vines have made a lot of new shoots this year*; *after pruning, the roses will send out a lot of strong new shoots*

2 *verb*

(a) to fire a gun; *soldiers were shooting into the woods*

(b) to hit or kill by firing a gun; *one of the robbers was shot by a policeman when he tried to run away*; *we went out hunting and shot two rabbits*

(c) to go very fast; *when the bell rang she shot downstairs*; *he started the engine and the car shot out of the garage*

(d) to make a film; *they're shooting a gangster film in our street* (NOTE: **shoots - shooting - shot** [ʃɒt])

③ **shoot up**

['ʃuːt 'ʌp] *verb*

(a) to go up fast; *prices shot up during the strike*

(b) to grow fast; *these tomatoes have shot up since I planted them*; *she used to be such a small child but she's really shot up in the last couple of years*

① **shop**

[ʃɒp]

1 *noun*

(a) place where you can buy things; *quite a few shops are open on Sundays*; *I never go to that shop - it's much too expensive*; *the sweet shop is opposite the fire station*; **corner shop** = small general store in a town, sometimes on a street corner; *we buy all our food from the corner shop*; **shop assistant** = person who serves customers in a shop; *the shop assistant was very*

helpful when I bought my camera; **shop window** = large window in a shop where goods are displayed so that customers can see them; *the shop windows are all decorated for Christmas* (NOTE: American English usually uses **store** instead of **shop: a bookstore, a computer store, etc.**)

(b) workshop, a place where goods are made or repaired; **body shop** = workshop where car bodies are repaired; **repair shop** = small factory where machines are repaired

(c) closed shop = system whereby a company agrees to employ only union members in certain jobs; *the union is asking the management to agree to a closed shop*

(d) to talk shop = to talk about your business; *the dinner party was dull - the men all sat in a corner talking shop*

2 *verb*

to look for and buy things in shops; *she's out shopping for his birthday present*; *Mum's gone shopping in town*; *they went shopping in Oxford Street*; *do you ever shop locally?* (NOTE: **shopping - shopped**)

> COMMENT: in Britain, smaller shops usually open Monday to Saturday from 9 o'clock or 9.30 to 5.30; some close for lunch between 1 o'clock and 2. Some shops close early on Wednesday or Saturday, though this is less frequent that it used to be. Supermarkets and some larger stores are open longer hours, especially on Thursday and Friday evenings, and are also open from 10.00 to 4.00 on Sundays. In big cities there are stores which are open from 7.00 in the morning to midnight. A few supermarkets are open 24 hours a day

③ **shop around**

['ʃɒp ə'raʊnd] *verb*

to go to various shops to find which one has the cheapest goods before you buy what you want; *if you want a cheap TV set you ought to shop around*; *you should shop around before getting your car serviced*

④ **shopkeeper**

['ʃɒpkiːpə] *noun*

person who owns a shop; *he stood up for the rights of the small shopkeepers*; *it was natural for small shopkeepers to feel annoyed when the supermarket opened*; *the shopkeeper is angry with the schoolchildren because they broke his window*

④ **shoplifter**

['ʃɒplɪftə] *noun*

person who steals things from shops; *we saw the shoplifter put a tin of beans in her bag*; *we have installed cameras to deter shoplifters*

③ **shopper**
['ʃɒpɪ] *noun*
person who buys things in a shop; *the store stays open till midnight for late-night shoppers*; *Oxford Street was crowded with shoppers when the sales started*

② **shopping**
['ʃɒpɪŋ] *noun*
(a) buying things in a shop; *we do all our shopping at the weekend*; *he's gone out to do the weekly shopping*; **window shopping** = looking at goods in shop windows, without buying anything; **shopping bag** = bag for carrying your shopping in; **shopping basket** = basket for carrying shopping; *US* **shopping cart** = metal basket on wheels, used by shoppers to put their purchases in as they go round a supermarket (NOTE: the British English for this is **supermarket trolley**)
(b) things which you have bought in a shop; *put all your shopping on the table*; *she was carrying two baskets of shopping* (NOTE: no plural: **some shopping, a lot of shopping**)

③ **shopping centre** *or* **shopping mall**
['ʃɒpɪŋ 'sentɪ *or* 'mɒl] *noun*
building with several different shops and restaurants, together with a car park; *we must stop them from building any more out-of-town shopping centres*

④ **shore**
[ʃɔː]
1 *noun*
land at the edge of the sea or a lake; *she stood on the shore waving as the boat sailed away*; **to go on shore** = to go on to the land from a ship; *when we were on shore in Greece our cruise ship sailed without us*
2 *verb*
to shore something up = to hold something up which might fall down; *they had to put in metal beams to shore up the ceiling*; *the army is trying to shore up the president's regime*

① **short**
[ʃɔːt]
1 *adjective*
(a) *(size, length)* not long; *have you got a short piece of wire?*; **short-sleeved shirt** = shirt with short sleeves
(b) *(distance)* not far; *she only lives a short distance away*; *the taxi driver wanted to take me through the high street, but I told him there was a shorter route*; *the shortest way to the railway station is to go through the park*; **short wave** = radio frequency below 60 metres
(c) *(period of time)* not long, small; *he phoned a short time ago*; *we had a short holiday in June*; *she managed to have a short sleep on the plane*
(d) *(height)* not tall; *he is only 1m 40 - much shorter than his brother*

(e) not as much as there should be; *the delivery was three items short*; **when we counted the cash we were £10 short** = we had £10 less than we should have had
(f) **short of** = with not enough; *I can't offer you any tea as we're short of milk*; *can I pay later as I'm rather short of cash at the moment?*; **to run short of** = to have less and less of; *in the hot weather the pubs ran short of beer*
(g) **short for** = written or spoken with fewer letters than usual; *Ltd is short for Limited*; **for short** = as a shortened version; *his name is Jonathan but everyone calls him Jonty for short* (NOTE: **shorter - shortest**)
2 *adverb*
(a) suddenly; *I stopped short when I saw her walking towards me*
(b) **short of** = without doing something; *short of sacking her, I don't know what we can do*
3 *verb*
to make a bad connection in an electric circuit, making the electric current follow the wrong path; *he switched on TV and shorted the whole house*

④ **shortage**
['ʃɔːtɪdʒ] *noun*
lack of something; *a chronic shortage of skilled staff*; *what is the government going to do about the housing shortage?*; *during the war, there were food shortages*

③ **short-circuit**
[ʃɔːt'sɜːkɪt]
1 *noun*
bad connection in an electric circuit, making the electric current follow the wrong path; *the worn cable caused a short-circuit*
2 *verb*
(a) to make a short-circuit; *a faulty contact caused the system to short-circuit*
(b) to get through something complicated by using a simple short cut; *is there any way of short-circuiting some of the administrative procedures?*

④ **shorten**
['ʃɔːtn] *verb*
to make shorter; *smoking will shorten your life*; *I must have these trousers shortened*; *'telephone' is often shortened to 'phone'*

③ **shortly**
[ʃɔːtlɪ] *adverb*
soon; *he left his office shortly before 5 o'clock*; *don't worry, she'll be here shortly*

③ **shorts**
[ʃɔːts] *noun*
short trousers for men or women, that come down above the knees; *he was wearing a pair of green running shorts*; *they won't let you into the church in shorts*; **boxer shorts** = men's underwear shaped like sports shorts

④ **short-term**

[ʃɔːtˈtɜːm] *adjective*

for a short period only; *staying in a hotel is only a short-term solution*; *we have taken on more staff on a short-term basis*; *see also* LONG-TERM

① **shot**

[ʃɒt]

1 *noun*

(a) action of shooting; the sound of shooting; *the police fired two shots at the car*; *some shots were fired during the bank robbery*; *a neighbour said she'd heard a shot*

(b) like a shot = very rapidly; *he heard a noise and was off like a shot*

(c) *(informal)* attempt; *he passed the test at the first shot*; to have a shot at something = to try to do something; *I'd like to have a shot at driving a bus*

(d) mail shot *or* mailing shot = leaflets sent by post to possible customers; *our latest mail shot goes out on Monday*

(e) *(slang)* injection; *the doctor gave him a yellow fever shot*

(f) *(slang)* small drink of alcohol; *he poured himself a shot of whisky and sat down to wait*

(g) photograph; *I took several shots of the inside of the house*

(h) large heavy ball thrown in a sporting competition; *how much does the shot weigh?*; to put the shot = to throw a heavy ball in a competition

(i) person who shoots well or badly; *she's a first-class shot*; *he's a hopeless shot*

2 *past tense and past participle of* SHOOT

① **should**

[ʃʊd] *verb used with other verbs*

(a) *(used in giving advice or warnings, used to say what is the best thing to do)* *you should go to the doctor if your cough gets worse*; *I should have been more careful*; *she shouldn't eat so much if she's trying to lose weight*; *should I ask for more coffee?*; *why should I clean up the mess you've made?*

(b) *(used to say what you expect to happen)* *if you leave now you should be there by 4 o'clock*; *their train should have arrived by now*; *there shouldn't be any more problems now* (NOTE: in meanings (a) and (b) ought to can be used instead of should)

(c) *(indicating a possibility)* *if the President should die in office, the Vice-President automatically takes over*; *I'll be in the next room should you need me*

(d) *(used instead of* would*)*; *(old)* *we should like to offer you our congratulations*; *if I had enough money I should like to buy a new car* (NOTE: negative: should not, usually shouldn't. Note also that should is the past of shall: shall we go to an Indian restaurant? - I suggested we should go to an Indian restaurant)

② **shoulder**

[ˈʃəʊldə]

1 *noun*

(a) part of the body at the top of the arm; *the policeman touched me on the shoulder*; *he fell and hurt his shoulder*; *look over your shoulder, he's just behind you*; shoulder blade = one of two large flat bones covering the top part of your back; *he fell when skiing and broke his shoulder blade*; shoulder to shoulder = side by side; *the three men stood shoulder to shoulder blocking the way*; *see also* BAG, CHIP, COLD

(b) piece of clothing which covers the part between top of the arm and the neck; *there's an ink mark on the shoulder of your shirt*; *a captain has three stars on his shoulders*

(c) piece of meat from the top part of the front leg of an animal; *we had a shoulder of lamb and new potatoes*

(d) hard shoulder = extra inside lane on a major road, where you can stop in an emergency; *the engine was making a funny noise, so I pulled over onto the hard shoulder*

2 *verb*

to carry responsibility, blame, etc.; *he had to shoulder all the responsibility for the company's collapse*; *she was left to shoulder the blame for the accident*

② **shout**

[ʃaʊt]

1 *noun*

yell, loud cry; *she gave a shout and dived into the water*; *people came running when they heard the shouts of the children*

2 *verb*

to make a loud cry, to speak very loudly; *they stamped on the floor and shouted*; *I had to shout to the waitress to get served*; *they were shouting greetings to one another across the street*

③ **shove**

[ʃʌv]

1 *noun*

sudden push; *she gave the car a shove and it started to roll down the hill*

2 *verb*

to push roughly; *he shoved the papers into his pocket*; *stop shoving - there's no more room on the bus*; *(informal)* shove off! = go away!; *shove off and let me finish my meal*

④ **shovel**

[ˈʃʌvl]

1 *noun*

wide spade; *the workmen picked up shovels and started to clear the pile of sand*

2 *verb*

(a) to lift up with a shovel; *they were shovelling sand into the truck*; *he collapsed after shovelling snow from the path*

(b) *(informal)* to put a large amount of food into your mouth; *it wasn't very elegant, the way he was shovelling potatoes into his mouth* (NOTE: **shovelling - shovelled** but American spelling **shoveling - shoveled**)

① **show**
[ʃəʊ]
1 *noun*

(a) exhibition, things which are displayed for people to look at; *the Hampton Court Flower Show opens tomorrow; she has entered her two cats for the local cat show*; **show flat** *or* **show house** = new flat or house which is decorated and filled with furniture by the builders so that people can see how other flats or houses will look

(b) on show = displayed for everyone to see; *is there anything new on show in this year's exhibition?*

(c) something which is on at a theatre; *'Cats' is a wonderful show*; *we're going to a show tonight*; *the show starts at 7.30, so let's have dinner early*

(d) show of hands = vote where people show how they vote by raising their hands; *the motion was carried on a show of hands*

(e) *(informal)* planned activity or organization; *she's running the whole show by herself*
2 *verb*

(a) to let someone see something; *he wanted to show me his holiday photos; she proudly showed me her new car; you don't have to show your passport when you're travelling to Ireland*

(b) to point something out to someone; *show me where the accident happened; he asked me to show him the way to the railway station; the salesman showed her how to work the photocopier; my watch shows the date as well as the time*

(c) to prove; *the results show how right we were to invest in the USA*

(d) to show signs of = to be visible; *the wound doesn't show any signs of infection*

(e) to be seen, to be obvious; *the repairs were badly done and it shows; her rash has almost disappeared and hardly shows at all*

(f) *(informal)* **to show someone the door** = to make someone leave, to sack someone; *when we complained we were shown the door* (NOTE: **showing - showed - has shown** [ʃəʊn])

② **shower**
[ˈʃaʊə]
1 *noun*

(a) slight fall of rain, snow, etc.; *in April there's usually a mixture of sunshine and showers; there were snow showers this morning, but it is sunny again now*

(b) device in a bathroom for sending out a spray of water to wash your whole body; **power shower** = strong shower driven by an electric pump; **shower curtain** = curtain around a shower to prevent the water going everywhere; **shower room** = small bathroom with a shower in it

(c) bath taken in a spray of water from over your head; *she went up to her room and had a shower; he has a cold shower every morning; you can't take a shower now, there's no hot water*; **shower cap** = plastic cap to prevent your hair getting wet when taking a shower

(d) *US* party where presents are given to a girl about to get married or who has had a baby; *we are holding a shower for Liliane next Saturday*

(e) *(informal)* group of slow, useless people; *come on you shower, get a move on!*
2 *verb*

(a) to wash under a spray of water; *he showered and went down to greet his guests*

(b) to shower someone with something = to give large amounts of something to someone; *she was showered with presents*

③ **show in**
[ˈʃəʊ ˈɪn] *verb*
to bring someone into a room, etc.; *please show the next candidate in; he was shown into a comfortable room with a view over the sea*

③ **shown**
[ʃəʊn] *see* SHOW

③ **show off**
[ˈʃəʊ ˈɒf] *verb*

(a) to show how you think you are much better than others; *don't watch her dancing about like that - she's just showing off*

(b) to display something you are proud of; *he drove past with the radio on very loud, showing off his new car*

③ **show out**
[ˈʃəʊ ˈaʊt] *verb*
to take someone to the door when they are leaving; *let me show you out*

③ **show over** *or* **show round**
[ˈʃəʊ ˈəʊvə or ˈʃəʊ ˈraʊnd] *verb*
to lead a visitor round a place; *the old guide showed us over or round the castle; he showed the students round his laboratory; I have to go out now but my mother will show you round*

③ **show up**
[ˈʃəʊ ˈʌp] *verb*

(a) *(informal)* to come; *we invited all our friends to the picnic but it rained and only five of them showed up*

(b) to do something which shows other people to be worse than you; *she dances so well that she shows us all up*

(c) to be seen clearly; *when I ride my bike at night I wear an orange jacket because it shows up clearly in the dark*

④ **shrank**
[ʃræŋk] *see* SHRINK

④ **shred**
[ʃred]
1 *noun*

(a) strip torn off something; *she tore his newspaper to shreds*; *the curtains were on the floor in shreds*
(b) small amount; *there's not a shred of evidence against him*
(c) long thin strip of fruit, vegetables, etc.; *marmalade with shreds of orange peel in it*
2 *verb*
(a) to tear (paper) into thin strips, which can then be thrown away or used as packing material; *they sent a pile of old invoices to be shredded*; *she told the police that the manager had told her to shred all the documents in the file*
(b) to cut into very thin strips; *here's an attachment for shredding vegetables*; *add a cup of shredded carrot* (NOTE: **shredding - shredded**)

④ **shrink**
 [ʃrɪŋk]
 1 *verb*
(a) to make smaller; *the water must have been too hot - it's shrunk my shirt*
(b) to get smaller; *my shirt has shrunk in the wash*; *the market for typewriters has shrunk almost to nothing* (NOTE: **shrank** [ʃræŋk] - **shrunk** [ʃrʌŋk])
 2 *noun*
(slang) psychiatrist; *she's been to see a shrink but she's no better at all*

④ **shrub**
 [ʃrʌb] *noun*
small plant with stiff stems; *a flowering shrub would look lovely under that window*

③ **shrug**
 [ʃrʌg]
 1 *verb*
to shrug your shoulders = to move your shoulders up to show you are not sure, not interested, etc.; *when I asked him what he thought about it all, he just shrugged his shoulders and walked off*
 2 *noun*
moving your shoulders up to show you are not sure, not interested, etc.; *he just gave a shrug and walked on* (NOTE: **shrugging - shrugged**)

④ **shuffle**
 [ˈʃʌfl] *verb*
(a) to walk dragging your feet along the ground; *he shuffled into the room in his slippers*
(b) to mix playing cards; *I think he must have done something to the cards when he was shuffling them*; *he shuffled the pack and dealt three cards to each player*

① **shut**
 [ʃʌt]
 1 *adjective*
closed, not open; *some shops are shut on Sundays, but most big stores are open*; *we tried to get into the museum but it was shut*; *she lay with her eyes shut*; *come in - the door isn't shut!*

2 *verb*
(a) to close something which is open; *can you please shut the window - it's getting cold in here*; *here's your present - shut your eyes and guess what it is*
(b) to close for business; *in Germany, shops shut on Saturday afternoons*; *the restaurant shuts at midnight* (NOTE: **shutting - shut**)

③ **shut down**
 [ˈʃʌt ˈdaʊn] *verb*
(a) to close completely; *the factory shut down for the holiday weekend*
(b) to switch off an electrical system; *they had to shut down the power station because pollution levels were too high*

③ **shut in**
 [ˈʃʌt ˈɪn] *verb*
to lock inside; *the door closed suddenly and we were shut in*; *we shut the cat in the kitchen at night*

③ **shut off**
 [ˈʃʌt ˈɒf] *verb*
(a) to switch something off; *can you shut off the water while I mend the tap?*
(b) to stop access to; *we can shut off the dining room with folding doors*; *the palace is shut off from the road by a high wall*

③ **shut out**
 [ˈʃʌt ˈaʊt] *verb*
(a) to lock outside; *if the dog keeps on barking you'll have to shut him out*; *I was shut out of the house because I'd left my keys inside*
(b) to stop light getting inside; to stop people seeing a view; *those thick curtains should shut out the light*; *a high wall shuts out the view of the factory*
(c) to stop thinking about something; *try to shut out the memory of the accident*

④ **shuttle**
 [ˈʃʌtl]
 1 *noun*
(a) thing which moves from one place to another; *there's a shuttle bus from the hotel to the exhibition grounds*; **shuttle service** = bus or plane which goes regularly backwards and forwards between two places; *the ferry operates a shuttle service between the islands*; **shuttle diplomacy** = action of a diplomat going backwards and forwards between two countries to try to make them reach an agreement; *see also* SPACE SHUTTLE
(b) small device holding thread which goes backwards and forwards under and over the vertical threads when weaving
 2 *verb*
to go backwards and forwards regularly; *waiters were shuttling backwards and forwards from the kitchen to the dining room*

① **shut up**
 [ˈʃʌt ˈʌp] *verb*
(a) to close something inside; *I hate being shut up indoors on a sunny day*

(b) *(informal)* to stop making a noise; *tell those children to shut up - I'm trying to work*; *shut up! - we're tired of listening to your complaints*; *once he starts talking it's impossible to shut him up*

④ **shy**
[ʃaɪ]
1 *adjective*

(a) nervous and afraid to do something; *he's so shy he sat in the back row and didn't speak to anyone*; *once bitten twice shy* = once you have had a bad experience you will not want to do it again; *I'm not getting involved with him again - once bitten twice shy!*

(b) to fight shy of doing something = to avoid getting involved

2 *verb*

(of a horse) to jump in a nervous way; *his horse shied at the noise of the gun*

3 *noun*

coconut shy = place at a fair where you throw balls at coconuts balanced on posts, trying to knock them off; *you must have a go on the coconut shy*

① **sick**
[sɪk]
1 *adjective*

(a) ill, not well; *he's been sick for months*; *we have five staff off sick*; **sick leave** = time when a worker is away from work because of illness

(b) to be sick = to bring up partly digested food from the stomach into the mouth; *the last time I ate mushrooms I was sick all night*; **to feel sick** = to want to bring food up from the stomach into the mouth; *when I got up this morning I felt sick and went back to bed*; *the oily food made her feel sick*; *see also* SEASICK

(c) to be sick (and tired) of = to have had too much of; *I'm sick of listening to all his complaints*; *she's sick and tired of doing housework all day long*; **to make someone sick** = to make someone very annoyed; *all my friends earn more than I do - it makes me sick!*

(d) referring to something sad, disgusting; *he made some sick jokes about handicapped people*

2 *noun*

the sick = people who are ill; *nurses were looking after the sick and the dying*

② **sickness**
['sɪknɪs] *noun*

(a) feeling of wanting to bring up food from the stomach into the mouth; **morning sickness** = feeling of wanting to be sick, felt by pregnant women in the morning; **travel sickness** = sickness caused by the movement of a car, aircraft, bus or train, etc.; **travel sickness pills** = pills taken to prevent travel sickness

(b) not being well; *there is a lot of sickness about during the winter months*

① **side**
[saɪd]
1 *noun*

(a) one of the four parts which with the top and bottom make a solid object such as a box; *stand the box upright - don't turn it onto its side*

(b) one of the two parts which with the front and back make a building; *the garage is attached to the side of the house*

(c) one of the surfaces of a flat object; *please write on both sides of the paper*

(d) one of two parts or two edges of something; *our office is on the opposite side of the street to the bank*; *London Airport is on the west side of the city*; *the children were standing by the side of the road*; **to look on the bright side** = to be optimistic; *you should look on the bright side - you'll have plenty of free time now you've lost your job*; *see also* WRONG

(e) one of two parts separated by something; *she jumped over the fence to get to the other side*; *in England cars drive on the left-hand side of the road*

(f) sports team; *the local side was beaten 2 - 0*

(g) part of the body between the top of the legs and the shoulder; *I can't sleep when I'm lying on my right side*; *the policemen stood by the prisoner's side*; *they all stood side by side*

(h) one of the sides of an animal, used as a piece of meat; *a side of bacon*

(i) *(informal)* **on the side** = separate from your normal work, and sometimes hidden from your employer; *her salary is very low, so the family lives on what she can make on the side*

(j) *(informal)* aspect of something; *the car runs well but it's rather on the small side*; **the book is on the heavy side** = (i) the book is quite heavy; (ii) the book is fairly difficult to read

(k) to be on someone's side = to support someone in a battle or argument, to have the same point of view as someone; *don't attack me - I'm on your side*; *whose side is he on?*; **to take sides** = to say who you agree with; *he refused to take sides in the argument*

(l) family, ancestors; *on my mother's side everyone has blue eyes*

2 *adjective*

which is at the side; *there is a side entrance to the shop*; *can you take that bucket round to the side door?*; **side plate** = small plate placed next to your dinner plate; *they served the vegetables on side plates*

3 *verb*

to side against someone = to disagree with someone in an argument; *I can't understand why they all are siding against me*; **to side with someone** = to agree with someone in an argument; *why do you always side with the boss?*

◊ **on the right side**
[ɒn ðɪ 'raɪt saɪd] *phrase*

(a) in the correct relationship with; *you'll be in trouble if you don't keep on the right side of the law*

(b) *(informal)* not older than; *she's still on the right side of forty*

② **side effect**
['saɪd ɪ'fekt] *noun*
effect produced by a drug, treatment, etc., which is not the main effect intended; *one of the side effects of the treatment is that the patient's hair falls out; the drug is being withdrawn because of its unpleasant side effects*

③ **sidewalk**
['saɪdwɔːk] *noun*
US hard path for walkers at the side of a road; *a girl was cycling along the sidewalk; we sat at a sidewalk café* (NOTE: in British English this is **pavement**)

④ **sideways**
['saɪdweɪz] *adverb*
to the side or from the side; *take a step sideways and you will be able to see the castle; if you look at the post sideways you'll see how bent it is*

④ **siege**
[siːdʒ] *noun*
surrounding an enemy town or castle with an army to prevent supplies getting in, and so force it to surrender; *the army laid siege to the castle; the inhabitants almost starved during the siege of the town;* **under siege** = surrounded by an enemy; *the town has been under siege for several weeks; the pop star's hotel was under siege by photographers and reporters;* **siege mentality** = feeling that you are surrounded by enemies

④ **sigh**
[saɪ]
1 *noun*
long deep breath, showing sadness, etc.; *she gave a deep sigh and put the phone down; you could hear the sighs of relief from the audience when the heroine was saved*
2 *verb*
to breathe deeply showing you are sad, relieved, etc.; *he sighed and wrote out another cheque*

② **sight**
[saɪt]
1 *noun*
(a) one of the five senses, being able to see; *my grandfather's sight isn't very good any more;* **to lose your sight** = to become blind; *he lost his sight in the accident*
(b) seeing, view; *he can't stand the sight of blood; we caught sight of a bear up in the mountains; she kept waving until the car disappeared from sight; the fog cleared and the mountains came into sight; they waved until the boat was out of sight; the house is hidden from sight behind a row of trees; the little boy burst into tears at the sight of the dead rabbit;* **at first sight** = when you see something for the first time; *at first sight I thought he was wearing a pair of dark blue pyjamas*

(c) something (especially something famous) which you ought to see; *they went off on foot to see the sights of the town; the guidebook lists the main tourist sights in Beijing;* **to do the sights** = to visit the main tourist attractions; *we did the sights in Barcelona*
(d) to look a sight = to look awful; *she looks a sight in that old coat*
(e) sights = part of a gun which you look through to aim; *he spent so long adjusting the gun's sights that the deer had disappeared;* **to set your sights on** = to aim for; *she's set her sights on becoming an actress*
2 *verb*
to see something a long way away; *we often sight rare birds on the lake; the helicopter sighted some pieces of wood from the boat* (NOTE: do not confuse with **cite, site**)

② **sign**
[saɪn]
1 *noun*
(a) movement of the hand which means something; *he made a sign to us to sit down*
(b) drawing, notice, etc., which advertises something; *the office has a big sign outside it saying 'for sale'; a 'no smoking' sign hung on the wall;* **(road) sign** = panel by the side of a road, giving instructions or warnings; *go straight on until you come to a sign pointing left, marked 'to the sea'*
(c) something which shows something; *there is no sign of the rain stopping; the economy is showing signs of improvement; the police can find no sign of how the burglars got into the office; he should have arrived by now, but there's no sign of him*
(d) printed character; *the pound sign (£) the dollar sign ($) the hash sign (#)*
2 *verb*
to write your name in a special way on a document to show that you have written it or that you have approved it; *the secretary brought him all the letters to sign; sign on the dotted line, please; the letter is signed by the managing director; a cheque is not valid if it has not been signed*

② **signal**
['sɪgnl]
1 *noun*
(a) sign or movement which tells someone to do something; *I'll give you a signal to start playing 'Happy Birthday'*
(b) device used to tell someone to do something; *the signal was at red so the train had to stop*
(c) electronic sound heard on a radio receiver; *we heard a faint signal coming from the mountains*
2 *verb*
to make signs to tell someone to do something; *the driver signalled to show that he was turning right; she signalled to me that we were running*

out of time (NOTE: British English is **signalling - signalled** but American English is **signaling - signaled**)

3 *adjective*

(formal) remarkable; *the conference was a signal success*

④ **signature**

['sɪgnɪtʃɪ] *noun*

(a) name written in a special way by someone to show that a document has been authorized or accepted; *he found a pile of cheques on his desk waiting for his signature; her signature doesn't look like her name at all; the shopkeeper looked very closely at her signature and compared it with the one on the credit card*

(b) **signature tune** = tune which is used to identify a radio or TV broadcast; *that programme has had the same signature tune for over 30 years*

③ **sign for**

['saɪn 'fɔː] *verb*

(a) to sign a document to show that you have received something; *he signed for the parcel*

(b) *(of footballer)* to transfer to a new club; *he signed for Chelsea yesterday*

② **significance**

[sɪg'nɪfɪkɪns] *noun*

(a) meaning; *what is the significance of your logo of a ship?*

(b) importance; *there was no significance in the fact that her temperature was higher than usual*; **of great significance** = very important; *the contents of the letter were of great significance; his remarks were of little significance*

① **significant**

[sɪg'nɪfɪkɪnt] *adjective*

important, full of meaning; *it is highly significant that everyone else was asked to the meeting, but not the finance director; there has been a significant improvement in his condition*

② **significantly**

[sɪg'nɪfɪkɪntlɪŋ] *adverb*

in a significant way; *my home town has not altered significantly in 20 years; the company has employed her again but on a significantly lower salary*

③ **sign on**

['saɪn 'ɒn] *verb*

(a) to start work; *he signed on and started work immediately*

(b) to start drawing unemployment benefit; *she signed on for her benefits*

② **silence**

['saɪlɪns]

1 *noun*

quiet, absence of noise; *I love the silence of the countryside at night; the crowd of tourists waited in silence; the chairman held up his hand and asked for silence; there was a sudden silence as she came in; there will be a minute's*

silence at 11 o'clock; **wall of silence** = plot by everyone to say nothing about what has happened; *the police investigation met with a wall of silence*

2 *verb*

to stop someone saying or writing something; *he tried to silence his critics by taking them to court; she refused to be silenced and continued to write her articles about government corruption*

③ **silent**

['saɪlɪnt] *adjective*

not talking, not making any noise; *he kept silent for the whole meeting; she seems rather silent today; a very silent and reserved young man; the house was cold and silent; this new washing machine is almost silent; they showed some old silent films*; **the silent majority** = the majority of people who do not protest, who are not members of political parties, etc., but who vote according to their beliefs

④ **silk**

[sɪlk] *noun*

(a) cloth made from threads produced by caterpillars living in trees; *she was wearing a beautiful silk scarf; I bought some blue silk to make a dress*

(b) *(informal)* **a silk** = a Queen's Counsel; **to take silk** = to become a Queen's Counsel

③ **silly**

['sɪlɪ] *adjective*

stupid, not thinking; *don't be silly - you can't go to the party dressed like that!; she asked a lot of silly questions; of all the silly newspaper articles that must be the silliest* (NOTE: **sillier - silliest**)

③ **silver**

['sɪlvɪ]

1 *noun*

(a) precious white metal; *gold is worth more than silver; how much is an ounce of silver worth?* (NOTE: Chemical element: chemical symbol: **Ag**; atomic number: **47**)

(b) coins made of white metal; *he held out a handful of silver*

(c) **silver foil** *or* **silver paper** = thin sheet of shiny metal which looks like silver, used for wrapping food in; *chocolate bars are wrapped in silver paper*

(c) knives, forks and spoons made of silver; *she's in the kitchen, polishing the silver; don't worry, all the silver is securely locked away*

(d) **silver (medal)** = medal given to someone who finishes in second place in a race or competition; *England won ten silver medals at the Olympics; see also* BRONZE, GOLD

(e) shiny white colour, like silver; *the car has been sprayed in silver*

(f) **silver wedding** = celebration when two people have been married for twenty-five years

2 *adjective*

of a shiny white colour, like silver; *the car has been sprayed with silver paint; she wore silver shoes to match her handbag*

① **similar**
['sɪmɪlɪ] *adjective*
very alike but not quite the same; *here is the old lampshade - do you have anything similar to replace it?; the two cars are very similar in appearance; our situation is rather similar to yours*

② **similarity**
[sɪmɪ'lærɪti] *noun*
being similar; *he bears an astonishing similarity to the Prince of Wales; there is no similarity whatsoever between the two cases; the two children are fair with blue eyes, but the similarity stops there* (NOTE: plural is **similarities**)

③ **similarly**
['sɪmɪlɪli] *adverb*
in a similar way; *all these infections must be treated similarly; he always writes a nice thank you letter, and similarly so does his sister*

④ **simmer**
['sɪmɪ] *verb*
(a) to cook by boiling gently; *we left the soup to simmer gently*
(b) **to simmer down** = to become calmer after being very annoyed; *will you try to simmer down and listen to me, please?*

① **simple**
['sɪmpl] *adjective*
(a) easy; *the machine is very simple to use; she described the accident in a few simple words; it turned out to be a simple job to open the door; they say the new tax forms are simpler than the old ones*
(b) ordinary, not very special, not complicated; *they had a simple meal of bread and soup; it's a very simple pattern of lines and squares* (NOTE: **simpler - simplest**)

③ **simple interest**
['sɪmpl 'ɪntrɪst] *noun*
interest calculated on the capital only, and not added to it; *the loan will be cheaper because it only attracts simple interest* (NOTE: the opposite is **compound interest**)

① **simply**
['sɪmpli] *adverb*
(a) in a simple way; *he described very simply how the accident had happened; she always dresses very simply*
(b) only; *he did it simply to annoy everyone; she gave a new look to the room simply by painting one wall red*
(c) *(to emphasize)* your garden is simply beautiful; it's simply terrible - what shall we do?*

④ **simultaneous**
[sɪml'teɪnɪs] *adjective*
happening at the same time as something else; *there will be simultaneous radio and TV*

broadcast of the concert; **simultaneous translation** = translation of a speech into another language done at the same time as a person is speaking

② **sin**
[sɪn]
1 *noun*
(a) wicked action which goes against the rules of a religion; *envy is one of the seven deadly sins*; **to live in sin** = to live together without being married
(b) something bad; *it would be a sin to waste all that food*
2 *verb*
to commit a sin, to do something wicked; *the priest told him he had sinned* (NOTE: **sinning - sinned**)

① **since**
[sɪns]
1 *preposition*
during the period after; *she's been here since Monday; we've been working non-stop since 4 o'clock - can't we have a rest?*
2 *conjunction*
(a) during the period after; *he has had trouble borrowing money ever since he was rude to the bank manager; since we got to the hotel, it has rained every day*
(b) because; *since he's ill, you can't ask him to help you; since it's such a fine day, let's go for a walk*
3 *adverb*
during the period until now; *she phoned on Sunday and we haven't heard from her since; he left England in 1990 and has lived abroad ever since*

③ **sincere**
[sɪn'sɪɪ] *adjective*
very honest and genuine; *a politician needs to appear sincere; we send you our sincere best wishes for a rapid recovery*

③ **sincerely**
[sɪn'sɪɪli] *adverb*
really, truly; *I sincerely wanted to see her at Christmas; he believed most sincerely that she would come immediately*; **Yours sincerely** US **Sincerely yours** = used as an ending to a letter addressed to a named person

① **sing**
[sɪŋ] *verb*
to make music with your voice; *she was singing as she worked; please sing another song; he always sings in the bath; she sang a funny song about elephants* (NOTE: **singing - sang** [sæŋ] - **has sung** [sʌŋ])

③ **singer**
['sɪŋɪ] *noun*
person who sings; *she's training to be a professional singer; I'm not a very good singer*

① **single**
['sɪŋgl]
1 *adjective*

(a) one alone; *he handed her a single sheet of paper*; *there wasn't a single person I knew at the party*; *the single most important fact about him is that he has no money*; **every single (one)** = each one; *you will need every single penny you have to pay for the house*; *every single time I asked her out, she refused*
(b) for one person only; *have you got a single room for two nights, please?*; *we prefer two single beds to a double bed*
(c) not married; *she's twenty-nine and still single*; *are there any single men on the course?*; **single parent** = one parent (mother or father) who is bringing up a child alone
(d) single ticket = ticket for a journey in one direction only; *two single tickets cost more than a return*
(e) in single figures = less than ten; *inflation was over 20% but now it is down to single figures*
2 *noun*
(a) ticket for one journey; *two singles to Oxford Circus, please*
(b) record with one piece of music on it; *the group's first single went into the top ten*
(c) *(in cricket)* one run; *he scored a single and won the match*

① **singles**
['sɪŋglz] *noun*
(a) singles = tennis game played between two people; *the men's singles champion*
(b) singles = people who are not married; *they went to a singles bar*

④ **singular**
['sɪŋgjʊlɪ]
1 *adjective*
(a) *(formal)* odd, strange; *we found ourselves in a really singular position*
(b) showing that there is only one thing or person; *'she' is a singular pronoun*
2 *noun*
form of a word showing that there is only one; *'child' is the singular, and 'children' is the plural*; *the singular of 'they have' is 'he has'*; *the singular of 'bacteria' is 'bacterium'*

④ **sinister**
['sɪnɪstɪ] *adjective*
which looks evil, which suggests that something bad will happen; *there's nothing sinister about their getting together*; *the sinister atmosphere of the castle*; *his colleague is a sinister character who never smiles*

③ **sink**
[sɪŋk]
1 *noun*
fixed washbasin for washing dishes, etc., in a kitchen; *the sink was piled high with dirty dishes*; *he was washing his hands at the kitchen sink*; **sink unit** = arrangement of cupboard, sink, taps, waste pipes, etc., forming a single piece of furniture
2 *verb*

(a) to go down to the bottom (of water, mud, etc.); *the ferry sank in 30m of water*; *the paper boat floated for a few minutes, then sank*; *you should tie a piece of lead to your fishing line to make it sink*
(b) to drop suddenly; *she was so upset that she just sank into an armchair and closed her eyes*; *my heart sank when I heard the news*; *inflation has sunk to the lowest point ever*
(c) to invest money in something; *he sank all his savings into a car-hire business* (NOTE: **sinking - sank** [sæŋk] - **sunk** [sʌŋk])

③ **sink in**
['sɪŋk 'ɪn] *verb*
to become fixed in the mind; *the speaker waited a moment for the meaning of what he had said to sink in*

④ **sip**
[sɪp]
1 *noun*
little drink; *she took a sip of water, and went on with her speech*
2 *verb*
to drink taking only a small amount of liquid at a time; *the girl was sipping her drink quietly* (NOTE: **sipping - sipped**)

③ **sir**
[sɜː] *noun*
(a) *(usually used by someone serving in a shop or restaurant)* polite way of referring to a man; *would you like a drink with your lunch, sir?*; *please come this way, sir*
(b) *(in letters)* **Dear Sir** = polite way of addressing a man you do not know; **Dear Sirs** = polite way of addressing a company
(c) *(way of addressing a male teacher, in Britain)* *please sir, I forgot to bring my homework*
(d) title given to a knight

COMMENT: the title is always used with the man's Christian name, and, in formal address, with the surname as well: you can say 'good morning, Sir George', but 'may I introduce Sir George Smith?'

① **sister**
['sɪstɪ]
1 *noun*
(a) girl or woman who has the same father and mother as someone else; *his three sisters all look alike*; *my younger sister Louise works in a bank*; *do you have any sisters?*
(b) senior female nurse in charge of a ward; *the sister told me my son was getting better* (NOTE: can be used with names as a title: **Sister Jones**. Note also that the male equivalent is a **charge nurse**)
2 *adjective*
sister company = company which forms part of the same group as another company; **sister ship** = ship which is of the same design and belongs to the same company as another ship

① **sit**
[sɪt] *verb*
(a) to be resting with your behind on something; to move in into this position; *mother was sitting in bed eating her breakfast; there were no seats left, so they had to sit on the floor*
(b) to take a test; *she failed her English exam and had to sit it again*
(c) to sit for a picture = to pose, to stand or sit still while someone paints or photographs you; *she sat for her portrait; he sat for her in his uniform*
(d) *(of Parliament, a council, etc.)* to be in session; *a light shines at the top of Big Ben when the House of Commons is sitting*
(e) *(of bird)* to rest; *the pigeon always comes and sits on the fence when I'm sowing seeds*
(f) to look after children, to baby-sit; *I'm looking for someone to sit for me tomorrow evening* (NOTE: **sits - sitting - sat** [sæt] **- has sat**)

① **sit back**
['sɪt 'bæk] *verb*
(a) to rest your back against the back of a chair when sitting; *just sit back and enjoy the film*
(b) to do nothing; *he just sat back and watched everyone else do the work*

① **sit down**
['sɪt 'daʊn] *verb*
to sit on a seat; *if everyone will sit down, the meeting can start; they all sat down and the film began; come and sit down next to me*

④ **sit-down**
['sɪtdaʊn]
1 *adjective*
(a) sit-down meal = meal where you sit at a table; *we'd rather have sandwiches in the bar than a sit-down meal*
(b) sit-down protest *or* **sit-down strike** = strike where the workers stay in their place of work and refuse to work or to leave; *the factory has been occupied by workers staging a sit-down strike*
2 *noun*
(informal) little rest; *I've been on my feet all day - I think I deserve a sit-down*

② **site**
[saɪt]
1 *noun*
(a) place where something is or will be; *this is the site for the new factory*; **building site** *or* **construction site** = place where a building is being built; *all visitors to the site must wear safety helmets*; **camping site** *or* **camp site** = place where you can camp; **green field site** = site for a factory which is in the country, and not surrounded by other buildings
(b) place where something happened, where something once existed; *this was the site of the Battle of Hastings in 1066; they're trying to find the site of the old Roman town*

(c) *(Internet)* **web site** = collection of pages on the web which have been produced by one company and are linked together; *how many hits did we have on our site last week?*
2 *verb*
to be sited = to be placed on a particular piece of land; *the hotel will be sited between the airport and the new exhibition centre* (NOTE: do not confuse with **cite, sight**)

④ **situated**
['sɪtjʊeɪtɪd] *adjective*
placed, in a certain situation; *the factory is situated next to the railway station; the tourist office is situated in the town centre*

① **situation**
[sɪtjuˈeɪʃn] *noun*
(a) position, way in which something is placed; *what's your opinion of the company's present situation?; I wonder how she got herself into this situation*
(b) job; *I'm looking for a more permanent situation*; **situations vacant** = list of job vacancies in a newspaper
(c) place where something is; *the hotel is in a very pleasant situation by the sea*

① **sit up**
['sɪt 'ʌp] *verb*
(a) to sit with your back straight; *sit up straight!*
(b) to move from a lying to a sitting position; *he's too weak to sit up; he sat up in bed to eat his breakfast*
(c) to stay up without going to bed; *we sat up playing cards until 2 a.m.*

① **six**
[sɪks]
(a) number 6; *he's six (years old) we're having some people round for drinks at six (o'clock) there are only six chocolates left in the box - who's eaten the rest?*; **the six hundreds** = the years from 600 to 699 AD (NOTE: compare **the sixth century**)
(b) *(in cricket)* score of six runs for sending the ball over the boundary without touching the ground; *he scored a century, including four fours and two sixes*
(c) six-pack = pack containing six bottle or cans; *they brought a six-pack of beer to the party*

① **sixteen**
[sɪksˈtiːn]
number 16; *he'll be sixteen next month; the train leaves at seventeen sixteen (17.16)* **the sixteen hundreds (1600s)** = the years from 1600 to 1699 (NOTE: compare **the sixteenth century**)

① **sixteenth (16th)**
[sɪksˈtiːnθ] *adjective & noun*
she came sixteenth in the race; the sixteenth of July or July the sixteenth (July 16th) her sixteenth birthday is on Tuesday; **the sixteenth century** = the years from 1500 to 1599 (NOTE: compare **the sixteen hundreds;** Note also that

with dates **sixteenth** is usually written **16th: July 16th, 1935; October 16th, 1991** (American style is **October 16, 1991**), say 'the sixteenth of October' or 'October the sixteenth' (American style is 'October sixteenth'); with names of kings and queens **sixteenth** is usually written **XVI: King Louis XVI** (say: 'King Louis the Sixteenth')

① **sixth (6th)**
[sɪksθ] *adjective & noun*
his office is on the sixth floor; what is the sixth letter of the alphabet?; ten minutes is a sixth of an hour; the sixth of August or August the sixth (August 6th) tomorrow is her sixth birthday; **sixth form** = top class in a school, with students between 16 and 18 years old; **the sixth century** = the period from 500 to 599 AD (NOTE: in dates **sixth** is usually written **6th: October 6th 1923; January 6th, 1984** (American style is **January 6, 1984**), say 'the sixth of January' or 'January the sixth' (American style is 'January sixth'); with names of kings and queens **sixth** is usually written **VI: King Edward VI:** say 'King Edward the Sixth')

① **sixtieth (60th)**
['sɪkstɪɪθ] *adjective & noun*
he was sixtieth out of 120 people who entered the race; a minute is a sixtieth of an hour and a second is a sixtieth of a minute; don't forget - it's dad's sixtieth birthday tomorrow

① **sixty**
['sɪksti]
number 60; *she's sixty (years old) the table cost more than sixty pounds (£60)* **she's in her sixties** = she's between 60 and 69 years old; **the (nineteen) sixties (1960s)** = the years from 1960 to 1969 (NOTE: **sixty-one (61), sixty-two (62),** etc., but **sixty-first (61st), sixty-second (62nd),** etc.)

① **size**
[saɪz]
1 *noun*
measurements of something, how big something is, or how many there are of something; *their garage is about the same size as our house; the school has an Olympic size swimming pool; he takes size ten in shoes; what size collars do you take?; the size of the staff has doubled in the last two years*
2 *verb*
to size someone up = to judge someone's qualities; *she quickly sized him up*

③ **skate**
[skeɪt]
1 *noun*
a pair of skates = a pair of boots with sharp blades attached for sliding on ice; *(informal)* **to put your skates on** = to hurry, to get going; *you'll have to put your skates on if you want to catch that train*
2 *verb*
(a) to move on ice wearing skates; *she skated across the lake; we're going skating tomorrow*

(b) to skate around something = to try to avoid mentioning something; *they skated around the subject of salaries*

③ **skater**
['skeɪtɪ] *noun*
person who goes on skates; *there were dozens of skaters on the frozen lake*

③ **skating**
['skeɪtɪŋ] *noun*
sport of sliding on ice on skates; *skating is very popular in Canada;* **skating rink** = special area for ice skating, or for playing ice hockey, etc.; *there used to be an indoor skating rink in Richmond*

③ **skeleton**
['skelɪtn] *noun*
(a) all the bones which make up a body; *they found the skeleton of a rabbit in the garden shed; he demonstrated using the skeleton in the biology lab; (informal)* **the skeleton in the cupboard** = embarrassing secret that a family is trying to keep hidden; *after the newspaper report, I wonder how many more skeletons they have hidden in the cupboard*
(b) skeleton staff = a few staff left to carry on with essential work while most of the workforce is away; *only a skeleton staff will be on duty over the Christmas period*
(c) skeleton key = key which will fit several different doors in a building; *I've locked myself out of my office - could you let me have the skeleton key, please?*

③ **skeptical**
US = SCEPTICAL

④ **sketch**
[sketʃ]
1 *noun*
(a) rough quick drawing; *he made a sketch of the church*
(b) short comic situation on TV or radio; *the show takes the form of a series of short sketches* (NOTE: plural is **sketches**)
2 *verb*
to make a quick rough drawing of something; *she was sketching the old church; he sketched out his plan on the back of an envelope*

④ **ski**
[skiː]
1 *noun*
one of two long flat pieces of wood, etc., which are attached to your boots for sliding over snow; *we always hire skis when we get to the ski resort; someone stole my new pair of skis;* **ski instructor** = person who teaches people how to ski; **ski boots** = boots to wear when skiing; **ski resort** = town in the mountains where people stay when on a skiing holiday; **water skis** = larger pieces of wood for attaching under your feet for sliding over water
2 *verb*

to travel on skis; *the mountain rescue team had to ski to the site of the accident*; *we skied down to the bottom of the slope without falling*; *she broke her arm skiing*; **to go skiing** = to slide over snow on skis as a sport; *we go skiing in Switzerland every winter* (NOTE: **skis - skiing - skied**)

③ **skiing**
['ski:ɪŋ] *noun*
the sport of sliding on skis; *skiing is a very popular sport*; *have you ever done any skiing?*

④ **skilful** *US* **skillful**
['skɪlful] *adjective*
showing a lot of skill; *he's a very skilful painter*

① **skill**
[skɪl] *noun*
ability to do something well; *portrait painting needs a lot of skill*; *he acquired management skills through running his own business*; *he's a chair maker of great skill*

① **skilled**
[skɪld] *adjective*
(a) being able to do something well, using a particular skill; *she's a skilled dance instructor*; *we need skilled computer analysts*; **skilled workers** *or* **skilled labour** = workers who have special skills or who have had a long period of training
(b) needing a particular skill; *nursing and other skilled professions*

② **skin**
[skɪn]
1 *noun*
(a) outer surface of the body; *the baby's skin is very smooth*; **to be just skin and bones** = to be extremely thin
(b) outer surface of a fruit or vegetable; *this orange has a very thick skin*; *you can cook these new potatoes with their skins on*
(c) thin layer on top of a liquid; *I don't like the skin on the top of chocolate pudding*
(d) *(informal)* **to have a thick skin** = to be able to stand a lot of criticism; *luckily he has a thick skin or he would get very annoyed at what the newspapers say about him*; **by the skin of your teeth** = only just; *he escaped from the enemy by the skin of his teeth*; **to jump out of your skin** = to be very frightened or surprised; *the bang made her jump out of her skin*
2 *verb*
to remove the skin from an animal, fish, etc.; *ask the butcher to skin the rabbit for you* (NOTE: **skinning - skinned**)

③ **skinny**
['skɪnɪ] *adjective*
(informal) very thin; *a tall skinny guy walked in*; *she has very skinny legs* (NOTE: **skinnier - skinniest**)

③ **skip**
[skɪp]
1 *noun*

large metal container for rubbish; *the builders filled the skip with old bricks and stones*
2 *verb*
(a) to run along partly hopping and partly jumping; *the children skipped happily down the lane*
(b) to jump over a rope which you turn over your head; *the boys played football and the girls were skipping*
(c) to miss part of something; *she skipped the middle chapters and went on to read the end of the story*; *I'm not hungry, I'll skip the pudding* (NOTE: **skipping - skipped**)

③ **skipper**
['skɪpɪ]
1 *noun*
(a) captain of a ship; *we reported to the skipper that there was water in the ship's engine room*
(b) *(informal)* captain of a team; *he's the youngest skipper ever of the national rugby team*
2 *verb*
to be the captain of a team; *the youngest man ever to skipper the English rugby team*

④ **skirt**
[skɜ:t]
1 *noun*
piece of clothing worn by women covering the lower part of the body from the waist down; the lower part of a dress starting at the waist; *she started wearing jeans to work, but the supervisor told her to wear a skirt*
2 *verb*
(a) to go round; *the main road skirts (round) the town*
(b) not to touch; *he only skirted round the subject, and didn't deal with it in depth at all*

④ **skull**
[skʌl] *noun*
the bones which form the head; *they found a human skull when they were digging*; *the scan showed a fracture of the skull or a skull fracture*

② **sky**
[skaɪ] *noun*
space above the earth which is blue during the day and where the moon and stars appear at night; *what makes the sky blue?*; *it's going to be a beautiful day - there's not a cloud in the sky*; *the wind carried the balloon high up into the sky*

④ **skyscraper**
['skaɪskreɪpɪ] *noun*
very tall building; *did you like the scene in the film where he is trying to climb up the skyscraper?*; *they're planning a 100-storey skyscraper near the park*

④ **slam**
[slæm]
1 *noun*

grand slam = winning a series of competitions, such as all the main tennis competitions held in a year; *a grand slam winner*; *the French rugby team are aiming for the grand slam*

2 *verb*

(a) to bang a door shut; to shut with a bang; *when he saw me, he slammed the door in my face*; *the wind slammed the door and I was locked out*

(b) to slam on the brakes = to apply the brakes fast when driving; *he slammed on the brakes and just stopped in time to avoid an accident* (NOTE: **slamming - slammed**)

③ **slander**
['slɑːndɪ]

1 *noun*

spoken statement which is not true and which damages a person's reputation; *what she said about me is slander*; *to sue somebody for slander*; **action for slander** *or* **slander action** = case in a law court where someone says that another person has slandered them

2 *verb*

to damage someone's reputation by saying things about him or her which are not true; *they slandered him at yesterday's press conference*; *compare* LIBEL

③ **slang**
[slæŋ] *noun*

popular words or phrases used by certain groups of people but which are not used in correct style; *'banger' is slang for an old car and also for a sausage*; *don't use slang in your essay*; *slang expressions are sometimes difficult to understand*

② **slap**
[slæp]

1 *noun*

(a) blow given with your hand flat; *she gave him a slap in the face*; **a slap on the wrist** = small punishment, slight criticism; *the department had a slap on the wrist from the inspectors, but nothing serious*

(b) friendly gesture; *he congratulated her with a slap on the back*

2 *verb*

(a) to hit with your hand flat; *she slapped his face*

(b) to tap as a friendly gesture; *they all slapped him on the back to congratulate him*

(c) to put something down flat on a surface; *she slapped the notes down on the table*; *they just slapped some paint on the wall to cover up the dirty marks* (NOTE: **slapping - slapped**)

3 *adverb*

to run slap (bang) into something = to run right into something; *he rode his bike slap into the middle of the procession*

④ **slash**
[slæʃ]

1 *noun*

(a) long cut with a knife; *he had a nasty slash on his arm*; *she took a knife and made a slash across the painting*

(b) printing sign (/) used to show an alternative (NOTE: plural is **slashes**)

2 *verb*

(a) to make a long cut with a knife; *he slashed the painting with a kitchen knife*

(b) to reduce a price, the number of something, sharply; *the management has slashed the number of staff*; *prices have been slashed in all departments*

④ **slate**
[sleɪt]

1 *noun*

(a) dark blue or grey stone which splits easily into thin sheets; *slate is used for making roofs*

(b) thin piece of this stone used to cover a roof; *the slates were already piled up ready to be fixed on the roof*

(c) list of candidates for a position; *the Democratic slate in the state elections*

2 *verb*

to criticize sharply; *the whole plan was slated by the chairman of the committee*

④ **slaughter**
['slɔːtɪ]

1 *noun*

(a) killing of animals; *these lambs will be ready for slaughter in a week or so*

(b) killing of many people; *the wholesale slaughter of innocent civilians* (NOTE: no plural)

2 *verb*

(a) to kill animals (usually for meat); *here's the shed where the cattle are slaughtered*; *the infected pigs have been slaughtered*

(b) to kill many people at the same time; *thousands of civilians were slaughtered by the advancing army*

④ **slave**
[sleɪv]

1 *noun*

person who belongs to someone legally and works for him; *in the old days, slaves worked on the tobacco plantations*; *(informal)* **slave driver** = boss who makes his staff work too hard

2 *verb*

to slave (away) = to work hard; *here am I slaving away over a hot stove, and you just sit and watch TV*

① **sleep**
[sliːp]

1 *noun*

rest (usually at night) with your eyes closed, and when you are not conscious of what is happening; *I need eight hours' sleep a night*; *try to get a good night's sleep - there's a lot of work to be done tomorrow*; *he always has a short sleep after lunch*; **to go to sleep** *or* **to get to sleep** = to start sleeping; *don't make all that noise - Daddy's trying to get to sleep*; *she put the light out and went to sleep* (NOTE: you can also say **to fall asleep**); **to send someone to sleep** = to make someone go to sleep; *her boring speeches would send anyone to sleep*; **to put someone to sleep** = to give someone an anaesthetic; **to put an animal to sleep** = to kill an animal that is old or ill; **my foot has gone to sleep** = my foot has lost all feeling; **not to lose any sleep over something** = not to worry about something; *it's such a tiny sum that I won't lose any sleep over it*

2 *verb*

(a) to be asleep, to rest with your eyes closed not knowing what is happening around you; *she never sleeps for more than six hours each night*; *he slept through the whole of the TV news*; *don't make any noise - Daddy's trying to sleep*; *(informal)* **to sleep like a log** = to sleep very deeply; *after his 12-mile walk he slept like a log*

(b) **a cottage that sleeps four** = a cottage with enough beds for four people

(c) *(informal)* **to sleep with someone** *or* **to sleep together** = to have sexual relations with someone; *they say he's slept with almost all the girls in the office* (NOTE: **sleeps - sleeping - slept** [slept])

④ **sleeping**
['sli:pɪŋ]
1 *adjective*

(a) who is asleep; *the firemen picked up the sleeping children and carried them to safety*

(b) **sleeping bag** = warm bag for sleeping in a tent, etc.; **sleeping car** = carriage on a train with beds where passengers can sleep; *there are three sleeping cars on the overnight express*; **sleeping partner** = partner who has a share in a business but does not work in it; **sleeping pill** *or* **sleeping tablet** = medicine which makes you go to sleep; **sleeping policeman** = hump in the road to stop cars going too fast

④ **sleepy**
['sli:pɪ] *adjective*

(a) feeling ready to go to sleep; *sitting in front of the TV made him sleepier and sleepier*; *the children had a busy day - they were getting very sleepy by 8 o'clock*; *some cough medicines make you feel sleepy*; *if you feel sleepy, don't try to drive the car*

(b) quiet; *a sleepy little country town* (NOTE: **sleepier - sleepiest**)

④ **sleeve**
[sli:v] *noun*

(a) part of a piece of clothing which covers your arm; *the sleeves on this shirt are too long*; *he was wearing a blue shirt with short sleeves*

(b) *(informal)* **to keep something up your sleeve** = to have a plan which you are keeping secret; **to laugh up your sleeve** = to laugh in secret at something

③ **slept**
[slept] *see* SLEEP

④ **slice**
[slaɪs]
1 *noun*

(a) thin piece cut off something to eat; *can you cut some more slices of bread?*; *have a slice of chocolate cake*; *would you like another slice of chicken?*

(b) *(in sports)* way of hitting a ball, which makes it go in a different direction

2 *verb*

(a) to cut into slices; *she stood at the table slicing the joint for lunch*; **sliced bread** = loaf of bread which has already been cut into slices before you buy it; *(informal)* **the best thing since sliced bread** = the most wonderful new invention in the world

(b) to hit a ball so that it spins off to one side; *he sliced the ball into the net*

③ **slid**
[slɪd] *see* SLIDE

③ **slide**
[slaɪd]
1 *noun*

(a) metal or plastic structure for children to go down lying or sitting; *there are swings and a slide in the local playground*

(b) small piece of film which can be projected on a screen; *she put the screen up and showed us the slides of her last trip*; *there will be a slide show in the village hall*; **slide projector** = apparatus for showing pictures from slides onto a screen

(c) steady fall; *the government must act to stop the slide in the pound*

(d) clip which goes into the hair to hold it in place; *she had two red slides in her hair*

2 *verb*

(a) to move without difficulty over an even surface; *the drawer slides in and out easily*; *the car slid to a stop*; *the children were sliding on the ice when it broke*; *the van has a sliding door which doesn't shut properly*

(b) to move something easily; *he slid the money over the table*

(c) to move down steadily; *the pound slid after interest rates were lowered*; **to let things slide** = to allow things to get worse, not to bother if things get worse; *she doesn't look after herself - she's just letting things slide* (NOTE: **sliding - slid** [slɪd])

② **slight**
[slaɪt]
1 *adjective*

not very big; *their daughter's a slight young girl*; *all you could see was a slight movement of the cat's tail*; *there was a slight improvement in his condition during the night*; *she wasn't the slightest bit nervous* (NOTE: **slighter - slightest**)

2 *noun*

(formal) insult; *I treat that remark as a slight on our reputation*

slightly
['slaɪtlɪ] *adverb*

not very much; *he was only slightly hurt in the car crash*; *the American bank is offering a slightly better interest rate*; *I only know him slightly*

slim
[slɪm]

1 *adjective*

thin, not fat; *how do you manage to stay so slim?*; *a slim, fair-haired boy*; *she looks slimmer in that dress* (NOTE: **slimmer - slimmest**)

2 *verb*

to diet in order to become thin; *she started slimming before her summer holidays* (NOTE: **slimming - slimmed**)

slip
[slɪp]

1 *noun*

(a) mistake; *he made a couple of slips in adding up the bill*; **a slip of the tongue** = a mistake in speaking

(b) small piece of paper; *as she opened the book a small slip of paper fell out*; *he handed her the green slip with the reference number on it*; **compliments slip** = piece of paper with the name of the company printed on it, sent with documents, gifts, etc., instead of a letter; **deposit slip** = piece of paper stamped by the bank clerk to prove that you have paid money into your account; **pay slip** = piece of paper showing the full amount of a worker's pay, and the money deducted as tax, pension and insurance contributions; **paying-in slip** = printed form which is filled in when money is being deposited in a bank; **sales slip** = paper showing that an article was bought at a certain shop on a certain day; *goods can be exchanged only on production of a sales slip*

(c) **pillow slip** = cloth bag to cover a pillow; *the girl had forgotten to change the pillow slips*

(d) small person; *she was just a slip of a girl*

(e) woman's underwear like a thin dress or skirt, worn under other clothes; *she bought a black slip*

(f) men's underwear which is very short; *he wore a white vest and slip*

2 *verb*

(a) to slide (and fall) by mistake; *he slipped and dropped all his shopping*; *he was using the electric saw when it hit something hard and slipped*; **slipped disc** = painful state where one of the discs in the spine has moved out of place

(b) to slide out of something which is holding you tight; *the dog slipped its lead and ran away*

(c) to push something without being seen; *the postman slipped the letters through the letter box*; *he slipped the keys into his pocket*

(d) to go down to a lower level; *profits slipped badly last year*; *the pound slipped on the foreign exchanges* (NOTE: **slipping - slipped**)

slip on
['slɪp 'ɒn] *verb*

(a) to slip because you step on something; *he slipped on the wet leaves and broke his ankle*

(b) to put clothes on quickly; *she slipped on her dressing gown and ran into the street*

slippers
['slɪpəz] *noun*

light comfortable shoes worn indoors; *he ran out into the street in his dressing gown slippers*; *put your slippers on if your shoes hurt*

slogan
['sləʊgn] *noun*

phrase which is easy to remember and is used in publicity for a product or for a political party, etc.; *we are using the slogan 'Smiths can make it' on all our publicity*; *the walls of the factory were covered with election slogans*

slope
[sləʊp]

1 *noun*

(a) surface or piece of ground which is not level, and rises or falls; *the land rises in a gentle slope to the church*; *they stopped halfway down the slope*; **ski slope** = specially prepared and marked slope for skiing down a mountain; **nursery slopes** = gentle snow-covered mountain slopes where people learn to ski

(b) angle at which something slopes; *the hill has an slope of 1 in 10, put the car in low gear*

2 *verb*

to go upwards or downwards; *the path slopes upwards*

slot
[slɒt]

1 *noun*

(a) long thin hole; *a coin has got stuck in the slot of the parking meter*; *put the system disk into the left-hand slot on the front of your computer*; **slot machine** = machine for gambling, or which provides drinks, cigarettes, plays music, etc., when you put a coin into a slot

(b) set time available for doing something; *the airline has asked for more takeoff and landing slots at the airport*

2 *verb*

to slot into = to fit into a slot; *the car radio slots easily into the space next to the clock* (NOTE: **slotting - slotted**)

slow
[sləʊ]

1 *adjective*

(a) not fast, needing a long time to do something; *luckily, the car was only going at a slow speed*; *she is the slowest walker of the group*; *the company is very slow at answering my letters*; *sales got off to a slow start but picked up later*; **slow train** = train which stops at each station

(b) showing a time which is earlier than the right time; *the office clock is four minutes slow* (NOTE: **slower - slowest**)

2 *verb*

to go slowly; *the procession slowed as it reached the cathedral*

3 *adverb*

not fast; *(of workers)* **to go slow** = to protest by working slowly or driving slowly; *they are threatening to go slow if their demands are not met*

ⓘ **slow down**

['sləʊ 'daʊn] *verb*

(a) to go more slowly; *the van had to slow down as it came to the traffic lights; please slow down, I can't keep up with you*

(b) to make something go more slowly; *the snow slowed the traffic down on the motorway*

(c) to work less hard; *you should slow down a bit - you're doing too much*

② **slowly**

['sləʊli] *adverb*

not fast; *luckily, the car was going very slowly when it hit the fence; the group walked slowly round the exhibition; speak more slowly so that everyone can understand; see also* SURELY

④ **slump**

[slʌmp]

1 *noun*

(a) rapid fall; *there has been slump in sales*

(b) period of economic collapse with high unemployment and loss of trade; *economists argued about the reasons for the slump;* **the Slump** = the world economic crisis of 1929 - 1933

2 *verb*

(a) to sit or to lie down in a clumsy way; *he sat slumped on a chair doing his homework; at the end of the meal, she just slumped down onto the sofa*

(b) to fall fast; *the pound slumped on the foreign exchange markets*

④ **smack**

[smæk]

1 *noun*

hitting someone with your hand flat as a punishment; *if you pull the cat's tail you'll get a smack*

2 *verb*

(a) to punish someone by hitting them with your hand flat; *she smacked the little girl for being rude*

(b) to put something down noisily; *she smacked the report down on the table and walked out of the room*

(c) to smack your lips = to make a loud noise with your lips to show you are hungry or would like to have something; *she smacked her lips as he mentioned diamonds*

(d) to show signs of; *the whole affair smacks of fraud*

3 *adverb*

straight, directly; *the bus ran smack into a tree*

ⓘ **small**

[smɔːl]

1 *adjective*

(a) little, not big; *small cars use less petrol than large ones; the house is too big for us, so we're selling it and buying a smaller one; she only paid a small amount for that clock; the guidebook isn't small enough to carry in your pocket; these trousers are already too small for him;* **small business** = little company with a low turnover and few employees; **small businessman** = man who runs a small business; **small change** = loose coins; *do you have any small change, I only have notes?*

(b) young; *big farm animals can frighten small children*

(c) a small fortune = a lot of money; *those shoes cost me a small fortune; she earns a small fortune selling postcards*

(d) the small hours = early in the morning; *we went on talking until the small hours (of the morning)* (NOTE: **smaller - smallest**)

2 *noun*

the small of the back = the middle part of your back below and between the shoulder blades; *something is tickling me in the small of my back*

③ **small-scale**

['smɔːlskeɪl] *adjective*

working in a small way, with few staff and not much money; *it is a small-scale operation with only 3 full-time staff;* **a small-scale enterprise** = a small business; *compare* LARGE-SCALE

② **smart**

[smɑːt]

1 *adjective*

(a) well-dressed or elegant; *a smart young man asked me if he could use my mobile phone; he looked very smart in his uniform*

(b) clever; *it was smart of her to note the car's number plate; he's the smartest of the three brothers;* **smart card** = plastic credit card with a computer chip in it

(c) sharp (blow); *she gave a smart knock on the door*

(d) rapid; *the horse set off at a smart pace; (informal)* **look smart!** = hurry up! (NOTE: **smarter - smartest**)

2 *verb*

to hurt with a burning feeling; *the burn on my hand is still smarting*

3 *noun*

sharp pain from a blow; *he remembered the smart of the slap on his cheek*

④ **smash**

[smæʃ]

1 *verb*

(a) to break into pieces; *he dropped the plate and it smashed to pieces*

(b) to break something to pieces; *demonstrators smashed the windows of police cars*

(c) to break a record, to do better than a record; *she smashed the world record*; *six records were smashed at the Olympics*

(d) to go violently; *the train smashed into the car*; *the crowd smashed through the railings*

(e) *(in tennis)* to play a fast stroke, sending the ball down to the ground (NOTE: **smashing - smashed**)

2 *noun*

(a) sound of something breaking into pieces; *we could hear the smash of plates being dropped in the kitchen*

(b) bad accident; *six people are feared killed in the train smash*

(c) *(in tennis)* fast stroke, sending the ball down to the ground

③ **smash up**
['smæʃ 'ʌp] *verb*
to break everything in a place; *the fans smashed up the pub*

② **smell**
[smel]
1 *noun*

(a) one of the five senses, which you can feel through your nose; *animals have a better sense of smell than humans*; *these dogs have a very keen sense of smell and can sniff out even a minute quantity of drugs*

(b) something which you can sense with your nose; *I love the smell of coffee coming from the restaurant*; *he can't stand the smell of fried onions*; *there's a smell of burning* or *there's a burning smell coming from the kitchen*; *she noticed a smell of gas downstairs*

(c) unpleasant thing which you can sense with your nose; *there's a smell* or *a funny smell* or *a nasty smell in the shed*

2 *verb*

(a) to notice the smell of something; *can you smell gas?*; *wild animals can smell humans*; *my nose is blocked - I can't smell anything*; *just smell these roses!*; *Mmm! - I can smell fish and chips!*; *(informal)* **to smell a rat** = to suspect that something wrong is happening; *why is he being so nice all of a sudden - I smell a rat!*

(b) to make a smell; *I don't like cheese which smells too strong*; *what's for dinner? - it smells very good!*; *there's something which smells funny in the bathroom*; *it smelt of gas in the kitchen*

(c) to bring your nose close to something to smell it; *she bent down to smell the roses* (NOTE: **smelling - smelled** or **smelt** [smelt])

① **smile**
[smail]
1 *noun*
way of showing that you are pleased, by turning your mouth up at the corners; *the dentist gave me a friendly smile*; *she had a big smile as she told them the good news*

2 *verb*

to show that you are pleased by turning your mouth up at the corners; *that girl has just smiled at me*; *everyone smile please - I'm taking a photo!*; *see also* CHEESE

② **smoke**
[sməuk]
1 *noun*

(a) white, grey or black cloud, given off by something that is burning; *the restaurant was full of cigarette smoke*; *clouds of smoke were pouring out of the upstairs windows*; *two people died from breathing toxic smoke*; *smoke alarms are fitted in all the hotel rooms*

(b) *(informal)* time when you are smoking a cigarette; *cigarettes aren't allowed in the office, so everyone goes outside for a quick smoke*; *I'm dying for a smoke!*

(c) **to go up in smoke** = (i) to be burnt; (ii) to fail, not to work; *his entire art collection went up in smoke in the fire*; *all her plans for buying a bigger house have gone up in smoke*

2 *verb*

(a) to give off smoke; *two days after the fire, the ruins of the factory were still smoking*

(b) to breathe in smoke (from a cigarette, pipe, etc.); *everyone was smoking even though the signs said 'no smoking'*; *she doesn't smoke much - only one or two cigarettes a day*; *you shouldn't smoke if you want to play football*; *I've never seen her smoking a pipe before*; **he smokes like a chimney** = he smokes a lot of cigarettes

(c) *(in a house)* **the chimney smokes** = the fire sends smoke into the room instead of taking it up the chimney

(d) to preserve food (such as meat, fish, bacon, cheese) by hanging it in the smoke from a fire; *a factory where they smoke fish*; **smoked salmon** = salmon which has been cured by smoking, and is served in very thin slices; *a plate of smoked salmon sandwiches*

④ **smoker**
['sməukı] *noun*
person who smokes cigarettes; *we only have two members of staff who are smokers*; **heavy smoker** = person who smokes a lot of cigarettes; *he was a heavy smoker and died of lung cancer*

② **smoking**
['sməukıŋ] *noun*
action of smoking cigarettes, etc.; *smoking is bad for your health*; *smoking is not allowed on the London Underground*; **'no smoking'** = do not smoke here; *I always sit in the 'no smoking' part of the restaurant*

③ **smooth**
[smu:ð]
1 *adjective*

(a) with no bumps, with an even surface; *the smooth surface of a polished table*; *the baby's skin is very smooth*; *velvet has a smooth side* *and a rough side*; **to take the rough with the smooth** = to accept that there are bad times as well as good times

(b) with no sudden movements; *dirt in the fuel tank can affect the smooth running of the engine*; *the plane made a very smooth landing*

(c) *(person)* too polite, with manners which are too good; *that car salesman's a bit too smooth for my liking* (NOTE: **smoother - smoothest**)

2 *verb*

(a) to make something smooth with a tool or with your hand; *she smoothed the sheets and adjusted the pillows*; *the edge of the shelf needs smoothing, it's still quite rough*; **to smooth the way for someone** *or* **something** = to make things easy for someone *or* something; *the retiring president cut taxes to smooth the way for his successor*; **to smooth things over** = to settle an argument; *after the quarrel, I called round at her house to try and smooth things over*

(b) to spread something gently over a surface; *smooth the cream over your face and let it dry*

④ **smuggle**
['smʌgl] *verb*

(a) to take goods into a country without declaring them to customs; *they tried to smuggle cigarettes into the country*; *we had to smuggle the spare parts over the border*

(b) to take something into or out of a place illegally; *the knives were smuggled into the prison by a someone visiting a prisoner*; *we'll never know how they smuggled the letter out*

③ **snack**
[snæk]

1 *noun*

a light meal, a small amount of food; *we didn't have time to stop for a proper lunch, so we just had a snack on the motorway*

2 *verb*

to eat a snack; *she never eats proper meals, she just snacks all the time*

③ **snack bar**
['snæk 'bɑː] *noun*

small simple restaurant where you can buy a light meal; *he met the girl by chance at a snack bar at Waterloo Station*

③ **snake**
[sneɪk]

1 *noun*

long animal which has no legs and moves along the ground by moving from side to side; *is this snake safe to handle?*; **snakes and ladders** = children's board game, played with dice, in which landing on a ladder moves you forward and landing on a snake moves you back

2 *verb*

to bend and twist; *the Great Wall of China snakes over the mountains*

COMMENT: only three species of snake are native to Britain: the grass snake and smooth snake which are harmless, and the adder, which is poisonous, though its bite is rarely fatal. There are no snakes in Ireland

③ **snap**
[snæp]

1 *noun*

(a) photograph taken quickly; *she showed me an old black-and-white snap of the house*; *he took a lot of snaps of his children*

(b) **cold snap** = short period of sudden cold weather; *a cold snap can have disastrous effects on my tomatoes*

(c) card game where you shout 'snap' if two similar cards are played at the same time; *do you want a game of snap?*; *they played snap all afternoon*

(d) US *(informal)* little metal fastener for clothes, in two parts which you press to attach together (NOTE: British English is **popper**)

2 *adjective*

sudden; **a snap decision** = a decision taken in a hurry; *they carried out a snap check or a snap inspection of the passengers' luggage*; *the government called a snap election*

3 *verb*

(a) to say something in a sharp angry tone; *he was tired after a long day in the office, and snapped at the children*; *the manager snapped at the shop assistant, but it wasn't her fault*

(b) to break sharply with a dry noise; *the branches snapped as he walked through the wood*

(c) **to snap your fingers** = to make a clicking noise with your middle finger and thumb; *they sat snapping their fingers in time to the music*; **to snap into place** = to make a click when fitting together; *push gently on the film cassette until it snaps into place*; *(informal)* **to snap out of it** = to stop being depressed; *he told her to snap out of it* (NOTE: **snapping - snapped**)

④ **snatch**
[snætʃ]

1 *noun*

little piece of something heard; *in the evening, I heard snatches of song from across the lake* (NOTE: plural is **snatches**)

2 *verb*

to grab something rapidly; *he came beside her on his bike and snatched her handbag*; *I didn't have time for a proper meal, but I snatched a sandwich*; *she snatched a few hours' sleep in the transit lounge*

④ **sneak**
[sniːk]

1 *verb*

(a) to go quietly without being seen; *she sneaked into the room; the burglar sneaked up to the house, hidden by the trees;* **to sneak up on someone** = to creep up behind someone without being noticed

(b) *(informal)* **to sneak on someone** = to tell an adult that another child has done something wrong; *he promised not to sneak on me to my mum* (NOTE: the past tense in British English is **sneaked** and in American English **snuck**)

2 *noun*

(informal) person who tells an adult what another child has done; *you promised not to say anything, you little sneak!*

④ **sneeze**
[sniːz]
1 *noun*

automatic action to blow air suddenly out through your mouth and nose because the inside of your nose tickles; *coughs and sneezes spread diseases*

2 *verb*

to make a sneeze; *the smell of roses makes me sneeze; he has hayfever and can't stop sneezing; (informal)* **it's not to be sneezed at** = you should not refuse it; *it's a good offer and not to be sneezed at*

④ **sniff**
[snɪf]
1 *noun*

breathing in air through your nose; *the dog gave a sniff at the plate before licking it; he gave a little sniff and walked out of the shop*

2 *verb*

(a) to breathe in air through your nose; *he sniffed and said 'I can smell fish and chips'; the customs inspection is very strict, a dog is taken round to sniff (at) each bag and suitcase; (informal)* **it's not to be sniffed at** = you should not refuse it; *a free ticket with Air Canada is not to be sniffed at;* **to sniff something out** = to discover something by smelling; *the dogs sniffed out drugs hidden in her bag*

(b) to breathe in air through your nose because you have a cold; *he's coughing and sniffing and should be in bed; don't sniff, use your hanky*

(c) to breathe in gas from glue; *the police caught them sniffing glue; see also* GLUE

③ **snooker**
['snuːkɪ] *noun*

game for two players, similar to billiards, played on a table with twenty-two balls of various colours; *would you like a game of snooker?; they played snooker all evening; he's the world snooker champion;* **snooker table** = table on which snooker is played

COMMENT: there are 15 red balls (worth 1 point each), a yellow ball (worth 2 points), a green (3 points), a brown (4 points), a blue (5 points), a pink (6 points), a black (7 points) and one white cue ball which the players use to hit the other balls. Each player in turn uses his cue to hit the one white cue ball against one of the 15 red balls in an attempt to send it into one of the pockets round the table; having done this he may choose any other ball which is not red to pot and score points according to its value; every time one of these balls is sent into a pocket it is replaced in (or as near as possible to) its special position on the table while the red balls which are sent into pockets are never put back on the table. When all the red balls have been removed, the rest of the balls must be hit into pockets in strict sequence according to their value (finishing with the black); the object is to score more points than your opponent

③ **snow**
[snəʊ]
1 *noun*

water which falls as light white ice crystals in cold weather; *two metres of snow fell during the night; the highest mountains were always covered with snow; children were out playing in the snow; we went for a skiing holiday and there was hardly any snow;* **snow tyres** = special tyres with thick treads, for use when driving on snow (NOTE: no plural: **some snow, a lot of snow**)

2 *verb*

to fall as snow; *look! - it's started to snow!; it snowed all day, and the streets were blocked; they say it's going to snow tomorrow; it hardly ever snows here in March* (NOTE: **to snow** is always used with the subject **it**)

③ **snowball**
['snəʊbɔːl]
1 *noun*

ball made with snow; *they were throwing snowballs at passing cars; I tried to make a snowball but the snow was too dry*

2 *verb*

to get steadily bigger; *the protests started slowly and then snowballed into mass demonstrations*

③ **snowed in**
['snəʊd 'ɪn] *adjective*

blocked by snow and not able to travel; *we were snowed in, and sat indoors playing cards*

③ **snowed under**
['snəʊd 'ʌndɪ] *adjective*

(informal) with too much work; *we're snowed under with orders; he's snowed under with work*

③ **snowman**
['snəʊmæn] *noun*

model of a man made of snow; *the children made a snowman in the school playground; when the sun came out the snowman melted* (NOTE: plural is **snowmen**)

snowstorm
['sniustɔːm] *noun*
storm when the wind blows and snow falls; *all flights are delayed because of the snowstorm*

snuck
[snʌk] *US see* SNEAK

so
[siʊ]
1 *adverb*
(a) *(showing how much)* *it's so cold that the lake is covered with ice; we liked Greece so much that we're going there again on holiday next year; the soup was so hot that I couldn't eat it*
(b) very much; *she was so kind to us when we were children; the film was not so boring - some parts were very exciting*
(c) also; *she was late and so was I; the children all caught flu, and so did their teacher; I like apples - so do I; he's a good cook and so is his wife; the teacher will be late and so will everyone else*
(d) *(showing that the answer is 'yes')* *does this train go to London? - I think so; was your car completely smashed? - I'm afraid so; will you be coming to the party? - I hope so!; are they going to be at the meeting? - I suppose so*
2 *conjunction*
(a) and this is the reason why; *it was snowing hard so we couldn't go for a walk; she's got flu so she can't come to the office*
(b) **so that** = in order that; *people riding bikes wear orange coats so that drivers can see them easily;* **so as to** = in order to; *they had to run to the station so as not to miss the train*
3 *adjective*
(a) *(informal)* **just so** = exactly as it should be; *she always wants everything to be just so*
(b) *(to emphasize, replacing an adjective)* *he's very rude, and his wife is even more so; see also* AND SO ON

◊ **so far**
['siʊ 'fɑː] *adverb*
until now; *he said he would lend me his book but so far he hasn't done so; how do you like your new job so far?*

◊ **so there!**
[sɪ 'ðeɪ] *phrase; (making a decision)*
that's my opinion, and it's none of your business; *if you don't want to come with me, I'll go all by myself, so there!*

◊ **so what**
[siʊ 'wɒt] *phrase*
what does it matter; *he may be annoyed - so what?; so what if I fail my exam, I can always take it again*

soak
[siʊk]
1 *noun*
action of lying in a bath for a long time; *after a game of rugby it is good to have a soak in a hot bath*

2 *verb*
(a) to put something in a liquid for a time; *the dry beans should be soaked in cold water overnight*
(b) to get or to make very wet; *I forgot my umbrella and got soaked; the rain soaked the soil*

soap
[siʊp]
1 *noun*
(a) substance which you wash with, made from oils and usually with a pleasant smell; *there's no soap left in the bathroom; I've put a new bar of soap in the kitchen; there is a liquid soap dispenser in the men's toilet* (NOTE: no plural in this meaning: **some soap, a bar** or **a cake** or **a piece of soap**)
(b) **soap (opera)** = serial story on television about the daily lives of a set of characters; *he sat in bed watching Australian soaps*
2 *verb*
to cover with soap; *there's no need to soap yourself all over, just your legs and feet*

soar
[sɔː] *verb*
(a) to fly high up into the sky; *the rocket went soaring into the night sky*
(b) *(of a bird)* to fly high in the sky without moving its wings; *we watched the big bird soaring above the mountain*
(c) to go up very quickly; *food prices soared during the cold weather* (NOTE: do not confuse with **sore**)

sober
['siʊbi] *adjective*
(a) not drunk; *I wasn't drunk after the party - I was stone cold sober*
(b) serious; *the sober truth is that we can't afford it; it was a very sober gathering, nobody laughed or made a joke*
(c) dark with no bright colours; *she was wearing a sober dark grey suit*

so-called
['siʊkɔːld] *adjective*
called by a wrong name; *one of her so-called friends stole her watch*

soccer
['sɒki] *noun*
football, a game played between two teams of eleven players with a round ball which can be kicked or headed, but not carried; *he played soccer at school and then joined his local team; they went to a soccer match last Saturday; let's have a game of soccer; he spends all his time watching soccer on TV; rival soccer fans fought in the street* (NOTE: the game is called **football** in most countries, but is generally called **soccer** in the USA to distinguish it from American football)

social
['siʊʃl]
1 *adjective*

(a) referring to human society; *the demand for equal treatment for all classes can lead to social conflict*; *an area with very serious social problems*; **social science** = study of people and the society they live in, including history, economics, etc.; **social security** = money or help provided by the government to people who need it; *he lives on social security payments*; **social services** = state services to help people with family problems; *the children are being looked after by social services*; **the social system** = the way in which a society is organized; **social worker** = person who works to help people with family or financial problems; *the old people get a weekly visit by a social worker*; see also EXCLUSION

(b) referring to friendly contact with other people; *we are organizing some social events for the visiting students*; *not being able to make conversation is a terrible social handicap*; **social life** = life involving other people, going to parties, films, etc.; *with two babies under two years old, they have no social life whatsoever*; *we don't have much social life nowadays*

2 *noun*

(old) party for the members of an organization; *the old people's club is holding a social next Saturday*

④ **socialism**
['sɪʊʃɪlɪzm] *noun*

(a) ideas and beliefs of socialists, that the means of production and distribution should belong to the people, that people should be cared for by the state and that all wealth should be shared equally; *his book explains the principles of socialism*

(b) political system where the state is run on these principles; *under socialism, this factory was owned by the state*

④ **socialist**
['sɪʊʃɪlɪst]

1 *adjective*

believing in socialism, being in favour of social change, wider sharing of wealth and of industry and welfare run by the state; **Socialist Party** = political party which follows the principles of socialism; *the Socialist Party won the last elections*

2 *noun*

person who believes in socialism; *he's been a socialist all his life*

④ **socialize**
['sɪʊʃɪlaɪz] *verb*

to meet people for friendly talk and activities; *the outing is an opportunity for people to socialize and get to know each other better*; *we don't socialize much with the people in our street*

① **society**
[sɪ'saɪtɪ] *noun*

(a) a large group of people, usually all the people living in a country, considered as an organized community; *society needs to be protected against criminals*; *a free and democratic society*; *a member of society*; a **consumer society** = type of society where consumers are encouraged to buy goods

(b) club or association of people who have the same interests; *he belongs to the local drama society* (NOTE: plural is **societies**)

③ **sock**
[sɒk]

1 *noun*

(a) piece of clothing worn on your foot inside a shoe; *he's almost ready - he only has to put on his socks and shoes*; *I've just bought a pair of socks*; **football socks** = special socks for playing football; **knee socks** = long socks which go up as far as the knees; *(informal)* **to pull your socks up** = to try to do better; *he'll have to pull his socks up or he'll lose his job*

(b) *(informal)* punch; *she gave him a sock in the jaw*

2 *verb*

(informal) to hit someone hard; *she socked the mugger on the jaw*

④ **socket**
['sɒkɪt] *noun*

(electric) socket = device in a wall with holes into which a plug can be fitted; *there is a socket on the wall that you can plug the vacuum cleaner into*; *this plug doesn't fit that socket*; **light socket** = part of a lamp where the bulb is fitted

④ **sofa**
['sɪʊfɪ] *noun*

long comfortable seat with a soft back; *he was asleep on the sofa*

① **soft**
[sɒft] *adjective*

(a) not hard, which moves easily when pressed; *there are big soft armchairs in the lobby of the hotel*; *I don't like soft seats in a car*; *do you like soft ice cream?*

(b) not loud; *when she spoke, her voice was so soft that we could hardly hear her*; *soft music was playing in the background*

(c) not bright; *soft lighting makes a room look warm*

(d) **soft on** = not severe towards; *judges were accused of being soft on crime*; **to have a soft spot for** = to like very much; *she has a soft spot for her gym instructor* (NOTE: **softer - softest**)

③ **soft drink**
['sɒft 'drɪŋk] *noun*

drink which is not alcoholic; *I'll just have a soft drink because I'm driving*; *we've got soft drinks for the children*

④ **soften**
['sɒfn] *verb*

to make something soft, to become soft; *heat the chocolate gently to soften it*; *her voice softened when she spoke to the children*; **to soften someone up** = to make someone weaker before asking for something, or before launching an attack; *can you try and soften him up a bit before I ask to borrow the car?*; *bombing raids were made to soften up the enemy defences*

④ **softly**
['sɒflɪ] *adverb*
(a) in a gentle way; *I touched her arm softly*
(b) quietly, not loudly; *she spoke so softly that we couldn't hear what she said*; *the burglars crept softly up the stairs*

② **software**
['sɒftweɪ] *noun*
computer programs which are put into a computer to make it work, as opposed to the machine itself; *what word processing software do you use?*; *compare* HARDWARE (NOTE: no plural)

② **soil**
[sɔɪl]
1 *noun*
earth in which plants grow; *put some soil in the plant pot and then sow your flower seeds*; *this soil's too poor for growing fruit trees*; *the farm has 150 hectares of rich black soil*
2 *verb*
to make dirty; *his overalls were soiled by black oil and rust*; *use more washing powder if the clothes are heavily soiled*

④ **solar**
['sɪʊlɪ] *adjective*
referring to the sun; **solar energy** *or* **solar power** = electricity produced from the radiation of the sun; *my calculator runs on solar power*; *solar power is a renewable source of energy*; **solar system** = the sun and the planets which orbit round it; *there are nine planets in the solar system*

③ **sold**
[sɪʊld] *see* SELL

② **soldier**
['sɪʊldʒɪ]
1 *noun*
person serving in the army; *here's a photograph of my father as a soldier*; *we were just in time to see the soldiers march past*; *enemy soldiers blew up the bridge*; *the children are playing with their toy soldiers*
2 *verb*
to soldier on = to continue doing something, in spite of difficulties; *even though sales are down, we must soldier on*; *she's soldiering on, revising for the exam*

③ **sold out**
['sɪʊld 'aʊt] *adjective*
no longer in stock, because all the stock has been sold; *the book was sold out within a week*

③ **sole**
[sɪʊl]
1 *adjective*
only; belonging to one person; *their sole aim is to make money*; *she was the sole survivor from the crash*; *I have sole responsibility for what*

goes on in this office; *he has the sole right to it* = he is the only person allowed to use it; **sole agency** = agreement to be the only person to represent a company or to sell a product in a certain area; *he has the sole agency for Ford cars*; **sole trader** = person who runs a business by himself but has not registered it as a company
2 *noun*
(a) the underneath side of your foot; *he tickled the soles of her feet*
(b) main underneath part of a shoe, but not the heel; *these shoes need mending - I've got holes in both soles*
(c) small flat white sea fish; *he ordered grilled sole* (NOTE: plural in this meaning is **sole**)
2 *verb*
to put a new sole on a shoe; *I want these shoes soled and heeled, please* (NOTE: do not confuse with **soul**)

④ **solely**
['sɪʊlɪ] *adverb*
(a) only; *the machine was designed solely for that purpose*
(b) without other people being involved; *he was solely to blame for what happened*

③ **solemn**
['sɒlɪm] *adjective*
(a) serious and formal, when it would be wrong to laugh; *the doctor looked very solemn and shook his head*; *at the most solemn moment of the ceremony someone's mobile phone rang*
(b) that should be treated as very serious and not to be broken; *he made a solemn promise never to smoke again*; **solemn and binding agreement** = agreement that is not legally binding, but which all parties are supposed to obey

② **solicitor**
[sɪ'lɪsɪtɪ] *noun*
(a) qualified lawyer who gives advice to members of the public and acts for them in legal matters; *I went to see my solicitor about making a will*; *she works as a clerk in a solicitor's office*
(b) *US* person who comes to the door collecting for charity

③ **solid**
['sɒlɪd]
1 *adjective*
(a) hard, not liquid; *the water in the tank had frozen solid*; *she is allowed some solid food*
(b) firm, strong; *is the table solid enough to stand on?*; *his wealth is built on a solid base of property and shares*
(c) made only of one material; *the box is made of solid silver*
(d) **for six hours solid** = for six hours without stopping; *negotiations went on for nine hours solid* (NOTE: **solider - solidest**)
2 *noun*
(a) hard substance which is not liquid; *many solids melt when heated, and become liquids*

(b) food, as opposed to drink; *the baby is beginning to eat solids*

④ **solo**

['sɪʊlɪʊ]

1 *noun*

piece of music played or sung by one person alone; *she played a piano solo* (NOTE: plural is **solos**)

2 *adjective*

carried out by one person alone; *she gave a solo performance in the Albert Hall*; *a piece for solo trumpet*; *he crashed on his first solo flight*

3 *adverb*

done by one person alone; *he flew solo across the Atlantic*

① **solution**

[sɪ'luːʃn] *noun*

(a) action of solving a problem; *the solution of the problem is taking longer than expected*

(b) answer to a problem; *the manager came up with a solution to the computer problem*; *we think we have found a solution to the problem of where to stay on holiday*; *the solutions to the puzzle are at the back of the book*

(c) mixture of a solid substance in a liquid; *wash your eye in a weak salt solution*

② **solve**

[sɒlv] *verb*

to find an answer to; *the loan will solve some of his financial problems*; *we have called in an expert to solve our computer problem*; *he tried to solve the puzzle*

① **some**

[sʌm]

1 *adjective & pronoun*

(a) a certain number of; *some young drivers drive much too fast*; *some books were damaged in the fire*; *some days it was so hot that we just stayed by the swimming pool all day*; *can you cut some more slices of bread?*; *she bought some oranges and bananas*; *we've just picked a basket of apples - would you like some?*; *some* **of** = a few; *some of the students are ill*; *some of these apples are too green*

(b) a certain amount; *can you buy some bread when you go to town?*; *can I have some more coffee?*; *to some extent it's an interesting problem*; *her illness is of some concern to her family*

(c) *(followed by a singular noun)* referring to a person or thing you cannot identify; *some man just knocked on the door and tried to sell me a magazine*; *I read it in some book I borrowed from the library*; *we saw it in some shop or other in Regent Street*

(d) *(referring to a period of time or a distance)* *don't wait for me, I may be some time*; *their house is some way away from the railway station* (NOTE: **some** is used with plural nouns and with nouns which have no plural: **some people, some apples, some bread**, etc.)

2 *adverb; (formal)* approximately, more or less; *some fifty people came to the meeting*; *the house is some sixty years old*

① **somebody** *or* **someone**

['sʌmbɪdi or 'sʌmwʊn] *pronoun*

a certain person; *somebody is sitting on my chair*; *I can't talk any longer - there's someone waiting outside the phone box*; *somebody phoned about an order*; *I know someone who can fix your car*

① **somehow**

['sʌmhaʊ] *adverb*

by some means, although you don't know how; *somehow we must get back home by 6 o'clock*; *the work has to be done somehow*

① **someone**

['sʌmwʊn] *see* SOMEBODY

③ **someplace**

['sʌmpleɪs] *adverb*

US somewhere; *haven't I seen you before someplace?*; *is there someplace else we can talk?*

① **something**

['sʌmθɪŋ] *pronoun*

(a) a certain thing; *there's something soft at the bottom of the bag*; *something's gone wrong with the TV*; *can I have something to drink, please?*; *there's something about her that I don't like*

(b) important thing; *come in and sit down, I've got something to tell you*

(c) approximate amount; *it cost us something around fifty pounds*; *something like 20% of the students can't spell*

(d) approximate name; *he's called Nick or Dick, or something like that*; *it's a fish or shellfish or something, anyway it lives in salt water*

① **sometimes**

['sʌmtaɪmz] *adverb*

occasionally, at various times; *sometimes it gets quite cold in June*; *sometimes the car starts easily, and sometimes it won't start at all*; *she sometimes comes to see us when she's in town on business*

② **somewhat**

['sʌmwɒt] *adverb; (formal)*

more than a little, rather; *it's a somewhat difficult question to answer*; *their system is somewhat old-fashioned*; *we were somewhat surprised to see him there*

① **somewhere**

['sʌmweɪ] *adverb*

(a) in or at a certain place which is not specified; *I left my umbrella somewhere when I was in London*; *let's go somewhere else, this pub is full*; *his parents live somewhere in Germany* (NOTE: American English also uses **someplace**: **we can go someplace else**)

(b) somewhere around *or* somewhere between *or* somewhere in the region of = approximately; *somewhere between 50 and 60* people turned up for the meeting; he has collected somewhere in the region of 25,000 books

① **son**
[sʌn] *noun*
male child of a father or mother; *they have a large family - two sons and four daughters; her son has got married at last; their youngest son is in hospital*

② **song**
[sɒŋ] *noun*
(a) words which are sung; *she was singing a song in the bath; the group's latest song has just come out on CD; the soldiers marched along, singing a song*
(b) *(informal)* **for a song** = for very little money; *she bought it for a song in the local market;* **he made a great song and dance about it** = he made a great fuss about it; *they made a terrible song and dance about having to wait for a taxi*
(c) special sound made by a bird; *I'm sure that's the song of a blackbird - look, he's over there!*

① **soon**
[suːn] *adverb*
(a) in a short time from now; *don't worry, we'll soon be in Oxford; it will soon be time to go to bed; can't we meet any sooner than that?; the fire started soon after 11 o'clock*
(b) **as soon as** = immediately; *please phone the office as soon as you get to the hotel; as soon as I put the phone down it rang again; the boss wants to see you as soon as possible*
(c) **just as soon** = would rather, would prefer; *I'd just as soon stay at the office than go to the party; see also* RATHER, SOONER (NOTE: **sooner - soonest**)

② **sooner**
['suːnɪ] *adverb*
(a) **sooner or later** = at some time in the future; *sooner or later, they will realize that they need to save as much money as possible; she drives so fast that sooner or later she'll have an accident;* **sooner rather than later** = quickly rather than taking a long time; *it would be wise to reduce the staff sooner rather than later*
(b) **the sooner the better** = it would be better to do it as soon as possible; *she should consult a lawyer, and the sooner the better*
(c) **would sooner do something** = would prefer to do something; *do you want to come with us? - no, I'd sooner stay at home; we'd sooner live in Chicago than Detroit;* **would sooner +;** *pronoun =* would prefer that; *I'd sooner she stayed at home than went out with her friends; see also* RATHER, SOON

④ **soothe**
[suːð] *verb*
to relieve pain, to make something less painful, to calm; *the chemist gave me a cream to soothe the rash; she managed to soothe their hurt feelings*

④ **soothing**
['suːðɪŋ] *adjective*
which relieves pain, which calms; *the nurse put some soothing cream on my rash; I find this piece by Mozart very soothing*

③ **sophisticated**
[sɪ'fɪstɪkeɪtɪd] *adjective*
(a) knowing a lot about the way people behave, and what is the current fashion; *they think smoking makes them look sophisticated*
(b) cleverly designed, complicated (machine); *his office is full of the latest and most sophisticated computer equipment*

③ **sore**
[sɔː]
1 *adjective*
(a) rough and sensitive; painful; *he can't play tennis because he has a sore elbow;* **sore throat** = infected throat, which is red and hurts when you swallow or speak; *she's got a sore throat and has lost her voice; (informal)* **to stick out like a sore thumb** = to be easily seen
(b) *US* angry; *he's sore at her for telling the boss about him* (NOTE: **sorer - sorest**)
2 *noun*
small wound on the skin; *he had sores on his back from lying in bed for a long time;* **cold sore** = infected spot on the lips caused by a virus (NOTE: do not confuse with **soar**)

① **sorry**
['sɒrɪ]
1 *adjective*
to be sorry = to be sad about; *I'm sorry I can't stay for dinner; he trod on my foot and didn't say he was sorry; everyone was sorry to hear you had been ill;* **not to be sorry** = to be quite happy; *we weren't sorry to see him go* = we were glad when he left; **to feel sorry for someone** = to be sympathetic about someone's problems; to pity someone; *we all feel sorry for her - her family is always criticizing her;* **to feel sorry for yourself** = to be miserable; *he's feeling very sorry for himself - he's just been made redundant* (NOTE: **sorrier - sorriest**)
2 *interjection; used to excuse yourself;* **sorry!** *I didn't see that table had been reserved; can I have another chocolate, please? - sorry, I haven't any left*

① **sort**
[sɔːt]
1 *noun*
(a) type, kind; *there were all sorts of people at the meeting; I had an unpleasant sort of day at the office; what sorts of ice cream have you got?; do you like this sort of TV show?*
(b) *(informal)* **sort of** = rather, more or less; *she was sort of expecting your phone call; we're all feeling sort of upset*
(c) *(informal)* **of sorts** = not very good; *he made a speech of sorts at the ceremony*
2 *verb*

(a) to arrange in order or groups; *the apples are sorted according to size before being packed*; *the votes are sorted then counted*; **sorting office** = department in a post office where letters are put in order according to their addresses

(b) to put things in order; *she is sorting index cards into the order of their dates*

① **sort out**
['sɔːt 'aʊt] *verb*

(a) to settle a problem; *did you sort out the hotel bill?*

(b) to put things in order or in groups; *I must sort out the papers in this drawer; until they're sorted out, we shan't know which are our files and which are theirs*

(c) to collect or select things of a particular kind from a mixed group of things; *sort out all the blue forms and bring them to me, please*

③ **sought**
[sɔːt] *see* SEEK

③ **soul**
[sɪʊl] *noun*

(a) the spirit in a person, the part which is believed by some people to go on existing after a person dies; *do you believe your soul lives on when your body dies?*; *from the depths of his soul he longed to be free*

(b) **to be the life and soul of a party** = to make a party go well

(c) person; *she's a cheerful old soul; poor soul! he sits at home all day, and doesn't have anyone to go to see him* (NOTE: do not confuse with **sole**)

① **sound**
[saʊnd]

1 *noun*

noise, something which you can hear; *sounds of music came from the street; I thought I heard the sound of guns; please can you turn down the sound on the TV when I'm on the phone?*; *she crept out of her bedroom and we didn't hear a sound*; **the speed of sound** = the rate at which sound travels; *Concorde flies faster than the speed of sound*; **I don't like the sound of that** = I do not think that is a very good idea

2 *verb*

(a) to make a noise; *sound your horn when you come to a corner; they sounded the alarm after two prisoners escaped*

(b) to seem; *it sounds as if he's made an unfortunate choice; the book sounds interesting according to what I've heard*; **that sounds strange** = it seems strange to me; **that sounds like a car** = I think I can hear a car; **that sounds like my father** = (i) that is like the way my father talks; (ii) I think I can hear my father coming; (iii) that's typical of the way my father usually behaves

3 *adjective*

(a) in good condition, not rotten; *most of the walls of the house are sound*; **sound in wind and limb** = fit and healthy; **he is of sound mind** = he is not mad

(b) sensible, which can be trusted; *he gave us some very sound advice*

(c) deep (sleep); *I was awoken from a sound sleep by the ringing of the telephone* (NOTE: **sounder - soundest**)

4 *adverb*

deeply; *the children were sound asleep when the police came*

③ **sound out**
['saʊnd 'aʊt] *verb*

to sound someone out about something = to ask someone's opinion about something; *I'll sound out the other members of the committee to see what they think*

③ **soup**
[suːp] *noun*

liquid food which you eat hot from a bowl at the beginning of a meal, usually made from meat, fish or vegetables; *we have onion soup or mushroom soup today; does anyone want soup?; a bowl of hot soup is always welcome on a cold day; if you're hungry, open a tin of soup*; **soup bowl** *or* **soup plate** *or* **soup spoon** = special bowl *or* plate *or* spoon for eating soup (NOTE: no plural: **some soup, a bowl of soup**)

④ **sour**
[saʊr]

1 *adjective*

(a) with a sharp bitter taste; *if the lemonade is too sour, add some sugar; nobody likes sour milk*; *(informal)* **sour grapes** = feeling bitter about something which you want but can't have; *he said that the latest model was no better than the older ones, but that was just sour grapes*

(b) **to go sour** = (i) to take on a sharp taste; (ii) to stop work and become unpleasant; *the cream has gone sour; after a few weeks, the whole deal began to go sour* (NOTE: **sourer - sourest**)

2 *verb*

to make unpleasant; *relations between the two countries have been soured by the incident*

① **source**
[sɔːs] *noun*

(a) place where something comes from; *I think the source of the infection is in one of your teeth; the source of the river is in the mountains; you must declare income from all sources to the tax office*; **income which is taxed at source** = income where the tax is removed before the income is paid

(b) person or thing which is the cause of something; *the children are a constant source of worry; polluted water is a possible source of disease*

① **south**
[saʊθ]

1 *noun*

(a) direction facing towards the sun at the middle of the day, direction to your left when you are facing the direction where the sun sets; *look south from the mountain, and you will see the city in the distance*; *the city is to the south of the mountain range*; *the wind is blowing from the south*
(b) part of a country to the south of the rest; *the south of the country is warmer than the north*; *she went to live in the south of England*
2 *adjective*
referring to the south; *the south coast is popular for holidays*; *cross to the south side of the river*; **south wind** = wind which blows from the south
3 *adverb*
towards the south; *many birds fly south for the winter*; *go due south for two kilometres, and you will see the village on your left*; *the river flows south into the Mediterranean*

③ **South America**
['sauθ ə'merɪkə] *noun*
southern part of the American continent containing Brazil, Argentina, Chile and several other countries; *Brazil is the largest country in South America*; *he is hiding from the police somewhere in South America*

③ **south-east**
[sauθ'i:st] *adjective, adverb & noun*
direction between south and east; *South-East Asia is an important trading area*; *house prices are higher in the south-east than anywhere else in England*; *the river runs south-east from here*

② **southern**
['sʌðɪn] *adjective*
of the south; *the southern part of the country is warmer than the north*

③ **South Pole**
['sauθ 'pɪul] *noun*
furthest point at the south of the earth; *they were trying to reach the South Pole*

③ **south-west**
[sauθ'west] *adjective, adverb & noun*
direction between south and west; *we need to head south-west for two miles*; *Arizona is in the south-west of the United States*

④ **souvenir**
[su:vɪ'nɪɪ] *noun*
thing bought which reminds you of the place where you bought it; *I bought a scarf as a souvenir of my holiday in Scotland*; *keep it as a souvenir of your visit*; *they were selling souvenir programmes of the Test Match*; **souvenir shop** = shop which sells souvenirs; *there are too many souvenir shops on the seafront*

④ **sow**
[sɪu] *verb*
to put seeds into soil so that they send out shoots and become plants; *peas and beans should be sown in April*; *sow the seed in fine soil* (NOTE: do not confuse with **sew**; note also: **sowing - sowed - has sown** [sɪun])

③ **soya** *or* **soy**
['sɔɪɪ *or* sɔɪ] *noun*
plant which produces beans which have a high protein and fat content; *meat substitutes are often made from soya*; **soya sauce** *or* **soy sauce** = dark sauce with a salt flavour, made from soya beans; *Chinese dishes are often seasoned with soya sauce*

① **space**
[speɪs]
1 *noun*
(a) empty place between other things; *there's a space to park your car over there*; *write your name and reference number in the space at the top of the paper*
(b) area which is available for something; *his desk takes up too much space*; **floor space** = area of the floor in a building; **office space** = area available for offices or used by offices; *we are looking for extra office space for our new staff*
(c) **(outer) space** = area beyond the earth's atmosphere; *the first man in space was the Russian Yuri Gagarin*; *this is a photograph of the Earth taken from space*; *could someone be sending messages from outer space?*; **space shuttle** = type of plane which is launched by a rocket, then flies in space and returns eventually to earth so that it can be used for another trip; *the space shuttle will be launched next week*; **space station** = satellite which goes round the earth and in which people can live and carry out scientific experiments
(d) **open spaces** = open country, with no buildings; *Canada's wide open spaces*
(e) **in a short space of time** = in a little time; *you can't do that in a short space of time, you'll need several weeks at least*; *in a very short space of time the burglars had filled their van with furniture*
2 *verb*
to space things out = to place things at intervals, with gaps between them; *repayments can be spaced out over a period of ten years*; *make sure the text is correctly spaced out on the page*

③ **space bar**
['speɪs 'ba:] *noun*
long bar at the bottom of a typewriter or computer keyboard which inserts a single space into text; *I use my thumb on the space bar when I type*

③ **spade**
[speɪd] *noun*
(a) common gardening tool with a wide square blade at the end of a long handle, used for digging; *he handed me the spade and told me to start digging*; **to do the spade work** = to do the less interesting work in advance before the main work is done; *I get my assistant to do most of the spade work*; **to call a spade a spade** = to say exactly what you think without trying to hide

your opinions by being polite; *if she's not satisfied, she's not afraid to call a spade a spade*

(b) small tool, used by children to play in sand; *the children took their buckets and spades to the beach*

(c) spades = one of the black suits in a pack of cards; *my last two cards were the ten and the ace of spades*; *she played the king of spades* (NOTE: the other black suit is **clubs**; **hearts** and **diamonds** are the red suits)

④ **spaghetti**
[spɪˈgeti] *noun*

long thin strips of pasta, cooked and eaten with a sauce; *I ordered spaghetti with a special cream sauce*

① **Spain**
[speɪn] *proper noun*

country in southern Europe, to the south of France and the east of Portugal; *lots of people go to Spain for their holidays*; *we are going to Spain next July* (NOTE: capital: **Madrid**; people: **the Spanish** or **the Spaniards**; language: **Spanish**; currency: **peseta, euro**)

④ **span**
[spæn]
1 *noun*

(a) width of wings, of an arch, etc.; *each section of the bridge has a span of fifty feet*

(b) length of time; *over a span of five years* or *over a five-year span*

2 *verb*

to stretch across space or time; *her career spanned thirty years*; *the bridge will span the river* (NOTE: **spanning - spanned**)

① **Spanish**
[ˈspænɪʃ]
1 *adjective*

referring to Spain; *I want to change my pounds into Spanish money*

2 *noun*

language spoken in Spain and many countries of Latin America; *he's studying French and Spanish as part of his business course*

② **spare**
[speə]
1 *adjective*

extra, not being used; *I always take a spare pair of shoes when I travel*; **spare parts** = pieces used to put in place of broken parts of a car, etc.; *I can't get spare parts for that type of washing machine*; **spare time** = time when you are not at work; *he built himself a car in his spare time*; **spare wheel** = fifth wheel carried in a car to replace one that has a puncture; *when he took it out, he found the spare wheel had a puncture as well*

2 *noun*

spares = spare parts, pieces used to mend broken parts of a car, etc.; *we can't get spares for that make of washing machine*; *it's difficult to get spares for the car because they don't make this model any more*

3 *verb*

(a) *(asking someone if they can do without something)* *can you spare your assistant to help me for a day?*; *can you spare about five minutes to talk about the problem?*; *if you have a moment to spare, can you clean the car?*; *can you spare 50p for a cup of tea?*

(b) not to show or give; *the driving test was awful, but I'll spare you the details*

(c) to spare someone or **someone's life** = not to kill someone; *he pleaded with the soldiers to spare his life*; *no one was spared, all the people in the village were killed*

④ **spark**
[spɑːk]
1 *noun*

little flash of fire or of light; *sparks flew as the train went over the junction*

2 *verb*

to spark (off) = to make something start; *the shooting of the teenager sparked off a riot*; *the proposal to close the station sparked anger amongst travellers*

③ **sparking plug** *US* **spark plug**
[ˈspɑːkɪŋ ˈplʌg] or [ˈspɑːk ˈplʌg] *noun*

(in an engine) device which is screwed into the top of a cylinder and produces a spark to light the fuel; *if the sparking plugs are dirty the engine won't run very well*

④ **sparkle**
[ˈspɑːkl]
1 *noun*

bright light; *there was a sparkle in her eyes as she answered the phone*

2 *verb*

(a) to shine brightly; *her jewels sparkled in the light of the candles*; *his eyes sparkled when he heard the salary offered*

(b) *(of person)* to be lively; *she was sparkling with enthusiasm*

④ **spat**
[spæt] *see* SPIT

① **speak**
[spiːk] *verb*

(a) to say words, to talk; *she spoke to me when the meeting was over*; *he walked past me without speaking*; *he was speaking to the postman when I saw him*; *the manager wants to speak to you about sales in Africa*; **to speak your mind** = to say exactly what you think; *(informal)* **speak for yourself** = that's what you think, I don't agree; *as we are both quite fat... - speak for yourself!*

(b) to be able to say things in (a foreign language); *we need someone who can speak Russian*; *he speaks English with an American* *accent; you will have to brush up your Japanese as my mother speaks hardly any English*

(c) to make a speech; *do you know who is speaking at the conference?*

(d) **so to speak** = as you might say; *he's a very close friend, we're like brothers, so to speak* (NOTE: **speaking - spoke** [spɪʊk] **- has spoken** [ˈspɪʊkn])

② **speaker**
[ˈspiːkɪ] *noun*

(a) person who speaks; *we need an Arabic speaker to help with the tour;* **he is a popular speaker** = many people come to hear him give speeches at meetings

(b) loudspeaker; *one of the speakers doesn't work; see also* LOUDSPEAKER

(c) *(in Parliament)* person who presides over a meeting of Parliament; *the Speaker called on the Prime Minister to speak*

COMMENT: the Speaker of the House of Commons is an ordinary MP who is elected by other MPs; similarly in the US House of Representatives, the Speaker is elected by other Congressmen

③ **speak up**
[ˈspiːk ˈʌp] *verb*

(a) to speak louder; to say what you have to say in a louder voice; *can you speak up please - we can't hear you at the back!*

(b) to make your opinions known strongly; *he's not afraid to speak up when he thinks someone has been badly treated;* **to speak up for** = to show your support for; *he was the only person who spoke up for me at the inquiry*

④ **spear**
[ˈspɪɪ]
1 *noun*

long pointed throwing stick, used as a weapon; *they kill fish with spears*

2 *verb*

to push something sharp into something to catch it; *spearing fish is not easy; she managed to spear a sausage on the barbecue with her fork*

① **special**
[ˈspeʃl]
1 *adjective*

(a) referring to something or someone who is not ordinary but has a particular importance or use; *this is a very special day for us - it's our twenty-fifth wedding anniversary; a report from our special correspondent in Beijing; he has a special pair of scissors for cutting metal*

(b) **nothing special** = very ordinary; *there is nothing special about his new car; did anything happen at the meeting? - no, nothing special*

2 *noun*

particular dish on a menu; **today's special** *or* **special of the day** = special dish prepared for the day and not listed in the printed menu; *I'll have the special, please*

③ **specialist**
[ˈspeʃlɪst]
1 *noun*

(a) person who knows a lot about something; *you should go to a tax specialist for advice*

(b) doctor who specializes in a certain branch of medicine; *he was referred to a heart specialist*

2 *adjective*

specialized; *does he have any specialist knowledge of international currency transactions?*

③ **specialize**
[ˈspeʃlaɪz] *verb*

to specialize in something = to study one particular subject; to produce one thing in particular; *at university, she specialized in Roman history; the company specializes in electronic components*

③ **specially**
[ˈspeʃli] *adverb*

in particular, more than usual; *the weather has been specially wet this weekend; he is specially good at designing furniture; aren't you tired? - not specially; see also* ESPECIALLY

③ **species**
[ˈspiːʃɪz] *noun*

group of living things, such as animals or plants, which can breed with each other; *several species of butterfly are likely to disappear as the weather becomes warmer* (NOTE: plural is **species**)

① **specific**
[spɪˈsɪfɪk] *adjective*

referring precisely to something; *can you be more specific about what you're trying to achieve?; I gave specific instructions that I was not to be disturbed; is the money intended for a specific purpose?*

② **specifically**
[spɪˈsɪfɪkli] *adverb*

particularly; *I specifically said I didn't want a blue door; the advertisement is specifically aimed at people over 60*

④ **specification**
[spesɪfɪˈkeɪʃn] *noun*

detailed information about what is needed; *she gave full specifications about how she wanted the kitchen to be laid out;* **the finished product is not up to specification** *or* **does not meet our specifications** = the product is not made in the way which was stated; **job specification** = very detailed description of what is involved in a job; *there was nothing about word-processing in my job specification*

③ **specify**
[ˈspesɪfaɪ] *verb*

to give clear details of what is needed; *please specify full details of the address to which the goods must be sent; do not include VAT on the invoice unless specified*

④ **specimen**
['spesɪmɪn] *noun*
(a) sample of something taken as standard; *the bank asked for a specimen signature for their records*
(b) example of a particular kind of creature or thing; *he has some very rare specimens in his butterfly collection; this is a fine specimen of this kind of tree*

③ **specs**
[speks] *noun*
(informal) = SPECTACLES; *I can't see anything without my specs!*

③ **spectacle**
['spektɪkl] *noun*
(a) something very impressive to look at; show; *the flower display is a spectacle not to be missed; for sheer spectacle you can't beat a military parade*
(b) spectacles = two pieces of plastic or glass in a frame which you wear in front of your eyes to help you see better; *have you seen my spectacles anywhere?; she has to wear spectacles to read; I can't remember where I put my spectacles; he's worn spectacles since he was a child* (NOTE: **spectacles** are also called **glasses**)

④ **spectacular**
[spek'tækjʊlɪ]
1 *adjective*
very impressive to see or watch; *the parade of tanks was even more spectacular than last year; she was very ill, but has made a spectacular recovery*
2 *noun*
impressive show; *a musical spectacular featuring over a hundred singers and dancers*

④ **spectator**
['spekteɪtɪ] *noun*
person who watches a football match, a horse show, etc.; *thousands of spectators watched the tennis match*

④ **speculate**
['spekjʊleɪt] *verb*
(a) to speculate about = to make guesses about; *we are all speculating about what's going to happen*
(b) to take a risk in business which you hope will bring profit; *he made a lot of money by speculating on the Stock Exchange*

③ **sped**
[sped] *see* SPEED

② **speech**
[spiːtʃ] *noun*
(a) formal talk given to an audience; *he made some notes before giving his speech; he wound up his speech with a story about his father; who will be making the speech at the prize giving?*; **speech day** = day when children are given prizes at school for good work, etc. (NOTE: plural in this meaning is **speeches**)

(b) speaking, making sounds with the voice which can be understood; *teaching speech to deaf children can be a very slow process*
(c) spoken language; *this word is more often used in speech than in writing*; **freedom of speech** = being able to say what you want; *the protesters demanded freedom of speech*; the **parts of speech** = different types of words, such as nouns, verbs, etc., which are classified according to their use; *nouns, adjectives and verbs are different parts of speech*

① **speed**
[spiːd]
1 *noun*
rate at which something moves or is done; *the coach was travelling at a high speed when it crashed; your car will use less petrol if you go at an even speed of 56 miles per hour; the speed with which they repaired the gas leak was incredible; the train travels at speeds of over 200 km per hour*
2 *verb*
(a) to move quickly; *the ball sped across the ice*
(b) to go too fast; *he was arrested for speeding in the centre of town* (NOTE: **speeding - sped** [sped] *or* **speeded - has sped**)

③ **speed limit**
['spiːd 'lɪmɪt] *noun*
fastest speed at which cars are allowed to go legally; *the speed limit in towns is 30 miles per hour; what is the speed limit on German motorways?*

③ **speed up**
['spiːd 'ʌp] *verb*
(a) to go faster; *she speeded up as she came to the traffic lights*
(b) to make something happen faster; *can't we speed up production?; we are aiming to speed up our delivery times*

② **spell**
[spel]
1 *noun*
(a) short period; *there was a spell of cold weather over the bank holiday weekend; the warm spell will last until Thursday*
(b) words which the person speaking hopes will have a magic effect; *her wicked sister cast a spell on the princess*
2 *verb*
to write or say correctly the letters that make a word; *how do you spell your surname?; we spelt his name wrong on the envelope*; *W-O-R-R-Y spells 'worry'*; **to spell out** = to explain very clearly; *let me spell out the consequences of this course of action* (NOTE: **spelling - spelled** *or* **spelt** [spelt] **- has spelled** *or* **has spelt**)

② **spelling**
['spelɪŋ] *noun*
correct way in which words are spelt; *she is a good journalist, but her spelling is awful*

① spend

[spend] *verb*

(a) to pay money; *I went shopping and spent a fortune*; *why do we spend so much money on food?*

(b) to use time doing something; *he wants to spend more time with his family*; *she spent months arguing with the income tax people*; *don't spend too long on your homework*; *why don't you come and spend the weekend with us?* (NOTE: **spending - spent** [spent])

① spending

['spendɪŋ] *noun*

paying money; *government spending on health has increased by 10%*; **consumer spending** = spending by consumers; *interest rates were increased to control consumer spending*; **spending money** = money for ordinary personal expenses; *how much spending money are you taking on holiday?*

④ sperm

[spɜːm] *noun*

male sex cell which fertilizes the female eggs; *out of millions of sperm only one will fertilize an egg* (NOTE: plural is **sperm**)

④ sphere

['sfɪə] *noun*

(a) object which is perfectly round like a ball; *the earth is not quite a perfect sphere*

(b) general area; *it's not a sphere of activity that we know very well*; **sphere of influence** = area of the world where a strong country can influence smaller or weaker countries; *some Latin American countries fall within the USA's sphere of influence*

④ spice

[spaɪs] *noun*

1 *noun*

(a) substance made from the roots, flowers, seeds or leaves of plants, used to flavour food; *pepper and mustard are the main spices I use*; *you need lots of spices for Indian cookery*

(b) thing which excites interest; *I included a murder scene to add a bit of spice to the story*

2 *verb*

to spice something up = (i) to add spices to something; (ii) to make something more exciting or interesting; *a pinch of mustard will spice up the sauce*; *we need something to spice up the scene where the hero and heroine meet in the rain*

④ spicy

['spaɪsi] *adjective*

with a lot of spices; *he loves spicy Indian food*; *Mexican cooking is hot and spicy* (NOTE: **spicier - spiciest**)

④ spider

['spaɪdə] *noun*

small animal with eight legs, which makes a web and eats insects; *it is fascinating to watch a spider making its web*

④ spike

[spaɪk] *noun*

(a) sharply pointed piece of metal; *the wall was topped with a row of metal spikes*

(b) **spikes** = sharp points in the soles of running shoes; *spikes give a runner a much better grip on the track*

③ spill

[spɪl]

1 *noun*

pouring of a liquid by accident; *the authorities are trying to cope with the oil spill from the tanker*

2 *verb*

(a) to pour liquid, powder, etc., out of a container by mistake; *that glass is too full - you'll spill it*; *he spilt soup down the front of his shirt*; *she dropped the bag and some of the flour spilled out onto the floor*

(b) *(informal)* **to spill the beans** = to reveal a secret (NOTE: **spilling - spilled** *or* **spilt** [spɪlt])

③ spilt

[spɪlt] *see* CRY, SPILL

③ spin

[spɪn]

1 *noun*

(a) turning movement of a ball as it moves, of a car out of control; *he put so much spin on the ball that it bounced sideways*; *he jammed on the brakes and the car went into a spin*

(b) *(informal)* **to put a spin on something** = to give something a special meaning; *the PR people have tried to put a positive spin on the sales figures*; *(informal)* **spin doctor** = person who explains news in a way that makes it better for the person or organization employing him; *government spin doctors have been having some difficulty in dealing with the news items about the minister's family*

(c) *(informal)* short ride in a car; *let's go for a spin in my new car*

2 *verb*

(a) to move round and round very fast; *the earth is spinning in space*; *the plane was spinning out of control*

(b) to make something turn round and round; *the washing machine spins the clothes to get the water out of them*; *he spun the wheel to make sure it turned freely*; **to spin a coin** = to make a coin turn round and round, so as to decide (by guessing which side of the coin will end up on top) which team plays first in a competition, etc.

(c) to twist raw wool, cotton, etc., to form a thread; *a spinning wheel*

(d) *(of a spider)* to make a web; *the spider has spun a web between the two posts* (NOTE: **spinning - spun** [spʌn])

④ **spine**
[spaɪn] *noun*
(a) a series of bones linked together to form a flexible support from the base of the skull to the hips; *he injured his spine playing rugby*
(b) sharp part like a pin, on a plant, animal, fish, etc.; *some animals have dangerous spines*; *did you know that lemon trees had spines?*
(c) back edge of a bound book, usually with the title printed on it; *the title and the author's name are printed on the front cover of the book and also on the spine*

③ **spin out**
['spɪn 'aʊt] *verb*
to make something last as long as possible; *I managed to spin the lecture out to last a full hour*

③ **spin round**
['spɪn 'raʊnd] *verb*
(a) to turn round and round very fast; *the earth spins round in space*
(b) to turn round fast to face in the opposite direction; *I tapped him on the shoulder and he spun round to face me*

④ **spiral**
['spaɪrɪl]
1 *noun*
(a) shape which is twisted round and round like a spring; *he drew a spiral on the sheet of paper*
(b) thing which turns, getting higher or lower all the time; *smoke was rising in spirals from the top of the chimney*
2 *adjective*
which twists round and round; *a spiral staircase leads to the top of the tower*
3 *verb*
(a) to move up or down in a spiral; *the rocket spiralled up into the air*; *the leaves dropped off the tree and spiralled down to the ground*
(b) to move rapidly upwards; *prices of imported goods are spiralling*; **spiralling inflation** = inflation where price rises make workers ask for higher wages which then increase prices again (NOTE: **spiralling - spiralled** but the American spelling is **spiraling - spiraled**)

② **spirit**
['spɪrɪt]
1 *noun*
(a) energy and determination; *I like her because she has got such spirit*; *she fought her case with great spirit*
(b) feelings which are typical of a particular occasion; *a good salesman needs to have the spirit of competition*; *I don't think she approached the task in the right spirit*; **to enter into the spirit of** = to take part in something with enthusiasm; *the managing director entered into the spirit of the party*; **Christmas spirit** = excitement and friendly feeling which are supposed to exist at Christmas; *making us all redundant on December 24th didn't show*

much Christmas spirit; **public spirit** = feeling that you belong to a certain part of society and have to do things to help others in the group
(c) ghost of someone dead; *the spirits of the dead*; **evil spirit** = wicked ghost which harms people; **Holy Spirit** = the third person of the Christian Trinity
(d) real intention of something; *that's not really in keeping with the spirit of the agreement*
(e) alcohol; **surgical spirit** = pure alcohol with an unpleasant taste, used as an antiseptic; *see also* SPIRITS
2 *verb*
to spirit away = to remove as if by magic; *they spirited her away before the photographers could get to her*

③ **spirits**
['spɪrɪts] *noun*
(a) strong alcoholic drink (whisky, etc.); *the club is licensed to sell beers, wines and spirits*
(b) mood; *the news had an excellent effect on our spirits*; *their spirits sank when they realized they had no chance of winning*; **in high spirits** = in a very excited mood; *she's been in high spirits since she passed her test*

④ **spit**
[spɪt]
1 *noun*
(a) metal rod pushed through meat over a fire, which is turned so that the meat is cooked all through; *they roasted pieces of lamb on spits*; *a spit-roasted lamb*
(b) thin piece of land which goes out into the sea; *the nature reserve is sited at the end of a spit of land*
(c) liquid which forms in your mouth; *(informal)* **spit and polish** = vigorous cleaning
(d) **he is the dead spit of his father** = he looks like an exact copy of his father
2 *verb*
(a) to push liquid or food out of your mouth; *he took a mouthful and immediately spat it out*
(b) **to spit on** = to send liquid out of the mouth to show contempt; *he spat on the car as it drove away*
(c) *(informal)* **he is the spitting image of his father** = he looks like an exact copy of his father
(d) to rain a little; *it isn't really raining - it's just spitting* (NOTE: **spitting - spat** [spæt])

③ **spite**
[spaɪt]
1 *noun*
(a) bad feeling; *they sprayed his car with white paint out of spite*
(b) **in spite of** = although something happened or was done; *in spite of all his meetings, he still found time to ring his wife*; *we all enjoyed ourselves, in spite of the awful weather*; *see also* DESPITE
2 *verb*
to annoy someone on purpose; *he did it purely to spite his sister*

④ **splash**
['splæʃ]
1 *noun*

(a) sound when something falls into a liquid or when a liquid hits something hard; *she fell into the pool with a loud splash*; *listen to the splash of the waves against the rocks*

(b) sudden show; *the red flowers make a bright splash of colour in the front garden*

(c) *(informal)* **to make a splash** = to do something which attracts a lot of publicity; *his new show made a splash on Broadway*

2 *verb*

(a) *(of liquid)* to make a noise when something is dropped into it or when it hits something; *I missed the ball and it splashed into the pool*; *the rain splashed against the windows*; *the little children were splashing about in the pools of water*

(b) to make someone wet by sending liquid on to him; *the car drove past through the rain and splashed my trousers*

(c) to move through water, making a noise; *he splashed his way through the shallow water to the rocks*

③ **splash out**
['splæʃ 'aut] *verb*

(informal) to spend a lot of money at one time; *we splashed out on a holiday in Tenerife*

④ **splendid**
['splendid] *adjective*

magnificent, which impresses; *after a splendid lunch we all had a short sleep*; *it was absolutely splendid to see your father again*

② **split**
[split]
1 *verb*

(a) to divide something into parts; *he split the piece of wood into three*; **to split the difference** = to agree on a figure which is half way between two figures suggested; *you are offering £20 and he wants £40, so why don't you split the difference and settle on £30?*; *see also* HAIR

(b) to divide or to come apart; *my trousers were too tight - they split when I bent down*; *after they lost the election, the party split into various factions*; *(informal)* **my head is splitting** *or* **I have a splitting headache** = I have a very bad headache (NOTE: **splitting - split**)

2 *noun*

(a) division; *they are trying to hide the split between the two factions of the party*

(b) banana split = dessert made of a banana cut in half, whipped cream, ice cream, chocolate sauce and nuts

(c) *(in dancing)* **to do the splits** = to put yourself on the floor, with your legs spread in opposite directions

3 *adjective*

which has been broken in half; **split ends** = hair problem, when the end of each hair splits into different strands; *my hair needs to be cut because of my split ends*; **split peas** = dried peas split in half; **in a split second** = very rapidly; *everything happened in a split second*; **to have a split personality** = mental condition where you react from time to time in two totally different and opposing ways

③ **split up**
['split 'ʌp] *verb*

(a) to divide; *we must try to split up the class into groups of three or four*

(b) to start to live apart; *they had a row and split up*

④ **spoil**
[spɔil]
1 *verb*

(a) to ruin something which was good; *we had such bad weather that our camping holiday was spoilt*; *half the contents of the warehouse were spoiled in the flood*; **to spoil your appetite** = to make you not want to eat; *don't eat so many crisps - they'll spoil your appetite for lunch*

(b) to be too kind to someone, especially a child, so that he or she sometimes becomes badly behaved; *you'll spoil that child if you always give in to him*; *grandparents are allowed to spoil their grandchildren a little*

(c) to be spoiling for a fight = to be eager to get into a fight; *the socialists were spoiling for a fight with the liberals*

(d) to go bad; *if we don't eat this meat today it will spoil* (NOTE: **spoiling - spoilt** [spɔilt] *or* **spoiled**)

2 *noun*

(formal)

(a) spoils = goods taken by soldiers from a defeated enemy; *their spoils filled several train wagons*

(b) *(humorous)* things bought; *she came back from the January sales with her spoils*

(c) spoil heap = heap of rubbish from a mine; *the countryside is littered with spoil heaps from old tin mines*

③ **spoke**
[spɪuk]
1 *noun*

rod which connects the centre of a wheel to the outside edge; *the wheel isn't turning straight because one of the spokes is bent*

2 *verb*

see also SPEAK

① **spoken**
['spɪukɪn] *see* SPEAK

② **spokesman** *or* **spokeswoman** *or* **spokesperson**
['spɪuksmɪn *or* 'spɪukswuːmɪn *or* 'spɪukspɜːsɪn]
noun

person who speaks on behalf of a party, group, politician, etc.; *a spokesman for the government or a government spokesman* (NOTE: plural is **spokesmen** or **spokeswomen**)

④ **sponsor**
['spɒnsɪ]
1 *noun*
(a) person or company that pays to help a sport, an exhibition, a music festival, etc., financially in return for the right to advertise at sporting events, on sports clothes, programmes, etc.; *the company is the sponsor of the premier division football*
(b) company which pays part of the cost of making a TV or radio programme by advertising on the programme
(c) person who pays money to a charity when someone else walks, swims, runs, a certain distance; *he's taking part in the school sports day and wants sponsors*
(d) person who takes responsibility for someone; *she acted as his sponsor when he applied for membership of the club*
2 *verb*
to be a sponsor; *the company has sponsored the football match*; *will you sponsor me if I apply to join the club?*; *I sponsored her to take part in a marathon for charity*

④ **spontaneous**
[spɒn'teɪnɪɪs] *adjective*
which happens of its own accord, which is not forced or prepared in advance; *in a spontaneous show of affection, she flung her arms round him and kissed him*; *what he said sounded more like a prepared statement than a spontaneous comment*

④ **spoon**
[spu:n]
1 *noun*
(a) object with a handle at one end and a small bowl at the other, used for eating liquids and soft food, or for stirring food which is being cooked; *use a spoon to eat your pudding*; *we need a big spoon to serve the soup*; **coffee spoon** = little spoon used for stirring coffee; **soup spoon** = special larger spoon for eating soup; *see also* DESSERT SPOON, TEASPOON, WOODEN SPOON
(b) amount held in a spoon; *add two spoons of sugar*
2 *verb*
to move something with a spoon; *she spooned sugar onto her plate*; **to spoon something into something** = to put something in with a spoon; *they were spooning soup out into each bowl*

③ **spoonful**
['spu:nful] *noun*
amount which a spoon can hold; *she always takes her coffee with two spoonfuls of sugar*; *put a spoonful of tea into the pot and add boiling water*

② **sport**
[spɔːt]
1 *noun*
(a) any game; all games taken together; *do you like watching sport on TV?* or *do you like the sports programmes on TV?*; *the world of sport is celebrating his record win*; **sports facilities** = equipment and buildings for playing sports, such as tennis courts, swimming pools, etc.; *the club has extensive sports facilities*
(b) game which you play; *the only sport I play is tennis*; *she doesn't play any sport at all*
(c) **good sport** = person who doesn't mind being teased; *he's a good sport*
2 *verb*
to wear something proudly; *he was sporting a red and orange tie*

③ **sports car**
['spɔːts 'kaː] *noun*
fast open car; *he bought a dark green sports car to impress his girlfriend*

③ **sportsman, sportswoman**
['spɔːtsmɪn or spɔːtswʊmɪn] *noun*
person who plays a sport; *she's an Olympic sportswoman* (NOTE: plurals are **sportsmen, sportswomen**)

② **spot**
[spɒt]
1 *noun*
(a) particular place; *this is the exact spot where Anne Boleyn was executed*; **black spot** = section of road where accidents often happen; *this road junction is a notorious black spot*; **on the spot** = at a particular place where something happens; *I happened to be on the spot when the incident took place*; *we had twenty policemen on the spot to make sure there was no trouble*; **to put someone on the spot** = to place someone in a position where he or she has to do something difficult; *he was put on the spot when they asked him if had ever smoked drugs*
(b) coloured mark, usually round; *her dress has a pattern of white and red spots*; *he wore a blue tie with white spots*; *(informal)* **to knock spots off someone** = to be easily better than someone; *she sang a little song which knocked spots off all the others*; *see also* SOFT
(c) small round mark or bump on the skin; *she suddenly came out in spots after eating fish*
(d) *(informal)* small amount; *would you like a spot of lunch?*; *we had a spot of luck*; *he's had a spot of bother with the tax people*
(e) *(finance)* buying something for immediate delivery; **spot price** = price for something which is delivered immediately
(f) **TV spot** = short period on TV which is used for commercials; *we are running a series of TV spots over the next three weeks*
2 *verb*
to notice; *the teacher didn't spot the mistake*; *we spotted him in the crowd* (NOTE: **spotting - spotted**)

④ **spotlight**
['spɒtlaɪt] *noun*

(a) bright light which shines on one small area; *she stood in the spotlights on the stage*

(b) **to turn the spotlight on something** = to draw attention to something; *the TV programme turns the spotlight on the problem of refugees*

④ **spouse**
['spaʊz] *noun*

(formal) husband or wife; *members of the club may be accompanied by their spouses*

③ **sprain**
[spreɪn]
1 *verb*

to tear a joint, such as your ankle; *he sprained his ankle jumping over the fence; he sprained his wrist and can't play tennis tomorrow*

2 *noun*

condition where the parts of a joint which hold the bones together are torn because of a sudden movement; *he is walking with a stick because of an ankle sprain*

③ **sprang**
[spræŋ] *see* SPRING

③ **spray**
[spreɪ]
1 *noun*

(a) mass of tiny drops of liquid; *the waves crashed against the sea wall sending spray over the road; we used a spray to kill the flies; she uses a spray to clear her blocked nose*

(b) **spray (can)** = container that sends out liquid in a spray; *this paint is sold in ordinary tins or as a spray*

(c) little branch of a plant with flowers on it; *the room was decorated with sprays of orange flowers*

2 *verb*

to send out liquid in fine drops; *he sprayed water all over the beds of flowers; they sprayed the room to get rid of the insects*

② **spread**
[spred]
1 *noun*

(a) soft paste of meat, fish or cheese; *as snacks, they offered us water biscuits with cheese spread*

(b) range; *there is a wide spread of abilities in the class; she has a wide spread of interests*

(c) *(informal)* attractive mass of food; *you should have seen the spread at her wedding reception!*

(d) action of moving over a wide area; *doctors are trying to check the spread of the disease*

2 *verb*

(a) to arrange over a wide area; *spread the paper flat on the table*

(b) to move over a wide area; *the disease has spread to the main towns*

(c) to cover with a layer of something; *she spread a white cloth over the table; he was spreading butter on a piece of bread*

(d) **to spread payments over several months** = to make payments over several months, not all at once (NOTE: **spreading - spread**)

③ **spread out**
['spred 'aʊt] *verb*

(a) to arrange things over a wide area; *she spread out the clothes on her bed; he spread out the plans on the MD's desk*

(b) to move away from others over a wide area; *the demonstrators spread out across the square; the policemen spread out to search the woods*

② **spring**
[sprɪŋ]
1 *noun*

(a) season of the year between winter and summer; *in spring all the trees start to grow new leaves; we always go to Greece in the spring; they started work last spring or in the spring of last year and they still haven't finished; you should come to England in April and see the beautiful spring flowers!*

(b) wire which is twisted round and round and which goes back to its original shape after you have pulled it or pushed it; *the bed is so old the springs have burst through the mattress; there's a spring to keep the door shut*

(c) strong pieces of special metal which absorb energy and allow a vehicle to travel easily over different surfaces; *the springs in the car are starting to squeak*

(d) place where a stream of water rushes out of the ground; *the town of Bath was built in Roman times around hot springs*

(e) quick jump into the air; *a little spring and he had reached the window ledge*

2 *verb*

(a) to move suddenly; *everyone sprang to life when the officer shouted; the door sprang open without anyone touching it*

(b) **to spring from** = to come suddenly from; *where on earth did you spring from?*

(c) *(informal)* **to spring something on someone** = to surprise someone; *she sprang the question on him and he didn't know how to answer it* (NOTE: **springing - sprang** [spræŋ] **- has sprung** [sprʌŋ])

④ **sprinkle**
['sprɪŋkl] *verb*

to scatter around; *sprinkle a little water on the shirt before you iron it; sprinkle the top of the pie with sugar*

④ **sprint**
[sprɪnt]
1 *noun*

fast run, especially at the end of a race; *he must save some energy for the final sprint*

2 *verb*

to run very fast over a short distance; *I had to sprint to catch the bus*; *she sprinted down the track*

④ **sprout**
[spraʊt]
1 *noun*
new shoot of a plant; **bean sprouts** = little shoots of beans, eaten especially in Chinese cooking; **Brussels sprouts** = shoots which look like tiny cabbages
2 *verb*
to produce new shoots; *throw those old potatoes away, they're starting to sprout*; *the bush had begun to sprout fresh green leaves*

③ **sprung**
[sprʌŋ] *see* SPRING

③ **spun**
[spʌn] *see* SPIN

④ **spur**
[spɜ:]
1 *noun*
(a) sharp metal point attached to the heel of a rider's boot which makes the horse go faster; *he put on his spurs and went to saddle up his horse*
(b) to win your spurs = to show your qualities for the first time; *it's a chance for this young player to win his spurs at international level*
(c) thing which stimulates; *the letter from the university was the spur that encouraged him to work harder*
(d) on the spur of the moment = without being planned in advance; *we decided on the spur of the moment to go to France*
(e) hill which leads from a higher mountain; *the hill we climbed was a spur of the Rockies*
(f) minor road or railway line leading off a main one; *a spur road runs off to the power station*
2 *verb*
to urge someone on; *the runners were spurred on by the shouts of the crowd* (NOTE: **spurring - spurred**)

④ **spy**
[spaɪ]
1 *noun*
person who is paid to try to find out secret information about the enemy, a gang, a rival firm; *he was executed as a Russian spy* (NOTE: plural is **spies**)
2 *verb*
to spy on someone = to watch someone in secret, to find out what they are planning to do; *we discovered that our neighbours had been spying on us*; **to spy for someone** = to find out secret information and pass it back to someone; *he was accused of spying for the Americans*

③ **squad**
[skwɒd] *noun*
(a) small group of soldiers who perform duties together; *Corporal, take your squad and guard the prisoners*; **firing squad** = group of soldiers whose duty is to shoot someone who has been sentenced to death
(b) department in the police service; *he's the head of the drug squad*; *she's investigating on behalf of the Fraud squad*; **squad car** = police car on patrol duty
(c) group of players from whom a sports team will be chosen; *the England squad for the World Cup has been selected*

② **square**
[skweɪ]
1 *noun*
(a) shape with four equal sides and four corners with right angles; *boards used for playing chess are divided up into black and white squares*; *graph paper is drawn with a series of small squares*; *(informal)* **back to square one** = to start again from the point you originally started from; *the test plane crashed, so it's back to square one again*
(b) open space in a town, with big buildings all round; *the hotel is in the main square of the town, opposite the town hall*; *tourists like feeding the pigeons in Trafalgar Square*; *Red Square is in the middle of Moscow*
(c) *(mathematics)* result when a number is multiplied by itself; *9 is the square of 3*
2 *adjective*
(a) shaped like a square, with four equal sides and four corners with right angles; *you can't fit six people round a small square table*; *an A4 piece of paper isn't square*; **a square peg (in a round hole)** = someone whose character means that he does not fit easily into a job, etc.
(b) making a 90° angle; *there's not one corner in the room that is square*
(c) honest and fair; *are you being square with me?*; **square deal** = honest treatment in business; *they didn't get a square deal from the tax office*; **a square meal** = a good substantial meal; *(informal)* **now we're all square** = we do not owe each other anything
(d) multiplied by itself; **square metre** = area of one metre multiplied by one metre; **ten square metres** = space of 2 metres x 5 metres; *the room is 5m by 9m, so its area is 45 square metres (45m²)* (NOTE: **ten square metres** is usually written **10 m²**)
3 *verb*
(a) to make something square; **squared paper** = paper with squares drawn on it, for making graphs, etc.
(b) to pay someone what is owed; to pay someone a bribe; *they had to square a couple of local officials before the deal went through*
(c) *(informal)* **to square it with someone** = to see that someone gives approval; *let me deal with it - I'll square it with the inspector*
(d) to square your shoulders = to straighten your shoulders; **to square up to someone** = to prepare to fight; *instead of running away, he squared up to the mugger looking very fierce*

(e) *(mathematics)* to multiply a number by itself; *3 squared is 9*

③ **squash**
[skwɒʃ]
1 *verb*
to crush, to squeeze; *hundreds of commuters were squashed into the train*; *he sat on my hat and squashed it flat*
2 *noun*
(a) a situation where a lot of people are crowded in a small space; *it's rather a squash with twenty people in the room*
(b) drink made of concentrated fruit juice to which water is added; *do you want some orange squash?* (NOTE: no plural)

③ **squeak**
[skwiːk]
1 *noun*
high little noise like that of a mouse or a door; *you can tell when someone comes into the garden by the squeak of the gate*; *(informal)* **narrow squeak** = a near miss, a narrow escape; *we had a narrow squeak when a lorry just missed crashing into our car*
2 *verb*
to make a squeak; *that door squeaks - it needs oiling*

④ **squeeze**
[skwiːz]
1 *noun*
(a) act of pressing or crushing; *I gave her hand a squeeze*; **a tight squeeze** = a situation where there is very little space to get into or through; *you can get through the hole, but it's a tight squeeze*
(b) amount pushed out; *he put a squeeze of toothpaste on his brush*; **a squeeze of lemon** = a few drops of lemon juice
(c) **credit squeeze** = period when lending by the banks is restricted by the government
2 *verb*
(a) to press on something; to press or crush a fruit, a tube, etc., to get something out of it; *she squeezed my arm gently*; *he squeezed an orange to get the juice*; *she squeezed some toothpaste onto her brush*
(b) to crush, to force into a small space; *you can't squeeze six people into that little car*; *more people tried to squeeze on the train even though it was full already*; *the cat managed to squeeze through the window*

③ **St**
see SAINT, STREET

④ **stab**
[stæb]
1 *noun*
(a) deep wound made by the point of a knife; *he died of stab wounds*
(b) **stab in the back** = attack by someone who is thought to be loyal; *his speech was a stab in the back for the party leader*

(c) *(informal)* **to have a stab at something** = to try to do something; *I'm keen to have a stab at driving a bus*
2 *verb*
(a) to wound by pushing with the point of a sharp knife; *he was stabbed in the chest*
(b) **to stab someone in the back** = to do something nasty to someone who thinks you are his friend; *she was stabbed in the back by people who owed their jobs to her* (NOTE: **stabbing - stabbed**)

④ **stabilize**
['steɪbɪlaɪz] *verb*
(a) to make firm; *we need more weight on this side of the boat to stabilize it*; *the United Nations is sending in troops to try to stabilize the situation*
(b) to become steady; *prices have stabilized*

③ **stable**
['steɪbl]
1 *noun*
(a) building for keeping a horse; *my horse is not in his stable, who's riding him?*
(b) **stables** = place where horses are kept for breeding, racing, etc.; *she enjoys working in the stables because she loves horses*
2 *adjective*
(a) steady, which does not shake; *the ladder is not very stable, will you hold it for me?*; *put a book under one leg of the desk to keep it stable*
(b) which does not change; *the hospital said his condition was stable*

④ **stack**
[stæk]
1 *noun*
(a) pile of things one on top of the other; *there was a stack of replies to our advertisement*
(b) *(informal)* **stacks of** = lots of; *you can charge tourists what you like - they've got stacks of money*
2 *verb*
(a) to pile things on top of each other; *the skis are stacked outside the school*; *she stacked up the dirty plates*; *the warehouse is stacked with boxes*
(b) *(of aircraft)* to circle round waiting in turn for permission to land at a busy airport; *we have had aircraft stacking for over fifteen minutes on busy days*

④ **stadium**
['steɪdiːm] *noun*
large building for sport, with seating arranged around a sports field; *our sports stadium was packed with spectators*; *they are building an Olympic stadium for the next Games* (NOTE: plural is **stadiums** or **stadia**)

② **staff**
[stɑːf]
1 *noun*
(a) all the people who work in a company, school, college, or other organization; *she's on the school staff*; *only staff can use this lift*; *a*

quarter of our staff are ill; that firm pays its staff very badly; he joined the staff last Monday; three members of staff are away sick; **kitchen staff** = people who work in a kitchen; **office staff** = people who work in offices; **staff room** = room for teachers in a school (NOTE: **staff** refers to a group of people and so is often followed by a verb in the plural)

(b) the general staff = group of senior army officers who work in headquarters

(c) (formal) long stick; the police attacked the protesters and beat them with staffs

2 verb

to provide workers for an organization; they are planning to staff the office with part-time sales people; the bar is staffed by Australians

① **stage**
[steɪdʒ]
1 noun

(a) raised floor in a theatre where the actors perform; the pop group came onto the stage and started to sing

(b) the stage = the profession of acting; she is planning to go on the stage; he has chosen the stage as a career

(c) one of several points of development; the first stage in the process is to grind the rock to powder; the different stages of a production process; **the contract is still in the drafting stage** = the contract is still being drafted; **in stages** = in different steps; the company has agreed to repay the loan in stages

(d) section of a long journey; stage one of the tour takes us from Paris to Bordeaux; **in easy stages** = not doing anything very difficult; we did the walk in easy stages; the tour will cross India by easy stages

(e) landing stage = wooden platform for boats to tie up to allow goods or people to be taken off; the ferry tied up at the landing stage

2 verb

(a) to put on, to arrange a play, a show, a musical, etc.; the exhibition is being staged in the conference centre

(b) to show; **to stage a recovery** = to recover; she has staged a remarkable recovery after her accident

④ **stagger**
['stægɪ]
1 noun

movement when someone walks but is not steady on his feet; he walked with a noticeable stagger

2 verb

(a) not to walk in a steady way, to walk almost falling down; she managed to stagger across the road and into the police station; three men staggered out of the pub

(b) to surprise enormously; I was staggered at the amount they charge for service

(c) to arrange holidays, working hours, so that they do not all begin and end at the same time; staggered holidays help the tourist industry; we have to stagger the lunch hour so that there is always someone on the switchboard

③ **stain**
[steɪn]
1 noun

(a) mark which is difficult to remove, such as ink or blood; it is difficult to remove coffee stains from the tablecloth; there was a round stain on the table where he had put his wine glass

(b) liquid paint used to give a different colour to wood; we bought some dark green stain for the garden furniture

2 verb

(a) to make a mark of a different colour on something; if you eat those berries they will stain your teeth; the tablecloth was stained with strawberry jam; his shirt was stained with blood

(b) to colour something with a stain; to put a stain on a surface; the door will be stained light brown

③ **stair**
[steɪ] see STAIRS

④ **staircase**
['steɪkeɪs] noun

set of stairs which go from one floor in a building to another; a spiral staircase leads to the top of the tower; the staircase is at the back of the building

② **stairs**
[steɪz] noun

steps which go up or down inside a building; you have to go up three flights of stairs to get to my office; he slipped and fell down the stairs; see also DOWNSTAIRS, UPSTAIRS (NOTE: **stair** is sometimes used in the singular meaning one step: he was sitting on the bottom stair)

③ **stake**
[steɪk]
1 noun

(a) strong pointed piece of wood or metal, pushed into the ground to mark something, or to hold something up; they hammered stakes into the ground to put up a wire fence; the apple trees are attached to stakes

(b) money which has been bet or invested; with a £5 stake he won £100; **the stakes are high** = a lot of money could be won or lost; **he has a stake in the company** = he has invested money in the company

(c) at stake = which may be lost if what you do fails; you must reply to the story in the paper, the reputation of the family is at stake! (NOTE: do not confuse with **steak**)

2 verb

(a) to put sticks in the ground to mark an area; we staked out the area where the riding events were to take place

(b) to stake your claim to something = to say in public that you have the right to take something; *as soon as we arrived at the hotel she staked her claim to the only room with a view of the sea*

(c) to risk; *he risked his reputation on the libel action*; *I'd stake my life on it, he's not guilty*; *they had staked everything on the success of this product*; **to stake money on something** = to risk or bet money on something; *she staked £10,000 on a throw of the dice*

④ **stalk**
[stɔːk]
1 *noun*

(a) stem of a plant which holds a leaf, a flower, a fruit, etc.; *roses with very long stalks are more expensive*; *cherries often come attached to stalks in pairs*

2 *verb*

(a) to walk in a stiff, proud or angry way; *she stalked into the committee room*

(b) to follow someone *or* something secretly in order to catch them; *the hunters stalked the deer*; *the photographers stalked the film star*; *the TV presenter was being stalked by a local fan*

② **stall**
[stɔːl]
1 *noun*

(a) small wooden stand in a market, where a trader displays and sells his goods; *he has a flower stall at Waterloo Station*; *we wandered round the market looking at the fruit stalls*

(b) stalls = seats on the ground floor in a theatre or cinema; *seats in the stalls are expensive, let's get tickets for upstairs*; *see also* ORCHESTRA

(c) separate section for one animal in a building such as a stable; *each horse had its own stall with its name on it*

(d) (choir) stalls = rows of seats for the choir in a church

2 *verb*

(a) *(informal)* to put off answering a question, making a decision, etc.; *have they got genuine doubts about the plan or are they simply stalling?*

(b) *(of a car engine)* to stop, often when trying to drive off; *if he takes his foot off the pedal, the engine stalls*; *the car stalled at the traffic lights and he couldn't start it again*

(c) *(of an aircraft)* to go so slowly that the engine stops and it falls

① **stamp**
[stæmp]
1 *noun*

(a) little piece of paper with a price printed on it which you stick on a letter, postcard, etc., to show that you have paid for it to be sent by the post; *you need a 27p stamp for that letter*; *she forgot to put a stamp on the letter before she posted it*; *he wants to show me his stamp collection*

(b) machine for making a mark on something; *we have a stamp for marking invoices when they come into the office*; **date stamp** = device with rubber numbers which can be moved, used for marking the date on documents or on food for sale

(c) mark made on something; *the invoice has the stamp 'received with thanks' on it*; *the customs officer looked at the stamps in his passport*

2 *verb*

(a) to stick a stamp on a letter or parcel; *all the envelopes need to be sealed and stamped*

(b) to mark something with a stamp; *they stamped my passport when I entered the country*

(c) to walk in a heavy way, banging your feet on the ground; *they stamped on the insects to kill them*; *he was so angry that he stamped out of the room*

(d) to make a noise by banging your feet on the ground; *the audience stamped on the floor in time to the music*

③ **stamp out**
['stæmp 'aut] *verb*

to stop or to remove; *the police are trying to stamp out corruption*

① **stand**
[stænd]
1 *verb*

(a) to be upright on your feet, the opposite of sitting or lying down; *she stood on a chair to reach the top shelf*; *they were so tired they could hardly keep standing*; *if there are no seats left, we'll have to stand*; *don't just stand there doing nothing - come and help us*

(b) to be upright; *only a few houses were still standing after the earthquake*; *the jar was standing in the middle of the table*

(c) to get up from a seat; *she stood and rushed to the door*

(d) to put upright; *stand the lamp over in the corner*; *he stood the pot on the table*

(e) to tolerate, to put up with; *the office is filthy - I don't know how you can stand working here*; *she can't stand all this noise*; *he stopped going to French lessons because he couldn't stand the teacher*

(f) to stand for election = to offer yourself as a candidate in an election; *he has stood for parliament several times but has never been elected*; **to stand against someone** = to put yourself against someone in an election; *she is standing against the leader in the election*

(g) to pay for; *he stood us all a round of drinks*
(NOTE: **standing - stood** [stud])

2 *noun*

(a) seats where you sit to watch a football match, etc.; *the stands were full for the international*; *we have tickets for the North Stand*

(b) something which holds something up; *the pot of flowers fell off its stand*

(c) display stand = special set of shelves for displaying goods for sale; **exhibition stand** = separate section of an exhibition where a company shows its products or services; *we must book a bigger stand next year - this one is too small* (NOTE: the American English for this is a **booth**); **news stand** = small wooden shelter on a pavement, used for selling newspapers

(d) position; *his stand against the party leader earned him a term in prison*; *she was criticized for her stand against government policy*; **to take a stand against** = to protest against; *they are taking a strong stand against corruption in the party*

(e) *US* **witness stand** = place in a courtroom where the witnesses give evidence (NOTE: British English is usually **witness box**)

② **standard**
['stændɪd]
1 *noun*

(a) the level of quality achieved by something; *the standard of service in this restaurant is very high*; *this piece of work is not up to your usual standard*

(b) excellent quality which is set as a target; *this product does not meet our standards*; *she has set a standard which it will be difficult to match*; **standard of living** *or* **living standards** = quality of personal home life (such as amount of food or clothes bought, size of the family car, etc.); *they can't complain about their standard of living, they're really quite well off*

(c) tree or bush grown with a tall trunk; *do you prefer an ordinary rose bush or a standard?*

(d) large official flag; *the royal standard flies over Buckingham Palace*

2 *adjective*

(a) usual, normal; *she joined on a standard contract*; *you will need to follow the standard procedure to join the association*; **standard authors** = the main classical authors, the authors that everyone usually has to study; **standard pronunciation** = pronunciation of educated speakers; **standard rate** = normal charge for something, such as a phone call or income tax; *the standard rate of income tax is 20p in the pound*; **standard work** = book which is the recognized authority on a subject; *he's the author of the standard work on mountain birds*

(b) on a tall pole; **standard lamp** = room lamp on a tall pole standing on the floor (NOTE: American English is **floor lamp**); **standard rose** = rose grown with a tall stem

(c) standard time = time which applies everywhere within a certain area of the world

③ **stand around**
['stænd ə'raʊnd] *verb*
to stand, and not do anything; *they just stood around and watched us working*

③ **stand aside**
['stænd ə'saɪd] *verb*
to step to one side; *we stood aside to let the ambulance crew pass*

③ **stand back**
['stænd 'bæk] *verb*
to take a step or two backwards; *stand well back, the marathon runners are coming*

③ **stand by**
['stænd 'baɪ] *verb*
(a) to confirm, to refuse to change; *I stand by what I said in my statement to the police*
(b) to stand and watch, without getting involved; *several people just stood by and made no attempt to help*
(c) to be ready; *we have several fire engines standing by*
(d) to support, to give help; *she stood by him while he was in prison*

③ **stand down**
['stænd 'daʊn] *verb*
to agree not to stay in a position or not to stand for election; *the mayor decided to stand down after several years in office*

① **stand for**
['stænd 'fɔː] *verb*
(a) to have a meaning; *what do the letters BBC stand for?*
(b) to be a candidate in an election; *she's standing for parliament*
(c) to accept; *they will never stand for that*; *I won't stand for any naughty behaviour from the children*

③ **stand in for**
['stænd 'ɪn fɔː] *verb*
to take the place of someone; *she's standing in for the chairman who is ill*

④ **standing**
['stændɪŋ]
1 *adjective*

(a) upright, not lying or sitting; *after the earthquake, the few buildings left standing needed to be repaired*

(b) permanent; *we have a standing agreement with our supplier to send back items we don't want*; **standing order** = order written by a customer asking a bank to pay money regularly to an account, or to a company to send something regularly; *I pay my subscription by standing order*; *we have a standing order for two dozen eggs every Friday*; **it is a standing joke with us** = it is something we always make jokes about; *his style of dancing is a bit of a standing joke with us*

2 *noun*

(a) being upright on your feet; *standing all day at the exhibition is very tiring*

(b) good reputation; *his standing in the community has never been higher*; *a hotel of good standing*

(c) **long-standing customer** or **customer of long standing** = person who has been a customer for many years

① **stand out**
['stænd 'aʊt] verb

(a) to be easily seen; *their house stands out because it is painted pink*; *her red hair makes her stand out in a crowd*

(b) to be very clear against a background; *that picture would stand out better against a white wall*

(c) to be much better than others; *two of the young musicians stood out for their interpretations of Bach*

① **stand up**
['stænd 'ʌp] verb

(a) to get up from sitting; *when the teacher comes into the room all the children should stand up*; *he stood up to offer his seat to the old lady*

(b) to stand upright, to hold yourself upright; *stand up straight and face forward*

(c) to put something in an upright position; *stand the books up on the shelf*; *she stood her umbrella up by the door*

(d) (informal) to stand someone up = not to meet someone even though you had arranged to; *we were going to have dinner together and he stood me up*

③ **stand up for**
['stænd 'ʌp fɔː] verb

to try to defend someone or something in an argument; *he stood up for the rights of the small shopkeepers*; *no one stood up for her when she was sacked*

③ **stank**
[stæŋk] see STINK

④ **staple**
['steɪpl]

1 noun

(a) piece of wire which is pushed through papers and bent over to hold them together; *he used some scissors to take the staples out of the papers*

(b) main food in a diet; *rice is the staple of the Chinese diet*

2 adjective

main; **staple product** = main product of a country, town, etc.; *corn is the staple crop of several American states*; **staple diet** = main part of what you eat; *rice with fish is the staple diet of many people in the Far East*

3 verb

to fasten papers together with a staple or with staples; *don't staple the cheque to the order form*; **to staple papers together** = to attach various papers with a staple or with staples; *all these papers need to be stapled together and filed*

④ **stapler**
['steɪplɪ] noun

little device used to attach papers together with staples; *the stapler has run out of staples*

② **star**
[stɑː]

1 noun

(a) bright object which can be seen in the sky at night like a very small bright light; *on a clear night you can see thousands of stars*; *the pole star shows the direction of the North Pole*

(b) famous person who is very well known to the public; *who is your favourite film star?*; *the film has an all-star cast*; *the Chelsea football star*

(c) **star sign** = the sign of the stars and planets which marks your birth; (informal) **thank your lucky stars** = consider yourself very lucky; *thank your lucky stars that you were not on that plane*

(d) shape that has several points like a star; *draw a big star and colour it red*

(e) a printing symbol shaped like a star; *a star next to a word refers you to the notes at the bottom of the page*

(f) classification sign for hotels, restaurants, etc.; **three-star hotel** = hotel which has been classified with three stars, under a classification system; *we stayed in a two-star hotel and found it perfectly comfortable*

2 verb

(a) to appear as a main character in a film or play; *she starred in 'Gone with the Wind'*; *he has a starring role in the new production of 'Guys and Dolls'*

(b) to mark a text with a star; *read the starred instructions carefully* (NOTE: **starring - starred**)

② **stare**
[steɪ]

1 verb

(a) to look at someone or something for a long time; *she stared sadly out of the window at the rain*

(b) (informal) **to stare someone in the face** = to be very obvious; *he couldn't find the answer even if it was staring him in the face*

2 noun

long fixed look; *he gave her a stare and walked on*

② **start**
[stɑːt]

1 verb

(a) to begin to do something; *the babies all started to cry* or *all started crying at the same time*; *he started to eat* or *he started eating his dinner before the rest of the family*; *take an umbrella - it's starting to rain*; *when you learn Russian, you have to start by learning the alphabet*; *we must start packing now or we'll miss the plane*; *at what time does the match start?*; **to start with** = first of all; *we have lots to do but to start with we'll do the washing up*

(b) to leave on a journey; *we plan to start at 6 o'clock*

(c) *(of a machine)* to begin to work; *the car won't start - the battery must be flat; the engine started at my first attempt*

(d) to make something begin to work; *I can't start the car; it is difficult to start a car in cold weather*

(e) to make something begin; *he fired a gun to start the race; the police think that the fire was started deliberately*

(f) to jump with surprise; *she started when she heard the bang*

1 *noun*

(a) beginning of something; *building the house took only six months from start to finish; things went wrong from the start; let's forget all you've done up to now, and make a fresh start; for a start = as the first point; for a start, tell me the exact time when you made the phone call*

(b) leaving for a journey; *we're planning on a 6 o'clock start; let's make an early start tomorrow = let's leave early*

(c) place where a race begins; *the cars were lined up at the start*

(d) being in advance of other competitors; *we'll never catch them, they have three hours' start on us; I'll give you four metre's start*

(e) sudden jump of surprise; *she gave a start when he put his hand on her shoulder*

③ **starter**

['stɑːtɪ] *noun*

(a) *(informal)* first part of a meal; *what do you all want as starters?; I don't want a starter - just the main course*

(b) person who starts doing something; *there were sixty starters in the race, but only twenty finished*

(c) person who organizes the start of something; *the starter fired a gun and the race started;* **under starter's orders** = ready to run just before the start

(d) starter (motor) = electric motor in a car which sets the main engine going; *your battery's OK, so maybe the starter isn't working*

④ **startle**

['stɑːtl] *verb*

to make someone suddenly surprised; *I'm sorry, I didn't mean to startle you; she looked up startled when she heard the knock at the door; we were all startled to hear about his getting married*

④ **startling**

['stɑːtlɪŋ] *adjective*

suddenly surprising; *everyone was talking about the startling election results*

② **start off**

['stɑːt 'ɒf] *verb*

(a) to begin; *we'll start off with soup and then have a meat dish*

(b) to leave on a journey; *you can start off now, and I'll follow when I'm ready*

② **start out**

['stɑːt 'aʊt] *verb*

(a) to leave on a journey; *she started out for home two hours ago, so I am surprised she hasn't arrived*

(b) to begin; *I'd like to start out by saying how pleased I am to be here*

② **start up**

['stɑːt 'ʌp] *verb*

(a) to make a business begin to work; *she started up a restaurant, but it failed*

(b) to make an engine start to work; *he started up the truck; from here you can hear the noise of the racing cars starting up*

④ **starvation**

[stɑːˈveɪʃn] *noun*

lack of food which results in illness; *people are dying of starvation in parts of Africa*

③ **starve**

[stɑːv] *verb*

(a) not to have enough food; *many people starved to death in the desert*

(b) to starve someone of something = not to give enough supplies to someone; *the health service is being starved of funds*

② **state**

[steɪt]

1 *noun*

(a) condition (often a bad condition), the way something or someone is; *the children are in a state of excitement; they left the house in a terrible state; look at the state of your trousers; she's not in a fit state to receive visitors*

(b) condition where you are depressed, worried, etc.; *she's in such a state that I don't want to leave her alone; he was in a terrible state after the phone call*

(c) state of health = being well or sick; *his state of health has improved with treatment;* **state of mind** = a person's feelings at a particular time; *he's in a very miserable state of mind; in her present state of mind she's unlikely to be able to decide what to do*

(d) government of a country; *we all pay taxes to the state; the state should pay for the museums;* **state-owned** = owned by the country or government and not by private individuals

(e) independent country; *the member states of the European Union;* **head of state** = official leader of a country, though not necessarily the head of the government

(f) one of the parts of a federal country; *the State of Arizona; New South Wales has the largest population of all the Australian states; see also* UNITED STATES OF AMERICA

2 *adjective*

referring to the state; **state enterprise** = company run by the state

3 *verb*

to give information clearly; *please state your name and address*; *it states in the instructions that you must not open the can near a flame*; *the document states that all revenue has to be declared to the tax office*

① **statement**
['steɪtmɪnt] *noun*

(a) clearly written or spoken description of what happened; *she made a statement to the police*

(b) list of invoices and credits and debits sent by a supplier to a customer at the end of each month; *I want to query something in last month's statement*; **bank statement** = written document from a bank showing the balance of an account; **monthly** *or* **quarterly statement** = statement which is sent every month *or* every quarter

③ **States**
['steɪts] *noun*

(informal) the United States of America; *we've lost touch with him now that he's gone to live in the States*; *they hitched their way across the States*

④ **statesman**
['steɪtsmɪn] *noun*

important political leader or representative of a country; *a meeting of world statesmen to agree to a nuclear test ban treaty* (NOTE: plural is **statesmen**)

① **station**
['steɪʃn] *noun*

(a) (railway) **station** = place where trains stop, where passengers get on or off, etc.; *the train leaves the Central Station at 14.15*; *this is a fast train - it doesn't stop at every station*; *we'll try to get something to eat at the station sandwich bar*

(b) bus station *or* **coach station** = place where coaches or buses begin or end their journeys; *coaches leave Victoria Coach Station for all parts of the country*; **underground station** *or* **tube station** = place where underground trains stop, where passengers get on or off; *there's an underground station just a few minutes' walk away*

(c) large main building for a service; *the fire station is just down the road from us*; *he was arrested and taken to the local police station*; **power station** = factory which produces electricity; *the power station chimneys can be seen from across the river*; **service station** = garage which sells petrol and repairs cars; *luckily I broke down right outside a service station*; **TV station** *or* **radio station** = building where TV or radio programmes are broadcast; *the station broadcasts hourly reports on snow conditions*

(d) (*in Australia*) **sheep station** = very large farm, specializing in raising sheep

2 *verb*

to place someone officially in a place; *soldiers were stationed in the border towns*; *police were stationed all along the route of the procession*

④ **stationary**
['steɪʃnri] *adjective*

not moving, standing still; *he collided with a stationary vehicle*; *traffic is stationary for six kilometres on the motorway into London* (NOTE: do not confuse with **stationery**)

④ **stationery**
['steɪʃnri] *noun*

materials used when writing, such as paper, envelopes, pens, ink, etc.; *the letter was typed on his office stationery* (NOTE: no plural; do not confuse with **stationary**)

③ **station wagon**
['steɪʃn 'wægɪn] *noun*

US large car with a flat space behind the seats where parcels or suitcases can be put (NOTE: British English for this is an **estate car**)

② **statistics**
[stɪ'tɪstɪks] *noun*

facts given in the form of figures; *we examined the sales statistics for the previous six months*; *government statistics show an increase in heart disease*

④ **statue**
['stætʃuː] *noun*

figure of a person or animal carved from stone, made from metal, etc.; *the statue of King John is in the centre of the square*

② **status**
['steɪtɪs] *noun*

(a) general position; **status inquiry** = check on a customer's credit rating; **legal status** = legal position

(b) social importance when compared to other people; *he has a low-status job on the Underground*; *his status in the company has been rising steadily*; **status symbol** = thing which you use which shows that you are more important than someone else; **the chairman's car is a just status symbol** = the size of his car shows how important he or his company is; **loss of status** = becoming less important in a group (NOTE: no plural)

④ **statutory**
['stætʃutri] *adjective*

imposed by law; *there is a statutory period of thirteen weeks before new employees are given permanent jobs*; **statutory holiday** = holiday which is fixed by law; **statutory sick pay** = payment made each week by an employer to an employee who is away from work because of sickness

① **stay**
[steɪ]

1 *verb*

(a) to remain, not to change; *the temperature stayed below zero all day*; *in spite of the fire, he stayed calm*; *I won't be able to stay awake until midnight*

(b) to stop in a place; *they came for lunch and stayed until after midnight; I'm rather tired so I'll stay at home tomorrow; he's ill and has to stay in bed*

(c) to stop in a place as a visitor; *they stayed two nights in Edinburgh on their tour of Scotland; where will you be staying when you're in New York?; my parents are staying at the Hotel London*

2 *noun*

(a) time during which you live in a place; *my sister's here for a short stay; did you enjoy your stay in London?*

(b) stay of execution = delay in putting a legal order into effect; *the judge granted a stay of execution*

③ **stay away**
['steɪ ə'weɪ] *verb*
not to come or go to something; *she doesn't like parties, and stayed away; many voters are bored with elections and stayed away from the polls*

③ **stay in**
['steɪ 'ɪn] *verb*
to stop at home instead of going out; *we prefer to stay in rather than go and queue for hours to get into the cinema*

③ **stay out**
['steɪ 'aut] *verb*
to remain away from home; *the girls stayed out until two o'clock in the morning*

③ **stay put**
[s'teɪ 'put] *phrase*
to stay where you are, not to move; *I'm not going to resign - I'm staying put!; stay put! - I'll go and get a doctor*

③ **stay up**
['steɪ 'ʌp] *verb*
not to go to bed; *we stayed up late to see the New Year in; little children are not supposed to stay up until midnight watching TV*

④ **steadily**
['stedɪlɪ] *adverb*
not changing; regularly or continuously; *things have been steadily going from bad to worse; sales have increased steadily over the last two years*

③ **steady**
['stedɪ]
1 *adjective*
(a) firm, not moving or shaking; *you need a steady hand to draw a straight line without a ruler; he put a piece of paper under the table leg to keep it steady*
(b) continuing in a regular way; *there is a steady demand for computers; the car was doing a steady seventy miles an hour; she hasn't got a steady boyfriend* (NOTE: steadier - steadiest)
2 *interjection*
(a) *(starting a race)* ready! steady! go!
(b) steady on! = be careful; *steady on! - you almost hit that car*

3 *verb*
(a) to calm; *she took a pill to steady her nerves*
(b) to keep firm; *he put out his hand to steady the ladder*

④ **steak**
[steɪk] *noun*
(a) thick slice of beef; *he ordered steak and chips; I'm going to grill these steaks*
(b) thick slice cut across the body of a big fish; *a grilled salmon steak for me, please!* (NOTE: do not confuse with **stake**)

③ **steal**
[stiːl] *verb*
(a) to take something which belongs to another person; *someone tried to steal my handbag; she owned up to having stolen the jewels; did the burglar steal all your CDs? - I'm afraid so; he was arrested for stealing, but the judge let him off with a fine*
(b) to steal the show = to do better than a star actor; *it was the little dog that stole the show; see also* THUNDER
(c) to move quietly; *he stole into the office and tried to find the safe*; to steal away = to go away very quietly; *he stole away under cover of darkness*; to steal a glance at = to look at quickly and secretly at; *while the boss wasn't looking she stole a glance at the papers on his desk* (NOTE: stealing - stole [stəʊl] - stolen ['stəʊlɪn] ; do not confuse with **steel**)

③ **steam**
[stiːm]
1 *noun*
(a) moisture which comes off hot or boiling water; *clouds of steam were coming out of the kitchen*; steam engine = engine which runs on pressure from steam
(b) *(informal)* to let off steam = to get rid of energy by doing something vigorous; *we sent the children out to play football in the garden to let off steam*
2 *verb*
(a) to send off steam; *the kettle is steaming - the water must be boiling*
(b) to cook over a pan of boiling water by allowing the steam to pass through holes in a container with food in it; *how are you going to cook the fish? - I'll steam it*
(c) to move by steam power; *the ship steamed out of the harbour*
(d) to go fast in a certain direction; *we were steaming along at 70 miles an hour when we had a flat tyre*

② **steel**
[stiːl]
1 *noun*
strong metal made from iron and carbon; *steel knives are best for the kitchen; the door is made of solid steel*; steel band = band which plays West Indian music on steel drums of different sizes which make different notes; *we spent the*

evening dancing to music from a steel band; **steel grey** = the colour of steel; *steel grey will be fashionable next winter*
2 *verb*
to steel yourself to do something = to get ready to do something which is going to be unpleasant; *he steeled himself for a very awkward interview with the police* (NOTE: do not confuse with **steal**)

③ **steep**
[stiːp]
1 *adjective*
(a) which rises or falls sharply; *the car climbed the steep hill with some difficulty*; *the steps up the church tower are steeper than our stairs at home*
(b) very sharp increase or fall; *a steep increase in interest charges*; *a steep fall in share prices*
(c) *(informal)* too much; *their prices are a bit steep*; *that's a bit steep! - I was trying to help you* (NOTE: **steeper - steepest**)
2 *verb*
(a) to soak in a liquid; *leave the clothes to steep in soap and water to get the stains out*
(b) to soak in a liquid to absorb its flavour; *the meat must steep in red wine and herbs for 24 hours*
(c) steeped in history = full of history, where many historical events have taken place; *Windsor Castle is steeped in history*

④ **steer**
[ˈstɪɪ] *verb*
(a) to make a car, a ship, etc., go in a certain direction; *she steered the car into a ditch*; *the pilot steered the ship into harbour*
(b) to steer clear of = to avoid; *I steer clear of fat food*

③ **steering wheel**
[ˈstiːrɪŋ ˈwiːl] *noun*
wheel which is turned by the driver to control the direction in which a vehicle travels; *in British cars the steering wheel is on the right-hand side*

④ **stem**
[stem]
1 *noun*
(a) stalk, the tall thin part of a plant which holds a leaf, a flower, a fruit, etc.; *trim the stems before you put the flowers in water*
(b) main stalk of a plant or tree; *a standard rose bush with a tall stem*
(c) part of a wine glass like a column; *wine glasses with coloured stems*
(d) from stem to stern = from the front of a boat to the back; *the boat was packed from stem to stern with tourists*
2 *verb*
(a) to stem from = to be caused by; *his health problems stem from an infection*
(b) to try to prevent something flowing or spreading; *first, try to stem the flow of blood*; *the police are trying to stem the rising tide of crime* (NOTE: **stemming - stemmed**)

② **step**
[step]
1 *noun*
(a) movement of your foot when walking; *I wonder when the baby will take his first steps*; *take a step sideways and you will be able to see the castle*
(b) to take one step forward and two steps back = not to advance very quickly; **step by step** = gradually, a little at a time; *it's better to introduce the changes step by step*; *the book takes you step by step through French grammar*
(c) regular movement of feet at the same time as other people; **in step** = moving your feet at the same rate as everybody else; **out of step** = moving your feet at a different rate from everybody else; *I tried to keep in step with him as we walked along*; *the recruits can't even march in step*; *one of the squad always gets out of step*; **in step with something** = at the same rate or speed as something; *house prices have risen in step with salaries*; **out of step with something** = moving at a different rate or speed from something; *wages have got out of step with the rise in the cost of living*
(d) the sound made by a foot touching the ground; *we heard soft steps outside our bedroom door*; *I can always recognize your father's step*
(e) one stair, which goes up or down; *there are two steps down into the kitchen*; *I counted 75 steps to the top of the tower*; *be careful, there's a step up into the bathroom*
(f) one thing which is done or has to be done out of several; *the first and most important step is to find out how much money we can spend*; **to take steps to prevent something happening** = to act to stop something happening; *the museum must take steps to make sure that nothing else is stolen*
2 *verb*
to move forwards, backwards, etc., on foot; *he stepped out in front of a bicycle and was knocked down*; *she stepped off the bus into a pool of water*; *don't step back, there's a child behind you*; **to step on the brakes** = to push the brake pedal hard; *(informal) US* **to step on the gas** = to drive faster; *step on the gas - we'll miss the train!*; *(informal)* **step on it!** = hurry up! (NOTE: **stepping - has stepped**)

③ **step in**
[ˈstep ˈɪn] *verb*
(a) to enter; *please step in and see what we have to offer*
(b) to do something in an area where you were not involved before; *everything was working fine until the manager stepped in*; *fortunately a teacher stepped in to break up the fight*

③ **stereo**
[ˈsteriɪʊ]
1 *adjective*
= STEREOPHONIC; *a stereo disk*

2 *noun*

(a) machine which reproduces sound through two different loudspeakers or headphones; *I bought a new pair of speakers for my stereo*; **personal stereo** = small stereo set which you can carry around and listen to as you walk; *she was listening to her personal stereo as she was jogging*

(b) in stereo = using two speakers to give an impression of depth of sound; **car stereo** = system in a car which reproduces sound in stereo

③ **stereophonic**

[sterɪɪˈfɒnɪk] *adjective*

referring to sound which comes through from two different channels and loudspeakers

④ **stereotype**

[ˈsterɪɪtaɪp] *noun*

typical sort of person; *he fits the stereotype of the mad professor*

④ **sterling**

[ˈstɜːlɪŋ]

1 *noun*

British currency; *the prices are quoted in sterling*; **the pound sterling** = official term for the British currency

2 *adjective*

(a) sterling silver = silver which has been tested to show that it has a standard high quality; *we gave her six sterling silver spoons*

(b) of a certain standard, especially of good quality; *she has many sterling qualities*; *this old coat has done sterling service over the years*

④ **stern**

[stɜːn]

1 *adjective*

serious and strict; *the judge addressed some stern words to the boys* (NOTE: **sterner - sternest)**

2 *noun*

back part of a ship; *the stern of the ship was damaged*; *see also* STEM (NOTE: the front part is the **bow)**

④ **steward**

[ˈstjuːɪd] *noun*

(a) man who looks after passengers, and serves meals or drinks on a ship, aircraft, train, or in a club; *the steward served us tea on deck*

(b) shop steward = elected trade union representative who reports workers' complaints to the management; *most of the shop stewards favour strike action*

(c) person who organizes public events such as horse races, etc.; *the stewards will inspect the course to see if the race can go ahead*

④ **stewardess**

[stjuːɪˈdes] *noun*

woman who looks after passengers and serves food and drinks on a ship or aircraft; *the stewardess demonstrated how to put on the life jacket* (NOTE: plural is **stewardesses)**

① **stick**

[stɪk]

1 *verb*

(a) to glue, to attach with glue; *can you stick the pieces of the cup together again?*; *she stuck the stamp on the letter*; *they stuck a poster on the door*

(b) to be fixed or not to be able to move; *the car was stuck in the mud*; *the door sticks - you need to push it hard to open it*; *he was stuck in Italy without any money*

(c) to push something into something; *he stuck his hand into the hole*; *she stuck her finger in the jam to taste it*; *she stuck the ticket into her bag*; *she stuck a needle into her finger*

(d) to stay in a place; *stick close to your mother and you won't get lost*; **to stick together** = to stay together; *if we stick together they should let us into the club*; **to stick to your guns** = to keep to your point of view even if everyone says you are wrong

(e) *(informal)* to bear, to put up with; *I don't know how she can stick working in that office*; *I'm going, I can't stick it here any longer* (NOTE: **sticking - stuck** [stʌk])

2 *noun*

(a) thin piece of wood, thin branch of a tree; *he pushed the pointed stick into a hole*; *I need a strong stick to tie this plant to*; *see also* WRONG

(b) (walking) stick = strong piece of wood with a handle used as a support when walking; *since she had the accident she gets around on two sticks*; *at last mother has agreed to use a walking stick*

(c) a hockey stick = curved piece of wood for playing hockey

(d) anything long and thin; *a stick of rock*; *a stick of chewing gum*

③ **sticker**

[ˈstɪkɪ] *noun*

small piece of paper or plastic which you can stick on something to show a price, as a decoration or to advertise something; *the salesman charged me more than the price on the sticker*; *she stuck stickers all over the doors of her wardrobe*; **airmail sticker** = blue sticker with the words 'air mail', which can be stuck on an envelope or parcel to show that it is to be sent by air

③ **sticking plaster**

[ˈstɪkɪŋ ˈplɑːstɪ] *noun*

small strip of cloth which can be stuck to the skin to cover a wound; *I want a piece of sticking plaster to put on my heel* (NOTE: American English calls this by a trade name: **BandAid)**

① **stick out**

[ˈstɪk ˈaʊt] *verb*

(a) to push something out; **to stick your tongue out at someone** = to make a rude gesture by putting your tongue out of your mouth as far as it will go; *that little girl stuck out her tongue at me!*

(b) to be further forward or extended away from something; *your wallet is sticking out of your pocket; the roof sticks out over the path*

(c) *(informal)* **to stick out a mile** *or* **to stick out like a sore thumb** = to be easily seen; *their house sticks out a mile because it is painted pink*

③ **stick up**
['stɪk 'ʌp] *verb*

(a) to be further up above a surface or to extend beyond a surface; *the rack sticks up above the roof of the car*

(b) to put up a notice, etc.; *she stuck up a notice about the village flower festival*

(c) *(informal)* **stick 'em up!** = put your hands up!

(d) **to stick up for someone** *or* **something** = to defend someone *or* something against criticism; *he stuck up for his rights and in the end won the case; will you stick up for me if I get into trouble at school?*

③ **sticky**
['stɪkɪ] *adjective*

(a) covered with something which sticks like glue; *my fingers are all sticky; this stuff is terribly sticky - I can't get it off my fingers*

(b) with glue on one side so that it sticks easily; **sticky label** = label with sticky glue on one side which you can stick without licking; **sticky tape** = plastic strip with glue on one side, used to stick things together, etc.; *she did the parcel up carefully with sticky tape*

(c) *(informal)* difficult or embarrassing; *I'm in a rather sticky situation here;* **he came to a sticky end** = he was put in prison, was ruined, killed, etc.; *see also* WICKET (NOTE: **stickier - stickiest**)

③ **stiff**
[stɪf]

1 *adjective*

(a) which does not move easily; *the lock is very stiff - I can't turn the key; I've got a stiff neck; she was feeling stiff all over after running in the race*

(b) *(brush)* hard; *you need a stiff brush to get the mud off your shoes*

(c) **bored stiff** = very bored; *he talked on and on until we were all bored stiff; I'm bored stiff with sitting indoors, watching the rain come down*

(d) difficult; *he had to take a stiff test before he qualified*

(e) formal, not friendly; *his attitude was very stiff towards her*

(f) strong, not weak; *they face stiff competition; a stiff breeze was blowing across the bay; his book received some stiff criticism in the press;* **stiff drink** = alcoholic drink with very little water added (NOTE: **stiffer - stiffest**)

2 *noun*

US (informal) dead body; *someone called to say there was a stiff on the sidewalk*

① **still**
[stɪl]

1 *adjective*

(a) not moving; *stand still while I take the photo; if you want to see the rabbits keep still and don't make any noise; there was no wind, and the surface of the lake was completely still*

(b) *(of drinks)* not fizzy; *can I have a glass of still mineral water, please?*

2 *adverb*

(a) continuing until now; which continued until then; *I thought he had left, but I see he's still there; they came for lunch and were still sitting at the table at eight o'clock in the evening; weeks afterwards, they're still talking about the accident*

(b) *(with comparative)* *we've had a cold autumn, but they expect the winter will be colder still;* **still more** = even more; *there were at least twenty thousand people in the football stadium and still more queuing to get in*

(c) in spite of everything; *it wasn't sunny for the picnic - still, it didn't rain; he still insisted on going on holiday even though he had broken his leg*

④ **stimulate**
['stɪmjʊleɪt] *verb*

to encourage someone or an organ to be more active; *we want to stimulate trade with the Middle East; I'm trying to stimulate the students; this drug stimulates the heart*

④ **stimulus**
['stɪmjʊlɪs] *noun*

thing that encourages someone *or* something to greater activity; *what sort of stimulus is needed to get the tourist trade moving?; a nerve which responds to stimuli* (NOTE: plural is **stimuli** ['stɪmjʊlaɪ])

④ **sting**
[stɪŋ]

1 *noun*

(a) wound made by an insect or plant; *bee stings can be very painful; have you anything for wasp stings?*

(b) tiny needle, part of an insect or plant which injects poison into your skin; *he pulled out the sting which was stuck in her arm*

2 *verb*

(a) to wound with an insect's or plant's sting; *I've been stung by a wasp; she walked bare-legged through the wood and got stung by nettles; see also* NETTLE

(b) to give a burning feeling; *the antiseptic may sting a little at first*

(c) *(informal)* **to sting someone (for)** = to charge someone a lot of money; *he was stung for parking on a yellow line; they stung me for £100* (NOTE: **stinging - stung** [stʌŋ])

③ **stink**
[stɪŋk]
1 *noun*
(a) very nasty smell; *there's a terrible stink in the kitchen*
(b) *(informal)* **to create** *or* **make** *or* **kick up** *or* **raise a stink about something** = to complain vigorously about something; *the neighbours will kick up a stink if you damage their fence*
2 *verb*
(a) to make a nasty smell; *the office stinks of gas*
(b) *(informal)* to seem to be dishonest; *the whole affair stinks* (NOTE: **stank** [stæŋk] - **stunk** [stʌŋk])

③ **stir**
[stɜː]
1 *noun*
(a) action of mixing the ingredients of something, or something which is cooking; *add the sugar and give the mixture a stir; you should give the sauce a stir from time to time*
(b) excitement; *the exhibition caused a stir in the art world*
2 *verb*
(a) to move a liquid or powder or something which is cooking, to mix it up; *he was stirring the sugar into his coffee; keep stirring the sauce, or it will stick to the bottom of the pan of the pan*
(b) to move about; *the baby slept quietly without stirring; I didn't stir from my desk all day*
(c) to stir someone to do something = to make someone feel that they ought to do something; *we must try to stir the committee into action* (NOTE: **stirring - stirred**)

③ **stir up**
['stɜː 'ʌp] *verb*
to stir up trouble = to cause trouble; *the fans came with the deliberate intention of stirring up trouble*

④ **stitch**
[stɪtʃ]
1 *noun*
(a) little loop of thread made with a needle in sewing or with knitting needles when knitting; *she uses very small stitches when sewing children's clothes; very fine wool will give you more stitches than in the pattern*
(b) *(informal)* clothes; *how can I go to the party - I haven't a stitch to wear;* **with not a stitch on** = completely naked; *I can't come now, I haven't a stitch on*
(c) small loop of thread used by a surgeon to attach the sides of a wound together to help it to heal; *she had three stitches in her arm; come back in ten days' time to have the stitches removed*
(d) sharp pain in the side of the body after you have been running; *I can't go any further - I've got a stitch*

(e) in stitches = laughing out loud; *his story about the school play had us all in stitches* (NOTE: plural is **stitches**)
2 *verb*
(a) to attach with a needle and thread; *she stitched the badge to his jacket*
(b) to sew the sides of a wound together; *after the operation, the surgeon stitched the wound; his finger was cut off in an accident and the surgeon tried to stitch it back on*

③ **stock**
[stɒk]
1 *noun*
(a) supply of something kept to use when needed; *I keep a stock of typing paper at home; our stocks of food are running low; the factory has large stocks of coal*
(b) quantities of goods for sale; **stock control** = making sure that enough stock is kept and that quantities and movements of stock are noted (NOTE: the word 'inventory' is used in American English where British English uses the word 'stock'. So, the British 'stock control' is 'inventory control' in American English)
(c) in stock = available in the shop or warehouse; *we hold 2,000 items in stock;* **out of stock** = not available in the shop or warehouse; *we are out of stock of this item or this item is out of stock;* **to take stock** = to count the items in a warehouse; *they take stock every evening after the store closes;* **to take stock of a situation** = to assess how bad a situation is; *we need to take stock of the situation and decide what to do next*
(d) investments in a company, represented by shares; **stocks and shares** = shares in ordinary companies; **government stocks** = government securities, bonds issued by a government (NOTE: in the UK, the term **stocks** is generally applied to government stocks and **shares** to shares of commercial companies. In the USA, shares in commercial corporations are usually called **stocks** while government stocks are called **bonds**. In practice, **shares** and **stocks** are terms that are used without always being precise, and this can lead to some confusion)
(e) liquid made from boiling bones, etc., in water, used as a base for soups and sauces; *fry the onions and pour in some chicken stock*
(f) on the stocks = being worked on; *she's finished writing one book and now has another on the stocks*
2 *verb*
to keep goods for sale in a warehouse or shop; *they don't stock this book; we try to stock the most popular colours*
3 *adjective*
normal, usually kept in a store; **stock size** = normal size; *we only carry shoes in stock sizes;* **stock argument** = argument which is frequently used; *she used the stock argument about higher salaries leading to fewer jobs*

① **Stock Exchange**
['stɒk ɪks'tʃeɪndʒ] *noun*

place where stocks and shares are bought and sold; *he works on the Stock Exchange; shares in the company are traded on the London Stock Exchange*

② **stockholder**
['stɒkhɪʊldɪ] *noun*

person who holds shares in a company; *the stockholders voted against the merger*

④ **stocking**
['stɒkɪŋ] *noun*

long light piece of women's clothing which covers all the leg and your foot; *she was wearing black shoes and stockings; the robbers wore stockings over their faces;* **Christmas stockings** = large coloured stockings, which children hang up by their beds or under the Christmas tree, and which are filled with presents on Christmas Eve; **stocking filler** = little gift which can be put into a Christmas stocking

③ **stock market**
['stɒk 'mɔːkɪt] *noun*

place where shares are bought and sold (i.e., a stock exchange); *the stock market crash of 1929;* **stock market value** = value of a company based on the current market price of its shares

③ **stock up with**
['stɒk 'ʌp wɪð] *verb*

to buy supplies for use in the future; *we'll stock up with food to last us over the holiday weekend*

③ **stole, stolen**
[stɪʊl or 'stɪʊlɪn] *see* STEAL

③ **stomach**
['stʌmɪk]

1 *noun*

(a) part of the inside of the body shaped like a bag, into which food passes after being swallowed; *I don't want anything to eat - my stomach's upset or I have a stomach upset; he has had stomach trouble for some time; his eyes were bigger than his stomach* = he took too much food and couldn't finish it

(b) the middle of the front of the body; *he had been kicked in the stomach*

2 *verb*

to put up with, to tolerate; *they left the meeting because they couldn't stomach any more arguments*

① **stone**
[stɪʊn]

1 *noun*

(a) very hard material, found in the ground, used for building; *all the houses in the town are built in the local grey stone; the stone carvings in the old church date from the 15th century; stone floors can be very cold* (NOTE: no plural in these meanings: **some stone, a piece of stone, a block of stone**)

(b) small piece of stone; *the children were playing at throwing stones into the pond; the beach isn't good for bathing as it's covered with very sharp stones*

(c) **precious stones** = stones, such as diamonds, which are rare and very valuable

(d) British measure of weight (= 14 pounds or 6.35 kilograms); *she's trying tried to lose weight and so far has lost a stone and a half; he weighs twelve stone ten (i.e. 12 stone 10 pounds)* (NOTE: no plural in this meaning: **he weighs ten stone;** note also that in the USA, human body weight is always given only in pounds)

(e) single hard seed inside a fruit; *count the cherry stones on the side of your plate*

2 *adverb*

completely; **stone cold** = very cold; *no wonder you're freezing, the radiators are stone cold;* **stone deaf** = completely deaf; *it's no use shouting - she's stone deaf;* US **stone broke** = with no money at all

① **stood**
[stʊd] *see* STAND

① **stop**
[stɒp]

1 *noun*

(a) end of something, especially of movement; *the police want to put a stop to car crimes;* **to come to a stop** *or* **to a full stop** = to stop moving; *the car rolled on without the driver, and finally came to a stop at the bottom of the hill; all the building work came to a stop when the money ran out*

(b) place where you break a journey; *we'll make a stop at the next service station*

(c) place where a bus or tram lets passengers get on or off; *we have been waiting at the bus stop for twenty minutes; there are six stops between here and Marble Arch*

(d) **full stop** = printed mark like a small dot, showing the end of a sentence or an abbreviation; *when reading, you should take a breath when you come to a full stop* (NOTE: American English is **period**); *see also* FULL STOP

(e) *(informal)* **to pull out all the stops** = to make every effort; *they pulled out all the stops to make sure the work was finished on time*

2 *verb*

(a) not to move any more; *the motorcycle didn't stop at the red lights; this train stops at all stations to London Waterloo; the people in the queue were very annoyed when the bus went past without stopping*

(b) to make something not move any more; *the policeman stopped the traffic to let the lorry back out of the garage; stop that boy! - he's stolen my purse*

(c) not to do something any more; *the office clock has stopped at 4.15; at last it stopped raining and we could go out; she spoke for two* hours without stopping; we all stopped work and went home; the restaurant stops serving meals at midnight

(d) **to stop someone** or **something (from) doing something** = to make someone or something not do something any more; the rain stopped us from having a picnic; how can the police stop people stealing cars?; can't you stop the children from making such a noise?; the builder couldn't stop the tap dripping

(e) to stay at a place for a short time; can you stop at the newsagent's on your way home and buy the evening paper?

(f) to stay as a visitor in a place; they stopped for a few days in Paris; I expect to stop in Rome for the weekend

(g) **to stop at nothing** = to do everything, whether good or bad, to succeed; he'll stop at nothing to get that job; **to stop short of doing something** = to stop just in time to avoid doing something; he stopped short of admitting he was guilty

(h) **to stop an account** = to stop supplying a customer until he has paid what he owes; **to stop a cheque** US **to stop payment on a check** = to ask a bank not to pay a cheque that you have written; **to stop someone's wages** = to take money out of someone's wages as a punishment; we stopped £25 from his pay because he was late (NOTE: **stopping - stopped**)

① **stop by**
['stɒp 'baɪ] verb
(informal) to visit someone for a short time; he said he might stop by on his way home

① **stop off**
['stɒp 'ɒf] verb
to stop for a time in a place before going on with your journey; we stopped off for a couple of nights in Dallas on our way to Mexico

① **stop up**
['stɒp 'ʌp] verb
(a) not to go to bed; we stopped up late to see the New Year in; I'm go to stop up to watch the golf on TV
(b) to block; he tried to stop up the hole in the pipe with some kind of cement

③ **storage**
['stɔːrɪdʒ] noun
(a) keeping in a store or warehouse; we put our furniture into storage; we don't have enough storage space in this house; **storage capacity** = space available for storage; **storage facilities** = equipment and buildings suitable for storage; **cold storage** = keeping food, etc., in a cold store to prevent it going bad; **to put a plan into cold storage** = to postpone work on a plan, usually for a very long time
(b) cost of keeping things in store; storage costs us 10% of the value of the items stored
(c) facility for storing data in a computer; a hard disk with a storage capacity of 200Mb

① **store**
[stɔː]
1 noun
(a) shop, usually a big shop; you can buy shoes in any of the big stores in town; does the store have a furniture department?; **department store** = large store, with different sections for different types of goods; **general store** = small (country) shop which sells a wide range of goods (NOTE: British English usually uses **shop** for small businesses; American English uses **store** for any kind of shop)
(b) supplies kept to use later; we keep a big store of coal for the winter; they bought stores for their journey
(c) place where goods are kept; the goods will be kept in store until they are needed; **cold store** = warehouse or room where supplies can be kept cold; **to be in store for someone** or **to have something in store for someone** = to be going to happen to someone; she's got a big surprise in store; we didn't know what would be in store for us when we surrendered to the enemy
2 verb
(a) to keep food, etc., to use later; we store (away) all our vegetables in the garden shed
(b) to put something in a warehouse for safe keeping; we stored our furniture while we were looking for a house to buy
(c) to keep something in a computer file; we store all our personnel records on computer

③ **storey** US **story**
['stɔːrɪ] noun
whole floor in a building; a twenty-storey office block; the upper storeys of the block caught fire

③ **storm**
[stɔːm]
1 noun
(a) high wind and very bad weather; several ships got into difficulties in the storm; how many trees were blown down in last night's storm?; March and October are the worst months for storms; **snowstorm** = storm when the wind blows and snow falls; **thunderstorm** = storm with rain, thunder and lightning; (informal) **storm in a teacup** = lot of fuss about something which is not important; **a storm of applause** = loud burst of cheering; a storm of applause greeted the orchestra
(b) **by storm** = (i) in a sudden rush or attack; (ii) with a great deal of excitement; the soldiers took the enemy castle by storm; the pop group has taken the town by storm
2 verb
(a) to rush about angrily; he stormed into the shop and demanded to see the manager; **to storm off** or **out** = to go away or out in anger; she stormed out of the meeting and called her lawyer
(b) to attack suddenly and capture; our troops stormed the enemy camp

④ **stormy**

['stɔːmɪ] *adjective*

(a) when there are storms; *they are forecasting stormy weather for the weekend*

(b) **stormy meeting** = meeting where there is a lot of argument (NOTE: **stormier - stormiest**)

② **story**

['stɔːrɪ] *noun*

(a) description that tells things that did not really happen but are invented by an author; *the book is the story of two children during the war*; *she writes children's stories about animals*

(b) description that tells what really happened; *she told her story to the journalist*; **it's a long story** = it is difficult to describe what happened

(c) lie, something which is not true; *nobody will believe such stories*

(d) *US* = STOREY (NOTE: plural is **stories**)

③ **stove**

[stəʊv] *noun*

apparatus for heating or cooking; *the shed is heated by an oil stove*; *the milk boiled over and made a mess on the kitchen stove* (NOTE: British English is also **cooker** for the cooking apparatus)

① **straight**

[streɪt]

1 *adjective*

(a) not curved; *Edgware Road is a long straight street*; *the line under the picture isn't straight*; *she has straight black hair*; *stand up straight!*

(b) not sloping; *is the picture straight?*; *the shelf should be perfectly straight but it slopes slightly to the left*; *your tie isn't straight*

(c) clear and simple; *I want you to give me a straight answer*; **a straight fight** = an election contest between two candidates only

(d) tidy; *can you get the room straight before the visitors arrive?*

(e) **to get something straight** = to understand clearly the meaning of something; *before you start, let's get this straight - you are not going to be paid for the work* (NOTE: **straighter - straightest**)

2 *adverb*

(a) going in a straight line, not curving; *the road goes straight across the plain for two hundred kilometres*; **to go straight on** *or* **to keep straight on** = to continue along this road without turning off it; *go straight on past the road junction and then turn left*; *keep straight on and you'll find the hospital just after the supermarket*; *the church is straight in front of you*

(b) immediately, at once; *wait for me here - I'll come straight back*; *if there is a problem, you should go straight to the manager*

(c) without stopping or changing; *she drank the milk straight out of the bottle*; *the cat ran straight across the road in front of the car*; *he looked me straight in the face*; *the plane flies straight to Washington*

(d) (alcohol) with no water or any other liquid added; *he drinks his whisky straight* (NOTE: British English also uses **neat** in this sense)

(e) *(informal)* **to go straight** = to stop committing crimes; *after he left prison he went straight for six or seven months*

3 *noun*

(on a racetrack) part of the track which is straight; *the runners are coming into the final straight*

④ **straighten**

['streɪtn] *verb*

(a) to make straight; *she had surgery to straighten her nose*; *he straightened his tie and went into the meeting*

(b) **to straighten up** = to stand straight after bending down; *he straightened up and looked at me*

③ **straightforward**

[streɪt'fɔːwəd] *adjective*

(a) honest and open; *she refused to give a straightforward answer*

(b) easy, not complicated; *if you follow the instructions carefully, it's quite a straightforward job*

③ **straight off**

['streɪt 'ɒf] *adverb*

immediately, at once; *I'll start straight off with the most important question*

③ **straight out**

['streɪt 'aʊt] *adverb*

directly, without hesitating; *she told him straight out that she didn't want to see him again*

④ **strain**

[streɪn]

1 *noun*

(a) nervous tension and stress; *can she stand the strain of working in that office?*

(b) condition where a muscle has been stretched or torn by a sudden movement; *she dropped out of the race with muscle strain*

(c) force of pulling something tight; *can that small rope take the strain of the boat?*

(d) **to put a strain on** = to make something more difficult; *the strong pound will put a strain on our exports*; *his drinking put a strain on their marriage*

(e) music, part of a tune; *they all sang to the strains of the guitar*

(f) variety, breed; *they are trying to find a cure for a new strain of the flu virus*; *he crossed two strains of rice to produce a variety which is resistant to disease*

2 *verb*

(a) to injure part of your body by pulling too hard; *he strained a muscle in his back* *or* *he strained his back*; *the effort strained his heart*

(b) to make great efforts to do something; *they strained to lift the piano into the van*

(c) to put pressure on something, to make something more difficult; *the mortgage repayments will strain our budget*; *the argument strained our relations*

(d) to pour liquid away, leaving any solids behind; *boil the peas for ten minutes and then strain*

④ **strand**
[strænd]
1 *noun*
one piece of hair, thread, etc.; *strands of hair kept blowing across her face*
2 *verb*
to leave someone *or* something alone and helpless; *her handbag was stolen and she was stranded without any money*; *the captain stranded the ship on a beach*

③ **stranded**
['strændɪd] *adjective*
alone and unable to move; *the tube strike left thousands of people stranded in central London*; *the airlines are trying to bring back thousands of stranded tourists*

② **strange**
[streɪnʒ] *adjective*
(a) not usual; *something is the matter with the engine - it's making a strange noise*; *she told some very strange stories about the firm she used to work for*; *it felt strange to be sitting in the office on a Saturday afternoon*; *it's strange that no one spotted the mistake*; *a strange-looking young man was with her*
(b) which you have never seen before or where you have never been before; *I find it difficult getting to sleep in a strange room*; *we went to Japan and had lots of strange food to eat*
(NOTE: **stranger - strangest**)

② **strangely**
['streɪnʒli] *adverb*
in a strange way; *your face seems strangely familiar, have we met before?*; *strangely enough, my birthday's on the same day as his*

③ **stranger**
['streɪnʒə] *noun*
(a) person whom you have never met; *I've never met him - he's a complete stranger to me*; *children are told not to accept lifts from strangers*
(b) person in a place where he has never been before; *I can't tell you how to get to the post office - I'm a stranger here myself*

④ **strap**
[stræp]
1 *noun*
long flat piece of material used to attach something; *can you do up the strap of my backpack for me?*; *I put a strap round my suitcase to make it more secure*
2 *verb*

(a) to fasten something with a strap; *he strapped on his oxygen cylinder*; *the patient was strapped to a stretcher*; *make sure the baby is strapped into her seat*
(b) to wrap a bandage tightly round a limb; *she strapped up his ankle and told him to lie down*
(NOTE: **strapping - strapped**)

③ **strategic** *or* **strategical**
[strɪ'tiːdʒɪkl] *adjective*
referring to strategy; **strategic advantage** = position which gives an advantage over the enemy; *breaking the enemy's secret code gave us an enormous strategic advantage*; **strategic planning** = planning the future work of an organization

② **strategy**
['strætɪdʒi] *noun*
planning of actions in advance; *their strategy is to note which of their rival's models sells best and then copy it*; *the government has no long-term strategy for dealing with crime*; **business strategy** = planning of how to develop your business

③ **straw**
[strɔː] *noun*
(a) dry stalks and leaves of crops left after the grain has been harvested; *you've been lying on the ground - you've got bits of straw in your hair*; *the farm workers picked up bundles of straw and loaded them onto a truck*
(b) thin plastic tube for sucking up liquids; *she was drinking orange juice through a straw*
(c) **straw poll** = rapid poll taken near voting day, to see how people intend to vote; *a straw poll of members of staff showed that most of them were going to vote for the council's plan*
(d) *(informal)* **the last straw** = the final and worst problem in a series; *the children had been ill one after another, but the last straw was when the eldest girl caught measles*; *that's the last straw = I can't stand any more of this*

③ **strawberry**
['strɔːbri] *noun*
common soft red summer fruit growing on low plants; *I picked some strawberries for dessert*; *a pot of strawberry jam* (NOTE: plural is **strawberries**)

④ **stray**
[streɪ]
1 *adjective*
(a) which is wandering away from home; *we found a stray cat and brought it home*
(b) not where it should be; *he was killed by a stray bullet from a gunman*
2 *verb*
to wander away; *the sheep strayed onto the golf course*; *the children had strayed too far onto the rocks and couldn't get back*
3 *noun*
animal which is lost and wandering far away from home; *we have two female cats at home and they attract all the strays in the district*

④ **streak**
[striːk]
1 *noun*

(a) line of colour; *she's had blonde streaks put in her hair*

(b) particularly characteristic type of behaviour; *she has a ruthless streak in her*; *it's his mean streak which makes him not buy any Christmas cards*

(c) streak of lightning = a flash of lightning

(d) period when a series of things happens; *I was on a winning streak, I won three times in a row*; *I hope our unlucky streak is coming to an end*; **a streak of luck** = a period when you are lucky; *his streak of luck continued as he won the lottery yet again*

2 *verb*

(a) to go very fast; *the rocket streaked across the sky*

(b) *(informal)* to run about naked in public

③ **stream**
[striːm]
1 *noun*

(a) little river; *can you jump across that stream?*

(b) things which pass continuously; *crossing the road is difficult because of the stream of traffic*; *we had a stream of customers on the first day of the sale*; *streams of refugees tried to cross the border*

(c) to come on stream = to start production; *output will be doubled when the new factory comes on stream*

2 *verb*

to flow continuously; *blood was streaming down his face*; *cars streamed out of the park*; *children streamed across the square*; **he has a streaming cold** = he has a cold where his nose is running all the time

① **street**
[striːt] *noun*

(a) road in a town, usually with houses on each side; *it is difficult to park in our street on Saturday mornings*; *her flat is on a noisy street*; *the school is in the next street*; **street map** *or* **street plan** = diagram showing the streets of a town, with their names; *you will need a street map to get round New York*

(b) *(used with names)* *what's your office address? - 16 Cambridge Street*; *Oxford Street, Bond Street and Regent Street are the main shopping areas in London* (NOTE: when used in names, **Oxford Street**, **Regent Street**, etc., it is usually written **St: Oxford St**)

(c) High Street = the main shopping street in a town; *his shop is on the High Street* (NOTE: the American English equivalent is **Main Street**)

(d) the man in the street = the ordinary person, who represents what most people think; *the government's message is not getting through to the man in the street*; *the man in the street isn't interested in Europe*

(e) at street level = at the same height as the street; *the main entrance is at street level*

(f) *(informal)* **streets ahead** = much more advanced or successful; *Japanese firms are streets ahead of us in computer technology*; *(informal)* **it's right up my street** = it's something I know a lot about and can do well; *you're the gardening expert - this job should be right up your street*

② **strength**
[streŋθ] *noun*

(a) being strong; *she hasn't got the strength to lift it*; *you should test the strength of the rope before you start climbing*

(b) being at a high level; *the strength of the demand for the new car is surprising*; *the strength of the pound increases the possibility of higher inflation*

(c) in strength = in large numbers; *the police were there in strength*; **at full strength** = with everyone present; *the department had several posts vacant, but is back to full strength again*; **in a show of strength** = to show how strong an army is; *in a show of strength, the government sent an aircraft carrier to the area*; **to go from strength to strength** = to get stronger and stronger; *under his leadership the party went from strength to strength*; **on the strength of** = because of; *they employed him on the strength of the references from his previous employer* (NOTE: the opposite is **weakness**)

② **strengthen**
['streŋθn] *verb*

(a) to make something stronger; *the sea wall is being strengthened to prevent another flood*; *this will only strengthen their determination to oppose the government*; *we are planning to strengthen airport security*

(b) to become stronger; *the wind is strengthening from the south-west* (NOTE: the opposite is **weaken**)

③ **stress**
[stres]
1 *noun*

(a) nervous strain caused by an outside influence; *she has difficulty coping with the stress of the office*; *people in positions of responsibility often have stress-related illnesses*

(b) force or pressure on something; *stresses inside the earth create earthquakes*; **stress fracture** = fracture of a bone caused by excessive force, as in some types of sport

(c) strength of your voice when you pronounce a word or part of a word; *in the word 'emphasis' the stress is on the first part of the word* (NOTE: plural is **stresses**)

2 *verb*

to put emphasis on something; *I must stress the importance of keeping the plan secret*

③ **stressed**
[strest] *adjective*
worried and tense; when you're feeling stressed it's better to try to get to bed early; if you feel stressed, just close your eyes and listen to some relaxing music; (*informal*) **stressed out** = very worried and tense; *he's stressed out with his new job*

③ **stretch**
[stretʃ]
1 *noun*
(a) long piece of land, road, etc.; *for long stretches of the Trans-Siberian Railway, all you see are trees; stretches of the river have been so polluted that bathing is dangerous;* the **final stretch** *or* the **home stretch** = the last stage of a race or journey; *he was far ahead of the other runners when they came to the final stretch*
(b) long period of time; *for long stretches we had nothing to do;* **at a stretch** = without a break; *he played the piano for two hours at a stretch*
(c) action of putting out your arms and legs as far as they will go; *I love to lie in bed and have a good stretch before I get up*
(d) (*informal*) time in prison; *he did a stretch in Wormwood Scrubs*
(e) **by no stretch of the imagination** = no one can possibly believe that; *by no stretch of the imagination can you expect him to win* (NOTE: plural is **stretches**)
2 *verb*
(a) to spread out for a great distance; *the line of cars stretched for three miles from the accident; the queue stretched from the door of the cinema right round the corner; white sandy beaches stretch as far as the eye can see*
(b) to push out your arms or legs as far as they can; *the cat woke up and stretched; the monkey stretched out through the bars and grabbed the little boy's cap;* (*informal*) **to stretch your legs** = to go for a short walk after sitting for a long time; *in the coffee break I went out into the garden to stretch my legs*
(c) to pull out so that it becomes loose; *don't hang your jumper up like that - you will just stretch it; these trousers are not supposed to stretch*
(d) to make someone work or think hard; **he is not fully stretched** = his work is too easy and does not make him think as hard as he could

③ **stretch back**
['stretʃ 'bæk] *verb*
to go back over a long period; *his interest in music stretches back to when he was at primary school*

④ **stretcher**
['stretʃɪ] *noun*
folding bed with handles, on which an injured person can be carried by two people; *some of the injured could walk, but there were several*

stretcher cases; the rescue team brought him down the mountain, strapped to a stretcher; **stretcher bearer** = person who helps to carry a stretcher

③ **stretch to**
['stretʃ 'tuː] *verb*
to be enough for; *will your money stretch to paying for a cab ride to the airport?;* **dinner won't stretch to seven** = there won't be enough food for seven people; **to stretch something to the limit** = to be almost too much for; *the new car is going to stretch my finances to the limit*

③ **strict**
[strɪkt] *adjective*
(a) exact (meaning); *the files are in strict order of their dates*
(b) which must be obeyed; *I gave strict instructions that no one was to be allowed in; the rules are very strict and any bad behaviour will be severely punished*
(c) insisting that rules are obeyed; *our parents are very strict with us about staying up late* (NOTE: **stricter - strictest**)

③ **strictly**
['strɪktli] *adverb*
(a) in a strict way; *all staff must follow strictly the procedures in the training manual*
(b) **strictly confidential** = completely secret; *what I am going to tell you is strictly confidential*
(c) **strictly speaking** = really, in reality; *strictly speaking, she's not my aunt, just an old friend of the family*

④ **stride**
[straɪd]
1 *noun*
long step; *in three strides he was across the room and out of the door;* **to make great strides** = to advance quickly; *doctors have made great strides in the treatment of cancer;* **to take something in your stride** = to deal with something easily; *other people always seem to have problems, but she just takes everything in her stride*
2 *verb*
to walk with long steps; *she strode into the room carrying a whip; we could see him striding across the field* (NOTE: **striding - strode** [strʊd])

③ **strike**
[straɪk]
1 *noun*
(a) stopping of work by workers because of lack of agreement with management or because of orders from a trade union; *they all voted in favour of a strike; the danger of a strike was removed at the last minute;* **general strike** = strike of all the workers in a country; **sit-down strike** = strike where the workers stay in their place of work and refuse to leave; **to take strike action** = to go on strike; *the workers voted to*

take strike action; **strike ballot** *or* **strike vote** = vote by workers to decide if a strike should be held

(b) to come out on strike *or* **to go on strike** = to stop work; *the workers went on strike for more money*; *the stewards and stewardesses are on strike for higher pay*; **to call the workforce out on strike** = to tell the workers to stop work; *the union called its members out on strike*

(c) military attack; *they launched an air strike against the enemy positions*

2 *verb*

(a) to stop working because of disagreement with management; *the workers are striking in protest against bad working conditions*

(b) to hit something hard; *he struck her with a bottle*; *she struck her head on the low door*; *he struck a match and lit the fire*

(c) *(of a clock)* to ring to mark an hour; *the church clock had just struck one when she heard a noise outside her bedroom door*

(d) to come to someone's mind; *a thought just struck me*; *it suddenly struck me that I had seen him somewhere before*; **it strikes me that** = I think that; *it strikes me that we may be charging too much*

(e) to surprise someone; *he was struck by the poverty he saw everywhere*

(f) to attack; *the police are afraid the killer may strike again*; *the illness struck without warning*

(g) to come to an agreement; *we expect to strike a deal next week*; *they struck a bargain and decided to share the costs* (NOTE: **striking - struck** [strʌk])

③ **strike off**
['straɪk 'ɒf] *verb*

to remove a name from a list because of bad behaviour; *he was struck off the register of doctors*

④ **striker**
['straɪkɪ] *noun*

(a) worker who is on strike; *strikers surrounded the factory*

(b) football player whose main task is to score goals; *his pass back to the goalkeeper was stopped by the opposition striker who then scored*

③ **striking**
['straɪkɪŋ]

1 *adjective*

noticeable, unusual; *she bears a striking similarity to Queen Elizabeth I*; *it is a very striking portrait of Winston Churchill*

2 *noun*

hitting; **within striking distance** = quite close, near enough to hit; *the capital is within striking distance of the enemy guns*

② **string**
[strɪŋ] *noun*

(a) strong thin thread used for tying up parcels, etc.; *this string isn't strong enough to tie up that big parcel*; *she bought a ball of string*; *we've run out of string* (NOTE: no plural in this meaning: **some string; a piece of string**)

(b) long series of things, events; *she's been plagued with a string of illnesses*; *I had a string of phone calls this morning*

(c) thread on a musical instrument which makes a note when you hit it; *he was playing the violin when one of the strings broke*; *a guitar has six strings*; **string instrument** = musical instrument with strings which make the notes

④ **string along**
['strɪŋ ə'lɒŋ] *verb*

(a) to walk along in a line behind someone; *the teachers walked in front and the children strung along behind*

(b) to promise someone something to get him or her to cooperate with you; *he was just stringing her along - he never intended to marry her, but just wanted to get at her money*

③ **strings**
[strɪŋz] *noun*

(a) *(informal)* hidden conditions; **are there any strings attached?** = are there any hidden conditions?; *the bank loaned us the money with no strings attached*; *(informal)* **to pull strings** = to use your influence to make something happen; *her father pulled strings to get her the job*

(b) the strings = section of an orchestra with string instruments; *the work provides a lot of scope for the strings*; *see also* BRASS, WIND

(c) members of an orchestra who play string instruments; *the strings sit at the front of the orchestra, near the conductor*

③ **strip**
[strɪp]

1 *noun*

(a) long narrow piece of cloth, paper, etc.; *he tore the paper into strips*; *houses are to be built along the strip of land near the church*; **magnetic strip** = layer of magnetic material on a plastic card, used for recording data

(b) strip cartoon *or* **comic strip** = cartoon story made of a series of small drawings inside little boxes side by side

(c) particular clothes worn by football players and fans; *he was wearing the Arsenal strip*

(d) landing strip = rough place for planes to land; *the soldiers cut a landing strip in the jungle*

2 *verb*

(a) to take off your clothes; *strip to the waist for your chest X-ray*; *he stripped down to his underpants*

(b) to remove completely; *the wind stripped the leaves off the trees*; *first we have to strip the old paint off the cupboards*; *he was stripped of his title following the scandal about bribes* (NOTE: **stripping - stripped**)

④ **stripe**

[straɪp] *noun*

(a) long line of colour; *he has an umbrella with red, white and blue stripes*

(b) piece of coloured cloth sewn to a soldier's jacket to show his rank; *he has just got his sergeant's stripes*

③ **stroke**

[strəʊk]

1 *noun*

(a) gentle touch with your hand; *she gave the dog a stroke*

(b) sudden loss of consciousness; *she had a stroke and died*

(c) movement of a pen, brush, etc., which makes a line; *she can draw a cartoon with just a few strokes of the pen*

(d) printing sign (/) used to show an alternative; *all members/visitors must sign the register* (NOTE: say 'all members stroke visitors' or 'all members or visitors')

(e) act of hitting something, such as a ball; *it took him three strokes to get the ball onto the green*; **to put someone off his stroke** = to distract someone's attention so that he does something wrong; *people kept on shouting while the minister was speaking and that put him off his stroke*

(f) sound made when hitting something (such as a bell); *on the stroke of midnight* = when the clocks are striking twelve

(g) stroke of luck = piece of luck; *I had a stroke of luck yesterday - I found my purse which I thought I had lost*; *it was a stroke of luck that you happened to come along at that moment*; *he hasn't done a stroke of work all day* = he hasn't done any work at all

(h) style of swimming; *she won the 200m breast stroke*

(i) person rowing who sits at the back of the boat and sets the pace for the others; *see also* BOW

2 *verb*

to run your hands gently over; *she was stroking the cat as it sat in her lap*

④ **stroll**

[strəʊl]

1 *noun*

short relaxing walk; *we went for a stroll by the river after dinner*

2 *verb*

to walk slowly to relax; *people were strolling in the park*; *on Sunday evenings, everyone strolls along the bank of the river*

① **strong**

[strɒŋ]

1 *adjective*

(a) (person) with a lot of strength; *I'm not strong enough to carry that box*

(b) which has a lot of force or strength; *the string broke - we need something stronger*; *the wind was so strong that it blew some tiles off*

the roof; **strong currency** = currency which is high against other currencies (NOTE: the opposite is a **weak currency**)

(c) with a powerful smell, taste, etc.; *I don't like strong cheese*; *you need a cup of strong black coffee to wake you up*; *there was a strong smell of gas in the kitchen*

(d) strong drink = alcohol; *have an orange juice, or would you prefer something stronger?* (NOTE: **stronger - strongest**)

2 *suffix; (used to show a number of people)* **a 50-strong party of marines landed on the beach**; **a 20-strong group of shift workers**

3 *adverb; going strong* = still very active, still working; *she had a heart operation ten years ago and is still going strong*

④ **strongly**

['strɒŋli] *adverb*

in a strong way; *the castle is strongly defended*; *they objected very strongly to the plan*

③ **struck**

[strʌk] *see* STRIKE

③ **structural**

['strʌktʃrəl] *adjective*

referring to a structure; *the inspector reported several structural defects*; **structural unemployment** = unemployment caused by the changing structure of an industry or of society

② **structure**

['strʌktʃə]

1 *noun*

(a) way in which things are organized; *a career structure within a corporation*; *the company is reorganizing its discount structure*

(b) *(formal)* way in which something is built; *the structure of the bridge had been weakened by constant traffic*

2 *verb*

to arrange according to a certain system; *we've tried to structure the meeting so that there is plenty of time for discussion*

③ **struggle**

['strʌgl]

1 *noun*

(a) fight; *after a short struggle the burglar was arrested*

(b) hard effort to do something because of difficulties; *setting up a new company during a recession was always going to be a struggle*; *her constant struggle to bring up her children*; *their struggle against illness*

2 *verb*

(a) to fight with an attacker; *two men were struggling on the floor*

(b) to try hard to do something difficult; *she's struggling with her maths homework*; *she struggled to carry all the shopping to the car*; **to struggle to your feet** = to stand up with great difficulty; *after the blast from the bomb she struggled to her feet and started running*

④ **stubborn**
['stʌbɪn] *adjective*
(a) not willing to change your mind; *he's so stubborn - he only does what he wants to do*
(b) difficult to remove; *to get rid of really stubborn stains you will need to use something stronger than ordinary soap*

③ **stuck**
[stʌk] *see* STICK

① **student**
['stju:dɪnt] *noun*
(a) person who is studying at a college or university; *all the science students came to my lecture*; *she's a brilliant student*; *two students had to sit the exam again*; **student card** = identification card, showing that you are a student, which allows you special discounts on certain items; **students' union** = (i) building where university students meet to drink, eat, see films, etc.; (ii) group representing the students at a university
(b) *US* boy or girl studying at high school

③ **studio**
['stju:dɪʊ] *noun*
(a) place where films, broadcasts, recordings, etc., are made; *the TV series was made at Teddington Studios*; *and now, back to the studio for the latest news and weather report*; *they spent the whole day recording the piece in the studio*
(b) very small flat for one person, usually one room with a small kitchen and bathroom; *you can rent a studio overlooking the sea for £300 a week in high season*
(c) room where an artist paints; *she uses this room as a studio because of the good light*; **design studio** = independent firm which specializes in creating designs for companies
(d) place where photographers take photographs; *a studio photograph of the bride and bridegroom* (NOTE: plural is **studios**)

② **study**
['stʌdi]
1 *noun*
(a) work of examining something carefully to learn more about it; *the company asked the experts to prepare a study into new production techniques*; *the review has published studies on the new drug*; **nature study** = learning about plants and animals at school
(b) room in which someone reads, writes, works, etc.; *when he says he is going to his study to read, it usually means he's going to have little sleep*
(c) **studies** = attending college or university; *she interrupted her studies and went to work in Kenya for two years*; *he has successfully finished his studies*
2 *verb*

(a) to learn about a subject at college or university; *he is studying medicine because he wants to be a doctor*; *she's studying French and Spanish in the modern languages department*
(b) to examine something carefully to learn more about it; *we are studying the possibility of setting up an office in New York*; *the government studied the committee's proposals for two months*; *doctors are studying the results of the screening programme*

① **stuff**
[stʌf]
1 *noun*
(a) substance, especially something unpleasant; *you've got some black stuff stuck to your shoe*
(b) *(informal)* things, equipment; *dump all your stuff in the living room*; *take all that stuff and put it in the dustbin*; *all your photographic stuff is still in the back of my car*
(c) ideas; *she talked about the dangers of smoking and all that stuff about lung cancer*
(d) *(informal)* **to do your stuff** = to do what you are supposed to do or what you're good at; *come on, England, do your stuff!*; *everyone must do their stuff quickly if we want the work to be finished tonight*; **to know your stuff** = to know your subject well, to be good at what you are doing; *it was fascinating to listen to him, he really knows his stuff*
2 *verb*
(a) to push something into something to fill it; *he stuffed his pockets full of sweets for the children*; *the banknotes were stuffed into a small plastic bag*
(b) to put chopped onions, chopped meat, etc., inside meat or vegetables before cooking; *they served stuffed vine leaves as a starter*; *we had roast lamb stuffed with mushrooms*
(c) *(informal)* **to stuff yourself** = to eat a lot; *they were stuffing themselves on chocolate pudding*
(d) to fill the skin of a dead animal so that it looks alive; *there was a stuffed bear at the top of the stairs in the old castle*
(e) *(informal, rude)* **(go and) get stuffed** = go away, stop interfering; *you can tell the manager to go and get stuffed*

④ **stumble**
['stʌmbl] *verb*
(a) to trip, to almost fall by hitting your foot against something; *he stumbled as he tried to get down the stairs in the dark*
(b) to walk about, staggering; *he was stumbling around in the basement, looking for the light switch*
(c) **to stumble across something** = to find something by accident; *I stumbled across this letter which someone had hidden*

(d) to make mistakes when reading; *he managed to stumble through the reading test*; *she read the TV news without stumbling over any of the foreign words*

④ **stump**
[stʌmp]
1 *noun*
(a) short piece of something left sticking up, such as the trunk of a tree that has been cut down; *after cutting down the trees, we need to get rid of the stumps*
(b) one of the three sticks placed in the ground as a target in cricket; *the ball hit the stumps and the last man was out*; *stumps were drawn* = the game of cricket came to an end (temporarily)
2 *verb*
(a) to stump along = to walk along with heavy steps; *he stumped angrily out of the shop*
(b) *(informal)* to ask someone a difficult question which he can't answer; *the MD was stumped when the committee asked him how many hours the average employee worked*; *today's puzzle has stumped me completely* or *has got me stumped*

④ **stun**
[stʌn] *verb*
(a) to knock someone out, to make someone lose consciousness with a blow to the head; *the blow on the head stunned him*
(b) to shock someone completely; *she was stunned when he told her that he was already married* (NOTE: **stunning - stunned**)

③ **stung**
[stʌŋ] *see* STING

③ **stunk**
[stʌŋk] *see* STINK

④ **stunning**
['stʌnɪŋ] *adjective*
extraordinary, wonderful and beautiful; *this is a stunning photograph of your mother*; *they have a stunning house in the country*

① **stupid**
['stju:pɪd] *adjective*
(a) not very intelligent; *what a stupid man!*
(b) not showing any sense; *it was stupid of her not to wear a helmet*; *he made several stupid mistakes*

① **style**
[staɪl] *noun*
(a) way of doing something, especially way of designing, drawing, writing, etc.; *the room is decorated in Chinese style*; *the painting is in his usual style*; *that style was fashionable in the 1940s*
(b) elegant or fashionable way of doing things; *she always dresses with style*; *they live in grand style*
(c) way someone behaves, thinks or lives; *it's not her style to forget an appointment*; *their style of life wouldn't suit me*

④ **stylish**
['staɪlɪʃ] *adjective*
attractive and fashionable; *he drives a stylish sports car*; *we ate in a very stylish new restaurant*

③ **sub**
[sʌb] *(informal)* = SUBMARINE, SUBSCRIPTION, SUBSTITUTE

① **sub-**
[sʌb] *prefix meaning*
below, under

② **subject**
['sʌbdʒɪkt] *noun*
(a) thing which you are talking about or writing about; *he suddenly changed the subject of the conversation*; *the newspaper has devoted a special issue to the subject of pollution*
(b) thing shown in a painting, etc.; *the same subject is treated quite differently in the three paintings*
(c) area of knowledge which you are studying; *maths is his weakest subject*; *you can take up to five subjects at 'A' Level*
(d) to be the subject of = to be the person or thing talked about or studied; *the painter Chagall will be the subject of our lecture today*; *advertising costs are the subject of close examination by the auditors*
(e) *(grammar)* noun or pronoun which comes before a verb and shows the person or thing that does the action expressed by the verb; *in the sentence 'the cat sat on the mat' the word 'cat' is the subject of the verb 'sat'*
(d) person who is born in a country, or who has the right to live in a country; *she is a British subject but a Canadian citizen*

④ **subjective**
[sʌb'dʒektɪv] *adjective*
seen from your own point of view, and therefore possibly biased; *this is a purely subjective impression of what happened* (NOTE: the opposite is **objective**)

② **subject to**
1 *adjective*
['sʌbdʒɪkt 'tu:]
(a) depending on something; *we want you to go on a study tour to France, subject to getting your parents' permission*; *the contract is subject to government approval* = the contract will be valid only if it is approved by the government; *sale subject to contract* = sale which is not legal until a proper contract has been signed
(b) affected by; *the timetable is subject to change without notice*; *this jewellery is subject to import tax*; *after returning from the tropics he was subject to attacks of fever*
2 *verb*
[sʌb'dʒekt 'tu:]

to subject to = to make something *or* someone suffer something unpleasant; *the guards subjected the prisoners to physical violence*; *we were subjected to a mass of questions by reporters*

④ **submarine**
[sʌbmɪˈriːn]
1 *noun*
special type of ship which can travel under water; *the submarine dived before she was spotted by enemy aircraft*
2 *adjective*
which is under the water; *a submarine pipeline*

② **submission**
[sʌbˈmɪʃn] *noun*
(a) state of giving in or having to obey someone; *their plan was to starve the enemy into submission* (NOTE: no plural in this meaning)
(b) evidence, document, argument used in court; *in his submission, he stated that the council had always acted within the law*

② **submit**
[sʌbˈmɪt] *verb*
(a) to submit to = to yield to; *he definitely won't submit to pressure from the committee*
(b) to put something forward for someone to examine; *you are requested to submit your proposal to the planning committee*; *he submitted a claim to the insurers*; *reps are asked to submit their expenses claims once a month*
(c) to plead in court; *the defence submitted that there was no case to answer* (NOTE: submitting - submitted)

④ **subordinate**
1 *adjective*
[sɪˈbɔːdnɪt]
(a) under the control of someone else; less important; **subordinate to** = which is under the control of; *the new arrangement will make our department subordinate to yours*
(b) subordinate clause = clause in a sentence which depends on the main clause
2 *noun*
[sɪˈbɔːdnɪt] person who is under the direction of someone else; *his subordinates find him difficult to work with*
3 *verb*
[sɪˈbɔːdneɪt]
to subordinate something to = to put something in a less important position than something else; *we were taught to subordinate our personal feelings to the needs of the state*

④ **subscription**
[sʌbˈskrɪpʃn] *noun*
(a) money paid to a club for a year's membership; *he forgot to renew his club subscription*
(b) money paid in advance to a magazine for a series of issues; *did you remember to pay the subscription to the computer magazine?*; **to take out a subscription to a magazine** = to start paying for a series of issues of a magazine; **to cancel a subscription to a magazine** = to stop paying for a series of issues
(c) subscription to a new share issue = offering new shares in a company for sale

② **subsequent**
[ˈsʌbsɪkwɪnt] *adjective*
(formal) which comes later; *the tropical storm and the subsequent floods stopped the cricket match*; *all subsequent reports must be sent to me immediately they arrive*

③ **subsequently**
[ˈsʌbsɪkwɪntli] *adverb; (formal)*
afterwards; *I subsequently discovered that there had been a mistake*; *what happened subsequently proved that our forecast had been correct*

④ **subsidize**
[ˈsʌbsɪdaɪz] *verb*
to help by giving money; *the government has agreed to subsidize the coal industry*

④ **subsidy**
[ˈsʌbsɪdi] *noun*
money given to help pay for something which is not profitable; *the government has increased its subsidy to the coal industry* (NOTE: plural is **subsidies**)

③ **substance**
[ˈsʌbstɪns] *noun*
(a) solid or liquid material, especially one used in chemistry; *a secret substance is added to the product to give it its yellow colour*; *toxic substances got into the drinking water*
(b) truth behind an argument; *there is no substance to the rumour that his business was controlled by a criminal gang*; *she brought documents to add substance to her claim*
(c) *(formal)* **a man of substance** = a rich man
(d) *(formal)* drug; *he was found to have certain illegal substances in his suitcase*

② **substantial**
[sʌbˈstænʃl] *adjective*
(a) large, important; *she was awarded substantial damages*; *he received a substantial sum when he left the company*; *a substantial amount of work remains to be done*
(b) large, which satisfies; *we had a substantial meal at the local pub*
(c) solid, strong; *this wall is too thin, we need something much more substantial*

③ **substantially**
[sʌbˈstænʃili] *adverb*
(a) mainly, mostly; *their forecast was substantially correct*
(b) by a large amount; *the cost of raw materials has risen substantially over the last year*

④ **substitute**
[ˈsʌbstɪtjuːt]
1 *noun*
person or thing that takes the place of someone *or* something else; *this type of plastic can be used as a substitute for leather*; *meat*

substitutes are often made from soya; I thought the substitute teacher was better than our normal teacher; when the goalkeeper was injured they sent on a substitute

2 *verb*

to substitute something or someone for something or someone else = to put something *or* someone in the place of something *or* someone else; *he secretly substituted the fake diamond for the real one*; **to substitute for someone** = to replace someone; *who will be substituting for the sales manager when she's away on holiday?*

④ **subtle**

['sʌtl] *adjective*

(a) not obvious or easily seen; *there's a subtle difference between the two political parties*

(b) difficult to analyze because of being complicated or delicate; *a sauce with a subtle taste of lemon; a subtler shade would be better than that bright colour* (NOTE: **subtler - subtlest**)

③ **subtract**

[sʌb'trækt] *verb*

to take one number away from another; *subtract 10 from 33 and you get 23* (NOTE: subtracting is usually shown by the minus sign - : **10 - 4 = 6:** say 'ten subtract four equals six')

④ **suburb**

['sʌbɜ:b] *noun*

residential area on the edge of a town; *he lives in a quiet suburb of Boston*; **the suburbs** = area all round a town where a lot of people live; *people who live in the suburbs find the air quality is better than in the centre of town*

③ **suburban**

[sɪ'bɜ:bɪn] *adjective*

referring to the suburbs; *this is a very a suburban area - almost everyone commutes to London every day*; **suburban line** = railway line between the suburbs to the centre of a town; *services on suburban lines have been affected by the strike*

③ **subway**

['sʌbweɪ] *noun*

(a) passage under ground along which people can walk (as under a busy road); *there's a subway from the bus station to the shopping centre*

(b) *US* underground railway system; *the New York subway; it will be quicker to take the subway to Grand Central Station* (NOTE: the London equivalent is the **tube** *or* **Underground**)

② **succeed**

[sʌk'si:d] *verb*

(a) to do well or to be profitable; *his business has succeeded more than he had expected*

(b) to succeed in doing something = to do what you have been trying to do; *she succeeded in passing her driving test; I succeeded in getting them to agree to my plan*

(c) *(informal, humorous)* to manage to do something which is rather stupid; *they succeeded in getting lost in the centre of London*

(d) to follow on after someone who has retired, left the job, etc.; *Mr Smith was succeeded as chairman by Mr Jones*

① **success**

[sʌk'ses] *noun*

(a) achieving what you have been trying to do; *she's been looking for a job in a library, but without any success so far*

(b) doing something well; *her photo was in the newspapers after her Olympic success; the new car has not had much success in the Japanese market*

(c) somebody *or* something that succeeds; *the launch of the new model was a great success; he wasn't much of a success as a manager; the heart operation was a complete success* (NOTE: plural is **successes**)

① **successful**

[sʌk'sesfʊl] *adjective*

who *or* which does well; *he's a successful business man; she's very successful at hiding her real age; their selling trip to German proved successful*

① **successfully**

[sʌk'sesfɪli] *adverb*

achieving what was intended; *the new model was successfully launched last week; she successfully found her way to the British Museum*

③ **succession**

[sɪk'seʃn] *noun*

(a) series of the same sort of thing; *I had a succession of phone calls from my relatives*

(b) in succession = one after the other; *three people in succession have asked me the same question; he won the title five times in succession*

④ **successive**

[sɪk'sesɪv] *adjective*

which come one after the other; *successive delays have meant that we are now ten months behind schedule; in three successive matches the goalkeeper was injured*

③ **successor**

[sɪk'sesɪ] *noun*

person who takes over from someone; *Mr Smith's successor as chairman will be Mr Jones; he handed the keys of the safe over to his successor*

① **such**

[sʌtʃ]

1 *adjective*

(a) of this sort; *the police are looking for such things as drugs or stolen goods*

(b) no such = not existing; *there is no such day as April 31st; someone was asking for a Mr Simpson but there is no such person working here*

(c) such as = like; *some shops such as food stores are open on Sundays*

(d) very; so much; *there was such a crowd at the party that there weren't enough chairs to go round; it's such a shame that she's ill and has to miss her sister's wedding; she's such a slow worker that she produces about half as much as everyone else; these days, people can't afford to buy such expensive meals*

2 *pronoun*

this type of person or thing; *she's very competent, and is thought of as such by the management; the noise was such that it stopped me sleeping*

③ **suck**

['sʌk] *verb*

(a) to hold something with your mouth and pull at it (with your tongue); *the baby didn't stop sucking his thumb until he was six*

(b) to have something in your mouth which makes your mouth produce water; *he bought a bag of sweets to suck in the car*

(c) to pull liquid into your mouth by using the muscles in your mouth; *she sucked the orange juice through a straw; she carries a bottle of apple juice everywhere and the baby sucks some when she's thirsty*

③ **suck up**

['sʌk 'ʌp] *verb*

(a) to swallow; *the new vacuum cleaner sucks up dust very efficiently*

(b) *(informal)* **to suck up to someone** = to say nice things to someone so as to get good treatment; *you should see the way he sucks up to the boss*

② **sudden**

['sʌdɪn] *adjective*

(a) which happens very quickly or unexpectedly; *the sudden change in the weather caught us without any umbrellas; the bus came to a sudden stop; his decision to go to Canada was very sudden*

(b) all of a sudden = suddenly, quickly, giving you a shock; *all of a sudden the room went dark*

① **suddenly**

['sʌdɪnli] *adverb*

quickly and giving you a shock; *the car in front stopped suddenly and I ran into the back of it; suddenly the room went dark; she suddenly realized it was already five o'clock*

④ **sue**

[suː] *verb*

to take someone to court, to start legal proceedings against someone to get compensation for a wrong; *she is suing the driver of the other car for damages; he sued the company for $50,000 compensation; we are still debating whether to sue or not*

① **suffer**

['sʌfɪ] *verb*

(a) to be in a bad situation, to do badly; *the harvest has suffered because of the bad weather; exports have suffered during the last six months*

(b) to receive an injury; *he suffered serious injuries in the accident*

(c) to feel pain; *he didn't suffer at all, and was conscious until he died*

(d) to suffer from = to have a disease or a fault; *she suffers from constant headaches; the company's products suffer from bad design; our car suffers from a tendency to use too much oil*

(e) not to suffer fools gladly = to be impatient with stupid people; *her main problem when answering customer complaints is that she doesn't suffer fools gladly*

④ **sufferer**

['sʌfrɪ] *noun*

person who has a certain disease; *a new drug to help asthma sufferers or sufferers from asthma*; **fellow sufferer** = person who suffers from the same thing as you; *she often gets headaches and likes to talk with fellow sufferers*

④ **suffering**

['sʌfrɪŋ] *noun*

feeling pain over a long period of time; *the doctor gave him an injection to relieve his suffering*; **to put an animal out of its suffering** = to kill an animal which is very ill

② **sufficient**

[sɪ'fɪʃɪnt] *adjective*

(formal) as much as is needed; *does she have sufficient funds to pay for her trip?; there isn't sufficient room to put the big sofa in here; allow yourself sufficient time to get to the airport*

③ **suffix**

['sʌfɪks] *noun*

letters added to the end of a word to make another word; *the suffix '-ly' can be added to an adjective to form an adverb such as 'partially' or 'suddenly'* (NOTE: plural is **suffixes;** the opposite, letters which are added in front of a word, is a **prefix**)

② **sugar**

['ʃʊgɪ] *noun*

(a) substance that you use to make food sweet; *how much sugar do you take in your tea?; a spoonful of sugar will be enough; can you pass me the sugar, please?*; **brown sugar** = sugar which has not been made pure; **white sugar** = sugar which has been made pure; **icing sugar** = fine powdered white sugar, used to cover cakes; *if you're in a hurry, just dust the cake with icing sugar*; **sugar lump** *or* **lump of sugar** = cube of white sugar (NOTE: no plural: **some sugar; a bag of sugar; a lump of sugar; a spoonful of sugar**)

(b) *(informal)* a spoonful of sugar; *how do you take your coffee? - milk and one sugar, please*

① **suggest**
[sɪ'dʒest] *verb*
to mention an idea to see what other people think of it; *the chairman suggested that the next meeting should be held in October; might I suggest a visit to the museum this afternoon?; what does he suggest we do in this case?*

① **suggestion**
[sɪ'dʒestʃn] *noun*
idea that you mention for people to think about; *we have asked for suggestions from passengers; the company acted upon your suggestion; whose suggestion was it that we should go out in a boat?; I bought those shares at the suggestion of the bank*

④ **suicide**
['su:ɪsaɪd] *noun*
(a) act of killing yourself; *whether her death was murder or suicide is not yet known*; **to commit suicide** = to kill yourself; *he killed his two children and then committed suicide*; **suicide note** = letter left by someone who has committed suicide; *her suicide note was left on the kitchen table*; **attempted suicide** *or* **suicide attempt** = trying to kill yourself, but not succeeding; *she is still in hospital after her suicide attempt*
(b) political suicide = action which ends your political career; *by voting against the government he effectively committed political suicide*

② **suit**
[su:t]
1 *noun*
(a) set of pieces of clothing made of the same cloth and worn together, such as a jacket and trousers or skirt; *a dark grey suit will be just right for the interview; the pale blue suit she was wearing was very smart;* **shell suit** = jacket and trousers for jogging; **ski suit** = one-piece suit, or jacket and trousers, for skiing
(b) one of the four sets of cards with the same symbol in a pack of cards; *clubs and spades are the two black suits and hearts and diamonds are the two red suits*
(c) to follow suit = to do what everyone else does; *she jumped into the pool and everyone else followed suit*
(d) = LAWSUIT
2 *verb*
(a) to look good when worn by someone; *green usually suits people with red hair; that hat doesn't suit her*
(b) to be convenient; *he'll only do it when it suits him to do it; Thursday at 11 o'clock will suit me fine*

② **suitable**
['su:təbl] *adjective*
which fits or which is convenient; *the most suitable place to meet will be under the big clock at Waterloo Station; we advertised the job again because there were no suitable candidates; a blue dress would be more suitable for an interview; I'm looking for a suitable present for her 30th birthday; is this a suitable moment to discuss the office move?*

③ **suitcase**
['su:tkeɪs] *noun*
box with a handle which you carry your clothes in when you are travelling; *I never pack my suitcase until the last minute; the customs officer made him open his three suitcases; (informal)* **to live out of a suitcase** = to travel so frequently, that you don't spend much time at home

④ **suite**
[swi:t] *noun*
(a) set of rooms, especially expensive rooms; *their offices are in a suite of rooms on the eleventh floor; they booked a suite at the Savoy Hotel;* **honeymoon suite** = specially attractive hotel rooms for honeymoon couples; **VIP suite** = specially luxurious suite at an airport or in a hotel, for very important people; *see also* EN-SUITE
(b) set of pieces of furniture; **bathroom suite** = bath, washbasin and toilet; *a new bathroom suite could cost over £3000;* **bedroom suite** = bed, chest of drawers and other furniture for a bedroom; **living room suite** = sofa and matching armchairs
(c) several short pieces of music played together as one item; *the 'Planets Suite' by Gustav Holst*
(NOTE: do not confuse with **sweet**)

② **sum**
[sʌm] *noun*
(a) quantity of money; *he only paid a small sum for the car; a large sum of money was stolen from his office; we are owed the sum of £500;* **lump sum** = money paid in one payment, not in several small payments; *you can take part of your pension as a lump sum*
(b) simple problem in maths; *she tried to do the sum in her head; see also* SUMS
(c) total of two or more figures added together; *the sum of all four sides will give you the distance around the field*
(d) sum total = total amount of something which may not be as much as you want; *the Royal Palace and the National Museum were closed, so we went to the Museum of the Army and that was the sum total of what we saw*

④ **summary**
['sʌmɪri]
1 *noun*
short description of what has been said or written, or of what happened, without giving all the details; *she gave a summary of what happened at the meeting; here's a summary of the book in case you don't have time to read it; it is 7.30 and here is a summary of the news*
(NOTE: plural is **summaries**)

2 *adjective*

which happens immediately; *he was given a summary trial*

① **summer**

['sʌmɪ] *noun*

hottest time of the year, the season between spring and autumn; *next summer we are going to Greece*; *the summer in Australia coincides with our winter here in England*; *I haven't any summer clothes - it's never hot enough here*; **Indian summer** = warm period in early autumn; *we had an Indian summer this year in late September*; **the summer holidays** = period during the summer when children do not go to school; holidays taken by workers during the period from June to September; *I'm starting my summer holidays on July 20th*; *the weather was awful during our summer holidays*; **summer school** = classes held at a school, college or university during the summer holiday; *she is organizing a summer school in Florence on 'Fifteenth Century Italian Art'*

③ **summer time**

['sʌmɪ 'taɪm] *noun*

system where the clocks are put forward one hour in March to take advantage of the longer period of daylight; *summer time begins at the end of March and ends in October*

③ **summertime**

['sʌmɪtaɪm] *noun*

the time of year when it is summer; *it's summertime, and the farmers are out in the fields all day long*

③ **summit**

['sʌmɪt] *noun*

(a) top of a mountain; *it took us three hour's hard climbing to reach the summit*

(b) **summit (meeting or conference)** = meeting of heads of state or government leaders to discuss international problems; *the question was discussed at the last European summit*

④ **summon**

['sʌmɪn] *verb*

(a) *(formal)* to tell people to come to a meeting; *the president summoned a meeting of the supreme council*; *she was summoned to appear before the committee*

(b) **to summon up courage** = to force yourself to be brave enough to do something; *he summoned up enough courage to do his first flight all by himself*; **to summon up strength** = to manage to have enough strength to do something; *he summoned up all his strength and climbed the last few metres to the top*

③ **sums**

[sʌmz] *noun*

maths, making simple calculations with figures; *she is much quicker at sums than her sister*

③ **sum up**

['sʌm 'ʌp] *verb*

(a) to make a summary of what has been said; *I'd just like to sum up what has been said so far*; *can you sum up the most important points in the speech for me?*

(b) *(of a judge)* to speak at the end of a trial and review all the evidence and arguments for the benefit of the jury; *I was surprised the judge did not mention that when he summed up* (NOTE: **summing - summed**)

① **sun**

[sʌn]

1 *noun*

(a) very bright star round which the earth travels and which gives light and heat; *the sun was just rising when I got up*; *I'll try taking a photograph now that the sun's come out*; *don't stare at the sun, even with sunglasses on*

(b) light from the sun; *I'd prefer a table out of the sun*; *we're sitting in the shade because the sun's too hot*; *she spent her whole holiday just sitting in the sun*; **sun cream** = cream which you put on your skin to avoid getting burnt by the sun; *it you're going to the beach don't forget to take the sun cream*; **everything under the sun** = absolutely everything; *we talked about everything under the sun*

2 *verb*

to sun yourself = to sit in the sun and get warm; *the cat was sunning herself on the window ledge* (NOTE: **sunning - sunned**)

① **Sunday**

['sʌndi] *noun*

the seventh day of the week, the day between Saturday and Monday; *last Sunday we went on a picnic*; *most shops are now open on Sundays*; *can we fix a lunch for next Sunday?*; *the 15th is a Saturday, so the 16th must be a Sunday*; *today is Sunday, November 19th*; **in your Sunday best** = wearing your smartest clothes; *all the children came in their Sunday best*

③ **sung**

[sʌŋ] *see* SING

③ **sunglasses**

['sʌnglɑːsɪz] *noun*

dark glasses worn to protect your eyes from the sun; *I always wear sunglasses when I'm driving*

③ **sunk**

[sʌŋk] *see* SINK

④ **sunlight**

['sʌnlaɪt] *noun*

light which comes from the sun; *sunlight was pouring into the room*; *there's not really enough sunlight to take a picture*; *sunlight is essential to give the body Vitamin D* (NOTE: no plural)

④ **sunny**
['sʌni] *adjective*
(a) with the sun shining; *another sunny day!*; *they forecast that it will be sunny this afternoon*
(b) where the sun often shines; *we live on the sunny side of the street*; *their sitting room is bright and sunny, but the dining room is dark*
(c) *US (informal)* **sunny side up** = (egg) fried on one side without being turned over, so you can see the yellow centre (NOTE: **sunnier - sunniest**)

④ **sunset**
['sʌnset] *noun*
time when the sun goes down in the evening; *at sunset, bats come out and fly around*

③ **sunshine**
['sʌnʃaɪn] *noun*
pleasant light from the sun; *we have had very little sunshine this July*; *the west coast of France has more than 250 days of sunshine per year* (NOTE: no plural)

② **super**
['suːpɪ] *adjective*
(informal) very good; *we had a super time in Greece*; *thank you for being such super hosts*; *let's go away for the weekend - what a super idea!*

④ **superb**
[suːˈpɜːb] *adjective*
marvellous, wonderfully good; *he scored with a superb shot from just outside the penalty area*; *I'll have another helping of that superb chocolate cake*

③ **superficial**
[suːpɪˈfɪʃl] *adjective*
(a) which affects only the top surface; *the damage was only superficial; she suffered a few superficial grazes but nothing serious*
(b) dealing only with the most obvious and simple matters; *I can't answer your question because I only have a very superficial knowledge of the subject*

④ **superintendent**
[suːpɪrɪnˈtendɪnt] *noun*
(a) person who is responsible for work, or for a place; *go and see the building superintendent about the leaking pipe*
(b) **police superintendent** = senior police officer, above a chief inspector

④ **superior**
[suːˈpɪriɪ]
1 *adjective*
(a) of very high quality; *he gave her a very superior box of chocolates*; **superior to** = better than; *our products are superior to theirs*; *their distribution service is much superior to ours*
(b) in a higher rank; *soldiers should always salute superior officers*; **superior to someone** = of a higher rank than someone; *she is superior to him in the office management system*

(c) thinking you are better than other people; *he gives himself such superior airs*
2 *noun*
person in a higher rank; *each manager is responsible to his superior* (NOTE: the opposite is **inferior**)

③ **superlative**
[suːˈpɜːlɪtɪv]
1 *noun*
form of an adjective or adverb showing the highest level when compared with another; *'biggest' is the superlative of 'big'*; *put a few superlatives in the ad to emphasize how good the product is*
2 *adjective*
extremely good; *he's a superlative goalkeeper*

COMMENT: superlatives are usually formed by adding the suffix -est to the adjective: 'quickest' from 'quick', for example; in the case of long adjectives, they are formed by putting 'most' in front of the adjective: 'most comfortable', 'most expensive', and so on. Some superlatives are not regular, such as 'worst' and 'best'. You can also form superlatives by adding phrases like 'as possible': 'as big as possible'

③ **supermarket**
['suːpɪmɑːkɪt] *noun*
large store selling mainly food and household goods, where customers serve themselves and pay at a checkout; *we've got no tea left, can you buy some from the supermarket?*; *we do all our shopping in the local supermarket*; **supermarket trolley** = metal basket on wheels, used by shoppers to put their purchases in as they go round a supermarket (NOTE: American English for this is **shopping cart**)

③ **supervise**
['suːpɪvaɪz] *verb*
to watch carefully, to see that work is well done; *she supervises all the new staff*; *our move to the new house was supervised by my wife*

④ **supervision**
[suːpɪˈvɪʒn] *noun*
act of supervising; *prisoners are allowed out under strict supervision to work on the prison farm*; *new staff work under supervision for the first three months*; *she is very experienced and can be left to work without any supervision*

③ **supervisor**
['suːpɪvaɪzɪ] *noun*
person who supervises work, a student, etc.; *if you have any questions, ask your supervisor*; *my supervisor says I am getting on very well*

④ **supper**
['sʌpɪ] *noun*
light meal which you eat in the evening; *what do you want for your supper?*; **to have supper** = to eat an evening meal; *we'll have supper outside*

as it is still hot; we usually have supper at about 7 o'clock; come and have some supper with us tomorrow evening; see note at DINNER

④ **supplement**

1 *noun*

['sʌplɪmɪnt]

(a) thing which is in addition, especially an additional amount; *the company gives him £200 per month as a supplement to his pension; you need to take a vitamin supplement every morning*

(b) additional section at the back of a book; *there is a list of Prime Ministers in the supplement at the back of the book*

(c) magazine which is part of a newspaper; *I read his article in the Sunday supplement*

2 *verb*

['sʌplɪment]

to add to; *we will supplement the ordinary staff with part-time people during the Christmas rush*

④ **supplier**

[sɪ'plaɪɪ] *noun*

person, company, or country which supplies; *they are major suppliers of spare parts to the car industry; a supplier of fertilizers or a fertilizer supplier*

② **supply**

[sɪ'plaɪ]

1 *noun*

(a) stock of something which is needed; *we have two weeks' supply of coal;* **in short supply** = not available in large enough quantities to meet the demand; *fresh vegetables are in short supply during the winter;* **the law of supply and demand** = general rule that the amount of something which is available is linked to the amount wanted by potential customers

(b) supplies = stock of food, etc., which is needed; *after two months at sea, their supplies were running out; the government sent medical supplies to the disaster area; we buy all our office supplies from one firm*

(c) something which is needed, such as goods, products or services; *the electricity supply has failed again; they signed a contract for the supply of computer equipment; rebel forces have cut off the town's water supply*

2 *verb*

to provide something which is needed; *details of addresses and phone numbers can be supplied by the store staff; he was asked to supply a blood sample; she was asked to supply the names of two referees; they have signed a contract to supply data;* **to supply someone with something** = to provide something to someone; *he supplies the hotel with cheese or he supplies cheese to the hotel*

3 *adjective*

supply teacher = teacher who takes the place of a permanent teacher who is away

② **support**

[sɪ'pɔːt]

1 *noun*

(a) thing which stops something from falling; *they had to build wooden supports to hold up the wall*

(b) something which helps keep something else in place; *the strap will provide some support for your knee*

(c) encouragement; *the chairman has the support of the committee; she spoke in support of our plan*

(d) financial help, money; *we have had no financial support from the bank;* **income support** = payments from the government to people with very low incomes

2 *verb*

(a) to hold something up to stop it falling down; *the roof is supported on ten huge pillars*

(b) to provide money to help; *we hope the banks will support us during the expansion period*

(c) to encourage; *which football team do you support?; she hopes the other members of the committee will support her*

(d) to accept; *the public will not support another price increase*

(e) to give help, to help to run; *the main computer system supports six PCs*

② **supporter**

[sɪ'pɔːtɪ] *noun*

person who encourages; *it sounds a good idea to me - I'm surprised it hasn't attracted more supporters;* **football supporter** = person who encourages a football team; *he's a Liverpool supporter*

④ **supportive**

[sɪ'pɔːtɪv] *adjective*

who supports or gives encouragement to someone; *he is very supportive of his children*

① **suppose**

[sʌ'pɪuz] *verb*

(a) to think something is probable; *where is the secretary? - I suppose she's going to be late as usual; I suppose you've heard the news?; what do you suppose they're talking about?; will you be coming to the meeting this evening? - I suppose I'll have to; I don't suppose many people will come*

(b) *(showing doubt)* what happens if?; *suppose it rains tomorrow, do you still want to go for a walk?; he's very late - suppose he's had an accident?; suppose I win the lottery!; (giving a doubtful yes) please can I go on the roundabout? - oh, I suppose so; (giving a doubtful no) it doesn't look as though anyone is coming to the meeting - I suppose not*

◊ **supposed to be**

[sɪ'pɪuzd tɪ 'biː] *phrase*

(a) should, ought to; *the children were supposed to be in bed; how I am supposed to know where he is?*

(b) believed to be; *he's supposed to be a good dentist; the film is supposed to be awful*

④ **supposedly**

[sɪ'pɪʊzɪdli] *adverb*

as you suppose; *she's supposedly going to phone us later*

④ **supposing**

[sɪ'pɪʊzɪŋ] *conjunction* what happens if?; *supposing it rains tomorrow, do you still want to go for a walk?; he's very late - supposing he's had an accident?*

④ **suppress**

[sɪ'pres] *verb*

(a) to limit something, such as a person's freedom; *the government suppressed the opposition movement and executed its leaders*

(b) to stop something being made public; *all opposition newspapers have been suppressed; they tried to suppress the evidence but it had already got into the newspapers*

(c) to stop yourself showing what you really feel; *she suppressed her feeling of disgust and tried to look happy; he couldn't suppress a smile*

④ **supreme**

[su'pri:m] *adjective*

(a) greatest, in the highest position; *her dog was supreme champion; it meant one last supreme effort, but they did it*

(b) **Supreme Court** = highest court in a country; *the Supreme Court was asked to rule on his case*

① **sure**

[ʃʊɪ]

1 *adjective*

(a) certain; *is he sure he can borrow his mother's car?; I'm sure I left my car keys in my coat pocket; it's sure to be cold in Russia in December; make sure or be sure that your computer is switched off before you leave; when taking a shower, please make sure that the shower curtain is inside the bath*

(b) which can be relied on; *it's a sure remedy for flu*

(c) **sure of yourself** = confident that what you do is right; *he's only just starting in business, so he's still not very sure of himself* (NOTE: **surer - surest**)

2 *adverb*

(a) *(mainly US) (meaning yes)* *can I borrow your car? - sure, go ahead!; I need someone to help with this computer program - sure, I can do it*

(b) *US (as emphasis)* *he sure was mad when he saw what they'd done to his car*

(c) **for sure** = certainly; *if you sell the house you'll regret it, and that's for sure!*

(d) **sure enough** = as was expected; *no one thought he would pass his exams and sure enough he failed*

① **surely**

['ʃʊɪli] *adverb*

(a) (used mostly in questions where a certain answer is expected) of course, I'm certain; *surely they can't expect us to work on Sundays?; but surely their office is in London, not Oxford?; they'll surely complain if we give them more work to do*

(b) carefully; **slowly but surely** = gradually; *slowly but surely he caught up with the leading car in the race*

① **surface**

['sɜ:fɪs]

1 *noun*

top part of something; *when it rains, water collects on the surface of the road; the surface of the lake was completely still; he stayed a long time under water before coming back to the surface; he seemed calm but under the surface he was furious; birds first appeared on the surface of the earth millions of years ago*

2 *verb*

(a) to come up to the surface; *the bird dived and then surfaced a few metres further on; his fear of failure has surfaced again*

(b) to cover a road, etc., with hard surface material; *we've had the drive surfaced with concrete; the kitchen floor is supposed to be surfaced with material which doesn't stain*

(c) *(informal)* to get up or wake up; *if you haven't surfaced by 8.30, I'll come and wake you up*

④ **surge**

[sɜ:dʒ]

1 *noun*

(a) sudden increase in the quantity of something; *the fine weather has brought a surge of interest in camping; the TV commercials generated a surge of orders*

(b) sudden rising up of water; *the surge of the sea between the rocks*

(c) sudden increase in electrical power; *power surges can burn out computer systems*

(d) sudden rush of emotion; *he felt a sudden surge of anger at the thought of having been cheated*

2 *verb*

(a) to rise suddenly; *the waves surged up onto the rocks*

(b) to move in a mass; *the crowd surged (forward) onto the football pitch; the fans surged around the pop star's car*

④ **surgeon**

['sɜ:dʒɪn] *noun*

doctor who specializes in surgery; *she has been sent to see an eye surgeon;* **house surgeon** = young surgeon working in a hospital in his or her last year of training; **dental surgeon** = DENTIST; *see also* PLASTIC

surgery

['sɜːdʒɪɪ] *noun*

(a) treatment of disease which requires an operation to cut into or remove part of the body; *she had surgery to straighten her nose*; *the patient will need surgery to remove the scars left by the accident* (NOTE: no plural in this meaning)

(b) room where a doctor or dentist sees and examines patients; *I phoned the doctor's surgery to make an appointment* (NOTE: American English is **doctor's office**)

(c) time when an MP receives visitors who ask him to solve their problems; *instead of writing to your MP why don't you go to one of her surgeries?* (NOTE: plural is **surgeries**)

surgical

['sɜːdʒɪkl] *adjective*

referring to surgery; **surgical gloves** = thin rubber gloves worn by a surgeon; *see also* SPIRIT

surname

['sɜːneɪm] *noun*

name of someone's family, shared by all people in the family; *her Christian name or first name is Anne, but I don't know her surname*; *Smith is the commonest surname in the London telephone directory*

surplus

['sɜːpləs]

1 *adjective*

extra, left over; *surplus butter is on sale in the shops*; *we are holding a sale of surplus stock*; **surplus to requirements** = more than is needed; *these copper pipes are surplus to our requirements*

2 *noun*

extra stock; material left over; *the problem of agricultural surpluses in the EU* (NOTE: plural is **surpluses**)

surprise

[sɪ'praɪz]

1 *noun*

(a) feeling when something happens which you did not expect to happen; *he expressed surprise when I told him I'd lost my job*; *to his great surprise, a lot of people bought his book*; *what a surprise to find that we were at school together!*

(b) unexpected event; *they baked a cake for her birthday as a surprise*; *what a surprise to see you again after so long!*

(c) to take someone by surprise = to shock someone by saying or doing something which they did not expect; *her question took him by surprise and he didn't know how to answer*

2 *adjective*

which is unexpected; *a surprise fall in the value of the dollar*; *they gave a surprise party for the retiring college principal*

3 *verb*

(a) to make someone surprised; *it wouldn't surprise me if it rained*; *what surprises me is that she left without saying goodbye*

(b) to find someone unexpectedly; *she surprised the two boys smoking in the yard*

surprised

[sɪ'praɪzd] *adjective*

astonished; *she was surprised to see her former boyfriend at the party*; *we were surprised to hear that he's got a good job*

surprising

[sɪ'praɪzɪŋ] *adjective*

astonishing, which you do not expect; *there was a surprising end to the story*; *wasn't it surprising to see the two sisters together again?*; *it's hardly surprising she doesn't want to see you again after what you said*

surprisingly

[sɪ'praɪzɪŋli] *adverb*

in a way which surprises; *considering she's just had an operation she looks surprisingly fit*; *not surprisingly, goods of this quality are very expensive*; *the magistrate was surprisingly soft on the youths*

surrender

[sɪ'rendɪ]

1 *noun*

(a) giving in to an enemy because you have lost; *the surrender of the enemy generals led to the end of the war*

(b) giving up of an insurance policy before the final date when it should mature; **surrender value** = money which an insurer will pay if an insurance policy is given up

2 *verb*

(a) to give in to an enemy because you have lost; *our troops were surrounded by the enemy and were forced to surrender*

(b) *(formal)* to give up a ticket, insurance policy, etc.; *he was asked to surrender his passport to the police*

surround

[sɪ'raʊnd] *verb*

to be all round someone *or* something; *the Prime Minister has surrounded himself with a group of advisers*; *floods had surrounded the village*

surrounded

[sɪ'raʊndɪd] *adjective*

with something all around; *the villa is outside the town, surrounded by vineyards*; *the surgeon, surrounded by his team of experts, started the operation at 9.30*; *the government collapsed, surrounded by scandals*

surroundings

[sɪ'raʊndɪŋz] *noun*

area around a person or place; *the surroundings of the hotel are very peaceful*; *she found herself in very unpleasant surroundings*

survey

1 *noun*

['sɜːveɪ]

(a) general report on a subject; general investigation by asking people questions; *we carried out a survey among our customers*; *the government has produced a survey of education needs*

(b) careful examination of a building to see if it is in good enough condition; *they asked for a survey of the house before buying it*; *the insurance company is carrying out a survey of the damage caused by the storm*; **a damage survey** = a report on damage done

(c) taking accurate measurements of land, so as to produce a plan or map

(d) quantity survey = calculating the cost of materials and labour needed for a building project

2 *verb*
[sɪ'veɪ]

(a) to ask people questions to get information about a subject; *roughly half the people we surveyed were in favour of the scheme*

(b) to make a survey of a building; *the insurance company brought in experts to survey the damage caused by the fire*

(c) to measure land in order to produce a plan or map; *they're surveying the area where the new airport will be built*

(d) to look at something so that you see all of it; *he stood on the roof of the palace surveying the crowd in the square*

③ **survival**
[sɪ'vaɪvl] *noun*

continuing to exist; *the survival of the crew depended on the supplies carried in the boat*; *the survival rate of babies has started to fall*; **the survival of the fittest** = the process of evolution of a species, by which the characteristics that help it to survive are passed on to its young, and those characteristics which do not help survival are not passed on

② **survive**
[sɪ'vaɪv] *verb*

(a) to continue to be alive after an accident, etc.; *it was such a terrible crash, it was miracle that anyone survived*; *the President has survived two bomb attacks this year*; *he survived a massive heart attack*; *not all the baby pigs survived more than a few days*

(b) to continue to exist; *it is one of the three surviving examples of his work*

(c) to live longer than someone else; *he survived his wife by ten years*; *she had no surviving relatives*; *he is survived by his only son*

④ **survivor**
[sɪ'vaɪvə] *noun*

person who is still alive after an accident, etc.; *helicopters were sent out to look for survivors*

② **suspect**
1 *adjective*
['sʌspekt]

which might be dangerous; *don't eat any of that fish - it looks a bit suspect to me*; **suspect package** = package which might contain a bomb

2 *noun*
['sʌspekt]

person who is thought to have committed a crime; *the police arrested several suspects for questioning*

3 *verb*
[sɪ'spekt]

(a) to suspect someone of doing something = to think that someone may have done something wrong; *I suspect him of being involved in the robbery*; *they were wrongly suspected of taking bribes*

(b) to guess, to think that something is likely; *I suspect it's going to be more difficult that we thought at first*; *we suspected all along that something was wrong*

④ **suspend**
[sɪ'spend] *verb*

(a) to hang something; *the ham is suspended in the smoke over a fire for some time, which gives it a particular taste*

(b) to stop something for a time; *work on the construction project has been suspended*; *sailings have been suspended until the weather gets better*

(c) to stop someone from doing something, such as working; *he has been suspended on full pay while investigations are continuing*

③ **suspenders**
[sʌ'spendɪz] *noun*

US straps which go over your shoulders to hold up your trousers; *he wore bright red suspenders with his jeans* (NOTE: British English for this is **braces**)

④ **suspicion**
[sɪ'spɪʃn] *noun*

(a) feeling that something is wrong, that someone has committed a crime; *his actions immediately aroused suspicion on the part of the police*; *the bank regards his business deals with considerable suspicion*; *they were arrested on suspicion of exporting stolen goods*

(b) general feeling that something is going to happen; *I have a suspicion that he's coming to see me because he wants to borrow some money*; *her suspicions proved to be correct when she saw the wedding announced in the paper*

③ **suspicious**
[sɪ'spɪʃɪs] *adjective*

(a) which seems to be wrong, dangerous or connected with a crime; *the police found a suspicious package on the station platform*; *that the secretary seemed to know all about the deal before everyone else was very suspicious*; *we became suspicious when we realized we hadn't seen him for three days*

(b) suspicious of = not trusting; *I'm suspicious of people who tell me they know a way of getting rich quickly*

③ **sustain**
[sɪ'steɪn] *verb*
(a) to make something continue; *how long can this level of activity be sustained?*
(b) to receive an injury; *he sustained severe head injuries*
(c) to give you strength; *you need a good breakfast to sustain you through the day*

③ **swallow**
['swɒləʊ]
1 *verb*
(a) to make food or liquid pass down your throat from your mouth to the stomach; *he swallowed his beer and ran back to the office*; *she swallowed hard and knocked on the door to the interview room*
(b) to accept something; *he finds being made redundant hard to swallow*
2 *noun*
common bird with pointed wings and tail, which flies fast; *there are several swallows' nests under the roof*

③ **swallow up**
['swɒləʊ 'ʌp] *verb*
to make something disappear inside; *he stepped out of the door and was swallowed up in the crowd*; *more than half my salary is swallowed up in mortgage repayments*

③ **swam**
[swæm] *see* SWIM

④ **swamp**
[swɒmp]
1 *noun*
area of land that is always wet, and the plants that grow in it; *you can't build on that land - it's a swamp*
2 *verb*
(a) to cover something with water; *the waves nearly swamped our little boat*
(b) swamped with = having so much, that it is impossible to deal with it all; *the office is swamped with work*; *the switchboard has been swamped with calls*

④ **swan**
[swɒn]
1 *noun*
large white water bird with a long curved neck; *there are swans on the Thames near Windsor*; *the swans stood by the edge of the water, flapping their wings*
2 *verb*
(informal) **to go swanning off** *or* **around** = to go off or travel about lazily, not doing any work; *instead of going to university he spent a year swanning around the Pacific islands*

COMMENT: in England, all swans belong to the crown. The swans on the Thames are counted every year

③ **swap** *or* **swop**
[swɒp]
1 *verb*
to exchange something for something else; *can I swap my tickets for next Friday's show?*; *let's swap places, so that I can talk to Susan*; *after every game the players swapped shirts with the other team*; *they swapped jobs* = each of them took the other's job (NOTE: **swapping** *or* **swopping - swapped** *or* **swopped**)
2 *noun*
(a) exchange of one thing for another; *I'll do a swap with you - one of my CDs for your T-shirt*
(b) swaps = things, such as stamps, coins, etc., which you have ready to exchange for others; *I have a few swaps left but nobody wants them*

④ **sway**
[sweɪ]
1 *verb*
(a) to move, bending in a smooth way from side to side; *the crowd swayed in time to the music*; *the palm trees swayed in the breeze*
(b) to have an influence on; *the committee was swayed by a letter from the president*
2 *noun*
to hold sway over someone = to hold power over someone; *he held sway in Russia for several years*

② **swear**
['sweə] *verb*
(a) to make a solemn public promise; *he swore he wouldn't touch alcohol again*; *the witnesses swore to tell the truth*; **to swear someone to secrecy** = to make someone swear not to tell a secret; *he was sworn to secrecy*
(b) to take an oath; **to swear someone in** = to make an official take an oath; *he was sworn in as governor*
(c) *(informal)* **I could have sworn** = I was totally sure; *I could have sworn I put my keys in my coat pocket*
(d) to shout curses; *they were shouting and swearing at the police*; *don't let me catch you swearing again!*
(e) *(informal)* **to swear by** = to believe completely in something; *he swears by an old Chinese medicine* (NOTE: **swearing - swore** [swɔː] **- sworn** [swɔːn])

④ **sweat**
[swet]
1 *noun*
drops of salt liquid which come through your skin when you are hot or when you are afraid; *after working in the field all day he was covered in sweat*; *he broke out into a cold sweat when they called his name*; **sweat gland** = gland in the body that produces sweat
2 *verb*
to produce sweat; *he ran up the hill, sweating and red in the face*; *see also* LABOUR

④ **sweater**
['sweti] *noun*
knitted pullover with long sleeves; *you'll need a sweater in the evenings, even in the desert*

④ **sweatshirt**
['swetʃɜːt] *noun*
thick cotton shirt with long sleeves; *a sweatshirt is comfortable if the evening is cool*

① **Swede**
[swiːd] *noun*
person from Sweden; *the Swedes have a very high standard of living*

① **Sweden**
['swiːdn] *noun*
country in northern Europe, between Norway and Finland; *we went for a camping holiday in Sweden*; *summer evenings in Sweden can be quite cool* (NOTE: capital: **Stockholm**; people: **the Swedes**; language: **Swedish**; currency: **the Swedish krona**)

① **Swedish**
['swiːdɪʃ]
1 *adjective*
coming from Sweden; referring to Sweden; *have you bought the new Swedish stamps?*; *Swedish roads do not have as much traffic as ours*
2 *noun*
language spoken in Sweden; *can you translate this letter into Swedish, please?*; *their children spoke Swedish with their grandmother*

③ **sweep**
[swiːp]
1 *verb*
(a) to clear up dust, dirt, etc., from the floor with a brush; *have you swept the kitchen floor yet?*
(b) to sweep the board = to win completely; *the British team swept the board in the Grand Prix*
(c) to move rapidly; *she swept into the room, with a glass of wine in her hand*; *the party swept to power in the general election*; *a feeling of anger swept through the crowd*; to sweep past = to go past quickly; *the president's car swept past*; *she swept past without saying a word*
(d) to follow a curve; *the motorway sweeps round the mountain*; *the road sweeps down to the harbour*
(e) to sweep something away = to carry something rapidly away; *the river flooded and swept away part of the village*; *she was swept away by the powerful current* (NOTE: sweeping - swept [swept])
2 *noun*
(a) act of clearing things with a brush; *I'll just give the hall floor a sweep*
(b) to make a clean sweep of something = (i) to clear something away completely; (ii) to win everything; *he made a clean sweep of all the old files*; *they made a clean sweep at the local government elections*

(c) wide open area; *the green sweep of the lawn running down to the lake*
(d) wide movement of your arm; *with a sweep of his arm he knocked all the glasses off the table*

② **sweet**
[swiːt]
1 *adjective*
(a) tasting like sugar, and neither sour nor bitter; *these apples are sweeter than those green ones*; to have a sweet tooth = to like sweet food; *he's very fond of puddings - he's got a real sweet tooth!*
(b) charming, pleasant; *he sent me such a sweet birthday card*; *it was sweet of her to send me flowers*; *what a sweet little girl!*; *how sweet of you to help me with my luggage!* (NOTE: **sweeter - sweetest**)
2 *noun*
(a) small piece of sweet food, made with sugar; *she bought some sweets to eat in the cinema*; *he likes to suck sweets when he is driving* (NOTE: American English for this is **candy**); cough sweets = sweet pills which you suck to cure a cough
(b) last course in a meal, sweet food eaten at the end of a meal; *what's on the menu for sweet?*; *we haven't had our sweet yet*; *I won't have any sweet, thank you, just some coffee*; sweet trolley = trolley with different sweet dishes, brought to your table in a restaurant for you to choose from; *the waiter brought a sweet trolley to our table*
(c) *(old term used to someone you love)* yes, my sweet, I'll be with you in a minute (NOTE: do not confuse with **suite**)

④ **swell**
[swel]
1 *verb*
to get bigger, to make bigger; *more and more people arrived to swell the crowd outside the palace gates*; to swell (up) = to become larger or to increase in size; *she was bitten by an insect and her hand swelled (up)* (NOTE: **swelling - swollen** ['swəʊlɪn] **- swelled**)
2 *adjective*
US (informal) very good; *we had a swell time in New York City*; *that sounds like a swell idea*
3 *noun*
movement of large waves in the open sea; *the boat rose and fell with the swell*; *there's a heavy swell running*

③ **swept**
[swept] *see* SWEEP

④ **swift**
[swɪft]
1 *adjective*
rapid; *their phone call brought a swift response from the police* (NOTE: **swifter - swiftest**)
2 *noun*
little bird like a swallow but with shorter wings and tail, which flies very fast

④ **swim**

[swɪm]

1 *noun*

moving in the water, using your arms and legs to push you along; *what about a swim before breakfast?*; *it's too cold for a swim*

2 *verb*

(a) to move in the water using your arms and legs to push you along; *she can't swim, but she's taking swimming lessons*; *she swam across the English Channel*; *salmon swim up the rivers in spring time*

(b) my head is swimming = I feel dizzy; *my head was swimming after working at the computer all day*

(c) to swim against the tide = to do things differently from everyone else; *carry on as you are, even if you think you're swimming against the tide*

(d) swimming in *or* swimming with = in a lot of liquid; *a plate of lamb swimming in sauce*; *sausages swimming in hot fat* (NOTE: swimming - swam) [swæm] - has swum [swʌm])

② **swimming**

['swɪmɪŋ] *noun*

action of swimming; **swimming costume** = clothing worn by women when swimming; *we forgot to bring our swimming costumes*; **swimming trunks** = short trousers worn by men and boys when swimming

② **swimming pool**

['swɪmɪŋ 'puːl] *noun*

large pool for swimming; *the school has an indoor swimming pool*; *she swam two lengths of the swimming pool*

③ **swing**

[swɪŋ]

1 *noun*

(a) movement of your arm forwards and backwards; **to take a swing at someone** = to try to hit someone; *someone took a swing at him with a stick*

(b) change in opinion which can be measured; *there was a swing of 10% to the socialists in the elections*

(c) to go with a swing = to go very well, to be very enjoyable; *the party went with a swing*; **to get into the swing of things** = to enjoy being involved; *he'd never been to a night club before but soon got into the swing of things*; **in full swing** = going very well; *when we arrived the party was in full swing*

(d) seat held by ropes or chains, to sit on and move backwards and forwards, usually outdoors; *she sat on the swing and ate an apple*

2 *verb*

(a) to move from side to side or forwards and backwards, while hanging from a central point; *she picked up the baby and swung him round and round*; *he swung up and down on the garden swing*; *a window swung open and a man looked out*

(b) to change direction or opinion; *the car swung off the road into the hotel car park*; *the voters swung to the right in Sunday's elections*; *he swung round to face the crowd*

(c) to move with a swing; *they were swinging the bags one after the other into the rubbish van*; *he swung his suitcase up onto the rack* (NOTE: swinging - swung [swʌŋ])

① **Swiss**

[swɪs]

1 *adjective*

(a) referring to Switzerland; *we eat a lot of Swiss cheese*; *the Swiss banking system protects the identity of its customers*

(b) Swiss roll = cake made by rolling up a thin sheet of cake covered with jam or cream (NOTE: American English is **jelly roll**)

2 *noun*

a Swiss = a person from Switzerland; **the Swiss** = people from Switzerland; *the Swiss celebrate their national day on August 1st*

② **switch**

[swɪtʃ]

1 *noun*

(a) small device that you push up or down to stop or start an electrical device; *the switch to turn off the electricity is in the cupboard*; *there is a light switch by the bed*

(b) sudden change in opinion; *a switch in government policy* (NOTE: plural is **switches**)

2 *verb*

(a) to do something quite different suddenly; *we decided to switch from gas to electricity*

(b) to exchange; *let's switch places*; *he switched flights in Montreal and went on to Calgary*; *the job was switched from our British factory to the States*

③ **switchboard**

['swɪtʃbɔːd] *noun*

central point in a telephone system, where all lines meet; *you should phone the switchboard if you can't get the number you want*; *we have to stagger the lunch hour so that there is always someone on the switchboard*

③ **switch off**

['swɪtʃ 'ɒf] *verb*

(a) to make an electrical device stop; *don't forget to switch off the TV before you go to bed*; *she forgot to switch her car lights off or switch off her car lights*; *the kettle switches itself off automatically when it boils*

(b) *(informal)* to stop listening to what someone is saying; *if you talk too slowly, everyone starts to switch off*; *I just switched off once the discussion started getting too technical*

③ **switch on**

['swɪtʃ 'ɒn] *verb*

(a) to make an electrical device start; *can you switch the radio on - it's time for the evening* *news?*; *when you put the light on in the bathroom, the fan switches itself on automatically*

(b) *(informal)* **switched on** = with it, knowing all that is happening; *she's very switched on to what is happening on the fashion scene*

③ **switch over to**
['swɪtʃ 'ʊʊvɪ tuː] *verb*
to change to something quite different; *we have switched over to gas for our heating*

① **Switzerland**
['swɪtzɪlænd] *noun*
European country, south of Germany, east of France and north of Italy; *many people go on skiing holidays in Switzerland*; *we went to Switzerland last summer* (NOTE: capital: **Berne**; people: **the Swiss**; languages: **French, German, Italian**; currency: **the Swiss franc**)

③ **swollen**
['swɪʊlɪn] *adjective*
much bigger than usual; *she can't walk with her swollen ankle*; *the swollen river burst its banks*; *see also* SWELL

③ **swop**
[swɒp] *noun & verb*
see SWAP

④ **sword**
[sɔːd] *noun*
weapon with a handle and a long sharp blade; *he rushed onto the stage waving a sword*

③ **swore**
[swɔː] *see* SWEAR

③ **sworn**
[swɔːn] *adjective*
under oath; *in his sworn statement he said something quite different*; **sworn enemies** = people who will always be enemies; *see also* SWEAR

③ **swum**
[swʌm] *see* SWIM

③ **swung**
[swʌŋ] *see* SWING

③ **symbol**
['sɪmbl] *noun*
sign, letter, picture or shape which means something or shows something; *they use a bear as their advertising symbol*; *the crown was the symbol of the empire*; *the olive branch is a symbol of peace*; *Pb is the chemical symbol for lead*

④ **symbolic** *or* **symbolical**
[sɪm'bɒlɪk or sɪm'bɒlɪkl] *adjective*
used as a symbol; *an olive branch is symbolic of peace*

③ **sympathetic**
[sɪmpɪ'θetɪk] *adjective*
showing that you understand someone's problems; *I'm very sympathetic to her problems*; *he wasn't very sympathetic when I told him I felt ill*

④ **sympathize**
['sɪmpɪθaɪz] *verb*
to sympathize with someone = to show that you understand someone's problems; *I sympathize with you, my husband snores too; I get back pains, and I sympathize with all fellow sufferers*

④ **sympathy**
['sɪmpɪθi] *noun*
(a) feeling of understanding for someone else's problems, or after someone's death; *we received many messages of sympathy when my wife died; I find it difficult to express my sympathy when someone whom I hardly know dies*; *he had no sympathy for his secretary who complained of having too much work*

(b) agreement with or support for someone *or* something; *I have a good deal of sympathy with the idea*; **to come out on strike in sympathy** = to stop work to show that you agree with another group of workers who are on strike; *the postal workers went on strike and the telephone engineers came out in sympathy* (NOTE: plural is **sympathies**)

④ **symphony**
['sɪmfɪni] *noun*
long piece of music in several parts, called 'movements', played by a full orchestra; *a performance of Beethoven's Fifth Symphony*; *Smetana included themes from folk music in his symphonies* (NOTE: plural is **symphonies**)

③ **symptom**
['sɪmptɪm] *noun*
(a) change in the way the body works, or change in the way the body looks, showing that a disease is present and has been noticed by the patient or doctor; *he has all the symptoms of measles*

(b) visible sign which shows that something is happening; *rubbish everywhere on the pavements is a symptom of the cash facing the town*

④ **syndicate**
1 *noun*
['sɪndɪkɪt]
group of people or companies working together to make money; *a German investment syndicate*

2 *verb*
['sɪndɪkeɪt]
to produce an article, a cartoon, etc., which is then published in several newspapers or magazines; *his cartoon strip is syndicated across the US*; *she writes a syndicated column on personal finance*

④ **syndrome**
['sɪndrɪʊm] *noun*
(a) group of symptoms which taken together show that a particular disease or condition is present; *their daughter has Down's syndrome*

(b) general feeling or way of approaching a problem, etc.; *it's an example of the 'let's go home early on Friday afternoon' syndrome*

① **system**
['sɪstɪm] *noun*
(a) group of things which work together; *the system of motorways or the motorway system; the London underground railway system;* **computer system** = set of programs, commands, etc., which run a computer; **central nervous system** = the brain and the cord running down the spine, which link together all the nerves
(b) the body as a whole; *being made redundant gives a serious shock to the system*

(c) way in which things are organized; *I've got my own system for dealing with invoices;* **filing system** = way of putting documents in order for easy reference

④ **systematic**
[sɪstɪ'mætɪk] *adjective*
organized in a good way; *a more systematic approach is needed; he organized a systematic attempt to bring down the government; she ordered a systematic report on the distribution service*

Tt

③ **T, t**
[ti:]
twentieth letter of the alphabet, between S and U; *don't forget - you spell 'attach' with two Ts;* **to dot the i's and cross the t's** = to settle the final details of an agreement; **T-junction** = junction where one road joins another at right angles; *go down the road and turn right at the T-junction*

① **table**
['teɪbl]
1 *noun*
(a) piece of furniture with a flat top and legs, used to eat at, work at, etc. ; *we had breakfast sitting round the kitchen table; he asked for a table by the window; she says she booked a table for six people for 12.30;* **to lay the table** *or* **to set the table** = to put knives, forks, spoons, plates, etc., on a table ready for a meal; *can someone set the table please, the food's almost ready; the table was laid for six;* **to clear the table** = to take away the dirty knives, forks, spoons, plates, etc., after a meal; *the waitress cleared a table for us and we sat down*
(b) list of figures, facts, information set out in columns; **table of contents** = list of contents in a book
(c) list of numbers to learn by heart how each number is multiplied; *he's learnt his nine times table*
2 *verb*
to put items of information on the table before a meeting; *the report of the finance committee was tabled;* **to table a motion** = to put forward a proposal for discussion by putting details of it on the table at a meeting

③ **tablecloth**
['teɪblklɒθ] *noun*
cloth which covers a table during a meal; *put a clean tablecloth on the table; the coffee stains on the tablecloth won't come out*

④ **tablespoon**
['teɪblspu:n] *noun*
(a) large spoon for serving food at table
(b) amount held in a tablespoon; *add two tablespoons of sugar*

④ **tablet**
['tæblɪt] *noun*
small round pill taken as medicine; *take two tablets before meals*

③ **table tennis**
['teɪbl 'tenɪs] *noun*
game similar to tennis, but played on a large table with a net across the centre, with small round bats and a very light white ball; *do you want a game of table tennis?* (NOTE: also called ping pong)

④ **tack**
[tæk]
1 *noun*
small nail with a wide head; **carpet tack** = nail for attaching a carpet to the floor; *(informal)* **to get down to brass tacks** = to start discussing the real problem
(b) movement of a sailing boat in a certain direction as it sails against the wind; **to change tack** = to start doing something different; *originally he offered to pay the all costs of the party and then changed tack and asked everyone to pay for themselves*
2 *verb*

(a) to nail something down using tacks; *he tacked down the edge of the carpet*

(b) *(in a sailing ship)* to change direction so that wind blows the sails from the other side; **they were tacking up the river =** they sailed up the river changing direction all the time because the wind was against them

③ **tackle**
['tækl]
1 *noun*

(a) equipment; *he brought his fishing tackle with him*

(b) *(in football, etc.)* trying to take the ball from an opposing player; *(in Rugby)* grabbing an opposing player so that he falls down and drops the ball

2 *verb*

(a) to grab someone to stop him doing something; *he tried to tackle the burglar himself*

(b) to try to deal with a problem or job; *you can't tackle a job like changing the central heating system on your own*; *you start cleaning the dining room and I'll tackle the washing up*

(c) *(in football, etc.)* to try to get the ball from an opposing player; *(in Rugby)* to grab hold of an opposing player so that he falls down and drops the ball; *he was tackled before he could score*

④ **tactic**
['tæktɪk] *noun*
(often plural)

(a) way of doing something so as to get an advantage; *his tactic is to wait until near closing time, when the supermarket reduces the price of all types of food*

(b) way of fighting a war; *guerrilla tactics were successful against the advancing army*

④ **tag**
[tæg]
1 *noun*

(a) label, a piece of paper, plastic, etc., attached to something to show a price, contents, someone's name and address, etc.; **gift tag =** little label put on a parcel to show who it is for and who it is from; **name tag =** label with a name printed on it; *visitors to the factory are given name tags*; **price tag =** label with the price printed on it; *the car has a £50,000 price tag*

(b) children's game where the first child has to try to touch another one who then chases the others in turn; *they were playing tag in the school playground*

2 *verb*

(a) to attach a label to something; *these coats need to be tagged before you put them on the racks*; *we tag birds so that we can study their migration routes*

(b) *(informal)* **to tag along behind someone =** to follow close behind someone; *whenever we go out for a walk my sister insists on tagging along*

(c) **to tag something on to something =** to attach something at the end of something else; *he tagged on an extra section at the end of the letter* (NOTE: **tagging - tagged**)

② **tail**
[teɪl]
1 *noun*

(a) long thin part at the end of an animal's body, which can move; *all you could see was a slight movement of the cat's tail*; **to turn tail =** to turn round and run away; *as soon as they heard the dog barking, the burglars turned tail and ran off* (NOTE: do not confuse with **tale**)

(b) end or back part of something; *the tail of the queue stretched round the corner and into the next street*; *they say it is safer to sit near the tail of an aircraft*

(c) **tails =** the side of a coin without the head of a king, etc., on it; **heads or tails =** throwing a coin in the air to see which side comes down on top; *let's toss heads or tails for the bill!*

(d) long back part of a coat or shirt; *he tucked the tail of his shirt back into his trousers*

(e) **tails =** man's evening dress, a black coat with a long tail, black trousers, white bow tie, etc.; *all the men wore white ties and tails to the ball*

2 *verb*

to follow close behind someone; *the police tailed the lorry from the harbour to the warehouse*

③ **tail off**
['teɪl 'ɒf] *verb*

to become fainter or less; *he started speaking, but his voice tailed off into a whisper*; *the number of overseas visitors starts to tail off in September*

④ **tailor**
['teɪlə]
1 *noun*

person who makes clothes for men, such as suits, coats, etc.; *he gets all his clothes made by a tailor in Oxford Street*

2 *verb*

(a) to make clothes which fit closely; *she wore a tailored jacket*

(b) to adapt something to fit a special need; *the payments can be tailored to suit your requirements*; *this course is tailored to the needs of women going back to work*

① **take**
[teɪk]
1 *verb*

(a) to lift and move something; *she took the pot of jam down from the shelf*; *the waiter took the tablecloth off the table*

(b) to carry something to another place; *can you take this cheque to the bank for me, please?*

(c) to go with someone or something to another place; *he's taking the children to school*; *they took the car to the garage*; *we took a taxi to the hotel*

(d) to steal; *someone's taken my watch*

(e) to go away with something which someone else was using; *someone has taken the newspaper I was reading; who's taken my cup of coffee?*

(f) to use or occupy; *sorry, all these seats are taken;* **to take your seats** = to sit down; *please take your seats, the play is about to start*

(g) to do a test; *you must go to bed early because you'll be taking your exams tomorrow morning; she had to take her driving test three times before she finally passed*

(h) to eat or to drink (often); *do you take sugar in your tea?; how do you take your coffee - black or white?; take the medicine three times a day after meals*

(i) to accept; *if they offer you the job, take it immediately*

(j) to do certain actions; *we took our holiday in September this year; she's taking a shower after going to the beach; she took a photograph or took a picture of the Tower of London; she needs to take a rest;* **to take action** = to do something; *you must take immediate action if you want to stop people stealing from the shop;* **to take a call** = to answer the telephone; *I was out of the office so my secretary took the call;* **to take the chair** = to be chairman of a meeting; *in the absence of the chairman his deputy took the chair;* **to take dictation** = to write down what someone is saying; *the secretary was taking dictation from the managing director;* **to take place** = to happen; *the reception will take place on Saturday;* **to take stock** = to count the items in a warehouse; **to take stock of a situation** = to examine the state of things before deciding what to do; *when we had taken stock of the situation, we decided the best thing to do was to sell the house*

(k) to need; *it took three strong men to move the piano; they took two days or it took them two days to get to London; when he wants to watch a TV programme it never seems to take him long to finish his homework*

(l) to accept or to hold; *the ticket machine takes 10p and 20p coins; the lift can take up to six passengers*

(m) to be successful, to have the right effect; **his kidney transplant has taken** = the transplant has been successful (NOTE: **taking - took** [tʊk] **- has taken** ['teɪkn])

2 *noun*

(a) money received in a shop; *today's take was less than yesterday's*

(b) scene which has been filmed; *the actors took a break between takes*

⓪ take after
['teɪk 'ɑːftə] *verb*
to look like a parent or relative; *she takes after her mother*

⓪ take away
['teɪk ə'weɪ] *verb*
(a) to remove something *or* someone; *take those scissors away from little Nicky - he could cut himself; the ambulance came and took her away; the police took away piles of documents from the office*

(b) to subtract one number from another (NOTE: **take away** is usually shown by the minus sign - : **10 - 4 = 6:** say 'ten take away four equals six')

⓪ takeaway
['teɪkɪweɪ] *noun & adjective; (informal)*
(a) shop where you can buy cooked food to eat somewhere else; *there's an Indian takeaway round the corner*

(b) hot meal which you buy to eat back home; *we had a Chinese takeaway* (NOTE: American English is **takeout**)

⓪ take back
['teɪk 'bæk] *verb*
(a) to go back with something; *if the trousers are too short you can take them back to the shop; if you don't like the colour, you can take it back and change it*

(b) to accept something which someone has brought back; *I took my trousers to the shop where I had bought them, but they wouldn't take them back because I didn't have a receipt*

(c) to withdraw something which has been said, and apologize for it; *I take it all back - they're a marvellous team*

⓪ take down
['teɪk 'daʊn] *verb*
(a) to reach up and bring something down; *I took the jar down from the shelf*

(b) to bring something down which had been put up; *on January 6th we take down the Christmas decorations; they have finished the roof and are taking down their ladders*

(c) to write down; *the policeman took down his name and address*

⓪ take in
['teɪk 'ɪn] *verb*
(a) to bring inside something which was outside; *the boat was taking in water; in October they took in the lemon trees from the gardens*

(b) to understand; *I don't think she took in anything of what you said*

(c) to deceive; *thousands of people were taken in by the advertisement*

(d) to make a piece of clothing smaller; *can you take these trousers in? - they're much too loose round the waist* (NOTE: the opposite in this meaning is to **let out**)

⓪ take off
['teɪk 'ɒf] *verb*
(a) to remove, especially your clothes; *he took off all his clothes or he took all his clothes off; take your dirty boots off before you come into the kitchen; see also* HAT

(b) to remove or to deduct; *he took £25 off the price*

(c) *(of plane)* to leave the ground; *the plane took off at 4.30*

(d) to remove someone in a plane or helicopter; *the ship was listing badly and the crew had to be taken off by helicopter*

(e) to start to rise fast; *sales took off after the TV commercials*

(f) she took the day off = she decided not to work for the day

(g) to imitate someone in a funny way; *he likes to make everyone laugh by taking off the head teacher*

③ **takeoff**
['teɪkɒf] *noun*
(of an aircraft) leaving the ground; *I always ask for a seat by the window, so that I can watch the takeoff*

③ **take on**
['teɪk 'ɒn] *verb*
(a) to agree to do a job; *she's taken on a part-time job in addition to the one she's already got*

(b) to agree to have someone as a worker; *the shop has taken on four youngsters straight from school; we need to take on more staff to cope with the extra work*

(c) to fight someone; *it seems he is taking on the whole government*

① **take out**
['teɪk 'aut] *verb*
(a) to pull something out; *he took out a gun and waved it around; the dentist had to take his tooth out*

(b) to invite someone to go out; *I'm taking all the office staff out for a drink*

(c) to take out insurance against theft = to pay a premium to an insurance company, so that if a theft takes place the company will pay compensation; to take out £50 = to remove £50 in cash from a bank account

(d) the hot weather takes it out of you = the hot weather makes you very tired; to take it out on someone = to make someone suffer because you are upset or worried; *he keeps on taking it out on his secretary*

③ **takeout**
['teɪkaut] *noun*
US hot meal which you buy to eat back home; *we had a takeout Chinese meal* (NOTE: British English is **takeaway**)

① **take over**
['teɪk 'əuvə] *verb*
(a) to start to do something in place of someone else; *Miss Black took over from Mr Jones on May 1st; thanks for looking after the switchboard for me - I'll take over from you now; when our history teacher was ill, the English teacher had to take over his classes; the Socialists took over from the Conservatives*

(b) to buy a business by offering to buy most of its shares; *the company was taken over by a big group last month*

① **takeover**
['teɪkəuvə] *noun*
(a) buying of a controlling interest in a business by buying more than 50% of the shares; *the takeover may mean that a lot of people will lose their jobs*; takeover bid = offer to buy all or most of the shares of a business so as to control it; to make a takeover bid for a company = to offer to buy most of the shares in a company; hostile takeover = takeover where the board of the company being bought do not recommend the sale and try to fight it

(b) occupying a capital city and removing the government; *many people were killed during the military takeover*

③ **take to**
['teɪk 'tu:] *verb*
(a) to start to do something as a habit; *he's taken to looking under his bed every night to make sure no one is hiding there; she's recently taken to wearing trousers to work;* he took to drink = he started to drink alcohol regularly

(b) to start to like someone; *she took to her boss right away*

③ **take up**
['teɪk 'ʌp] *verb*
(a) to occupy or to fill a space; *this sofa takes up too much room; being in charge of the staff sports club takes up too much of my time*

(b) to remove something which was down; *you will need to take up the carpets if you want to polish the floor*

(c) to start to do a certain activity, sport, etc.; *she was over fifty when she took up long-distance running*

(d) to take someone up on something = to accept an offer made by someone; *he asked me if I wanted two tickets to Wimbledon and I took him up on his offer*

③ **tale**
[teɪl] *noun*
(literary) story; *a tale of a princess and her wicked sisters;* old wives' tale = old, and often silly, idea; *eating carrots won't make you see in the dark - that's just an old wives' tale* (NOTE: do not confuse with **tail**)

③ **talent**
['tælɪnt] *noun*
(a) natural ability or skill; *she has a talent for getting customers to spend money*

(b) people with natural ability; *the club is always on the lookout for fresh talent;* talent contest = contest to find new performers, singers, etc.

④ **talented**
['tælɪntɪd] *adjective*
with a lot of talent; *she's a very talented musician*

① **talk**
[tɔ:k]
1 *noun*

(a) conversation, discussion; *we had a little talk, and she agreed with what the committee had decided*; *I had a long talk with my father about what I should study at university*

(b) **talks** = negotiations; *we have entered into talks with the union leaders*

(c) lecture about a subject; *he gave a short talk about the history of the town*

(d) general rumour; *there has been talk of a change of government*

2 *verb*

to say things, to speak; *the guide was talking French to the group of tourists*; *I didn't understand what he was talking about*; *we must talk to the neighbours about their noisy dog - he kept me awake again last night*; *they're talking of selling their house and going to live by the sea*

③ **talk into**
['tɔːk 'ɪntuː] *verb*

to talk someone into doing something = to persuade someone to do something; *the salesman talked us into buying a new car*

③ **talk over**
['tɔːk 'əʊvɪ] *verb*

to discuss; *we've talked it over and decided not to leave*; *if you want to borrow money, go and talk it over with the bank manager*; *why don't you come and talk it over with your mother?*

③ **talk round**
['tɔːk 'raʊnd] *verb*

to persuade someone to change his or her mind; *he wanted to resign immediately, but I managed to talk him round*

② **tall**
[tɔːl] *adjective*

(a) high, usually higher than normal; *the bank building is the tallest building in London*; *can you see those tall trees over there?*; *he's the tallest boy in his class*; *how tall are you? - I'm six foot two (6' 2")*

(b) *(informal)* **tall order** = difficult task; *asking all the staff to move house is a really tall order* (NOTE: **taller - tallest.** Note also the use with figures: **the tree is two metres tall**; **he's six foot tall**; **tall** is used with people and thin things like trees or skyscrapers; for things which are a long way above the ground use **high: high clouds, a high mountain**)

④ **tan**
[tæn]

1 *adjective*

with a brown and yellow colour; *he was wearing tan shoes*

2 *noun*

(a) brown and yellow colour; *have you got the same shoes, but in tan?*

(b) brown colour of the skin after being in the sun; *she got a tan from spending each day on the beach*

3 *verb*

to get brown from being in the sun; *she tans easily - just half an hour in the sun and she's quite brown* (NOTE: **tanning - tanned**)

④ **tangle**
['tæŋgl]

1 *noun*

mass of threads, string, hair, etc., all mixed together; *the tangle of shrubs in the back garden needs clearing*; **in a tangle** = all mixed up; *all my wool is in a tangle*

2 *verb*

(a) to get things mixed together in knots; *her hair is so tangled that it's impossible to comb it*

(b) **to tangle with someone** = to get into an argument with someone; *tourists are advised not to tangle with the local football supporters*

② **tank**
[tæŋk] *noun*

(a) large container for liquids; *how much oil is left in the tank?*; **petrol tank** = container built into a car, truck, etc., for holding petrol; **water tank** = tank for holding water

(b) armoured vehicle with caterpillar tracks and powerful guns; *tanks rolled along the main streets of the town*

④ **tanker**
['tæŋkɪ] *noun*

ship or truck for carrying liquids, especially oil; *an oil tanker ran onto the rocks in the storm*; *a petrol tanker broke down on the motorway*

③ **tap**
[tæp]

1 *noun*

(a) device with a knob which, when you twist it, lets liquid or gas come out; *he washed his hands under the tap in the kitchen*; *she forgot to turn the gas tap off*; **tap water** = water which comes through pipes into a building and not from a well; *we haven't got any bottled water, will tap water be all right?*; **cold tap** = tap which produces cold water; **hot tap** = tap which produces hot water; **on tap** = available when you need it; *we should have all this information on tap*; **to turn a tap on** = to allow water to run; **to turn a tap off** = to stop water running (NOTE: American English is also **faucet**)

(b) little knock; *as a signal, he gave three taps on the door*

2 *verb*

(a) to hit something gently; *she tapped him on the knee with her finger*; *a policeman tapped him on the shoulder and arrested him*

(b) to attach a secret listening device to a telephone line; *the police tapped his phone because they thought he was a spy*

(c) to take liquid out of something; *they tap the rubber trees in the plantations*; *he's going down to the cellar to tap a new barrel of beer*

(d) to take energy or resources and use them; *the resources of Northern Siberia have not yet been tapped* (NOTE: **tapping - tapped**)

⑩ **tape**
[teɪp]
1 *noun*
(a) long narrow strip of cloth, plastic, etc.; *she stitched tape along the bottom of his trousers to stop them fraying*; **tape measure** *or* **measuring tape** = long strip of plastic marked in centimetres or inches, etc., used for measuring; *he took out a tape measure and measured the length of the table*; **sticky tape** = strip of plastic with glue on one side, used to stick things together, etc.
(b) **magnetic tape** = special plastic tape on which sounds and pictures can be recorded, also used for recording computer data; **audio tape** = special magnetic tape on which sounds can be recorded; *she lent me her Beatles tape*; *I play a lot of tapes when I'm driving by myself*; **on tape** = recorded on magnetic tape; *we have the whole conversation on tape*; **tape deck** = part of a stereo system, which plays tapes
2 *verb*
(a) to record something on tape or on video; *the whole conversation was taped by the police*; *I didn't see the programme because I was at work, but I've taped it*
(b) to attach with sticky tape; *she taped up the box before taking it to the post office*

⑫ **target**
['tɑːgɪt]
1 *noun*
(a) object which you aim at with a gun, etc.; *his last shot missed the target altogether*; *she hit the target three times in all*; **target practice** = practising at shooting at a target; *he put an old tin can on top of the post and used it for target practice*
(b) goal which you try to reach; **to set targets** = to fix amounts or quantities which workers have to produce; **to meet a target** = to produce the quantity of goods or sales which are expected; *we need to set targets for our salesmen to meet*; **to miss a target** = not to produce the amount of goods or sales which are expected; *the factory missed its production targets again this year*; **target language** = language which a student is learning, the language into which something is translated; **target market** = market to which a company is planning to sell its service
2 *verb*
to aim at customers, possible markets, etc.; *the advertising campaign is targeting the student market*

⑭ **tariff**
['tærɪf] *noun*
(a) tax to be paid for importing or exporting goods; **to impose a tariff on something** = to make a tax payable when you buy something; **to lift tariff barriers** = to reduce import taxes
(b) list of prices for electricity, gas, water, etc.; *the new winter tariff will be introduced next week*

⑩ **task**
[tɑːsk] *noun*
(a) job of work which has to be done; *there are many tasks which need to be done in the garden*; *he had the unpleasant task of telling his mother about it*; **task force** = special group of people chosen to carry out a difficult task; *they sent in a task force to sort out the problem school*
(b) **to take someone to task for** = to criticize someone for; *she took him to task for not cleaning the bathroom*

⑫ **taste**
[teɪst]
1 *noun*
(a) one of the five senses, by which you can tell differences of flavour between things you eat, using your tongue; *I've got a cold, so I've lost all sense of taste*
(b) flavour of something that you eat or drink; *the pudding has a funny or strange taste*; *do you like the taste of garlic?*; *this milk shake has no taste at all*
(c) being able to appreciate things that are beautiful; *my taste in music is quite different from hers*; *I don't share his taste for bright green shirts*; *she showed great taste in decorating her dining room*; **to someone's taste** = in a way that someone likes; *modern jazz is not to everyone's taste*
(d) very small quantity of food or drink, or other things; *this is a taste of what the country will be like under the new ruler*; **he's had a taste of prison** = he has been in prison once
2 *verb*
(a) to notice the taste of something with your tongue; *can you taste the onions in this soup?*; *she's got a cold so she can't taste anything*
(b) to have a certain taste; *this cake tastes of soap*; *what is this green stuff? - it tastes like cabbage*; *the pudding tastes very good*
(c) to try something to see if you like it; *would you like to taste the wine?*; *she asked if she could taste the cheese before buying it*

⑬ **taught**
[tɔːt] *see* TEACH

① **tax**
[tæks]
1 *noun*
money taken by the government from incomes, sales, etc., to pay for government services; *the government is planning to introduce a tax on food*; *you must pay your tax on the correct date*; *the newspaper headline says 'TAXES TO GO UP'*; **airport tax** = tax added to the price of an air ticket to cover the cost of running an airport; **income tax** = tax which is paid according to how much you earn; *income tax is deducted from your salary every month*; **value added tax (VAT)** = tax on goods and services, added as a percentage to the invoiced sales price; *see also* ROAD TAX; **exclusive of tax** = not including

tax; **inclusive of tax** = including tax; *all prices are shown inclusive of value added tax* (NOTE: plural is **taxes**)

2 *verb*

(a) to put a tax on something *or* someone; *income is taxed at 25%*

(b) to pay tax on something; *the car is for sale, taxed till next April*

(c) to demand a great deal; *moving all this furniture taxed her strength*

(d) *(formal)* to tax someone with something = to accuse someone of doing something; *she taxed him with neglecting her*

③ **taxation**

['tæk'seɪʃn] *noun*

action of imposing taxes; *money raised by taxation pays for all government services*; **direct taxation** = taxes (such as income tax) which are paid direct to the government; **indirect taxation** = taxes (such as VAT) which are added to the price of goods and not paid directly to the government

③ **tax disk**

['tæks 'dɪsk] *noun*

round piece of paper which is attached to a car windscreen to show that you have paid tax on the car for the current year; *his tax disk has expired*

③ **taxi**

['tæksi] *noun*

car which you can hire with a driver; *can you call a taxi to take me to the airport?*; *why aren't there any taxis at the station today?*; *there are no buses on Sunday afternoons, so we had to take a taxi to the party* (NOTE: also often called a **cab** and sometimes **taxicab**)

2 *verb*

(of an aircraft) to go slowly along the ground before taking off or after landing; *the aircraft taxied out onto the runway*

③ **taxi driver**

['tæksi 'draɪvɪ] *noun*

person who drives a taxi; *the taxi driver helped me with my luggage*

④ **taxpayer**

['tækspeɪɪ] *noun*

person who pays tax, especially income tax; *I don't think the government's plan will be very popular with taxpayers*

① **tea**

[tiː] *noun*

(a) drink made from hot water which has been poured onto the dried leaves of a tropical plant; *can I have another cup of tea or some more tea?*; *I don't like tea - can I have coffee instead?*

(b) a cup of tea; *can we have two teas and two cakes, please*

(c) the dried leaves of a tropical plant used to make a warm drink; *we've run out of tea, can you put it on your shopping list?*; *put a spoonful of tea into the pot and add boiling water*

(d) dried leaves or flowers of other plants, used to make a drink; *mint tea*

(e) **(afternoon) tea** = afternoon meal at which you drink tea and eat bread, cake, etc.; *why don't you come for tea tomorrow?*; *the children have had their tea*; *we've been asked out to tea by my sister or my sister has asked us to tea*; *tea is served at 4 o'clock in the hotel lounge*; **cream tea** = afternoon tea with cakes, thick cream and jam

(f) *(in the North of England and Scotland)* **(high) tea** = early evening meal; *they arrived just in time for tea*; *I'm having a baked potato for my tea* (NOTE: generally no plural: **teas** means **cups of tea**, or the **meals**)

③ **teabag** *or* **tea bag**

['tiːbæg] *noun*

small paper bag with tea in it which you put into the pot with hot water; *I don't like weak tea - put another teabag in the pot*

① **teach**

[tiːtʃ] *verb*

(a) to give lessons, to show someone how to do something; *she taught me how to dance*; *he teaches maths in the local school*; *she taught herself to type*; *who taught her to swim?*

(b) *(informal)* to teach someone a lesson = to punish someone for doing something wrong; *I've locked up her bike - it will teach her a lesson not to go out when she should be doing her homework*; **that'll teach you** = that will be a punishment for you; *that'll teach you for forgetting to do the washing up* (NOTE: **teaching - taught** [tɔːt])

① **teacher**

['tiːtʃɪ] *noun*

person who teaches, especially in a school; *Mr Jones is our maths teacher*; *the French teacher is ill today*; *he trained as a primary school teacher*; *see also* PET

① **teaching**

['tiːtʃɪŋ] *noun*

(a) work of being a teacher, of giving lessons; *the report praised the high standard of teaching at the college*; *he was working in a bank, but has decided to go into teaching instead*; **the teaching profession** = all teachers, taken as a group; *the teaching profession is often blamed by parents if their children do badly at school*

(b) **teachings** = political or moral ideas which are taught; *Christianity is based on the life and teachings of Jesus Christ*; *the teachings of Gandhi*

④ **teacup**

['ti:kʌp] *noun*

cup for drinking tea; *she put the teacups and saucers out on a tray*; *(informal)* **storm in a teacup** = lot of fuss about something which is not important

① **team**

[ti:m]

1 *noun*

(a) group of people who play a game together; *there are eleven people in a football team and fifteen in a rugby team*; *he's a fan of the local football team*; *our college team played badly last Saturday*

(b) group of people who work together; *they make a very effective team*; *in this job you have to be able to work as a member of a team*; **management team** = all the managers who work together in a company; **sales team** = all representatives, salesmen and sales managers working together in a company; *he has a sales team of twenty salesmen* (NOTE: the word **team** is singular, but can be followed by a singular or plural verb: **the team has** *or* **have come out of the changing room**)

2 *verb*

to team up with someone = to join someone to work together; *I teamed up with George to tackle the German project*

④ **teapot**

['ti:pɒt] *noun*

pot which is used for making tea; *put two teabags into the teapot and add boiling water*

② **tear**

1 *noun*

(a) [tɪə] drop of salt water which forms in your eye when you cry; *tears were running down her cheeks*; **in tears** = crying; *all the family were in tears*; **she burst into tears** = she suddenly started crying

(b) [teə] place where something has a hole in it from being ripped; *can you mend the tear in my jeans?*; *see also* WEAR AND TEAR

2 *verb*

[teə]

(a) to make a hole in something by pulling; *he tore his trousers climbing over the fence*; *my jacket is torn - can it be mended?*

(b) to pull something into bits; *he tore the letter in half*; *she tore up old newspapers to pack the cups and saucers*

(c) to go very fast; *he tore across the platform, but just missed his train*; *she grabbed the dress and tore out of the shop* (NOTE: **tearing - tore** [tɔː] **- torn** [tɔːn])

③ **tear down**

['teə 'daun] *verb*

(a) to knock something down; *they tore down the old town hall and replaced it with a supermarket*

(b) to remove a piece of paper or cloth which is hanging up; *the crowd tore down the pictures of the president*; *the police tore down the opposition party's election posters*

③ **tear gas**

['tɪə 'gæs] *noun*

gas which makes your eyes burn, used by police to control crowds; *in the end the police had to resort to using tear gas*; *the police used tear gas to clear demonstrators from in front of the Parliament building*

④ **tease**

[ti:z] *verb*

to say or do something to annoy someone on purpose; *he teased her about her thick glasses*; *stop teasing that poor cat*

③ **teashop**

['ti:ʃɒp] *noun*

small restaurant which serves mainly tea, coffee, sandwiches and cakes; *our village teashop serves the best chocolate cake I've ever tasted*

④ **teaspoon**

['ti:spu:n] *noun*

(a) small spoon for stirring tea or other liquid; *can you bring me a teaspoon, please?*

(b) the amount contained in a teaspoon; *I take one teaspoon of sugar in my coffee*

③ **teatime**

['ti:taɪm] *noun*

time when tea is served (between 4 and 5.30 p.m.); *hurry up, it'll soon be teatime!*; *the children's TV programmes are on at teatime*

③ **tech**

[tek] *noun*

(informal) technical college, further education college for older students and adults; *he's doing an engineering course at the local tech*; *see also* HIGH TECH

② **technical**

['teknɪkl] *adjective*

referring to industrial processes or practical work; *don't bother with the technical details of how the machine works, just tell me what it does*; *the instructions are too technical for the ordinary person to understand*; **technical college** = further education college for older students and adults, teaching technical skills and other subjects such as languages; **technical subjects** = practical skills taught in schools or colleges, such as car maintenance, electrical engineering, etc.; **technical term** = specialized word used in a particular science, or trade

③ **technically**

['teknɪkli] *adverb*

(a) in a technical way; *it's technically possible to make a light bulb that would never wear out*

(b) **technically (speaking)** = according to the exact meaning; *technically he isn't a member of the club because he hasn't paid this year's subscription*

④ **technician**
[tek'nɪʃn] *noun*

person who is a specialist in a particular area of industry or science; *she's a computer technician*; *we have a team of technicians working on the project*; **laboratory technician** = person who deals with practical work in a laboratory

① **technique**
[tek'ni:k] *noun*

way of doing something; *he developed a new technique for processing steel*; *she has a specially effective technique for dealing with complaints from customers*

③ **technological**
[teknɪ'lɒdʒɪkl] *adjective*

referring to technology; *the company has reported making an important technological discovery*

① **technology**
[tek'nɒlɪdʒɪ] *noun*

use or study of industrial or scientific skills; *we already have the technology to produce such a machine*; *the government has promised increased investment in science and technology*; **the introduction of new technology** = putting new electronic equipment into a business or industry; *see also* INFORMATION TECHNOLOGY

③ **teddy (bear)**
['tedɪ 'beɪ] *noun*

child's toy bear; *she won't go to bed without her teddy bear*; *the little boy held his old teddy tight* (NOTE: the plural is **teddies**)

④ **teen**
[ti:n] *noun*

(a) **teens** = age between 13 and 19; *she joined the bank when she was still in her teens*
(b) *US* = TEENAGER

④ **teenage**
['ti:neɪdʒ] *adjective*

(a) *(also* **teenaged**) aged between 13 and 19; *he has two teenage(d) daughters*
(b) referring to young people aged between 13 and 19; *the government is trying to deal with the problem of teenage crime*; *the teenage market for the pop group's records is enormous*

③ **teenager**
['ti:neɪdʒ] *noun*

young person aged between 13 and 19; *most of the people who come to the club are teenagers*

③ **teeshirt** *or* **T-shirt**
['ti:ʃɜ:t] *noun*

light shirt with no buttons or collar, usually with short sleeves; *no wonder you're cold if you went out in just a teeshirt*; *she was wearing jeans and a T-shirt*

② **teeth**
[ti:θ] *see* TOOTH

④ **telecommunications**
[telɪkɪmju:nɪ'keɪʃnz] *noun*

communication system using telephone, radio, TV, satellites, etc.; *thanks to modern telecommunications, the information can be sent to our office in Japan in seconds* (NOTE: also shortened to **telecoms** ['telɪkɒmz])

① **telephone**
['telɪfɪʊn]

1 *noun*

machine which you use to speak to someone who is some distance away; *can't someone answer the telephone - it's been ringing and ringing*; *I was in the garden when you called, but by the time I got to the house the telephone had stopped ringing*; *she lifted the telephone and called the ambulance*; **by telephone** = using the telephone; *he booked his plane ticket by telephone*; *she reserved a table by telephone*

2 *verb*

to call someone using a telephone; *your wife telephoned when you were out*; *can you telephone me at ten o'clock tomorrow evening?*; *I need to telephone our office in New York* (NOTE: **telephone** is often shortened to **phone: phone call, phone book,** etc., but not in the expressions **telephone switchboard, telephone operator, telephone exchange**)

◊ **on the telephone**
['ɒn ðɪ 'telɪfɪʊn]

(a) speaking by telephone; *don't make such a noise - Daddy's on the telephone*; *William! - there's someone on the telephone who wants to speak to you*; *the sales manager is on the telephone all the time*
(b) with a telephone in the house; *don't look for their address in the phone book - their cottage isn't on the telephone*

③ **telephone book** *or* **telephone directory**
['telɪfɪʊn 'bʊk *or* daɪ'rektɪrɪ] *noun*

book which gives the names of people in a town with their addresses and telephone numbers; *the restaurant must be new - it isn't in the telephone book*; *look up his number in the telephone directory* (NOTE: is often shortened to **phone book**)

③ **telephone box**
['telɪfɪʊn 'bɒks] *noun*

shelter with windows round it containing a public telephone; *call me from the telephone box outside the station, and I'll come and pick you up*; *there was a queue of people waiting to use the telephone box* (NOTE: often shortened to **phone box**)

① **telephone number**
['telɪfɪʊn 'nʌmbɪ] *noun*

number of one particular telephone; *what's the telephone number of the garage?*; *his telephone number's Birmingham 987 1234* (NOTE: is often shortened to **phone number**)

COMMENT: British telephone numbers are formed of a town or area code followed by the number of the actual telephone. Area codes always start with 0, and may have three further figures for large towns (Central London is 020 7, Liverpool is 0151) or several figures for smaller towns (Oxford is 01865). The number for the actual telephone usually has eight figures. The numbers are spoken as area code + four + four: so 020 8943 1673 is spoken as 'oh two oh, eight nine four three, one six seven three'

④ **telescope**

['telɪskɪʊp]

1 *noun*

tube with a series of lenses for looking at objects which are very far away; *with a telescope you can see the ships very clearly; he discovered a satellite using the telescope in his back garden*; **optical telescope** = telescope which uses mirrors and lenses to make the image and light coming from stars very much larger; **radio telescope** = telescope which uses radio waves to find or see stars and other objects in the sky

2 *verb*

to push together, so that one piece slides into another; *in the crash, several of the carriages of the express train were telescoped*

④ **televise**

['telɪvaɪz] *verb*

to broadcast something by television; *the debates in parliament are now televised*; **the show is being televised live** = the show is being broadcast on TV as it takes place, and not recorded and broadcast later

① **television (TV)**

[telɪ'vɪʒn] *noun*

(a) sound and pictures which are sent through the air or along cables and appear on a special machine; *we don't watch television every night - some nights we go to the pub; is there any football on television tonight?*; *Saturday evening television programmes are never very interesting; he stayed in his room all evening, watching television*; **cable television** = television system, where pictures are sent by cable

(b) piece of electrical equipment which shows television pictures; *we can't watch anything - our television has broken down; switch off the television - that programme's stupid; when my husband comes home in the evening he just pours himself a beer, turns on the television and goes to sleep* (NOTE: **television** is often written or spoken as **TV** ['ti: 'vi:])

③ **television set (TV)**

[telɪ'vɪʒn 'set] *noun*

piece of electrical equipment which shows television pictures; *my father has bought a new television set or a new TV*

① **tell**

[tel] *verb*

(a) to communicate something to someone, for example a story or a joke; *she told me a long story about how she got lost in London; I don't think they are telling the truth*

(b) to give information to someone; *the policeman told them how to get to the post office; he told the police that he had seen the accident take place; don't tell my mother you saw me at the pub; nobody told us about the picnic*

(c) to tell someone what to do = to give someone instructions; *the teacher told the children to stand in a line; give a shout to tell us when to start*

(d) to notice; *he can't tell the difference between butter and margarine; you can tell he is embarrassed when his face goes red* (NOTE: **telling - told** [tɪʊld])

③ **tell off**

['tel 'ɒf] *verb*

(informal) to speak to someone angrily about something wrong he or she has done; *the students were told off for being late; the teacher will tell you off if you don't do your homework*

④ **temper**

['tempɪ]

1 *noun*

(a) state of becoming angry; *you have to learn to control your temper; he has a violent temper; she got into a temper*

(b) general calm state of mind; **he lost his temper** = he became very angry; **she tried to keep her temper** = she tried to stay calm and not get angry

2 *verb*

(a) *(formal)* **to temper something with** = to make something have a less harsh effect; *we try to temper the strict prison regime with sports and educational activities*

(b) to make a metal hard by heating and cooling; *a tempered steel blade*

② **temperature**

['temprɪtʃɪ] *noun*

(a) heat measured in degrees; *the temperature of water in the swimming pool is 25°, temperatures in the Arctic can be very low; I can't start the car when the temperature is below zero; put the thermometer in the patient's mouth - I want to take her temperature*

(b) illness where your body is hotter than normal; *she's off work with a temperature; the doctor says he's got a temperature and has to stay in bed*

④ **temple**

['templ] *noun*

(a) building for worship, usually Hindu or Buddhist, or ancient Greek or Roman, but not Christian or Muslim; *we visited the Greek temples on the islands*

(b) flat part of the side of the head between the top of the ear and the eye; *he had a bruise on his right temple*

④ **temporarily**
['temprırıli] *adverb*

for a short time only; *at the moment, he's temporarily unemployed*; *I'm staying at my mother's temporarily while my flat is being decorated*

② **temporary**
['tempriri] *adjective*

which is not permanent, only lasting a short time; *she has a temporary job with a construction company*; *this arrangement is only temporary*; **temporary employment** = work which does not last for more than than a few months; **temporary staff** = staff who are appointed for a short time; *we usually hire about twenty temporary staff during the Christmas period*

③ **tempt**
[temt] *verb*

(a) to try to persuade someone to do something, especially something pleasant or wrong; *can I tempt you to have another cream cake?*; *they tried to tempt him to leave his job and work for them*

(b) **to be tempted to** = to feel like doing something; *he was tempted to send the food back to the kitchen*; *I am tempted to accept their offer*

(c) **to tempt fate** = to do something which could have bad results; *it would be tempting fate to buy that car without having had it checked by a garage*

④ **temptation**
[tem'teıʃn] *noun*

being tempted; thing which tempts; *putting chocolates near the cash desk is just a temptation for little children*; *the temptation is just to do nothing and hope the problem will simply go away*

① **ten**
[ten]

(a) number 10; *in the market they're selling ten oranges for two dollars*; *she's ten (years old) next week*; *the next plane for Paris leaves at 10 (o'clock) in the evening*; **the ten hundreds (1000s)** = the years from 1000 to 1099 (NOTE: compare **the tenth century**)

(b) *(informal)* **ten to one** = very likely; *ten to one he finds out about the payment*

(c) *(informal)* **tens** = £10 notes or $10 bills; *he gave me two twenties and four tens*

④ **tenant**
['tenınt] *noun*

person or company that rents a room, flat, house, office, land, etc., in which to live or work; *the previous tenants left the flat in a terrible state*; **sitting tenant** = person who is living in a

property and paying rent for it when the property is sold; *he bought the flat with a sitting tenant in it*

① **tend**
[tend] *verb*

(a) **to tend to do something** = to be likely to do something; *she tends to lose her temper very easily*

(b) **to tend towards something** = to lean in a certain direction; *he's certainly not a Conservative - if anything, he tends towards the Liberals*

(c) to look after something; *his job is to tend the flower beds in front of the town hall*

③ **tendency**
['tendınsı] *noun*

way in which someone *or* something is likely to act; *the photocopier has a tendency to break down if you try to do too many copies at the same time*; *at parties, he has an unfortunate tendency to sit in a corner and go to sleep*

④ **tender**
['tendı]

1 *adjective*

(a) (food) which is easy to cut or chew; *a plate of tender young beans*; **tender meat** = which can be chewed or cut easily; *the meat was so tender, you hardly needed a knife to cut it* (NOTE: the opposite is **tough**)

(b) delicate, easily damaged; *the baby has very tender skin*

(c) showing love; *the plants need a lot of tender loving care*

(d) which cannot stand frost; *keep the tender young plants in the warm greenhouse until June*

2 *noun*

(a) offer to do something at a certain price; **to put in a tender** *or* **to submit a tender for a job** = to offer to do work at a certain price

(b) **legal tender** = coins or notes which can be legally used; *old pound notes are no longer legal tender in England* (NOTE: no plural in this meaning)

(c) *(old)* coal wagon attached to a steam locomotive

3 *verb*

(a) **to tender for a job** = to offer to do work at a certain price; *the company is tendering for a construction job in Saudi Arabia*

(b) *(formal)* to offer; *he tendered his resignation*

(c) *(formal)* to offer money; *please tender the correct fare*

③ **tennis**
['tenıs] *noun*

(a) game for two or four players who use rackets to hit a ball backwards and forwards over a net; *he's joined the local tennis club*; *would you like a game of tennis?*; *I won the last two tennis matches I played*; *tennis players have to be fit*; **tennis ball** = ball for playing tennis; *that* *onion's the size of a tennis ball*; **tennis court** = specially marked area for playing tennis; **tennis racket** = racket used to play tennis; **tennis shoes** = special light shoes worn when playing tennis **(b) real tennis** = original medieval form of tennis, played by two players inside a court with high walls

> COMMENT: a game starts with one player hitting the ball over the net; this is the only time during a game when the ball must bounce before being hit. The strange way of counting the score comes from the ancient game of real tennis: the first point won by a player is 15, the second is 30 and the third 40; a fourth point wins the game unless the score reaches 40 - 40 (called 'deuce'); after the next point, the umpire calls 'advantage' to the player who has won the point, and if they also win the next point, they win the game; if not, the score goes back to deuce. The first player to win 6 games wins the 'set'. A men's match is played over the best of 3 or 5 sets; women's and mixed doubles competitions are always played over the best of 3 sets

④ **tense**
[tens]
1 *adjective*

nervous and worried; *I always get tense before going to a job interview; the atmosphere in the hall was tense as everyone waited for the result of the vote* (NOTE: **tenser - tensest**)
2 *noun*

(grammar) form of a verb which shows the time when the action takes place; **future tense** = form of a verb which shows that something will happen; *'he will eat' and 'he is going to eat' are forms of the future tense of the verb 'to eat'*; **past tense** = form of a verb which shows that it happened before the present time; *'sang' is the past tense of the verb 'to sing'*; **present tense** = form of a verb which shows the time we are in now; *the present tense of 'to sit' is 'he sits' or 'he is sitting'*
3 *verb*

to become nervous and worried; *he tensed suddenly, as he heard a sound outside the window*

② **tension**
['tenʃn] *noun*

(a) being tight; *you need to adjust the tension in your tennis racket before starting a game*
(b) state of nervous anxiety; *tension built up as we waited for the result*
(c) situation between countries or races who may be enemies; *there is tension in the area caused by fighting between different religious groups*

④ **tent**
[tent] *noun*

shelter made of cloth, held up by poles and attached to the ground with ropes; *we went camping in the Alps and took our tent in the back of the car; their tent was blown away by the wind; the flower show was held in a tent in the grounds of the castle*; **to pitch a tent** = to put up a tent; *we pitched our tent in a field by a little mountain stream*

④ **tentative**
['tentɪtɪv] *adjective*

which has been suggested but not accepted, done in an uncertain way because you are not sure what will happen; *this is only a tentative suggestion; we suggested Wednesday May 10th as a tentative date for the wedding*; **tentative proposal** = proposal made to find out what the response is; *we put forward a tentative proposal for the committee to consider*

① **tenth (10th)**
[tenθ] *adjective & noun*

the tenth of April or April the tenth (April 10th) that's the tenth phone call I've had this morning; we spend a tenth of our income on food; **the tenth century** = the period from 900 to 999 (NOTE: compare **the ten hundreds**; Note also that with dates **tenth** is usually written **10th: July 10th, 1935; April 10th, 1991** (American style is **April 10, 1991**), say 'the tenth of April' or 'April the tenth' (American style is 'April tenth'); with names of kings and queens **tenth** is usually written **X: King Charles X:** say: 'King Charles the Tenth')

① **term**
[tɜːm]
1 *noun*

(a) official length of time; *his term as President was marked by a lot of disagreement; she was sent to prison for a term of three years*; **in the long term** = for a long period from now; **in the short term** = for a short period from now; *in the long term, this investment should be very profitable*; **term of office** = period of time when someone has a position; *during his term of office as President; see also* LONG-TERM, SHORT-TERM

(b) one of the parts of a school or university year; *a school year has three terms: autumn, spring and summer; cricket is played during the summer term only, and football in both the autumn and spring terms; the autumn term ends on December 15th; next term I'll be starting to learn the piano*; **half-term** = short holiday in the middle of a school term; *we took a few days' holiday at half-term*

(c) word or phrase which has a particular meaning; *he used several technical terms which I didn't understand; some people use 'ducks' as a term of affection*

(d) *see also* TERMS

2 *verb*

(formal) to call something by a certain word; *you say it is acceptable behaviour - I would term it shocking*

④ **terminal**
['tɜːmɪnl]
1 *adjective*
(a) in the last period of a fatal illness; *he has terminal cancer*; **terminal illness** = illness from which the patient will soon die
(b) at the end; **terminal shoot** = shoot at the end of a branch
2 *noun*
(a) building at an airport where planes arrive or depart; *the flight leaves from Terminal 4*
(b) building where you end a journey; **air terminal** = building in the centre of a town where passengers arrive from an airport; **bus terminal** *or* **coach terminal** = place where coaches or buses begin or end their journeys; *coaches leave the terminal every fifteen minutes*
(c) **electric terminal** = connecting point in an electric circuit; *the positive terminal of a battery is indicated by a plus sign*
(d) **computer terminal** = keyboard and monitor, attached to a main computer system

④ **terminate**
['tɜːmɪneɪt] *verb*
(formal) to finish, to come to an end; *the offer terminates on July 31st*; *the flight from Paris terminates in New York*

① **terms**
[tɜːmz] *noun*
(a) conditions which are agreed before something else is done; *we bought the shop on very favourable terms*; *what are the terms of the agreement?*
(b) **to come to terms** = to reach an agreement; *when it became obvious that neither side would win, they came to terms*; **to come to terms with something** = to accept that something has happened and cannot be changed; *it took him some time to come to terms with the fact that he would never walk again*
(c) **terms of payment** = condition for paying something; *the terms of payment are 50% discount, with 60 days' credit*; *our terms are cash with order* = we will supply the goods you want if you pay cash at the same time as you place the order
(d) **terms of reference** = areas which a committee has to examine or discuss; *the terms of reference of the committee do not extend to EU policy*
(e) way of getting on with someone; *they're on bad terms with the people next door*; *the company is on good terms with all its suppliers*; **they're not on speaking terms** = they refuse to talk to each other
(f) **in terms of** = (i) expressed as; (ii) as regards; *how much is 5% per month in terms of an annual percentage rate?*; **we are talking in terms of a salary plus bonuses** = the job is offered with a salary plus bonuses

① **terrible**
['terɪbl] *adjective*
(a) very bad; *we shouldn't have come to this party - the music's terrible*; *there was a terrible storm last night*
(b) frightening; *it must have been terrible to be in the car which plunged into the river*

② **terribly**
['terɪblɪ] *adverb; (informal)*
(a) very; *I'm terribly sorry to have kept you waiting*; *the situation is terribly serious*
(b) in a very bad way; *the farmers are suffering terribly from drought*

③ **terrific**
[tɪ'rɪfɪk] *adjective*
(informal)
(a) wonderful; *we had a terrific time at the party*
(b) very big or loud; *there was a terrific bang and the whole building collapsed*

④ **terrify**
['terɪfaɪ] *verb*
to make someone very frightened; *the sound of thunder terrifies me*

④ **territorial**
[terɪ'tɔːriːl] *adjective*
referring to territory; *they made territorial gains at the end of the war*; **territorial waters** = sea waters near the coast of a country, which are part of that country and which are governed by the laws of that country

② **territory**
['terɪtrɪ] *noun*
(a) large stretch of land; land which belongs to a country; *they occupied all the territory on the east bank of the river*; *a group of soldiers had wandered into enemy territory*
(b) area visited by a salesman; *his territory covers all the north of the country*
(c) area which an animal or bird thinks belongs only to it; *animals often fight to defend their territories* (NOTE: plural is **territories**)

④ **terror**
['terɪ] *noun*
(a) great fear; *they live in constant terror of racist attacks*; **reign of terror** = period when law and order have broken down and people live in a continual state of fear
(b) (informal) naughty child; *their daughter's a little terror*
(c) (informal) **a terror for** = who insists on; *the new manager is a terror for smart uniforms in the shop*

④ **terrorism**
['terɪrɪzm] *noun*
policy of using violence in a political cause; *acts of terrorism continued during the whole summer*; *the government has said that it will not give in to terrorism*

④ **terrorist**
['terɪrɪst]
1 *noun*

person who practises terrorism; *terrorists stormed the plane and told the pilot to fly to Rome*

2 *adjective*

referring to terrorism; *terrorist attacks have increased over the last few weeks*

① **test**

[test]

1 *noun*

(a) examination to see if you know something, etc.; *we had an English test yesterday*; *she passed her driving test*

(b) examination to see if something is working well; *the doctor will have to do a blood test*; *it is a good test of the car's ability to brake fast*

(c) = TEST MATCH; *England lost the third test against Pakistan*

2 *verb*

(a) to try to see if you can do something, etc.; *the teacher tested my spoken German*

(b) to try to see if everything is working well; *we need to test your reactions to noise and bright lights*; *he has to have his eyes tested*; *she tested her new car in the snow*

④ **testament**

['testɪmənt] *noun*

(a) last will and testament = document written by someone which says what they want to happen to their property after they die; *this is the last will and testament of James Smith*

(b) the Old Testament = the first part of the Bible, which deals with the origins and history of the Jewish people; the New Testament = the second part of the Bible, which deals with the life of Jesus Christ, his teachings, and the early Christian church

④ **testify**

['testɪfaɪ] *verb*

to give evidence in court; *she testified against her former boss*; *he refused to testify because he was afraid*

④ **testimony**

['testɪmɪni] *noun*

statement given in court about what happened; *the defence lawyers tried to persuade the jury that the manager's testimony was false*

④ **testing**

['testɪŋ]

1 *adjective*

which is difficult to deal with; *this has been a testing time for the whole family*; *in the second interview they will ask you more testing questions*

2 *noun*

examining something to see if it works well; *during the testing of the engine several defects were corrected*

③ **test match**

['test 'mætʃ] *noun*

international cricket or rugby match; *England beat Australia in the last test match*

① **text**

[tekst] *noun*

(a) main written section of a book, not the notes, index, pictures, etc.; *it's a book for little children, with lots of pictures and very little text*; text processing = using a computer to produce, check and change documents, reports, letters, etc.

(b) original words of a speech; *the text of the Gettysburg Address*

④ **textile**

['tekstaɪl] *noun*

cloth; *they export textiles all over the world*; *the textile industry is influenced by world commodity prices*

④ **texture**

['tekstʃɪ] *noun*

(a) the way in which a surface can be felt; *the soft texture of velvet*

(b) the way a substance is formed; *this bread has a light texture*; *the heavy texture of clay soil*

① **than**

[ðæn or ðɪn]

1 *conjunction; (used to indicate an action or state which is being compared with something else) it's hotter this week than it was last week*

2 *preposition; (used to link two parts of a comparison) his car is bigger than mine*; *she was born in London, so she knows it better than any other town*; *you can't get more than four people into this lift*; *it's less than five kilometres to the nearest station*

① **thank**

[θæŋk] *verb*

(a) to say or do something that shows you are grateful to someone for doing something for you; *she thanked the policeman for helping her to cross the street*; *don't forget to thank Aunt Ann for her present*; *'Thank you for your letter of June 25th'*

(b) thank goodness! *or* thank God! *or* thank heavens! = expressions used to show relief; *thank goodness it didn't rain for the school sports day!*; *thank God the ambulance turned up quickly!*

④ **thankful**

['θæŋkfʊl] *adjective*

glad because a worry has gone away; *we'll all be thankful to get back into harbour safely*; *I'm thankful that the firemen arrived so quickly*; *see also* MERCY

① **thanks**

[θæŋks]

1 *noun*

word showing that you are grateful; *we sent our thanks for the gift*; *we did our best to help but got no thanks for it*; *the committee passed a vote of thanks to the secretary for having organized the meeting*; *many thanks for your letter of the 15th*

2 *interjection showing you are grateful*

do you want some more tea? - no thanks, I've had two cups already; anyone want a lift to the station? - thanks, it's a long walk from here

ⓘ **Thanksgiving**

[θæŋks'gɪvɪŋ] *noun*

American festival, celebrating the first harvest of the pilgrims who settled in the United States (celebrated on the fourth Thursday in November); *all the family will be here for Thanksgiving*

> COMMENT: the traditional menu for Thanksgiving dinner is roast turkey, with sauce made from cranberries (a red berry), followed by pumpkin pie

ⓘ **thanks to**

['θæŋks 'tuː] *preposition*

because of, as a result of; *thanks to the map which he faxed to us, we found his house without any difficulty; thanks to the fog, all planes were diverted to Manchester*

ⓘ **thank you**

['θæŋk juː]

1 *interjection showing that you are grateful; thank you very much for your letter of the 15th; did you remember to say thank you to your grandmother for the present?; would you like another piece of cake? - no thank you, I've had enough;* **thank-you letter** = letter written to thank someone for something

2 *noun*

words which show you are grateful; *let's say a big thank you to the people who organized the show*

ⓘ **that**

[ðæt]

1 *adjective*

(used to show something which is further away) *can you see that white house on the corner over there?; do you remember the name of that awful hotel in Brighton?* (NOTE: the opposite is **this**; the plural is **those**)

2 *pronoun*

that's the book I was talking about; do you know who that is sitting at the next table?

3 *relative pronoun*

where is the parcel that she sent you yesterday?; can you see the man that sold you the ticket?; there's the suitcase that you left on the train! (NOTE: when it is the object of a verb **that** can be left out: **where's the letter he sent you? here's the box you left in the bedroom.** When it is the subject, **that** can be replaced by **which** *or* **who: a house that has red windows** *or* **a house which has red windows; the man that stole the car** *or* **the man who stole the car**)

4 *conjunction*

(a) *(after verbs like* **hope, know, tell, say;** *and adjectives like* **glad, sorry, happy);** *they told me that the manager was out; she said several times that she wanted to sit down; I*

don't think they knew that we were coming; I'm glad that the weather turned out fine; I am sorry that you have been kept waiting

(b) *(after* **so** *or* **such;** *+ adjective or noun) the restaurant was so expensive that we could only afford one dish; it rained so hard that the street was like a river; we had such a lot of work that we didn't have any lunch; there was such a long queue that we didn't bother waiting* (NOTE: **that** is often left out: **he didn't know we were coming; it's so hot in here we all want a drink of water**)

5 *adverb; (usually with negative)*

so, to such an extent; *you must remember him, it's not all that long ago that we had a drink with him; his new car is not really that big*

ⓘ **thaw**

[θɔː]

1 *verb*

(a) to melt; *the ice is thawing on the village pond*

(b) to warm something which is frozen; *can you thaw the frozen peas?*

(c) to become less formal; *after a period of tension, relations between the two countries have begun to thaw*

2 *noun*

warm weather which makes snow and ice melt; *the thaw came early this year*

ⓘ **the**

[ðɪ] *before a vowel* [ðiː] *article*

(a) *(meaning something in particular) where's the book you brought back from the library?; that's the cat from next door; the town centre has been made into a pedestrian zone*

(b) *(used with something of which only one exists) the sun came up over the hills; they want to land scientists on the moon*

(c) *(meaning something in general) there's nothing interesting on the television tonight; she refuses to use the telephone; the streets are crowded at lunchtime; many people were out of work during the 1990s*

(d) [ðiː] *(meaning something very special) it's the shop for men's clothes; she's the doctor for children's diseases; that's not the Charlie Chaplin, is it?*

(e) *(used to compare) the more he eats the thinner he seems to get; the sooner you do it the better; this is by far the shortest way to London; she's the tallest person in the office*

② **theatre** *US* **theater**

['θɪtɪ] *noun*

(a) building in which plays are shown; *I'm trying to get tickets for the theatre tonight; what is the play at the local theatre this week?; we'll have dinner early and then go to the theatre*

(b) *US* **movie theater** = building where films are shown (NOTE: British English for this is only **cinema**)

(c) the theatre = (i) art of presenting plays on the stage; (ii) business of presenting plays on the stage; *I like the theatre better than the cinema*; *she wants to work in the theatre as a designer*

(d) operating theatre = special room in a hospital where surgeons carry out operations; *they rushed him straight into the operating theatre* (NOTE: American English is operating room)

④ theft
[θeft] *noun*

(a) stealing (in general); *we have brought in security guards to protect the hotel against theft*; *they are trying to stop theft by members of the public*

(b) act of stealing; *thefts in supermarkets have increased enormously*

① their
[ðeɪ] *adjective*

(a) belonging to them; *after the film, we went to their house for supper*

(b) referring to them; *the family were eating their dinner when the fire broke out* (NOTE: do not confuse with there, they're)

① theirs
[ðeɪz] *pronoun*

the one that belongs to them; *which car is theirs - the Ford?*; *she's a friend of theirs*; *the girls wanted to borrow my car - theirs wouldn't start*

① them
[ðem] *object pronoun*

(a) *(referring to a people or things which have been mentioned before)* *do you like cream cakes? - no, I don't like them very much*; *there's a group of people waiting outside - tell them to come in*

(b) *(referring to a singular, used instead of* him; *or* her*)*; *if someone phones, ask them to call back later*

② theme
[θiːm] *noun*

(a) the main subject of a book or article; *the theme of the book is how to deal with illness in the family*

(b) main idea; *the theme of the exhibition is 'Europe in the twenty-first century'*

(c) main tune in a piece of music; *the theme comes again at the end of the piece*; theme park = amusement park based on a single theme (such as Disneyland, etc.); *a visit to the theme park is included in the package tour*; theme tune *or* theme song = tune or song played several times in a film or TV serial by which you can recognize it

① themselves
[ðɪmˈselvz] *pronoun*

(a) *(referring to the same people or things that are the subject of the verb)* *cats always spend a lot of time cleaning themselves*; *it's no use going to the surgery - the doctors are all ill themselves*

(b) by themselves = all alone; *the girls were all by themselves in the tent*; *they did it all by themselves*

① then
[ðen]
1 *adverb*

(a) at that time in the past or future; *he had been very busy up till then*; *ever since then I've refused to eat pigeons*; *we're having a party next week - what a pity! I'll be in Scotland then*

(b) after that, next; *we all sat down, and then after a few minutes the waiter brought us the menu*; *it was a busy trip - he went to Greece, then to Italy and finally to Spain*

(c) and so, therefore; *if there isn't any fish on the menu, then we'll have to have a vegetarian dish*; *then he was already at home when you phoned?*

2 *adjective*

who or which existed at a certain time in the past; *the then head teacher was a man called Jones*

④ theoretical
[θɪˈretɪkl] *adjective*

not proved or done in practice; *she has the theoretical power to dismiss any of the staff*

① theory
[ˈθɪɪri] *noun*

(a) explanation of something which has not been proved but which you believe is true; *I have a theory which explains why the police never found the murder weapon*

(b) careful scientific explanation of why something happens; *Galileo put forward the theory that the earth turns round the sun*; the theory of evolution = theory, explained by Charles Darwin, that species develop by a process of natural selection

(c) statement of general principles which may not apply in practice; in theory = in principle, though maybe not in practice; *in theory the treatment should work, but no one has ever tried it*; *in theory the results should be the same every time you do the experiment* (NOTE: plural is theories)

④ therapist
[ˈθerɪpɪst] *noun*

person who is specially trained to give therapy; *the therapist said I should rest my leg as much as possible*; occupational therapist = person who treats patients by making them do certain activities and exercises

④ therapy
[ˈθerɪpi] *noun*

treatment of a patient to help cure a disease or condition; *they use heat therapy to treat muscle problems*; group therapy = type of treatment where a group of people with the same disorder meet together with a therapist to discuss their condition and try to help each other; occupational therapy = treating patients by using activities to help them deal with problems or disabilities, used especially for handicapped patients or patients suffering from mental illness; **speech therapy** = treatment to cure a disorder in speaking; *see also* HORMONE

① **there**
[ðeɪ]
1 *adverb*
(a) in that place; *is that black van still there parked outside the house?*; *where have you put the tea? - there, on the kitchen counter*
(b) to that place; *we haven't been to the British Museum yet - let's go there tomorrow; have you ever been to China? - yes, I went there last month*
(c) *(used when giving something to someone)* *there you are: two fish and chips and a pot of tea* (NOTE: do not confuse with their, they're)
2 *interjection*
(a) *(showing pity)* *there, there, don't get upset; there, sit down for a little while and you'll soon feel better*
(b) *(showing you were right)* *there, what did I say? the plane's late*
(c) *(making a decision)* *if you don't want to come with me, I'll go all by myself, so there!*
3 *pronoun; (used usually with the verb* to be,; *when the real subject follows the verb)*
there's a little door leading into the garden; there's someone at the door asking for you; there are some pages missing in my newspaper; were there a lot of people at the cinema?; there seems to have been a lot of rain during the night; there isn't any jam left in the cupboard (NOTE: when there comes at the beginning of a sentence, the following subject comes after the verb if the subject is a noun and not a pronoun: there goes the bus but there it goes)

③ **thereby**
[ðeɪˈbaɪ] *adverb; (formal)*
by doing that; *a truck crashed into the bridge, thereby blocking the road; the company lowered its prices, thereby winning market share from its competitors*

① **therefore**
[ˈðeɪfɔː] *adverb*
for this reason; *I therefore have decided not to grant his request; they have reduced their prices, therefore we should reduce ours if we want to stay competitive*

④ **thermometer**
[θɪˈmɒmɪtɪ] *noun*
instrument for measuring temperature; *put the thermometer in your mouth - I want to take your temperature; the thermometer outside shows 20°*

① **these**
[ðiːz] *see* THIS

① **they**
[ðeɪ] *pronoun*
(a) *(referring to people or things)* *where do you keep the spoons? - they're in the right-hand drawer; who are those people in uniform? - they're traffic wardens; the children played in the sun and they all got red*
(b) *(referring to people in general)* *they say it's going to be fine this weekend*
(c) *(referring to a singular, used after someone, etc.)* *if someone else joins the queue, they'll just have to wait* (NOTE: when it is the object, them is used instead of they: we gave it to them; the police beat them with sticks; also when it follows the verb to be: who's that? - it's them!)

③ **they're**
[ðeɪ] = THEY ARE (NOTE: do not confuse with their, there)

② **thick**
[θɪk]
1 *adjective*
(a) bigger than usual when measured from side to side, not thin; *he cut a slice of bread which was so thick we couldn't toast it; the walls of the castle are three metres thick; some oranges have very thick skins; he took a piece of thick rope*
(b) close together; *they tried to make their way through thick jungle; the field was covered with thick grass; (informal)* **through thick and thin** = together, even when things are going badly; *she stuck with him through thick and thin; (of two people)* **they're as thick as thieves** = they are great friends, they share each other's secrets
(c) *(of liquids)* which cannot flow easily; *if the paint is too thick add some water; a bowl of thick soup is just what we need on a cold day like this*
(d) which you cannot see through easily; *thick fog had closed the airport*
(e) *(informal)* stupid, not very intelligent; *he's a bit thick; it's a bit thick* = it's not very fair; *it's a bit thick, having to work on Saturdays when everyone else has the day off* (NOTE: thicker - thickest)
2 *adverb*
in a thick way; *put the plaster on thick so that it covers up the cracks; (informal)* **to lay it on thick** = to praise someone excessively; *it was laying it on a bit thick to say that she plays the violin like Menuhin;* **thick and fast** = rapidly and often; *the faxes came in thick and fast*

④ **thief**
[θiːf] *noun*
person who steals; *the police are certain they will catch the thief; see also* THICK (NOTE: plural is thieves [θiːvz])

④ **thigh**
[θaɪ] *noun*
part at the top of the leg between your knee and your hip; *she was wearing a very short skirt and everyone could see her thighs*

② **thin**
[θɪn]
1 *adjective*

(a) not fat; *the table has very thin legs*; *he's too thin - he should eat more*; **as thin as a rake** = very thin; *she's a model and is as thin as a rake*

(b) not thick; *a plate of thin sandwiches*; *the book is printed on very thin paper*; *the parcel was sent in a thin cardboard box*

(c) not placed or growing close together; *the audience is a bit thin tonight*; *the hill was covered with thin grass*; *see also* VANISH

(d) *(of liquid)* which flows easily, which has too much water; *all we had for lunch was a bowl of thin soup*; *add water to make the paint thinner*

(e) which you can see through; *they hung thin curtains in the windows*; *a thin mist covered the valley* (NOTE: **thinner - thinnest**)

2 *adverb*

in a thin way; *don't spread the butter too thin*

3 *verb*

(a) to make more liquid; *if you want to thin the soup just add some water*

(b) to become fewer; *the crowds began to thin by evening*

(c) **to thin out** = to make plants grow less close together; *these lettuces need to be thinned out*

① **thing**
[θɪŋ] *noun*

(a) something which is not living, which is not a plant or animal; *can you see that black thing in the soup?*; *what do you use that big blue thing for?*

(b) usually kind way of talking to or about a person or animal; *the lady in the sweet shop is a dear old thing*; *you silly thing! - why on earth did you do that?*

(c) something in general; *they all just sat there and didn't say a thing*; *the first thing to do is to call an ambulance*; *that was a stupid thing to do!*; **a good thing** = something lucky; *it's a good thing there was no policeman on duty at the door*; **first thing in the morning** = as soon as you get up; **last thing at night** = just before you go to bed; *first thing in the morning, he does his exercises*

(d) problem, worry; *I can't relax, it's just one thing after another*

(e) *(informal)* **to have a thing about something** = to have strong feelings about something; *he has a thing about spiders*; *she's got a thing about men with beards*

(f) *(informal)* **to do your own thing** = to be independent, to do what you want to do; *he listens to what the manager says but then goes away and quietly does his own thing*

① **things**
[θɪŋz] *noun*

(a) clothes, equipment; *did you bring your tennis things?*; *she left her painting things in the car*

(b) general situation; *things aren't going well at the office*; *he always takes things too seriously*

① **think**
[θɪŋk]
1 *verb*

(a) to use your mind; *we never think about what people might say, we always do what we think is right*; **to think twice** = to consider very carefully; *think twice before you sign that contract*

(b) to have an opinion; *I think London is a nicer town to live in than Frankfurt*; *everyone thinks we're mad to go on holiday in December*; *according to the weather forecast, they think it's going to rain*; *he didn't think much of the film*; *the gang is thought to be based in Spain*

(c) to make a plan to do something; *we're thinking of opening an office in New York* (NOTE: **thinking - thought** [θɔːt])

2 *noun*

period when you think, the act of thinking; *let me have a little think and I'll tell you what we should do*; *have a think about what I've just said*; *we really need to have another think about the plan*; *(informal)* **to have another think coming** = to have to change your plans; *if he thinks he's going to tell me how to do my job, he's got another think coming*

② **think about**
['θɪŋk ə'baʊt] *verb*

(a) to have someone *or* something in your mind; *I was just thinking about you when you phoned*; *all she thinks about is food*

(b) to consider a plan in your mind; *have you ever thought about writing children's books?*; **to think twice about** = to consider very carefully; *I'd think twice about spending all the money you've saved*

(c) to have an opinion about something; *what do you think about the government's plans to increase taxes?*

③ **think back**
['θɪŋk 'bæk] *verb*

to remember something in the past; *think back to last Wednesday - do you remember seeing me sign the letter?*

④ **thinking**
['θɪŋkɪŋ] *noun*

process of reasoning about something; *I don't understand the thinking behind the decision*; **to my way of thinking** = my opinion is; *to my way of thinking, it shouldn't be allowed*

① **think of**
['θɪŋk 'ɒv] *verb*

(a) to consider a plan in your mind; *we are thinking of going to Greece on holiday*

(b) to remember something; *now I think of it, he was at the party last week*

(c) to have an opinion about something; *what do you think of the government's plans to increase taxes?*; *I didn't think much of the play*; *she asked him what he thought of her idea*; **to tell someone what you think of something** = to criticize; *he went up to her and told her exactly what he thought of her stupid idea*; **to think highly of someone** = to have a high opinion of someone; **to think nothing of doing something** = to consider something normal, easy; *she thinks nothing of working ten hours a day*; *(as a response to an apology)* **think nothing of it!** = please don't bother to thank me for it; **he thought better of it** = he changed his mind; *he was going to pay the whole bill himself, and then thought better of it*

③ **think out**
['θɪŋk 'aʊt] *verb*
to consider something carefully in all its details; *have you thought out all the implications of the plan?*; *they submitted a well thought-out design*

③ **think over**
['θɪŋk 'əʊvɪ] *verb*
to consider a plan or proposal very carefully; *that's the proposal: think it over, and tell me what you decide tomorrow*

③ **think up**
['θɪŋk 'ʌp] *verb*
to invent a plan or new idea; *he thought up a mad plan for making lots of money*

① **third (3rd)**
[θɜːd]
1 *adjective*
(a) referring to three; *she came third in the race*; *the cake shop is the third shop on the right*; *it will be her third birthday next Friday*; *her birthday is on the third of March or March the third (March 3rd)* **the third century** = the period from 200 to 299 (NOTE: with dates **third** is usually written **3rd: May 3rd, 1921**: **June 3rd, 1896** (American style is **June 3, 1896**), say 'the third of June' or 'June the third' (American style is 'June third'); with names of kings and queens **third** is usually written **III: King Henry III**: say 'King Henry the Third')
(b) third party = any third person, in addition to the two main parties involved in a contract; *if possible we want to prevent third parties becoming involved in the dispute*; **third party insurance** = insurance which pays compensation if someone who is not the insured person suffers a loss or injury
(c) *(followed by a superlative)* only two others are more; *this is the third longest bridge in the world*; *he's the third highest paid member of staff*
2 *noun*
one part out of three equal parts; *a third of the airline's planes are made in Europe*; *two-thirds of the staff work part-time*

④ **thirsty**
['θɜːstɪ] *adjective*
feeling that you want to drink; *it's so hot here that it makes me thirsty*; **are you thirsty?** = would you like a drink?; **thirsty work** = hard

work which makes you want to drink; *moving all this furniture is thirsty work* (NOTE: **thirstier - thirstiest**)

① **thirteen**
[θɜː'tiːn]
number 13; *he's only thirteen (years old), but he can drive a car*; *she'll be thirteen next Monday*; **the thirteen hundreds (1300s)** = the period form 1300 to 1399 (NOTE: compare **the thirteenth century**)

① **thirteenth (13th)**
[θɜː'tiːnθ] *adjective & noun*
the thirteenth of September or September the thirteenth (September 13th) *it's her thirteenth birthday on Monday*; **Friday the thirteenth (Friday 13th)** = day which many people think is unlucky; **the thirteenth century** = the period from 1200 to 1399 (NOTE: compare **the thirteen hundreds**; Note also that with dates **thirteenth** is usually written **13th: July 13th, 1935**; **October 13th, 1991** (American style is **October 13, 1991**), say 'the thirteenth of October' or 'October the thirteenth' (American style is 'October thirteenth'); with names of kings and queens **thirteenth** is usually written **XIII: King Louis XIII** (say: 'King Louis the Thirteenth')

① **thirtieth (30th)**
['θɜːtɪɪθ] *adjective & noun*
he came thirtieth out of thirty-five in the race; *the thirtieth of March or March the thirtieth (March 30th)* *it was my thirtieth birthday last week* (NOTE: with dates **thirtieth** is usually written **30th: May 30th, 1921**: **June 30th, 1896** (American style is **June 30, 1896**), say 'the thirtieth of June' or 'June the thirtieth' (American style is 'June thirtieth')

① **thirty**
['θɜːtɪ]
number 30; *he's thirty (years old)* *she must have more than thirty pairs of shoes*; *she and her partner are both in their thirties* = they are both aged between 30 and 39 years old; **the (nineteen) thirties (1930s)** = the period from 1930 to 1939 (NOTE: **thirty-one** (31), **thirty-two** (32), etc., but **thirty-first** (31st), **thirty-second** (32nd), etc.)

① **this**
[ðɪs]
1 *adjective & pronoun*
(a) *(used to show something which is nearer - in contrast to* **that**); *this is the shop that was mentioned in the paper*; *this little girl is a friend of my daughter*; *I think we have been to this pub before*; *this is Angela Smith, our new sales manager*
(b) *(used to refer to a part of today, the recent past or a period of time which will soon arrive)* *I saw him on the train this morning*; *my mother is coming for tea this afternoon*; *I expect to hear from him this week*; *he's retiring this August*; *this year, our sales are better than last year*; *they're going to Spain this summer* (NOTE: plural is **these**)

2 *adverb; (informal)*

so much; *I knew you were going to be late, but I didn't expect you to be this late*

④ **thorough**

['θʌrɪ] *adjective*

(a) very careful and detailed; *the police have carried out a thorough search of the woods*

(b) total; *they made a thorough mess of it; it was a thorough waste of time*

④ **thoroughly**

['θʌrɪli] *adverb*

(a) in a complete and careful way; *we searched the garden thoroughly but couldn't find his red ball*

(b) totally; *I'm thoroughly fed up with the whole business*

③ **those**

[ðɪʊz] *see* THAT

① **though**

[ðɪʊ] *adverb & conjunction*

(a) in spite of the fact that; *though tired, she still kept on running*; *we don't employ any accounting staff, though many companies do*; **odd though it may seem** = although it may seem odd

(b) as though = as if; *his voice sounded strange over the telephone, as though he was standing in a cave*; *that shirt doesn't look as though it has been ironed*; *it looks as though there is no one in*

(c) even though = in spite of the fact that; *he didn't wear a coat, even though it was snowing*; *he wouldn't come with us, even though we asked him twice*; *we managed to make ourselves understood, even though no one spoke English*

① **thought**

[θɔːt]

1 *noun*

(a) idea which you have when thinking; *he had an awful thought - suppose they had left the bathroom taps running?*

(b) process of thinking; *he sat deep in thought by the window*

(c) opinion; *he expressed his thoughts on the subject in a letter to the newspaper*; **to have second thoughts about something** = to change your mind about something; *I think she's beginning to have second thoughts about accepting the job*; **on second thoughts** = having thought about it again; *I asked for coffee, but on second thoughts I think I'll have tea*

2 *verb*

see THINK

④ **thoughtful**

['θɔːtfʊl] *adjective*

(a) being sensitive to what other people want; *it was very thoughtful of you to come to see me in hospital*

(b) thinking deeply; *he looked thoughtful, and I wondered if there was something wrong*

① **thousand**

['θaʊzɪnd]

number 1000; *we paid two hundred thousand pounds (£200,000) for the house*; *thousands of people had their holidays spoilt by the storm* (NOTE: after numbers **thousand** does not take the plural ending **-s: two thousand, ten thousand**)

① **thousandth (1000th)**

['θaʊzɪnθ]

1 *adjective*

referring to a thousand; *the tourist office gave a prize to their thousandth visitor*

2 *noun*

one part out of a thousand; *a thousandth of a second*

④ **thread**

[θred]

1 *noun*

(a) long strand of cotton, silk, etc.; *a spider spins a thread to make its web*; *wait a moment, there's a white thread showing on your coat*

(b) to lose the thread of a conversation = to miss what the conversation is about

(c) ridge going round and round a screw or the inside of a nut; *it's difficult to tighten the nut because the thread is very worn*

2 *verb*

(a) to put a piece of cotton through the eye of a needle; *my eyesight is getting so bad, I can't even thread a needle*

(b) to make something go through a hole; *put the reel on the projector and then thread the end of the film through this slot*

(c) to thread your way = to go carefully between things; *she threaded her way through the piles of boxes*; *we threaded our way through the crowds of Christmas shoppers*

② **threat**

[θret] *noun*

(a) warning that you are going to do something unpleasant, especially if someone doesn't do what you want; *her former husband had been making threats against her and the children*; *the police took the threat to the Prime Minister very seriously*; *do you think they will carry out their threat to bomb the capital if we don't surrender?*; **death threat** = warning to someone that he or she will be killed

(b) person or thing which may harm; *fast sports cars are a threat to other road users*

② **threaten**

['θretn] *verb*

(a) to warn that you are going to do something unpleasant, especially if someone doesn't do what you want; *she threatened to go to the police*; *the teacher threatened her with punishment*

(b) to be likely to have a bad effect on something; *the collapse of the stock market threatened the exchange rate*

③ threatening

['θretnɪŋ] *adverb*

suggesting that something unpleasant will happen; *the weather looks threatening*; *the crowd made threatening gestures at the referee*

① three

[θriː]

number 3; *she's only three (years old), so she can't read yet*; *come and see me at three (o'clock) three men walked into the bank and pulled out guns* (NOTE: **three** (3) but **third** (3rd))

③ three-quarters

[θriːˈkwɔːtɪz]

1 *noun*

three fourths of one whole; *I'm three-quarters of the way through the book*; *about three-quarters of the members are in favour*; **three-quarters of an hour** = forty-five minutes; *we had to wait an hour and three-quarters*

2 *adverb*

75%, three fourths; *the bottle was three-quarters full*

③ threw

[θruː] *see* THROW (NOTE: do not confuse with **through**)

④ thrift

[θrɪft] *noun*

(a) saving money and spending it carefully; *through hard work and thrift the family became rich* (NOTE: no plural in this meaning)

(b) *US* private local bank which accepts and pays interest on deposits from small investors

④ thrill

[θrɪl]

1 *noun*

feeling of great excitement; *it gave me a thrill to see you all again after so many years*; *the thrill of driving through a group of elephants*

2 *verb*

to make someone very excited; *we were thrilled to get your letter*

③ throat

[θrɪʊt] *noun*

(a) tube which goes from the back of your mouth down the inside of your neck; *she got a fish bone stuck in her throat*; **sore throat** = infected throat, which is red and hurts when you swallow or speak; *she's got a sore throat and has lost her voice*; **to clear your throat** = to give a little cough; *he cleared his throat and started to speak*; **a lump in your throat** = feeling unable to speak because you are so upset or so happy; *she had a lump in her throat as she saw her little girl dance across the stage*

(b) your neck, especially the front part; *he put his hands round her throat and pressed hard*

④ throne

[θrɪʊn] *noun*

chair on which a king or queen sits during ceremonies; **to succeed to the throne** = to become king or queen; *he succeeded to the throne when his grandfather died* (NOTE: do not confuse with **thrown**)

① through

[θruː]

1 *preposition*

(a) across the inside of something; going in at one side and coming out of the other; *she looked through the open door*; *cold air is coming in through the broken window*; *the street goes straight through the centre of the town*; *she pushed the needle through the ball of wool*

(b) during a period of time; *they insisted on talking all through the film*

(c) by; *we sent the parcel through the ordinary mail*; *we heard of his wedding through the newspaper*

(d) caused by; *we marked him as absent through illness*; *we missed the deadline through her forgetting to mark it in her diary*

(e) *US* up to and including; **Monday through Friday** = from Monday to Friday inclusive

2 *adverb*

(a) going in at one side and coming out of the other side; *someone left the gate open and all the sheep got through*

(b) speaking by telephone; *I can't get through to New York*; *can you put me through to the person who deals with customer complaints?*

(c) **to see something through** = to make sure that something is finished (NOTE: do not confuse with **threw**; **through** is often used after verbs: **to go through, to fall through, to see through**, etc.)

3 *adjective*

(a) not stopping; **through traffic** = traffic which is going through a town and doesn't stop; *through traffic is being diverted to the bypass*

(b) **through with something** = finished using something, not wanting something any more; *are you through with the newspaper?*; *she's through with her boyfriend*

① throughout

[θruːˈaʊt] *preposition & adverb*

everywhere, all through; *throughout the country floods are causing problems on the roads*; *heavy snow fell throughout the night*

① throw

[θrɪʊ]

1 *verb*

(a) to send something through the air; *how far can he throw a cricket ball?*; *they were throwing stones through car windows*; *she threw the letter into the wastepaper basket*; *he was thrown into the air by the blast from the bomb*

(b) **to throw a party** = to organize a party; *they threw a reception for the prize winners*

(c) *(informal)* to shock; *what the boss said threw me* (NOTE: **throwing - threw** [θruː] - **has thrown** [θrɪʊn]])

2 *noun*

(a) act of throwing; *her throw beat the world record*; *he hurt his back after a throw from his horse*

(b) only a stone's throw from = very near; *the hotel is only a stone's throw from the beach*

(c) piece of material which you put over a chair, use as a carpet, etc.; *she gave me a piece of old Chinese silk as a throw to cover the sofa*

① **throw away**
['θrəυ ə'weɪ] *verb*
to get rid of something which you don't need any more; *don't throw away those old newspapers - they may come in useful*; *she threw away all her winter clothes*

③ **thrown**
[θrəυn] *see* THROW

① **throw out**
['θrəυ 'aυt] *verb*
(a) to push someone outside; *when they started to fight, they were thrown out of the restaurant*
(b) to get rid of something which you don't need; *I'm throwing out this old office desk*
(c) to refuse to accept; *the proposal was thrown out by the planning committee*

③ **throw up**
['θrəυ 'ʌp] *verb*
(a) *(informal)* to be sick, to bring up partly digested food from the stomach into the mouth; *the cat threw up all over the sofa*
(b) to give up something; *she's thrown up her job and gone to live in Australia*

③ **thru**
[θru:] *preposition, adverb & adjective*
US (informal) = THROUGH

④ **thrust**
[θrʌst]
1 *noun*
force which pushes; *the thrust of the rocket's engines pushed him back in his seat*
2 *verb*
to push suddenly and hard; *he thrust the newspaper into his pocket*; *she thrust the documents into her briefcase* (NOTE: **thrusting - thrust**)

④ **thumb**
[θʌm]
1 *noun*
(a) short thick finger which is slightly apart from the other four fingers on each hand; *the baby was sucking its thumb*; *she cried when she hit her thumb with the hammer*
(b) his fingers are all thumbs = he is awkward when trying to do something with his hands; *can you help me untie this knot, my fingers are all thumbs!*; rule of thumb = easily remembered way of doing a simple calculation; *divide by eight and multiply by five is a useful rule of thumb when converting kilometres into miles*
(c) *(informal)* thumbs up (sign) = gesture to show that you approve, that things are all right; *he gave us the thumbs up to show that we were through to the next stage of the competition*;

(informal) thumbs down (sign) = gesture to show you disapprove; *the project got the thumbs down from the minister*
(d) under someone's thumb = dominated by someone; *she's got him under her thumb* = he has to do what she tells him to do
2 *verb*
(a) to thumb a lift = to ask a car driver or truck driver to take you as a passenger, usually by signalling with the thumb while holding a sign with your destination written on it; *her car broke down and she thumbed a lift from a passing motorist*
(b) to thumb through = to turn over pages; *I was just thumbing through this old accounts book*

③ **thumbtack**
['θʌmtæk] *noun*
US pin with a large flat head, used for pinning papers to a wall or a surface; *she used thumbtacks to pin the poster to the door*; *he put a thumbtack on the teacher's chair* (NOTE: British English is **drawing pin**)

④ **thunder**
['θʌndɪ]
1 *noun*
(a) loud noise in the air following a flash of lightning; *a tropical storm accompanied by thunder and lightning*; *he was woken by the sound of thunder*
(b) loud noise; *the thunder of horses on the road outside the house*; *he took his bow to a thunder of applause*; *(informal)* to steal someone's thunder = to spoil what someone is planning to do by doing it first, and so getting applauded for it
2 *verb*
(a) to make a loud noise in the air following lightning; *it thundered during the night*
(b) to make a loud noise like thunder; *lorries thundered past on the motorway all night*
(c) to speak in a very loud voice; *'shut up' he thundered to the little boy in the back row*

③ **thunderstorm**
['θʌndəstɔːm] *noun*
storm with rain, thunder and lightning; *there was a terrible thunderstorm last night and our house was struck by lightning*; *don't shelter under a tree during a thunderstorm*

① **Thursday**
['θɜːzdeɪ] *noun*
day between Wednesday and Friday, the fourth day of the week; *last Thursday was Christmas Day*; *shall we arrange to meet next Thursday?*; *today is Thursday, April 14th*; *the club meets on Thursdays or every Thursday*; *the 15th is a Wednesday, so the 16th must be a Thursday*

① **thus**
[ðʌs] *adverb; (formal)*
(a) in this way; *the two pieces fit together thus*
(b) as a result; *she is only fifteen, and thus is not eligible for the over-sixteens competition*

tick

[tɪk]

1 *noun*

(a) mark written to show that something is correct; *put a tick in the box marked 'R'* (NOTE: American English for this meaning is **check**)

(b) sound made every second by a clock; *the only sound we could hear in the room was the tick of the grandfather clock*

(c) *(informal)* a short moment; *wait a tick, my shoe has come undone*; *wait there, I'll be with you in a tick*

(d) *(informal)* credit; *all the furniture in the house is bought on tick*

(e) small insect which lives on the skin and sucks blood; *sheep can be affected by ticks*

2 *verb*

(a) to mark with a tick to show that you approve; *tick the box marked 'R' if you require a receipt* (NOTE: American English for this meaning is **check**)

(b) to make a regular little noise; *all you could hear was the clock ticking in the corner of the library*; *watch out! that parcel's ticking!*

ticket

['tɪkɪt] *noun*

(a) piece of paper or card which allows you to travel; *they won't let you get on to Eurostar without a ticket*; *we've lost our plane tickets - how can we get to Chicago?*; **season ticket** = ticket which can be used for any number of journeys over a period (usually one, three, six or twelve months); **single ticket** *US* **one-way ticket** = ticket for one journey from one place to another; **return ticket** *US* **round-trip ticket** = ticket for a journey from one place to another and back again

(b) piece of paper which allows you to go into a cinema, an exhibition, etc.; *can I have three tickets for the 8.30 show please?*; *we tried several theatres but there were no tickets left anywhere*

(c) **parking ticket** = paper which you get when you leave a car parked wrongly, telling you that you will have to pay a fine; *if you leave your car on the yellow line you'll get a ticket!*

(d) label, piece of paper which shows something; *keep the ticket in case you want to change the trousers later*; **price ticket** = piece of paper showing a price

(e) *US* a party's list of candidates for election to political office; *he ran for governor on the Republican ticket*

ticket office

['tɪkɪt 'ɒfɪs] *noun*

office where tickets can be bought (either for travel or for theatres or cinemas, etc.); *there was a long queue at the ticket office*; *if the ticket office is shut you can buy a ticket on the train*

tickle

['tɪkl]

1 *noun*

something in your throat which makes you cough; *I've got a nasty tickle in my throat*

2 *verb*

to touch someone in a sensitive part of the body to make them laugh; *she tickled his toes and he started to laugh*; *something is tickling me in the small of my back*; *(informal)* **tickled pink** = very much amused; *we were tickled pink to get our first letter from our little granddaughter*

tick off

['tɪk 'ɒf] *verb*

(informal) **to tick someone off** = to say that you are annoyed with someone; *the policeman ticked them off for running across the road in front of a bus*

tide

[taɪd]

1 *noun*

(a) regular rising and falling movement of the sea; *the tide came in and cut off the children on the rocks*; *the tide is out, we can walk across the sand*; **high tide** *or* **low tide** = points when the level of the sea is at its highest *or* at its lowest; *high tide is at 6.05 p.m. today*; **the tide has turned** = the tide has started to go up or down

(b) **the tide of public opinion** = the general trend of feeling among the public

2 *verb*

to tide someone over = to help someone get through a difficult period; *can you lend me £50 to tide me over until pay day?*

tidy

['taɪdi]

1 *adjective*

(a) neat, in order; *I want your room to be completely tidy before you go out*; *she put her clothes in a tidy pile*

(b) *(informal)* quite large amount or sum; *when he dies his children will inherit a tidy sum* (NOTE: **tidier - tidiest**)

2 *verb*

to tidy up = to make everything completely tidy; *mother asked us to help her tidy up after the party*; *he tidied up his room before he went to school*

tie

[taɪ]

1 *noun*

(a) long piece of coloured cloth which men wear round their necks under the collar of their shirts; *he's wearing a blue tie with red stripes*; *they won't let you into the restaurant if you haven't got a tie on*; **old school tie** = tie with a special design which shows which school you went to (NOTE: American English prefers **necktie**)

(b) result in a competition or election where both sides have the same score; *the result was a tie and the vote had to be taken again*; **there was a tie for second place** = two people were equal second (NOTE: also **draw** in a game)

(c) cup tie = sports match between two teams as a result of which one goes out of the competition; *we're expecting a big crowd for the cup tie next week*

(d) thing which prevents you from doing what you want to do; *the big house has become something of a tie to my parents*

2 *verb*

(a) to attach with string, rope, etc.; *the parcel was tied with a little piece of string*; *he tied his horse to the post*; *the burglars tied his hands behind his back*; *he's tied to his work* = he can never get away from it

(b) to have the same score as another team in a competition; *they tied for second place*

(c) to make a knot; *he tied a knot in his handkerchief to remind him*

② tie up
['taɪ ʌp] *verb*

(a) to put string or rope round something; *the parcel was tied up with thick string*; *you should tie that dog up or it will bite someone*

(b) to be tied up = to be busy; *I'm rather tied up at the moment - can we try to meet next week some other time?*

④ tiger
['taɪgɪ] *noun*

large wild animal of the cat family living mainly in India and China; it is yellow in colour, with black stripes; *I bet you wouldn't dare put your hand into the cage and stroke that tiger*

② tight
[taɪt]

1 *adjective*

(a) fitting too closely; *these shoes hurt - they're too tight*

(b) packed close together; **a tight fit** = situation where there is not enough space to fit; *we can get one more person into the taxi but it will be a tight fit*; **a tight schedule** = a schedule where many meetings are very close together; *the doctor has a very tight schedule today and cannot fit in any more appointments*

(c) *(informal)* **money is tight** = there is not very much money available

(d) holding firmly; *keep a tight hold of the bag, we don't want it stolen*

(e) *(informal)* drunk; *he got rather tight at the Christmas party* (NOTE: **tighter - tightest**)

2 *adverb*

(a) closely, firmly (shut); *make sure the windows are shut tight*

(b) to hold tight = to hold something firmly; *hold tight - we're about to take off*

④ tighten
['taɪtn] *verb*

to make tight; to become tight; *I tightened the straps on my rucksack*; **to tighten your belt** = to be ready to spend less, eat less, etc.; *the government warned that we must tighten our belts*

② tightly
['taɪtlɪ] *adverb*

in a tight way; *she kept her eyes tightly shut*; *tie the string as tightly as you can*

③ tights
[taɪts] *noun*

piece of clothing made of thin material, covering your hips, and your legs and feet separately, worn by girls, women, dancers, etc.; *look - you've got a hole in your tights!*

③ tile
[taɪl]

1 *noun*

(a) flat piece of baked clay used as a covering for floors, walls or roofs; *the floor is covered with red tiles*; *we are putting white tiles on the bathroom walls*

(b) similar piece of another kind of material used to cover a floor, etc.; *they put cork tiles on the walls*; **carpet tiles** = square pieces of carpet which can be put down on the floor like tiles

2 *verb*

to cover the surface of a roof, a floor or a wall with tiles; *they have tiled the kitchen with red floor tiles*; *a white-tiled bathroom*

① till
[tɪl]

1 *preposition & conjunction*

until, up to the time when; *I don't expect him to be home till after nine o'clock*; *they worked from morning till night to finish the job*; *we worked till the sun went down*

2 *noun*

drawer for keeping cash in a shop; *there was not much money in the till at the end of the day*

3 *verb*

(formal) to plough and cultivate soil, to make it ready for growing crops; *in some parts of the country farmers are still using horses to till the land*

④ tilt
[tɪlt]

1 *noun*

(a) sloping position; *the table has a noticeable tilt*

(b) (at) full tilt = at full speed; *he was going full tilt when he tripped over*; *the car ran full tilt into a tree*

2 *verb*

(a) to slope; *the shelf is tilting to the right*; *you'll have to change places - the boat is tilting*

(b) to put in a sloping position; *he tilted the barrel over to get the last drops of beer out*

③ timber
['tɪmbɪ] *noun*

(a) *(general)* wood cut ready for building; *these trees are being grown to provide timber for houses* (NOTE: no plural: for one item say **a piece of timber**)

(b) timbers = large pieces of wood used in building; *the roof was built with timbers from old ships*; *some of the timbers are rotten and need to be replaced*

① **time**

[taɪm]

1 *noun*

(a) particular point in the day shown in hours and minutes; *what time is it? or what's the time?*; *can you tell me the time please?*; *the time is exactly four thirty*; *departure times are delayed by up to fifteen minutes because of the volume of traffic*; **to tell the time** = to read the time on a clock or watch; *she's only three so she can't tell the time yet*

(b) hour at which something usually happens; *the closing time for the office is 5.30*; *it's must be nearly time for dinner - I'm hungry*; *is it time for the children to go to bed?*; *see also* BEDTIME, DINNERTIME, LUNCHTIME, TEATIME

(c) amount of hours, days, weeks, etc.; *there's no need to hurry - we've got plenty of time*; *do you have time for a cup of coffee?*; *he spent all that time watching the TV*; *if the fire alarm rings, don't waste time putting clothes on - run out of the hotel fast*; *see also* FIND TIME

(d) certain period; *we haven't been to France for a long time*; *we had a letter from my mother a short time ago*; **in ... time** = during a period from now; *we're going on holiday in four weeks' time*; **to take time** = to need a certain amount of time; *it didn't take you much time to get dressed*; **to take your time** = to do something carefully and slowly; *don't hurry me, I like to take my time*; **your time's up** = the amount of time allocated to you is over; *bring back your boat, your time's up*; *(informal)* **to do time** = to serve a prison sentence; *he's doing time for theft*

(e) system of hours on the clock; **Summer Time** *or* **Daylight Saving Time** = system of putting the clocks forward one hour in summer to provide extra light in the evening; **time difference** = difference in time between one time zone and another; *there is two hours time difference between Moscow and London*

(f) particular moment when something happens; *they didn't hear anything as they were asleep at the time*; *by the time the ambulance arrived the man had died*; *you can't do two things at the same time*; **for the time being** = temporarily; *for the time being I'm staying at my mother's while my flat is being decorated*; **at times** = on some occasions; *at times I think he's quite mad*; *see also* SOMETIMES

(g) period when things are pleasant or bad; *everyone had a good time at the party*; *we had an awful time on holiday - the hotel was dreadful, and it rained without stopping for ten whole days*

(h) one of several moments or periods when something happens; *I've seen that James Bond film on TV four times already*; *that's the last time I'll ask them to play cards*; *next time you come, bring your swimming things*; **time after time** = again and again; *I've told her time after time not to do it*

(i) times = multiplied by; *six times twenty is one hundred and twenty*; *this book is three times as expensive as that one*; *she's a hundred times more efficient than the old secretary*

(j) times = a period in the past; *in Elizabethan times, most men carried swords*; **behind the times** = not up-to-date, old-fashioned; **he's way behind the times** = he's very old-fashioned

2 *verb*

(a) to count in hours, minutes and seconds; *I timed him as he ran round the track*; *don't forget to time the eggs - they have to cook for only three minutes*; *the police cameras timed the car - it was going at more than 100 miles an hour*

(b) to choose the right moment; *she timed her holiday right - its was the hottest week of the year*

◊ **in time**

[ɪn ˈtaɪm] *phrase*

not late; *they drove fast and got to the station just in time to catch the train*; *you'll have to hurry if you want to be in time for the meeting*; *we got to Buckingham Palace just in time to see the Changing of the Guard*; **in good time** = early, before the time needed; *we drove fast and got to the airport in good time*

◊ **on time**

[ˈɒn ˈtaɪm] *phrase*

happening at the expected time; *the plane arrived on time*; *she's never on time for meetings*; *you will have to hurry if you want to get to the wedding on time or if you want to be on time for the wedding*

③ **time limit**

[ˈtaɪm ˈlɪmɪt] *noun*

point in time by which something should be done; *we will set a time limit of two weeks for the project to be completed*

④ **timetable**

[ˈtaɪmteɪbl]

1 *noun*

printed list which shows the times of classes in school, of trains leaving, etc.; *we have two English lessons on the timetable today*; *the airline has issued its summer timetable, and all the times have changed*; *according to the timetable, there should be a train to London at 10.22*

2 *verb*

to schedule, to arrange the times for something; *you are timetabled to speak at 4.30*

③ time zone
['taɪm ˌzɪʊn] *noun*

one of 24 bands in the world in which the same standard time is used; when you fly across the USA you cross several time zones

④ timing
['taɪmɪŋ] *noun*

controlling the time at which something happens; *the timing of the conference is very convenient, as it comes just before my summer holiday; that was good timing - to arrive just as I was opening a bottle of wine!*

⑤ tin
[tɪn] *noun*

(a) metal container in which food is sold and can be kept for a long time; *I'm lazy - I'll just open a tin of soup; she bought three tins of cat food; we'll need three tins of white paint for the ceiling* (NOTE: in British English also called **can**, especially for drinks; American English is only **can**)

(b) any metal box; *keep the biscuits in a tin or they'll go soft; she puts her spare coins into a tin by the telephone*

(c) soft metal with a colour like silver; *bronze is a mixture of copper and tin; there have been tin mines in Cornwall since Roman times* (NOTE: Chemical element: chemical symbol: **Sn**; atomic number: 50)

③ tinned
[tɪnd] *adjective*

preserved and sold in a tin; *I like tinned pineapple better than fresh*

⑤ tin opener
['tɪn ˌɪʊpnɪ] *noun*

device for opening tins of food; *we took several tins of soup with us when we went camping, but forgot the tin opener!* (NOTE: American English is **can opener**)

② tiny
['taɪnɪ] *adjective*

very small; *can I have just a tiny bit more pudding?; the spot on her forehead is so tiny you can hardly see it; she lives in a tiny village in the Welsh mountains* (NOTE: **tinier - tiniest**)

② tip
[tɪp]

1 *noun*

(a) end of something long; *she reads Braille by touching the page with the tips of her fingers; he pushed the piece of wood into the river with the tip of his walking stick; (informal)* **it's on the tip of my tongue** = I'll remember it in a moment, I'm trying hard to remember it; **it's the tip of iceberg** = it's only a small part of something (usually unpleasant) while the rest is hidden; *those errors in the accounts were just the tip of the iceberg - the staff had been stealing money and stock for years*

(b) money given to someone who has provided a service; *the taxi driver was annoyed because I only gave him a 20p tip; the service hasn't been very good - should we leave a tip for the waiter?; the staff are not allowed to accept tips*

(c) advice on something which could be profitable; *he gave me a tip about a horse which was likely to win; she gave me a tip about a cheap restaurant just round the corner from the hotel*

(d) place where household rubbish is taken to be thrown away; *I must take these bags of rubbish to the tip*

(e) *(informal)* dirty place; *just look at your bedroom - it's a tip!*

2 *verb*

(a) to pour something out; *he picked up the box and tipped the contents out onto the floor; she tipped all the food out of the bag*

(b) to give money to someone who has helped you; *I tipped the waiter £1; should we tip the driver?*

(c) to predict that something may happen, especially who will win; *he's tipped to win the election; which horse are you tipping in the next race?* (NOTE: **tipping - tipped**)

② tip over
['tɪp 'ɪʊvɪ] *verb*

(a) to lean and fall over; *the lorry tipped over in the wind; my cup tipped over and all the coffee spilled on to the tablecloth*

(b) to make something lean so that it falls over; *the wind was so strong that it tipped over the caravan*

② tip up
['tɪp ʌp] *verb*

(a) to lean and fall over; *the cup tipped up and all the tea went into the saucer*

(b) to turn something over so that the contents fall out; *he tipped up the bottle to see if there was any tomato sauce left inside*

④ tire
[taɪɪ]

1 *noun*

US see TYRE

2 *verb*

(a) to become tired; to make someone become tired; *he is getting old and tires easily; we went for a long cycle ride to tire the children out*

(b) to tire of = to lose interest in something; *the children soon tired of playing with their toy soldiers*

① tired
['taɪɪd] *adjective*

(a) feeling sleepy; *I'm tired - I think I'll go to bed; if you feel tired, lie down on my bed*

(b) feeling that you need rest; *we're all tired after a long day at the office*

(c) to be (sick and) tired of something = to be bored with something, to have had enough of something; *I'm sick and tired of waiting for the doctor; they're tired of always having to do all* *the washing up*; **to get tired of something** = to become bored with something; *can't we do something else - I'm getting tired of visiting museums*

③ **tired out**
['taɪd 'aʊt] *adjective*
feeling very sleepy, feeling that you must have rest; *they were tired out after their long walk*; *come and sit down - you must be tired out*

③ **tissue**
['tɪʃuː] *noun*
(a) soft paper handkerchief; *there is a box of tissues beside the bed*
(b) **tissue paper** = thin soft paper used for wrapping glass and other delicate objects; *wrap the glasses in tissue paper before you put them away in the box*
(c) groups of cells which form an animal or plant; *animal tissue grown in a laboratory*; *they took a sample of tissue from the growth*

① **title**
['taɪtl] *noun*
(a) name of a book, play, painting, film, etc.; *he's almost finished the play but hasn't found a title for it yet*; **title page** = page at the beginning of a book, which gives the title (usually in large letters), the name of the author and the name of the publisher; **title role** = part in a play or film which gives the name to the play or film; *she played the title role in 'Mrs Warren's Profession'*
(b) *(in sport)* official position of champion; *what are his chances of keeping the Formula One title for a second year running?*
(c) word (such as Dr, Mr, Professor, Lord, Sir, Lady, etc.) put in front of a name to show an honour or a qualification
(d) right to own a property; *he holds the title to the property*; **title deeds** = document showing who is the owner of a property

① **to**
[tuː]
1 *preposition*
(a) *(showing direction or place)* *they went to the police station*; *do you know the way to the beach?*; *the river is to the north of the town*; *everyone take one step to the right, please*
(b) *(showing a period of time)* *the office is open from 9.30 to 5.30, Monday to Friday*; *she slept from 11.30 to 8.30 the following morning*
(c) *(showing time in minutes before an hour)* *get up - it's five to seven*; *the train leaves at a quarter to eight* (NOTE: **to** is used for times between the half hour and o'clock: **3.35** = twenty-five to four; **3.45** = a quarter to four; **3.55** = five minutes to four. For times after the hour see **past**)
(d) *(showing person or animal that receives something)* *take the book to the librarian*; *pass the salt to your grandfather*; *you must be kind to cats*

(e) *(showing connection)* *they lost by twelve to nine*; *the exchange rate is ten francs to the pound*; *there are four keys to the office*; *in this class there are 28 children to one teacher*

(f) *(showing that you are comparing)* *do you prefer butter to margarine?*; *you can't compare tinned pineapple to fresh fruit*

2 *(used before a verb)*

(a) *(following verbs)* *did you remember to switch off the light?*; *the burglar tried to run away*; *she agreed to go to work in Australia*; *they all decided to go home early*

(b) *(showing purpose)* *the nurses came to help at the scene of the accident*; *the doctor left half an hour ago to go to the hospital*

(c) *(used after adjectives)* *I'd be glad to help*; *is the water OK to drink?*; *I'm sorry to be so late for the meeting*

(d) *(used after a comparison)* *she was too tired to do anything except sit down*

(e) *(used after nouns)* *this is the best way to do it*; *she had a sudden desire to lie down and go to sleep*

3 *adverb*

(a) **to come to** = to become conscious again; *when he came to, he was lying on the floor of the church*

(b) **to pull a door to** = to pull a door until it is shut but not locked; *when you go out, just pull the door to*

③ **toast**
[təʊst] *noun*

(a) slices of bread which have been cooked at a high temperature until they are brown; *can you make some more toast?*; *she asked for scrambled eggs on toast*; **brown toast** *or* **white toast** = toast made from brown bread *or* white bread; *I always have a piece of brown toast and marmalade for breakfast*; see also **WARM** (NOTE: no plural in this meaning: **some toast, a piece of toast** *or* **a slice of toast**)

(b) **to drink a toast to someone** = to take a drink and wish someone success; *let's drink a toast to the bride and bridegroom!*; *we all drank a toast to the future success of the company*

2 *verb*

(a) to cook bread, etc., in a toaster or under a grill, until it is brown; *we had toasted tomato sandwiches*

(b) to wish someone success and drink at the same time; *they all toasted the happy couple in champagne*

④ **toaster**
['təʊstə] *noun*

electric device for toasting bread; *that slice of bread is too thick to fit in the toaster*

④ **tobacco**
[tɪˈbækɪʊ] *noun*
dried leaves of a plant used to make cigarettes and for smoking in pipes; *he bought some pipe tobacco*; *tobacco causes lung cancer* (NOTE: no plural)

① **today**
[tɪˈdeɪ]
1 *noun*
(a) this day; *today's her sixth birthday*; *what's the date today?*; *there's a story in today's newspaper about a burglary in our road*
(b) this present time; *the young people of today have far more money than I had when I was their age*
2 *adverb*
on this day; *he said he wanted to see me today, but he hasn't come yet*; *today week or a week today* = in exactly seven days' time; *a week today, and we'll be sitting on the beach* (NOTE: no plural. Note also that when you refer to the morning or afternoon, etc., of **today**, you say **this morning, this afternoon**, etc.; the day before today is **yesterday** and the day after today is **tomorrow**)

③ **toe**
[tɪʊ]
1 *noun*
one of the five parts like fingers at the end of the foot; *she trod on my toe and didn't say she was sorry*; **big toe** = the largest of the five toes; **little toe** = the smallest of the five toes; **to keep someone on their toes** = to keep someone ready or alert; *my job is to make sure the staff are always on their toes*
2 *verb*
to toe the line = to do what you are told to do; *he was sacked because he refused to toe the line* (NOTE: do not confuse with **tow**)

① **together**
[tɪˈgeðɪ] *adverb*
(a) doing something with someone else or in a group; *tell the children to stay together or they'll get lost*; *if you're going to the cinema, and we're planning to go too, why don't we all go together?*
(b) joined with something else, or with each other; *tie the sticks together with string*; *do you think you can stick the pieces of the cup together again?*; *if you add all the figures together, you'll get the total sales*; *we've had three sandwiches and three beers - how much does that come to all together?*; *compare* ALTOGETHER

② **toilet**
[ˈtɔɪlɪt] *noun*
(a) bowl with a seat on which you sit to get rid of waste matter from your body; *there is a shower and toilet in the bathroom*; **to go to the toilet** = (i) to use a toilet to remove waste matter from the body; (ii) to remove waste matter from the body; *the children all want to go to the toilet at the same time*; *Mum! the cat's been to the toilet on the sitting room carpet*; **toilet paper** = soft paper for wiping your bottom after going to the toilet; **toilet roll** = roll of toilet paper; **to flush a toilet** = to press a handle to make water flow through the toilet bowl to clear it; *don't forget to flush the toilet*
(b) room with this toilet bowl in it; *the ladies' toilet is at the end of the corridor*; *the men's toilets are downstairs and to the right*; *there's a public toilet at the railway station*

④ **token**
[ˈtɪʊkɪn] *noun*
(a) thing which is a sign or symbol of something; *please accept this small gift as a token of our thanks*; **by the same token** = in the same way; *you have every right to complain about him, but, by the same token, you mustn't get upset if he complains about you*; **token charge** = small charge which does not cover the real costs; **token gesture** = small action done to show that you intend to deal with a problem; *the motion criticizing the government was simply a token gesture by the opposition parties*; **token payment** = small payment to show that a payment is being made; **token strike** = short strike to show that the workers want to make a complaint about something; **token woman** *or* **token black** = woman *or* black person appointed to a position on a committee, etc., in an attempt to show that there is no sexual or racial discrimination
(b) piece of paper, card, etc., which is used in the place of money; *you can use these tokens to pay for meals*; **book token** *or* **flower token** = card which is bought in a shop and given as a present: it can only be exchanged for books or flowers; **gift token** = card bought in a shop which is given as a present and which must be exchanged in that shop for goods
(c) plastic or metal disk, used instead of money; *she put a token into the slot machine*

③ **told**
[tɪʊld] *see* TELL

④ **tolerance**
[ˈtɒlɪrɪns] *noun*
(a) tolerating unpleasant behaviour, etc.; *the police showed great tolerance faced with a crowd of youths throwing bottles and stones*
(b) allowing something to exist which you do not agree with; *tolerance of other people's views*
(c) ability of the body to stand the effect of a drug or a poison; *he has been taking the drug for so long that he has developed a tolerance to it*
(d) amount by which something can vary from a particular size; *the specifications allow for a tolerance of 0.005mm*

④ **tolerate**
['tɒlɪreɪt] *verb*
(a) to allow something which you do not like to happen without complaining about it; *she does not tolerate singing in the classroom*
(b) to allow something which you do not agree with to exist; *opposition parties are not tolerated in that country; he is not known for tolerating people with opposing views to his*
(c) to accept the effect of a drug or a poison; *the body can tolerate small amounts of poison*

④ **toll**
[tɒʊl]
1 *noun*
(a) payment for using a service, usually a road, bridge or ferry; *you have to pay a toll to cross the bridge; there's an office at the bridge where the man collects the tolls;* **toll bridge** = bridge where you have to pay a toll to cross
(b) number of people hurt, of buildings damaged, etc.; **to take a toll of** = to destroy or damage; *the storm took a heavy toll of ships in the harbour; the wind took a toll of trees in the park;* **death toll** = number of people who have died; *the death toll in the disaster has risen to three hundred*
(c) solemn ringing of a bell; *the toll of the great bell could be heard across the fields*
2 *verb*
to ring a bell slowly, as for a funeral; *the bell was tolling as the coffin arrived at the church*

③ **toll call**
['tɒʊl 'kɔːl] *noun*
US long-distance telephone call; *I made a toll call to Seattle*

③ **toll free**
['tɒʊl 'friː] *adjective & adverb*
US without having to pay the charge for a long-distance telephone call; *a toll-free number; to call someone toll-free*

③ **tomato**
[tɪ'mɑːtɪʊ US tɪ'meɪtɪʊ] *noun*
(a) small, round red fruit used in salads and cooking; *tomatoes cost 30p per kilo; we had a salad of raw cabbage and tomatoes; someone in the crowd threw a tomato at the speaker on the platform;* **tomato sauce** = sauce made with tomatoes and herbs; *do you want tomato sauce with your fish and chips?*
(b) tomato plant, plant which produces tomatoes; *he planted six tomatoes in his back garden* (NOTE: plural is **tomatoes**)

① **tomorrow**
[tɪ'mɒrɪʊ]
1 *adverb*
referring to the day after today; *are you free for lunch tomorrow?; I mustn't forget I have a dentist's appointment tomorrow morning; we are going to an Italian restaurant tomorrow evening*
2 *noun*

the day after today; *today's Monday, so tomorrow must be Tuesday; tomorrow is our tenth wedding anniversary;* **the day after tomorrow** = two days after today; *we're going to Paris the day after tomorrow*

③ **ton**
[tʌn] *noun*
(a) measure of weight equal to 2240 pounds; *a ship carrying 1000 tons of coal;* **metric ton** = 1000 kilograms (NOTE: also called a **tonne**)
(b) *(informal)* **it weighs a ton** = it is very heavy; *your suitcase weighs a ton, what have you got in it?; (informal)* **tons of** = lots of; *I've tons of work to do; she had tons of cards on her twenty-first birthday*
(c) *(slang)* **to do a ton** = to drive at 100 miles per hour; *he was doing a ton on the motorway when the police stopped him*

② **tone**
[tɪʊn]
1 *noun*
(a) way of saying something, or of writing something, which shows a particular feeling; *his tone of voice showed he was angry; she said hello in a friendly tone of voice; you could tell from the tone of his letter that he was annoyed*
(b) *(on the phone)* special noise which indicates something; *please speak after the tone;* **dialling tone** = noise made by a telephone to show that it is ready for you to dial a number; **engaged tone** = sound made by a telephone when the line dialled is busy; *every time I call her number I get the engaged tone*
(c) slight difference in colour; *she prefers soft tones like pink or pale blue*
(d) **muscle tone** = normal slightly tense state of a healthy muscle; *exercising every day will improve muscle tone*
(e) general spirit of an area, a meeting, etc.; *having all those rusty old fridges and cookers in their front garden lowers the tone of the neighbourhood*
(f) *(in music)* the difference in pitch between pairs of notes
2 *verb*
to tone in with = to fit in well or to be in harmony with; *the colour of the carpet tones in well with the curtains*

③ **tongue**
[tʌŋ] *noun*
(a) organ in your mouth, which can move and is used for tasting, swallowing and speaking; *the soup was so hot it burnt my tongue;* **to say something with your tongue in your cheek** *or* **to say something tongue in cheek** = to say something which you do not mean seriously; **it's on the tip of my tongue** = I'll remember it in a moment, I'm trying hard to remember it
(b) similar part in an animal, used for food; *we had tongue and salad*
(c) way of speaking; *she can have a sharp tongue when she wants to*

(d) language; **mother tongue** or **native tongue** = language which you spoke when you were a little child; *she speaks English very well, but German is her mother tongue*

① **tonight**
[tɪ'naɪt] *adverb & noun*
the night or the evening of today; *I can't stop - we're getting ready for tonight's party; I'll be at home from eight o'clock tonight; I don't suppose there's anything interesting on TV tonight*

③ **tonne**
[tʌn] *noun*
metric ton, weight of one thousand kilograms; *they harvested over one hundred tonnes of apples*

① **too**
[tu:] *adverb*
(a) more than necessary; *there are too many people to fit into the lift; I think we bought too much bread; it's too hot for us to sit in the sun*
(b) *(often at the end of a clause)* also; *she had some coffee and I had some too; she, too, comes from Scotland* or *she comes from Scotland too*

① **took**
[tʊk] *see* TAKE

② **tool**
[tu:l] *noun*
instrument which you hold in the hand to do certain work, such as a hammer, spade, etc.; *a set of tools for mending the car*

② **tooth**
[tu:θ] *noun*
(a) one of a set of hard white objects in the mouth which you use to bite or chew food; *children must learn to clean their teeth twice a day; I'll have to see the dentist - one of my back teeth hurts; the dentist took one of her teeth out;* **false teeth** = artificial plastic teeth which fit inside the mouth and take the place of teeth which have been taken out; **milk teeth** = a child's first twenty teeth, which are gradually replaced by permanent teeth; *see also* WISDOM TOOTH
(b) **to have a sweet tooth** = to like sweet food; *he's very fond of puddings - he's got a real sweet tooth!; don't put the chocolates next to her - she's got a very sweet tooth;* **long in the tooth** = old; *she's getting a bit long in the tooth for riding a motorcycle*
(c) **in the teeth of something** = in spite of some problem or obstacle; *the housing development was approved in the teeth of violent opposition from the local residents;* **armed to the teeth** = carrying lots of weapons; *the robbers were armed to the teeth*
(d) one of the row of pointed pieces on a saw, comb, zip, etc.; *throw that comb away, half its teeth are broken* (NOTE: plural is **teeth** [ti:θ])

④ **toothpaste**
['tu:θpeɪst] *noun*
soft substance which you spread on a toothbrush and then use to clean your teeth; *she squeezed some toothpaste onto her brush; I must buy a small tube of toothpaste to take when I'm travelling* (NOTE: no plural: **some toothpaste, a tube of toothpaste**)

① **top**
[tɒp]
1 *noun*
(a) highest place, highest point of something; *he climbed to the top of the stairs and sat down; the bird is sitting on the top of the apple tree; look at the photograph at the top of page four; Manchester United are still at the top of the premier league*
(b) flat upper surface of something; *do not put coffee cups on the top of the computer; the desk has a black top; a birthday cake with sugar and fruit on the top*
(c) cover for a jar, bottle, etc.; *take the top off the jar, and see what's inside; she forgot to screw the top back on the bottle*
(d) best position in a contest, a profession, etc.; *she came top in the competition*
(e) child's toy which turns very rapidly on a point; *when a spinning top slows down, it wobbles and finally falls over*
(f) *(informal)* **big top** = very large circus tent
2 *adjective*
(a) in the highest place; *the restaurant is on the top floor of the building; jams and marmalades are on the top shelf*
(b) best; *she's one of the world's top tennis players*
3 *verb*
(a) to put something on top; *strawberry cake topped with whipped cream*
(b) to do better than; *I don't think anyone else will top his score; (informal)* **to top it all** = on top of everything else; *to top it all, a pipe burst in the bathroom and the whole house was flooded* (NOTE: **topping - topped**)

◊ **on top**
phrase
on; *a birthday cake with sugar and fruit on top*

◊ **on top of**
phrase
(a) on; *he put the book down on top of the others he had bought; there is a roof garden on top of the hotel; do not put coffee cups on top of the computer*
(b) in addition to; *on top of all my office work, I have the clean the house and look after the baby*

② **topic**
['tɒpɪk] *noun*
subject of a discussion or conversation; *can we move on to another topic?;* **to bring up a topic** = to start to discuss something; *she brought up the topic of where to go on holiday*

topical

['tɒpɪkl] *adjective*

interesting at the present time; *the question of global warming is very topical*

topple

[tɒpl] *verb*

(a) to fall down; *he lost his balance and toppled forwards*

(b) to make a government or dictator lose power; *the government was toppled after three days of street fighting*

topple over

['tɒpl 'ʊvɪ] *verb*

to fall down; *the bottle toppled over and smashed onto the floor*

top up

['tɒp 'ʌp] *verb*

to add liquid to fill completely something which is half empty; *let me top up your glass*; *I topped the bottle up with tap water*

torch

[tɔːtʃ]

1 *noun*

(a) small portable electric lamp; *take a torch if you're going into the cave*; *I always carry a small torch in the car* (NOTE: American English only uses **flashlight**)

(b) burning light, carried in the hand; *the demonstrators marched through the streets carrying torches* (NOTE: plural is **torches**)

2 *verb*

to set fire to something on purpose; *rioting students torched the police station*

tore

[tɔː] *see* TEAR

torn

[tɔːn] *see* TEAR

torture

['tɔːtʃɪ]

1 *noun*

making someone suffer pain as a punishment or to make them reveal a secret; *they accused the police of using torture to get information about the plot*

2 *verb*

to inflict mental or physical pain on someone; *the soldiers tortured their prisoners*; *the policeman tortured the girl by refusing to tell her where her mother was*

toss

[tɒs]

1 *verb*

(a) to throw something up into the air, or to someone; *she tossed me her car keys*; **to toss a coin** = to throw a coin to decide something according to which side is on top when it comes down; *we tossed a coin and I had to do the washing up*; **let's toss for it** = let's throw a coin in the air and the person who guesses right starts to play first or has first choice

(b) to move something about; *the waves tossed the little boat up and down*; **the horse tossed its head** = made a sharp movement of the head

2 *noun*

(a) act of throwing something into the air; *(in sport)* **to win the toss** = to guess correctly which side of the coin comes down on top and so have first choice or play first

(b) sharp movement up and down of the head; *with a toss of its head, the horse raced off*

toss up

['tɒs 'ʌp] *verb*

to throw a coin to see which side is on top when it comes down; *we tossed up, and I had to do the washing up*; *let's toss up to see who pays for the taxi*

total

['tɪʊtɪl]

1 *adjective*

complete, whole; *the expedition was a total failure*; *their total losses come to over £400,000*

2 *noun*

whole amount; *the total comes to more than £1,000*; **grand total** = final total made by adding several items

3 *verb*

to add up to; *the bill totalled £600*; *he was declared bankrupt, with debts totalling more than £1m* (NOTE: British English **totalling - totalled** but American English spelling is **totaling - totaled**)

totally

['tɪʊtɪli] *adverb*

completely; *the house was totally destroyed in the fire*; *I had totally forgotten that I had promised to be there*; *he disagrees totally with what the first speaker said*

touch

[tʌtʃ]

1 *noun*

(a) one of the five senses, the sense of feeling with the fingers; *the sense of touch is very strong in blind people*

(b) contact, the passing of news and information; **to get in touch with someone** = to contact someone; *I'll try to get in touch with you next week*; **to lose touch with someone** = to lose contact with someone; *they used to live next door, but we've lost touch with them now that they've moved to London*; **to put someone in touch with someone** = to arrange for someone to have contact with someone; *the bank put us in touch with a local lawyer*; **to stay in touch with someone** = to keep contact with someone; *we met in Hong Kong thirty years ago but we have still kept in touch*; *see also* OUT OF TOUCH (NOTE: no plural in meanings (a) and (b))

(c) gentle physical contact; *I felt a light touch on my hand*

(d) very small amount; *he added a few touches of paint to the picture*; *there's a touch of frost in the air this morning*; **finishing touches =** final work to make something perfect; *we're just putting the finishing touches to the exhibition before we open tomorrow morning* (NOTE: plural in meanings (c) and (d) is **touches**)

2 *verb*

(a) to feel with your fingers; *the policeman touched him on the shoulder*; *don't touch that cake - it's for your mother*

(b) to be so close to something that you press against it; *his feet don't touch the floor when he sits on a big chair*; *there is a mark on the wall where the sofa touches it*

(c) to eat or drink; *I never touch coffee*; *we never touch fruit which has not been washed*

(d) to make someone feel sad; *his sad song touched all the people in the church*

(e) *(informal)* **to touch someone for =** to try and get someone to lend or give you money; *how much did he touch you for?*

③ **touch down**
['tʌtʃ 'daʊn] *verb*

(a) to land; *the plane touched down at 13.20*

(b) to score a try in Rugby, by touching the ground behind the opponents' line with the ball; *he touched down behind the posts*

③ **touched**
[tʌtʃt] *adjective*

grateful, pleased with; *she was touched to get your phone call on her birthday*

③ **touching**
['tʌtʃɪŋ] *adjective*

which affects the emotions; *a touching letter from my sister*

③ **touch up**
['tʌtʃ 'ʌp] *verb*

to add a small amount of paint; *you will need to touch up the car where it has been scratched*

② **tough**
[tʌf] *adjective*

(a) difficult to chew or to cut; *my steak's a bit tough - how's yours?*; *(informal)* **this meat is as tough as old boots =** it is extremely tough (NOTE: the opposite is **tender)**

(b) difficult; *the exam is extremely tough* (NOTE: the opposite is **easy)**

(c) strict; *the police are getting tough on drunk drivers*

(d) *(informal)* unfortunate; *it's tough that you can't come to the party*; *having three little children to look after is tough on the parents*; **tough luck! =** I'm sorry you have a problem, that you didn't win, that you didn't do well, etc., but there's nothing I can do to help you; *you've missed the last bus? - tough luck, you'll just have to walk* (NOTE: **tougher - toughest)**

② **tour**
[tuːr]
1 *noun*

(a) holiday journey to various places coming back in the end to the place you started from; *there are so many tours to choose from - I can't decide which one to go on*; *she gave us a tour round the old castle*; **conducted tour** *or* **guided tour =** tour with a guide who shows places to tourists; **package tour =** tour where everything (hotel, food, travel, etc.) is arranged and paid for before you leave

(b) journey on business to various places coming back in the end to the place you started from; *he is leading a group of businessmen on a tour of Italian factories*

(c) journey round various places where you perform, speak, etc.; *the pop group is on an American tour*; *the Prime Minister went on a tour of the North East*

2 *verb*

(a) to go on holiday, visiting various places; *they toured the south of France*

(b) to visit various places to perform or speak; *the opera company toured Eastern Europe last year*

④ **tourism**
['tuːrɪzm] *noun*

business of providing travel, accommodation, food and entertainment for tourists; *tourism is the country's main source of income*

③ **tourist**
['tuːrɪst] *noun*

person who goes on holiday to visit places away from his home; *the tourists were talking German*; *there were parties of tourists visiting all the churches*; *Trafalgar Square is always full of tourists*; **tourist bureau** *or* **tourist information office** *or* **tourist information centre =** office which gives information to tourists about the place where it is situated; *you can get a map of the town from the tourist bureau*; **tourist class =** type of seating in an aircraft which is cheaper than first class; *he always travels first class, because he says tourist class is too uncomfortable*; *the tourist class fare is much less than the first class*; **tourist trap =** place which charges tourists too much; *it used to be a quiet little town, but now it's just a tourist trap*

④ **tournament**
['tuːnɪmɪnt] *noun*

sporting competition with many games where competitors who lose drop out until only one is left; *the Wimbledon tennis tournament*; *the golf tournament starts on Saturday*

④ **tow**
[təʊ]
1 *verb*

to pull a car or a ship which cannot move by itself; *the motorways were crowded with cars towing caravans*; *they towed the ship into port*

2 *noun*

action of pulling something; *we got a tractor to give us a tow to the nearest garage* (NOTE: do not confuse with **toe**)

① **towards** *US also* **toward**
[tɪˈwɔːdz] *preposition*
(a) in the direction of; *the crowd ran towards the police station*; *the bus was travelling south, towards London*; *the ship sailed straight towards the rocks*
(b) near (in time); *do you have any free time towards the end of the month?*; *the exhibition will be held towards the middle of October*
(c) as part of the money to pay for something; *he gave me £100 towards the cost of the hotel*
(d) in relation to; *she always behaved very kindly towards her father*

④ **towel**
[ˈtaʊɪl] *noun*
large piece of soft cloth for drying; *there's only one towel in the bathroom*; *after washing her hair, she wound the towel round her head*; *I'll get some fresh towels*; **to throw in the towel** = to give up, not to continue a contest; **bath towel** = very large towel for drying yourself after having a bath; **beach towel** = coloured towel used to dry yourself after swimming in the sea, and also for sitting on; **tea towel** = cloth which you use for drying plates, dishes, etc.; **towel rail** = bar of metal or wood in a bathroom on which you can hang a towel

③ **tower**
[ˈtaʊɪ]
1 *noun*
(a) tall construction; *the castle has thick walls and four square towers*; **tower block** = very tall block of flats; *they live in a tower block south of the Thames*; **control tower** = tall building at an airport where the radio station is
(b) **the Tower of London** = castle in London, built by William the Conqueror; *there is a picture of the Tower of London on the front of the book*
2 *verb*
to tower over = to rise very high above; *he towers over his wife who is very small*

① **town**
[taʊn] *noun*
place, larger than a village, where people live and work, with houses, shops, offices, factories, etc.; *there's no shop in our village, so we do our shopping in the nearest town*; *the town is known for its chocolate*; *they moved their office to the centre of town*; **town centre** = central part of a town, where main shops, banks and places of interest are situated; *the traffic in the town centre has got so bad that I walk everywhere* (NOTE: this is called **downtown** in American English); **town plan** *or* **town map** = diagram showing the streets of a town with their names; **market town** = town which has a regular market; **seaside town** = town by the sea; *(informal)* **to go to town on something** = to

spend a lot of money or time on something; *she really went to town on buying furniture for the new house*; *(informal)* **to paint the town red** = to go out drinking and going to parties in town

④ **toxic**
[ˈtɒksɪk] *adjective*
poisonous, harmful; *caution: this product is toxic*; **toxic waste** = waste which is poisonous or harmful to the environment; *environmentalists want to ban the dumping of toxic waste in the sea*

④ **toy**
[tɔɪ]
1 *noun*
thing for children to play with; *we gave him a box of toy soldiers for Christmas*; *the children's toys are all over the sitting room floor*; *she won't let me play with any of her toys*
2 *verb*
to toy with something = to play with something (not seriously); *she wasn't hungry and only toyed with her food*

③ **trace**
[treɪs]
1 *noun*
(a) something which shows that something existed; **without trace** = leaving nothing behind; *the car seems to have vanished without trace*
(b) very small amount; *there was a trace of powder on his coat*; *she showed no trace of anger*
2 *verb*
(a) to follow an animal's tracks; *we traced the fox back to its hole*
(b) to find where someone *or* something is; *they couldn't trace the letter*; *the police traced him to Dover*
(c) to copy a drawing, etc., by placing a sheet of transparent paper over it and drawing on it; *she traced the map and put it into her project on the history of the village*

③ **trace element**
[ˈtreɪs ˈelɪmɪnt] *noun*
chemical element which a plant or animal needs to grow properly, but only in very small amounts

> COMMENT: plants require traces of copper, iron, manganese and zinc; human beings need chromium, cobalt, copper, magnesium, manganese, molybdenum, selenium and zinc, but all in tiny quantities

② **track**
[træk]
1 *noun*
(a) **tracks** = series of marks left by an animal's feet, marks left by wheels, etc.; *we followed the car tracks to the forest*; *those are the tracks of a deer*; **to make tracks for** = to go towards; *they made tracks for the nearest hotel*
(b) **to be on someone's track** = to follow someone; *the police are on his track*

(c) to keep track of = to keep an account, to keep yourself informed about; *I like to keep track of new developments in computer technology*; **to lose track of someone** *or* **something** = not to know where someone *or* something is; *we lost track of him after he went to work in Turkey*; **we lost track of the time** = we didn't know what time it was

(d) rough path; *we followed a track through the forest*; **off the beaten track** = in a place which is away from main roads and not normally visited by many people; *our village is off the beaten track and so is very quiet*; **you're on the right track** = you're working the right way in order to succeed, you're doing the right thing; *we haven't solved the problem yet, but we're certainly on the right track*; **you're on the wrong track** = you're working in the wrong way

(e) path for races; **track events** = running competitions; **track shoes** = running shoes

(f) line of parallel rails for trains; *the trains will be late because of repairs to the track*; **single-track railway** = railway where trains go up and down the same rails but with places where two trains can pass; *(informal)* **to have a one-track mind** = to think about only one thing or to have only one thing which interests you

(g) one of the sections of music on a disk; *one of the tracks from their disk has been released as a single*

2 *verb*

to follow someone *or* an animal; *the hunters tracked the bear through the forest*; *we tracked the fox back to its hole*; *the police tracked the gang to a flat in south London*

ⓘ **track down**
['træk 'daun] *verb*

to track someone down = to follow and catch (a criminal); **to track something down** = to manage to find something; *I finally tracked down that file which you were looking for*

ⓘ **tracksuit**
['træksuːt] *noun*

pair of matching trousers and top, in warm material, worn when practising sports; *the runners were warming up in their tracksuits*

ⓘ **tractor**
['træktɪ] *noun*

heavy vehicle with large back wheels, used for work on farms; *he was driving a tractor down the village street*; *we got a tractor to pull the car out of the ditch*

ⓘ **trade**
[treɪd]
1 *noun*

(a) business of buying and selling; *Britain's trade with the rest of Europe is up by 10%*; **export trade** = the business of selling to other countries; **import trade** = the business of buying from other countries; **free trade** = system where goods can go from one country to another without any restrictions; **to do a good trade in a range of products** = to sell a large number of a range of products; **to do a roaring trade** = to sell a lot very fast; *the ice cream sellers have been doing a roaring trade during the hot weather*

(b) people or companies that deal in the same type of product or service; *he is in the secondhand car trade*; **trade price** = special wholesale price paid by a retailer to a wholesaler or manufacturer

2 *verb*

(a) to buy and sell, to carry on a business; *the company has stopped trading*; *they trade in tobacco*

(b) to exchange something for something; *I'll trade the car for your motorbike*

ⓘ **trade in**
['treɪd 'ɪn] *verb*

to give in an old item, such as a car or washing machine, as part of the payment for a new one; *he traded in his old Rolls Royce for a new model*

ⓘ **trademark** *or* **trade name**
['treɪdmɑːk or 'treɪd 'neɪm] *noun*

particular name, design, etc., which has been registered by the manufacturer and which cannot be used by other manufacturers; *Acme is a registered trademark*; *their trademark is stamped on every item they produce*

ⓘ **trader**
['treɪdɪ] *noun*

person who does business; *Arab traders crossed into India by boat*

ⓘ **trade union** *or* **trades union**
['treɪd 'juːnɪn or 'treɪdz 'juːnɪn] *noun*

organization which represents workers who are its members in discussions with employers about wages and conditions of employment; *the staff are all members of a trades union or they are trade union members* (NOTE: American English is **labor union**)

ⓘ **tradition**
[trə'dɪʃn] *noun*

beliefs, customs and stories which are passed from one generation to the next; *it's a family tradition for the eldest son to take over the business*; *according to local tradition, two murderers were hanged where the two roads meet*

ⓘ **traditional**
[trɪ'dɪʃnl] *adjective*

according to tradition; *on Easter Day it is traditional to give chocolate eggs to the children*; *villagers still wear their traditional costumes on Sundays*

ⓘ **traffic**
['træfɪk]
1 *noun*

(a) cars, lorries, buses, etc., which are travelling on a street or road; *I leave the office early on Fridays because there is so much traffic* *leaving London*; *the lights turned green and the traffic moved forward*; *rush-hour traffic is worse on Fridays*; **traffic-calming measures** = ways used to reduce the amount of traffic or to make it go slower, such as imposing speed limits, making narrow places in roads, etc.; **traffic offences** = offences committed by drivers of vehicles; **traffic police** = branch of the police force dealing with traffic on roads

(b) *US* **traffic circle** = place where several roads meet, and traffic has to move in a circle round a central area (NOTE: British English is **roundabout**)

(c) **air traffic** = aircraft flying around; *air traffic round London will increase when they build the new airport*

(d) illegal trade; *the South American drugs traffic* (NOTE: no plural: **some traffic**; **a lot of traffic**)

2 *verb*

to deal in drugs, weapons, etc., illegally; *he made a fortune trafficking in guns* (NOTE: **trafficking - trafficked**)

③ **traffic jam**
['træfik 'dʒæm] *noun*

situation where cars, lorries, etc., cannot move forward on a road because there is too much traffic, because there has been an accident, because of repair works to roads, etc.; *a lorry was blown over, causing a big traffic jam*; *there are traffic jams on the roads out of London every Friday evening*

③ **traffic lights**
['træfik 'laits] *noun*

red, green and orange lights for making the traffic stop and start; *to get to the police station, you have to turn left at the next traffic lights*; *he drove across the junction when the traffic lights were red* (NOTE: often shortened to just **lights**)

③ **traffic warden**
['træfik 'wɔːdin] *noun*

person whose job it is to see that cars are legally parked, and to give parking tickets to those which are not legally parked; *I'm just going to the post office - shout if you see a traffic warden coming*

③ **tragedy**
['trædʒidi] *noun*

(a) serious play, film, or novel which ends sadly; *Shakespeare's tragedy 'King Lear' is playing at the National Theatre*

(b) very unhappy event; *tragedy struck the family when their mother was killed in a car crash* (NOTE: plural is **tragedies**)

③ **tragic**
['trædʒik] *adjective*

(a) very sad; *a tragic accident on the motorway*

(b) referring to a tragedy; *one of the greatest tragic actors*

③ **trail**
[treil]

1 *noun*

(a) tracks left by an animal, by a criminal, etc.; *we followed the trail of the bear through the forest*; *the burglars left in a red sports car, and a police car was soon on their trail*

(b) path or track; *keep to the trail otherwise you will get lost*; **mountain trail** = path through mountains; **nature trail** = path through the countryside with signs to showing interesting features, such as plants, trees, birds or animals

(c) something that follows behind; *the car left a trail of blue smoke*; *the dogs followed the trail of drops of blood to a warehouse*; *the storm left a trail of destruction across the south of the country*

2 *verb*

(a) to follow the tracks left by an animal or a person; *the police trailed the group across Europe*

(b) **to trail behind** = to follow slowly after someone; *she came third, trailing a long way behind the first two runners*; *the little children trailed behind the older ones*

(c) **trailing plant** = plant whose stems hang down or lie along the ground

(d) to let something drag behind; *she stormed out, trailing her coat on the floor behind her*

③ **trailer**
['treilɪ] *noun*

(a) small goods vehicle pulled behind a car; *we carried all our camping gear in the trailer*

(b) *US* van with beds, table, washing facilities, etc., which can be towed by a car; **trailer park** = place where trailers are kept, usually permanently (NOTE: also called a **mobile home**; British English is **caravan**)

(c) parts of a full-length film shown as an advertisement for it; *we saw the trailer last week, and it put me off the film*

① **train**
[trein]

1 *noun*

(a) engine pulling a group of coaches on the railway; *the train to Paris leaves from platform 1*; *hundreds of people go to work every day by train*; *the next train to London will be in two minutes*; *to get to Glasgow, you have to change trains at Crewe*; **stopping train** = train which goes slowly, stopping at each station; **suburban train** = train which goes from the centre of a town to the suburbs; **train set** = child's toy train with engines, coaches and rails; **train timetable** = list showing times of arrivals and departures of trains

(b) series of things, one after the other; *the police are trying to piece together the train of events which led to the accident*; **train of thought** = series of thoughts, one after the other; *my wife asked me to help with the baby, thus breaking my train of thought*

2 *verb*

(a) to teach someone or an animal how to do something; *she's being trained to be a bus driver*; *guide dogs are trained to lead blind people*

(b) to make a plant grow in a certain way; *we've trained the climbing rose up the wall*

(c) to become fit by practising for a sport; *he's training for the 100 metres*; *she's training for the Olympics*

③ **trainer**

['treɪnɪ] *noun*

(a) person who trains a sportsman or a team; *his trainer says he's in peak condition for the fight*

(b) trainers = light sports shoes; *she needs a new pair of trainers for school*; *he comes to work every morning in trainers*; *she came to the interview wearing a pair of dirty trainers*

① **training**

['treɪnɪŋ] *noun*

(a) being taught a skill; *the shop is closed on Tuesday mornings for staff training*; *there is a ten-week training period for new staff*

(b) practising for a sport; **to be in training** = to practise for a sport; *she's in training for the Olympics*

③ **training college**

['treɪnɪŋ 'kɒlɪdʒ] *noun*

college where teachers are trained; *after university she took an education course at a training college*

③ **transaction**

[træn'zækʃn] *noun*

piece of business; *the whole transaction was conducted in French*; **cash transaction** = business which is paid for in cash

② **transfer**

1 *noun*

['trænsfɪ]

(a) action of moving something *or* someone to a new place; *I've applied for a transfer to our London branch*; **on the transfer list** = on the list of footballers who can move to other teams

(b) changing to another form of transport; **transfer passenger** = traveller who is changing from one aircraft or train or bus to another, or to another form of transport

2 *verb*

[træns'fɜ:]

(a) to move something *or* someone to another place; *the money will be transferred directly to your bank account*; *she transferred her passport from her handbag to her jacket pocket*; *he's been transferred to our Manchester office*

(b) to change from one type of travel to another; *when you get to London airport, you have to transfer onto an internal flight* (NOTE: **transferring - transferred**)

③ **transform**

[trænz'fɔ:m] *verb*

to change the appearance of someone *or* something completely; *after her marriage she was transformed*; *the frog was transformed into a handsome prince*

③ **transit**

['trænzɪt] *noun*

movement of passengers or goods on the way to a destination; *some of the party's luggage was lost in transit*; **goods in transit** = goods being transported from one place to another; **transit lounge** = waiting room in an airport where passengers wait for connecting flights; **transit passengers** = travellers who are changing from one aircraft to another

③ **transition**

[træn'zɪʃn] *noun*

process of moving from one state to another; *she easily made the transition from being a poor student to a rich executive*

④ **translate**

[trænz'leɪt] *verb*

to put words into another language; *can you translate what he said?*; *he asked his secretary to translate the letter from the German agent*; *she translates mainly from Spanish into English, not from English into Spanish*

④ **translation**

[trænz'leɪʃn] *noun*

text which has been translated; *I read Tolstoy's 'War and Peace' in translation*; *she passed the translation of the letter to the accounts department*; **translation bureau** = office which translates documents for companies

④ **translator**

['trænsleɪtɪ] *noun*

person who translates; *she works as a translator for the European Parliament*

④ **transmission**

[trænz'mɪʃn] *noun*

(a) radio or TV broadcast; *we interrupt this transmission to bring you a news flash*

(b) *(formal)* passing of disease from one person to another; *patients must be isolated to prevent transmission of the disease to the general public*

(c) *(in a car)* series of moving parts which pass the power from the engine to the wheels; *there's a strange noise coming from the transmission*

④ **transmit**

[trænz'mɪt] *verb*

(a) to pass a disease from one person to another; *the disease was transmitted to all the people he came into contact with*; *the disease is transmitted by fleas*

(b) to send out a programme or a message by radio or TV; *the message was transmitted to the ship by radio* (NOTE: **transmitting - transmitted**)

④ **transparent**
[trænz'peɪrɪnt] *adjective*
(a) which you can see through; *the meat is wrapped in transparent plastic film*
(b) which is completely obvious; *his explanation was a transparent lie*
(c) clear and open about official actions; *the government insists on the importance all its actions being transparent*

④ **transplant**
1 *noun*
['trɑːnsplɑːnt]
(a) act of taking an organ such as the heart, or tissue such as a piece of skin, and putting it into a patient to replace an organ or tissue which is not working properly or is damaged; *he had a heart transplant*
(b) organ or piece of tissue which is transplanted; *the kidney transplant was rejected*
2 *verb*
[træns'plɑːnt]
(a) to move a plant from one place to another; *you should not transplant trees in the summer*
(b) to put an organ or piece of tissue into a patient to replace an organ or tissue which is not working properly or is damaged; *they transplanted a kidney from his brother*

② **transport**
1 *noun*
['trænspɔːt]
movement of goods or people in vehicles; *air transport is the quickest way to travel from one country to another*; *rail transport costs are getting lower*; *what means of transport will you use to get to the hotel?*; **public transport** = transport (such as buses, trains) which can be used by anyone; *its quicker to go by public transport into central London than by car*; *the government's policy is to persuade people to use public transport instead of their cars*; *how can we get to Kew Gardens by public transport?*
2 *verb*
[træn'spɔːt]
to move goods or people from one place to another in a vehicle; *the company transports millions of tons of goods by rail each year*; *the visitors will be transported to the factory by helicopter*

③ **transportation**
[trænspɔː'teɪʃn] *noun*
action or means of moving goods or people; *the company will provide transportation to the airport*; **ground transportation** = buses, taxis, etc., available to take passengers from an airport to the town

③ **trap**
[træp]
1 *noun*
(a) device to catch an animal; *there is a mouse in the kitchen so we will put down a trap*

(b) device to catch a person by surprise; **police radar trap** = small radar device by the side of a road which senses and notes details of cars which are travelling too fast
(c) **trap door** = door in a floor or in a ceiling; *there's a trap door leading to the roof*
(d) *(informal)* mouth; **keep your trap shut!** = don't say anything
2 *verb*
to catch or hold; *several people were trapped in the wreckage of the plane*; *he was trapped on video as he tried to break into the bank* (NOTE: **trapping - trapped**)

③ **trash**
[træʃ]
1 *noun*
(a) useless things; *throw out all that trash from her bedroom* (NOTE: British English prefers **rubbish**)
(b) *US (informal)* poor useless people; **white trash** = poor white people (NOTE: no plural)
2 *verb*
(a) to smash up; *someone trashed the telephones*
(b) to ruin someone's reputation; *she wrote an article trashing the pop singer*

③ **trashcan**
['træʃkæn] *noun*
US large plastic or metal container for household rubbish; *they come to empty the trashcans once a week*; *she put the rest of the dinner in the trashcan* (NOTE: also called a **garbage can**; British English for this is **dustbin**)

④ **trauma**
['trɔːmɪ] *noun*
mental shock caused by a sudden unpleasant experience, which was not expected to take place; *she was in trauma after the crash*; *in court, he had to live through the trauma of the accident again*

④ **traumatic**
[trɔː'mætɪk] *adjective*
which gives a sharp and unpleasant shock; *witnessing an accident can be as traumatic as being involved in it*; *I will never forget our traumatic arrival in India*

② **travel**
['trævɪl]
1 *noun*
(a) action of moving from one country or place to another; *air travel is the only really fast method of going from one country to another*; **travel insurance** = insurance taken out by a traveller against accident, loss of luggage, illness, etc.; **travel sickness** = sickness caused by the movement of a car, aircraft, bus or train, etc. (NOTE: no plural in this meaning)
(b) **travels** = long journeys abroad; *she is someone he met on his travels in India*
2 *verb*

to move from one country or place to another; *he travels fifty miles by car to go to work every day*; *he has travelled across the United States several times on his motorbike*; *the bullet must have travelled several metres before it hit the wall* (NOTE: **travelling - travelled** but American spelling is **traveling - traveled**)

④ **traveller** *US* **traveler**
['trævlɪ] *noun*

(a) person who travels; *travellers on the 9 o'clock train to London*; *travellers to France are experiencing delays because of the dock strike*

(b) person who has no fixed home and who travels around the country; *the music festival was full of travellers*

④ **traveller's cheque** *US* **traveler's check**
['trɪvlɪz 'tʃek] *noun*

cheque which you buy at a bank before you travel and which you can then use in a foreign country; *most shops in the USA accept traveller's cheques*; *the hotel will cash traveller's cheques for you*

④ **tray**
[treɪ] *noun*

(a) flat board for carrying food, glasses, cups and saucers, etc.; *he had his lunch on a tray in his bedroom*; *she bumped into a waitress carrying a tray of glasses*

(b) flat open container on a desk for documents which have to be dealt with; *there was a pile of letters in my tray when I returned to work*

④ **tread**
[tred]
1 *noun*

(a) top part of a stair or step which you stand on; *the carpet on the bottom tread is loose*; *metal treads are noisy*

(b) pattern of lines cut into the surface of a tyre; *you need to change your tyres - the tread's worn*

(c) way of walking; *he walked up to the door with a firm tread*

2 *verb*

to step, to walk; *she trod on my toe and didn't say she was sorry*; *watch where you're treading - there's broken glass on the floor* (NOTE: **treading - trod** [trɒd] **- has trodden** ['trɒdɪn])

④ **treasure**
['treʒɪ]
1 *noun*

jewels, gold, or other valuable things; *the treasures in the British Museum*; *buried treasure* = gold, silver, etc., which someone has hidden; *they are diving in the Caribbean looking for Spanish treasure*; **treasure hunt** = game where clues lead you from place to place until you come to a hidden prize; *we organized a treasure hunt for the children's party*

2 *verb*

to value something; *I treasure the calm life of the fishing village where I live*; *she treasures her three cats and wouldn't part with them for anything*

④ **treasury**
['treʒri] *noun*

(a) **the Treasury** = government department which deals with the country's finance; *all government departments have to have their spending plans approved by the Treasury* (NOTE: the term is used in both the UK and the USA; in most other countries this department is called the **Ministry of Finance**); *US* **Secretary of the Treasury** *or* **Treasury Secretary** = member of the government in charge of finance (NOTE: in most countries, the equivalent is the **Finance Minister**; in the UK, it is the **Chancellor of the Exchequer**)

(b) place where treasure is kept; *robbers broke into the royal treasury and stole boxes of gold*

① **treat**
[triːt]
1 *noun*

special thing which gives pleasure; *it's always a treat to sit down quietly at home after a hard day working in the shop*; **a treat in store** = special pleasant experience in the future; *if you've never seen this film before you've got a treat in store*; **this is our treat** = we are paying the bill

2 *verb*

(a) to deal with someone; *she was badly treated by her uncle*; *it you treat the staff well they will work well*

(b) **to treat someone to something** = to give someone a special meal or outing as a gift; *come along - I'll treat you all to ice creams!*

(c) to look after a sick or injured person; *after the accident some of the passengers had to be treated in hospital for cuts and bruises*; *she is being treated for rheumatism*

(d) to process in some way to make safe or to protect; *waste water from households is treated by the council*; *the wood has been treated to make it resistant to rot*

① **treatment**
['triːtmɪnt] *noun*

(a) way of behaving towards something or someone; *the report criticized the treatment of prisoners in the jail*; *what sort of treatment did you get at school?*; *we got VIP treatment when we visited China*

(b) way of looking after a sick or injured person; *he is having a course of heat treatment*; *the treatment for skin cancer is very painful*

② **treaty**
['triːti] *noun*

(a) written legal agreement between two or more countries; *the treaty was signed in 1845*; *countries are negotiating a treaty to ban nuclear weapons*

(b) legal agreement between individual persons; **to sell a house by private treaty** = to sell by an agreement between the person who is selling and the person who is buying, and not by auction (NOTE: plural is **treaties**)

① **tree**
[tri:] *noun*

(a) very large plant, with a thick trunk, branches and leaves; *the cat climbed up an apple tree and couldn't get down*; *in autumn, the trees in our park turn brown and red*; *he was sheltering under a tree and was struck by lightning*

(b) family tree = table showing a family going back over many generations; *he's going through the local parish records to try to establish his family tree*; *they can trace their family tree back to the Norman invasion of 1066*

④ **tremble**
['trembl]
1 *noun*

shaking movement; *there was a tremble in her voice*

2 *verb*

to shake because you are cold or afraid; *she was trembling with cold*; *I tremble at the thought of how much the meal will cost*

② **tremendous**
[trɪ'mendɪs] *adjective*

(a) enormous, very big; *there was a tremendous explosion and all the lights went out*; *there's tremendous excitement here in Trafalgar Square as we wait for the election result*

(b) wonderful; *it would be absolutely tremendous if you won*; *her birthday party was tremendous fun*

② **trend**
[trend] *noun*

general tendency; *there is a trend away from old-established food stores*; *the government studies economic trends to decide whether to raise taxes or not*

② **trial**
['traɪl] *noun*

(a) court case held before a judge; *the trial will be heard next week*; **to stand trial** *or* **to be on trial** = to appear in court; *she stood trial, accused of murder*; *he's on trial for theft*

(b) act of testing something; *the new model is undergoing its final trials*; **on trial** = being tested to see if it is acceptable; *the system is still on trial*; **trial period** = time when a customer can test a product before buying it; *at the end of the trial period we weren't satisfied and sent the machine back*; **trial and error** = testing and rejecting various things until you find the one which works; *we found out the best way of working was simply by trial and error*

(c) game played to select the best players for a team; *trials to select the England Rugby team will be held this weekend*

④ **tribal**
['traɪbl] *adjective*

referring to tribes; *according to tribal custom the women sit in a different area from the men*; *their tribal lands were occupied by people from a neighbouring tribe*

④ **tribe**
[traɪb] *noun*

(a) group of people with the same race, language and customs; *she went into the jungle to study the jungle tribes*

(b) *(informal)* large family group; *they came with all their tribe of children*

④ **tribunal**
[traɪ'bjuːnl] *noun*

specialist court which examines special problems and makes judgements; *a special tribunal has been set up to investigate these complaints*; **industrial tribunal** = court which decides in disputes between employers and workers; *the case of unfair dismissal went to the industrial tribunal*; **rent tribunal** = court which decides in disputes about rents and can decide a fair rent

④ **tribute**
['trɪbjuːt] *noun*

(a) words, flowers or gifts, etc., to show respect to someone, especially someone who has died; *tributes to the dead president have been received from all over the world*

(b) to pay tribute to = to praise; *speaker after speaker paid tribute to her work for charity*

③ **trick**
[trɪk]
1 *noun*

clever act to deceive or confuse someone; *the recorded sound of barking is just a trick to make burglars think there is a dog in the house*; **to play a trick on someone** = to deceive or confuse someone; *he played a mean trick on his sister*; *my memory seems to be playing tricks on me*; *(informal)* **that should do the trick** = that should do what we want to be done; *'there, that should do the trick' he said as he tightened the last screw*; **Trick or Treat** = children's game at Halloween, where children visit houses asking for fruit, sweets, etc., otherwise they will do something naughty; *see also* HAT TRICK

2 *adjective*

which deceives; *trick photography makes a tiny insect look like a giant monster*; **trick question** = question which is intended to deceive people

3 *verb*

to deceive, to confuse someone; *we've been tricked, there's nothing in the box*; **to trick someone into doing something** = to make someone do something which he did not mean to do by means of a trick; *he tricked the old lady into giving him all her money*; **to trick** someone out of something = to get someone to lose something by a trick; *she tricked the bank out of £100,000*

③ **tricky**
['trɪkɪ] *adjective*
(a) difficult to do; *getting the wire through the little hole is quite tricky*
(b) *(informal)* who cannot be trusted; *he's a tricky individual* (NOTE: trickier - trickiest)

③ **tried, tries**
[traɪd or traɪz] *see* TRY

④ **trigger**
['trɪgɪ]
1 *noun*
little lever which you pull to fire a gun; *he pointed the gun at her and pulled the trigger*
2 *verb*
to trigger something (off) = to start something happening; *the police are afraid the demonstration may trigger off a full-scale riot; the explosion was triggered by a spark*

④ **trillion**
['trɪljɪn] *noun*
(a) one million millions
(b) trillions of = a huge number of; *there were trillions of tiny fish in the lake*

④ **trim**
[trɪm]
1 *adjective*
(a) tidy, cut short; *she always keeps her hedges trim*
(b) slim and fit; *he keeps himself trim by going for a long walk every day* (NOTE: trimmer - trimmest)
2 *verb*
(a) to cut something to make it tidy; *he trimmed the hedge in front of the house; ask the hairdresser to trim your beard*
(b) to cut back; to reduce; *to trim expenditure*
(c) to decorate; *she wore a white blazer trimmed with blue* (NOTE: trimming - trimmed)
3 *noun*
(a) being fit; *he's in very good trim after a week at the health farm*
(b) cutting of your hair, a plant, etc.; *he went to the hairdresser's for a trim; can you give my beard a trim, please?*
(c) decoration on a car, a piece of clothing, etc.; *the car is white with a dark blue trim*

④ **trio**
['triːʊ] *noun*
(a) group of three people, especially a group of three musicians
(b) piece of music for three instruments (NOTE: plural is trios)

② **trip**
[trɪp]
1 *noun*

(a) short journey; *our trip to Paris was cancelled; we're going on a trip to the seaside;* **business trip** = journey to visit business contacts; **coach trip** = journey by coach; **day trip** = journey lasting one day
(b) *(slang)* sensation experienced after taking drugs; *she had a bad trip*
2 *verb*
to catch your foot in something so that you stagger and fall down; *she tripped as she was coming out of the kitchen with a tray of food; see also* TRIP OVER, TRIP UP (NOTE: tripping - tripped)

④ **triple**
['trɪpl]
1 *verb*
to become three times as large; to make something three times as large; *output has tripled over the last year; we've tripled the number of visitors to the museum since we reduced the entrance fee*
2 *adjective*
with three parts; *the three brothers are marrying three sisters in a triple wedding*

② **trip over**
['trɪp 'ʊvɪ] *verb*
(a) to catch your foot in something so that you stagger and fall; *she was running away from him when she tripped over and fell down*
(b) to trip over something = to catch your foot in something so that you stagger and fall; *she tripped over the wire and fell down the stairs*

② **trip up**
['trɪp 'ʌp] *verb*
(a) to trip someone up = to make someone fall down; *she put her foot out and deliberately tripped the waiter up*
(b) *(informal)* to make a silly mistake; *we tripped up badly in not inviting her to the party;* to trip someone up = to force someone to make a mistake; *he tried to trip me up by asking a question on a completely different subject*

④ **triumph**
['traɪʊmf]
1 *noun*
great victory, great achievement; *they scored a triumph in their game against the French; the bridge is a triumph of modern engineering;* **in triumph** = celebrating a great victory; *after the battle the army entered the city in triumph*
2 *verb*
(a) to win a victory, to achieve something; *she triumphed in the 800 metres*
(b) to triumph over something = to be successful in spite of difficulties which could have stopped you; *he triumphed over his disabilities to become world champion;* to triumph over someone = to win a victory over someone; *our local team triumphed over their old rivals*

① triumphal

[traɪˈʌmfl] *adjective*

referring to triumph; *the team made a triumphal return to their home town*; **triumphal arch =** large building over a road, to celebrate a victory; *there are the ruins of a triumphal arch in the centre of the square*

① trod, trodden

[trɒd or ˈtrɒdn] *see* TREAD

① trolley

[ˈtrɒli] *noun*

small cart on wheels; *they put the piano onto a trolley to move it out of the house*; **drinks trolley =** trolley on an aircraft, with various drinks which are served by stewards or stewardesses; **luggage trolley =** small cart with wheels, for carrying luggage at an airport or railway station (NOTE: American English for this is **baggage cart**); **supermarket trolley =** small cart with wheels for pushing round a supermarket (NOTE: American English for this is **shopping cart**); **dessert trolley** or **sweet trolley =** table on wheels on which desserts are taken to each table in a restaurant

② troop

[truːp]

1 *noun*

(a) troops = soldiers; *enemy troops occupied the town*

(b) large group of people; *she took a troop of schoolchildren to visit the museum*

2 *verb*

to go all together in a group; *after the play the whole cast trooped off to the local restaurant*; *all the students trooped into the hall*

3 *adjective*

referring to soldiers; **troop ship** or **troop train =** ship or train which transports soldiers

④ trophy

[ˈtrɪʊfɪ] *noun*

prize given for winning a competition; *he has a display of trophies which he won at golf*; *our team carried off the trophy for the third year in a row* (NOTE: plural is **trophies**)

④ tropic

[ˈtrɒpɪk] *noun*

(a) Tropic of Cancer = parallel running round the earth at 23°28N; **Tropic of Capricorn =** parallel running round the earth at 23°28S

(b) the tropics = the hot areas of the world lying between these two parallels; *he lived in the tropics for ten years*; *people work more slowly in the tropics*

② tropical

[ˈtrɒpɪkl] *adjective*

(a) referring to hot countries; *in tropical countries it is always hot*; **tropical storm =** violent storm occurring in the tropics

(b) tropical fish = brightly coloured little fish coming from hot countries; *I'm going to the library to find out how to look after tropical fish*

① trouble

[ˈtrʌbl]

1 *noun*

(a) problems, worries; *the trouble with old cars is that sometimes they don't start*; *looking after your cat is no trouble - I like animals*; *the children were no trouble at all*; *we are having some computer trouble* or *some trouble with the computer*; *he's got his old back trouble again*; **it's asking for trouble =** it is likely to cause problems; *if you don't take out insurance, it's just asking for trouble*

(b) to get into trouble = to start to have problems with someone in authority; *he and his friends got into trouble with the police*; *she got her best friend into trouble*

(c) to take the trouble to = to make an extra effort and do something; *he didn't even take the trouble to write to thank us*; *if you had taken the trouble to look at the train timetable, you would have seen that there aren't any trains on Sundays*

2 *verb*

(a) to cause inconvenience; *can I trouble you for a light?*; *I'm sorry to have to trouble you with this, but I don't know how to switch my computer off*; **not to trouble to do something =** to make no effort to do something; *he didn't even trouble to tell us he was going to cut down the tree*

(b) to make someone worried; *I can see that there's something troubling him but I don't know what it is*

(c) to make an extra effort to do something; *he didn't even trouble to thank us for our gift*

④ troubled

[ˈtrʌbld] *adjective*

(a) where there are problems; *he comes from a troubled family background*; *we live in troubled times*

(b) worried; *he has a troubled look on his face*; *they seem troubled but I don't know why*

② trousers

[ˈtraʊzɪz] *noun*

clothes which cover your body from the waist down, split in two parts, one for each leg; *he tore his trousers climbing over the fence*; *she was wearing a red jumper and grey trousers*; *he bought two pairs of trousers in the sale*; *(informal)* **who wears the trousers in that family? =** who makes the decisions in the family? (NOTE: plural; to show one piece of clothing say **a pair of trousers**)

④ truce

[truːs] *noun*

agreement between two armies or enemies, etc., to stop fighting for a time; *when it got dark, they decided to call a truce*

② truck

[trʌk]

1 *noun*

goods vehicle for carrying heavy loads; *trucks thundered past the house all night*; *they loaded the truck with bricks* (NOTE: British English also uses **lorry**)

2 *verb*

to transport in a truck; *they trucked supplies to the refugees in the mountains*

Ⓓ **truck driver** *or* **trucker**

['trʌk 'draɪvɪ or 'trʌkɪ] *noun*

person who drives a truck; *a truck driver gave us a lift into town* (NOTE: British English also uses **lorry driver**)

Ⓐ **true**

[truː] *adjective*

correct, right; *what he says is simply not true*; *it's quite true that she comes from Scotland*; *is it true that he's been married twice?* (NOTE: **truer - truest**)

Ⓓ **truly**

['truːli] *adverb*

(a) really; *he truly believes that was what happened*; *I'm truly grateful for all your help*; *do you love me, really and truly?*

(b) Yours truly *US* **Truly yours** = words written at the end of a slightly formal letter; *(informal)* **yours truly** = me myself; *who had to pay for all the damage, why yours truly, of course!*

Ⓓ **trumpet**

['trʌmpɪt] *noun*

(a) brass musical instrument which is played by blowing; *he plays the trumpet in the school orchestra*; *she practises the trumpet in the evenings*

(b) *(informal)* **to blow your own trumpet** = to boast about what you have done; *he's always blowing his own trumpet*

Ⓓ **trunk**

[trʌŋk] *noun*

(a) thick stem of a tree; *he tried to measure round the trunk of the old oak tree*

(b) an elephant's long nose; *the elephant picked up the apple with its trunk*

(c) large box for storing or sending clothes, etc.; *they sent a trunk of clothes in advance to the new house*

(d) *US* space at the back of a car, where you put luggage; *they packed all the boxes in the trunk* (NOTE: British English is **boot**)

(e) swimming trunks = short trousers worn by men and boys when swimming

Ⓐ **trust**

[trʌst]

1 *noun*

(a) belief that something or someone is strong, will work well, etc.; *don't put too much trust in his skills as a driver*; **to take something on trust** = to take something without looking to see if it is all right; *we took his statement on trust*

(b) legal arrangement to pass valuables or money to someone to look after; *he left his property in trust for his grandchildren*

(c) company which manages money for its clients; *see also* UNIT TRUST

2 *verb*

(a) to be sure of someone, to be confident that someone is reliable; *you can trust his instructions - he knows a lot about computers*; *I wouldn't trust him farther than I could kick him*

(b) *(informal)* **trust you to** = it is typical of you to; *trust him to be late!*; *trust them to forget to bring the food!*

(c) *(formal)* to hope or to believe; *I trust she will not get lost*

(d) to trust someone with something = to give something to someone to look after; *can she be trusted with all that cash?*

Ⓑ **trustee**

[trʌs'tiː] *noun*

person who administers a trust or who directs a charity or other public institution; *the lease has to be agreed with the trustees of grandfather's estate*; *the director is appointed by the trustees of the museum*

Ⓐ **truth**

[truːθ] *noun*

thing which is true, a true story; *do you think he is telling the truth?*; *the police are trying to work out the truth about what happened*; *I don't think there is any truth in his story*

Ⓐ **try**

[traɪ]

1 *verb*

(a) to make an effort to do something; *the burglar tried to climb up the tree*; *don't try to ride a motorbike if you've never ridden one before*; *why don't you try to get a ticket yourself?*

(b) to test, to see if something is good; *you must try one of my mother's cakes*; *I tried the new toothpaste and I didn't like the taste*; *have you ever tried eating cheese with fruit?*

(c) to hear a civil or criminal case in court; *the case will be tried by a judge and jury*

2 *noun*

(a) making an effort to do something; *she's going to have a try at water skiing*; *he had two tries before he passed his driving test*; **let's give it a try** = let's see if it works

(b) goal scored in rugby; *they scored two tries* (NOTE: plural is **tries**)

Ⓓ **try on**

[traɪ 'ɒn] *verb*

(a) to put on a piece of clothing to see if it fits; *you must try the trousers on before you buy them*; *did you try on the shoes at the shop?*

(b) *(informal)* **to try it on** = to try to trick someone; *don't believe him - he's just trying it on*

Ⓐ **try out**

['traɪ 'aʊt] *verb*

to test something, to see if it is good; *it's best to try a car out before you buy it*

② **T-shirt** or **teeshirt**
['tiːʃɜːt] *noun*

light shirt with no buttons or collar, usually with short sleeves; *she was wearing jeans and a T-shirt*; *no wonder you're cold if you went out in just a T-shirt*

③ **tube**
[tjuːb] *noun*

(a) long pipe for carrying liquids or gas; *he was lying in a hospital bed with tubes coming out of his nose and mouth*; *air flows down this tube to the face mask*; **inner tube** = rubber tube which is filled with air inside a tyre

(b) soft container with a screw top which contains paste, etc.; *I forgot to pack a tube of toothpaste*; *she bought a tube of mustard*

(c) *(in London)* the underground railway system; *it's quicker to take the tube to Oxford Circus than to go by bus*; *you'll have to go by bus because there's a tube strike* (NOTE: the American English equivalent is **subway**)

(d) *(in Australia)* can of beer

④ **tuck**
[tʌk]
1 *verb*

to put into a narrow or small place; *the shop is tucked away down a little lane*; *I offered him a £10 note, which he tucked away into his shirt pocket*
2 *noun*

little fold in a piece of cloth; *I put a tuck in the shirt to make it fit better round the waist*

③ **tuck in**
['tʌk 'ɪn] *verb*

(a) to fold something around and push the ends in; *she tucked the blanket in around the baby* or *she tucked the baby in*; *he tucked his trousers into his boots*

(b) *(informal)* to start eating in an enthusiastic way; *come on, the food's ready, everyone can tuck in*; *after our long walk we all tucked in to a huge lunch*

③ **tuck up**
['tʌk 'ʌp] *verb*

to tuck someone up in bed = to push the edge of the sheets and blankets around someone to keep them warm; *by eight o'clock the children were all tucked up in bed*

① **Tuesday**
['tjuːzdeɪ] *noun*

day between Monday and Wednesday, the second day of the week; *I saw him in the office last Tuesday*; *the club always meets on Tuesdays*; *shall we meet next Tuesday evening?*; *today is Tuesday, April 30th*; *the 15th is a Monday, so the 16th must be a Tuesday*

④ **tug**
[tʌg]
1 *verb*

to pull hard; *he tugged on the rope and a bell rang* (NOTE: **tugging - tugged**)
2 *noun*

(a) sudden pull; *he felt a tug on the line - he had caught a fish!*

(b) powerful boat which pulls other boats; *two tugs helped the ship get into the harbour*

④ **tumble**
['tʌmbl]
1 *verb*

to fall; *he tumbled down the stairs head first*; *she arrived home late after the party and just tumbled into bed*
2 *noun*

fall; *she took a tumble on the ski slopes*

④ **tumour** *US* **tumor**
['tjuːmɪ] *noun*

swelling or growth of new cells in the body; *the doctors discovered a tumour in the brain* or *a brain tumour*; *the hospital diagnosed a tumour in the stomach*

③ **tune**
[tjuːn]
1 *noun*

(a) series of musical notes which have a pattern which can be recognized; *he wrote some of the tunes for the musical*; *she walked away whistling a little tune*

(b) **to change your tune** = to change your way of thinking; *he used to say that managers had an easy life, but when he was promoted he soon changed his tune*; *(informal)* **to the tune of £100** = at least £100; *we are paying rent to the tune of over £500 a week*

(c) **in tune** = with the correct musical tone; *the various sections of the orchestra weren't playing in tune*; **in tune with** = fitting in with, similar to; *his speech was in tune with the changing policies of the party*; **out of tune** = not fitting in with; *the wind instruments seem to be playing out of tune*
2 *verb*

(a) to adjust a radio to a particular station; *he keeps the radio tuned to Radio 4*

(b) to adjust a musical instrument so that it plays at the correct pitch; *the man has come to tune the piano*

(c) to adjust a car engine so that it works as efficiently as possible; *you'd use less petrol if you had the engine properly tuned*

③ **tunnel**
['tʌnl]
1 *noun*

long passage under the ground; *the Channel Tunnel links Britain to France*; *the road round Lake Lucerne goes through six tunnels*; *they are digging a new tunnel for the underground railway*; *taking the tunnel through the Alps is quicker than driving up the roads over the mountains*; **tunnel vision** = (i) seeing only the area immediately in front of the eye; (ii) having the tendency to concentrate on only one aspect of a problem; *(informal)* **there's light at the end of the tunnel** = there is some hope that everything will be all right in the end

2 *verb*

to dig a long passage underground; *they decided to tunnel under the hill rather than build the road round it* (NOTE: **tunnelling - tunnelled** but American spelling is **tunneling - tunneled**)

Ⓣ **Turkey**

['tɜːki] *noun*

country in the eastern Mediterranean, south of the Black Sea; *Turkey lies partly in Europe and partly in Asia; we're going sailing off the coast of Turkey this summer* (NOTE: capital: **Ankara**; people: **the Turks**; language: **Turkish**; currency: **Turkish lira**)

Ⓣ **turkey**

['tɜːki] *noun*

(a) large farm bird, similar to a chicken but much bigger, often eaten at Christmas; *we had roast turkey and potatoes; who's going to carve the turkey?*

(b) *US (informal)* failure; *his latest film was a complete turkey*

> COMMENT: roast turkey is served with roast potatoes, bread sauce, Brussels sprouts and forms the main part of the traditional Christmas or Thanksgiving meal

Ⓣ **turn**

[tɜːn]

1 *noun*

(a) movement in a circle; *he gave the bottle top a couple of turns; don't forget to give the key an extra turn to lock the door*

(b) change of direction, especially of a vehicle; *the bus made a sudden turn to the left; see also* U-TURN

(c) road which leaves another road; *take the next turn on the right*

(d) doing something in order, one after the other; *you have to wait for your turn to see the doctor; it's my turn on the piano now; let me go now - no, it's my turn next;* **in turn** = one after the other in order; *each of the children will sing a song in turn;* **out of turn** = not in the correct order; *people don't like it if you go out of turn*

(e) to take turns *or* **to take it in turns** = to do something one after the other, to help each other; *they took it in turns to push the car or they took turns to push the car*

(f) the meat is done to a turn = properly cooked all through

(g) performance in a show; *their song and dance act is one of the most popular turns of the evening*

(h) to do a good turn = to do something to help; **one good turn deserves another** = if you do something to help someone they should do something to help you

2 *verb*

(a) to go round in a circle; *the wheels of the train started to turn slowly; be careful - the blades go on turning for a few seconds after the engine has been switched off*

(b) to make something go round; *turn the handle to the right to open the safe*

(c) to change direction, to go in another direction; *turn left at the next traffic lights; the car turned the corner too fast and hit a tree; the path turns to the right after the pub;* **the tide has turned** = the tide has started to go up or down

(d) to move your head or body so that you face in another direction; *can everyone turn to look at the camera, please*

(e) to change into something different; *leaves turn red or brown in the autumn; when he was fifty, his hair turned grey*

(f) to go past a certain time; *it's turned nine o'clock, and they still haven't come home;* **she's turned sixty** = she is more than 60 years old

(g) to find a page in a book; *please turn to page 65*

Ⓣ **turn away**

['tɜːn ə'weɪ] *verb*

(a) to send people away; *the restaurant is full, so we have had to turn people away*

(b) to turn so as not to face someone; *he turned away because he didn't want to be photographed*

Ⓣ **turn back**

['tɜːn 'bæk] *verb*

(a) to go back in the opposite direction; *the path was full of mud so we turned back and went home*

(b) to tell someone to go back; *the police tried to turn back the people who had no tickets*

Ⓣ **turn down**

['tɜːn 'daʊn] *verb*

(a) to refuse something which is offered; *he was offered a job in Australia, but turned it down; she has turned down a job or turned a job down in the town hall*

(b) to make less noisy, less strong; *can you turn down the radio - I'm trying to work; turn down the gas or turn the gas down - the soup will burn*

Ⓣ **turn in**

['tɜːn 'ɪn] *verb*

(a) to take someone *or* something to someone in authority; *everyone was asked to turn in their guns; he caught the thief and turned him in to the police*

(b) *(informal)* to go to bed; *it's after eleven o'clock - time to turn in!*

Ⓣ **turn into**

['tɜːn 'ɪntʊ] *verb*

(a) to change to become something different; *the wicked queen turned the prince into a frog; we are planning to turn this room into a museum*

(b) to change direction and go into something; *we went down the main road for a short way and then turned into a little lane on the left*

① turn off

['tɜːn 'ɒf] *verb*

(a) to switch off; *don't forget to turn the TV off when you go to bed*; *turn off the lights* or *turn the lights off - father's going to show his holiday films*

(b) to leave a road you are travelling on; *you can turn off the High Street into one of the car parks*; *when you get to the next crossroads turn off the main road and go down a little path towards the river*

① turn on

['tɜːn 'ɒn] *verb*

(a) to switch on; *can you turn the light on* or *turn on the light - it's too dark to read*; *turn on the TV* or *turn the TV on - it's time for the news*

(b) to attack someone suddenly; *the dog suddenly turned on the girl*; *the newspapers suddenly turned on the prime minister*

① turn out

['tɜːn 'aʊt] *verb*

(a) to force someone to go out; *they were turned out of their house when they couldn't pay the rent*

(b) to produce or make; *the factory turns out more than 10,000 cars a week*

(c) to switch off; *turn out the lights* or *turn the lights out - father's going to show a film of our holidays*

(d) to happen in the end; *we got talking, and it turned out that she was at school with my brother*; *the party didn't start very well, but everything turned out all right in the end*

(e) to come out; *the whole town turned out to watch the cycle race*

① turn over

['tɜːn 'əʊvə] *verb*

(a) to roll over; *the lorry went round the corner too fast and turned over*; *their boat turned over in the storm*

(b) to turn the page of a book; *turn over the page* or *turn the page over*; *she turned over two pages together*

(c) to have a certain amount of sales; *we turn over about three million pounds per annum*

③ turnover

['tɜːnəʊvə] *noun*

(a) amount of sales of goods or services by a business; *our turnover is rising each year*

(b) staff turnover = changes in staff, with some leaving and new people coming; *high staff turnover is a sign that a company is in trouble*

(c) type of small sweet pie made with pastry and a fruit filling; *an apple turnover*

④ turnpike

['tɜːnpaɪk] *noun*

US motorway where you have to pay tolls

① turn round

['tɜːn 'raʊnd] *verb*

to move your head or body so that you face in another direction; *he turned round when the policeman touched his shoulder*; *she turned round to see who was following her*

① turn up

['tɜːn 'ʌp] *verb*

(a) to arrive; *the food was spoiled because half the guests didn't turn up until nine o'clock*; *he turned up unexpectedly just as I was leaving the office*

(b) to be found; *the police searched everywhere, and the little girl finally turned up in Edinburgh*; *the keys turned up in my coat pocket*

(c) to make louder, stronger; *can you turn up the radio* or *turn the radio up - I can't hear it*; *turn up the gas* or *turn the gas up, the potatoes aren't cooked yet*

(d) to unfold; *to keep warm he turned up his coat collar*

④ tutor

['tjuːtə]

1 *noun*

teacher, especially a person who teaches only one student or a small group of students; *his first job was as private tutor to some German children*

2 *verb*

to teach a small group of students; *she earns extra money by tutoring foreign students in English*

② TV

['tiː 'viː] *noun*

(a) television; *they watch TV every night*; *the TV news is usually at nine o'clock*; *some children's TV programmes are very dull*; *the daughter of a friend of mine was on TV last night*; **cable TV** = television system where the programmes are sent along underground cables; **satellite TV** = television system, where pictures are sent via space satellites; **TV lounge** = room in a hotel, college, hospital, etc., where residents can watch TV

(b) television set; *he's bought a portable TV*; *our TV is broken so we had to listen to the radio instead*; *we have a TV in our bedroom*

① twelfth (12th)

[twelfθ] *adjective & noun*

he came twelfth out of two hundred in the competition; *today is the twelfth of August* or *August the twelfth (August 12th) it's her twelfth birthday next week*; **the twelfth century** = the period from 1100 to 1199 (NOTE: compare **the twelve hundreds**; Note also that with dates **twelfth** is usually written **12th**: July 12th, 1935; October 12th, 1991 (American style is **October 12, 1991**), say 'the twelfth of October' or 'October the twelfth' (American style is 'October twelfth');

with names of kings and queens **twelfth** is usually written **XII**: King Louis XII (say: 'King Louis the Twelfth')

① **twelve**
[twelv]
number 12; *she's twelve (years old) tomorrow*; *come round for a cup of coffee at twelve o'clock*; *there are twelve months in a year*; the **twelve hundreds** = the period from 1200 to 1299 (NOTE: **twelve o'clock at night** is midnight)

① **twentieth (20th)**
['twentɪɪθ] *adjective & noun*
she was twentieth out of twenty in the race; *today is the twentieth of June or June the twentieth (June 20th) it's her twentieth birthday on Wednesday*; **the twentieth century** = the period from 1900 to 1999 (NOTE: with dates **twentieth** is usually written **20th**: July 20th, 1935; October 20th, 1991 (American style is **October 20, 1991**), say 'the twentieth of October' or 'October the twentieth' (American style is 'October twentieth')

① **twenty**
['twenti]
number 20; *she's twenty (years old) next week*; **he's in his twenties** = he is between 20 and 29 years old; **the (nineteen) twenties (1920s)** = the years from 1920 to 1929; **the twenty-first century** = the period from the year 2000 to 2099; *(informal)* **twenties** = £20 notes or $20 bills; *he gave me two twenties and four tens*; *see also* VISION (NOTE: **twenty-one (21)**, **twenty-two (22)**, etc., but **twenty-first (21st)**, **twenty-second (22nd)**, etc.)

③ **twice**
[twaɪs] *adverb*
two times; *turn it off - I've seen that programme twice already*; *twice two is four*, *twice four is eight*; *I'm fifteen, she's thirty, so she's twice as old as I am*

④ **twin**
[twɪn]
1 *adjective & noun*
(a) one of two babies born at the same time to the same mother; *he and his twin brother*; *she's expecting twins*; **identical twins** = twins who look exactly alike; *I'm not surprised you were confused, they're identical twins*
(b) **twin beds** = two single beds placed in a bedroom; **twin room** = room for two people with two beds
2 *verb*
to twin one town with another town = to arrange a special relationship between a town in one country and a similar town in another country, to encourage international understanding; *Richmond is twinned with Fontainebleau* (NOTE: **twinning - twinned**)

③ **twist**
[twɪst]
1 *verb*

(a) to turn in different directions; *the path twisted between the fields*
(b) to wind something round something; *she twisted the string round a piece of stick*
(c) to bend a joint in the wrong way; *she twisted her ankle running to catch the bus*; *(informal)* **to twist someone's arm** = to put pressure on someone to persuade them to do what you want; *I had to twist his arm to get him to lend me his car*
2 *noun*
(a) thing which has been twisted; *put a twist of lemon (peel) in the drink*; *the twists and turns of the road through the mountains*; *it is difficult to follow the twists and turns of government policy*
(b) different way of telling a story; *he put a new twist on the story about the princess*

① **two**
[tuː]
number 2; *there are only two peppermints left in the box*; *his son's only two (years old), so he can't read yet*; *she didn't come home until after two (o'clock)* **one or two** = some, a few; *only one or two people came to the exhibition* (NOTE: **two (2)** but **second (2nd)**)

③ **tying**
['taɪɪŋ] *see* TIE

① **type**
[taɪp]
1 *noun*
(a) sort or kind; *this type of bank account pays 10% interest*; *what type of accommodation are you looking for?*; **blood type** = classification of blood into a certain group
(b) characters used in printing; *the chapter headings are in bold type* (NOTE: no plural in this meaning)
2 *verb*
to write with a typewriter; *please type your letters - your writing's so bad I can't read it*; *she only typed two lines and made six mistakes*

③ **typed**
[taɪpd] *adjective*
written on a typewriter; *we prefer to get typed applications rather than handwritten ones*

④ **typewriter**
['taɪpraɪtə] *noun*
machine which prints letters or figures on a piece of paper when keys are pressed; *keep a cover over your typewriter when you are not using it*; **typewriter ribbon** = thin strip of material or plastic, with ink or carbon on it, used in a typewriter

③ **typhoon**
[taɪˈfuːn] *noun*
the name for a violent tropical storm in the Far East; *the typhoon caused immense damage in the regions along the coast* (NOTE: in the Caribbean it is called a **hurricane**)

② typical
['tɪpɪkl] *adjective*

having the usual qualities of a particular group or occasion; *describe a typical day at school*; *he's definitely not a typical bank manager*; **that's typical of him** = that's what he always does; *it's typical of them to be late*

② typically
['tɪpɪkli] *adverb*

in a typical way; *I want to buy something which is typically Welsh*; *typically, he arrived for dinner a hour late*

① tyre *US* tire
[taɪɪ] *noun*

ring made of rubber and a hard case, which is put round a wheel and which is filled with air; *check the pressure in the tyres before starting a journey*; *they used an old tyre to make a seat for the garden swing*; **flat tyre** = a tyre which has lost all the air in it; *he pulled up at the side of the road to change a flat tyre*; *my bike got a flat tyre and I had to walk home* (NOTE: American English is simply a **flat**); **snow tyres** = special tyres with thick treads, for use when driving on snow; *when hiring a car in the winter, check if it has snow tyres*; **spare tyre** = (i) extra tyre carried in a car in case you have a flat tyre; (ii); *(informal)* roll of fat round your waist

Uu

① U, u
[juː]

twenty-first letter of the alphabet, between T and V; *the letter 'q' is always followed by a 'u'*; **U-bend** = bend in a pipe shaped like a U; *see also* U-TURN

④ ugly
['ʌgli] *adjective*

(a) not beautiful, not pleasant to look at; *what an ugly pattern!*; *the part of the town round the railway station is even uglier than the rest*; *the possibility of inflation reared its ugly head*; **ugly as sin** = very ugly

(b) **ugly mood** = dangerous mood; *the mood of the crowd turned ugly* (NOTE: **uglier - ugliest**)

④ uh huh
[ə'hə] *interjection showing that you agree or that you have been listening*; *'Want to come?' - 'Uh huh!'*

③ UK
[juː'keɪ] *abbreviation for* United Kingdom; *exports from the UK* or *UK exports rose last year*

③ ultimate
['ʌltɪmɪt]
1 *adjective*
last, final; *this is the ultimate game in the series*
2 *noun*
the most valuable or desirable thing; *our first-class cabins are the ultimate in travelling luxury*

③ ultimately
['ʌltɪmɪtli] *adverb*
in the end; *ultimately, the manager had to agree to refund her money*

③ umbrella
[ʌm'brelɪ] *noun*

(a) round frame covered with cloth which you hold over your head to keep off the rain; *can I borrow your umbrella?*; *the company gives away umbrellas with red, green and white spots*; *as it was starting to rain, he opened his umbrella*; *the wind blew my umbrella inside out*; **beach umbrella** = a large umbrella to protect you from the sun

(b) **umbrella organization** = large organization which includes several other smaller ones

④ umpire
['ʌmpaɪɪ]

1 *noun*

person who acts as a judge in a game to see that the game is played according to the rules; *the umpire ruled that the ball was out*; *he was fined for shouting at the umpire* (NOTE: umpires judge in tennis and cricket, but in most other games the person in charge is a **referee**)

2 *verb*

to act as umpire; *we don't think he umpired the match very fairly*

④ UN
['juː'en] *abbreviation for*

United Nations; *UN peacekeeping forces are in the area*; *the British Ambassador to the UN spoke in the debate*

② unable
[ʌn'eɪbl] *adjective*

(formal) not able to (do something); *I regret than I am unable to accept your suggestion; she was unable to come to the meeting* (NOTE: be unable to is rather formal; otherwise use **can't** or **couldn't**)

④ **unacceptable**
[ʌnɪkˈsɛptɪbl] *adjective*
which you cannot allow because it is too bad; *there were an unacceptable number of errors in the test; the terms of the contract are quite unacceptable*

④ **unanimous**
[juˈnænɪmɪs] *adjective*
with everyone agreeing; *there was a unanimous vote against the proposal; the jury reached a unanimous verdict of not guilty*

④ **unarmed**
[ʌnˈɑːmd] *adjective*
with no weapons; *should policemen who patrol the streets be armed or unarmed?*; **unarmed combat** = fighting an enemy without using weapons; *soldiers practise unarmed combat*

④ **unaware**
[ʌnɪˈweɪ] *adjective*
unaware of or **unaware that** = not knowing; *he said he was unaware of any rule forbidding animals in the restaurant; she walked out of the restaurant with her boyfriend, unaware that the photographers were waiting outside*

③ **unbelievable**
[ʌnbɪˈliːvɪbl] *adjective*
incredible, which is difficult to believe; *it's unbelievable that she didn't know that the drugs were hidden in her suitcase; he has an unbelievable number of pop records*

④ **uncertain**
[ʌnˈsɜːtɪn] *adjective*
(a) doubtful, not sure; *she is uncertain as to whether her father will come to stay; their plans are still uncertain*
(b) **in no uncertain terms** = rudely; *he told him in no uncertain terms what he could do with his offer*
(c) which will probably change for the worse; *she faces an uncertain future*

③ **uncle**
[ˈʌŋkl] *noun*
brother of your father or mother; husband of an aunt; *he was brought up by his uncle in Scotland; we had a surprise visitor last night - old Uncle Charles*

④ **unclear**
[ʌnˈklɪə] *adjective*
not clear; *the result of the election is still unclear - the two parties are neck and neck*

④ **uncomfortable**
[ʌnˈkʌmftɪbl] *adjective*
(a) not comfortable, not soft and relaxing; *what a very uncomfortable bed!*; *plastic seats are very uncomfortable in hot weather*

(b) **to feel uncomfortable about** = to feel worried about; *I still feel uncomfortable about asking her to carry all that cash to the bank*

④ **uncommon**
[ʌnˈkɒmɪn] *adjective*
strange or odd; rare; *it's a very uncommon bird in the north of Scotland; it's not uncommon for us to have hundreds of phones calls during the morning* (NOTE: uncommon - uncommonest)

④ **unconscious**
[ʌnˈkɒnʃɪs]
1 *adjective*
not conscious, not aware of what is happening; *he was found unconscious in the street; she was unconscious for two days after the accident*; **unconscious of something** = not realizing something; *he was quite unconscious of how funny he looked*
2 *noun*
the unconscious = the part of the mind which stores thoughts, memories or feelings which you are not conscious of, but which influence what you do

④ **uncover**
[ʌnˈkʌvɪ] *verb*
(a) to take a cover off something; *leaving the pots of jam uncovered will simply attract wasps*
(b) to find something which was hidden; *they uncovered a secret store of gold coins; the police have uncovered a series of secret financial deals*

① **under**
[ˈʌndɪ]
1 *preposition*
(a) in or to a place where something else is on top or above; *we all hid under the table; my pen rolled under the sofa; she can swim under water*
(b) less than a number; *no one wanted the old table - it was sold for under £10; it took under two weeks to sell the house; the train goes to Paris in under three hours; under half of the members turned up for the meeting*
(c) younger than; *she's a managing director and she's still under thirty*
(d) according to; *under the terms of the agreement, the goods should be delivered in October*
(e) controlled by a ruler; *the country enjoyed a period of peace under the rule of the British* (NOTE: under is often used with verbs: **to look under, to go under,** etc.)
2 *adverb*
(a) in a lower place; **to go under** = to fail, to go bankrupt; *the company went under during the recession*
(b) *(informal)* **down under** = in Australia and New Zealand; *we get a lot of tourists from down under*

③ **underclothes**
['ʌndɪkluðz] *noun*
clothes which you wear next to the skin, under other clothes; *he ran out of the house in his underclothes*; *the doctor asked him to strip down to his underclothes*

④ **underestimate**
1 *noun*
[ʌndɪr'estɪmɪt] estimate which is less than the actual figure; *the figure of £50,000 was a considerable underestimate*
2 *verb*
[ʌndɪr'estɪmeɪt] to think that something is smaller or not as bad as it really is; *he underestimated the amount of time needed to finish the work*; *don't underestimate the intelligence of the average voter*

④ **undergo**
[ʌndɪ'gɪu] *verb*
to suffer, to have something happen to you; *she will probably have to undergo another operation soon* (NOTE: **underwent** [ʌndɪ'went] - **undergone** [ʌndɪ'gɒn])

③ **underground**
['ʌndɪgraʊnd]
1 *adverb*
(a) under the ground; *the ordinary railway line goes underground for a short distance*; *worms live all their life underground*; *if power cables were put underground they wouldn't spoil the scenery*
(b) to go underground = to go into hiding; *they had to go underground for a time until the police called off their search*
2 *adjective*
(a) under the ground; *there's an underground passage to the tower*; *the hotel has an underground car park*
(b) secret, hidden; *he was a member of an underground terrorist organization in the 1970s*
3 *noun*
railway in a town, which runs under the ground; *thousands of people use the underground to go to work*; *take the underground to go to Oxford Circus*; *it's usually quicker to get to Waterloo by underground*; *mobile phones won't work in the London Underground* (NOTE: the London Underground is often called the **tube**. In the USA, an underground railway is called a **subway**)

④ **underline**
['ʌndɪlaɪn] *verb*
(a) to draw a line under a word, a figure; *he wrote the title and then underlined it in red*
(b) to emphasize; *this just underlines the urgent need for more medical supplies*; *I want to underline the fact that we need an experienced sales force*

③ **underlying**
[ʌndɪ'laɪɪŋ] *adjective*
which is the reason for everything; *it is difficult to solve the underlying problem of bad housing*

④ **undermine**
[ʌndɪ'maɪn] *verb*
to make weaker; *the documents undermined his case*; *our heavy industry has been undermined by the low labour costs in the Far East*

② **underneath**
[ʌndɪ'niːθ]
1 *preposition*
under; *she wore a long green jumper underneath her coat*; *can you lie down and see if my pen is underneath the sofa?*
2 *adverb*
under; *he put the box of books down on the kitchen table and my sandwiches were underneath!*
3 *noun*
base, the part of something which is under; *the underneath of the car is showing signs of rust*

④ **underpants**
['ʌndɪpænts] *noun*
men's short underwear for the part of the body from the waist to the top of the legs; *the doctor told him to strip down to his underpants*; *his wife gave him a pair of bright red white and blue underpants for his birthday*

③ **undershirt**
['ʌndɪʃɜːt] *noun*
US light piece of underwear for the top half of the body; *he wears a thick undershirt in winter*; *if you don't have a clean undershirt, wear a T-shirt instead* (NOTE: British English is **vest**)

① **understand**
[ʌndɪ'stænd] *verb*
(a) to know what something means; *don't try to talk English to Mr Yoshida - he doesn't understand it*; *I hardly speak any Japanese, but I managed to make myself understood*
(b) to have information, to think something is true because someone has told you so; *we understand that they're getting married next month*; *it was understood that the group would meet at the pub*
(c) to have sympathy for someone; *she's a good teacher - she really understands children*
(d) to know why something happens or how something works; *I can easily understand why his wife left him*; *I still don't understand how to operate the new laser printer* (NOTE: **understanding - understood** [ʌndɪ'stʊd])

④ **understandable**
[ʌndɪ'stændɪbl] *adjective*
normal, which is easy to understand; *her response was quite understandable in the circumstances*

③ **understanding**
[ʌndɪ'stændɪŋ]
1 *noun*
(a) ability to understand something; *my understanding of how the Internet works is severely limited*

(b) sympathy for someone else and their problems; *the boss showed no understanding when she told him about her financial difficulties*; *the aim is to promote understanding between the two countries*

(c) private agreement; *we reached an understanding with the lawyers*; *the understanding was that we would all go to the office after lunch*

(d) on the understanding that = on condition that, provided that; *we accept the terms of the treaty, on the understanding that it has to be passed by Parliament*

2 *adjective*

sympathetic; *his understanding attitude was much appreciated*

① **understood**
[ʌndɪ'stʊd] *see* UNDERSTAND

③ **undertake**
[ʌndɪ'teɪk] *verb*

(a) to agree to do something; *he has undertaken to pay her £100 a week for twelve weeks*

(b) to do something; *they undertook a survey of the market on our behalf* (NOTE: **undertook** [ʌndɪ'tʊk] - **has undertaken**)

④ **under way**
['ʌndɪ 'weɪ] *adverb*

in progress; *the show finally got under way after a lot of delays*

③ **underwear**
['ʌndɪweɪ] *noun*

clothes worn next to your skin under other clothes; *it's December, so I'd better get out my winter underwear*; *the nurse asked her to strip to her underwear and put on a hospital gown*; *each child will need to bring a change of underwear* (NOTE: no plural)

③ **underwent**
[ʌndɪ'went] *see* UNDERGO

③ **undid**
[ʌn'dɪd] *see* UNDO

③ **undo**
[ʌn'duː] *verb*

(a) to make something loose, which is tied or buttoned; *the first thing he did on getting home was to undo his tie*; *undo your top button if your collar is too tight*; *wait a tick, my shoe has come undone*

(b) to upset the good effect of something; *his remarks on TV undid all the good work done to increase racial cooperation* (NOTE: **undid** [ʌn'dɪd] - **has undone** [ʌn'dʌn])

③ **undoubted**
[ʌn'daʊtɪd] *adjective*

certain, true; *his undoubted enthusiasm for the project helped get it off the ground*

④ **undress**
[ʌn'dres] *verb*

to take your clothes off; *the doctor asked the patient to undress or to get undressed*; *he undressed and got into the bath*; *they carried him upstairs, undressed him and put him to bed*

④ **uneasy**
[ʌn'iːzɪ] *adjective*

nervous and worried; *I'm rather uneasy about lending her so much money* (NOTE: **uneasier - uneasiest**)

② **unemployed**
[ʌnɪm'plɔɪd]

1 *adjective*

without a job; *the government is encouraging unemployed teenagers to apply for training grants*

2 *noun*

the unemployed = people with no jobs; *the government is offering special grants to help the unemployed*

② **unemployment**
[ʌnɪm'plɔɪmɪnt] *noun*

lack of work; *the unemployment figures or the figures for unemployment are rising*; **mass unemployment** = situation where large numbers of people are out of work; **unemployment benefit** = money paid by the government to someone who is unemployed

④ **unexpected**
[ʌnɪk'spektɪd] *adjective*

which is surprising and not what was expected; *we had an unexpected visit from the police*; *his failure was quite unexpected*

④ **unexpectedly**
[ʌnɪk'spektɪdlɪ] *adverb*

in an unexpected way; *just as the party was starting his mother walked in unexpectedly*

③ **unfair**
[ʌn'feɪ] *adjective*

not right, not fair; *it's unfair to expect her to do all the housework while her sisters don't lift a finger to help*; **unfair dismissal** = removing of a person from his job for reasons which do not appear to be reasonable; *he appealed to the tribunal on the grounds of unfair dismissal*

③ **unfortunate**
[ʌn'fɔːtʃɪnɪt] *adjective*

(a) which is not lucky; *he made some rather unfortunate purchases on the stock exchange*
(b) which makes you sad; *it was very unfortunate that she couldn't come to see us*
(c) embarrassing; *he made some very unfortunate friendships when he was in the army*; *she made some unfortunate remarks about the bride's feet*

① **unfortunately**
[ʌn'fɔːtʃɪntlɪ] *adverb*

sadly, which you wish was not true; *unfortunately the train arrived so late that she missed the meeting*

unhappy
[ʌnˈhæpi] *adjective*

sad, not happy; *he's unhappy in his job because his boss is always criticizing him*; *she looked very unhappy when she came out of the hospital*; *the children had an unhappy childhood* (NOTE: unhappier - unhappiest)

unidentified
[ʌnaɪˈdentɪfaɪd] *adjective*

which you do not recognize, which you cannot identify; *the photograph stayed in a drawer unidentified for years*

uniform
[ˈjuːnɪfɔːm]
1 *noun*

special clothes worn by all members of an organization or group; *he went to the fancy dress party dressed in a policeman's uniform*; *who are those people in French army uniform?*; *what colour is her school uniform?*; *the holiday camp staff all wear yellow uniforms*; **in uniform** = wearing a uniform; *the policeman was not in uniform at the time*
2 *adjective*

all the same, never changing; *the supermarket wants vegetables of uniform size and colour*

unify
[ˈjuːnɪfaɪ] *verb*

to join separate countries or groups together to form a single one; *the country was finally unified after years of civil war*

union
[ˈjuːniən] *noun*

(a) **(trade)** **union** = organization which represents workers who are its members in discussions with employers about wages and conditions of employment; *the staff are all members of a union or they are (trade) union members*; *the union called a meeting to discuss the company's takeover by a German company* (NOTE: American English for **trade union** is **labor union**)

(b) state of being joined together; *we support the union of these various groups under one umbrella organization*

(c) group of countries or independent states which are linked into a federation; *the union between England and Scotland is over 300 years old*; *Union Flag*; *see* UNION JACK; *see also* EUROPEAN UNION

(d) *(specifically)* the United States of America; *the President will give his State of the Union message in January*

(e) *(formal)* marriage; *their union will be celebrated on 1st November*

Union Jack
[ˈjuːniən ˈdʒæk] *noun*

national flag of the United Kingdom; *the Union Jack was flying over the embassy* (NOTE: also called the **Union Flag**)

unique
[juːˈniːk] *adjective*

different to everything else, the only one that exists; *the stamp is unique, and so worth a great deal*; *he's studying the unique wildlife of the island*

unit
[ˈjuːnɪt] *noun*

(a) one part of something larger; *if you pass three units of the course you can move to the next level*

(b) one piece of furniture, such as a cupboard, or set of shelves, etc., which can be matched with others; *the kitchen is designed as a basic set of units with more units which can be added later*; **wall unit** = cupboard which matches other units and is attached to the wall; **corner unit** = unit which matches other units and fits into a corner

(c) **monetary unit** = main item of currency of a country (such as the dollar, peseta, pound, etc.); *the pound is the monetary unit in Britain*

(d) **unit trust** = organization which takes money from small investors and invests it in stocks and shares under a trust deed, the investment being in the form of units or shares in the trust

(e) specialized section of a hospital; *she is in the intensive care unit*; *the burns unit was full after the plane crash*

unite
[juːˈnaɪt] *verb*

to join together into a single body; *the office staff united in asking for better working conditions*; *workers of the world, unite!*

united
[juːˈnaɪtɪd] *adjective*

joined together as a whole; *relief workers from various countries worked as a united team*; *they were united in their desire to improve their working conditions*

United Kingdom (UK)
[juːˈnaɪtɪd ˈkɪŋdəm] *noun*

independent European country, formed of England, Wales, Scotland and Northern Ireland; *he came to the United Kingdom to study*; *does she have a UK passport?*; *French citizens do not need work permits to work in the United Kingdom*; *see also* BRITISH, ENGLISH (NOTE: capital: **London**; people: **British**; language: **English**; currency: **pound sterling (£)**)

United Nations (UN)
[juːˈnaɪtɪd ˈneɪʃnz] *noun*

international organization including almost all independent states in the world, where member states are represented at meetings; *see also* GENERAL ASSEMBLY, SECURITY COUNCIL

United States of America (USA)
[juːˈnaɪtɪd steɪts ʌv əˈmerɪkə] *noun*

independent country, a federation of states (originally thirteen, now fifty) in North America, south of Canada and north of Mexico; *she now lives in the United States with her husband and two sons*; **as a student, I worked in the USA during my summer holidays**; **which is the largest city in the United States?**; **we went across to the United States by ship**; **he never had the chance to visit the United States**; *see also* AMERICAN (NOTE: capital: **Washington DC**; people: **Americans**; language: **English**; currency: **US dollar**)

③ **unity**
['ju:nɪti] *noun*
being one whole; *the aim of the government is to preserve national unity*

③ **universal**
[ju:nɪ'vɜ:sɪl] *adjective*
which is understood or experienced by everyone; *there is a universal desire for peace in the region*; **universal product code** = bar code, printed lines which can be read by a computer

③ **universe**
['ju:nɪvɜ:s] *noun*
all space and everything that exists in it, including the earth, the planets and the stars; *scientists believe the universe started as an explosion of matter*

① **university**
[ju:nɪ'vɜ:sɪti] *noun*
highest level of educational institution, which gives degrees to successful students, and where a wide range of specialized subjects are taught; *you need to do well at school to be able to go to university* (NOTE: plural is **universities**)

② **unknown**
['ʌnnɪʊn] *adjective*
(a) not known; *she was killed by an unknown attacker*; *the college received money from an unknown donor*
(b) an **unknown quantity** = person whose ability and track record you know nothing about; *the new boss is something of an unknown quantity* (NOTE: the opposite is a **known quantity**)

① **unless**
[ʌn'les] *conjunction* if not; except if; *unless we hear from you within ten days, we will start legal action*; *I think they don't want to see us, unless of course they're ill*

③ **unlike**
['ʌnlaɪk] *adjective & preposition*
(a) totally different from; *he's quite unlike his brother*
(b) not normal, not typical; *it is unlike him to be rude* = he is not usually rude

② **unlikely**
[ʌn'laɪkli] *adjective*
(a) not likely; *it's unlikely that many people will come to the show*
(b) (story) which is probably not true; *he told some unlikely story about how his train ticket had been eaten by a dog*

④ **unlucky**
[ʌn'lʌki] *adjective*
not lucky, which brings bad luck; *many people think Friday 13th is unlucky*; *they say it's unlucky to walk under a ladder* (NOTE: **unluckier - unluckiest**)

④ **unnecessary**
[ʌn'nesɪsɪri] *adjective*
which is not needed, which does not have to be done; *it is unnecessary for you to wear a suit to the party*; *she makes too many unnecessary phone calls*

④ **unofficial**
[ʌnɪ'fɪʃl] *adjective*
not approved by an administration or by people in power; *we have had some unofficial meetings with people from the ministry*; **unofficial strike** = strike by local workers which has not been approved by the union

④ **unpleasant**
[ʌn'plezɪnt] *adjective*
not nice, not pleasant; *there's a very unpleasant smell in the kitchen*; *the boss is a very unpleasant man and shouts at his secretary all the time*; *try not to be unpleasant to the waitress*

④ **unpopular**
[ʌn'pɒpjʊli] *adjective*
not liked by other people; *the new working hours were very unpopular with the staff*

④ **unrest**
[ʌn'rest] *noun*
protest by people to try to get political or industrial change; *the announcement of the election followed a period of unrest*; *the government has sent in troops to deal with the unrest in the south of the country* (NOTE: no plural)

③ **unsealed**
['ʌnsi:ld] *adjective*
which is not closed or stuck down; **unsealed envelope** = envelope where the flap has not been stuck down but is simply tucked inside; *the information was sent in a unsealed envelope* (NOTE: an envelope where the flap is stuck down is a **sealed envelope**)

③ **unsuccessful**
[ʌnsɪk'sesfil] *adjective*
which does not succeed; *he was unsuccessful in his attempt to get elected to Parliament*; *your application for the job was unsuccessful*

④ **untidy**
[ʌn'taɪdi] *adjective*
not tidy; *his bedroom is untidier than ever*; *he'll never be promoted, he always looks so untidy* (NOTE: **untidier - untidiest**)

④ **untie**
[ʌn'taɪ] *verb*
to undo something which is tied with a knot; *since her shoelaces are always untied, she'd be better off wearing boots*; *someone untied the boat and it drifted away down the river*; *can you help me untie this knot, it is very tight!*

① until

[ʌn'tɪl]

1 *conjunction*

up to the time when; *she was perfectly well until she ate the strawberries*; *he blew his whistle until the police came*

2 *preposition & conjunction*

up to the time when; *I don't expect to be back until after ten o'clock*; *until yesterday, I felt very well* (NOTE: the word till has the same meaning)

② unusual

[ʌn'juːʒʊɪl] *adjective*

strange, not normal; *it is unusual to have rain at this time of year*; *she chose a very unusual colour scheme for her sitting room*

③ unusually

[ʌn'juːʒʊɪlɪ] *adverb*

strangely, not as normal; *the weather is unusually warm for January*; *unusually, she didn't say very much at the dinner*

④ unveil

[ʌn'veɪl] *verb*

(a) to take a cover off something, so as to open it formally to the public; *the statue was unveiled by the mayor*

(b) to reveal details of a new plan, etc.; *the committee will unveil its proposals next week*

③ unwell

[ʌn'wel] *adjective*

sick, ill, not well; *she felt unwell and had to go home* (NOTE: not used before a noun: the baby was unwell but a sick baby)

④ unwilling

[ʌn'wɪlɪŋ] *adjective*

not wanting to do something; *he was unwilling to pay any more*; *she was an unwilling member of the crew*

① up

[ʌp]

1 *adverb*

(a) in or to a high place; *put your hands up above your head*; *what's the cat doing up there on the cupboard?*

(b) to a higher position; *his temperature went up suddenly*; *the price of petrol seems to go up every week*

(c) not in bed; *the children were still up when they should have been in bed*; *they stayed up all night watching films on TV*; *he got up at six because he had an early train to catch*; *it's past eight o'clock - you should be up by now*; *she's getting better - the doctor says she will be up and about quite soon*

(d) towards the north; *I'll be going up to Scotland next week*

(e) in London; *give me a call next time you're up in town*; *I'm up in London next week for a meeting*

(f) your time's up = you have had all the time allowed

(g) *(informal)* happening in an unpleasant or dangerous way; *something's up - the engine has stopped!*; *what's up?* = what's the matter?; *what's up with him?* = what is the matter with him?; *what's up with the cat? - it won't eat anything*

2 *preposition*

(a) in or to a high place; *they ran up the stairs*; *she doesn't like going up ladders*

(b) along; *go up the street to the traffic lights and then turn right*; *the house is about two hundred metres up the road* (NOTE: that up is often used after verbs: to keep up, to turn up, etc.)

3 *verb*

(a) to raise prices, etc.; *they upped their offer to £1000*

(b) *(informal)* to stand up, to get up; *she upped and left him when she heard he had been seen with her best friend* (NOTE: upping - upped)

4 *noun*

the ups and downs of life in the army = the good and bad periods

③ up-and-coming

[ʌpɪn'kʌmɪŋ] *adjective*

(informal) becoming fashionable and likely to succeed; *they live in a very up-and-coming part of town*; *he's one of the most up-and-coming young MPs*

③ up and down

['ʌp ənd 'daʊn]

1 *preposition*

in one direction, then in the opposite direction; *the policeman was walking up and down in front of the bank*; *she looked up and down the street but couldn't see her little boy*

2 *noun*

ups and downs = the times of good luck and bad luck; *his book describes the ups and downs of life in the army*

③ up and running

['ʌp ənd 'rʌnɪŋ] *adjective*

(informal) working; *he played an important role in getting the project up and running*; *the project is up and running at long last*

④ update

1 ['ʌpdeɪt] *noun*

latest information; *the manager gave us an update on the latest sales figures*

2 [ʌp'deɪt] *verb*

to add the latest information to something so that it is quite up-to-date; *she was asked to update the telephone list*; *the figures are updated annually*; *they have updated their guidebook to Greece to include current prices*

③ up for

['ʌp 'fɔː] *preposition*

(a) ready for; *my house insurance is up for renewal*

(b) up for sale = on sale, going to be sold; *he's put his flat up for sale*

③ **up front**
[ʌp ˈfrʌnt] *adverb*
in advance; **money up front** = payment in advance; *they are asking for £100,000 up front before they will consider the deal; we had to put money up front before we could get them to sign the deal*

④ **upgrade**
[ʌpˈgreɪd] *verb*
(a) to improve the quality of something; *she has upgraded her computer*
(b) to put someone into a more important job; *his job has been upgraded to senior manager*

④ **uphold**
[ʌpˈhɪʊld] *verb*
(a) **to uphold the law** = to make sure that laws are obeyed
(b) *(legal)* to reject an appeal and support an earlier judgement; *the appeal court upheld the decision of the lower court* (NOTE: upholding - upheld [ʌpˈheld])

④ **upkeep**
[ʌpˈkiːp] *noun*
cost of keeping a house, a car, etc., in good order; *we're forced to sell the house because its upkeep is so expensive; the upkeep of the car costs me more than £50 a week; how much are you getting from your former husband for the upkeep of the children?* (NOTE: no plural)

① **upon**
[ʌˈpɒn]
(a) *(formal)* on; *the church was built upon a low hill*
(b) likely to happen soon; *the summer holidays will soon be upon us again*

② **upper**
[ˈʌpɪ]
1 *adjective*
(a) higher or further up; *the upper slopes of the mountain are covered in snow;* **upper arm** = part of the arm from the shoulder to the elbow; *he had a rash on his right upper arm*
(b) more important; *(in a school)* **the upper forms** = classes with older pupils; **upper house** *or* **upper chamber** = more senior of the two houses in a parliament (in Britain, the House of Lords, in the USA, the Senate); *the bill has been passed in the lower house and now goes to the upper house for further discussion* (NOTE: opposite is **lower**)
2 *noun*
top part of a shoe; *a pair of shoes with leather uppers and plastic soles*

③ **upright**
[ˈʌpraɪt]
1 *adjective*
standing straight up, vertical; *he got dizzy as soon as he stood upright; put your seats into the upright position for landing; she picked up the bottle and placed it upright on the table*
2 *noun*

(a) vertical post; *the goalkeeper was leaning against one of the uprights*
(b) piano with a vertical body (NOTE: the other type of piano, with a large horizontal body, is called a **grand piano**)

④ **uprising**
[ˈʌpraɪzɪŋ] *noun*
revolt; *an uprising against the government; the uprising was crushed by the army*

② **upset**
[ʌpˈset]
1 *adjective*
(a) very worried, unhappy, anxious; *she gets upset if he comes home late*
(b) slightly ill; *she is in bed with an upset stomach*
2 *noun*
(a) slight illness; **stomach upset** = slight infection of the stomach; *she is in bed with a stomach upset*
(b) unexpected defeat; *there was a major upset in the tennis tournament when the number three seed was beaten in the first round*
3 *verb*
(a) to knock over; *he upset all the coffee cups*
(b) to make someone worried or unhappy; *don't upset your mother by telling her you're planning to go to live in Russia*

③ **upside down**
[ˈʌpsaɪd ˈdaʊn] *adverb*
(a) with the top underneath; *don't turn the box upside down - all the papers will fall out; the car shot off the road and ended up upside down in a ditch; bats were hanging upside down from the branches*
(b) in disorder; *while he was out someone had searched his room, turning the place upside down*

② **upstairs**
[ʌpˈsteɪz]
1 *adverb*
on or to the upper part of a building, bus, etc.; *she ran upstairs with the letter; I left my glasses upstairs; let's go upstairs onto the top deck - you can see London much better*
2 *adjective*
on the upper floors of a building; *we have an upstairs kitchen; we let the one of the upstairs offices to an accountant*
3 *noun*
the upper floors of a building; *the upstairs of the house needs decorating*; compare DOWNSTAIRS

② **up to**
[ˈʌp ˈtuː] *preposition*
(a) as many as; *the lift will take up to six people*
(b) **what are you up to these days?** = what are you doing?
(c) **it's up to you** = it is your responsibility
(d) capable of doing something; *it's a very demanding job and I wonder if she's up to it*

② up to date or up-to-date
['ʌp tɪ' deɪt]

1 *adverb*

with the latest information; *I keep myself up to date on the political situation by reading the newspaper every day*

2 *adjective*

with very recent information; *I don't have an up-to-date timetable*

③ upward
['ʌpwɪd]

1 *adjective*

moving towards a higher level; *the rocket's engines generate enormous upward thrust*

2 *adverb*

US = UPWARDS

③ upwards *US* upward
['ʌpwɪdz] *adverb*

(a) towards the top; *the path went upwards for a mile then levelled off*

(b) upwards of = more than; *upwards of a thousand people answered the advertisement*

④ uranium
[jʊ'reɪniɪm] *noun*

radioactive metal used in producing atomic energy (NOTE: Chemical element: chemical symbol: **U**; atomic number: **92**)

② urban
['ɜːbɪn] *adjective*

(a) referring to towns; *they enjoy an urban lifestyle*

(b) living in towns; *the urban fox has become common in many parts of London*

③ urge
[ɜːdʒ]

1 *noun*

strong wish to do something; *she felt an urge to punch him on the nose*

2 *verb*

(a) to advise someone strongly to do something; *he urged her to do what her father said*; *I would urge you to vote for the proposal*; *our lawyer urged us to be careful and avoid breaking the law*

(b) to urge someone on = to encourage someone to do better, to do more; *the runners were urged on by their supporters*

④ urgency
['ɜːdʒɪnsɪ] *noun*

being very important, needing to be done quickly; *there was a note of urgency in his voice*; *the police seem to have no sense of urgency*; **there's no great urgency** = there's no need to rush

③ urgent
['ɜːdʒɪnt] *adjective*

which is important and needs to be done quickly; *he had an urgent message to go to the police station*; *she had an urgent operation*; *the leader of the council called an urgent meeting*; *this parcel is urgent and needs to get there tomorrow*

④ urine
['jʊɪrɪn] *noun*

waste water which is passed out of the body; *he was asked to produce an urine sample for testing*

① us
[ʌs] *object pronoun; (meaning me and other people)* mother gave us each 50p to buy ice cream; who's there? - it's us!; the company did well last year - the management have given us a bonus

① US or USA
['juːes or 'juːes'eɪ] *see* UNITED STATES; *they're thinking of going to the US on holiday next year*; *we spent three weeks travelling in the USA*

① use
1 *verb*

[juːz]

(a) to take a tool, etc., and do something with it; *did you use a sewing machine to make your curtains?*; *the car's worth quite a lot of money - it's hardly been used*; *do you know how to use a computer?*; *can I use this knife for cutting meat?*

(b) to take a service; *guests used the fire escape to get out of the building*; *she used the money she had saved to pay for a trip to Greece*; *I don't use the underground much because I can walk to the office*; *we use second-class mail for all our correspondence*

(c) to take a substance and do something with it; *don't use the tap water for drinking*; *does this car use much petrol?*; *turn down the heating - we're using too much gas*

(d) to take advantage of someone; *he works every evening until late - I think they're just using him*

2 *noun*

[juːs]

(a) purpose, being useful for something; *can you find any use for this piece of cloth?*

(b) being used; *the coffee machine has been in daily use for years*

(c) possibility of using something; *room 51 has no bathroom, but you have the use of the bathroom next door*; *the lounge is for the use of the hotel guests*; *don't worry, he'll soon recover the use of his arm*

(d) being useful; *he kept the old chair, thinking it might be of use some day*; *what's the use of telling the children to shut up - they never do what I say*; *it's no use just waiting and hoping that someone will give you a job*

(e) to make use of something = to use something; *he didn't make use of his phrase book once*; *you should make more use of your bicycle*

① used
[juːzd] *adjective*

which is not new; *a shop selling used clothes*; *a used car salesman*

① **used to**
['ju:zd 'tu:] *phrase*
(a) to be used to something *or* **to doing something** = not to worry about doing something, because you do it often; *farmers are used to getting up early; we're used to hard work in this office; I'm not used to eating such a large meal at lunchtime*
(b) to get used to something *or* **to doing something** = to do something often or for a period of time, so that it is not a worry any more; *she'll soon get used to her new job; we lived in Canada for six years, so we got used to very cold temperatures; even though he had to catch the 6.15 train for years, he never got used to getting up early*
(c) *(showing that something happened often or regularly in the past)* there used to be lots of *small shops in the village until the supermarket was built; when we were children, we used to go to France every year for our holidays; the police think he used to live in London; he used not to smoke a pipe; didn't she use to work in London?* (NOTE: the forms used in the negative and questions: he used to work in London; he didn't use to work in London *or* he used not to work in London; didn't he use to work in London?)

① **useful**
['ju:sful] *adjective*
who *or* which can help you do something; *I find these scissors very useful for opening letters; she's a very useful person to have in the office;* **to make yourself useful** = to do something to help

③ **useless**
['ju:slis] *adjective*
which is not useful, which doesn't help; *these scissors are useless - they won't cut anything; I found it useless to try to persuade her to do something different;* **she's useless at numbers** = she is no good at mathematics

③ **user**
['ju:zɪ] *noun*
person who uses a tool or a service; *we have mailed the users of our equipment about the possible design fault;* **road user** = motorist, cyclist, etc., who uses the road; **user's guide** *or* **handbook** = book showing someone how to use something; *I find the computer user's guide very useful*

① **use up**
['ju:z 'ʌp] *verb*
to use all of something; *she's used up all the glue; paying for the house has used up all my savings*

② **usual**
['ju:ʒʊl]
1 *adjective*

(a) which is done or used often; *she took her usual bus to the office; we'll meet at the usual time, usual place; his usual practice is to get up at 6.30 and run round the park; the usual hours of work are from 9.30 to 5.30*
(b) as usual = as is normal, in the usual way; *the post was late today as usual; as usual, it rained for the school sports day;* **business as usual** = everything is still working in the normal way in spite of difficulties; *although their warehouse burnt down within twenty-four hours it was business as usual*
2 *noun*
(informal) drink or food which someone has most often in a restaurant, pub, etc.; *a pint of the usual, please; will you have your usual, sir?*

① **usually**
['ju:ʒɪlɪ] *adverb*
very often, mostly; *there's usually someone in the office at 9 o'clock; we usually have sandwiches for lunch; the restaurant is usually full on Friday evenings*

④ **utility**
[ju:'tɪlɪti] *noun*
(a) how useful something is; **utility van** = small van for carrying goods; **utility room** = room in a house where you put the washing machine, freezer, etc.
(b) utilities = essential public services (such as electricity, gas, water, etc.)

④ **utilize**
['ju:tɪlaɪz] *verb*
(formal) to make use of something; *he's looking for a job where he can utilize his programming skills*

④ **utter**
['ʌtɪ]
1 *adjective*
complete, total; *the exhibition was an utter waste of time; he's an utter fool*
2 *verb*
to speak; to make a sound; *she only uttered a few words during the whole evening*

④ **utterly**
['ʌtɪlɪ] *adverb*
completely; *he was utterly worn out after the test*

③ **U-turn**
['ju:tɜ:n] *noun*
(a) turning round to go back in the opposite direction; *the police car did or made a U-turn and went back to the hotel; U-turns are not allowed on motorways*
(b) to do a U-turn = to change policy completely; *the newspapers were surprised at the government's U-turn on defence expenditure; the government has done a complete U-turn on pensioners' rights*

Vv

① V, v
[viː]
twenty-second letter of the alphabet, between U and W; *I know his name's Stephen but I don't know if it is spelt with a 'ph' or a 'v' (Stephen or Steven)*

③ vacancy
['veɪkɪnsɪ] *noun*
(a) job which is not filled; *we have vacancies in several departments*; *we advertised a vacancy for a secretary in the local paper*; **job vacancies** = jobs which are empty and need people to do them
(b) empty place, empty room; *all the hotels had signs saying 'No vacancies'*

③ vacant
['veɪkɪnt] *adjective*
(a) empty, available for you to use; *there are six rooms vacant in the new hotel wing*; *is the toilet vacant yet?*; **with vacant possession** = empty, with no one living in it; *the house is for sale with vacant possession*
(b) **situations vacant** *or* **appointments vacant** = list in a newspaper of jobs which are available
(c) *(expression)* not showing any interest; *he sat with a vacant expression on his face*

② vacation
[vɪ'keɪʃn]
1 *noun*
(a) *(especially US)* holiday; *the family went on vacation in Canada*
(b) *GB* period when the universities and law courts are closed; *I'm spending my vacation working on a vineyard in Italy*; **long vacation** = summer holiday in a British university; **vacation job** = job taken by a student during the vacation to earn money to help pay for the costs of a university or college course
2 *verb*
US to take a holiday; *they are vacationing in Mexico*

④ vaccine
['væksiːn] *noun*
substance which contains the germs of a disease and which is injected into a patient to prevent him or her getting the disease; *the hospital is waiting for a new batch of vaccine to come from the laboratory*; *new vaccines are being developed all the time*

④ vacuum
['vækjuːm]
1 *noun*

(a) space which is completely empty of all matter, including air; *the experiment has to be carried out in a vacuum*; **vacuum-packed food** = food packed in a plastic envelope from which all air has been removed; *vacuum-packed cheese will keep for months*
(b) **to create a vacuum** = to empty a space completely; **power vacuum** = situation where there is no one left in control; *the death of the Foreign Minister creates a power vacuum in the government*
(c) **working in a vacuum** = working in a situation where you have no connection with anyone else
(d) *US* = VACUUM CLEANER
2 *verb*
(informal) to clean using a vacuum cleaner; *she vacuums the hall every day*; *I must vacuum the living room before my mother arrives*

③ vacuum cleaner
['vækjuːm 'kliːnɪ] *noun*
machine which cleans by sucking up dust; *our cat hides under the bed when she hears the vacuum cleaner*

③ vague
[veɪg] *adjective*
not clear, with no precise details; *he's very vague about what he wants to do after university*; *we've made some vague plans to go to Greece in August*; *she hadn't the vaguest idea what to do* = she had no idea at all (NOTE: **vaguer - vaguest**)

④ vain
[veɪn] *adjective*
(a) which does not succeed; *she went to the pub in the vain hope of finding him there*
(b) **in vain** = without any success; *we waited in vain for a bus and had to walk home*; *he did not die in vain* = his death had an immense effect on the people
(c) very proud of your appearance, clothes, achievements, etc.; *he's very vain, and is always combing his hair* (NOTE: do not confuse with **vein**; note: **vainer - vainest**)

③ valid
['vælɪd] *adjective*
(a) which is acceptable because it is true; *that is not a valid argument or valid excuse*; *she made several valid points in her speech*

(b) which is legal and can be used for a time; *travellers must have a valid ticket before boarding the train; I have a season ticket which is valid for one year; he was carrying a valid passport*

③ **valley**
['vælɪ] *noun*
long piece of low land through which a river runs; *fog forms in the valleys at night; a lot of computer companies are based in the Thames Valley*

③ **valuable**
['væljuːbl]
1 *adjective*
worth a lot of money; *be careful, that glass is valuable!; the burglars stole everything that was valuable*
2 *noun*
valuables = items which are worth a lot of money; *you can deposit valuables in the hotel safe*

① **value**
['væljuː]
1 *noun*
(a) amount of money which something is worth; *he imported goods to the value of £500; the fall in the value of the yen; items of value can be deposited in the hotel safe overnight;* **to rise in value** = to become worth more; **to fall in value** = to become worth less; *houses have fallen in value in some parts of the country;* **good value (for money)** = a bargain, something which is worth the price paid for it; *that restaurant gives value for money; holidays in Italy are good value because of the exchange rate*
(b) quantity shown as a number; *what is the pressure value at the moment?*
(c) practical value = being useful; *the device is of no practical value at all*
2 *verb*
(a) to estimate the value of something in money; *the jewels have been valued at £5000*
(b) to consider something as being valuable; *she values her friendship with him*

① **value added tax (VAT)**
['væljuː 'ædɪd tæks] *noun*
tax imposed on the value of goods or services; *see* VAT

④ **valve**
[vælv] *noun*
(a) device in a tube (in a machine) which allows air or liquid to pass through in one direction only; *the problem was caused by a faulty valve;* **safety valve** = valve which allows liquid, gas, steam, etc., to escape if the pressure becomes too high
(b) piece of tissue in the heart, in a blood vessel, or other organ, which opens and closes to allow liquid to pass in one direction only; *surgery was needed to repair a valve in the heart*

③ **van**
[væn] *noun*
covered goods vehicle; *a delivery van ran into the back of my car; our van will call this afternoon to pick up the goods;* **van-load** = amount of goods carried in a van; *when we moved we had three van-loads of books;* **security van** = specially protected van for delivering cash and other valuable items; *six gunmen held up the security van*

④ **vanish**
['vænɪʃ] *verb*
to disappear suddenly; *the rabbit vanished down a hole;* **to vanish into thin air** = to disappear completely; *all the money the investors had put into the company simply vanished into thin air*

④ **variable**
['veɪriːbl]
1 *adjective*
which may change frequently; *the weather forecast is for variable winds; the weather can be very variable on the coast*
2 *noun*
thing which varies; *we have to take a great many variables into account*

② **variation**
[veɪriˈeɪʃn] *noun*
(a) change from one state or level to another; *the variation in colour or the colour variation is because the cloth has been dyed by hand; there is a noticeable variation in temperature in the desert regions; the chart shows the variations in price over a period of six months*
(b) variations = short pieces of music which take the same theme but repeat it in different styles

② **varied**
['veɪrɪd] *adjective*
made up of different sorts and kinds; *the menu isn't very varied - there are only three starters and two main courses; a varied programme of music*

① **variety**
[vɪˈraɪtɪ] *noun*
(a) differences; *her new job, unlike the old one, doesn't lack variety;* **a variety of** = a lot of different sorts of things or people; *she's had a variety of boyfriends; we had a variety of visitors at the office today; we couldn't go on holiday this year for a variety of reasons;* **variety is the spice of life** = if you meet lots of different people, visit lots of different places, etc., then this makes your life exciting
(b) different type of plant or animal in the same species; *do you have this new variety of rose?; is this a new variety of potato?*
(c) type of entertainment which includes several different short performances by different types of artist (such as singers, dancers, etc.); *at Christmas, the TV has nothing but a series of variety shows*

① various
['veɪrɪɪs] *adjective*

different; *the shop sells goods from various countries*; *I'll be out of the office today - I have to see various suppliers*

② vary
['veɪri] *verb*

(a) to change what you do often; *it will help your digestion if you vary your diet*

(b) to be different; *prices of flats vary from a few thousand pounds to millions*

② vast
[vɑːst] *adjective*

enormous, very large; *the plain was vast - it stretched as far as the eye could see*; *a vast tanker suddenly appeared out of the fog*

① VAT
[væt or viːeɪ'tiː]

abbreviation for Value Added Tax, a tax imposed as a percentage of the invoice value of goods or services; *VAT is an indirect tax*; *the invoice includes VAT at 17.5%*; *hotels and restaurants have to charge VAT like any other business*; *in Britain there is no VAT on books*; **VAT inspector** = government official who checks that VAT is being paid; **VAT invoice** = invoice which shows VAT separately

④ veal
[viːl] *noun*

meat from a calf; *we had roast veal for lunch*; **veal cutlet** = flat cake of minced veal, fried

③ vegetable
['vedʒɪtɪbl] *noun*

(a) plant grown to be eaten, but not usually sweet; *we grow potatoes, carrots and other sorts of vegetables in the garden*; *what vegetables do you want with your meat? - beans and carrots, please*; *the soup of the day is vegetable soup*; **green vegetables** = vegetables which are green, especially cabbage, etc.; *green vegetables are a good source of fibre in the diet*; **root vegetables** = vegetables, such as carrots, of which you eat the roots

(b) **vegetable oil** = oil which is extracted from plants

④ vegetarian
[vedʒɪ'teɪrɪɪn]

1 *noun*

person who eats only fruit, vegetables, bread, eggs, etc., but does not eat meat, and sometimes not fish; *our children are all vegetarians*; **strict vegetarian** = person who does not eat any animal products, including eggs and milk

2 *adjective*

not eating meat; *he is on a vegetarian diet*; *she asked for the vegetarian menu*; **vegetarian dish** = dish which does not contain meat

② vehicle
['viːɪkl] *noun*

(formal) car, truck, bus, etc., a machine which carries passengers or goods; *a three-wheeled vehicle*; *goods vehicles can park at the back of the building*; **commercial vehicle** = vehicle which carries passengers or goods; **heavy goods vehicle (HGV)** = very large truck

④ vein
[veɪn] *noun*

(a) small tube in the body which takes blood from the tissues back to the heart; *the veins in her legs are swollen*; *compare* ARTERY

(b) mood shown in speaking or writing; *he went on in the same vein for twenty minutes*

(c) thin tube forming part of the structure of a leaf; *the veins are easily seen if you hold the leaf up to the light*

(d) thin layer of mineral in rock; *they struck a vein of gold* (NOTE: do not confuse with **vain**)

④ velvet
['velvɪt] *noun*

cloth made from silk, with on one side a soft surface like fur; *he wore a velvet jacket for dinner*

④ venture
['ventʃɪ]

1 *noun*

business or commercial deal which involves risk; *the venture failed and all the partners lost money*; *she has started a new venture - a computer shop*

2 *verb*

(formal)

(a) to risk doing something dangerous; *she ventured into the cave*; *they ventured out into the snowstorm*

(b) to say something, even though other people may criticize you for saying it; *at last he ventured to say that the whole thing was a failure*

④ venue
['venjʊ] *noun*

agreed place where a meeting will be held; *what is the venue going to be for the exhibition?*; *the meeting will be held on Wednesday, 10th May, but the venue has not been fixed yet*

③ verb
[vɜːb] *noun*

(grammar) word which shows an action, being or feeling, etc.; *in the sentence 'she hit him with her fist' the word 'hit' is a verb*

④ verbal
['vɜːbl] *adjective*

(a) spoken; not written down; *the head teacher gave the boys a verbal warning*; **verbal agreement** = agreement which is spoken (such as one made over the phone)

(b) *(grammar)* referring to a verb; *when you say 'to X-ray' the noun has taken a verbal form*; **verbal noun** = noun formed from a verb (NOTE: in English, verbal nouns are formed from the '-ing ' form of verbs, as in **cycling is good exercise**; **singing is very popular in Wales**)

④ **verdict**

['vɜːdɪkt] *noun*

(a) decision of a magistrate or jury; *the jury returned a guilty verdict after one hour*; **to come to a verdict** *or* **to reach a verdict** = to decide whether the accused is guilty or not

(b) *(informal)* opinion, what you think about something; *she gave her verdict on the soup*

④ **verge**

[vɜːdʒ]

1 *noun*

(a) border of grass along the side of a road; *you can park on the verge outside the house*; *wild flowers were growing all along the motorway verges*

(b) edge; **on the verge of** = near to; *the company is on the verge of collapse*; *she was on the verge of a nervous breakdown*

2 *verb*

to verge on = to be close to; *his comments about her clothes verged on the offensive*

④ **versatile**

['vɜːsɪtaɪl *US also* 'vɜːsɪtl] *adjective*

(a) *(person)* good at doing various things equally well; *he's very versatile - he can play the piano, the guitar and he's the lead singer as well*

(b) *(machine, material, etc.)* which is suitable for various uses; *the car is extremely versatile: it can be used on rough mountain tracks, but is equally suitable for town use*

④ **verse**

[vɜːs] *noun*

(a) group of lines which form a part of a song or poem; *we sang all the verses of the school song*; *she read the first verse to the class*

(b) poetry, writing with words carefully chosen to sound attractive, set out in lines usually of a regular length; *he published a small book of verse*; *compare* PROSE (NOTE: no plural in this meaning)

(c) one short sentence from the Bible, each of which has a number; *the reading in church was some verses from St John's Gospel*; **to give** *or* **to quote chapter and verse for something** = to say exactly where to find a piece of information

① **version**

['vɜːʃn] *noun*

(a) description of what happened as seen by one person; *the victim told her version of events to the jury*

(b) type of a work of art, model of car, etc.; *this is the film version of the novel*; *he bought the cheapest version available*

(c) translation; *here is the Chinese version of the book*

④ **versus**

['vɜːsɪs or viː] *preposition; (in a sports match, a civil court case)*

against (NOTE: usually written **v: Manchester United v Arsenal; Smith v the Inland Revenue**, sometimes also written **vs**)

④ **vertical**

['vɜːtɪkl]

1 *adjective*

standing or rising straight up; *he drew a few vertical lines to represent trees*

2 *noun*

the vertical = position of something pointing straight up and down; *the ship was listing several degrees from the vertical*

① **very**

['veri]

1 *adverb; (used to make an adjective or adverb stronger) it's very hot in the car - why don't you open a window?*; *can you see that tall pine tree over there?*; *the time seemed to go very quickly when we were on holiday*

2 *adjective*

exactly the right one, exactly the same; *she's the very person you want to talk to*; *the scene takes place at the very beginning of the book*; *he did his very best to get tickets*

◊ **very many**

['veri 'meni] *adjective*

a lot of; *very many small birds failed to survive the winter*; **not very many** = not a lot of; *there weren't very many visitors at the exhibition* (NOTE: **not very many** is used with things you can count: **not very many cars**)

◊ **very much**

['veri 'mʌtʃ]

1 *adverb*

greatly; *I don't like chocolate very much*; *thank you very much for your cheque*; *it's very much hotter today than it was yesterday*

2 *adjective*

not very much = not a lot of; *she doesn't have very much work to do at the office*; *they haven't got very much money* (NOTE: **not very much** is used with things which you cannot count: **not very much money**)

④ **vessel**

['vesl] *noun*

(a) *(formal)* container for liquid; *experts on the Roman period think it was a form of ancient drinking vessel*; **blood vessel** = any tube which carries blood round the body; *arteries and veins are both blood vessels*

(b) ship; *vessels from all countries crowded into the harbour*; **merchant vessel** = commercial ship which carries a cargo

④ **vest**

[vest] *noun*

(a) light piece of underwear for the top half of the body; *he wears a thick vest in winter*; *if you don't have a clean vest, wear a T-shirt instead* (NOTE: American English is **undershirt**)

(b) *US* short coat with buttons and without any sleeves, which is worn over a shirt and under a jacket; *he wore a pale grey vest with a black jacket* (NOTE: British English is **waistcoat**)

③ vet

[vet]

1 *noun*

(informal) veterinary surgeon; *we have to take the cat to the vet*; *the vet has a surgery in the High Street*

2 *verb*

to examine carefully; *all candidates have to be vetted by the managing director* (NOTE: **vetting - vetted**)

④ veteran

['vetrɪn]

1 *noun*

(a) soldier, sailor, etc., who has fought in a war; *the veterans visited war graves on the 50th anniversary of the battle*

(b) person who has a lot of experience; *he is a veteran of many takeover bids*

2 *adjective*

who has a lot of experience; *she's a veteran war correspondent*; *the veteran American film director died this week*; **veteran car** = car made before 1905 (or, according to some people, before 1916); *compare* VINTAGE

③ veterinary

['vetrɪnri] *adjective*

referring to the treatment of sick animals; *he always wanted to study veterinary medicine*; **veterinary surgeon** = doctor who specializes in treating sick animals; *the sign over the door says 'Veterinary Surgeon'* (NOTE: always shortened to **vet** when speaking)

④ veto

['vi:tɪʊ]

1 *noun*

ban, order not to allow something to become law; *the president exercised his veto*; *the UK used its veto in the Security Council*; **power of veto** = power to forbid something; *the President has (the) power of veto over bills passed by Congress* (NOTE: plural is **vetoes**)

2 *verb*

to forbid; *the proposal was vetoed by the president*; *the council has vetoed all plans to hold protest marches in the centre of town*

② via

['vaɪɪ] *preposition*

through; *we drove to London via Windsor*; *we are sending the payment via our office in New York*; *the shipment is going via the Suez Canal*

④ viable

['vaɪɪbl] *adjective*

able to work in practice; *the project is certainly viable*; **not commercially viable** = not likely to make a profit; *it is no longer viable to extract tin from these mines*

④ vicar

['vɪkɪ] *noun*

(in the Church of England) priest in charge of a parish; *we have to see the vicar to arrange a date for the wedding*; *the vicar is in his element when he's talking about cricket*

③ vice

[vaɪs] *noun*

(a) wicked way of living, especially involving sex; **vice squad** = police department dealing with sexual offences, etc.

(b) particular form of being wicked; *jealousy is a vice*

(c) bad habit; *I have all the usual vices - I smoke, I drink, I drive too fast*

(d) tool that screws tight to hold something, so that a workman can work on it; *he put the piece of wood in a vice before cutting it* (NOTE: spelled **vise** in American English in this meaning)

③ vicious

['vɪʃɪs] *adjective*

(a) cruel and wicked; *a vicious attack on an elderly lady*

(b) **vicious circle** = situation where one problem leads to another which is worse than the first; *he found it hard to break out of the vicious circle of drugs, followed by crime and imprisonment*

② victim

['vɪktɪm] *noun*

person who is attacked, who is in an accident; *the victims of the train crash were taken to the local hospital*; *she was the victim of a brutal attack outside her front door*; *earthquake victims were housed in tents*

④ victimize

['vɪktɪmaɪz] *verb*

to treat someone less fairly than others; *the prison governor was accused of victimizing young prisoners*; *she was victimized at school because she was fat*

④ victor

['vɪktɪ] *noun*

(formal) person who wins a fight, game or battle; *the victor ran round the track waving a flag*

② victory

['vɪktri] *noun*

winning of a battle, a fight, a game, etc.; *they won a clear victory in the general election*; *the guerrillas won a victory over the government troops*; *the American victory in the Olympics*

① video

['vɪdɪʊ]

1 *noun*

(a) electronic system which records, stores and reproduces pictures and sound; *using video, it is possible to show students the mistakes they have made and get them to correct them*

(b) text, film or graphics which can be viewed on a television or monitor; *he was watching a video of the film*; *she borrowed the video from the public library*

2 *verb*

to record pictures, a TV programme or film, etc., on tape; *I didn't see the programme because I was at work, but I've videoed it*

④ **videotape**
['vɪdiːəʊteɪp]
1 *noun*
magnetic tape on which pictures and sound can be recorded for playing back on a television set; *he made a videotape of the film*
2 *verb*
= VIDEO

① **view**
[vjuː]
1 *noun*
(a) what you can see from a certain place; *you can get a good view of the sea from the church tower; we asked for a room with a sea view and were given one looking out over the railway station*
(b) photograph or picture; *here is a view of our house taken last year*
(c) way of thinking about something; *in his view, the government ought to act now;* **point of view** = way of thinking; *try to see it from a teacher's point of view;* **to take a dim view of something** = not to think very highly of something; *he takes a dim view of members of staff turning up late for work*
(d) **in view of** = because of; *in view of the stormy weather, we decided not to go sailing; (formal)* **with a view to** = with the aim of; *they bought the shop with a view to converting it into a restaurant;* **on view** = exhibited for people to look at; *the final year students' work is on view in the college art gallery*
2 *verb*
(a) to watch; *the Queen viewed the procession from a special stand; she viewed the display on TV*
(b) to consider; *he views the change of government as a disaster for the country*

③ **viewer**
['vjuːə]
noun
(a) person who watches TV; *the programme attracted ten million viewers*
(b) small device through which you can look at colour slides; *she bought a little viewer to look at her slides*

④ **viewpoint**
['vjuːpɔɪnt]
noun
particular way of thinking about things; *his viewpoint is not the same as mine; she looks at the project from the viewpoint of a mother with young children*

④ **vigorous**
['vɪɡrəs] *adjective*
very energetic, very strong; *he went for a vigorous run round the park; the plant has put out some vigorous shoots*

④ **villa**
['vɪlə] *noun*
large country house or seaside house, usually in a warm country; *he is staying in a villa on the Mediterranean; they are renting a villa in Greece for August*

① **village**
['vɪlɪdʒ] *noun*
small group of houses in the country, like a little town, with a church, and usually some shops; *they live in a little village in the Swiss Alps; the village shop sells just about everything we need; they are closing the village school because there aren't enough children*

④ **vine**
[vaɪn] *noun*
climbing plant which produces grapes; *the sides of the hills along the Moselle are covered with vines*

④ **vinegar**
['vɪnɪɡə] *noun*
liquid with a sharp taste, made from sour wine, used in cooking; *French dressing is a mixture of oil and vinegar*

④ **vineyard**
['vɪnjəd] *noun*
area planted with vines for making wine; *there are some vineyards in southern England; we visited vineyards along the Moselle and bought some wine*

③ **vintage**
['vɪntɪdʒ] *noun*
(a) fine wine made in a particular year; *1995 was a very good vintage; what vintage is it? - it's a 1968;* **vintage wine** = fine, expensive old wine made in a good year
(b) year when something was made; **vintage car** = one made between 1917 and 1930 (NOTE: compare **veteran car**)
(c) of typical high quality associated with a certain person; *the film is vintage Laurel and Hardy*

④ **vinyl**
['vaɪnl] *noun*
type of strong plastic sheet which can be made to look like other materials such as leather, tiles, etc.; *they covered the floor with vinyl tiles to look like marble*

④ **violate**
['vaɪəleɪt] *verb*
to break a rule, to go against the law; *the council has violated the planning regulations; the rebels violated the conditions of the peace treaty; the country has violated the international treaty banning the testing of nuclear weapons*

② **violence**
['vaɪələns] *noun*
(a) action which is intended to hurt someone; *acts of violence must be punished*
(a) great force; *the violence of her reaction surprised everyone*

② **violent**
['vaɪələnt] *adjective*
(a) very strong; *the discussion led to a violent argument; a violent snowstorm blew all night*
(b) very severe; *he had a violent headache*

(c) who commits acts of violence; *he husband was a very violent man*; **violent death** = death caused by an act of violence; *she died a violent death*

③ **violently**
['vaɪəlntli] *adverb*

(a) roughly, with force; *this horse threw him violently onto the ground*; *she rolled the bottle violently across the table*

(b) strongly, with great feeling; *she violently rejected the accusations made against her*; *he reacted violently to the injection*; *the mushrooms made her violently sick*

③ **violin**
[vaɪə'lɪn] *noun*

string instrument played with a bow; *everyone listened to him playing the violin*

③ **VIP**
[viːaɪ'piː] = **VERY IMPORTANT PERSON**; *seats have been arranged for the VIPs at the front of the hall*; *we laid on VIP treatment for our visitors*; *we got VIP treatment when we visited China*; **VIP lounge** = special room at an airport for important travellers; **VIP suite** = specially luxurious suite at an airport or in a hotel, for very important people

③ **virtual**
['vɜːtʃuəl] *adjective*

almost, nearly; *the company has a virtual monopoly of French wine imports*

② **virtually**
['vɜːtʃuəli] *adverb*

almost; *the price of these shirts has been reduced so much that we're virtually giving them away*; *it's virtually impossible to get tickets for the concert*

③ **virtue**
['vɜːtjuː] *noun*

(a) particularly good character; good quality; *hard work is his principal virtue*

(b) special thing which gives you an advantage; *the virtue of the train link to France is that you arrive right in the centre of Paris*

(c) *(formal)* **by virtue of** = as a result of; *by virtue of his father who was born in Newcastle he can claim British nationality*

④ **virus**
['vaɪrəs] *noun*

(a) tiny cell which can only develop in other cells and often destroys them; *scientists have isolated a new flu virus*

(b) hidden routine placed in a computer program, which corrupts or destroys files; *you must check the program for viruses* (NOTE: plural is **viruses)**

COMMENT: many common diseases such as measles or the common cold are caused by viruses; these diseases cannot be treated with antibiotics

④ **visa**
['viːzɪ] *noun*

special stamp on a passport allowing you to enter a country; *she filled in her visa application form*; *he applied for a tourist visa*; *you will need a visa to go to China*; **entry visa** = visa allowing someone to enter a country; **multiple entry visa** = visa allowing someone to enter a country many times; **tourist visa** = visa which allows a person to visit a country for a short time on holiday; **transit visa** = visa which allows someone to spend a short time in one country while travelling to another country

③ **vise**
[vaɪs] *noun*
US see VICE (d)

③ **visible**
['vɪzɪbl] *adjective*

which can be seen; *the marks of the bullets were clearly visible on the car*; *everywhere in the forest there are visible signs of the effects of acid rain*; **visible imports** *or* **exports** = real products which are imported *or* exported; *compare* INVISIBLE

④ **visibly**
['vɪzɪbli] *adverb*

in a way which everyone can see; *she was visibly annoyed by the television cameras outside her house*

② **vision**
['vɪʒn] *noun*

(a) eyesight, your ability to see; *after the age of 50, the many people's vision begins to fail*; **field of vision** = area which you can see over clearly; **tunnel vision** = (i) seeing only the area immediately in front of the eye; (ii) having the tendency to concentrate on only one aspect of a problem; **twenty/twenty vision (20/20 vision)** = perfectly normal eyesight

(b) what you can see from where you are; *from the driver's seat you have excellent all round vision*

(c) ability to look and plan ahead; *her vision of a free and liberal society*; *we need a man of vision as college principal*

(d) thing which you imagine; *he had visions of himself stuck in London with no passport and no money*; *she had visions of him being arrested for drug smuggling*

① **visit**
['vɪzɪt]
1 *noun*

short stay with someone, short stay in a town or a country; *they had a visit from the police*; *we will be making a short visit to London next week*; *the manager is on a business visit to China*; **to pay a visit to** = to go and see; *while we're in town, let's pay a visit to the local museum*; *we will pay my sister a visit on her birthday*
2 *verb*

to stay a short time with someone, to stay a short time in a town or country; *I am on my way to visit my sister in hospital*; *they are away visiting friends in the north of the country*; *the group of tourists are going to visit the glass factory*; *he spent a week in Scotland, visiting museums in Edinburgh and Glasgow*; **visiting hours** *or* **visiting times** = times of day when friends are allowed into a hospital to visit patients; **visiting team** = opposing team that have come to play against the home team

② **visitor**

['vɪzɪtɪ] *noun*

(a) person who comes to visit; *how many visitors come to the museum each year?*; *we had a surprise visitor yesterday - the bank manager!*; **visitors' book** = book in which visitors to a museum or guests at a hotel write comments about the place; **visitors' bureau** *or* **visitor information centre** = office which deals with visitors' questions; **health visitor** = nurse who visits people in their homes to check their health; **prison visitor** = member of a group of people who visit, inspect and report on conditions in a prison; **summer visitor** = person or a bird that only comes to this country in the summer; *the swallow is a summer visitor to Britain*

(b) the visitors = VISITING TEAM

③ **visual**

['vɪʒuɪl] *adjective*

referring to seeing; **visual aids** = maps, slides, films, etc., used to illustrate a lecture; *using slides or other visual aids would make the lecture more interesting*; **visual arts** = arts such as painting, sculpture, etc., which can be seen, as opposed to music which is listened to; *photography is one of the visual arts*

④ **visualize**

['vɪʒuɪlaɪz] *verb*

to have a picture of something in your mind; *I can just visualize myself driving a sports car down the motorway*; *can you visualize her as manager of the shop?*

② **vital**

['vaɪtl] *adjective*

(a) very important; *it is vital that the murderer should be caught before he commits another crime*; *oxygen is vital to human life*

(b) vigorous, energetic; *his vital energy comes out in his paintings*

(c) vital organs = the most important organs in the body (such as the heart, lungs or brain) without which a human being cannot live

④ **vitamin**

['vɪtəmɪn] *noun*

essential substance which is found in food and is needed for growth and health; *make sure your diet contains enough vitamins*

④ **vivid**

['vɪvɪd] *adjective*

(a) very lively, very like the real thing; *she has a vivid imagination*; *the play is a vivid picture of country life*; *I had a really vivid dream last night*; *she gave a vivid account of her experiences at the hands of the kidnap gang*

(b) very bright; *a field of vivid yellow flowers*; *the vivid colours of a Mediterranean beach*

④ **vocabulary**

[vɪ'kæbjʊlɪrɪ] *noun*

(a) words used by a person or group of persons; *reading stories to little children helps them expand their vocabulary*; *she reads a lot of French newspapers to improve her vocabulary*; *the dictionary will give you some of the specialist legal vocabulary you will need in your job*

(b) printed list of words; *there is a German-English vocabulary at the back of the book* (NOTE: plural is **vocabularies**)

④ **vocal**

['vɪʊkl] *adjective*

(a) referring to the voice; *singers need to do vocal exercises daily*; **vocal cords** = folds in the throat which are brought together to make sounds when air passes between them

(b) very loud (in protest); *the protesters were very vocal at the demonstration*

④ **vogue**

[vɪʊg] *noun*

fashion; *are those silver shoes the latest vogue?*; *the vogue for wearing bright red braces seems to have disappeared*; **in vogue** = fashionable; *this year, black is back in vogue again*

① **voice**

[vɔɪs]

1 *noun*

(a) sound made when you speak or sing; *I didn't recognize his voice over the telephone*; *the chairman spoke for a few minutes in a low voice*

(b) to lose your voice = not to be able to speak; *she's got a sore throat and has lost her voice*; **to raise your voice** = to start to shout; **at the top of your voice** = very loudly; *the little boy suddenly said 'look at her funny hat' at the top of his voice*

2 *verb*

to tell what you think; *she voiced her objections to the plan*

④ **voice mail**

['vɔɪs 'meɪl] *noun*

type of telephone answering system, where messages can be left for a person; *he wasn't in his office, so I left a message on his voice mail*

④ **volcano**

['vɒl'keɪnɪʊ] *noun*

mountain with a hole on the top through which red hot rocks, ash and gas can come out; *the volcano erupted last year* (NOTE: plural is **volcanoes**)

> COMMENT: volcanoes occur along faults in the earth's surface and exist in well-known chains. Some are extinct (they no longer erupt), but some are always active, in that they send out gas and smoke all the time. Volcanoes are popular tourist attractions: the best-known in Europe are Vesuvius, Stromboli and Etna in Italy and Helgafell in Iceland; the best-known in North America is Mount St Helen's in Washington State. There are no volcanoes in the British Isles

② **volume**

['vɒlju:m] *noun*

(a) one book, especially one in a series; *have you read the third volume of his history of medieval Europe?*

(b) amount of sound; *she turned down the volume on the radio; he drives with the car radio on at full volume*

(c) capacity, amount which is contained inside something; *what is the volume of this barrel?*

(d) amount of something; *the volume of traffic on the motorway was far more than usual*

④ **voluntarily**

['vɒlɪntrɪli] *adverb*

willingly; *he surrendered voluntarily to the police*

③ **voluntary**

['vɒlɪntri] *adjective*

(a) done because you want to do it, and without being paid; *many retired people do voluntary work*; **voluntary organization** = organization which does not receive funds from the government but relies on contributions from the public or from business

(b) done willingly, without being forced; *he made a voluntary contribution to the fund*; **voluntary redundancy** = situation where a worker asks to be made redundant, usually in return for a large payment

④ **volunteer**

[vɒlɪn'tɪɪ]

1 *noun*

(a) person who offers to do something without being paid or being forced to do it; *the school relies on volunteers to help with the sports day; the information desk is manned by volunteers*

(b) soldier who has asked to join the army, without being forced to do so; *the volunteers had two weeks' training and then were sent to the front line*

2 *verb*

(a) to offer to do something without being paid or being forced to do it; *he volunteered to collect the entrance tickets*; *will anyone volunteer for the job of washing up?*

(b) to join the armed services because you want to, without being forced; *he volunteered for the Royal Navy*

(c) to give information without being forced to do so; *she volunteered a statement to the police*

③ **vote**

[vɪʊt]

1 *noun*

(a) marking a paper, holding up your hand, etc., to show your opinion or who you want to be elected; *how many votes did you get?*; *there were only ten votes against the plan*; **to take a vote on a proposal** *or* **to put a proposal to the vote** = to ask people present at a meeting to say if they agree or do not agree with the proposal; **to cast a vote** = to vote; *the number of votes cast in the election was 125,458*

(b) act of voting; **vote of no confidence** = vote to show disapproval of the government, etc.; *they passed a vote of no confidence in the chairman*; **postal vote** = election where the voters send in their voting papers by post; *the result of the postal vote will be known next week*

(c) the right to vote in elections; *only in 1928 were women given the vote*

(d) number of votes made by a group of voters; *no one knows where the youth vote will go*

2 *verb*

to mark a paper, to hold up your hand, etc., to show your opinion or who you want to be elected; *fifty per cent of the people voted in the election; we all voted to go on strike*; **to vote for a proposal** *or* **to vote against a proposal** = to say that you agree *or* do not agree with a proposal; *twenty people actually voted for the proposal to knock down the old church*

③ **vote of thanks**

['vɪʊt əv 'θæŋks] *noun*

situation where someone has done something and is given an official thank you by a vote of a whole committee; *she proposed a vote of thanks to the outgoing chairman*

④ **voter**

['vɪʊtɪ] *noun*

person who votes or who has the right to vote; *voters stayed at home because of the bad weather; the voters were queuing outside the polling stations from early morning*; **floating voter** = person who is not sure which party to vote for in an election

③ **voucher**

['vaʊtʃɪ] *noun*

paper which is given instead of money; *enclosed is a voucher to be presented at the reception desk of the hotel when you arrive; with every £20 of purchases, the customer gets a cash voucher to the value of £2*; **gift voucher** = card bought in a store, which you give as a present and which must be exchanged in that store for goods; *it will be simpler to give her a gift voucher since we can't decide on a present*

④ **vow**
[vaʊ]
1 *noun*

solemn promise; *he made a vow to visit the holy places in the Near East*; *she vowed to have her revenge but she died before she could keep her vow*
2 *verb*

(formal) to make a solemn promise to do something; *he vowed to pay the money back*

④ **vowel**
['vaʊl] *noun*

one of the five letters (a, e, i. o, u) which represent sounds made without using the teeth, tongue or lips; *'b' and 't' are consonants, while '*e*' and '*i*' are vowels* (NOTE: the letters representing sounds which are not vowels are **consonants**; note also that in some languages 'y' is a vowel)

④ **voyage**
['vɔɪdʒ] *noun*

long journey, especially by ship; *the voyages of Sir Francis Drake*

③ **vs**
['vɜːsɪs] *see* VERSUS

③ **vulnerable**
['vʌlnɪrɪbl] *adjective*

who or which can easily be hurt; *the government is vulnerable to criticism*; *children of that age are particularly vulnerable*; *small babies are vulnerable to infection*

Ww

③ **W, w**
['dʌbl juː]

twenty-third letter of the alphabet, between V and X; *'one' is pronounced as if it starts with a W*

③ **wage** *or* **wages**
[weɪdʒ *or* 'weɪdʒɪz]
1 *noun*

money paid, usually in cash each week, to a worker for work done; *all work came to a stop when the firm couldn't pay the workers' wages*; *her wages can't keep up with the cost of living*; *the company pays quite good wages*; *she is earning a good wage or good wages in the pizza restaurant*; **wage freeze** = period when wages are not allowed to increase; **basic wage** = normal pay without any extra payments; *the basic wage is £110 a week, but you can expect to earn more than that with overtime*; **hourly wage** *or* **wage per hour** = amount of money paid for an hour's work; *they are paid by the hour and the hourly wage is very low*; **a living wage** = enough money to live on; *he doesn't earn a living wage*; **minimum wage** = lowest hourly wage which a company can legally pay its workers; *a statutory minimum wage has existed in some countries for years* (NOTE: used both in the singular and the plural: he doesn't earn a living wage; her wages are £500 a week)
2 *verb*

to wage war on = to fight against; *the government is waging war on poverty*; *the police are waging war on drug dealers*

④ **wagon**
['wægn] *noun*

(a) railway truck used for carrying heavy loads; *the container wagons are leaving the freight terminal*

(b) *(informal)* **on the wagon** = not drinking alcohol; *he's been on the wagon for the last three months*

(c) *(old)* heavy cart pulled by horses (NOTE: also spelt **waggon** in British English)

③ **waist**
[weɪst] *noun*

(a) narrower part of the body between the bottom of the chest and the hips; *she measures 32 inches round the waist or she has a 32-inch waist*

(b) part of a piece of clothing such as a skirt, trousers or dress, that goes round the middle of the body; *the waist of these trousers is too small for me* (NOTE: do not confuse with **waste**)

③ **waistcoat**
['weɪskɪʊt] *noun*

short coat with buttons and without any sleeves, which is worn over a shirt and under a jacket; *a three-piece suit has a jacket, trousers and waistcoat*; *he wore a bright silk waistcoat to the wedding* (NOTE: American English is **vest**)

① **wait**
[weɪt]
1 *verb*

(a) to stay where you are or not do anything until something happens or someone comes; *wait here while I call an ambulance*; *they had been waiting for half an hour in the rain before the bus finally arrived*; *wait a minute, my shoe is undone*; *don't wait for me, I'll be late*; *we gave our order half an hour ago, but are still waiting for the first course*; *the man didn't come on Friday, so we had to wait until Monday to have the fridge repaired*

(b) to keep someone waiting = to make someone wait because you are late; *the boss doesn't like being kept waiting*; *sorry to have kept you waiting!*

(c) to wait on someone = to serve food and drink to someone, especially in a restaurant; to wait on someone hand and foot = to do everything for someone; *he just sits around watching TV, and his mother waits on him hand and foot*

(d) to wait a meal for someone = not to serve a meal at the usual time because you are waiting for someone to arrive; *don't wait dinner for me, I'm going to be late*

2 *noun*

time spent waiting until something happens or arrives; *you've just missed the bus - you will have a very long wait for the next one*; to lie in wait for someone = to hide and wait for someone to come so as to attack him; *the lions were lying in wait in the long grass* (NOTE: do not confuse with **weight**)

④ **waiter**

['weɪtə] *noun*

man who brings food and drink to customers in a restaurant; *the waiter still hasn't brought us the first course*; *shall we give the waiter a tip?*; **head waiter** = person in charge of other waiters; *see also* WAITRESS

③ **waiting list**

['weɪtɪŋ 'lɪst] *noun*

list of people waiting for a service or medical treatment; *we have been put on the waiting list for a council flat*; *there is a waiting list of people hoping to get on the flight*; *hospital waiting lists are going to be reduced*

③ **waiting room**

['weɪtɪŋ 'ruːm] *noun*

room where you wait at a doctor's, dentist's or at a railway station; *take a seat in the waiting room - the dentist will be free in a few minutes*

④ **waitress**

['weɪtrɪs] *noun*

woman who brings food and drink to customers in a restaurant; *the waitress brought us the menu*; *how much shall we give the waitress as a tip?*; *see also* WAITER (NOTE: plural is **waitresses**)

③ **wait up**

['weɪt 'ʌp] *verb*

not to go to bed because you are waiting for someone; *don't wait up for us - we'll be very late*

② **wake**

[weɪk]

1 *verb*

(a) to stop someone's sleep; *the telephone woke her* or *she was woken by the telephone*; *I banged on her door, but I can't wake her*; *he asked to be woken at 7.00*

(b) to stop sleeping; *he woke suddenly, feeling drops of water falling on his head* (NOTE: waking - woke [wʊk] - has woken)

2 *noun*

(a) white waves following a boat as it goes through the water; *the ferry's wake rocked the little boat*

(b) in the wake of = following something, immediately after something; *the management has to decide what to do in the wake of the sales director's resignation*

(c) meeting of people before a funeral

② **wake up**

['weɪk 'ʌp] *verb*

(a) to stop someone's sleep; *he was woken up by the sound of the dog barking* or *the barking of the dogs woke him up*

(b) to stop sleeping; *she woke up in the middle of the night, thinking she had heard a noise*; *come on, wake up! it's past ten o'clock*; *he woke up to find water coming through the roof of the tent*; **wake-up call** = phone call from the hotel switchboard to wake a guest up

(c) to wake up to = to realize; *when is he going to wake up to the fact that he is never going to be promoted?*

① **Wales**

[weɪlz] *noun*

country to the west of England, forming part of the United Kingdom; *there are some high mountains in North Wales*

① **walk**

[wɔːk]

1 *verb*

(a) to go on foot; *the baby is ten months old, and is just starting to walk*; *she was walking along the high street on her way to the bank*; *the protesters walked across Westminster Bridge*; *the visitors walked round the factory*; to walk someone home = to go with someone who is walking home; *it was getting late, so I walked her home*

(b) to take an animal for a walk; *he's gone to walk the dog in the fields*

2 *noun*

(a) usually pleasant journey on foot; *let's all go for a walk in the park*

(b) going on foot; *it's only a short walk to the beach; it's only a five minutes' walk from the office to the bank or the bank is only a five minutes' walk from the office*

(c) path where you can walk; *we spent three days walking along one of the long-distance walks in the hills*

(d) organized route for walking; *we went on a walk round Dickens' London; are you coming on the sponsored walk for refugees?*

③ **walk about**
['wɔːk ə'baʊt] *verb*
to walk in various directions; *we walked about looking for a restaurant*

③ **walker**
['wɔːkɪ] *noun*
person who goes walking for pleasure and exercise; *he's a keen walker, and goes walking in Scotland every summer*

③ **walk off**
['wɔːk 'ɒf] *verb*
(a) to go away on foot; *she walked off and left him holding the shopping; the builders walked off the site because they said it was too dangerous*
(b) to walk off your dinner = to go for a walk to help you digest your dinner

③ **walk off with**
['wɔːk 'ɒf wɪð] *verb*
(a) to win; *she walked off with first prize*
(b) to steal; *the burglar walked off with all my silver cups*

① **walk out**
['wɔːk 'aʊt] *verb*
(a) to go out on foot; *she walked out of the house and down the street*
(b) to go out angrily; *he walked out of the restaurant, saying that the service was too slow*
(c) *(of workers)* to go on strike, to stop working and leave your office or factory; *the office staff walked out in protest*
(d) to walk out on someone = to leave someone suddenly; *she walked out on her husband and went to live with her mother; our head salesman walked out on us just as we were starting our autumn sales campaign*

① **walk up**
['wɔːk 'ʌp] *verb*
(a) to climb on foot; *I never take the lift - I always walk up the three flights of stairs to my office*
(b) to walk up to someone = to come or go up to someone on foot; *she walked up to me and asked if I needed any help*

① **wall**
[wɔːl] *noun*
(a) bricks, stones, etc., built up to make one of the sides of a building, of a room or to surround a space; *the walls of the restaurant are decorated with pictures of film stars; there's a*

clock on the wall behind my desk; he got into the house by climbing over the garden wall; the garden is surrounded by an old stone wall*
(b) *(informal)* **to drive or send someone up the wall** = to make someone very annoyed; *the noise of the drilling in the road outside the office is sending me up the wall*
(c) wall of silence = plot by everyone to say nothing about what has happened; *the police investigation met with a wall of silence*
(d) walls = thick stone construction round an old town; *you can walk all round York on the old town walls*

④ **wallet**
['wɒlɪt] *noun*
small flat leather case for credit cards and banknotes, carried in your pocket; *someone stole my wallet in the crowd; his wallet was stolen from his back pocket; do not leave your wallet on the car seat*

④ **wallpaper**
['wɔːlpeɪpɪ]
1 *noun*
paper with different patterns on it, covering the walls of a room; *the wallpaper was light green to match the carpet*
2 *verb*
to stick wallpaper on walls; *she spent the weekend wallpapering the dining room*

① **Wall Street**
['wɔːl 'striːt] *noun*
(a) street in New York where the Stock Exchange is situated; *he walked along Wall Street, looking for the company's offices*
(b) American finance centre in New York; *Wall Street reacted cautiously to the interest rise*
(NOTE: here the name of the street is used to mean the American financial markets in general)

③ **wander**
['wɒndɪ] *verb*
(a) to walk around without any particular aim; *they wandered round the town in the rain;* **to wander away or wander off** = to walk away from where you are supposed to be; *two of the party wandered off into the market*
(b) to stop thinking about the current problem and think about something else; *sorry - my mind was wandering, thinking about the garden;* **he is old and his mind is wandering** = he no longer thinks clearly

① **want**
[wɒnt]
1 *verb*
(a) to hope that you will do something, that something will happen, that you will get something; *she wants a new car for her birthday; where do you want to go for your holidays?; he wants to be a teacher; do you want any more tea?*
(b) to ask someone to do something; *the manager wants me to go and see him; I want those windows painted*

(c) to need; *with five children, what they want is a bigger house; the kitchen ceiling wants painting*

(d) to look for someone; *the bank manager has disappeared and is wanted by the police*

2 *noun*

(a) lack of something; **in want of something** = needing something; *the kitchen is in want of a good clean; he looks as though he's in want of a good meal*; **for want of something better** = as something better is not available; *for want of something better to do we went to the cinema*

(b) something that you want very much; *their greatest want is for warm clothes*; **wants** = things needed; *their wants are too numerous to count*; **to draw up a wants list** = to make a list of things which you need

① **war**

[wɔ:] *noun*

(a) fighting between countries; *millions of soldiers and civilians were killed during the war; in 1914 Britain was at war with Germany or Britain and Germany were at war*; **to declare war on a country** = to state formally that a war has begun against a country; **civil war** = situation inside a country where groups of armed people fight against each other or against the government; **prisoner of war (POW)** = member of the armed forces captured by the enemy in time of war

(b) strong action against something; *the police have declared war on the drug dealers*

(c) argument between companies; **price war** *or* **price-cutting war** = competition between companies to get a larger market share by cutting prices; *at the moment there's a price war between the two airlines*

③ **ward**

[wɔ:d]

1 *noun*

(a) room or set of rooms in a hospital, with beds for patients; *the children's ward is at the end of the corridor; she was taken into the accident and emergency ward*

(b) division of a town for administrative purposes; **an electoral ward** = area of a town represented by a councillor on a local council; *Councillor Smith represents Central Ward on the council; the ballot boxes from each ward were brought to the council offices* (NOTE: the American equivalent is a **precinct**)

(c) young person protected by a guardian or a court; **ward of court** = young child who is under the protection of the High Court; *the High Court declared the girl a ward of court*

2 *verb*

to ward something off = to keep something away; *they keep a flock of geese in the warehouse to ward off thieves*

③ **warden**

['wɔ:dɪn] *noun*

(a) person in charge of an institution, an old people's home, a college, etc.; *ask the warden if we can visit on Sundays*

(b) person who looks after or guards something; **park warden** *or* **forest warden** = person who looks after a park or forest; *the park warden told us not to let our dog run loose*

(c) **traffic warden** = person whose job it is to see that cars are legally parked, and to give parking tickets to those which are parked illegally; *move your car - there's a traffic warden coming; I'm just going to the post office - shout if you see a traffic warden coming*

④ **wardrobe**

['wɔ:drʊb] *noun*

(a) clothes; *she bought a whole new wardrobe for her holiday*

(b) tall cupboard in which you hang your clothes; *he moved the wardrobe from the landing into the bedroom*

④ **warehouse**

['weɪhaʊs]

1 *noun*

large building where goods are stored; *our products are dispatched from the central warehouse to shops all over the country*

2 *verb*

to store goods in a warehouse; *they have offered to warehouse for us on a temporary basis*

④ **warfare**

['wɔ:feɪ] *noun*

fighting a war, especially the method of fighting; *the arguments between the countries soon developed into open warfare; the enemy resorted to guerrilla warfare; governments are trying to ban chemical warfare*

② **warm**

[wɔ:m]

1 *adjective*

(a) quite hot; *the temperature is below freezing outside but it's nice and warm in the office; the children tried to keep warm by playing football; are you warm enough, or do you want another blanket?; the winter sun can be quite warm in February*; *(informal)* **warm as toast** = nice and warm; *it may be snowing outside, but we're as warm as toast in our little cottage*

(b) pleasant and friendly; *we had a warm welcome from our friends; she has a really warm personality* (NOTE: **warmer - warmest**)

2 *verb*

(a) to make hotter; *come and warm your hands by the fire; if you're cold, I'll warm some soup; the greenhouse effect has the result of warming the general temperature of the earth's atmosphere*

(b) to become interested in something, to start to like someone; *she never really warmed to the subject of her college course*; *I think everyone is warming to the new boss*

3 *noun*

place where it is warm; *I'm not going out for a walk - I'm staying here in the warm*

③ **warming**
['wɔːmɪŋ] *noun*

making warmer; **global warming** = gradual rise in temperature over the whole of the earth's surface, caused by the greenhouse effect

④ **warmly**
['wɔːmli] *adverb*

in a warm way; *they greeted us very warmly when we arrived*; *I warmly welcome the result of the election*; *wrap up warmly if you're going for a walk in the snow*

④ **warmth**
[wɔːmθ] *noun*

(a) being or feeling warm; *it was cold and raining outside, and he looked forward to the warmth of his home*

(b) enthusiasm for something; *the management's lack of warmth for the project*

③ **warm up**
['wɔːm 'ʌp] *verb*

(a) to make hotter; *a cup of coffee will soon warm you up*; *I'll just warm up some soup for supper*

(b) to practise or exercise; *the orchestra is warming up before the concert*; *the runners were warming up in their tracksuits*

② **warn**
[wɔːn] *verb*

(a) to inform someone of a possible danger; *we were warned to boil all drinking water*; *children are warned not to play on the frozen lake*; *the group was warned to look out for pickpockets*; *the guide warned us that there might be snakes in the ruins*

(b) to inform someone in advance; *the railway has warned that there will be a strike tomorrow*; *the weather forecast warned of storms in the English Channel* (NOTE: you warn someone **of** something, or **that** something may happen)

② **warning**
['wɔːnɪŋ]

1 *noun*

(a) information about a possible danger; *he shouted a warning to the children*; *the government issued a warning about travelling in some countries in the area*; *each packet of cigarettes has a government health warning printed on it*

(b) written or spoken notice to an employee telling him or her that they will be dismissed or punished if they don't stop behaving in a certain way; *when he was late for the third time this week, he got a written warning*

(c) without warning = unexpectedly; *the car in front braked without warning and I couldn't stop in time*

2 *adjective*

which informs about a danger; *red warning flags are raised if the sea is dangerous*; *warning notices were put up round the building site*

④ **warrant**
['wɒrɪnt]

1 *noun*

official document from a court permitting someone to do something; *the magistrate issued a warrant for her arrest*

2 *verb*

(a) to guarantee that something is of good quality, will work properly, etc.; *all the spare parts are warranted for six months*

(b) to be a good reason for; *our sales in France do not warrant six trips a year to Paris by the sales director*

④ **warranty**
['wɒrɪnti] *noun*

guarantee, a legal document which promises that goods purchased will work properly or that an item is of good quality; *the car is sold with a twelve-month warranty*; *the warranty covers spare parts but not labour costs* (NOTE: plural is **warranties**)

④ **warrior**
['wɒriɪ] *noun*

(formal) person who fights in battle; *thousands of warriors charged at the enemy, waving spears*

④ **wary**
['weɪri] *adjective*

careful because of possible problems; *I am very wary of any of his ideas for making money*; *you should be wary of going on the ice in the spring* (NOTE: **warier - wariest**)

③ **was**
[wɒz] *see* BE

① **wash**
[wɒʃ]

1 *verb*

(a) to clean using water; *cooks should always wash their hands before touching food!*; *I must wash the car before we go to the wedding*; *the moment I had washed the windows it started to rain*; *his football shirt needs washing*

(b) to wash your hands of someone *or* **something** = to refuse to be responsible for something; *she's washed her hands of her son since he was put in prison for drugs dealing*; *he's washed his hands of the whole affair*

(c) to be washed overboard = to be pulled off a boat by waves; *he was washed overboard during the night*

2 *noun*

(a) action of cleaning, using water; *the car needs a wash*; *give the car a good wash before you put the polish on*; *he's in the bathroom, having a quick wash*

(b) **to do a wash** = to wash some clothes in a washing machine; *I'll do a wash this morning*; **in the wash** = (i) being washed; (ii) in a pile of things waiting to be washed; *all my T-shirts are in the wash*; **to come out in the wash** = to lose colour; *all the colour of my pyjamas came out in the wash*; *(informal)* **it will all come out in the wash** = everything will work out correctly, in spite of various mistakes having been made; *don't worry too much about the mistakes in your report - it'll all come out in the wash*

(c) the wake of a ship, the waves made by a ship moving through water; *the little boat rocked in the wash of the ferry*

(d) mixture of paint and water; *they started to put a pale yellow wash on the front of the house*

(e) **car wash** = place where cars are taken to be washed automatically; *why do you wash the car yourself, when you could easily take it to the car wash?*

① **wash away**
['wɒʃ ə'weɪ] *verb*
to remove with water; *use a bucket of water to wash away the mud from under the car*; *several houses were washed away by the floods*

③ **washbasin**
['wɒʃbeɪsn] *noun*
container, with taps, for holding water for washing your hands and face, usually attached to the wall of a bathroom; *each bedroom in the hotel has a washbasin*

① **wash down**
['wɒʃ 'daʊn] *verb*
(a) to wash with a large amount of water; *they washed down the van with buckets of water*; *the sailors were washing down the deck*

(b) to have a drink with food; *he had a pizza washed down by a glass of beer*

② **washing**
['wɒʃɪŋ] *noun*
(a) clothes which have been washed, or which are ready to be washed; *put the washing in the washing machine*; *she hung out her washing to dry*; *washing left out in the morning will be delivered to your room within 12 hours*; **to do the washing** = to wash dirty clothes; *I'm not doing the washing today*

(b) action of washing; **washing powder** = soap in powder form, used in washing machines or dishwashers; *can you buy some washing powder next time you go to the supermarket?* (NOTE: no plural)

② **washing machine**
['wɒʃɪŋ mɪ'ʃiːn] *noun*
machine for washing clothes; *he took the clothes out of the washing machine and hung them up to dry* (NOTE: a machine for washing plates and glasses is a **dishwasher**)

② **washing up**
['wɒʃɪŋ 'ʌp] *noun*
(a) cleaning of dirty dishes, glasses, knives and forks, etc., with water; *can someone help with the washing up?*; *it took us hours to do the washing up after the party*; *use this little brush for the washing up*; **washing-up liquid** = liquid soap used for washing dirty dishes; *don't put so much washing-up liquid into the bowl*

(b) dirty dishes, glasses, cutlery, etc., waiting to be cleaned; *there is a pile of washing up waiting to be put into the dishwasher*

① **wash off**
['wɒʃ 'ɒf] *verb*
to take off by washing; *wash the mud off your shoes before you come into the house*; *the stain won't wash off*

① **wash up**
['wɒʃ 'ʌp] *verb*
(a) to clean dirty cups, plates, knives, forks, etc., with water; *it took us hours to wash up after the party*; *my brother's washing up, while I'm sitting watching the TV*

(b) *(of the sea)* to bring something up onto the beach; *it's interesting to walk along the shore to see what has been washed up onto the beach during the night*

(c) *US* to wash your face and hands; *he went into the bathroom to wash up*

① **wasn't**
['wɒznt] *see* BE

③ **wasp**
[wɒsp] *noun*
insect with black and yellow stripes, which can sting; *wasps buzzed around the kitchen as she was making jam*

② **waste**
[weɪst]
1 *noun*
(a) unnecessary use of time or money; *it is a waste of time asking the boss for a rise*; *that computer is a waste of money - there are plenty of cheaper models*

(b) rubbish, things which are no use and are thrown away; *put all your waste in the rubbish bin*; *the dustmen collect household waste once a week*; **industrial waste** = rubbish from industrial processes; *the company was fined for putting industrial waste into the river*; **kitchen waste** = rubbish from the kitchen, such as bits of vegetables, tins, etc.; **nuclear waste** = radioactive waste from a nuclear reactor; *the disposal of nuclear waste is causing problems worldwide*; **waste pipe** = pipe which takes used or dirty water to the drains; *the waste pipe from the kitchen sink is blocked* (NOTE: no plural; do not confuse with **waist**)

2 *verb*
to use more of something than you need; *don't waste time putting your shoes on - jump out of the window now*; *we turned off all the heating so as not to waste energy*; *(old saying)* **waste**

not, want not = if you don't waste anything, you will never lack things when you really need them

3 *adjective*

(a) useless, ready to be thrown away; *we have heaps of waste paper to take to the dump*; *waste products should not be dumped in the sea*

(b) *(of land)* not used for cultivation or building; **waste ground =** area of land which is not used for any purpose; *the plan is to build houses on the waste ground by the railway station*; **to lay waste =** to destroy the crops and buildings in an area, so that it cannot be used again

ⓐ **wastepaper basket** *US* **wastebasket**
[weɪstˈpeɪpɪ ˈbɑːskɪt] *noun*

small box or basket where useless papers can be put; *he threw the letter into the wastepaper basket*

① **watch**
[wɒtʃ]

1 *noun*

(a) device like a little clock which you wear on your wrist; *she looked at her watch impatiently*; *what time is it? - my watch has stopped* (NOTE: plural in this meaning is **watches**)

(b) looking at something carefully; *visitors should be on the watch for pickpockets*; *keep a watch on the potatoes to make sure they don't burn* (NOTE: no plural for this meaning)

(c) period when a soldier or sailor is on duty; *the men on the night watch didn't see anything unusual*

2 *verb*

(a) to look at and notice something; *did you watch the TV news last night?*; *we went to the sports ground to watch the football match*; *everyone was watching the children dancing*

(b) to look at something carefully to make sure that nothing happens; *watch the saucepan - I don't want the potatoes to burn*; *can you watch the baby while I'm at the hairdresser's?*

① **watch out**
[ˈwɒtʃ ˈaʊt] *verb*

(a) to be careful; *watch out! there's a car coming!*

(b) **to watch out for =** to be careful to avoid; *you have to watch out for children playing in the road*; *watch out for pickpockets!*

① **water**
[ˈwɔːtɪ]

1 *noun*

(a) common liquid (H_2O) which forms rain, rivers, lakes, the sea, etc., and which makes up a large part of the bodies of organisms, and which you drink and use in cooking, in industry, etc.; *can we have three glasses of water please?*; *cook the vegetables in boiling water*; *is the tap water safe to drink?*; *you are advised to drink only bottled water*; *the water temperature is $60°$*; **drinking water =** water which you can drink safely; **running water =** water which is available in a house through water mains and

taps; *I'm not sure that all the houses in the village have running water*; *there is hot and cold running water in all the rooms*; **under water =** (i) swimming under the surface of water; (ii) covered by floods; *she can swim well, even under water*; *parts of the town are under water after the river flooded*

(b) *(phrases)* **to keep your head above water =** (i) to swim with your head out of the water; (ii) to be able to keep out of trouble; **to spend money like water =** to spend large amounts of money; *when they were furnishing the house they just spent money like water*; *(informal)* **it's all water under the bridge =** a long time has passed and the situation has changed completely; **like water off a duck's back =** having no effect at all; *he was told off several times for being late, but it was like water off a duck's back*

(c) mass of water forming a lake, river, sea, etc.; *they live right on the water's edge*; *when you fly across Finland, you realize how much water there is*; *living surrounded by water, they became good sailors* (NOTE: no plural for meanings (a), (b) and (c): **some water; a drop of water**)

(d) **waters =** areas of sea; **territorial waters =** sea near the coast of a country, which is part of that country and governed by the laws of that country; **in international waters** *or* **outside territorial waters =** in that part of the sea which is outside any country's jurisdiction; *the attack happened in British territorial waters*

2 *verb*

(a) to pour water on the soil round a plant to make it grow; *because it is hot we need to water the garden every day*; *she was watering her pots of flowers*

(b) *(of your eyes)* to fill with tears; *(of your mouth)* to fill with water; *peeling onions makes my eyes water*; **to make your mouth water =** to look so good that your mouth fills with water; *those cakes make my mouth water*; *his new car made her mouth water*

(c) **to water something down =** to make a statement less radical; *their proposals were watered down a lot*

④ **watercolour** *US* **watercolor**
[ˈwɔːtɪkʌlɪ] *noun*

(a) paint which is mixed with water and used by artists; *he prefers using watercolours to oils*

(b) picture painted using watercolours; *there is an exhibition of Turner's watercolours in the Tate Gallery*; *she bought a watercolour of the village church*

② **wave**
[weɪv]

1 *noun*

(a) ridge of water on the surface of the sea, a lake or a river; *waves were breaking on the rocks*; *watch out for big waves on the beach*; *the sea was calm, with hardly any waves*

(b) up and down movement of your hand; *she gave me a wave* = she waved her hand to me
(c) regular curve on the surface of hair; *his hair has a natural wave*
(d) sudden increase in something; *a wave of anger surged through the crowd*; **crime wave** = increase in the number of crimes; **heat wave** = sudden spell of hot weather; *the temperature went up to 40° during the heat wave in Athens*
(e) groups of people, machines, etc., rushing forwards; *wave after wave of soldiers attacked the fort*; *they sent in waves of planes to bomb the harbour*
(f) **air waves** = way in which radio signals move through the air; *see also* LONG WAVE, MEDIUM WAVE, SHORT WAVE

2 *verb*
(a) to move up and down in the wind; *the flags were waving outside the town hall*
(b) to make an up and down movement of the hand (usually when saying goodbye); *they waved until the car was out of sight*; *they waved goodbye as the boat left the harbour*; **to wave to someone** = to signal to someone by moving your hand up and down; *when I saw him I waved to him to cross the road*; **to wave someone on** = to tell someone to go on by a movement of the hand; *the policeman waved the traffic on*
(c) *(of hair)* to have a wave; *I wish my hair would wave naturally*

④ **wax**
[wæks]
1 *noun*
(a) solid substance made from fat or oil, used for making candles, polish, etc.; *she brought a tin of wax polish and started to polish the furniture*
(b) soft yellow substance made by bees to build their nests; *he separated the honey from the wax and put it into jars*
(c) soft yellow substance that forms in your ears
2 *verb*
(a) to put wax polish on furniture, etc.; *she was waxing the dining room table*
(b) *(informal)* **to wax lyrical about something** = to be full of enthusiasm about something; *the reviewer waxed lyrical about the young painter*

① **way**
[weɪ]
1 *noun*
(a) path or road which goes somewhere; *they are our neighbours from across the way*; *I'll walk the first part of the way home with you*
(b) correct path or road to go somewhere; *do you know the way to the post office?*; *she showed us the way to the railway station*; *they lost their way and had to ask for directions*; *I'll lead the way - just follow me*
(c) **on the way** = during a journey; *I'll stop at the post office on my way to the restaurant*; *she's on her way to the office*; **well on the way to** = nearly; *the repairs to the house are well on*

the way to being finished; **to go out of your way to help someone** = to make a special effort to help someone
(d) to make your way = to go to (a place) with some difficulty; *can you make your way to passport control?*; *he made his way to the tourist information office*
(e) particular direction from here; *a one-way street*; *can you tell which way the wind is blowing?*; *this way please, everybody!*
(f) means of doing something; *my mother showed me the way to make marmalade*; *isn't there any other way of doing it?*; *he thought of a way of making money quickly*; *the way she said it implied it was my fault*; *(informal)* **to get your own way** = to do what you want to do, even if other people don't want you to do it; *she always seems to get her own way*
(g) to have it both ways = to take advantage from two courses of action; *he wants to have it both ways, but he'll soon realize he can't*; *you can't have it both ways - going out to the club every evening and saving money*; **in many ways** = almost completely; *in many ways, I think she is right*; **in some ways** = not completely; *in some ways she may be wrong*
(h) manner of behaving; *he spoke in a pleasant way*; *you will have to get used to the manager's funny little ways*
(i) distance; *the bank is quite a long way away*; *he's got a long way to go before he qualifies as a doctor*
(j) space where someone wants to be or which someone wants to use; *get out of my way - I'm in a hurry*; *it's best to keep out of the way of the police for a moment*; *I wanted to take a short cut, but there was a lorry in the way*
(k) progress, forward movement; **under way** = moving forwards; *the project is under way at last*
(l) in a bad way = very ill; *she's in hospital and in a really bad way*

2 *adverb; (informal)*
far, a long distance away; *the bank is way beyond the Post Office*; *their financial problems started way back in 1992*; *the price was way too high for me*; **way over your head** = difficult to understand; *the book was way over my head*

◊ **by the way**
['baɪ ðɪ 'weɪ] *(used to introduce something which is not very important or to change the subject which is being talked about)* *by the way, have you seen my keys anywhere?*

◊ **no way**
['nɪʊ weɪ]
not at all; *can I have a table for lunch? - no way!*; *there's no way that the government is going to get involved*

◊ **out of the way**
['ɪʊt əv ðə 'weɪ]

(a) not near any large town; *the village is a bit out of the way*

(b) strange, unusual; *what she proposed was nothing out of the way*

① **way in**
['weɪ 'ɪn] *noun*
entrance; *this is the way in to the theatre; the way in is through the gates by the park*

① **way out**
['weɪ 'aʊt] *noun*
(a) exit; *this is the way out of the car park; he couldn't find the way out of the cinema in the dark*

(b) **a way out of a difficulty** = a solution to a problem; *the leave the country and live abroad was probably the easiest way out*

③ **way up**
['weɪ 'ʌp] *noun*
way in which something stands; *keep the jar the right way up or the contents will spill; he was pretending to read the book, but was holding it the wrong way up*

① **we**
[wiː] *pronoun*
(a) *(used by a speaker referring to himself and others)* *he said we could go into the exhibition; we were not allowed into the restaurant in jeans; we had a wonderful holiday - we all enjoyed ourselves enormously* (NOTE: when it is the object **we** becomes **us**: **we** gave it to him; he gave it to us; when it follows the verb to **be**, **we** usually becomes **us**: who is it? - it's us!)

(b) *(used instead of I)* **the royal we** = using 'we' instead of 'I'; *Queen Victoria said 'we are not amused'*

② **weak**
[wiːk] *adjective*
(a) not strong; *after his illness he is still very weak; I don't like weak tea - put another teabag in the pot*

(b) not good at, not having knowledge or skill; *she's weaker at science than at maths; French is his weakest subject; she gave the weakest of excuses for not finishing the work on time* (NOTE: do not confuse with **week**; note: **weaker - weakest**)

④ **weaken**
['wiːkn] *verb*
to make or to become weak; *she was very weakened by the disease; if you remove that wall you'll weaken the whole structure; living outside the borough weakens his chances of getting a place in that school* (NOTE: the opposite is **strengthen**)

③ **weakness**
['wiːknɪs] *noun*
(a) state of being weak; *the doctor noticed the weakness of her pulse* (NOTE: the opposite is **strength**)

(b) *(informal)* **weakness for** = liking for; *she has a weakness for tall men with dark hair; I have a weakness for Danish pastries*

③ **wealth**
[welθ] *noun*
riches, a large amount of money; *his wealth wᴏ⸴ inherited from his grandfather* (NOTE: no plural)

④ **wealthy**
['welθi] *adjective*
very rich (person); *is she really wealthy, or just rich?; 50% of the land is in the hand of the ten wealthiest families* (NOTE: **wealthier - wealthiest**)

② **weapon**
['wepɪn] *noun*
object such as a gun or sword, which you fight with; *the crowd used iron bars as weapons*

① **wear**
[weə]
1 *verb*
(a) to have (especially a piece of clothing) on your body; *what dress are you wearing to the party?; when last seen, he was wearing a blue raincoat; she's wearing her mother's earrings; she wears her hair very short*

(b) to become damaged or thin through being used; *the tread on the car tyres is worn; I've worn a hole in the heel of my sock*

(c) *(informal)* **not to wear something** = not to allow or put up with something; *you can't put that picture up in the office - the female staff will never wear it* (NOTE: **wearing - wore** [wɔː] **- has worn** [wɔːn])

2 *noun*
(a) *(formal)* clothes; *the menswear department is on the ground floor*

(b) action of wearing clothes; *this jacket is suitable for summer wear; a little black dress is perfect for evening wear*

(c) amount of use which something may have; *the carpet on the stairs will have a lot more wear than the one in the bedroom*

(d) action of damaging something through use; **fair wear and tear** = damage through normal use which is accepted by an insurance company; *the policy covers most forms of damage but not wear and tear to the machine*

① **wear off**
['weə 'ɒf] *verb*
to disappear gradually; *the effects of the drug wore off after a few hours*

① **wear out**
['weə 'aʊt] *verb*
(a) to use something so much that it is broken and useless; *walking across the USA, he wore out three pairs of boots*

(b) **to wear yourself out** = to become very tired through doing something; *she wore herself out looking after the old lady; see also* WORN OUT

④ **weary**
['wɪərɪ] *adjective*
(formal) very tired; *we were all weary after a day spent walking round London; (formal)* **to**

grow weary of (doing) something = to get tired of doing something; *we grew weary of always eating in the same restaurant* (NOTE: wearier - weariest)

① **weather**
['weðı]
1 *noun*
(a) conditions outside, i.e., if it is raining, hot, cold, windy, sunny, etc.; *what's the weather going to be like today?*; *the weather in Iceland is usually colder than here*; *rain every day! - just normal English summer weather!*; *if the weather gets any better, then we can go out in the boat*
(b) to make heavy weather of something = to make something you are doing more difficult and complicated than it need be; *we asked him to sort out the invoices but he's really making heavy weather of it*
(c) under the weather = miserable or unwell; *she's feeling a bit under the weather* (NOTE: no plural; do not confuse with **whether**)
2 *verb*
(a) *(of sea, frost, wind, etc.)* to wear down rocks, to change the colour of wood, etc.; *the rocks have been weathered into curious shapes*; *the wooden fence was dark brown but now it has weathered to a light grey colour*
(b) to survive a storm, crisis; *I don't know if we can weather this crisis without any extra cash*

④ **weave**
[wiːv] *verb*
(a) to make cloth by winding threads in and out; *the cloth is woven from the wool of local sheep*; *the new weaving machines were installed last week*
(b) *(informal)* **get weaving!** = get going!, start now!; *if you don't get weaving you'll never finish on time*; *come on, don't just sit around, let's get weaving*
(c) to make something by a similar method, but using straw, etc.; *she learnt how to weave baskets* (NOTE: **wove** [wɪʊv] - **has woven** [wɪʊvn])

③ **web**
[web] *noun*
(a) net made by spiders to catch flies; *the garden is full of spiders' webs in autumn*
(b) *(internet)* **the Web** = the World Wide Web, the thousands of web sites and web pages in the Internet, which users can visit; **web page** = single file of text and graphics, forming part of a web site; **web site** = collection of pages on the web which have been produced by one company or person and are linked together; *how many hits did we have on our site last week?*

④ **wed**
[wed] *verb*
(formal, used mainly in newspapers) to marry; *'PRINCESS TO WED POP STAR'*; *he wed his childhood girlfriend* (NOTE: **wedding** - **wed** or **wedded**)

② **wedding**
['wedɪŋ] *noun*
marriage ceremony, when two people are officially made man and wife; *they rang the church bells at the wedding*; *don't count on having fine weather for your wedding*; *the film ends with a wedding*; *this Saturday I'm going to John and Mary's wedding*; **a church wedding** = a wedding held in a church, and performed by a priest; **a registry wedding** *or* **a civil wedding** = wedding held in a registry office or other place, but not a church, which is performed by a registrar; **silver wedding** = celebration when two people have been married for twenty-five years; **golden wedding** = celebration when two people have been married for fifty years; *it's my parents' golden wedding next Tuesday*; **white wedding** = wedding where the bride wears a white dress; **wedding anniversary** = date which is the date of a wedding in the past; *don't tell me that for once you remembered our wedding anniversary!*; **wedding breakfast** = special meal for the bride, the bridegroom, their families and guests, eaten after the wedding ceremony; **wedding cake** = special cake made with dried fruit, covered with icing, eaten at a wedding reception; *did you get a piece of wedding cake?*; **the 'Wedding March'** = piece of music by Mendelssohn played at weddings; *the organ played the 'Wedding March' as the bride and bridegroom walked out of the church*; **wedding reception** = party held after a wedding, including the wedding breakfast, drinks, toasts, etc.; *the wedding reception was held in the gardens of the hotel*; **wedding ring** = ring which is put on the finger during the wedding ceremony

COMMENT: at a wedding, the bride is usually assisted by bridesmaids (young girls) and pages (little boys). The bridegroom is always helped by his best man, who is usually an old school friend. The bride is 'given away' by her father, that is, she goes into the church on his arm, and leaves the church on the arm of her new husband. Weddings are often on Saturdays; weddings are always followed by the wedding breakfast, and then the bride and bridegroom go away on honeymoon. The costs of the wedding are usually borne by the parents of the bride, and the parents of the bridegroom have very little to do with the organization of the wedding, apart from being there

④ **wedge**
[wedʒ]
1 *noun*
(a) solid piece of wood, metal, rubber, etc., that has a V-shape; *put a wedge under the door to hold it open*
(b) piece of anything with a V-shape; *a wedge of cheese*

(c) the thin end of the wedge = something which seems small and not very important but which will make things change in a dramatic way later; *allowing the children to stay out till 10.30 is just the thin end of the wedge - in a couple of years' time they'll not come home until after midnight!*

2 *verb*

(a) to put a wedge under something fix it firmly open or shut; *she wedged the door open with a piece of wood*

(b) to force something into a small space; **to become wedged** *or* **to get wedged** = to become tightly stuck; *he got his head wedged between the bars of the cage*

① **Wednesday**
['wenzdi] *noun*
day between Tuesday and Thursday, the third day of the week; *she came for tea last Wednesday*; *Wednesdays are always busy days for us*; *can we meet next Wednesday afternoon?*; *Wednesday the 24th would be a good date for a meeting*; *the 15th is a Tuesday, so the 16th must be a Wednesday*

④ **weed**
[wi:d]
1 *noun*
wild plant that you do not want in a garden; *weeds grew all over the strawberry beds while he was on holiday*

2 *verb*

(a) to pull out plants which you do not want from a garden; *she spent all afternoon weeding the vegetable garden*

(b) to weed out = to remove something which is not wanted; *weed out any old newspapers you don't want and take them to the paper bank*

① **week**
[wi:k] *noun*

(a) period of seven days, usually from Monday to Sunday; *there are 52 weeks in the year*; *the firm gives us two weeks' holiday at Easter*; *it's my aunt's 80th birthday next week*; *I go to the cinema at least once a week*; **a week from now** *or* **a week today** = this day next week; *a week from now or in a week's time, I'll be on holiday*; **a week tomorrow** = in eight days' time; *a week tomorrow I'll be in Greece*; **yesterday week** = a week ago yesterday; *they came back from holiday yesterday week*; **what day of the week is it today?** = is it Monday, Tuesday, etc.?

(b) part of a seven day period, when people work; *he works a 35-hour week or he works 35 hours every week* (NOTE: do not confuse with **weak**)

④ **weekday**
['wi:kdeɪ] *noun*
any of the days from Monday to Friday, when most offices are open (but not Saturday or Sunday); *the banks are only open on weekdays*; *there are many more trains on weekdays than on Sundays*

① **weekend**
['wi:kend] *noun*
Saturday and Sunday, or the period from Friday evening to Sunday evening; *we're going to Brighton for the weekend*; *why don't you come to spend next weekend with us in the country?*; *at weekends, we try to spend time in the garden*; **long weekend** = weekend, including Friday night and Sunday night; *we took a long weekend in Paris*; **weekend break** = short holiday over a weekend; *we went away for a weekend break in Brighton*

③ **weekly**
['wi:klɪ]
1 *adjective & adverb*
which happens or is published once a week; *we have a weekly paper which tells us all the local news*; *the weekly rate for the job is £250*; *do you pay the newspapers weekly?*

2 *noun*
magazine published once a week; *he gets a gardening weekly every Friday* (NOTE: plural is **weeklies**)

④ **weep**
[wi:p] *verb*
(formal) to cry, to have tears coming out of your eyes; *seeing them cut down the trees to make a new motorway is enough to make you weep*; *my mother wept with joy when I came back safe and sound*; *crowds of weeping relatives followed the coffin* (NOTE: **weeping - wept** [wept])

③ **weigh**
[weɪ] *verb*

(a) to use scales or a weighing machine to measure how heavy something is; *can you weigh this parcel for me?*; *they weighed his suitcase at the check-in desk*; *I weighed myself this morning*; **weighing machine** = device for weighing someone or something; *she placed the bag of sweets on the weighing machine*

(b) to have a certain weight; *this piece of meat weighs 100 grams*; *the packet weighs twenty-five grams*; *how much do you weigh?*; *he weighs 120 pounds*; *she only weighs 40 kilos*

① **weight**
[weɪt]
1 *noun*

(a) how heavy something is; *what's the maximum weight of parcel the post office will accept?*; **to sell fruit by weight** = to sell for a certain price per pound or kilo; **gross weight** = weight of both the container and its contents; **net weight** = weight of goods without the packing material and container

(b) how heavy a person is; *his weight is less than it was a year ago*; **to lose weight** = to get thinner; *he's trying to lose weight*; **to put on weight** = to get fatter; *she's put on a lot of weight since her holiday*

(c) to pull your weight = to work as hard as everyone else; *the manager has the reputation for being ruthless with employees who don't pull their weight*; (informal) **to throw your weight about** = to use your authority to tell people what to do in a rude way; *she loves to throw her weight about at management meetings*; **she's worth her weight in gold** = she's a very useful person and we couldn't do without her

(d) something which is heavy; *if you lift heavy weights like big stones, you can hurt your back*; *have you got a weight to put on the papers to stop them blowing away?*; **that's a weight off my mind!** = that is something I need not worry about any longer

2 *verb*

(a) to attach something heavy to something; *they weighted down the sack with bricks and threw it into the river*

(b) to add an amount to a total to produce a certain result; *the figures are weighted to take account of seasonal variations* (NOTE: do not confuse with **wait**)

② **weird**
['wɪɪd] *adjective*

strange, different from what is normal; *I don't like her new boyfriend - he's really weird*; *wasn't it weird that he phoned just when we were talking about him?*; *this meat has a weird taste* (NOTE: **weirder - weirdest**)

② **welcome**
['welkʌm]

1 *adjective*

(a) met or accepted with pleasure; *the rain was welcome after months of drought*; *a bowl of warm soup would be welcome*; *after a game of rugby he had a welcome hot shower or a hot shower was very welcome*

(b) welcome to = willingly allowed to; *you're welcome to use the library whenever you want*

(c) (informal) (as a reply to 'thank you') thanks for carrying the bags for me - *you're welcome!*

2 *verb*

(a) to greet someone in a friendly way; *the staff welcomed the new secretary to the office*; *when we arrived at the hotel we were welcomed by a couple of barking guard dogs*

(b) to be glad to hear news; *I warmly welcome the result of the election*; *I would welcome any suggestions as to how to stop the water coming through the roof*

3 *noun*

action of greeting someone; *there was not much of a welcome from the staff when we arrived at the hotel*; **a warm welcome** = a friendly welcome; *they gave me a warm welcome*

② **welfare**
['welfeɪ] *noun*

(a) providing comfort and freedom from want; *the club looks after the welfare of the old people in the town*; *we take the children to a child welfare clinic*; *the government has taken measures to reform the welfare system*

(b) money paid by the government to people who need it; *he exists on welfare payments*; *the family is on welfare*

① **well**
[wel]

1 *adverb*

(a) in a way that is satisfactory; *he doesn't speak Russian very well*; *our business is small, but it's doing well*; *is the new computer working well?*

(b) a lot (more); *he got back from the office late - well after eight o'clock*; *you should go to the Tower of London - it's well worth a visit*; *there were well over sixty people at the meeting*; *she's well over eighty*

(c) as well = also; *when my aunt comes to stay she brings her two cats and the dog as well*; *you can't eat fish and chips and a meat pie as well!*; **as well as** = not only, but also; *some newsagents sell food as well as newspapers*; *she ate a slice of chocolate cake as well as two scoops of ice cream*

(d) (to emphasize) *he may well be right*; *she's well aware of how serious the situation is*

2 *adjective*

healthy; *she's looking well after her holiday!*; *the secretary's not very well today - she's had to stay off work*; *it took him some weeks to get well after his flu*

3 *interjection;* (which starts a sentence, and often has no meaning) *well, I'll show you round the house first*; *well now, we've done the washing up so we can sit and watch TV*; (showing surprise) *well, well! what is Mr Smith doing here!*

4 *noun*

very deep hole dug in the ground with water or oil at the bottom; *we pump water from the well in our garden*; *Middle Eastern oil wells*

① **well done**
['wel 'dʌn]

1 *interjection* showing congratulations; *well done, the England team!*; *well done to all of you who passed the exam!*

2 *adjective*

(meat) which has been cooked a long time; *can I have my steak well done, please?*

③ **well-earned**
[wel'ɜːnd] *adjective*

which you have deserved; *after doing all that gardening I think I can take a well-earned rest*

③ **wellingtons** (informal) **wellies**
['welɪŋtɪnz or 'welɪz] *noun*

long rubber boots which go almost up to your knees, often c∧loured green; *put your wellies on - it's pouring down*

② **well-known**
[wel'nɪʊn] *adjective*

famous, known by a lot of people; *she lives next door to a well-known TV star*

② **well-off**
[wel'ɒf] *adjective*
(informal) rich; *I thought his wife came from a well-off family; our neighbours have always been better off than us*

② **well-paid**
['wel'peɪd] *adjective*
earning a good salary; *well-paid secretaries can earn really high salaries; what I want is not just a well-paid job but one that is interesting*

① **Welsh**
[welʃ]
1 *adjective*
referring to Wales; *we will be going climbing in the Welsh mountains at Easter*; **Welsh rarebit** = slice of bread with toasted cheese on top
2 *noun*
(a) the Welsh = the people of Wales; *the Welsh are proud of their language; the Welsh are magnificent singers*
(b) language spoken in Wales; *Welsh is used in schools in many parts of Wales*

③ **went**
[went] *see* GO

③ **wept**
[wept] *see* WEEP

③ **were, weren't**
[wɜː or wɜːnt] *see* BE

① **west**
[west]
1 *noun*
direction of where the sun sets; *the sun sets in the west and rises in the east; we live in a village to the west of the town; their house has a garden that faces west or a west-facing garden*
2 *adjective*
in or to the west; *she lives on the west coast of the United States; the west part of the town is near the river*; **west wind** = wind which blows from the west; *a wet west wind is blowing from the Atlantic*
3 *adverb*
towards the west; *go west for about ten kilometres, and then you'll come to the national park; the river flows west into the ocean*

② **western**
['westɪn]
1 *adjective*
from or in the west; *Great Britain is part of Western Europe; the Western part of Canada has wonderful mountains*; *see also* COUNTRY
2 *noun*
film about cowboys; *she likes watching old westerns on TV*

② **wet**
[wet]
1 *adjective*

(a) covered in water or other liquid; *she forgot her umbrella and got wet walking back from the shops; the chair's all wet where he knocked over his beer; the baby is wet - can you change her nappy?*; **wet through** *or* **soaking wet** = very wet; *change your shirt - it's wet through; I was soaking wet after falling into the river*
(b) when it is raining; *the summer months are the wettest part of the year; there's nothing I like better than a wet Sunday in London*
(c) not yet dry; *watch out! - the paint's still wet*
(d) *(informal)* always attacked by others, not able to take decisions; *don't be so wet - phone the manager and tell him what you think!*
(NOTE: **wetter - wettest**)
2 *verb*
(a) to make something wet; *the rain didn't really wet the soil*
(b) to sprinkle with water; *wet the shirt before you iron it*
(c) *(of child)* to wet the bed = to pass waste water from the body in bed and make it wet; *she's started to wet her bed*
3 *noun*
(informal) person, especially a politician, who prefers compromise instead of taking decisions; *she got rid of all the wets in her cabinet*

③ **we've**
[wiːv] = WE HAVE

④ **whale**
[weɪl] *noun*
(a) huge animal that lives in the sea; *you can take a boat into the mouth of the river to see the whales*
(b) *(informal)* to have a whale of a time = to enjoy yourself very much; *the children had a whale of a time at the zoo*

④ **wharf**
[wɔːf] *noun*
place by the sea where a ship can tie up to take on or put off cargo; *the fishing boats were tied up at the wharf* (NOTE: plural is **wharfs** *or* **wharves** [wɔːvz])

① **what**
[wɒt]
1 *adjective*
(asking a question) *what time is it?; what type of food does he like best?*
2 *pronoun*
(a) the thing which; *did you see what was in the box?; what we like to do most on holiday is just to visit old churches*
(b) *(asking a question) what's the correct time?; what did he give you for your birthday?; what's the name of the French restaurant in the High Street?; what's the Spanish for 'table'?; what happened to his car?*
3 *adverb*
(a) *(showing surprise) what a huge meal!; what beautiful weather!*

(b) *(giving a reason)* *what with the children being ill one after another, and my husband being away, I've got my hands full at the moment*

4 *interjection; (showing surprise)*
what! the restaurant's full?; what! did you hear what he said?; I won the lottery! - What! (NOTE: after **what** used to ask a question, the verb is put before the subject: **what's the time** but **they don't know what the time is**)

③ **what about**
[wɒt ə'baut] *phrase; (showing a suggestion)*
what about having some lunch?; they invited everybody - are you sure, what about Fiona?

① **whatever**
[wɒt'evɪ] *pronoun; (form of 'what' which emphasizes)*
(a) *it doesn't matter what; you can have whatever you like for Christmas; she always does whatever she feels like doing; I want that car whatever the price*
(b) *(in questions) what, why; whatever made him do that?; whatever does that red light mean?; I've sold the car - whatever for?*

③ **what for**
['wɒt 'fɔ:] *phrase*
(a) *why; what are they all shouting for?; he's sold his car - what for?; what did he phone the police for?*
(b) *for what use; what's this red button for?*

② **whatsoever**
[wɒtsɪu'evɪ] *adjective & pronoun; (form of 'whatever' which emphasizes) there is no truth whatsoever in the report; the police found no suspicious documents whatsoever;* **none whatsoever** = *none at all; do you have any idea why the computer suddenly stopped working? - none whatsoever* (NOTE: always used after a noun and after a negative)

③ **wheat**
[wi:t] *noun*
cereal plant of which the grain is used to make flour; *after the storms much of the wheat lay flat on the ground; my mother uses wheat flour to make bread* (NOTE: no plural)

② **wheel**
[wi:l]
1 *noun*
(a) round piece which turns round a central point and on which a bicycle, a car, etc., runs; *the front wheel and the back wheel of the motorbike were both damaged in the accident; we got a flat tyre so I had to get out to change the wheel;* **on wheels** = with wheels attached; *hospital beds are on wheels so they are easy to move; see also* MEALS
(b) any similar round piece for turning; **steering wheel** = wheel which is turned by the driver to control the direction of a vehicle; *the steering wheel is on the right-hand side of the car in British cars;* **to be at the wheel** = to be driving; *she was at the wheel when the car went off the*

road; **to take the wheel** = to start to drive a car; *she took the wheel because her husband was falling asleep*
2 *verb*
(a) to push something along that has wheels; *he wheeled his motorbike into the garage; she was wheeling her bike along the pavement; the waiter wheeled in a sweet trolley*
(b) to wheel round = to turn round suddenly; *she wheeled round and went straight back to the counter*
(c) to fly in circles; *birds were wheeling above the fishing boats*
(d) to wheel and deal = to negotiate to make business deals

④ **wheelchair**
['wi:ltʃeɪ] *noun*
chair on wheels which people who cannot walk use to move around; *he manages to get around in a wheelchair; she has been confined to a wheelchair since her accident;* **wheelchair entrance** = special entrance with a slope instead of steps, which can be used by people in wheelchairs

① **when**
[wen]
1 *adverb; (asking a question)*
at what time; *when is the last train for Paris?; when did you last go to the dentist?; when are we going to get paid?; since when has he been wearing glasses?; I asked her when her friend was leaving* (NOTE: after **when** is used to ask a question, the verb is put before the subject: **when does the film start?** but **he doesn't know when the film starts; when is he coming?** but **they can't tell me when he is coming**)
2 *conjunction*
(a) at the time that; *when he was young, the family was living in London; when you go on holiday, leave your key with the neighbours so they can feed the cat; do you remember the day when we all went for a picnic in Hyde Park?; let me know when you're ready to go*
(b) after; *when the speaker had finished, he sat down; wash up the plates when you've finished your breakfast*
(c) even if; *the salesman said the car was worth £5000 when he really knew it was worth only half that*
(d) although; *I said I knew nothing about it when in fact I'd known about it for some time*

① **whenever**
[wen'evɪ] *adverb*
(a) at any time that; *come for tea whenever you like; we try to see my mother-in-law whenever we can or whenever possible*
(b) *(form of 'when' which emphasizes) whenever did she learn to drive?*

① **where**
[weɪ] *adverb*
(a) *(asking a question) in what place, to what place; where did I put my glasses?; do you*

know where the restaurant is?; where are the knives and forks?; where are you going for your holiday?

(b) *(showing place)* in a place in which; *stay where you are and don't move*; *they still live in the same house where they were living twenty years ago*; *here's where the wire has been cut*

(c) whenever; *use fresh tomatoes where possible* (NOTE: after **where** used to ask a question, the verb is put before the subject: **where is the bottle?** but **he doesn't know where the bottle is**)

② **whereas**
[weɪrˈæz] *conjunction*

(a) if you compare this with the fact that; *he likes tea whereas she prefers coffee*

(b) *(formal)* taking the following fact into consideration; *whereas the contract between the two parties states that either party may withdraw at six months' notice*

③ **whereby**
[weɪˈbaɪ] *adverb; (formal)*

by which; according to which; *a deed whereby ownership of the property is transferred*; *a teaching method whereby students can measure their own progress*

② **wherever**
[weɪˈevɪ] *adverb*

(a) to or in any place; *you can sit wherever you want*; *wherever we go on holiday, we never make hotel reservations*; *the police want to ask her questions, wherever she may be*

(b) *(form of 'where' which emphasizes)* wherever did you get that hat?

① **whether**
[ˈweðɪ] *conjunction*

(a) *(showing doubt, or not having reached a decision)* if; *do you know whether they're coming?*; *I can't make up my mind whether to go on holiday now or later*

(b) *(applying to either of two things)* both; *all employees, whether managers or ordinary staff, must take a medical test* (NOTE: do not confuse with **weather**)

① **which**
[wɪtʃ] *adjective & pronoun*

(a) *(asking a question)* what person or thing; *which dress are you wearing to the wedding?*; *which boy threw that stone?*

(b) **which is which** = what is the difference between the two; *there are two switches, one for the light and one for the fan, but I don't know which is which*

(c) *(only used with things, not people)* that; *the French restaurant which is next door to the office*; *they've eaten all the bread which you bought yesterday*

(d) in which case = if that is the case; *he's ill, in which case he'd better stay at home* (NOTE: with an object, **which** can be left out: **here's the bread we bought yesterday**)

③ **whichever**
[wɪtʃˈevɪ]

1 *pronoun*

(a) anything that; *you can take several routes, but whichever you choose, the journey will still take three hours*

(b) *(form of 'which' which emphasizes)* no matter which; *take whichever one you want*

2 *adjective*

no matter which; *whichever newspaper you read, you'll get the same story*

① **while**
[waɪl]

1 *noun*

(a) some time; *it's a while since I've seen him*; **in a while** = in a short time, soon; *I'll be ready in a while*; **a little while** = a short period of time; *do you mind waiting a little while until a table is free?*; **quite a while** = a longer period of time; *he changed jobs quite a while ago*; **once in a while** = from time to time, but not often; *it's nice to go to have an Indian meal once in a while*

(b) it is worth while = it is good to do, it may be profitable; *it's worth while keeping copies of your work, in case your computer goes wrong*; *it's well worth while trying to get a ticket for the show*; **to be worth someone's while** = to be worth doing; **it is worth your while** = it is worth the effort; *it's worth your while keeping copies of your work, in case your computer goes wrong*; **I'll make it worth your while** = I'll pay you a lot to do it; *it's an awful job, but if you agree to do it I'll make it worth your while*; *see also* WORTHWHILE

2 *conjunction*

(a) when, at the time that; *he tried to cut my hair while he was watching TV*; *while we were on holiday someone broke into our house*; *shall I clean the kitchen while you're having a bath?*

(b) *(showing difference)* he likes meat, while his sister is a vegetarian; *she only earns £120 a week while everyone else in the office earns twice that*; *everyone is watching TV, while I'm in the kitchen making the dinner*

(c) *(formal)* although; *while there may still be delays, the service is much better than it used to be*

② **whilst**
[waɪlst] *conjunction; (formal)*

while; *she went to London whilst he remained in their cottage in the country*

④ **whip**
[wɪp]

1 *noun*

(a) long, thin piece of leather with a handle, used to hit animals to make them do what you want; *riders use the whip to make their horses run faster*

(b) to crack the whip = to make everyone do what you want; *the boss had to crack the whip to get the job finished on time*

(c) MP who controls other MPs of his party at the House of Commons and who makes sure that all MPs vote; **Chief Whip** = main whip, who organizes the other whips; *the Government Chief Whip made sure the MPs were all present for the vote*
(d) sweet pudding made with whipped cream or eggs and fruit or chocolate; *she made a chocolate whip*
2 *verb*
(a) to hit someone or an animal with a whip; *he whipped the horse to make it go faster*
(b) to beat cream, eggs, etc., until firm; *whip the eggs and milk together*; *it is easier to whip cream if it is cold*
(c) to go quickly; *he whipped round to the newsagent's to buy some cigarettes*
(d) to do something quickly; *he whipped off his hat when he saw her coming towards him*; *she whipped out her chequebook*
(e) *(slang)* to steal; *someone's whipped my newspaper!* (NOTE: whipping - whipped)

④ **whisk**
[wɪsk]
1 *noun*
kitchen tool used for whipping cream, eggs, etc.; *she was looking for the whisk to beat some eggs*
2 *verb*
(a) to move something very fast; *she whisked the plate of cakes away before I could take one*; *they came in, said hello to us, and whisked our daughter off to the restaurant*
(b) to beat cream, eggs, etc., very quickly; *next, whisk the mixture until it is smooth and has no lumps*; *I always whisk egg whites by hand*

④ **whiskey**
['wɪski] *noun*
Irish or American whisky

③ **whisky**
['wɪski] *noun*
(a) alcoholic drink, made in Scotland from grain; *the factory produces thousands of bottles of whisky every year*; *I don't like whisky - I prefer beer*
(b) a glass of this drink; *two whiskies, please* (NOTE: plural is whiskies; note also that the spelling whiskey is used when it is made in Ireland or the United States)

③ **whisper**
['wɪspə]
1 *noun*
quiet voice, words spoken very quietly; *she spoke in a whisper*
2 *verb*
to speak very quietly, to make a very quiet sound; *he whispered instructions to the other members of the gang*; *she whispered to the nurse that she wanted something to drink*

④ **whistle**
['wɪsl]
1 *noun*

(a) high-pitched sound made by blowing through your lips when they are almost closed; *she gave a whistle of surprise*; *we heard a whistle and saw a dog running across the field*
(b) simple instrument which makes a high-pitched sound, played by blowing; *the referee blew on his whistle to stop the match*
2 *verb*
(a) to blow through your lips to make a high-pitched sound; *they marched along, whistling an Irish song*; *the porter whistled for a taxi*
(b) to make a high-pitched sound using a small metal instrument; *the referee whistled to stop the match*

① **white**
[waɪt]
1 *adjective*
of a colour like snow or milk; *a white shirt is part of the uniform*; *a white car will always look dirty*; *her hair is now completely white*; **white Christmas** = Christmas when there is snow on the ground; **white coffee** = coffee with milk added; *do you take your coffee black or white?*; **white goods** = large household electrical equipment like fridges and washing machines; **white meat** = pale meat like breast of chicken or turkey, opposed to red meat like beef; **white wine** = wine which is clear or slightly yellow; *I'll have a glass of white wine with the fish*; *(informal)* **white as a sheet** = completely white, very pale; *are you all right? - you look as white as a sheet* (NOTE: whiter - whitest)
2 *noun*
(a) colour of snow or milk; *the white of the mountains stood out against the deep blue of the sky*
(b) person whose skin is pale; *whites are in the minority in African countries*
(c) pale-coloured meat (on a chicken); *do you want a leg or some white?*
(d) white part of something; *the white of an egg*; *the whites of his eyes were slightly red*; *(informal)* **wait until you see the whites of their eyes** = wait until they are very close to you
(e) *(informal)* white wine; *a glass of house white, please*

① **White House**
['waɪt 'haʊs] *noun*
(a) building in Washington D.C., where the President of the USA lives and works; *the President invited the Prime Minister to lunch at the White House*; *the new First Lady is planning to change the decorations in only a few rooms in the White House*
(b) *(informal)* the US government, the president himself; *a White House spokesman gave a statement to the press*; *White House officials refused to confirm the report*

① **who**
[hu:] *pronoun*

(a) *(asking a question)* which person or persons; *(who was it) who phoned?*; *who are you talking to?*; *who was she going home with?*; *who spoke at the meeting?*

(b) the person or the people that; *the men who came yesterday morning work for the electricity company*; *anyone who didn't get tickets early won't be able to get in*; *there's the taxi driver who took us home last night*; *do you remember the girl who used to work here as a waitress?* (NOTE: with an object, **who** can be left out: **there's the man I saw at the pub**. Note also that when **who** is used as an object, it is sometimes written **whom** [huːm] : **whom are you talking about? the man whom I saw in the office**, but this is not common. After **who** used to ask a question, the verb is put before the subject: **who is that man over there?** but **I don't know who that man is over there**)

② **whoever**
[huːˈevɪ] *pronoun; (form of 'who' which emphasizes)* no matter who, anyone who; *whoever finds the umbrella can keep it*; *go home with whoever you like*

① **whole**
[hɪʊl]

1 *adjective*

all of something; *she must have been hungry - she ate a whole apple pie*; *we spent the whole winter in the south*; *a whole lot of people went down with flu*

2 *noun*

all, everything; *she stayed in bed the whole of Sunday morning and read the newspapers*; *the whole of the north of the country was covered with snow*; *did you watch the whole of the programme?* (NOTE: do not confuse with **hole**)

3 *adverb*

in one piece; *the penguin swallowed the fish whole*

④ **wholesale**
[ˈhɪʊlseɪl]

1 *adverb*

buying goods from manufacturers and selling them in large quantities to traders who then sell them in smaller quantities to the general public; *he buys wholesale* (NOTE: the opposite is **retail**)

2 *adjective*

(a) in large quantities; *we get a wholesale discount from the manufacturer*

(b) on a large scale; *the wholesale killing of wild birds*

③ **wholesaler**
[ˈhɪʊlseɪlɪ] *noun*

person who buys goods in large quantities from manufacturers and sells them to retailers; *the shop doesn't buy direct from the manufacturer but from a wholesaler*

④ **wholly**
[ˈhɪʊlɪ] *adverb; (formal)*

completely, totally; *I don't think she has wholly recovered from her illness*; *we were talking about two wholly different subjects* (NOTE: do not confuse with **holy**)

① **whom**
[huːm] *see* WHO

① **who's**
[huːz] = WHO IS, WHO HAS

① **whose**
[huːz] *pronoun*

(a) *(asking a question)* which belongs to which person; *whose is that car?*; *whose chequebook is this?*; *whose money was stolen?*

(b) of whom; *the family whose car was stolen*; *the girl whose foot you trod on* (NOTE: do not confuse with **who's**)

① **why**
[waɪ]

1 *adverb*

(a) *(asking a question)* for what reason; *why did he have to phone me in the middle of the TV film?*; *I asked the ticket collector why the train was late*

(b) *(giving reason)* she told me why she couldn't go to the party*

(c) *(showing something else is preferred)* why go by plane to Paris when you can take the train?*; *why don't we go for a picnic as it's fine?* (NOTE: after **why** used to ask a question, the verb is put before the subject: **why is the sky blue?** but **I don't know why the sky is blue**)

2 *interjection showing surprise*
why, if it isn't old Mr Smith!

④ **wicked**
[ˈwɪkɪd] *adjective*

(a) very bad; *what a wicked thing to say!*; *it was wicked of them to steal the birds' eggs*

(b) naughty; *she gave a wicked little laugh*

(c) *(informal)* very good; *they do a wicked line in French pastries*

④ **wicket**
[ˈwɪkɪt] *noun*

(a) *(in cricket)* set of three sticks put in the ground with two small sticks on top, used as the target; *the first ball hit his wicket*

(b) *(in cricket)* main playing area between two sets of these sticks; **fast wicket** = wicket where the ball moves fast off the ground; **slow wicket** = wicket where the ball moves slowly off the ground; *(informal)* **to be on a sticky wicket** = to be in an awkward situation; *the new sales assistant is on a very sticky wicket - the customer turned out to be the wife of the owner of the store*

(c) US position or opening with a window at a post office, bank, etc.

① **wide**
[waɪd]

1 *adjective*

(a) which measures from side to side; *the table is three foot or three feet wide; the river is not very wide at this point*

(b) extensive, enormous; *the shop carries a wide range of imported goods; she has a wide knowledge of French painting* (NOTE: **wider - widest**)

2 *adverb*

(a) as far as possible, as much as possible; *she opened her eyes wide; the door was wide open so we just walked in;* **wide apart** = separated by a large space; *he stood with his legs wide apart;* **wide awake** = very much awake; *at eleven o'clock the baby was still wide awake*

(b) not on the target; *the shells fell wide of their target;* **to be wide of the mark** = to be very wrong; *he's wide of the mark when he says that the old car is worth £2000*

3 *noun*

(in cricket) ball which goes too far to one side of the wicket

② **widely**

['waɪdli] *adverb*

(a) by a wide range of people; *it is widely expected that he will resign*

(b) over a wide area; *pollution spread widely over the area round the factory; she has travelled widely in Greece;* **he is very widely travelled** = he has travelled in many places

④ **widen**

['waɪdn] *verb*

(a) to make wider; *we need to widen the road to take larger lorries*

(b) to become wider; *further along, the road widens to allow two cars to pass*

③ **widespread**

['waɪdspred] *adjective*

over a large area; *there were widespread floods in the south of the country; there is a widespread idea that exercise is good for you*

④ **widow**

['wɪdəʊ] *noun*

woman whose husband has died and who has not married again; *she was left a widow at a very early age*

④ **widower**

['wɪdəʊə] *noun*

man whose wife has died and who has not married again; *she married again, this time a widower aged 62*

③ **width**

[wɪdθ] *noun*

(a) measurement of something from one side to another; *I need to know the width of the sofa; the width of the garden is at least forty feet* or *the garden is at least forty feet in width*

(b) distance from one side to another of a swimming pool; *she swam three widths easily*

① **wife**

[waɪf] *noun*

woman who is married to a man; *I know Mr Jones quite well but I've never met his wife; they both came with their wives;* see also TALE (NOTE: plural is **wives** ['waɪvz])

④ **wig**

[wɪg] *noun*

false hair worn on the head; *she wore a green wig for the party; in the play, he wears a grey wig to make him look older*

② **wild**

[waɪld]

1 *adjective*

(a) living in nature, not in a zoo; *wild dogs wander over parts of Australia;* **wild animals** = animals which are living in natural surroundings, as opposed to pets or farm animals; *we watched a TV programme on wild animals in Africa;* **wild flower** = flower which grows naturally, not a garden plant; *the book has several pictures of wild flowers*

(b) **wild mountain scenery** = mountains with high rocks, waterfalls, etc.

(c) *(informal)* very angry; very excited; *he will be wild when he sees what I have done to the car; the fans went wild at the end of the match;* *(informal)* **to be wild about something** = to be very interested in something; *she's wild about motorbikes;* **beyond your wildest dreams** = even better than you could expect; *the results exceeded our wildest dreams*

(d) not thinking carefully; *she made a few wild guesses, but didn't find the right answer; they had the wild idea of walking across the Sahara*

2 *noun*

(a) **in the wild** = living in nature; *in the wild, elephants can live to a great age*

(b) **the wilds of** = the remote parts of; *they have a cottage in the wilds of the Scottish mountains*

3 *adverb*

(a) freely; *in this zoo, animals can run wild in fields*

(b) without any control; *the crowds were running wild through the centre of the town*

④ **wilderness**

['wɪldɪnɪs] *noun*

wild country or desert, which is not cultivated and which has no inhabitants; *he spent years exploring the Arctic wilderness*

③ **wild goose chase**

[waɪld 'guːs 'tʃeɪs] *noun*

hopeless search; *they set off on a wild goose chase for new kitchen furniture*

③ **wildlife**

['waɪldlaɪf] *noun*

birds, plants and animals living free and not controlled by humans; *they spent the summer studying the wildlife in the national park;* **wildlife park** = large park surrounded by high fences, where wild animals are kept and are allowed to run wild inside (NOTE: no plural)

② **wildly**

['waɪldlɪ] *adverb*

(a) in a wild way; *the crowd cheered wildly as the pop group started to sing*

(b) wildly wrong = completely wrong; *his prediction of a fine summer was wildly wrong*

① **will**

[wɪl]

1 *verb, used with other verbs*

(a) *(to form the future) the party will start soon*; *will they be staying a long time?*; *we won't be able to come to tea*; *if you ask her to play the piano, she'll say 'no'*

(b) *(emphasizing) the dog will keep eating the cat's food*

(c) *(polite way of asking someone to do something) will everyone please sit down?*; *will someone close the curtains?*; *(formal) won't you sit down?*

(d) *(showing that you are keen to do something) don't call a taxi - I'll take you home*; *the car will never start when we want it to*; *don't worry - I will do it* (NOTE: the negative: **will not** is usually written **won't** [wɪʊnt]. The past is: **would**, negative: **would not**, usually written **wouldn't**. Note also that **will** is often shortened to **'ll: he'll =** he will)

2 *noun*

(a) power of the mind and character; **to work with a will =** to work very hard and willingly; **with the best will in the world =** however much you want to do something; *even with the best will in the world, I don't see how we can finish it in time*

(b) wish; **against your will =** without your agreement; *he was forced to sign the document against his will*; **of your own free will =** willingly, without being forced; *he signed the document of his own free will*; **at will =** whenever you want to; *visitors can wander around the gardens at will*

(c) legal document by which a person gives instructions as to what should happen to the property after he or she dies; *he wrote his will in 1984*; *according to her will, all her property is left to her children*; *has she made a will yet?*

COMMENT: to make a valid will, a person must not be mad, and the will must be signed and witnessed by two witnesses who will not benefit from the will. In English law, you have complete freedom to leave your property as you wish. You may, for example, not leave anything to your children, but leave your fortune to a home for cats, although in this case, your children would probably contest the will in the courts

② **willing**

['wɪlɪŋ]

1 *adjective*

keen to help; *is there anyone who is willing to drive the bus?*; *I need two willing helpers to wash the car*

2 *noun*

being eager to help; **to show willing =** to show you are eager to help

③ **willingly**

['wɪlɪŋlɪ] *adverb*

readily, in a eager way; *I would willingly do the shopping but my foot hurts too much*

① **win**

[wɪn]

1 *noun*

beating someone in a game; *the local team has only had two wins so far this year*; *we're disappointed, we expected a win*

2 *verb*

(a) to beat someone in a game; to be first in a race; *I expect our team will win tomorrow*; *the local team won their match yesterday*; *she won the race easily*

(b) to get (a prize, etc.); *she won first prize in the art competition*; *he won two million pounds on the lottery*; *she's hoping to win a new car in a competition in the paper* (NOTE: **winning - won** [wʌn])

① **wind**

1 [wɪnd] *noun*

(a) air moving fast outdoors; *the wind blew two trees down in the park*; *there's no point trying to use an umbrella in this wind*; *there's not a breath of wind - the sailing boats aren't moving at all*; **to run like the wind =** to run very fast; *he ran like the wind and won the race*

(b) being able to breathe; **to get your wind back =** to breathe properly again after running fast; *just give me a moment to get my wind back and I'll give you the message*

(c) **wind instruments =** musical instruments which you have to blow to make a note; *he doesn't play any wind instrument, just the piano*; **the wind section =** section of an orchestra with wind instruments; *the work provides a lot of scope for the wind section*; *see also* BRASS, STRINGS

(d) gas which forms in the stomach; *the baby is suffering from wind*

(e) **to get wind of something =** to hear a rumour about something; *somehow, our rivals got wind of our plan to expand our chain of stores*

2 [waɪnd] *verb*

(a) to turn a key, etc., to make a machine work; *do you need to wind (up) the clock twice a week?*

(b) to twist round and round; *he wound the towel round his waist*; *she wound the string into a ball* (NOTE: **winding - wound** [waʊnd])

③ **wind down**

['waɪnd 'daʊn] *verb*

to turn a handle to make something go down; *you can wind down the window if it is too hot*

① **window**

['wɪndɪʊ] *noun*

(a) opening in a wall, door, etc., which is filled with glass; *when I fly, I always ask for a seat by*

the window, so that I can watch the landing and takeoff; I looked out of the kitchen window and saw a fox; it's dangerous to lean out of car windows; the burglar must have got in through the bathroom window; **shop window** = large window in a shop where goods are displayed so that customers can see them; she bought the dress she had seen in the shop window
(b) window of opportunity = short moment when the conditions for something are especially favourable
(c) section of a computer screen used to display special information; open the command window to see the range of possible commands

③ **window box**
['wɪndɪʊ 'bɒks] noun
long narrow box for plants which is put on a ledge outside a window; she has a beautiful display of flowers in her window boxes

④ **windscreen**
['wɪnskriːn] noun
glass window in the front of a car, bus, truck, etc.; the windscreen broke when a stone hit it; I can't see through the windscreen - it's so dirty (NOTE: the American English is **windshield**)

④ **windshield**
['wɪnʃiːld] noun
(a) screen on the front of a motorcycle; the windshield protects the rider from the rain
(b) US glass window in the front of a car, bus, truck, etc. (NOTE: British English is **windscreen**)

③ **wind up**
['waɪnd 'ʌp] verb
(a) to turn a key to make a machine work; when did you wind up the clock or wind the clock up?
(b) to turn a handle to make something go up; wind up your window if it starts to rain
(c) to end up, to be finally; they wound up owing the bank thousands of pounds; we tried several restaurants and wound up in one by the railway station
(d) to finish; the meeting wound up at five o'clock
(e) to wind up a company = to close down company and sell its assets to pay its debts; the court ordered the company to be wound up
(f) (informal) to make someone annoyed; he only did it to wind you up

③ **windy**
['wɪndi] adjective
when a strong wind is blowing; we have a lot of windy weather in March; dress warmly, it's a cold windy day outside (NOTE: **windier** - **windiest**)

② **wine**
[waɪn]
1 noun
alcoholic drink made from grapes; we had a bottle of French red wine; two glasses of white wine, please; should we have some white wine with the fish?; **house wine** = special wine selected by a restaurant, cheaper than other

wines on the wine list; **wine list** = list of wines and other drinks available in a restaurant (NOTE: usually singular: **some wine, a glass of wine.** Note that the plural **wines** means different sorts of wine)
2 verb
to wine and dine someone = to invite someone for an expensive meal; he seems to spend most of his time wining and dining potential customers

③ **wine glass**
['waɪn 'glɑːs] noun
glass for serving wine; these wine glasses are very expensive

② **wing**
[wɪŋ] noun
(a) one of the two parts of the body which a bird or butterfly, etc., uses to fly; the birds were soaring in the warm air currents, hardly moving their wings; which part of the chicken do you prefer, a leg or a wing?
(b) (informal) **to take someone under your wing** = to help someone by showing them what to do, especially someone who is new to the work or who is in training
(c) one of the two flat parts sticking from the side of an aircraft, which hold the aircraft in the air; he had a seat by the wing, so could not see much out of the window
(d) part of a large building which leads off to the side of the main building, often built as an extension; they are building a new wing for the hospital
(e) body panel over the wheel of a car, which protects against splashing water and mud; the front wing was dented in the crash (NOTE: American English for this is **fender**)
(f) side of a football or hockey pitch; he ran along the left wing
(g) (in sport) player who plays on the wing; he passed the ball out to the wing
(h) part of a political party which has a certain tendency; she is on the right wing of the Conservative party

④ **wink**
[wɪŋk]
1 verb
to shut and open one eye quickly, as a signal; she winked at him to try to tell him that everything was going well
2 noun
(a) opening and shutting one eye quickly; she gave him a wink to show that she had seen him take the last piece of cake
(b) (informal) **forty winks** = a very short sleep; he closed his eyes and had forty winks; **hardly sleep a wink** = almost not to sleep at all; we hardly slept a wink last night because of the noise of the traffic outside

② **winner**
['wɪnɪ] noun
(a) person who wins; the winner of the race gets a silver cup

(b) something which is successful; *his latest book is a winner*

③ **winning**
['wɪnɪŋ] *adjective*
(a) which has won; *the winning team go on to the next stage of the tournament; she had the winning lottery ticket;* **winning post** = post which indicates the end of a horse race; *the first past the winning post was 'White Lady'*
(b) pleasant, attractive; *she has a very winning smile*

③ **win over**
['wɪn 'ɪʊvɪ] *verb*
to persuade someone who was previously reluctant; *we argued with them, but finally won them over*

② **winter**
['wɪntɪ]
1 *noun*
the coldest season of the year, the season between autumn and spring; *in some countries winter usually means snow; it's too cold to do any gardening in the winter; we're taking a winter holiday in Mexico;* **winter sports** = sports which are done in the winter, such as skiing, skating, etc.
2 *verb*
to spend the winter in a place; *these birds normally winter in Southern Portugal*

③ **wipe**
[waɪp]
1 *verb*
to clean or dry with a cloth; *wipe your shoes with a cloth before you polish them; here's a tissue to wipe your nose; use the blue towel to wipe your hands; I'll do the washing up, but someone else must wipe*
2 *noun*
action of cleaning or drying with a cloth; *she gave the table a quick wipe*

③ **wipe out**
['waɪp 'aʊt] *verb*
(a) to kill, to destroy; *the huge waves wiped out half the villages along the coast*
(b) to remove completely; *the costs of moving to the new office have completely wiped out our profits*

③ **wipe up**
['waɪp 'ʌp] *verb*
to clean liquid which has been spilt, with a cloth; *wipe up that milk which you spilt on the floor*

③ **wire**
['waɪɪ]
1 *noun*
(a) thin piece of metal or metal thread; *he used bits of wire to attach the apple tree to the wall; the basket is made of woven wire*
(b) **(electric) wire** = thin metal thread along which electricity flows, usually covered with coloured plastic; *the wires seem to be all right,*

so there must be a problem with the dishwasher itself; **live wire** = wire with electricity running through it; *be careful - that's a live wire*
(c) *(informal)* **to get your wires crossed** = to get two messages confused; *we seem to have got our wires crossed - I thought we were meeting today, and he thought it was tomorrow*
2 *verb*
to put in wires to carry electricity round a building; *the office has been wired for computers*

④ **wisdom**
['wɪzdɪm] *noun*
general common sense; *I doubt the wisdom of allowing her to go out alone at night;* **words of wisdom** = sound advice; *just a few words of wisdom: don't get involved!*

③ **wisdom tooth**
['wɪzdɪm 'tuːθ] *noun*
one of the four back teeth which only grow after the age of 20, or sometimes not at all

③ **wise**
[waɪz] *adjective*
(a) having intelligence and being sensible; *I don't think it's wise to ask her to invest all that money in his business; it was a wise decision to cancel the trip*
(b) **to be none the wiser** = to know no more about it than you did before; *I read his report, and I'm still none the wiser; his complicated explanation left us none the wiser about how the system would work* (NOTE: **wiser - wisest**)

① **wish**
[wɪʃ]
1 *noun*
(a) desire; *I have no wish to get involved*
(b) what you want to happen; **to make a wish** = to think of something you would like to have or to see happen; *close your eyes and make a wish; make a wish when you blow out the candles on your birthday cake;* **her wish came true** = what she wanted to happen did happen
(c) greetings; *best wishes for the New Year!; please give my good wishes to your family* (NOTE: plural is **wishes**)
2 *verb*
(a) to want something (which is almost impossible to have); *I wish I were blonde; I wish we didn't have to go to work on Christmas Day; I wish my birthday wasn't in June when I'm taking exams*
(b) to want something to happen; *she sometimes wished she could live in the country; I wish some of you would help me with housework;* **I wouldn't wish it on anyone** = it is so awful, I wouldn't want anyone, even someone I don't like, to have it; *this flu is awful, it's not something I would wish on anyone*
(c) to hope something good will happen; *she wished him good luck in his interview; he wished me a Happy New Year; wish me luck - it's my exam tomorrow*

(d) *(formal)* to want; *the headmaster wishes to see you in his study*

④ **wit**
[wɪt] *noun*
(a) being able to say clever and funny things; *his wit comes out all through his book*
(b) wits = intelligence; **at your wits' end** = not knowing what to do next; *they were at their wits' end when the builders reported even more structural problems in the house;* **to keep your wits about you** = to keep calm in a difficult situation and think hard what to do next; *don't panic, keep your wits about you, and everything will be all right*

④ **witch**
[wɪtʃ] *noun*
(in children's stories) wicked woman believed to have magic powers; *the wicked witch turned the prince into a frog* (NOTE: plural is **witches**)

① **with**
[wɪθ or wɪð] *preposition*
(a) *(showing things or people that are together)* *she came here with her mother; my sister is staying with us for a few days*
(b) *(showing something which you have)* *he went into the church with his hat on; you know the girl with blue eyes who works in the accounts department; they live in the house with the pink door*
(c) *(showing something which is used)* *he was cutting up wood with a saw; since his accident he walks with a stick; the crowd attacked the police with stones and bottles*
(d) because of; *her little hands were blue with cold; half the people in the office are ill with flu*
(e) and; *he always has ice cream with apple pie; I want a sheet of paper with an envelope* (NOTE: **with** is used with many adjectives and verbs: **to agree with, to be pleased with**, etc.)

② **withdraw**
[wɪθ'drɔ:] *verb*
(a) to move back; *the crowd slowly withdrew as the soldiers advanced; he talked to the guests for a few moments, then withdrew into his library*
(b) to take back; *the old coins have been withdrawn from circulation*
(c) to take money out of a bank account; *you can withdraw up to £100 from any cash machine*
(d) to take back something which has been said; *she withdrew her offer to provide the food for the party* (NOTE: **withdraw** [wɪθ'dru:] - **withdrawn**)

③ **withdrawal**
[wɪθ'drɔ:l] *noun*
(a) removing money from a bank account; *she made three withdrawals last week*
(b) going back, doing the opposite of what you had said you would do; *his withdrawal from the election surprised his friends*

(c) withdrawal symptoms = unpleasant physical condition which occurs when someone stops taking a drug; *she is trying to give up smoking, and is having difficulty in coping with the withdrawal symptoms*

④ **withhold**
[wɪθ'hiuld] *verb*
to refuse to let someone have something; *they suspect him of withholding important information from the police* (NOTE: **withholding - withheld** [wɪθ'held])

① **within**
[wɪ'ðɪn] *preposition*
(a) *(in space or time)* in; *the house is within easy reach of the station; we are within walking distance of the shop; I must go back for a checkup within three months; they promised to deliver the sofa within a week;* **within sight** = able to be seen; *we are almost there, the house is within sight; the ship sank within sight of land*
(b) within the law = legal; *is parking on the pavement within the law?*

③ **with it**
['wɪð ɪt] *phrase; (informal)*
knowing all about something; *she's very with it when it comes to what is happening on the fashion scene; I'm just not very with it today - I seem to be forgetting everything*

① **without**
[wɪ'ðaut] *preposition*
(a) not with; *they came on a walking holiday without any boots; she managed to live for a few days without any food; he was stuck in Germany without any money; they were fined for travelling without a ticket*
(b) not doing something; *she sang for an hour without stopping; they lived in the hut in the forest without seeing anybody for weeks*
(c) without doubt = certainly; *it is, without any doubt, his best film ever*

② **witness**
['wɪtnɪs]
1 *noun*
(a) person who sees something happen or who is present when something happens; *the witness happened to be outside the house when the fire started*
(b) person who appears before a court or committee to give evidence; *the secretary appeared as a witness in the libel case*
(c) person who is present when someone signs a document; *the contract has to be signed in front of two witnesses; his sister signed as a witness*
(d) *(formal)* **to bear witness to** = to be evidence of; *his reaction bore witness to his interest in the matter* (NOTE: plural is **witnesses**)
2 *verb*
(a) to be present when something happens, and see it happening; *did anyone witness the accident?*

(b) to sign a document to show that you guarantee that the other signatures on it are genuine; *one of his colleagues witnessed his signature*

③ **witness box** US **witness stand**
['wɪtnɪs 'bɒks or 'wɪtnɪs 'stænd] *noun*
place in a courtroom where the witnesses give evidence; *he was called to the witness box to answer questions from the prosecuting counsel*

④ **witty**
['wɪti] *adjective*
clever and funny; *he made a witty speech at the wedding; she made some witty remarks which helped to keep everyone amused* (NOTE: **wittier - wittiest**)

③ **wives**
[waɪvz] *see* WIFE

③ **wobble**
['wɒbl]
1 *verb*
to move from side to side; *the children made the jelly wobble in their bowls; don't wobble the table when I'm pouring coffee*
2 *noun*
shaking movement; *the front wheel has a wobble*

③ **wobbly**
['wɒbli] *adjective*
(a) shaking from side to side; *his bike has a wobbly back wheel; she sat on a wobbly armchair*
(b) *(of person)* not very steady; *she's a lot better, but still a bit wobbly on her feet*

③ **woke** *or* **woken**
[wəʊk or wəʊkn] *see* WAKE

① **woman**
['wʊmɪn] *noun*
adult female person; *the manageress is an extremely capable woman; there were two middle-aged women in the seats next to ours; there are more and more women bus drivers; he still has no woman in his life* (NOTE: plural is **women** ['wɪmɪn])

③ **won**
[wʌn] *see* WIN

① **wonder**
['wʌndɪ]
1 *verb*
(a) to want to know something; *I wonder why the room has gone quiet; she was wondering how many French francs you get for a pound; if you don't ring home, your parents will start wondering what has happened*
(b) to think about something; *I wonder how I can earn more money; he's wondering what to do next;* **to wonder about** = (i) to think about; (ii) to worry about; *we've been wondering about moving house; I'm wondering about the children, they look very pale*

(c) *(asking a question politely)* *we were wondering if you would like to come for dinner on Saturday*
2 *noun*
(a) amazing thing; **to do wonders for** = to help make something better; *an evening out would do wonders to cheer him up; the cream did wonders for her skin problem;* **no wonder** = it isn't surprising; *it's no wonder you had difficulty in getting tickets for the show with so many tourists in London*
(b) admiring feeling of surprise; *the little girl stared at the elephant in wonder*

① **wonderful**
['wʌndɪful] *adjective*
very good, splendid; *they had a wonderful holiday by a lake in Sweden; the weather was wonderful for the whole holiday; you passed your driving test first time? - wonderful!*

④ **wonderfully**
['wʌndɪfuli] *adverb*
in a wonderful way; *the experiment worked wonderfully well*

③ **won't**
[wəʊnt] *see* WILL NOT

② **wood**
[wʊd] *noun*
(a) hard material which comes from a tree; *the kitchen table is made of wood; she picked up a piece of wood and put it on the fire; a wood floor would be just right for this room* (NOTE: no plural for this meaning: **some wood, a piece of wood**)
(b) many trees growing together; *the path goes straight through the wood; their house is on the edge of the woods; (informal)* **not to see the wood for the trees** = not to see what is important because you are concentrating only on details; **we're not out of the wood(s) yet** = we still have problems; *there's still so much to do to the house, we're not out of wood yet*
(c) large wooden ball, used in bowls; *she picked up the wood and stepped up to take her turn*
(d) heavy wooden club, used in golf to hit the ball as far as possible; *he's trying a new wood* (NOTE: do not confuse with **would**)

③ **wooden**
['wʊdɪn] *adjective*
(a) made out of wood; *in the market we bought little wooden dolls for the children*
(b) *(of an actor, etc.)* being awkward and not natural when acting; *he was very wooden on stage*

③ **wooden spoon**
['wʊdɪn 'spuːn] *noun*
(a) spoon made of wood, used when cooking; *she used a wooden spoon to stir the sauce*
(b) silly prize given to someone who is last in a competition; *the wooden spoon goes to the team from the Police Force*

④ **woodland**
['wʊdlɪnd] *noun*
area of land covered in woods; *they walked through the woodlands to the lake; woodland birds are affected by climate change*

④ **wool**
[wʊl] *noun*
(a) long threads of twisted animal hair, used to make clothes or carpets, etc.; *the carpet is made of wool; I need an extra ball of wool to finish this pullover*
(b) to pull the wool over someone's eyes = to deceive someone by not telling them the true facts; *the estate agent tried to pull the wool over our eyes about the house;* see also COTTON WOOL

① **word**
[wɜːd] *noun*
(a) separate piece of language, either written or spoken; *this sentence has five words; he always has difficulty in spelling words like 'though'; a word-for-word translation often doesn't make any sense*
(b) something spoken; *she passed me in the street but didn't say a word; I'd like to say a few words about Mr Smith who is retiring today;* to have a word with = to speak to; *I must have a word with the manager about the service; the waitress had made so many mistakes, I had to have a word with her;* to have words with someone = to argue with someone; *he had words with his neighbour about the fence;* without a word = without saying anything; *she went out of the room without a word*
(c) something written; *we had a postcard with a few words from my sister in Canada; we've not heard a word from the lawyers*
(d) promise which you have made; to give your word = to promise; *he gave his word that the matter would remain confidential;* to keep your word = to do what you promised to do; *he kept his word, and the cheque arrived the next day;* to take someone's word for it = to accept what someone says as being true; *OK, I'll take your word for it, this is all the cash you have in the house*
(e) to breathe a word = to mention something; *we want to keep the plan secret, so don't breathe a word to anyone;* in other words = to that is to say; *it's seven o'clock - in other words, time for dinner; I'm going on holiday next month, in other words I'll be away from the office for about four weeks;* you took the words out of my mouth = you've said exactly what I was going to say

③ **wore**
['wɔː] *see* WEAR

① **work**
[wɜːk]
1 *noun*

(a) something done using your strength or your brain; *there's a great deal of work still to be done; there's too much work for one person; she tries to avoid doing too much work in the house; if you've finished that piece of work, there's plenty more to be done; cooking for two hundred people every day is hard work;* to have your work cut out to do something = to find it difficult to do something; *they'll have their work cut out to get the job finished on time;* he hasn't done a stroke of work all day = he hasn't done any work at all
(b) job done regularly to earn money; *he goes to work every day on his bicycle; work starts at 9 a.m. and finishes at 5 p.m.; her work involves a lot of travelling; he is still looking for work*
(c) at work = working; *the builders are still hard at work; she's at work today, but will have the day off tomorrow;* out of work = without a job; *hundreds of people were put out of work when the factory closed; she has been out of work for six months* (NOTE: no plural for meanings (a) and (b): **some work, a piece of work**)
(d) something which has been made, painted, written, etc., by someone; *an exhibition of the work of local artists; the complete works of Shakespeare;* standard work = book which is the recognized authority on a subject; *he's the author of the standard work on mountain birds*
2 *verb*
(a) to use your strength or brain to do something; *I can't work in the garden if it's raining; he's working hard at school, we're very pleased with his progress; work well and you'll soon get a better job;* to set to work = to start working; *if we all set to work early, we should finish the job this evening*
(b) to have a job; *she works in an office in London; he used to work in his father's shop; she had to stop working when her mother was ill*
(c) *(of machine)* to run; *the computers aren't working; the machine works by electricity*
(d) to make a machine run; *she works the biggest printing machine in the factory; do you know how to work the washing machine?*
(e) to succeed; *will the plan work?; if the cough medicine doesn't work, you'll have to see a doctor*
(f) to move a little; to work loose = to become loose by constant movement; *the nut holding the wheel must have worked loose*

③ **work at**
['wɜːk 'æt] *verb*
to work at something = to work hard; *if you want to become a tennis professional you will have to work at it*

① **worker**
['wɜːkɪ] *noun*
(a) person who works in a certain way; *she's a good worker; he's a fast worker*

(b) person who works, especially in a certain job; *the factory closed when the workers went on strike*; *office workers usually work from 9.30 to 5.30*

(c) female bee which goes out to find honey for the queen

④ **workforce**

['wɜːkfɔːs] *noun*

all the workers in an office or factory; *the management has made an increased offer to the workforce*; *the company cannot continue production with half its workforce off sick* (NOTE: no plural)

① **working**

['wɜːkɪŋ] *adjective*

referring to a job or to work; *the working population of a country*; *the unions have complained about working conditions in the factory*; *he came to the party in his working clothes*; **working breakfast** = breakfast where you discuss business; **working class** = group in society consisting of people who work with their hands, usually earning wages not salaries; **working life** = the years a person has worked; *I was a commuter all my working life*; **working party** = group of experts who study a problem and report on how to deal with it; *a working party was set up to study the question of building a new airport*; **working week** = the part of the work when people usually go to their jobs; *the government is planning to reduce the working work to 35 hours*

③ **workings**

['wɜːkɪŋz] *noun*

(a) way or ways in which something works; *the workings of a car engine are a complete mystery to him*; *I wish I could understand the workings of local government!*

(b) **workings** = place where mineral has been dug; *that hole is the entrance to some old iron workings*

③ **workman**

['wɜːkmɪn] *noun*

man who works with his hands; *two workmen came to mend the gas heater* (NOTE: plural is **workmen**)

① **work on**

['wɜːk 'ɒn] *verb*

to work hard to make something better; *you'll have to work on your French if you want to get through the exam*

① **work out**

['wɜːk 'aʊt] *verb*

(a) to calculate; *I'm trying to work out if we've sold more this year than last*; *the waiter couldn't work out the total bill*

(b) to succeed; *everything worked out quite well in the end*

(c) to do exercises; *he works out every morning in the gym*

④ **workplace**

['wɜːkpleɪs] *noun*

place where work is done; *more work will get done if the workplace is in pleasant surroundings*

① **works**

['wɜːks] *noun*

(a) factory; *the steel works will be closed next week for the Christmas holidays*

(b) parts of a machine; *I looked inside the clock and there seems to be dust in the works*

(c) **public works** = constructions done by a government or local council; **road works** = repairs to a road

(d) *(informal)* **the works** = everything; *they have laid out new gardens in front of the town hall with pools, coloured lights, fountains - the works!*

③ **workshop**

['wɜːkʃɒp] *noun*

very small factory where things are made or repaired; *he runs a workshop for repairing bicycles*; *the chairs are made in the workshop behind the shop*

③ **work up**

['wɜːk 'ʌp] *verb*

(a) to develop; *I find it difficult to work up any enthusiasm for my job*

(b) to do some hard work to make something happen; *I'm doing some digging to work up an appetite*

(c) **to work yourself up into a state** = to make yourself annoyed and worried by something; *he's worked himself up into such a state about his exams*

① **world**

['wɜːld] *noun*

(a) the earth on which we live; *here is a map of the world*; *she flew round the world twice last year*; *he has to travel all over the world on business*; *a round-the-world ticket allows you to stop in several places*; **the Old World** = Europe, Asia and Africa; **the New World** = North and South America; **the Third World** = countries of Africa, Asia and South America which do not have highly developed industries; **World War** = war in which many countries all over the world take part

(b) **to come into the world** = to be born; **to bring a child into the world** = to give birth to a baby; **to be all alone in the world** = to have no family; *he isn't married, an only child, both his parents are dead, so he's all alone in the world*; *(informal)* **to be on top of the world** = to feel very happy; *she's got a new boyfriend and is on top of the world*; **out of this world** = magnificent; *the cooking in the restaurant was out of this world*; **to think the world of someone** = to respect or love someone; *they think the world of their daughter*; **to do**

someone a world of good = to make someone feel much better; *his holiday has done him a world of good*

(c) *(making a question stronger)* who in the world is John Sparrow? = do you have any idea who John Sparrow is?

(d) people with a particular interest or who work in a particular business; *he's very interested in the world of music*; *she wants to get into the world of big business*

(e) particular group of animals, etc.; *the insect world*

④ **worldwide**
[wɜːld'waɪd] *adjective & adverb*

over the whole world; *the company has a worldwide network of distributors*; *a worldwide energy crisis*; *the TV news programme is available worldwide*

④ **worm**
[wɜːm]
1 *noun*

(a) small animal which has no bones or legs and lives in the soil; *birds were on the grass looking for worms*; *the early bird catches the worm* = if you are the first to do something you will beat your rivals (NOTE: also called **earthworm**)

(b) similar tiny animal living inside an animal's body; *we had to give the dog a tablet to get rid of its worms*

2 *verb*

(a) to get through by twisting and turning; *they managed to worm their way into the exhibition*

(b) to worm something out of someone = to get information out of someone by continually asking questions; *they managed to worm the information out of her*

(c) to get worms out of an animal; *the cat needs to be wormed*

③ **worn**
[wɔːn] *see* WEAR

③ **worn out**
[wɔːn 'aʊt] *adjective*

(a) very tired; *he was worn out after the game of rugby*; *she comes home every evening, worn out after a busy day at the office*

(b) old and which has been used a lot; *the tyres on the back wheels are worn out*; *she was wearing a pair of worn out trainers*; *see also* WEAR OUT

② **worried**
['wʌrɪd] *adjective*

anxious; *he had a worried look on his face*; *she's looking worried*; *I'm worried that we may run out of petrol*; worried to death = extremely worried; *they were worried to death about her*

③ **worry**
['wʌrɪ]
1 *noun*

(a) something which makes you anxious; *go on holiday and try to forget your worries*

(b) being anxious; *she is a great source of worry for her family*

2 *verb*

to be anxious because of something; *he's worrying about his driving test*; *I worry when the children stay out late*; *don't worry, I'll be back on time*; *she's always pale and that worries me*

③ **worrying**
['wʌrɪɪŋ] *adjective*

which makes you worried; *there has been a worrying increase in the number of thefts*

① **worse**
[wɜːs]
1 *adjective*

(a) less good (as compared to something else); *it rained for the first week of our holidays, and the second week was even worse*; *I think this film is worse than the one I saw last week*; *both children are naughty - but the little girl is worse than her brother*; *both children are ill, and to make matters worse, their mother has broken her arm*

(b) more ill; *he's much worse since he started taking his medicine*

2 *adverb*

not as well; *he drives badly enough but his sister drives even worse* (NOTE: **worse** is the comparative of **bad, badly** and **ill**)

3 *noun*

something which is worse; *they thought their problems were over, but worse was to follow*; to take a turn for the worse = to suddenly become more ill; *everyone thought she was getting better and then she took a turn for the worse*

④ **worsen**
['wɜːsn] *verb*

to become worse; *I think the pain has worsened today*; *we are watching the worsening situation carefully*

③ **worse off**
['wɜːs 'ɒf] *adjective*

with less money than before; *the family is much worse off since he was made redundant*

④ **worship**
['wɜːʃɪp]
1 *noun*

(a) praise and respect to God; *prayer is the most important part of worship*; an act of worship = a religious ceremony

(b) praise and love for someone or something; *her worship of her boss isn't healthy*; hero worship = excessive praise and love for someone who is considered a hero

2 *verb*

(a) to praise and respect God; *the ancient peoples worshipped stone statues of their gods*

(b) to take part in a church service; *they worship regularly in the parish church*

(c) to praise and love someone very much; *she absolutely worships her boyfriend* (NOTE: **worshipping - worshipped**)

worst

[wɜːst]

1 *adjective*

worse than anything else; *this summer is the worst for fifty years*; *I think this is the worst film he's ever made*

2 *adverb*

less well than anything or anyone else or than at any other time; *it's difficult to say which team played worst in the tournament*; *she works worst when she's tired*

3 *noun*

very bad thing; *the worst of the bad weather is past now*; **to prepare for the worst** = to get ready to have bad news; *your father was very badly injured - you must prepare for the worst* (NOTE: **worst** is the superlative of **bad** and **badly**)

worth

[wɜːθ]

1 *adjective*

(a) to be worth = to have a certain value or price; *this ring's worth a lot of money*; *gold is worth more than silver*; *the house is worth more than £250,000*; *the car is worth £6,000 on the secondhand market*

(b) for all you are worth = with as much effort as possible; *they dug for all they were worth to try to find people trapped by the explosion*

(c) to be worth doing something = to find something good or helpful to do; *it's worth taking a map with you, as you may get lost in the little streets*; *his latest film is well worth seeing*; *the old castle is well worth visiting or is well worth a visit*; *see also* WHILE

2 *noun*

value; *its worth will increase each year*; *can you give me twenty pounds' worth of petrol?*

worthwhile

[wɜːθˈwaɪl] *adjective*

which is worth the effort spent on it; *taking handicapped children to the seaside is a very worthwhile project*; *was your trip to London worthwhile?*

worthy

[ˈwɜːðɪ] *adjective*

deserving; *it's a worthy cause, and I'm ready to help*; *the plan is worthy of careful consideration* (NOTE: **worthier - worthiest**)

would

[wʊd] *verb used with other verbs*

(a) *(polite way of asking someone to do something)* *would you please stop talking?*; *would someone please tell me where the library is?*; *would you like some more tea?*

(b) *(past of 'will')* *he said he would be here for lunch*; *she hoped she would be well enough to come*; *he wouldn't go even if I paid him*

(c) *(past of 'will', showing something which often happens)* *he would bring his dog with him, even though we asked him not to*; *naturally the car wouldn't start when we were in a hurry*; *my husband forgot my birthday again this year - he would!*

(d) *(showing something which often happened in the past)* *every morning she would go and feed the chickens*; *he would always be there waiting outside the station*; *they would often bring us flowers*

(e) *(following a condition)* *I'm sure that if they could come, they would*; *I would've done it if you had asked me to*; *if she were alive, she would or she'd be a hundred years old today*; *if it snowed we would or we'd go skiing* (NOTE: the negative **would not** is usually written **wouldn't**. Note also that **would** is often shortened to **'d: she'd be a hundred, he'd stay at home.** Note also that **would** is only used with other verbs and is not followed by **to**)

would rather

[ˈwʊd ˈrɑːðə] *verb*

to prefer; *I would rather live in London than anywhere else*; *are you all going to pay? - we'd rather not*; *they'd rather we stayed at home than go with them*

wound

1 [wuːnd] *noun*

(a) cut made on someone's body, usually in fighting; *the soldier had a bullet wound in his leg*; *he was admitted to hospital with a knife wound in his chest*

(b) hurt to someone's feelings; *the wounds caused by the divorce will take years to heal*

2 [wuːnd] *verb*

(a) to hurt someone badly in a fight, a war; *two of the gang were wounded in the bank robbery*; *as a young soldier he was badly wounded in the battle of the Somme*

(b) to hurt someone's feelings; *she was deeply wounded by what he said*

3 [waʊnd] *see* WIND

wove, woven

[wəʊv or ˈwəʊvn] *see* WEAVE

WPC

= WOMAN POLICE CONSTABLE

wrap

[ræp]

1 *verb*

(usually **wrap up**)

(a) to cover something all over; *we're wrapping up the Christmas presents for the children*; *the parcel is wrapped (up) in brown paper*; *if you're cold, wrap yourself (up) in your blanket*

(b) to wear warm clothes; *wrap up warmly if you're going for a walk in the snow*

(c) *(informal)* to finish off; *that just about wraps up the points we have to make*

(d) to wrap round = to put right round something; *she wrapped her arms around the little boy*; *it's cold - wrap your scarf round your neck* (NOTE: **wrapping - wrapped** [ræpt])

2 *noun*

(a) piece of cloth that is put round the shoulders or the top part of the body; *she pulled her wrap closer around her*

(b) *(informal)* to keep something under wraps = to keep something secret; *the whole project is still under wraps*

Ⓘ **wrapped up in**
['wræpt 'ʌp ɪn] *adjective*
busy doing something, so that you don't notice anything else; *she is so wrapped up in her work she sometimes forgets to eat*

Ⓘ **wrapping**
['ræpɪŋ] *noun*
paper, cardboard, plastic, etc., used to wrap something up; *the children tore the wrapping off the box; remove the wrapping before putting the dish in the microwave;* **wrapping paper** = brightly coloured paper used to wrap presents; *I bought two rolls of Christmas wrapping paper*

Ⓘ **wreck**
[rek]
1 *noun*
(a) ship which has been sunk or badly damaged; *divers have discovered the wreck of a Spanish treasure ship; the wreck of the 'Mary Rose' was found in the sea near Southampton*

(b) anything which has been damaged and cannot be used; *the police towed away the wreck of the car; their new car is now a total wreck*

(c) *(informal)* nervous, tired and worried person; *after the interview with the boss he was a nervous wreck; spend just two hours manning the complaints desk and you're reduced to a wreck*

2 *verb*
(a) to damage something very badly; *the ship was wrecked on the rocks in the storm; the building was wrecked by the explosion*

(b) to ruin something; *the children have caught measles and that has wrecked our plans to go to Greece*

Ⓘ **wreckage**
['rekɪdʒ] *noun*
what is left of a building, ship, plane, etc., after it has been wrecked; *wreckage of the cars and lorries covered the motorway; the rescue team searched the wreckage of the hotel looking for survivors; clearing the wreckage from the railway track will take several days* (NOTE: no plural)

Ⓘ **wrist**
[rɪst] *noun*
joint between the arm and the hand; *he sprained his wrist and can't play tennis tomorrow; see also* SLAP

Ⓘ **write**
[raɪt] *verb*
(a) to put words or numbers on paper, etc., with a pen, computer, etc.; *she wrote the address on the back of an envelope; someone wrote 'down*

with the management' on the wall of the bank; write the reference number at the top of the letter; did you know she used to write for the 'Sunday Times'?; he wrote a book on keeping tropical fish

(b) to write a letter and send it to someone; *have you written to your MP yet?; she writes to me twice a week; don't forget to write as soon as you get to your hotel; he wrote a letter to the management to complain about the service; don't forget to write a postcard when you get to New York; (informal)* **it's nothing to write home about** = it's not very special; *the food in the hotel was nothing to write home about* (NOTE: **writing - wrote** [rəʊt] **- has written** ['rɪtn])

Ⓘ **write back**
['raɪt 'bæk] *verb*
to answer by letter; *she got my postcard, and wrote back immediately*

Ⓘ **write down**
['raɪt 'daʊn] *verb*
to write on paper, etc.; *she wrote down the registration number of the car; please write down all the necessary details on a piece of paper*

Ⓘ **write in**
['raɪt 'ɪn] *verb*
(a) to write a letter to an organization; *hundreds of people wrote in to complain about the programme*

(b) US to vote for a candidate whose name does not appear on the ballot paper, by writing his or her name there

Ⓘ **write off**
['raɪt 'ɒf] *verb*
(a) to cancel a debt; *the bank couldn't trace him so they had to write the debt off*

(b) to remove an asset from a company's accounts because it no longer has any value; **the car was written off** = the insurance company considered the car a total loss

Ⓘ **write out**
['raɪt 'aʊt] *verb*
to write something in full; *can you write out a list of all the things you want?;* **to write out a cheque** = to write the words and figures on a cheque and then sign it

Ⓘ **writer**
['raɪtɪ] *noun*
person who writes; *who is the writer of this letter?; she's the writer of books on gardening*

Ⓘ **write up**
['raɪt 'ʌp] *verb*
to write a text in full from notes which you have taken; *I took masses of notes, and now I have to write them up for the local newspaper*

Ⓘ **writing**
['raɪtɪŋ] *noun*
(a) something which is written; *please don't phone, reply in writing; put everything in writing, then you have a record of what has been done*

(b) *(informal)* **the writing is on the wall** = there are signs that a disaster is about to happen; *the writing is on the wall for old-fashioned butcher's shops*

(c) words written by hand; *his writing's so bad I can't read it; see also* HANDWRITING

(d) being a writer; *he earns his living from writing*

(e) *(formal)* **writings** = serious things written; *we studied the writings of Karl Marx*

③ **written**
['rɪtn] *adjective*
which has been put in writing; *he had a written reply from the Prime Minster's office; see also* WRITE

① **wrong**
[rɒŋ]
1 *adjective*
(a) not correct; *he gave three wrong answers and failed the test; that's not the right time, is it? - no, the clock is wrong; you've come to the wrong house - there's no one called Jones living here; there is something wrong with the television; I must have pressed the wrong key - a message flashed up on the screen;* **wrong number** = telephone number which is not the one you wanted to dial; *we tried dialling several times, but each time got a wrong number; I want to speak to Mr Cousin please - sorry, you've got the wrong number*
(b) to start on the wrong foot = to start to do things the wrong way; **to get out of bed on the wrong side** = to start the day badly; **to get the wrong end of the stick** = not to understand correctly what someone is saying

(c) not suitable; *you came just at the wrong time, when we were bathing the children; she was wearing the wrong sort of dress for a wedding*

(d) bad; *it's wrong to talk like that about her; cheating in exams is wrong*

(e) making someone worried; **what's wrong?** = what is the matter?; *what's wrong with my handwriting? - there's nothing wrong with it, it's just that I find it difficult to read;* **I hope nothing's wrong** *or* **there's nothing wrong, is there?** = I hope there is no problem

2 *adverb*

badly; *everything went wrong yesterday; she spelt my name wrong;* **don't get me wrong** = don't put the wrong meaning on what I'm trying to say; *don't get me wrong, I love him more than anyone else but at times he can be very annoying*

3 *noun*

(a) thing which is not right; *the group is campaigning against wrongs done to children in care*

(b) to be in the wrong = to have made a mistake; *I apologize - I was clearly in the wrong*

◊ **on the wrong side of**
[ɒn ðɪ 'rɒŋ saɪd ɒv] *phrase*
(a) going against; *he got on the wrong side of the law*
(b) *(informal)* older than; *she's on the wrong side of fifty*

③ **wrote**
[rʊt] *see* WRITE

Xx

③ **X, x**
[eks]
(a) twenty-fourth letter of the alphabet, between W and Y
(b) *(sign showing that something is multiplied)* 3 $x\ 3 = 9$ (NOTE say 'three times three equals nine')
(c) *(sign showing size)* **the table top is 24 x 36cm** (NOTE: say 'twenty-four by thirty-six centimetres')
(d) *(sign used to indicate an unknown person)* *let's take the example of Mrs X, who is a widow, 40 years old*
(e) mark of a cross; *to find the treasure, you have to find the spot marked 'X' on the map*

③ **Xmas**
['krɪsmɪs or 'eksmɪs] *noun*
(informal) = CHRISTMAS

④ **X-ray**
['eksreɪ]
1 *noun*
(a) **X-rays** = rays which go through the soft tissue, and allow the bones and organs in the body to be photographed; *the dentist took X-rays of his teeth; an X-ray examination showed the key inside the baby's stomach; the X-ray department is closed for lunch*
(b) photograph taken with X-rays; *the X-ray showed that the bone was broken in two places; they will take an X-ray of his leg; she was sent to hospital for an X-ray*
2 *verb*
to take an X-ray photograph of someone; *there are six patients waiting to be X-rayed; they X-rayed my leg to see if it was broken*

Yy

① Y, y
[waɪ]
twenty-fifth letter of the alphabet, between X
and Z; *not many words begin with a Y*

④ yacht
[jɒt] *noun*
(a) sailing boat, used for pleasure and sport;
yacht club = private club for people who sail
yachts
(b) large luxurious motor boat; *she spent her
holiday on a yacht in the Mediterranean*

② yard
[jɑːd] *noun*
(a) measurement of length, 36 inches (= 0.914
metres); *the police station is only yards away
from where the fight took place; can you move
your car a couple of yards as it is blocking the
entrance to our garage?*; **square yard** =
measurement of area measuring one yard on
each side
(b) area of concrete at the back or side of a
house; *we keep our bikes in the yard*
(c) *US* garden round a house; *we're having a
barbecue in the back yard*
(d) large area where stores are kept outside,
where lorries can pick up or put down loads; *he
went to the builder's yard to buy some bricks*
(e) Scotland Yard; *(informal)* **the Yard** =
headquarters of the London Metropolitan
Police; *they called in the Yard to investigate;
Scotland Yard officers were called in*

④ yeah
[jeɪ] *interjection; (informal meaning)* YES

① year
[jɜː] *noun*
(a) period of time, lasting twelve months, from
January 1st to December 31st; *Columbus
discovered America in the year 1492; the great
celebrations which took place in the year 2000;
last year we did not have any holiday; next year
she's going on holiday in Australia; the
weather was very bad for most of the year;* **year
in, year out** *or* **year after year** = every year,
over a long period of time; *year in, year out he
sends me a plant for my birthday;* **all year
round** = working or open for the whole year; *the
museum is open all year round; see also* NEW
YEAR, NEW YEAR'S DAY
(b) *(informal)* **since the year dot** = for a very
long time; *we've been going on holiday to
Wales since the year dot*

(c) a period of twelve months from a particular
time; *we spent five years in Hong Kong; he died
two hundred years ago today; she'll be eleven
years old tomorrow; how many years have you
been working for the company?*
(d) **years** = a long time; **I haven't seen him for
years** = I haven't seen him for a very long time
(e) *(in Britain)* **school year** *or* **academic year** =
period which starts in September and finishes in
July; *the school year starts in September; it's
her last year at college;* **tax year** = the
twelve-month period which starts on April 6th,
used to calculate personal tax; *see also*
CALENDAR, FINANCIAL, LEAP YEAR

④ yell
[jel]
1 *verb*
to shout very loudly; *the policeman yelled to
her to get out of the way*
2 *noun*
loud shout; *he gave a yell and everyone came
running to see what he had found*

② yellow
['jeləʊ]
1 *adjective*
of a colour like that of the sun or of gold; *his
new car is bright yellow; she's wearing yellow
shoes; at this time of year the fields are full of
yellow flowers* (NOTE: **yellower - yellowest**)
2 *noun*
the colour of the sun or gold; *do you have any
hats of a lighter yellow than this one?; the
yellow of the flowers against the rocks makes a
very beautiful photograph*
3 *verb*
to become yellow; *the pages of the diary have
yellowed with time but you can still read it*

③ yellow line
['jeləʊ 'laɪn] *noun*
line painted along the side of a street, showing
that you are not allowed to park; *he got a ticket
for parking on a double yellow line*

③ yellow pages
['jeləʊ 'peɪdʒɪz] *noun*
section of a telephone directory printed on
yellow paper, which lists businesses under
various headings, such as computer shops,
newsagent's, etc.; *he looked up 'airlines' in the
yellow pages*

yen
[jen] *noun*
(a) currency used in Japan; *it cost two thousand yen* (NOTE: no plural; usually written ¥ after figures: **2000¥**
(b) *(informal)* strong desire; *he has a yen to go walking along the Great Wall of China*

yes
[jes] *adverb; (word showing that you agree, accept, etc., the opposite of 'no')* *they asked her if she wanted to come and she said 'yes'; anyone want more coffee? - yes, please; you don't like living in London? - yes I do!; didn't you work in Scotland at one time? - yes, I did; I need a clear answer - is it 'yes' or 'no'?*

yesterday
['jestɪdeɪ] *adverb & noun*
the day before today; *yesterday was March 1st so today must be the 2nd; she came to see us yesterday evening;* **the day before yesterday =** two days before today; *it rained the day before yesterday; the shop only opened the day before yesterday*

yet
[jet]
1 *adverb*
(a) already, until now; *has the manager arrived yet?; I haven't seen her yet this morning; don't throw the newspaper away - I haven't read it yet*
(b) **as yet =** up till now; *they have not managed to repair the fault as yet; as yet, he hasn't given me any explanation for being late*
(c) still, even; *the police charged and yet more fans were arrested; she ate yet another piece of cake*
(d) *(formal)* in the future; *all hope is not lost, we may yet win the championship*
2 *conjunction*
but, still; *he's very small and yet he can kick a ball a long way; it was starting to snow, and yet he went out without a coat*

yield
[jiːld]
1 *noun*
(a) interest produced by an investment; *the yield on these bonds is higher than average*
(b) quantity of a crop or a product produced from a plant or from an area of land; *what is the normal yield per hectare?*
2 *verb*
(a) to produce money; *the investment has yielded a good interest until now*
(b) to produce a crop or a product; *this variety of rice can yield up to 2 tonnes per hectare; the North Sea oil deposits yield 100,000 barrels a month*
(c) to produce a result; *their researches finally yielded the information they were looking for*
(d) **to yield to someone =** to give up, to give way; *(of traffic)* **to yield to another car =** to allow another car to go first; **to yield to pressure =** to give in to pressure; *the government yielded to pressure from the unions and did not proceed with the planned legislation*

yoghurt *or* **yogurt**
['jɒgɪt] *noun*
milk which has become slightly sour after bacteria are added, often flavoured with fruit; *a pot of strawberry yoghurt;* **plain yoghurt =** yoghurt without any flavouring

yolk
[jɪʊk] *noun*
yellow part inside an egg; *in my boiled egg, the yolk was soft and the white was hard; beat the yolks of three eggs and add sugar*

you
[juː] *pronoun*
(a) *(referring to someone being spoken to)* *are you ready?; you look tired, you should rest a bit; if I give you my address will you give me yours?; hello, how are you?; are you both keeping well?*
(b) *(referring to anybody)* *you never know when you might need a pair of scissors; you have to be very tall to be a policeman*
(c) *(addressing someone directly)* *you with the red scarf over there, I need to see your ticket!; hey you! leave my bicycle alone* (NOTE: **you** is both singular and plural)

you'd
[juːd] = YOU HAD, YOU WOULD

you'll
[juːl] = YOU WILL

young
[jʌŋ]
1 *adjective*
not old; *she's very young, she's only six; he became Prime Minister when he was still a young man; my little brother's much younger than me or much younger than I am; in the afternoon there are TV programmes for very young children; this is where your Daddy used to live when he was a young boy; your new haircut makes you look younger* (NOTE: **younger - youngest**)
2 *noun*
(a) young animals or birds; *animals fight to protect their young*
(b) **the young =** young people; *today, the young have great need of moral teaching* (NOTE: no plural)

youngster
['jʌŋstɪ] *noun*
young person; *the youngsters went to the park to play football*

your
[jɔː] *adjective*
belonging to you; *I hope you didn't forget to bring your toothbrush; this letter is for your brother*

① **yours**

[jɔːz] *pronoun*

(a) belonging to you; *this is my car - where's yours?*; *my car's in the garage, can I borrow yours?*; **a friend of yours** = one of your friends; *you said she was a friend of yours, but she says she's never met you*

(b) *(greetings used at the end of a letter)* **Yours faithfully** = used as an ending for business letters, when addressed to no specific person; **Yours sincerely** *US* **Sincerely yours** = used as an ending to a letter addressed to a named person; **Yours truly** *US* **Truly yours** = words written at the end of a slightly formal letter; *(informal)* **yours truly** = me myself; *who had to pay for all the damage, why yours truly, of course!*

① **yourself**

[jɔːˈself] *pronoun*

(a) *(referring to 'you' as a subject)* *why do you wash the car yourself, when you could easily take it to the car wash?*; *watch out for the broken glass - you might hurt yourself*; *I hope you are all going to enjoy yourselves*

(b) *(for emphasis)* *did you yourself see what happened?*

(c) **by yourself** = alone, with no one to help you; *will you be all by yourself at Christmas?*; *did you find your way back to the hotel all by yourself?* (NOTE: the plural **yourselves** refers to **you** as a plural subject)

② **youth**

[juːθ] *noun*

(a) young man; *gangs of youths were causing trouble in the village*; *a youth, aged 16, was arrested for possessing drugs*; **youth club** = club where young people meet; *she runs the youth club attached to the church*

(b) period when you are young, especially the time between being a child and being an adult; *in his youth he was a great traveller*; *I haven't done that since the days of my youth!*

③ **you've**

[juːv] = YOU HAVE

Zz

③ **Z, z**

[zed *US* ziː]

last and twenty-sixth letter of the alphabet; *he can say his alphabet from A to Z*

③ **zebra**

[ˈzebrɪ or ziːbrɪ] *noun*

(a) African animal like a horse, with black and white stripes; *zebras' stripes help them hide in the long grass of the African bush* (NOTE: usually no plural: **a herd of zebra**)

(b) **zebra crossing** = place marked with black and white lines where you can walk across a road; *it's safer to use a zebra crossing when you're crossing a main road*

③ **zero**

[ˈzɪrɪʊ] *noun*

(a) number 0; *to make an international call you dial zero zero, followed by the number of the country*

(b) freezing point of water on a thermometer; *the temperature outside stayed below zero for days*

(c) score of no points; *they lost ten - zero* (NOTE: plural is **zeros**)

④ **zinc**

[zɪŋk] *noun*

hard bright light-coloured metal; *iron coated with zinc is used for shed roofs* (NOTE: Chemical element: chemical symbol: **Zn**; atomic number: 30)

④ **zip**

[zɪp]

1 *noun*

device for closing openings on trousers, dresses, bags, etc., consisting of two rows of teeth which lock together; *the zip of my coat is broken*; *can you do up the zip at the back of my dress?* (NOTE: also called a **zip fastener**; in American English it is a **zipper**)

2 *verb*

(a) **to zip up** = to close something using a zip; *she zipped up her coat*; *he zipped up his bag*

(b) to go fast; *cars were zipping past us on the motorway* (NOTE: **zipping - zipped**)

③ **zip code**

[ˈzɪp ˈkɪʊd] *noun*

US numbers used to indicate a postal delivery area in an address on an envelope; *don't forget the zip code - it's a very important part of the address* (NOTE: the British English for this is **postcode**)

Ⓞ **zipper**
['zɪpɪ] *see* ZIP

Ⓞ **zone**
[zɪʊn]
1 *noun*
area or part which is different from others, or which has something special; *police cars are patrolling the inner city zones*; **pedestrian zone** = part of a town where cars are not allowed; *the town centre has been made into a pedestrian zone*; **time zone** = one of 24 bands in the world in which the same standard time is used; *when you fly across the USA you cross several time zones*
2 *verb*
to divide a town into parts for planning purposes; *the land is zoned for industrial use*

Ⓞ **zoo**
[zuː] *noun*
place where wild animals are kept, and where people can go to see them; *let's go to the zoo this afternoon*; *we went to the zoo to see the lions and elephants*

Ⓞ **zoom**
[zuːm]
1 *noun*
= ZOOM LENS
2 *verb*
(a) to go very fast; *cars were zooming past me on the motorway*
(b) *(of prices, etc.)* to rise suddenly and sharply; *the exchange rate zoomed up last month*
(c) **to zoom in on something** = to focus a camera lens so that it makes a distant object appear to come closer; *he zoomed in on the yacht*

Ⓞ **zoom lens**
['zuːm 'lenz] *noun*
camera lens which allows you to change quickly from distant to close-up shots while still keeping in focus; *using a zoom lens can give you close-ups of lions from quite a long way away*

SUPPLEMENT

You say

Numbers

one, two, three, four	1, 2, 3, 4
five, six, seven, eight	5, 6, 7, 8
nine, ten, eleven, twelve	9, 10, 11, 12
thirteen, fourteen	13, 14
fifteen, sixteen	15, 16
seventeen, eighteen	17, 18
nineteen, twenty	19, 20
twenty-one, twenty-two, twenty-three	21, 22, 23
thirty, thirty-one, thirty-two	30, 31, 32
forty, fifty, sixty	40, 50, 60
seventy, eighty, ninety	70, 80, 90
one hundred, a hundred and one	100, 101
two hundred, three hundred	200, 300
four hundred, five hundred	400, 500
six hundred, seven hundred	600, 700
eight hundred, nine hundred	800, 900
one thousand	1,000
ten thousand	10,000
one million	1,000,000
one billion	1,000,000,000
one trillion	1,000,000,000,000

Decimals

0.5	zero point five
0.23	zero point two three
2.5	two point five

Money

£1	one pound
30p	thirty pence *or* thirty pee
£1.25	one pound twenty-five *or* one twenty-five
£27.36	twenty-seven pounds thirty-six (pee)
$1	one dollar
10¢	ten cents *or* a dime
25¢	twenty-five cents *or* a quarter
30¢	thirty cents
$1.25	one dollar twenty-five *or* one twenty-five

continued...

You say ...*continued*

Telephone numbers

0171-921 3567   oh-one-seven-one, nine-two-one,
                                          three-five-six-seven

Year

1998   nineteen ninety-eight
2000   the year two thousand
1905   nineteen five *or* nineteen hundred and
                                          five *or* nineteen oh five

Date

2.1.98 or 2/1/98   the second of January nineteen ninety
                                          eight *or* (*US*) February first nineteen
                                          ninety eight

NOTE: American dates are written as: month/day/year
                    European & British dates as: day/month/year

Weights and Measures - Metric Measures

Length
1 millimetre (mm)		= 0.0394 in
1 centimetre (cm)	= 10 mm	= 0.3937 in
1 metre (m)	= 100 cm	= 1.0936 yds
1 kilometre (km)	= 1000 m	= 0.6214 mile

Weight
1 milligramme (mg)		= 0.0154 grain
1 gramme (g)	= 1000 mg	= 0.0353 oz
1 kilogramme (kg)	= 1000 g	= 2.2046 lb
1 tonne (t)	= 1000 kg	= 0.9842 ton

Area
$1 cm^2$	$= 100 mm^2$	= 0.1550 sq.in.
$1 m^2$	$= 10,000 cm^2$	= 1.1960 sq.yds
1 are (a)	$= 100 m^2$	= 119.60 sq.yds
1 hectare (ha)	= 100 ares	= 2.4711 acres
$1 km^2$	= 100 hectares	= 0.3861 sq. mile

Capacity
$1 cm^3$	= 0.0610 cu. in	
$1 dm^3$	$= 1000 cm^3$	= 0.0351 cu. ft
$1 m^3$	$= 1000 dm^3$	= 1.3080 cu. yds
1 litre	$= 1 dm^3$	= 0.2200 gallon
1 hectolitre	= 100 litres	= 2.7497 bushels

continued...

Weights and Measures ...*continued*

Imperial Measures

Length

1 inch		= 2.54 cm
1 foot	= 12 inches	= 0.3048 m
1 yard	= 3 feet	= 0.9144 m
1 rod	= 5.5 yards	= 4.0292 m
1 chain	= 22 yards	= 20.117 m
1 furlong	= 220 yards	= 201.17 m
1 mile	= 1760 yards	= 1.6093 km

Weight

1 ounce	= 437.6 grains	= 28.350 g
1 pound	= 16 ounces	= 0.4536 kg
1 stone	= 14 pounds	= 6.3503 kg
1 hundredweight	= 112 pounds	= 50.802 kg
1 ton	= 20 cwt	= 1.0161 tonnes

Area

1 sq.inch		= 6.4516 cm^2
1 sq.foot	= 144 sq.ins	= 0.0929 m^2
1 sq. yard	= 9 sq.ft	= 0.8361 m^2
1 acre	= 4840 sq.yds	= 4046.9 m^2
1 sq.mile	= 640 acres	= 259.0 hectares

Capacity

1 cu.inch		= 16.387 cm^3
1 cu.foot	= 1728 cu.ins	= 0.0283 m^3
1 cu.yard	= 27 cu.ft	= 0.7646 m^3
1 pint	= 4 gills	= 0.5683 litre
1 quart	= 2 pints	= 1.1365 litres
1 gallon	= 8 pints	= 4.5461 litres
1 bushel	= 8 gallons	= 36.369 litres
1 fluid ounce	= 8 fl.drachms	= 28.413 cm^3
1 pint	= 20 fl.oz	= 568.26 cm^3

Visit the dedicated website for this
English Study Dictionary
www.StudyDictionary.com

English Dictionary for Students

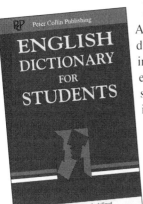

A comprehensive, up-to-date general English dictionary for upper-intermediate students. It includes over 25,000 main entries, each with example sentences and a clear definition. A student's thesaurus is also available to help improve vocabulary.

Dictionary:
ISBN 1-901659-06-2
924pages, paperback

Thesaurus:
ISBN 1-901659-31-3
280 pages, paperback

The Guide to Better English

A new concise guide that clearly explains how to write (and speak) better English. Packed with examples from newspapers and magazines that show how best to - and how not to - use English.
A witty and informative book for anyone who needs to write in English.
ISBN 1-901659-66-6   240pages
paperback

For details of our range of over 80 English and bilingual study material, visit our website: www.PeterCollin.com
Peter Collin Publishing, 1 Cambridge Road, Teddington, TW11 8DT, UK
email: info@petercollin.com